THE ANCIENT SYNAGOGUE

◈ THE ANCIENT
◈ SYNAGOGUE

The First Thousand Years

LEE I. LEVINE

YALE UNIVERSITY PRESS / NEW HAVEN & LONDON

Published with the assistance of the Ronald and Betty Miller Turner Publication Fund and the Lucius N. Littauer Foundation.

Designed by Nancy Ovedovitz and set in Janson type by Tseng Information Systems, Inc. Printed in the United States of America by Edwards Brothers, Ann Arbor, Michigan.

Library of Congress Cataloging-in-Publication Data
Levine, Lee I.
The ancient synagogue : the first thousand years / Lee I. Levine.
p.   cm.
Includes bibliographical references and index.
ISBN 0-300-07475-1 (alk. paper)
1. Synagogues—History—To 1500.
2. Judaism—History—Post-exilic period,
586 B.C.–210 A.D.   3. Judaism—History—
Talmudic period, 10–425.   I. Title.
BM653.L38   1999
296.6'5'0901—dc21   98-52667
                                          CIP

A catalogue record for this book is available from the British Library.

The paper in this book meets the guidelines for permanence and durability of the Committee on Production Guidelines for Book Longevity of the Council on Library Resources.

10 9 8 7 6 5 4 3 2 1

To Mira

CONTENTS

PART II: THE SYNAGOGUE AS AN INSTITUTION

PREFACE

This volume is the fruit of years of teaching and research connected with the ancient synagogue. It was only after living in Israel for several years and seeing firsthand the steady stream of archeological discoveries associated with this institution—the buildings as well as their artistic and epigraphical remains—that this subject first engaged my attention. The opportunity to share this fascinating material with students further stimulated my interest and curiosity. This led to the editing of several volumes on the subject in the 1980s, *Ancient Synagogues Revealed* and *The Synagogue in Late Antiquity*—the former a series of articles presenting the latest findings of archeological excavations of synagogues, the latter a collection of the papers delivered at an international conference sponsored by the Jewish Theological Seminary in New York. Since then, I have published a number of articles on a range of topics dealing with various aspects of the ancient synagogue.

The subject matter in this volume has been organized both diachronically and synchronically. The primary division is chronological, with the destruction of the Temple in the year 70 serving as a watershed. The reason for this division is twofold. First, the presence of the Temple and its subsequent destruction were powerful factors in shaping the religious role of the synagogue. As long as the Temple existed, no institution could compete with its prominence, sanctity, or religious authenticity. The Temple was the Jewish religious institution par excellence, and its demise created a vacuum in Jewish life, which was filled in large part by the synagogue.

A second factor in choosing the year 70 as a watershed is related to the disparate nature of the sources at our disposal before and after that year. The literary sources change dramatically, and the quality and quantity of the archeological and epigraphical material for late antiquity far exceeds that which was available earlier.

Following the Introduction and a chapter on the origins of the synagogue, we shall focus on the synagogues of Judaea and the Diaspora, and then on the role of these synagogues in Jewish society in the first century C.E. Such an arrangement allows for the initial presentation and analysis of the relevant data, followed by a synthesis of the material and a discussion of a variety of issues relating to the functioning of the synagogue in the late Second Temple period.

The remainder of the book is devoted to the post-70 era. After a series of chapters on the synagogue's development in late antique Palestine and the Diaspora, our attention focuses on the synagogue as an institution—the physical dimension of the building, its communal aspects, and its leadership, as well as a number of specific groups within Jewish society that played a significant role in this institution: the Patriarchs, the rabbis, women, and priests. A chapter is devoted to the liturgical developments within the synagogue, an aspect richly addressed by rabbinic and other material. There I describe how the Jewish worship context evolved in late antiquity until it reached a form quite similar to that which exists in most liturgical contexts today. Another chapter deals with the interpretation of Jewish art and examines what can and cannot be ascertained given the evidence available, and a final chapter discusses the internal and external (i.e., diachronic and synchronic) forces that shaped the synagogue of late antiquity.

A few words regarding the use of this book are in order. Owing to its size, an attempt has been made to keep footnotes as unencumbered as possible. Therefore, shortened references have been used throughout, with full bibliographical details appearing at the end of the volume. Translations of verses from the Old Testament are taken from *The Holy Scriptures According to the Masoretic Text* of the Jewish Publication Society of America (Philadelphia, 1917); a number of emendations have been made in the translations at the discretion of the author. Translations of verses from the New Testament follow the Revised Standard Version (RSV). Page references to critical editions appear in parentheses; full references to these editions appear in a designated section of the bibliography. On rare occasions, several editions of a single work are cited. For example, Lieberman's edition is used when citing the first four *sedarim* of the Tosefta, and Zuckermandel's edition for the last two. However, when no pagination appears, the standard uncritical edition is being cited. When relevant information appears in the printed, and not the critical, edition, the former is cited without a page reference. At times I have cited an older critical edition rather than a newer one, in which case the name of the edition is cited as well (e.g., for Tanḥuma or Pesiqta de Rav Kahana). Translations of Greek and Latin sources have been taken from the Loeb Classical Library unless otherwise indicated. In citing collections of epigraphical material, reference is made to the inscription number ("no.")

in a given corpus; whenever a number appears alone (not preceded by "p."), the reference is to a page in that edition.

Several of the chapters in this book have appeared as articles, although each has undergone extensive revision and expansion. Chapter 9, on the synagogue's physical dimension, originally appeared in the Hebrew journal *Cathedra* in 1990, while Chapter 13, a study of the relationship between the sages and the synagogue, was originally published in *The Galilee in Late Antiquity* in 1992. Chapter 2, on the origins of the synagogue, is a revision of an article that appeared in the *Journal of Biblical Literature* in 1996. All appear here with the permission of the publishers.

Since I began working on this volume several years ago, I have enjoyed the support of several institutions and academic frameworks. The Rockefeller Foundation made it possible for me to spend six weeks at its magnificent academic center in Bellagio, Italy. My sabbatical stay at Yale University and the Jewish Theological Seminary, along with grants from the Hebrew University of Jerusalem and the Memorial Foundation for Jewish Culture, afforded me further opportunities to make substantial progress in my research.

I also have benefited immensely from the comments and suggestions of many colleagues who were kind enough to read parts of the manuscript: Professors G. Blidstein, S. Fine, G. Foerster, I. Gafni, R. Jacoby, R. Kalmin, S. Reif, A. Shinan, P. van der Horst, B. Visotzky, and Z. Weiss. My thanks are also due to a number of graduate students who helped in the final stages of the research: Jill Borodin, Joshua Kulp, and Jennifer Tobenstein. I am indebted to Ḥani Davis for her superb editing skills and meticulous reading of the manuscript in its many versions. Her insights and suggestions are found throughout this book. Finally, I thank Charles Grench, Mary Pasti, and the staff of Yale University Press for the professional and supportive attention given to every phase of this book's production.

CHRONOLOGY

37–4	Herod's reign
6 C.E.	Direct Roman rule in Judaea, with prefects and procurators
26–36	Pontius Pilate in Judaea
40	Caligula's attempt to place his statue in the Jerusalem Temple
66–74	First revolt against Rome
69–96	Flavian dynasty
70	Destruction of the Second Temple
74	Conquest of Masada
ca. 70–225	Tannaitic age
70–132	Yavnean era
ca. 70–80	Era of Yoḥanan ben Zakkai in Yavneh
ca. 90–120	Era of Rabban Gamaliel II
132–135	Second revolt against Rome (Bar-Kokhba revolt)
ca. 140–180	Ushan era
ca. 180–225	Era of R. Judah I
193–235	Severan era
ca. 200–220	Codification of the Mishnah
ca. 220–500	Amoraic age
279	Death of R. Yoḥanan bar Napḥa, a leading Palestinian *amora*
306–337	Reign of Constantine I
324	Recognition of Christianity as the official religion of the Roman Empire
ca. 326	Discovery of the cross and Golgotha
351	Gallus revolt
361–363	Reign of Julian
379–395	Reign of Theodosius I
438	Publication of the Theodosian (II) Code
614	Persian conquest of Palestine
638	Arab conquest of Jerusalem

THE ANCIENT SYNAGOGUE

one INTRODUCTION

The synagogue, one of the unique and innovative institutions of antiquity, was central to Judaism and left indelible marks on Christianity and Islam as well.[1] The building was always the largest and most monumental in any given Jewish community and was often located in the center of the town or Jewish neighborhood.

In the Hellenistic and early Roman periods, the term "synagogue" was used to refer to the community as well as its central building. Luke uses the term in both meanings in the same chapter (Acts 13:14, 43), as do the Jews of Berenice in one inscription. In Egypt, Rome, and Judaea "synagogue" referred to a building, but in a number of inscriptions from Bosphorus, the community was clearly intended (in these latter cases, the word *proseuche* [προσευχή, house of worship] refers to the building).

Here, the term "synagogue" will be used to refer to the communal framework that evolved sometime in the Persian or Hellenistic period and constituted the focus of Jewish community life in antiquity. In the early stages, it is entirely possible that some communities met on premises other than a "synagogue" building or called their central institution by another name. By the second century C.E., however, "synagogue" had become a universal term for the building in which communal activities were held.[2]

---

1. See, for example, Krinsky, *Synagogues of Europe*, 15–20.

2. On the differences between the two most widespread terms of the first century, *synagoge* and *proseuche*, see below, Chap. 5. Neither of these terms was uniquely Jewish, as both were borrowed from the

In comparison to the Jerusalem Temple, which it replaced as the central religious institution in Jewish life, the synagogue was nothing short of revolutionary in four major areas.[3]

Location. The synagogue was universal in nature. Not confined to any one place, as were the "official" Jewish sacrifices of the post-Josianic era, the synagogue enabled Jews to organize their communal life and worship anywhere.

Leadership. The functionaries of the synagogue were not restricted to a single caste or socioreligious group. In principle, anyone could serve at its head. Priests might play a central role in its religious affairs as well, owing to their competence and experience in liturgical matters and not necessarily to their priestly lineage. Synagogue leadership was—in theory, at least—open and democratic.

Participation. The congregation was directly involved in all aspects of synagogue ritual, whether scriptural readings or prayer service. This stands in sharp contrast to the Jerusalem Temple setting, where people entering the sacred precincts might never witness the sacrificial proceedings unless they themselves were offering a sacrifice. In many cases, visitors to the Temple remained in the outer Women's Court without partaking in or viewing what transpired in the inner Israelite or Priestly Courts.[4] Moreover, non-Jews were explicitly banned from the Temple precincts under penalty of death (inscriptions giving due warning were set up around the sacred precincts), whereas the synagogue was open to all; in many places, particularly in the Diaspora, non-Jews attended the synagogue regularly and in significant numbers.

Worship. The most distinct aspect of the synagogue, however, was that it provided a context in which a form of worship alternative to that of the Jerusalem Temple developed. The synagogue eventually came to embrace a wide range of religious activities, including scriptural readings, prayers, hymns, sermons, and liturgical poetry. In place of the silence and passivity characterizing the Temple's official sacrificial cult, the synagogue placed a premium on public recitation—communal prayer, as well as the reading, translation, and exposition of sacred texts.

The centrality of the text in the synagogue's liturgical agenda was indeed revolutionary; the communal reading and study of sacred texts made the synagogue, from its inception, radically different from other Jewish religious frameworks of antiquity. The Jerusalem Temple, the temples of Elephantine and Leontopolis, and the liturgy of Qumran all had entirely different foci. The synagogue was also unique vis-à-vis contemporary

---

surrounding pagan culture. However, in the course of time, and certainly by the first century C.E., they had become largely associated with the Jewish community.

3. On the uniqueness of the synagogue as a religious institution, see Elbogen, *Jewish Liturgy*, 188; Heinemann, *Prayer*, 13-19; S. Safrai, "Synagogue," 908-9; Fleischer, "Beginnings of Obligatory Jewish Prayer," 400-401; L. Levine, "Second Temple Synagogue," 7.

4. Pagan temples sometimes barred people from entering; at times they were open to all, see Stambaugh, "Functions of Roman Temples," 571; MacMullen, *Paganism*, 44.

pagan religious contexts, wherein hymns, prayers, and recitations formed the primary nonsacrificial liturgy.

The synagogue did not emerge at first as a quintessentially religious institution, although some dimension of religious activity was undoubtedly present from the outset. Only in the course of the first five hundred years of the Common Era, after 70 C.E., did the religious component develop and expand to become the decisive feature of the synagogue. Whereas the Jerusalem Temple had served as the main focus of Jewish national and religious life, after its destruction many of its customs and prerogatives were gradually absorbed by the synagogue.

However, the synagogue's primary importance throughout antiquity lay in its role as a community center. By the first century C.E., the synagogue had become the dominant institution on the local Jewish scene throughout the Diaspora and Judaea, with the sole exception of pre-70 Jerusalem. No other communal institution that might conceivably have competed with the synagogue for communal prominence is ever mentioned in our sources. Within the confines of the synagogue the Jewish community seems to have not only worshipped regularly, but also studied, held court, administered punishment, organized sacred meals, collected charitable donations, housed the communal archives and library, and assembled for political and social purposes.

As a communal institution, the synagogue was fundamentally controlled and operated by the local community. Running such an institution may have been the concern of the community as a whole, as was most likely the case in villages and towns, or of the local urban aristocracy, which often assumed responsibility for the building and maintenance of such structures.[5] In contrast to pagan temples and Christian churches, for which models used throughout the Roman and Byzantine Empires were the norm, local synagogues were generally autonomous. As a result, we can see a broad range of styles and practices associated with this institution throughout antiquity. All these features—from architectural patterns, artistic expression, and inscriptions to prayer, Torah-reading, sermons, *targum* (תרגום, translation and interpretation of Scriptures), and *piyyut* (פיוט, synagogue poetry)—characterized the synagogue of antiquity, constituting what Peter Brown has called in another context an "exuberant diversity."[6]

The extent of this diversity has become abundantly clear over the past generation or two with the dramatic increase in archeological material and greater sophistication in the analysis and evaluation of our literary sources. As a result, we are aware of striking regional differences even within tiny Palestine, not to speak of the far-flung Diaspora. In several cases we have become aware of very different types of synagogues even within a given city.

Despite this diversity, the institution exhibited a remarkable unity. Its basic role as a

---

5. Baron, *Jewish Community*, I, 53–54, 134–41. See below, Chap. 10.

6. Brown, "Art and Society," 18.

community center and the range of activities and types of religious functions conducted therein, as well as orientation, ornamentation, symbolism, and sanctity, were in varying degrees common to synagogues throughout antiquity. These shared characteristics invariably appear in both archeological and literary sources.

The synagogue evolved significantly during late antiquity. For all its continuity as a communal institution between the first and seventh centuries C.E., it was the religious component of the institution that changed dramatically in scope and prominence. The synagogue evolved from a community center with a religious component into a house of worship that included an array of communal activities. This transformation is most strikingly attested to by the synagogues in Palestine, although, despite the relative paucity of evidence, such developments may be detected in the Diaspora as well. The synagogue had become—according to R. Isaac, borrowing a phrase from the prophet Ezekiel (11:16)—a *miqdash me'at* (מקדש מעט), a "lesser" or "diminished" sanctuary.

The impetus for these changes came from several quarters. Certainly, internal Jewish developments, first and foremost among which was the destruction of the Temple, played a significant role. No less important, however, were the evolving Empire-wide social and religious contexts in which the synagogue operated. Greco-Roman influences were clearly in evidence in many physical aspects of the synagogue, as were Christian models by late antiquity. With regard to the church, an ironic reversal took place between the first and seventh centuries C.E. Whereas nascent Christianity drew heavily on religious and liturgical elements derived from contemporary Jewish life, this trend was largely reversed after the ascendancy and dominance of the church in the Byzantine period, when Jewish life generally, and the synagogue in particular, began absorbing influences from contemporary Christian practice.

The synagogue, more than any other Jewish institution of antiquity, demonstrates a fascinating synthesis of Jewish and non-Jewish elements within a single framework. While some features of the synagogue reflect earlier Jewish customs and beliefs, others, as just noted, derive from the surrounding pagan and later Christian worlds. The integration of these elements in every aspect of the institution—from the physical dimension of art and architecture to the spiritual dimension of liturgy—offers a glimpse into the diverse and dynamic nature of Jewish life at the time, socially, religiously, and culturally. As we shall see, the Jewish world was far from monolithic in its response to these stimuli; while many elements were adopted and adapted, others were ignored by some communities.

The various ways these external models were combined with practices identified at the time as Jewish are intriguing. Often they coexisted with no apparent tension, and we can only speculate on how a community might have understood such a combination. For example, the zodiac motif depicting the four seasons and Helios riding a chariot is invariably found on the mosaic floors of synagogues alongside panels depicting distinctively Jewish symbols, such as the Torah shrine, menorah, *lulav*, and shofar. In the recently discovered synagogue at Sepphoris, biblical scenes and hitherto unattested Temple-related items are featured together with the zodiac pattern. Clearly, many Jewish communities integrated non-Jewish models into their synagogue framework without feeling threatened or compromised in any way.

Because of its centrality and importance in the community, the synagogue played an integrative role in ancient Jewish society. The inclusiveness of its activities, ranging from social to religious and from political to educational, underscores this fact. An impressive array of religious forms found expression within its walls, some of older Second Temple-period vintage (scriptural readings, sermons, and *targumim*), some of post-70 origin (communal prayer, *piyyut*, and religious art). Moreover, all segments of the community came within the purview of the synagogue in one way or another—the common folk of all genders and ages, village and town leaders, the wealthy urban aristocracy, various economic and social associations, the Patriarchate and those associated with that office, the rabbis, and other religious figures within the community.

The study of the synagogue has far-reaching implications in addition to establishing the important role of this institution in Jewish society. Given its centrality, there is much to learn about the community per se via this institution: How did the community define itself? What was the nature of its leadership? What was the community's relationship with its pagan and Christian surroundings, as well as with the Roman and Byzantine authorities (both secular and religious)?

In light of the growing wealth of information regarding the ancient synagogue, many conceptions regarding Jewish history of late antiquity have undergone serious revision. The location of synagogue remains, for example, has afforded a much more complete picture of Jewish settlement in Byzantine Palestine than was heretofore known. At times, these remains have confirmed much of what we knew from other sources, i.e., that post-70 Jewish settlement was particularly concentrated in the Galilee, as well as in other large urban centers of the country. In other cases, however, archeological finds have supplemented extant literary sources by indicating that Jewish settlement flourished in other areas, e.g., the eastern, southern, and western peripheries of Judaea and the Golan, which have been largely ignored in literary sources.

Moreover, our assessment of the sociological, political, and cultural dimensions of Jewish life in late antiquity has been totally transformed by the cumulative finds relating to the ancient synagogue. Until recently it was almost universally assumed, in the historiographical tradition reaching back to the nineteenth century, that the Jewish communities of late antiquity suffered ever-increasing persecution and discrimination and that, as a result, these communities, particularly those in Byzantine Palestine, were severely reduced in status and diminished in size. On the basis of the data now available, this picture must be seriously revised. Synagogues, in fact, were to be found the length and breadth of Byzantine Palestine and the Diaspora; some were built anew; others underwent periodic renovation. Jewish cultural activity—far from being stifled—continued to flourish throughout these centuries: artistic expression was extensive, synagogue prayer and poetry were refined and expanded, sermonic and targumic materials were compiled and edited, new halakhic and liturgical forms were created, new types of apocalyptic literature were written, and new forms of synagogue poetry and mystical experiences crystallized.

Finally, synagogue studies have opened up new vistas regarding our understanding of the nature of Judaism throughout late antiquity. It was once assumed (and, as it turns out, quite gratuitously) that the synagogue and Jewish religious life generally followed rabbinic dictates: what the rabbis legislated, the community accepted. Reality, however, appears to have been far more complex. Synagogue remains offer a variety of cultural, artistic, and religious expressions, some of which appear far from compatible with rabbinic dicta. That the rabbis were a significant factor in Jewish society by late antiquity is indisputable; that they wielded definitive authority or that their influence was normative in communal affairs, even in religious matters, does not appear to have been the case very often. Only now are we beginning to realize the many different currents at play in Jewish life at the time, resulting in a rich mosaic of beliefs and practices.

SOURCES AND METHODOLOGY

Given its centrality in Jewish life, it is not surprising that the synagogue is mentioned frequently in a wide variety of sources. Nevertheless, while literary and archeological materials abound, both in absolute terms and in comparison to other institutions in Jewish life of antiquity, our understanding of the synagogue is hampered by the diverse types of sources available, by their varying foci, and by the resultant discontinuity of information from one locale to another and from one period of time to the next.

For example, our knowledge of Diaspora synagogues in the pre-70 era rests primarily on literary remains, but for late antiquity (Babylonia excepted), the evidence is drawn almost exclusively from archeological material. Thus, the discrepancy in the sources available for the two periods is sharp. The situation regarding continuity is only slightly more promising with respect to Roman Palestine. The limited amount of sources for the pre-70 period is replaced by a plethora of material from the late Roman and Byzantine eras. Both rabbinic sources and archeological data offer a relatively detailed picture of the synagogue in its late antique Palestinian setting. The former is a particularly rich source in this regard, although utilizing this material presents not a few methodological challenges. In addition to the usual issues relating to the reliability of textual traditions and attributions, the late editing of many rabbinic works, and the dating of unattributed statements, we must constantly question how reflective this material is of the synagogue in general. Do rabbinic traditions preserve unique cases that may have been of interest to the sages but that were not necessarily reflective of the institution as a whole? If so, how limited are they? Perhaps they are more representative of "rabbinic" synagogues, those in which the rabbis tended to congregate, than of the majority of synagogues serving the community at large. Or are these sources merely an indication of what the rabbis wished to see rather than what was usually the case? Complicating this matter further is the issue of the nature and extent of rabbinic influence on this institution. As we can no longer assume that the rabbis ipso facto wielded authority over synagogue affairs, their comments about the institution and its leadership must be treated with a measure of circumspection.

With the exception of Babylonia, rabbinic material does not relate to the Diaspora. As a result, we possess only vague notions about the Diaspora from the rabbinic perspective, and little idea as to the ties between the rabbis themselves and this vast array of Jewish communities.

Regarding our sources generally, we are faced with the fact that each corpus of evidence has its own particular raison d'être, with the synagogue often playing only a very tangential role. Each type of source tends to concentrate on certain dimensions of the institution without making any attempt to offer a more inclusive picture. Rabbinic literature, for example, focuses on the synagogue's liturgical and, at times, social aspects, Josephus on its political role, and the New Testament on the synagogue within the context of Jesus' and Paul's missions. Nevertheless, even if only partial, the information offered by each source is invaluable. When these sources are taken together, a fairly comprehensive picture of the synagogue does emerge. As the range of sources is impressive both geographically and chronologically, so, too, are the subjects addressed both directly and indirectly: the physical aspects of the synagogue; artistic expression; cultural proclivities; communal activities; leadership roles; and liturgical expressions.

Let us review the main sources to which we will have recourse throughout our study, beginning with the pre-70 era.

Josephus notes the existence of synagogues in Judaea within the context of his political narrative of the first century. In both Dor and Caesarea, the synagogue became a center of controversy during the political struggles between Jews and pagans; in Tiberias, the synagogue (here called *proseuche*) served the Jewish community as a meeting place for its political deliberations at the outset of the revolt in 66–67 C.E. Regarding the Diaspora, Josephus cites a series of Roman documents affecting Jewish communities in a number of locales, particularly Asia Minor. The rights accorded the Jews under Roman rule are clearly articulated in these *privilegia*, and on several occasions the *privilegia* make explicit reference to the synagogue; more often, they mention activities and functions which we can safely assume took place in this institution.

Philo makes only a few passing references to the synagogue or *proseuche*. In the course of describing the pogroms of 38 C.E., he notes the existence of Alexandrian synagogues, and particularly a monumental, lavishly ornamented one. On several occasions, he mentions certain aspects of the Sabbath morning scriptural liturgy, as well as the worship practices of the Therapeutae and Essenes.

A number of books in the New Testament speak of synagogue-related matters. All the gospels recount Jesus' activity in Galilean synagogues, but Luke is especially expansive in his opening account of Jesus' preaching in Nazareth. The information in Acts on the synagogue, in both Jerusalem and the region of Asia Minor and Greece, is of primary importance to our understanding of the pre-70 institution.

Rabbinic material has preserved a number of traditions which presumably describe pre-70 synagogues; however, some of them are quite late and are of questionable historical value. Of particular importance, however, is the Tosefta's rather elaborate description of a first-century Alexandrian synagogue.

Although the pre-70 archeological material is scanty, it is of cardinal importance. Remains of at least four synagogue buildings are attested—three in Judaea and one in the Diaspora (Delos)—yet inscriptions provide the bulk of archeological evidence from this period. The Theodotos inscription from Jerusalem, that of Julia Severa from Acmonia in Asia Minor, a number of catacomb inscriptions from Rome, three synagogue inscriptions from Berenice (Cyrene), five from Delos, six from the Bosphorus, and sixteen (or parts thereof) from Egypt offer us a varied and far-ranging picture of the institution in the first century C.E.

This situation changes dramatically in the post-70 era. As noted, archeological material for the Diaspora is far more abundant than previously. Twelve buildings have been identified as synagogues of late antiquity; nine additional sites are less certain. Hundreds of inscriptions have been found, most dedicatory in nature and deriving from the synagogue buildings themselves, others stemming from a funerary context and mentioning someone associated in his or her lifetime with a synagogue. A similar situation of abundant archeological evidence holds true with regard to Roman-Byzantine Palestine. To date, well over one hundred synagogues have been identified and close to two hundred inscriptions retrieved, almost two-thirds of which are in Hebrew or Aramaic, the remainder in Greek. The score of amulets found in synagogue contexts are likewise of great value, not to speak of the dozens of mosaic floors, some of which have been remarkably well preserved.

Literary remains relating to the synagogue in this period are scattered among the writings of Byzantine authors (e.g., *Scriptores Historiae Augustae*), church fathers (Epiphanius, John Chrysostom), the Theodosian Code, and Justinian's *Novellae*. However, the overwhelming preponderance of literary material derives from rabbinic sources. More than four hundred pericopes explicitly mention the synagogue from either a historical, communal, or liturgical perspective; many hundreds, if not thousands, more deal with the religious activities which took place within the walls of this institution. Other Jewish texts relating to synagogue matters include the mystical Hekhalot texts, the various *targumim*, early Byzantine *piyyutim*, and Byzantine halakhic material, such as the list of practices differing in Palestine and Babylonia.

The methodological problems mentioned above with regard to rabbinic literature hold true—mutatis mutandis—with regard to other sources. Many of the statements preserved are problematic because of their selectivity, tendentiousness, or fragmentary nature. Even if a report appears to be accurate in and of itself, we are rarely certain whether the instance described was a localized phenomenon or one reflective of other times and places as well. Nevertheless, with the required modicum of caution and awareness of the issue of validation, a not insignificant amount of information about the synagogue may indeed be retrievable.

HISTORY OF RESEARCH

To attempt to reconstruct the history of research on the ancient synagogue is, in essence, to relate the histories of research in each of the various corpora of material pertaining to the various aspects of this institution. One may trace the history of research on the synagogue building by focusing on archeological reports, on its worship dimension by following publications treating liturgy, and on its artistic and sociocultural dimensions by reviewing those works which have concentrated on Jewish art and epigraphical remains. Only on rare occasion has there been an attempt to synthesize and integrate the various strands into a historical account of the institution.

Despite the enormous diversity in the various fields of research, they very often share many characteristics. Until the mid-twentieth century, a small handful of scholars mastered each of these disciplines. The assumption shared by most of them was that the development of the synagogue underwent a steady progression from stage to stage in a more or less linear fashion, and thus much of their work focused on tracing this evolution. Let me offer two examples of this phenomenon.

The first concerns the synagogue building. In its classical expression within the realm of archeology, the regnant theory was that the outward physical appearance of the synagogue developed in three separate and distinct phases during late antiquity. This particular theory crystallized over the first half of the twentieth century, beginning with the first serious study of the ancient synagogue, Kohl and Watzinger's *Antike Synagogen in der Galilaea* (in 1916). Based upon brief surveys and probes they carried out between the years 1905 and 1907 in eleven Galilean and Golan buildings (including one on the Carmel), these two scholars established criteria which became axiomatic in synagogue studies for decades: the Galilean synagogues were built in the late second and early third centuries, constituted a recognizable architectural group, and were modeled architecturally and artistically after buildings in Roman Syria, especially the Roman basilica.

Several decades later, in 1934, Sukenik published his Schweich lectures under the title *Ancient Synagogues in Palestine and Greece*, in which he added a second tier to this theory by identifying a series of Christian basilica–like synagogue structures (e.g., Naʿaran, Bet Alpha, Gerasa) as originating in the sixth and seventh centuries. These, he claimed, belonged to a later synagogue type, in contrast to the earlier Galilean one. In 1949, Sukenik further developed this distinction, adding Ḥammat Gader, Ḥuseifa, and Jericho to the list. Finally, in the 1950s, a third type was added by Goodenough and Avi-Yonah, who posited the broadhouse or transitional stage.

The basis of the above approach was the assumption that synagogue typology is linked to its chronology: different types of synagogues were built at different times. Thus, at any given moment one particular type was regnant, although there may have been some overlap in the transition from stage to stage.

The second example concerns a similar approach that characterized the study of Jewish liturgy, particularly with regard to the development of the *'Amidah* (עמידה), which was the primary focus of many early studies. Already in the nineteenth century, a number of scholars began setting the parameters for the subject when they posited a linear development for this prayer, i.e., that it evolved from a shorter, simpler version into a longer, more complex one. Zunz was the first to address the subject, and was followed in the first half of the twentieth century by Kohler, Finkelstein, Elbogen, and others. The core of the *'Amidah* was generally traced back to the Persian or early Hellenistic periods and was described as having developed incrementally in response to internal and external influences (e.g., competing Jewish ideologies, external political and cultural influences, persecutions, the destruction of the Temple) until it was standardized under Rabban Gamaliel of Yavneh ca. 100 C.E.

The liturgical dimension of the synagogue was revolutionized by the findings from the Cairo Genizah, not the least of which was an awareness of the liturgical diversity in the first millennium C.E. Not only did this affect our understanding of the development of the prayer ritual, but it also related to the cycles of scriptural readings for the Sabbath and festivals. Inspired and facilitated by the texts from the Cairo Genizah, scholars such as Mann and Büchler wrote extensively on the triennial Torah and prophetic readings as reflected in these early documents.

The first half of the twentieth century also produced several formidable works aimed to be systematic compilations of much of the known data on the synagogue. Krauss's *Synagogale Altertümer* (1922) focused primarily on the material culture of the institution as reflected in rabbinic literature and the limited archeological evidence then available. Elbogen's still definitive *Der jüdische Gottesdienst in seiner geschichtlichen Entwicklung* (1913; Hebrew version 1972; English version 1993) focused on the synagogue's liturgical and, secondarily, physical and communal dimensions.

Since the mid-twentieth century and, more precisely, since the 1950s and early 1960s, a veritable explosion has taken place in synagogue studies. The reasons for this wave of activity are multifold.

(1) Synagogue-related finds began surfacing dramatically, particularly in the archeological realm. Buildings were discovered in urban centers such as Caesarea, Tiberias, and Bet Shean, as well as in more rural settings such as Ma'on (Nirim). Following the 1967 Arab-Israeli war, synagogues were found in Gaza, Susiya, and 'En Gedi, as were a host of structures and related remains in the Golan and the southern Judaean hills. At the

same time, the number of synagogues discovered in the Diaspora, or those now securely identified as such, has almost doubled, including the monumental edifice at Sardis. All of these finds have generated a renewed interest in the synagogue building per se, as well in numerous related areas.

(2) New fields of inquiry have been created, particularly as a result of a series of seminal studies, foremost among which is the thirteen-volume work of Goodenough, *Jewish Symbols in the Greco-Roman Period*, published between 1953 and 1968. In fact, his efforts at collecting a hitherto unimagined array of Jewish artistic works from late antiquity spurred the creation of the field of ancient Jewish art. Goodenough, however, had aimed to do much more, hoping that his collection of material would serve a much grander design of reconceptualizing the nature and form of Judaism in late antiquity.

The study of Jewish art was given a significant boost with the publication of the final excavation report in 1956 of the synagogue at Dura Europos. Discovered in 1932, this building is by far the most sensational and revolutionary ancient synagogue ever unearthed. Kraeling's official publication on the site was followed soon after by Goodenough's detailed and controversial analysis in volumes 9–11 of his *Jewish Symbols* (1964). These two monumental works ushered in a plethora of studies in a host of fields, the ramifications of which continue to our own day.

Similar groundbreaking efforts were taking place in epigraphical studies. The first major corpus of Jewish inscriptional evidence was published by Frey. While volume 1 of his *Corpus Inscriptionum Judaicarum* had already appeared in 1936, the publication of volume 2, including inscriptions from the eastern Mediterranean (Asia Minor, Syria, and Palestine) and North Africa, appeared only posthumously, in 1952. For all its inadequacies—in no small part probably due to the exigencies surrounding its publication—this singular achievement provided the springboard for many other collections that appeared in the coming decades, each of which focused on specific geographical areas or types of inscriptions. Such studies include the corpus of catacomb inscriptions which provided the basis for Leon's *History of the Jews of Ancient Rome* (1960), the corpus of Egyptian inscriptions appended to volume 3 of *Corpus Papyrorum Judaicarum*, edited by Tcherikover, Fuks, and Stern (1964), Lifshitz' *Donateurs et fondateurs dans les synagogues juives* (1967), and the three volumes of the Jewish Inscriptions Project of the Faculty of Divinity at the University of Cambridge: Horbury and Noy's *Jewish Inscriptions of Graeco-Roman Egypt* (1992) and Noy's two-volume *Jewish Inscriptions of Western Europe* (1993–95).

(3) This era also witnessed methodological breakthroughs which breathed new life and insight into fields which had lain dormant for decades. Some of these studies, such as Heinemann's *Prayer in the Talmud: Forms and Patterns*, which appeared originally in Hebrew (1964; English trans. 1977), were conceptual in nature. Heinemann introduced into the study of Jewish prayer a form-critical approach widely used in biblical studies, and he single-handedly revitalized the historical study of Jewish prayer over the past thirty years. Heinemann espoused the theory that various prayer forms developed in dif-

ferent contexts and were transmitted orally; thus, a plethora of versions were in circulation simultaneously. As a result of his influence, the linear approach to the development of Jewish prayer has generally been abandoned.

As noted, a similar development subsequently took place in the archeological realm. With the discovery of the remains of scores of additional structures, the older concept of a linear development from one architectural type of synagogue to another has generally become passé and has been replaced by the assumption that different architectural types were in use at one and the same time (see below, Chap. 9).

(4) An abundance of newly published material has revolutionized a number of areas in the study of Jewish liturgy. We have already taken note of the extraordinary documentation provided by the Cairo Genizah, which affected practically every area of synagogue studies. Renewed interest in targumic studies has also been generated by new finds from several other sources. On the one hand, the Qumran discoveries revealed fragments of Aramaic *targumim* already in use in the pre-70 era; on the other, the sensational discovery of the Neofiti manuscript of the Torah in the Vatican library in 1949 provided the earliest, most complete *targum* text known to date. This latter discovery was particularly instrumental in generating a renaissance in targumic studies.

The increased interest in the study of midrash over the past generation has led to renewed scholarly attention given to the homiletical material found in rabbinic literature. Heinemann's form-critical approach to Jewish prayer has reawakened interest in the *Sitz im Leben* of other rabbinic genres as well; he himself—until his death in 1978—devoted numerous studies to the rabbinic homily, particularly the proem. This renewed interest in early Jewish liturgy spilled over to the field of scriptural lectionary, an area which had not been seriously addressed since the early part of the century. Attention was directed toward uncovering traces of the triennial lectionary cycle in extant literary works, and studies such as Guilding's *The Fourth Gospel and Jewish Worship* (1960), though controversial, have often been quoted in this regard.

The area of *piyyut* has received increasing scholarly attention since the 1960s. Building on the earlier work of Schirmann and Zulay, major contributions have been made in this field by Mirsky, Rabinovitz, Yahalom, and especially Fleischer. The study of this religious and literary genre was begun by Zunz over a century ago; however, the increased availability of Genizah material has revolutionized this field. Instead of assuming a medieval origin in a Muslim context for the *piyyut*, it is universally conceded today that this genre crystallized in Byzantine Palestine, when literally thousands of such poems were written. To date, we know of perhaps as many as twenty *paytanim* (poets) who flourished at the time, not to speak of other anonymous ones. Unknown several generations ago, Yannai is now identified as a sixth-century poet who penned at least two thousand poems, as probably did the greatest of ancient *paytanim*, El'azar Ha-Qallir (or Qillir).

(5) The flurry of activity in synagogue studies is also an outcome of the worldwide expansion in Jewish studies within institutions of higher learning over the past three de-

cades. This has been noticeable in Israel since 1967 with the dramatic increase in the number and size of the country's universities; in the United States, where Jewish studies began growing geometrically in the mid-1960s; and in England, Germany, and Canada. As a result, the sheer quantity of scholarly material being produced in studies related to the synagogue is far greater now than it was a generation or two ago.

(6) Finally, it is important to note that the increased interest in the ancient synagogue is in no small measure due to the attention Christian scholars have accorded the Jewish background of the New Testament and early Christianity. Although such interest was already apparent at the outset of the century in Schweitzer's *The Quest for the Historical Jesus* (1906), a much greater openness and receptivity has been evident from the 1950s and 1960s onward. Although the reasons for this are undoubtedly many, I should mention influential works such as Davies' *Paul and Rabbinic Judaism* (1948), the post-Holocaust Christian reassessment of attitudes toward Jews and Judaism, the impact made by the creation of the State of Israel, the exploration of Christian roots within Judaism stimulated by the Qumran evidence, and, finally, the effects of the new atmosphere of tolerance and understanding generated by the changes in Catholic policy in the decisions of Vatican II. The increased interest and resultant contributions of Christian scholars to Jewish studies over the last generation have consequently been of major importance in bringing synagogue-related studies to the fore.

The heightened interest of late in synagogue studies has spurred a number of attempts to summarize the institution's history in broad outline, including Levy's *The Synagogue: Its History and Function* (1963), Hruby's *Die Synagoge: Geschichtliche Entwicklung einer Institution* (1971), and Schrage's extensive entry on the synagogue in volume 7 of the *Theological Dictionary of the New Testament* (1964; English trans. 1971).

This explosion in synagogue-related research persists today. Not only does material continue to issue forth—be it new primary data from excavations, Genizah material, or secondary studies—but more refined methodological approaches and different assumptions underpin most scholarly works. We have already noted that the neat linear approach has largely been replaced by a more multifaceted and complex one. It is now generally agreed that institutional developments such as that of the synagogue were not necessarily determined by authorities from above, nor did they occur in a monolithic fashion; rather, a more diversified and dynamic approach is to be preferred, one which is far more reflective of the actual historical processes.

A greater sensitivity to methodological questions also stands at the forefront of recent scholarly deliberations. These include a more sophisticated use of literary sources, especially the New Testament and rabbinic literature, and, in the case of the latter, one which distinguishes more systematically between earlier and later material and between that of Palestinian and Babylonian provenance. Not only are the possible tendentiousness and selectivity of all literary sources more widely acknowledged, so, too, are the literary and theological agendas of each of these writings. At the same time, a growing number of scholars are more inclined to search out the possible social and cultural implications of archeological finds, and interdisciplinary studies, although still in their infancy in this area, are in evidence of late.

Moreover, scholarly treatments are now generally more attuned to external influences on Jewish society than had hitherto been the case. Rather than questioning whether such influences existed, efforts are now directed at determining the degree of such influence, in what areas of Jewish life, in which geographical regions, among which classes of society, and under what historical circumstances. Once again, the mid-twentieth century was pivotal in redefining this field of inquiry. Lieberman's works (*Greek in Jewish Palestine*, 1942; *Hellenism in Jewish Palestine*, 1950) and Hengel's magnum opus (*Judentum und Hellenismus*, 1969; English trans. 1974) framed an era in which a series of pathbreaking studies, including those of Goodenough, M. Smith, Scholem, Bickerman, Schalit, and Tcherikover, were written.[7]

In recent decades, new aspects of the ancient synagogue have been addressed in addition to the older, more traditional ones. The role of women in the synagogue (Brooten, *Women Leaders in the Ancient Synagogue*, 1982), the place and authority of the rabbis (L. Levine, Goodman, and S. J. D. Cohen, in *The Galilee in Late Antiquity*, 1992), the symbolic versus decorative interpretation of artistic motifs, Jewish borrowing of pagan and Christian motifs and symbols (Foerster, Ovadiah, and Hachlili) and their meaning in a Jewish context—these subjects and more have attracted scholarly attention of late.

Also noteworthy is the increasing number of studies focusing on the Diaspora synagogue. While Sukenik, Goodenough, and Kraeling had occasion to address this subject earlier,[8] it was the discovery of the Sardis building, following the final publication of the Dura Europos excavations, that ushered in a remarkably fruitful era of research and inquiry about this Diaspora institution. The main catalyst in this thrust has been Kraabel, who himself participated in the Sardis dig and has since written a plethora of studies on various aspects of the Diaspora synagogue, including a summary of the building remains which is still standard.[9] Other notable contributors to this field include Hengel, Seager, Foerster, Ovadiah, White, Feldman, and Rutgers.[10]

---

7. See my *Judaism and Hellenism*.

8. Sukenik, *Ancient Synagogues*; Goodenough, *Jewish Symbols*, II, 70–100; Kraeling, *Dura: Synagogue*.

9. See the following studies by Kraabel: "Judaism in Western Asia Minor"; "*Hypsistos* and the Synagogue at Sardis," 81–93; "Melito and the Synagogue at Sardis," 77–85; "Paganism and Judaism," 13–33; "Diaspora Synagogue," 477–510; "Jews in Imperial Rome," 41–58; "Social Systems of Diaspora Synagogues," 79–91; "Excavated Synagogues," 227–36; "Roman Diaspora: Six Assumptions," 445–64; "Impact of the Discovery," 178–90; "*Synagoga Caeca*," 219–46; "Unity and Diversity," 49–60; (and A. Seager), "Synagogue and Jewish Community," 178–90. Many of these studies have been collected in a festschrift in his honor; see Overman and MacLennan, *Diaspora Jews and Judaism*.

10. *Hengel*: "Proseuche und Synagoge," 27–54; "Synagogeninschrift von Stobi," 110–48. *Seager*: "Building History," 425–35; "Architecture of Dura and Sardis Synagogues," 149–93; "Synagogue at Sardis," 178–84; "Recent Historiography," 39–47; (and A. T. Kraabel), "Synagogue and Jewish Com-

The increased activity in the study of the ancient synagogue has been facilitated by an ever growing corpus of scholarly aides. Recent decades have witnessed the appearance of convenient handbooks on ancient synagogues, such as those of Saller, Chiat, and Ilan.[11] Up-to-date summaries of archeological finds have been made available in the *New Encyclopedia of Archaeological Excavations in the Holy Land*,[12] as well as in a collection of rabbinic material relating to synagogue sites by Hüttenmeister and Reeg.[13] Hachlili's volumes, *Ancient Jewish Art and Archaeology in the Land of Israel* (1988) and *Ancient Jewish Art and Archaeology in the Diaspora* (1998), provide a broad overview of synagogue material, particularly the artistic dimension, and, in effect, serve in many ways to update Goodenough's major work. Several computer data bases have made much of rabbinic literature available on-line;[14] in recent years at least eleven volumes of essays on the ancient synagogue have appeared, offering overviews of the subject and detailed studies of the synagogue in its many manifestations.[15]

The appearance of basic compendia is nowhere more evident than in the field of epigraphy. A number of important corpora have appeared over the past twenty years: Naveh's collection of Hebrew and Aramaic inscriptions from Palestine, *On Stone and Mosaic* (1978), Roth-Gerson's *Greek Inscriptions from Ancient Synagogues in Eretz-Israel* (1987), the volumes of Horbury and Noy mentioned above, as well as Kant's discussion of ancient Jewish inscriptions in Greek and Latin in his "Jewish Inscriptions in Greek and Latin" (1987).

Finally, new synagogue-related fields have emerged. Of cardinal importance are the studies on ancient Jewish mysticism. Many of the compositions contain prayers and incantations identical (or almost identical) to prayers known from synagogue liturgy. What the precise relation was between these mystical circles, the rabbis, and the actual synagogue prayers at the time is far from certain, but some sort of tie clearly seems to have existed.

---

munity," 168–78. *Foerster:* "Survey of Diaspora Synagogues," 164–71; "Synagogue at Corinth," 185; "Synagogue in Leptis Magna," 53–58. *Ovadiah:* "Ancient Synagogues in Asia Minor," 857–66; "Ancient Synagogues from Magna Grecia," 9–20. *White:* "Delos Synagogue Revisited," 133–60; *Building God's House*, 60–101. *Feldman:* "Diaspora Synagogues," 48–66. *Rutgers:* "Diaspora Synagogues," 67–95. Mention should also be made of Trebilco's *Jewish Communities*, which, while not dealing with the synagogue per se, still contains an enormous amount of relevant material.

11. Saller, *Catalogue of Ancient Synagogues;* Chiat, *Handbook of Synagogue Architecture;* Z. Ilan, *Ancient Synagogues.*

12. E. Stern, *NEAEHL.*

13. Hüttenmeister and Reeg, *Antiken Synagogen.*

14. *Bar-Ilan University Responsa Project; Davka CD-ROM Judaic Classics Library.*

15. L. Levine, *Ancient Synagogues Revealed;* idem, *Synagogue in Late Antiquity;* Gutmann, *Dura-Europos Synagogue;* idem, *The Synagogue;* idem, *Ancient Synagogues;* Oppenheimer et al., *Synagogues in Antiquity;* Z. Safrai, *Ancient Synagogue;* Hachlili, *Ancient Synagogues in Israel;* Klil-Hahoresh, *Synagogues;* Urman and Flesher, *Ancient Synagogues;* Fine, *Sacred Realm.*

Another important field in synagogue-related studies is Jewish magic. Beginning with the publication of *Sepher Ha-Razim* in 1966 by Margalioth and continuing with the volumes by Naveh and Shaked (*Amulets and Magical Bowls: Aramaic Incantations of Late Antiquity*, 1985; *Magic Spells and Formulae: Aramaic Incantations of Late Antiquity*, 1993), the scholarly world has been presented with a convenient collection of Jewish magical material from late antiquity. To these we must add the texts on magic from the Genizah of late antiquity edited by Schiffman and Swartz (*Hebrew and Aramaic Incantation Texts from the Cairo Genizah*, 1992).

Despite this prodigious display of research, almost all these studies have been directed to one or another specific field of research: archeology, liturgy, epigraphy, art history, etc. Most are highly specialized, concentrating on a particular dimension of the synagogue or on a particular type of evidence.[16] The aim of the present study is to integrate the data from these various fields into a comprehensive account of this pivotal Jewish institution as a whole over a thousand-year period. It is an attempt to trace the synagogue's growth and development from a wide variety of perspectives in light of the forces at play within the Jewish community and impacting upon it from without.

---

16. An exception to the above are the integrative studies regarding sacred space that have recently appeared; see Branham, "Sacred Space under Erasure"; idem, "Vicarious Sacrality"; Fine, *This Holy Place.*

part I THE HISTORICAL DEVELOPMENT
OF THE SYNAGOGUE

two ORIGINS

Determining the origin and early development of the synagogue has presented modern scholarship with a seemingly insurmountable challenge. As often happens with institutions, movements, and ideas of revolutionary proportions, the forces which shape new initiatives, especially in their embryonic stages, remain shrouded in mystery. For a period of time these initiatives crystallize outside the limelight of history, only to appear later in our sources in a relatively developed form. Such, indeed, was the case with the ancient synagogue. Despite our understandable interest in knowing when such an institution first appeared, what factors were decisive in its development, who was responsible for it, and where exactly this "creation" took place, the sources at our disposal are oblivious to these issues—either because they are not as historically oriented as we would have wished or perhaps because these early formative stages simply were not worthy of comment at the time.

The earliest "hard" evidence we have for the existence of a synagogue appears in a number of inscriptions from Ptolemaic Egypt which mention a *proseuche*, commencing with the third century B.C.E. To date, about twelve such inscriptions and papyri have been discovered from the Hellenistic period, and the earliest archeological remains of a synagogue building on the island of Delos in the Aegean indicate a late second-century or possibly mid-first-century B.C.E. date of construction.[1]

---

1. For a detailed presentation of the evidence, see below, Chap. 4.

It is not until the first century C.E. that the synagogue emerges into the full light of history as the central communal institution of Jewish communities throughout Judaea and the Diaspora. Major cities, such as Jerusalem, Alexandria, Rome, and probably Antioch, boasted a number of such institutions, not to speak of villages, towns, and cities throughout the Roman Empire, which undoubtedly had at least one. The number and range of both literary and archeological sources referring to the synagogue at this time are indeed impressive.[2]

The existence of a *proseuche* in third-century B.C.E. Egypt indicates that the synagogue's roots in the Diaspora go back at least to this time. But how far back can we assume the institution's existence in either the Diaspora or Judaea? Are we to follow this evidence alone and posit a Ptolemaic Egyptian origin? Or are we to assume a history of several hundred years, back to the Exilic or Restoration periods? Or perhaps even earlier, to First Temple times?

STATE OF RESEARCH

As might be expected, the theories propounded to explain the emergence of the synagogue range far and wide. Some scholars date its origins as early as the ninth or eighth century B.C.E., and some look to the late seventh century. Most have opted for either a sixth-century date, at the time of the Babylonian exile, or a fifth-century date and a Judaean setting, wherein the synagogue emerged as an outgrowth of the reforms of Ezra and Nehemiah. Still others posit dates ranging from the fourth down to the first centuries B.C.E. This wide spectrum of opinion differs not only chronologically, but also geographically. Some place the first appearance of the synagogue in a Babylonian or Egyptian setting, while others assume that Judaea provided the original social and religious context.

The reasons for this variety of opinions are many. First and foremost, of course, is the sheer absence of data. With no clear-cut references at hand, the only recourse has been to speculate on the time, place, and reasons for the synagogue's emergence. Such efforts have been guided by one or more of the following considerations: (1) determining a major event in Jewish history which may have given rise to such a new and revolutionary institution; (2) discovering a reference in the Bible which may point to the existence of a framework that can be termed a protosynagogue or a synagogue-in-the-making; (3) construing the absence of references to synagogues, particularly in Judaean literature of the Hellenistic period, as an indication of a late date of origin there; (4) following only the hard evidence, i.e., that of third-century B.C.E. Egypt or first-century C.E. Palestine, as the decisive factor in accounting for origins.

Secondly, it is not always clear what is meant by the term "synagogue" and, consequently, what characteristics and developments ought to determine its time and place

---

2. See below, Chaps. 3–5.

of origin. As noted above, the term can be taken to refer to a congregation, a group of people (*qahal* or *'edah* [קהל, עדה] in the Septuagint, Ben Sira, and *targumim*), or a building.[3] And even if congregation is meant, the "synagogue of Ḥasidim" (συναγωγὴ Ασιλαίων— I Macc. 2:42) and the "synagogue of scribes" (συναγωγὴ γραμματέων—ibid., 7:12) were probably no more than groups of like-minded pious individuals, thus rendering the term "synagogue" here meaningless for our purposes. On the other hand, a building qua build-ing also might not be an adequate indication, for many different settings could have been used for a synagogue: a public building built expressly for the purpose, a multipurpose communal building, a residence, or part of a private home converted for public use. Alter-natively, perhaps the synagogue should be defined on the basis of its functions, status, or role within a community.

Thirdly, how does one define the essential nature of this institution at its beginning? Was the nascent synagogue primarily a social-communal institution, or was it, first and foremost, a religious one? And if the latter function was considered primary, which par-ticular religious activity was focal—listening to a prophet? praying? fasting? reading the Torah?

Fourthly, how does one define the emergence of the synagogue, or of any other in-stitution, for that matter? Is this to be determined by the first appearance of any of the aforementioned activities? If so, then what about the issue of continuity? Perhaps a par-ticular phenomenon surfaced in an early context but then disappeared for a long period of time, leaving no trace in Jewish religious practice other than an isolated literary ref-erence? For example, could the Torah-reading ceremony described in Neh. 8–10 be con-sidered the beginning of the synagogue, since it may have been the origin of the practice of Torah-reading? Or was the ceremony of Ezra and Nehemiah only a onetime occur-rence conducted under very special circumstances? The Torah-reading ceremony of the later synagogue, then, would have been the outcome of other factors, with the earlier setting serving, at best, as some sort of historical precedent for a later development.

Finally, one is faced with the issue of whether to place credence in later rabbinic tradi-tions. What should one make of the rabbinic claims that the *miqdash me'at* of Ezek. 11:16 and the *ma'on* (מעון, "dwelling place") of Ps. 90:1 are indeed evidence for the synagogue's existence?[4] Such traditions are of highly questionable value to begin with and are even more compromised by the contradictory claims made throughout rabbinic literature re-garding the origins of several fundamental synagogue practices. For example, various sources maintain that the weekly scriptural readings originated with either Moses, a body

---

3. See above, Chap. 1; and *TDNT*, VII, 802–10.

4. B Megillah 29a. See also the reference in Pesiqta Rabbati 26 (p. 129b) to the prophet Zephaniah preaching in the synagogue, as Jeremiah did in the marketplace and as Ḥuldah did to the women. So, too, with regard to the *targumim*, which frequently associate biblical figures with the synagogue; see, for example, Targum Jonathan of Ex. 18:12; Judg. 5:9, as well as the *targumim* of I Chr. 16:31 and Is. 1:13.

of prophets and elders, the Men of the Great Assembly, a group of former prophets, or early Ḥasidim.[5] With regard to the *'Amidah*, various claims have been made that this prayer originated with the biblical Patriarchs, Moses, a group of 120 elders and prophets, or the Yavnean Simeon Hapaquli.[6] In view of these disparate notions, it seems certain that such traditions are little more than anachronistic musings, perhaps for homiletical purposes, and are of little historical worth.

Given such a formidable array of issues, it should come as no surprise that the theories regarding synagogue origins are diverse and, at times, far afield. In the absence of explicit references, scholars have clutched at any and all hints and allusions, utilizing them as evidence for the institution's emergence. The more important of these theories may be briefly summarized.[7]

An increasing number of scholars over the past several decades have focused on the later First Temple period as the context for synagogue origins. Several have pointed to Solomon's references to the Temple as a place of prayer, others to the custom of regularly visiting a prophet on the Sabbath and New Moon.[8] Of greater attraction has been the presumed impact of Josiah's reforms in 621 B.C.E., which prohibited worship in shrines and altars outside Jerusalem. This is considered by many to have been the crucial factor which led to the creation of a new religious framework based on non-sacrificial worship.[9] Finally, the use of certain terms, such as *bet ha'am* (בית העם, Jer. 39:8) and *mo'ade el* (מועדי אל, Ps. 74:8), have also been invoked to substantiate a pre-Exilic date of origin.[10]

---

5. *Moses:* Y Megillah 4, 1, 75a. *Prophets and elders:* Mekhilta of R. Ishmael, Beshalaḥ, 1 (p. 154); Mekhilta de R. Šimʿon b. Jochai, Beshalaḥ 15:22 (p. 103). *Great Assembly:* B Berakhot 33a. *Former prophets:* Sifre-Deuteronomy 343 (p. 395). *Ḥasidim:* Midrash on Psalms 17:4 (p. 64a).

6. *Biblical patriarchs:* B Berakhot 26b; Midrash Hagadol, Genesis 19:27, 28:11 (pp. 324, 498). *Moses:* Y Berakhot 7, 11c; Y Megillah 3, 8, 74c; Midrash on Psalms 19:22 (p. 82b). *120 elders, prophets, and Simeon Hapaquli:* B Megillah 17b–18a.

7. For useful surveys regarding the origins of the synagogue, see Weingreen, "Origin of the Synagogue," 68–84; Rowley, *Worship*, 213–45; Hruby, *Synagoge*, 19–30; Gutmann, "Origin of the Synagogue," 36–40; idem, "Synagogue Origins," 1–6; L. Levine, "Second Temple Synagogue," 8–10; and the recent Hachlili, "Origin of the Synagogue: A Reassessment."

8. I Kgs. 8; II Kgs. 4:23; Finkelstein, "Origin of the Synagogue," 49–59; idem, *Pharisees*, 563; Weingreen, "Origin of the Synagogue," 68–84; I. Levy, *Synagogue*, 12. See also Levenson, "From Temple to Synagogue," 143–66.

9. Morgenstern, "Origin of the Synagogue," 192ff.; Weingreen, "Origin of the Synagogue," 68–84; Weinfeld, *Deuteronomy*, 44. Some have argued that the synagogue was a presupposition of Josiah's reforms (von Waldow, "Origin of the Synagogue Reconsidered," 269–84); others have opined that it was a consequence of them (Wellhausen, *Geschichte*, 184). Yet other scholars claim to have discerned early sermons and catechetical instruction in the books of Jeremiah and Deuteronomy; Judaean and Babylonian settings have also been suggested (Nicholson, *Preaching to the Exiles*).

10. So, for example, Löw, *Gesammelte Schriften*, IV, 5ff.; idem, "Synagogale Rituus," 97ff. See also Donner, "Argumente zur Datierung des 74. Psalms," 41–50; Gelston, "Note on Psalm lxxiv 8," 82–86; Rowley, *Worship*, 218–21 and literature cited there; and, for vigorous reservations, Haran, "Priest, Temple and Worship," 181 n. 11.

A second approach, which, as noted, has been preferred by most scholars over the years, places the origin of the synagogue in a sixth-century Babylonian Exilic setting.[11] The destruction of the First Temple and the subsequent exile have been viewed as traumatic and decisive factors leading to the creation of an alternative form of religious worship. The gathering of elders to hear the words of the prophet (Ezek. 8:1; 14:1) and, to a lesser extent, the later rabbinic interpretation of Ezekiel's " 'lesser' or 'diminished' sanctuary" (B Megillah 29a) as referring to the synagogue have been invoked to substantiate this dating.[12]

Another view regards the Restoration period, particularly the activities of Ezra and Nehemiah in fifth-century Jerusalem, as the time of the synagogue's beginnings.[13] Given the centrality of the Torah-reading and its concomitant exposition in a later synagogue context, some have viewed the public reading of the Torah by Ezra in the month of Tishri, 444 B.C.E., as the catalyst in the emergence of the synagogue. Proponents of this view often seek support by invoking later rabbinic traditions which view the age of Ezra as the critical period in the development of synagogue liturgy.[14]

Over the past century, scholarly opinion has generally been divided over these last three options: a seventh-century B.C.E. date focusing on the Josianic reforms, a sixth-century Babylonian Exilic venue, or a fifth-century B.C.E. Jerusalem Torah-reading framework. All three relate to the synagogue primarily as a religious institution, the first two as a worship context (prayer, prophetic discourse) in lieu of sacrifices, the last as a liturgical-scriptural context, with the Torah-reading ceremony serving as its focus.

Another event sometimes invoked as a catalyst for the creation of the synagogue is the desecration of the Temple by King Manasseh in the course of his reign (687-642 B.C.E.; II Kgs. 21:4-7). It is assumed that under these circumstances alternative secretive religious frameworks were sought (Finkelstein, "Origin of the Synagogue," 52-53). See also Janssen, who, in *Juda in der Exilszeit*, 156ff., opines that the beginnings of the synagogue may have been in the meetings of prophetic disciples in the pre-Exilic period.

11. A view already propounded by the tenth-century Sherira Gaon of Pumbeditha (Iggeret Rav Sherira Gaon [pp. 72ff.]; see also Gutmann, "Sherira Gaon," 209-12) and by Sigonio in the sixteenth century in his *De republica Hebraeorum* (63ff.; reprinted in Ugolino, *Thesauris antiquitatum sacrarum*, IV, p. ccxci). See also Schürer, *History*, II, 426; Wellhausen, *Geschichte*, 196ff.; Bacher, "Synagogue," 619; Elbogen, *Jewish Liturgy*, 189; Herford, *Pharisees*, 89-91; S. Krauss, *Synagogale Altertümer*, 52-66; G. F. Moore, *Judaism*, I, 283; Baron, *Jewish Community*, I, 59-63, 73; idem, *Social and Religious History of the Jews*, I, 126; Landsberger, "House of the People," 153-54; Janssen, *Juda in der Exilszeit*; Rowley, *Worship*, 224-25; Sandmel, *Judaism and Christian Beginnings*, 143; Shanks, *Judaism in Stone*, 21ff.; Levenson, "From Temple to Synagogue," 143-66.

12. Another line of argument dates the synagogue to sixth-century Judaea, associating it with either the fast days then being commemorated (Zech. 8) or the institution of the *ma'amadot*, assumed by some to have crystallized around that time (Landman, "Origin of the Synagogue," 322-25). On the *ma'amadot*, see below.

13. Mentioned as a possibility by both Schürer (*History*, II, 426) and Bacher ("Synagogue," 619), but advocated by S. Safrai ("Synagogue," 909-13) and M. Smith ("Jewish Religious Life," 258-60). See also Weinfeld, "Biblical Roots," 547-63.

14. Y Megillah 4, 1, 75a; B Bava Qama 82a; B Megillah 3a. See also Elbogen, *Jewish Liturgy*, 191-92.

Whatever their popularity, these options far from exhaust the scope and variety of views on the subject, particularly in recent decades. In 1931, Zeitlin proposed a fourth-century setting, viewing the synagogue primarily as a communal institution, as indicated by its name, *synagoge* (place of assembly). According to Zeitlin, the inhabitants of the towns and villages in Persian-Hellenistic Judaea would congregate to discuss communal affairs; these "town meetings," at first convened primarily for social and political purposes, gradually assumed a religious stamp under Pharisaic influence.[15] A similar idea had already been put forth by Löw, although he himself dated the synagogue's emergence to the First Temple period.[16]

More recently, Hengel has argued for a Hellenistic Egyptian setting.[17] Following a line of argument articulated earlier by Bousset, Gressmann, Friedländer, and others,[18] Hengel bases his claim on several considerations. First of all, he follows the existing evidence, namely, that the first clear-cut indication of the existence of synagogues appears in inscriptions from third-century B.C.E. Hellenistic Egypt. Secondly, he argues that the synagogue community was, in fact, a Jewish form of the Hellenistic religious association prevalent in Ptolemaic Egypt. The emergence of the synagogue, then, was not only an outcome of developments within the Jewish community, but also the product of forces from without.

Griffiths carried Hengel's argument one step further, claiming an Egyptian origin for the synagogue on the basis of architectural and functional parallels between the Egyptian Jewish *proseuche* and Egyptian pagan temples.[19] Beyond citing various parallels meticulously enumerated by Dion some years earlier,[20] e.g., the existence of a *pylon* (i.e., gateway) at the entrance to the building, a double colonnade, an adjacent grove, its status as a place of asylum, Griffiths points to the association of a place of worship with a place of learning—*Per Ankh*, "the House of Life," a library and place of special rites)—a feature which he claims links the Egyptian and Jewish institutions.[21]

---

15. Zeitlin, *Studies*, 1-13 (= "Origin of the Synagogue," 69-81). A variation of Zeitlin's approach is offered in Landman, "Origin of the Synagogue," 317-25. Zeitlin (*Studies*, 7) dates the book of Esther to this period and associates the word כנס, which appears only here in biblical literature, with the synagogue (*bet knesset*).

16. See above, note 10.

17. Hengel, "Proseuche und Synagoge," 161-80 (= Gutmann, *Synagogue*, 31-50).

18. According to Bousset and Gressmann (*Religion des Judentums*, 172) and Friedländer (*Synagoge und Kirche*, 56ff.), the synagogue first appeared in the Diaspora, i.e., Egypt, in the pre-Hasmonean period.

19. Griffiths, "Egypt and the Rise of the Synagogue," 1-15.

20. Dion, "Synagogues et temples," 45-75.

21. The weakness of Griffiths' argument is not only due to the very limited evidence available for Egyptian temples. Even if one were to suppose that the *Per Ankh* served as a place of instruction, it appears to have been confined to priestly circles. On this institution as a priestly framework for medical and cultic education, see Grabbe, *Judaism*, I, 95. This is indeed a far cry from the weekly scriptural readings of the Jewish community in the *proseuche*. Moreover, such a suggestion ignores any earlier tra-

Returning to a Judaean setting, Rivkin has suggested that the synagogue was a creation
of the Pharisees in the Hasmonean era.[22] Given the far-ranging upheavals within Jewish society resulting from a successful revolt and the attainment of political sovereignty
several decades later, Rivkin argued that the synagogue reflects many of the new trends
in Hasmonean society: Pharisaic ascendancy, emerging individualism, and democratiza-
tion. Furthermore, he has tried to turn the absence of any prior concrete data regarding
the synagogue in Judaea to his advantage, asserting that Ben Sira's failure to mention a
synagogue at the beginning of the second century B.C.E. is a telling indication that such
an institution did not exist at that time. Ben Sira's description of contemporary Jewish
religious leadership and institutions is so detailed, he claims, as to validate this *argumentum ex silentio.*

Also relying heavily on the silence of Hellenistic Jewish sources, Grabbe revived a suggestion made earlier by, inter alia, Jost, Zunz, and Friedländer, namely, that the Judaean
synagogue is a late, post-Maccabean phenomenon.[23] Since the Judaean synagogue is attested only in the late first century B.C.E., at the very earliest, Grabbe concludes that the
institution itself is a post-Maccabean phenomenon.

Indeed, both Jewish and pagan sources of this period fail to mention the existence of
a synagogue. None of the authors who describe Jewish society during the Hellenistic era
notes the existence of such an institution—neither Hecataeus of Abdera, Manetho, nor
Mnaseas of Patara.[24] Agatharchides (second century B.C.E.), in his description of religious practices in the Jerusalem Temple, observes the following:

> The people known as Jews, who inhabit the most strongly fortified of cities, called by the
> natives Jerusalem, have a custom of abstaining from work every seventh day; on those occa-
> sions they neither bear arms nor take any agricultural operations in hand, nor engage in any
> other form of public service, but pray with outstretched hands in the temples until the eve-
> ning.[25]

The above reference to "temples" ($\tau o \hat{\iota} s \ \dot{\iota} \epsilon \rho o \hat{\iota} s$) has been interpreted by some to mean
synagogues. However, it is more likely that the reference was indeed to the Jerusalem
Temple and that the use of the plural here was inadvertent; pagan writers would have

---

ditions which the Jews might have brought with them from Judaea regarding the reading of Scriptures,
e.g., Deuteronomy or Neh. 8. See in this regard the interesting remark of Hecataeus, that the high priest
Ezekias read to his friends from Scriptures which he brought from Judaea to Egypt in the late fourth
century (Josephus, *Against Apion* 1, 187-89, and comments in Kasher, *Josephus, Against Apion*, I, 179-81).

22. Rivkin, "Ben Sira and the Non-Existence of the Synagogue," 320-48. This approach has also been
adopted by Gutmann, "Synagogue Origins," 3-4.

23. Jost, *Geschichte des Judenthums*, III, 136; Zunz, *Gottesdienstlichen Vorträge der Juden*, 3; Friedländer,
Synagoge und Kirche, 53ff. (noting the synagogue's first appearance in Judaea); Grabbe, "Synagogues in
Pre-70 Palestine," 401-10; idem, *Judaism*, II, 529.

24. See M. Stern, *Greek and Latin Authors*, passim.

25. Ibid., I, 107. See also S. J. D. Cohen, "Pagan and Christian Evidence," 161-62.

considered the use of the plural, "temples," most natural. In any case, a religious setting in Jerusalem at that time could only have been the Temple, and praying all day with outstretched hands is rather unusual and would make some sense, if at all, in the Temple and not a synagogue setting. The only other possibility is that Agatharchides was referring to certain Diaspora synagogues, where Sabbath worship (but not necessarily praying with outstretched hands) might have lasted most of the day.[26] However, this was most unlikely, and thus a Temple setting was undoubtedly intended.

THE CITY-GATE AS SYNAGOGUE FORERUNNER

Having thus reviewed the more salient suggestions put forth by scholars regarding the origins of the ancient synagogue, I wish to propose a different approach.[27] In addressing this issue in the past, scholars have almost invariably tried to pinpoint a historical context or event which led to the emergence of this institution. Given the state of our sources or, more precisely, the lack of any solid evidence, such efforts have clearly become exercises in studied guesswork; as a result, prevailing theories on this subject have ranged over a period of more than eight hundred years.

The theories, with but few exceptions, share several assumptions: that the religious component of the ancient synagogue was primary and that dramatically new religious circumstances gave rise to this institution. Implicit in most of these theories is the view that some kind of liturgical activity, be it listening to God's word from a prophet, the recital of public prayer, or the introduction of scriptural readings, played a crucial and definitive role in the formation of the early synagogue. However, as noted at the outset of this chapter, in the formative stages of a new phenomenon there is very often no one moment marking a dramatic innovation. The synagogue may not have resulted from a crisis or a specific decision by any one person or community to initiate something boldly new. We may well be dealing with a much more subtle and gradual process, one that took place over decades, if not centuries, and at a different pace depending on the specific locale. Only at a later stage, when the synagogue had more or less crystallized, could one look back with the advantage of hindsight and say that a novel institution had indeed been created.

Thus, it may be helpful to revisit the question of origins from a different perspective. Instead of combing the earlier sources for clues regarding the time and place of the synagogue's origins, I would suggest a different starting point, namely, a period from which we have some solid evidence about what the synagogue was and how it functioned. Armed with what we know about the synagogue when it appears in the full light of history, we may then look to an earlier period and ask ourselves where those activities performed in the synagogue took place in earlier periods. We may then have some clue as to how, why,

---

26. See, for example, Philo's *Hypothetica* 7, 13; and below, Chap. 4.
27. See also L. Levine, "Nature and Origin," 425–48, here modified; see below.

and from where the institution referred to in the first century as a synagogue (or as a *pros-euche*, somewhat earlier in Egypt) first developed. A more sociological and institutional approach may thus be warranted in trying to understand the synagogue's origins rather than searching for a moment of religious crisis or innovation that sparked its creation.

Let us turn for a moment to the first-century C.E. synagogue. In the following chapters we will discuss the characteristic features of the Second Temple synagogue in detail. Suffice it to say for our present purposes that both the synagogue and the *proseuche* of this period were first and foremost communal institutions where the gamut of activities of any Jewish community found expression. As documented in contemporary sources, the building might have been used as a courtroom, school, or hostel, or for political meetings, social gatherings, keeping charity funds, slave manumissions, meals (sacred or otherwise), and, of course, religious-liturgical functions.[28]

On the assumption, then, that the first-century synagogue served as a center for a variety of communal as well as religious functions and activities, we now are in a position to look for the framework which served the same (or similar) purposes in earlier centuries. When seen in this light, it becomes clear that the setting for most, if not all, of these activities in previous eras was the city-gate, the main communal setting in cities and towns in the First Temple period.[29]

The city-gate as the focal point of communal activity is well attested in biblical and non-biblical literature.[30] It served as a marketplace (II Kgs. 7:1), as well as a setting where

---

28. See below, Chap. 5; and Horsley, *Galilee*, 222–33.

29. This suggestion was first broached by Silber in his doctoral thesis at the University of Denver and was summarized by the same author in a pamphlet entitled *Origin of the Synagogue* (1915). Silber, however, following Löw, dates this transition to the Solomonic period and further concludes that the synagogue was secular in origin, only later acquiring a distinct religious character. Decades later, the city-gate thesis was revisited by Hoenig ("Ancient City-Square," 448–76), who, however, confused the town square of Greco-Roman times with the city-gate of a Near Eastern setting (on this, see Ward-Perkins, *Cities of Ancient Greece and Italy*, 12) while freely utilizing later rabbinic material to supplement what little is known on the subject from pre-70 times. Moreover, much of his argument rests on the very problematic reading of *reḥov ha-ʿir* (רחוב העיר) in place of the not uncommon reference to *ḥever ha-ʿir* (חבר העיר) in rabbinic literature. See also Löw, *Gesammelte Schriften*, IV, 5ff.

On the city-gate in biblical times, see Köhler, *Hebräische Mensch*, 143–71; de Vaux, *Ancient Israel*, 152–53; *Encyclopaedia Biblica*, VIII, 231; Frick, *City in Ancient Israel*, 78–91; Kenyon, *Royal Cities*, 57–61; and esp. Fritz, *City in Ancient Israel*, 35–37, 138–40.

30. *CAD*, A/1, 82–88, s.v. "abullu"; ibid., B, 19–20, s.v. "babu"; Frick, *City in Ancient Israel*, 83–84, 114–27; *Encyclopaedia Biblica*, VIII, 232–36; McCown ("City," 634) has summarized the phenomenon thusly: "For the ancient Hebrew, the city gate was much more than a means of ingress and egress, much more than an important part of the city's defenses. It was also the 'center' (even though at one side) of the city's social, economic and judicial affairs." G. Evans (" 'Gates' and 'Streets,' " 1–12) has collected much valuable material in this regard: "A study of the texts in which the term appears shows clearly that the gate, together with the street which lay behind it, just within the walls, was a centre of political and legal

a ruler would hold court and where prophets would speak (I Kgs. 22:10; Jer. 38:7).[31] As
the gate was a popular meeting-place for public gatherings, a variety of communal activities were conducted there. So, for example, Hezekiah "appointed battle officers over
the people; then, gathering them to him in the square of the city-gate [רחוב שער העיר], he
rallied them" (II Chr. 32:6).[32] Those who came regularly to the gate were the populace
at large (see Ruth 3:11) and the town elders and leaders.[33] The transaction between Abraham and Ephron the Hittite took place at the city-gate (Gen. 23:10, 18), and a number of
legal documents from Nuzi conclude with the formula "the tablet was written after the
proclamation at the gate."[34]

Announcement of a settlement at the gate afforded it maximum publicity and signified
the assent of the entire community, and certain meals marking the fulfillment of a commandment were eaten there.[35] Moreover, prophetic activity often took place there so as
to reach the greatest number of people (Is. 29:21; Amos 5:10).

One of the primary events at the city-gate was judiciary.[36] City elders would assemble
there to dispense justice: "His father and mother shall take hold of him and bring him
out to the elders of his town at the public place [i.e., the gate] of his community" (Deut.
21:19; 17:5; 22:24; see also Ps. 69:13). The prophet Amos advised: "Hate evil and love
good, and establish justice at the gate" (5:15; see also Zech. 8:16).

The importance of the city-gate as a place for settling personal affairs in the presence
of the community is vividly reflected in Ruth 4:1-2: "Meanwhile, Boaz had gone to the
gate and sat down there. And now the redeemer whom Boaz had mentioned passed by.
He called, 'Come over and sit down here, So-and-so.' And he came over and sat down.
Then [Boaz] took ten elders of the town and said, 'Be seated here,' and they sat down."[37]
These ten elders (referred to by Speiser as "city-fathers") undoubtedly convened there

---

activity, as well as of trade. . . . the gate was the scene of many activities which, in a western city, were
carried on in a central square" (p. 1).

31. Other references to rebuking the people at the gates include Is. 29:21 and Amos 5:10. On the communal significance of the city-gate, see Eph'al and Naveh, "Jar of the Gate," 59-65.

32. On the discovery of such a square between the main and outer gates at the biblical site of Tel Dan,
see Biran, "Tel Dan: Five Years Later," 177; idem, "Dan," 327-31; and below, notes 41 and 42.

33. See Prov. 31:23: "Her husband is renowned at the city-gate [lit., gates], sitting with the elders of
the land." See also ibid., 31:31.

34. See, for example, Pfeiffer and Speiser, *Nuzi Texts*, 115. See also de Vaux, "Patriarches hébreux,"
25 and n. 1. The references to "gates" in Deut. 6:9 and 11:20 may mean city-gates; see Tigay, *Deuteronomy*, 79.

35. According to Deut. 26:12, the tithes given to the Levite, stranger, orphan, and widow on the third
year of a sabbatical cycle were to be eaten at the city-gate.

36. See McKenzie, "Judicial Procedure at the Town Gate," 100-104. For rabbinic interpretations of
biblical references to judicial proceedings at the city-gate, see HaLivni (Weiss), "Location of the Bet
Din," 181-91.

37. The concept of "ten" as a quorum appears in Josephus' description of the Essenes (*War* 2, 146), at
Qumran (CD 13, 1; 1QS 6:3; 6, 7; 10:14), and, of course, in later rabbinic literature (e.g., M Megillah 4:3).

regularly to officiate as judges, arbitrators, and witnesses to business transactions.[38] They were the civil judiciary—as opposed to the priestly judiciary of the Jerusalem Temple and the local sanctuaries.[39]

The gate as the "heart" of a city is also reflected in the fact that a conqueror might place his throne there as a sign of subjugation. Nebuchadnezzar's officers did so (Jer. 39:3) and thus fulfilled the prophet's dire prediction (ibid., 1:15-16): "For I am summoning all the peoples of the kingdoms of the north, declares the Lord. They shall come and shall each set up a throne before the gates of Jerusalem, against its walls round about and against all the towns of Judah. And I will argue my case against them for all their wickedness. They have forsaken me and sacrificed to other gods and worshiped the works of their hands."[40]

A king might sit at the city-gate to hear the people's grievances. So, for example, following Absalom's death, Joab urged David to terminate his mourning and to sit at the gate so that "all the people may come before the king" (II Sam. 19:8-9). On another occasion, Ahab, king of Israel, and Jehoshaphat, king of Judah, sat at the gate of Samaria prior to a battle in Gilead, summoning the prophets to support their venture (I Kgs. 22:10). Similarly, according to II Chr. 32:6, Hezekiah assembled the people at the city-gate in order to strengthen their resolve in the face of Sennacherib's imminent attack; a century or so later, we are told, Zedekiah also sat at a city-gate called Benjamin (Jer. 38:7).

Finally, the city-gate was also a place for performing religious functions. In the ancient Near East, people often gathered at the city-gate to worship gods, as is evidenced by the cultic objects found near the gates of Megiddo Va, Beersheba IV, and Tel Dan.[41] Regarding the latter site, Biran, following Barnett, notes the following about the city-gate as a possible place for holding religious ceremonies in antiquity: "We may consider this to be also a ceremonial route. This could depend to a certain extent on the interpretation of the unique structure found in the square between the outer and main gates. This structure is rectangular with an open space where a throne or pedestal was set. Two decorated column-bases were found in situ, a third in the debris and of the fourth only an imprint was left. . . . Our suggested reconstruction shows a canopied structure which could have served the king when he sat at the gate (e.g., II Kgs. 22:10) or it could have served as a pedestal for the statue of a god."[42]

---

38. As in the story of Abraham and Ephron in Gen. 23. See Speiser, "'Coming' and 'Going,'" 20-23; Reviv, "Early Elements and Late Terminology," 190-91; and, for a dissenting opinion, G. Evans, "'Coming' and 'Going,'" 28-33.

39. Weinfeld, *Deuteronomy*, 235. One of the gates of Jerusalem under Josiah was named after Joshua, governor of the city (II Kgs. 23:8).

40. On the meting out of punishment against an entire city, see Deut. 13:17.

41. See *NEAEHL*, I, 172 (Beersheba), 327-329 (Dan). On Megiddo, see Herzog, *Stadttor in Israel*, 164. On this subject generally, see Dever, *Recent Archaeological Discoveries*, 128-62.

42. Biran, "'To the God Who Is in Dan,'" 143; see also Barnett, "Bringing the God into the Temple," 10-20; and the recent Biran, *Biblical Dan*, 238-45. The role of the city-gate in religious processions and

In terms of explicit biblical evidence, II Kgs. 23:8 has the following to say about Josiah's reforms of 621 B.C.E.:

> He brought all the priests from the town of Judah [to Jerusalem] and defiled the shrines where the priests had been making offerings—from Geba to Beer-sheba. He also demolished the shrines of the gates, which were at the entrance of the gate of Joshua, the city prefect— which were on a person's left [as he entered] the city gate.

In the post-Exilic period, the area of the city-gate was utilized by Ezra and Nehemiah: "The entire people assembled as one man in the square before the Water Gate, and they asked Ezra the scribe to bring the scroll of the Teaching of Moses with which the Lord had charged Israel" (Neh. 8:1).

Archeological data confirm the fact that the biblical (i.e., Iron Age) gate was the site of many communal functions. In contrast to the early Middle Bronze Age II gate, which appears to have fulfilled much more of a defensive role, the twenty or so known Iron Age II gate complexes (ca. 1000–580 B.C.E.) differed significantly.[43] Whereas gates in the second millennium had rooms usually separated by partition walls that served as independent units, chambers of the Iron Age II opened onto the main passageway. These chambers were either two, four, or six in number, at times of a large size (in one instance, reaching 9 m. long), and often contained benches and stone water-basins.[44] These areas and, even more important, the adjacent open spaces usually inside but at times outside the gate (in which case there was often another circumvallating wall) provided the setting for the many civilian functions noted above.[45] A striking example of a complex gate system may be found at Tel Dan, where three gates (outer, main, and upper) were preceded by a paved square, a courtyard, and a royal processional way, respectively (fig. 1). The

---

ritual may well be reflected in the words of Ps. 24:7–9: "Lift up your heads, O gates . . . so the king of glory may come in."

43. The subject has been addressed over the past several decades by Herzog in a series of studies, first in Hebrew (*The City-Gate in Eretz-Israel and Its Neighboring Countries*), then in German translation (see above, note 41), and more recently in English ("Settlement and Fortification Planning in the Iron Age," 265–74; *Archaeology of the City*). See also E. Stern, "Hazor, Dor and Megiddo," 233–48.

44. Six-chambered gates have been discovered at Megiddo, Hazor, Gezer, Lachish, and Ashdod. Four-chambered gateways were found at Ashdod, Dan, Beersheba, Megiddo, and Dor, while two-chambered gateways were excavated at Dor, Mt. Gerizim, and Megiddo. See *NEAEHL*, passim; Fritz, *City in Ancient Israel*, 77–78 (Dan), 81 (Hazor), 88–96 (Megiddo), 104 (Lachish), 111 (Beersheba). See also E. Stern and Sharon, "Tel Dor, 1986," 203–7; and Magen, "Mount Gerizim," 73–76. On the controversial question, whether there are any chronological implications to the different-numbered chambers, see above, note 43.

On the earlier Mesopotamian gate and its development in the third to first millennia B.C.E., see Damerji, *Architecture of Doors and Gates*, 181–98.

45. See also *Encyclopaedia Biblica*, VIII, 237–43; and A. Mazar, *Archaeology of the Land of the Bible*, 467–70.

1. Model of the city-gate at Tel Dan (Tel Dan Museum).

latter two gates had four sentry rooms each. The entire network was built sometime in the ninth century B.C.E., presumably by Ahab.[46]

THE EMERGENCE OF THE SYNAGOGUE IN THE SECOND TEMPLE PERIOD

The results of recent and not-so-recent excavations indicate that a major change seems to have taken place in the gate area in the Hellenistic period. Traditions that had held sway for centuries were now being revised, in part owing to sustained and intensive contact with the Hellenistic world.[47] From the available data—and one must admit that the evidence here is fragmentary, at best—it is clear that Hellenistic gates had no accompanying rooms and usually no adjacent open area or square.[48] Instead, they were usually flanked—as earlier—by round or square towers. The gate itself was no more than

---

46. Biran, *Biblical Dan*, 235–53.

47. E. Stern, "Excavations at Tell Mevorakh," 17-27; idem, "Walls of Dor," 11-14; idem, *Dor*, 206-8; Sharon, "Fortification of Dor," 105-13; see also idem, "Local Traditions," 5. See also van Beek, "Canaanite-Phoenician Architecture," 70*-77*.

a passageway between these towers. This change may have been inspired by developments in Greek fortification systems in general, which themselves appear to have resulted from technological advances in the art of warfare, particularly the introduction of ballistae, catapults, and siege engines.[49]

While the gate area of third-century B.C.E. Marisa, on the southern coastal plain of Judaea, still boasted a square surrounded by buildings (an area evidently used for assorted religious, administrative, and military activities),[50] gate areas from other Hellenistic sites in Israel reflect this new design. So, for example, the gate at Dor changed dramatically, from the casemate-type wall, which had been in vogue for five hundred years, to a simpler Hellenistic style having no adjacent open areas, rooms, or separate buildings.[51] Hellenistic building techniques are also evidenced in the Hellenistic town of Samaria-Sebaste;[52] by the first century B.C.E., Herod used this Hellenistic gate model at both Sebaste and Caesarea (fig. 2).[53] Although meagerly preserved, the "Ginat" gate in Jerusalem, discovered by Avigad, may also reflect a similar Hellenistic model.[54]

On the basis of the above discussion, it therefore becomes evident that most of the activities carried out within the context of the first-century synagogue are already documented for the city-gate area in the First Temple period. By the Hellenistic period, the functions previously associated with the city-gate and adjacent square were relocated to a building that came to be known as a synagogue, a change required when the biblical city-gate complex was transformed from a center of urban activity into a simple, functional gate for entrance and exit.

An important caveat is in order here. A change in the function of the city-gate took place during the Hellenistic period at certain sites located primarily in the coastal area of Judaea and relate almost exclusively to the pagan cities of this region (e.g., Dor, Marisa).

---

48. Arav, *Settlement Patterns*, 159.

49. See Shatzman, "Ballistra Stones from Tel Dor," 94-104; Sharon, "Fortification of Dor," 105-13; and, more generally, Winter, *Greek Fortifications*, 222-33, 324-32. See also Shatzman, "Artillery in Judaea," 461-82.

50. Avi-Yonah and Kloner, "Maresha," 948-51. The transitional character of Hellenistic Marisa — with a heavy emphasis on its pre-Hellenistic oriental elements — is argued by G. Horowitz, "Town Planning of Hellenistic Marisa," 93-111.

51. E. Stern, *Excavations at Dor*, I, 277-78. See also idem, "Walls of Dor," 11-13; Sharon, "Phoenician and Greek Ashlar Construction Techniques," 21-42.

52. Crowfoot, Kenyon, and Sukenik, *Buildings in Samaria*, 24-27.

53. *Samaria-Sebaste:* Crowfoot, Kenyon, and Sukenik, *Buildings in Samaria*, 31, 39-41; Avigad, "Samaria (City)," 1307. On a round Hellenistic tower at Akko, similar to the one found at Samaria, see Dothan, "Fortifications of Ptolemais," 71-74. *Caesarea:* Frova, *Caesarea Maritima*, 249-71.

54. Avigad, *Discovering Jerusalem*, 50, 69; see also Arav, *Settlement Patterns*, 159. At times, a freestanding gate was built with no accompanying walls, as in first-century C.E. Tiberias; see *NEAEHL*, IV, 1470-71.

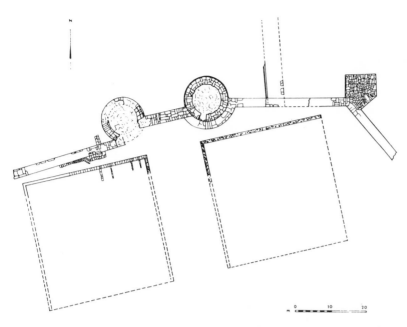

2. Plan of the northern city-gate of Herodian Caesarea.

Whether other parts of the country were similarly affected at this time is unknown. We lack any kind of significant archeological evidence for Jewish settlements in Judaea in the Persian and Hellenistic periods. The fact that Jerusalem had a wall at this time is amply documented (e.g., Neh. 2–3; Josephus, *War* 5, 142–55), and we already have had occasion to note that Ezra and Nehemiah gathered the people at the city's Water Gate for the public reading of Scriptures. Nevertheless, we have no inkling what this Jerusalem gate area might have looked like or if, in fact, it was a city-gate rather than one serving the Temple precincts. Other than for Jerusalem, we have no information regarding Judaean towns or villages.[55] It is quite possible that these places had no fortifications at this time and that communal activities were already taking place in some other outdoor framework or even inside a public building, i.e., a synagogue.[56]

The implications of the above discussion point to the fact that—in contrast to the *communis opinio*—the emergence of the Judaean synagogue was not the outcome of any specific event or crisis, but rather a gradual development during the Persian and Hellenis-

---

55. On the paucity of archeological material for this period, especially in the hinterland, and on Persia's general policy of limiting urban fortifications, see E. Stern, "Cities," 25–26; idem, "Fortifications," 327.

56. Here I am modifying the suggestion for a Hellenistic dating of the synagogue's origin argued in my article "Nature and Origin." The import of the lack of physical evidence for specifically Jewish centers was not fully realized then.

3. Remains of the Gamla synagogue abutting the city wall.

tic periods. It is impossible to offer a specific date for what was a process that transpired in various locales sometime between the fifth and first centuries B.C.E.[57]

What may be no more than a fortuitous indication of a synagogue setting continuing the earlier city-gate tradition (albeit not at that particular Hellenistic site) can be found in the structure at Gamla, which has been generally regarded as the earliest known synagogue building in Judaea, dating to the first century B.C.E. or the turn of the first century C.E. (fig. 3). This synagogue was located neither in the middle of the settlement nor on a particularly high spot, as were many village synagogues in the centuries following the destruction of the Temple. Rather, it was situated at the eastern edge of the town

---

57. The assumption that the synagogue evolved from a communal setting such as the biblical city-gate may also explain the association of the *ḥazzan* with this institution—at least as attested in later rabbinic sources. In the ancient Near East the *ḥazzan* functioned as a city administrator, a chief magistrate or mayor; he is also mentioned as a religious functionary in early antiquity, e.g., the Babylonian *ḥazzanu* of a temple, although this position appears to have been derivative. It is possible that the *ḥazzan*, who became a permanent fixture in the later synagogue, was formerly associated with a village or town (i.e., city-gate) context, but no explicit source makes this connection. On the *ḥazzanu* in the ancient Near East, see Weisberg, *Guild Structure*, 93; Kaufman, *Akkadian Influences*, 55; Menzel, *Assyrische Tempel*, I, 289; II, 232 nn. 3864–65; *CAD*, II, 163–65. For an example of the religious dimension of this term, see Waterman, *Royal Correspondence*, I, 254–55 (Letter 366).

between two main streets and near what was undoubtedly the entrance to the city.[58] Had Gamla existed centuries earlier, a city-gate area almost certainly would have been located there. The structure at Gamla perhaps preserves vestiges of the earlier tradition, while its synagogue fulfilled the functions performed earlier in the city-gate area.

BETWEEN CITY-GATE AND SYNAGOGUE

The Torah-reading ceremony, the central religious component of Second Temple synagogue ritual (see below, Chap. 5), may have taken place initially at the city-gate. When precisely this custom emerged as a common practice within the Jewish community is unknown. No Greek author of the Hellenistic period, nor any author of the apocryphal and pseudepigraphal books of the last centuries B.C.E., refers to such a practice; however, such an *argumentum ex silentio* is of limited value. References to any kind of institutional practice—even in the Jerusalem Temple—are not all that numerous for these centuries, and it is quite possible that for a long period of time the practice of reading the Torah may not have merited comment.

There are certainly enough biblical passages that might have influenced the development of the Torah-reading custom (e.g., Deut. 6:7; 31:9-13) or at least legitimized it ex post facto. Earlier theories have considered the original Torah-reading ceremony as either a polemic against undesirable foreign influences (Samaritans or Hellenism) or simply, following Deuteronomy, a means of teaching the ordinary Jew about his tradition and religion.[59] It has also been suggested that exposure to the Greek world and Greek models may have played a role in crystallizing or, alternatively, strengthening the communal Torah-reading ceremony (this may well have been the case in the Diaspora).[60]

Most scholars have considered the Torah-reading ceremony a substitute for Temple worship deriving from the Babylonian Diaspora.[61] In fact, however, it may well have developed parallel to, and not in opposition to or as a substitute for, the sacrificial cult; rather, it constituted an additional form of worship and increased communal participation. Indeed, the earliest reference we have to a Torah-reading ceremony is that of the

---

58. Gutman, "Synagogue at Gamla," 30-34; idem, "Gamala," 459-63. As can be seen at the site, the synagogue is located adjacent to the city fortifications. However, the latter were only added in the mid-first century C.E. in preparation for the war against Rome.

59. *Samaritans:* Büchler, "Reading of the Law and Prophets," 424. Similarly, Büchler regards the Hellenistic decrees referred to by Josephus as reflective of the Jewish-Samaritan controversy of the late Second Temple period; see idem, *Tobiaden und Oniaden,* 143-71. *Hellenism:* Leszynsky, *Sadduzäer,* 133ff. *Jewish tradition:* J. Mann, *Bible as Read,* I, 4: "Rather the positive aim and need of familiarizing the ordinary Jew on the leisure days of the Jewish calendar with a knowledge of his religion should be regarded as the main raison d'être of this institution." See also Elbogen, *Jewish Liturgy,* 130-31.

60. Kugel and Greer, *Early Biblical Interpretation,* 56.

61. Fishbane, *Biblical Interpretation,* 113.

maʿamadot, a local ceremony held when a region's priests (and other lay representatives) officiated in the Temple during an assigned week.[62] According to the Mishnah—a late source for our purposes but, in this instance, clearly reflecting Second Temple practice—a portion of the Scriptures was read publicly in the town or village on each day of that week: "The ordinary Jews [non-priests and non-Levites] associated with each priestly division would gather in their towns and read [the sciptural section dealing with] the creation story [Gen. 1–2:4]."[63]

This mishnah is valuable to our discussion on three counts: (1) it attests to the early practice of Torah-reading in a local setting;[64] (2) it tells us that the reading was performed by those unable to participate in the Temple worship in Jerusalem; (3) a synagogue per se is not mentioned, but a general reference is made to gathering in "towns." Although later renditions of this tradition, followed by most commentators, freely introduce the notion that these scriptural readings took place in the local synagogue,[65] such interpretations are wholly gratuitous. The mishnah mentions only "towns," and the specific *Sitz im Leben* may have been the city-gate area or some other public space.[66]

---

62. On the division into twenty-four courses of priests, Levites, and Israelites, see Schürer, *History*, II, 245–50; S. Safrai, *Pilgrimage*, 217–20; Sperber, "Mishmarot and Maʿamadot," 89–93; see also Elbogen, *Jewish Liturgy*, 190–92. On the formative period of this institution, see also Liver, *History of the Priests and Levites*, 33–52, esp. pp. 49–52. On one of the Temple roles of the head of a *maʿamad*, see M Tamid 5:6 (cf. also M Sotah 1:5).

63. M Taʿanit 4:2; see comments by Albeck, *Mishnah*, II, 495–96. At first glance, there seems to be little connection between the reading of the creation story and the Temple service. Two possible explanations come to mind.

1. The association may derive from the apparent connection between the building of the Tabernacle (Ex. 25–40) and the creation story, on the one hand, i.e., the subdivision of the former into seven parts (six dealing with creation and the last with the Sabbath law), and, on the other hand, the completion of the Tabernacle on New Year's Day (Ex. 40:17). In other verses as well there is an association of the Sabbath with the Temple (Lev. 19:30; 26:2). Such a connection—already made in rabbinic sources—may also explain why the period of service for each priestly course extended from Sabbath to Sabbath, reminiscent of the week of creation. See Cassuto, *Commentary on Exodus*, 334–35, 447ff.; Sarna, *Exploring Exodus*, 196–220.

2. In rabbinic literature, there is a tradition that the creation of the world began on the Temple Mount, on its foundation stone (אבן השתייה). In addition, a related tradition speaks of Adam being created from the dust of the Temple Mount, where he was later buried. The Christians knew of this tradition and subsequently transferred Adam's burial spot to Golgotha, in reaction to which later rabbinic sources claim he was buried in the Cave of Machpelah in Hebron. See Ginzberg, *Legends of the Jews*, I, 12; V, 14–16, 125–26; Gafni, "Pre-Histories of Jerusalem," 10–16. See also Terrien, "Omphalos Myth," 315–38.

64. The division into *maʿamadot* was already known to the author of I Chronicles (24:1–18) in the fourth or third century B.C.E., and the customs described in the mishnah may well have crystallized as early as this time.

65. See, for example, B Taʿanit 27b. See also Albeck, *Mishnah*, II, 341; Schürer, *History*, II, 293.

66. Many scholars have viewed the *maʿamadot* ceremony as the setting from which the synagogue as

Of particular interest in the above-cited mishnah is the fact that the local Torah-reading ceremony of the *ma'amad* was clearly parallel to the Temple ritual, a substitute for those unable to be in Jerusalem. In the past, the emergence or evolution of the synagogue during the Second Temple period has often been viewed as competitive with the development of the Jerusalem Temple. Many have characterized the synagogue as a "Pharisaic" institution that emerged in response to the Sadducean-run Temple.[67] However, the Phar-

---

we know it emerged. See, for example, Hruby, *Synagoge*, 16–17; Bowker, *Targums and Rabbinic Literature*, 9–10; Zeitlin, *Rise and Fall of the Judaean State*, I, 179; Petuchowski, "Liturgy of the Synagogue," 46.

Another early rabbinic tradition which may have a bearing on the role of a public area in the Second Temple period is found in M Bikkurim 3:2, where the following ritual of bringing firstfruits to the Temple is described: "How do they bring up [to Jerusalem] the firstfruits? All the villages in the [area of the] *ma'amad* gather together in the *ma'amad*'s city and lodge in the city square [plaza or gate area, רחובה של עיר] and they would not enter the houses and early in the morning the person in charge would say, 'Let us arise and go up to Zion, to [the house of] the Lord our God'" (Jer. 31:5). Perhaps of significance is the fact that the Tosefta (Bikkurim 2:8 [p. 292]) speaks of the *ḥazzanim* of the synagogue accompanying the processions to Jerusalem.

Finally, the mishnaic tradition of public fast-day ceremonies conducted in the public square may also have a bearing on the question at hand (M Ta'anit 2; T Ta'anit 1:8–13 [pp. 325–28]; and later parallels). However, the specific literary tradition that has been preserved appears to be a second-century C.E. version, to wit, the mention of a *Nasi* and *av bet din*, the recitation of an elaborate 'Amidah prayer (M Ta'anit 2:2–4), and the reference to a specific incident and specific personalities of this time (ibid., 2:5; T Ta'anit 1:13 [pp. 327–28]).

67. The list of scholars making this assumption is long and impressive. For a sampling, see Herford, *Pharisees*, 88–109; R. M. Grant, *Historical Introduction to New Testament*, 274–75; Hengel, *Judaism and Hellenism*, I, 82; idem, *Paul*, 57; Hengel and Deines, "Sanders' 'Common Judaism,'" 32–33; Gutmann, "Synagogue Origins," 4; Hanson, *The People Called*, 353. Flesher ("Palestinian Synagogues," 68–69) has similarly posited a sharp contrast between the priestly Temple cult and the synagogue, although without Pharisaic-Sadducean overtones. Cf., however, Saldarini, *Pharisees, Scribes and Sadducees*, 52–53; Grabbe, "Synagogues in Pre-70 Palestine," 408–9; Herford, *Pharisees*, 88–103; G. F. Moore, *Judaism*, 286–87; Finkelstein, *Pharisees*, 568–69; and Perrot, "Reading of the Bible," 150. Given the assumed spiritual prominence of the Pharisees in Jewish life of the Second Temple period and the universality of the synagogue as a religious institution, it was more than natural in the past to posit Pharisaic dominance and influence over the synagogue. In no small part, the polemics of the New Testament were responsible for this misconception, pitting Jesus against the Pharisees, often in a synagogal context (Matt. 12:14; 23:1–6). Primarily, however, these views reflect the ongoing belief that the Pharisees determined the normative religious tradition in the Second Temple period. This point of view has in large measure been rejected today; see, for example, M. Smith, "Palestinian Judaism," 73–81; Aune, "Orthodoxy in First Century Judaism?" 1–10; S. J. D. Cohen, *From Maccabees to Mishnah*, 160–64; Grabbe, "Synagogues in Pre-70 Palestine," 408–9; E. P. Sanders, *Judaism*, 47–72, 380–412. If, then, Pharisaic Judaism was not normative, and if many literary compositions of the Second Temple period often ascribed to them by modern scholars are, in fact, not theirs (e.g., on the Psalms of Solomon; see O'Dell, "Religious Background of Psalms," 241–57; see also E. P. Sanders, *Paul*, 402–4), then there is little justification in speaking of their control over the local synagogues. See now S. J. D. Cohen, "Pharisees and Rabbis," 99–114.

isees had little or nothing to do with the early synagogue, and there is not one shred of evidence pointing to such a connection. No references associate the early Pharisees (the "Pairs") with the synagogue, nor is there anything in early synagogue liturgy that is particularly Pharisaic.

Early evidence connecting the judicial process once conducted at the city-gate with the synagogue may be found in the book of Susannah. The focus of this story is a town meeting attended by the elders and townspeople alike for the purpose of adjudication. According to the Septuagint version, the trial took place in "the synagogue" (συναγωγή); the revised version of Theodotian merely states that "the people assembled."[68] Scholars generally regard the Septuagint tradition as older and assume that it had a Semitic *Vorlage* of Palestinian provenance and was composed in the Persian or, more likely, Hellenistic period.[69] Thus, we may have here an early attestation of the term "synagogue" referring either to a separate building or perhaps to an outdoor area that served as the setting for a major communal activity.[70]

An advanced stage in the transition to a synagogue building could perhaps justifiably be dated to the late Hellenistic–early Roman period, that is, the first century c.e. Our argument here—unfortunately, but of necessity—rests heavily on the lack of evidence. Had the synagogue been a known and recognized institution in Palestinian Jewish life, one might well have expected it to be mentioned at least once in the many literary works of the third and second centuries b.c.e.[71] Yet, despite the numerous references to Jewish elites and religious institutions of the day, Ben Sira takes no note of it. We also might have expected I and II Maccabees to note the impact of Antiochus' persecutions on the functioning of the synagogue, had it existed; they do not. Purity laws, circumcision, the Sabbath, festivals, kashrut, and, of course, the Temple are all mentioned, but not a word is said about the synagogue.[72] Compare this silence to descriptions of first-century c.e. pogroms and anti-Jewish incidents in both Judaea and the Diaspora, where the synagogue featured prominently in the writings of both Josephus and Philo.[73]

---

68. Charles, *Apocrypha and Pseudepigrapha*, I, 649; C. A. Moore, *Daniel, Esther and Jeremiah: Additions*, 101–4.

69. C. A. Moore, *Daniel, Esther and Jeremiah: Additions*, 91–92.

70. The reference in Matt. 6:5 to those who "pray in the synagogues and on the street corners" is intriguing. The use of a synagogue or, alternatively, the street corner, as a place of worship may reflect a stage of development between the city-gate area and that of organized, "housed" places of worship when both locales were being utilized. Then, again, the passage in Matthew may be referring to private, and not communal, prayer.

71. For the literature dating to this period, see Nickelsburg, *Jewish Literature*, 71–160; Hengel, *Judaism and Hellenism*, I, 110ff.; M. Stone, "Apocalyptic Literature."

72. I Macc. 1:41–64; II Macc. 6.

73. See below, Chaps. 3 and 4. This line of argument must, however, be tempered for pre-first-century c.e. Egyptian Jewish literary sources likewise make no mention of a *proseuche*, although that institution is well attested in epigraphical and papyrological sources.

The same silence permeates the books of Tobit and Jubilees, the Letter of Aristeas, the Testaments of the Twelve Patriarchs, the book of Enoch, and others. The synagogue as a place of worship or central institution in Jewish life is nowhere to be detected. Similarly, third- and second-century B.C.E. non-Jewish writers who describe the Jewish scene—particularly its religious component—omit all reference to this institution.[74] When the word "synagogue" does, in fact, appear in the late second-century B.C.E. book of I Maccabees, it refers to a group of people: an assembly of Ḥasidim (2:42), an assembly of scribes (7:12), or the large "national" assembly (ἐπὶ συναγωγῆς μεγάλης) which acclaimed Simon the Maccabee as ruler in 141 B.C.E. (14:28). In the Septuagint, the term invariably refers to a congregation as a whole and not a meeting-place.[75]

We may thus conclude that the synagogue as a distinct and recognizable institution began to crystallize owing to a shift in urban planning. The previous setting of this institution's many functions was well rooted in biblical society. City-gates, with their manifold activities, existed throughout Palestine and other Near Eastern settings for centuries, if not for a millennium or more. The Jews were perpetuating a well-known model. The later move into a building in place of the open-air city-gate setting was likewise a familiar phenomenon in the Hellenistic age. Within Jewish society, this move constituted the beginnings of the institution known as the synagogue.

The shift from the city-gate as a center of various activities to a setting within the city may have affected Jerusalem and its Temple as well. One of the striking aspects of the first-century Jerusalem Temple is the fact that it had become the center of activity for those living within the city and in many ways for Jews throughout Judaea and beyond. More precisely, it was on the Temple Mount that a wide variety of social, political, religious, judicial, and economic functions took place.[76] Never before had the Temple area functioned in such a comprehensive capacity. We have already seen that in biblical times the Jerusalem city-gates were a focal point for many of these activities, including the Torah-reading ceremony organized by Ezra and Nehemiah in the fifth century B.C.E.

When did this plethora of functions move to the Temple Mount area? It, too, may have occurred with the disappearance of the city-gate and the concomitant embellish-

---

74. This point has already been noted on numerous occasions in the previous two centuries, at the very least from the time of Bauer (*Beschreibung*, II, pp. 125ff.). The interpretation of Ps. 74:8 ("they have burned all the assembly places of God") as a reference to the destruction of synagogues during the Antiochan persecutions is hardly accepted today (see Goldstein, *I Maccabees*, 138 n. 208).

75. See *TDNT*, VIII, 805. It may be precisely for this reason, i.e., the association in Second Temple literature of the word "synagogue" with "congregation," that the word became applied to a building that housed communal activities. That the synagogue building belonged to the community as a whole is clearly attested in early rabbinic tradition; see, for example, M Nedarim 5:5; T Bava Metzia 11:23 (p. 125); Lieberman, *TK*, IX, 320; Y Megillah 3, 2, 74a; Y Yevamot 12, 13a; Genesis Rabbah 81:1 (pp. 969–72); and below, Chap. 11.

76. Jeremias, *Jerusalem in the Time of Jesus*, 40, 54–57; L. Levine, *Caesarea under Roman Rule*, 181–85.

ment of the Temple area. There can be little doubt that the Hasmonean renovations on the Temple Mount and certainly Herod's enlargement of the area to twice its former size were done not only to increase the number of pilgrims or to satisfy personal ambitions, but also to accommodate the new functions of the Temple Mount. When Herod planned this area architecturally as a Hellenistic *temenos* (sacred area) on the one hand and as the equivalent of a Greek agora or Roman forum on the other, he was, in fact, centralizing in this public area activities once conducted in other parts of the city, primarily the city-gate area. This development thus coincided with the wider relocation of communal functions to other settings, as was the trend elsewhere in the Hellenistic East.

If this assumption be granted, namely, that the Temple Mount area inherited many of the functions once associated with the Jerusalem city-gate at about the same time that the synagogue emerged in various towns and villages throughout Palestine and the Diaspora, it might explain a number of interesting and hitherto enigmatic phenomena, such as the ceremonial reading of the Torah within the Temple precincts. This was the only formal liturgical activity not specifically associated with sacrifices (in contrast with the levitical psalms, which were) that took place there. Annually on Yom Kippur, as well as on the Sukkot festival at the end of each sabbatical year, the high priest would read from the Torah in public (הקהל, *Haqhel*, in Deut. 31).[77] Such proceedings were clearly ancillary to the Temple's main agenda and, as such, were conducted in the Women's Court and not in the Priests' Court. They were intended for all the people gathered in the Temple precincts. Might this practice have been a carryover from former city-gate practices?

The puzzling reference to two functionaries, the *rosh knesset* (ראש כנסת) and *ḥazzan knesset* (חזן כנסת), with regard to these particular ceremonies may also gain a measure of clarity. In references to the synagogue from the first centuries C.E., rabbinic literature specifically notes these two officials in connection with the Torah-reading ceremony.[78] Might they earlier on have held pivotal roles in city-gate affairs, including religious activities, and could these roles have been subsequently carried over to the Temple and synagogue?

The proposed reconstruction for the evolution of the synagogue has implications regarding its relationship with the Temple. As noted above, it is totally unwarranted to view the synagogue as a rival of the Temple.[79] Throughout the Second Temple period, at least in Palestine, the synagogue was never endowed with any special sanctity or halakhic

---

77. M Yoma 7:1; M Sotah 7:8; see also M Tamid 5:3.

78. T Megillah 3:21 (p. 359); T Sukkah 4:6 (p. 273). In the Temple setting, both the *ḥazzan knesset* and *rosh knesset* were subordinate to the priestly hierarchy; in the newly developing synagogue, these roles were destined to become central. For literature in this regard, see above, note 57.

79. Contra Flesher, in "Palestinian Synagogues," 27–39, whose hypothesis flies in the face of incontrovertible evidence. Too much has to be explained away for his thesis of an inherent conflict between these two institutions to be credible.

importance.[80] Moreover, several sources indicate the prominence of priests even in the synagogue setting.[81] Thus, there seems to have been no inherent conflict between these two institutions, and priestly participation and leadership in synagogues simply reflect their wider role as religious and communal leaders in this era.

The suggestion that the synagogue fully crystallized sometime in the Hellenistic period would also go a long way toward explaining the development of the Jewish *proseuche* in Egypt and some of its salient features, including the considerable influence of Ptolemaic models. The Jews who settled in Egypt and elsewhere in the early Hellenistic period had no viable or established framework for communal activities, which in Judaea had taken place at the city-gate. In adapting to a new environment and in seeking a setting for their communal functions, the Jews in Egypt and throughout the Diaspora looked to their immediate surroundings for suitable models.[82]

There is little to be gained in arguing whether the synagogue originated in Judaea or the Diaspora. In fact, the institution evolved in both places more or less simultaneously, but for very different reasons. For the Jews of Palestine, there was a need to find an alternative to the city-gate or open public space now fast disappearing. For Jews in the Hellenistic and later Roman Diaspora, use of the pagan city-gate (if one still existed in its earlier community-oriented form) was out of the question; it was thus imperative to create a framework to preserve and give expression to their communal identity in an alien environment.

Under such circumstances were the *synagoge* and *proseuche* born.

---

80. S. J. D. Cohen, "Temple and Synagogue," 151–74.
81. See E. P. Sanders, *Judaism*, 170–82; and below, Chaps. 3–5.
82. See below, Chap. 4.

three PRE-70 JUDAEA

No pre-70 source addresses the nature or functions of the Judaean synagogue in any systematic way.[1] In contrast to the Temple, the synagogue merited relatively little attention; we have few sources on how synagogues functioned, where they were located, or how they looked—aspects about which Josephus and the Mishnah supply a plethora of information with regard to the Temple.[2] As noted, the synagogue at this time had no halakhic or religious standing;

1. We have been using the name Judaea for the pre-70 period, as this was the official title of the Roman province at the time. Only in the wake of the Bar-Kokhba revolt in 135 C.E. did Hadrian change the name to Syria-Palaestina, a change that will be followed in later chapters by using the name Palestine. It should be noted that the name Judaea had a dual meaning in the pre-70 era—a limited reference to the southern part of the country (as against Samaria, Galilee, and Peraea) and a broader one to the entire province. See M. Stern, *Greek and Latin Authors*, I, 233-34, 290; II, 11-15, 168-70, 217-20; Feldman, "Observations on the Name of Palestine," 6-14; and Schürer, *History*, I, 514.

2. Josephus, *War* 5, 184-237; idem, *Antiquities* 15, 380-425; M Middot; M Sheqalim. Studies on the Jerusalem Temple based on these sources are abundant; see, for example, Hollis, *Archaeology of Herod's Temple*; Simons, *Jerusalem in the Old Testament*; Vincent and Stève, *Jérusalem de l'Ancien Testament*; Busink, *Tempel von Jerusalem*; and L. Levine, "Josephus' Description of the Jerusalem Temple," 233-46.

An interesting example of this imbalance is the Roman practice of offering gifts to the Jerusalem Temple; no comparable gesture is known regarding the pre-70 synagogue. See, for example, Philo, *Embassy* 157, 297, 319; Josephus, *War* 5, 562; idem, *Antiquities* 16, 14; 18, 122.

it was a communal institution and, as such, merited no special status and consequently little attention.[3] Nevertheless, the picture is not entirely bleak. Almost a score of synagogues in first-century C.E. Judaea are known, those from literary sources, which are mentioned only on occasion and always en passant within the given agenda of a particular source.[4] These include literary references in Josephus' writings (Tiberias, Dor, and Caesarea), the New Testament (Nazareth, Capernaum, and Jerusalem), rabbinic literature (Jerusalem), and the Damascus Document (Qumran and presumably elsewhere as well). Four sites have yielded unequivocal archeological evidence for the first century (Gamla, Masada, Herodium, and Jerusalem), and a recently discovered building at Qiryat Sefer near Modi'in may well provide us with a fifth instance. The designation of several other archeological sites as synagogues is less certain (Capernaum, Migdal, Chorazim, northern Jerusalem, and Jericho). Although this material is scattered throughout the entire province of Judaea, a concentration of finds exists in the Galilee (including the Golan), Jerusalem, and the Judaean Desert, with three additional examples in the coastal area. Let us review this evidence region by region.

GALILEE

Some Methodological Considerations

Because much of our information regarding the Galilee derives from the New Testament accounts of Jesus, determining the historical reliability of this material is of paramount importance. All gospels refer to Jesus' activity in Galilean synagogues. Mark and Luke speak of Jesus' preaching and healing in synagogues throughout the region, Matthew of teaching, preaching, and healing there, and John of speaking openly in synagogues and in the Temple.[5] The towns and villages which Jesus frequented (as has often been noted, he seems to have studiously avoided contact with cities)[6] all appear to have

---

3. S. J. D. Cohen, "Temple and Synagogue," 152–74.

4. It is difficult to view the term *hieroi* in *War* 4, 408, as referring to synagogues. That the Sicarii would carry out a general destruction of synagogues would be strange indeed, as is the coupling of such buildings with cities, as a reference in the text does. Despite the difficulty in assuming that there were such pagan temples in Judaea, it is more likely that Josephus did, in fact, have such buildings in mind and that greater Judaea—including pagan areas—was intended. Another possible reference to such structures may be found in *War* 1, 277, and its parallel in *Antiquities* 14, 374.

5. Evidence from each gospel is referred to respectively: Mark 1:21–28, 39; 3:1; 6:2 (for other settings in Jesus' ministry according to Mark, see Rhoads and Michie, *Mark as Story*, 63–72); Matt. 4:23; 9:35; Luke 4:15–44; 13:10–21; John 6:35–59; 18:20. See also Schwartzman, "Synoptic Evangelists," 115–32.

6. Freyne, *Galilee, Jesus and the Gospels*, 135–55; R. A. Horsley, *Galilee*, 158–255; Edwards, "Socio-Economic and Cultural Ethos," 53–73. See also Freyne, "Urban-Rural Relations," 75–91. On urban-rural relations generally in the Empire, see MacMullen, *Roman Social Relations*, 28–56.

had synagogues, whatever their size, location, or social-religious configuration. Jesus' visits to these synagogues on the Sabbath were clearly timed so as to afford him maximum exposure to the local population—or at least the gospel narratives purport to convey this message.

Unique among first-century sources, the gospel narratives focus on the healing effected within the synagogue. Miracle-working activity was far from uncommon in antiquity generally and in Judaea specifically.[7] Exorcising demons, performing wonders, making miraculous signs, and healing the sick within the context of the synagogue would not have been considered unusual given the institution's centrality in Jewish communal life. What is highlighted in these narratives, however, is not only the nature and extent of this practice, but also the fact that it took place on the Sabbath. It is this timing which was controversial and thus became a bone of contention between Jesus and some of those present. In one case he is reportedly criticized by the archisynagogue, in another by the Pharisees.[8] The gospel authors appear to have highlighted a not uncommon phenomenon in rural areas in order to account for Jesus' charisma and popularity.

The historical value of this New Testament literature regarding the first-century Judaean synagogue has been called into question of late. It has been suggested that all the gospels—Matthew perhaps excepted—were written in the Diaspora and, as such, may reflect the late first-century C.E. Diaspora synagogue familiar to the authors, who then projected this setting onto the first-century Galilee.[9]

However, caution against such extreme skepticism should be maintained. Although the gospels and Acts—those writings most relevant to the subject at hand—may have originated in the Diaspora, chronologically they are not so distant from Jesus' setting; the difference between the latter part of the first century C.E. and ca. 30 C.E. is only a generation or two. Furthermore, it is not at all clear that a Diaspora setting had an impact on these accounts. All the gospels, no matter when or where written, report much the same information regarding the Galilean synagogues. How might we explain this coincidence? Are we to assume—as per the above-noted assumption—that all Diaspora synagogues, whether in Rome, Alexandria, Antioch, or elsewhere, shared identical features? This, as we will see below (Chap. 4), was certainly not the case; Diaspora synagogues varied considerably from region to region. Even were we to assume the existence of some sort of overriding unity among the far-flung first-century Diaspora synagogues, might it not be warranted to assume that Judaean synagogues shared in that commonality?

Moreover, there is a significant amount of corroboration between the New Testa-

---

7. Kee, *Miracle in the Early Christian World*, 146–70; Freyne, *Galilee, Jesus and the Gospels*, 227–39; and especially Aune, "Magic in Early Christianity," 1507–57. See also E. P. Sanders, *Jesus and Judaism*, 157–73; M. Smith, *Jesus the Magician*, 68–93; and the recent Crossan, *Historical Jesus*, 303–32.

8. Luke 13:14; Matt. 12:14, respectively.

9. See, for example, Kee, "Transformation of the Synagogue," 18.

ment evidence and other information relating to first-century Judaea.[10] For example, Acts refers to Diaspora Jewry's synagogues in Jerusalem, and this presence is reflected in rabbinic literature and the Theodotos inscription as well (see below). The centrality of scriptural readings in the synagogue (viz., Luke 4) is echoed in the Theodotos inscription, Philo, Josephus, and some early rabbinic traditions (e.g., T Megillah 3 [p. 359]). Finally, we might wonder why New Testament writers would attribute a Diaspora synagogue setting to Jesus' time if such an institution had no place in the Galilee. It appears rather unlikely that all the gospel writers would refer time and again to Jesus' activity in an institution which never existed in his time.[11]

Such an assumption, that there were no synagogue buildings in Galilean towns and villages in the first century, thus appears unwarranted.[12] That such buildings existed in Judaea at the time is attested for Jerusalem (the Theodotos inscription), Masada, Gamla, and Capernaum (Luke 7:5). Moreover, the recent archeological discovery at Qiryat Sefer, a village in the Modi'in region, seems to provide us with an example of a village synagogue in western Judaea. Whether such evidence is to be found in every village is unknown, but probably not. Smaller settlements may have made do with a village square or someone's home, but this is mere speculation.

Nazareth

Jesus' appearance in his hometown synagogue is mentioned in each of the synoptic gospels.[13] It was a memorable occasion, and it is precisely the fact that Jesus was appearing in his *patris* that determined the nature and course of this particular narrative. The accounts in Matthew (13:53–58) and Mark (6:1–6)[14] are similar: Jesus teaches at the local synagogue; those gathered are astonished by his words and deeds; he is immediately identified by those assembled as the carpenter's son, the son of Mary, brother of James,

---

10. See a thorough review of the evidence—and a refutation of Kee's theory—in Oster, Jr., "Supposed Anachronism," 178–208; see also E. P. Sanders, *Jewish Law*, 341–43; Riesner, "Synagogues in Jerusalem," 179–210; van der Horst, "Was the Synagogue a Place of Sabbath Worship?"

11. That the gospel writers have emerged of late less as historians and more as theologians and literary writers should not be given undue weight for our purposes; see Conzelmann, *Theology of St. Luke*, 34–38; Talbert, *Literary Patterns*, contra Anderson, "Broadening Horizons," 261–74. It is rather safe to assume that writers using "historical" data for biographical or historical narrative (e.g., Luke-Acts) would not consciously distort or concoct basic information dealing with Jesus' synagogue experiences. See, for example, Luke 1:1–4: "It seems good to me . . . to write an orderly account."

Regarding the inclusion of very early (and thus authentic and historical) material in much of Luke's narrative, see Schurmann, *Lukasevangelium*, 223ff.; Ringe, *Jesus, Liberation and the Biblical Jubilee*, 42–45, 107–9; and Chilton, "God in Strength," 121–32.

12. See Groh, "Stratigraphic Chronology," 57–60; R. A. Horsley, *Galilee*, 225–26.

13. Temple, "Rejection at Nazareth," 229–42.

14. See Perrot, "Jésus à Nazareth," 40–49.

Joseph, Simon, Judas, and his sisters. We are told that those gathered were highly offended, although the reason for this is not made clear. Jesus' reply that "a prophet is not without honor except in his own country [i.e., hometown] and in his own house" (Mark adds: "among his own kin") may well be what triggered the above account. Both gospel pericopes add that owing to his townsmen's disbelief, Jesus did not succeed in performing miracles there. Mark notes, however, that Jesus nevertheless managed to heal some sick people.

Luke's account of Jesus' visit to the Nazareth synagogue is markedly different, so much so that it has been suggested that Jesus made two different visits to Nazareth, one described in Mark and Matthew, the other in Luke.[15] Whatever the case, the importance of Luke's pericope cannot be overestimated for our understanding of the first-century Judaean synagogue. It has attracted a great deal of scholarly attention.[16]

> And he came to Nazareth, where he had been brought up: and, as was his custom, he went into the synagogue on the Sabbath day and stood up to read. And he was handed the book of the prophet Isaiah. And when he had opened the book, he found the place where it was written, "The Spirit of the Lord is upon me, because He has anointed me to preach the gospel to the poor; He has sent me to proclaim release to the captives, and recover the sight to the blind, to set at liberty those that are oppressed, to proclaim the acceptable year of the Lord" [Is. 61:1–2].[17]

> And he closed the book, and he gave it back to the attendant, and sat down. And the eyes of all those in the synagogue were fixed on him. And he began to say unto them, "Today this scripture is fulfilled in your ears." And all spoke well of him, and wondered at the gracious words which proceeded out of his mouth. And they said, "Is this not Joseph's son?" And he said unto them, "You will surely quote me the proverb, 'Physician, heal yourself': what we have heard you did in Capernaum, do also here in your own country." And he said, "Truly, I say to you, no prophet is accepted in his own country. But I tell you in truth, many widows were

---

15. Luke 4:16–30; Perrot, "Jésus à Nazareth," 47. See also Lagrange, *L'évangile*, 123, 201. The gospels themselves do not know of two visits. Alternatively, the account in Luke may be a rewriting or reworking of Mark 1–6 (see Leaney, *Commentary of the Gospel According to St. Luke*, 51–52; Bultmann, *History of Synoptic Tradition*, 31–32), honed to fit Luke's theology (Conzelmann, *Theology of St. Luke*, 34–38) or part of Luke's programmatic agenda (Brawley, *Luke-Acts and the Jews*, 11–12; cf. J. T. Sanders, *Jews in Luke-Acts*, 164–68). See also Kümmel, *Introduction*, 130–51.

16. See, for example, Finkel, "Jesus' Sermon at Nazareth," 106–15; idem, "Jesus' Preaching," 325–41; Anderson, "Broadening Horizons," 259–75; Combrink, "Structure and Significance of Luke 4:16–30," 27–47; Perrot, "Luc 4:16–30 et la lecture biblique," 324–40 and bibliography in n. 11; J. T. Sanders, "From Isaiah 61 to Luke 4," 75–106; Chilton, "Announcement in Nazara," 147–72; C. A. Evans, *Luke*, 70–76; Monshouwer, "Reading of the Prophet," 90–99; Tyson, *Images of Judaism*, 59–62. On the date and authorship of Luke, see Fitzmyer, *Luke*, 35–62.

17. This passage is used also in Matt. 11:4–5 and Luke 7:22. The verses in our present context have been carefully edited by excluding some phrases, incorporating a clause from Is. 58:6, and generally following the Septuagint version. See R. A. Horsley, *Jesus and the Spiral of Violence*, 250–51.

in Israel in the days of Elijah, when the heaven was shut up three years and six months, when great famine was throughout the land; but to none of them was Elijah sent, except to Sarepta, in the territory of Sidon, to a woman who was a widow. And many lepers were in Israel in the time of Elisha the prophet; and none of them was cleansed, save Naaman the Syrian."

And all those in the synagogue, upon hearing these things, were filled with anger, and rose up, and thrust him out of the city, and led him unto the edge of the hill on which their city was built, that they might cast him down headlong. But passing through the midst of them, he went away.[18]

This passage is far longer and more detailed than its parallels and was deliberately placed by Luke at the very beginning of Jesus' career. Mark and Matthew, in contrast, place their versions of the Nazareth incident later in Jesus' Galilean ministry.[19] Thus, the positioning of this tradition is clearly of significance, and its importance for the Lucan account is thus unquestionable.[20]

As regards the synagogue itself in this account, a number of details are noteworthy. According to Luke, Jesus was apparently accustomed to go to the synagogue on the Sabbath, either as an ordinary participant or as an itinerant preacher or healer; other gospel traditions bear this out. Certain stages of the synagogue liturgy are carefully noted: Jesus stood up to read from the Prophets, was handed the book of Isaiah, read several verses, returned the book to the synagogue official, sat down, and proceeded to address the congregation.

Surprisingly, reading from the Torah is omitted. However, rather than conclude that we have here an exceptional practice, it is more reasonable to assume that Luke omitted the Torah-reading and noted only that of the Prophets, because this alone was relevant to his purpose (i.e., Jesus' subsequent sermon).[21] The selection of the prophetic reading described by Luke is enigmatic. Was it the prescribed reading for that particular Sabbath? Who made that decision? Of no less interest is the selection of the specific passage. Luke's account seems to allude to the fact that Jesus himself chose the passage. If so, was

---

18. Luke 4:16-30.

19. Finkel, "Jesus' Sermon at Nazareth," 115.

20. Luke obviously intends to use Jesus' "inaugural address" in Nazareth to set forth the main themes of his gospel and its companion volume, Acts. These can be summarized as follows: (1) Jesus' message is rooted in Jewish tradition—the synagogue setting, reading from Scriptures, and preaching the power of the Spirit; (2) his mission is of a distinctly social, humanitarian nature—helping the poor, releasing captives, curing the blind, and freeing the oppressed—with a distinctly miracle-oriented component; (3) fulfillment is to take place imminently, and Jesus himself is the messianic prophet; (4) having been rejected and persecuted by the Jews, Jesus' mission will turn to the gentiles, as did those of Elijah and Elisha (see also Luke 17:7-24). See Combrink, "Structure and Significance of Luke 4:16-30," 39-42; Brawley, *Luke-Acts and the Jews*, 1-27; J. T. Sanders, "From Isaiah 61 to Luke 4," 75-106; Siker, " 'First to the Gentiles,' " 73-90.

21. In Acts 13:15-16, the readings from both the Torah and the Prophets are noted.

this Luke's invention, or was it indeed an accepted practice in the Galilee, and in most contemporary synagogues, for that matter? Given the absence of parallels, no definitive answer is possible.

The sudden and dramatic change in the people's attitude toward Jesus (vv. 22, 28) may have resulted from his message on this occasion, or it may reflect several radically different attitudes toward him, ranging from sympathetic acceptance to hostile rejection, on the part of fellow-townsmen. Luke may well have condensed these reactions into his account of Jesus' programmatic sermon.[22]

Capernaum

Jesus' activity in the Capernaum synagogue is mentioned in all the gospels.[23] For Mark, followed by Matthew, this was, in essence, the beginning of his ministry. The synoptic gospels focus primarily on Jesus' healing activity there while, according to John, Jesus delivered a long exposition regarding his divinity, the Eucharist, and Mystical Body —clearly a speech setting forth the author's theological agenda. In contrast, nothing explicit is reported in the synoptic gospels about the content of his teaching in Capernaum, other than the fact that all who heard him were amazed. Jesus taught with authority and not, Mark adds, as did the scribes. He reputedly exorcised an unclean spirit and healed a withered hand there.[24] Whereas in Nazareth Jesus' words caused an uproar, in Capernaum his deeds did so.

A noteworthy aspect is the congregation's reaction to Jesus' act of healing on the Sabbath.[25] The Pharisees (as well as the scribes, according to Luke, and the Herodians, according to Mark) found his behavior objectionable and sought ways to counter his influence and activity.[26] The historicity of any or all of these particular groups' opposition is questionable but not impossible. Why such traditions developed specifically with regard to Capernaum, rather than elsewhere, is unclear.

Of further interest regarding Capernaum is the tradition reported by Luke that a Roman centurion stationed in the town built this synagogue.[27] Although this claim is found only in Luke, Matthew, for his part, highlights the Roman officer's piety and faith.

---

22. Opinions vary regarding the reasons for this anger. See Brawley, *Luke-Acts and the Jews*, 16–18 and bibliography cited there. See Bruce, *Acts of the Apostles*, 15–18.

23. Mark 1:21–29; Matt. 12:9–14; Luke 4:31–38; John 6:35–59.

24. Matt. 11:5; Luke 7:22; Mark 3:1–5.

25. Mark 3:1–6; Luke 6:6–11. See *TDNT*, VII, 20–26.

26. On the identity of these groups and how they function in each gospel, see, inter alia, Schürer, *History*, II, 322ff.; Cook, *Mark's Treatment of Jewish Leaders*; Saldarini, *Pharisees, Scribes and Sadducees*; Malbon, "Jewish Leaders in Mark," 259–81; D. R. Schwartz, *Jewish Background of Christianity*, 89–101. On the constantly recurring thesis that the Herodians were Essenes, see the judicious comments of Braun, "Were the New Testament Herodians Essenes?" 75–88 and bibliography cited there.

27. Luke 7:1–5. For possible archeological remains of a first-century synagogue building at Capernaum, see below.

Matthew focuses on the man's personal faith, Luke on his worthiness as a gentile.[28] Luke's reference to the Roman centurion fits neatly into his overriding interest in portraying the openness and receptivity of the gentiles to Jesus' message, even from the very outset of his ministry. Thus, the centurion's faith and humility, along with his generosity and support of the synagogue, are most suitable traditions for Luke to include. Did Luke himself invent this account of the centurion's building of the Capernaum synagogue? Was it a product of an earlier tradition which he inherited, or is it, in fact, a valid piece of historical evidence?[29] Once again, the question of historicity remains moot.

Tiberias

In anticipation of a Roman invasion following the outbreak of the revolt in Jerusalem, Josephus was sent to organize the Galilee in 66–67 C.E. Tiberias figures prominently in Josephus' writings owing either to the city's pivotal role in the region or Josephus' particular need in the 90s to refute personal attacks by Justus of Tiberias regarding his conduct of the war, or both.[30] Whatever the reasons, Josephus' movements in and around the city, his meetings, speeches, and escapes, as well as the names of local leaders, leave us with a much more detailed picture of Tiberias than of any other Galilean city of the time.[31]

Josephus mentions a Tiberian *proseuche* on three occasions. The first time it is described as a very large building ($\mu\acute{\epsilon}\gamma\iota\sigma\tau o\nu$ $o\H{\iota}\kappa\eta\mu\alpha$) that could accommodate a large crowd ($\pi o\lambda\grave{v}\nu$ $\H{o}\chi\lambda o\nu$)[32] and where deliberations were held on that Sabbath morning. Nothing is said about worship, which presumably took place beforehand and was either assumed or considered unimportant by Josephus for his narrative. The meeting itself consisted of a series of speeches, and the participants disbanded only at midday, when, Josephus notes, the Sabbath meal was served.[33] Another meeting was set for the next day, when very early that morning, at the first hour,[34] people again gathered in the *proseuche* to resume discussions. A third meeting was called for the following day, which was also proclaimed a day of public fast.[35] The proceedings began with the usual ($\tau\grave{\alpha}$ $\nu\acute{o}\mu\iota\mu\alpha$) service for a fast day, but soon thereafter a confrontation ensued, which quickly became heated and violent.

---

28. Matt. 8:5–13. On this narrative in its Matthean and Lucan contexts, see Martin, "Pericope of the Healing of the 'Centurion's' Servant/Son," 14–22.

29. For the acceptance of this tradition, see White, *Building God's House*, 86. Moreover, it may be that Luke exaggerated the size of the centurion's gift, given the fact that it came from an army officer; in fact, the Roman may have made only a modest contribution.

30. S. J. D. Cohen, *Josephus in Galilee and Rome*, 114–70.

31. Ibid., 216–21; see also Schürer, *History*, II, 178–82; Avi-Yonah, "Founding of Tiberias," 160–69; Hoehner, *Herod Antipas*, 91–100; Freyne, *Galilee, Jesus and the Gospels*, 129–34; R. A. Horsley, *Galilee*, 78–80, 169–74, 271–75.

32. *Life* 277.

33. Ibid., 279.

34. Ibid., 280.

35. Ibid., 290–303.

Josephus' references to the Tiberian *proseuche* and the events there are noteworthy on several counts. First is the term itself. This is the only instance in which a Judaean synagogue is referred to as a *proseuche* (although an equivalent Hebrew term does appear in the Damascus Document—see below). In Josephus' other accounts, as well as in the gospel traditions, the Theodotos inscription, and rabbinic literature, the term used for this Judaean communal institution is invariably *synagoge*. Why, then, was Tiberias different? If, indeed, *proseuche* was used primarily with regard to the Diaspora, especially—though not exclusively—in Egypt, then possibly there was some tie between this Tiberias building and the Diaspora.

In the absence of firm evidence, we can only speculate. Perhaps it was owing to the fact that, in many ways, the city was almost certainly modeled after a Hellenistic *polis* by its founder, Herod Antipas. It had been named for an emperor; its local government was structured as a *polis*, replete with archons, *boule* and *demos;* the city boasted a stadium and, later on, had been given an additional name, Claudiopolis, possibly following Claudius' death in 54.[36] The *proseuche* building may well have been constructed by Antipas himself or, alternatively, during the reign of Agrippa I. The latter's contact with the Diaspora, and particularly with Alexandrian Jewry, is well known, especially with regard to the events surrounding the anti-Jewish outbreaks of 38 C.E. Finally, it may not be coincidental that a later rabbinic source describes a third- or fourth-century Tiberian synagogue as a *dyplastoon* (דיפליא סטיא)—the identical term used for the first-century Alexandrian synagogue (דפלסטטון).[37]

A second noteworthy feature is the purportedly large size of this *proseuche* building. Josephus specifically mentions this, and his statement is reinforced by the fact that when not meeting in the *proseuche*, Tiberians would gather in the local stadium, much as the *demos* of Ephesus and Antioch were wont to meet in their respective theaters.[38] To date, monumental synagogue buildings are known only from the Diaspora: one (perhaps two) in Alexandria described by Philo and the Tosefta and another in Sardis, dating from the late third century C.E. and excavated in the 1960s.[39]

Finally, the Tiberias *proseuche* in this Josephan context served, inter alia, as a forum for

36. See, for example, Josephus, *War* 2, 641 (βουλή of 600); idem, *Life* 69, 296 (δέκα πρῶτοι); 134, 271, 278, 294; idem, *War* 2, 599 (ἄρχων); 2, 615 (ὑπάρχοι); idem, *Antiquities* 18, 149 (ἀγορανόμος). See also Avi-Yonah, "Tiberias in the Roman Period," 154–62; Kasher, "Founding of Tiberias," 3–11; D. R. Schwartz, *Agrippa I*, 137–40.

37. *Tiberian synagogue:* Midrash on Psalms 93 (p. 416). *Alexandrian synagogue:* T Sukkah 4:6 (p. 273); and below, Chap. 4.

38. *Tiberias: Life* 91; 331. See also Hengel, "Proseuche und Synagoge," 177–78 (= Gutmann, *Synagogue,* 47–48). *Ephesus:* Acts 19:29. *Antioch:* Josephus, *War* 7, 47.

39. See below, Chap. 4. On the Sardis synagogue, see Seager, "Building History," 425–35; Seager and Kraabel, "Synagogue and Jewish Community," 168–90; Kraabel, "Diaspora Synagogue," 483–88; and below, Chap. 8.

4. Plan of the Gamla synagogue
(Qatzrin Museum).

discussing burning political issues of the day, thus indicating the pivotal role played by this institution in communal affairs. In Josephus' report, at least, its religious dimension was decidedly secondary, and on these occasions the Sabbath as well as fast-day rituals were apparently dwarfed by the pressures of the political agenda.

Gamla

Gamla is the earliest synagogue structure to have been discovered in Judaea to date.[40] The building may have been erected as late as the turn of the first century C.E., although a mid-first century B.C.E. foundation, sometime between Alexander Jannaeus (103–76 B.C.E.) and Herod (37–4 B.C.E.), has also been suggested.

The Gamla building is architecturally impressive (fig. 4). It is the only public building thus far excavated in that town and may well be the only one that ever existed there. Located adjacent to the eastern wall, the building has an axis that runs northeast to southwest and is 25.5 meters long and 17 meters wide. The hall itself measures 13.4 by 9.3 meters. In the northwestern corner of this hall is a niche, possibly used for storage. Two entrances are located to the southwest, one giving access to the northern aisle or platform and a second, larger one leading directly into the main hall. Another entrance from

---

40. Gutman, *NEAEHL*, II, 460–62; Ma'oz, "Architecture of Gamla," 152–54; and Z. Ilan, *Ancient Synagogues*, 73–74. The building's dimensions differ somewhat in each of the above publications; I will follow those in *NEAEHL*. On the recent discovery of the Jericho building, see below.

the east opens onto the eastern aisle. Below these elevated aisles was a series of benches surrounding the main hall on all four sides, and in front of each line of benches stood a row of columns. The columns surrounded an open space in the middle of the hall. This central area was unpaved, with the exception of a row of stones running in an east-west direction. A single bench ran along the eastern wall of the building, and similar benches may have run along the northern and southern walls as well. A small basin (for washing hands?) in the eastern aisle was fed by a channel that cut through the eastern wall. No inscriptions were discovered in the building, and the only depiction is a stylized palm tree carved in a stone block. A stepped cistern just west of the synagogue's main entrance may have been used as a *miqveh*, but it dates only from the period of the revolt (66–67 C.E.). East of the synagogue's main hall are several rooms, one of which may have had some sort of opening into the main hall. This room also contains benches, leading the excavator to suggest that it may have served as a study room.

If our assumptions are correct, namely, that the synagogue at this time was first and foremost a communal institution and that the structure at Gamla is the only public building in the town (it is the only one found to date), then, indeed, it must have served as the local synagogue. The building's internal plan is reminiscent of Hellenistic public halls, e.g., a *bouleuterion* or *ecclesiasterion*, and is similar in its overall plan to the structures at Masada and Herodium that have been identified as synagogues (see below). There can be little doubt as to the structure's identity.[41] The uniqueness of Gamla lies in the fact that it has the only building that can be safely identified as a synagogue from the pre-70 Galilee-Golan region.

JERUSALEM

The existence of a number of synagogues in Jerusalem is clearly attested in several New Testament passages. In one instance, Paul makes the following statement upon being apprehended by the Roman authorities: "They did not find me in the Temple disputing with anyone, or stirring up a crowd, neither in the synagogues nor in the city."[42]

However, there is no more unequivocal testimony for the existence of synagogues in Jerusalem than Acts 6:9, which notes a series of such institutions, all associated with Diaspora Jewry.[43] After describing a conflict within the nascent Jerusalem church, between Greek-speaking (possibly meaning Diaspora-born) and Aramaic-speaking Jews (6:1–7),[44] Acts goes on to note the opposition to Stephen (6:8–9):

---

41. As noted above in Chap. 2, further indication of this building's function as a synagogue may be evidenced from its location between two main east-west streets near the town's eastern entrance.

42. Acts 24:12; see also ibid., 22:19 and 26:11. See Cadbury, *Acts*, 86–89.

43. See *TDNT*, VII, 837–38.

44. Although the Greek speaks of "Hebraisti," the term probably refers to a Semitic language, and

Full of grace and power, Stephen worked great wonders and signs among the people. And some of those from the synagogue of the Freedmen [Libertines], and of the Cyreneans and of the Alexandrians, and of those from Cilicia and Asia came forward and disputed with Stephen.

Discussion of this passage has at times focused on the exact number of synagogues referred to, since the text itself is somewhat ambiguous. Opinions range from one or two to five. However, given what we know of the extensive Diaspora presence in the city and given the significant differences between these various communities, the last option appears the most likely.[45]

The existence of Jews in Jerusalem from each of the above-mentioned communities finds confirmation elsewhere. That Jews of Cyrene frequented Jerusalem is attested in Mark and Luke as well as Acts.[46] Alexandrian Jews' presence is documented in a variety of sources, including one rabbinic tradition which specifically mentions an Alexandrian synagogue in the city.[47] Paul himself hailed from Cilicia, and his sister's son also may have lived in Jerusalem.[48] Regarding Asia, Acts speaks of an Ephesian who lived in the city. Funerary inscriptions take note of Jews from Alexandria, Cyrene, Cilicia, and elsewhere in Asia Minor who were buried in the city.[49]

The term "Freedmen" or "Libertines" in this passage has attracted much attention. Many have identified the synagogue of the Libertines with that mentioned in the Theo-

---

in this case Aramaic is a far more likely candidate. The evidence for Aramaic's widespread use in first-century Judaea is overwhelming; see Fitzmyer, "Languages of Palestine," 501-31; Gundry, "Language Milieu," 404-8; Rabin, "Hebrew and Aramaic," 1007-39; Schürer, *History*, II, 20-26; and L. Levine, *Judaism and Hellenism*, 80-84.

45. *One synagogue:* Jeremias, *Jerusalem in the Time of Jesus*, 62-66; Bruce, *Acts of the Apostles*, 156; Conzelmann, *Acts of the Apostles*, 47; Riesner, "Synagogues in Jerusalem," 204-5. *Two synagogues*—the freedmen synagogue, composed of Cyrenean and Alexandrian Jews, and a synagogue of Jews from Asia Minor. Denton, *Commentary on Acts of the Apostles*, 187-88; Foakes-Jackson and Lake, *Beginnings of Christianity*, 1, 4, 66; *TDNT*, VII, 837 n. 252; Bruce, *Commentary on Acts*, 133 n. 24; *Expositor's Bible Commentary*. *Five synagogues:* Schürer, *History*, II, 428 and n. 8; S. Safrai, *Pilgrimage*, 57.

On the Diaspora presence in Jerusalem, see Jeremias, *Jerusalem in the Time of Jesus*, 58-71; and generally, S. Safrai, "Relations," 184-204. Moreover, there were individual Diaspora Jews who were quite prominent in the Temple. Many high priests' families hailed originally from abroad (particularly Egypt—see M. Stern, "Reign of Herod," 274), and a number of Diaspora Jews contributed significant gifts to the Temple: Alexander, father of Tiberius (Alexandria—Josephus, *War* 5, 205); Nicanor (Alexandria—M Yoma 3:10; T Kippurim 2:4 [p. 231]; Horbury and Noy, *Jewish Inscriptions*, 243-45); Helena and Monobaz (Adiabene—M Yoma 3:10); and elsewhere (T Kippurim 2:5 [p. 231]).

46. Mark 15:21; Luke 23:26; Acts 2:10; 11:20.

47. T Megillah 2:17 (p. 352) and parallels; see below. See, however, B Megillah 26a, which substitutes "Tarsian" for "Alexandrian."

48. Acts 23:16.

49. Ibid., 21:29; Rahmani, *Catalogue*, 17.

dotos inscription (see below) on the basis of passages from Tacitus and Philo, which indicate that the Jews brought to Rome in captivity were soon freed.[50] Theodotos' family apparently hailed from Rome as the Roman name, Vettenos, seems to indicate; in all probability they were descendants of Jews taken captive by Pompey in 63 B.C.E.[51] Alternatively, some scholars, following several ancient manuscripts and commentaries of Acts, read "Libyans" instead of "Libertines," a name which would fit the North African setting of the following two geographical names on the list.[52] Finally, in line with rabbinic evidence, Jeremias has suggested reading "Synagogue of the Alexandrians" or "Synagogue of the Tarsians" here.[53]

The significance of the above passage is twofold. The list of Diaspora Jewish communities in Jerusalem is impressive. In contrast to Acts 2:5-11, which attests to a large and multifarious gathering "from every nation" on a festival,[54] our passage speaks of the institutionalized presence of Diaspora Jews in the city. We do not know how these synagogues functioned: Were they established on the initiative of those who settled in Jerusalem, or were they sponsored (in whole or in part) by the various Diaspora communities themselves? The latter alternative is quite possible, that these Diaspora communities established synagogues in Jerusalem not only to serve their former residents but also to attend to the needs of those compatriots visiting the city on pilgrimage.[55]

Undoubtedly, the single most important piece of evidence relating to the pre-70 Judaean synagogues generally, and Jerusalem synagogues in particular, is the Theodotos inscription, found by Weill during the City of David excavations in 1913-14 (fig. 5).[56] Discovered in a cistern along with other building fragments, the slab of stone bearing this inscription came in all probability from a nearby structure, traces of which were

---

50. Tacitus, *Annals* 2, 85; Philo, *Embassy* 155; Jeremias, *Jerusalem in the Time of Jesus*, 65-66; Goodenough, *Jewish Symbols*, I, 179; *TDNT*, IV, 265-66; Riesner, "Synagogues in Jerusalem," 204-6.

51. The Roman connection has been suggested by Clermont-Ganneau ("Découverte," 196-97) on the basis of: (1) *gens Vettia* or *Vectia* being associated with that city and (2) a person by the name of Vettienus mentioned by Cicero. This suggestion has been accepted by some (e.g., Schwabe, "Greek Inscriptions," 363-64), though there have been reservations as well; see S. Safrai, *Pilgrimage*, 56-57 and n. 147; M. Stern, "Jewish Diaspora," 17; Roth-Gerson, *Greek Inscriptions*, 78. Cf. Riesner, "Synagogues in Jerusalem," 198.

52. Bruce, *Acts of the Apostles; idem, Commentary on Acts*, 133 n. 24.

53. Jeremias, *Jerusalem in the Time of Jesus*, 65-66.

54. On the possible origins of this list in either astrological or geographical circles, see Brinkman, "'Catalogue of Nations,'" 418-27.

55. On Acts' possible theological agenda in this account, see J. T. Sanders, *Jews in Luke-Acts*, 245.

56. FitzGerald, "Theodotus Inscription," 175-81; Deissmann, *Light from the Ancient East*, 10. The inscription has usually been dated to the first century C.E. (Schwabe, "Greek Inscriptions," 362-65) and, of late, to the late first century B.C.E. (Roth-Gerson, *Greek Inscriptions*, 76-86). However, Kee ("Transformation of the Synagogue," 1-24; idem, "Early Christianity in the Galilee," 4-7), following Vincent ("Chronique," 247-77), has opted for a post-70 date.

5. Theodotos inscription.

claimed to have been found. The inscription, written in Greek and dating from the first century C.E., is ten lines long and reads as follows:

> Theodotos, the son of Vettenos, priest and *archisynagogos*, son of an *archisynagogos*, grandson of an *archisynagogos*, built this synagogue [τὴν συναγωγήν] for the reading of the Law [i.e., the Torah] and the study of the commandments, and a guesthouse and rooms and water installations for hosting those in need from abroad, it [i.e., the synagogue], having been founded by his fathers, the presbyters, and Simonides.[57]

As noted, the name Vettenos appears to place this inscription among Jews who came from Rome. Of singular importance in this inscription is the listing of three synagogue activities: reading the Torah, studying the commandments, and providing rooms and water for itinerant pilgrims.[58] Whether the hostel services were intended only for Jews

---

57. See comments in Roth-Gerson, *Greek Inscriptions*, 76–86; White, *Social Origins*, 294–95. On the extensive hellenization reflected in the language, names, and titles in this inscription, see the comments in Roth-Gerson, *Greek Inscriptions*, 76–86, and L. Levine, *Judaism and Hellenism*, 72–84.

Hereditary positions such as those in the inscription are not uncommon in Jewish life in antiquity. The Hasmonean and Herodian dynasties, not to mention the high priestly office (at least until the time of Herod), are cases in point, as is the family of Judah the Galilean, founder of the Fourth Philosophy (or Sicarii); see Urbach, "Class Status and Leadership," 43–45. From the first century C.E. onward, the Hillelite family of Patriarchs likewise constituted a hereditary office, and this practice also seems to have been known among the sages in the talmudic era; see ibid., 62–63; Alon, *Jews, Judaism and the Classical World*, 436–57. This question has been addressed by Beer on several occasions; see his "Hereditary Principle," 149–57; idem, "Sons of Eli," 79–93. An inscription from the Smyrna synagogue dating to the fourth century C.E. notes that one Irenopolis, a presbyter and *pater* of the community, was the son of Joub, likewise a presbyter in his time; see Tcherikover et al., *CPJ*, II, 9, no. 739; Lifshitz, *Donateurs et fondateurs*, 22–23.

58. Jeremias, *Jerusalem in the Time of Jesus*, 60–61. On synagogue functions in first-century synagogues, see below, Chap. 5.

from Rome in the context of a *Landsmannschaft* or whether they were available to others as well is unknown.[59]

The number of buildings referred to in this inscription is difficult to assess. Are we speaking of a single, all-inclusive structure, resembling those from later periods, for example, Dura and Ḥammam Lif? Or were there perhaps two separate buildings, one for worship and one for lodging? It is conceivable, though unlikely in light of the functions listed, that there were even more rooms involved (and perhaps an additional structure). The answer depends on how we understand the function of the water installations of this complex. Whom did they serve? If they were only meant to service the needs of the lodgers, then they may have been part of the hostel itself. If, perhaps, they were used for ritual and purification purposes for the general public, as were those adjacent to the southern Temple entrance, then we may well be dealing with yet another structure.

Also of interest in the above inscription is the nature of the institution's leadership, which was familial and is documented as such over three generations. Those in charge were of priestly lineage, but it is very unlikely that this had anything to do with the synagogue's proximity to the Temple. Rather, Vettenos was probably the head of a wealthy Roman Jewish family which had taken the initiative in maintaining this institution for generations. The title of archisynagogue was clearly of importance in this particular institution and is known from other first-century synagogues as well.[60]

Finally, the concluding phrase of the Theodotos inscription has been taken to refer either to the building of this particular synagogue several generations earlier by Theodotos' ancestors, the elders, and Simonides or to the original congregation. Whether the earlier institution, dating to the first century B.C.E., was in Jerusalem or Rome is unclear, although given the time frame involved it may conceivably have been the latter. In that case, the Jerusalem synagogue referred to by the inscription would have been, in effect, the continuation of an earlier institution established for the purpose of serving visitors and perhaps the Roman Jewish community of the city in particular.

Rabbinic sources have preserved a number of traditions of varying historical reliability with regard to the Second Temple synagogue, and specifically those in Jerusalem. One of the earliest is a Toseftan tradition reported by the second-century R. Simeon b. Gamaliel concerning several disputes between the Houses of Shammai and Hillel (first century C.E.) over synagogue practices permissible on the Sabbath: "The House of Shammai says: Charity for the poor is not to be announced [or determined—פוסקין] on the Sabbath in the synagogue, even [if it is a matter of collecting money in order] to arrange a marriage for orphans . . . and one does not pray for the sick on the Sabbath; and the House of Hillel permits [these things to take place]."[61] The House of Shammai seems to have made

---

59. See, for example, Schwabe, "Greek Inscriptions," 363.

60. See below, Chaps. 5 and 11.

61. T Shabbat 16:22 (p. 79); according to MS Erfurt, the tradent is R. Simeon b. Elʿazar, also of the second century.

a clear and unequivocal distinction between what is proper and what is improper activity in the synagogue on the Sabbath; the Hillelites probably did not differ, in principle, but simply made allowance for extenuating circumstances, such as those noted.[62] It seems safe to conclude that the Houses of Shammai and Hillel were not conducting a theoretical discussion but rather were commenting upon current practice in Palestinian synagogues. Otherwise, it is difficult to understand why such an issue would arise.[63] Healing the sick (and not merely reciting a prayer) on the Sabbath in some synagogues is clearly attested in New Testament pericopes (see above). Whether such a debate between these schools had any effect is unknown. Even within Pharisaic circles, the issue remained unresolved.

Another Toseftan tradition reports that a first-century synagogue of Alexandrian Jews located in Jerusalem was purchased by R. Eli'ezer b. R. Zadoq and used for private purposes.[64] This source appears in a relatively early rabbinic compilation dealing with laws and practices pertaining to the synagogue, many of which are clearly of older vintage. As already noted, the reality reflected in this tradition, i.e., of Diaspora synagogues in first-century Jerusalem, is corroborated in other sources as well.

More problematic, however, are several rabbinic traditions which refer to a synagogue on the Temple Mount itself.[65] The most explicit one in this regard is a reference in the Tosefta, which describes the Simḥat Bet Hashoeva ceremony on the holiday of Sukkot: "R. Joshua b. Ḥanania said: We would not sleep all the days of Simḥat Bet Hashoeva. We would arise early for the morning Tamid sacrifice and from there go to the synagogue and then to the additional sacrifices."[66]

In contrast to this tradition, which refers to a synagogue,[67] the two parallel versions in the Bavli (Sukkah 53a) and Yerushalmi (Sukkah 5, 2, 55b) do not. The former refers only to prayer, while the latter omits all reference to an interim stage between the morning and the additional sacrifices. Although the Toseftan tradition is chronologically the earliest, and thus might have been assumed to preserve a more authentic account, these other conflicting traditions tend to mitigate its historical value.[68]

---

62. Gilat, "Development of *Shevut* Prohibitions of Shabbat," 114.

63. It is not clear whether the second issue discussed by the Houses in this source concerned a synagogue-related activity.

64. T Megillah 2:17 (pp. 352–53); Y Megillah 3, 1, 73d; B Megillah 26a. On the reading in the Babylonian Talmud, see above, note 47.

65. Hoenig, "Supposititious Temple-Synagogue," 115–31. See also Bacher, "Synagogue," 620; G. F. Moore, *Judaism*, II, 12; E. Levy, *Foundations of Prayer*, 74.

66. T Sukkah 4:5 (p. 273). On the Simḥat Bet Hashoeva festivities in the Second Temple, see Rubenstein, *History of Sukkot*, 131–45.

67. Here, too, the manuscripts differ. MS London of the Tosefta reads "academy" (*bet midrash*) for "synagogue," while the editio princeps and MS Erfurt add "academy" after "synagogue"; see Lieberman, *TK*, IV, 888–89. In another Toseftan tradition (Ḥagigah 2:9 [p. 383]) only the term "academy" appears in the Temple Mount ritual on Sabbaths and holidays. See parallels in T Sanhedrin 7:1 [p. 425]; see also Y Sanhedrin 1, 4, 19c.

68. Chronological priority is, of course, no guarantee of historical accuracy. Early, even contempo-

While the above tradition is inconclusive in and of itself regarding the presence of a synagogue on the Temple Mount, a no less important consideration here is the absence of a synagogue in several important descriptions of the Temple precincts. In Josephus' description of the Temple and Temple Mount,[69] he never mentions the existence of a synagogue. Nor does the Mishnah, with its very detailed listing of the dimensions of buildings, courtyards, and Temple-related appurtenances, ever make reference to a synagogue.[70] Furthermore, the one time the Mishnah mentions a regular daily prayer service in the Temple, conducted by and for the administering priests, it does not refer to a synagogue. Rather, these prayers appear to have been recited somewhere in the area of the Court of the Priests.[71] Thus, we have little basis for assuming the existence of a synagogue on the Temple Mount.

Several other rabbinic sources report on the number of synagogues to be found in Jerusalem. One often cited source speaks of 480; another, probably a corrupt reading, speaks of 460, and yet another notes 394.[72] These numbers—all appearing in later amoraic compilations—appear to be incredibly exaggerated, and in one case, at least, undoubtedly symbolic (viz., the number 480). Truth to tell, the unusual figure of 394 appearing in the Babylonian Talmud is baffling.[73] What these traditions do evidence, however, is the assumption by later generations that late Second Temple Jerusalem abounded in such institutions. More than that, however, we cannot say.

JUDAEAN DESERT

Masada

Undoubtedly, the most famous synagogue remains from the Second Temple period are those from Masada (figs. 6-7). Although the original function of this building in

---

rary sources can also be tendentious and incomplete. Nevertheless, being aware of what can happen to traditions in the process of being transmitted from generation to generation (and at times in entirely different cultural and social contexts), we ought to give some weight to a source's proximity to events or institutions in judging its historicity.

69. *War* 5, 184-237; see also Busink, *Tempel von Jerusalem*, 1062ff.; Hildesheimer, "Beschreibung der herodianischen Tempels," 1-32.

70. M Middot 1-4. See Busink, *Tempel von Jerusalem*, 1529-74; Hollis, *Archaeology of Herod's Temple*, 103-231.

71. M Tamid 5:1.

72. *480 synagogues:* Y Megillah 3, 1, 73d; PRK 15:7 (p. 257); Song of Songs Rabbah 5:12; Lamentations Rabbah 2:4 (p. 50b) and Proem 12 (p. 6a); Yalqut Shim'oni, Isaiah, 390 (481 synagogues). *460 synagogues:* Y Ketubot 13, 1, 35c. *394 synagogues:* B Ketubot 105a. See Miller, "Number of Synagogues," 51-55.

73. On the tendency in rabbinic literature to exaggerate data from the Second Temple period, see T Pesaḥim 4:15 (p. 166); and Lieberman, *TK*, IV, 568. See also B Pesaḥim 64b; Lamentations Rabbah 1:49 (p. 23a); Josephus, *War* 6, 423-27.

6. Masada synagogue, looking north. The room with the parchment remains is to the left.

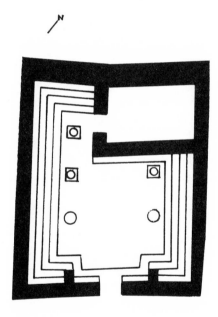

7. Plan of the Masada synagogue.

Herod's time is unclear, it was converted into a synagogue during the occupation of the fortress by the Sicarii (an extreme revolutionary faction) between 66 and 74 C.E.[74] Surrounded on all four sides by benches arranged in four tiers (with a single bench adjacent

74. Yadin, *Masada*, 181–91; idem, "Synagogue at Masada," 19–23; and now Netzer, *Masada*, 402–13. Yadin once suggested that the hall also functioned as a synagogue in Herod's time as well, but this idea has not been generally accepted. Foerster describes the room in this earlier stage as a vestibule and hall similar to those of Herodium, while Netzer identifies it as a stable (see Yadin, "Synagogue at Masada," 20–21; Foerster, "Synagogues at Masada and Herodium," 24–29; Netzer, *Masada*, 410–13).

to the northern room—see below), the rectangular hall measured 15 by 12 meters and had a single door 1.35 meters wide in the middle of its southeastern wall. Unique to Masada is a small room (5.7 by 3.5 meters) protruding into the northern corner of the hall. It is in this room that fragments of scrolls from the books of Deuteronomy and Ezekiel, containing passages undoubtedly used in synagogue liturgy at the time, were discovered. It would appear that the main hall (compared by Yadin to an *ecclesiasterion*, by Avigad to a Hellenistic basilica, by Foerster to a *pronaos* of a temple at Dura Europos, and by Ma'oz to a hypothetical Alexandrian assembly house) served the revolutionaries of Masada for meeting purposes generally as well as for religious services—i.e., it functioned as a first-century synagogue.[75]

Herodium

The 15-by-10.5-meter hall at Herodium, which apparently functioned earlier as a *triclinium* in Herod's fortress palace, was apparently used by the revolutionaries during the First Revolt against Rome.[76] Four columns and several rows of benches were introduced into this rectangular hall. As at Masada, its plaster walls were simple and unornamented. Entrance was gained through three portals in the east, and just outside the hall was a stepped cistern which may have served as a *miqveh*, a juxtaposition similar to that at Gamla in its last stage.

Qumran

The situation at Qumran is indeed intriguing. The Qumran scrolls and various literary descriptions of the Essenes (and I am assuming that the Essenes and Qumran sect were closely associated, perhaps in a broad-based movement which may have included the Therapeutae as well) indicate that the concept of worship was well developed by this group. On numerous occasions, community rules and practices relating to the form and content of the sect's worship were prescribed, as this realm encompassed much of its life. Proof of this can be found in the remains of over two hundred non-biblical prayers, psalms, and hymns which have been recovered from among the Qumran manuscripts.[77] Priests played a central role in these worship settings, and collections of blessings and

---

75. Yadin, "Synagogue at Masada," 20 n. 1; Avigad, "On the Form of Ancient Synagogues," 95-98; Foerster, "Synagogues at Masada and Herodium," 26-29; Ma'oz, "Judaean Synagogues as a Reflection," 195. Thus, the positioning of the small room in the direction of Jerusalem, opposite the synagogue's entrance, would have been merely coincidental, as Netzer also seems to indicate (*Masada*, 410-12).

76. Foerster, "Synagogues at Masada and Herodium," 24.

77. See, for example, 1QS 6:3-8; Josephus, *War* 2, 128-29; Fraade, "Interpretive Authority," 56-58; Weinfeld, "Prayer and Liturgical Practice in Qumran," 160-75; idem, "Morning Prayers in Qumran," 481-94; Chazon, "Prayers from Qumran," 265-84.

prayers seem to have been in circulation there.[78] Various opinions have been put forth regarding the required number of times for daily prayer (ranging from two to six).[79]

Talmon, on the one hand, has argued that these liturgical modes were more a continuation of biblical models than variations of forms which later found expression in rabbinic literature, a conclusion likewise reached by Nitzan in her study of Qumran prayer.[80] Weinfeld, Schiffman, and Chazon, on the other hand, have argued for a closer tie between Qumran and later Jewish practices, particularly those recorded in rabbinic literature.[81]

Nevertheless, despite the centrality of liturgical settings as reflected in the scrolls, nothing whatsoever is said about the public reading of Scriptures. Could there have been a conscious aversion to imitating what was being done in contemporary synagogues—yet another expression of the Qumran sect's desire to maintain biblical precedents while rejecting models which had evolved within the Jewish community in the post-biblical era? Alternatively, did the ongoing practice of study carried out within the Qumran community render such public readings superfluous? Interestingly, it appears that another breakaway group of the Second Temple period, the Samaritans, also did not include the reading of Scriptures as part of its communal ritual at this stage. They, too, may have tried to remain within biblical parameters as much as possible or, alternatively, distance themselves from current Jewish practice.[82]

What might have been the setting for communal worship in Qumran? The Damascus Document mentions a בית השתחות (= house or place of prostration):

> And no one entering a "house of prostration" shall come in a state of uncleanness requiring washing. And at the sounding of the trumpets for assembly, he shall have done it [i.e., the washing] before or he shall do it later, but they (the impure) shall not interrupt the whole service; for it is a holy house [בית קודש].[83]

---

78. On priests at Qumran, see, for example, 1QS 2:19-20; 6:4-5, 8; 9:7; and comments in Cross, *Ancient Library of Qumran*, 128ff.; Gartner, *Temple and Community in Qumran*, 4-15; Licht, *Rule Scroll*, 110-15; Leaney, *Rule of Qumran*, 91-95, 165, 184; Gaster, *Dead Sea Scriptures*, 332-35; Weinfeld, *Organizational Pattern*, 19; Schiffman, *Eschatological Community*, 68-71; Fraade, "Interpretive Authority," 46-69, esp. 56-57. For a suggested additional dimension of Qumran's priestly orientation focusing on basic ideological issues, see D. R. Schwartz, "Law and Truth," 229-40. On the blessings and prayers found at Qumran, see Baillet, *Qumran Grotte 4*, 73-86; Schiffman, "Dead Sea Scrolls and Jewish Liturgy," 35-42; Goshen-Gottstein, "*Psalms Scroll* (11QPs²)," 22-33.

79. Schiffman, "Dead Sea Scrolls and Jewish Liturgy," 39-40; Talmon, *World of Qumran*, 215.

80. Talmon, *World of Qumran*, 11-52; Nitzan, *Qumran Prayer and Religious Poetry*, passim.

81. Weinfeld, "Prayer and Liturgical Practice in Qumran," 241-58 and bibliography cited there; Schiffman, "Dead Sea Scrolls and Jewish Liturgy," 33-45; Chazon, "Prayers from Qumran," 265-84.

82. Weinfeld, "Prayer and Liturgical Practice in Qumran," 241-42.

83. CD 11, 21-12, 1; interpretation follows Steudel, "Houses of Prostration," 66; but see also Vermes, *Dead Sea Scrolls*, 110, and Schiffman, *Reclaiming*, 291, for somewhat different renditions of this passage. Talmon (*World of Qumran*, 241-42) and Nitzan (*Qumran Prayer and Religious Poetry*, 62-63) concur that

The term "house of prostration," reminiscent, on the one hand, of the Diaspora *proseuche*, may also hark back to biblical precedents, where such a term, together with the designation בית ה', refers to worship in general and possibly even to prayer.[84] The nature and structure of this worship setting is never made explicit, but it undoubtedly consisted of prayers, blessings, and hymns described in other Qumran writings. It is such a setting that Josephus may have had in mind when he described the main Essene worship service (and communal meal) near midday.[85]

Where at Qumran would such a liturgical setting have been? The most reasonable guess is room 77, the largest at the site (fig. 8). This room may have functioned not only as a dining area but also as a place of worship. In this regard, a platform at the western end of the room may have had some significance.[86]

If indeed public worship at Qumran included hymns, prayers, and blessings, as well as a sacred communal meal, then paradoxically the "synagogue" at Qumran—for all its uniqueness in setting, function, and liturgy—conforms in certain ways with the ordinary Judaean synagogue. The liturgical dimension was neither set apart nor assigned a special place; rather, it found expression in the main assembly hall of the congregation, as did other communal activities.

Let us turn now to the literary evidence regarding the Essenes. Philo offers us an interesting description of their Sabbath worship in contrast to the description in the Qumran scrolls. Essene worship, according to Philo, consists of the reading and expounding of Scriptures in synagogues. Regarding their Sabbath worship, he notes: "For that day has been set apart to be kept holy and on it they abstain from all other work and proceed to sacred spots which they call synagogues [συναγωγαί]. There, arranged in rows according to their ages, the younger below the elder, they sit decorously as befits the occasion with attentive ears. Then one takes the books and reads aloud and another of especial proficiency comes forward and expounds what is not understood."[87] Whether this description is reflective of Essene settings generally, perhaps even in Qumran (although admittedly ignored in the scrolls) or, alternatively, everywhere except Qumran, is impossible to de-

---

the reference is to a place of worship in Qumran; Falk, however, demurs, claiming that the reference is to the Jerusalem Temple (*Prayers*, 243–45). In general, he argues for close liturgical ties between Qumran and the Temple (ibid., 253–55).

84. II Sam. 12:20; Jer. 26:2.

85. *War* 2, 129–31.

86. Talmon, *World of Qumran*, 62. Alternatively, the author of the Damascus Document may not have had Qumran in mind, but rather the various sectarian communities scattered throughout the country which may have set aside a special בית השתחות expressly for liturgical purposes; see Schiffman, "Dead Sea Scrolls and Jewish Liturgy," 35. For a recent attempt to view the Qumran texts as reflecting the practices of a "synagogue community" closely related to Hellenistic associations, see Klinghardt, "Hellenistic Associations," 251–67.

87. Philo, *Every Good Man Is Free* 81.

8. Room 77 at Qumran,
looking west, possibly
used for meals
and liturgical gatherings.

termine. It is entirely possible that Essene groups in Judaea adopted certain practices regnant in the wider community, and it is these that Philo highlighted.

THE COASTAL AND SHEPHELAH REGIONS

Dor

The first mention of a Judaean synagogue by Josephus is with reference to Dor, in the aftermath of Emperor Caligula's attempt to erect his statue in the Jerusalem Temple (40-41 C.E.). Following this traumatic episode, and the subsequent ascent of Claudius as emperor, policy regarding the Jews reverted to its earlier, more tolerant posture. Claudius promptly issued a series of decrees protecting Jewish rights and privileges, including their right to worship in accordance with their ancestral custom.[88] One very concrete expression of this Imperial support was awarding Agrippa I rule over Judaea and Samaria, in addition to the regions already under his control.[89]

It is in reaction to these developments that some young men in Dor desecrated the local synagogue by erecting a statue of the emperor there. Agrippa appealed to Petronius, governor of Syria, who quickly intervened by dispatching a harsh letter to the leaders of the city (τοῖς πρώτοις) demanding the apprehension of the perpetrators of this deed. In the course of this letter quoted by Josephus, Petronius makes the following points regarding the synagogue:[90]

---

88. *Antiquities* 19, 279-91. On Claudius' edict and other decrees, see Tcherikover, *Hellenistic Civilization*, 409-15. See also D. R. Schwartz, *Agrippa I*, 30-31. Imperial protection extended to holy objects as well. See Josephus, *War* 2, 231, and idem, *Antiquities* 20, 115-17, where we are told that a Roman soldier was executed by the procurator Cumanus for tearing a Torah scroll.

89. *Antiquities* 19, 292-96. See Schürer, *History*, I, 442-54.

90. *Antiquities* 19, 300-311.

(1) the inviolability of the synagogue is considered a time-honored Jewish privilege, i.e., "laws of the fathers" (πατρίων . . . νόμων);

(2) setting up a statue in a synagogue is prohibited (lit., is a sacrilege—ἀσέβειαν);

(3) the synagogue is the realm of the God of Israel; no other deity or statue can be put there without destroying the institution ("each [god] must be lord over his own place, in accordance with Caesar's decree").[91]

By responding quickly and firmly, Petronius hoped to squelch any overt hostilities between local Jewish youth and their pagan counterparts.[92] We never learn what transpired thereafter, since Josephus' narrative then moves on to other events. There can be little doubt, however, given the stability of Imperial rule and Agrippa's firm control over his kingdom, that order was quickly restored and the statue removed.[93]

That a synagogue should be the target of attack by resentful pagan youth in the wake of Caligula's abortive attempt to desecrate the Jerusalem Temple is not difficult to imagine, although it may be entirely fortuitous that such an incident took place in Dor and not elsewhere. In contrast to the mobs in Alexandria a few years earlier (38 C.E.), the pagan youth made no attempt to destroy the synagogue building at Dor, much less Jewish homes and shops.[94] The Dor incident appears to have been the work of a small group of young men (νεανίσκοι) perhaps resentful of Jewish particularism and its recognized status, frustrated by the failure of Caligula's plan, or apprehensive about the restoration of Jewish political sovereignty in the guise of Agrippa.[95]

Caesarea

Some twenty-five years later, ca. 65–66, Josephus mentions a synagogue in Caesarea at the height of a conflict over the status of the Jews in that city.[96] The synagogue apparently adjoined land owned by a gentile; either the synagogue was located in a predominantly non-Jewish neighborhood, or a non-Jew happened to own land in an area

91. Ibid., 305.

92. Ibid., 309–11. On the history of such tensions between Jews and pagans during the Hellenistic and early Roman periods in Palestine, see J. H. Levy, *Studies in Jewish Hellenism*, 60–78.

93. D. R. Schwartz, *Agrippa I*, 135.

94. Philo, *Flaccus* 44–96; idem, *Embassy* 132–37; Smallwood, *Jews under Roman Rule*, 235–42. Likewise, extreme measures, such as the scourging, torturing, and hanging evidenced in Alexandria, were not invoked in Dor.

95. Josephus himself refers to them as "young men of Dor, who set a higher value on audacity than on holiness and were by nature recklessly bold" (*Antiquities* 19, 300). By way of contrast, see the recently published honorific dedication from second-century Dor to a Roman governor, presumably of Syria, in Gera and Cotton, "Dedication from Dor," 258–66.

96. *War* 2, 266–70, 284–92; *Antiquities* 20, 173–78, 182–84. See also L. Levine, "Jewish-Greek Conflict," 381–97. Opinions have varied regarding the nature of this conflict and the Jews' demands; see ibid.; Kasher, "*Isopoliteia* Question in Caesarea," 16–27; D. R. Schwartz, "Felix and Isopoliteia," 265–86.

where many Jews lived, or there were no distinct neighborhood boundaries between Jews and non-Jews in first-century Caesarea. Unfortunately, there is no way of determining which of the above is a true reflection of the reality, although the implications of each of the above possibilities are fascinating. When the Jewish community attempted to buy the plot, the proprietor not only refused to sell but proceeded to build workshops on the site, leaving the Jews only a narrow, difficult, and perhaps noisy passageway to the building. Some Jewish youth—referred to by Josephus as hotheads (θερμότεροι)—decided to take matters into their own hands and tried to halt construction, but were prevented from doing so through the intervention of the procurator Florus.[97]

According to Josephus, when the Jews had congregated inside the synagogue on the following day, the Sabbath, someone sacrificed a bird on an overturned pot at the building's entrance. The Jews were outraged; the mock sacrifice was clearly perceived to be a desecration of their building and may also have constituted an insidious reference to a well-known pagan accusation that the Jews were expelled from Egypt because they were lepers.[98] Although the Romans intervened and removed the offensive object, matters by then had gotten out of hand. Violence broke out and the Jews fled to nearby Narbatta.[99]

Qiryat Sefer (Modi'in Region)

In the course of the building of a new town, Qiryat Sefer (located in the foothills of the Judaean mountains, about fifteen kilometers east of Lod), an ancient settlement has been excavated since the summer of 1995.[100] To date, private dwellings and an industrial quarter have been uncovered, and in the middle of this complex a small building, 8 by 8 meters, was found (fig. 9). The structure is oriented on a northwest-southeast axis, and its northwestern facade—with an entranceway—was built of hewn stones. Outside the building a large gabled lintel was found with traces of a rosette and diagonal lines, perhaps indicating a Syrian gable. The floor of the hall was paved with flagstones, and there were benches and a footrest on three sides (northeast, southeast, and southwest). Behind the benches was an aisle (about 1.8 meters), similar to that at Gamla (and, later

97. *War* 2, 285–88. To achieve the same end, Jewish leaders gave the Roman official a bribe, whereupon Florus promptly fled the city, leaving the Jews to pursue their ends unobstructed.

98. *Against Apion* 1, 279 (in refutation of Manetho's claim; see M. Stern, *Greek and Latin Authors*, I, 81). According to the Torah (Lev. 14:1–7), the purification rites for a leper included the sacrifice of a bird on an earthen vessel. A similar calumny was also perpetrated by Pompeius Trogus and Lysimmachus; see M. Stern, *Greek and Latin Authors*, I, 335–37, 383–85, 533, and his comments on pp. 84–85. On the accusations of leprosy made by Philo of Byblos, Ptolemy Chennus, and Helladius regarding Moses in particular, see ibid., I, 533; II, 144–45, 149, 491.

99. According to the sixth-century historian Malalas, Vespasian destroyed a synagogue in Caesarea and built an odeum in its place (*Chronicle* 10, 261 [p. 138]), as he did in Antioch, replacing the synagogue there with a theater (see below, Chap. 4, note 225).

100. My thanks to the excavator of Qiryat Sefer, Y. Magen, for his personal communication about this site, a report which has not yet been published.

9. Qiryat Sefer (Modi'in region). The entrance leads to a hall surrounded by columns and a wide aisle. The structure stands apart from surrounding buildings.

on, Arbel). The hall contained four columns with Doric-like capitals. The building itself was set off from the surrounding complex. On the basis of the pottery, coins, and stone vessels, which date primarily to the later first and early second centuries C.E., it appears that the site was abandoned in the aftermath of the Bar-Kokhba revolt (132–135 C.E.).

Although a final report has not yet been published, it seems that we have here a small building serving this settlement and perhaps the immediate area as well. Given its central location in the settlement, its careful construction, and its public character, the structure appears to be a convincing candidate as the first village synagogue ever found in Judaea. The synagogue building itself seems to have been constructed in the second half of the first century.

OTHER SUGGESTED SITES

Buildings at a number of sites have been identified as synagogues, but these identifications are either tentative or have met with serious reservations.

Capernaum. In the course of excavating the fourth- to fifth-century C.E. synagogue, Corbo and Loffreda noted black basalt stone walls under the building's white limestone walls although with a slight discrepancy in the southwest corner. In 1981, following the excavation of trenches to clarify the dating and function of these basalt walls and others under the later building's stylobates, Corbo claimed to have discovered an earlier, first-century synagogue.[101] Measurements of the earlier building approximate those of the later one, ca. 24.50 by 18.70 meters, and its walls are 1.20–1.30 meters thick and thus seem most likely to have been part of a public, rather than private, building. The dating of the earlier building is based on pottery found in and under a cobbled pavement of basalt stone some 1.3 meters below the level of the later synagogue floor.

It is thus possible that there was a first-century building at this site. Such an assumption rests on the supposition that the basalt walls were not built merely to support the later building, but belonged to an earlier structure later utilized to provide foundation courses for the limestone synagogue building. The excavators have assumed that the layer of basalt stones constituted the floor of an earlier building, although no connection to the walls has been attested. No doors or benches have been identified. If, nevertheless, one assumes the existence of an earlier building, then its identification as a synagogue becomes compelling. A large building located in the center of town fits the bill for a first-century synagogue, although it would have been different in its location and size from the structure at Gamla. According to the excavators, for example, this building would have been about 50% larger than the one at Gamla and more than twice the size of the Masada and Herodium buildings. However, given the meager remains, there is little to be learned about the overall plan of this building.

Migdal (Magdala). In the course of excavating Migdal or Magdala, north of Tiberias, in 1971–74, Corbo and Loffreda discovered a building from the first centuries C.E. which they identified as a synagogue in its first stage.[102] The building has an unusual shape; it is a small structure (8.2 by 7.2 meters, the inner hall measuring 6.6 by 5.5 meters) having five rows of benches to the north and seven columns along the other three walls. Five columns were round and two were heart-shaped corner columns. The original floor was made of basalt slabs, but most of these were removed in the building's second stage, when the floor was raised. Corbo identified this building as a first-century synagogue which was converted into a water installation in the second century. Netzer, however, on the basis of the published findings, has concluded that the water channels on three sides of the hall were built at the same time as the earlier floor, i.e., that the original first-century building was also a water facility and that it functioned as a *nymphaeum* in both stages. The floor of the second stage was raised in order to correct a problem of flooding.[103]

---

101. Corbo, "Resti dello sinagoga," 313–57. For an English summary of these excavations, see Strange and Shanks, "Synagogue Where Jesus Preached," 25–31. Cf. also the reservations of Tsafrir, "Synagogues of Capernaum and Meroth," 155–57.

102. Corbo, "La città romana di Magdala," 364–72; Groh, "Stratigraphic Chronology of the Galilean Synagogue," 58–59.

103. Netzer, "Water Installation in Magdala," 165–72. Cf. also Ma'oz, "Synagogue of Gamla and Typology of Second-Temple Synagogues," 39.

Chorazim. In 1926, Ory reported the discovery of a synagogue at Chorazim, some two hundred meters west of the later building visible today on the site. Ory's unpublished report states the following: "A square colonnaded building of small dimensions, of a disposition similar to the interior arrangement of the synagogue, 7 columns, 3 on each side (the entrance was afforded through the east wall), were supporting the roof, and the whole space between the colonnade and walls on three sides was occupied with sitting benches in 5 courses." Unfortunately, these remains have never been verified. Visits to the site have yielded no clues as to the whereabouts of this structure. Ory's report has been included on occasion in surveys of first-century synagogues, but the use of such data seems unwarranted for the present.[104]

Northern Jerusalem. In 1991, while excavating an agricultural settlement in the northern part of the city, archeologists found a large agricultural building complex. First reports spoke of a niche in the southern wall, benches along the walls, an adjacent courtyard also lined with benches, and nearby *miqva'ot.* They suggested that this complex was, in fact, a synagogue or, at the very least, a prayer room. The complex was built in the first century B.C.E. and abandoned following the earthquake of 31 B.C.E.[105]

However, this identification has been greeted with general skepticism. The niche and benches were rather crudely made and did not seem to indicate any type of public building. Moreover, the claims made in a very brief report published several years later were severely reduced, and some details enigmatically altered or eliminated.[106] The case for a synagogue or prayer hall at this site appears to have evaporated.

Jericho. In the winter of 1998, Netzer announced the discovery in Jericho of a synagogue dating to the first half of the first century B.C.E.[107] In its final stages, the complex measured ca. 28 by 20 meters. Located next to the Hasmonean palace, its eastern section consists of seven rooms and a courtyard; its western part includes a hall (16.2 by 11.1 meters) running from east to west and surrounded by twelve pillars with benches connecting them, and aisles. Adjacent to this building on the south is a *miqveh;* the channel bringing water to it from the conduit to the north also fed a basin inside the hall itself. At a later building stage, an additional space was added on the western part of the hall,

---

104. Foerster, "Synagogues at Masada and Herodium," 26.

105. Josephus, *Antiquities* 15, 121–22.

106. On and Rafyunu, "Jerusalem—Khirbet a-Ras," 61: "At the next stage [i.e., the first century B.C.E.—L.L.] the complex was renovated; along the southern wall of the northern tower, a new wing was built which spread over a large part of the courtyard. In the middle of this new wing, a *miqve* together with a courtyard in the shape of [the Hebrew letter] 'resh' were discovered, and to the south a rectangular room (4m × 5m) divided by a low wall of hewn stones. In the eastern [*sic*—L.L.] wall of this room was a square niche in front of which was a stone-slabbed floor. It is quite possible that at this stage, which ended with the destruction caused by the earthquake of 31 B.C.E., this complex served as an assembly place for worship purposes." See also the note on this excavation in Riesner, "Synagogues in Jerusalem," 192.

107. Netzer, "Synagogue from Hasmonean Period" (forthcoming).

where a U-shaped bench was placed to serve as a *triclinium* (dining room). In the north-eastern corner of the hall a niche was found which may have contained a cupboard.

If Netzer's identification of the building is correct, it would constitute the earliest known synagogue from Second Temple Judaea. Moreover, some of the interior elements found in this building—a triclinium in the main hall and the niche with its cupboard (which Netzer suggests might have held Torah scrolls)—would clearly constitute finds of revolutionary proportions. Perhaps future excavations will allow him to further solidify this suggestion.

THE JUDAEAN SYNAGOGUE IN PERSPECTIVE

Despite the scattered and fragmentary nature of synagogue-related material, some interesting information may be gleaned regarding the first-century Judaean synagogue. Certain basic features recur in a number of cases, others can be discerned in only one or another of them, and some interesting distinctions and differences also appear, especially from region to region.

The public, communal dimension is clearly one of the most prominent features of the first-century Judaean synagogue. This is strikingly borne out in the archeological finds at Gamla, and perhaps at Qiryat Sefer as well; these are the only public buildings to have been discovered at those sites to date. This public dimension is likewise in evidence, albeit in a negative context, at Dor and Caesarea, where the synagogue became the focus of anti-Jewish activity. The fact that charity monies were collected in the synagogue, as per one rabbinic tradition, reinforces the impression of this building's centrality. Finally, the events in Tiberias emphasize in no uncertain terms the pivotal role that the local *proseuche* played in the critical deliberations of the community at the outbreak of the revolt. Interestingly, the synagogue here filled a number of roles at one and the same time; it was both a place of worship and a setting for critical political debates.

Thus, it is not at all strange that the synagogue buildings identified to date have adopted, each in its own way, an architectural style befitting a community-oriented framework. Gamla, Masada, Herodium, and Qiryat Sefer each have a square or rectangular area surrounded by columns and benches, an arrangement facilitating communal participation, be it for political, religious, or social purposes. The model chosen for these settings consciously or unconsciously approximated Hellenistic *bouleuteria* or *ecclesiasteria*, which likewise catered to an assembly of people empowered to make decisions.

The religious dimension, too, was an important component on the synagogue's agenda. However, this must be placed in perspective given the nature of our sources, which have a clear propensity to emphasize this aspect of the synagogue's activities, often to the exclusion of others. The gospel accounts focus on Jesus' preaching and teaching, and the description of his Sabbath-morning appearance in a Nazareth synagogue is extremely valuable; the Theodotos inscription likewise mentions the religious-educational aspects of the synagogue before its social-communal ones; the Sabbath assembly of Caesarean Jews in their synagogue provides the setting for a demonstrative anti-Jewish act; and the Tiberian *proseuche* was the scene of Sabbath and fast-day worship within a period of three days. Given this penchant on the part of the literary sources, synagogue remains from this period prove to be an important corrective. The buildings themselves are neutral communal structures with no notable religious components—neither inscriptions, artistic representations, nor the presence of a Torah shrine. The first-century synagogue did not have the decidedly religious profile that it was to acquire by late antiquity.

However, one component of a religious nature, the presence of a nearby *miqveh*, seems to have been fairly ubiquitous among Judaean synagogues. Such was the case at Gamla in its last stage, Masada, Herodium, and Jerusalem (assuming that some of the water installations noted in the Theodotos inscription refer to this usage as well). While there is nothing in Jewish law (then or now) that would require the use of a *miqveh* for synagogue worship (and, in fact, it all but disappears in synagogues of late antiquity), its presence reflects the communal, inclusive nature of the building. Purity concerns were of enormous importance in many circles of Jewish society in the late Second Temple period, commencing in the mid-second century B.C.E. with the rise of the Hasmoneans. Early rabbinic legal traditions, the Qumran scrolls, and the discovery of hundreds of *miqva'ot* in and around Jerusalem all attest to the emphasis on purity, which was a prerequisite for entering the Temple precincts or selling foodstuffs, wine, and oil to the Temple authorities.[108] It is no coincidence that the Mishnah reports only two instances over a thousand-year period before the second century B.C.E. when the red heifer (for purifying those with corpse impurity) was offered as a sacrifice, but no fewer than seven instances (according to another tradition: five) in the last 250 years of the Second Temple period (M Parah 3:5).

Despite the paucity of material, enough has survived to enable us to appreciate the wide diversity which characterized the pre-70 Judaean synagogue. Many, perhaps even most, synagogues in Jerusalem were linked to Jews from various Diaspora communities, which undoubtedly maintained diverse customs and practices. In fact, Jesus may have operated differently in various synagogue settings, as is indeed depicted in the various gospels, and the *proseuche* of Tiberias, physically and functionally, stands in striking contrast to what we know of other Judaean synagogues. The Caesarea synagogue, located in the midst of other buildings (even those belonging to non-Jews), is clearly quite different in situation from the synagogue at Gamla, not to speak of those at Masada and Herodium. And, of course, the Qumran worship setting was sui generis with regard to its name and its location, as indeed were most other aspects of this community.

This diversity holds true architecturally as well. Of the three best-known buildings from pre-70 Judaea commonly identified as synagogues (Gamla, Masada, and Herodium), the differences are no less salient than the similarities. Yet several attempts have

---

108. E. P. Sanders, *Judaism*, 214–30.

been made to delineate a typology for the Second Temple synagogue on the basis of these buildings: columns in the center, benches on all four sides with a focus on the center of the room, and the proximity of ritual baths.[109]

Such attempts, however, are unconvincing. Whatever elements were held in common can be attributed to Greco-Roman architectural traditions and not a particular synagogue model. Moreover, the differences between these buildings are not insignificant, e.g., the location of entrances, internal plans, positioning and number of benches, shape of the hall, and overall setting vis-à-vis surrounding structures.[110] Even the synagogues created by the revolutionaries at Masada and Herodium following the outbreak of hostilities in 66 differ from one another, although this is primarily due to the earlier buildings which they replaced. Thus, it is unjustified to speak of a single model of the Second Temple Judaean synagogue. Essentially, what we have is a variety of buildings that served the myriad purposes and functions of the first-century institution. The great variety of synagogue buildings of later antiquity had a precedent in the first century.

One of the most striking differences among Judaean synagogues may have been due to regional diversity, and this is particularly evident when comparing the coastal area with the rest of the country. The synagogues at both Dor and Caesarea had extremely high profiles: they were central institutions and were recognized as such by both Jews and non-Jews alike. Such visibility had its disadvantages, for it made these buildings vulnerable to attack by hostile mobs and groups. The events at Dor and Caesarea, as indeed at Alexandria somewhat earlier, point to a phenomenon that recurred not infrequently in late antiquity as well, either in times of political stress or in charged religious circumstances. Synagogues were desecrated, destroyed, outlawed, and at times even converted into churches by local firebrands and agitated mobs.[111]

Clearly, these coastal synagogues, located in pagan urban centers, had to deal with issues familiar to Diaspora Jewry but relatively unknown in areas where Jews formed the majority. In contradistinction to the Jews living in the interior of Judaea, those living in the coastal area as well as in the Diaspora came to accord their synagogues a degree of sanctity similar to that associated with pagan temples. Petronius' letter regarding the Dor synagogue certainly takes note of this characteristic, and apparently even those who perpetrated the desecration by placing the emperor's statue there likewise assumed that there was some sort of sanctity inherent in this place. While the religious dimension of Judaean synagogues was not a decisive factor in shaping the institution at the time, this may not

---

109. Foerster, "Synagogues at Masada and Herodium," 26–29; Maʿoz, "Synagogue of Gamla and Typology of Second-Temple Synagogues," 35–41; idem, "Judaean Synagogues as a Reflection," 10–12.

110. L. Levine, "Second Temple Synagogue," 10–13; Chiat, "First-Century Synagogue Architecture," 49–60; idem, "Synagogue and Church Architecture," 49–56.

111. Parkes, *Conflict of Church and Synagogue*, s.v. "synagogues"; Simon, *Verus Israel*, 265–70. See also below, Chap. 7.

have been as true of the hellenized, largely non-Jewish coastal region. It might well be that in this area the Jews, living as they did among a dominant pagan population, sought to enhance their communal institution with a religious dimension, much as was being done by their Diaspora coreligionists (see below, Chap. 4). Within the strictly political realm, this kind of quasi-Diaspora orientation held with regard to events in first-century Caesarea.[112]

As a communal institution, the synagogue in each and every region of Second Temple Judaea was clearly being shaped by local needs and customs. This was certainly the case with regard to Jerusalem. Given the presence of the Temple, there can be little doubt that what were considered usual synagogue activities elsewhere often found expression within the precincts of Jerusalem's Temple Mount. Mutatis mutandis, we might also assume that a Judaean village synagogue would have differed in some ways from its Galilean counterpart—whether urban or rural. The Qiryat Sefer building varies in some ways from the building at Gamla, as the one at Masada does from the one at Herodium, and as the Tiberian *proseuche* undoubtedly did from Jerusalem's Theodotos synagogue or from the synagogues at Dor and Caesarea.

In the same vein, the gospels' accounts of the healing and miracles that purportedly occurred in first-century Galilean synagogues are invaluable pieces of information. Other sources ignore this aspect of synagogue life, possibly because it was too common a phenomenon to require comment, or too embarrassing, or was simply one of the many items not addressed in these sources. Whatever the case, and despite its unusualness, there is no reason to question the reports' validity. In diatribes delivered some three centuries later, the Antiochan John Chrysostom made the same points while attempting to dissuade fellow-Christians from attending synagogue services and following other Jewish practices (see below, Chap. 8). It is difficult to assess the extent of such healings and miracle workings. Was this activity confined to the Galilee? to rural synagogues? to the lower strata of society? This seems doubtful, but owing to the limited evidence being what it is, not much more can be said in this regard.

We can see in late Second Temple Judaean society two contrasting developments. On the one hand, the Temple was assuming an ever more central role in Jewish life not only because of the growth of Jerusalem as an urban center and as a focus of significant pilgrimage, but also because of the accumulation of power by the priesthood and the enhanced role of the Temple Mount (at least since Herod's time) as the setting for a wide range of social, economic, religious, and political activities. On the other hand, as we have seen, the synagogue had been evolving as a distinct and defined institution, having fully replaced the earlier city-gate as the forum for communal activity in Second Temple Judaea. Centralization in the Temple was paralleled by decentralization in the local synagogues. Prior to 70, the Temple was recognized as the central institution in Jewish life;

---

112. L. Levine, "Jewish-Greek Conflict," 381–97.

nevertheless, the newly emerging role of the synagogue transformed it into the pivotal institution for local Jewish affairs. This development was indeed fortuitous. Though no one could have foreseen this in the early first century, the seeds of Jewish communal and religious continuity were already sown during the generations prior to the destruction of the Temple.

four THE PRE-70 DIASPORA

Ancient Diaspora communities, particularly those of Alexandria and Egypt, have provided us with a significant amount of material regarding the Hellenistic and early Roman synagogue, or *proseuche*. Epigraphical evidence hails from as early as the third century B.C.E., papyrological and archeological data from the second century B.C.E., and literary sources from the first century C.E. Together they afford an intriguing, if only partial, picture of the role and status of this institution throughout the Hellenistic-Roman Diaspora. Regarding external appearance and internal organization, there were some significant differences between the synagogues in Alexandria, North Africa, and Asia Minor. Even the various names by which communities referred to the synagogue may well reflect different perceptions of the institution and its place in society. Nevertheless, the Diaspora synagogue fulfilled much the same function as a communal and religious center within each Jewish community. Roman authorities clearly articulated the rights and privileges of this institution in a number of contemporary decrees and edicts.

By the first century C.E., Jewish communities were to be found the length and breadth of the Roman Empire, with the possible exception of the northern and western provinces.[1] Despite the well-known problems in estimating demographic statistics for an-

---

1. The widespread Jewish dispersion is attested, for example, by Diodorus Siculus (*Bibliotheca Historica* 40, 3, 8) for the Hellenistic period and, for the Roman era, by Strabo as quoted by Josephus in

tiquity, it appears quite certain that the Jewish population of the Diaspora, ranging perhaps between three and five million, outnumbered that of Judaea well before 70 C.E.[2] It
is reasonable to assume that almost any Jewish community would have had its own *topos*
(per Josephus),[3] i.e., synagogue. Thus, the number of such institutions throughout the
Empire undoubtedly reached into the many hundreds, if not thousands. However, the
information available regarding the pre-70 Diaspora synagogue relates only to a very
small percentage of these places and, what is more, varies greatly in what is presented,
and how. The geographical distribution of evidence for this institution is likewise imbal-
anced. While the large Jewish center in Egypt is relatively well documented, information
about an important region such as Syria is practically nonexistent; Asia Minor merits
considerable attention in several sources, particularly Josephus and Acts, but only limited information is available regarding Greece, Italy, North Africa, and the Bosphorus
region. Nevertheless, taken together, what we have is far from negligible, and it is to an
examination of this material that we now turn. Given the extensive geographical distribution, the variety of sources, and the fact that the sources tend to focus on particular
communities, each locale will be discussed individually.

EGYPT

Epigraphical and Papyrological Evidence

No synagogue building has yet been discovered in Egypt. However, the epigraphical material that has been recovered, supplemented by a number of papyri,[4] has contributed enormously to the study of this institution in the Ptolemaic-Roman era. This material is considerably earlier than any other Diaspora evidence known to date.[5] Altogether,
the synagogue is mentioned explicitly in fifteen documents and is implied in five more.[6]

Two inscriptions date from the reign of Ptolemy III Euergetes (246–221 B.C.E.) and

---

Antiquities 14, 115; Philo, *Moses* 2, 232; idem, *Flaccus* 45–46; idem, *Embassy* 214, 245, 281–82. See also Acts
2:9–11; and *Antiquities* 4, 115–16, in Josephus' recasting of Bil'am's prophecy.

2. Baron, *Social and Religious History of the Jews*, I, 167–71, 369–72. See also M. Stern, "Jewish Diaspora," 117–83; Smallwood, *Jews under Roman Rule*, 356–88; Kasher, "Jewish Migration and Settlement,"
65–91.

3. *Antiquities* 14, 235, 260.

4. Tcherikover et al., *CPJ*, I, 8.

5. The evidence for a significant Jewish presence in Egypt at the outset of the Hellenistic period is
persuasive. What is less clear is whether this presence was forced, i.e., because of captivity, or was the
result of free choice—or both. There are conflicting reports not only in the sources (*Letter of Aristeas* 12–
14 and Josephus, *Antiquities* 12, 11–33; contra idem, *Against Apion* 1, 186–89), but also among historians
(Tcherikover, *Hellenistic Civilization*, 273; Modrzejewski, "How to Be a Jew," 75–76).

6. The epigraphical material has been conveniently collected and extensively analyzed by Horbury
and Noy, *Jewish Inscriptions*. Previously, most of these inscriptions had appeared in Frey's *CIJ* and were

his wife Berenice, three from the reign of Ptolemy VII (143–117 B.C.E.) and his two wives named Cleopatra, three from the second or first century B.C.E., and one from the first century C.E.[7] Two other inscriptions are more difficult to date and stem from the late Hellenistic or early Roman eras.[8] One inscription from Leontopolis may be referring to a *proseuche*, and fragmentary remains of four inscriptions make mention of a *temenos* (holy place), probably also referring to synagogues.[9] Finally, four papyri dating from the late third century B.C.E. to the beginning of the second century C.E. note local synagogues in a variety of contexts.[10] Altogether, this evidence sheds light on many important aspects of the early Egyptian synagogue.

The most common type of inscription, the dedicatory inscription, appears (with minor differences) some eight times throughout the Ptolemaic era. To cite two examples:

> On behalf of king Ptolemy and queen Berenice his sister and wife and their children, the Jews [dedicated] the *proseuche*.[11]

> On behalf of king Ptolemy and queen Cleopatra the sister and queen Cleopatra the wife, Benefactors, the Jews in Nitriai [dedicated] the *proseuche* and its appurtenances.[12]

Such inscriptions clearly reflect the common Egyptian Jewish practice of dedicating synagogues to the ruling family. The geographical and chronological distribution of these inscriptions indicates that this practice was accepted by all of Egyptian Jewry. The implications of such a practice are fairly obvious: it expresses the loyalty and gratitude of the Jewish community toward the king and queen, as well as the Jews' dependence upon them. The status of the Jews in Ptolemaic Egypt as part of the class of "Hellenes" (i.e., resident aliens and not native Egyptians) was due to their protection by and service to the king.[13] In a strikingly similar fashion, Onias IV, who fled Judaea and sought asylum in Egypt, proposed to Ptolemy VI that he be granted permission to build a temple to the God of Israel at Leontopolis "in the likeness of that at Jerusalem and with the same dimensions on behalf of you and your wife and children."[14]

---

later re-edited by Lewis in vol. III of *CPJ*. The last-mentioned work remains basic for papyrological material. See also Tcherikover, "Prolegomenon," 10.

7. Horbury and Noy, *Jewish Inscriptions*, nos. 22, 117 (Ptolemy III); nos. 24, 25, 125 (Ptolemy VII); nos. 13, 27, 28 (second to first centuries B.C.E.); no. 126 (first century C.E.).

8. Ibid., nos. 9, 20.

9. *Proseuche:* ibid., no. 105. *Temenos:* ibid., nos. 16, 17, 127, 129.

10. Tcherikover et al., *CPJ*, I, nos. 129, 134, 138; II, no. 432.

11. Horbury and Noy, *Jewish Inscriptions*, no. 22.

12. Ibid., no. 25.

13. See Bickerman, *Jews in the Greek Age*, 83–85; Modrzejewski, *Jews of Egypt*, 73–87.

14. Josephus, *Antiquities* 13, 67. On this episode, see Tcherikover et al., *CPJ*, I, 44–46; Grabbe, *Judaism*, I, 266–67; Modrzejewski, *Jews of Egypt*, 121–33; Gruen, "Origins," 47–70.

Egyptian Jewry was dependent upon royal recognition and support for its communal institutions, its right to own and administer property and assets, as well as the legitimacy and authority of its communal activities and decisions. Such royal backing is reflected in a number of inscriptions: the ruling couple are referred to as "benefactors," they declare a synagogue "inviolate" (ἄσυλος), and they order an earlier dedicatory inscription to be restored.[15]

In terms of synagogue practice generally, the Egyptian custom of dedicating a synagogue to a ruler is most unusual, and only two other parallels are known: a dedicatory inscription from Qatzion in the Upper Galilee from the year 197 C.E. (although the identity of that building is far from clear) and a fragmentary inscription from late second-century C.E. Osijek, Hungary.[16] Several instances from Italy approximate Egyptian practice in that a number of synagogues in Rome were named after prominent Romans, including Augustus.[17] An Ostia inscription notes "the well-being of Augustus,"[18] and a late midrash speaks of a synagogue in Rome named after Severus.[19] These possible similarities are few in number, and thus the concentration of dedicatory inscriptions in Egypt is indeed unique. This was undoubtedly due to the centralized control exercised by the Ptolemies; as a result, religious (and other) buildings often required the sanction and authorization of the ruler.[20] Evidence of this pattern in pagan Egypt is not lacking, and the practice apparently carried over to the Jewish community.[21]

Nevertheless, it is important to note that despite the clear and unequivocal imitation of this Ptolemaic dedicatory practice, the Jews adapted it so as not to compromise their own religious sensibilities. For example, in contrast to pagan practice, the avoidance of

---

15. Horbury and Noy, *Jewish Inscriptions*, nos. 25 and 125, respectively. See also Kasher, "Three Jewish Communities," 115–16.

16. The inscription from Qatzion is quite explicit as to the dedicatees (Septimius Severus and his sons, Caracalla and Geta), the date (197 C.E.), and the donors (the Jews). However, whether the building (as yet not fully excavated) in which it was found was a synagogue or some other building continues to be debated. Advocates of such an identification are Schürer (*History*, III, 93), S. Klein (*Galilee*, 127), Avi-Yonah (*Days of Rome and Byzantium*, 49), and Roth-Gerson (*Greek Inscriptions*, 125–29), while those who question this identification include Kohl and Watzinger (*Antike Synagogen*, 209) as well as Lifshitz, who excludes this inscription from his collection of Greek dedicatory inscriptions (*Donateurs et fondateurs*). Regarding the inscription from Hungary, see Scheiber, *Jewish Inscriptions*, 53–55; and below, Chap. 8.

17. From the catacomb inscriptions, we learn of a synagogue of the Augustesians, Agrippesians, and perhaps also Volumnesians; see Leon, *Jews of Ancient Rome*, 140–42, 157–59; and below, note 132.

18. Dating from the first or second century, the fragmentary inscription reads: *pro salute aug[usti]"* (For the well-being of the emperor); see Fortis, *Jews and Synagogues*, 118; White, *Social Origins*, 392–94.

19. Genesis Rabbati 45:8 (p. 209).

20. Fraser, *Ptolemaic Alexandria*, I, 190; Kasher, *Jews in Egypt*, 134–38.

21. *Pagans:* Fraser, *Ptolemaic Alexandria*, I, 190–91, 226ff., 282–84. See also Tcherikover, *Hellenistic Civilization*, 349; Hengel, "Synagogeninschrift von Stobi," 174 n. 97; idem, "Proseuche und Synagoge," 159. *Jews:* Dion, "Synagogues et temples," 45–75.

divine epithets (especially θεός) was an elegant way of not acknowledging royal divinity.[22] Philo makes a point of noting Jewish sensitivities in this regard.[23] According to Josephus, Onias IV was also careful in his expression of obeisance to the Egyptian king when negotiating the building of the Leontopolis temple, as were the Jewish and Samaritan protagonists before Ptolemy Philometer.[24]

The terms used with regard to the Egyptian synagogue are of interest. The overwhelming majority of references in Egypt are to a *proseuche*, appearing ten times in the inscriptions and four times in the papyri.[25] The word *synagoge* appears once and a reference to synagogue officials twice; the designation *eucheion* appears on one occasion.[26] The Jews of Ptolemaic Egypt also borrowed terminology associated with pagan contexts in other instances as well. The phrase used to describe the God of Israel (θεὸς ὕψιστος— *theos hypsistos*, the Most High God) is documented in pagan as well as Jewish contexts, as are various terms for synagogue officials, such as the archisynagogue and *nakoros*.[27]

The religious dimension of these *proseuchae* is reflected in the sanctity accorded them. A number of inscriptions specifically refer to the "holy" or "great place";[28] another source associates the institution with the "Most High God."[29] The sanctity of one *proseuche* was expressed as follows: "On the orders of the queen and king, in place of the previous plaque about the dedication of the *proseuche*, let what is written below be written up:

---

22. Hengel, "Proseuche und Synagoge," 161–62; Fraser, *Ptolemaic Alexandria*, I, 283.

23. Philo, *Embassy* 134–49.

24. *Onias IV: Antiquities* 13, 67. *Jews and Samaritans:* ibid., 13, 74–76.

25. Horbury and Noy, *Jewish Inscriptions*, nos. 9, 13, 22, 24, 25, 27, 28, 117, 125, 126. For references in the papyri, see above, note 10. On the term *proseuche* with reference to the Jewish community, see Levinskaya, *Acts in Its Diaspora Setting*, 207–25.

26. *Synagogue:* Horbury and Noy, *Jewish Inscriptions*, no. 20. Papyrus no. 138 (Tcherikover et al., *CPJ*, I) seems to refer to a meeting of a Jewish (burial?) association in the *proseuche*. *Synagogue officials:* Horbury and Noy, *Jewish Inscriptions*, nos. 18, 26. *Eucheion:* Tcherikover et al., *CPJ*, II, no. 432.

27. *Theos hypsistos:* C. Roberts et al., "Gild of Zeus," 55–72; Fraser, *Ptolemaic Alexandria*, I, 282; II, 440 nn. 764–65; *TDNT*, VIII, 614–19; Simon, "Theos Hypsistos," 372–85; Levinskaya, *Acts in Its Diaspora Setting*, 51–103. This phrase was already widely used in the Septuagint (e.g., Gen. 18:20; Ps. 7:8; 17:14), Egyptian Jewish inscriptions (Horbury and Noy, *Jewish Inscriptions*, 274–75; and above), and contemporary Jewish Hellenistic literature (II Macc. 3:31; III Macc. 7:9). It appears often in the Delos synagogue (Frey, *CIJ*, I, nos. 727–29; Schürer, *History*, III, 70–71; and below), and the Bosphorus kingdom (ibid., 72; Frey, *CIJ*, I, 690, 690a; Lifshitz, "Prolegomenon," 67; Levinskaya, *Acts in Its Diaspora Setting*, 229–46; Goodenough, "Bosphorus Inscriptions," 221–45; and below). See also Kraabel, "*Hypsistos* and the Synagogue at Sardis," 81–93. *Archisynagogos:* Horbury and Noy, *Jewish Inscriptions*, no. 18, and comments on p. 29. See also Rajak and Noy, "*Archisynagogoi*," 75–93. *Nakoros* (attendant): Tcherikover et al., *CPJ*, I, no. 129; see also the material gathered in Dion, "Synagogues et temples," 65–73; G. H. R. Horsley, *New Documents*, IV, 49–52.

28. Horbury and Noy, *Jewish Inscriptions*, nos. 16, 17, 127. Although the term *proseuche* does not appear in these fragmentary inscriptions, there can be little doubt that such a building was intended.

29. Ibid., nos. 19, 27, 105.

King Ptolemy Euergetes [proclaimed] the *proseuche* inviolate [ἄσυλον]. The queen and king gave the order."[30] This inscription, usually dated to the latter part of the second century B.C.E., thus attests to the holy status enjoyed by an Egyptian synagogue from an early period.[31] Such a status may be paralleled in a papyrus from Alexandrou-Nesos in the Fayyum dated to 218 B.C.E., where it is stated that a Jew named Dorotheus was accused of stealing a cloak and took refuge in a *proseuche* (for purposes of asylum?). Only after the intervention of a third party did Dorotheus agree to leave the cloak with the *nakoros* of the synagogue until final adjudication.[32]

A further indication, albeit indirect, of the synagogue's sanctity is reflected in the use of terms such as τέμενος and ἱερον περίβολον for "sacred precinct" in connection with a *proseuche*.[33] Finally, a second-century papyrus describes a plot of land attached to a *proseuche* in Arsinoe-Crocodilopolis as a "sacred grove or garden" (ἱερὰ παράδεσος).[34] All the above would thus seem to imply that the synagogue building itself was considered sacred. Philo, too, alludes to the sacredness and inviolability of *proseuchae* on a number of occasions (see below).[35]

Epigraphical evidence makes it quite clear that the *proseuche* might include other buildings or structures in addition to the "sacred precinct" (i.e., land or courtyards) noted above. Several inscriptions mention τὰ συγκύροντα, which may refer to ancillary buildings, annexes to the main building, or landholdings.[36] Other structures may have included

---

30. Ibid., no. 125; Tcherikover et al., *CPJ*, I, no. 125; Dion, "Synagogues et temples," 57–59; Modrzejewski, *Jews of Egypt*, 97–98; Rigsby, *Asylia*, 571–73.

31. Dion prefers to date this inscription to the days of Ptolemy VIII Euergetes (145–116 B.C.E.) and notes the interesting but not particularly compelling parallel act of granting asylum to Jonathan the Hasmonean and the Jerusalem Temple by Demetrius in 152 (I Macc. 10:43). See also Horbury and Noy, *Jewish Inscriptions*, 214.

32. Tcherikover et al., *CPJ*, I, no. 129. See also Kasher, "Synagogues as 'Houses of Prayer' and 'Holy Places,'" 215. On the office in general, see Llewelyn and Kearsley, *New Documents*, VI, 203–6.

33. Horbury and Noy, *Jewish Inscriptions*, nos. 9, 129; Frey, *CIJ*, II, 1433; Lifshitz, *Donateurs et fondateurs*, no. 87; Dion, "Synagogues et temples," 59–60.

34. Tcherikover et al., *CPJ*, I, no. 134. See also Kasher, *Jews in Egypt*, 138–39. Cf., however, an alternative suggestion of Modrzejewski (*Jews of Egypt*, 89), who views this term as "a well-known technical term for one category of landed property."

35. Another indication of the holiness of a *proseuche* is reflected in III Macc. 7:19–20: "And when they finished their voyage in peace with appropriate thanksgivings, there, too, in like manner they determined to celebrate these days also as festive for the duration of their community. They inscribed them as holy on a pillar and dedicated a house of prayer [*proseuche*] at the site of the banquet." That a *proseuche* was built as a memorial to the miraculous salvation of a community is noteworthy. Unfortunately, the historicity of much of this book's narrative is questionable. See, for example, Nickelsburg, "Stories," 80–84; Modrzejewski, *Jews of Egypt*, 141–53.

36. Horbury and Noy, *Jewish Inscriptions*, nos. 9, 25. On the various meanings of συγκύροντα, see ibid., 14; Kasher, "Three Jewish Communities," 121. On the appearance of this term in a fragmentary inscription from Cyrene, see Fraser, "Inscriptions of Cyrene," 115–16.

a gateway (πυλών), such as the one from second-century Xenephyris, which is noted as having been part of a *proseuche*, or an exedra, such as the one from second- or first-century B.C.E. Athribis.[37] One papyrus mentions what appears to be a rather high water bill owed by two local synagogues; we can only conjecture that this may have been due to the use of water for guests, communal needs (e.g., sacred meals), or ritual purposes. It is also conceivable that some water may have been used for domestic purposes by Jews whose homes were located in close proximity to the *proseuche*.[38]

A number of other interesting details regarding Egyptian synagogues emerge from our data. Dedicatory inscriptions are about evenly divided between the community as a whole and wealthy individuals. *Proseuchae* were built by the Jewish communities of Arsinoe-Crocodilopolis, Schedia, Nitriai, Xenephyris, and Athribis; all of these originated in the Hellenistic period and are dedicated to the royal couple.[39] Among the seven inscriptions mentioning individual donations, two speak of donating the entire building, the others of donating parts thereof: an exedra, a sundial, and a well.[40] The remaining inscriptions are fragmentary and make no mention of the objects involved.[41] Of these seven inscriptions, two were in honor of the royal couple.[42] In only two cases is the donor's name mentioned, while in two others the donor's wife and children are also included.[43] Although the dating of these inscriptions is uncertain, they appear to be somewhat later, ranging from the second century B.C.E. down to possibly the late Roman period (i.e., the second–third centuries C.E.).

The *proseuche*'s centrality to the Jewish community is reflected not only in the number of dedicatory inscriptions or buildings and property associated with it but also by the fact that it was the meeting-place for various Jewish associations (σύνοδος). So, for example, we read of one such group (a burial society?) meeting in a *proseuche*.[44] Less clear

---

37. *Xenephyris*: Horbury and Noy, *Jewish Inscriptions*, no. 24. *Athribis*: ibid., no. 28. This was apparently an annex (partially open?) to the main hall or building, itself used for a variety of purposes. On the exedra, see ibid., 49; Kasher, *Jews in Egypt*, 112–13; and S. Krauss, *Synagogale Altertümer*, 349–50. See also Goodenough's suggestion (virtually ignored subsequently) to read "cathedra" instead of "exedra," thus turning this into a reference to a bench or perhaps a Seat of Moses (*Jewish Symbols*, II, 85). See Fraser, *Ptolemaic Alexandria*, II, 443 n. 773; Griffiths, "Egypt and the Rise of the Synagogue," 9–10.

38. Tcherikover et al., *CPJ*, II, no. 432; Fuks, in ibid., 221; and Kasher, *Jews in Egypt*, 143–44.

39. Horbury and Noy, *Jewish Inscriptions*, nos. 117, 22, 25, 27, and 24 (which mentions only the exedra).

40. *Building*: ibid., nos. 13, 126. *Exedra*: ibid., no. 28; for possible meanings of the term "exedra," see Tcherikover et al., *CPJ*, III, 143, no. 1444; Horbury and Noy, *Jewish Inscriptions*, 49–50; and, more generally, Modrzejewski, *Jews of Egypt*, 96. *Sundial and well*: Horbury and Noy, *Jewish Inscriptions*, no. 115.

41. Horbury and Noy, *Jewish Inscriptions*, nos. 16, 17, 20, 27, 129.

42. Ibid., nos. 13, 28.

43. Ibid., nos. 13, 20; and ibid., nos. 28, 126, respectively. See Noy, "Jewish Place of Prayer," 118–22.

44. Tcherikover et al., *CPJ*, I, no. 138. On the *dekany* as a possible burial association, see Noy, *JIWE*, II, no. 440. On the meaning of *dekany* in the Aphrodisias inscription, see Reynolds and Tannenbaum, *Jews and God-Fearers*, 28–30; and below, Chap. 8.

is a reference to a meeting of a Sambathic association, perhaps in Naucratis.[45] While the identification of this latter group (and whether it was even Jewish) and its precise venue remain unclear, from what we know of Ptolemaic Egypt generally, a temple—or, in this case, the Jewish *proseuche*—would have been an obvious choice.[46]

Several papyri from Arsinoe contain some interesting details regarding local synagogues. One second-century C.E. document dealing with water distribution, referred to above, notes two such institutions, one called a *proseuche*, the other an *eucheion*.[47] The former is identified as having belonged to Theban Jews; the latter presumably belonged to the indigenous population. If this was the case, then we have here an interesting example of Theban Jews organizing their own synagogue, which served as their *Landsmannschaft*. A second papyrus, from the second century B.C.E., is a land survey noting that the synagogue was located on the outskirts of the town and bordered by private estates and a canal—possibly indicating that a (the?) Jewish quarter of the town was there.[48]

One inscription refers to a gold crown, presumably a token of honor bestowed on someone.[49] This well-known pagan practice was adopted by Diaspora Jews in both Cyrene and Asia Minor (see below), and apparently in Egypt as well. A papyrus notes a "Jewish communal archive" ('Ιουδαίων ἀρχεῖον) in Abusin el-Meleq which may well have been located in the local synagogue, and it is here that documents of importance—contracts, records of priestly lineage, wills, official statements, etc.—were deposited.[50] Local synagogues must also have had arrangements for the safekeeping of communal monies earmarked for local use or for the Jerusalem Temple.[51]

Finally, there is evidence that several Egyptian synagogues, one in Alexandria and the other in Naucratis, had statues. Statue bases were discovered in each, one with the explicit inscription "to the synagogue," the second mentioning a Sambathic association.[52] Despite an attempt to explain away this phenomenon (both inscriptions deal with Judaizers and not full-fledged Jews: these were people who "did not share the sensibilities of some Jews about images"; this was a pagan institution), we may well have here evidence

45. Horbury and Noy, *Jewish Inscriptions*, no. 26 and comments on pp. 44–45.

46. C. Roberts et al., "Gild of Zeus," 72–87. Compare this to the meeting of a *dekany* in the Aphrodisias inscription; see below, Chap. 8; and White, *Building God's House*, 88.

47. See above, note 38; and Tcherikover et al., *CPJ*, II, no. 432.

48. Tcherikover et al., *CPJ*, I, no. 134 and comments by Tcherikover on pp. 247–48; Kasher, *Jews in Egypt*, 138–39.

49. Horbury and Noy, *Jewish Inscriptions*, no. 129; see also Goodenough, *Jewish Symbols*, VII, 148–71; and below.

50. Tcherikover et al., *CPJ*, II, no. 143; see also Frey, *CIJ*, II, no. 775. On the importance of documents proving priestly lineage which were stored in communal archives, see Josephus, *Against Apion* 1, 31–36; idem, *Life* 6.

51. See, for example, Philo, *Embassy* 156–57, 216, 291, 312–16; idem, *Special Laws* 1, 77. See also Josephus, *Antiquities* 14, 112–13, 214–16, 260, 261; 16, 160–72.

52. Horbury and Noy, *Jewish Inscriptions*, nos. 20, 26.

of communities whose conception of Judaism did not preclude such images, not unlike those who built a synagogue in third-century Nehardea which also had a statue.[53]

Philo

The writings of Philo are of inestimable importance as a source for Alexandrian Jewry generally and for the synagogue in particular. Living at the height of this Jewry's power and prosperity and through traumatic—even cataclysmic—events that shook the community to its foundations, Philo was far from being a dispassionate and objective bystander. This commitment, added to his natural penchant for conveying a definite religious and cultural message to readers and listeners, means that one must exercise caution in evaluating many of his claims.[54]

For example, Philo speaks of Jews in Rome conducting regular weekly meetings on "sacred Sabbaths," when they are "trained" in their ancestral philosophy.[55] He refers to *proseuchae* as schools (*didaskaleia*) for the inculcation of virtue, emphasizing the instructional dimension of these synagogue gatherings, which were based on scriptural readings.[56] These sessions were led by a priest or elder and may have lasted for a good part of the day;[57] Philo himself mentions the late afternoon as a terminus ad quem.[58] With regard to the Therapeutae, Philo describes the solemnity surrounding their Sabbath observance, which likewise featured an extensive discourse offered by the senior member of the group.[59]

Philo portrays the synagogue's religious agenda as an intensive intellectual experience, and there may be some truth to his claim. Similar frameworks for serious philosophical discussions and study sessions were not an uncommon feature in the Roman world, and some Jews—particularly in the various sects—may well have created similar settings.[60] The real question, however, is how widespread such a practice was. Did it reflect the existence of a Jewish intellectual elite in Alexandria, or was it typical of many

53. B Rosh Hashanah 24b. See Rajak, "Jews as Benefactors," 27–28.

54. Opinions regarding the reliability of Philo as a historian and commentator on current events are seriously divided; see, for example, Smallwood, "Philo and Josephus," 114–29; and, for an opposite view, D. R. Schwartz, "Josephus and Philo," 26–45. See also idem, "On Drama and Authenticity in Philo and Josephus," 113–29.

55. *Embassy* 156.

56. *Moses* 2, 215–16; *Special Laws* 2, 62, 63; *Embassy* 312.

57. See *Letter of Aristeas* 310.

58. *Hypothetica* 7, 13: "And indeed they do always assemble and sit together, most of them in silence except when it is the practice to add something to signify approval of what is read. But some priest who is present or one of the elders reads the holy laws to them and expounds them point by point till about the late afternoon, when they depart having gained both expert knowledge of the holy laws and considerable advance in piety." See also below, note 61.

59. *Contemplative Life* 31. On Therapeutae generally, see Schürer, *History*, II, 591–97.

60. See Mason, "Greco-Roman, Jewish, and Christian Philosophies," 12–18.

Egyptian *proseuchae*, both in Alexandria and the *chora*? I am inclined to prefer the former alternative, as Philo's emphasis is too unique and extreme: he alone calls the synagogue a *didaskaleion!* To assume that ordinary Jews would be interested in such intensive study sessions or would be willing to stay in the synagogue for much of the day flies in the face of all we know of human nature and Jewish practice de facto.[61]

Philo also notes that the *proseuche* functioned as a repository where funds for the Temple were collected and stored until their transfer to Jerusalem. Presumably, funds for local communal use were deposited there as well.[62]

Within his dramatic account of the Alexandrian pogroms of 38 C.E. and their aftermath, Philo takes note of Alexandrian synagogues on a number of occasions.[63] These buildings were located in every section of the city, and there was one especially magnificent *proseuche* which he describes in somewhat greater detail. Besides being large, the building was lavishly decorated with, inter alia, insignia, shields, golden crowns, stelae, and inscriptions honoring the emperor.[64] By specifically mentioning these accoutrements, Philo may have been indicating the loyalty of the Jewish community to Rome, thereby discounting one of the main charges brought by Flaccus and the Alexandrians against the Jews. Emphasizing the legal and recognized status of these buildings (Philo claims that only the Jews were so privileged by Augustus), he excoriates those perpetrating the violence and destruction as guilty of desecration and abominable acts heretofore unheard of.[65] According to Philo, the desecration reached such proportions that, not only were the synagogues despoiled and in some cases destroyed, but statues of the emperor as well as other images were introduced in direct violation of the status quo enshrined by earlier Ptolemaic and Roman rulers.[66]

One final comment on Philo's terminology is in order. In line with Egyptian Jewish practice, as noted above, Philo almost always (nineteen times) uses the term *proseuche* or

---

61. In first- and second-century Palestine, Jews abandoned liturgical study sessions or intense political discussions for their Sabbath midday meal; see, for example, Josephus, *Life* 279; B Betzah 15b. Cf., however, Kasher ("Synagogues as 'Houses of Prayer' and 'Holy Places,'" 211), who suggests that the extended scriptural readings in Egyptian synagogues, as described by Philo, originated in the desire to imitate the original reading of the Septuagint as described in the *Letter of Aristeas*, implying that this was practiced widely.

62. *Embassy* 156–57, 216, 312–16. See also Kasher, "Synagogues as 'Houses of Prayer' and 'Holy Places,'" 217 n. 44.

63. On events in Alexandria, see Tcherikover et al., *CPJ*, I, 55–74; Smallwood, *Jews under Roman Rule*, 220–55; Modrzejewski, *Jews of Egypt*, 161–83.

64. *Embassy* 133.

65. *On the recognized status:* ibid., 138–39, 311ff. See also Josephus, *Antiquities* 14, 213–16. *On the violence:* Philo, *Flaccus* 41ff.; idem, *Embassy* 132ff.

66. *Flaccus* 43; *Embassy* 134–35, 138. It is not clear, however, whether the desecration caused by the introduction of statues meant that the *proseuche* per se was considered sacred by the Jews, as has sometimes been claimed.

a derivative.[67] Nevertheless, he does use the term *synagoge* on two occasions.[68] Moreover, Philo, too, alludes to the institution's sanctity, invoking the terms τεμένος and ἱερός and ἱεροί περίβολοι.[69]

A Rabbinic Tradition

The number of sources in rabbinic literature relating to the pre-70 Roman Diaspora is almost negligible; even rarer are the references to the Diaspora synagogue. Nevertheless, we have one extremely rich pericope, and if its historicity is upheld, it will constitute a source of major importance to the subject at hand. First appearing in the early third-century Tosefta, this tradition is subsequently cited, with variations, in both the Yerushalmi and the Bavli.[70] Owing to its importance, I quote the Toseftan tradition in full:

> R. Judah [b. Ilai] said: "Whoever has not seen the double stoa [i.e., colonnade] of Alexandria has never in his life seen the glory of Israel. It is a kind of large basilica, a stoa within a stoa, holding, at times, twice the number of those who left Egypt. And seventy-one cathedrae [i.e., honorary chairs or thrones] of gold were there for the seventy-one elders, each of them [worth] 25 talents of gold, and a wooden platform [במה] was in the middle. And a *ḥazzan* of the synagogue [lit., assembly] stood on it with kerchiefs in his hand. When one took hold [of the Torah scroll] to read, he would wave the kerchiefs and they [i.e., those congregated] would answer "Amen" for each benediction; and he would again [wave the kerchiefs] and they would [again] respond "Amen." And they would not sit indiscriminately, but goldsmiths would sit by themselves, silversmiths by themselves, weavers by themselves, Tarsian weavers by themselves, and blacksmiths by themselves. And why to such an extent [i.e., why the rigid division]? So that if a visitor comes he can [immediately] make contact with his trade, and thus he will be able to make a living [ומשם פרנסה יוצאה].[71]

According to the above tradition, this Alexandrian building was of enormous proportions. The statement that it could "hold twice the number of those who left Egypt" was, of course, never intended to be taken literally; rather, it is a stock phrase in rabbinic literature denoting a very large number of people.[72] In this case, the reference is to an assembly hall of such monumental size that kerchiefs were required in order to signal the congregation when to respond. The description of the golden chairs, each worth twenty-five tal-

---

67. Mayer, *Index Philoneus*, 247. See also Hengel, "Proseuche und Synagoge," 169; Kasher, "Synagogues as 'Houses of Prayer' and 'Holy Places,' " 210.

68. *Embassy* 311; *Dreams* 2, 127. With respect to the Essenes, see Philo's *Every Good Man Is Free* 81; idem, *Special Laws* 3, 171.

69. *Embassy* 137; *Flaccus* 48; *Special Laws* 3, 171.

70. T Sukkah 4:6 (p. 273); Y Sukkah 5, 1, 55a–b; B Sukkah 51b.

71. On this source, see the comments in Lieberman, *TK*, IV, 889–92; S. Krauss, *Synagogale Altertümer*, 261–63; Fraser, *Ptolemaic Alexandria*, I, 284–85; Kasher, *Jews in Egypt*, 349–55. See also Gordon, "Basilica and Stoa," 359–62.

72. Lieberman, *TK*, IV, 890 n. 8.

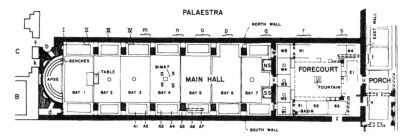

10. Plan of the Sardis synagogue.

ents, is probably exaggerated as well. Nevertheless, the above description is so detailed and unique that it ought not be rejected out of hand as totally fanciful, especially in light of the fact that archeological excavations at Sardis have revealed a synagogue building of monumental dimensions—its assembly hall alone measuring sixty meters in length (fig. 10).[73]

This rabbinic tradition immediately calls to mind the large Alexandrian synagogue which Philo describes in his narrative of the events of 38 C.E.; he speaks of this building as "the largest and most magnificent [μεγίστη καὶ περισημοτάτη] in the city," one in which the pagan mobs erected a bronze statue of a man riding a quadriga.[74] Thus, it is quite plausible that both the rabbinic tradition and Philo are referring to the very same building. The rabbinic description of the main hall as a kind of basilica, *dyplastoon* (a stoa within a stoa or a double stoa), is compatible with the architectural traditions of the period. The hall may have had rows of columns, perhaps two deep, on two, three, or four sides, thus forming a series of aisles, examples of which can be seen in the Basilica Aemilia and the Basilica Julia in Rome.[75] An example of such a multi-aisled synagogue has been discovered in Byzantine Gaza (seventh century C.E.).[76] As noted above, the first-century *proseuche* in Tiberias must also have been of large proportions if meetings of the city's residents could be conducted there in place of the city's stadium.[77] Another Tiberian synagogue of the third or fourth century (perhaps it was the same as the first-century one) was described in rabbinic sources in the same way as the one in Alexandria, namely, as a *dyplastoon*.[78]

Regarding the elders mentioned in the above Toseftan tradition, the number of those so honored is far from unusual. While "seventy" clearly has a symbolic ring, the fact is

73. Seager, "Building History," 425; Seager and Kraabel, "Synagogue and Jewish Community," 169; and below, Chap. 8.

74. *Embassy* 134.

75. Boethius and Ward-Perkins, *Etruscan and Roman Architecture*, 192–94. On monumental buildings in the East, particularly the Alexandrian *kaisareion*, see ibid., 459–60.

76. Ovadiah, "Synagogue at Gaza," 195.

77. Josephus, *Life* 92, 276–80, 331.

78. Midrash on Psalms 93:8 (p. 208b).

that this number was adopted by many ruling bodies during this period.[79] Rabbinic literature reports seventy (or seventy-one) members in the Jerusalem sanhedrin; Josephus appointed seventy leaders when organizing the Galilee in 66–67 C.E.; there were seventy prominent persons who represented the Jews residing in Batanaea, and the Zealots appointed seventy members to a high court in Jerusalem during the revolt.[80]

From an archeological perspective, the only evidence which may possibly relate to this Alexandrian tradition of seventy-one elders comes from Sardis in late antiquity. At the western end of the hall were three semicircular benches, clearly intended for people of rank within the congregation. These Sardis elders faced eastward toward the center of the hall and the Torah shrine (or shrines) located at its eastern end, and the building's excavators have estimated that some seventy people could have been seated comfortably on these benches.[81] Thus, the number of leaders in these two communities may well have been identical, although the seating arrangement in Sardis was different from that indicated by the individual Alexandrian cathedrae described in the Tosefta.

In the above-quoted Toseftan tradition, reference is made to a wooden platform (במה, *bima*) in the center of the hall which was used for the reading of Scriptures. Once more, the finds at Sardis prove enlightening, as a stone table was found in the middle of the hall, toward its western end, and what may have been traces of a platform or canopy were found toward the middle.[82] This custom of having a table or *bima* in the center of the hall was thus not uncommon in synagogues of the Roman world. In synagogues of Second Temple Judaea, such as those at Gamla, Masada, and Herodium, the reading of Scriptures would also have been carried out in the center of the hall since the benches and columns on all four sides left no room for a platform at one end.[83] In third-century Dura Europos as well, benches on all four sides of the room would have required setting up a table or platform in the center of the hall. In fact, the final excavation report notes a

---

79. Num. 11:16. On the council of elders (γέροντες) heading the Alexandrian community in the first century, see Philo, *Flaccus* 74; Schürer, *History*, III, 93–94; Smallwood, "Jews under Roman Rule," 227–33; M. Stern, "Jewish Community and Institutions," 168–69. For other representative bodies numbering seventy in the biblical period, see Judg. 9:2; II Kgs. 10:1.

80. M Sanhedrin 1:6; *War* 2, 570; *Life* 14, 79; *War* 2, 482; *Life* 11, 56; and *War* 4, 336, respectively. Equally interesting is the fact that later on the Samaritans, too, had a governing council of seventy (lit., "Family of Seventy"), which was well established in Samaritan life at the time of Baba Rabba's reforms in the third century. See J. M. Cohen, *Samaritan Chronicle*, 70, 228–29. On the number "seventy" in later rabbinic sources, see Ginzberg, *Legends*, VII, 429.

81. Seager and Kraabel, "Synagogue and Jewish Community," 169; Seager, "Building History," 426. Interestingly enough, this seating arrangement is very different from that prescribed in T Megillah 3:21 (p. 360), where the elders were to face the congregation with their backs to the holy, i.e., the Torah shrine or the direction of Jerusalem.

82. Seager and Kraabel, "Synagogue and Jewish Community," 169–70.

83. See the articles of Yadin, Foerster, Gutman, and Ma'oz in L. Levine, *Ancient Synagogues Revealed*, 19–41; and L. Levine, "Second Temple Synagogue," 10–19.

number of depressions found in the floor in the center of the room, perhaps made by the legs of a platform which once stood there.[84]

One element of the above tradition which has proven as intriguing as it has elusive is the concluding section dealing with the seating arrangements within the synagogue. Each professional group seems to have sat separately. Why should professional affiliation have proven so critical in this synagogue? One can indeed point to the inscriptions in Rome, where at least one synagogue appears to have been organized around a professional group,[85] although most Jews, both in Rome and elsewhere, seem to have based their affiliation on other criteria.

Several scholars have attempted to place this Alexandrian synagogue in a setting that would explain its economic dimension. Krauss, followed by Fraser, has suggested that the building itself was a basilica-marketplace, a merchants hall used mainly for economic purposes but also for worship and judicial proceedings.[86] Alternatively, one might posit that this Alexandrian synagogue included members of all groups but that only the artisans—for whatever reason—sat in this fashion.

Once again, the Sardis synagogue offers an interesting parallel. Located on the main street of the city, it stood adjacent to a row of shops, many of which appear to have been owned by Jews.[87] One side entrance of this synagogue even joined its atrium to these shops. Might there have been a similar situation in Alexandria, and might this in some way explain the unique seating arrangements specifically affecting the artisan class there?

However, it may be that we ought to be looking elsewhere—to the non-Jewish world—for at least a partial explanation of this phenomenon. There is a great deal of evidence, both literary and archeological, attesting to highly structured and differentiated seating arrangements in Roman theaters and amphitheaters. Even during the late Republic, but especially after Augustus, there were set places for different Roman social and political groupings, not to speak of distinctions among foreigners, *collegia*, soldiers, circus factions, women, and others.[88] It might well be, then, that as regards seating, the Alexandrian synagogue reflected current Roman practice in large places of assembly and that rabbinic tradition noted this fact in its description.

---

84. Kraeling, *Dura: Synagogue*, 256.

85. Leon, *Jews of Ancient Rome*, 142–44.

86. S. Krauss, *Synagogale Altertümer*, 261–63; Fraser, *Ptolemaic Alexandria*, I, 285. Goodenough (*Jewish Symbols*, II, 86) repeats this claim, although he is skeptical about the value of the entire tradition.

87. On representations of *menorot* on shops adjacent to the synagogue, see Seager and Kraabel, "Synagogue and Jewish Community," 176–87; Hanfmann et al., "Roman and Late Antique Period," 166.

88. See Suetonius, *Augustus* 44. For a discussion of the various social groups, see Rawson, "Discrimina Ordinvm: The Lex Julia Theatralis," 83–114; Small, "Social Correlations to the Greek Cavea," 85–93; Rouèche, *Aphrodisias in Late Antiquity*, 218ff.; Edmondson, "Dynamic Arena," 81–111; Van Nijf, *Civic World*, 209–40. My thanks to Zeev Weiss for bringing several of these references to my attention. See also MacMullen, *Roman Social Relations*, 71–79.

One final issue to be addressed concerns the basic historicity of the above-quoted rabbinic tradition. It is quite obvious that many phrases in this source recall descriptions of the Jerusalem Temple found in Josephus as well as elsewhere in rabbinic literature. On the Temple Mount, we are told, there was a large area enclosed by a double stoa ("a stoa within a stoa"), at one end of which was a basilica (i.e., a royal stoa) of colossal proportions.[89] The placing of the platform in the center of the Alexandrian synagogue and the custom of waving kerchiefs are likewise reminiscent of Temple practice. At the *Haqhel* celebration held in the Temple every seven years, a special wooden platform was constructed for the reading of the Torah;[90] whenever the high priest would officiate in the daily ritual, a Temple functionary (סגן) would stand by the altar and signal by waving a kerchief.[91] Even the opening phrase of the above-quoted tradition ("Whoever has not seen the double stoa . . . of Alexandria has never in his life seen the glory of Israel") is remarkably reminiscent of the hyperboles occasionally used in rabbinic literature when introducing Temple-related matters.[92] Therefore, it is quite in place to ask whether the literary parallels do not, in effect, undermine the historical veracity of our source. Perhaps the transmitter of the Alexandrian synagogue description, R. Judah b. Ilai (or someone before him), had collected all sorts of phrases which were originally related to the Temple and merely appended them to his description of the well-known Alexandrian synagogue, even though they had no basis in reality.[93]

I think not. In the first place, why would someone (presumably in Palestine) need to invent such an exaggerated depiction? If it was, indeed, such a blatant fabrication, why would R. Judah even bother to report it? Furthermore, the parallels noted above, from both Philo and Sardis, lend a measure of plausibility to the assumption that such a building could have existed in as powerful and wealthy a community as that of first-century Alexandria. The fact that there are so many allusions to the Jerusalem Temple in the description of this synagogue may not necessarily be owing to literary style but to historical reality resulting from either a common architectural tradition which influenced both Alexandrian and Jerusalem Jews or, what seems more likely, a conscious attempt by Alexandrian Jews to emulate the form and patterns of Herod's Temple in their large

---

89. Y Sukkah 5, 1, 55a; Y Ta'anit 3, 11, 66d; B Sukkah 45a. See also Josephus, *War* 5, 190; idem, *Antiquities* 15, 396, 411–16.

90. M Sotah 7:8.

91. M Tamid 7:3.

92. For instance: "Whoever has not seen the Temple standing has never seen a magnificent building"—B Sukkah 51b; "Whoever has not seen Herod's Temple has never seen a beautiful building"—B Bava Batra 4a.

93. The tendency to project descriptions of the Temple onto the synagogue (not to speak of Temple practices) is widespread in rabbinic literature. See, for example, R. Isaac's assertion that the phrase *miqdash me'at* in Ezek. 11:16 refers to the synagogue (B Megillah 29a). The difference, of course, is that in our case the reference relates to a particular place and time.

synagogue. It should be remembered that this may be what Onias IV did when building his temple in Leontopolis in the second century B.C.E.[94] There may be other indications of the adoption of Temple-related practices by Egyptian synagogues,[95] and if this be the case, then the Toseftan literary parallels point to a very significant historical reality: the imitation of Temple forms in at least one important Diaspora synagogue.

BERENICE (CYRENE)

Three important communal inscriptions relating to the synagogue were found in this North African city, and together they contain not a few surprises.[96] First and foremost is the very nature of these Greek inscriptions, which are decrees of the local Jewish *politeuma* honoring various individuals who had benefited the community in one way or another. These decrees not only refer to the same community but span a period of approximately sixty-five years, thus offering a repeated glimpse into the workings and concerns of this synagogue. Moreover, the inscriptions refer to the synagogue as an institution (or, as we shall see, they use an alternative term) and therefore furnish precious information regarding this institution.[97]

The earliest of these inscriptions, discovered several centuries ago, is the most poorly preserved of the three. It records a resolution of the Jewish community (here called *politeuma*) and its archons to honor one Decimus Valerius Dionysios in gratitude for his benefactions. The following is the text of the inscription:

> In the year [?] 3, on the 5th of Phamenoth, in the archonship of Arimmas son of . . . , Dorion son of Ptolemaios, Zelaios son of Gnaius, Ariston son of Araxa . . . , Sarapion son of Andromachos, Nikias son of . . . , . . . son of Simon. Whereas Dec[i]mus Valerius Dionysios son of Gaius . . . remains a noble and good man in word and deed . . . , doing whatever good he can, both in a public capacity and as a private individual, to each one of the citizens, and in particular plastering the floor of the amphitheater and painting its walls, the archons

94. Josephus, *Antiquities* 12, 388; 13, 63, 67, 72; 20, 236; idem, *War* 1, 33. Cf., however, ibid., 7, 427.

95. See Kasher, "Synagogues as 'Houses of Prayer' and 'Holy Places,'" 205–20. Moreover, the claim that R. Judah was using a current Palestinian model anachronistically is difficult. That something as monumental as the building described here existed or was under construction in second-century Palestine, in the wake of the various unsuccessful rebellions and the resultant economic and social upheavals, seems rather far-fetched, to say the least. In all probability, Jews at that time would not have been able to afford such a structure, nor is the assumption that Galilean-type synagogues were being built around that time any longer valid. Therefore, a claim for anachronism is hardly credible; see Krautheimer, "Constantinian Basilica," 123–24 and n. 22; Gutmann, "Archaeological Fact," 226–27; Fine, *This Holy Place*, 43–45.

96. On the history of the Jewish community of Cyrene generally, see Applebaum, *Jews and Greeks*, 130ff.; Hirschberg, *Jews in North Africa*, I, 21–86.

97. Published originally by Roux ("Décret de politeuma des juifs," 281–96), these inscriptions have been analyzed by Reynolds ("Inscriptions," 242–47) and Lüderitz (*Corpus jüdischer Zeugnisse aus der Cyrenaika*, 147–58). See also G. H. R. Horsley, *New Documents*, IV, 202–9; White, *Social Origins*, 296–300.

and the *politeuma* of the Jews at Berenice resolved to register him in the . . . of the . . . and [resolved] that he be exempted from liturgies of every kind; and likewise [they resolved] to crown him with an olive wreath and a woolen fillet, mentioning his name at each assembly and at the new moon. After engraving this resolution on a stele of Parian marble the archons are to set it in the most visible place in the amphitheater.

All [the stones cast were] white [i.e., the decision was unanimous]. Dec[i]mus Valerius Dionysios son of Gaius plastered the floor of the amphitheater and painted [its walls] at his own expense as a contribution to the *politeuma*.[98]

Dating to the end of the first century B.C.E.,[99] this inscription is remarkable on a number of counts. We learn that the Jewish community was led by archons and organized as a *politeuma*.[100] Though once acknowledged as the usual form of Jewish communal organization in the Greco-Roman Diaspora, this view has been called into question of late, particularly with regard to the Alexandrian and the larger Egyptian community.[101] Nevertheless, the evidence, from Berenice at least, is clear-cut; such a form of communal organization did, in fact, exist there. That archons often stood at the head of a Jewish community is well attested throughout antiquity in all parts of the Diaspora.[102] Moreover, four of the six preserved personal names of these archons are Greek; of the patronyms, four are in Greek, two are entirely missing, and one (Simon) is of Jewish derivation.

The honoree, Decimus Valerius Dionysios, son of Gaius, bears a Roman name and thus appears to have been a Roman citizen. If so, then a number of other issues connected with his name are unclear: Why is no tribal status noted? Was his father also a Roman citizen? Was he a freedman? What was his connection (official or otherwise) to the Jewish community?[103]

It appears certain that Decimus was a member of the *politeuma*, since the decree notes that he was to be exempt from communal liturgies. The honor accorded him consisted of an olive crown and a fillet, and the mention of his name at each "assembly" and on the New Moon. This "assembly" may well refer to the Sabbath gathering, well known in first-century sources. However, taking special note of a monthly meeting is unusual, as New Moon celebrations are unknown elsewhere in the Diaspora.[104]

---

98. Translation based on Horsley, *New Documents*, IV, 203, with some changes.

99. Roux ("Décret de politeuma des juifs," 288–89) dates this inscription to 8–6 B.C.E., assuming the missing letter is *iota* (= 10) or, more likely, *kappa* (= 20) and that the era is that of Actium (31 B.C.E.).

100. Cf., however, the recent suggestion by Lüderitz ("What Is the *Politeuma?*" 183–225), who defines *politeuma* here as the Jewish oligarchy or ruling body, and not the community as a whole.

101. See, for example, Tcherikover et al., *CPJ*, I, 6, 9, 32, 61; Smallwood, *Jews under Roman Rule*, 225–33, 359–60; Kasher, *Jews in Egypt*, 29ff. See the recent discussion and bibliography on this issue in Zuckerman, "Hellenistic *Politeumata* and the Jews," 171–85; Hönigman, "Birth of a Diaspora," 93–98; Lüderitz, "What Is the *Politeuma?*" 183–225.

102. See below, Chap. 11.

103. See Reynolds, "Inscriptions," 246–47; Lüderitz, *Corpus jüdischer Zeugnisse aus der Cyrenaika*, 151.

104. The juxtaposition of regular (i.e., Sabbath) meetings and those of the New Moon in this and the following inscription is intriguing, but elusive; see Judith 8:6; McKay, *Sabbath and Synagogue*, 11–42.

The reference to Decimus' significant impact on a great many people (the citizens of Berenice generally? the Jewish community only?) may have been the result of his holding public office. In particular, he is recognized as having contributed to the Jewish community by plastering the floor of the amphitheater and painting its walls.

Of the two specific benefactions noted, the painting of walls is most intriguing. The Greek word ζωγραφέω can convey two possible meanings: to paint generally or to paint figures (human or animal). If the former was intended, then the paintings may have been similar to those at Pompeii, Herodian Jerusalem, or Masada.[105] If the latter was intended, then the amphitheater would have boasted more striking decorations, and if it indeed served as a synagogue, as will be argued below, then the decorations might have been similar to those in other Diaspora synagogues, such as on the third-century walls at Dura Europos or the sixth-century mosaic floor at Ḥammam Lif in North Africa.[106] At this juncture, certitude is elusive.

Perhaps the most significant detail in this inscription is the thrice-mentioned term "amphitheater": To what does it refer? Was it a civic building which served all citizens as a place of sports, entertainment, or assembly? Or was this the synagogue of the *politeuma?* Among those who have addressed the issue, three distinct approaches have been adopted. Schürer, Goodenough, Caputo, Gabba, Horsley, and Zuckerman assume that this was a regular Roman amphitheater;[107] Robert, Applebaum, Cohen, M. Stern, Rajak, and Barclay assume it was a Jewish public building;[108] Hirschberg, Roux, Reynolds, Lüderitz, and White are less commital.[109]

The major arguments in favor of regarding the amphitheater as a civic building are as follows: the term itself suggests that interpretation; the decorations involved are attested in public entertainment buildings elsewhere in North Africa; Jews are known to have frequented theaters and amphitheaters and thus may well have contributed funds to them; the inscription also notes Decimus Valerius Dionysios' benevolence to all citizens of the city; the Jews of Cyrene were quite hellenized, and therefore erecting a stele in a

---

105. *Pompeii:* Brion, *Pompeii and Herculaneum*, 201–30. *Jerusalem:* Avigad, *Discovering Jerusalem*, 81ff. *Masada: NEAEHL*, III, 973ff.

106. See below, Chap. 8. On the murals in the first-century synagogue at Acmonia (Asia Minor), see below. The same root, ζωγράφος, appears on a third- or fourth-century sarcophagus from Rome to designate the profession of Eudoxius (Noy, *JIWE*, II, no. 277).

107. Schürer, *History*, III, 104; Goodenough, *Jewish Symbols*, II, 143–44; XII, 52 n. 11; Caputo, "Edifici teatrali della Cirenaica," 283–85; Gabba, *Iscrizioni Greche e Latine*, 63ff.; G. H. R. Horsley, *New Documents*, IV, 208–9; Zuckerman, "Hellenistic *Politeumata* and the Jews," 179.

108. Robert, *Gladiateurs*, 34 n. 1; Applebaum, *Jews and Greeks*, 164–67; idem, "Organization of Jewish Communities," 486–88; S. J. D. Cohen, *From Maccabees to Mishnah*, 109–10; M. Stern, "Jewish Diaspora," 135; Rajak, "Jews as Benefactors," 28–30; Barclay, *Jews in the Mediterranean Diaspora*, 237.

109. Hirschberg, *Jews in North Africa*, I, 26; Roux, "Décret de politeuma des juifs," 290–92; Reynolds, "Inscriptions," 247; Lüderitz, *Corpus jüdischer Zeugnisse aus der Cyrenaika*, 155; White, *Social Origins*, 297 n. 36. Cf., however, Lüderitz's comments in "What Is the *Politeuma?*" 213, where he seems much more comfortable with a Jewish identification.

civic building might constitute but one more example of their acculturation; the amphi-theater was probably a well-enough-established institution in the late first century B.C.E. as to preclude applying the name to a different type of building.

On the other hand, the following considerations argue for identifying the amphi-theater as a specifically Jewish building: Why should a prominent Jew have been respon-sible for or have seen fit to repair and plaster the floor of a city amphitheater? The usual Roman amphitheater is not known to have had plastered floors, in any case. Would the Jews have been able to place a stele in a civic institution? And if Dionysios' beneficence was not related to them, why would the Jewish community have honored him for it? Why would Jews have placed their communal inscriptions in a public arena? The amphi-theater was still not a well-defined institution functionally at this time, and consequently the name could well have been used for other institutions, in this case a synagogue.[110] Moreover, the last lines of the inscription indicate that Decimus Valerius Dionysios' gift was given to the *politeuma*, thus confirming that this was most probably a Jewish building. A second inscription from Berenice (see below) likewise associates the Jewish commu-nity with an amphitheater, further reinforcing this connection. If, on the other hand, the amphitheater was a civic institution, then why were the Jews using it regularly for their communal purposes?[111] Certitude in this matter is impossible. We read of no remotely similar occurrence elsewhere in antiquity. While we are dealing here with obviously Jew-ish communal matters, that the term "amphitheater" might refer to a Jewish building is most unusual, to say the least. However, to assume that this inscription refers to honors bestowed by the Jews on one of their own in return for benefactions to the city's amphi-theater, and then to call this a contribution (ἐπίδομα) to the *politeumata*, would require an enormous stretch of the imagination.

It seems, therefore, that the most likely interpretation is that we are indeed dealing here with a Jewish institution.[112] We cannot be sure why exactly it was called an amphi-theater. The most likely explanation is that the name was related to the shape of the building. The word ἀμφιθέατρον seems to indicate a circular or elliptical arena where

---

110. On the architectural fluidity of the Roman amphitheater prior to the Flavian era and the building of the colosseum, see Golvin, *L'amphithéâtre romain*, I, 268–72. Humphrey ("Hippo-Stadia," 122) writes: "In the Late Republic and early Empire, the terminology for Roman entertainment buildings, and espe-cially for the building that we would later know as the 'amphitheater,' was still in flux." Welch, in "Roman Amphitheatres Revived," 273, notes: "The Colosseum canonized the Roman amphitheatre as an archi-tectural form. Amphitheatres securely dated after it (e.g., Capua) self-consciously refer to it in the same way that circuses throughout the empire looked back to the Circus Maximus." On the early evolution of the amphitheater, however, Welch adopts a different approach; see idem, "Arena in Late-Republican Italy," 69.

111. On the other hand, theaters, amphitheaters, and stadiums were often used for meetings of the citizenry as a whole, as in *Alexandria*—Josephus, *War* 2, 490-91; *Antioch*—ibid., 7, 47; *Ephesus*—Acts 19:29; *Tiberias*—Josephus, *Life* 331.

112. See M. Stern, "Jewish Diaspora," 135.

people sit in the round, or, as per Dionysios of Halicarnassus, it could refer to a U-shaped building with seating on three sides.[113] Serving as a meeting place for the community, this amphitheater qua synagogue had to have adequate seating arrangements. We possess no information regarding its location in the city. Applebaum once suggested a site outside the city wall to the south, but he later retracted this in light of subsequent excavations.[114]

The second Berenice inscription, from 24–25 C.E., contains a further resolution of the community—this time in the name of nine archons and the *politeuma* at large—taken on the festival of Sukkot. The inscription notes the honors bestowed upon a Roman official, Marcus Tittius, for his support of the Jewish community, as well as for his kindness to the Greek citizens of the city.

> Year 55. Phaoph 25. At the gathering of the Festival of Tabernacles during the terms of office of the archons:
>
> Cleandros son of Stratonicos
> Euphranor son of Ariston
> Sosigenes son of Sosippos
> Andromachos son of Andromachos
> Marcus Laelius Onasion son of Apollonios
> Philonides son of Hagemon
> Autochles son of Zenon
> Sonicos son of Theodotos
> Josephos son of Straton
> Since Marcus Tittius[115] son of Sextus [from the tribe of] Aemilia, a goodly and worthy man, who has assumed the responsibility of government in public affairs and who has exercised management of these matters benevolently and rightly, and has always displayed in his conduct a gentle character on all occasions; and not only does he give of himself unstintingly in these matters to those citizens [of the city generally] who entreat him in private, but also to the Jews of our *politeuma*, publicly and privately, he has been supportive in his governance and has not ceased, in his own noble goodness, behaving in a worthy manner. Now, therefore, the archons and *politeuma* of the Jews in Berenice have decided to praise him by name and dedicate to him at each assembly and new moon [celebration] a crown of olive branches and a woolen fillet; and [it has been decided] that the archons are to record this resolution on a stele of Parian marble and set it up in the most prominent place in the amphitheater.
>
> All [the stones cast] were white.[116]

---

113. See, for example, his description of the old Circus Maximus as a U-shaped building in *Roman Antiquities* 3, 68, 3; and comments by Cary, LCL, II, 242–43 n. 2. See also Humphrey, "Hippo-Stadia," 122–23. It is interesting to note that in the fourth century C.E. Epiphanius speaks of Samaritans imitating the Jews by building a synagogue "which is shaped like a theater and thus is open to the sky" (*Panarion* 80, 1, 6).

114. Applebaum, "Jewish Community in Cyrenaika," 159–62; idem, *Jews and Greeks*, 194.

115. On the spelling of this name, see Reynolds, "Inscriptions," 245.

116. For the Greek text, see above, note 97.

The dating of this document is certain: the year 55 of the Actium era, i.e., 24–25 C.E.[117] The document is clearly a Jewish one. It begins with a list of archons and a decree taken on the Sukkot holiday.[118] The benefactions of Marcus Tittius to the Jews may have been appreciably more significant than those he bestowed on the Greeks; at least the Jews seem to have thought so. That such a declaration was made by the Jewish community at its regular weekly (?) and monthly meetings in the amphitheater once again suggests that we are dealing with a Jewish building.

The inscription provides clear evidence of the salutary rapport enjoyed by the Jewish community with this Roman official. Moreover, the community's efforts to publicly proclaim these excellent relations, orally and in writing, is striking evidence of a sense of self-confidence vis-à-vis the authorities. The fact that the favors bestowed by Marcus Tittius do not appear to have been at the expense of, or opposed by, the general citizenry but were part of his overall policy reinforces the impression that—at this juncture, at least—the Jews were on good terms with their Greek neighbors and Rome's representatives. This had not always been the case, as a letter from Marcus Agrippa to the *polis* of Cyrene some four decades earlier attests.[119]

The use of crowns and fillets indicates the continued use of Greek customs in bestowing honors, as does dedicating a stele in a public building. There is no more powerful indication of this acculturation than the names of the nine archons and their fathers. Of the twenty names which appear, nineteen are Greek or Roman and only one (Josephos) is Jewish. Noteworthy is the fact that these Greek names (as in the other two inscriptions) were popular in pagan Cyrene.[120] Together with the Greek language, the other elements in this inscription—the year and month, the voting process (casting white stones), its formulary announcement, the designation *politeuma*, and the ways in which honor was bestowed—all point to a community comfortably ensconced in its larger Greco-Roman milieu.[121]

Once again, we are informed of the set meeting times of the community when Tittius was to be honored. It would seem that the regular assembly was on the Sabbath, and additional meetings were held at the beginning of each month. At least part of these assemblies undoubtedly included a liturgical element; to what extent, if at all, these gatherings included "secular" communal matters is unknown. If they did, then such a combination

---

117. Lüderitz ("What Is the *Politeuma?*" 212) has suggested a much earlier date—43 B.C.E.

118. Might this Sukkot meeting time be related to a note appearing in a later Christian source, stating that Jewish archons were elected annually in September (Tishri)? See Schürer, *History*, III, 99; and below, Chap. 8. See also Burtchaell, *From Synagogue to Church*, 235 n. 61.

119. Josephus, *Antiquities* 16, 160–61, 169–70. Hirschberg's suggestion, that Tittius was honored because he implemented the Imperial edicts recorded by Josephus, is problematic owing to the time gap between the decree and the writing of the inscription; see his *Jews in North Africa*, I, 25–26.

120. Reynolds, "Inscriptions," 244–45; Applebaum, "Jewish Community in Cyrenaika," 163.

121. See Fraser, *Ptolemaic Alexandria*, II, 484 and n. 781.

would be reminiscent of Josephus' account of events in Tiberias at the outbreak of the revolt in 66 C.E.[122] It is of significance that major gatherings of the community took place on the Sukkot festival, when important decisions such as the one recorded in the above inscription were made.

A third inscription, from the year 55 C.E., commemorates a series of donations made by at least eighteen individuals (part of the slab is broken and part is missing) for restoring their synagogue (here referred to as a συναγωγή):

> The year 2 of Nero Claudius Caesar Drusius Germanicus Imperator on 6 Choiak:
> It has been decided by the community [συναγωγή] of Jews in Berenice that those donating towards the restoration of the synagogue building [συναγωγή] be inscribed on a stele of Parian marble:
>
> | | | |
> |---|---|---|
> | Zenion son of Zoilos | archon | 10 dr[achmae] |
> | Isidoros son of Dositheos | archon | 10 dr. |
> | Dositheos son of Ammonios | archon | 10 dr. |
> | Pratis son of Jonathan | archon | 10 dr. |
> | Karnedas son of Cornelius | archon | 10 dr. |
> | Heracleides son of Heracleides | archon | 10 dr. |
> | Thaliarchos son of Dositheos | archon | 10 dr. |
> | Sosibios son of Jason | archon | 10 dr. |
> | Pratomedes son of Socrates | archon | 10 dr. |
> | Antigonos son of Straton | archon | 10 dr. |
> | Kartisthenes son of Archias | priest | 10 dr. |
> | Lysanias son of Lysanias | | 25 dr. |
> | Zenodoros son of Theuphilos | | 28 dr. |
> | Mar . . . [son of] | | 25 dr. |
> | Alexander son of Euphranor | | 5 dr. |
> | Isidora daughter of Serapion | | 5 dr. |
> | Zosima daughter of Terpolios | | 5 dr. |
> | Polon son of Dositheos | | 5 dr.[123] |

Compared with the two previous inscriptions, this one is unique in a number of ways. The list of donors reveals a wealth of names unmatched in the other Cyrenian inscriptions. Once again, Greek names predominate, with many characteristic Greek Cyrenian (Karnedas, Kartisthenes, Pratis, Pratomedes), Egyptian (Ammonios, Serapion), Roman (Cornelius), and Hebrew (Jonathan) names.

Of the eighteen donors, the first ten are archons—as compared to seven and nine in the two earlier inscriptions—a factor which may indicate growth in the local Jewish community or perhaps only an administrative reorganization that had taken place in the three

---

122. *Life* 276–303; and above, Chap. 3.

123. For the Greek text, see above, note 97; and Lifshitz, *Donateurs et fondateurs*, no. 100. See Reynolds, "Inscriptions," 244; Applebaum, "Jewish Community in Cyrenaika," 163 and esp. n. 152.

decades between the second and third inscriptions. Either of these possibilities is likely in light of the fact that the word *synagoge* appears twice here, once in relation to the community itself (instead of the previously used term, *politeuma*) and once with reference to the community building (instead of amphitheater).

At the very least, the above terms (*politeuma*-synagogue; amphitheater-synagogue) may have been synonymous,[124] and thus no great significance is to be attributed to the change in nomenclature. It is less likely that these terms refer to two distinct Jewish frameworks existing side by side in the city.[125] If the community decided to change its nomenclature, as seems mostly likely, we can only speculate as to the reasons for such a change. Was the community assuming a more "Jewish" posture; i.e., were these new terms now considered more Jewishly identifiable and significant? This line of reasoning, however, is not borne out by the names of the community leaders or the language of the inscription, where the Greek component remains strong. Perhaps the Jews lost their right to be called a *politeuma?* Or, in the case of the building, was the term "amphitheater" now associated more with a sports arena and therefore inappropriate for a Jewish public building? It may also be the case that the Jewish community underwent some far-reaching changes—internally and externally—in the first century C.E., but any such changes remain unknown.[126] In any case, we can assume rather confidently that in all three inscriptions we are dealing with the main body of Jews in Cyrene and not some marginal group; each appears to speak on behalf of the entire Jewish community of the city.

The third inscription also raises several points of interest with regard to the people and sums of money mentioned. First among the non-archons on the list is a priest, perhaps significant owing to his status in the community, which would be reminiscent of Philo's reference to a priest presiding over Sabbath instruction as well as of Jerusalem's Theodotos inscription.[127] Several Jewish women are mentioned as donors, a phenomenon attested for first-century Asia Minor and one that recurs with greater frequency in later antiquity in both the Diaspora and Palestine.[128] Finally, the sums of money recorded are generally quite modest. Whether this is of import regarding the economic and political status of the Jewish community in the mid-fifties is impossible to tell.

---

124. See Kasher, *Jews in Egypt*, 181.

125. Perhaps, as in second-century B.C.E. Memphis, where the terms *politeuma* and *synagoge* appear simultaneously; see Rappaport, "Iduméens en Egypte," 73–82. See also Applebaum, *Jews and Greeks*, 162 n. 149.

126. See Applebaum, "New Jewish Inscription," 172.

127. See above; and Chap. 3.

128. See below, Chap. 14.

ITALY

Ostia

Although the Ostia synagogue as it stands today dates from the fourth century c.e., there are several earlier stages in the building's history.[129] Most of the extant building existed from the beginning: the main hall, adjacent areas to the east, the kitchen, and parts of other walls. All underwent extensive renovations over time. The masonry of a large auxiliary room, built in *opus vittatum* as opposed to the *opus reticulatum* of the synagogue hall, was clearly an addition, as were the monumental apsidal *aedicula* and massive columns which later dominated the main hall. Moreover, these last-noted additions, i.e., the *aedicula* and the columns, seem to have required the removal of a second floor and the sealing of upper-story windows. Unfortunately, the absence of a detailed excavation report makes it impossible to delineate the synagogue's earliest building stage with any degree of certainty.

Nonetheless, there is general agreement that the earliest traces of the building go back to the first century c.e. The synagogue then consisted primarily of the 24.9-by-12.5-meter hall,[130] which, along with several other rooms, served the needs of the local community. The room may already have had a *bima* along its curved western wall and may have been lined with benches.

The synagogue itself was located on the outskirts of the city, near the city wall and close to the sea, a pattern widely adopted by Diaspora Jewish communities.

Rome

Our knowledge of synagogues in Rome derives primarily from the rich epigraphical evidence found in the local Jewish catacombs. Originally attributed to the first centuries c.e., these finds have been reevaluated over the past decade, resulting in a general consensus that dates them to the third to fifth centuries c.e.[131] Nevertheless, some of the synagogues referred to may have already existed in the first century c.e. There are four likely candidates, three of which were apparently named after prominent first-century Romans: Augustus, Agrippa, and Volumnius. The fourth is called the synagogue of the Hebrews, perhaps so-named owing to the fact that it was the first Jewish congregation in the city.[132]

---

129. On the earlier stages of this building, see Squarciapino, *Synagogue of Ostia*, 25; Fortis, *Jews and Synagogues*, 124–25; Kraabel, "Diaspora Synagogue," 498–99; White, *Building God's House*, 69; idem, *Social Origins*, 379–82; idem, "Synagogue and Society," 27–38.

130. Following the measurements in the Italian (and not the English) section of Squarciapino's report (p. 7). See also Kraabel, "Diaspora Synagogue," 497.

131. Rutgers, "Jüdischen Katakomben," 140–57.

132. La Piana, "Foreign Groups," 354–56; Leon, *Jews of Ancient Rome*, 140–42, 147–49, 157–59; M. Stern, "Jewish Diaspora," 166–67; van der Horst, *Ancient Jewish Epitaphs*, 86–89. Synagogues of the

In addition, there is one literary source that clearly relates to the first-century syna-gogues of Rome, i.e., Philo's description of the Roman community in his *Embassy*. In noting the beneficence of Augustus to the Jews generally, and to those in the capital city in particular, Philo notes the following:

> How then did he [Augustus] show his approval? He was aware that the great section of Rome on the other side of the Tiber is occupied and inhabited by Jews, most of whom were eman-cipated Roman citizens. For having been brought as captives to Italy they were liberated by their owners and were not forced to violate any of their native institutions. He knew there-fore that they have houses of prayer [προσευχάς] and meet together in them, particularly on the sacred sabbaths when they receive as a body a training in their ancestral philosophy. He knew, too, that they collect money for sacred purposes from their first-fruits, and send them to Jerusalem by persons who would offer the sacrifices. Yet, nevertheless, he neither ejected them from Rome nor deprived them of their Roman citizenship because they were careful to preserve their Jewish citizenship also, nor took any violent measures against the houses of prayer, nor prevented them from meeting to receive instructions in the laws, nor opposed their offerings of the first-fruits.[133]

Philo's description of the Roman *proseuchae* is fascinating. The problem, of course, is de-termining how much here is Philo's projection of Alexandrian practices and terminology onto Rome's Jewry and how much actually accords with the Jewish scene in the Imperial capital during the first century. If later catacomb evidence can provide a clue, it would seem that Philo's use of the term *proseuche* is out of place here. Epigraphical evidence from the catacombs indicates that the Jews of Rome used the term *synagoge* with but rare exception.[134] But since these inscriptions date by and large to the third to fifth centuries, it is also possible that the nomenclature had changed by then. In this vein, we should also note that Juvenal, in the early second century, likewise uses the term *proseuche* with reference to the local Jewish community.[135] Nevertheless, Philo's description of Roman Jewish synagogues and practices seems to correspond with what we know about other Jewish communal frameworks at the time: the Jews possessed a communal building, met

---

Hebrews were also found in Philadelphia in Lydia (see Frey, *CIJ*, II, no. 754; Trebilco, *Jewish Communi-ties*, 162) and in Corinth (Frey, *CIJ*, I, no. 718), and a synagogue of the Jews is attested in Reggio di Cala-bria (ibid., no. 635b; Noy, *JIWE*, I, no. 139). For a review of the interpretations of the term "Hebrews," see Harvey, "Synagogues of the Hebrews," 132–47.

That Jews would name their synagogues after prominent Romans is indeed unusual; even in Ptole-maic Egypt, *proseuchae* were dedicated to rulers but not named after them. The high regard in which the Jews held these rulers (and perhaps were dependent upon them) is certainly reflected in this practice, just as it is in Philo's encomium to Augustus cited above. See now Richardson ("Augustan-Era Syna-gogues in Rome," 17–29), who suggests that there were perhaps five early synagogues, including that of the "Herodians."

133. *Embassy* 155–57.
134. Frey, *CIJ*, I, no. 531; Leon, *Jews of Ancient Rome*, 139.
135. *Satires* III, 296 (M. Stern, *Greek and Latin Authors*, II, 99).

regularly, especially on the Sabbaths, designated study as the focal liturgical activity, and sent funds to Jerusalem (i.e., the firstfruits).[136] In short, although we cannot be certain of Philo's accuracy, neither should this information be rejected out of hand.

In fact, Philo's description of the status of Rome's Jewish community, in its general outline, is corroborated by Josephus. In a decree directed to the citizens of Delos, he notes the following: "For example, Gaius Caesar, our consular *praetor*, by edict forbade religious societies to assemble in the city [i.e., Rome itself], but these people alone he did not forbid to do so or to collect contributions of money or to hold common meals."[137] The rights thus enjoyed by Rome's Jewish community were firmly fixed and were the basis of Jewish communal life—the rights to assemble, collect monies, and hold communal meals. Moreover, the granting of such rights was an exception to general policy. According to this document at least, only the Jews were accorded such recognition, at first by Julius Caesar and later by Julius Gaius.[138] In reality, however, many groups in Rome functioned similarly in the first century C.E., whether officially or unofficially. For example, some political and religious *collegia* were forbidden in Rome from the time of Caesar and Augustus; others were declared *licita*, and still others existed surreptitiously, although the above decree gives quite a different impression.[139]

Of interest regarding Rome's synagogues is another statement made by Philo. He indicates that the Jews tended to live together in the Transtiberine (Trastevere) region, much as Alexandrian Jewry concentrated in two of that city's five quarters.[140] It appears that of the eleven or more synagogues mentioned in the catacomb inscriptions, at least seven were located in the Transtiberene area.[141] But just as some Alexandrian Jews were to be found in other quarters of the city as well,[142] such seems to have been the case in Rome, too. In fact, the discovery of Jewish catacombs in different directions outside the city walls might argue for such a spread, at least later on.[143]

---

136. Philo may have accorded his last point special prominence given the overall agenda of *Embassy*, i.e., to demonstrate the sanctity and centrality of the Jerusalem Temple for Jews everywhere. Still, it is doubtful whether Philo would have invented such practices rather than merely highlighting certain existing customs for his purposes. See also *Embassy* 312-16.

137. *Antiquities* 14, 214-15; and comments in Smallwood, *Jews under Roman Rule*, 135 n. 52; Rajak, "Jewish Rights," 23-24.

138. See below, p. 104. On Caesar's attitude to *collegia* generally, see Suetonius, *Iulius* 42, 3: "He dissolved all guilds, except those of ancient foundation."

139. See La Piana, "Foreign Groups," 183ff. On Jewish rights, especially in comparison with those of other peoples, see Pucci Ben Zeev, "Caesar and Jewish Law," 28-37.

140. Philo, *Flaccus* 55. Cf., however, Josephus, *War* 2, 495, where Josephus claims that the Jews were particularly concentrated in the Delta quarter, a claim indirectly borne out in the papyri; see Tcherikover et al., *CPJ*, II, nos. 194, 200, 202, 209, 212, 213, 221.

141. M. Stern, "Jewish Diaspora," 167; and below, Chap. 8.

142. Philo, *Embassy* 132.

143. M. Stern, "Jewish Diaspora," 165-68; and below, Chap. 8.

DELOS

Discovered in the early part of the twentieth century, the building at Delos, an Aegean island lying to the south and east of the Greek mainland, has for decades been a subject of debate. Only since the 1970s has a consensus emerged that views the building as a synagogue, the earliest known to date and the only building complex identified as such with certitude from the pre-70 Diaspora.[144]

It is unclear when precisely the local Jewish community built or occupied this building as a synagogue. The terminus a quo is the second century B.C.E., the terminus ad quem the mid-first century B.C.E. The building continued to function as a synagogue down to the second century C.E. It was located on the eastern shore of the island, some distance from the harbor and city center and near a stadium, gymnasium, and residential area.[145] In fact, the synagogue building itself may have originally been a private home, later transformed by the local Jewish community into its religious and social center. A similar phenomenon held true for several pagan associations in Delos;[146] it also seems to have been the case in other Jewish communities of the Diaspora in subsequent centuries.[147] Utilizing a building originally intended as a private home may be a reflection of the (limited) size of a community and, secondarily perhaps, of the economic resources at its disposal.

The Delos synagogue (fig. 11) included a courtyard to the east, fronting the sea (C). The building itself was divided into three parts: the southern part (D) contained a series of small rooms, one giving access to a cistern; the middle room (B), having a triportal entrance, functioned as the main point of entry into the assembly hall (A), located to the north. Benches lined at least two walls of this last room, and a carved marble chair was positioned in the middle of the western wall, facing the single entrance from the east.[148]

The identification of the Delos building as a synagogue is based on a number of factors, some of secondary importance, others more primary. In the former category are the following considerations: Jews were already living in Delos in the later Hellenistic period; the building was located close to the sea, as was customary for synagogues in many communities; the building plan has some characteristics reminiscent of Galilean-type synagogues; the marble chair was possibly a Seat of Moses; the building faced east,

---

144. Overviews of the history of this debate have been offered on a number of occasions; see, for example, Bruneau, *Cultes de Délos*, 486ff.; idem, " 'Israélites de Délos'," 489-95; Kraabel, "Diaspora Synagogue," 491; White, "Delos Synagogue Revisited," 137-40; idem, *Social Origins*, 332-42. See also Goodenough, *Jewish Symbols*, II, 71-75.

145. Bruneau, *Cultes de Délos*, pl. A; idem, " 'Israélites de Délos,' " 466; White, "Delos Synagogue Revisited," 156.

146. Bruneau, *Cultes de Délos*, 622-30; idem, " 'Israélites de Délos,' " 494; White, "Delos Synagogue Revisited," 152; idem, *Building God's House*, 66. See also Picard, *L'établissement des Poseidoniastes de Bérytos*.

147. So, for example, in Ostia, Priene, Dura, and Stobi. See White, *Building God's House*, 62ff.; and below, Chap. 8.

148. For a description of the remains, see Plassart, "Synagogue juive de Délos," 201-5; Bruneau, *Cultes de Délos*, 481-84; White, "Delos Synagogue Revisited," 147-52.

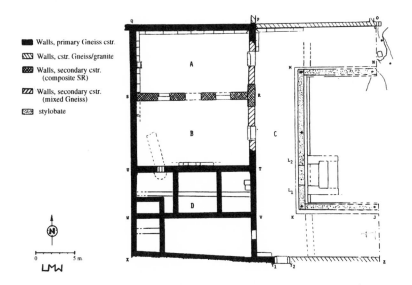

11. Plan of the Delos synagogue. Room A functioned as the main assembly hall. Note the benches along two walls and the chair in the middle of the western wall.

toward Jerusalem; and the cistern found there might have functioned as a *miqveh*. However, the above considerations are not of equal weight; some are inconsequential, speculative, or wrong.

The most telling evidence with respect to the building's identification as a synagogue is the inscriptions found in or near the building. Four were inscribed on column bases found in rooms A and B, each mentioning "Theos Hypsistos":

[1] Zosas of Paras to Theos Hypsistos [gave this in fulfillment of] a vow.

[2] Laodice to Theos Hypsistos, saved by His treatments, [gave this in fulfillment of] a vow.

[3] Lysimachus, on behalf of himself, [made] a thanks-offering to Theos Hypsistos.

[4] To Hypsistos, a vow, Marcia.[149]

A fifth inscription found in a house nearby mentions a *proseuche:* "Agathocles and Lysimachus [have made a contribution] to the *proseuche.*"[150]

As noted above, both terms—*proseuche* and *theos hypsistos*—could have been used in a pagan context, but this was not usually the case.[151] Thus, when combined with the an-

---

149. These inscriptions appear in Frey, *CIJ*, I, nos. 727–30; Lifshitz, *Donateurs et fondateurs*, nos. 4–7; Bruneau, *Cultes de Délos*, 484; White, "Delos Synagogue Revisited," 139 n. 25; idem, *Social Origins*, 338–40.

150. Frey, *CIJ*, I, no. 726; Lifshitz, *Donateurs et fondateurs*, no. 3; White, "Delos Synagogue Revisited," 140 n. 28. A sixth, very fragmentary inscription (Frey, *CIJ*, I, no. 731) contributes nothing in this regard.

151. See, for example, M. Stern, *Greek and Latin Authors*, II, 294–95, 569. See also C. Roberts et al., "Gild of Zeus," 55–72.

cillary considerations mentioned before, an identification of the building as a Jewish *proseuche* becomes compelling.[152] The absence of Jewish symbols and a Torah shrine has rightfully been dismissed as irrelevant. There is no reason to assume that such an early synagogue building would have had them; in places like Gamla, Masada, and Herodium they did not.[153]

The likelihood that this building was, in fact, a Jewish *proseuche* was significantly enhanced by the discovery and publication in the early 1980s of two inscriptions found about one hundred meters to the north. Inscribed on marble stelae, they reveal the existence of a Samaritan community as early as the third or second century B.C.E. Calling themselves the "Israelites on Delos," who make offerings to the sacred Mount Gerizim (lit., Argarizein), these Samaritans honored several benefactors of their community:

[1]   The Israelites on Delos, who make offerings on hallowed Argarizein, crown with a gold crown Sarapion, son of Jason, of Knossos, for his benefactions toward them.

[2]   The Israelites [on Delos], who make offerings to hallowed, consecrated Argarizein, honor Menippos son of Artemidoros, of Herakleion, both himself and his descendants, for having constructed and dedicated at their expense the *proseuche* of God, the [. . . .] and the [. . . .] [and they crowned him] with a gold crown and [. . .].[154]

It is not clear whether these benefactors were fellow-Samaritans honored by their coreligionists on Delos or prominent pagans who had contributed to the local Samaritan community.[155] In the first inscription, the donation of Sarapion of Knossos was unspecified; in the latter, Menippos of Herakleion built the *proseuche* and perhaps other parts of the complex as well, though this part of the inscription is mutilated. If, indeed, these

---

152. See Hengel, "Proseuche und Synagoge," 175; Robert, "Inscriptions grecques de Sidé," 44.

153. See above, Chap. 3; and the summaries of Bruneau, Goodenough, and Kraabel cited above, note 144.

154. For interpretations of "the *proseuche* of God," see Bruneau ("for a vow" — "'Israélites de Délos,'" 488) and White ("to the *proseuche*" — "Delos Synagogue Revisited," 142–44). I have adopted White's interpretation.

These inscriptions were first published in Bruneau, "'Israélites de Délos,'" 467–75. See also Kraabel, "New Evidence," 331–32; idem, "*Synagoga Caeca*," 220–24; White, "Delos Synagogue Revisited," 141–44; idem, *Social Origins*, 340–42; Llewelyn, *New Documents*, VIII, 148–51.

Use of the name "Israelites" by the Delos Samaritans is undoubtedly part of the same phenomenon as the appearance of the name "Jeroboam" on coins from Samaria at about this time (Meshorer, *Ancient Jewish Coinage*, I, 31, 160). In both instances, the implicit claim is that the Samaritans are the successors of the true Israel, i.e., the northern kingdom. For a Jewish polemic against the Samaritans contrasting the virtuous woman of Judah with the compromised "daughters of Israel," see Moore, *Daniel, Esther and Jeremiah: Additions*, 114.

155. Bruneau prefers to consider them Samaritans; Kraabel leaves the question open, though he leans toward a Samaritan identification; White concludes that they were, in fact, pagans (Bruneau, "'Israélites de Délos,'" 481; Kraabel, "New Evidence," 334; and esp. idem, "*Synagoga Caeca*," 222–23; White, "Delos Synagogue Revisited," 142 n. 36, 144; and, for a more decisive view, idem, *Building God's House*, 66–67).

men were pagans, then the reason for their benefaction is unclear: Were they maintaining political or economic ties with the Samaritans? Or perhaps they had other kinds of bonds (familial?) with members of this community? The fact that pagans would contribute to synagogues is not, in and of itself, unusual. We have already come across one such example (i.e., Capernaum according to Luke 7:5), and others will follow below. Interestingly, the Samaritans, like numerous Diaspora Jewish communities, chose to honor those benefactors with golden crowns and public inscriptions.

No less important for our purposes is the mention of a Samaritan *proseuche*. This would seem to clinch the fact that the other Samaritan inscription refers to a synagogue as well. The fact that Samaritans lived in the vicinity only strengthens the likelihood that this residential area may have served Jews as well. In second-century Ptolemaic Egypt, both of these communities lived side by side and even shared the same charity funds.[156] Whether we are dealing with two separate *proseuchae* (one Jewish and one Samaritan), as seems likely, or perhaps one *proseuche* serving both communities is an intriguing question. However, nothing more definitive can be forthcoming at present.[157]

The main reservation in identifying the Delos building as a synagogue—besides the absence of explicit evidence—has always been due to the lamps found there, some of which are decorated with pagan motifs. Of late, this evidence has been either ignored or dismissed. Earlier in the century, it was assumed that Jews throughout antiquity were united in their opposition to figural representation. Over the past generation, however, this view has been dramatically altered by both the endless stream of archeological finds and a more nuanced understanding of the literary sources. Jewish communities of late antiquity were far from monolithic in this regard, and there is no reason to assume that in an earlier period all Jews were of one mind. Delos may very well reflect a different cultural and artistic norm from that of late Second Temple Judaea. Taken in conjunction with the statue bases from Egypt and with the synagogue of Berenice from the years 8–6 B.C.E., which boasted wall decorations, perhaps even of animals and humans (see above), as well as the third-century C.E. Dura Europos synagogue, the figural representations may have been quite acceptable to use, at least in some parts of the Diaspora.

A significant degree of hellenization within the local Jewish community is also attested by the language and prosopography evidenced in the above inscriptions. Like the Jews of Egypt and Cyrene, those of Delos used Greek exclusively (at least as far as our limited evidence indicates), and their Greek names likewise reflect a hellenized cultural milieu. From Josephus we learn that many Delian Jews were also Roman citizens (see below).[158]

---

156. *Antiquities* 13, 74–79.

157. See Kant, "Jewish Inscriptions," 707–8 n. 9.

158. *Antiquities* 14, 231–32. This phenomenon was so widespread that their exemption from military service became an issue for other Delians.

The building used by the Jews for communal purposes followed the pattern established by other Delian associations, whose premises also included a porticoed courtyard and a lavish marble chair.[159] The chair, similar to those reserved for priests in pagan temples, may be our earliest evidence of the "Seat [cathedra] of Moses," a chair or bench found in a number of synagogues of late antiquity and mentioned in both the New Testament and rabbinic literature.[160]

Finally, some information regarding the Delos community generally, and indirectly its synagogue, has been preserved in Roman decrees relating to a number of Diaspora communities and included by Josephus in his *Antiquities*. Pertinent to our present discussion is the following:

> Julius Gaius, Praetor, Consul of the Romans, to the magistrates, council and people of Parium,[161] greeting. The Jews in Delos and some of the neighboring Jews, some of your envoys also being present, have appealed to me and declared that you are preventing them by statute from observing their national customs and sacred rites. Now it displeases me that such statutes should be made against our friends and allies and that they should be forbidden to live in accordance with their customs and to contribute money to common meals and sacred rites, for this they are not forbidden to do even in Rome. For example, Gaius [Julius] Caesar, our consular praetor, by edict forbade religious societies to assemble in the city, but these people alone he did not forbid to do so or to collect contributions of money or to hold common meals. Similarly do I forbid other religious societies but permit these people alone to assemble and feast in accordance with their native customs and ordinances. And if you have made any statutes against our friends and allies, you will do well to revoke them because of their worthy deeds on our behalf and their goodwill toward us.[162]

The above document reveals a number of important matters. As noted, the Jews of Rome seem to have enjoyed extensive communal privileges; and Roman officials expected this practice to be followed elsewhere as well.[163] Secondly, the Delos Jewish community had obviously encountered considerable difficulties with its neighbors. The Jews were forced to appeal to Rome because Delian authorities were perceived to be undermining Jewish communal life. Presumably, laws had been enacted to prevent the Jews from observing their traditions and collecting monies to finance activities such as common meals and sacred rites (τὰ ἱερά). The severity of the matter is underscored by the simultaneous appearance in Rome of a counterdelegation who presented arguments against the Jews.

In a second decree from about the same time, Delian officials acknowledged (though

---

159. It should be noted that such models differed considerably in elaborateness, depending on the material circumstances of each group; see Bruneau, *Cultes de Délos;* White, *Building God's House,* 26ff.

160. See below, Chap. 9.

161. On suggestions for the identification of this site, see comments by Marcus in Josephus, *Antiquities,* LCL, VII, 561 n. *f.*

162. *Antiquities* 14, 213–16. Pucci Ben-Zeev ("A Letter Concerning Delian Jews," 237–43) dates this decree to 43 B.C.E., claiming that it was authored by Octavian.

163. See above, notes 137 and 138.

not very happily, it seems) that Jews were to be exempt from military service by orders of a Roman official.[164] Privileges of this sort could not but have had a souring effect on the relations between the Jews and their neighbors, with the latter, in turn, attempting to reduce (if not eliminate) the Jews' preferred status. In light of these documents, the location of the Delian Jewish community in a relatively isolated part of the island takes on additional significance. Not only could it have served Jewish interests to be somewhat isolated, but it may already reflect (or have subsequently contributed to) a degree of social alienation, and perhaps even hostility, between the Jewish and pagan residents on the island.

ASIA MINOR AND GREECE

We are probably as well informed about the Jewish communities and their synagogues in Asia Minor and Greece as in any other part of the Diaspora.[165] Not only does the pre-70 material begin to rival that of Egypt, but archeological data (buildings and inscriptions) from Asia Minor supply extensive information about these communities in late antiquity as well.

These two provinces will be treated together since the sources of information are the same for both. Josephus and Acts supply the bulk of data for the pre-70 era, and practically all of the archeological remains come from late antiquity alone. The material here is organized by source and not by individual locale.

Josephus

Josephus has preserved a series of Imperial edicts relating to the first century B.C.E., each reaffirming the rights and privileges of various Jewish communities in Asia Minor in the face of local opposition and hostility.[166] Each edict presumes that the Jews were

---

164. Josephus, *Antiquities* 14, 231-32: "Decree of the Delians. 'In the archonship of Boeotus, on the twentieth day of the month of Thargelion, response of the magistrates. The legate Marcus Piso, when resident in our city, having been placed in charge of the recruiting of soldiers, summoned us and a considerable number of citizens and ordered that if there were any Jews who were Roman citizens, no one should bother them about military service, inasmuch as the consul Lucius Cornelius Lentulus had exempted the Jews from military service in consideration of their religious scruples. We must therefore obey the magistrate.'" Similar to this was the decree which the people of Sardis passed.

165. On the numerous Jewish communities in this area, see, inter alia, Philo, *Embassy*, 245, 281; M. Stern, "Jewish Diaspora," 143-55; Trebilco, *Jewish Communities*, 5-36; Levinskaya, *Acts in Its Diaspora Setting*, 137-66; Lichtenberger, "Organisationsformen," 23-27.

166. Josephus, *Antiquities* 14, 213-64; 16, 160-73. On these edicts, see Schürer, *History*, III, 114ff.; Juster, *Juifs*, I, 391ff.; II, 1-27; La Piana, "Foreign Groups," 348-51; Smallwood, *Jews under Roman Rule*, 120-43; Applebaum, "Legal Status," 420-63; Moehring, *"Acta pro Judaeis,"* 124-58; Rajak, "Roman Charter," 107-23; idem, "Jewish Rights," 19-35; Pucci Ben Zeev, "Caesar and Jewish Law," 28-37; idem, "Jewish Rights," 39-53.

These decrees stem from the basic recognition extended by Julius Caesar to the Jews in the Empire, in no small part in gratitude for the support he received from Antipater, Hyrcanus II, and the Jews of

well organized, having formed their own communal framework, and possessed their own social and religious mores.[167] Undoubtedly, this also meant the presence of a place of worship, i.e., a *proseuche* or synagogue, although, admittedly, in only a few of these edicts is such a place specifically mentioned. It is to this evidence that we now turn.

Josephus records a decree regarding the Jews of Halicarnassus,[168] in which it is carefully noted that the community was assured the inviolability of their holy days and gatherings: "We have also decreed that those men and women who so wish may observe their Sabbaths and perform their sacred rights in accordance with the Jewish laws, and many built places of prayer [*proseuchae*][169] near the sea, in accordance with their native custom."

Of especial interest here is the explicit statement that many Jews built synagogues near bodies of water, a phenomenon we have already encountered in Egypt, Delos, and Ostia.[170] A similar reference appears in Acts.[171] The reason for this practice is not entirely clear, although one obvious possibility is the need to be close to water for purification purposes, a practice already attested in the *Letter of Aristeas*.[172] There may also have been other reasons for this preference, e.g., the Jews' desire to distance themselves from the pagan city generally in order to avoid, or at least reduce, tensions with their neighbors

---

Judaea in his struggle against Pompey (Josephus, *Antiquities* 14, 211-12). At the same time, these privileges also continued the earlier Hellenistic tradition of religious and ethnic tolerance with regard to the Jews. Josephus makes this claim in an exaggerated form on several occasions; see his *Antiquities* 12, 119-20; 16, 160-61; and below.

167. Scholars have long debated the precise framework of these privileges. Were the Jews categorized by the Romans as an association (*collegium*), a private religious fraternity (*thiasos*), an independent body parallel to the local *polis* (*politeuma*), or simply a group with the right to assemble regularly (*synodos, koinon*)? It may be, however, that there was no single rubric for all Jewish communities. Just as there was a great deal of heterogeneity from one Diaspora community to the next, there may also have been variety in the rubrics of their communal organization. Local contexts and precedents were undoubtedly decisive. See Schürer, *History*, III, 107-14; Juster, *Juifs*, I, 409-24; La Piana, "Foreign Groups," 348-51; Applebaum, "Legal Status," 460; Smallwood, *Jews under Roman Rule*, 133-36; Rabello, "Legal Condition," 719-20; Rajak, "Roman Charter," 107-23.

168. *Antiquities* 14, 258.

169. E. P. Sanders, *Jewish Law*, 259, 341 n. 26.

170. See above; see also Lauterbach, "Tashlik," 207ff.; Goldin, *Studies in Midrash*, 346.

171. Acts 16:13. See also Philo, *Flaccus* 122-23.

172. *Letter of Aristeas* 304-6. The idea that the sea was valid for purification purposes is reflected in the following:

"All seas are valid as a *miqveh* . . . so [says] R. Meir. R. Judah says: The Great Sea is valid as a *miqveh*. . . . R. Yosi says: All seas render clean by virtue of being flowing waters" (M Miqva'ot 5:4).

"And it happened that Rabban Gamaliel and Onqelos the Proselyte would come to Ashkelon, and Rabban Gamaliel immersed himself in a bath and Onqelos the Proselyte in the sea. R. Joshua b. Qabusai said: I was with them and Rabban Gamaliel immersed himself in the sea" (T Miqva'ot 6:3 [p. 658]).

Regarding the waters of a river, see T Makhshirin 2:12 (p. 674); T Miqva'ot 4:5 (p. 656). See also E. P. Sanders, *Judaism*, 223-24.

stemming from their different practices and behavior or to allow for a less "polluted" worship environment, far from pagan places of idolatry.[173]

Several of the decrees regarding Sardis which Josephus has preserved are likewise pertinent to our discussion. One document explicitly notes that the Jews had a place ($\tau o\pi \acute{o}s$) where they decided their affairs, being organized, as they were, in an association ($\sigma \acute{v} vo\delta ov$) governed by ancestral laws.[174] In another decree, the Jews were granted both the right to organize their communal life, including self-adjudication, and a place ($\tau o\pi \acute{o}s$) for the practice of their ancestral customs, which included prayer and sacrifice.[175]

A general edict of Augustus to the Jews of Asia Minor from the year 12 B.C.E. is of especial importance: "And if anyone is caught stealing sacred books or sacred monies from a Sabbath-house [$\sigma \alpha \beta \beta \alpha \tau \epsilon \hat{\iota} ov$] or a banquet hall [$\dot{\alpha} v\delta \rho \acute{\omega} v$], he shall be regarded as sacrilegious, and his property shall be confiscated to the public treasury of the Romans." [176] Many, if not most, of the synagogues referred to had a banquet hall in addition to a place for Sabbath assembly. Sacred communal meals are documented in a number of first-century Jewish contexts (Pharisaic *ḥavurot*, Essenes [Qumran], Therapeutae, and the early church), mostly in connection with religious associations. However, it would appear that such communal meals were not foreign to the wider Jewish community, as reflected in the decree regarding Delian Jews.[177] Such banquet halls could have served other functions as well, and smaller facilities may have consisted of a single room utilized for several purposes. Finally, the reference to a synagogue as a repository for sacred books (i.e., Scriptures) and sacred monies is invaluable. As in other Diaspora communities, these monies were probably donated for local use as well as for the Jerusalem Temple, a practice which, as we have seen, was widespread among first-century Diaspora communities.[178]

---

173. See Mekhilta of R. Ishmael, Bo, 1 (p. 2); and Sukenik, *Ancient Synagogues*, 49ff., where being near water is associated with the rabbinic concept of "impurity of gentile lands." See also Alon, *Jews, Judaism in the Classical World*, 146–89.

174. *Antiquities* 14, 235.

175. Ibid., 260: "they may, in accordance with their accepted custom, come together and have a communal life and adjudicate suits among themselves, and that a place be given them in which they may gather together with their wives and children and offer their ancestral prayers and sacrifices to God." The reference to Jewish sacrifices is enigmatic; see below, Chap. 5, note 31.

176. Josephus, *Antiquities* 16, 164. See M. Stern, "Jewish Diaspora," 146. On a similar term in Syriac, בית שבתא דיהודי, see Payne Smith, *Thesaurus Syriacus*, I, col. 497. There is also a reference to a *sabbateion* in an early second-century inscription from Thyatira in Asia Minor, where a synagogue is probably intended (Frey, *CIJ*, II, no. 752; van der Horst, *Ancient Jewish Epitaphs*, 150–51). For a reference to a "house of the Sabbath" in Rabbat Moab which was destroyed by Barsauma between 419–22 C.E., see Nau, "Deux épisodes," 188. On the *andron* generally, see C. Roberts et al., "Gild of Zeus," 47–48.

177. See above, note 162.

178. *Antiquities* 14, 213–16. Regarding the sending of money to Jerusalem by the Jews of Ephesus, see Philo, *Embassy* 315. Regarding the Jerusalem church and contributions from various "diaspora" churches, see, inter alia, Rom. 15:25–26; I Cor. 16:1–4; Meeks, *First Urban Christians*, 110.

New Testament

As was the case with the Second Temple Judaean synagogue, the New Testament has preserved invaluable material relating to the Diaspora synagogue in Asia Minor and Greece. The account in Acts of Paul's journeys attests to the density of Jewish settlement and the subsequent development of Christianity throughout the eastern Mediterranean in general and in Asia Minor and Greece in particular. In all, Acts mentions the synagogue nineteen times, almost always referring to the institution as "synagogue," with the one exception being for Philippi, where the term *proseuche* is used. Acts informs us of synagogues in Damascus (9:2, 20), Salamis (13:5), Antioch of Pisidia (13:14), Iconium (14:1), Thessalonica (17:1), Berea (17:10), Athens (17:17), Corinth (18:7, 8), Ephesus (18:19ff.), and Philippi (16:13).

The frequent reference to synagogues in Acts is not fortuitous. According to Luke, this institution was a critical factor in the spread of Christianity in its early stages. Almost every reference to a synagogue is related to Paul's missionary activity;[179] at first he addresses the Jews and only later the gentiles. The pattern appearing in Luke is almost inexorable: visit to a synagogue, effective preaching, Jewish hostility, and expulsion.[180] This recurrent phenomenon goes to the heart of Acts' theological and political message. Paul is rebuffed time and again by the Jews, and only then devotes himself fully and unequivocally to the gentile mission. The theological basis of this schema is clearly spelled out in Acts 13:46: "And Paul and Barnabas spoke out boldly, saying, 'It was necessary that the word of God should be spoken first to you. Since you thrust it from yourselves, thereby judging yourselves unworthy of eternal life, behold, we turn to the gentiles.' "[181]

As for the historical reliability of Acts, much has been written and a range of positions adopted—from the more skeptical to the largely accepting. Theological agendas aside, one may assume that the specific events reported, especially those relating to the synagogue, are largely credible. Luke was certainly familiar with the Jewish Diaspora and wrote for Christian Diaspora communities. It is hard to imagine that he would invent accounts for a population that knew a great deal about the synagogue, its workings, and Paul's activities. At the very least, even were one to doubt the specific details included in Acts, one would have to admit that such events could well have taken place, even if not precisely in the manner recorded.

Many interesting and important details regarding the synagogue emerge from the ac-

---

179. The one exception is the reference to an Alexandrian Jew named Apollos, who spoke in the synagogue of Ephesus (Acts 18:26).

180. So, for example, Acts 9:20-22; 13:44-48; 14:1-6; 14:19; 17:1-9, 16ff.; 18:18-21.

181. See also Kee, "Jews in Acts," 183-95. Despite a rather skeptical approach to the historical validity of many New Testament traditions concerning the synagogue, McKay (*Sabbath and Synagogue*, 165-71) seems to accept most of Acts' accounts as reliably reflecting the synagogues that Luke knew. See also Segal, *Paul*, 267-73.

counts in Acts. For instance, the antiquity of the custom of reading Scriptures in the synagogue on the Sabbath is considered here, as in other sources, to derive from Moses himself (Acts 15:21). In fact, it is Sabbath worship which regularly provides the setting for Paul's encounters (e.g., Acts 13:42; 16:13; 17:2; 18:4). Clearly, the Sabbath was the primary occasion for the community to congregate, particularly in a worship context.[182] As noted, this phenomenon may be alluded to in two Berenice inscriptions, where the regular (as opposed to monthly) gathering seems to refer to the Sabbath, and Josephus' reference to the σαββατεῖον of Asia Minor Jewry.[183]

While most cities appear to have had one synagogue, the plural "synagogues" is used on several occasions, probably reflecting a large local Jewish population that required more than one building.[184] The only synagogue official specifically named in these accounts is the *archisynagogos*. In one instance, this official invited Paul to speak to the congregation in Antioch of Pisidia following the reading of the Torah and Prophets; clearly the position entailed a degree of responsibility and authority.[185] In a second instance, Acts notes that Crispus, the archisynagogue of the Corinthian synagogue, became a believer (18:8). That his whole household followed suit is not surprising. However, the fact that immediately afterward many other Corinthians, having heard Paul, began to believe in Jesus and were then baptized may attest to the impact of Crispus' conversion on his fellow-citizens and thus to his prominence in the community.

Two synagogue scenes described in Acts are especially noteworthy. One (16:12–13) has to do with Paul's first encounter with the Jews of Philippi in Macedonia. He came to the city in midweek and waited several days for the Sabbath and his first encounter with the local Jewish community. He then went to the riverside, "where we supposed there was a place of prayer [*proseuche*],"[186] and there met a group of women. The presence of women, some of high standing, in Paul's audience at Berea is also noted.[187]

Acts singles out gentiles, both men and women, as also having frequented Diaspora synagogues.[188] The attraction of many pagans to Judaism in antiquity is well docu-

---

182. Regarding the Christians of Berea, Acts notes that some Jews would gather daily to learn Scriptures, particularly in response to Paul's message. Clearly, the intent here is to describe an emerging Christian community whose fervor and commitment led to daily study, a practice reminiscent of the daily study among various sects, such as the Essenes, Therapeutae, and, undoubtedly, the Pharisees. The author of Acts describes these Jews as "more noble" than those of nearby Thessalonica (Acts 17:11).

183. *Antiquities* 16, 164.

184. Acts 9:2, 20; 13:5.

185. Ibid., 13:15. See Chap. 5.

186. Alternatively: where prayer was carried out.

187. Acts 17:12. The special attraction of women to Judaism is attested elsewhere as well (e.g., *War* 2, 560); see below, Chap. 14.

188. So, for example, Acts 13:43; 14:1–2; 17:4, 12; 18:4; as well as Josephus, *War* 7, 45. See also ibid., 2, 463; idem, *Against Apion* 2, 123; and Trebilco, *Jewish Communities*, 145–66, esp. 164–66.

mented.[189] Although the nature of this missionary phenomenon has been vigorously debated of late, the issue in dispute concerns the extent of the phenomenon in the first century and the degree of active missionizing on the part of the Jews.[190] What is to be noted in the present context is the central role played by the synagogue in this phenomenon. It was not only the place where Judaism was most visible, thus drawing the sympathetic and curious, but, once they were won over, it became a focus of identification and affiliation. These gentiles, of many stripes and referred to by different terms, may have played a prominent role in some Diaspora synagogues (see below, Bosphorus), a phenomenon which appears at times to have been the case in late antiquity as well.[191] In fact, the status enjoyed by many Diaspora communities may have been due, at least in part, to the presence and support of many pagan sympathizers.

The second account of importance described in Acts (13:15) offers us a fleeting glimpse at the Sabbath-morning liturgy in the Antioch of Pisidia synagogue. Four elements are featured in this schema: a selection from the Torah is recited; then a selection from the Prophets is read; the archisynagogue invites Paul to speak; Paul addresses the congregation. This order generally parallels Luke's earlier description of the synagogue service at Nazareth.[192] Perhaps the remarkable fact in this account is the receptivity of the local community to the participation of outsiders. Paul's appearance in Antioch was unannounced; he was, for all intents and purposes, a stranger. Nevertheless, he was asked to address the congregation. How widespread this custom was is impossible to assess, although we may note that something similar happened at Ephesus. According to Acts 18:24–26, an Alexandrian Jew named Apollos came to the local synagogue there and spoke effectively

---

189. So, for example, Josephus, *Antiquities* 14, 110; see Schürer, *History*, III, 150–76; Juster, *Juifs*, I, 253–337; Stern, "Sympathy for the Jews," 155–67 (= M. Stern and S. Safrai, *Jewish History in the Second Temple Period*, 505–17); Feldman, "Proselytes and 'Sympathizers,'" 265–305; idem, *Jew and Gentile*, 177–445; McKnight, *Light among the Gentiles;* Figueras, "Epigraphic Evidence," 194–206.

190. See, for example, S. J. D. Cohen, "Was Judaism in Antiquity a Missionary Religion?" 14–23 (cf. Feldman's very different emphasis in the same volume, "Was Judaism a Missionary Religion in Ancient Times?" 24–37); Goodman, "Jewish Proselytizing," 53–78; idem, *Mission and Conversion*, 60–90. For a more strident denial of the *sebomenoi* phenomenon, now seriously undermined by the publication of the Aphrodisias inscription, see MacLennan and Kraabel, "God-Fearers," 46–53; Kraabel, "Disappearance of the 'God-Fearers,'" 113–26. See also Gager, "Jews, Gentiles, and Synagogues," 91–99; Feldman, *Jew and Gentile*, 342–82.

191. On the gentiles and Diaspora synagogues, see S. J. D. Cohen, "Respect for Judaism," 409–30; idem, "Crossing the Boundary," 13–33; see also Trebilco, *Jewish Communities*, 145–66, esp. 164–66; Georgi, *Opponents of Paul*, 83–117. Regarding late antiquity, see Wilken, *John Chrysostom and the Jews*, 66–94; Meeks and Wilken, *Jews and Christians*, 83–127; Smelik, "John Chrysostom's Homilies." On the Aphrodisias inscription in this regard, see Reynolds and Tannenbaum, *Jews and God-Fearers*, 43–92. See below, Chap. 8.

192. Luke 4:16–21. It has sometimes been claimed that this similarity really indicates Luke's projection of the synagogue liturgy he knew from the late first-century Diaspora onto Jesus' Galilee; however such skepticism seems unwarranted. See my comments in this regard, above, Chap. 3.

and fervently about Jesus from a distinctively non-Pauline perspective. Once again, the synagogue served as an open forum for Jews of different backgrounds and persuasions.

The Acmonia Inscription

The region of Asia Minor and Greece has left us with an unusually rich trove of epigraphical evidence. While the total number of Jewish inscriptions stands at about one hundred, the inscriptions relating to the synagogue or its officials comprise almost half this number. Most are dedicatory inscriptions from synagogue buildings; a few are epitaphs which mention a synagogue affiliation. Although practically all these inscriptions date from late antiquity, one of the most important among them comes from first-century c.e. Acmonia. Located inland in Phrygia, this city has an importance in large measure due to its strategic position on the Persian Royal Road. The inscription reads as follows:

> The edifice was constructed by Julia Severa. Publius Tyrronios Clados, archisynagogos for life, Lucius son of Lucius, archisynagogos, and Popilios Zoticos, archon, have renovated [the building] from their own funds and from the community treasury. They decorated the walls and the ceiling, and they made the windows secure and [made] all the rest of the decoration. The synagogue honors these individuals with a gold shield on account of their excellent leadership and their kindly feelings toward and zeal for the congregation.[193]

The items of interest here are manifold. Most striking, of course, is the fact that the synagogue building itself was built by one Julia Severa a number of years prior to the date of this inscription, which itself deals with the restoration of the structure. Even more unusual than the nature of this woman's benefaction is the fact that she was a well-known pagan who came from "a nexus of leading families." The local coinage celebrates Julia Severa as politically active in the mid-first century, holding the positions of *agonothete* and ἀρχιέρεια (high priestess) of the local Imperial cult.[194] Pagan donations to synagogues

---

193. The translation of this inscription has been adapted from White, *Social Origins*, 308-10, and Trebilco, *Jewish Communities*, 58-59. See also Frey, *CIJ*, II, no. 766 (= *MAMA*, VI, no. 264); Lifshitz, *Donateurs et fondateurs*, no. 33. A major issue here is whether Julia Severa donated a building to the Jews for use as a synagogue or simply built an edifice which later was transferred to, or bought by, the Jewish community. The term οἶκος (lit., house or building) has been used in both ways (see the Phocaea and Stobi inscriptions in White, *Social Origins*, nos. 68, 73). From the inscription here it seems most likely that a synagogue building was intended. Why else should the fact that Julia erected a building be mentioned at all in this context? If one assumes that the building was originally earmarked for some other purpose, and only later was given or sold to the Jews, why, then, is this fact not noted? It seems very plausible that the edifice had been intended from the beginning as a gift of a synagogue to the Jewish community and only later was renovated by the three leaders named.

194. Levick, *Roman Colonies*, 107. Julia's husband, Lucius Servenius Capito, was a decurion in Acmonia in the time of Nero, and her son, L. Servenius Cornutus, held many offices—he was, for example, a senator under Nero and a *legatus* to the proconsul of Asia. For the numismatic evidence, see Ramsay,

are known in other places in Asia Minor as well, but donating an entire building was indeed rare.[195] It was once suggested that Julia was, in fact, a Jew; however, this claim has been controverted by her now well documented pagan affiliations.[196]

Sometime—perhaps several decades—after the initial contribution by Julia, repairs of the synagogue were undertaken by three leading officials—two *archisynagogoi* and one archon.[197] How Popilios Zoticos, as archon, was related to the synagogue is unknown. The two *archisynagogoi*—bearing Greek and Latin names—may not have held identical positions. One was head for life (διὰ βίου); whether this was a purely honorary title following years of service or, indeed, a reflection of a continuous term of office is difficult to determine. The second one, Lucius, is simply noted as an *archisynagogos*. Whether his father, of the same name, also held this position is unknown; it will be remembered that retaining such an office for generations within a single family is attested in the Theodotos inscription from first-century Jerusalem.[198]

The funds used for restoration of the building appear to have been matching grants (whatever the relative percentages) from these three leaders and the community at large. The wall and ceiling paintings are noteworthy, though the nature of these paintings —geometrical, floral, or figural motifs—is unknown. Depending on the lavishness of the ornamentation, this synagogue may have been similar to the one in contemporary Berenice or the ones in Sardis and Dura Europos later on.

The three major donors were honored in ways typical for Greek donors generally. Not only did they merit the above inscription, but they were awarded a gold shield.[199]

Cities and Bishoprics, 638–39; see also Schürer, *History*, III, 31. On the positions Julia held in the Imperial cult, see Ramsay, *Cities and Bishoprics*, 639; Trebilco, *Jewish Communities*, 59.

195. See below, Chap. 8. A parallel phenomenon from the fourth century may be the building of a *proseuche* by the Imperial governor in Panticapaeum (Levinskaya, *Acts in Its Diaspora Setting*, 229–31). It is interesting to note that relations between the Jews and their neighbors in this region appear to have been particularly close; see Sheppard, "Jews, Christians and Heretics," 169–80; Crawford, "Multiculturalism at Sardis," 38–47. On this phenomenon generally, see M. Stern, "Sympathy for the Jews," 505–17.

196. See, for example, White, *Social Origins*, 308–9; Ramsay, *Cities and Bishoprics*, 648–51, 673–75; and the somewhat ambiguous note in Juster, *Juifs*, I, 430–31. On the opposite phenomenon, namely, Jews contributing to pagan shrines, see the examples cited in Barclay, *Jews in the Mediterranean Diaspora*, 321–22.

197. A similar synagogue inscription, of undetermined date, was found in Olbia, along the shores of the Black Sea. It, too, speaks of synagogue officials restoring the building: "The society under the presidency of [? . . .] Pourthaios Achilleus son of Demetrius, Dionysodoros son of Eros [?], Zobeis son of Zobeis, the archons, have restored by their own care the synagogue from the foundations till . . . and have roofed it." See the translation and comments of Lifshitz, "Prolegomenon," 64; idem, *Donateurs et fondateurs*, no. 11; Frey, *CIJ*, I, no. 682.

198. See above, Chap. 3. White (*Social Origins*, 309–10 n. 48) has speculated that the synagogue officials named Tyrronios and Lucius were Jewish freedmen (or their descendants) in the service of Julia Severa, and this would therefore explain her involvement with the Jewish community.

199. See Robert, "Inscriptions grecques de Sidé," 41 n. 1, 254. On the phenomenon of such dedications in Asia Minor and some of their social and political implications, see Rogers, "Gift and Society," 188–99.

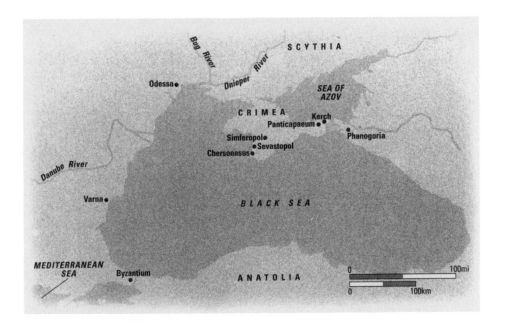

12. Area of the Bosphorus kingdom.

THE KINGDOM OF BOSPHORUS

Jews probably reached the Kingdom of Bosphorus on the northern shore of the Black Sea via Asia Minor owing to the political and economic ties between these two regions (fig. 12).[200] By the first century C.E., with Bosphorus serving as a vassal kingdom of Rome, the presence of Jews as well as the influence of Judaism are well attested. This religious influence continued to grow until the fourth century at least, when the cult of Theos Hypsistos became one of the most popular in the region.[201] Excavations now under way in Chersonesus in southwestern Crimea have uncovered remains of what may be a synagogue from the first century C.E.[202] Throughout the region, seven inscriptions dating from the first and early second centuries have been found, each referring to the manumission of slaves. This procedure appears to have been regularly carried out in the local *proseuche;* in one instance, the synagogue itself (in this case, the term refers to the congregation) was appointed guardian.[203]

200. Minns, *Scythians and Greeks,* 620–22.

201. Schürer, *History,* III, 37–38; Goodenough, "Bosphorus Inscriptions," 221–45; Lifshitz, "Bosphorean Kingdom," 130–33; Levinskaya, *Acts in Its Diaspora Setting,* 105–16; Levinskaya and Tokhtas'yev, "Jews and Jewish Names," 55–73.

202. MacLennan, "In Search of the Jewish Diaspora," 49–51.

203. These inscriptions are to be found in one or more of the following collections: Frey, *CIJ,* I, nos.

To date, three inscriptions, from 41 C.E., 59 C.E., and 67 C.E., have been discovered in Gorgippia (modern Anape). The first of these translates as follows:

> To the Most High God, Almighty, blessed, in the reign of the king Mithridates, the friend of [?] and the friend of the fatherland, in the year 338 [= 41 C.E.], in the month Deios, Pothos, the son of Strabo, dedicated to the prayer-house, in accordance with the vow, his house-bred slave-woman, whose name is Chrysa, on condition that she should be unharmed and unmolested by any of his heirs under Zeus, Ge, Helios.[204]

Noteworthy, in the first place, is the threefold invocation of God, in typical Jewish form (θεῶι ὑψίστωι παντοκράτορι εὐλογητῶι).[205] The Greek names of the Jews, both father and son, should not surprise us, for elsewhere in the Diaspora Jews adopted the nomenclature regnant in their surroundings as a matter of course.[206] The fact that this and similar manumission ceremonies were performed in the synagogue is indeed unique. Clearly, this was an act with religious as well as social implications, as the manumission formula itself attests.

At first there was some skepticism about the Jewishness of this text owing to the pagan formula summoning Jupiter, the earth, and the sun to witness the transaction.[207] However, such usage should not be overly surprising; similar formulas appear frequently in Bosphoran documents (and in other Jewish ones as well—see below) and undoubtedly had become so common that they had lost all blatantly pagan associations.[208] Moreover, in many other instances, from fifth-century Elephantine through Josephus' writings and down to third-century C.E. Bet She'arim and Hungary, we find Jews utilizing formulas with distinct pagan connotations.[209]

Three other inscriptions from the first and early second centuries come from the area

---

683, 684, 690; *CIRB*, nos. 64, 70, 71, 72, 73, 985, 1123, 1124; Lifshitz, "Prolegomenon," 65–69. See also Levinskaya, *Acts in Its Diaspora Setting*, 231–42. For a manumission document from Roman Egypt in 291 C.E., see Tcherikover et al., *CPJ*, III, no. 473. In this case, Jewish slaves were freed and the Jewish community ("the synagogue of the Jews") paid their ransom. See also Harrill, *Manumission of Slaves*, 172–78. On the manumission of Jewish slaves at Delphi, see Frey, *CIJ*, I, nos. 709–11; on the manumission of slaves in Roman Italy generally, see Dyson, *Community and Society*, 199–203.

204. Levinskaya, *Acts in Its Diaspora Setting*, 239–40. See also Frey, *CIJ*, I, no. 690, with some minor variations.

205. See also Horbury and Noy, *Jewish Inscriptions*, no. 116 and comments, p. 200.

206. Lifshitz, "Prolegomenon," 68.

207. Westermann, *Slave Systems*, 124–26.

208. Nock, *Conversion*, 63; Lieberman, *Hellenism in Jewish Palestine*, 214; Minns, *Scythians and Greeks*, 516, 616; Lifshitz, "Bosphorean Kingdom," 130; MacLennan, "In Search of the Jewish Diaspora," 48; M. Stern, "Jewish Diaspora," 156.

209. Schürer, *History*, III, 37; Lieberman, *Hellenism in Jewish Palestine*, 214; Levinskaya, *Acts in Its Diaspora Setting*, 222; Scheiber, *Jewish Inscriptions*, 37ff.

around the ancient city of Panticapaeum (near modern-day Kerch).[210] While similar in many ways to the inscriptions from Gorgippia (i.e., with a manumission ceremony in the synagogue and a promise that the slave will not be reclaimed), they nevertheless display several unique features. To cite one example: "I release in the *proseuche*, Elpias the son [?] of my slave, bred in my house; he shall remain undisturbed and unassailed by any of my heirs, except for [his duty] to visit the *proseuche* regularly; the community [*synagoge*] of the Jews and the God-fearers [?] will be [together with me] guardian [of the enfranchised]."[211] We note here use of both *proseuche* and *synagoge*; the first clearly refers to the building, as in other inscriptions from the region, the latter to the community. Unique to these Panticapaeum inscriptions are two stipulations: that the emancipated slave is to frequent the synagogue in the future and that the synagogue (i.e., the community) is to assume responsibility as a guardian (ἐπιτροπευούσης) for the act of manumission. All of these elements appear in each of the Panticapaeum inscriptions, as well as in a more fragmentary one from Phanagoria, dating, perhaps, to 16 C.E.[212]

Of interest here is the reference to a group of "God-fearers" (θεὸν σέβων) mentioned together with the Jews. If this interpretation is correct, it would indicate that God-fearers held a legally recognized position in the synagogue alongside the regular Jewish community, a presence even more institutionalized then than later on, in third-century Aphrodisias.[213] Such a situation has far-reaching implications regarding these God-fearers' numbers as well as their social and political standing.[214]

---

210. Frey, *CIJ*, I, nos. 683, 684; Lifshitz, "Prolegomenon," 65–66; MacLennan, "In Search of the Jewish Diaspora," 44–47.

211. Lifshitz, "Prolegomenon," 66; Trebilco, *Jewish Communities*, 155–56.

212. Another Panticapaeum inscription, dating to 80 C.E., reads as follows: "During the reign of Tiberius Julius Rhescuporius friend of Caesar and of the Romans, dutiful in the 377th year the 12th of Peretou, I Chreste, formerly wife of Drusus, release to the *proseuche* my slave Heraclas, a free person once and for all according to my vow; he shall remain untouched and undisturbed by all my heirs as I have vowed. He may go where he wants unrestricted except that he must adhere devoutly to the *proseuche*. This agreement is made by my heirs Heraclides and Helikoniados, and under the joint guardianship of the community of the Jews." See Frey, *CIJ*, I, no. 683; translation, with some modifications, in MacLennan, "In Search of the Jewish Diaspora," 47. On the fragmentary inscription from Phanagoria, see Frey, *CIJ*, I, no. 691; Lifshitz, "Prolegomenon," 69; Levinskaya, *Acts in Its Diaspora Setting*, 236–37, where there is a slightly different rendition. Lifshitz, following Nadel, has suggested that these emancipated slaves may have been obligated to work (in the fields?) for the synagogues ("Bosphorean Kingdom," 128).

213. Lifshitz, "Prolegomenon," 66. See also Figueras, "Epigraphic Evidence," 202–3. Note also the Miletus inscription, which arguably may be read: "A place for Jews and God-fearers" (Frey, *CIJ*, II, no. 748); see below, Chap. 8.

214. Levinskaya (*Acts in Its Diaspora Setting*, 74–76) rejects this reading and suggests the following toward the end of the inscription: "that he (the freed slave) works for the prayer-house under the guardianship of the Jewish community, and honours God." She thus assumes that there is no reference here to a class of God-fearers, although she herself accepts the fact of their existence in large numbers

SYRIA

Despite its large size and relatively long history, the Jewish community of Syria generally, and of Antioch in particular, is only very partially known.[215] Ironically, of all the Diaspora communities, this one offers us some important literary data from late antiquity (Chrysostom, Malalas, and several rabbinic traditions—see below, Chap. 8); for the pre-70 period, however, we must rely almost exclusively on Josephus and several traditions preserved by the sixth-century chronicler Malalas.[216] Antioch and its kings played a central role in the Jewish affairs of Judaea during its Seleucid period, particularly in the century following Jason's Hellenistic reforms in Jerusalem (ca. 175–75 B.C.E.),[217] and it is in this context that some information is forthcoming.

Josephus writes the following: "For, although Antiochus surnamed Epiphanes sacked Jerusalem and plundered the Temple, his successors on the throne restored to the Jews of Antioch all such votive offerings as were made of brass, to be laid up in their synagogue, and, moreover, granted them citizen rights on an equality with the Greeks. Continuing to receive similar treatment from later monarchs, the Jewish colony grew in numbers, and their richly designed and costly offerings formed a splendid ornament to the holy place [τὸ ἱερόν]. Moreover, they were constantly attracting to their religious ceremonies multitudes of Greeks, and these they had in some measure incorporated with themselves."[218]

Given Josephus' claim that Jews lived in Antioch from its very foundation under Seleucus I or, at the latest, from the reign of Antiochus III,[219] then the existence of a synagogue in this community at an early date is more than likely. In the above source, Josephus claims that one of Antiochus IV's successors gave the city's synagogue all the brass ornaments and gifts that had been plundered from the Jerusalem Temple. If this is true, then this must have occurred between 163 and 65 B.C.E., i.e., after the death of

---

in the Bosphorus at the time (ibid., 113–16). Most scholars, however, have accepted the suggested reading. See, for example, Schürer, *History*, III, 166–68; Reynolds and Tannenbaum, *Jews and God-Fearers*, 54–56; Trebilco, *Jewish Communities*, 155–56.

215. Perhaps the size and importance of this community influenced Herod's generous contribution to the city; see Josephus, *War* 1, 328, 425.

216. On Jews of Antioch in this period, see S. Krauss, "Antioche," 27–49; Kraeling, "Jewish Community at Antioch," 130–60; Meeks and Wilken, *Jews and Christians*, 2–13; M. Stern, "Jewish Diaspora," 137–42; Levinskaya, *Acts in Its Diaspora Setting*, 127–35. On Jewish-Christian relations in first-century Antioch, see Hahn, "Judaism and Jewish Christianity," 341–66. See also Downey, *History of Antioch*.

217. See, for example, II Macc. 4:4ff.; I Macc. 11:42–44; Josephus, *Antiquities* 13, 377ff., 387ff.

218. *War* 7, 44–45. On the tension between the Syrian pagan and Jewish populations throughout this period, see Roth-Gerson, "Anti-Semitism in Syria," 301–21.

219. *Antiquities* 12, 119; *Against Apion* 2, 39 (Seleucus I). Cf., however, Josephus' statement in *War* 7, 44–45 (Antiochus IV); and the comments by Marcus, Josephus, *War*, LCL, 737–42. See also Kraeling, "Jewish Community at Antioch," 138–39.

Antiochus IV and prior to the Roman conquest of Syria by Pompey.[220] Moreover, if Josephus is correct that later Seleucid kings showered further benefactions on the Jews and their synagogue, then the original gifts must have been granted early on in this period, probably in the mid-second century, under Alexander Balas or Demetrius, when relations with the Jews of Judaea had improved considerably.

The above source is also noteworthy in what it tells us about the centrality and prominence of this synagogue; for whatever reason, when a Seleucid king wished to restore the Temple treasures to the Jewish people, he turned to the Antioch synagogue, and not to Jerusalem itself. Thus, the term τὸ ἱερόν undoubtedly refers to the local synagogue and not, as is sometimes assumed, to the Jerusalem Temple. As a result of these gifts, and perhaps the local community's contributions as well, the Antioch synagogue became quite ornate and lavish, perhaps rivaling that of Alexandria as described by Philo and the Tosefta (see above).

As in Asia Minor and Greece, Greeks in Syria were drawn to Judaism in significant numbers. After describing the grandeur of the local synagogue, Josephus notes the attraction of Jewish religious ceremonies for Antiochan gentiles. He seems to allude to the fact that many of these Greeks identified with Judaism, but either they had not fully committed themselves to the religion or the Jews had not fully accepted them: the Jews "had in some measure incorporated [these Greeks] with themselves."[221]

Malalas reports the existence of a tomb of the Maccabean martyrs in Antioch;[222] a medieval source (Nissim ibn Shahin of Qairuon) notes the existence of a Ḥashmunit synagogue in the city which was later converted into a church.[223] The synagogue was allegedly named after the mother of the Maccabean martyrs.[224] Finally, Malalas reports that, during the first Jewish revolt, Vespasian had destroyed a synagogue at Daphne and replaced it with a theater: "He built the theater of Daphne, inscribing on it, *ex praeda Iudaea* ('from the spoils of Judaea'). The site of the theater had formerly been a Jewish

---

220. See, however, comments by Downey (*History of Antioch*, 109), who has doubts regarding the reliability of this report.

221. For a strikingly similar phenomenon in Antioch several centuries later, in the time of John Chrysostom, see below, Chap. 8.

222. Malalas, *Chronicle* 8, 206-7 (pp. 108-9). According to Malalas, Antiochus IV brought the Maccabean remains to Antioch, and a few years later Judah Maccabee (*sic*) requested and received the bones from Demetrius; he then proceeded to bury them near a synagogue in the Kerateion section of Antioch. See J. Obermann, "Sepulchre of Maccabean Martyrs," 250-65; Bickerman, "Maccabées de Malalas," 63-83; Simon, *Recherches*, 147-53; Downey, *History of Antioch*, 110-11. The source for the tradition of the Maccabean martyrs is II Macc. 6:18-7:42. See also Schatkin, "Maccabean Martyrs," 97-113.

223. Kraeling, "Jewish Community at Antioch," 140; Downey, *History of Antioch*, 544. For a Samaritan tradition describing a synagogue built over the tomb of Baba Rabba in Constantinople, see *Chronicle* II, 25, 16 (p. 109).

224. See Nau, *Martyrologe*, 19, 52, 106, 123, 131 (*PO* 10.1).

synagogue."[225] The report, at first blush, appears strange indeed. Interestingly, Malalas reports a similar instance in Caesarea: "Vespasian also built in Caesarea in Palestine out of the spoils from Judaea a very large odeum, the size of a large theater; its site, too, had formerly been that of a Jewish synagogue."[226] Might we have in these two reports not later Christian fantasies but rather evidence for Roman practice in several places following their successful resolution of the Jewish revolt of 66?

We have additional information regarding Syrian synagogues from Damascus. Acts (9:1–2) speaks of the existence of a budding Christian community within the city's synagogues. Paul was incensed by what he considered a perversion and gained permission to bring these Christians to Jerusalem. Following his conversion, he preached in these very synagogues (9:20–23). Moreover, the synagogues of Damascus, as in Antioch and elsewhere, were known for attracting pagan sympathizers and converts. Of especial noteworthiness in Josephus' account is the fact that women were singled out as being particularly prominent among these Damascan pagans.[227]

THE DIASPORA SYNAGOGUE IN PERSPECTIVE

The range of sources relating to pre-70 Diaspora synagogues is varied. All three major categories are represented—literary, archeological, and epigraphical—and within each category there are substantial differences in the nature of the evidence and its historical value. The literary material, for example, ranges from references in Philonic religious monographs and historical accounts, to the edicts cited by Josephus, and finally to Acts' accounts of Paul's synagogue visitations.

Similarly with regard to the epigraphical material: some inscriptions are major communal documents (Berenice) or shorter contracts of manumission (Bosphorus), others are brief statements of individual (Delos, Acmonia, Egypt) or communal (Egypt) contributions, while still others are epitaphs noting synagogue affiliation (Rome). Of the two archeological remains, one dates to the first centuries B.C.E. and C.E. (Delos), while the other is primarily a fourth-century C.E. structure which originated in the first century (Ostia).

For each Diaspora community there is a combination of these sources. Epigraphical evidence is our sole source for Cyrene and the Bosphorus kingdom; literary and epigraphical testimony, for Egypt, Asia Minor, Rome, and Greece; archeological, epigraphical, and limited literary material, for Delos and Italy; and literary evidence, for Syria.

---

225. Malalas, *Chronicle* 10, 261 (p. 138); Downey, *History of Antioch*, 206–7. See also Malalas' report (*Chronicle* 10) that Titus had erected a gate of cherubs in Antioch from the spoils of the Jerusalem Temple.

226. Malalas, *Chronicle* 10, 261 (p. 138). See also L. Levine, *Roman Caesarea*, 25–26.

227. *War* 2, 560. As often happened, widespread attraction was matched by extensive hostility. This, too, found expression in Damascus at the outbreak of the revolt in 66 C.E. See ibid., 2, 259–61; 7, 368; Josephus, *Life* 27.

Given this broad range of primary material at our disposal, a number of features common to the pre-70 Diaspora synagogue become evident. All sources are in agreement as to the centrality of this institution throughout the Roman world. Each may express this reality in a different way, given the particular medium and the specific subject at hand, but the implication is always the same. As with Judaean communities, this point is driven home by the fact that no other Jewish communal institution or building is ever noted in these sources. And while a number of these communities boasted larger communal frameworks, such as a *politeuma* or *gerousia* (Berenice, Alexandria), no specific place is ever mentioned as housing these bodies. The synagogue building seems to have played a central role in this regard as well.

Thus, the synagogue (or *proseuche*) became the focus of communal activity, fulfilling the needs of its local community and serving as a setting for all aspects of communal life. For those seeking to preserve their Jewish way of life—and most Jews in antiquity wished to do so, however they might define that task—such an institution was a sine qua non. Moreover, it served to distinguish them from the surrounding society. Familial and ethnic ties were deepened by common historical roots and memories, enhanced by the special ties to Jerusalem and its Temple, strengthened by a network of customs and ceremonies, and bolstered by a set of beliefs which at times contrasted sharply with those of their neighbors.[228] In its functions, the Diaspora synagogue closely paralleled the contemporary Judaean one, as well as many non-Jewish frameworks throughout the Empire, and it filled the multiple purposes that a religious and ethnic minority such as the Jews would have needed—religious, educational, social, political, and economic.

Nevertheless, although linked by a distinct (though not always easily defined) religious and ethnic heritage, these Diaspora communities reflected a striking degree of diversity. The various names given the synagogues may reflect diverse perceptions of just what this institution was and how it was to function within the community. The most widespread terms, *proseuche* and *synagoge*, have been noted and—even in the Diaspora—may well point to varying emphases in each, at least in the formative stages.[229] However, as we have already had occasion to note, other terms were being used in the first century: ἱερόν (holy place), εὐχεῖον (place of prayer), σαββατεῖον (Sabbath meeting-place), and διδασκαλεῖον (place of instruction).[230] More unusual terms, such as "amphitheater" and *templum*, were

---

228. Gafni, "Punishment, Blessing or Mission," 229-50.

229. L. Levine, "Second Temple Synagogue," 13-14. The situation may be somewhat analogous to the twentieth-century American Jewish scene, where a synagogue might be called a "temple," "synagogue," "shul," or "community center." While to most Jews there may be little or no difference between these various names, they can reflect very different ideological and functional notions about the institution in the eyes of the founders and those it served in subsequent stages.

230. ἱερόν: Josephus, *War* 7, 44-45; III Macc. 2:28. εὐχεῖον: Tcherikover et al., *CPJ*, II, 223. σαββατεῖον: Josephus, *Antiquities* 16, 164; Tcherikover et al., *CPJ*, III, 46. See also S. Krauss, *Synagogale Altertümer*, 26-27; and above, note 176. διδασκαλεῖον: Philo, *Special Laws* 2, 62.

also invoked, as was the word οἶκος.[231] The synagogues of Rome—some early, others late—are of a unique order, having been named after famous people or places of origin.[232]

A limited, though striking, example of both the unity and diversity among these synagogues may be gleaned from even the small amount of archeological evidence hailing from this period, i.e., the buildings of Delos and Ostia (first stage). On the one hand, they are both close to the sea and located in a relatively remote area vis-à-vis the rest of the city; both may even have been oriented toward Jerusalem.[233] On the other hand, the Delos building was similar to other villa-like structures on the island; its marble chair was unmatched at Ostia. The first-century Ostia synagogue probably resembled other local buildings, but too little remains from this early stage to be certain. The types of inscriptions and artistic representations found at Delos (e.g., lamps) are not found at Ostia, even with regard to its later synagogue. Delos inscriptions feature *theos hypsistos* and there are blatantly pagan symbols on the lamps, whereas an Ostia inscription notes the welfare of the emperor, and the artistic expression there is almost nonexistent.

One of the major reasons for this diversity was that the Jews emigrating from Hellenistic and early Roman Judaea did not have any set form of communal organization. Another reason was the powerful forces impacting upon each community. In this respect, we have noted numerous examples of Jewish practices that followed patterns of the wider culture. Years ago, Kraabel called attention to this phenomenon, and with the passage of time, together with new discoveries and studies, this perception has only been strengthened.[234] The names used by members of the community often imitate those generally popular on the local scene. Julia Severa's contribution of a synagogue building seems to reflect a particular social and religious context unique to this part of Asia Minor; the organization and functioning of the Jewish *politeuma* in Berenice may well have derived, in part at least, from Cyrenian models;[235] the type of building renovated and used by Delian Jews was similar to those of other associations on that island; and the manumission decrees from Bosphorus, with their formulary components, are well known in that

---

231. *Amphitheater:* see above, notes 97 and 98. *Templum:* Tacitus, *Hist.* 5, 5, 4; see M. Stern, *Greek and Latin Authors*, II, 43. οἶκος: see above, note 218, as well as later examples; cf. Lifshitz, *Donateurs et fondateurs*, nos. 13, 21, 22, 61.

232. Leon, *Jews of Ancient Rome*, 135–66.

233. Both synagogues featured entrances on the eastern side. This direction was emphasized in Delos by placing the ornamental chair along the western wall facing the entrance and in Ostia by placing a raised *bima* along the western wall.

234. Kraabel, *Diaspora Jews and Judaism*, 257-67 (= "Social Systems," 79-91). See also Price, "Jewish Diaspora," 176-77. More recently, White has carried this argument even further, suggesting that almost every Diaspora synagogue was a private home converted into a communal institution; see his *Building God's House*, 60-61, 64, 78; and esp. his "Delos Synagogue Revisited," 135-36, with regard to the Delos synagogue.

235. See Lüderitz, "What Is the *Politeuma?*" 219-22.

particular region. We have seen time and again that Jews in the Diaspora freely borrowed different types of frameworks from their surroundings, adapting them to their
own use. Associations ranged from the more officially recognized *politeuma* and *collegium*
to less-defined groupings (*synodos, koinon, thiasos, communitas*), which might be based on
common geographical origins, commercial interests, religious affiliation, mutual aid, or
dining and burial societies.[236]

Studies focusing on the Egyptian synagogue have further confirmed this perception,
highlighting the many links between the Jewish *proseuche* on the one hand and the surrounding Egyptian culture on the other. Such parallels include dedications on behalf of
the ruling family, the *proseuche*'s status as a place of asylum, the names and functions of
synagogue officials, and various architectural components.

Significant local influence points to another characteristic of these Diaspora synagogues—namely, a high degree of hellenization. Diaspora synagogues employed Greek
terms for their institutions and officials, and they often referred to the God of Israel as the
Greeks did to Zeus (i.e., *theos hypsistos*). They almost always wrote in Greek, bore Greek
and, at times, Latin names, honored fellow-Jews and benevolent pagans with crowns,
shields, woolen fillets, and inscriptions, and built and decorated their buildings in ways
customary in Hellenistic-Roman society.

The interest of pagans in the synagogue is indicative of the institution's accessibility
as well as its importance and centrality in the Jewish community. Evidence for pagan
sympathizers and converts has been noted throughout the Diaspora, and in a number of
instances these people chose to be actively supportive of the local Jewish community.
The God-fearers of Bosphorus are an interesting example of this, as are Julia Severa's
involvement and benefaction. Especially noteworthy in this regard is the presence of
women among those attracted to Judaism, a phenomenon attested to throughout the
Roman world and in a variety of sources.[237]

Acceptance by many elements in the wider society notwithstanding, the Jews of the
Diaspora were continually seeking to gain and maintain recognition of their rights, as
well as confirmation of the status of their central institution. Synagogue evidence reveals
the extent to which this occurred. This would seem to have been at least part of the reason why the Jews of Berenice honored the Roman official Marcus Tittius in 24-25 C.E.

---

236. See Schürer, *History*, III, 87-137; Waltzing, *Étude historique*, passim; Juster, *Juifs*, I, 413-24;
Smallwood, *Jews under Roman Rule*, 133-38; Kraabel, *Diaspora Jews and Judaism*, 23-26 (= "Unity and
Diversity," 51-54); Meeks, *First Urban Christians*, 34-36; L. Levine, "Second Temple Synagogue," 20-23.
See also A. Baumgarten, "City Lights," 56-58; Wilson, "Voluntary Associations," 1-15; Kloppenborg,
"Collegia and *Thiasoi*," 16-30; idem, "Early Synagogues as Collegia," 90-109 (with some rather exagger-
ated claims).

237. See, for example, Josephus, *War* 2, 560-61 (Damascus); Acts 13:50 (Antioch, Pisidia); ibid., 16:13
(Philippi, Macedonia); Martial, *Epigrammata*, IV, 4 (M. Stern, *Greek and Latin Authors*, I, 524). See also
van der Horst, *Ancient Jewish Epitaphs*, 109-13; and below, Chap. 14.

and why the Acmonia community gave prominence to Julia Severa's gift years—if not decades—after the original donation.

Sometimes this recognition came quite naturally, nurtured as it was within a diverse society.[238] Throughout the course of Jewish history, the more diverse and pluralistic a society, the greater its acceptance of the Jewish community within it. The Roman Empire provided such a multicultural setting. For much of the Hellenistic period, Ptolemaic Egypt provided a classic example of such a setting, as the Jews, like their neighbors, dedicated building after building in honor of the reigning king and queen. However, we have also noted numerous occasions on which the Jews were forced to seek official Roman confirmation of their rights in face of attacks and hostility from their neighbors. In such cases, their minority status and distinctive customs proved as irritating and intolerable to some as they were attractive to others. Such a reality may well lie behind much of Philo's apologetics, as well as Josephus' inclusion of edicts issued on behalf of numerous Diaspora communities. The dimension of Jewish marginality may also have found expression in the not-uncommon location of the synagogue (and perhaps also the community) on the outskirts of a city. Such was the case over a wide geographical area, and we have noted such instances in Delos, Ostia, Macedonia, and Egypt.[239]

When all is said and done, the Diaspora synagogue was indeed the product of a creative synthesis between Jewish tradition, the requirements of each community, and the influence of the surrounding culture. The Jews succeeded in creating an institution which expressed and reflected their needs as individuals and as a community, and did so within the parameters of the cultural and social contexts in which they found themselves. They borrowed, yet always within limits; Ptolemaic *proseuchae* were not dedicated "to" Ptolemy but "on behalf of" the king. They honored the ruler as was customary in other dedicatory inscriptions to Greek and Egyptian deities at the time.[240] The Jewish place of worship was not identical to the pagan sanctuary or any other place of sacrifice; rather, it was a *proseuche*, a place for prayer and communal study.

Thus, for all its borrowing and diversity, the Jewish communal institution remained quintessentially Jewish. It served the Jewish community and housed its rites and observances, which were influenced first and foremost—though far from exclusively—by a common Jewish past and present. The Jews had brought their own *patria* to the Diaspora, a cultural and religious tradition that pagans could either respect, resent, or ignore but of which the Jews themselves were proud. They were committed to honoring and perpetuating this heritage, and, for the most part, the surrounding world was supportive. To safe-

---

238. On the multicultural, social, and religious mix in Ptolemaic Egypt, see Fraser, *Ptolemaic Alexandria*; Walbank, "Hellenistic World," 99-102; Samuel, *From Athens to Alexandria*, 105-17.

239. Even in Alexandria, the major Jewish residential area, Delta, was on the coast, in the northeastern section of the city.

240. Fraser, *Ptolemaic Alexandria*, 226-27, 282. See also Nock, *Conversion*, 61-62.

guard and transmit one's traditional customs was an undisputed value in Roman society,[241] and on the communal level the synagogue was the main vehicle for achieving this goal.

We have noted that the Jewish community regarded their synagogues as holy places. The very term *proseuche* may be indicative of this fact, but even more so are specific references to the synagogue as a place of asylum, as a "sacred precinct" (Egypt), or as a "holy place" (Antioch; Philo's reference to Essenes).[242] The manumission of slaves in the synagogues of the Bosphorus kingdom also appears to indicate the sanctity associated with these buildings. The intention seems to have been that this ceremony be carried out in the presence of the Jewish God, as may have been the case with regard to Apollo in Delphi.[243]

The reasons for this attribution of sanctity to some (many? all?) Diaspora synagogues is worthy of comment. It seems most likely that such status was an attempt on the part of Jewish communities to accord their synagogues and *proseuchae* the prestige enjoyed by many temples and cities throughout the Hellenistic and early Roman worlds. Moreover, it was precisely at this time that granting temples the title of "sacred and inviolable" (ἱερὸς καὶ ἄσυλος) increased markedly and was viewed as a mark of high honor.[244] As a consequence, Diaspora communities also adopted this status (whether formally or not), thus enhancing, in their own eyes as well as in the eyes of others, the prestige of their main communal institution.

The tenacity with which the Jews defended the integrity of this institution, its functions, and their rights generally is a reflection of these commitments and loyalties. From within and without, attempts to undermine what they perceived as their fundamental interests and rights were met head-on. So, for example, Paul encountered fierce resistance within Diaspora synagogues,[245] and Jews frequently appealed to Rome in order to overcome attempts by municipal authorities to undermine their status. The fact that Diaspora Jewry continued to thrive for centuries in many of these cities and regions attests to the overall success of its efforts.

---

241. See, for example, *Antiquities* 16, 44; 19, 290; *Against Apion* 2, 232-35, and comments in Kasher, *Josephus, Against Apion*, II, 519-21; and, generally, MacMullen, *Paganism*, 2-4.

242. See Goodman, "Sacred Space," 4-6.

243. Frey, *CIJ*, I, nos. 709-11.

244. Rigsby, *Asylia*, 1-29.

245. Acts 18:6 and esp. 19:9.

THE SECOND TEMPLE SYNAGOGUE—
five ITS ROLE AND FUNCTIONS

B y the first century C.E., the synagogue was playing a pivotal institutional role within the Jewish communities of Judaea and the Diaspora. This centrality is particularly evident in the wide range of activities which took place there. Though many first-century sources focus on particular events relating to a specific synagogue, several—e.g., the Theodotos inscription and a number of documents cited by Josephus—list some of the varied activities that transpired there. Rabbinic traditions speak of the synagogue as the venue for various educational and other activities, and while this material primarily reflects the circumstances of later antiquity, some information may be relevant for the first century as well.[1] The synagogue was also the logical setting in which a Jewish community would honor one of its prominent members by placing a commemorative inscription therein, often in recognition of a generous donation.[2]

The range of functions within the synagogue is similar to the gamut of activities which found expression in many contemporary pagan temples. Frequently surrounded by courtyards and ancillary rooms, these buildings or complexes might also function as libraries, markets, banks, and at times venues for study and learning. As a meeting place

---

1. See below, Chap. 10.
2. As in the case of Decimus Valerius Dionysios at Berenice; see above, Chap. 4.

for *collegia* or *sodalitates*, the temple would also serve some of the religious, social, political, and economic needs of members.[3]

The synagogue's centrality was also recognized by the outside world. Hostility of pagans toward Jews was vented primarily, if not exclusively, through violent attacks on local synagogues.[4] Contrastingly, when a ruler wished to honor or express support for a Jewish community, this, too, was often done within the context of the local synagogue. Thus, Seleucid rulers are reported as having donated spoils from the Jerusalem Temple to a synagogue in Antioch,[5] and the many privileges enjoyed by Jewish communities throughout the Diaspora were invariably linked, directly or indirectly, to this institution.

Jewish communities, for their part, chose to honor kings and emperors in the synagogue, as, for example, the Egyptian *proseuchae*, which were dedicated to Ptolemaic rulers, and the Alexandrian synagogue, which displayed tributes to the emperor.[6] Rome's Jews named synagogues after Augustus and his viceroy, Agrippa, the Jews of Berenice honored a Roman official in their amphitheater at weekly (?) and monthly meetings, and those of Acmonia recalled the benefactions of the pagan noblewoman Julia Severa.[7]

Moreover, the fact that these various activities are documented for synagogues and *proseuchae* throughout the Empire argues for a basic similarity in the role of both institutions at this time. If, as we have argued, these institutions served, first and foremost, the needs of a community, then it is most likely that such needs—be they of an economic, social, political, or religious nature—did not differ significantly from Judaea to the Diaspora, nor among the communities in Egypt, Asia Minor, or Rome.

Some degree of commonality among first-century synagogues is related, for example, to leadership positions within this institution. While information is severely limited owing to the scarcity of epigraphical evidence, two kinds of leaders appear to have been especially prominent in the first century: the priest and the *archisynagogos*.[8] The Theo-

---

3. Stambaugh, "Functions of Roman Temples," 580–91. See also C. Roberts et al., "Gild of Zeus," 76–79, 83; Meeks, *First Urban Christians*, 31–32.

4. Josephus, *Antiquities* 19, 299–305; idem, *War* 2, 285–92; Philo, *Embassy*, 132–34. On the nature and extent of anti-Jewish sentiments in antiquity, see Daniel, "Antisemitism," 45–65; Gager, *Origins of Anti-Semitism*, 35–112.

5. Josephus, *War* 7, 44. In the early third century C.E., an emperor referred to in rabbinic literature as Antoninus (in all probability, Caracalla, 211–17 C.E.) allegedly donated a menorah to a synagogue; see Y Megillah 3, 2, 74a.

6. Horbury and Noy, *Jewish Inscriptions*, nos. 22, 24, 25, 27, 28, 117; Philo, *Embassy* 133.

7. Leon, *Jews of Ancient Rome*, 140–42. The Roman official was Marcus Tittius, son of Sextus Aemilia; see above, Chap. 4; Lifshitz, *Donateurs et fondateurs*, no. 33.

8. However, we have also had occasion to note other official titles associated with the synagogue: νακόρος (=νεωκόρος), חזן, and προστάτης (Egypt); ἄρχων (Berenice, Antioch); and ὑπηρέτης (Galilee) —all of which have parallels in contemporary pagan contexts; see Oster, Jr., "Supposed Anachronism," 202–4.

dotos inscription presents these two leadership roles in tandem over a period of three generations, and this combination reappears at third-century Dura Europos, where the priest Samuel bar Yed'ayah served as archon and elder.[9] Other first-century evidence focuses on one role or the other. Philo speaks of priests in Egyptian synagogues who instructed the congregation during Sabbath-day meetings, and one of the Berenice inscriptions mentions a priest, Cartisthenes, son of Archias, at the head of a list of donors who were not community officers.[10] We have noted the centrality of priests in Qumran generally, especially with regard to the ritual of prayer and study.[11] Thus, these four examples drawn from Judaea and the Diaspora may indeed be reflective of the role that priests often played in the first-century synagogue.

The title *archisynagogos* is well documented in our literary and epigraphical material, particularly with regard to the post-70 era. Used by pagans as well,[12] this title is attested in a variety of first-century sources and locales. Besides in the Theodotos inscription, the term is used by Luke with regard to the Galilee (13:14) and Antioch in Pisidia (Acts 13:15), in the Julia Severa inscription from Acmonia, and in an inscription from Egypt of less certain first-century dating than the Theodotos inscription.[13] Here, too, we are dealing with a series of examples which together embrace urban and rural communities in both Judaea and the Diaspora. The prominence of this office is fairly well attested early on in rabbinic tradition. A number of sources refer to the Hebrew equivalent of *archisynagogos*, the *rosh knesset*, with respect to the Torah-reading ceremonies in the Temple as well as with regard to the second- and third-century synagogue (and possibly the first-century synagogue, too).[14] On the basis of the evidence at hand, we may conclude that the *archisynagogos* was not only a communal leader (Acmonia, Galilee), but also a wealthy member of the community (Acmonia) who participated in the ritual, administrative, and financial aspects of the institution.[15]

---

9. Frey, *CIJ*, II, nos. 828–29.

10. Philo, *Hypothetica* 7, 13. *Berenice inscription:* above, Chap. 4; and Applebaum, *Jews and Greeks*, 163–64. In the post-70 era as well, priests appear to have played a prominent role in many synagogues over a wide geographical area—Susiya, Eshtemoa, Na'aran, and Naveh in Palestine; Dura Europos (as noted) and Sardis in the Diaspora—as well as in the towns and villages mentioned in the list of priestly courses. See Roth-Gerson, *Greek Inscriptions*, 78–79 n. 11; Seager and Kraabel, "Synagogue and Jewish Community," 189; and below, Chap. 15.

11. See above, Chap. 3, note 78; and, more generally, Burtchaell, *From Synagogue to Church*, 253–56.

12. *TDNT*, VII, 844–45. See also G. H. R. Horsley, *New Documents*, IV, 214–16.

13. *Acmonia:* Lifshitz, *Donateurs et fondateurs*, no. 33. *Egypt:* Horbury and Noy, *Jewish Inscriptions*, no. 26. An *archisynagogos* appears in a later Alexandrian inscription from the third century C.E.; see ibid., no. 18.

14. M Yoma 7:1; M Sotah 7:7–8; T Megillah 3 (pp. 353–64).

15. On the *archisynagogos* in the later Empire, see below, Chap. 11. Others contributed to the synagogue as well, although material regarding individual gifts is limited. Aside from the Theodotos inscription from Jerusalem, two inscriptions from first-century Egypt refer explicitly to Jews (Alypus and Pa-

The apparent commonality shared by these far-flung Jewish communities did not preclude the fact that a great deal of diversity also prevailed. As we have already had occasion to note, local influences often shaped the synagogue in its physical appearance, leadership positions, legal standing, and specific customs and practices. Were we better informed, we might also detect subtle—and not so subtle—cultural and religious differences among the various communities. Yet, notwithstanding this diversity, there clearly was a broad-based common agenda and range of activities for most, if not all, of these first-century institutions.

Diversity among Diaspora and Judaean synagogues has usually been claimed on the basis of the different nomenclature used for the synagogue building. In the former, the term *proseuche* was dominant; in the latter, *synagoge*. Indeed, all but two references to the Judaean institution refer to it by the term "synagogue."[16] Of the fifty-nine references to the Diaspora institution, thirty-one, i.e., some 53%, refer to a *proseuche*.[17] It has been claimed that not only was the geographical factor of importance, but a chronological one was important as well—i.e., the term *proseuche* predominated until the first century C.E. and seems to have been replaced thereafter by the term *synagoge*.[18] This last claim, although having some basis in fact, rests on somewhat shaky ground owing to the paucity of evidence. True enough, the term *proseuche* is used almost exclusively in Hellenistic Egypt, the Bosphorus, and Delos, which account for almost all of the relevant synagogal evidence for the first-century C.E. Diaspora and earlier. Nevertheless, one should be cautious about overgeneralizing on the basis of such limited data. These three regions may have preferred such nomenclature; elsewhere (e.g., Rome, Greece, Asia Minor, and Cyrene), "synagogue" and other terms were in vogue.[19]

Regarding the reasons for using these two terms, it may well be that the terms *proseuche* and *synagoge* reflect a somewhat different emphasis in each institution. The former seems to indicate a desire by Diaspora synagogues to highlight a religious dimension; as

---

pous) who built *proseuchae* (Horbury and Noy, *Jewish Inscriptions*, nos. 13, 126), while several others, only partially preserved, appear to refer to some sort of gift (ibid., nos. 16, 20, 127, 128, 129). Of interest in this regard is a second-century B.C.E. inscription which speaks of a military commander named Eleazar who contributed a sundial, probably to a synagogue (ibid., no. 115 and commentary; see also no. 129). On the first-century Acmonia inscription referring to Julia Severa's gift of a building to the local Jewish community and the restoration by synagogue officials, see above, Chap. 4.

16. The Tiberian *proseuche* and the Qumran בית השתחות.

17. Oster, Jr., "Supposed Anachronism," 186. On the suggestion that the *proseuche* in these and other instances refers to a Jewish institution, see Lifshitz, "Prolegomenon," 64–69; M. Stern, "Jewish Diaspora," 155–57; Levinskaya, "Jewish or Gentile Prayer House?" 154–59; idem, *Acts in Its Diaspora Setting*, 207–25. Some, however, have expressed reservations; see, for example, G. H. R. Horsley, *New Documents*, I, 25–28; Kraemer, "Jewish and Christian Fish," 144–47.

18. Hengel, "Proseuche und Synagoge," 169–78; Horbury and Noy, *Jewish Inscriptions*, 33; G. H. R. Horsley, *New Documents*, IV, 219–20.

19. For other names of the synagogue, see above, Chap. 4, note 230.

noted, many of these institutions seem to have acquired a measure of sanctity unknown in most contemporary Judaean synagogues.[20] Such a development may have been due to the Diaspora synagogue's unique context, being distant from the Jerusalem Temple and surrounded by pagan religious models. Moreover, the greater need of Diaspora Jews to define themselves in religious-communal terms vis-à-vis their pagan surroundings may also have had a bearing on the nature of and emphasis within their synagogues.[21] The Judaean synagogue, on the other hand, was unique not only because it was referred to almost exclusively by one term, "synagogue," but also because this word was bereft of any religious connotation. The synagogue in Judaea was thus designated by a term denoting a place of gathering; it was primarily a communal institution whose religious profile was perhaps less prominent than that of its Diaspora counterpart.

THE SYNAGOGUE AS A COMMUNITY CENTER

The role of the synagogue as the focal communal framework is reflected in its function as a venue for public gatherings. Tiberias in 66–67 C.E. provides a striking example of such a function. In debating whether to join the rebellion then in progress, the populace convened in either the city's stadium or the local *proseuche*.[22] In addition, several decrees quoted by Josephus regarding Jewish rights and privileges in Asia Minor make the association of a synagogue as a community center quite clear:

> Jewish citizens of ours have come to me and pointed out that from the earliest times they have had an association of their own in accordance with their native laws and a place of their own, in which they decide their affairs and controversies with one another.[23]

> It has therefore been decreed by the council and people that permission shall be given them to come together on stated days to do those things which are in accordance with their laws,

---

20. As we noted in Chap. 3 with respect to the Dor incident, it is quite likely that coastal synagogues may have been influenced by Diaspora models, as, for example, in the sanctity ascribed to it by Jew and non-Jew alike.

21. L. Levine, "Second Temple Synagogue," 21–22. What is the significance of the term *proseuche?* The word itself appears some 114 times in the Septuagint as a translation of the Hebrew word for prayer, *tefillah* (תפילה). However, it is doubtful, as we shall see below, whether the prayer component was the dominant feature of Egyptian Jewry's liturgy. As in Judaea, the Torah-reading ceremony appears to have been central. Thus, it is unlikely that the term *proseuche* would have been chosen solely owing to this factor.

Another consideration which may have come into play here in opting for a term such as *proseuche* instead of *synagoge* is the fact that the latter had been (or was being) appropriated in the Septuagint to designate the community, a translation of the Hebrew terms *qahal* and *'edah*. Therefore, not only was the term "synagogue" more neutral or "secular" (to invoke modern parlance), but it was also being used for other biblical concepts.

22. Josephus, *Life* 271–98, 331; and above, Chap. 3.

23. *Antiquities* 14, 235; see also the decree of the people of Halicarnassus, where the religious component of Jewish rights is emphasized (discussed above, Chap. 4).

and also that a place shall be set apart by the magistrates for them to build and inhabit, such as they may consider suitable for this purpose.[24]

There is also some indirect evidence that Egyptian synagogues served a wider communal purpose. As will be recalled, several inscriptions mention τὰ συγκύροντα when referring to the *proseuche*.[25] What precisely is intended remains unclear, but it may well be a reference to ancillary rooms used for a variety of purposes, as in contemporary pagan temples.[26] Moreover, the building(s) mentioned in the Theodotos inscription, together with the Gamla and Delos buildings and the inscription from Cyrene, seem to indicate that these structures functioned in a similar fashion.

In addition to serving as a meeting place for the community as a whole, the synagogue also hosted various subgroups within the community. Several papyri from Hellenistic Egypt indicate that a burial society once met in a local *proseuche*; another papyrus indicates that an association in Apollonopolis Magna organized a series of banquets, probably in the local synagogue.[27] This may also have been the case with regard to the Sambathic association in Naucratis, although the precise nature of this group (Jews? *sebomenoi?*) remains unclear.[28] The various professional guilds mentioned in the Tosefta[29] in connection with the Alexandrian synagogue may have used the premises for professional gatherings as well as for worship purposes.

One of the most intriguing functions of the ancient synagogue which is mentioned on a number of occasions was to provide a place for communal meals. Once again, Josephus provides us with the clearest statements of this activity. In an edict issued by Julius Caesar (cited above), the following rights are confirmed: "Now it displeases me that such statutes should be made against our friends and allies, and that they should be forbidden to live in accordance with their customs and to contribute money to common meals and sacred rites. . . . I forbid other religious societies but permit these people alone to assemble and feast in accordance with their native customs and ordinances."[30] The edict is a general recognition of two basic rights which the Jews enjoyed: to assemble according to their ancestral tradition and to collect monies for communal meals. Similarly, in writing to the Jews of Asia Minor, Augustus makes reference to their sacred books and sacred

---

24. *Antiquities* 14, 259–61. Communal use of the synagogue is likewise attested for a later period; see B Shabbat 150a; B Ketubot 5a.

25. Horbury and Noy, *Jewish Inscriptions*, nos. 9, 25.

26. Tcherikover et al., *CPJ*, III, no. 1433; Lifshitz, *Donateurs et fondateurs*, no. 87. See also Hengel, "Synagogeninschrift von Stobi," 165 n. 68; Dion, "Synagogues et temples," 60.

27. Tcherikover et al., *CPJ*, I, nos. 138–39. Similar societies or individuals are mentioned in rabbinic literature with regard to Second Temple Jerusalem; see T Megillah 3:15 (p. 357); Tractate Semaḥot 12:5 (p. 81); and Ginzberg, *Commentary*, II, 55–56. However, whether they convened in a synagogue setting is not clear.

28. Horbury and Noy, *Jewish Inscriptions*, no. 26.

29. T Sukkah 4:5 (p. 273).

30. *Antiquities* 14, 214–16.

monies which are stored in the synagogue (here referred to as a *sabbateion*) and banquet hall (ἀνδρών).[31]

It is difficult to determine the nature of these meals. Were they holiday feasts, meals for transients and visitors, or events sponsored by local Jewish associations? Alternatively, might they have been regular communal gatherings on the Sabbath and perhaps New Moon? Or perhaps they were all of the above in various permutations over time and place. Whatever the answer, one fact remains eminently clear from the documents quoted by Josephus. These meals were recognized by Romans and Jews alike as important communal activities which played an integral part in the corporate life of the Jews.

Many Jewish sects in the Second Temple period, such as the Pharisaic *ḥavurah*, the Essenes or Qumran sectarians, and the Therapeutae in Egypt, featured communal meals.[32] A mishnaic passage may also indicate that meals were regularly eaten in synagogues.[33] Such meals, of course, became a central feature in the nascent Christian church.[34]

Although Jewish literary sources are mostly silent about this aspect of synagogue life,

31. Ibid., 16, 164. See comments in Marcus, Josephus, *Antiquities*, LCL, VIII, 273 n. *c*. It is possible that an edict issued to the Jews of Sardis, assuring them of their right to offer prayers and sacrifices to God (*Antiquities* 14, 260-61), may likewise point to a communal banquet. As noted above (Chap. 4), the reference to "sacrifices" is baffling. Does it mean "offerings" in general, and does the word "sacrifices" reflect a pagan misunderstanding of Jewish ritual; does it perhaps refer to actual sacrifices made by gentile worshippers to the God of Israel; or does it point to what we are discussing, i.e., communal meals or banquets of the Jewish community or parts thereof? On the above, see Marcus, Josephus, *Antiquities*, LCL, VII, 589, n. *d*; Bickerman, "Altars of Gentiles," 151; S. J. D. Cohen, "Pagan and Christian Evidence," 166. It may be that the word "sacrifices" refers simply to the monies sent by Sardis Jews to Jerusalem, as per Josephus, *Antiquities* 16, 171. Might the interpretation find substantiation in ibid., 12, 10?

32. *Pharisaic ḥavurah:* Lieberman, "Discipline," 199-200 (= *Texts and Studies*, 200-207); Neusner, "Fellowship," 125-42; Oppenheimer, *'Am Ha-aretz*, 118-69. *Essenes or Qumran sectarians: War* 2, 128-33; 1QS 6:4-5; 1QSa 2:17-21, CD 13, 2-3. Regarding the Essenes, Philo writes: "They live together, formed into clubs, bands of comradeship, with common meals, and never cease to conduct all their affairs to serve the general weal" (*Hypothetica* 11, 5). See Delcor, "Repas cultuels," 401-25. See also van der Ploeg, "Meals of the Essenes," 163-75; Klinghardt, "Hellenistic Associations," 261-62. On the general identification of the Essenes with the Qumran sect, despite recent reservations by some, see Vermes and Goodman, *Essenes According to Classical Sources*, 12-14. *Therapeutae:* Philo, *Contemplative Life* 64-90.

33. M Zavim 3:2. See comments of Rabin, *Qumran Studies*, 34. The mishnah of the Babylonian Talmud as well as of Lowe's MS reads בית הכנסת instead of בני הכנסת.

Inscriptions from later synagogue buildings in Caesarea and Stobi specifically mention a dining hall (*triclinium*); see Roth-Gerson, *Greek Inscriptions*, 115-17; Lifshitz, *Donateurs et fondateurs*, no. 10; and Hengel, "Synagogeninschrift von Stobi," 167-68. It is interesting to note that the building at Ostia (from its fourth-century stage, at the very least) had kitchen facilities; see White, *Building God's House*, 69 n. 24; and Hengel, "Synagogeninschrift von Stobi," 167-72. On Netzer's claim to have discovered a *triclinium* in a Jericho synagogue, see above, Chap. 3.

34. Kuhn, "Lord's Supper and Communal Meal at Qumran," 65-93; Black, *Scrolls and Christian Origins*, 102-18. See also Alon, *Studies*, I, 286-91.

comparative pagan material is not lacking. Communal meals within temple precincts are well known in the Roman world.[35] At times, such repasts were intimately connected to cultic acts, as was the Passover sacrifice in the Jerusalem Temple. Moreover, temple settings were well suited to provide space for either large family affairs (space not ordinarily available in private homes) or various kinds of fraternities.[36] As at the Ostia synagogue, temples, too, were at times outfitted with kitchens for such purposes. Archeological remains of banquet areas within temple precincts have been found throughout Greece, Asia Minor, and Syria, in Nabatean temples, and in the Caesarea Maritima *mithraeum*.[37]

In addition to the pagan temples, Hellenistic and Roman religious associations likewise sponsored such meals. Aelius Aristides describes a gathering of Serapis worshippers at which the icon of the god was brought into the banquet hall and set on a chair in order to participate in the festivities.[38] Devotees of Isis, Asclepius, Jupiter, Heracles, and others are noted as having incorporated communal meals into their religious practice.[39] Thus, it would appear that Jewish communities throughout the Empire were adopting (and undoubtedly adapting) widespread practices of the Hellenistic and Semitic worlds, incorporating them in one way or another into their organized communal life. So central were these meals in Jewish life that they, along with several other activities, became subjects of controversy and hostility between the Jews and their neighbors (see above).

Among its communal functions, the synagogue also served as a place for administering justice. Attested already in the Septuagint version of Susannah (see Chap. 2), adjudication was one of the basic privileges granted to Diaspora communities,[40] and in Judaea this right was for the most part exercised on a local level. New Testament evidence is helpful in this regard. One tradition, appearing in each of the synoptic gospels, makes this point rather clearly: "Beware of men; for they will deliver you up to councils and flog you in their synagogues; and you will be dragged before governors and kings for my sake, to bear testimony before them and the Gentiles."[41] Two stages of adjudication are indicated: (1) sentences were meted out in the synagogue, and, in all probability, the trial itself was conducted there as well; and (2) at times, such procedures may have constituted but a first

---

35. Nock, *Early Gentile Christianity*, 72–76; C. Roberts et al., "Gild of Zeus," 77–79; Kane, "Mithraic Cultic Meal," 313–51; Meslin, "Convivialité ou communion sacramentelle?" 295–306; Lipiński, "Le repas sacré," 130–34*; Burkert, "Oriental Symposia," 7–24.

36. MacMullen, *Paganism*, 36–39, esp. n. 24.

37. See above, notes 32 and 33; Negev, "Nabataean Necropolis," 111, 127–29; Bull, "Mithraeum of Caesarea," 79.

38. *Oratio* 8, 54, 1.

39. C. Roberts et al., "Gild of Zeus," 47–48; MacMullen, *Paganism*, 38–39. At Petra, meals were held in rock-hewn chambers, and a participant was referred to as *ḥbr*; see Cantineau, *Nabatéen*, II, 63.

40. On Susannah, see Chap. 2, notes 68–70. See also C. A. Moore, *Daniel, Esther and Jeremiah: Additions*, 104: "So they went to the synagogue of the city where they were living, and all the sons of Israel who were there sat in judgment." On rights, see *Antiquities* 14, 235, 259–61; and above, note 23.

41. Matt. 10:17–18; Mark 13:9; Luke 21:12. See also Luke 12:11.

stage. More serious cases might then have been referred or appealed to higher authorities, while others might have been heard from the outset by these higher authorities, whether Jewish or Roman. That flogging was carried out regularly in the synagogue is further indicated by another passage in Matthew, following Jesus' famous "Woe" speech: "Therefore I send you prophets and wise men and scribes, some of whom you will kill and crucify, and some you will scourge in your synagogues and persecute from town to town."[42]

Paul's speech on the steps of the barracks in Jerusalem (Acts 22:19) once again recalls this phenomenon. His words are especially poignant, for he is presumably speaking from personal experience: "I said: 'Lord, here of all places they know that I imprisoned those who believed in You, or beat them in the synagogues.'"[43]

That the synagogue continued to function as a court and place of punishment for centuries to come is explicitly indicated in later rabbinic sources as well as by Epiphanius.[44] Undoubtedly, all sorts of judicial matters were addressed within the synagogue framework, one of which—the manumission of slaves—is well attested in the epigraphical evidence, albeit primarily in one particular region. As noted above (Chap. 4), a number of first-century inscriptions from the Bosphorus relate to this public procedure in a *proseuche* setting, some stipulating that the freed slave must continue to visit the synagogue and that the latter would protect him or her from re-enslavement.[45]

The first-century synagogue also provided for visitors and transients. While most evidence in this regard comes from the post-70 period,[46] the one clear and explicit pre-70 source is the Theodotos inscription, which notes that this synagogue also functioned as a hostel (τὸν ξενῶνα).[47] How unique this function was to Jerusalem, the focus of Temple pilgrimage, is unclear. However, the fact that later synagogues also served such a purpose may point to similar needs in the pre-70 era as well.

It appears that a wide range of charitable activities were housed in the synagogue. As noted above (Chap. 3), the two Pharisaic schools, Bet Hillel and Bet Shammai, disagreed over the propriety of making decisions regarding charity to the poor in the synagogue on the Sabbath, and Matthew may refer to the same phenomenon when he has Jesus "caution his followers not to 'trumpet' their gifts as do the hypocrites in the synagogues and streets that they may be praised by men."[48] In all likelihood, these funds were kept

---

42. Matt. 23:24.

43. Acts 22:19. Elsewhere (II Cor. 11:24), Paul speaks of being flogged by Jews thirty-nine times on five different occasions; see Trebilco, *Jewish Communities*, 20–21.

44. M Makkot 3:12; Y Bikkurim 1, 3, 64a; Epiphanius, *Panarion* 30, 11; and below, Chap. 10.

45. See above, Chap. 4, notes 211 and 212.

46. For example, B Pesaḥim 100b–101a; Y Megillah 3, 74a; the multiroom synagogue complexes as at Dura, Ostia, 'En Gedi, and Ḥammat Tiberias may indicate a provision for lodging accommodations.

47. Frey, *CIJ*, II, no. 1404; Lifshitz, *Donateurs et fondateurs*, no. 79; Roth-Gerson, *Greek Inscriptions*, 76–86; and above, Chap. 3.

48. T Shabbat 16:22 (p. 79); Matt. 6:2.

somewhere on the synagogue premises, and the actual distribution of monies likewise took place there—again, as was the case later on.[49] We have seen that in the Diaspora, the right to collect funds for a variety of purposes was specifically guaranteed, as in the general privilege issued by Julius Caesar.[50]

Although evidence for schools in synagogues is negligible for the pre-70 period, there is reason to believe that synagogue premises served in such a capacity in many, if not most, places in this era. One late rabbinic tradition speaks of 480 synagogues in pre-70 Jerusalem, each of which had a primary school (בית ספר) and an advanced school (בית תלמוד).[51] Despite this exaggerated and schematic number, the assumption that many children studied in some sort of formal setting at this time is not entirely far-fetched. In the Greco-Roman world, educational frameworks for children were well known.[52] Moreover, rabbinic material attributes the introduction of some sort of public schooling to some personalities in the Second Temple period, Simeon b. Shataḥ (first century B.C.E.) and the high priest Joshua b. Gamala (first century C.E.).[53] Even though such attributions are highly questionable (although, truth to tell, it is hard to fathom why the latter, a relatively unknown figure, would have been singled out for no reason), some sort of educational system may already have been formalized in this pre-70 period. The well-established and widespread local educational apparatus already reflected in rabbinic discussions from the second century onward (see below, Chap. 10) was probably not created overnight. Nor were they under rabbinic auspices; these schools seem to have been a communal responsibility and thus might well have existed much before the time the editors of rabbinic literature began including such material.

Josephus, for his part, emphasizes the instruction received by Jewish children, presumably reflecting, at the very least, the situation in the first century.[54] Even discounting his proclivity to exaggerate in matters of Jewish piety, there probably is some truth to his claims. Although Josephus does not specify a public setting, one seems to be implied by his far-reaching claims for Jewish literacy; and if a public institution was involved, it in all probability was the local synagogue. The Theodotos inscription as well may allude to such a framework of instruction when it refers to study of the commandments, but we cannot

---

49. See, for example, T Terumot 1:10 (p. 109); T Bava Batra 8:14 (p. 158).

50. *Antiquities* 14, 215.

51. Y Megillah 3, 1, 73d; Y Ketubot 13, 35c; B Ketubot 105a.

52. Marrou, *Education in Antiquity*, 199–209, 335–36.

53. Y Ketubot 8, 32c; B Bava Batra 21a. See also Schürer, *History*, II, 417–21; Ebner, *Elementary Education*, 38–50, 105–7; S. Safrai, "Education," 946ff.

54. *Against Apion* 2, 204: "Again the Law . . . orders that they [i.e., the children] shall be taught to read and shall learn both the laws and the deeds of their forefathers, in order that they may imitate the latter, and, being grounded in the former, may neither transgress nor have any excuse for being ignorant of them." See Josephus' further comments in this regard in *Against Apion* 1, 42–43; 2, 151ff.; as well as A. Baumgarten, "Torah as a Public Document," 17–24.

be sure of its precise implication. Other forms of instruction within the context of the synagogue took place on the Sabbath and included the community as a whole (see below).

Until now, we have focused on the communal "non-worship" dimension of the early synagogue. Although information in this area is limited, there can be little doubt that this aspect of the synagogue constituted the very essence of the institution at this time. Serving as a "place of gathering" on a regular (i.e., daily) basis, the synagogue functioned first and foremost as a community center with a broad and varied agenda.

THE SYNAGOGUE AS A RELIGIOUS INSTITUTION

In the first century, worship in the synagogue seems to have been limited to Sabbaths and holidays. Pre-70 sources speak almost exclusively about the Sabbath and in several instances, both in Berenice, to New Moon and Sukkot gatherings. Other holiday gatherings—although unattested—can reasonably be assumed. Most extant sources—given their particular agendas—focus on the religious dimension of the synagogue, and it is to this aspect that we now turn.[55]

Information regarding the religious agenda of the synagogue is uneven. Some activities are well documented, and there is a virtual consensus as to their centrality; others remain more elusive with respect to both their form and content, while still others are the subject of scholarly debate as to whether they, in fact, existed at all during this period and, if so, in what form. The first category for which documentation is comparatively rich includes the reading and study of Scriptures (the Torah and Prophets) on Sabbaths and holidays. The second includes related Torah-reading activities such as the sermon or *targum*. The last category refers to communal prayer, the existence of which at this time is far from clear. We will examine each separately.

---

55. What follows is an implicit rejection of the main thesis of McKay's *Sabbath and Synagogue*, wherein she argues that Sabbath worship only made its appearance in a synagogue setting from the third century C.E. onward. Her argument relies on a series of methodological and conceptual errors: making an arbitrary and artificial distinction between the terms *proseuche* and *synagoge* and thus not relating to the plain meaning of the former (i.e., a place of prayer); explaining away contradictory evidence as not reflecting contemporary Jewish norms (e.g., Qumran); positing a difference between weekday and Sabbath rituals (thus dismissing the Tiberias evidence); ignoring the sacred status attributed to a number of pre-70 buildings (which would obviously be connected with their religious dimension), and more. Most crucial of all is her narrow definition of what exactly constituted worship in the ancient synagogue. I would claim— evidence for prayer aside—that the reading of sacred texts and the accompanying instruction were recognized and valid forms of worship in the Jewish community. To define worship simply as the recitation of prayers and psalms is quite arbitrary. For more extensive critiques of her thesis, see Reif, "*Sabbath and Synagogue*" (review), 610–12; and esp. van der Horst, "Was the Synagogue a Place of Sabbath Worship?"

Torah-Reading

By the first century C.E., the Torah had become the holiest object in Judaism besides the Temple itself. As early as the second century B.C.E., the *Letter of Aristeas* had spelled out the sanctity of the Torah, in this case in its Greek translation. When the seventy-two emissaries from Judaea had completed their translations and presented Ptolemy Philadelphus with a copy of the Torah, the king reputedly stood for a moment in silence and then bowed seven times, saying: "I thank you, good sirs, and him [i.e., the Jerusalem high priest] that sent you even more, but most of all I thank God, whose holy words these are."[56]

At about the same time, I Maccabees notes that on several occasions prior to battle, the Maccabees had the Torah read aloud in order to invoke divine aid and gain scriptural support, and in a letter from Jonathan to Sparta reference is made to "the Holy Books in our possession."[57] Josephus relates two incidents in the mid-first century which highlight this very special status. Around the year 50, while searching a Judaean village, a Roman soldier found a Torah scroll which, according to the account in *War*, he tore and threw into a fire. Enraged by this blasphemy, the Jews demanded (and received) retribution.[58]

The second instance is a fascinating aside which Josephus relates while reporting on the events in Caesarea ca. 66 C.E. He notes that when fleeing the city, the Jews made sure that they took their Torah scroll with them. However, this angered the governor, Florus, and the Jews were arrested and put into chains because they had dared to remove it from the city.[59] This account clearly reflects the sanctity in which the Torah scroll was held by both Jews and non-Jews. But why were the Romans outraged by the removal of a Torah scroll (or scrolls) from the city? It would appear that the Torah was regarded as the holiest object which the local Jewish community possessed, and for the Romans it was the Jewish equivalent of a statue of a pagan deity. Its presence served as added insurance for the protection of the city, and its absence increased its vulnerability.

The association of the sanctity of the Torah scroll with that of the statue of a pagan deity is further indicated in two—albeit later—Diaspora sources, one literary and one

---

56. *Letter of Aristeas* 176–77. The letter goes on to describe the elaborate reception accorded the completed Greek translation of the Torah by the Alexandrian Jewish community and Ptolemy himself (ibid., 308–21).

57. I Macc. 3:48; II Macc. 8:23; I Macc. 12:9.

58. *War* 2, 229–31: "At that the Jews were roused as though it were their whole country which had been consumed in the flames; and, their religion acting like some instrument to draw them together, all on the first announcement of the news hurried in a body to Cumanus at Caesarea, and implored him not to leave unpunished the author of such an outrage on God and on the law." See also the parallel account in *Antiquities* 20, 115–17. On this incident and its larger context during Cumanus' governorship, see Schürer, *History*, I, 458–60; Smallwood, *Jews under Roman Rule*, 263–69; Aberbach, "Conflicting Accounts," 1ff.; M. Stern, *Greek and Latin Authors*, II, 78–80.

59. *War* 2, 292. See also L. Levine, *Roman Caesarea*, 22–33.

architectural. The first is a papyrus from second-century Egypt describing an event at the time of Trajan; we learn of two disputing delegations, one representing the Jewish community, the other the pagan, which were dispatched from Alexandria to Rome, each to present its case before the emperor. The pagans, we are told, brought with them a statue of their god, the Jews some other object. Here, unfortunately, the papyrus is damaged and the object which the Jewish delegation brought is unknown. Tcherikover has surmised, with a good deal of plausibility, that the Jews brought a Torah scroll as their source of divine protection and support, with it playing much the same role as that played by the statue accompanying the pagan delegation.[60]

The second example comes from third-century Dura Europos, whose synagogue, well known for its stunning wall paintings, was heavily influenced in its architecture and art by other Duran and eastern religious buildings.[61] One clear link is the centrality and prominence of the shrine (i.e., *aedicula*) in the *naos* of the temples and in the synagogue. The *aediculae* of the temples each contained a statue of a deity; the *aedicula* of the synagogue, a Torah scroll.[62]

Finally, as in Caesarea, the Torah's sanctity was clearly acknowledged by non-Jews. Josephus notes four main components in the triumphal procession in Rome following the victory over the Jews and Jerusalem in 70 C.E. The Temple vessels, which included the menorah and the golden table, were followed by a Torah scroll, images of victory (made of ivory and gold), and, finally, Vespasian, Titus, and Domitian.[63]

Thus, the centrality of the Torah-reading ceremony in Jewish worship of the pre-70 synagogue should come as no surprise.[64] In fact, each of the following sources from the Second Temple period indicates this explicitly.

---

60. Tcherikover et al., *CPJ*, II, 82–87 and also 85–86 and n. 17.

61. Rostovzeff, *Dura and Its Art*, 68–99; Kraeling, *Dura: Synagogue*, 348–49; Goodenough, *Jewish Symbols*, IX, 29–37; Perkins, *Art of Dura*, 10ff., 33–69, 114–26. On Torah scrolls in the first centuries C.E., see Haran, "Torah Scrolls," 93–106.

62. Rostovtzeff, *Dura and Its Art*, s.v., "aedicula"; Kraeling, *Dura: Synagogue*, 16; Goodenough, *Jewish Symbols*, IX, 65–67.

63. *War* 7, 148–52.

64. On the public dimension of the Torah—that it belonged to the Jewish people as a whole—see A. Baumgarten, "Torah as a Public Document," 17–24. An interesting account of the utilization of a Torah scroll in order to lend dramatic effect to a speech is offered by Josephus when describing one of his archrivals who harangued the Tiberian populace: "The principal instigator of the mob was Jesus, son of Sapphias, at that time chief magistrate of Tiberias, a knave with an instinct for introducing disorder into grave matters, and unrivalled in fomenting sedition and revolution. With a copy of the laws of Moses in his hands, he now stepped forward and said: 'If you cannot, for your own sakes, citizens, detest Josephus, fix your eyes on your country's laws, which your commander-in-chief intended to betray, and for their sakes hate the crime and punish the audacious criminal'" (*Life* 134–35).

Josephus:

He [Moses] appointed the Law to be the most excellent and necessary form of instruction, ordaining, not that it should be heard once for all or twice or on several occasions, but that every week men should desert their other occupations and assemble to listen to the Law and to obtain a thorough and accurate knowledge of it, a practice which all other legislators seem to have neglected.[65]

Philo:

He [Augustus] knew therefore that they have houses of prayer [*proseuche*] and meet together in them, particularly on the sacred Sabbaths when they receive as a body training in their ancestral philosophy.[66]

He required them to assemble in the same place on these seventh days and, sitting together in a respectful and orderly manner, hear the laws read so that none should be ignorant of them.[67]

Philo also describes Essene practice on the Sabbath:

They use these laws [of the Torah] to learn from at all times, but especially each seventh day, since the seventh day is regarded as sacred. On that day they abstain from other work and betake themselves to the sacred places which are called synagogues. They are seated according to age in fixed places, the young below the old, holding themselves ready to listen with the proper good manners. Then one of them takes the books and reads. Another, from among those with most experience, comes forward and explains anything that is not easy to understand.[68]

New Testament:

And he came to Nazareth, where he had been brought up; and he went to the synagogue, as his custom was, on the Sabbath day. And he stood up to read; and there was given to him the book of the prophet Isaiah. He opened the book and found the place where it was written . . .[69]

But when they departed from Perga, they came to Antioch in Pisidia, and went into the synagogue on the Sabbath day, and sat down. And after the reading of the law and the prophets the rulers of the synagogue sent unto them.[70]

For Moses of old time has in every city those that preach him, being read in the synagogues every Sabbath day.[71]

---

65. *Against Apion* 2, 175. See also *Antiquities* 16, 43, a passage purportedly taken from a speech delivered by Nicolaus of Damascus before Agrippa on behalf of the Jews.

66. *Embassy* 156. See also Philo's comment in his *Dreams* 2, 127.

67. *Hypothetica* 7, 12.

68. *Every Good Man Is Free* 81–82. Suetonius (*Tiberius* 32:2) notes one Diogenes who lectured every Sabbath in Rhodes.

69. Luke 4:16–22.

70. Acts 13:14–15.

71. Ibid., 15:21.

Rabbinic literature:

And a wooden *bima* was to be found in the center [of the hall, referring to an Alexandrian synagogue], and the *ḥazzan* of the synagogue would stand in the corner [of the *bima*] with kerchiefs in his hand. When one came and took hold of the scroll to read [a section from the Torah], he [the *ḥazzan*] would wave the kerchiefs and all the people would answer "Amen" for each blessing. He would [again] wave the kerchiefs and all the people would respond "Amen."[72]

Archeology:

Theodotos, son of Vettenos, a priest and *archisynagogos*, son of an *archisynagogos* and grandson of an *archisynagogos*, built the synagogue for reading the Law and studying the commandments.[73]

Thus, there can be little question that scriptural readings constituted the core of contemporary Jewish worship in the synagogue. A remarkable—though very late—rabbinic tradition articulates the highest possible religious value of such activity. On the verse "and Moses gathered all the congregation of Israel" (Ex. 35:1), the midrash continues: "The Holy one, Blessed be He, said to Israel: 'If you congregate each Sabbath in your synagogues and read Torah, I will accredit you as if you bore witness on me that I am your King.'"[74] As already noted, there is no firm evidence for the early development of this custom.[75] Whether we are dealing with a strictly internal phenomenon or one stimulated from without—or both—must remain moot for the present.

The form and frequency of the Torah-reading ceremony, once introduced, are likewise uncertain. Did Torah-reading constitute a regular Sabbath practice from the outset, as rabbinic literature would have it and as a number of modern scholars hold?[76] Or did the custom begin as Sabbath readings in preparation for the festivals, especially Passover, a theory which seems to be indicated in a number of rabbinic sources and which has found modern adherents as well?[77] Or, perhaps, at the very outset there were sections of

---

72. T Sukkah 4:6 (p. 273); and Lieberman, *TK*, 891–92.

73. Frey, *CIJ*, II, no. 1404; and above, Chap. 3.

74. Midrash Hagadol, Exodus 35:1 (p. 722).

75. See above, Chap. 2.

76. Rabbinic literature ascribes the weekly Sabbath readings to Moses and the weekday readings (Mondays and Thursdays) to Ezra or the prophets and elders (Y Megillah 4, 1, 75a; B Bava Qama 82a). See also S. Safrai, "Synagogue," 912–13.

77. M Megillah 3:6; Sifra, Emor, 17 (ed. Weiss, p. 103a); Sifre-Deuteronomy 127 (p. 185). See also B Megillah 32a. According to this theory, the earliest readings were taken from Pentateuchal sections relating to a specific Sabbath or festival and deal with the laws and rituals associated with each. This seems to be reflected in the earliest stage of festival readings, as preserved in the Mishnah, where, inter alia, the four special Sabbaths before Passover are noted (M Megillah 3:4–5). Similarly, on the Day of Atonement, the high priest would not only perform the prescribed ritual, but also read the scriptural section detailing these ceremonies (M Yoma 1:3). Thus, Thackeray has suggested (*Septuagint and Jewish Worship*,

the Torah deemed especially meaningful that were chosen to be read, irrespective of the calendar?[78]

Whatever the early stages of the Torah-reading ceremony, the question arises as to when it became fully institutionalized as the central component in the non-sacrificial liturgy. The chronological parameters are probably to be fixed between the fifth and third centuries B.C.E. On the one hand, the terminus post quem is undoubtedly the period of Ezra and Nehemiah, when the first public Torah-reading ceremony appears to have been held. By the third century, on the other hand, the existence of a regular communal Torah-reading framework was probably a prime factor in the creation of the Septuagint. Whatever its primary motivation, such a translation would have served, inter alia, the liturgical needs of the Alexandrian Jewish community.[79] This liturgical practice was probably brought to Egypt from Judaea and was not the creation of the fledgling Diaspora community; there is no evidence of such a custom in the earlier Elephantine community, which flourished in Upper Egypt in the fifth century B.C.E. The brief account of the high priest Ezekias reading to his friends from the Torah (lit., scroll) upon his arrival in Egypt may well point to such a practice.[80]

By the first century, a weekly ceremony featuring the communal reading and study of holy texts had become a universal Jewish practice. It was a unique liturgical feature in the ancient world; no such form of worship was known in paganism. True enough, certain mystery cults in the Hellenistic-Roman world produced sacred texts that were read on occasion.[81] However, it was indeed sui generis for an entire community to devote regular meetings to such an activity. This, it appears, is the context within which to understand the above-quoted sources (especially Josephus and Philo). While their tone may have been self-laudatory, there is cause. They were indeed trumpeting a form of worship which set the Jewish community apart from the surrounding cultures.[82]

43ff.) that holiday readings per Lev. 23, as well as those relating to the four special Sabbaths, eventually led to regular weekly readings and, ultimately, the triennial cycle. Assuming a gradual introduction of these readings, one might guardedly suggest that, of the special pre-Passover Sabbath readings, Shabbat Sheqalim (dealing with the half-sheqel tax) and Shabbat Parah (dealing with purity matters) were introduced in the Hasmonean period, when priestly and Temple concerns came much more to the fore in Jewish society. See also Elbogen, *Jewish Liturgy*, 130-31.

78. For example, Deut. 32, as suggested in McNamara, *New Testament and Palestinian Targum*, 112ff. See also Elbogen, *Jewish Liturgy*, 132.

79. Schürer, *History*, III, 474-76; Kahle, *Cairo Geniza*, 132-33. Cf., however, Bickerman (*Jews in the Greek Age*, 102-5), who views the Ptolemaic court's initiative as the main impetus for the translation.

80. *Against Apion*, I, 183-89.

81. See, for example, Nock, *Conversion*, 26-32; Momigliano, *On Pagans, Jews and Christians*, 89-91 n. 10; Patte, *Early Jewish Hermeneutic*, 36; Thackeray, *Septuagint and Jewish Worship*, 43ff.; Elbogen, *Jewish Liturgy*, 119.

82. See Momigliano, *On Pagans, Jews and Christians*, 89-91. This unique practice was already adumbrated in Deut. 31:9-13; see Tigay, *Deuteronomy*, 499-502.

It is generally acknowledged that the regnant custom, in Palestine at least, was to complete the Torah-reading cycle within a three- to three-and-a-half-year period. This custom is explicitly documented for Roman-Byzantine Palestine but is generally presumed to have been operative in the pre-70 period as well.[83] These later sources regularly contrast the Palestinian practice with that of Babylonia, where the Torah-reading was completed in one year and was marked by the holiday of Simḥat Torah. Fleischer, on the other hand, suggests that the one-year cycle also originated in Palestine and, in fact, that it predated the triennial practice.[84] Even though his suggestion rests on a series of rather dubious

83. On the triennial Torah-reading cycle in pre-70 Palestine, see, for example, the classic studies of Büchler, "Reading of the Law and Prophets," 420–68; Heinemann, "Triennial Cycle," 41–48; Perrot, *Lecture de la Bible*, 147ff.; idem, "Reading of the Bible," 137–59. According to Guilding (*Fourth Gospel and Jewish Worship*, 24–57, 229–33), not only is the triennial cycle an early phenomenon, but the literary form of the gospel of John, and even the Pentateuch itself, was based on such a cycle. For a critique of this thesis, especially as it relates to the Pentateuch, see Porter, "Pentateuch and Triennial Lectionary Cycle," 163–74. For a later dating of the triennial cycle, see Wacholder, "Prolegomenon," xvii–xliii.

According to Modrzejewski (*Jews of Egypt*, 95–96), the first-century Cairo scroll of Deuteronomy (Papyrus Fouad 266) may indicate a triennial reading cycle.

On the triennial Torah-reading cycle in Roman-Byzantine Palestine, see B Megillah 29b; *Differences in Customs*, no. 48 (ed. Margalioth, pp. 172–73; ed. Lewin, pp. 98–99). Indirect rabbinic evidence for this practice may be found in M Megillah 3:4; Leviticus Rabbah 3:6 (p. 69); Tractate Soferim 16:8 (pp. 291–92); see also Y Shabbat 16, 5, 15c; Esther Rabbah, Proem 3; comments by A. Epstein, *Meqadmoniot Hayehudim*, 54ff.; and below, Chap. 16.

Similar traces of the triennial cycle have been detected in the presumed divisions of various midrashic works and *targumim*; see, for example, Albeck, "Midrash Wayyiqra Rabba," 25–43; Theodor and Albeck, *Genesis Rabbah*, 97ff. (introduction); J. Mann, *Bible as Read*, 11 (introduction); Elbogen, *Jewish Liturgy*, 132; Fried, "List of Sedarim," 103–13; Shinan, "Numerical Proem," 89ff.

Ancient *piyyutim* likewise reflect a triennial division; see Heinemann, "Triennial Lectionary Cycle," 41–48; Zulay, "Studies on Yannai," 213ff. Later reports of this practice, from twelfth-century Egypt, are to be found in Benjamin of Tudela (pp. 62–63), Genizah fragments (Fleischer, *Prayer and Prayer Rituals*, 220), and Maimonides, *Laws of Prayer* 13:1.

84. Fleischer, "Annual and Triennial Torah Reading," 25–43. Fleischer's theory rests primarily on a statement in B Megillah 31b by the Palestinian sage R. Simeon b. Elʿazar (late second century): "Ezra established for Israel [i.e., the Jews] that they should read the sections from Leviticus containing curses before (the holiday of) ʾAtzeret (i.e., Shavuʿot or the Pentecost) and those from Deuteronomy before Rosh Hashanah." Fleischer assumes that this reflects an annual cycle. This may be; however, it is not the only, or even the most probable, way to understand this statement. It could very well be that R. Simeon was establishing two special readings for these two Sabbaths which had nothing whatsoever to do with a regular cycle, much as was the case with the special readings in the weeks preceding Passover. On the other hand, if this statement reflects an annual cycle and the normative practice at the time was such, as Fleischer suggests, then why make the statement at all? His assumption, that this statement is a defense of the annual cycle in face of a triennial "takeover" at the time, is wholly gratuitous. See the reservations of Bar Ilan, "Blessings and Curses," 29–35 (and Fleischer's rejoinder, "Annual and Triennial Torah Reading," 39 n. 38; and, further, Bar Ilan, "Regarding a Baraita," 126–34). See also the much later (seventh-

assumptions, an original Palestinian provenance for the annual cycle is nevertheless conceivable.[85]

Our information available regarding Torah-reading in specific settings is spotty. Presumably, the Torah was read twice a year in the towns and villages whose local priestly courses were officiating in the Jerusalem Temple. To the best of our knowledge, regular readings did not take place in the Temple, even at the end of the Second Temple period, or at Qumran as part of the communal liturgy. Philo describes Essene Sabbath gatherings in synagogues replete with Torah-reading and instruction;[86] it appears that he is referring here to Essene communities throughout Judaea and not specifically to the Qumran community.[87] In these dispersed communities, the Sabbath celebration included scriptural readings, as in other local synagogues. Presumably, these village- or town-dwelling Essenes did not have the same time available on a daily basis for continuous study as did their peers at Qumran, and thus the Sabbath offered an opportunity for more concentrated study. If this assumption is granted, then what we have here is evidence for significant liturgical variation, even within this sect, one that was linked to geographical and social considerations.

Similar to the Essene practice throughout Judaea is that of the Therapeutae in Egypt. As Jews likewise devoted themselves to a life of piety, purity, and learning, they spent their Sabbaths studying scriptural readings.[88] The same also may have been true of the Samaritans, but reliable contemporary sources are unavailable in this regard. Not until the third and fourth centuries C.E., with the communal and religious revival under Baba Rabba, do we have substantive material on which to base historical assessments. At that time, some Samaritans spent the entire day in the synagogue, where the reading and study of Scriptures had become a fixed routine. If we assume, as appears likely, that Baba Rabba basically revived old customs rather than instituting totally new ones, then we may conjecture that such scriptural readings existed beforehand, perhaps as early as the first

---

to eighth-centuries) Tractate Soferim, 17:1, 2, and 6 (pp. 297, 298, and 305, respectively), where an annual cycle might also be indicated.

85. Admittedly, assuming the existence of two parallel and contemporaneous systems for Torah-reading (whether pre- or post-70) would raise a number of intriguing questions: Why two customs? Did they always exist simultaneously? If not, which came first, and why did the other develop? Fleischer, for example, has suggested that the difference between the two practices is that the system of shorter readings (i.e., the triennial cycle) was adopted in places that had a more expansive Torah-related liturgy, i.e., sermons and *targumim*. The longer, annual, reading held sway where there were fewer concomitant activities. This is an interesting but highly speculative theory even for the later period (Fleischer, "Annual and Triennial Torah Reading," 27).

86. *Every Good Man Is Free* 81–83.

87. Ibid., 75–76; *Hypothetica* 11, 1; Josephus, *War* 2, 124.

88. Philo, *Contemplative Life* 30–31; idem, *Every Good Man Is Free* 81–84. See also Vermes, "Essenes and Therapeutai," 495–504; Vermes and Goodman, *Essenes According to Classical Sources*, 15–17.

centuries C.E.[89] This, however, is quite speculative. Regarding Samaritan practices, anything earlier than the third or fourth centuries C.E. becomes a matter of guesswork.[90]

Reading from the Prophets (Haftarah)

By the first century C.E. at the very latest, readings from the Torah were accompanied by readings from the Prophets. The New Testament evidence here is crucial; Jesus was asked to read from the book of Isaiah when he visited a Nazareth synagogue, and Paul delivered a sermon in the synagogue in Antioch in Pisidia following readings from the Torah and the Prophets.[91] The third-century Tosefta has preserved a list of haftarah readings for (and prior to) holidays and a list of passages not to be read at all in public, as well as a series of norms governing such readings.[92] How much of this Tosefta material is relevant to the pre-70 era is difficult to assess. Probably some of it is; much of the material in the chapter appears to reflect practices of the first two centuries C.E.

Regarding the actual procedure for reading from the Prophets, it appears that only Luke might shed some light on the custom: "And there was given to him the book of the prophet Isaiah. And when he had opened the book, he found the place where it was written. . . . And he closed the book, and he gave it again to the attendant, and sat down. And the eyes of all those in the synagogue were fastened on him. And he began to say unto them, 'This day is this Scripture fulfilled in your ears.' "[93] According to Luke, following the Torah-reading Jesus was handed a scroll containing the book of Isaiah. Later rabbinic literature assumes that the Prophetic readings were fixed and usually related in some fashion to the Torah-reading.[94] Was this true even at this early stage? The impression from the above passage is that Jesus chose at least the particular passage to be read. Might he have chosen the book as well?[95] Furthermore, the Prophetic reading seems to

---

89. *Samaritan Chronicle* 16, 1–2 (p. 85); Crown, "Byzantine and Moslem Period," 57–59; Boid, "Use, Authority and Exegesis," 604–5; Pummer, "Samaritan Rituals and Customs," 677–78.

90. Similarly, the problem of determining first-century Christian liturgy is likewise formidable; see Meeks, *Early Urban Christianity*, 144–50.

91. Luke 4:17–19 and Acts 13:14–15, respectively. On the regularity of the prophetic readings in the context of the first-century Sabbath liturgy, see Acts 13:27: "For those who live in Jerusalem and their rulers, because they did not recognize him nor understand the utterances of the prophets which are read every Sabbath, fulfilled these [words] by condemning him."

92. T Megillah 3:1–9 (pp. 353–55).

93. Luke 4:17–21.

94. B Megillah 29b: "one that resembles it [i.e., the Torah-reading]." For a suggestion regarding the relevance of Philonic writings for determining the haftarah cycle, see N. Cohen, "Earliest Evidence," 225–49.

95. Scholarly opinion is divided over the reader's degree of freedom in this regard. Some opine that the selections were predetermined, others that the reader had autonomy in this matter, and still others that the book read from was chosen earlier but the choice of the exact passages was left to the reader. For a summary of such opinions, see Crockett, "Luke IV: 16–30 and the Jewish Lectionary Cycle," 26–27.

have consisted of only a few verses, and those quoted in Luke might indeed be indicative of the usual portion that was read.[96] Nevertheless, it is clear from Luke that, in this case at least, it was the Prophetic reading—and not that from the Torah—which determined the nature of the sermon subsequently delivered.[97]

It is impossible to say when these readings from the Prophets were introduced into synagogue worship. Since they followed and presumably related to the Torah portion,[98] they would seem to postdate the introduction of the Torah-reading liturgy, which was in the third century B.C.E. at the latest. Abudraham (fourteenth century) dates the institution of the reading from the Prophets to the time of Antiochus IV's persecutions.[99] While this medieval source has little historical value for our purposes, the period designated may, in fact, not be far off the mark. Both Ben Sira and II Maccabees already speak of books of the Prophets as sacred literature alongside the Torah.[100] The Hasmonean era—with its many upheavals and dramatic political, military, social, and religious developments—gave rise to messianic expectations and hopes of renewed grandeur in certain circles; apocalyptic speculation emerged, and eschatological groups such as the Dead Sea sect combed the Prophets for contemporary allusions.[101] The use of the prophetic corpus—or variations of it, as the apocalyptic mode appears to be—seems to have flourished at the time, and it may well have been this climate that gave rise to such institutionalized recitations.

---

96. Luke 4:18-19. The Tosefta (Megillah 3:18 [p. 358]) speaks of three, four, or five verses for the haftarah. Amoraic sources expand this (in theory at least) to twenty-one verses; see Y Megillah 4, 2, 75a; B Megillah 23a. See also Tractate Soferim 13:15 (pp. 250-51). And see Büchler, "Reading of the Law and Prophets," 7, 13. According to M Megillah 4:2-4, the reading from the Prophets was to consist of at least three verses, the Torah-reading itself of at least ten (on weekdays) or twenty-one (on Sabbaths).

97. It was this very idea that formed the basis of J. Mann's monumental *Bible as Read*. Despite much criticism, this approach has been refined and nuanced in Bregman, "Triennial Haftarot," 74-84. Elbogen (*Jewish Liturgy*, 143) suggests that the term "haftarah" refers to the end of the scriptural-reading segment of the liturgy, parallel to the term אשלמתא (= "completion"). It has also been suggested that the term means "dismissed"; this prophetic reading, along with its related homily, may have concluded the communal worship service. On the haftarah generally, see Perrot, *Lecture de la Bible*, 175-93; J. Mann, *Bible as Read*, I, 555-60; Rappaport, *Erech Millin*, I, 328-50; Schürer, *History*, II, 452, following Bacher, *Exegetische Terminologie*, II, 14.

98. B Megillah 29b: "[one] that resembles it."

99. Siddur Abudraham (p. 172). On persecution as a factor in medieval (and modern) explanations of liturgical changes, see J. Mann, "Changes in the Divine Service," 241-302.

100. Ben Sira, Prologue; II Macc. 2:13; 15:9.

101. Schürer, *History*, II, 488ff.; M. Stone, "Apocalyptic Literature," 383-441. See also J. J. Collins, "Apocalyptic Literature," 345-70; idem, "Jewish Apocalypses," 21-59. On the Dead Sea sect, see Dimant, "Qumran Sectarian Literature," 514-22.

Study and Instruction

It is eminently clear from all sources that Torah-reading in the early synagogue was more than ceremonial in character—i.e., more than the mere recitation of a holy text. No matter what the provenance—Judaea or the Diaspora—the Torah-reading (and the reading from the Prophets) served as a springboard for further instruction and edification.

Philo—as might be expected, given his philosophical bent—aggrandizes these Sabbath sessions, claiming that a great deal of time was spent in expounding the portion read, so much so that the synagogue was aptly described as a school (διδασκαλεῖον) for the learning of virtues: "Even now this practice is retained, and the Jews every seventh day occupy themselves with the philosophy of their fathers, dedicating that time to the acquiring of knowledge and the study of the truths of nature. For what are our places of prayer throughout the cities but schools of prudence and courage and temperance and justice, and also of piety, holiness, and every virtue by which duties to God and men are discerned and rightfully performed." [102] Or, as he states elsewhere:

> So each seventh day there stand wide open in every city thousands of schools of good sense, temperance, courage, justice and the other virtues in which the scholars sit in order quietly with ears alert and with full attention, so much do they thirst for the draught which the teacher's words supply, while one of special experience rises and sets forth what is the best and sure to be profitable and will make the whole of life grow to something better. But among the vast number of particular truths and principles there studied, there stand out practically high above the others two main heads: one of duty to God as shown by piety and holiness, one of duty to men as shown by humanity and justice, each of them splitting up into multiform branches, all highly laudable. These things show clearly that Moses does not allow any of those who use his sacred instruction to remain inactive at any season. [103]

Josephus also attests to a similar devotion to study when quoting a speech of Nicolaus of Damascus delivered to Marcus Agrippa on behalf of Ionian Jewry. In an attempt to explain certain Jewish customs viewed unfavorably by their neighbors, Nicolaus proclaims: "There is nothing hostile to mankind in our customs, but they are all pious and consecrated with saving righteousness. Nor do we make a secret of the precepts that we use as guides in religion and in human relations; we give every seventh day over to the study of our customs and law, for we think it necessary to occupy ourselves, as with any other study, so with these through which we can avoid committing sins." [104]

The statements of Philo and Josephus should not, of course, be taken as evidence of what happened in all synagogues in their day, not in Alexandria and certainly not throughout the rest of the Diaspora and Judaea. The nature and extent of biblical exposition on

---

102. *Moses* 2, 216.

103. *Special Laws* 2, 62–63.

104. *Antiquities* 16, 43.

any given Sabbath undoubtedly varied from place to place. The educational bent of Galilean villagers or of Jews from the Egyptian *chora* was undoubtedly much less than that of the Essenes, Therapeutae, or Alexandrian intellectuals, whose entire Sabbath might have been spent in either self-study or communal study.[105] Nevertheless, what is clear is that in some places, and probably not only in certain Alexandrian circles, Sabbath morning worship developed into a serious learning session. For the ordinary Jew who attended Sabbath worship, however, this kind of rigor seems most improbable. The element of study in the typical synagogue was undoubtedly much more curtailed in scope.

Sermons

The New Testament evidence makes it crystal clear that the sermon (i.e., the exposition of an idea that appears in the scriptural reading) was a recognized component of the Sabbath service. Jesus preached in Nazareth, as did Paul in Antioch in Pisidia.[106]

Philo has left us several descriptions of communal Sabbath observances among at least some Alexandrian Jews, and on each occasion he focuses on the sermon or exposition of the Torah:

> For it was customary on every day when opportunity offered, and pre-eminently on the seventh day, as I have explained above, to pursue the study of wisdom with the ruler expounding and instructing the people what they should say and do, while they received edification and betterment in moral principles and conduct.[107]

> And indeed they do always assemble and sit together, most of them in silence except when it is the practice to add something to signify approval of what is read. But some priest who is present or one of the elders reads the holy laws to them and expounds them point by point till about the late afternoon, when they depart, having gained both expert knowledge of the holy laws and considerable advance in piety.[108]

Clearly, the instruction accompanying the reading of Scriptures was predominant, lasting, according to Philo, almost the entire day. In contrast to the episodes recorded in the New Testament, where the preacher is described as having spoken spontaneously, here Philo talks about a "priest" (ἱερός), "elder" (γερός), or "leader" (ἡγεμών) who fulfilled this function. The goals of such expositions—the acquisition of moral principles, a knowledge of the laws, and piety—are singled out.[109]

---

105. On the "philosophizing" aspect of ancient Judaism, see Mason, "Greco-Roman, Jewish, and Christian Philosophies," 12–18; on the study dimension as crucial to the Qumran sect's self-identity, see Fraade, "Interpretive Authority," 51–69; on the intellectual climate of Alexandria at this time, see Wolfson, *Philo*, I, 55–86; Mendelson, *Secular Education in Philo*, 81–84.

106. Luke 4:20–21 and Acts 13:15, respectively.

107. *Moses* 2, 215.

108. *Hypothetica* 7, 13.

109. For comparative material from the surrounding Greco-Roman world, see Malherbe, *Moral Ex-*

The focus of Sabbath worship for the Therapeutae of Egypt was likewise a sermon delivered by their leader and teacher. Philo offers a brief description of the setting,[110] although he avoids touching upon the contents of these homilies. Nevertheless, given the fact that members of this community spent the entire week studying Scriptures individually, there can be little doubt that the Sabbath sermon dealt with matters pertaining to their studies. Philo has the following to say: "Then the senior among them who also has the fullest knowledge of the doctrines which they profess comes forward and with visage and voice alike quiet and composed gives a well-reasoned and wise discourse. He does not make an exhibition of clever rhetoric like the orators or sophists of today but follows careful examination by careful expression of the exact meaning of the thoughts, and this does not lodge just outside the ears of the audience but passes through the hearing into the soul and there stays securely. All the others sit still and listen, showing their approval merely by their looks or nods."[111]

That the sermon or exposition of scriptural readings became central to Jewish worship —in Egypt and elsewhere—in the first century may be reflected in an interesting remark made by Josephus when recounting the story of the translation of the Torah into Greek. The *Letter of Aristeas* (305–8) reports that its focus was a festive reading of Scriptures; Josephus remarks that the text was also interpreted for the benefit of those assembled.[112]

We have no way of knowing for certain the forms and styles of rhetoric used by preachers in the first century. On the basis of later analogies, and assuming that some speeches in first-century sources may derive from—or were at least influenced by—a synagogue setting, various suggestions have been proposed. Some have assumed that IV Maccabees is, in fact, a series of synagogue sermons, that Philo's questions and answers originated in a synagogue setting, or that the speeches in Acts are testimony to Hellenistic Jewish sermon patterns and presage later homiletical patterns.[113] All such hypotheses, however intriguing, remain inconclusive.

In conclusion, let me say a word about several other aspects of the sermon. From the

---

hortation. Note should be taken of Kasher's suggestion ("Synagogues as 'Houses of Prayer' and 'Holy Places,'" 211) that much of Philo's description and a good part of Egyptian synagogue practice derived from the memories and traditions surrounding the ceremony that concluded the translation of the Torah into Greek, an event of major historical and religious importance to that Jewish community.

110. *Contemplative Life* 28.

111. Ibid., 31. Interestingly, this scenario took place in the sect's sanctuary (σεμεῖον), in which there was a strict separation of men and women (ibid., 32–33). The term μοναστήριον is likewise used for individual cells used by members of the sect during the week (ibid., 25). See Daniel-Nataf, *Philo—Writings*, 188 n. 25.

112. *Letter of Aristeas* 305–8; *Antiquities* 12, 107–8.

113. *IV Maccabees*: Freudenthal, *Flavius Josephus (IV Makkabäerbuch)*; see also Siegert, *Drei hellenistisch-jüdische Predigten*, II. *Philo*: Runia, "Structure of Philo's Allegorical Treatises," 230; idem, "Further Observations," 107, 112; and Wolfson, *Philo*, I, 95–96. *Acts*: Wills, "Form of the Sermon," 277–99; Black II, "Rhetorical Form of the Sermon," 1–18; Bowker, "Speeches in Acts," 96–111.

accounts concerning Jesus and Paul, it is clear that a sermon probably followed the Prophetic reading and related to it. This would seem to have very often been the case with oppositional, messianically oriented groups, such as early Christians and members of the Qumran sect. The books of the Prophets lend themselves to revolutionary messages, be they of a political, social, or religious nature. More mainstream synagogues undoubtedly focused (though by no means exclusively) on the Torah-reading itself, as per Philo and Josephus, but we have no information in this regard.[114]

Later synagogue sermons often preceded the scriptural readings, but this type of sermon remains unattested for the first century. However, it is safe to assume that whenever a sermon preceded the readings, it invariably related to, and prepared the way for, the Torah-reading itself.

Even within the limited material at our disposal, we find contrasting practices with regard to the location of the preacher in the synagogue when delivering his sermon. Luke describes Jesus as sitting when he preached; Paul stood.[115] Might this reflect a change in the position of the preacher between the early and mid first century? Or perhaps this marked a difference in practices of delivery between Judaea and the Diaspora? While certitude in this matter is elusive, neither of these options is compelling. In fact, we may simply have two alternative coexisting practices with no geographical or chronological implications. This last assumption is bolstered by the fact that in subsequent centuries we find both positions in use in synagogue settings.[116]

Targumim

Another activity which appears to have accompanied the Torah-reading was the recitation of a *targum*. It is generally assumed that the custom of translating Scriptures into the vernacular at the synagogue service already existed in the Second Temple period.[117] Given the increasing dominance of Aramaic throughout the Near East from the Persian period onward, and the concomitant fact that this language was used in books, official documents, personal names, and the speech of Jews in the late Second Temple

---

114. Hengel ("Scriptures and Their Interpretation," 159) has estimated that 96% of Philo's quotations come from the Torah, an emphasis characteristic of other Jewish-Hellenistic writings as well. If there is a correlation between Philo's writings and his synagogue sermons, then the centrality of the Torah for sermonic material is clearly established, in his case at least.

115. Luke 4:20 and Acts 14:14-16, respectively.

116. See below, Chap. 16.

117. See the introductory remarks on the subject in McNamara, *Palestinian Judaism and the New Testament*, 17-89, 171-210; le Déaut, *Introduction à la littérature targumique;* Alexander, "Jewish Aramaic Translations," 242-50; Grossfeld, "Targum Onqelos," 241-46; S. A. Kaufman, "Dating the Language of the Palestinian Targums," 129-30; Wilcox, "Aramaic Background," 362-78. See however, Z. Safrai ("Origins of Reading the Aramaic Targum," 187-93) who, following rabbinic evidence closely, dates this practice to the second century C.E.

period, it is not at all surprising that a need arose to make the reading and study of Scriptures accessible to the people at large.[118] This phenomenon had been preceded by similar though accelerated developments within the Jewish communities of Greek-speaking countries during the Hellenistic and early Roman periods. It was in Egypt, in the wake of the large-scale settlement of Jews there, that the Torah was translated into Greek, and this was closely followed by the translation of other biblical books.[119] Thus, it appears that in many, if not most, places in the Roman Diaspora no *targum* was necessary, as the readings themselves may have been in the vernacular. This, however, is far from certain, and it may be that the Septuagint translation (or variations thereof) was used after the Hebrew reading, parallel to the Aramaic *targum* practice in Judaea.[120]

It is impossible to assess when the first Aramaic translations made their appearance, although both Moore and Bloch have suggested very early dates in the Second Temple period.[121] The difficulty is that all extant manuscripts of the *targumim* (Onqelos, Targum Jonathan of the Prophets, Targum Pseudo-Jonathan, Neofiti, Fragments, etc.) derive from anytime between the seventh and the sixteenth centuries.[122] Moreover, there is evidence of late interpolation, such as the oft-quoted reference to Muhammad's wife and daughter (Targum Pseudo-Jonathan of Gen. 21:21), the mention of Constantinople (ibid., of Num. 24:24), and reference to the six orders of the Mishnah (ibid., of Ex. 26:9). Given the presence of clearly late material, why should we assume the antiquity of the *targum* genre at all? The answer is fourfold.

(1) We have evidence of written *targumim* for the pre-70 period. Fragments of an Aramaic *targum* of Leviticus (4Q tgLev) and Job (11Q tgJob; 4Q tgJob) have been found at

---

118. Rabin, "Hebrew and Aramaic," 1007-39 and the extensive bibliography there; Fitzmyer, "Languages of Palestine," 501-31; Schürer, *History*, II, 20 n. 68 and bibliography cited there; McNamara, *Palestinian Judaism and the New Testament*, 54-68.

119. The Jews of Alexandria, at least, viewed their translation as divinely inspired, celebrating the anniversary of its completion with an imposing public ceremony (*Letter of Aristeas* 310; Philo, *Moses* 2, 41-42; *Antiquities* 12, 107-8).

120. See generally on this issue Perrot, "Lecture dans la diaspora hellénistique," 118-21. On Greek in Diaspora liturgy, see Fraser, *Ptolemaic Alexandria*, I, 284; Schürer, *History*, III, 140-42; Tcherikover, "Prolegomenon," 30-32; van der Horst, "Greek Evidence," 277-96.

On the suggestion that the various Greek versions of the Septuagint are, in fact, Greek *targumim*, see Kahle, *Cairo Geniza*, 213-14; Modrzejewski, *Jews of Egypt*, 100-101. Cf., however, the objections raised in Wevers, "Barthélemy and Proto-Septuagint Studies," 58-77. This may have been the case in certain locales in Judaea as well, even in the pre-70 era.

121. See G. F. Moore (*Judaism*, I, 302-3), who suggests that such translations may have been coterminus with the scriptural reading itself. R. Bloch ("Methodological Note," 60-61) opines that the *targum* genre "is much closer to the Midrash. . . . It is even probable that it originally was a homiletic midrash, or simply a series of homilies on Scripture, read in the synagogue after the public reading of the Torah."

122. Kahle, *Masoreten des Westens*, II, 3. For an overall introduction to targumic studies, see McNamara, *New Testament and Palestinian Targum*, 5-37. See also Black, "Aramaic Studies and the Language of Jesus," 17-28.

Qumran; and rabbinic literature as well makes reference to a *targum* of Job found in the time of Rabban Gamaliel II, at the turn of the second century.[123] This last source also cites an earlier tradition that a fragment of the *targum* of Job was found during repair (or reconstruction) work on the Temple Mount in the days of Rabban Gamaliel the Elder (flourished ca. 25–45 C.E.).[124]

(2) Over the last century, there have been many studies comparing targumic traditions with those found in Josephus, the writings of the Qumran sect, the Septuagint, apocryphal literature, the New Testament, and rabbinic literature.[125] The similarities are often striking and may lead to the conclusion that some *targum* traditions date to the same (i.e., the late Second Temple) period as well.

(3) Various studies—focusing especially on the *targumim*, on the one hand, and on Qumran Aramaic, on the other—have demonstrated linguistic affinities between these different types of literature.[126] To explain such ties, a common historical setting has been deemed logical and necessary.

(4) The *targum* as an integral part of the synagogue liturgy is well known from later antiquity. Detailed laws relating to this practice, as well as accounts of people who functioned in the capacity of delivering the *targum*, along with the translations and interpretations on such occasions, abound in the rabbinic sources.[127] Even second-century authorities were already well aware of this practice and discussed many regulations associated therewith.[128] These tannaitic sages were not initiating a new practice, but rather were commenting upon, critiquing, and shaping an already existing institution. Thus, it

---

123. T Shabbat 13:2 (p. 57) and parallels in Y Shabbat 16, 1, 15c; B Shabbat 115a; and Tractate Soferim 5:17 (p. 161). See also comments by Lieberman, *TK*, III, 203–4; and Sokoloff, *Targum to Job*.

124. Sokoloff, *Targum to Job*. Rabbinic claims to the antiquity of *targum* in the days of Ezra (e.g., B Megillah 3b; B Nedarim 37b; B Sanhedrin 21b) have not constituted a serious factor in this debate, and rightfully so.

125. *Josephus:* see references in McNamara, *New Testament and Palestinian Targum*, 269. In the classic work of Rappaport (*Agada und Exegese*, xx–xxii), the author discusses the many parallels between rabbinic tradition and Josephus, suggesting that an early written Aramaic *targum* stood behind both. *Qumran sect:* A number of scholars have pointed out the affinities between the *targum* genre and other Qumran writings, i.e., the *pesher* commentaries—especially Habbakuk—and the Genesis Apocryphon. See, for example, Vermes, "Commentaires bibliques à Qumran," 95–103; Brownlee, "Habakkuk Midrash and Targum of Jonathan," 169–86; Wieder, "Habakkuk Scroll and Targum," 14–18; Lehmann, "1Q Genesis Apocryphon," 251–52; Fitzmyer, *Genesis Apocryphon*, 26–34. *Septuagint:* already suggested in Frankel, *Vorstudien zur der Septuaginta*, 185–91; idem, *Über den Einfluss der Palästinischen Exegese*, 81, followed by Churgin, "Targum and Septuagint," 41–65. *Apocrypha:* Marmorstein, *Studien zum Pseudo-Jonathan Targum*, I. *New Testament:* McNamara, *New Testament and Palestinian Targum*, 70ff.; idem, *Palestinian Judaism and the New Testament*, 91–169; Wilcox, "Aramaic Background," 377. *Rabbinic literature:* McNamara, "Some Early Rabbinic Citations," 1–15.

126. See Diez-Macho, "Recently Discovered Palestinian Targum," 60.

127. See below, Chaps. 13 and 16.

128. For example, T Megillah 3:31–41 (pp. 362–64).

is quite likely that the practice goes back at least to the late Second Temple period. Moreover, the reference in Targum Jonathan to the Hasmonean ruler John Hyrcanus is often cited as proof of the existence of early material.[129]

On the basis of the above considerations, it has generally been assumed that the editing process of the *targumim* occurred over centuries in late antiquity and beyond, into the early Middle Ages. Much material was added and adapted over time, although some traditions may well be early, deriving from the first century C.E., if not beforehand.[130] While differences among scholars still exist regarding how much early material is, in fact, embedded in the *targumim*, there is a consensus regarding two matters. For one, the *targumim* already existed in the first century C.E. in both written and oral form.[131] The fact that an Aramaic *targum* of Job was found on the Temple Mount in the days of Rabban Gamaliel the Elder (first half of the first century C.E.) would indicate that other such works of the Torah and the Prophets were undoubtedly also in circulation, and not only at Qumran. The other matter of consensus is that much of the material in the extant *targumim* originated in the synagogue setting.[132] No one doubts that some of these traditions had their origin in a later, literary, bet midrash context, but others are quite different in both form and content[133] and are best explained as having a more popular, synagogal *Sitz im Leben*.

Thus, we are left with both certitude and perplexity. *Targumim* were in use in the first century,[134] first and foremost (though by no means exclusively) in a synagogue setting.

---

129. The historical reference to the Hasmonean John Hyrcanus is from Targum Jonathan of Deut. 33:11.

130. See Schürer, *History*, I, 99-114; Kahle, *Cairo Geniza*, 191-208; McNamara, *New Testament and Palestinian Targum*; idem, *Palestinian Judaism and the New Testament*; Diez-Macho, "Recently Discovered Palestinian Targum," 60. See also Alexander, "Targumim and Early Exegesis," 60-71; Bowker, *Targums and Rabbinic Literature*; and above, note 117.

131. See, for example, in this regard the statement by Goshen-Gottstein, "Aspects of Targum," 36: "I am afraid that in spite of the Qumran material of targumic character and more sophisticated approaches in Aramaic dialectology, the gap between dicta on targumic origins and extant Targumim remains unbridged. It is one thing to talk about 'Targum' as an institution, possibly hailing back to the early times of the Second Temple—i.e., its prehistory being shrouded in the general traditions about the 'Men of the Great Assembly.' It is another to analyse actual Targumim. More than ever we are aware that the institution in the abstract and exegetical traditions must not be mixed up with an actual protoformulation in literary standard Aramaic, say first-century B.C.E., even less so with the final fixation of the text on Babylonian soil, four centuries later. If we have learned anything in the past quarter of a century it is this: we may at best connect isolated exegetical traditions; we can never overcome a gap of eight centuries."

132. See Kasher, "Aramaic Targumim and Their *Sitz im Leben*," 75-85; York, "Targum in Synagogue and School," 74-86.

133. York, "Targum in Synagogue and School." See Shinan, "Aggadah of Palestinian Targums," 203-17.

134. For a more cautious approach regarding the early dating of targumic traditions, see York, "Dating of Targumic Literature," 49-62; Grabbe, "Jannes/Jambres Tradition," 393-401; as well as the more gen-

However, the content of these *targumim*, how they were delivered, how literal or flexible they were in their renditions, and, most important, what their ideological viewpoints were are all issues which, for the present, must remain unanswered.

Communal Prayer

The most problematic area in the study of synagogue worship in the Second Temple period is that of communal prayer. On the one hand, private prayer was a well-known phenomenon in biblical and Second Temple times;[135] on the other hand, it is universally acknowledged that steps were taken within rabbinic circles at Yavneh soon after the destruction of the Temple to institutionalize communal prayer.[136] The question today, however, is whether communal prayer as a regular and obligatory worship framework already existed in the pre-70 era and, if so, to what degree. For the most part, discussion in this regard has focused on the *Shemoneh 'Esreh* or *'Amidah*, the central prayer in Jewish liturgy.

Over the past century and more, a broad consensus has prevailed, i.e., that the activity of Rabban Gamaliel and his colleagues in Yavneh was one of editing and organizing an already extant public prayer. Scholars differ on the degree of editing involved, from a minimalist position of "touching up" or slightly reformulating an already existing version to a position advocating a serious reworking of earlier materials by the Yavnean sages.[137]

Many have attempted to determine earlier versions of the *'Amidah*, usually by focusing on sources which purportedly preserve embryonic forms of this prayer. A unilinear view of the development of Jewish prayer was once axiomatic among scholars, and attempts have frequently been made to trace the evolution of the urtext of this prayer. Its various layers were attributed to different historical contexts, ranging from the Restoration period in the sixth to fifth centuries B.C.E. to the post-70, Yavnean era.[138] Earlier traces of the *'Amidah* were supposedly detected in a wide range of sources: Psalms, Ben Sira, the Psalms of Solomon, and the Dead Sea Scrolls.[139] Bickerman went a step further, suggest-

---

eral critiques in S. A. Kaufman, "Methodology in the Study of the Targums," 117–24; idem, "Dating the Language of the Palestinian Targums," 118–41.

135. M. Greenberg, "Refinement of the Conception of Prayer," 57–92; idem, *Biblical Prose Prayer*; idem, "Tefilla," cols. 896–922; Kaufmann, *Religion of Israel*, 160–61, 366–67; Weinfeld, *Deuteronomy*, 32–45. See also Johnson, *Prayer in the Apocrypha and Pseudepigrapha*; Flusser, "Psalms, Hymns and Prayers," 551–77; Charlesworth, "Prolegomenon," 265–85; idem, "Jewish Hymns, Odes and Prayers," 411–36.

136. See B Berakhot 27b–28b; B Megillah 17b–18a; Heinemann, *Prayer*, 13–36; Elbogen, *Jewish Liturgy*, 195–203; G. F. Moore, *Judaism*, I, 292.

137. See the range of positions, from, for example, the minimalist position of N. Cohen ("Shim'on Hapakuli's Act," 547–55) through the intermediary ones of Elbogen (*Jewish Liturgy*, 201–2) and Heinemann (*Prayer*, 13ff.) to the maximalist position of Zahavy (*Studies in Jewish Prayer*, 95–101).

138. So, for example, Kohler, *Origins of Synagogue and Church*, 18ff., 206ff.; idem, "Origin and Composition," 410–25; Finkelstein, "Development of the Amidah," 1–43, 127–70.

139. Mirsky, *Piyyut*, 18–29; Liebreich, "Impact of Nehemiah 9:5–37," 227–37; Liber, "Structure and

ing that many of the *'Amidah*'s formulations first appearing in Ben Sira were subsequently incorporated into a civic prayer of Jerusalem and were finally adopted and adapted by the Yavnean sages following the destruction.[140] Common to all the above is the assumption that the *'Amidah* crystallized as a communal prayer at some point in the late Second Temple period. Even the pioneering study of Heinemann, which posited at this stage a multiplicity of orally transmitted forms, assumed that the basic outlines of the *'Amidah* prayer (the number of blessings, their content, and order) had taken shape before 70.[141] The work at Yavneh was thus one of editing and perhaps reformulation.

Until recently, the lone dissenting voice to this consensus was that of Zeitlin. Decades ago, he argued that, in fact, no public prayer was known in Judaea in the pre-70 period and that the institution of communal synagogue prayer is only a post-70 phenomenon.[142] Of late, this line of argument has been adopted by me and, subsequently, by Fleischer and Reif.[143]

The case against the existence of institutionalized communal prayer in the Second Temple synagogue rests squarely on the evidence at hand (or lack thereof) for communal Jewish prayer-worship in the pre-70 period. With all their diversity, extant sources are unanimous in this respect; as we have seen above, Philo, Josephus, the New Testament, the Theodotos inscription, and what appear to be early rabbinic traditions speak only of scriptural readings and sermons.[144] None mentions public communal prayer. Moreover, the few extant buildings usually identified as synagogues would seem to indicate not only a range of plans and styles, but the lack of any discernible or distinctive orientation toward Jerusalem.[145] The Judaean examples are all focused on the center of the hall, with benches on four sides. This is of significance, as it was the physical orientation of the devotee, i.e., facing Jerusalem, which was associated with prayer early on and with all prayer halls in late antiquity.[146]

History," 353–57; Marmorstein, "Oldest Form of Eighteen Benedictions," 137–59; Lévi, "Dix-huit benedictions," 161–78; and Weinfeld, "Prayers for Knowledge, Repentance and Forgiveness," 186–200; idem, "Traces of *Kedushat Yozer*," 15–26; idem, "Morning Prayers in Qumran," 481–94; Talmon, *World of Qumran*, 200–43; idem, "Manual of Benedictions," 475–500; Flusser, "Second Benediction," 331–34; Kohler, "Essene Version."

140. Bickerman, "Civic Prayer," 163–85; idem, *Jews in the Greek Age*, 280. See also Baer (*Israel among the Nations*, 32–36), who claimed that Greek prayers provided the model for the *'Amidah*.

141. Heinemann, *Prayer*, 1–36.

142. Zeitlin, "Tefillah," 208–49 (= *Studies*, I, 92–133).

143. L. Levine, "Second Temple Synagogue," 19–20; Fleischer, "Beginnings of Obligatory Jewish Prayer," 397–425; Reif, *Judaism and Hebrew Prayer*, 44–52, 82–87.

144. It may be of significance that Luke, who incorporates prayer pericopes more than any other gospel writer, speaks of prayer in the Temple and in private homes—but never in the synagogue. See Falk, "Jewish Prayer Literature," 269–76.

145. L. Levine, "Second Temple Synagogue," 10–19.

146. See Dan. 6:11; and below, Chap. 9.

Recently, Fleischer has pursued this line of reasoning to an extreme, arguing against the existence of any formal public prayer in either Second Temple Judaea or the Diaspora.[147] On the face of it, the basis for his argument would appear self-evident; the above-noted written sources invariably speak of a Torah-reading ceremony and never of prayer. Thus, according to Fleischer, the evidence indicates that the Diaspora situation was much the same as that in Judaea, namely, that prayer was not yet a recognized communal form of worship.

However, Fleischer's claim is too absolute and monolithic, leaving little room for diversity and nuances. Regarding the Diaspora, the difficulty with Fleischer's claim rests primarily in the very name used for the Diaspora synagogue: *proseuche*, literally, "house of prayer." On the basis of the name alone, it has been commonly assumed that prayer functioned as a significant element in Jewish worship outside Judaea. Nevertheless, on the basis of the references to Torah-reading in Diaspora sources, Fleischer dismisses the prayer factor, claiming that the name *proseuche* was invoked by Diaspora Jews for the purpose of ascribing a measure of sanctity to their institution and thus asserting its inviolability in the face of pagan attack.[148]

To dismiss a name used for hundreds of years in a wide variety of geographical locales as being a kind of ruse to demonstrate self-confidence and, at the same time, mislead the gentiles, is most problematic. Non-Jews visited Diaspora synagogues in large numbers during the first century C.E. and undoubtedly knew very well what went on inside. To assume that the institution was called by a name which had nothing whatsoever to do with what actually transpired therein is stretching credulity to the limit. Indeed, if Jews desired to create an aura of sanctity for their place of worship, many other terms were available (and some were, in fact, used) which would have conveyed this message no less poignantly.[149] Moreover, if Fleischer is correct, why is it that only some Diaspora communities invoked the term *proseuche* and not others? The Jews of Berenice apparently had no qualms about using the name "amphitheater" and later "synagogue," nor did the Jews of Rome and Asia Minor about regularly using the term *synagoge*.

Nevertheless, Fleischer has rightly pointed to a sharp discrepancy between the name *proseuche* on the one hand and the activities recorded as having transpired therein on the other. One emphasizes prayer, the other the reading of the Torah. Perhaps, however,

---

147. Fleischer, "Beginnings of Obligatory Jewish Prayer," 402ff. and esp. 424–25. Note, furthermore, Fleischer's rather rigid definition of communal prayer (ibid., 401, 414, 426).

148. Ibid., 409. The argument that the term *proseuche* was invoked to offer an extra measure of protection to the synagogue would seem to be undermined by the fact that it was used as early as the third and second centuries B.C.E., when Jewish life flourished in Hellenistic Egypt.

149. For example, the synagogue could have been referred to as ἱερόν ("holy place"), as seems to have been the case on occasion; see Josephus, *War* 7, 45 (Antioch); III Macc. 2:28 (Egypt). See also Josephus, *Against Apion* 1, 209 on Agatharchides' reference to ἐν τοῖς ἱεροῖς in Jerusalem; however, the reference here is undoubtedly to the Jerusalem Temple itself (despite the plural).

an answer is to be sought—not in denying the prayer dimension—but in another direction. Rather than explain away the term *proseuche*, as Fleischer sought to do, it may be simpler instead to explain why the Torah-reading ceremony was singled out as so central by Diaspora writers. Several factors seem to have been involved. Firstly, it may well be that the Torah service was indeed the focus (though not exclusively) of Jewish worship in the Diaspora, as it was in Judaea. Secondly, this part of the service was undoubtedly the most dramatic and participatory component of the Jewish worship context and thus the one most likely to be described. Thirdly, not only was the Torah-reading important in its own right, but it also served as a focus around which most, if not all, other liturgical elements revolved, i.e., the *targum*, sermon, and haftarah. Fourthly, as noted above, the Torah-reading ceremony and its related components reflected what was most unique and distinctive in the synagogue worship context in comparison with other religious institutions in the Greco-Roman world. As a place of religious worship, the synagogue was fundamentally a place of study and instruction, and since such an emphasis was sui generis in antiquity, it was only natural for this facet to be highlighted in descriptions of Jewish worship.

Thus, owing to its centrality, ancient authors made use of the Torah-reading ceremony, each for his own purpose: the author of Acts, to set the stage for Paul's preaching to Jews and non-Jews; Philo, to expound on the didactic, philosophical, and moral lessons imbibed by Jews on the Sabbath; and rabbinic tradition, to describe a hall so huge and magnificent that the only way the congregation could respond was by the *ḥazzan* waving kerchiefs.

In sum, it would appear unjustifiable to deny the existence of prayer as an integral part of Diaspora worship, although, admittedly, not the dominant element. The name *proseuche* accorded to many Diaspora institutions is simply too telling to be dismissed.[150] Nevertheless, we admittedly have no way of determining the exact nature, composition, and extent of Jewish prayer in the Diaspora during the Second Temple period. Some have tried to identify specific compositions in extant Jewish and Christian literature that may have stemmed from a pre- or post-70 Diaspora *proseuche* setting.[151] Such suggestions, however, remain tentative at best.[152]

---

150. Moreover, it may be of more than passing interest that in the only Palestinian synagogue which Josephus refers to as a *proseuche*, namely, the one in Tiberias, the recitation of prayers is specifically mentioned. However, in this case Josephus was speaking not of an ordinary Sabbath but of a fast day, which may explain the predominance of prayers there (*Life* 290–95).

151. *Letter of Aristeas* 305. See Kasher ("Synagogues as 'Houses of Prayer' and 'Holy Places,'" 211), who claims that the story "provided an important paradigm for imitation." See also Charlesworth, *Old Testament Pseudepigrapha*, II, 671–97; idem, "Jewish Hymns, Odes and Prayers," 411–36. See also Flusser, "Psalms, Hymns and Prayers"; Fiensy, *Prayers Alleged to Be Jewish*; idem, "Hellenistic Synagogal Prayers," 17–27.

152. The one possible example of a *proseuche* prayer may be preserved in the famous Nash papyrus from

As to why communal prayer played a more prominent role in Diaspora synagogues than in those of Judaea, several reasons may be suggested. The use of hymns and prayers was central to pagan religious frameworks, much more so than in Jerusalem, where silence accompanied the actual sacrificial rite.[153] Thus, exposure to these pagan forms may well have stimulated local Diaspora communities to imitate these practices in some way. The distance from the Jerusalem Temple and its manifold and impressive ceremonies seems to have played a role as well. Diaspora communities may have felt a need to compensate for this distance by embellishing their own liturgy.[154]

If, however, Torah-reading was, in fact, dominant in the *proseuche* setting, why did so many of these communities choose the term *proseuche* to designate their communal building? As noted some time ago[155]—and Fleischer has reemphasized this as well—it is reasonable to assume that the name *proseuche* did indeed bestow an aura of holiness and sanctity on these Diaspora institutions. Given their minority status and the distance from the sacred center of Jewish life, i.e., the Jerusalem Temple, Diaspora Jews might well have desired to enhance their local institutions with this additional religious dimension—in name as well as in fact.

On the Judaean scene, the issue of communal prayer fares differently, and a nuanced approach is required. While there is no evidence for communal prayers in the typical synagogues of Judaea throughout this period,[156] such prayers did, in fact, exist in certain specific settings. It is clear from extant literary sources (Josephus and Philo) and from the Qumran scrolls that the Essenes and related groups conducted regular communal prayer sessions. It is understandable that a group which consciously distanced itself from the remainder of the Jewish community and from the Temple itself would find it necessary to develop some sort of prayer mode as its primary form of worship. The efficacy and validity of the sacrificial cult in Jerusalem were denied, and into this void substitute worship elements were introduced.[157] As noted, the Essenes throughout Judaea, accord-

---

second-century B.C.E. Egypt. The prayers listed there (the Ten Commandments and the *Shema*ʿ) may reflect Hebrew prayers current in at least some Egyptian *proseuchae*, but there is no way to prove this. See Albright, "Biblical Fragment," 15–39; Fraser, *Ptolemaic Alexandria*, II, 443 n. 777; Bickerman, *Jews in the Greek Age*, 86. Cf. Lacheman, "Matter of Method," 15–39. See also *Liber Antiquitatum Biblicarum* 11, 8: "Take care to sanctify the Sabbath day . . . to praise the Lord in the assembly of the elders and to glorify the Mighty One in the council of the older men."

153. *Pagan ritual*: MacMullen, *Paganism*, 16, 44. *Temple ritual*: for example, *Letter of Aristeas* 92, 95. For differing interpretations of the reason for the silence in Jerusalem's two Temples, see Kaufmann, *Religion of Israel*, 301–4; Knohl, *Sanctuary of Silence*, 148–52; idem, "Between Voice and Silence," 17–30.

154. Hengel, "Proseuche und Synagoge," 33–35.

155. L. Levine, "Second Temple Synagogue," 22.

156. Ibid., 19–20.

157. According to Talmon (*World of Qumran*, 202–6, 237ff.), Qumran was influenced by biblical verses stressing the importance of prayer, while its communal prayer stemmed from the "commune ideology" and "corporate personality" of the sect.

ing to Philo, would gather in their own synagogues for regular worship and at Qumran a
בית השתחות is mentioned as the setting for worship services.[158]

There is some indication that certain prayers found in the scrolls may have originated
before Qumran was established, hailing from groups with which the sect had affinities.[159]
In addition, prayer services were held in the Temple every morning by the officiating
priests, many elements of which later found their way into later normative Jewish prayer.
The Mishnah records the following: "The appointed [official] said to them: 'Recite one
blessing.' And they blessed and read the Ten Commandments, the *Shema*ʿ [Deut. 6:4-
9], 'If, then, you obey' [ibid., 11:13-21], 'And He spoke' [Num. 15:37-41]. They blessed
the people with three blessings: 'True and certain,' Temple sacrifice [*Avodah*], and the
priestly blessing. And on the Sabbath, they would add a blessing for the departing priestly
course."[160]

Bet Hillel and Bet Shammai are said to have disputed the precise number of blessings
which were to be recited on holidays and Rosh Hashanah which fell on the Sabbath. In
the context of that discussion, the Tosefta refers to a specific incident that took place in
the presence of the elders of Bet Shammai and Ḥoni Haqatan.[161]

Acts speaks of ninth-hour prayers in the Temple, and other occasions—public and
private, daily, and on holidays—are mentioned in a variety of other sources.[162] The evidence in Matthew regarding prayer in the synagogue and on street corners is equivocal:
"And when you pray, you must not be like the hypocrites; for they love to stand and pray
in the synagogues and on the streetcorners, that they may be seen."[163] It would appear
that Matthew is responding critically not to communal prayer in synagogues, but to the
ostentatious display of piety by individuals, and is advocating devotions in private and
not demonstrative prayer in public, which he associates with hypocrites.

Nevertheless, it is quite possible that some blessings were recited in synagogues in both
Judaea and the Diaspora. Although only finding expression in the Mishnah and Tosefta, a

---

158. *Judaea*: Philo, *Contemplative Life* 81-83. *Qumran*: CD 11, 21; Talmon, *World of Qumran*, 241-
42; Steudel, "Houses of Prostration," 49-68; Chazon, "Special Character of Sabbath Prayer," 1-21; and
above, Chap. 3.

159. See idem, "Prayers from Qumran," 271-73; idem, "Special Character of Sabbath Prayer," 1-21;
Knohl, "Between Voice and Silence," 30.

160. M Tamid 5:1. See comments of Zeitlin, "Morning Benediction and Readings in the Temple,"
330-36; Hammer, "What Did They Bless?" 305-24; Kimelman, "*Shema*ʿ and Its Rhetoric," 135-43; and
below, Chap. 16. In the case of this Temple prayer as well, Fleischer attempts to neutralize the evidence
of communal prayer by assuming that this tradition is anachronistic ("Beginnings of Obligatory Jewish
Prayer," 414-15, 419-24). For a recent suggestion that the recitation of the *Shema*ʿ was first introduced
in the Hasmonean era, see A. Baumgarten, "Invented Traditions," 202-9.

161. T Rosh Hashanah 2:17 (pp. 320-21); and below, Chap. 16.

162. Acts 3:1; Falk, "Jewish Prayer Literature," 285-98. See the interesting though problematic tradition in T Sukkah 4:5 (p. 273); and comments in Lieberman, *TK*, IV, 888-89; and above, Chap. 3.

163. Matt. 6:5; McKay, *Sabbath and Synagogue*, 172.

blessing before and after the Torah-reading may have already been a customary practice in the first century.[164] In addition to the Torah blessings, there is some evidence that the priestly benediction may have been recited in pre-70 synagogues. The Mishnah records the following: "In the province it was pronounced as three blessings, but in the Temple as a single blessing; in the Temple they [i.e., the priests] pronounced the Name as it was written, but in the province by substituted terms; in the province the priests raised their hands only as high as their shoulders, but in the Temple above their heads, except for the High Priest who raised his hands only as high as the frontlet."[165]

Thus, according to this tradition, the priestly blessing was recited not only in the Temple itself,[166] but also outside Jerusalem. The term used in this last regard is quite vague; in juxtaposition with the Temple, this tradition speaks of "outlying areas" (מדינה) or, in a parallel version, "borders" (גבולין).[167] This source, however, poses a number of questions. Can we regard it as historically reliable, and, if so, to which communal framework does it refer? Assuming a modicum of credibility for this tradition does not appear unwarranted, and it would seem most likely that the synagogue is the venue being discussed. What is not at all clear, however, is whether the two practices noted as taking place in the Temple and synagogue were contemporaneous. Were there similar rituals being conducted simultaneously in the Temple and contemporary synagogues, or does this tradition in reality compare pre-70 Temple practice with that of the post-70 synagogue? The answer to this is not clear. Only by assuming the former can we posit the recitation of priestly blessings in the Second Temple synagogue. However, since this mishnaic pericope may well derive from the Ushan era (ca. 140–180 C.E.), some three generations after the Temple's destruction, it is very possible that the comparison being made is between pre-70 Temple practice and the practice in contemporary synagogues, with which these *tannaim* were familiar.[168]

Thus, we may conclude that the place of prayer in the Second Temple synagogue in Judaea varied considerably. Prayer appears to have played little or no role in the typical Judaean synagogue.[169] Whether some places distant from Jerusalem (e.g., in the Galilee) may have introduced this component in some limited fashion is a moot issue. Nevertheless, there was a short, fixed morning prayer service for officiating priests in the Temple but, interestingly enough, this framework was separate from their sacrificial routine.[170] The various sects may have developed communal prayer patterns; evidence regarding Qumran, the Essenes, and the Therapeutae is clear-cut thanks to the scrolls, Josephus,

---

164. M Megillah 4:2; T Sukkah 4:6 (p. 273).

165. M Sotah 7:6. See also M Tamid 7:2.

166. M Tamid 5:1.

167. Sifre Zuta 6:27 (p. 250). On גבולין as outlying areas, see B Berakhot 12a.

168. On the use of the term גבולין for post-70 practice, see T Kippurim 1:9 (pp. 223–24); B Yoma 19b.

169. See Talmon, *World of Qumran*, 267–68.

170. M Tamid 4:3–5:1.

and Philo. Moreover, there is some indication that the Pharisees knew of a fixed prayer mode (possibly communal), at least on holidays. Outside Judaea, however, the prayer component seems to have been considerably more developed, although, unfortunately, we are in no position to determine its nature, form, or content.

On the basis of the subject matter treated in this chapter and the two previous chapters, several basic features of the first-century synagogue have become clear. Firstly, the institution was essentially a communal one, although given the nature of our literary sources, its religious component is often emphasized. While the communal feature of the synagogue—the universal public Jewish institution par excellence—would continue until the end of antiquity, its religious component, as we shall see, gradually became more predominant.

Secondly, the sacred character of the synagogue was first discernible in the pre-70 Diaspora; it was this institution that had acquired a measure of sanctity in this period, much before the synagogue in Judaea. We read of sacred meals, sacred monies, sacred books, sacred precincts, and even a sacred grove in connection with the Diaspora synagogue. True enough, Philo also attributes sanctity to Essene synagogues of Judaea, but even if we assume the accuracy of this characterization (as against its being the projection of a Diaspora writer), we would still claim, on the basis of the evidence available, that in this respect (as in many others) the Essenes did not reflect wider Judaean practice. Only much later, in the post-70 era, do the synagogues of Roman-Byzantine Palestine gradually evolve in this direction.

Thirdly, in the two previous chapters, which focused on the synagogues of Judaea and the Diaspora, it was natural to take note of the extensive diversity among these institutions, one which stemmed from differing regional contexts and local influences. This diversity is evident in both the physical remains of synagogues (Delos, Gamla, and Masada) and the various names (*proseuche, synagoge, didaskaleion*, amphitheater, etc.) accorded the institution. Recognition of the diversity in Second Temple synagogues is certainly a valid, and indeed crucial, component for understanding the nature of the synagogue at this time. However, it ought not stand alone, but should be regarded as necessary—but not sufficient—for a full appreciation of the institution. This present chapter has highlighted the unity within this diversity. For all its variety, the first-century synagogue exhibited many common features—both communal and religious. Despite all the different nuances between the various communities, these common denominators were far from inconsequential.

With the notable exception of the pre-70 Jerusalem institution, the synagogue incorporated Jewish communal life within its walls: the political and liturgical, the social and educational, the judicial and spiritual. It is this inclusiveness that made the first-century synagogue a pivotal institution in Jewish life, one that played a major role in enabling communities throughout the world to negotiate the trauma and challenges created by the Temple's destruction in 70 C.E. For all the very important comparisons which have been made between the synagogue and comparable Greco-Roman associations (*thiasos, koinon, collegia*, etc.),[171] no analogy does justice to the unique role of this institution within Jewish society. Given the Jews' special needs, together with the willingness and ability of Roman society to tolerate and, for the most part, even support such differences, the synagogue assumed a role unmatched in contemporary pagan frameworks, even though it clearly borrowed much from them.

---

171. Surveyed by Poland in his *Geschichte des griechischen Vereinswesen*.

LATE ROMAN PALESTINE
six # (70–FOURTH CENTURY C.E.)

The impact of Jerusalem's destruction in 70 C.E. on the Jews of Roman Palestine, and the concomitant elimination of the leadership and institutions associated with the city, cannot be underestimated.[1] Suddenly, the major national and religious focus of Jewish life—the Jerusalem Temple—had been eliminated, along with the rituals and ceremonies which had constituted the warp and woof of divine worship in Israel. True enough, there was already a historical precedent for coping with such a loss. The destruction of Jerusalem and the First Temple in 586 B.C.E. did not spell the demise of Judaism or the disappearance of the Jewish people; life went on, adaptations were made, and the Temple was eventually restored.[2] Moreover, Diaspora

---

1. On the response to 70 C.E., see L. Levine, "Judaism from the Destruction of Jerusalem," 125–48, 338–40, and literature cited therein; Baron, *Social and Religious History of the Jews*, II, 110–28; S. J. D. Cohen, "Significance of Yavneh," 45–51; idem, *From Maccabees to Mishnah*, 214–31; Goldenberg, "Broken Axis," 869–82; Bokser, "Wall Separating God and Israel," 349–74; idem, "Rabbinic Responses to Catastrophe," 37–61; Kirschner, "Apocalyptic and Rabbinic Responses," 27–46; Avery-Peck, "Judaism without the Temple," 409–31.

2. Whether and to what degree the destruction of the First Temple was remembered and commemorated during the Second Temple period is an intriguing question with little scholarly consensus. Discussion often centers around the nature and extent of observance of the Ninth of Av and other related fasts, a practice apparently indicated by M Rosh Hashanah 1:3; T Ta'anit 3:6 (p. 338); Y Betzah 2, 2, 61b (= B Ta'anit 13a). See also J. Rosenthal, "Four Fast Days," 446–59.

communities long before 70 C.E. had come to terms with their geographical distance from the Temple, which, for all practical purposes, no longer impacted on their daily lives. Some sects of the Second Temple period had created alternative forms of worship to supplement and, at times, even replace Temple ritual. Nevertheless, the tragedy of 70, following an era of dramatic Jewish demographic, religious, and social growth, undoubtedly caused serious reverberations throughout the Jewish world. A new reality had now emerged.

Generally speaking, one can assume that those living closest to Jerusalem and the Temple were most affected by the destruction, the Jews of the region of Judaea proper more than those of the Galilee, and the last more than those living in the Diaspora. In most cases, geographical propinquity probably correlated with a sense of attachment, dependence, and loss. No other Jewish institution was more affected by the events of 70 than the synagogue. In a religious vein, the synagogue had come to play an important, though limited, role on the local level; now, in the post-70 era, it would begin to acquire an increased centrality in Jewish religious life. Here, too, however, geographical distinctions are in order. As noted earlier, the religious component of the Second Temple synagogue differed from place to place, and it appears that there may have been a correlation between distance from the Temple and the degree of liturgical development in the synagogue of a given area. The Diaspora synagogue seems to have had a more elaborate ritual than its Palestinian counterpart, and there may have been some differences between worship in the Galilean synagogue as compared to the Judaean. Synagogues located in Jerusalem itself may have had a more limited religious agenda than elsewhere. Nevertheless, whatever differences might have existed, there is little question that Palestinian synagogues as a whole were deeply affected by the destruction and that the institution's subsequent development was in no small measure a response to this catastrophe.

Although the year 70 thus provides us with a clear watershed, the subsequent periodization of the post-70 era is less easily defined. The fourth century has been chosen as a convenient dividing line for two reasons, one external and one internal; the former relates to more general historical circumstances, the latter to the primary sources at our disposal. The fourth century marked the official demise of the pagan Roman political order and its replacement by Christianity beginning with Constantine and culminating under Theodosius I. The passing of the relatively tolerant pagan rule, with its generally respectful attitude toward the Jews and Jewish tradition, and the concomitant rise of its Christian successor under the influence, in varying degrees, of an often hostile clergy, is an obvious benchmark which could not but affect Jewish life.[3]

There is no precise date for this transition. Formally, we can point to 324 C.E. and Constantine's official recognition of Christianity. However, this event did not automati-

---

3. Christian hostility will be discussed below, in Chap. 7. For an example of pagan tolerance, see Minucius Felix, *Octavius* 6, 1–3.

cally inaugurate a dramatic shift in the attitude toward the Jews and Judaism. The fourth century was a period of transition and fluidity, when the fate of the Jews and Jewish institutions was far from clear. On occasion they were negatively affected, but more often they found support, and in some respects even gained in stature, under the Imperial authorities.[4] Thus, the full import of the Christianization of the Empire on the Jews became clear only at the end of a process which began in the early fourth century but required generations to complete (on the part of the church and Imperial authorities) and be assimilated (on the part of the Jews). Between such dates as 324 (Constantine's recognition of Christianity), the 330s (the reshaping of Jerusalem as a Christian city and the beginning of extensive church building throughout the country), 363 (the abandonment of Julian's plans to rebuild the Temple), and 381 (Christianity's becoming the official religion), most Jews, it is safe to assume, became fully aware of the momentous changes that were taking place and possibly even cognizant of some of their long-range implications.

The second major change of the fourth century was the close of the talmudic era in Palestine. The last sages mentioned in the Yerushalmi and *midrashim* lived in the third quarter of the fourth century and the final editing of the Talmud took place soon thereafter. Thus, sometime in the second half of the fourth century, all recording of specific attributions and names in the Palestinian rabbinic corpus ceased.[5] With but rare exception, then, every attributed saying or story regarding Palestinian sages in rabbinic literature predates the mid-fourth century, with the overwhelming bulk of the material associated with sages from the second and third centuries. Similarly, although the aggadic *midrashim* were not compiled until subsequent centuries, the ascribed material, i.e., the names of people, places, and events, refers to the fourth century and earlier. Thus, specific references in the most important literary sources at our disposal regarding the ancient synagogue—i.e., rabbinic literature—terminate sometime in the latter half of that century. Historiographically as well as in the overall historical context, the fourth century appears to have been a watershed.

In terms of archeology, the fourth century also marks a hiatus of sorts in the building of synagogues in Palestine. Based on the evidence to date, there appears to have been a building spurt in the third and fourth centuries. Most excavations carried out over the past generation, the Golan region excepted, indicate that the first stages of a synagogue edifice can be dated no earlier than the mid-third or fourth century. Such is the case in the Galilee, for example, at Ḥorvat ʿAmmudim, Gush Ḥalav, Khirbet Shemaʿ, Meiron, Nevoraya, Ḥammat Tiberias, Ḥammat Gader, Maʿoz Ḥayyim, Reḥov, Bet Shean (north), and perhaps Chorazim; in the Golan at Qatzrin; on the Carmel range at Ḥorvat Sumaqa;

---

4. Goodman, *State and Society*, 116–18; Linder, *Jews in Roman Imperial Legislation*, 67–78; S. J. D. Cohen, "Pagan and Christian Evidence," 170–75; Millar, "Jews of the Graeco-Roman Diaspora," 97–112; L. Levine, "Status of the Patriarch," 28–32.

5. Ginzberg, *Jewish Law and Lore*, 26–27; Sussmann, "Once Again Yerushalmi Neziqin," 101–3 and esp. 132–33. See also Strack and Stemberger, *Introduction to Talmud and Midrash*, 188–89.

in the Shephelah at Ḥorvat Rimmon; and in Judaea at ʿEn Gedi and Eshtemoaʾ.[6] The fourth and fifth centuries, with but few exceptions (e.g., Merot, Capernaum, and Sepphoris), are somewhat more problematic with regard to building activity. Few sites offer a firm dating for this period, in part owing to the uncertainty of the numismatic and ceramic evidence. A renewed surge in synagogue building is in evidence from the turn of the sixth century.[7]

Of no less import is the fact that the rich artistic and epigraphical material from ancient Palestinian synagogues dates for the most part from the fourth century onward. The information to be derived from all of the above fields of research—architecture, art, and epigraphy—is thus far more detailed and comprehensive toward the end of late antiquity than for the late Roman Empire (i.e., the third and fourth centuries), and this fact, too, would warrant separate treatment of the synagogue in this later period.

Our focus in this and the next chapter, and indeed for much of the remainder of this study is primarily the synagogues of Palestine. The evidence for this institution is so extensive as to dwarf Diaspora-related material for late antiquity. The many hundreds of literary references to the synagogue itself, and the hundreds, if not thousands, more in Palestinian rabbinic legal and homiletic works referring to its liturgical functions, far outweigh comparable references to the Diaspora synagogue. The archeological material from Roman-Byzantine Palestine is likewise predominant, though to a lesser degree. To date, remains of over 100 buildings throughout Roman Palestine have been identified, and some estimates go as high as 180 (fig. 13).[8] With regard to the epigraphical evidence, Palestinian synagogue remains have yielded some 130 inscriptions in Aramaic and Hebrew and about 70 in Greek, as compared to 13 buildings and over 170 inscriptions from the Diaspora.[9] To this last number we should add well over 100 funerary inscriptions, deriving mostly from the catacombs of Rome, which refer to deceased synagogue officials.

---

6. Groh, "Stratigraphic Chronology of the Galilean Synagogue," 60-69; Foerster, "Dating Synagogues with a 'Basilical' Plan," 87-94. See also Bloedhorn ("Capitals of the Synagogue of Capernaum," 49-54), who suggests a late third-century date for the early stage of the Capernaum synagogue, as does Fischer (*Korinthische Kapitell*).

7. For the above sites, as well as others referred to below, see—unless otherwise indicated—the relevant entries in E. Stern, *NEAEHL*. On renewed synagogue construction in the sixth century, see Foerster, "Basilical Plan as a Chronological Criterion," 173-79; idem, "Dating Synagogues with a 'Basilical' Plan," 92.

8. For the higher estimate, see Z. Ilan, *Ancient Synagogues*.

9. Regarding epigraphical remains from Palestine, see Naveh, *On Stone and Mosaic*. Roth-Gerson lists thirty inscriptions, but does not include in her calculations sixteen inscriptions from the Beth Sheʿarim synagogue (*Greek Inscriptions*, 134-44; Schwabe and Lifshitz, *Beth Sheʿarim*, II, 90-94) or three Greek inscriptions from Ḥammat Gader (Roth-Gerson, *Greek Inscriptions*, 131-33). She also refers to the eight dedicatory inscriptions found at the northern end of the Ḥammat Tiberias synagogue as if they were one. Finally, nine as yet unpublished Greek inscriptions have been discovered at the Sepphoris synagogue, and several more in Tiberias.

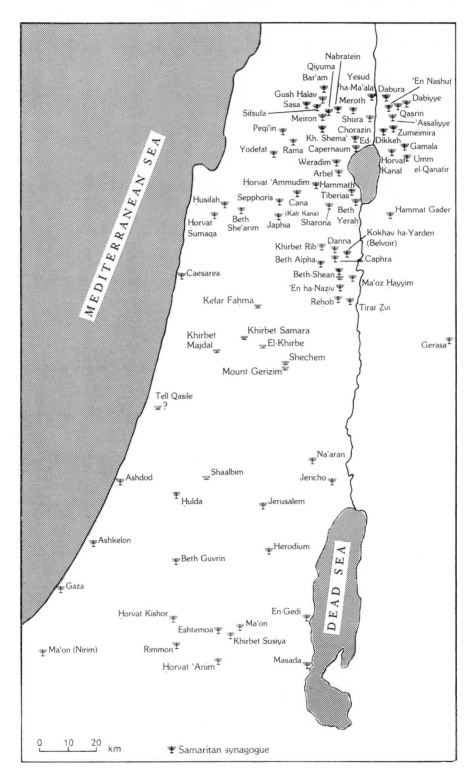

MEDITERRANEAN SEA

DEAD SEA

Nabratein
Qiyuma
Bar'am
Yesud
Gush Halav   ha-Ma'ala   Dabura   'En Nashut
Sasa   Meroth   Dabiyye
Sifsufa   Qasrin
Meiron   Shura   'Assaliyye
Peqi'in   Chorazin   Zumeimira
Kh. Shema'   Ed-Dikkeh
Yodefat   Rama   Capernaum   Gamala
Weradim   Horvat   Umm
Arbel   Kanaf   el-Qanatir
Horvat 'Ammudim   Hammath
Husifah   Sepphoris   Cana   Tiberias   Hammat Gader
Horvat   Beth   (Kafr Kana)   Beth
Sumaqa   She'arim   Japhia   Sharona Yerah
Khirbet Rib   Danna   Kokhav ha-Yarden
Beth Alpha   (Belvoir)
Caesarea   Caphra
Beth-Shean
'En ha-Naziv   Ma'oz Hayyim
Kefar Fahma   Rehob   Tirat Zvi

Khirbet   Khirbet Samara
Majdal   El-Khirbe   Gerasa
Shechem
Mount Gerizim

Tell Qasile
?

Na'aran
Shaalbim   Jericho
Ashdod
Hulda   Jerusalem

Ashkelon   Herodium

Beth Guvrin

Gaza

Horvat Kishor   En-Gedi
Eshtemoa   Ma'on
Ma'on (Nirim)   Rimmon   Khirbet Susiya
Horvat 'Anim   Masada

0   10   20   km

Samaritan synagogue

13. Map of excavated synagogues of Roman-Byzantine Palestine.

SOURCES AND METHODOLOGY

In addressing the history of the synagogue in late Roman Palestine, we are confronted by a number of baffling issues, in part owing to the sources at our disposal. These sources are problematic in their own right; they are both plentiful and scanty, in evidence for one period and absent for another, at times corroborating each other and on occasion at striking variance. Let us consider these issues one by one.

Rabbinic Material—Abundance and Scarcity

For all the richness of rabbinic material with respect to our subject, it is devoid of any overall picture of the synagogue as an institution. Instead, these sources focus on certain liturgical components of synagogue (and private) worship, i.e., key prayers and the Torah-reading, as well as the use of the synagogue as a place of study. Material relating to other aspects of the institution—communal functions, synagogue officials, benefactors, interior and exterior design, furnishings, etc.—is relatively sparse and noted only en passant.

Given the institution's centrality in the post-70 era, one might expect it to have received great attention in the various rabbinic writings. After all, the Temple merited a mishnaic tractate on its physical dimensions alone, in addition to other tractates or parts thereof that describe ceremonies and rituals conducted therein.[10] Moreover, the Sanhedrin, which, according to non-rabbinic accounts at least, was far from being a Pharisaic institution, was thoroughly "Pharisaized" or "rabbinized" in the Mishnah and Talmud; to wit, an entire tractate was so named.[11] Even a facility such as the *miqveh*, which played a significant role in Temple and sectarian ritual in the pre-70 era, merited tractates in the Mishnah and Tosefta, although no later compilation exists in either Talmud.[12]

Thus, for all its centrality in Jewish life following the destruction of the Temple, the synagogue per se merits minimal attention in the Mishnah and in tannaitic *midrashim*, though somewhat more in the Tosefta, the two *talmudim*, and later *midrashim*. Prayer (Tractate Berakhot) and, to a lesser extent, the Torah- and haftarah-readings (Tractate Megillah) are discussed more fully than other worship activities, but even here the former often does not necessarily refer to a synagogue setting. In Mishnah Berakhot, for example, the synagogue is never mentioned in relation to the two main prayers (the *Shema'* and *'Amidah*) that are discussed in the tractate's first five chapters. The prayer settings

---

10. Aside from Middot describing the Temple and Temple Mount, the rest of the order of Qodashim (an additional ten tractates) is devoted to Temple-related matters. In addition, many tractates in the order of Mo'ed (e.g., Yoma, Sukkah, Rosh Hashanah, Sheqalim, Pesaḥim, as well as Bikkurim in the order of Zera'im) focus in varying degrees on Temple ritual.

11. On the difficulties in defining the pre-70 Sanhedrin, its activities, composition, and authority, see Mantel, *Studies*, 54–101; Efron, *Studies*, 287–338; Bickerman, "On the Sanhedrin," 356–59; L. Levine, *Judaism and Hellenism*, 87–90; idem, *Rabbinic Class*, 76–83; and Goodblatt, *Monarchic Principle*, 103–30.

12. See Reich, "Synagogue and Ritual Bath," 205–12.

noted include riding on animals, traveling on a ship, and working in a tree or on a wall.[13] The prescriptions in rabbinic literature regarding prayers may equally have applied to settings such as an academy, a private home, an open square, or a field. Indeed, obligatory prayer at this time may have been, to a large degree, private.

While the apparent lack of attention given to the synagogue in rabbinic literature is at first glance surprising, upon further consideration the phenomenon should not be regarded as strange. Once we bear in mind that rabbinic literature was never intended to be a balanced documentation of Jewish life in antiquity, we may regain some perspective on not only how to evaluate what has been preserved, but also—and no less important— how to judge what, in fact, has been omitted. Rabbinic literature is, first and foremost, an account of laws, homilies, and stories that the rabbis deemed important to discuss and transmit and that later generations of sages saw fit to preserve. From this mass of material, one can cull a great deal of information about contemporary Jewish society and even about certain aspects of the Roman world generally, even though this clearly was not the intention of the editors of these sources. If information extraneous to the rabbinic agenda does, in fact, appear, it is usually because it was in some way linked to a halakhic or homiletic context. What has been omitted in this literature regarding Jewish and even rabbinic society far outweighs, of course, what has been preserved—a truism, indeed, but one that must always be borne in mind. Moreover, even what has been preserved must be treated with a measure of caution. This material has been filtered through many hands before reaching its final form in a particular compilation, and it often reflects the welt-anschauung and prejudices of those who transmitted and edited the material.[14]

It is clear, for example, that the rabbis were not interested in reporting on the synagogue per se, nor, for that matter, on any other communal framework. Regarding pre-70 institutions, what little has been preserved are merely random traditions, some more idealized and tendentious than others, which the sages considered to be of significance. Perhaps some of this material was intended to serve as a blueprint for the future. However, even with respect to their own day, i.e., the second to fourth centuries c.e., rabbinic sources regarding non-rabbinic frameworks are of limited value. We know very

---

13. These examples raise the important question regarding the degree to which mishnaic rulings represent a systematic treatment of a given subject and thus deal with fundamental issues or the degree to which they treat exceptions to the rule and problematic situations. It would appear that both dimensions are in evidence with regard to prayer. The presentation of the principal prayers in the first part of Berakhot is general and universally prescriptive, although some pericopes may indeed deal with very specific and problematic issues whose more general applicability can only be guessed.

14. For various perspectives on the historical value of rabbinic literature and how it should be used, see, inter alia, Herr, "Conception of History," 132–42; Neusner, *Formative Judaism*, 99–144; Green, "Context and Meaning," 97–111; Goodblatt, "Towards a Rehabilitation of Talmudic History," 31–44; Goldenberg, "History and Ideology," 159–71; L. Levine, *Rabbinic Class*, 16–22; Gafni, "Concepts of Periodization and Causality," 21–38.

little about Roman and Jewish municipal institutions,[15] and nothing systematic has been recorded regarding schools and charitable frameworks of the Jewish community—two institutions certainly of interest to the sages. What does exist is at best anecdotal and fragmentary.[16] Even as regards the rabbinic academy, an institution of prime importance and concern to the sages, our information happens to be even more limited than that relating to the synagogue.[17] Information is woefully scant with regard to where rabbinic academies were located, how they looked inside and out, how they functioned, who was in charge, how learning frameworks were organized, who the students were, and what role, if any, the institution played in the larger community.

Nevertheless, for all the limitations in the nature and variety of sources on the synagogue, there is a real distinction to be made between second-century tannaitic material on the one hand and that of the third- and fourth-century amoraic sources on the other.[18] The former corpus is generally much more restricted in scope, and its agenda is fixed by either the halakhic emphasis and parameters set by R. Judah I in his Mishnah, on which the Tosefta expands, or the biblical text which the tannaitic *midrashim* address.[19] Amoraic material, which includes the *talmudim* as well as aggadic *midrashim*, is far richer in evidence regarding the synagogue.[20]

This increase in material may not be coincidental. It reflects a very profound transformation that was taking place within rabbinic circles. More rabbis were now involved in issues and institutions relating to the Jewish community generally and, as a result, became more responsive to its needs.[21] This attitudinal and behavioral change is reflected in

---

15. Juster, *Juifs*, I, 438–56; II, 243ff.; Baron, *Jewish Community*, I, 133–40.

16. Baron, *Jewish Community*, 124–26, 130–31; S. Safrai, "Education," 945–70; Bergman, *Charity in Israel*, 13–38.

17. Baron, *Jewish Community*, I, 150–55; Urman, "House of Assembly and House of Study," 238–55. See also idem, "Location of the Academy," 163–72.

18. On this distinction and its ramifications, see Strack and Stemberger, *Introduction to Talmud and Midrash*; *EJ*, II, 865–75; XV, 798–803; Halivni, *Midrash, Mishnah and Gemara*, 38–75; Goldberg, "Mishna," 211–51; idem, "Palestinian Talmud," 303–19.

19. B. Cohen, *Mishnah and Tosefta*, 37–58; *EJ*, XII, 93–110; Goldberg, "Tosefta," 283–301.

20. Albeck, *Introduction to the Mishnah*, 79–143.

21. I have written elsewhere about the greater involvement of the rabbis in the Jewish community in the third and fourth centuries. The rabbis of Yavneh inherited a basically sectarian tradition, which was gradually transformed only in subsequent generations. Throughout much of the second century, the rabbis' involvement in the larger society, their acceptance of other forms of behavior, and their involvement with other institutions were generally quite limited.

A watershed was reached in the lifetime of R. Judah I, whose influence on Jewish society generally and the rabbis in particular was profound. The rabbis became more and more involved with their surroundings, their academies became fixed institutions in various locales and were not dependent on any one particular sage, and more rabbis began undertaking communal tasks and relating to the public at large. Certain classic sectarian interests—strict observance of tithing and sabbatical year laws, hostility toward other Jews with different types or degrees of observance, and disdain for the less educated—were

a statement by R. Isaac of the third century with regard to the teaching required of sages in his generation: "At first, when money was available [lit., a *perutah* was to be found], one would desire to study Mishnah and Talmud [i.e., halakhic material]; now that money is not available, and, what is more, we suffer from the [gentile] kingdoms, one desires to hear Bible or aggadic teachings." [22]

In this light, then, it is not surprising that we find much more material relating to various facets of the synagogue as an institution included in later sources. The mid-third-century Tosefta is richer than the Mishnah and all the tannaitic *midrashim* combined, and the *talmudim* and amoraic *midrashim* are even more inclusive of such material.

In sum, the relative absence of second-century synagogue material in rabbinic litera-ture may be less related to historical fact (i.e., the synagogue's relative unimportance in society) than to contemporary rabbinic attitudes toward and relations with that institu-tion and to the process of selection by the editors of these compilations.

Post-70 Synagogues: The Archeological Evidence?

The archeological issues concerning synagogues in this period are as fascinating as they are perplexing. To date, there is meager evidence, at best, of synagogue buildings for almost two centuries following the destruction of the Temple. The assumption made by earlier archeologists, that many of the monumental Galilean synagogue buildings are to be dated to the period of R. Judah the Prince and the Severan dynasty, has yet to be stratigraphically substantiated.[23] With but one or two possible exceptions, none of the scores of post-70 buildings excavated to date stems from this period,[24] and this applies

---

modified by the new reality. Within this context, therefore, it is not at all unexpected that some rabbis at least would begin addressing communal issues more earnestly and that the editors of rabbinic com-positions would subsequently choose to include some of this material. The increased data available from the third and fourth centuries should be understood against this backdrop. See L. Levine, *Rabbinic Class*, 23–42; idem, "Sages and Synagogue"; S. J. D. Cohen, "Place of the Rabbi," 157–73; Goodman, *State and Society*, 93–118; and below, Chap. 13.

22. PRK 12:3 (p. 205).

23. This date was already posited in the monumental study by Kohl and Watzinger (*Antike Synagogen*, 204–18) and became axiomatic among archeologists through the writings of Sukenik (*Ancient Synagogues*, 68) and Avi-Yonah ("Synagogue Architecture," 67–73). See also Avigad and Foerster (in L. Levine, *An-cient Synagogues Revealed*, 42–43 and 47–48, respectively), Hüttenmeister and Reeg (*Antiken Synagogen*, I, viii–ix), and Tsafrir ("Source of Architectural Design," 70–79), who tend to prefer a third-century dating. Recently, Ma'oz ("When Were the Galilean Synagogues First Constructed?" 416–26) has attempted to revive the Kohl and Watzinger thesis, but cites no new hard evidence.

24. The earliest stratum at Nevoraya (north of Safed) is dated by E. M. Meyers ("Second Preliminary Report on Excavations at en-Nabratein," 40; *NEAEHL*, III, 1077–78; "Torah Shrine," 317–18) to the mid-second century. However, these remains are fragmentary and the published report is preliminary; the evidence has yet to be presented fully and systematically. Thus, there is some hesitation to view this phase as definitive evidence for a second-century Galilean synagogue. Another possible candidate for a second-century synagogue is some sort of public building which was erected by the Jews of Qatzion,

to archeological data from all parts of Roman Palestine: the Galilee and Golan, the Bet Shean area, the Jordan Valley, southern Judaea, and the coastal region.

No less striking than the absence of archeological evidence following the destruction in 70 is the burst of synagogue building in the Galilee and elsewhere from the mid-third century onward.[25] Excavations over the past generation have indicated that numerous synagogues were erected at this time. What is so unusual about this phenomenon is that it seems to have occurred when least expected. Given the heretofore generally accepted picture of the third century as a time of economic, social, and political instability, one could not have anticipated so intense a period of synagogue building.[26] In fact, Mac-Mullen has claimed that it is precisely at this time that pagan culture was on the wane, owing in part to the inability or unwillingness of wealthy benefactors to subsidize the pomp, performances, sacrifices, and public feasting that had been the norm for centuries. Such contributions were essential for the maintenance of pagan temple ritual. Third-century instability claimed a heavy toll in this regard, and across the Empire, whether in Ostia, Asia Minor, or Antioch, this century has invariably been characterized as one of decline and decay.[27]

Let us address each of these issues separately. The fact that no synagogue remains have been found for some two centuries after 70 is indeed surprising. It has been suggested that the absence of synagogues may have been caused by their destruction in the wake of the various revolts throughout Palestine between 66 and 135 C.E., especially that of Bar-Kokhba (132–135 C.E.). We have already taken note of Malalas' report of Vespasian's (perhaps Titus') conversion of the synagogues of Caesarea and Daphne into an odeum and theater respectively, and to this we might also add the destruction of a major Alexandrian synagogue as a result of the 115–117 Diaspora revolt.[28] Rabbinic literature knows of one such case in Roman Palestine. The following is recorded in the Bavli:

---

in the eastern Upper Galilee, in honor of Septimius Severus and his sons in 197 C.E. The nature of this building, however, remains a mystery. The preserved dedicatory inscription in stone may have once been affixed to a synagogue, but it also could have belonged to some other public building; see Roth-Gerson, *Greek Inscriptions*, 125–29.

25. So, for example, at Gush Ḥalav, Nevoraya, Khirbet Shema', Meiron, Ḥorvat 'Ammudim, and 'En Gedi. A similar phenomenon recurs at this time with respect to the Jewish catacombs in Rome. Those discovered date from the late second through the fifth centuries. Where, then, are the remains of Jews from the first century B.C.E. or the first and second centuries C.E.? And why were the existent catacombs of late antiquity in use precisely at this time? No convincing answers to these questions have been forthcoming to date. See Rutgers, *Jews in Late Ancient Rome*, 96–99, 267–68.

26. A typical description of this era can be found in Avi-Yonah, *Jews of Palestine*, 89–114.

27. MacMullen, *Paganism*, 127–30; see also, for example, Meiggs, *Roman Ostia*, 83–85 (deterioration and decline); Magie, *Roman Rule in Asia Minor*, 688–723 (decay and chaos); Downey, *History of Antioch*, 252–53 (strife, uncertainty, a disordered and difficult period).

28. On Malalas, see above, Chap. 4, notes 225 and 226. On the destruction of Alexandrian synagogue(s) as a result of the revolt in 115–117 C.E., see Y Sukkah 5, 1, 55b; Tcherikover et al., *CPJ*, I, 93.

R. El'azar [third-century *amora*] proceeded to relate a halakha in the academy and did not say it in the name of R. Yoḥanan. R. Yoḥanan heard [of this] and became angry. R. Ami and R. Asi came to visit him [and] said: "Was there not an incident in the Tiberian synagogue [regarding] a lock with a fastening device [גלוסטרא] at its tip which was a subject of dispute between R. El'azar and R. Yosi [second century] until they tore a Torah scroll in their anger? Do you actually imagine [that they, in fact, tore a scroll]? Rather, say: 'A Torah scroll was torn in their anger.' And R. Yosi b. Qisma was there [and] said: 'I would be surprised [i.e., I predict] if this synagogue [where such an incident occurred] did not become [a place of] idolatry.' And so it happened."[29]

Despite the problematic chronological issues connected with this source, as well as its citation only in the Bavli,[30] there may be embedded here some memory (following R. Yosi b. Qisma's statement) of a Tiberian synagogue being converted into a pagan temple sometime in the early second century. Might this possibly be a reference to the building of a Hadrianeum in Tiberias, as reported by Epiphanius?[31] The issue must remain moot for the present.

Regarding the post-135 Hadrianic persecutions, there is no way of verifying whether these measures included the obliteration of existing synagogues; no substantiation of such a claim exists in either rabbinic or archeological material. No source mentions or even alludes to the closing or dismantling of synagogues,[32] and no archeological excavation has uncovered a destruction layer beneath a third-century building. Even if we were to ignore this negative evidence, there is little to substantiate the claim that the revolt or its aftermath affected the Galilee in any measurable way.[33] Thus, the Hadrianic persecutions—while perhaps explaining the lack of evidence in several locales—clearly do not account for the absence of remains throughout the country.

A second theory explains the scarcity of archeological remains for this period as owing to the fact that the synagogue, like the contemporary church, was not an identifiable public building, but rather a private home, a *domus ecclesiae*.[34] Remains of such private

---

29. B Yevamot 96b, and variations in Y Sheqalim 2, 7, 47a. On the word גלוסטרא, see Jastrow, *Dictionary*, loc. cit.

30. See the comments in Eliav, *Sites, Institutions and Daily Life*, 68–71.

31. Epiphanius, *Panarion*, 30, 12.

32. On the Hadrianic persecutions following the Bar-Kokhba revolt, see Lieberman, "Persecution of the Jews," 213–45; Herr, "From the Destruction of the Temple," 365–67; Mor, *Bar-Kochba Revolt*, 238–40. The comments of R. Judah b. Ilai (mid-second century C.E.) regarding what is to be done with a synagogue that has been destroyed may be relevant here (M Megillah 3:3); however, this comment stands alone and indeed may be only theoretical.

33. Goodman, *State and Society*, 137–38; Mor, *Bar-Kochba Revolt*, 103–21; Oppenheimer, *Galilee*, 37–44; and the discussion of this issue in Oppenheimer et al., "Jewish Community in the Galilee," 51–83.

34. Tsafrir, "Source of Architectural Design," 79–80. The term *domus ecclesiae* in this context is somewhat problematic. It may be understood to refer to a "religious community building," much as was found at Dura or Capernaum. However, it may refer to a "house church" which did not entail interior

buildings are notoriously hard to identify. However, this theory, too, is not without its problems. To compare the synagogue with the *domus ecclesiae* is to assume that the synagogue congregation invariably met in an ordinary home. While this may have been the case at times in the Diaspora, it would contradict everything we know about Palestinian synagogues. In the first century synagogues were essentially communal buildings and were constructed (or restored) as such—separate edifices with columns as well as benches on four sides, as found at Gamla or Masada. Literary sources likewise confirm the public character of synagogue buildings. At Caesarea, Dor, Tiberias, as well as according to the Theodotos inscription from Jerusalem, Judaean synagogues appear to have been separate, identifiable buildings. Synagogues from the third century onward were also public Jewish buildings, with a presence and prominence analogous to those of the first century. Both rabbinic sources and archeological finds confirm this picture (see below). Moreover, there is no reason to assume that late first-century to mid-third-century synagogues "went underground" and were ensconced in private dwellings, as the church was forced to do owing to its status as a *religio illicita*. A hiatus of approximately two hundred years in the building of public Jewish communal institutions appears most unlikely. Indeed, for all its limitations, rabbinic literature indicates just the opposite. The evidence points to the continued centrality of the synagogue as a multifaceted communal institution.

A third explanation, however, may be the most plausible. Generally speaking, synagogue remains prior to late Roman and Byzantine strata are hard to come by. At site after site, in cities or villages, public or private buildings, the extensive rebuilding from late antiquity or, for that matter, from any period thereafter has almost entirely obliterated earlier remains. Our knowledge, for example, of pre-Byzantine Caesarea or pre-Severan Sebaste, Bet Shean, or even Gerasa is limited and fragmentary.[35] As regards Second Temple Jerusalem, the extensive and monumental building program carried out by Herod and his successors during the last one hundred years of this era almost entirely obliterated earlier remains. Given the large-scale construction of synagogues and other structures in late antiquity, a similar situation may have held true for previous structures as well. Only the synagogue remains at Nevoraya and perhaps Capernaum (as interpreted by the Franciscan excavators) may possibly be construed as examples of later structures replacing earlier ones lying beneath them.

Nevertheless, despite the lacunae in our sources, there can be no doubt that the synagogue continued to function as a central communal institution in Jewish communities

---

alterations for use by the community and was thus architecturally indistinguishable from other private buildings. The Dura church is thus not a *domus ecclesiae*, but rather a private dwelling that was converted into an identifiable church building; see White, *Social Origins*, 25. On the conversion of private homes into synagogues in many Diaspora communities, see idem, *Building God's House*, 62–77.

35. Interestingly, the same holds true with respect to Diaspora synagogues. Those of late antiquity cannot be traced before the second century C.E. Regarding first-century Judaea, see Sanders, *Historical Figure*, 100.

everywhere after 70 and throughout the ensuing centuries. As noted, tannaitic sources are too explicit in this regard for us to assume otherwise. Moreover, the centrality and prominence of the synagogue in the first century are matched by a similar status in the third and fourth centuries; there is hardly time for dramatic changes in such a relatively short interim. Take, for example, the revealing exchange between two rabbis in Lydda in the first half of the third century c.e.:

> And R. Ḥama bar Ḥanina and R. Hoshaya were walking among the synagogues of Lydda. R. Ḥama bar Ḥanina said to R. Hoshaya: "How much money have my ancestors [lit., my fathers] invested here?" The other responded: "How many souls have your ancestors lost here [lit., have they sunk here]? There are no people to study Torah!"[36]

Here, then, we have two very contrasting rabbinical reactions to the impressive synagogue buildings in Lydda from the first half of the third century: one takes pride in the material remains; the other is sharply critical of this use of communal funds. Of interest for our purposes is the fact that synagogue structures were standing at this time, and it is clear from the exchange that we are dealing with imposing edifices. Moreover, this report is far from sui generis; other sources report many synagogue buildings in third-century Palestine—e.g., the reputed eighteen synagogues in Sepphoris and its environs at the time of Rabbi Judah I's funeral (ca. 225). Broader contextual circumstances would also argue for a similar conclusion, i.e., an increased role, prestige, and sanctity for the synagogue following the Temple's disappearance. Thus, any attempt to base far-reaching conclusions regarding the nature and importance of the synagogue in the post-70 period on the availability or absence of archeological material is fraught with danger. Only an assessment that balances the archeological and literary remains within the historical context of the late Roman era can hope to achieve some degree of credibility.

Synagogue Building in the Mid-Third Century

Just as the absence of archeological material in the post-70 era raises perplexing questions, so does the unexpected reappearance of evidence in the mid-third century. Prior to the wave of excavations over the past few decades, the mid to late third century would not have seemed a likely time for such a spurt in synagogue building. Nevertheless, the archeological evidence exists and continues to grow. In addition, there are several rabbinic traditions from precisely this time which attest to contemporary synagogue building:

> The people of Bet Shean asked R. Ami [late third century]: "Is it permissible to take stones from one synagogue in order to build another?" He said to them: "It is forbidden." R. Ḥelbo said: "R. Ami only forbade this because of the sadness [that would be caused]."
>   R. Gorion said: "The people of Migdal [north of Tiberias] asked R. Simeon b. Laqish

---

36. Y Sheqalim 5, 6, 49b; Y Peah 8, 9, 21b. On the town of Lydda in this period, see J. J. Schwartz, *Jewish Settlement in Judaea*, 69–80; Oppenheimer, "Jewish Lydda," 115–36.

(mid-third century; died ca. 280): 'Is it permissible to take stones [of a synagogue] in one city and build in another?' He said to them: 'It is forbidden.'" R. Ami had taught: "Even from the eastern to the western [side of the city] it is forbidden because of the destruction [that would be evident] at that site [where a synagogue had once stood]."[37]

These traditions are indeed unique. Only for this period—and in these pericopes—does Palestinian rabbinic literature evidence a concern about rebuilding or relocating synagogue buildings.[38] For our purposes, these sources from the mid to late third century are relevant in that they attest to actual cases of Jewish communities interested in building new synagogues in locales where old ones once stood. Is it merely coincidental that these particular sources were preserved, and were there, in fact, other instances in late antiquity which simply were not recorded in rabbinic literature? Or, alternatively, are these sources reflective of a unique situation in third-century Palestine, in which older synagogues were being abandoned and new ones required elsewhere? If the latter is the case, then we might ask why this need emerged at this particular time? Was it merely a matter of relocation?[39] Had the community grown and did it now require newer and larger facilities? Or was there some sort of destruction or upheaval that eliminated the older buildings? The last alternative appears improbable, as we have no evidence of persecution or destruction from the third century.[40] Whatever the specific reasons for rebuilding, rabbinic literature fully corroborates the archeological evidence that such construction was being undertaken at this time.

An interesting parallel to this Jewish phenomenon may be found in extant Samaritan traditions which speak of a major religious revival in the third century under the leadership of the legendary Baba Rabba. The Samaritan chronicles relate a series of reforms carried out under his aegis, including the reorganization of Samaritan leadership around an appointed council of seven elders (three priests and four laymen) and the establishment of a system of regional officials in which one layman and one priest were assigned to each district.[41] The cornerstone of this reformation was the synagogue (fig. 14).[42] Baba

---

37. Y Megillah 3, 1, 73d.

38. The only other comparable traditions come from third- and fourth-century Babylonia and involve R. Ḥisda, R. Papa, and R. Huna; see B Megillah 26b.

39. According to the suggestion of E. Meyers regarding the influx of Judaean immigrants into the Galilee following the two Jewish revolts ("Galilean Regionalism," 99).

40. On third-century conditions in Palestine, see Lieberman, "Palestine in the Third and Fourth Centuries," 329-44 (= *Texts and Studies*, 112-27); Avi-Yonah, *Jews of Palestine*, 35-136.

41. Abu 'l-fath, in *Samaritan Documents* (pp. 142-46); *Kitab al-Tarikh* (pp. 177-86); Chronicle II, in *Samaritan Chronicle* (pp. 65-76); Adler, "Nouvelle Chronique," 87-96. On these reforms generally, see *Samaritan Chronicle* (pp. 228-38); Crown, "Byzantine and Moslem Period," 58-59; idem, "Samaritans in the Byzantine Orbit," 110-11; idem, "Samaritan Religion," 32-34, 41-43; Kippenberg, "Synagoge," 351-60. On the reforms in Samaritan leadership, see *Samaritan Chronicle* (pp. 66-74); *Kitab al-Tarikh* (pp. 184-85 [see also p. 181]); *Samaritan Documents* (pp. 143-45 and n. 170).

42. *Samaritan Documents* (pp. 142, 146); *Kitab al-Tarikh* (pp. 177, 183); *Samaritan Chronicle* (pp. 65, 71-72).

14. Torah shrine from the mosaic floor of the Samaritan synagogue at Khirbet Samara.

Rabba reputedly reopened numerous synagogues that had been closed, first by the emperor Commodus (180–92 C.E.) and later by Alexander Severus (222–35 C.E.).[43] Moreover, he built a large synagogue on Mt. Gerizim, opposite the site of the former Samaritan temple, and next to it a *miqveh* for purification purposes:

> Later, the priest Baba Rabba built a ritual bath for purification on the boundary of the chosen place, Mount Gerizim Beth-El, the Mountain of Inheritance and Divine Presence. . . . He further built a Synagogue, adjoining the Chosen Place, Mount Gerizim Beth-El, so that the people could pray in it opposite this holy mountain.[44]

Baba Rabba built eight additional synagogues in various Samaritan villages, seven of whose locations are specifically mentioned.[45] Most revealing, however, is the following

43. Adler, "Nouvelle Chronique," 85–87; *Kitab al-Tarikh* (pp. 166–72).

44. *Samaritan Chronicle* (p. 71). According to Abu 'l-fath: "On the periphery of the Holy Mountain Baba Rabba built a water pool for purification at prayer times, that is, before the rising of the sun and its setting. And he erected a prayer house for the people to pray in, opposite the Holy Mountain"; see *Kitab al-Tarikh* (pp. 182–83); see also *Samaritan Documents* (pp. 145–46).

45. *Samaritan Documents* (p. 146); *Kitab al-Tarikh* (p. 183); *Samaritan Chronicle* (pp. 71–72). These

information: "He built in them a place in which to read and to interpret, and to hear petitions, in the southern part of the house of prayer, so that anyone with a personal problem
could ask the *Ḥukama* [i.e., the sage] about it and be given a sound answer."[46] Thus, we
have here the familiar combination of a school and a setting for the *ḥukama* to deal with
issues brought to him by the people.

Few scholars have reservations regarding the historical basis of Baba Rabba's reforms.
However, the issue which has been vigorously debated of late is one of dating, and the
diversity of opinion in this regard has been fueled by the ambiguity and contradictory
nature of the sources themselves. While the various chronicles clearly place Baba Rabba's
activity in the mid-third century, under the emperors Alexander Severus, Gordianus, and
Philip, they also note the existence of Constantinople at the time as well as the fact that
Baba Rabba was incarcerated and died there. This would, of course, bring us to the fourth
century, for Constantinople was built in the 320s and dedicated by Constantine in 330.
Moreover, several names mentioned in connection with Baba Rabba have been arguably
identified with fourth-century figures.

It is little wonder, then, that the dating of Baba Rabba has been the subject of much
controversy. Early in this century, Montgomery advocated a fourth-century setting, more
specifically the era of Constantius (337–61), and many have since followed his lead.[47] In his
edition of Chronicle II, Cohen has recently suggested that Baba Rabba lived around the
turn of the fourth century and was publicly active for a twenty-year period, ca. 308–28.[48]
Of late, however, a number of scholars, including Crown, Hall, and Stenhouse, have opted
for the traditional Samaritan chronology, assuming a mid-third-century setting for these
reformations.[49] If this last suggestion is accepted, then Samaritan synagogue building

---

synagogues are said to have been built of stone (it is specifically mentioned that no timber was used), and
all had earthen floors. Chronicle II mentions the names of seven of the eight synagogues with earthen
floors, Abu 'l-fath the names of all eight. Magen, however, has suggested that these particular sites may,
in fact, date to the thirteenth century, when these chronicles were composed ("Samaritan Synagogues"
[Eng.], 226–27).

On the archeological discoveries of Samaritan synagogues, see ibid., 193–230; idem, "Samaritan Synagogues" (Heb.), 66–90; idem, "Samaritan Synagogues and Their Liturgy," 229–64. The recently discovered Samaritan synagogues at el-Khirbe and Khirbet Samara have been tentatively dated to the fourth
century c.e. See also Pummer, "Samaritan Synagogue," 24–35; Z. Safrai, "Samaritan Synagogues," 84–
112.

46. *Kitab al-Tarikh* (p. 183). See also *Samaritan Documents* (p. 146).

47. Montgomery, *Samaritans*, 101–4. See also Kippenberg, "Synagoge," 351; *Samaritan Documents*
(pp. 197–201 nn. 192, 204); Broadie, *Samaritan Philosophy*, 2; Isser, *Dositheans*, 43, 95; MacDonald, *Theology of the Samaritans*, 26; Pummer, *Samaritans*, 4; Hüttenmeister and Reeg, *Antiken Synagogen*, II, 534.

48. *Samaritan Chronicle* (pp. 224–28).

49. Crown, "Byzantine and Moslem Period," 56; idem, "Samaritans in the Byzantine Orbit," 105–108;
idem, "Samaritan Religion," 32–34; Hall, "Samaritan History," 52–54; idem, *Samaritan Religion*, 2–14;
Stenhouse, "Fourth-Century Date," 317–26; idem, "Baba Rabba," 327–32.

would constitute an interesting chronological parallel to the appearance of the late third-century Jewish synagogues and may even be related in some way to this development.[50]

Returning to the question of how one might explain the resurgence in the building of Jewish synagogues in the mid to late third century, given what we know of the period generally, our response can be only tentative. One approach would be to discount the literary and numismatic evidence regarding a third-century crisis in Palestine. Either the period of anarchy was not as severe as once assumed or, more likely, different regions of the Empire may have been affected in different ways.[51] Not all areas may have suffered to the same degree. While this last claim undoubtedly has a good deal of merit in and of itself, third-century Palestinian sages are rather unequivocal in their negative comparisons of conditions in their own day with those which prevailed a generation or two earlier.[52] Even if we discount part of these statements as hyperbole, it would be wholly gratuitous and arbitrary to disregard them completely.

A second approach toward solving this quandary is to accept both the historicity of the political and economic crisis at the time and the archeological evidence, but to assign each of these sets of data to a different period. The nadir of economic and political conditions was reached in the third quarter of the century, and this is apparently reflected in rabbinic sources. Toward the end of this century, however, specifically in its fourth quarter, during the reign of Diocletian (284–311), the economic and political situation of the Empire ameliorated, and the archeological material may reflect in the main this period of stabilization. Such a chronological division is certainly possible, but it may be just a little too neat and compartmentalized. Some archeological and literary evidence for synagogue building seems to point more toward the mid (and not late) third century, although, admittedly, precision regarding dating is unattainable, while certain literary traditions indicate a continued decline in the late third century, if not into the fourth as well.

A third approach would accept the evidence of both types of sources, archeological and literary, claiming that the building of synagogues was perhaps in direct response to the crisis of the third century. Having lost the Temple, Jerusalem, and much of the re-

---

50. A number of artistic similarities between Jewish and Samaritan synagogues of the third and fourth centuries have been noted by Amit (" 'Curtain,' " 571–75), to which one might add the cluster of religious symbols appearing almost simultaneously in the fourth-century synagogues at Ḥammat Tiberias (Jewish) and at el-Khirbe and Khirbet Samara (Samaritan). Crown has suggested significant Jewish influence on Samaritan practice at this time: "There are geographical, social and historical reasons for arguing that Jews and Samaritans lived in close symbiosis with a consequence that Rabbinic Judaism was a formative factor in Samaritanism despite Samaritan denials" ("Samaritan Religion," 35). On possible Samaritan influence on the rabbinic listings for names of Jerusalem about this time, see Shinan, "Seventy Names of Jerusalem."

51. Cameron, *Later Roman Empire*, 1–12; L. Levine, "Palestine in the Third Century," 119ff. and esp. 136–43. With regard to Sardis, see White, *Social Origins*, 317 n. 52.

52. White, *Social Origins*, 127–35; Avi-Yonah, *Jews of Palestine*, 89ff.; Sperber, *Roman Palestine—Land*, 11–99.

gion of Judaea following the unsuccessful rebellions in the first and second centuries, and now finding themselves in the throes of political and social instability, many Jewish communities may have striven to reassert their identity and demonstrate their cohesiveness by erecting communal buildings.[53] Moreover, the breakdown of a political order may have had economic ramifications, allowing people to avoid taxes and other payments and thus direct their monies toward local projects, such as the building of synagogues.

Building activity in the face of political and economic turmoil is not an unknown phenomenon and may be documented in other places in the third century. The drive to build transcended all boundaries, touching upon Jew and non-Jew alike across the Empire. Emperors, urban aristocracy, and villagers from Egypt, Libya, Asia Minor, Numidia, and Gaul undertook building projects at this time.[54] The third century witnessed the erection of walls and the refurbishing of buildings in cities such as Tiberias and Caesarea;[55] if the above Samaritan evidence is taken into account, then synagogues were also being restored and built anew in Samaria. Christians, too, were active at this time in building new churches. Porphyry refers to the "great buildings" of the Christians, which he says "imitate the construction of temples," and Eusebius describes the extensive building activity of Christians throughout the Empire even before the large-scale persecutions of 303.[56] Lactantius reports that in the year 303, at the beginning of the persecution of Christians, Diocletian ordered the destruction of a large church on a hill adjacent to his palace in Nicopolis (Asia Minor).[57] On this basis, White claims that the third century witnessed a spate of church building with larger and more formal structures than the *domus ecclesiae*, referring to these buildings as *aula ecclesiae*.[58]

This last-noted alternative—synagogue building as an act of reaffirmation in the face of economic and social stress—appears to be the most plausible explanation available. The third century, no less than other eras in the course of history, defies generalizations, which only tend to obliterate cross-currents, distinctions, and nuances.

CONTINUITY AND CHANGE

In one very fundamental way, the synagogue of late antiquity exhibited a marked continuity from the pre-70 era; both literary sources and archeological data indicate that it served as the central public framework for each Jewish community. Rabbinic litera-

---

53. Later on, Jews would express this need for self-identity through the massive use of Jewish symbols, a phenomenon which seems to make its first appearance at this time. See L. Levine, "Menorah."

54. MacMullen, *Response to Crisis*, 119–20.

55. *Tiberias:* B Bava Batra 7b. *Caesarea:* Holum et al., *King Herod's Dream*, 107–53; Levine, *Roman Caesarea*, passim.

56. Porphyry, *Adversos Christianos*, frag. 76; Eusebius, *Ecclesiastical History* 8, 1, 5–6.

57. Lactantius, *De mortibus persecutorum* 12, 4–5; see also Millar, "Paul of Samosata," 14–15.

58. White, *Building God's House*, 123–39.

15. Suggested reconstruction of the Meiron synagogue at the crest of the mountain.

ture, for its part, takes note of no other communal institution, and this is true of non-Jewish sources as well. The synagogue and its officials, along with the Patriarchate, are referred to by various church fathers and the Theodosian Code; contrastingly, the rabbinic academy, along with the rabbis, rarely merit attention in these sources.

The synagogue's centrality is persuasively conveyed by archeological remains. Throughout late Roman Palestine, many communities emphasized this centrality by erecting the building in the very center of town and out of all physical proportion to the surrounding structures. This is strikingly evident at Susiya, Chorazim, Qatzrin, and Ḥorvat 'Ammudim.[59] Additionally, the synagogue's prominence might be expressed topographically by placing it on an artificial podium, as at Capernaum,[60] high on a hill and overlooking the town, as at Khirbet Shema' and Ma'on (Judaea), or literally perched at the very peak of the mountain, towering over the village itself, as at Meiron (fig. 15). An elaborate facade, as at most Galilean-type synagogues (e.g., Bar'am), or an imposing interior, as at Ḥammat Tiberias, also gave expression to this prominence.[61]

A number of rabbinic sources emphasize the synagogue's centrality. The Tosefta is especially intriguing in this regard:

> One should not behave lightheartedly in a synagogue. One should not enter synagogues lightheartedly. One should not enter them in the heat because of the heat, nor in the cold because of the cold, nor in the rain because of the rain. And one should not eat in them nor drink in them nor sleep in them nor stroll in them, nor just relax [lit., enjoy oneself] in them, but [one should] read Scriptures and study laws [lit., Mishnah], and engage in midrash [i.e.,

---

59. For these and following sites, see E. Stern, *NEAEHL*, passim; and Z. Ilan, *Ancient Synagogues*, passim.

60. The Capernaum synagogue was especially prominent owing to the use of limestone in contrast to the local basalt.

61. On the variety of synagogue styles in the third and fourth centuries, see below, Chap. 9.

exegetical commentary] in them. A public eulogy may be delivered therein. R. Judah [b. Ilai] said: "The above relates to a standing synagogue, but if destroyed, they are to be left alone, and let grass grow there as a sign of sadness (or despair).[62]

This source is often mistakenly quoted as an indication of what did not take place in the synagogue. In reality, however, it indicates what was actually happening in the synagogue and that to which the rabbis objected; whether or not the sages were effective in influencing this objectionable behavior is another issue. As of the time of the above statement at least, these objectionable practices were still very much a part of synagogue activity and inspired the above apodictic declaration. By focusing on what the rabbis wished to prohibit, we may gain a clearer idea of how, in fact, many synagogues were then functioning.

The institution reflected in the above source was indeed a community center. It was a place of gathering and socializing, of conducting business (following one interpretation of the term "lightheartedly"),[63] of taking shelter from inclement weather, of camaraderie involving food and drink; it was a hostel and a place of relaxation; finally, it was a place for study and public eulogies. The sages were in agreement with regard to the two last-mentioned functions; however, the community at large apparently recognized the legitimacy of the other activities as well. Thus, the sages made the above declaration in an attempt to preserve the reverence they deemed befitting for such an institution. The Tosefta, in fact, describes an institution akin to the synagogue in Jerusalem per the Theodotos inscription, the Sardis and Halicarnassus synagogues as described in the edicts preserved by Josephus, and the archeological remains from the Dura Europos, 'En Gedi, Capernaum, and Ḥammat Tiberias (last stage) synagogues. The above-noted functions characterized the ancient synagogue throughout antiquity and across all geographical borders.[64]

A standard characteristic of all later synagogues which first made its appearance in third-century structures was the orientation toward Jerusalem.[65] Almost all synagogues of the period faced this direction, although the expression of this orientation might differ from building to building. With the exception of Arbel, Galilean-type synagogues faced their elaborate and ornate facades in the direction of the Holy City and the Temple ruins (fig. 16). The interior was oriented in this direction as well; most of these structures had three rows of columns, on the west, north, and east. Only the southern part, facing Jerusalem, had none, as this direction served as the hall's focus.[66] Other synagogues, at Khir-

---

62. T Megillah 2:18 (p. 353).

63. B Megillah 28b.

64. For somewhat similar roles of the pagan shrine in rural districts of late antiquity, see Libanius, *Pro templis* 30, 8.

65. See Landsberger, "Sacred Direction," 181–203; and below, Chap. 9. See also Wilkinson, "Orientation," 16–30 (to be used with caution). The uniqueness and sanctity of Jerusalem also found expression in a number of other tannaitic traditions; see, for example, M Kelim 1:6–9; M Ketubot 13:11.

66. Foerster, "Ancient Synagogues," 291ff.

16. Remains of the main entrance of the Chorazim synagogue.

bet Shema‘ and Gush Ḥalav, for instance, had a *bima* against the southern wall (fig. 17), and still others, as at Arbel, had a niche facing Jerusalem. Synagogues in the southern part of the country, e.g., Eshtemoa and Susiya, thus faced north. On occasion, the form of orientation in a given building changed over time. So, for example, the synagogues at Merot, Ḥammat Tiberias, and ‘En Gedi at first had doors facing Jerusalem; later on, these were replaced by a *bima*, and the doors were relocated in a different direction.[67]

Orienting oneself toward Jerusalem in prayer, clearly documented already in biblical literature, is emphatically articulated in contemporary rabbinic sources. "Those who stand outside Israel must direct their hearts [i.e., face] toward the Land of Israel, as it is written: 'And they will pray toward their land' [II Chr. 6:38]. And those standing in the Land of Israel direct their hearts toward Jerusalem and pray, as it is written: 'And they shall pray toward this city' [ibid.]. Those standing in Jerusalem shall direct their hearts toward the Temple, as it is written: 'And they shall pray toward this House' [ibid., 6:32]. Those standing in the Temple should direct their hearts toward the Holy of Holies and pray, as it is written: 'And they shall pray toward this place' [I Kgs. 8:30]. Thus, those who stand in the north will face south, those who stand in the south will face north, those in the east will face west and those in the west will face east. Thus, all Israel will be praying to the same place."[68]

The emphasis on physical orientation toward Jerusalem undoubtedly reflects profound changes transpiring within the Jewish community and its synagogues in late antiquity. On one level, it was a powerful statement of religious and ethnic particularism. No longer was the main communal institution to be a neutral gathering place, as were the first-century Judaean synagogue buildings. The synagogue was now meant to embody historical memories, a religious-communal attachment to the present, and perhaps

---

67. On these sites, see above, note 59.

68. T Berakhot 3:15–16 (pp. 15–16) and parallels. See also M Berakhot 5:5; Tanḥuma, Qedoshim, 10 (p. 39b). This last source emphasizes Jerusalem and the Temple as the center (*omphalos*) of the world.

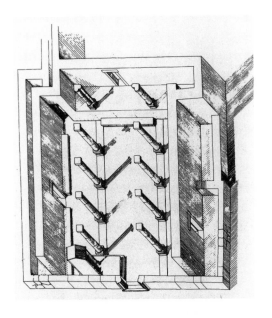

17. Suggested isometric reconstruction
of the Gush Ḥalav synagogue.
Note the Torah shrine below, to the left
of the entrance.

(messianic and other) hopes for the future.[69] This physical expression of attachment to Jerusalem and the Temple—despite the fact that each building's ornamentation and architectural style were almost exclusively borrowed, selected, and adapted from the material culture of the surrounding world—was expressed first and foremost via its orientation.

However, the synagogue's newly articulated orientation was also a function of a more profound change touching upon the very nature of the institution. It was in the post-70 period that the synagogues of Roman Palestine began to acquire an enhanced religious profile. While the synagogue's manifold communal functions continued unabated, the main assembly hall gradually became something more than a large gathering place; its liturgical role was now emphasized more than ever before. In some synagogues this new emphasis found expression only in the outward orientation and in the interior arrangement of columns; in others, a permanent *bima*, niche, or *aedicula* was placed in or against the Jerusalem-oriented wall to emphasize the desired liturgical focus.[70] Clearly, worship was becoming an increasingly important component of synagogue activities in Roman

---

69. See Gafni, *Land, Center and Diaspora*, 58–73. On the belief that the divine *Shekhinah* continues to reside in the Temple (as well as rival beliefs), see Ehrlich, "Place of the *Shekhina*," 315–29.

70. See Hachlili, *Art and Archaeology*, 166–87. See also idem, "Niche and Ark," 43–53. It is for this reason, perhaps, that the elders who had previously faced the congregation with their backs to Jerusalem (T Megillah 3:21 [p. 360]) now also faced in the direction of Jerusalem (*Differences in Customs*, no. 36 [p. 156]). For the continued development of this emphasis in the subsequent Byzantine period, see below, Chap. 7.

Palestine, as it already had been in the Diaspora. By the third century, this new emphasis was receiving due architectural expression.

The seven-branched menorah as a decorative (symbolic?) feature first appears in synagogues from the late third century. The large menorah incised on the northern lintel of the Khirbet Shemaʿ building is a case in point, as is the menorah inside a wreath at the center of the Nevoraya synagogue lintel. The possibility that an actual three-dimensional menorah may have been found in some synagogues is indicated by a number of rabbinic sources which state that such an object was, in fact, donated to a synagogue. Several of these traditions note that the legendary emperor Antoninus made such a donation. While the latter traditions concerning Antoninus may be of questionable historical value, the example cited by all these sources was undoubtedly drawn from the synagogue reality of the time and would thus attest to the presence of *menorot* in some synagogue buildings.[71]

Indeed, there is little question that the increasingly dominant religious dimension of the synagogue was the major factor in making the issue of orientation so pronounced in synagogue architecture of late antiquity. The Jews now began to imitate the widespread practice of a fixed orientation that was customary in pagan and, later, Christian buildings. For the most part, both pagan temples and Christian churches faced east,[72] as did the Tabernacle and both Jerusalem Temples for well over one thousand years. The Jews of late Roman Palestine, from the Galilee to southern Judaea (and in the Diaspora), altered this practice completely and dramatically. While they may well have been influenced by the earlier Jewish tradition of praying toward Jerusalem,[73] the communities may have done this also out of a demonstrative rejection of pagan practice or owing to their strongly felt religious and ethnic identification with Jerusalem.

The rabbis now began to claim that synagogue liturgy requiring ten male participants guaranteed God's presence (= *Shekhinah*) there. Invoking the verse "God stands in the congregation of the Lord" (Ps. 82:1), the sages asserted: "Wherever ten persons assemble in a synagogue, God's presence is with them."[74] It is this enhanced religious dimension of the synagogue in the rabbis' eyes that seems to have been behind their protest against using the synagogue for "secular" or non-worship purposes. That they did not approve of what they saw is clear; for that reason the above-quoted prohibition was articulated.

There were other types of protest as well. The second-century sage R. Ishmael b. Elʿazar declared that the *ʿam ha-ʾaretz* dies for two reasons: calling the holy ark a

---

71. On the Khirbet Shemaʿ and Nevoraya synagogues, see *NEAEHL*, loc. cit.; on the Antoninus menorah, see T Megillah 2:14 (p. 352); Y Megillah 3, 2, 74a; B ʿArakhin 6b. See also Chap. 9.

72. Cf., however, the comments in Wilkinson, "Orientation," 26–29; Herbert, "Orientation of Greek Temples," 31–34.

73. I Kgs. 8:44; II Chr. 6:34, 38; Dan. 6:11. See also M Berakhot 4:5.

74. Mekhilta of R. Ishmael, Baḥodesh, 11 (ed. Lauterbach, II, p. 287); B Berakhot 6a; see also Y Berakhot 5, 1, 8d–9a; PRK 5:8 (p. 91); Seder ʿOlam 15 (p. 64). On the *Shekhinah*'s presence in rabbinic literature and in Matthew, see Sievers, " 'Where Two or Three . . . ,' " 171–82.

"chest" (*'arana*) and calling the synagogue a "house of people" (*bet 'am*).[75] We will have occasion to return to this source in another context; what is eminently clear, however, is that any "secular" reference to the synagogue or its appurtenances was anathema to this sage (and probably others as well, certainly those who preserved and transmitted this particular statement). Whether such admonitions were effective is another issue. Several inscriptions indicate that in some communities this rabbinic dictum was either unknown or ignored. The term *'arana*, used to identify the Torah shrine, has been found at Naveh in the Hauran and at Dura Europos.[76]

The rabbinic desire that the synagogue evolve into a substantially different institution following the destruction of the Temple is reflected in a series of *taqqanot* (enactments) and comments which sought to enhance its religious and liturgical dimension. Immediately following the events of 70 C.E., R. Yoḥanan b. Zakkai issued a series of *taqqanot* aimed at transferring many Temple practices to this new setting.[77] While some of these enactments were directed toward Jewish courts, and although the synagogue is never specifically mentioned, it is the latter institution that was undoubtedly the primary context affected. Blowing the shofar on Rosh Hashanah, using the *lulav* and *ethrog* during the seven-day Sukkot festival, and following the priestly practice of not wearing sandals when blessing the people all point to a synagogue setting for their implementation. How many synagogues responded to R. Yoḥanan b. Zakkai's *taqqanot* is unknown. Some contemporaries viewed his moves with alarm.[78] The story of his outwitting the Sons of Bathyra regarding the blowing of the shofar on the Sabbath attests to the tradition's intent to demonstrate Yoḥanan's cleverness.[79] As it stands, however, the story attests not only to R. Yoḥanan's successful handling of the challenge to his authority, but also to the very opposition engendered by these measures.

Some rabbinic traditions were aimed at encouraging Jews to build synagogues in imitation of certain features of the Temple: "One does not build the entrances to the synagogue except toward the east, as we find with regard to the sanctuary [i.e., the Tabernacle], which was open toward the east, as is written: 'And those encamped before the Tabernacle toward the east, before the Tent of Meeting eastward' [Num. 3:38]. One does not build them except on the highest point of the city, as it is written: "at the height of . . . you will call" [Prov. 1:21]." [80] Just as the Temple portals faced east and the Temple edifice itself was located on the highest point along Jerusalem's eastern ridge, towering above the

---

75. B Shabbat 32a. On the term *'am ha-'aretz*, see below.

76. Kraeling, *Dura: Synagogue*, 269; Naveh, "Aramaic and Hebrew Inscriptions," 307.

77. M Rosh Hashanah 4:1–4; M Sukkah 3:12. On these enactments, see Alon, *Jews in Their Land*, I, 107–18; L. Levine, "Judaism from the Destruction of Jerusalem," 133–36.

78. On the opposition to R. Yoḥanan in a variety of areas, see Alon, *Jews, Judaism and the Classical World*, 314–43.

79. B Rosh Hashanah 29b.

80. T Megillah 3:22–23 (p. 360). See also Lieberman, *TK*, V, 1200–1201; Fine, *This Holy Place*, 41–49.

biblical City of David, so one should build a synagogue entrance facing east at the highest point in a town. Whether intended to be descriptive or prescriptive, evidence shows that the guidelines delineated in this tradition might be only sporadically implemented. While synagogues were often located on prominent sites in the city or village, more so in some than in others, the tradition that portals should face east found expression in only a handful of synagogues in the north (Arbel, Maʿoz Ḥayyim, Khirbet Sumaqa, and presumably Bet Shean [north] and Sepphoris) and in a number of synagogues in southern Judaea.[81] The builders of most structures, i.e., the overwhelming majority of archeological finds to date, were either unaware of this latter recommendation or ignored it.

Further links between the synagogue and Temple also find expression in tannaitic literature. One tradition claims that a synagogue and its quorum of ten men would assure God's attention for Israel, and this was similar to the recitation of the divine name in the Temple.[82] Another tie is reflected in a statement attributed to R. Judah. When prescribing what should not be done in a destroyed synagogue, this second-century sage invoked Lev. 26:31: "and I will leave waste your sanctuaries." Just as a sanctuary (i.e., the Temple) retains its sanctity when destitute, so, too, does a synagogue.[83]

Some time in the third or fourth century, additional steps were taken by the rabbis to link these two institutions. Memories of the Temple cult were introduced into synagogue liturgy. Thus, it was claimed that the ʿAmidah prayer was instituted in order to replace Temple sacrifices, and numerous sources from the amoraic period make the claim that prayer was considered a substitute for sacrifices as a means of atonement.[84] About this time, the content of the Additional ʿAmidah (Mussaf) recited on Sabbaths and holidays had also changed. Whereas a selection from Deut. 32 (the Song of Moses) was previously read, the Mussaf ʿAmidah now included recitation of the sacrifices that used to be offered in the Temple.[85] Finally, at some point in late antiquity, a supplementary Torah-reading (maftir) from Num. 29, where the sacrifices of each holiday are enumerated, was introduced on holidays.[86]

These last modifications in synagogue liturgy take us one step further in demonstrat-

---

81. The southern Judaean synagogues include Eshtemoa, Susiya, Maʿon, ʿAnim, and perhaps Ḥorvat Rimmon (first stage); see Amit, "Architectural Plans," 6–35; NEAEHL, passim.

82. B Berakhot 6a. See also Y Berakhot 5, 1, 8d–9a.

83. M Megillah 3:3. See also Fine, "Did the Synagogue Replace the Temple?" 18–26, 41.

84. B Berakhot 26a; Sifre-Deuteronomy 41 (p. 88); PRK 24:19 (p. 377); Tanḥuma, Korah, 12; Tanḥuma, Ki Tavo, 1 (p. 23a).

85. B Rosh Hashanah 31a; Y Berakhot 4, 6, 8c. See also Elbogen, Jewish Liturgy, 98; J. Hoffman, "Surprising History of Musaf ʿAmidah," 41–45; L. A. Hoffman, Canonization, 157.

86. Elbogen, Jewish Liturgy, 138. About this time (though precision here is impossible), the daily psalms once recited by the Levites in the Temple (M Tamid 7:4) were now transferred to the synagogue setting (B Rosh Hashanah 31a; Tractate Soferim 18:2 [pp. 310–13]). See also Maharshen, "Daily Psalm," 198–99.

ing explicitly what always had been implicit when associating the synagogue with the Temple, and especially when transferring Temple practices to the synagogue setting. It was at this time that the synagogue itself began assuming a degree of sanctity. This idea was new to the Palestinian setting and was not always easily assimilated, even within rabbinic circles.[87]

An important rabbinic source concerning the emerging sanctity of the synagogue—in rabbinic thought, at least—is found in Mishnah Megillah, wherein there is a sequence of items placed in hierarchical order:

> When the people of the city sell their town square,[88] they may only buy a synagogue with this money. If a synagogue [is sold], they may only buy a Torah chest. If a chest [is sold], they may only [buy] mantles for wrapping the scrolls. If the mantles [are sold], they may only buy [sacred] books [i.e., Prophets and Writings]. If the [sacred] books [are sold], they may only buy a Torah. However, if they sell a Torah, they may not buy [sacred] books; if [sacred] books [are sold], they may not buy mantles; if mantles [are sold], they may not buy a Torah chest; if a Torah chest [is sold], they may not buy a synagogue; if a synagogue [is sold], they may not buy a square. And so, too, with the remaining monies.[89]

Thus, the first part of the above source lists places and objects, one more sacred than the next. Monies made from the sale of a less holy object must be used to acquire something more holy, but not vice versa. According to the Talmud, the square's sanctity appears to be the sole opinion of R. Menahem b. Yose;[90] everything else seems to have been undisputed. Thus, the synagogue is less holy than the objects which it contains, objects which are all associated with the Torah scroll. It is clear from this list that the Torah scroll itself is considered the most holy object in the synagogue and that it bestows degrees of sanctity on other objects, depending on how close they are to it in kind (i.e., other sacred books) or how close they are physically (e.g., mantles, chests, synagogue).[91]

This mishnah regarding the sanctity of a synagogue while it is still functioning stands in marked contrast to the following mishnah, which offers a wide spectrum of opinion regarding the synagogue building's status once it ceases to function as such:

---

87. For a full discussion of the evolving sanctity of the synagogue in late antiquity, see Fine, *This Holy Place*, 35–126. Cf., however, the remarks of Goldberg, "Service of the Heart," 195–211.

88. The square acquired a modicum of sanctity since the Torah was occasionally read there: "R. Yohanan said: 'This [mishnaic tradition is to be ascribed] to R. Menahem b. R. Yose, for R. Menahem b. R. Yose said: "A town square has sanctity since they [sometimes] take out a Torah and read it publicly"'" (Y Megillah 3, 1, 73d; see also M Ta'anit 2:1).

89. M Megillah 3:1.

90. See above, note 88.

91. Ironically, the special status of the Torah is also reflected in the fast-day ceremony, for which the Torah scroll was taken into the public square. According to R. Hiyya bar Abba, this act was to demonstrate that "the one precious item we have has been humiliated because of our sins" (Y Ta'anit 2, 1, 65a). My thanks to David Levine for calling my attention to this source.

"A synagogue is only sold on condition that, if they wish, they can return it [to its former status as a synagogue]," says R. Meir. The sages say: "If sold, it is sold forever [i.e., there can be no such condition], except that it may not then be used as a bathhouse, a tannery, a place of immersion, and a urinal." R. Judah says: "They may sell it as a courtyard and the buyer may do with it as he pleases."[92]

This second-century debate, from the generation of Usha, focuses on the option of re-selling an abandoned synagogue building. It is unanimously agreed that it can be done; the only issue is whether there are any restrictions on such a transaction. The more con-servative R. Meir recommends a clause allowing its reclamation as a synagogue whenever desired; the sages stake out a more flexible position, allowing a permanent sale except in cases where its new use would discredit the building's former status. R. Judah, the most liberal of all, recommends that the building be regarded as a courtyard, thus allowing the buyer to do what he wishes with it. This is in contrast to the traditions, noted above, wherein several third-century rabbis would not even allow stones from one synagogue to be moved and reused to build another synagogue. We can see how dramatically the sacred status of the synagogue developed among the rabbis within the span of a century.[93]

What caused this profound transformation of the synagogue from a principally com-munal institution to one with an increasingly distinct religious stamp? Was there an idea, an object, or a practice which served as a catalyst for this change? No source addresses this issue head on and thus certainty is elusive. Nevertheless, there are a number of likely causes reflected in various rabbinic traditions. The ways in which the synagogue had begun to emulate the Temple have been noted, and, of course, the Temple was regarded as the sacred Jewish institution par excellence. Was it this increasing identification with the Temple, which was emphasized on a regular basis by the central role of the priestly blessing at this time, which bestowed sanctity on the synagogue?[94]

Moreover, the holiest object in the synagogue was the Torah scroll (or scrolls), which was to be found increasingly, and on a permanent basis, in the main halls of synagogues. This is evidenced by the appearance of *bimot*, apses, and niches in third- and fourth-century buildings (fig. 18). The presence of scrolls undoubtedly played a role in accord-ing an enhanced sanctity to the synagogue building itself. There is no better testimony to this fact than the diatribe of Chrysostom in one of his homilies against the Jews:

But since there are some who consider the synagogue to be a holy place, we must say a few things to them as well. Why do you reverence this place when you should disdain it, despise it and avoid it? "The Law and the books of the prophets can be found there," you say. What of

---

92. M Megillah 3:2.

93. Y Megillah 3, 1, 73d. See also Goldberg, "Heiligkeit des Ortes," 26–31. On the superiority of a number of extra-Temple religious practices over those associated with the Temple in amoraic literature, see Bokser, "Rabbinic Responses to Catastrophe," 37–61.

94. See, for example, M Megillah 4:3.

18. Qatzrin synagogue, looking southwest. Note the *bima* along the southern wall.

it? You say, "Is it not the case that the books make the place holy?" Certainly not! This is the reason I especially hate the synagogue and avoid it, that they have the prophets but do not believe in them, that they read these books but do not accept their testimonies. . . . Therefore stay away from their gatherings and from their synagogues and do not praise the synagogue on account of its books. Rather, hate it and avoid it for that very reason, for they have mangled the saints because they do not believe their words and they accuse them of extreme impiety.[95]

95. John Chrysostom, *Homily* 1, 5, trans. in Meeks and Wilken, *Jews and Christians*, 94-96. See also Meyers, "Torah Shrine," 303-38. Amoraic literature's preference for referring to the Torah cabinet as *'aron* and not *tevah*, as was the case earlier, is indicative of a change in perspective. The term *'aron* carries with it very clear associations with the biblical ark containing the tablets with the Ten Commandments that was placed in the holiest precinct of the Tabernacle and then of the Temple. Later on, the Karaites attacked the Rabbanites precisely because of this association; see Lieberman, *Midreshei Teiman*, 25. It is perhaps noteworthy that over a millennium earlier, it was the introduction into Jerusalem of the holy ark with the two tablets of stone which David perceived as essential to granting the city a sacred status (II Sam. 6). Moreover, the sanctity of the Torah is reflected in the dramatic account of Levi b. Sisi (early third century), who, upon the approach of Roman soldiers to his town, took a Torah scroll in hand, climbed onto a roof, and exclaimed: "Master of the universe, if I have ignored one word in this Torah scroll, let them [the soldiers] enter; if not, have them leave." (Y Ta'anit 3, 8, 66d). Compare this to the

Despite this poignant evidence, whether the presence of scrolls was the pivotal factor in the evolving synagogue sanctity is unclear.[96]

Several other possibilities also present themselves. According to rabbinic literature, prayer was becoming an ever more significant element in synagogue liturgy in late antiquity. Certainly the synagogue's orientation toward Jerusalem from the third century onward reflects an enhanced connection with the holy city, a connection linked to the requirement to turn toward Jerusalem in prayer. Thus, the growing role of congregational prayer in the synagogue liturgy may have contributed to the building's heightened sanctity.[97]

It is also possible that this newly emerging status of Palestinian synagogues was influenced in some measure by Diaspora models. We have seen that with regard to sanctity, the Diaspora synagogue preceded that of Palestine by generations, if not centuries. Already before 70, the Diaspora synagogue was not only a place for Torah-reading, as in its Palestinian counterpart, but also a setting for some sort of public prayer; the sanctity enjoyed by these Diaspora institutions may have been related, inter alia, to this prayer dimension.[98] Might this Diaspora model have helped shape, through channels as yet unknown to us, the later Palestinian one?

On the basis of the sources available, however, it is well nigh impossible to ascertain which of the above was the pivotal factor in the synagogue's transformation in status and role in late Roman Palestine. It is entirely possible, and indeed quite probable, that the change was not due to any one of the above, but rather to a combination of some, or all, of them. Moreover, the subsequent Byzantine era was also to contribute toward the movement in the direction of increasing synagogue sanctity (see below, Chap. 7).

Nevertheless, having seen the extent of rabbinic support for viewing the synagogue in a new religious light, particularly as regards the Temple, we should note that not all sages were comfortable with the conception that the synagogue and its practices should resemble those of the Temple. One tannaitic tradition quoted often in the Bavli offers the

---

use of a Torah scroll by Joshua, son of Sapphias, in first-century Tiberias (Josephus, *Life* 134–35), when he accused Josephus of betraying the city.

The process of introducing the Torah scrolls into the synagogue on a permanent basis was a long one. From the extant evidence, though limited, it is rather clear that pre-70 synagogues did not have any *bimot* or *aediculae*, and the Torah would have been brought into the hall for reading and then removed. By the third and fourth centuries, a permanent installation was becoming more common, and it was almost a universal fixture by the end of late antiquity. See, for example, T Megillah 3:21 (p. 360); B Soṭah 39b; below, Chap. 9.

96. As argued in Fine, *This Holy Place*; see also Lightstone, *Commerce of the Sacred*, 104.

97. For the emphasis on public prayer, see, for example, B Berakhot 32b; Tanḥuma, Ki Tavo, 1 (p. 23a); Pirqei de Rabbi Eliezer 5 (= Seder Eliyahu Zuta 23 [p. 42]). On the comparison of a prayer leader with one who offers a sacrifice, see Y Berakhot 4, 4, 8b; Genesis Rabbah 49:23 (pp. 506–7). Cf., however, Ginzberg, *Commentary*, III, 350–51. See also Bokser, "Rabbinic Responses," 47–57; Fine, *This Holy Place*, 62–67; Z. Safrai, "Communal Functions," 200; Urman, "House of Assembly and House of Study," 235–36.

98. See above, Chap. 4; as well as Goodman, "Sacred Space," 1–16.

following words of caution: "One should not make a house in the likeness of the Sanctuary; nor an exedra in the likeness of the Temple porch [אולם], nor a courtyard like the עזרה [i.e., the Temple courtyard], nor a table like the [Temple] table, nor a menorah like the [Temple] menorah. Rather, one may make [a menorah] of five, six, or eight [branches], but one of seven he shall not make."[99] Sages subscribing to such a tradition would probably have preferred to maintain a rigid distinction between synagogue and Temple, an emphasis quite different from—though not necessarily contradictory to—that reflected in the above-noted sources, which clearly attempted to create physical and psychological ties between the two institutions. The many archeological finds of seven-branched *menorot* from late antiquity, including a number of three-dimensional ones, indicate that many communities did not subscribe to (or perhaps know of) these rabbinic restrictions.[100] It is also possible—though difficult to substantiate—that the above prohibition may reflect in the main the attitudes between 70 and 135, when the hopes of the more messianically inclined were still high regarding the restoration of the Temple.[101]

The issue of imitating Temple practices gave rise to disagreements in other areas as well. Apparently, several second-century Galilean rabbis tried to conduct fast-day ceremonies as they were once carried out in the Temple:

> It once happened in the days of R. Ḥalafta and R. Ḥanina b. Teradion that someone led services and completed the entire benediction and no one else responded "Amen" [this being the case in the Temple as well. The *ḥazzan* called out:] "Blow [the *shofar*], priests, blow." [He recited:] "He who answered our father Abraham on Mt. Moriah, He will answer you and will listen to the voice of your cries this day." [The *ḥazzan* then said:] "Blow, sons of Aaron, blow." [He then continued to recite:] He who answered our fathers in the Sea of Reeds, He will answer you and listen to the voice of your cries this day." When the report [of what had happened] came before the sages, they said: "We would not have acted thusly except at the eastern gate of the Temple Mount."[102]

The more expanded Tosefta version adds that R. Ḥalafta instituted this practice in Sepphoris and R. Ḥanina b. Teradion in Sikhni (or Sikhnin).[103] It appears that these two sages were attempting to perpetuate Temple practices, although it is unclear just which com-

99. B Rosh Hashanah 24a-b; B ʿAvodah Zarah 43a; B Menaḥot 28b; Midrash Hagadol, Exodus 20:20 (pp. 410-11); Blidstein, "Prostration and Mosaics," 22.

100. Hachlili, *Art and Archaeology*, 236-56. See also Goodenough, *Jewish Symbols*, IV, 71-98; Sperber, "History of the Menorah," 135-59; Negev, "Chronology," 193-210; L. Levine, "Menorah." It may be significant that the above-noted prohibition was preserved in the Bavli and not in the Yerushalmi. Might this indicate that the Palestinian *amoraim* did not object to such representations or that they saw no reason to do so in light of the popular practice?

101. This line of reasoning finds interesting corroboration on a half-dozen lamps from southern Judaea dating to the period between 70 and 135 C.E. on which the menorah is displayed. Of these, five have more than seven branches (Sussman, *Ornamental Jewish Oil-Lamps*, nos. 1-6).

102. M Taʿanit 2:5.

103. T Taʿanit 1:13 (pp. 327-28). See also Lieberman, *TK*, V, 1075.

ponent(s) of this ceremony constituted a continuation: omitting the response "Amen," according priests a central role in the ritual, reciting these particular prayers, or prostrating oneself in the prayer setting.[104] The aversion of some other sages to perpetuating one or more of these customs in all probability stemmed from the desire to clearly differentiate between Temple and synagogue practice.[105]

Thus, from the various traditions cited above, it would seem that while there was general consensus within rabbinic circles over the synagogue's sanctity, there was less agreement as to the institution's precise status, degree of sanctity, and extent of identification with the Temple. As noted, this issue engaged the wider Jewish community as well. Steps were gradually being taken by various communities throughout the country to steer the synagogue toward sanctification, and it is in the third century that we see the first visible manifestations of this process. The change was indeed a giant step from what the synagogue had been in the pre-70 era, yet still a far cry from what would evolve in the subsequent centuries.

In what appears to be a quintessentially elegant formulation reflecting the ambiguity of the synagogue's new role and the ambivalence in identifying it with the Temple, the third-century R. Isaac defined the synagogue as a מקדש מעט, a diminished or small sanctuary.[106] This formulation gives eloquent expression to the ambiguity: there was indeed something sacred about the synagogue; it was comparable to the מקדש. Yet, it was only a replica of sorts, whose status was not to be confused with that of the Jerusalem Temple itself. In reality, it was diminished—מעט—less than the Temple, not quite as sacred and not quite as special.

SYNAGOGUES IN ROMAN PALESTINE— FURTHER OBSERVATIONS

We have explicit evidence for a large number of synagogues throughout the country in the late Roman era, especially the third and fourth centuries. As noted, remains of synagogues during this period have been discovered not only in the Galilee, but in Judaea and the Shephelah as well. Many cities and even villages undoubtedly had more than one synagogue, as did Alexandria, Rome, and Jerusalem before 70. Pre-135 Betar reputedly had more than 480 such institutions, although this is clearly an inflated figure; Tiberias had thirteen, Sepphoris and its environs possibly eighteen, and Lydda an un-

---

104. On prostration at fast-day ceremonies, see Y 'Avodah Zarah 4, 43d; B Megillah 22a; and comments in Ginzberg, *Commentary*, III, 119–22; Blidstein, "Prostration and Mosaics," 34–36.

105. Blidstein ("Prostration and Mosaics," 35–36) has suggested that opposition to the practice of prostration may also stem from the fact that this practice had become widespread in Christian circles by this time. See also ibid., 22, for several other examples of rabbinic opposition to imitating Temple practices.

106. B Megillah 29a, citing Ezek. 11:16.

defined (but large) number.[107] Even towns and villages such as Gush Ḥalav and Barʿam had at least several such buildings, as has been attested archeologically. Some synagogues were named after the professions of their founders or leading members, such as the Tarsian synagogues in Lydda;[108] others were named after a town or city, presumably the place of origin of those who founded the synagogue, such as the synagogues of the Alexandrians, Cyrenians, Cilicians, and Asians in pre-70 Jerusalem and those of Gophna, Babylonia, Sidon, Tyre, and perhaps Cappadocia attested in Sepphoris.[109] A synagogue may have been named after the section of a city, such as the Kifra and Hammat synagogues in Tiberias.[110] One Tiberian synagogue was named "Boule," either because *boule* members founded it and dominated its affairs, the building was located near the meeting place of the city's *boule*, or the building itself was (or had once been) the meeting place of the city's *boule*.[111] Finally, a synagogue may have been named because of its age (the Old Synagogue or Sarugnaia, south of Tiberias), its size (the Large or Great Synagogue of Sepphoris), or a historical event (the "Synagogue of [the] Rebellion" in Caesarea).[112]

In addition to the above, individual nameless synagogues are mentioned in connection with specific communities, such as those at Maʿon and Migdal near Tiberias and those at Sikhnin, Caesarea, Lydda, Tivʿon, Bet Shean, and Bostra.[113] We also read in rabbinic lit-

---

107. *Betar:* Y Taʿanit 4, 8, 69a; B Gittin 58a. *Tiberias:* B Berakhot 8a. See also B Ḥagigah 15a–b, as well as B Sotah 22a; and Miller, "Number of Synagogues," 55–58. In the eighth century, Tiberias reportedly boasted at least thirty synagogues, which were destroyed in the major earthquake of 749 C.E.; see Avissar, *Sefer Teveria*, 92. On the dating of this earthquake, see Tsafrir and Foerster, "Date of the 'Sabbatical Year Earthquake,'" 357–62. *Sepphoris:* Y Kilʾaim 9, 4, 32b; Y Ketubot 12, 3, 35a; Ecclesiastes Rabbah 7:11; but cf. reservations of Miller, in "Number of Synagogues," 59–63. *Lydda:* Y Sheqalim 5, 6, 49b; Y Peah 8, 21b.

108. Leviticus Rabbah 26:3 (pp. 830–31); B Nazir 53a.

109. *Jerusalem:* T Megillah 2:17 (pp. 352–53)—Alexandrians; Y Megillah 3, 1, 73d—Cyrenians; B Megillah 26a—Cilicians; Acts 6:9—Asians. *Sepphoris:* Y Berakhot 3, 6a; Y Nazir 7, 1, 56a—Gophna; Y Sanhedrin 10, 1, 28a; Y Shabbat 6, 8a; Y Berakhot 5, 1, 9a; Genesis Rabbah 33:3 (p. 305); PRK 25 (p. 381); see also Y Yoma 7, 5, 44b; Y Megillah 4, 5, 75b; and, for medieval evidence, Goitein, *Mediterranean Society,* II, 167—Babylonia; Roth-Gerson, *Greek Inscriptions,* 105–10—Sidon, Tyre; Y Sheviʿit 9, 5, 39a—Cappadocia.

110. *Kifra:* Y Megillah 1, 1, 70a; Pesiqta Rabbati, Supplement B (p. 196b). *Hammat Tiberias:* Y Sotah 1, 4, 16d.

111. Y Sheqalim 7, 3, 50c; Y Taʿanit 1, 2, 64a. Cf. S. Klein, *Galilee,* 99.

112. כנישתא עתיקתא דסרינגית: Y Kilʾaim 9, 32c; Leviticus Rabbah 22:4 (p. 511). PRK :כנישתא רבתה דציפורין 18:5 (p. 297). כנישתא מרדתא דקיסרין: Y Bikkurim 3, 3, 65d; Y Sanhedrin 1, 1, 18a; Y Nazir 7, 1, 56a; Midrash on Samuel 6 (p. 34b); Numbers Rabbah 12:3. A similar phenomenon may be noted in Bursa (Turkey), where a synagogue was named "Gerush" (lit., exile) after the Spanish exiles who founded it. As noted in Chaps. 4 and 8, the community in Rome used names for synagogues in each of the categories listed and also named them after leading historical figures.

113. *Maʿon:* B Yevamot 64b; B Shabbat 139a; B Zevaḥim 118b; see also Y Megillah 3, 2, 74a; B Ḥullin 97a. *Migdal:* Y Megillah 3, 1, 73d. *Sikhnin:* Y Megillah 4, 5, 75b. *Caesarea:* B Yevamot 65b. *Lydda:* Y Sheqalim 5, 6, 49b; Y Peah 8, 9, 21b; Leviticus Rabbah 35:12 (pp. 830–31). *Tivʿon:* T Megillah 2:5 (p. 349); Y Megillah 4, 1, 74c. *Bet Shean:* Y Megillah 3, 4, 74a. *Bostra:* B Shabbat 29b.

erature of synagogues that catered to Greek-speaking communities, presumably located in Palestine, such as the one in Caesarea where the Jews did not know enough Hebrew to recite even the most basic of prayers, the *Shemaʿ*.[114]

There were a number of synagogues in Roman Palestine organized around particular social constituencies, a practice to which the rabbis objected. Undoubtedly, Jewish-Christian communities had their own places of worship, although we know next to nothing about them.[115] Rabbinic traditions exhibit special hostility to the *ʿammei ha-ʾaretz* and their synagogues. This term had borne a series of meanings since biblical times, often strikingly different from one period to another.[116] While any consensus regarding the meaning of the term in the second and third centuries is illusive, it appears to have referred to a large segment of non-rabbinic Jewish society, those at whom the rabbis took umbrage on grounds of what was for them unacceptable religious observance and inadequate study of the Torah. The rabbis identified certain synagogues with these Jews and referred to these places in pejorative terms. In one tradition, the first-century R. Dosa b. Hyrcanus asserts that visiting such synagogues "takes one out of this world."[117] He also equates sitting in their synagogues with behavior such as sleeping in the morning, drinking wine in the afternoon, and engaging in children's talk. As noted above, one second-century source is no less disdainful of the *ʿam ha-ʾaretz*:

> R. Ishmael b. Elʿazar says: "The *ʿammei ha-ʾaretz* die because of two sins—because they call the holy ark *ʾarana* and because they call the synagogue a *bet ʿam* [house of people]."[118]

Clearly, some rabbis objected to what they viewed as a cheapening, perhaps a defilement, of the synagogue's sanctity by these people. Calling a holy ark simply an ark and using the vernacular (i.e., Aramaic), not to mention referring to a synagogue as a *bet ʿam*, obviously appeared to some as highly irreverent. It is hard to explain such hostility for what appears to be mildly deviant behavior;[119] death is not a light curse. Obviously, there is much more to R. Ishmael's attitude toward the *ʿam ha-ʾaretz* than meets the eye. Unfortu-

---

114. T Megillah 3:13 (p. 356); Y Sotah 7, 1, 21b.

115. See Visotzky, *Fathers of the World*, 129–49; Saldarini, "Gospel of Matthew," 26–27; A. Baumgarten, "Literary Evidence for Jewish Christianity," 50. On Jewish Christianity in rabbinic literature generally, see the important remarks of Visotzky, *Fathers of the World*, 129–49. With regard to the seven synagogues on Mt. Zion in the time of Aelia Capitolina, as reported by the Bordeaux Pilgrim (333 C.E.), which presumably belonged to Jewish Christians, see Taylor, *Christians and Holy Places*, 210–20; cf. Mimouni, "La synagogue judéo-chrétienne," 215–34.

116. See Oppenheimer, *ʿAm Ha-aretz*, passim; L. Levine, *Rabbinic Class*, 112–17, and the literature cited therein; Viviano, *Study as Worship*, 42–43.

117. M ʾAvot 3:10. The reading כנסיות in a number of manuscripts (Kaufman, Parma, and the Genizah fragments) amounts to basically the same thing. See my *Rabbinic Class*, 114.

118. B Shabbat 32a; Midrash Hagadol, Genesis 25:24 (p. 439).

119. The rabbis also urged one another never to sit together with these people (B Berakhot 47a) and not to associate with them in any manner (B Pesahim 49b). See above, note 117.

nately, however, there is little more to go on, although we have already noted that several communities (at Dura Europos and Naveh) did, in fact, refer to their ark as an *'arona* or *bet 'arona*. Thus, R. Ishmael's objections were not at all theoretical, and his contempt was similar to that felt at times by intellectual and religious elites toward the unschooled and unsophisticated masses. Such an attitude was widespread among the intelligentsia of antiquity and held true for pagans and Christians no less than for Jews.[120]

We have no way of assessing how widespread the synagogues of the *'ammei ha-'aretz* were. It may be that they were quite well known, certainly in this post-70 stage, and were perhaps even more reflective of what was generally taking place than those synagogues following rabbinic dicta.

Here and there in rabbinic writings we find other expressions of the sages' unhappiness with, and objections to, various synagogue practices. For instance, they excluded laborers from leading services and from participating in the priestly blessing (although the reasons for doing so are unclear), and they objected to inappropriately dressed prayer leaders and the inclusion of certain additions to the service which they considered sectarian.[121] Well known are the steps that the rabbis advocated against a range of sectarians. The introduction into the daily prayer of references to Jewish Christians and other heresies considered dangerous to the Jewish community was a significant step.[122] Rabbinic involvement in this innovation is explicitly documented;[123] what is unclear is whether they were taking the lead in initiating something totally new or merely perpetuating—and further developing—an already existing breach.[124]

Clearly, the rabbis could be quite judgmental of their surroundings. They would often record what they liked and would either criticize or ignore what displeased them. The reality of ancient synagogues, their forms, practices, and organization, is a subject far wider than rabbinic sources permit us to see. While this corpus is of enormous value with regard to the subject at hand, it is also restricted in scope and tendentious in outlook, touching only on limited—albeit important—aspects of the topic. It behooves us to be aware of these limitations.

---

120. See MacMullen, *Paganism*, 8 and nn. 33-36.

121. *Leading services:* T Berakhot 2:9 (pp. 7-8). *Priestly blessing:* B Berakhot 16a. See the explanation of Rashi, loc. cit. The rabbis often looked askance at such workers (see Ayali, *Workers and Artisans*, 95-97), and tensions appear to have been mutual; see Genesis Rabbah 65:15 (p. 728); and the comments of S. Klein, *Galilee*, 107-8. See also S. Krauss, *Synagogale Altertümer*, 194-96. *Inappropriate dress:* M Megillah 4:8. *Sectarian prayer additions:* M Berakhot 5:3; M Megillah 4:8-9.

122. Regarding references to Christians specifically in the synagogues, see John 9:22; 12:42; 16:2; Epiphanius, *Panarion* 29, 9, 2.

123. B Berakhot 28b-29a. See Kimelman, *"Birkat Ha-Minim,"* 226-44; Katz, "Separation of Judaism and Christianity," 63-76. See also Kalmin, "Christians and Heretics," 155-69.

124. See Lieberman, *TK*, I, 53-54; Flusser, "Jewish Religion," 23-24.

B yzantine Palestine (fourth to seventh centuries) witnessed the continued evolution and development of the synagogue and provided a rich context in which to
understand additional dimensions of this institution. Synagogue remains from
this period exist in greater numbers and in more geographical areas than do
those from earlier periods; indeed, this period constitutes a peak in synagogue development as reflected in its architectural, artistic, and epigraphical remains. The synagogue
building acquired an ever more distinctive religious character, and synagogue liturgy
continued to expand, becoming more inclusive as well as more standardized.

These changes were not merely a continuation of the past. Rather, a new element was
being introduced into Byzantine Palestine at this time which not only affected the climate
of Jewish life generally, but also had a significant impact on the synagogue, its appearance,
status, and modus operandi. This new element was Christianity, whose growing dominance in the course of the fourth century and whose dramatically expanding presence in
Palestine could not help but impact on Jewish life in a profound way. At best, it stimulated
and fructified various aspects of Jewish life; at worst, it was a disruptive, threatening, and
at times even destructive force. By the turn of the fifth century, and with increasing frequency in the sixth, Jews, Judaism, and the synagogue were being assaulted on a number
of fronts throughout the Empire. Church legislation attacked Jews and Jewish practices,
Imperial edicts became more restrictive, and Christian preachers fulminated against a

religion and people they regarded as anachronistic, loathsome, and rejected by God. On occasion, mobs were incited against the Jews, resulting in damage, loss of lives, and either the desecration or outright destruction of synagogues.[1] Imperial legislation was invoked on a regular basis to try to prevent such destruction.[2] In some cases, Christians confiscated synagogues and converted them into churches, as was the case, for example, in Stobi, Gerasa, and Apamea according to archeological remains and in Callinicum, Ravenna, and elsewhere in Italy, Mauretania, Spain, Gaul, Syria, and Minorca per our literary sources.[3]

Nevertheless, despite this litany of anti-Jewish words and deeds, we have become well aware that sermons were often not heeded nor legislation always enforced. Despite official restrictions, the Jews of Byzantine Palestine continued to build synagogues (e.g., Merot, Capernaum, Bet Alpha, Qatzrin), repair those already standing (e.g., Chorazim, Ḥammat Tiberias, 'En Gedi), and entirely rebuild and refurbish others after a period of abandonment and disrepair (Nevoraya). In many instances, it was only in its last stages (i.e., the sixth and seventh centuries) that a synagogue building reached its greatest dimensions (e.g., Ḥammat Tiberias, 'En Gedi, Nevoraya, Ḥorvat Rimmon, Ḥammat Gader). In several regions, synagogues were erected in large numbers where none, or at least very few, seem to have existed before. On the periphery of Judaea (to the east and west and especially in the southern part of the region) a dozen or so synagogues have been discovered

---

1. Baron, *Social and Religious History of the Jews*, II, 207-9; III, 4-18; Parkes, *Conflict of Church and Synagogue*, 163-95, 263-69; Simon, *Verus Israel*, 202-33; Avi-Yonah, *Jews of Palestine*, 208-31; Ben-Sasson, *Trial and Achievement*, 3-12.

2. The earliest such legislation was in evidence in 393 C.E. (*Cod. Theod.* 16, 8, 9 [Linder, *Jews in Roman Imperial Legislation*, 137-38]) and continued in 397 (16, 8, 12 [143-44]), 412 (16, 8, 20 [190-92]), 420 (16, 8, 21 [205-8]), and 423 (16, 8, 25 [208-9]). See also the law from 438 C.E. (Linder, *Jews in Roman Imperial Legislation*, 323ff.). That such legislation was often ineffective is clear not only from the need to reissue protective laws, but also from the numerous cases of synagogue destruction. Incidents are reported to have occurred in Rome, Constantinople, Edessa, Sicily, Sardinia, North Africa, Alexandria, Antioch, and northern Italy. See Parkes, *Conflict of Church and Synagogue*, 187, 212-14, 236-38, 250-51. In Palestine as well it is reported that the early fifth century witnessed the destruction of synagogues and temples as Barsauma and some forty other monks went on a rampage which supposedly lasted for some years (ibid., 230). See also Simon, *Verus Israel*, 225; Avi-Yonah, *Jews of Palestine*, 218; and below, Chap. 8. On the destruction of pagan shrines by zealous Christians, see Trombley, *Hellenic Religions and Christianization*, I, 123ff., 207ff., 342ff.; Liebeschuetz, *Antioch*, 237-39. On the other hand, Imperial restrictions on the building of synagogues were often not implemented, as was the case later on, in the Middle Ages, under Islamic rule (Assis, "Synagogues in Medieval Spain," 8).

3. Juster, *Juifs*, 464 n. 3; Parkes, *Conflict of Church and Synagogue*, 166-68, 187, 204-7, 225-29, 244, 263; Simon, *Verus Israel*, 225-29; Avi-Yonah, *Jews of Palestine*, 218-20; Bradbury, *Severus of Minorca*, 30, 2 (p. 123) and 130 n. 25. On the conversion of temples into churches, see Trombley, *Hellenic Religions and Christianization*, I, 108ff., 123ff.; II, 377ff. There were also instances where attempts were made to protect Jewish rights and to use Jewish synagogues, as was the case with Gregory and the Terracinan Jewish community; see Katz, "Pope Gregory and the Jews," 120-22. For a recent overview, see Braun, "Jews in the Late Roman Empire," 142-71.

to date.[4] Given Hadrian's prohibition of Jewish settlement in the Jerusalem environs,[5] the extensive destruction in Judaea in the aftermath of the Bar-Kokhba revolt, and the strong Galilean focus of rabbinic literature, the number of Judaean synagogues found to date is indeed surprising. The most unexpected discoveries, however, have been in the Golan, where all but one (Gamla) of the twenty-five synagogues uncovered to date appear to have flourished in the Byzantine era.[6] In fact, practically all Palestinian synagogues known to date from archeological excavations stem from the Byzantine period. Most were built at that time, but even those constructed earlier, in the third century, continued to function throughout most, if not all, of this period.[7]

The very existence of Byzantine synagogue remains at well over one hundred sites has been the main catalyst in reassessing this entire historical period regarding Jewish life in the Holy Land. Since the beginning of Jewish historiography in the nineteenth century, this era was considered the dawn of the "Dark Ages" for the Jews of Palestine. Jewish life was then viewed as being in steady decline after the destruction of the Temple in the first century. Crises in subsequent centuries served only to exacerbate this trend: the failure of the Bar-Kokhba revolt and Hadrian's persecutions in the second century; the Empire-wide anarchy and instability of the third century; the rise of Christianity and the beginning of anti-Jewish legislation in the fourth century; and, finally, the disappearance of the Patriarchate in the fifth.[8] Even the partially and perhaps hastily edited form of the Yerushalmi, especially when compared to its more polished Babylonian counterpart, has usually been interpreted as an indication of the sudden closure of this enterprise in the face of impending disaster.[9] Therefore, to find that Jews throughout the Byzantine era were building synagogues everywhere, often on a grand and imposing scale, requires a major reevaluation of this period.

There is probably no more striking example of the new perception of this period as one of relative stability and at times even of remarkable prosperity for the Jews than the synagogue at Capernaum (fig. 19). This building, monumental in size and ornate in decoration, was completed in the plan as we know it today only in the latter part of the fifth century, i.e., well into the Byzantine era.[10] The building's prominence was enhanced by

---

4. Z. Ilan, *Ancient Synagogues*, 254-321, which also includes a number of dubious identifications.

5. Eusebius, *Ecclesiastical History* 4, 6, 4; Justin, *Dialogue with Trypho* 16, idem, *First Apology* 47; Schürer, *History*, I, 553-55.

6. Z. Ilan, *Ancient Synagogues*, 61-113; Ma'oz, "Art and Architecture of the Synagogues of the Golan," 98-115; idem, *NEAEHL*, II, 538-45; Hachlili, Jewish Art from the Golan," 183-212. Cf., however, the assumption of an earlier, late Roman date for some synagogue sites by Urman (*Golan*, 80-116; Gregg and Urman, *Jews, Pagans and Christians*, 305-10).

7. The Second Temple synagogues that never survived the revolt of 66 are excluded.

8. See, for example, Graetz, *History of the Jews*, II, 559ff.; Baron, *Social and Religious History of the Jews*, II, 172-75, 209-14; Avi-Yonah, *Jews of Palestine*, 275.

9. Ginzberg, *Jewish Law and Lore*, 24-29.

10. Corbo, *Cafarnao*, 113-69.

19. Aerial view of the Capernaum synagogue, looking northeast. The courtyard lies to the east.

the artificially raised podium on which it stood, dwarfing the nearby church of St. Peter, which was also built in the fifth century.[11]

This picture of a dynamic and expansive Jewish community in Byzantine Palestine has received confirmation from an entirely unexpected source. Documents from the Cairo Genizah have established that many works formerly dated to the early Middle Ages were actually written in the Byzantine era, and certain literary genres—once thought to have been the products of later centuries—in reality made their first appearance at that time. Synagogue poetry, the *piyyut*, originated in Palestine between the fourth and fifth centuries; the earliest amoraic *midrashim* were edited then; the Hekhalot mystical traditions began crystallizing at about this time; a number of apocalyptic works were composed around the turn of the seventh century; and many targumic traditions took shape from the fourth century onward.[12]

11. Corbo, *House of St. Peter*, 16–18. See Brent, "Christianisierung," 15–28.

12. *Piyyut:* Heinemann and Petuchowski, *Literature of the Synagogue*, 207–8; Dan, *City in Eretz-Israel*, 32–40; *Midrash:* Strack and Stemberger, *Introduction to Talmud and Midrash*, 300ff. *Hekhalot:* Stemberger, "Non-Rabbinic Literature," 30–36. *Apocalyptic literature:* Ibn Shmuel, *Midreshei Geulah*; Baron, *Social and Religious History of the Jews*, III, 16–17. *Targum:* Hayward, "Date of Targum Pseudo-Jonathan," 7–30; Shinan, "Dating Targum Pseudo-Jonathan," 109–16; idem, *Embroidered Targum*, 11–15, 193–98.

Thus, synagogue finds are not the only component in this reevaluation. The Byzantine period generally is now accorded a far different appraisal than that which was normative earlier; it was not a post-Classical era of decline, but rather an era that generated new forms and institutions, as well as a new cultural and spiritual focus, while continuing many traditions from the past.[13] Many Palestinian cities, though perhaps less lavishly ornamented than their precursors, reached their apogee of physical growth precisely during late antiquity; the total number of settlements (villages, towns, and cities) increased significantly, and, in general, the eastern Mediterranean world flourished.[14] The earlier picture of a cultural wasteland characterized by political decline and economic decay has now been replaced by a radically different understanding of this era.

DIVERSITY

The flourishing Jewish life attested by synagogue finds reflects a rich diversity among the country's regions and communities. Beginning with the material remains, the vast majority of scholars today have eschewed the rigid classification of synagogues which once linked typology with chronology.[15] Whereas it was once assumed that synagogues built in the Byzantine period were basilical in form, following the contemporary church model, today not only are we aware of a far richer variety of such basilical types than before,[16] but we also know of other synagogue types that were either being refurbished or even built anew at this time. Merot, Nevoraya, and probably Chorazim and Capernaum were constructed between the fourth and sixth centuries following a "Galilean" model; broadhouse-type synagogues were being built in the third to fifth centuries (Susiya, Eshtemoa, Ma'on, 'Anim, Ḥorvat Rimmon, and perhaps Ḥammat Tiberias, Yafia, and Kefar Ḥananiah); and a variety of buildings, all more or less under Galilean influence, were being constructed in the Byzantine Golan.[17]

A striking example of this marked diversity among synagogues is evident in the Bet Shean area. To date, we know of five contemporaneous synagogue buildings that func-

---

13. See the companion volumes by Cameron, *Later Roman Empire* and *Mediterranean World*, as well as Brown's *World of Late Antiquity*, 22ff., 96ff., 137ff. For a critique of Gibbon's account of the Byzantine era (*Decline and Fall of the Roman Empire*) in light of the current understanding of late antiquity, see Vryonis, "Hellas Revisited," 92–118.

14. On Caesarea, see, for example, Holum et al., *King Herod's Dream*, 162–99; Tsafrir, "Notes on Settlement and Demography," 269–83; and Cameron, *Mediterranean World*, 152–86; Downey, *Antioch*, 317ff.

15. For a fuller discussion of the matter, see below, Chap. 9.

16. This is what Avi-Yonah ("Ancient Synagogues," 41) calls a "bewildering variety." See also Foerster, "Ancient Synagogues," 40–41; idem, "Dating Synagogues with a 'Basilical' Plan," 88–92; Tsafrir, *Archaeology and Art*, 285–99.

17. Ma'oz, "Art and Architecture of the Synagogues of the Golan," 98–115; and above, note 6.

tioned in the sixth-century Bet Shean region.[18] To date, no other urban setting boasts such a concentration of remains having not only geographical but also chronological propinquity. The synagogues referred to are Bet Shean A, just north of the city wall; Bet Shean B, near the southwestern city-gate; Bet Alpha, to the west; Ma'oz Ḥayyim, to the east; and Reḥov, to the south. However, despite the fact that all these buildings functioned at one and the same time, they are, in fact, remarkably different from one another in a variety of ways.

Let us compare three aspects of these buildings: architectural plan, art, and inscriptions (i.e., language and culture).

Architectural Plan. Three of these buildings (Bet Shean A, Bet Alpha, and Ma'oz Ḥayyim in its later stages) are apsidal basilicas; Reḥov is a basilica-type building, but with a raised *bima* at its southern end flanked by two side rooms; and Bet Shean B is a kind of chapel or prayer room—a simple, almost square room, possibly with a niche (of which little remains) in the direction of Jerusalem. Reḥov and Bet Alpha have a narthex in the north; Bet Shean A has auxiliary rooms on a number of sides, but no narthex has been recovered; and Ma'oz Ḥayyim has a side entrance and no narthex.

The most stunning variation, and indeed a striking exception to the norm at Bet Shean and elsewhere, is the orientation of Bet Shean A. This building faces northwest; i.e., its apse is in this direction, while its entrances face southeast. Various theories have been put forth to explain this apparent deviation, ranging from its being a Samaritan synagogue[19] or some kind of sectarian building to the congregation's aversion to facing the

---

18. Chiat, *Handbook of Synagogue Architecture*, 121–44; idem, "Synagogue and Church Architecture," 6–24; Z. Ilan, *Ancient Synagogues*, 169ff.; and, for specific sites, Hüttenmeister and Reeg, *Antiken Synagogen; NEAEHL*. See also Roth-Gerson, *Greek Inscriptions*, nos. 4–9. For a recent presentation of the Reḥov findings, see Vitto, "Interior Decoration," 293–97.

19. Whether this building is a Jewish or a Samaritan synagogue has been a subject of controversy for years. The excavator Zori ("Ancient Synagogue at Beth-Shean," 73) posits a Jewish identification of this building, while Hüttenmeister and Reeg (*Antiken Synagogen*, II, 574–75) as well as Foerster ("Ancient Synagogues of the Galilee," 313; cf. also *NEAEHL*, I, 234) argue for a Samaritan identification; a noncommittal position is espoused by Naveh (*On Stone and Mosaic*, 76–77). See also Chiat, *Handbook of Synagogue Architecture*, 131–32; Z. Ilan, *Ancient Synagogues*, 180–81. The Samaritan identification stems primarily from an inscription in Samaritan, i.e., in the paleo-Hebraic script used exclusively by the Samaritans at this time, that was discovered in a side room of the building. Jacoby ("Responses," 130–31) has added two further considerations in favor of this being a Samaritan synagogue: the absence of animal figures in the panel depicting the Torah shrine (especially when the decorations are compared to those in the nearby Bet Alpha synagogue, which was executed by the same artisans) and the absence of the *lulav* and *ethrog*. Both, she claims, reflect Samaritan beliefs. The first claim, however, is questionable, as panels depicting religious symbols in many Jewish synagogues (e.g., Ḥammat Tiberias) are also devoid of figural representation. Thus, the absence of figures in this particular context proves very little, other than indicating congregational preference. However, her second point, the absence of the *lulav* and *ethrog*, is more persuasive. Samaritans interpret the biblical reference to the four species (Lev. 23:39–44)

synagogue south, in the direction of Tel Bet Shean, where pagan temples and later a Byzantine church were located. However, it also may be that too much has been made of this apparent deviation. Then, as now, there may have been all sorts of extenuating circumstances (e.g., topography or the particular layout of the plot of land) that influenced the founders to so position the building and justified (in their eyes at least) such a deviation from the generally accepted practice. Whatever the reason, this building shares many characteristics with other known synagogues, and even its northwestern orientation has been duplicated by the newly discovered Sepphoris synagogue, which also faces in this direction.[20] Moreover, other synagogues display a variety of deviations from the generally accepted Jerusalem orientation; thus, the perception of the uniqueness of this synagogue's orientation has become somewhat attenuated over the years.[21]

Art. The range of artistic representation in the Bet Shean synagogues is about as broad as one could imagine, from strictly conservative to strikingly liberal. At the former end of the spectrum stands the Reḥov building, where the only decorations are of a geometric nature, except for one plaster fragment depicting the facade of a building (the Ark of the Covenant?) and a menorah.[22] In Bet Shean A, the geometric patterns on several panels are complemented by another one containing religious symbols of the Torah shrine (here resembling the entrance to a building more than other parallel designs), two *menorot*, *shofarot*, *lulavim*, *ethrogim*, and incense shovels. The Maʿoz Ḥayyim synagogue also features geometric patterns, several representations of birds, and a few religious symbols.

The mosaic floor in the prayer room of the Bet Shean B synagogue, with its inhabited scrolls, features figural representations of animals along with an elaborate floral motif

---

to mean not four separate items (which was the Jews' interpretation) but parts of the *sukkah*. Thus, their absence as independent items is not surprising, and we may well have here a distinctively Samaritan feature. Still and all, a Samaritan identification is not certain, and the latest excavations at el-Khirbe and Khirbet Samara by Magen ("Samaritan Synagogues" [Eng.], 193-230) have even further beclouded the issue. The newly discovered mosaic floors from these two Samaritan synagogues are quite different from the Bet Shean A panel. For example, at Bet Shean two *menorot* flank the ark, a *parokhet* (curtain) covers a portal and not an ark, and the *parokhet* is not gathered to one side, while a symmetrical display of a shofar and incense shovel is found alongside the *menorot*. None of these features is duplicated in the two newly discovered Samaritan buildings.

This Bet Shean synagogue will thus be included in the discussion, albeit with some reservations. In any case, neither its inclusion nor its exclusion will affect the overall picture of diversity, since—orientation aside—this building does not represent an extreme example of Jewish architectural, artistic, or cultural tendencies among the Bet Shean synagogues. The Samaritans were probably no less scrupulous about positioning their synagogues than were the Jews; thus, a northwesterly direction presents problems in either case.

20. Weiss and Netzer, *Promise and Redemption*, 12-13.

21. See below, Chap. 9. See also Naveh, *On Stone and Mosaic*, no. 26; Z. Ilan, *Ancient Synagogues*, 180-82; *NEAEHL*, loc. cit.; Chiat, *Handbook of Synagogue Architecture*, 128-32.

22. See Vitto, "Interior Decoration," 293-96.

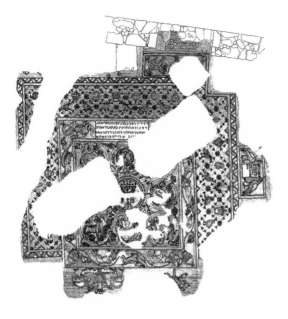

20. Mosaic floor of the prayer room
in Bet Shean B. Note the menorah
in the center.

(fig. 20). This prayer chapel and a large room nearby appear to have shared a common courtyard, leading many to assume that these rooms were part of either a large synagogue complex or a wealthy individual's home which also included a prayer room. If the latter, this situation might have been similar to that in Stobi,[23] where Claudius Tiberius Polycharmos designated a part of his house be used as a synagogue by the local Jewish community. These two sites may be examples of what rabbinic literature refers to as "the synagogue of an individual."[24] The mosaic floor of this large, nearby room is most unusual. One of its panels features scenes from Homer's *Odyssey*, while a second depicts the god of the Nile together with Nilotic motifs (i.e., a series of animals and fish) and a symbolic representation of Alexandria with its customary Nilometer. Between these two panels is a third one, containing a Greek dedicatory inscription naming one Leontis as the benefactor or owner of the building.

Sharing Bet Shean B's inclination toward expansive artistic representation is the Bet Alpha synagogue, rich in its diversity, Jewish content, and pagan motifs. Its well-known mosaic floor consists of three main panels surrounded by geometric borders. One of the panels includes the same religious motifs appearing in Bet Shean A, although here birds flank the shrine (as do lions in the inscription at the northern end of the pavement). The central panel depicts Helios, the zodiac signs, and the four seasons (fig. 21), while the

---

23. See below, Chap. 8.

24. בית הכנסת של יחיד—Y Megillah 3, 4, 74a.

21. The central panel in the Bet Alpha mosaic floor depicting the four seasons, zodiac signs, and Helios in the center.

third panel illustrates the biblical narrative of the Binding of Isaac (Gen. 22). Although the same artisans, Marianos and his son Ḥanina, laid the mosaic floors at both Bet Alpha and Bet Shean A, the style and content at each location are strikingly different. Clearly, various types of pattern books were in circulation, leading to very different floors.

Thus, the floors of these five contemporaneous Bet Shean synagogues demonstrate a wide diversity, ranging from the strictly aniconic on the one hand to elaborate representations of Jewish and non-Jewish figural motifs on the other.

Inscriptions. The linguistic and cultural ambience of these communities, as reflected in their inscriptions, also varies widely.[25] Not surprisingly, Reḥov is the most conservative, with primarily Hebrew and some Aramaic inscriptions. The inscription from Maʿoz Ḥayyim contains only one Hebrew word, *Shalom;* Bet Shean A has a number of Greek in-

---

25. For these inscriptions, see Naveh, *On Stone and Mosaic;* Roth-Gerson, *Greek Inscriptions.*

22. Greek (upper) and Aramaic (lower) inscriptions from the Bet Alpha synagogue.

scriptions and a paleo-Hebrew (Samaritan?) one, while Bet Shean B and Bet Alpha have Greek and Aramaic inscriptions (fig. 22). The Aramaic inscription at Bet Alpha preserves the date of construction, i.e., the time of Justin, probably referring to Justin I (518–27 C.E.). The Greek inscription at this site notes the names of Marianos and Ḥanina, artisans (τεχνῖτε) who, as noted above, are also named in an inscription at Bet Shean A.[26]

The differences in these communities' cultural proclivities are no less striking than their differences in languages. Not only did Reḥov avoid using Greek, but the contents of its inscriptions are quintessentially Jewish. As noted, fragmentary inscriptions found on the columns and walls appear to have been blessings for various occasions,[27] and the monumental twenty-nine-line, 365-word mosaic inscription in the narthex is entirely halakhic in content (fig. 23). An almost identical inscription (as yet unpublished) appears on the plaster of one of the synagogue's columns, making these two sui generis among synagogue epigraphical evidence anywhere. Contrast this with the Homeric and Alexandrian scenes on the Leontis floor or with the Helios and zodiac depictions from Bet Alpha. Moreover, the Bet Alpha mosaic presents an intriguing balance of Jewish motifs on the one hand and those drawn from the surrounding culture on the other. The zodiac panel is placed between two others, each having a distinctly Jewish bent—one with religious symbols and imagery and the other with the Binding of Isaac narrative. Taken together with the Alexandrian and Homeric motifs, Bet Shean B is probably the most hellenized of all these local synagogues. In fact, an Aramaic inscription in the prayer room itself contains a number of linguistic mistakes which, according to Kutscher, most likely reflect a highly acculturated stratum of Palestinian Jewry.[28]

There was undoubtedly a great deal of diversity among ancient synagogues outside of

26. Roth-Gerson, *Greek Inscriptions*, nos. 4, 5.

27. Z. Ilan, *Ancient Synagogues*, 186–87.

28. Kutscher, *Language of Isaiah Scroll*, 57–60.

23. The halakhic inscription from the Reḥov synagogue.

Bet Shean as well. This would have been especially true of synagogues in urban centers, which might have differed considerably from one another in their architectural styles, language, and use of motifs, given their varying constituencies. Archeological evidence from other urban centers, however, is sparse, and thus any comparisons with Bet Shean are almost impossible to make. The remains of three buildings have been excavated in Tiberias: the famous Severus synagogue excavated in 1961–63, another synagogue excavated by Slousch in 1921, and a third excavated by Berman and On in 1989. While the latter two are either poorly documented or poorly preserved, the few finds there seem to indicate that these buildings differed in plan, decorations, and other features.[29] Similarly with regard to Sepphoris. Aside from the recently discovered synagogue, with its mosaic floor rich in artistic motifs and inscriptions, we know of only one fifth-century Greek inscription which originated in another synagogue, probably located in another part of the city. It speaks of leaders from several communities in Phoenicia who settled in the city.[30] Finally, only one synagogue has been excavated in Caesarea, although a number

---

29. *NEAEHL*, II, 574–77; Z. Ilan, *Ancient Synagogues*, 139–43, 146–47.
30. Roth-Gerson, *Greek Inscriptions*, no. 24.

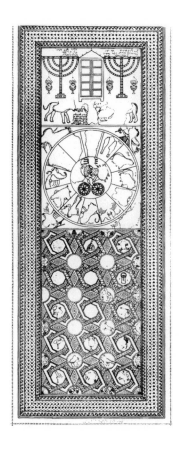

24. The mosaic floor at Naʿaran.

of inscriptions, as well as rabbinic sources relating to local synagogues, seem to point to other types of synagogues there.[31]

Even in a place like Jericho, there seem to have been striking differences between neighboring synagogues. A sixth-century synagogue there was demonstrably aniconic in its decorations, featuring geometric patterns and a stylized ark. Yet, several kilometers away and at about the same time, Naʿaran boasted a zodiac design, a representation of the biblical Daniel, and an assortment of animal depictions (fig. 24). Both synagogues, however, bore Aramaic or Hebrew inscriptions; Greek is not in evidence. The Golan region also reflects a variety of attitudes toward figural art and has a considerable amount of figural representation.[32]

Outside the main urban centers of Byzantine Palestine, one is struck by the very

---

31. Ibid., nos. 25–29; L. Levine, "Synagogue Officials."

32. Maʿoz, "Art and Architecture of the Synagogues of the Golan," 109–12; idem, *Jewish Art in the Golan*; Hachlili, "Jewish Art from the Golan," 183–212.

noticeable regional differences within the country. The structures which dominate the Galilee feature monumental facades facing Jerusalem, relief carvings, flagstone pavements, two or three rows of columns, few inscriptions or Jewish motifs, and occasionally a permanent *bima*. The Golan synagogues are built of basalt, oriented internally to either the south or the west, and characterized by a richly decorated single entrance (Dikke excepted), a limited repertoire of motifs (the menorah, geometric patterns, a variety of animals [eagles, lions, fish, snakes], as well as some human figures, including Nikes), and a score of inscriptions, mostly in Aramaic and Hebrew.[33] The synagogues further south, in the Jordan Valley, Hebron hills, and Shephelah, generally follow a basilical plan, although even here there was a great deal of diversity.[34] Some buildings had an apse, niche, or *bima*, or a combination thereof. The use of figural representation, as well as of Greek, Aramaic, and Hebrew, also varied considerably (fig. 25). By and large, it can be said that figural representations and use of Greek were ubiquitous in hellenized urban settings and much less common in rural and more isolated regions. Thus, the less accessible Upper Galilee was considerably more conservative in such matters than the Lower Galilee, with its cities and major roads,[35] and southern Judaea, including 'En Gedi, was generally less receptive to figural representations than were communities in the coastal region.

Diversity among synagogues, however, not only was external, but went well beyond facades, plans, art, and language. It is clear, for example, that synagogue liturgy likewise varied from region to region at this time. To date, we know of a number of different customs for reading the Torah and haftarah, and the prayer service may have differed from locale to locale, as was surely the case with the use of *piyyutim* or the types of *targumim* and sermons offered.[36]

FIGURAL ART

The abundance of Jewish art from the synagogues of the Byzantine period tells us much about the institution and its adaptation by different communities. The media of artistic expression utilized in these synagogues are varied and include stone moldings, mosaic floors, and frescoes. The forms of expression range from simple geometric and floral shapes to human and even mythological figures.[37]

The figural representations themselves are quite varied; at times they consist only of birds ('En Gedi, Ma'oz Hayyim), an assortment of animals (Ma'on-Nirim, Gaza, Bet

33. Hachlili, "Jewish Art from the Golan," 183–212.

34. Kloner, "Ancient Synagogues: Archeological Survey," 11–18; Foerster, "Ancient Synagogues," 38–42.

35. E. M. Meyers, "Galilean Regionalism," 93–101.

36. Shinan, "Sermons, Targums and Reading from Scriptures," 97ff.; see below, Chap. 16.

37. For this and what follows, see Hachlili, *Art and Archaeology-Israel*, 200–24. See also the detailed note of Baron, *Social and Religious History of the Jews* (1937 ed.), 51–53 n. 15.

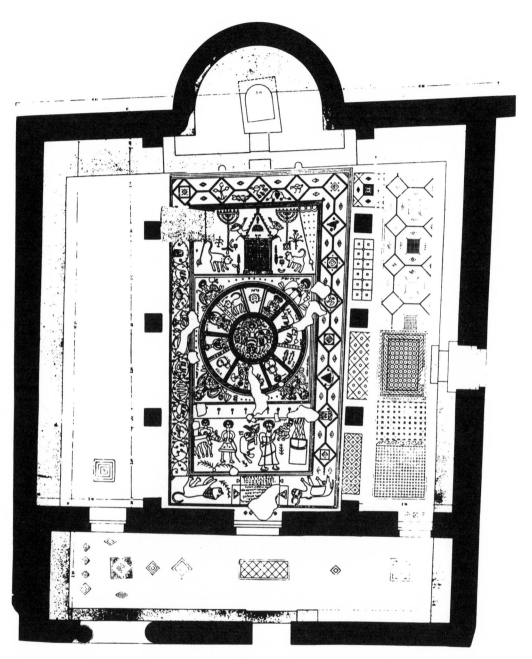

25. Plan and mosaics of the Bet Alpha synagogue.

Shean B, Yafia, Chorazim), and, not infrequently, human representations. A common pattern in this last category is that of the four seasons, zodiac signs, and a representation of the sun god appearing on a series of mosaic floors (Ḥammat Tiberias, Bet Alpha, Ḥuseifa, Naʿaran, and perhaps Susiya).[38] Zodiac depictions have been identified, albeit arguably, on stone fragments from Merot and Barʿam. Other human depictions appear in various biblical scenes (see below).

The ubiquity of such figural representations in synagogue art, as well as in the necropolis of Bet Sheʿarim, has indeed revolutionized our understanding of Jewish attitudes toward this type of artistic expression.[39] Before the deluge of archeological discoveries beginning with Bet Alpha (1928–29), Dura Europos (1932), and Bet Sheʿarim (beginning in 1936), it was assumed that Jews did not engage in figural art, or at least did so only on rare occasions. The apparent prohibition of the second commandment, together with a number of Josephus' accounts regarding Jewish aversion to figural representations in the late Second Temple period, particularly in Jerusalem,[40] essentially determined the matter. However, with the steady accumulation of archeological material over the past several generations, and particularly following the publication of Goodenough's monumental work on Jewish symbols in the 1950s and 1960s, this issue has been completely reevaluated, and the resulting picture is far more complex.[41]

Today, we can safely conclude that Jews in the biblical and early Second Temple periods did, in fact, make use of a variety of figural representations. Examples from the biblical period include the cherubs over the holy ark, those woven into the Tabernacle *parokhet*, the cherubs and animal figures used by Solomon in his Temple and palace decorations, and the twelve oxen supporting the large basin in the Temple courtyard.[42] Moreover, the bronze serpent attributed to Moses, the golden calves in the northern sanctuaries of Dan and Beth-el, and innumerable figurines and seal engravings (e.g., of lions, horses, gazelles, cocks, snakes, and monkeys) found at Israelite sites and dating primarily to the eighth and seventh centuries B.C.E. all point to a generally permissive attitude toward this art form in the First Temple era.[43] From the late Persian and early Hellenistic periods, the "Yehud" coins minted in Jerusalem feature a wide variety of figural representations, including owls, eagles, a winged leaping animal, a Persian king, a divine figure sitting on a winged wheel, a warrior, a governor, a high priest, and depictions of Ptolemy, Berenice,

---

38. Hachlili, *Art and Archaeology-Israel*, 301–9; idem, "Zodiac," 61–76; Goodenough, *Jewish Symbols*, VIII, 167–218. At Sepphoris, the sun is depicted above the chariot.

39. See L. Levine, "Finds from Beth-Shearim," 277–81.

40. See, for example, *Antiquities* 17, 149–63; 18, 55–59, 262ff.

41. Avigad, *Beth Sheʿarim*, III, 275–87. See also Schubert, "Jewish Pictorial Traditions," 147–59.

42. Ex. 25:20; 36:35; I Kgs. 7:23ff.

43. Num. 21:9; II Kgs. 18:4; I Kgs. 12:26–33; A. Mazar, *Archaeology of the Land of the Bible*, 501–7; Isserlin, "Israelite Art," 44–50.

26. An eagle appearing on a
Yehud coin (fourth century B.C.E.).

and Athena (fig. 26).⁴⁴ Even at the turn of the second century B.C.E., the Tobiad Hyrcanus used a variety of carved animal reliefs when building his estate east of the Jordan River.⁴⁵

However, beginning in the later Hellenistic or Hasmonean period, the pendulum swung sharply in the opposite direction. Strict avoidance of animal and human depictions became the norm in Jewish society for about three hundred years, commencing with the rise of the Hasmoneans and lasting until the aftermath of the Bar-Kokhba revolt (ca. 150 B.C.E.-150 C.E.).⁴⁶ The reasons for this radical about-face with respect to figural representation are not entirely clear (fig. 27). Various suggestions have been put forth: (1) a traumatic reaction to the 167 B.C.E. desecration of the Temple by Antiochus IV, which included coercive pagan worship; (2) a more stringent position in this regard reflecting the attitude of the Sadducees, who were generally in control of affairs in Jewish Palestine in the late Second Temple period (except for the era of Salome, 76-67 B.C.E., when the Pharisees dominated); (3) the result of Hasmonean policy, which aimed, in part, at cultivating unique Jewish modes of expression and may have included art as well; and (4) a Jewish reaction to hellenization and the threat of foreign influences.⁴⁷

44. Meshorer, *Ancient Jewish Coinage*, I, 13-34; idem, *Treasury*, 11-27; Barag, "Coin of Bagoas," 97-99; idem, "Silver Coin," 4-14. It is interesting to note that in the Persian period, although Jewish society was largely isolationist, at least as far as our literary sources indicate, Judaean coins were heavily influenced by foreign motifs, including what appear as rather daring figural representations. In contrast, the later Hasmonean era witnessed a great deal of Hellenistic influence, especially within the ruling elite, although its coins and other forms of artistic representation were strictly aniconic.

45. *NEAEHL*, II, 647-48.

46. This figural avoidance is evident first and foremost in the coins of the era; see Meshorer, *Ancient Jewish Coinage*, I, 35-98; II, 5-165. See also Avigad, *Discovering Jerusalem*, 144-50; Kon, "Jewish Art," 60-64; Hachlili, *Art and Archaeology-Israel*, 65-119.

47. M. Smith, "Goodenough's 'Jewish Symbols,'" 60. See also Simon (*Verus Israel*, 23), who writes as follows: "When the older Judaism therefore rigorously excluded *all* images, whatever their object, its

27. Coin of John Hyrcanus.
Obverse: paleo-Hebrew inscription.
Reverse: double cornucopias
with a pomegranate.

Thus, the reintroduction of figural representation beginning in the late second and third centuries C.E. first evidenced at Bet She'arim is far from exceptional in the wider perspective of Jewish history. It reflects yet another shift of the pendulum with regard to Jewish attitudes toward figural representation owing to internal needs and in response to the wider cultural, social, and political contexts in which the Jews of Palestine found themselves (fig. 28). Here, too, a number of suggestions (not necessarily mutually exclusive) have been offered to explain the reintroduction of figural motifs: the ever increasing hellenization of the Jewish population; the Jews' more defined minority status, which made the need for social, economic, and cultural accommodation to the outside world ever more pressing; and the decline of paganism and the acceptance of the view that such images were not necessarily a threat to Jews and Judaism.[48]

---

rigor was due in part to an excessive caution and to a desire to withhold all temptation, and in part to the need to distinguish its usage from that of the pagans, who made very free use of images. The prohibition was thus one of the means whereby Israel deliberately accentuated the difference between itself and the gentiles." See also Avi-Yonah, "Jewish Art and Architecture," 250–63; idem, *Oriental Art in Roman Palestine*, 13–27; Avigad, *Beth She'arim*, III, 277–78; B. Cohen, "Art in Jewish Law," 167.

Nevertheless, here, as elsewhere, exceptions are in evidence, especially from the Herodian era. A few depictions of fish and birds appear among the archeological remains from the Jewish quarter, while Herod (on one occasion) and some of his descendants (Philip and Agrippa I) used figures on some of their coins, as did Antipas in his palace in Tiberias. See Avigad, *Discovering Jerusalem*, 150, 169; Meshorer, *Ancient Jewish Coinage*, II, 29, 44–46, 60–61; Josephus, *Life* 65–66. Finally, an enigmatic statement in the Tosefta ('Avodah Zarah 5:2 [p. 468]) claims that stamps or seals bearing images—except of humans—were known in Jerusalem.

48. See Simon, *Verus Israel*, 23–27; Urbach, "Rabbinical Laws of Idolatry," 154ff., 236ff.; J. Baumgarten, "Art in the Synagogue," 198, 201, 206. Urbach has built his often quoted theory on this very assumption, namely, that it was the fear of idolatry which was behind the earlier aniconic posture, and that paganism's decline in the second and third centuries led to the rabbis' more liberal legislation vis-à-vis figural art. Such an assumption, however, is problematic. There is no evidence that at any time in the Second Temple period idolatry was perceived as a threat to the Jews. This view is attested in both rabbinic and non-rabbinic sources; see Song of Songs Rabbah 7:13 (p. 160); Judith 8:18; Josephus, *War* 2, 195–98. Thus, Jewish avoidance of figural art ought to be attributed to other causes, no less than their subsequent re-adoption of this form of representation. See also Hachlili, *Art and Archaeology-Israel*, 285–87.

28. Mosaic floor in the Ḥammat Tiberias synagogue.

Despite the apparent prohibition of the second commandment as understood previously, the exigencies of the time were ultimately the determining factors. Why and how this happened among the masses is not stated in our sources. However, we do have some indication of this impending shift within rabbinic circles. Flexibility among the sages in such matters often derived from a creative use of hermeneutics, which itself was driven by historical necessity and, at times, ideological convictions. A dramatic expression of this kind of flexibility regarding artistic expression is offered by the Mishnah with respect to Rabban Gamaliel II (flourished ca. 90–120 C.E.):

> Proklos, the son of Philosophos, asked [a question of] Rabban Gamaliel while the latter was bathing in the bath of Aphrodite in Acre, saying to him: "It is written in your Torah, 'and there shall not cleave to you any of the devoted [i.e., forbidden] thing' [Deut. 13:18]. Why do you thus bathe in the bath of Aphrodite?" He answered: "One may not give an answer in the bath." And when he came out he said: "(1) I did not come into her [Aphrodite's] area [lit., boundary], she came into mine. People do not say, 'Let us make a bath for Aphrodite,' but rather, 'Let us make a [statue of] Aphrodite as an adornment for the bath'; (2) moreover, even if they would offer you much money, you would not enter your place of worship [lit., idolatry] naked and suffering pollution and urinate in front of her [i.e., Aphrodite]. But she stands at the edge of the gutter, and everyone urinates in front of her; (3) the verse only refers to 'their gods'; that which they treat as a god is forbidden and that which they do not treat as a god is permitted." [49]

The response attributed to Rabban Gamaliel is as fascinating as it is far-reaching. He is quoted as offering three reasons for his frequenting a pagan-ornamented bathhouse. The first deals with the definition of the building's function: Was it built as a pagan sanctuary or as a bath? Is Aphrodite's presence inherent to the building's function, or was she merely a decorative addition? R. Gamaliel's answer is that her statue was brought in as ornamentation; the building itself was intended for a very different (we might say "secular") purpose. Secondly, the nature of a facility should also be judged by what people actually do there. When one walks around naked and urinates with no regard to the presence of a statue of a deity, the statue is quite clearly ancillary and of no real consequence for those present. Thus, the bathhouse is not to be regarded as something sacred or specifically pagan. The third claim, however, is the most far-reaching. One should regard a place or an object as idolatrous only if it is so regarded by the pagans themselves; if they do not consider something idolatrous, but rather solely ornamental, that ought to determine one's attitude and behavior. This last response is the most revolutionary precisely be-

---

49. M ʿAvodah Zarah 3:4. For a different dating of this story, to the time of R. Gamaliel III (early third century), see Wasserstein, "Rabban Gamliel and Proclus," 257–67. See also the story recorded in T Moʿed Qatan 2:15 (p. 372), recounting how R. Gamaliel sat on a bench of gentiles (perhaps ordinarily used for commercial purposes) on Shabbat, much to the chagrin of his Jewish hosts.

cause it is cast as a general principle. Nothing, not even a statue, is inherently forbidden; everything depends on its function and on the intention of those who placed it there.[50]

Such a transition, from an aniconic posture in the late Second Temple period to a less restrictive stance in late antiquity, was not always easy or smooth. Differences of opinion might often be sharp and even bitter, and this was true even within rabbinic circles.[51] However, it is only for Byzantine Palestine that our diverse sources furnish us with a detailed and nuanced picture of the varied attitudes toward figural art within Jewish society. The use of animal and human figures had become, on the one hand, quite acceptable in many Byzantine communities; some were clearly more daring than others, but the use of human or animal figures was widely practiced. On the other hand, our data also point to individual communities or entire regions that tended to be more conservative and studiously avoided any such representations. Predictably, many of the latter communities tended to be in rural districts or relatively isolated regions, such as the Upper Galilee and southern Judaea, although conservative communities might also be found in or near large urban centers, as, for example, the Reḥov synagogue in the Bet Shean area.

JEWISH MOTIFS

A survey of synagogue art in late antiquity reveals a seemingly endless variety of patterns, designs, and motifs of both Jewish and non-Jewish content. Jews borrowed heavily from the Byzantine world in this regard[52] and at times may have even used the same artisans or pattern books as did neighboring churches. In comparing the nearby synagogues of Gaza and Maʿon and the Shellal church, it is clear that the Jews substituted a menorah for a cross when adapting and judaizing a well-known Byzantine mosaic pattern for their own use.[53] Whether all these mosaics were produced in the same workshop

---

50. The same Rabban Gamaliel had various representations of the moon in his upper chamber, which he would make use of when cross-examining witnesses testifying to a new moon (M Rosh Hashanah 2:8). An analogous situation cropped up in the mid-third century regarding the use of the Bostra nymphaeum by Jews for drinking water. R. Yoḥanan overruled his friend and colleague Resh Laqish and permitted such usage, despite the presence of statues and the fact that the site was occasionally used for pagan ritual purposes. See Y Sheviʿit 8, 11, 38b–c; B ʿAvodah Zarah 58b–59a; and Blidstein, "R. Yohanan, Idolatry and Public Privilege," 154–61.

51. See J. Baumgarten, "Art in the Synagogue," 198–204; L. Levine, *Judaism and Hellenism*, 106–10; and esp. below, Chap. 13.

52. Ovadiah, "Art of the Ancient Synagogues," 301–18; Narkiss, "Pagan, Christian and Jewish Elements," 183–86; Hachlili, *Art and Archaeology-Israel*, 310ff., 366ff.

53. Avi-Yonah, *Art in Ancient Palestine*, 389–95; idem, "Mosaic Floor of Maʿon Synagogue," 77–85; Ovadiah, "Mosaic Workshop," 367–72; as well as the comments of Hachlili, "Gaza School of Mosaicists," 46–58; idem, *Art and Archaeology-Israel*, 310–16, 390; and N. Stone, "Shellal Mosaic," 207–14. On the situation in Rome, see Rutgers, *Jews in Late Ancient Rome*, 70–76, 83.

29. The *'Aqedah* scene in the Bet Alpha mosaic.

is a moot issue, although Rutgers has suggested the use of common workshops for Jews and Christians in Rome. Similarly, it appears that the Susiya synagogue adopted a pattern of the Temple facade which was also being used in a sixth-century Madeba church.[54] The raw material came from a limited menu of Jewish symbols and depictions as well as a much wider range of motifs offered by the Byzantine world. This was the setting for a series of creative syntheses in synagogal art as synagogues throughout the country created their own combinations from the options available.

An important facet of synagogue art in the Byzantine period is the greatly increased use of Jewish motifs and symbols as compared with earlier times. Biblical scenes or figures were only sparingly used.[55] The *'Aqedah* (Binding of Isaac) scene at Bet Alpha is the most elaborate example of biblical art (fig. 29); others include the figures of Daniel (Na'aran, Susiya), David (Gaza and possibly Merot; fig. 30), and Aaron, as well as fragmentary representations of the *'Aqedah* and possibly the visit of the three angels to Abraham and Sarah (Sepphoris) and what is arguably a depiction of the symbols for the twelve tribes

---

54. Foerster, "Allegorical and Symbolic Motifs," 546–47.

55. No less remarkable is the fact that there are no traces of biblical figures or scenes in Jewish funerary art in either Roman-Byzantine Palestine or the Diaspora.

30. Representation of David
from the Gaza synagogue.

(Yafia). Regarding Jewish symbols, the menorah is far and away the most common one, often appearing with a shofar, *lulav*, and *ethrog*. A frequent pattern in synagogue mosaics displays a Torah shrine flanked by pairs of *menorot, shofarot, lulavim, ethrogim,* and incense shovels.[56] Interestingly, these clusters of Jewish symbols frequently accompany the zodiac signs, although they might stand independently as well (e.g., Bet Shean A; fig. 31).

The meaning and significance of the above-mentioned cluster of symbols have long been debated (fig. 32). One popular theory maintains that they were primarily intended to recall the Jerusalem Temple (or possibly the Wilderness Tabernacle),[57] with the facade representing that of the Temple and the menorah, shofar, *lulav, ethrog,* and incense shovel symbolizing accouterments once used in this setting. If this interpretation is granted, then the clear implication is that remembering the Temple was of paramount importance in some Byzantine Jewish communities. The appearance of this motif in the synagogue,

---

56. Hachlili, *Art and Archaeology—Israel,* 234–300; Narkiss, "Representational Art," 366ff.

57. Narkiss, "Scheme of the Sanctuary," 13; Kühnel, "Jewish Symbolism," 147–49; Grossberg, "Reactions," 64–65. See also Branham, "Vicarious Sacrality," 319ff.; Z. Safrai, "From Synagogue to 'Little Temple,'" 23–28. For other possible explanations of the "incense shovel," see Narkiss, "Spice Box," 32.

31. Panel from the Bet Shean A synagogue exhibiting a series of Jewish symbols.

then, could be viewed, at the very least, as triggering a memory of that institution and, at the very most, as reflecting a desire that the synagogue be considered some sort of continuation of the Temple in terms of sanctity and religious significance.

A second approach regards these religious symbols within the context of the synagogue itself.[58] The facade is thus interpreted as representing the Torah shrine, while the other symbols are said to represent the various objects found in the synagogue or used in the synagogue service. By late antiquity, at the very latest, the shofar and *lulav* had become integral parts of synagogue festival worship.

Each of the above interpretations, however, has its weaknesses. To interpret the facade as a depiction of the Temple exterior is problematic. In no way does it resemble either what we know of the Temple facade (via Josephus or Mishnah Middot) or, in fact, depictions of the Temple facade in second- and third-century Jewish art (e.g., on the Bar-Kokhba coins or the Dura frescoes). Given this fact, it has been further suggested that the synagogue depictions refer to an inner portal of the Temple, but this, too, is not altogether convincing. The incense shovel and menorah are certainly appropriate for the Temple context, but one wonders why the shofar, *lulav*, and *ethrog* were so emphasized, since they appear to have been quite peripheral to official Temple worship. Moreover, with

58. Dothan, *Hammath Tiberias*, 33–39; Goodenough, *Jewish Symbols*, IV, 111–36; XII, 83–86; Hachlili, *Art and Archaeology-Israel*, 272–80. Amit, "Reactions and Comments," 65–66.

32. Cluster of Jewish symbols from the Ḥammat Tiberias synagogue.

the Temple in mind, one could readily suggest other items which would have been even more closely identified with the Temple ritual: the altars, showbread table, priestly garments, etc. On the other hand, the symbols depicted would seem to fit a synagogue context rather nicely, the one problematic element being the incense shovel. It patently does not apply to the synagogue or its liturgy, at least on the basis of what we know to date.[59]

A third approach, intriguing though not without its own problems, would interpret many of these symbols as referring to the major holiday season during the month of Tishri, when three major Jewish festivals occur in rapid succession: Rosh Hashanah (the New Year), Yom Kippur (the Day of Atonement), and Sukkot.[60] Thus, the above-noted symbols can easily be associated with one of these holidays: shofar—Rosh Hashanah; incense shovel—Yom Kippur;[61] *lulav* and *ethrog*—Sukkot. The last-mentioned holiday was

---

59. It seems, however, that at least some Jews used incense in tombs, as reported by the sixth-century Christian pilgrim Antoninus Martyr regarding the Cave of Machpelah in Hebron; see Toberler and Molinier, *Itinera Hierosolymitana,* 374; Antoninus Martyr, in *PPTS* (p. 24).

60. First suggested by Bratslavi ("Symbols," 115–18) and later espoused by Wirgin ("Menorah as Symbol of Judaism," 141–42); Eitan ("Menora as Symbol," 49); and Fine (*This Holy Place,* 121).

61. On the importance of the incense shovel for the Yom Kippur ceremony, see Lauterbach, *Rabbinic Essays,* 51–83.

considered the most popular and important of the pilgrimage festivals in the late Second Temple period, while Rosh Hashanah and Yom Kippur became known in rabbinic tradition as the Days of Awe (or in modern parlance, the High Holidays). These two holidays were greatly developed in scope and content by the rabbis following the destruction of the Second Temple, and they came to represent a wide range of ideological themes and religious values. Interestingly enough, these High Holidays were more exclusively synagogue-centered than other major holidays, and it may be for this reason that John Chrysostom chose to inveigh against them in his very first homily against the Jews: "What is this sickness? The festivals of the wretched and miserable Jews which follow one after another in succession—Trumpets, Booths, the Fasts—are about to take place. And many who belong to us and say that they believe in our teaching, attend their festivals, and even share in their celebrations and join their fasts. It is this evil practice I now wish to drive from the church."[62]

Elsewhere, Chrysostom rails at those Christians who are attracted to hearing the shofar (Rosh Hashanah), dancing (!) and fasting (Yom Kippur), and building booths (Sukkot).[63] Thus, it is not inconceivable that synagogues featured these particular symbols which were associated with the holidays of the month of Tishri and were recognized for their centrality by non-Jews as well. Interestingly, it is these very symbols which are often depicted on the Jewish gold glass fragments that were found in the catacombs of Rome.[64] The weakness of this theory, however, is that it relates to only three symbols which appear in these panels, and the smallest and most peripheral ones at that. The menorah and Torah shrine which dominate are not addressed (fig. 33).

Another interpretation of this cluster of Jewish symbols is more inclusive in nature. Rather than viewing all of these symbols as reflecting one particular institution or time framework, it is claimed that we may indeed be dealing with several allusions simultaneously. Thus, these symbols may actually point to the Temple and synagogue at one and the same time, identifying the two by amalgamating their representative symbols.

Finally, in a variation of the last-mentioned inclusive approach, one might view these symbols as representing two basic concepts in Judaism, the Temple and the Torah. Certain symbols are clearly associated with the Temple setting; others would seem to indicate the sanctity of the Torah shrine. Since these two dimensions were often associated with one another, starting with placing the two tablets of stone bearing the Ten Commandments together with Moses' Torah (Deut. 31:9, 26) in the Wilderness Tabernacle and later in the First Temple, this combination may have found expression here as well.

Whatever their specific significance and meaning, the widespread use of these sym-

62. *Adv. Iud.* 1, 1, 844 (also in Meeks and Wilken, *Jews and Christians*, 86).

63. See *Adv. Iud.* 1, 5, 851; 1, 2, 846; 7, 1, 915; and Wilken, *John Chrysostom and the Jews*, 75.

64. Goodenough, *Jewish Symbols*, II, 108–19; Leon, *Jews of Ancient Rome*, 218–24; Noy, *JIWE*, II, nos. 588–97; Rutgers, *Jews in Late Ancient Rome*, 81–85.

33. Torah shrine flanked by *menorot* and other symbols, from the Bet Alpha synagogue.

bols in a synagogue context certainly gave vivid expression to the institution's religious dimension and undoubtedly enhanced it.

THE RELIGIOUS DIMENSION

The Byzantine period witnessed very significant advances in the transformation of the synagogue building into a distinctively religious institution. What had begun to emerge during the later Roman period was now fully realized. The orientation of synagogue buildings toward Jerusalem (or the Holy Land, if in the Diaspora) was almost universally practiced, albeit with some exceptions already mentioned.

The Jerusalem orientation was now further emphasized by the almost universal practice of placing a platform, niche, or apse for the Torah shrine against the Jerusalem-oriented wall.[65] In the Galilean-type synagogue, such a podium would have been located between the entrance portals facing Jerusalem, either on one or both sides of the main

---

65. See Fine, *This Holy Place*, 105–11. For further discussion of synagogue orientation, see below, Chap. 9.

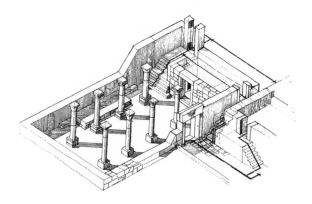

34. Reconstruction of the
Khirbet Shemaʿ synagogue.

entrance (e.g., Gush Ḥalav, Nevoraya, and Merot). In other types of buildings, the platform was situated in the center of the wall facing Jerusalem (as at Reḥov and Khirbet
Shemaʿ [fig. 34], and in one case there seem to have been two such podiums — Susiya). The
emphasis on a Jerusalem orientation was even more pronounced in synagogues which
adopted a basilical plan that incorporated a niche or apse. Architecturally, these installations riveted the synagogue participant in a specific direction, and if the prayer leader,
Torah-reading, or preaching were likewise positioned in or near the apse (or niche), as
seems likely, then this focus would have become even more pronounced.[66]

However, the appearance of a *bima* or apse as a permanent fixture in most synagogues
was not simply an architectural addition. It meant that the Torah shrine was now accorded central prominence within the hall. It will be remembered that Second Temple
synagogues had no such arrangement; Torah scrolls were kept elsewhere and introduced
into the assembly hall when needed. This arrangement began to change in the late Roman
period, and by late antiquity a permanent Torah shrine had become the norm. There can
be little doubt that the permanent presence of the Torah was an important component in
determining the ambience of the synagogue's main hall, wherein all those present faced
the Torah ark and the Jerusalem wall. This, of course, is in contradistinction to the earlier
custom, whereby all faced the center of the hall or the elders faced the congregation.[67]

Literary sources[68] and a number of inscriptions from this period refer to the synagogue as a "holy place" (אתרה קדישה or *hagios topos*) and to the community as a "holy congregation" (קהילה קדישה) or a holy *ḥavurah* (or association — חבורתה קדישה). References to a
"holy place" appear in synagogues throughout the country, in Hammat Tiberias (twice;

66. Hachlili, "Niche and Ark," 3–53.

67. See *Differences in Customs*, no. 36 (p. 156), contra T Megillah 3:21 (p. 360).

68. For example, Ecclesiastes Rabbah 8:10. See also Y Bikkurim 3, 3, 65d, where a Caesarean synagogue is likened to God's Temple.

35. Greek (upper) and
Aramaic (lower)
inscriptions from the
Ḥammat Tiberias synagogue.

fig. 35), Naʿaran (four times), Kefar Ḥananiah, Ashkelon, and Gaza, and to "the most
holy [place]" in Gaza and Gerasa.[69] Mention is made of a holy congregation or community in inscriptions from Bet Shean, Jericho, and Susiya.[70] The term "the language of the
holy house" (לישן בית קודשא) occurs frequently in Targum Pseudo-Jonathan and seems to
refer to the language used in the synagogue setting,[71] while in the same *targum* of Lev.
26:2, it is the synagogue which almost assuredly is referred to as a sanctuary.[72]

Thus, we are on safe ground in assuming that in the course of the Byzantine period,
the synagogue came to be widely viewed as a holy place,[73] a status clearly articulated in
fourth-century legislation. Valentinian I (ca. 370 C.E.) refers to the synagogue as a *religionum loca* when prohibiting soldiers from seizing quarters there.[74] Such a status is likewise
assumed in other edicts issued over the next half-century aimed at protecting synagogues
from violence.[75]

The tendency to associate synagogue and Temple, first noted in Palestine in the post-
Temple era, gained momentum in the Byzantine period. The appearance of plaques con-
taining lists of the twenty-four priestly courses—in Caesarea, Ashkelon, Reḥov, perhaps
Kissufim (near Gaza), Nazareth, and Yemen—may serve as evidence of the associations

---

69. *"Holy place":* Naveh, *On Stone and Mosaic*, nos. 16, 26, 60, 64, 65; Roth-Gerson, *Greek Inscriptions*,
nos. 3, 17, 23. *"The most holy place":* ibid., nos. 10, 21.

70. Naveh, *On Stone and Mosaic*, nos. 46, 69, 84.

71. Shinan, "Aramaic Targum as a Mirror," 248–49.

72. See comments in Blidstein, "Prostration and Mosaics," 37–39; and below, Chap. 13. On the issue
of synagogue sanctity, see Schubert, "Jewish Pictorial Traditions," 161–70; and esp., for a detailed treatment, Fine, *This Holy Place.*

73. In the early third century, the term "holy" appears on coins from Sepphoris with regard to the
city and its council (Meshorer, "Sepphoris and Rome," 168–69).

74. *Cod. Theod.* 7, 8, 2 (Linder, *Jews in Roman Imperial Legislation*, 116–18).

75. See above, note 2.

which were being forged at this time between the synagogue and the memory of the Temple.[76] In contemporary *piyyutim*, the subject of the twenty-four priestly courses became a frequent motif.[77] One Byzantine *paytan*, Hadutha (or Hadutaha), wrote *piyyutim* for each of the twenty-four priestly courses, and other synagogue poets were themselves priests and thus may have been inclined to focus on Temple-related matters as well.[78]

We noted in the previous chapter that during the third and fourth centuries Temple-related matters were being introduced into the synagogue liturgy, for example, the *Mussaf 'Amidah* and the *maftir* reading for holidays, both of which focus on the Temple sacrifices.[79] It was also about this time that the *'Avodah* service recalling the Temple ritual on Yom Kippur was added to that day's synagogue liturgy, as was the recitation of a psalm for each day of the week, a custom which had been associated with the priests in the Temple.[80] In truth, this latter practice is first explicitly mentioned as an element of synagogue worship only in a source from the seventh or eighth century, but it undoubtedly originated well before that.[81] The addition of this psalm not only served to expand the synagogue liturgy by adopting older patterns of Temple worship, but, in turn, reinforced the association made between these two institutions. Moreover, we recall the claim ascribed to R. Joshua b. Levi that the *'Amidah* prayer was introduced as a substitute for sacrifices (תפילות כנגד תמידין תקנום).[82] Finally, Temple terminology seems to have permeated other aspects of synagogue life as well. In a revealing account of Joseph collecting taxes for the Patriarch in Cilicia, Epiphanius refers to these monies as "tithes" and "firstfruits." If indeed accurate — and it would be difficult to imagine the motivation for inventing such

---

76. *Caesarea*: Avi-Yonah, "Caesarea Inscription," 24–28. *Ashkelon*: Sukenik, "Three Inscriptions," 16–17. *Reḥov*: Z. Ilan, *Ancient Synagogues*, 186. *Kissufim*: Z. Ilan, "Broken Slab," 225–26; *Nazareth*: H. Eshel, "Fragmentary Hebrew Inscription?" 159–61. *Yemen*: Degan, "Inscription of Twenty-Four Priestly Courses," 302–3. See also Naveh, *On Stone and Mosaic*, nos. 51, 52, 56, 106.

77. S. Klein, *Galilee*, 177–92; and the numerous articles on the subject by Fleischer, e.g., "Regarding the [Priestly] Courses," 142–61; "Piyyutim of Yannai," 176–84; see also idem, "Additional Data," 47–60.

78. Zulay, "History of Piyyut," 111–20; Fleischer, "Hadutha," 71–96. Some *paytanim* were priests, e.g., R. Pinḥas biribi Hakohen (Fleischer, "Early Paytanim of Tiberias," 370); R. Simeon bar Megas (Yahalom, *Priestly Palestinian Poetry*, 11). In addition, *piyyutim* written for the Ninth of Av often focus on the Temple priests, their roles, and the Temple cult; see Fleischer, "Qaliric Compositions," 1–40.

On the connection between *hekhalot* mysticism and Temple traditions, see Elior, "Earthly Temple," 217–67.

79. See above, Chap. 6.

80. On the *'Avodah* service, see B Yoma 36b and 56b. Although these traditions are from fourth-century Babylonia, there is little doubt that such a practice was current in Palestine as well, as attested by the scores of *piyyutim* which highlight the *'Avodah* service; see Elbogen, *Studien*, 49ff.; Goldschmidt, *Maḥzor*, xviii–xxv; L. A. Hoffman, *Canonization*, 107. On the daily recitation of psalms, see above, Chap. 6, note 79. See also 'Avot de R. Nathan, A, 1 (p. 3a).

81. Tractate Soferim 18:2 (pp. 310–13).

82. B Berakhot 26b. Y Berakhot 4, 1, 7b, ascribes this tradition to the sages generally (תפילות מתמידין גמרו). Cf. however, the comments of Blidstein, *Prayer*, 243 n. 26.

terms—then Temple-related expressions for obligatory donations were being invoked by the fourth-century Patriarchate.[83]

Two very different sources from late antiquity make this connection between the synagogue and Temple eminently clear. The first is a halakhic work from the end of the Byzantine period, referred to today as "the Book of Court Cases" (ספר המעשים) or "the Literature of Court Cases" (ספרות המעשים):

> And thus said the sages: "One must not enter the Temple Mount with his staff and shoes. And if, owing to our sins, the Temple Mount is no longer available to us, a lesser sanctuary is and we must behave in [it] in a spirit of holiness and fear, as is written: 'You must fear My sanctuary' [Lev. 19:30]. Therefore, our ancestors have determined that in all synagogue courtyards there would be a large living [i.e., fresh] water vessel for sanctifying [i.e., washing hands and feet]."[84]

A second source appears as fragments of a midrash on Deuteronomy, found in the Cairo Genizah:

> As long as the Temple existed, the daily offerings and sacrifices would atone for the sins of Israel. Nowadays, the synagogues of Israel replace the Temple, and as long as Israel prays in them, they, in effect, replace the daily offerings and sacrifices; and when prayers are recited [therein] at the proper times and [the Jews] direct their hearts [to God through their prayers], they gain merit and will see the rebuilding of the Temple and the sacrificing of the daily offering and [other] sacrifices, as it is written: "And I will bring them to My holy mountain, and I will rejoice in My house of prayer; your sacrifices and offerings are welcome on My altar, for My house will be called a house of prayer for all peoples" [Is. 56:7].[85]

In the former source, the synagogue is acknowledged as inferior to the Temple, yet it still has been assigned a sufficient degree of holiness to warrant a vessel being placed there for the washing of hands and feet. Purification, of course, was crucial for Temple visitors, and the purpose of this custom in the synagogue was undoubtedly to introduce a modicum of such purity. In the latter source, however, the synagogue is accorded an even higher status than before, and synagogue and prayer have replaced the Temple and sacrifices. Moreover, it is claimed that proper observance of prayer will lead to the reestablishment of the Temple, a situation already foreseen by the prophet Isaiah.

The addition of an eternal light (נר תמיד) to the synagogue at some point during these centuries further strengthened its association with the Temple. Although lighting fixtures for the synagogue are noted in tannaitic sources, there is no indication that these were intended for anything more than basic illumination within the building.[86] In several

---

83. *Panarion* 30, 11, 2.
84. Margoliot, *Palestinian Halakhah*, 131–32.
85. Ginzberg, *Geniza Studies*, I, 152–53.
86. M. Pesaḥim 4:4. See also Y Pesaḥim 4, 9, 31b; B Pesaḥim 53b.

late *midrashim*, however, the presence of an eternal light is clearly attested. Clearly, the association of synagogue and Temple had become so commonplace during this period that, at some point, a biblically ordained appurtenance of the latter was introduced into the former. Another tradition explains the commandment to have lights in synagogues in a very simple manner: "Synagogues and academies are like the Temple."[87]

Indicative of the Temple's memory in the synagogue is the mosaic floor in the fifth-century synagogue at Sepphoris, which portrays a series of Temple offerings.[88] Each offering is depicted graphically and is accompanied by the Hebrew term for that offering, e.g., the daily sacrifice (תמיד), the oil (שמן), and the meal offerings (סולת). Various items used in Temple ceremonies are likewise depicted, such as trumpets (חצוצרות), the table of the showbread, and a basket of firstfruits. No other synagogue, with the possible exception of Dura Europos, makes as clear a statement regarding the close association of synagogue and Temple.

Some of the reasons for the synagogue's evolution into an institution with an even more pronounced religious character were suggested in the previous chapter. We noted reasons such as the association of the synagogue with the Temple, the beginnings of a permanent presence of the Torah scrolls in the synagogue hall, the increasing importance of public prayer, and the possible influence of Diaspora models. This process continued into the Byzantine era with even greater impetus, and several additional factors appear to have played a significant role at the time. The first was the remarkable development in the concept of holiness throughout many parts of society in late antiquity. "Holiness" as a religious category characterizing places, people, and objects was becoming an ever greater concern in a wide variety of religious circles. The holy man had become a well-recognized phenomenon of late antiquity.[89] Brown's pathbreaking studies of the Christian holy man or saint have been followed by that of Fowden with regard to pagan holy figures and by Kirschner's comparison of pagan, Christian, and Jewish models.[90] It would be difficult to isolate the synagogue from these developments; rather, some sort of influence—the proverbial Zeitgeist—ought to be posited in this regard as well. A second and more immediate factor was the dramatic development and growing presence of Christianity throughout much of Palestine at this time.

---

87. Midrash Hagadol, Numbers 8:1 (p. 119).

88. Weiss and Netzer, *Promise and Redemption*, 20-25.

89. On the holy person in the Hellenistic and Roman worlds, see Anderson, *Sage, Saint and Sophist*. Regarding holiness in paganism, see Bowersock, *Hellenism*, 15-28.

90. Brown, *Society and the Holy*, 103-65; idem, "Saint as Exemplar," 1-25; Fowden, "Pagan Holy Man," 33-59; Kirschner, "Vocation of Holiness," 105-24. See also Valantasis, *Spiritual Guides*, 1-33; Markus, *End of Ancient Christianity*, 199-211; Philips, "Sociology," 2752-64. Regarding rabbinic tradition specifically, see L. Levine, *Rabbinic Class*, 105-9, and literature cited therein, to which I might now add Diamond, "Hunger Artists and Householders," 29-47.

THE IMPACT OF CHRISTIANITY

There is no doubt that the era of Constantine ushered in a period of profound change in the way Christians related ideologically and liturgically to Palestine, Jerusalem, and other holy sites, as well as to the increasingly widespread phenomenon of pilgrimage to the Holy Land.[91] There is no gainsaying the dramatic effect of Constantine's massive infusion of money and energy into recasting Jerusalem as a Christian city, first and foremost by building a series of magnificent churches, sometimes referred to as pilgrim-churches, in order to commemorate events in the life of Jesus, a shift from what J. Z. Smith has termed the "utopian" to the "locative" mode.[92] "Constantine created, for the first time, a Christian 'Holy Land,' laid palimpsest-like over the old, and interacting with it in complex ways, having for its central foci a series of Imperial-dynastic churches."[93]

The second component of this revolution concerned pilgrimage. As happens with regard to seminal and dramatic transformations, scholars have disputed whether this phenomenon was new and revolutionary in the fourth century or whether it was the continuation of a process which had originated a century or two earlier, only now increasing in intensity and scope owing to Imperial and church support.[94] While pilgrimage did exist earlier, in the second and third centuries, all evidence seems to point to the fact that this earlier phenomenon was different from that of the fourth century and later. Early

---

91. See Markus, *Christianity in the Roman World*, 87ff.; MacMullen, *Christianizing the Roman Empire*, 43–51. The revolution in Christian life that began unfolding in Byzantine Palestine in the fourth century could not have been foreseen. Whatever his motivations, Constantine initiated a process whereby Jerusalem was transformed into a focal point of Christian life throughout the Empire. Until then, Christianity had by and large shunned earthly, physical Jerusalem in favor of a heavenly, spiritual one (John 4:19–26). For Paul, places could not be holy: "The God who made the world and everything in it, being the Lord of heaven and earth, does not dwell in shrines made by men" (Acts 17:24). Christians believed, moreover, that if there was a real temple, it was within the believers themselves: "The temple of God is holy; you are that temple" (I Cor. 3:17; see also II Cor. 6:16). After taking a generally inhospitable posture (officially, at least) prior to the fourth century, Christianity had now become receptive to the idea of a *locus sanctus*. See Barnes, *Constantine and Eusebius*, 220–21; Hunt, *Holy Land Pilgrimage*, 32–35; Holum, "Hadrian and St. Helena," 71–77; Wilken, *Land Called Holy*, xiv, 83. See also Nibley, "Christian Envy," 97–123.

92. Hunt, *Holy Land Pilgrimage*, 6–27, 190–202; J. Z. Smith, *Map Is Not Territory*, 101–2, 147–51, 308–9.

93. J. Z. Smith, *To Take Place*, 79. Markus (*End of Ancient Christianity*, 139–55; "How on Earth Could Places Become Holy?" 257–71) has suggested that the sacred and holy in Christianity owe much to the veneration of martyrs and their tombs and relics, and that this can best account for the growing sanctity of place then appearing in the Byzantine Christian world.

94. Some scholars maintain the newness of this phenomenon; see, for example, Holum, "Hadrian and St. Helena," 66–81; Sivan, "Pilgrimage, Monasticism," 54–63; Taylor, *Christians and Holy Places*, 306–18, 329–31; Wilken, *Land Called Holy*, 82–100; Markus, "How on Earth Could Places Become Holy?" 261–62. Walker's study (*Holy City, Holy Places?* 36–41, 311–15) of the differences of opinion between Eusebius and Cyril of Jerusalem regarding the centrality and sanctity of Jerusalem and other holy places dramatizes

pilgrimage was limited by the distances the pilgrims traversed to reach their destinations, and it was limited to a religious elite whose goals seem to have been cognitive and exegetical—i.e., they visited biblical sites for the historical memories with which they were associated.[95] What distinguished the new wave of Christian pilgrims to Byzantine Palestine were not only the numbers involved, but also the spiritual and devotional experiences evoked. It is this ontological dimension which was most often primary, as these pilgrims sought traces of God in these holy places; such goals preoccupied pilgrims from the fourth century onward.[96]

A third element in the Byzantine Christian revolution—and one that relates to the above two—is the emergence of a vigorous monastic movement in Palestine in the fourth century. Pilgrims provided a constant source of recruits for the burgeoning monasteries of Jerusalem and the Judaean Desert, and one of the monks' functions was to provide these pilgrims with food, water, lodgings, and explanations of the holy sites, which might include prayer and scriptural readings. Indeed, the development of a vigorous monastic community in Palestine seems to have been closely connected with pilgrimage.[97]

Thus, from the fourth century on, the concept of "holiness" became associated with Christian sites, particularly Jerusalem and its new Temple, an association which benefited greatly from Imperial initiatives, an emerging Jerusalem-centered ideology (per Cyril of Jerusalem), and increased pilgrimage. Moreover, this newly discovered sanctity was institutionalized in the developing Christian liturgy, which ritualized these associations, a process that first took root in Jerusalem and which was often brought home to local

---

the transformation that was taking place in Christian thinking in the fourth century. See MacCormack, "Loca Sancta," 12–14.

Other scholars maintain continuity with the pre-Constantinian era; see Windisch, "Palästinapilger," 145–58; Hunt, *Holy Land Pilgrimage*, 2–5; Wilkinson, "Jewish Holy Places," 41–53. Common to these scholars is the assumption that Jewish veneration of tombs and holy places had spawned similar traditions in early Christianity, which then, almost organically, attained a more developed expression in the Byzantine period. See also Lane, *Pagans and Christians*, 476; MacCormack, "Loca Sancta," 20; Chadwick, *History and Thought*, 3–8.

95. MacCormack, "Loca Sancta," 20–21.

96. Walker, *Holy City, Holy Places?* 37–38; Holum, "Hadrian and St. Helena," 69; Wilken, *Land Called Holy*, 83–84; Taylor, *Christians and Holy Places*, 310ff.

97. Sivan, "Pilgrimage, Monasticism," 55: "neither the scholarly interest displayed by many of the early visitors nor the piety that imbued all pilgrims is sufficient in itself to explain the vast expansion of Christian topography in early Byzantine Palestine. Nor are imperial-sponsored projects, like those of Constantine, enough to account for the numerous localities shown to pilgrims toward the end of the 4th century. The renewal of biblical traditions and their association with specific contemporary localities appears to have been largely the unique result of the mutual interests and combined efforts of monks and pilgrims in the 4th century. Otherwise it would be difficult to explain the spread of monasticism in the area, the active involvement of monks and priests in hosting and guiding pilgrims, and the response of pilgrims to the wide-scale 'promotion' of the Holy Land." See also Hunt, *Holy Land Pilgrimage*, 50–106; Hirschfeld, "Holy Sites," 112–30.

churches throughout the Empire by pilgrims returning from the Holy Land.[98] Thus, the temporal and spatial dimensions of Christian Palestine were fast becoming inextricably intertwined with the sanctity of Jesus' words and deeds.

Moreover, sanctity was often ascribed to churches through their identification with the Jerusalem Temple. Eusebius refers to the Church of the Holy Sepulchre as a "New Jerusalem" and a "temple" (ναός), and he similarly applied the latter designation to the church built in Tyre ("a temple of God").[99] It is reported that in the sixth century, upon completion of his magnificent Hagia Sophia edifice in Constantinople, Justinian exclaimed: "Solomon, I have conquered you!"[100]

It is significant that much of the symbolism associated with the Temple and Temple Mount in Jewish tradition was now being transferred to Golgotha and the Church of the Holy Sepulchre. This "New Jerusalem built over against the one so famous of old"[101] was where Adam was created and Isaac was bound as a sacrifice, where Egeria saw King Solomon's ring and the horn from which the kings of Judah were anointed. The dedication of the Church of the Holy Sepulchre coincided (intentionally?) with the time of the completion of the First Temple by Solomon, and it was identified as the *omphalos*, or the navel, of the world.[102]

Given this monumental change in the status of Palestine, and particularly that of Jerusalem, for Christians, as well as the new Christian emphasis on the sanctity of space, we might well ask what effect this had on the local Jewish community. It is difficult to imag-

---

98. Hunt, *Holy Land Pilgrimage*, 107-27. See also Baumstark, *Abendländische Palästinapilger*, 80-83. See, however, the important reservations of Bradshaw ("Influence of Jerusalem"), that the city may have been as much an importer of liturgical traditions as an exporter. For this and other aspects of sanctity in Byzantine Christian life (e.g., community, liturgy, time), see Markus, *End of Ancient Christianity*, passim.

99. Eusebius, *Vita Constan.* 3, 33, 36, 45; idem, *Eccles. Hist.* 10, 4, 1-3, 25, 69. Regarding the use of *naos* for other churches, see idem, *Vita Constan.* 3, 45.

100. Referred to in Wilken, *Land Called Holy*, 93. See also Procopius, *Buildings*, 1. A Syriac hymn notes that the cathedral of Edessa was compared to the Wilderness Tabernacle built by Bezalel (Mango, *Art of the Byzantine Empire*, 57). Many Christian communities began to view their own local churches as holy places. Despite the above-noted insistence of church leaders following New Testament guidelines, i.e., that God is omnipresent and that buildings per se have no inherent sanctity, attitudes in many communities were very often strikingly different. As Crowfoot (*Early Churches*, 7) has commented, many church buildings in the eastern Mediterranean resembled to a large degree the church of Tyre, which Eusebius describes as a replica of the Jerusalem Temple. According to Markus: "new ways of speech were making their appearance in media which reflect more directly the instinctive habits of imagination: we have inscriptions that speak of 'the house of God,' 'the hall of Christ,' and the like; and visual imagery represented the saint in his shrine just as age-old representations showed the dead in his tomb. Before long 'locus sanctus narratives' would come to adorn churches" ("How on Earth Could Places Become Holy?" 264).

101. Eusebius, *Vita Constan.* 3, 33.

102. Wilken, *Land Called Holy*, 93-97; Kühnel, "Jewish Symbolism," 150-51; see also Alexander, "Jerusalem as the *Omphalos*," 104-19.

ine that the Jews, even those living in the Galilee and Golan—areas somewhat removed from the major arena of Christian activity, in Judaea and the larger urban centers—would or could be impervious to such changes. Here, however, our sources fail us. Very little is recorded in rabbinic literature about Christianity in general, and what there is stems basically from the second and third centuries. Nevertheless, a number of sources have been cited by scholars which seem to indicate an awareness of fourth-century Christian claims and a rabbinic attempt to counter them.[103] By necessity, these sources are only suggestive, each bearing a greater or lesser degree of probability. A number of Byzantine Aramaic *piyyutim*, however, contain fairly explicit barbs at a number of Jesus-related traditions.[104]

It is tempting to assume that the increase in the use of Jewish symbols in the Byzantine period resulted, at least in part, from this new Christian presence, which moved the Jews to reassert and reestablish their self-identity.[105] Moreover, it may well be that the synagogue assumed an increased spiritual and religious role for the Jews as a result of Christianity's emphasis on the sanctity of the land in general and specific sites in particular. The fact that churches were also being referred to as "holy" or compared to a temple (ναός) generally and to the Jerusalem Temple in particular may have stimulated Jews to make similar assertions regarding synagogue sanctity. In this case, the synagogue would have provided an avenue for the Jewish community to channel its disappointment and frustration on the one hand and its longings and hopes on the other. What they were powerless to realize in the political realm, Jews might have hoped to achieve within the confines of their synagogues, albeit in an associative and symbolic vein.

In a sense, the emphasis of most synagogue buildings (Galilean-type and Golan build-

---

103. See J. J. Schwartz, "*Encaenia*," 265–81; Yahalom, "Angels Do Not Understand Aramaic," 42–44; and the rich trove of material collected and analyzed by Visotzky in his *Fathers of the World* as well as his "Anti-Christian Polemic," 83–100. See also the material marshaled (at times, somewhat forced) by Avi-Yonah, *Jews of Palestine*, 166–74. One opportunity for at least some Jews to witness firsthand the power and grandeur of Christian Jerusalem was on the Ninth of Av, when they were allowed to visit the city and mourn the destruction of the Temple, a custom reported in *Itinerarium Burdigalense* (p. 22).

104. Lately, this influence of Byzantine Christianity on rabbinic Judaism generally has been emphasized by J. Neusner in a series of publications (*Judaism and Its Social Metaphors*, 21–204; *Judaism in the Matrix of Christianity*, 67–137; *City of God in Judaism*, 241–78). Neusner, however, seems to have posited an overly acute distinction between pre- and post-Constantinian developments. It is hard to see, for example, how one can confidently assume that a midrashic pericope (e.g., from Genesis or Leviticus Rabbah) reflects a Byzantine setting. Perhaps such statements originated earlier, as many of the texts indeed claim. Such a realization is already reflected in the study of Christian liturgy, where former assumptions regarding post-Constantine origins are being abandoned in favor of the realization that such practices arose, in fact, much earlier (Bradshaw, "Ten Principles," 6–7). Too radical a redactional approach (i.e., following solely the assumed time of compilation to date a tradition) has serious drawbacks, as does the assumption that assigned statements are unquestionably accurate.

105. See L. Levine, "Menorah." We are speaking of "increased" usage; all of the themes which became prominent in the Byzantine period (sanctity of the synagogue, representation of the Temple, use of religious symbolism, etc.) had already surfaced earlier in one form or another.

ings excluded) in this period on a modest exterior and relatively richly decorated interior may offer concrete expression of external political realities and internal communal needs. Galilean-type and Golan synagogues, with their impressive facades, were generally located in areas of relatively isolated Jewish settlement. Synagogue structures found in the area of the Sea of Galilee, Bet Shean, the coastal and Judaean regions—areas with a far greater Christian presence—were clearly fashioned with an eye toward the Christian basilica. This type of building provided an architectural model for many contemporary synagogues, which, inter alia, fit the social, political, and religious contexts now unfolding.[106]

It would be interesting to understand—origins aside—what the Jews of late antiquity might have meant when they used the terms "sacred" and "holy" with regard to their synagogues. Were the buildings holy because God was there, an idea already found in several statements in rabbinic literature from the second and third centuries but appearing with far greater frequency in both Palestine and Babylonia in the fourth?[107] Or did holiness derive from the "holy" congregation, from sacred objects or functions (i.e., the presence of Torah scrolls and the holding of prayers), or from the synagogue's increasing association with the Temple?[108] A definitive answer to this question is elusive, and it may well be that there is, in fact, no single answer. Various communities might have used the same term but with markedly different or overlapping connotations. Moreover, it is conceivable—and even quite likely—that all members of the same community did not relate to these terms in the same way.

Nevertheless, given the developments of the Byzantine era, we may hazard a guess that the sociopolitical context may have constituted no less a factor in the Jewish usage of "holy" than the spiritual or religious dimensions. With the Byzantine synagogue being associated with and related to Jerusalem and its Temple,[109] it may well be that the concepts of "holy" and "sacred" were now being mobilized to enhance and deepen this connection in light of Christian usage. Moreover, the fact that some churches at this time were

---

106. On the Byzantine synagogue's indebtedness to contemporary Christian models, see Tsafrir, "Byzantine Setting," 147–57.

107. *Second and third centuries:* Y Berakhot 5, 1, 8d–9a; B Berakhot 6a. See also Urbach, *Sages,* 55–63. *Fourth century:* B Berakhot 6a; Y Berakhot 5, 1, 9a; 9, 1, 13a; B Megillah 29a; PRK 5:8 (p. 90) and parallels; Deuteronomy Rabbah 7:2; Midrash on Psalms 84:4. PRK 28:8 (pp. 431–32) is instructive in this regard: "R. Judan [said] in the name of R. Isaac: 'Whenever the Jews [lit., Israel] close themselves up in synagogues and academies, the Holy One, Blessed be He, also closes Himself up with them. . . .' R. Ḥaggai [said] in the name of R. Isaac: 'Whenever the Jews [lit., Israel] gather in synagogues and academies, the Holy One, Blessed be He, gathers his *Shekhina* (= Divine Presence) there with them.'" See Ehrlich, "Place of the *Shekhina,*" 320–29.

108. See Y Berakhot 5, 1, 9a; B Berakhot 6a, where God's presence is directly linked to the congregation's constituting "an assembly of the Lord" (עדת אל). See also above, Chap. 6. On the different conception of sanctity in Judaism and Christianity, see Dan, *On Sanctity,* 11–30.

109. Narkiss, "Image of Jerusalem in Art," 11–20.

identified as replicas or substitutes for the Jerusalem Temple[110] is likewise of significance. It presented a challenge to the Jews and forced them to assert their claim that the synagogue was the legitimate continuation of Temple practice and presence. The midrash fragment quoted above focuses squarely on this issue, claiming that the synagogue and prayer have now replaced the Temple with its sacrifices.[111]

Churches at this time were also being referred to in inscriptions as "holy places," and this, too, is probably not unrelated to the contemporary synagogue usage.[112] Thus, the association of the synagogue with the Temple, Jerusalem, and holiness, a process which commenced well before Constantine (especially in rabbinic circles) but gained much impetus in the Byzantine era, was quite possibly spurred on by Christian models and polemical claims.[113]

Thus, the synagogue of Byzantine Palestine came to fill many more needs of the Jewish community than ever before, particularly in the religious and spiritual realms. What is clear is that this development cannot be viewed as a solely internal matter, divorced from the late Roman and particularly the Byzantine historical settings. Many features of the synagogue, both physical and liturgical, can be linked to patterns, models, and stimuli from the surrounding world.[114]

In reviewing the Byzantine synagogue, we have noted several major trends. One is the continued development of the institution throughout Palestine, evident to us as increasing numbers of synagogues dating to this period have been found throughout the country.[115] The ongoing Imperial legislation prohibiting the building and repair of synagogues

---

110. Cf. above, note 99; as well as Socrates, *Eccles. Hist.* 1, 17.

111. See above, note 85; as well as Chap. 6, note 82.

112. See, for example, the references to "holy place" in regard to the church on Mt. Nebo and twenty or so other sites in Byzantine Palestine in Piccirillo, *Mt. Nebo*, 36, 51.

113. An interesting synagogue practice unique to Palestine reflects in a vivid manner the awe and reverence for the holy ark and, perhaps, for Jerusalem. Among the series of customs which distinguished Palestinian from Babylonian Jewry, and which date to late antiquity, is the following: "Those [elders] in the east [i.e., Babylonia] face the congregation [when sitting in the synagogue], and their backs are toward the [Torah] ark; those living in Eretz-Israel face the [Torah] ark" (*Differences in Customs* 36 [ed. Margalioth, p. 156; ed. Lewin, pp. 75–76]). Palestinian elders faced the ark and thus also Jerusalem and the site of the Temple; the Babylonians did not. This practice also differs from that recorded in the T Megillah 3:21 (p. 360), where it is stated that the elders (here: Palestinians) sat with their backs toward the holy (ark? Jerusalem? both?) while facing the congregation. Babylonian Jewry thus continued this older Palestinian practice, while in Byzantine Palestine a new custom evolved that reflected more equality (the elders and the congregation sat facing the ark together) as well as greater reverence vis-à-vis the holiest object in the room. This renewed interest, if not fascination, with Jerusalem and the Temple on the part of Christians and Jews in the fourth century may throw additional light on Julian's revolutionary plan to rebuild the Jewish Temple.

114. See below, Chap. 18.

115. The abundance of archeological data for the Byzantine synagogue raises the intriguing method-

was apparently being honored in the breach. On the other hand, lurking behind the facade of growth and expansion was a disconcerting reality. With the rise of Christianity, forces were unleashed and restrictions introduced which threatened to limit the construction and functioning of synagogues and even destroy them.[116] The most dramatic example of this latter threat, as noted, were the activities of the fifth-century Barsauma, who, with his band of forty or so fanatic monks, reputedly destroyed synagogues and temples throughout the country. Indeed, these two trends may not be entirely unrelated. Perhaps it was the laxity, ineffectiveness, and perceived corruption of the Imperial bureaucracy in enforcing such decrees limiting non-Christian practice that led some elements within the church, from bishops to monks, to seize the initiative.[117]

These contradictory forces coexisted for generations. It was only the Arab conquest, with its far-reaching political, social, and economic consequences, which effectively began to constrict local Jewish life, one of the indications of which was the precipitous decline in the number of synagogues throughout the country.

---

ological question of whether this institution actually emerged and flourished in this period or whether it was the latest stage of a phenomenon that was true of earlier periods as well (except that we have no material remains for earlier periods). It is clear from our presentation that, given its role as the primary Jewish public institution, we have assumed the synagogue's centrality through the Hellenistic-Byzantine eras. The fact that we have so much evidence for late antiquity may be best explained as a quirk of archeology, namely, that the latest strata are those largely preserved, much as we argued in the previous chapter with respect to the absence of first- and second-century synagogues.

116. See Rubin, "Christianity in Byzantine Palestine," 107–8; Peters, *Jerusalem*, 158–61. Perhaps the destruction layer in the Reḥov synagogue is a result of this wave of attacks. See *NEAEHL*, IV, 1272. See also the decrees of 393 and 397 granting protection to synagogues (Linder, *Jews in Roman Imperial Legislation*, nos. 21, 25). On the destruction of synagogues generally or their conversion into churches, see below, Chaps. 8 and 9.

117. See also Fowden, "Bishops and Temples," 53–78; MacMullen, *Christianizing the Roman Empire*, 86–101; Rubin, "Christianity in Byzantine Palestine," 107–11.

eight # DIASPORA SYNAGOGUES

The evidence for the Diaspora synagogue in late antiquity invites comparison with the proverbial cup of water only partly full. On the one hand, we have material remains of twelve buildings (excluding Delos) as well as hundreds of inscriptions relating to the synagogue or its officials.[1] Moreover, literary sources note scores of synagogues throughout the Roman-Byzantine and Persian worlds, although in most cases nothing substantive is conveyed about the institution.[2] On the other hand, given the existence of an extensive and far-flung Diaspora, this evidence appears woefully fragmentary. There can be little doubt that what we have is but a small sample of what actually existed in late antiquity.

Archeological remains of synagogue buildings derive from all parts of the Empire, from Dura Europos (Syria) in the East to Elche (Spain) in the West. Between these geographical extremes, synagogue remains have been found at Gerasa in Provincia Arabia (Jordan), Apamea in Syria, Sardis and Priene in Asia Minor, Aegina in Greece, Stobi in Macedonia, Plovdiv (ancient Philippopolis) in Bulgaria, Ostia and Bova Marina in Italy,

---

1. For recent surveys of Diaspora synagogue remains, see Feldman, "Diaspora Synagogues," 48–66; Rutgers, "Diaspora Synagogues," 67–95; and esp. Hachlili, *Art and Archaeology—Diaspora*, passim.

2. See the listing of some sixty-six places in Feldman, "Diaspora Synagogues," 49. Rutgers offers the number of at least 150 without any enumeration ("Diaspora Synagogues," 67).

and Ḥammam Lif (Naro) in North Africa (fig. 36).[3] Inscriptions from these synagogues alone number about 150. Taken together with inscriptions found elsewhere (e.g., in Asia Minor), and especially those discovered in the catacombs of Rome and Venosa which mention the titles of synagogue officials,[4] the total number of synagogue-related inscriptions from the Diaspora is well over three hundred.[5] The buildings themselves have been discovered over the course of the past century. The earliest report, from the end of the nineteenth century, relates to the Ḥammam Lif synagogue. At the beginning of the twentieth century, synagogues were identified (at times arguably) at Priene, Aegina, and Elche. Between 1929 and 1934, four synagogues were discovered, at Stobi (1931), Gerasa (1929), Dura Europos (1932), and Apamea (1934). Three decades later, the synagogues at Ostia (1961) and Sardis (1962) were excavated, and in the 1980s, those at Bova Marina and Plovdiv came to light.

In contradistinction to the situation in the pre-70 period, for which literary sources (primarily Philo, Josephus, and Acts) are of inestimable value in any discussion of the Diaspora synagogue, the situation in late antiquity leaves much to be desired. There are no literary sources which offer any serious discussion or description of these synagogues and how they functioned. Jewish sources are limited almost exclusively to rabbinic literature, which addresses the situation in Babylonia only—and even then in a limited fashion. Regarding non-Jewish sources, the synagogue is indeed mentioned both in Roman Imperial sources and by church fathers, and many of these references are of immense value.

---

3. Excluded from this list are nine sites whose identification as synagogues remains uncertain. These include Athens; Miletus, Pergamum, and Mopsuestia in Asia Minor; Palmyra in Syria; Carthage and Leptis Magna in North Africa; Chersonesus in the Crimea; and Qana' in Yemen. On these sites, see Stavroulakis and DeVinney, *Jewish Sites*, 46-47; Goodenough, *Jewish Symbols*, II, 78; von Gerkin, "Synagoge in Milet," 177-81; Kraabel, "Diaspora Synagogue," 488-89; Avi-Yonah, "Mosaics of Mopsuestia," 186-90; Foerster, "Survey of Diaspora Synagogues," 165; Duval, "Art paléochrétien," 413-15; Lund, "Synagogue at Carthage?" 245-62 (see also Rives, *Religion and Authority in Roman Carthage*, 221-23); Foerster, "Synagogue in Leptis Magna," 53-58; MacLennan, "In Search of the Jewish Diaspora," 44-51 (see also E. Eshel, "Incised Hebrew Inscription"). Information on Qana' was communicated by A. V. Sadov. See also the comments in Hachlili, *Art and Archaeology—Diaspora*, 49-52, 209-16.

4. The number here could fluctuate between several score to well over one hundred, depending on whether one interprets certain offices as being connected to a synagogue, for example, those of presbyter and, more notably, archon, in Rome (this title alone is mentioned in almost fifty inscriptions). See Frey, *CIJ*, I, lxviiiff.; Leon, *Jews of Ancient Rome*, 167ff.; Noy, *JIWE*, I, 328-29. Given the fact that the synagogue was the basic communal institution in Rome, it can be assumed that all officials named were associated in one way or another with it (see below).

5. In addition to the aforementioned categories, mention should be made of other inscriptions listed by Lifshitz (*Donateurs et fondateurs*), several from Greece (Corinth, Athens), three from Hungary, at least a dozen more from western Europe, and the many known to us from literary sources. An example in the last category would be the inscriptions from the synagogue in Edessa, which was converted by the bishop Rabbula (died 435 or 436) into the church of St. Stephen; see J. B. Segal, *Edessa*, 182.

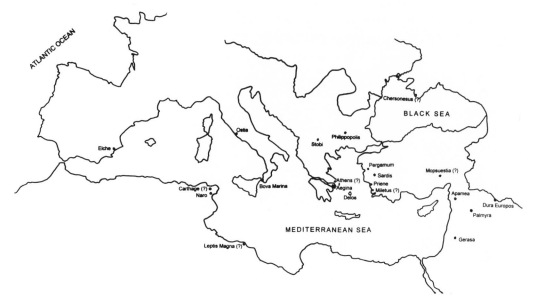

36. Map of the excavated Diaspora synagogues of late antiquity.

However, Roman sources are limited in number, and Christian material is often depre-catory in nature and intent, frequently reporting only a synagogue's destruction.

ARCHEOLOGICAL SITES

Let us begin with a survey of the Diaspora synagogue buildings that have been re-covered to date.

Dura Europos

Discovered in 1932, in the course of the extensive excavations carried out by Yale University and the Department of Antiquities of Syria, the synagogue at Dura Euro-pos is the most complete and important one yet recovered in the Diaspora.[6] The first of the synagogue's two stages dates from the late second or early third century; the second stage was built in 244-45 and destroyed in 256.

The building is unique in a number of ways. The entire complex in both its stages is

---

6. The bibliography on this synagogue is understandably extensive. The two basic works are Krael-ing, *Dura: Synagogue;* and Goodenough, *Jewish Symbols,* IX-XI. See also White, *Building God's House,* 93–97; idem, *Social Origins,* 272–93; Hachlili, *Art and Archaeology—Diaspora,* 96–197, 424–32. For a listing of many of the major contributors in this regard, see Gutmann, "Early Synagogue and Jewish Catacomb Art," 1338–42.

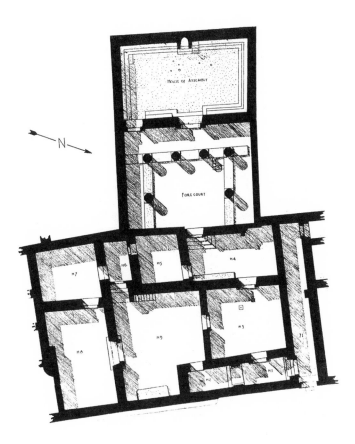

37. Plan of the Dura Europos synagogue.

clearly identifiable (fig. 37). Toward the middle of the third century, the synagogue community expanded significantly and additional facilities were required. A second building
was therefore acquired and integrated into the original synagogue complex, which itself
underwent extensive remodeling. Undoubtedly, the full range of synagogue functions
was carried out in the new complex, although it is impossible to designate which room
was assigned what function. In each stage, the focus of the building was the sanctuary
(house of assembly), with an *aedicula* serving as a Torah shrine located in its western wall.
Benches lined the four walls of the room, and there may have been some sort of *bima* or
table in the center.

The pièce de résistance of this building is its astounding display of Jewish art (fig. 38).
In its later stage, the synagogue walls were covered from floor to ceiling with frescoes.
Just above the *aedicula* on the western wall are Temple-associated representations, i.e.,
a menorah, the Temple facade, and an *'Aqedah* scene (since Mt. Moriah, at least from

38. Western wall of the Dura Europos synagogue with a Torah niche in the center.

the time of Chronicles, was identified with the Temple Mount). Above these depictions is a series of biblical scenes illustrating the bestowal of blessings—Jacob to his sons and grandsons—as well as one of a seated royal figure (David? the Messiah?) holding court. Also depicted is David, dressed as Orpheus and enchanting animals with his music. Flanking this upper panel are four large figures, one of which—on the upper right-hand side—is clearly identified as Moses. The identity of the others is unclear, and they have been subject to a number of possible identifications, including those of Goodenough, who views all of them as Moses.[7]

The remainder of the wall space in the synagogue illustrates an array of what must have been between fifty and sixty scenes taken from the biblical narrative. The finding of Moses, the exodus from Egypt, and Ezekiel's vision of the dry bones are the most extensive single representations preserved (figs. 39–40), but there are also several cycles of sequential events narrated in the Bible, as, for example, the loss of the ark at Even ha-ʿEzer and its sojourn in Philistine territory, a series of Elijah stories, and depictions of the Wilderness Tabernacle and Solomon's Temple.

---

7. The upper right-hand portrait is Moses at the burning bush and is so identified by an inscription. Based on this identification, Goodenough (*Jewish Symbols*, IX, 110–23) opines that the upper left-hand one may be Moses at Sinai; the bottom right-hand one, Moses reading the Law (per Deuteronomy); and the bottom left-hand one, Moses standing humbly, arms folded, before his death (see Midrash on Proverbs 14 [p. 118]). See also Kraeling, *Dura: Synagogue*, 227–39; Weitzmann and Kessler, *Frescoes*, 127–32, 170–73.

39. Panel on the western wall of the Dura Europos synagogue depicting Moses and the Children of Israel crossing the Sea of Reeds.

40. Panel on the northern wall of the Dura Europos synagogue depicting Ezekiel and the vision of the dry bones.

It has long been debated whether there is any overall pattern to these frescoes.[8] Are they arbitrary or is there an all-inclusive theme which informs all the different depictions? Barring this, is there any logic in the arrangement of each of the three registers in the room—i.e., does each represent a different idea, and, if so, how do they relate? Little consensus has been reached, and such questions may be assuming a far more ambitious agenda than the Duran Jews had ever dreamed of. It might well be, as Bickerman noted decades ago, that what is represented here is a kind of *Heilsgeschichte* drawing exclusively on biblical motifs. According to this approach, each individual depiction or set of depictions has its own meaning and significance, with no necessary assumption of one overall theme.[9]

Whatever the case, the implications of the Dura synagogue representations vis-à-vis Jewish art are enormous. Studies abound with regard to the paintings themselves, and the latter have also sparked renewed interest in the field of ancient Jewish art generally. The synagogue constitutes an impressive example of this art and presumably of "midrashic" traditions of the Bible, which almost certainly did not originate there. Lying on the fringes of the eastern Empire, the Dura community was too small and peripheral, and its history too short, to have created such a rich tradition ex nihilo. Clearly, these motifs were found elsewhere—in both Jewish and non-Jewish settings—and undoubtedly in many other synagogues of the Diaspora as well. If there were any doubts beforehand as to whether such an art once existed in antiquity, then Dura put them to rest. To date, however, nothing even remotely comparable has been recovered elsewhere. Thus, while the euphoria over the first revelations of Dura has dimmed somewhat in the almost seventy years that have passed since the original discovery, these finds clearly indicate that a wider Jewish artistic tradition must have existed,[10] one which will come to light sooner or later.

The uniqueness of the Dura synagogue also rests on the fact that its immediate urban context has also been extensively excavated and explored.[11] What has become evident is that the builders of this synagogue adapted local architectural and artistic models, thus fitting it neatly into patterns found throughout the city. The Torah shrine, for instance, was a close approximation of the *aediculae* found in local pagan temples, with the distinction that, in the Jewish context, it was intended to house a scroll (or scrolls) and not an idol. Linguistically as well, the Jews of Dura merged into the cultural milieu of their surroundings. Some of the nineteen Greek and twenty-two Aramaic inscriptions found are

---

8. L. Levine, "Synagogue at Dura-Europos," 172–77; Gutmann, "Programmatic Painting," 137–54; idem, "Early Synagogue and Jewish Catacomb Art," 1322–28; Hachlili, *Art and Archaeology—Diaspora*, 180–82.

9. Bickerman, "Symbolism in Dura Synagogue," 127–51. Carrying this idea even further, Wharton suggests that the Dura narratives are a "pastiche" and should be viewed "as postmodernist (deconstructive, circumstantial, local and multicultural)." See Wharton, "Good and Bad Images," 1–25; as well as idem, *Refiguring*, 38–51. Regarding other aspects of the Dura frescoes, see below, Chap. 17.

10. See Weitzmann and Kessler, *Frescoes*, 143–50.

11. Perkins, *Art of Dura*, 33–69; Gates, "Dura-Europos," 166–81.

41. Depiction from the Gerasa synagogue of animals marching to Noah's ark. Note also the menorah and the Greek inscription.

dedicatory; others identify figures and scenes depicted in the frescoes. The ten Iranian inscriptions are enigmatic graffiti, possibly documenting a series of visits to the synagogue by outsiders. No other site known to date is more illustrative of the adaptability of a Diaspora community to its social, religious, and cultural environment than that of Dura.

Gerasa

Excavated in 1929, the synagogue of Gerasa in Jordan was situated on a mound west of the centrally located Temple of Artemis, at the highest point of the city.[12] Remains of the synagogue's mosaic floor were found about fifteen centimeters beneath the floor of the church which replaced it.

East of the synagogue building are the remains of an atrium surrounded by a colonnade on its northern, eastern, and southern sides. On the basis of different-sized tesserae found in the center of the atrium, it has been conjectured that a basin for ablutions may have once stood there, although no actual remains were discovered. From this atrium, one approached the synagogue building by ascending a series of steps to the west. The floor of the vestibule was entirely covered with a mosaic pavement containing the familiar cluster of Jewish symbols (menorah, shofar, incense shovel, *lulav*, and *ethrog*), a Greek inscription surrounded by several animals (probably lions), and a scene from the Noah story. The last includes a depiction of animals exiting the ark; to its left are the heads of two young men, Noah's sons Shem and Yaphet (whose names appear in Greek), as well as a dove carrying an olive branch in its beak. The Greek inscription flanking the menorah reads: "To the most holy place, Amen, Selah. Peace upon the congregation" (fig. 41).

Three doors led into the building's interior, which was arranged in a basilical plan.

---

12. Crowfoot and Hamilton, "Discovery of a Synagogue at Jerash," 211-19; Kraeling, *Gerasa*, 236-39, 318-23; Goodenough, *Jewish Symbols*, I, 259-60; Roth-Gerson, *Greek Inscriptions*, no. 10; Naveh, *On Stone and Mosaic*, no. 50; Crowfoot, *Churches at Jerash*, 16-20.

Two rows of columns separated the nave from the side aisles, and at its western end, in the direction of Jerusalem, there appears to have been some sort of niche. The floor of the nave was paved with marble slabs, and the two side aisles were covered with mosaics. Although fragmentary, the mosaic remains indicate a high level of execution. The western part of the pavement was removed and destroyed when the building was converted into a church; only geometric designs and a guilloche border have been preserved. A five-line Hebrew inscription was found in the northern aisle: "Peace on Israel, Amen, Amen, Selah. Pinḥas son of Baruch, Yose son of Samuel, and Judan son of Ḥizqiyah." The synagogue dates from the fourth or fifth century and was replaced by a church in 530-31 C.E., i.e., the beginning of Justinian's reign, as we learn from an inscription found there.

Apamea

The building at Apamea, situated in the very heart of the city, on the *cardo maximus*, approximately one hundred meters south of the main intersection, was discovered during excavations carried out in the mid-1930s (fig. 42).[13] The local Jewish community was evidently of sufficient stature and prominence to have been able to acquire such a central location. The building was constructed in the late fourth century but appears to have existed for only a number of decades before it was destroyed and converted into a church in the early fifth century.

The main hall of the synagogue measured about 15.50 by 9 meters; it had a square niche for the Torah scrolls in its southern wall as well as a lavish mosaic floor with impressive carpet-like geometric patterns (fig. 43), as at Sardis (see below). The floor also had a menorah and contained twenty dedicatory inscriptions that often included not only the names of the donors, but also those of other family members.

Unique to these inscriptions was a listing of the number of feet of mosaic floor contributed by each person: Iliasios—150 feet, Sapricia—150 feet, Euthalis Scholastikos—140 feet, Alexandra—100 feet, Ambrosia—50 feet, Domitilla (or Domina, Domnina)—100 feet, Eupithis—100 feet, Diogenis—100 feet, Basilidas—100 feet, Thaumasis (along with his wife, Hesychios, and mother-in-law, Eustathia)—100 feet, Hierios (and his wife, Urania)—100 feet, Colonis—75 feet, Theodoros (and his wife, Hesychios)—35 feet.

Among those mentioned, either as donors or honorees, were the head of the Antioch council (*gerousiarch*), several *archisynagogoi*, a presbyter, a *ḥazzan*, and a deacon. Of special interest are several inscriptions which note the date of donation (i.e., the year 703 of the Seleucid era, or 391 C.E.), as well as the participation of community leaders in these endeavors:

---

13. Brenk, "Synagoge von Apamea," 1-25; Hachlili, *Art and Archaeology—Diaspora*, 32-34, 198-204, 402; Sukenik, "Mosaic Inscriptions," 541-51; Frey, *CIJ*, II, nos. 803-18; Lifshitz, *Donateurs et fondateurs*, nos. 38-56. See also Mayence, "Fouille à Apamée," 199-204. For the nave inscription mentioning women, see Brooten, *Women Leaders*, 158-59.

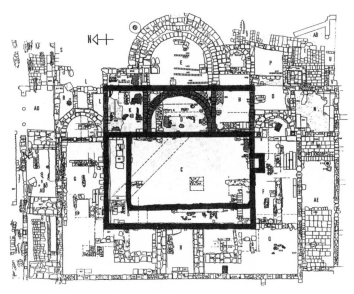

42. Plan of the Apamea synagogue with the niche to the south.
Remains of several Byzantine churches with apses facing east were
discovered on the synagogue ruins.

43. Mosaics from the Apamea synagogue.

> In the time of the most illustrious *archisynagogoi* Eusebios, Nemeos, and Phineos, and the gerousiarch Theodoros, and the most illustrious presbyters Isakios, Saulos, and the others, Iliasios, *archisynagogos* of the Antiochans, made the entrance of mosaic, 150 feet, in the year 703, the seventh day of the month of Audynaios [= January 7, 391]. Blessings upon all!

> Iliasios [son] of Isakios, *archisynagogos* of the Antiochans, for the welfare of Photios his wife, and of [their] children, and for the welfare of Eustathia his mother-in-law, and in memory of Isakios, Edesios, and Hesychios [his] ancestors, made the mosaic of the entrance. Peace and mercy upon all your holy people! [14]

The above inscriptions reflect very different types of dedications. The first records the gift of an archisynagogue of the Antiochan synagogue in Apamea, who contributed a sizable section of the floor in honor of his colleagues—three archisynagogues, a gerousiarch, and at least two presbyters. In contrast, the second inscription speaks of this same Iliasos honoring his family. The former type of inscription is most unusual and is sui generis among the inscriptions from this synagogue. On the other hand, thirteen other inscriptions from the Apamea synagogue were made by, or in honor of, a family. Nine of the inscriptions were donated by women, and in another three, wives are mentioned as benefactors along with their husbands. All the inscriptions are in Greek, as are the names of the donors, including those which are transliterated from the Hebrew: Nemeos, Phineas, Isakios, Saulos, and Hesychios.

Both Iliasos inscriptions were placed in the entranceway or portico of the synagogue. One other inscription was also found there; it states that an anonymous donation was made in the time of Nemeos, the *ḥazzan* and *diakonos* of the synagogue. This inscription refers to the synagogue building as a *naos*.

Sardis

Located in one of the major cities of western Asia Minor, the Sardis synagogue, discovered in 1962, has deservedly attracted a great deal of scholarly attention over the past generation, particularly through the articles of Kraabel and Seager and more recently Bonz.[15] The Sardis structure is by far the most monumental of all ancient synagogues. Its impressiveness stems from its prominent location, large dimensions, and rich remains. Located on the main street, at an important intersection of the city, the synagogue was housed in what formerly had been a wing of the city's *palaestra*, or gymnasium (fig. 44). Outside its southern wall, facing the main street, the building was fronted by a row of

---

14. Following Sukenik's transcription and translation in "Mosaic Inscriptions," 544–45.

15. For Kraabel's and Seager's contributions to this subject, see above, Chap. 1, note 9; as well as Bonz, "Jewish Community of Ancient Sardis," 343–59; idem, "Differing Approaches to Religious Benefaction," 139–54. See also Trebilco, *Jewish Communities*, 37–54; White, *Building God's House*, 98–101; idem, *Social Origins*, 310–23; Hachlili, *Art and Archaeology—Diaspora*, 58–63, 218–31, 410–12.

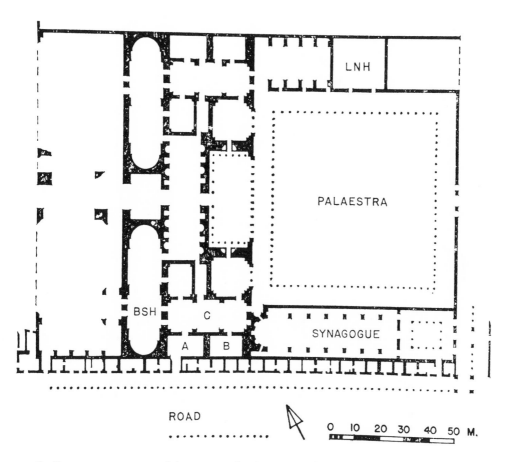

LNH

PALAESTRA

BSH   C

A   B

SYNAGOGUE

ROAD

0   10   20   30   40   50 M.

44. Sardis synagogue as part of the municipal *palaestra* complex.

shops, some of which were owned by Jews; a side entrance directly connected these shops
with the synagogue's atrium.[16]

No other extant ancient synagogue can match that of Sardis in sheer physical size.
The building itself was some 80 meters long; in its last stage it was divided into two
parts, an almost 60-meter-long sanctuary and a 20-meter-long atrium. Compare this to
the largest Palestinian synagogues known to date—Capernaum (24 meters), Meiron (27
meters), and Gaza (ca. 30 meters).

The building was completed sometime in the second century C.E. as part of the city's
immense gymnasium and bath complex (fig. 45).[17] The complex's southeastern wing, like

---

16. Crawford, *Byzantine Shops*, 17–18.

17. The following building history of the synagogue is based on Seager and Kraabel, "Synagogue and
Jewish Community," 171–73.

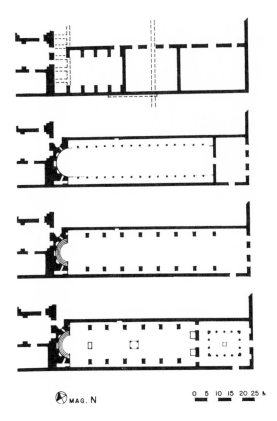

MAG. N

0 5 10 15 20 25 M

45. Four building stages at Sardis. The final two stages were occupied by the synagogue.

its northern counterpart, was divided into a series of rooms, which appear to have once been *apodyteria* (dressing rooms) or exercise rooms, each opening onto the *palaestra* area. However, when the building was converted into a civil basilica, its inner partitions were removed and entrances sealed, and a new entrance was made from the street to the east. The building had a forecourt in the east and an exedra with niches for statues of deities or emperors in the west. While there has been some discussion as to whether the building was used by the Jewish community at this juncture, that seems unlikely to have been the case, and the building probably served some public civic function for a period of time.

In its next stage, dated to the last half of the third century, the building was taken over by the local Jewish community of Sardis.[18] The wall separating the main hall and atrium

18. Adopting Seager's dating, Bonz ("Jewish Community of Ancient Sardis," 343–59; "Differing Approaches to Religious Benefaction," 139–54) offers an explanation of the local Jewish community's rise to prominence in the course of the third century, which allowed for the construction of the synagogue. For a suggestion that the synagogue building dates only to the fourth century, see Bottermann, "Synagoge von Sardis," 103–21.

was removed to create an 80-meter-long hall. At its western end, three-tiered semicircular benches were built, and the exedra was transformed into an apse.

The synagogue as revealed in the excavations and partially reconstructed on site was built in the fourth century. All stratified archeological evidence points to sometime in mid-century: the atrium was completed in 360–80 C.E.; the main hall, with its piers and elaborate mosaic floor, was completed in the second quarter of the fourth century; the wall inscriptions, along with the plaques and marble revetment on which they appear, date from the mid-fourth to the early fifth centuries.

Visitors to the building would have entered the atrium from either one of the streets to the east or south. The atrium was large and attractive, with porticoes surrounding an open courtyard which was lavishly decorated with a mosaic pavement of multicolored geometric patterns and had a chancel screen or balustrade between the columns supporting its roof. In the center of the atrium stood an impressive marble basin for washing and perhaps drinking. A reference to the "fountain of the Jews" in a municipal inscription may refer to this basin.[19]

Three portals—a large central door flanked by two smaller ones—led from the courtyard into the main sanctuary. Immediately inside the sanctuary, two *aediculae* on masonry platforms flanked the main entrance, at least one of which—probably the southern one, which was of a better quality—was intended to hold the Torah scrolls (fig. 46). The function of the second *aedicula* remains unknown; additional scrolls or possibly a menorah might have been kept there, or perhaps it served as a seat for an elder or some other community official. As was the case in a number of other places in the synagogue, the stones used for these *aediculae* originally came from pagan buildings in the city.

Toward the western end of the hall stood a massive stone table, which has been labeled the "eagle table" because of the two large Roman eagles engraved in relief on each of its two supporting stones (fig. 47). The table was flanked by two pairs of lions, each sitting back to back. Both the eagles and lions also appear in secondary use, the latter perhaps dating back to the city's Lydian period, i.e., the sixth to fifth centuries B.C.E.

According to the excavators' estimates, the semicircular benches at the western end of the sanctuary could have accommodated about seventy people (figs. 48–49). Directly in front of the apse is a delicately executed mosaic floor featuring vine tendrils extending from a vase or basin, similar, perhaps, to the one located in the atrium outside. The names of donors were incorporated into this mosaic. A stone parapet, perhaps a kind of chancel screen, separated the mosaic and the apse from the main hall.

Pillars divided the central nave and two side aisles of the main hall. As there were no traces of a balcony or stone benches, the congregation—which by some estimates might have numbered up to one thousand people—probably sat on mats or wooden benches, and some might have stood. The floor was lavishly decorated with geometric patterns

---

19. Seager and Kraabel, "Synagogue and Jewish Community," 169.

46. Reconstructed *aedicula* along the eastern wall of the Sardis synagogue, near the entrances.

47. "Eagle table" found in the center of the Sardis synagogue.

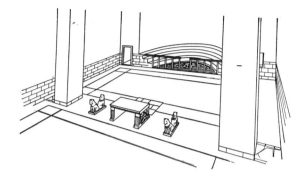

48. Drawing of the western section of the Sardis synagogue, with the "eagle table," two pairs of lions, and an apse with benches along the western wall.

49. Reconstruction of the western section of the Sardis synagogue.

and was divided into seven bays, while the lower parts of the walls were decorated with marble wall panels or revetments (*skoutlosis*), the upper parts with panels of brightly colored marble inlay.

The excavations also yielded a rich harvest of epigraphical material, which has yet to be systematically published. In all, over eighty inscriptions were reportedly found.[20] With but two or three exceptions,[21] these inscriptions are in Greek, as are the personal names mentioned in them. Of the thirty or so donors listed, only two names are Hebrew derivatives. The Sardis donors are identified either by profession, not uncommon in Jewish epigraphy, or by public office, which was far less common. Among the synagogue members were provincial and city officials, procurators, city councillors, *comes*, and members of the decurionate. Altogether, this synagogue boasted well-placed, prosperous, and influential members of the community, which would indeed account for the building's central location, size, and impressiveness, as well as the ability of the Jewish community to maintain such an imposing facility for centuries.

Of particular interest regarding the religious functioning of the synagogue is an inscription found in the very center of the mosaic floor mentioning one "Samoe, *hiereus* [priest] and *sophodidaskalos*," the latter title referring to a wise teacher or a teacher of wisdom. Given the prominent position of this inscription, it is clear that Samoe at one time occupied a central religious role within the community. It has also been suggested that this Samoe may have preached or taught from the very spot where the inscription was found.

Finally, synagogue inscriptions tell us something about the nature of the Judaism understood and practiced in this synagogue. One inscription refers to the Torah shrine as a *nomophylakion* (i.e., that which protects the Law); another bears the cryptic sentence "Having found, having broken,[22] read! observe!" These inscriptions were carefully executed and may once have been prominently displayed in the synagogue hall near the Torah shrines. Eleven inscriptions mention the Greek term *pronoia* (divine providence), and the appropriation of this cosmopolitan Greek philosophical-religious concept apparently reflects a significant degree of acculturation among the Jews.[23]

In addition, remains of some nineteen *menorot* were found, some incised in stone,

---

20. Interim publications include Robert, *Nouvelles inscriptions*; Lifshitz, *Donateurs et fondateurs*, nos. 17–27. Publication of the final report of these excavations, including the epigraphical material, is forthcoming (Seager et al., *Synagogue and Its Setting*).

21. In addition to a few full Hebrew names, one letter or parts of several letters were found in some nine fragments.

22. The term may refer to the "breaking open" of a text (i.e., to fathom its meaning) or to breaking a seal in order to open a scroll; see Kraabel, *Diaspora Jews and Judaism*, 289.

23. Kraabel, "*Pronoia* at Sardis," 75–96; and, more generally, Harrison, "Benefaction Ideology," 109–16.

brick, metal, or pottery. The most impressive is an ornate stone menorah which also bears the name of its donor, Socrates.[24]

It is little wonder that such synagogue finds have thrown into question many of the negative assumptions prevalent in early scholarship concerning late ancient Diaspora Jewish life. They have demonstrated, beyond all doubt, that at least some communities had achieved a high degree of recognition and status within their individual cities; in the case of Sardis, this continued for several centuries after the Christianization of the Empire, right up the Persian destruction of the city in 616.[25]

Priene

The synagogue at Priene, located on the Ionian coast of Asia Minor between Ephesus and Miletus, was identified as such only decades after it was excavated.[26] At first referred to as a "house-church," it appears that the building originally functioned in the Hellenistic period as a private residence and was transformed into a synagogue sometime in the second or third century.[27] The main hall was an irregular rectangle, measuring 10.20 meters (east to west) by 12.59–13.70 meters (north to south); two rows of stone slabs served as stylobates and were laid on an east-west axis; a niche 1.35 by 1.37 meters was cut into its eastern wall, thus indicating that this was a broadhouse-type synagogue (see Chap. 9) similar to the one at Dura Europos. The hall had benches along its northern wall, as well as a small forecourt. A series of rooms, undoubtedly serving a wide variety of congregational purposes, surrounded the hall.

The identification of this building as a synagogue became conclusive with the discovery of a number of smaller items bearing Jewish symbols.[28] A relief, which appears to originally have been affixed to the wall, was found on the floor in front of the niche; it depicted the usual Jewish symbols, with the menorah being flanked by peacocks. Nearby, a pillar incised with a menorah was found on the floor. Presumably, the carving was never completed, as only three branches of the menorah are represented. Another relief, featuring a menorah with a *lulav* and shofar on one side and an *ethrog* on the other, was found in a church next to the theater and may have originated in this synagogue. Finally, a large basin, almost a meter in diameter, was found in the synagogue building.

---

24. Seager and Kraabel, "Synagogue and Jewish Community," 176.

25. Crawford, "Multiculturalism at Sardis," 38–47.

26. Wiegand and Schrader, *Priene*, 480; Goodenough, *Jewish Symbols*, II, 77; Kraabel, "Diaspora Synagogue," 489–91; White, *Building God's House*, 67–68; idem, *Social Origins*, 325–32; Hachlili, *Art and Archaeology—Diaspora*, 56–58.

27. White, *Social Origins*, 328–30.

28. Wiegand and Schrader, *Priene*, 480; Foerster, "Survey of Diaspora Synagogues," 165; White, *Social Origins*, 332.

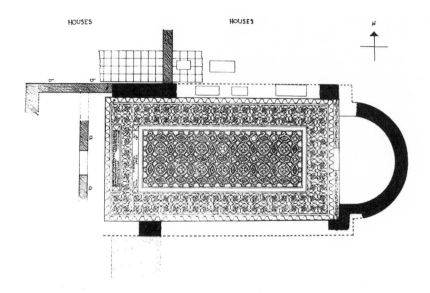

50. Mosaic floor of the Aegina synagogue.

Aegina

The synagogue of Aegina, an island in the Aegean Sea near Piraeus, the port of Athens, was located close to the local harbor.[29] Traces of ancillary rooms were found at the northern end of the building, which perhaps had a portico at its western end. The main hall measured 13.50 by 7.60 meters, and on its eastern end was an apse measuring 5.50 meters in diameter. The floor of the nave had a mosaic pavement with geometric designs (fig. 50). Dated to the fourth century, the synagogue appears to have been built over an earlier structure of unknown identity but identical plan. The following two Greek inscriptions were found at the western end of the mosaic floor.

> I, Theodoros, the *archisynagogos* who served for four years, built the synagogue from its foundations. Revenues [contributed] amounted to 85 gold pieces and offerings to God [i.e., from the synagogue treasury] [amounted] to 105 gold pieces.

> Theodoros the younger being in charge, the mosaic work has been done out of synagogue revenues. Blessings upon all who enter.[30]

---

29. Mazur, *Jewry in Greece*, 25–33; Sukenik, *Ancient Synagogues*, 44–45; Goodenough, *Jewish Symbols*, II, 75–76; Foerster, "Survey of Diaspora Synagogues," 166–67; White, *Social Origins*, 356–59; Hachlili, *Art and Archaeology—Diaspora*, passim.

30. Frey, *CIJ*, I, nos. 722–23; Lifshitz, *Donateurs et fondateurs*, nos. 1–2; Sukenik, *Ancient Synagogues*, 44; Wischnitzer, *Architecture of European Synagogue*, 4–5; Goodenough, *Jewish Symbols*, II, 75–76; White, *Social Origins*, 356–59.

51. Menorah from the mosaic floor in
the Plovdiv (Philippopolis) synagogue.

Plovdiv

Discovered in Bulgaria in 1981, this synagogue was located in the center of ancient Philippopolis (now Plovdiv), a city founded by Philip II of Macedonia.[31] It was located on a *cardo*, not far from the forum and close to other major public buildings (a large bath complex and a basilica). The synagogue hall itself is part of a larger complex which, although poorly preserved, clearly once included a number of other rooms and courtyards. The synagogue hall had a southern orientation toward Jerusalem and entrances in the north, where the atrium was also located. Although it appears to have been almost square, the hall had a basilical plan with two rows of columns. Measuring 13.5 meters (north to south) by 14.2 meters (east to west), its nave was 9 meters wide, and the two aisles each measured 2.6 meters wide. The total area of the entire synagogue complex is estimated to have been 600 square meters.

Remains of the building's mosaic floor indicate a tripartite division, with each panel measuring 3.0 by 3.8 meters. Geometric designs predominate alongside an array of ivy leaves. A large, highly ornate seven-branched menorah with a circular base adorned the central panel (fig. 51).

The mosaic floor contained two inscriptions in Greek; the better-preserved one was found in a side panel: "From his [resources], and according to design [or Providence],[32] Cosmianus, otherwise known as Joseph, made this decoration. Blessing to all." Dated on paleographic grounds to the third century, the inscription notes a wealthy benefactor's gift to the synagogue. The synagogue had presumably suffered, as did much of the city, during the Gothic incursions of the mid-third century, and the renovation recorded in

---

31. Danov and Kesjakova, "Unique Finding," 210–26; and, for somewhat more detail, Danov, "Neues aus der Geschichte von Philippopolis," 107–23; Koranda, "Menorah-Darstellungen," 218–39; Hachlili, *Art and Archaeology—Diaspora*, passim.

32. See Danov and Kesjakova, "Unique Finding," 212.

this inscription possibly came in their aftermath. It is unusual to see a Greek (or Latin) name together with a Hebrew (or Semitic) one, although the same phenomenon occurs in nearby Stobi as well. Nevertheless, each of these names is attested elsewhere for Jews.[33] An early third-century inscription from Intercisa (Hungary) mentions one Cosmius, a customs official who likewise contributed to a synagogue. Finally, the formula "Blessing to . . ." appears in other Jewish inscriptions, as, for example, ones from Italy, Syracuse, Aegina, and Bet She'arim.[34]

The second inscription, which is fragmentary and very poorly preserved ("made the arrangement and the decoration"), was found at the foot of the mosaic menorah, on either side of its base, and is dated to the fourth century. By the next century, the synagogue was no longer in use.

Stobi

Located in Macedonia, about 160 kilometers north of Salonika, the ancient town of Stobi was excavated extensively between the years 1924 and 1934.[35] Amid a cluster of buildings along one of the main streets between the Roman bridge and a church, a structure was identified as a synagogue on the basis of a monumental Greek inscription found therein.[36] However, excavations soon made clear that the building functioned as a church from sometime in the fifth or sixth century. The column on which the synagogue inscription appears was clearly in secondary usage.

For decades since the excavation of this building in 1931, the only evidence for a synagogue was this very impressive and informative inscription, arguably the most important one found to date in any Diaspora synagogue setting (fig. 52):

> The year 311 [?]. Claudius Tiberius Polycharmos, also named Achyrios, father [*pater*] of the synagogue at Stobi, having lived my whole life according to Judaism, have, in fulfillment of a vow, [given] the buildings to the holy place, and the *triclinium*, together with the *tetrastoon*, with my own means, without in the least touching the sacred [funds]. But the ownership and disposition of all the upper chambers shall be retained by me, Claudius Tiberius Polycharmos, and my heirs for life. Whoever seeks in any way to alter any of these dispositions of mine shall pay the Patriarch 250,000 denarii. For thus have I resolved. But the repair of the roof tiles of the upper chambers shall be carried out by me and my heirs.[37]

---

33. On the name "Joseph" in Jewish inscriptions, see Noy, *JIWE*, I, nos. 70, 79.

34. Ibid., 203.

35. Kitzinger, "Survey of Early Christian Town of Stobi," 81–161; Marmorstein, "Synagogue of Claudius Tiberius Polycharmus," 373–84; Kraabel, "Diaspora Synagogue," 494–97; White, *Social Origins*, 343–52; Hachlili, *Art and Archaeology—Diaspora*, 63–67, 231–33, 410. See also Moe, "Cross and Menorah," 148–57.

36. See, for example, Wischnitzer, *Architecture of European Synagogue*, 7–9.

37. Translation generally follows White, *Social Origins*, 352–56. See also Kitzinger, "Survey of Early Christian Town of Stobi," 141–42; Hengel, "Synagogeninschrift von Stobi"; Feldman, "Diaspora Synagogues," 62.

```
     .... ////
....../TIΕΞΡΙΣΕΡ.ΑΝ
ΧΑΡΜΟΣΟΚΑΙΑΧΥΡΙ
ΟΣΟΠΑΤΗΡΤΗΣΕΝ
ΣΤΟΒΟΙΣΣΥΝΑΓΩΓΗΣ
ΟΣΦΛΕΙΤΙΕΥΣΑΜΕ
ΝΟΣΠΑΣΑΝΠΟΛΕΙΤΕΙ
ΑΝΚΑΤΑΤΟΝΙΟΥΔΑΙ
ΣΜΟΝΕΥΧΗΣΕΝΕΚΕΝ
ΤΟΥΣΜΕΝ ΟΙΚΟΥΣΤΩ
ΑΓΙΩΤΟ ΠΩΚΑΙΤΟ
ΤΡΙΚΛΕΙΝΟΝΣΥΝΤΩ
ΤΕΤΡΑΣΤΟΩΕΚΤΩΝ
ΟΙΚΕΙΩΝΧΡΗΜΑΤΩΝ
ΜΗΔΕΝΟΛΩΣΠΑΡΑΨΑ
ΜΕΝΟΣΤΩΝΑΓΙΩΝΤΗ
ΔΕΕΞΟΥΣΙΑΝΤΩΝΥΠΕ
ΡΩΩΝΠΑΝΤΩΝΠΑΣΑΝ
ΚΑΙΤΗΝΔΕΣΠΟΤΕΙΑΝ
ΕΧΕΙΝΕΜΕΤΟΝΚΛΤΙΒΕΡΙ
ΟΝΠΟΛΥΧΑΡΜΟΝΚΑΙΤΟΥΣ
ΚΑΙΤΟΥΣΚΛΗΡΟΝΟΜΟΥΣ
ΤΟΥΣΕΜΟΥΣΔΙΑΠΑΝΤΟΣ
ΒΙΟΥΟΣΑΝΔΕΒΟΥΛΗΘΗ
ΤΙΚΑΙΝΟΤΟΜΣΑΙΠΑΡΑΤΑΥ
ΤΕΜΟΥΔΟΧΘΕΝΤΑΔΩΣΕΙΤΩ
ΠΑΤΡΙΑΡΧΗΔΗΝΑΡΙΩΝΝΥΡΙΑ
ΔΑΣΕΙΚΟΣΙΓΕΝΕΟΥΤΩΓΑΡ
ΜΟΙΣΥΝΕΔΟΞΕΝΗΝΔΕΕΠΙ
ΣΚΕΥΗΝΤΗΣΚΕΡΑΜΟΥΤΩΝ
ΥΠΕΡΩΩΝΠΟΙΕΙΣΘΑΙΕΜΕ
ΚΑΙΚΛΗΡΟΝΟΜΟΥΣ
ΕΜΟΥΣ
```

52. Stobi synagogue inscription engraved on a column.

This inscription is of enormous historical value. In the first place, it mentions the name of the donor and his office or title. The combination of Latin and Greek names would seem to indicate his position of prominence within the Jewish community and perhaps within the town as well. The title *pater* appears elsewhere in Jewish inscriptions, but its precise meaning remains elusive. Like the feminine *mater*, it clearly derives from the larger Greco-Roman world and may have been essentially honorific, although some have suggested that it may have referred to a member of the *gerousia*.[38]

Secondly, the inscription tells us something about the synagogue building itself. The main hall is referred to as a holy place, clearly indicating its high religious profile. In addition, Polycharmos built a series of other unspecified structures (τοὺς . . . οἴκους), perhaps referring to one or more of the other buildings found in the immediate vicinity of the synagogue. This may apply in particular to the building directly south of it, where there appears to have been an opening or doorway between the two. In addition to the

---

38. Noy, *JIWE*, I, 77–78; and below, Chap. 11.

general designation, the inscription also mentions a *triclinium*, or dining room, which probably served, at the very least, as a place for communal meals and possibly as a general meeting place for other communal purposes as well. The term *tetrastoon*, a four-sided stoa, seems to refer to a courtyard, or atrium, perhaps in some way connected to the *triclinium*. Finally, the building (or buildings) described in this inscription clearly had a second story, the upper chambers of which were reserved for use by Polycharmos' family.

Thus, it appears that Polycharmos was now ceding part of his original home to the community at large. The inscription discusses details governing the arrangement between these two parties. One of the stipulations of this agreement requires an offender to pay an enormous sum of money to the Patriarch—a reference, in all probability, to the Patriarch of Palestine. If so understood, and this has been the most widely accepted interpretation to date (as against a local patriarch, noted in several laws in the Theodosian Code), the inscription would constitute an extremely important piece of evidence regarding the status and prestige of this office toward the end of the third century, even in such a distant Diaspora community.[39] The association of the Patriarch with the Stobi synagogue raises interesting questions regarding the relation of this office to the synagogue as an institution, and we shall return to this issue in Chapter 12.

Finally, the Stobi inscription also contains a date, which, unfortunately, is partly obliterated. Over the years, scholarly consensus has focused on one of two alternatives, each dependent upon a different era as a basis for calculation: 163 C.E. or 280 C.E. Following Hengel's detailed study in 1966, the latter date has been generally preferred.[40]

However, in the early 1970s, excavations at the site were renewed after a forty-year hiatus, and it soon became clear that a synagogue building had once existed on this site.[41] In fact, it has been claimed that several stages of an earlier structure are discernible, including remains of an early second-century pavement; coins of Marcus Aurelius; a menorah-graffito; and frescoes bearing the name Polycharmos in *tabula ansata* frames. In addition, a bronze votive plaque with the name Posidonia was found; and another bronze plaque, bearing the name Eustathius, and a menorah were discovered in a sewage canal. What is not fully clear, however, is which stage should be associated with the above-mentioned monumental inscription: Are we dealing with a late second-, early third-, or—as usually assumed—a later third-century inscription and structure?[42] It would seem, moreover, that Polycharmos' house—and subsequently the synagogue—included the building to the south of the later church (referred to as the House of Psalms).

---

39. See L. Levine, "Status of the Patriarch," 1–32, esp. 13.

40. Hengel, "Synagogeninschrift von Stobi," 110–48. For a long period, the year 163 C.E. was widely preferred; see, for example, Frey, *CIJ*, I, 504–7; Alon, *Jews in Their Land*, II, 251–52, 672; Baron, *Jewish Community*, I, 84; III, 28 n. 24. More recently, Poehlman ("Polycharmos Inscription," 235–46) has again argued for a second-century date. See also White, *Social Origins*, 346–48.

41. Mano-Zissi, "Stratigraphic Problems," 208–9.

42. See White, *Social Origins*, 343–56.

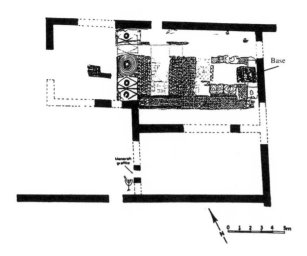

53. Plan of the Stobi synagogue, with the *bima* facing east.

The outlines of the interior plan of the third- to fourth-century synagogue are detectable but, as yet, far from clear (fig. 53). Its hall measured 7.9 by 13.3 meters, with the base of what was probably a *bima* along the eastern wall and the remains of a bench along the southern wall. The walls themselves appear to have been frescoed with geometric and floral motifs and perhaps given decorative stucco moldings. A mosaic floor pavement also has geometric motifs. In addition, per the synagogue inscription, other large communal areas included a *triclinium* and a *tetrastoon*.

Sometime in the later fourth or possibly fifth century, the synagogue was converted into a church.

Ostia

The synagogue of Ostia is located near the wall of this port city of Rome, not far from the harbor and adjacent to the important coastal artery, the Via Severiana.[43] The synagogue remains visible today date to the fourth century C.E., but there clearly were earlier stages dating as far back as the late first or early second century C.E. Several distinct stages of construction mark the building's history (fig. 54). It has generally been assumed that the building was erected as a synagogue from the outset and not, as was the case elsewhere, as a private home that was later converted into a synagogue. White, however, has recently suggested that the original structure was part of the insula complex and may not have served the Jewish community at this first stage. The walls of the main hall (ca. 12.5 by 24.9 meters) were built in *opus reticulatum*, typical of the Flavian and

---

43. Squarciapino, *Synagogue of Ostia*, 19-26; idem, "Synagogue at Ostia," 194-203; Fortis, *Jews and Synagogues*, 121-28; Kraabel, "Diaspora Synagogue," 497-500; White, *Building God's House*, 69-70; idem, *Social Origins*, 379-94; idem, "Synagogue and Society," 23-58 (the most detailed and comprehensive of all treatments); Hachlili, *Art and Archaeology—Diaspora*, 53-55, 216, 409; Noy, *JIWE*, I, no. 13; Fine and Della Pergola, "Synagogue of Ostia," 42-57. See also Wischnitzer, *Architecture of European Synagogue*, 5-7.

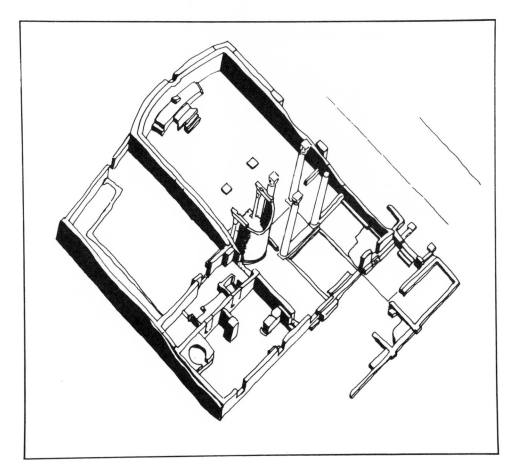

54. Plan of the Ostia synagogue.

early Antonine periods, and thus this room, adjacent anterooms, and perhaps also the adjoining kitchen date to this first period. Later stages featured the *opus vittatum* and *opus latericium*, which were common styles in the third and fourth centuries. A well covered with a small basin was found at the entrance to the building, and a *bima*, measuring 6.2 by 1.25 by 0.79 meters, was built against the northwestern wall of the main hall at this stage.

The Ostia synagogue was subsequently renovated, the kitchen was relaid with black and white mosaics, and a second story was removed, thereby creating a far more spacious main hall. The southeastern entrance to the hall was completely remodeled, and a *propylaeum* with four gray 4.7-meter-high marble columns with Corinthian capitals was introduced, along with the Torah *aedicula* (fig. 55). Some of the above-noted renovations are attested by an important inscription found in the course of excavations. The inscription consists of four lines in Greek and one (the first) in Latin (*"pro salute Aug . . ."*):

55. Monumental *aedicula*
of the Ostia synagogue.

For the well-being of the emperor!
    Mindi[u]s Faustos established and built [the synagogue] with his own funds and set up
the ark [κειβωτόν] of the sacred Law.[44]

The inscription is generally dated to the late second to early third centuries on paleographic grounds. It was found in secondary use in the synagogue vestibule of the subsequent fourth-century building. The inscription attests to a wealthy donor, Mindius
Faustos, who contributed to the remodeling of the synagogue. Moreover, it seems clear
that at this stage, i.e., at least a century before the final renovations of the fourth century
and beyond, the synagogue had a permanent Torah shrine.[45]

When the building assumed its present fourth-century form and plan, it measured
36.6 by 23.5 meters. The mosaic kitchen floor was replaced by one of earth, and it may
have been at this juncture that the windows in the main hall were blocked. A second wall
was constructed around the sanctuary's original one, and a large *opus vittatum* apse (3.62
meters wide) was introduced and served as an *aedicula* for Torah scrolls. Finally, three
small rooms were partitioned off east of the *propylaeum*, and a new entrance to the complex, together with a narthex and adjoining rooms, were completed. Either at this time,
or perhaps in the previous renovation, a large room with benches along two walls was
annexed to the kitchen.

Let us describe the synagogue complex as a visitor in the fourth century would have
seen it. Entering from the Via Severiana, one walked down a long vestibule paved with
black and white tesserae; a marble basin for washing was set over a well on the immedi-

44. Translation by R. Brilliant in V. B. Mann, *Gardens and Ghettoes*," 210–11. See also Noy, *JIWE*, I,
no. 13; G. H. R. Horsley, *New Documents*, IV, 112 (and, generally, 105–12); and White, "Synagogue and
Society," 39–42.

45. According to Noy's interpretation of this inscription, there may have even been a permanent ark
in the synagogue prior to Mindius Faustos' donation (*JIWE*, I, 24–26).

ate left. To the left of the vestibule was a series of rooms (now largely destroyed); there is no way of determining how they might have been used. The main rooms were off to the right of the vestibule. The first three entrances led into the sanctuary. This was a wide central entranceway flanked by two smaller ones, reminiscent of the tripartite entranceway at Sardis and Gerasa, as well as Palestinian synagogues. These portals led to several small rooms partitioned with thin walls. The right-hand room is reported to have contained traces of a ritual bath (*miqveh*).

The central room functioned as a passageway leading into the synagogue hall through a *propylaeum*. A raised *bima* stood in the back, i.e., the northwestern end of the hall, against a slightly curved wall; just to the south of the *propylaeum*, resting on a podium, was a large apsidal *aedicula* in which the Torah scrolls were undoubtedly kept. The symbols carved on two corbels (found at the ends of the architraves extending from the apse) include a menorah, shofar, *lulav*, and *ethrog*. A small fragment of a stone lion was found on the floor of the main hall; however, its original location is unknown. The floor of this hall was decorated in part with marble slabs (*opus sectile*) in secondary use (some of which bore older inscriptions, mostly from other buildings) and in part with a black and white mosaic floor featuring a Solomon's knot. Two columns stood near the middle of the hall.

South of the main hall was a kitchen with an oven and marble-topped table in which five lamps decorated with *menorot* were found. West of the kitchen was a large room with a mosaic floor and benches. Squarciapino has suggested that it may have served as a *bet midrash* or a hostel, but there is no firm evidence for either identification.

Finally, in 1969, an inscription mentioning a local *archisynagogos* was found at the southern end of the site, and it reads as follows: "Plotius Ampliatus, Plotius Secundinus, and Secunda, his children, and Ofilia Basilia, his wife, have done [this in honor of] Plotius Fortunatus, *archisynagogos*."[46]

Bova Marina

At the toe of the Italian peninsula, some fifty kilometers south of Reggio di Calabria, a synagogue was discovered in 1985.[47] Located near an already excavated Roman villa, northeast of which stood a small necropolis, it appears that the site had been inhabited since the second century C.E., although no architectural remains have survived. The excavators identified two distinct stages in the building's history. In the fourth century, a series of rectangular rooms and enclosed spaces adjoined a central hall; they probably constituted the synagogue's ancillary rooms (referred to by the excavators as service rooms) and entranceways. The central mosaic floor of the synagogue hall was decorated

46. Squarciapino, "Plotius Fortunatus," 183–91; V. B. Mann, *Gardens and Ghettoes*, 211; Noy, *JIWE*, I, no. 14.

47. Lattanzi, *Neapolis*, 419–21; Costamagna, "Seminari di archeologia cristiana," 313–17; Hachlili, *Art and Archaeology—Diaspora*, 34–35, 204–5.

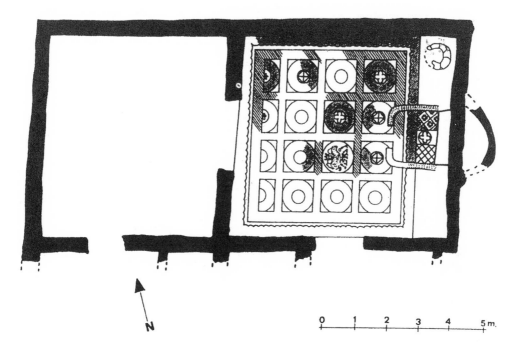

56. Plan of Bova Marina synagogue.

with geometric designs and plaited borders with wreath-like decorations. Rosettes and a Solomon's knot were also represented, along with the central design of menorah, shofar, *lulav*, and *ethrog*.

The synagogue complex was altered in the sixth century: many of the ancillary rooms and open spaces were redesigned, three of the rectangular spaces continued to adjoin the hall, and one of the floors to the south was retiled. It seems clear that the atrium of the synagogue was located in the south, and the entire complex appears to have opened toward the south. A number of rooms were also found northwest of the hall, as in the earlier stage. The central area of the synagogue, i.e., the main hall, was oriented in a northeast-southwest direction. It was significantly remodeled in this stage, with the addition of a semicircular niche, a *bima*, and what appears to be a parapet or chancel screen (fig. 56).

The menorah decoration continued to be featured in this stage as well. Though largely obliterated, it remains clearly recognizable. Its three-legged base was preserved, as were traces of some of its upper branches; other Jewish symbols flanked the menorah. Two amphora handles with menorah impressions were also found.

Over three thousand bronze coins were found in one of the ancillary rooms. The building ceased to exist around the year 600, when the entire area appears to have been abandoned.

Naro (Ḥammam-Lif)

Located about eighteen kilometers south of Tunis, this North African synagogue was discovered in 1883 by French soldiers stationed in the area.[48] The building, which was part of a villa complex, was constructed perhaps as early as the fourth or fifth century but possibly as late as the sixth. The complex had over a dozen rooms, with the main hall located in the south, at the end of an elaborate entranceway. The small synagogue hall (5.25 by 9 meters) was located in the center of the villa complex, with an apse set in the middle of its western wall. Ordinarily, one might assume, on this basis, that the synagogue was oriented to the west; however, in this case there are strong indications that prayer was directed toward the east. Two small rooms were located off the main hall to the east, one of which contained the following two-part mosaic inscription in Latin: "Instruments of Thy servant the Naronitian. / Instruments of Thy servant from Naro [?]." These lines are set in panels resembling opened books, perhaps a representation of Torah scrolls. It is quite possible that the Torah scrolls (*instrumenta*) were kept in this room.

The mosaic floors throughout the complex are generally plain, except for one elaborate pavement in the main hall having two outer panels with vines in the shape of acanthus leaves emanating in pairs from four vases, themselves shaped like acanthus leaves (fig. 57). Among the tendrils are animals (a lion, ducks, pelicans, other birds, etc.), and baskets of fruits or vegetables. Between these end panels are two more horizontally divided panels; the upper one features a partially preserved scene of fish, ducks, and water, with perhaps some land, plants, and a bull. Also depicted here is a wheel or star, with a spiked object at the top, interpreted by some as the hand of God. The lower panel contains two peacocks standing at the edge of an amphora-shaped fountain flanked by trees.[49] Some have interpreted these scenes as representing either heaven, paradise, the messianic days, or the creation story. Whatever the case, these panels display some remarkable parallels with mosaics from contemporary Christian churches in North Africa.[50] Between these last two panels, at the very center of the mosaic design, is the most prominent Latin inscription in this building: "Your servant Juliana p[?] at her own expense paved with mosaic the holy synagogue of Naro for her salvation." One final inscription, found in the entrance-

---

48. Goodenough, *Jewish Symbols*, II, 89–100; Hachlili, *Art and Archaeology—Diaspora*, 47–48, 207–9, 408–9. See also Biebel, "Mosaics of Hammam Lif," 541–51; Dunbabin, *Mosaics of Roman North Africa*, 194 n. 32; Foerster, "Survey of Diaspora Synagogues," 171; Le Bohec, "Inscriptions juives," nos. 13–15; and the recent Darmon, "Les mosaïques de la synagogue de Hammam Lif," 7–29. This building has not been seen since soon after its discovery. The floor was cut into panels and sold to museums and private collectors; a large part of the main mosaic is found today in the Brooklyn Museum. All subsequent descriptions derive from several early sketches, which are largely identical but have some discrepancies between them; see Goodenough, *Jewish Symbols*, III, nos. 887 and 888. On the fate of these mosaics, see Wharton, "Erasure."

49. For an eschatological interpretation of this scene, see Goodenough, *Jewish Symbols*, II, 96ff. See also Kanof, *Jewish Ceremonial Art*, 27.

50. Dunbabin, *Mosaics of Roman North Africa*, 194–95; see also Belz, *Marine Genre Mosaic Pavements*.

57. Mosaic floor in the Naro synagogue.

way, mentions one Asterius, son of the archisynagogue Rusticus, and his wife Margarita, daughter of Riddeus, who together paved part of the portico with mosaic.

Elche

Although first discovered in 1905 on the southeastern coast of Spain, the identification of this building as a church or synagogue has been a subject of controversy for some time.[51] Scholarly opinion has come around almost unanimously in recent decades to view the remains of this building as those of a synagogue, but the original identification as a church by excavator Pedro Ibarra still holds considerable weight, especially within Spanish academic circles.

The rectangular hall of this building measures 10.9 by 7.55 meters and is oriented in an east-west direction, with a portal in the west and an apse in the east (fig. 58). The apse, which is 3.0 meters wide and 2.1 meters deep and which is preserved to a height of ca. 1.0 meters, connects with the main synagogue mosaic on its southern side; near the western wall of the building, a basin was found set into the mosaic floor. This floor fea-

---

51. Fernández, *Ciudad Romana de Ilici*, 241–44; Burgos, *Sinagogas españolas*, 212–16; Rabello, "Iscrizioni ebraiche," 659–62 (= "Situation of Jews in Roman Spain," 182–86); Halperin, *Synagogues of the Iberian Peninsula*, 26–28; Hachlili, *Art and Archaeology — Diaspora*, 45–47, 205–7, 407–8. Varying numbers are given by Fernández, Burgos, and Hachlili for the sizes of the mosaic panels. We have followed Fernández. For a general survey of the Jews in Spain in late antiquity, see Rabello, "Situation of Jews in Roman Spain," 160–90.

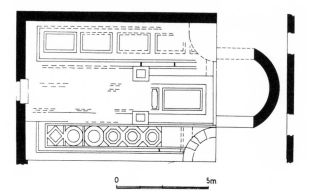

0   5m

58. Plan of the Elche synagogue.

tures many geometric designs (especially braids, mazes, and diamonds) and has rectangular, square, octagonal, and round frames interspersed throughout. One of its prominent motifs is a series of knots, including a Solomon's knot.

The mosaic floor appears to have been arranged in three parallel panels stretching over the length of the hall on an east-west axis. The northern panel is 2.45 meters wide; the central one is 3.2 meters wide; and the third, to the south, is 2.25 meters wide. This division corresponds with three inscriptions found in the main hall (see below) and thus may not have been fortuitous. One obvious explanation is that the three parts may have been contributed by different groups or individuals named in each inscription.

The arrangement of the mosaic floor, as well as its dominant patterns, is reminiscent of other Spanish mosaics of the late Roman era. At Palencia and Bobadilla, as well as at Elche itself, large villa pavements with the identical ornamentations and arrangements have been found. Because of this striking resemblance, it has been suggested that the mosaics at Elche and elsewhere may have been made by artisans of the same school. Thus, there is little justification for positing a late Byzantine date for this building, or for accounting for its decoration by assuming some external Byzantine influence. Its similarity to other mosaics from Roman Spain suggests dating this synagogue mosaic to a late Roman workshop and thus positing a fourth-century date for its creation. Presumably, the apse was added somewhat later, perhaps in the fifth century, and by the seventh century the building seems to have been converted into a church.

Identification of this building as a synagogue is based upon the three inscriptions found in the mosaic pavement.

1. "Place of prayer [*proseuche*] of the people . . ."
This inscription was found along the eastern edge of the mosaic floor, facing the congregation. The second line is illegible, but the term *proseuche* in this first line is a major factor in determining the Jewish identification of the building. The inscription is set in a *tabula ansata* frame, and a leaf, perhaps an *ethrog*, is incised on the right-hand side of this

line. Whether a similar design appeared on the left-hand side as well, or underneath it, at the extremities of the second, obliterated line, is unknown.

2. "Vow of the archons and presbyters"

This inscription was found on the northern side of the hall, also facing the congregation. Although the last word is somewhat mutilated (and is also blatantly misspelled), both Lifshitz and Noy agree that "presbyters" is the most likely reading. Both "archons" and "presbyters" appear very frequently in Jewish inscriptions, although the precise delineation between the functions of each might well vary from region to region. Wischnitzer has suggested that the seats of these synagogue officials may have, in fact, been located along this northern wall.[52]

3. "A good voyage to you, Sy [. . .], the fortunate"

This inscription is located on the southern edge of the mosaic pavement and runs east to west so that it, like the others, could be read by someone standing in the center of the hall. It was probably dedicated by an itinerant, who probably also contributed to the building. This kind of *euploia* (lit., "good voyage") inscription belongs to a well-known genre and, as might be expected, is especially ubiquitous in coastal areas.

One interesting find is a 45-centimeter-high stone base with a 9–10-centimeter-deep square cavity that was found in the area of the apse. It has been suggested that this stone may have been used as a charity box.

SYNAGOGUES OF ROME

While no synagogue building has survived from ancient Rome, the names of synagogues that once existed in the city, as well as the titles of numerous offices associated with them, have been preserved in the epigraphical evidence. The vast majority of these inscriptions were found in the Jewish catacombs (large burial sites) and hypogea (smaller burial sites) which were found in the southwestern, northeastern and southern parts of the city. Some six hundred inscriptions were recovered from various excavations, beginning with the discovery of the Monteverde catacomb in 1602; most of these discoveries, however, were made in the period between 1859 and 1919.[53] We know of three large communal catacombs: Monteverde, in Transtiberinum on the Via Portuense, in the southwestern section of Rome, near the Trastevere; Vigna Randanini, near the Via Appia, in the southern part of the city; and the Villa Torlonia, near the Via Nomentana, in the northeast.[54] Three hypogea were also found in the latter part of the nineteenth century.[55]

---

52. Lifshitz, *Donateurs et fondateurs*, no. 101; Noy, *JIWE*, II, no. 181; Wischnitzer, *Architecture*, 12.

53. Rutgers, *Jews in Late Ancient Rome*, 1–49.

54. Platner and Ashby, *Topographical Dictionary*, passim.

55. See especially Leon, *Jews of Ancient Rome*, 46–74; as well as Schürer, *History*, III, 95–98; Smallwood, *Jews under Roman Rule*, 519–25; M. Stern, "Jews of Italy," 143–48; Rutgers, *Jews in Late Ancient Rome*, 32–33.

In the past, these inscriptions were dated to the first centuries C.E.[56] Of late, however, a consensus has developed that the catacombs in which they were found date from the late second to fifth centuries C.E. Solin has proposed this date on the basis of epigraphical and paleographical considerations, Konikoff on the basis of the style and artistic work in the forty-odd sarcophagi, and Rutgers on the basis of the overall material culture of the catacombs, i.e., their plans, building techniques, burial styles, artwork (wall paintings, gold glass), and lamps, as well as the various types of sarcophagi and inscriptions found therein.[57]

The synagogues of Rome are mentioned in some forty inscriptions.[58] The precise number of attested Roman synagogues, however, is unclear and depends on the interpretation of a number of terms and the reconstruction of fragmentary references. Some identifications are universally acknowledged; others are problematic and controversial. The number eleven is most often cited, but estimates range between ten and sixteen.[59]

Of particular interest are the names of the various synagogues. Some of these date back to the first century and were either named after prominent individuals (Augustus, Agrippa, Volumnius, Herod?) or referred to as the "Synagogue of the Hebrews" or that of the "Vernaclesians" (native-born Jews). These latter names are usually understood as referring to some of the earliest synagogues in the city. In later centuries, synagogues might have been named after the congregants' place of origin (Tripoli? Rhodes? Elaea? Secenia? Arca of Lebanon?), trade (Calcaresians—limekiln workers), or local residential district (Campesians, Siburesians). One late midrash names a "synagogue of Severus" in Rome, which, if historical, would have honored one of the rulers of this dynasty, quite possibly Alexander Severus.[60]

Given the absence of actual buildings, we cannot be certain of the location of these synagogues. There is little doubt that many were situated on the right bank of the Tiber in Transtiberinum, one of the most crowded quarters of the city. Already in the first century,

---

56. See also above, Chap. 4; and M. Stern, "Jews of Italy," 144.

57. Solin, "Juden und Syrer," 654–721; Konikoff, *Sarcophagi*, 13–58; and Rutgers, "Jüdischen Katakomben," 140–57; idem, "Archeological Evidence," 101–18; and now the comprehensive *Jews in Late Ancient Rome*, also by Rutgers.

58. Noy, *JIWE*, II, 539–40.

59. For example, van der Horst (*Ancient Jewish Epitaphs*, 88) speaks of ten synagogues; Schürer (*History*, III, 96–98) of ten and possibly eleven; Leon (*Jews of Ancient Rome*, 135–66), Stern ("Jews of Italy," 144), Noy (*JIWE*, II, 539–40 and comments to no. 1), Williams ("Structure of Roman Jewry," 131; "Organisation of Jewish Burials," 166–68), Goodman ("Roman Identity," 90*), and Lichtenberger ("Organisationsformen," 17–19) of eleven; Penna ("Juifs à Rome," 327) of eleven and possibly thirteen; Vogelstein (*Rome*, 27) of twelve or thirteen; La Piana ("Foreign Groups," 352 n. 22), Momigliano ("Nomi delle prime sinagoghe," 284); Baron (*Jewish Community*, I, 81) and Westenholz ("Synagogues," 23–27) of thirteen; and Feldman ("Diaspora Synagogues," 51) of sixteen. See also Frey, "Communautés juives à Rome," 267ff.

60. Genesis Rabbati 45:8 (p. 209).

Philo indicates that this was where most Jews concentrated: "How then did he [Augustus] show his approval? He was aware that the great section of Rome on the other side of the Tiber is occupied and inhabited by Jews, most of whom were emancipated Roman citizens."[61] Inscriptions naming seven synagogues were found in the nearby Monteverde catacomb, and thus it appears quite certain that most, if not all, must have been located in this general vicinity. This would include those of the Augustesians, Agrippesians, Calcaresians, Hebrews, Vernaclesians, Volumnesians, and Tripolitans.[62] Two synagogues bear the names of sections of Rome and were most probably located there—that of the Siburesians (Subura was a congested quarter known for its squalor, prostitutes, trade activity, and—contrastingly—a few wealthy homes) and that of the Campesians (the Campus Martius was on the left bank of the Tiber).[63] Finally, a reference by Juvenal to the presence of Jews in the Grove of Camenae near the Porta Capena, in the southern part of the city at the beginning of the Via Appia, has raised speculation that a Jewish community might have been located there as well.[64] It is thus clear that most synagogues were located in the poorer, less desirable neighborhoods of the city, an indication of the relatively low socioeconomic status of most Jews—a fact that has been documented in literary sources as well.[65] Such locations are in marked contrast to the central location of the monumental Sardis synagogue and the epigraphical evidence attesting to the prominence and prosperity of its members.

Moreover, in contrast to Alexandria and other urban centers, where the Jews tended to congregate in particular neighborhoods or sections of the city,[66] Rome's Jews were widely scattered in disparate, autonomous synagogues. We know of no all-embracing *gerousia* in Rome, such as that which once controlled the affairs of Alexandrian Jewry or the *politeuma* of Berenice. The synagogues of Rome were thus self-sufficient units. Among all the inscriptions, there is no mention of a community-wide network, and in light of the large number of synagogues in the city, this absence is undoubtedly significant. The only possible hint of some overseeing body is when Paul reputedly summoned "the leading men of the Jews" (τοὺς ὄντας τῶν Ἰουδαίων πρώτους), those who were accustomed to

---

61. Philo, *Embassy* 155. On this neighborhood in later antiquity, see MacMullen, "Unromanized in Rome," 56–58, 63. Regarding the more conservative character of this quarter, cf., however, Rajak, "Inscriptions and Context," 230–33.

62. M. Stern, "Jews of Italy," 144–46.

63. See Noy, *JIWE*, II, map 1; as well as Platner and Ashby, *Topographical Dictionary*, 91–94, 500–501.

64. Juvenal, *Saturae*, 3, 10–18; M. Stern, *Greek and Latin Authors*, II, 97–98; idem, "Jews of Italy," 147; Platner and Ashby, *Topographical Dictionary*, 405. Cf., however, Leon, *Jews of Ancient Rome*, 137 n. 1.

65. See the statements of Martial and Juvenal, in M. Stern, *Greek and Latin Authors*, I, nos. 239, 246; II, no. 299; and Lichtenberger, "Organisationsformen," 16–17.

66. Philo, *Flaccus* 55; Josephus, *War* 2, 488; Tcherikover et al., *CPJ*, III, nos. 454, 468; and Trebilco, *Jewish Communities*, 79–80. Nevertheless, Philo does note that synagogues were located in many parts of the city, despite their concentration in the Delta quarter (Philo, *Embassy* 132; Josephus, *Against Apion* 2, 33–37).

receiving correspondence from Judaea.[67] However, no central body is alluded to elsewhere, and it may well be that the heads of various synagogues are intended.

Synagogue officials are mentioned in approximately 130 inscriptions. Most frequently noted is the archon (almost fifty times), whose duties were primarily administrative, political, and fiscal. In addition, the offices of *archisynagogos, pater, mater* (if indeed an office), scribe, gerousiarch, *prostates*, and others are noted. Judging by the number of officials mentioned in these inscriptions, a large number of Jews appear to have been involved in the synagogues' functioning.[68] Finally, a number of titles appear in catacomb inscriptions associated with children; these have no parallels in Jewish epigraphical evidence from elsewhere.[69]

The language of the Roman community, the names of synagogues, and the titles of officials all indicate the extent to which the Jews were integrated in the larger Roman scene.[70] Rather than viewing this community as distinct and isolated, scholars studying the material culture of the catacombs and their inscriptions have made eminently clear the extent to which the Jews had absorbed many practices appearing elsewhere in Rome into their material and organizational culture. Moreover, these Roman synagogues themselves were far from homogeneous, as was true of Greco-Roman associations generally. They were different not only in name, date of founding, and location, but also in their structure and organization, as attested by the many titles and combinations thereof among those who stood at their head.[71]

BABYLONIAN SYNAGOGUES

Unlike in Rome, the evidence for the existence of Babylonian synagogues is entirely literary; there are no archeological finds or, for that matter, literary works (Jewish or non-Jewish) other than the Bavli which attest to this institution in Babylonia. As a result, the information which does exist is severely limited in scope and reflects only a rabbinic perspective.

On the basis of this material, Gafni has developed an intriguing theory regarding the Babylonian synagogue. In contrast to what we have seen elsewhere, he assumes that this institution restricted its activity to the liturgical dimension, focusing almost exclusively on prayer and at times the reading of the Torah. Most other communal activities, ranging from the educational to the judicial and social, were associated with other institutions or officials (see below). The only synagogue official noted, and even then on rare occasion,

---

67. Acts 28:17, 21.

68. On these various offices generally, see below, Chap. 11.

69. Williams, "Structure of Roman Jewry," 131.

70. See Goodman, "Roman Identity," 85*–99*; Noy, "Writing in Tongues," 300–311.

71. See Williams, "Structure of Roman Jewry," 136–41, although her specific suggestions regarding synagogue officials and their roles remain hypothetical.

is the *ḥazzan*. The plethora of official synagogue titles known from both Palestine and the Roman Empire (especially that of the archisynagogue) are almost unknown.[72] Moreover, whereas the synagogue was often singled out for attack by Christian mobs in the West, such was not the case in Babylonia owing to the institution's much lower communal profile.[73]

In support of his argument, Gafni offers an explanation for a discrepancy between two versions of a tradition wherein R. Simeon b. Gamaliel reputedly thwarts a Babylonian attempt at gaining calendrical independence.[74] According to the Babylonian version, the confrontation between the Palestinian emissaries and Hananiah, leader of this Babylonian "revolt," took place in the *bet midrash*. The venue mentioned in the Yerushalmi is where the Torah and haftarah were read, i.e., the synagogue. Whereas the Palestinian source assumes that the synagogue might serve as a communal and political center, the Bavli knows of no such tradition, as such a setting was foreign to the Babylonian experience. The latter thus placed this encounter in an academy setting.

Another distinction is that the synagogue in the Roman Empire was considered public property, owned and controlled by the community either on a direct, democratic basis or via communal officials representing the entire congregation. However, the situation in Sassanian Babylonia appears to have been far different. Ownership of a synagogue is often associated with individuals, even among the rabbis themselves, and while not unknown in the West, this phenomenon seems to have been far more prevalent in Babylonia. At least five Babylonian sages are mentioned specifically in connection with synagogues clearly associated with themselves, institutions which they had either built or dominated in one way or another.[75] One statement, attributed to R. Ashi, is especially poignant in this regard. Commenting on the distinction between a village synagogue and an urban one, R. Ashi says: "The synagogue of Mata Meḥasiya [his place of residence], if I wish, I can sell it; even though people come from all over [and thus it might be considered part of the public domain], they come with my consent [i.e., because of my presence]."[76]

Gafni accounts for the unique Babylonian status of the synagogue by the fact that many functions assumed by synagogues in the West were being handled in Babylonia via a larger communal apparatus, either the Exilarch or the rabbinic academies. The court system, for example, operated for the most part under the latter's aegis.

Let us state at the outset that Gafni's thesis may indeed be valid, and Babylonia's synagogues may well have functioned differently from those everywhere else in late antiquity. However, there are several methodological issues which have to be addressed before any firm conclusion can be drawn. For one, can we assume that a comparison between the

---

72. See, however, Beer, *Babylonian Exilarchate*, 21–22, 228 n. 20; Gafni, *Jews of Babylonia*, 97.

73. Gafni, "Synagogues in Talmudic Babylonia," 221–31.

74. On the background of this tradition, see Oppenheimer, *Galilee*, 45–53.

75. B Megillah 26b; B Bava Batra 3b.

76. B Megillah 26a. On the location of the synagogue, see Oppenheimer, *Babylonia Judaica*, 415–21.

Babylonian setting and others to its west is a valid one on the basis of the data at hand? For the latter, we have a plethora of literary and archeological material which offers a fairly broad picture of the range of activities in these synagogues. In contrast to the imposing physical remains of some 150 buildings, as well as the many hundreds of inscriptions and the wealth of literary evidence from diverse sources for the Roman-Byzantine synagogue, the evidence for Babylonia is slim. Other than the Bavli, Babylonia boasts no archeological remains, no epigraphical evidence, no non-Jewish sources, no non-rabbinic sources, and not even another type of rabbinic source (e.g., a midrash). This imbalance, about which Gafni himself is quite aware,[77] is so pronounced that any comparison between the Roman and Sassanian settings would seem almost impossible.

If, nevertheless, one wishes to make a cogent comparison between Palestine and Babylonia, it might be preferable to compare the functioning of the synagogue in Babylonia on the basis of the Bavli with its functioning in Palestine on the basis of the Yerushalmi alone. We could then assume that there was some sort of parity between two similar corpora of information. Indeed, once this limitation is imposed, some of the above distinctions become far less compelling. Many communal functions of the Palestinian synagogue do not find expression in the Yerushalmi but do in other Palestinian sources: midrashic compilations, archeological material, and non-Jewish sources. No less than the Bavli, the Yerushalmi concentrates almost exclusively on the synagogue's liturgical activity. With regard to synagogue officials, we know very little from either source, and, as a matter of fact, it is actually the Bavli that often tells us more about this subject with regard to Palestine than does the Yerushalmi. On the basis of such a comparison, it is hard to claim that "the picture in the Bavli is dramatically different" from that in the Yerushalmi.[78]

Moreover, some of the information that we have in the Yerushalmi regarding non-liturgical synagogue matters in Palestine also finds expression in the Bavli with regard to Babylonia. This includes the presence of a *hazzan*, the existence of a school on synagogue premises, and several activities: serving meals, perhaps acting as a place of lodging, and recording synagogue destruction.[79]

But there is second basic issue which must be addressed when comparing the role of rabbis in Babylonia and Palestine generally, and with respect to the synagogue in particular. Gafni has correctly highlighted one basic distinction between the Bavli on the one hand and Palestinian rabbinic and non-rabbinic sources on the other in this regard. However, this distinction can be taken one step further. That the Bavli has undergone

---

77. Gafni, "Synagogues in Talmudic Babylonia," 224–26.

78. Ibid., 225.

79. *Ḥazzan:* B ʿEruvin 74b (cf. also 55b; B Yoma 11a); B Berakhot 53a; and perhaps B ʿArakhin 6b, though the term used here (חזני דפומבדיתא) does not appear in several MSS (see Oppenheimer, *Babylonia Judaica,* 357; Gafni, "Synagogues in Talmudic Babylonia," 226 n. 15). *School:* B Berakhot 17a (though the term "synagogue" does not appear in all manuscript traditions or in the parallel in B Sotah 21a). *Meals and lodging:* B Pesaḥim 101a. *Destruction of synagogue:* B Yoma 10a; Iggeret Rav Sherira Gaon (p. 97).

a far more sophisticated redaction than the Yerushalmi from a literary point of view is well known. In addition, one gets the distinct impression that this document also focuses much more exclusively on the rabbinic world than do its Palestinian counterparts. The Bavli seems to concentrate on rabbinic concerns and interests to a degree unknown in corresponding Palestinian sources, which appear to have had a wider scope and agenda. Examples of this proclivity are legion and can even be evidenced in some of the citations noted above. For example, when speaking of the Persian destruction of Jewish institutions, emphasis in the Bavli and Rav Sherira's letter is placed on the sages and their academies as well as on the Exilarch. Furthermore, in speaking of mothers who bring their children to study, it is the Bavli which notes that, at the same time, their husbands were studying in the academy.[80] Finally, an example from synagogue liturgical life might also be cited. With respect to public fast-day ceremonies as described in the Mishnah, the elder (זקן) who is to lead in prayer is identified in the Bavli as ideally being a sage.[81] In contrast, the Yerushalmi offers a definition that includes a far wider circle of people.[82]

If this is the case, then with regard to broader issues, such as the role of various non-rabbinic institutions in Babylonian society, one may ask to what extent the Bavli can be relied upon as offering any sort of balanced and accurate picture. It is not unlikely, given its tendentiousness, that it might well ignore or downplay these other frameworks in favor of a more focused rabbinic agenda, even though this would not have been representative of the larger community. And so with regard to the synagogue as a communal institution: the rabbis of Babylonia might not have had recourse to this institution except for worship (and even then not always), and thus the synagogue is given short shrift in the Bavli.

A number of scholars—Baron, Beer, and Neusner, as well as Gafni—have rightly pointed to some special characteristics of Babylonian Jewry, its sages, and, indirectly, its synagogue.[83] The presence of the Exilarchate, with the prestige and power accrued by this office, was a most unusual phenomenon in the Jewish world of late antiquity. Ranked high in the Persian court and granted extensive control over Jewish life and institutions, the Exilarch was recognized by all (although not always with equanimity) as the most prominent within the Jewish community. It was because of their generally privileged relationship with the Exilarch that the rabbis gained for themselves public prominence and recognition throughout the Babylonian Jewish world. They were often given official backing by him for their judicial decisions and seem to have enjoyed a high degree of recognition—religiously, politically, and very often materially.[84] This might explain one

---

80. See previous note; and Gafni, "Synagogues in Talmudic Babylonia," 226–29.

81. M Taʿanit 2:2; B Taʿanit 16a.

82. Y Taʿanit 2, 2, 65b.

83. Gafni, "Synagogues in Talmudic Babylonia," 229; idem, "Court Cases," 23–40; idem, *Jews of Babylonia*, 53ff. Similar discussions have appeared elsewhere: Baron, *Social and Religious History of the Jews*, II, 195–98; Beer, *Babylonian Amoraim*, 57–93; Neusner, *Talmudic Judaism*, 46ff.

84. See, for example, B Shabbat 119a; B Rosh Hashanah 31b; B Yevamot 95a; B Ketubot 85a; B Bava

of the most intriguing aspects of the Babylonian synagogue noted above—the ownership of synagogues by rabbis. This was certainly not the case with all, or even most, Babylonian rabbis, and the relatively few who are actually mentioned in this regard may possibly come close to exhausting the list. In any case, it admittedly is a most unique phenomenon.

However, this reality should not blur the fact that most synagogues in Babylonia may well have functioned as communal facilities. The Exilarch does not seem to have been involved in synagogue affairs, and the rabbis themselves related to the synagogue in much the same way as their Palestinian counterparts did.[85] They participated either by preaching or by answering queries regarding synagogue practice.[86] On the other hand, they do not seem to have been responsible for, or involved in, the actual running of these institutions.[87] In a number of instances, they were taken aback by unfamiliar local liturgical practices and acquiesced in situations that were not to their liking.[88] The most striking account in this regard tells of four third-century sages, Rav, Samuel, Samuel's father, and Levi, who used to pray in Nehardea, in the "Shaf ve-Yativ" synagogue, even though there was a statue there.[89]

Furthermore, the Bavli may allude—however fleetingly—to existing communal frameworks which might have something to do with the synagogue, as, for example, "the seven good men of the town" (שבעה טובי העיר)—if this was, in fact, a Babylonian institution) or the local town council (מעמד אנשי העיר) who had to give their assent to Ravina when he wanted to erect some sort of building on the lot of a former synagogue.[90] There is also the somewhat enigmatic distinction accorded to Ada bar Ahava by R. Joseph, that he should leave "worldly matters" to laymen while he attends to "heavenly matters."[91]

At times, Babylonian rabbis would praise the synagogue and strongly encourage their colleagues to attend, or they would openly declare their preference for praying within their own academies or at home and not in the synagogue. This was equally true of Palestinian sages, and in this respect at least the rabbinic elite differed little from one country to the next.

Thus, it is possible that synagogues were peripheral to the Babylonian sages and were thus largely ignored in the Bavli, not necessarily because the institution was of marginal importance in the life of the general community, but rather because the rabbis them-

---

Qama 113a; B Bava Batra 167a; B Sanhedrin 7b; B Makkot 16b; and Neusner, *History of Jews in Babylonia*, II, 111ff.; III, 126–30, 272ff.; IV, 125ff., 309–15; V, 244ff. See also Beer, *Babylonian Amoraim*, 222–57.

85. B Berakhot 6b, 7b–8a; B Megillah 26b; and below, Chap. 13.

86. B Megillah 21b; B Pesaḥim 117b; B Sukkah 55a.

87. Neusner, *Talmudic Judaism*, 87–91.

88. For example, B Megillah 22b; B Taʿanit 28b.

89. On this synagogue, see B Rosh Hashanah 24b; B ʿAvodah Zarah 43b; as well as Oppenheimer, *Babylonia Judaica*, 290–91; idem, "Babylonian Synagogues," 40–43.

90. B Megillah 26b.

91. B Qiddushin 76b. See also Gafni, *Jews of Babylonia*, 117ff.

selves were only minimally involved in its affairs. It must be remembered that the sages were relative latecomers to Babylonia. The Jewish community had already existed there for many centuries and undoubtedly had developed traditions of its own, including synagogue customs. The very old synagogues bearing names associated with events of Jewish history from the Exilic and post-Exilic periods is an indication of their alleged sanctity and of the deep roots that the local community claimed to have developed.[92] Moreover, the Babylonian sage Abbaye explicitly locates the *Shekhinah* in two specific synagogues in the towns of Hutzal and Nehardea.[93] The Babylonian sages, more so perhaps than their Palestinian counterparts, had other non-synagogal outlets for their communal activities. In addition to their academies, active rabbinic involvement in the local court system offered them the opportunity to affect communal life in a myriad of ways.[94] The synagogues thus appear to have played a minor role in their lives, and thus—in light of the sources at our disposal—we should be cautious in extrapolating from their particular circumstances and applying it to Babylonian Jewry in general.

THE CENTRALITY OF THE DIASPORA SYNAGOGUE

The synagogue continued to be the focal Jewish institution in the Diaspora of late antiquity, just as it was in earlier periods and in contemporary Roman-Byzantine Palestine. Communities organized themselves around this institution and gave expression to their communal life within its walls. We saw above that the synagogue sanctuary was part of a much larger complex (e.g., Dura, Stobi, Ostia). Sometimes the complex included an adjacent atrium (Sardis, Gerasa, and Phocaea[95]) or additional rooms (Bova Marina, Dura, Plovdiv, Naro), which might have included a kitchen, meeting or study hall (Ostia), or a *tetrastoon* and *triclinium* (Stobi). The inclusion of dining halls indicates the importance of communal meals in the synagogal agenda, as do the parchment fragments from Dura Europos containing what appears to be a form of *birkat hamazon* (grace after meals).[96] Another activity attested for Diaspora synagogues involves the collection of charity. It is explicitly noted in rabbinic literature for third-century Bostra, capital of Provincia Arabia,[97] and the charitable activity mentioned in the Aphrodisias inscription

---

92. On the synagogues of Shaf ve-Yativ, Daniel, and Hutzal, for example, see Oppenheimer, "Babylonian Synagogues," 41–42. Regarding Babylonian "local patriotism" generally, see Gafni, *Land, Center and Diaspora*, 52–57.

93. B Megillah 29a. On the sanctity ascribed to synagogues in the Bavli, see Fine, *This Holy Place*, 119–26.

94. Gafni, "Public Sermons," 121–29; idem, "Court Cases," 23–40. See also Goodblatt, *Rabbinic Instruction*, 171–96.

95. Lifshitz, *Donateurs et fondateurs*, no. 13.

96. Kraeling, *Dura: Synagogue*, 259.

97. Leviticus Rabbah 5:4 (pp. 113–14).

was associated almost assuredly with that community's synagogue (see below). It may be the collection of charity which accounts for the discovery of over three thousand bronze coins in the Bova Marina synagogue, and if the hollowed-out stone found at Elche indeed served as a charity box, it would provide additional evidence for such communal activity.

The synagogue may also have housed a library. Jerome reports that when in Rome in 384, he met a Jew (*Hebraeus*) with many books (*volumina*) which he had borrowed from the synagogue.[98] Similarly, in the small town of Mago in Minorca, the local synagogue purportedly possessed "silver" vessels and "sacred books," although the latter may refer to Torah scrolls or other biblical books only.[99]

Synagogues often gained a reputation as an effective place of healing. How many functioned in this capacity, and with what frequency, is unknown. If John Chrysostom is to be believed, the synagogue at Daphne, outside Antioch, provided such a setting and included a period of incubation (presumably overnight).[100] The process of healing was often accompanied by the appearance of the God of Israel in a dream in the course of the night. Commonly associated with the cult of Asclepius, the god of healing, this phenomenon, according to Chrysostom, was the means to, or an indication of, this cure.

The number of synagogues in each city was, of course, a function of the size and geographical concentration of the Jewish community. Larger communities undoubtedly boasted many more than one synagogue. The Diaspora communities of Alexandria and Rome had many *proseuchae* or synagogues, as was the case with Sepphoris, Tiberias, Lydda, and presumably Caesarea in Palestine.[101]

Not only was the synagogue central to internal Jewish communal life, but it attracted non-Jews as well. Church fathers repeatedly warn their flocks to distance themselves from Jews and Judaism. Ignatius so remonstrates with church members in Philadelphia (Asia Minor), and the author of the *Martyrdom of Pionius* admonishes Christians not to seek refuge in synagogues during persecutions.[102] Origen cautions Christians not to discuss on Sunday matters they had heard raised the previous day in the synagogue or to partake of meals in both church and synagogue.[103] Ephrem is distressed with members of the church who are attracted to Jewish customs and feasts,[104] and, finally, Jerome expresses dismay at Christians who turned to Jews for the correct interpretation of a passage from Jonah.[105]

---

98. Jerome, *Letters* 36, 1.

99. As reported by Severus, bishop of Minorca, in his *Epistula Severi* 9–10 (*PL* 41, 924–25). See also Bradbury, *Severus of Minorca*, 13, 13 (p. 95).

100. *Adv. Iud.* 1, 6; Wilken, *John Chrysostom and the Jews*, 97–98.

101. See above, Chap. 6.

102. *To the Philadelphians* 6, 1; *Martyrdom of Pionius* 13. For other examples, see Wilson, *Related Strangers*, 159–68.

103. *Hom. Lev.* 5, 8; *Select. Exod.* 12, 46.

104. Drijvers, "Syrian Christianity," 141. On the close relations between Jews and Christians in Asia Minor, see Sheppard, "Jews, Christians and Heretics," 169–80.

105. *Letters* 71, 5. See also Reynolds and Tannenbaum, *Jews and God-Fearers*, 85–89; Figueras, "Epi-

Two dramatic instances of this attraction to Judaism in late antiquity are attested in Aphrodisias and Antioch.[106] The monumental inscription found on a marble block in the former city records the names of Jews, proselytes, and gentile God-fearers who contributed to a memorial erected by their association (*dekany*) in the early third century.[107] The memorial ($\mu\nu\hat{\eta}\mu\alpha$) was presumably a building (or part of one) that was used as a *patella* (lit., dish), perhaps a soup kitchen "for relief of suffering in the community."[108] On one side of the stone the Jewish members of this *dekany* are listed, while on the other, following a break in the text, are the names of a few proselytes and fifty-four *theosebeis*, or gentile God-fearers, the first nine of whom are identified as city councillors ($\beta o\upsilon\lambda\epsilon\upsilon\tau\alpha\iota$). Thus, we have here conclusive proof of a group of gentile God-fearers, of high rank and significant number, who were publicly and actively associated with the local Jewish community. Similarly, according to one interpretation of a second-century inscription from Panticapaeum in the Crimea, God-fearers are noted alongside Jews as witnesses to manumission procedures in the local synagogue.[109]

No less revealing is the situation in Antioch toward the end of the fourth century. In 386–87, John Chrysostom, recently ordained as a priest, delivered a series of vituperative sermons against members of his church (and indirectly against Jews and Judaism) whom he accused of judaizing.[110] Chrysostom regards the synagogue (as well as Jewish souls) as

---

graphic Evidence," 198–203. The evidence from the Bosphorus in late antiquity is intriguing though inconclusive. Some fifteen inscriptions dating from the second and third centuries C.E. relate to religious associations (*thiasoi*) of *theos hypsistos*. Whether these were Jewish or pagan groups, or perhaps Jewishly-inspired associations of the Most High God consisting mainly, if not exclusively, of God-fearers, has been a matter of dispute. In all events, the dominance of this cult in third-century Tanais is clearly evidenced in the statement that "85% of all the dedications to the gods found in Tanais were made to the Most High God, while if we take into consideration private dedications only, the figure is even more impressive— 100%. The number of members of *thiasoi* in Tanais shows that nearly all the male population of the city in the IIIrd century were adherents of the Most High God." See Levinskaya and Tokhtas'yev, "Jews and Jewish Names," 73 n. 84; and, more generally, Levinskaya, *Acts in Its Diaspora Setting*, 111–16, 242–46.

106. For a broad overview of this phenomenon, see Feldman, *Jew and Gentile*, 383–445.

107. Reynolds and Tannenbaum, *Jews and God-Fearers*. See also Schürer, *History*, III, 25–26; White, *Building God's House*, 88–89; Rajak, "Jewish Community," 20–21; Feldman, *Jew and Gentile*, 367–69; J. J. Collins, "Feldman, *Jew and Gentile*" (review), 718; Mussies, "Jewish Personal Names," 255–76. A *dekany* is also mentioned in Rome; see Noy, *JIWE*, II, no. 440. For a contrast to the generally accepted third-century dating, see Bonz ("Jewish Donor Inscriptions," 285–91), who suggests a fifth-century setting.

108. Williams ("Jews and Godfearers," 304–10) suggests that the *dekany* was, in fact, a burial society and that the memorial in question was a *triclinium*.

109. Lifshitz, "Prolegomenon," 65–66. Cf., however, Levinskaya, *Acts in Its Diaspora Setting*, 74–76; and above, Chap. 4. The Miletus theater inscription has been variously interpreted to refer to Jews and God-fearers; Jews who were in fact also called God-fearers; God-fearers who were called Jews. See Schürer, *History*, III, 167–68.

110. Simon, *Recherches*, 140–53; Meeks and Wilken, *Jews and Christians*, 30–35; Wilken, *John Chrysostom and the Jews*, 66–94; Brändle, "Christen und Juden," 142–60; Harkins, "Prolegomenon," xxxviii–xlvii.

a "dwelling place of demons," a "hideout for thieves," and a "den of wild animals."[111] Jewish festivals seem to have had a seductive attraction for Christians; according to Chrysostom, many, especially women, were ensnared on those occasions.[112] Synagogues were compared to theaters, houses of prostitution, and idolatrous temples, where debauchery and drunkenness reigned supreme.[113] The synagogue's spell derives from what Wilken has referred to as its "numinous power,"[114] a trait apparently widely associated with this institution in Christian circles.

Much to Chrysostom's consternation,[115] Christians preferred taking oaths in synagogues. He tells the story of intercepting one Christian who was taking another into the synagogue for such a purpose and of remonstrating the former for his intentions. Chrysostom's version of the Christian's reply is telling: "Many had told him that oaths which were taken there were more awesome."[116]

As noted, the synagogue as a place of healing is vividly described with regard to Daphne, near Antioch. From Chrysostom's fulminations, it is clear that Christian recourse to the synagogue was a widespread phenomenon which served to anger church officials and undermine their authority.[117] Such "powers," of course, were intimately linked to Jewish healing procedures, which were closely associated in the ancient world with magic. Jewish involvement in this realm throughout later antiquity is well documented and has gained even further attention since the publication of *Sefer Harazim*, Jewish amulet and incantation texts, etc.[118]

No less irritating to Christian clergy was the flocking of the local population to the synagogue on Sabbaths and holidays. Their participation in synagogue rituals on Sabbaths, Rosh Hashanah, Yom Kippur, Sukkot, Passover, and fast days is castigated by Chrysostom.[119] Even the circumcision of Christians and their use of Jewish ritual baths are

---

111. *Adv. Iud.* 1, 3–4, 7.

112. Ibid., 2, 3; 4, 7; and Wilken, *John Chrysostom and the Jews*, 92–94. See Simon, *Verus Israel*, 326–27. Jerome also attests to this phenomenon (*In Matt.* 23, 5; *Letter* 121), and, as will be remembered, it occurred in first-century Damascus also (Josephus, *War* 2, 559–61; see above, Chap. 4).

113. *Adv. Iud.* 1, 3–4.

114. Wilken, *John Chrysostom and the Jews*, 94.

115. *Adv. Iud.* 1, 3: "Three days ago (believe me, I am not saying) I saw a noble and free woman, who is modest and faithful, being forced into a synagogue by a coarse and senseless person who appeared to be a Christian (I would not say that someone who dared to do such things was really a Christian). He forced her into a synagogue to make an oath about certain business matters which were in litigation" (Meeks and Wilken, *Jews and Christians*, 90).

116. *Adv. Iud.* 1, 3. See also Simon, *Verus Israel*, 355.

117. *Adv. Iud.* 1, 7.

118. Simon, *Verus Israel*, 339–68; Wilken, *John Chrysostom and the Jews*, 83–88. See also Schürer, *History*, III, 342–79; Margolioth, *Sepher Ha-Razim*; Naveh and Shaked, *Amulets and Magic Bowls*; idem, *Magic Spells and Formulae*.

119. Simon, *Verus Israel*, 326. Evidence to substantiate Chrysostom's concern can be found in the Jew-

noted.[120] There were few secrets, even in a city the size of Antioch, and people were well aware of the habits of their neighbors.[121] Wilken describes this situation rather pointedly:

> If Christians were going around the corner to attend the synagogue, this meant that the divine was more tangibly present in the synagogue than in churches. If churches were empty because the Jews were celebrating their high holy days, this suggested that the Jewish way was more authentic. If the Christians used the Jewish calendar to set the date of a Christian festival, this could only mean that the Jews had the true calendar. In such a setting there was no middle ground, no accommodation between Jews and Christians, because the claims of the two religions were being negotiated not in the tranquility of the scholar's study but in the din of the city's streets. When churches were empty and the synagogue filled, it was not a secret but public knowledge passed on in the shops and bazaars of the city.[122]

At the heart of this "numinous" attraction was the view that synagogues were indeed sacred places. Chrysostom mockingly calls them "sacred shrines." [123] This sacredness, he suggests, is derived from the presence of the Torah and the books of the Prophets.[124] Chrysostom attempts to counter this claim to sacredness by arguing that the Jews in reality deny, insult, and dishonor the prophets by ignoring their testimonies. Moreover, it is senseless to regard the Torah ark as holy, since it is a poor substitute for the original ark with its tablets of stone.[125]

Finally, the fascination of Antiochan Christians with Judaism and Jewish practices is evident in the transformation of an Antioch synagogue honoring the Maccabean martyrs into a Christian martyrium. As we have noted above,[126] it would seem that a synagogue had been built in or near the alleged burial site of these martyrs (see II Macc. 6–7). The veneration of these martyrs was subsequently adopted by Christians in various regions. Sometime in the fourth century, the Antioch synagogue was taken over by the local church, for by Chrysostom's time the relics therein were already in Christian hands. Thus, the Christians of the city were also attracted to Jewish martyrs! [127]

---

ish prayer (*'Amidah*) embedded in a Christian liturgical text as preserved in the *Apostolic Constitutions* (7, 33–38), a work often dated to fourth-century Syria.

120. *Adv. Iud.* 2, 2; *Catech.* 1, 2–3.

121. *Adv. Iud.* 8, 4.

122. Wilken, *John Chrysostom and the Jews*, 78.

123. *Adv. Iud.* 1, 3.

124. Ibid., 1, 5, where, inter alia, the following is said: "Therefore stay away from their gatherings and from their synagogues and do not praise the synagogue on account of its books. Rather, hate it and avoid it for that very reason, for they have mangled the saints because they do not believe their words and they accuse them of extreme impiety" (Meeks and Wilken, *Jews and Christians*, 96). See also Wilken, *John Chrysostom and the Jews*, 79–83.

125. Meeks and Wilken, *Jews and Christians*, 32.

126. See above, Chap. 4.

127. *In Sanctos Maccabaeos Homilia* 1, 1; Simon, *Recherches*, 158; Schatkin, "Maccabean Martyrs," 97–113; Wilken, *John Chrysostom and the Jews*, 88.

As was the case earlier in Egypt, the later Diaspora synagogue also gave expression to Jewish loyalties toward the Imperial authorities during this period. Two inscriptions from Hungary reflect this phenomenon; the one from Intercisa is most revealing:

> To the eternal god. For the salvation of our lord, Severus A[lexander], the pious, felicitous emperor an[d of Julia Mamaea] the empress, mother of the emperor, does Cosmius, the chief of the customs station, the flautist and *archisynagogos* of the Jews, gladly fulfill his vow.[128]

The benefactor in this inscription, Cosmius, was a Roman Jewish official in charge of the local customs office. He was also active in the local synagogue, serving as the *archisynagogos* and a musician. His dedication of a synagogue to the Imperial Severan family is noteworthy. As mentioned above, a similar dedication in honor of the emperor was made in Ostia by Mindius Faustos at about this time. It will be recalled that the first line of this latter inscription reads *"pro salute Aug."* Perhaps reciprocally, the emperor Alexander Severus himself was reputedly mocked by an Alexandrian mob as being a "Syrian *archisynagogos*," and this may be indicative of his pro-Jewish proclivities, although the historical value of this source generally is somewhat dubious.[129] The second inscription, from Mursa in Hungary, refers to Septimius Severus' family and joins the above evidence, as well as that from Rome and Qatzion (in the Upper Galilee) which likewise attests to the high regard in which Jews held members of this dynasty.[130]

Synagogues by their very location might reflect the prominence, or at least the acceptance, of the local Jewish community. Many were situated in or near the city center, as at Sardis, Apamea, and Plovdiv; sometimes they were located on a main, though not central, street, as at Priene and Stobi. Of course, in the larger cities, where more than one synagogue was to be found, there were locations of varying prominence.

If respectability and acceptance often characterized the synagogue in late antiquity, so, too, did the notion of transition. Even in Hellenistic and early Roman times, Jewish prominence and privilege were at times offset by anti-Jewish sentiments and actions. Conversion was matched by animosity, attractiveness by hostility. In fact, these were probably not unrelated sentiments. The privileged position of Jews and the distinctive-

---

128. Scheiber, *Jewish Inscriptions*, 29 and comments, 30-32. For a discussion of the interpretation of the term *spondill*, see below, p. 283.

129. *Scriptores Historiae Augustae–Alexander Severus* 28. Another instance of Imperial support, either official or unofficial, is attested by an inscription from Panticapaeum, dated to 306 C.E., which speaks of an Imperial governor of Theodosia, one Aurelius Valerius Sogus, who built a *proseuche* to the Most High God (*CIRB* 64; Levinskaya, "Jewish or Gentile Prayer House?" 154).

130. For the Mursa inscription, see Scheiber, *Jewish Inscriptions*, 53-55: "[For the salvation of the em]perors [Lucius Septimius Severus Pe]rtinax [and Marcus Aurelius Antoninus, the] Augusti [and Iulia Augusta, mother of the cam]ps . . . [Secu]ndus [. . . the Sy]nagogue [of the Jews?] [fallen from] age . . . [from the foun]dations [has restored]." See also Genesis Rabbati 45:8 (p. 209); Roth-Gerson, *Greek Inscriptions*, 125-29.

ness of Judaism were sources of admiration for some and of irritation for others. By the fourth century, these polar sentiments had come ever more sharply into focus. In both Sardis and Antioch, for example, the attractiveness of Judaism is clearly reflected. Yet, at the apparent height of prestige of the Antiochan Jewish community, and undoubtedly because of it, a local priest like Chrysostom vigorously castigated them in public sermons, and local Christians confiscated the synagogue honoring Maccabean martyrs.

Indeed, with the triumph of Christianity and the ever increasing power of the church, anti-Jewish sentiment found a sustained advocate. Yet even here a distinction has to be made between the fourth century on the one hand and the fifth and sixth on the other.[131] We have had occasion to note that a number of synagogues were destroyed or converted into churches during this period.[132] But what had been very sporadic throughout much of the fourth century—e.g., at Antioch, Tipasa (Mauretania), and Dertona (Spain)—became much more common from the late fourth century onward.[133] At a time when the synagogue at Callinicum, on the Euphrates, was destroyed (in 388, followed by the well-known confrontation between Ambrose and the emperor Theodosius I), when riots were led by Bishop Cyril of Alexandria (in 414), when synagogues elsewhere were frequently destroyed and replaced by churches and the Jews were expelled, when 540 Jews in the town of Mago in Minorca converted to Christianity and their synagogue was burnt and replaced by a church (in 418), and, finally, when Rabbula, the bishop of Edessa (died 435 or 436) consecrated a church to St. Stephen where a synagogue had once stood, a new dimension in Jewish-Christian relations was rapidly unfolding.[134]

Linder has perceptively pointed out the gradual shift in terminology regarding Judaism between the fourth and fifth centuries. Throughout most of the fourth century, the term *religio*, a neutral term denoting a system of beliefs and practices, was used to refer to Judaism. However, by the fifth century, the term had been replaced by *superstitio*, a

---

131. Wilken, *John Chrysostom and the Jews*, 49–55.

132. See above, Chap. 7.

133. Simon, *Verus Israel*, 224 ff. Of interest in this regard is Ambrose's accusation that Jews had done the same thing to Christians in the time of Julian: "And to be sure, if I were to talk in terms of the law of peoples [*iure gentium*] I would say how many basilicas of the Church the Jews burned in the time of Julian's rule: two at Damascus, of which one has barely been repaired, but at the expense of the Church, not the Synagogue; the other basilica lies in squalid ruins. Basilicas were burned in Gaza, Ascalon, Berytus, and almost everywhere in that area, and no one sought revenge. A basilica was also burned at Alexandria by pagans and Jews" (Millar, "Diaspora," 104). See also Parkes, *Conflict of Church and Synagogue*, 121–50.

134. *Callinicum:* Simon, *Verus Israel*, 226–27. *Alexandria:* Socrates, *Ecclesiastical History* 7, 13, 15. *Mago:* Bradbury, *Severus of Minorca*, 29, 2 (p. 123); Hunt, "St. Stephen in Minorca," 106–23; see also Miles, "Santa Maria Maggiore's Mosaics," 155–75. *Edessa:* J. B. Segal, *Edessa*, 182. Even in Palestine, there are reports of the destruction of synagogues at Rabbat Moab and elsewhere by Barsauma and fellow-monks in the early fifth century; see Nau, "Deux épisodes," 186–91.

pejorative word which referred to something different, hostile, and base.[135] This is how Judaism and its institutions were now becoming officially viewed.

BETWEEN UNITY AND DIVERSITY

One very blatant feature of the Diaspora synagogue in late antiquity was its rich variety, most clearly attested in the marked differences in the architectural styles of the various extant buildings.[136] The synagogue building at Sardis was worlds apart from the converted private home at Dura Europos, even after the latter had been transformed into an enlarged synagogue complex. The architectural plan of the Ostia synagogue was quite different from that of Naro, as was that of Aegina from the one in Priene.[137] Moreover, the location of the synagogues varied, ranging from the center of a town to its periphery (e.g., Ostia, Bova Marina, Dura); variation was also evident in the plan of the sanctuary and the shape of the entire complex. For example, most synagogues had some sort of atrium, but some clearly did not (Priene, Ostia).

The attitude toward figural art varied markedly from one Diaspora synagogue to the next. One community employed a full range of figural representation (Dura); another featured animals and fish only (Naro); still others bore no traces whatsoever of such art (Apamea, Stobi, Elche, and Bova Marina). The synagogue at Sardis reflects an interesting combination of these two modes. On the one hand, its extensive mosaic floors and marble revetments are geometric in pattern, with no trace of figural representation. Nevertheless, this congregation placed statues of two pairs of lions and table supports featuring stone replicas of majestic eagles in the center of the nave, at the very spot from which the Torah was read. Clearly, this community had no objection, in principle, to figural representation, yet for whatever reason this did not find expression on its floors and walls.[138]

Diaspora synagogues also varied in the quantity and nature of their epigraphical evidence. Although Aramaic, Latin, and even Hebrew were used at times, Greek is by far the predominant language of inscriptions, and not only because most extant remains have been found in the eastern part of the Empire, where Greek continued to dominate. Even in the Jewish catacombs in Rome, the overwhelming majority of inscriptions are in Greek (78%), with Latin accounting for 21%. This range of linguistic distribution was true of

---

135. Linder, *Jews in Roman Imperial Legislation*, 55–58.

136. See L. Levine, "Diaspora Judaism," 139–49.

137. See the above descriptions of these buildings; and esp. Kraabel, "Diaspora Synagogue," 477–510; White, *Building God's House*, 62–77; and Seager, "Architecture of the Dura and Sardis Synagogues," 79–116.

138. Mention should be made of Eudoxius the painter (ξωγράθος) from Rome. Whether his depictions of living things were exhibited in a local synagogue is unknown (Noy, *JIWE*, II, no. 277).

139. MacMullen, "Unromanized in Rome," 49–50.

other plebian and immigrant groups in the capital as well.[139] Nevertheless, in some synagogues in the West (e.g., at Naro, Ostia, Brescia, and Capua), Latin was more visible.[140] Finally, the titles and offices of leaders and governing bodies differ from synagogue to synagogue.[141]

The larger social, cultural, and religious contexts of each Jewish community probably had a decisive role in shaping not only its artistic and architectural features, but also the functions and practices within the various synagogues.[142] We have already noted the extent to which the Egyptian Jewish *proseuche* drew on pagan models: its proximity to a grove of trees; its function as a place of asylum; the use of known official titles; the dedication of buildings to the ruling family, etc.[143] In our survey of Diaspora synagogue sites from late antiquity, the local context was likewise very much in evidence, and this dimension will be addressed below.[144]

However, alongside the above-noted diversity there was also a great deal of unity and commonality among Diaspora synagogues. The centrality of this institution in the Diaspora of late antiquity is reflected, first and foremost, in the major expense required to build and maintain such facilities, which was the responsibility of each and every community. As noted already on several occasions, the synagogue was the Jewish communal building par excellence at this time.

Orientation of the synagogue interior toward Jerusalem was universally adhered to in Diaspora synagogues. The centrality of Jerusalem—whether linked to memories of the past or hopes for the future—thus found expression in the plans of each and every building.[145] Gerasa and Dura Europos were oriented to the west (and it may not be coincidental that the representations of Mt. Moriah [the Temple Mount] appear on the western wall of the latter site), Apamea and Plovdiv to the south, Stobi and Ostia to the southeast, and the others more or less to the east.

Another feature common to Diaspora synagogues of late antiquity was the promi-

---

140. Noy, *JIWE*, I, nos. 5, 14, 20.

141. Frey, *CIJ*, I, lxviii ff.; Leon, *Jews of Ancient Rome*, 167–94; Kant, "Jewish Inscriptions," 692–98; Williams, "Structure of Roman Jewry," 131; and below, Chap. 11.

142. Regarding outside influences on Jewish burial sites, see Rutgers, "Archaeological Evidence," 101–18.

143. Dion, "Synagogues et temples," 45–75; and above, Chap. 4.

144. See below, Chap. 18.

145. See the plans of Diaspora synagogues in Kraabel, "Diaspora Synagogue," 503–5; and White, *Building God's House*, 63–76. It has been much disputed as to whether the Holy Land is referred to in the famous Monteverde epitaph of Regina (*venerandi ruris*). See, for example, Goodenough, *Jewish Symbols*, II, 135–36; Leon, *Jews of Ancient Rome*, 248–49; van der Horst, *Ancient Jewish Epitaphs*, 112, 126 n. 42; Noy, *JIWE*, II, no. 103. On other possible ties to the Land of Israel in Diaspora archeological material, see Noy, "Letters Out of Judaea," 106–17.

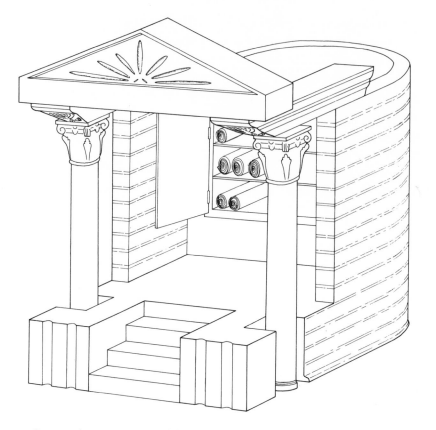

59. Suggested reconstruction of the Torah ark and *aedicula* in the Ostia synagogue.

nence of the Torah shrine. Almost every extant structure had this permanent fixture in its main hall. This took the form of an *aedicula* (Dura, Sardis, and Ostia—fig. 59), a niche (Priene, Gerasa, and Apamea), an apse (Elche, Aegina), or a *bima* (Bova Marina, Stobi). The only questionable instance to date is at Naro, but even there, inscriptions found in an adjacent room to the east of the main hall seem to indicate that the room served as a storage place for holy objects (*instrumenta*)—which we assume refers to the Torah scrolls.[146]

Moreover, Diaspora synagogues exhibit similar kinds of Jewish symbols, the most prominent among them being the menorah. In some synagogues, an elaborately styled menorah is depicted in the center of the nave (Bova Marina, Plovdiv). However, while far from rare, Jewish symbols do not seem to have been a dominant feature in Diaspora synagogue decoration. A somewhat more extensive use of Jewish symbols, particularly of the

---

146. Goodenough, *Jewish Symbols*, II, 89–92.

menorah, is evidenced at Diaspora burial sites, especially in the catacombs of Rome.[147]

Throughout late antiquity, Diaspora synagogues were regarded as religious institutions with a sacred status, such as that reflected in Valentinian's decree of ca. 370 defining the synagogue as a *religionum loca*.[148] This status is confirmed not only by inscriptions from Stobi, Philadelphia, Gerasa, and Hyllarima, but also by statements of Chrysostom in the fourth century and of Procopius in the sixth.[149] Chrysostom claimed that this sanctity was attributed to the presence of Torah scrolls. However, he concedes that it may also have derived from other "sacred" forms of worship, such as prayer, or from the synagogue's association with the Temple.[150]

Closely related to the subject of sanctity, and as early as the second century B.C.E., many Diaspora synagogues were clearly concerned with purification issues. This concern found expression in the letter of Aristeas and in the inclusion of basins, fountains, or wells in courtyards or entranceways in many Diaspora synagogues. Such finds have come to light in Sardis, Dura, Ostia, and Priene and are mentioned in inscriptions from Sidé and Pamphylia in Asia Minor.[151] Purity issues may have been a major factor in the location of a number of synagogues near bodies of water. As noted, the reasons for this concern with purification in a liturgical setting are unclear. Aristeas offers one reason; parallel pagan practices suggest another.[152]

RELIGIOUS LEADERSHIP

Little is known about the religious leadership in Diaspora synagogues. Only in isolated instances is the word "rabbi" used with regard to a non-Babylonian Diaspora leader. The term appears in a number of Jewish epitaphs from the fourth to sixth centuries in Cyprus (R. Attikos); Brusciano (R. Abba Maris), Venosa (rabbis), and Salerno (R. Abun-

---

147. Leon, *Jews of Ancient Rome*, 196–98; Rutgers, "Archeological Evidence," 107; idem, *Jews in Late Ancient Rome*, 93–95; Fine and Rutgers, "New Light on Judaism," 1–23.

148. *Cod. Theod.* 7, 8, 2 (Linder, *Jews in Roman Imperial Legislation*, no. 14).

149. *Inscriptions:* Lifshitz, *Donateurs et fondateurs*, nos. 10, 28, 32, 78; see also Robert, "Inscriptions grecques de Sidé," 43 n. 4; Hengel, "Synagogeninschrift in Stobi," 173 n. 95. *Chrysostom: Adv. Iud.* 1, 3; see Wilken, *John Chrysostom and the Jews*, 79–80. *Procopius: Buildings* 6, 2.

150. *Adv. Iud.* 1, 5. See Meeks and Wilken, *Jews and Christians*, 94–95; Goodman, "Sacred Space," 1–16; and esp. Fine, who has presented this material most comprehensively in his *This Holy Place*, 117–46, and more succinctly in "Holiness and the Ancient Synagogue," 39–47.

151. Lifshitz, *Donateurs et fondateurs*, nos. 28 and 37.

152. *Letter of Aristeas* 304–6; E. P. Sanders, *Jewish Law*, 262–63; and above, Chap. 4. Interestingly, there have been very few reports of ritual baths found near Diaspora synagogues. Ostia here is the exception. Whether this is due to the oversight of excavators or to the fact that Diaspora Jews had little use for such facilities is unclear. It should be noted that use of *miqva'ot* also declined in post-70 Palestine. See Reich, "Synagogue and Ritual Bath," 211.

danti) in Italy; Tortosa (R. Juda?), Tarragona (R. Latous), and Emerita (R. Samuel, R. Jacob) in Spain; Volubilis in Mauretania (R. Judah); and Cyrene (rabbi).[153]

We know of no talmudic rabbis who functioned in any capacity in a synagogue of the Roman Diaspora. Rabbinic literature makes no mention of rabbinic figures living there nor of any academies being established there, the sole exception being the school established by R. Mattiah b. Ḥeresh in Rome in the early second century.[154] However, this institution, mentioned only once in rabbinic sources, is never attested elsewhere. Thus, any rabbinic leadership in the Roman Diaspora was probably locally nurtured and had little or nothing to do with the contemporary rabbinic academies in Palestine and Babylonia.[155]

Mention of other Diaspora religious leaders (e.g., a priest or *didaskalos*—teacher) occurs only on rare occasions. The example of Samoe from Sardis has already been noted. In an inscription in his honor, located in the center of the synagogue's mosaic pavement, along with the titles "priest and *sophodidaskalos*," shows that Samoe played a leading role in the religious affairs of that community. A person described as a *didaskalos*, who might also have been an *archisynagogos*, is mentioned in an inscription from Corinth.[156] Other titles include *mathetes sophon* (a disciple of the wise), *nomomathes* (one learned in the Law), and possibly *nomodidaskalos* (teacher of the Law)—all of which appear in Rome—and *sophos* (a wise person), found in Argos.[157] In fifth-century Minorca, Theodorus was the recognized leader of the town (by Christians as well) and had functioned as a *defensor civitatis*, who enjoyed exemptions from all curial obligations and was the acknowledged *patronus*. This same Theodorus was also referred to as a *legis doctor*, which undoubtedly referred to

---

153. Millar, "Jews of the Graeco-Roman Diaspora," 111; Noy, *JIWE*, I, nos. 22, 36, 86, 183, 186; Lifshitz, "Prolegomenon," 57–58. See also Leon, *Jews of Ancient Rome*, 192–94; S. J. D. Cohen, "Epigraphical Rabbis," 2–3.

154. B Sanhedrin 32b; Toaff, "Matia ben Cheresh," 69–80; Segal, "R. Matiah Ben Heresh of Rome," 221–41. On the even more enigmatic figure of Todos or Theudas of Rome, see, inter alia, T Betzah 2:15 (p. 291); B Berakhot 19a; B Pesaḥim 53a–b; Y Pesaḥim 7, 1, 34a; and Bokser, "Todos and Rabbinic Authority," 117–30, where it is claimed that the earlier rabbinic traditions relating to Todos indicate that he possessed no real communal authority.

155. S. J. D. Cohen, "Epigraphical Rabbis," 16–17; van der Horst, *Ancient Jewish Epitaphs*, 97–98; Williams, "Jews and Godfearers," 297–310; cf. Reynolds and Tannenbaum, *Jews and God-Fearers*, 78–84. Any rabbinic figures known to us from Palestinian literature who ventured out to the Roman Diaspora did so for short visits. The case of R. Meir appears to have been most unusual. According to tradition, he fled to Asia Minor late in life and died there; see Y Kil'aim 9, 4, 32c; Alon, *Jews in Their Land*, II, 670–73. On the other hand, several sages noted in the Yerushalmi and Bavli are identified as having come from Carthage. See, for example, Y Demai 5, 2, 24c; B Bava Qama 114b. Cf. Simon, *Recherches*, 30–87; Rives, *Religion and Authority in Roman Carthage*, 219–20.

156. G. H. R. Horsley, *New Documents*, IV, 213–14. On the title *didaskalos* in a fifth- or sixth-century Spanish inscription from Tarragona, see Noy, *JIWE*, I, no. 186. Rabello ("Situation of Jews in Roman Spain," 174–75) suggests a fourth-century date.

157. Noy, *JIWE*, II, nos. 68, 270, 307, 374, 390 (?), 544.

someone knowledgeable in the Torah.[158] In a catacomb inscription from Rome, as well as in the Aphrodisias inscription, mention is made of a psalm singer, quite possibly referring to a synagogue functionary.[159] A *super orans* (chief cantor) is noted in a fifth- or sixth-century epitaph from Emerita, Spain.[160] Finally, although Scheiber renders the Greek term *spondill* in the inscription from Intercisa as a place-name, the term has often been interpreted as a reference to the Latin *spondalia*, meaning flautist.[161]

THE DIASPORA AND PALESTINE—SIMILARITIES AND DIFFERENCES

It would seem that Diaspora Judaism was not radically different from Palestinian Judaism, at least as far as the synagogue is concerned.[162] Many of the characteristics common to Diaspora synagogues hold true for Palestine as well.

The Torah shrine is prominent in most synagogues of late antiquity, appearing in a variety of settings in Palestine as well as in the Diaspora: a niche (Priene and Eshtemoa); an apse (Elche and Bet Alpha); an *aedicula* (Dura and Nabratein).[163] The centrality of the Torah to Jewish liturgy in antiquity is universally recognized; the Torah was read, expounded, and studied throughout the Jewish world, and these architectural remains reinforce this perception.

The purity concerns noted above for the Diaspora were likewise widespread among the Jews of Palestine, and water installations for this purpose have been found in all parts

---

158. Bradbury, *Severus of Minorca*, 6, 2 (p. 85); Hunt, "St. Stephen in Minorca," 109, 118–20; Millar, "Jews of the Graeco-Roman Diaspora," 119; see also Rabello, "Situation of Jews in Roman Spain," 167–70. For a term from Athens referring to a schoolteacher, see Lifshitz, "Prolegomenon," 83, no. 715b.

159. Noy, *JIWE*, II, 502; Reynolds and Tannenbaum, *Jews and God-Fearers*, 5 (line 15), 9, 46; see also G. H. R. Horsley, *New Documents*, I, 115–17.

160. Lifshitz, "Prolegomenon," no. 665a.

161. Scheiber, *Jewish Inscriptions*, 31; cf. Lifshitz, "Prolegomenon," no. 677; Kant, "Jewish Inscriptions," 696–97; Feldman, "Diaspora Synagogues," 61.

162. For a more extensive treatment of this subject, see my "Diaspora Judaism," 149–58. Here I wish to balance the somewhat engaging thesis offered by Kraabel in his "Unity and Diversity," 49–60: "Let me state the thesis at the outset: The Judaism of the synagogue communities of the Roman Diaspora is best understood, on the basis of the present evidence, as the grafting of a transformed biblical 'exile' ideology onto a Greco-Roman form of social organization" (49). Possible biblical influences aside, there seems to be no question that the Diaspora synagogue must be viewed primarily within a horizontal (i.e., Greco-Roman) context not only with regard to its non-Jewish components, but also with regard to its Jewish dimension. Judaism of the Second Temple period and its post-70 development affected Jewish communities both in Palestine and throughout the Diaspora. Any "biblical" influences were mediated through contemporary Jewish frameworks—institutional as well as ideological.

163. Kraabel, "Diaspora Synagogue"; Hachlili, *Art and Archaeology—Diaspora*, 166–82; L. Levine, "Interior of the Ancient Synagogue," 70–74.

of the country.[164] Moreover, synagogues in coastal cities in both Palestine and the Diaspora were often located near the shore (at Gaza and Caesarea, as well as Delos and Ostia).

Sacred status was common to synagogues in both Palestine and the Diaspora. Synagogues were defined as "holy" (and on occasion "most holy") throughout the Byzantine world. While the Diaspora synagogue was the first to acquire this status, already in the pre-70 period developments in Palestine in the late Roman and Byzantine periods elevated local synagogues to a similar position.

As will be spelled out in greater detail in the following chapter, the physical dimensions of synagogue buildings in both Palestine and the Diaspora varied in a similar fashion. Monumental structures were erected by some communities (Sardis, Capernaum), and far more modest structures by others (Khirbet Shemaʿ, Priene). In addition, the location of these buildings might have differed considerably, from the center of a city or village to its periphery.

Also common to Diaspora and Palestinian synagogues were the languages used. The primary languages of Palestine were those most in evidence throughout the East, i.e., Greek and Aramaic.[165] Hebrew played a distinctly minor role in inscriptional evidence, as it did in the Diaspora to an even lesser degree. As mentioned, Greek reigned supreme in the Diaspora, although Aramaic was also used in the East, as was Latin in the West. Thus, while rabbinic influence may have been a crucial factor in making Hebrew the primary language of communal prayer in Palestine and Babylonia, it seems that the local vernacular (usually Greek) was used for liturgical purposes in the Diaspora.[166] This would explain the tradition claiming that in Asia Minor R. Meir could not find a Megillah written in Hebrew and was thus forced to write one himself.[167]

In addition, there appears to have been just as broad a range of attitudes toward art and figural representation among the communities of Palestine as in the Diaspora. In the former, this is evident in the more conservative communities, such as ʿEn Gedi and Reḥov, as well as in the more hellenized ones, such as Ḥammat Tiberias and Bet Alpha. These last examples have been cited particularly with regard to the representation of the zodiac signs and Helios, which in the more conservative communities are either completely ignored (Reḥov) or noted only by name (ʿEn Gedi) but which in the more hellenized settings are fully represented.[168] The same range of attitudes toward figural representation, as noted, is found in the Diaspora, as we can see by comparing the strictly aniconic mosaic floors of the Apamea and Aegina synagogues and the full-blown pictorial cycles of biblical narratives depicted at Dura.

---

164. See E. P. Sanders, *Jewish Law*, 255–71; as well as two classic studies: Büchler, "Levitical Impurity," 1–81; and Alon, *Jews, Judaism and the Classical World*, 146–234. See below, Chap. 9.

165. Naveh, *On Stone and Mosaic*; Roth-Gerson, *Greek Inscriptions*.

166. De Lange, "Hebrew Language," 111–37.

167. T Megillah 2:5 (p. 349).

168. See Hachlili, "Zodiac," 61–77; L. Levine, "Interior of the Ancient Synagogue," 63–70.

The emphasis on local traditions, so clearly evident in Diaspora buildings, was of consequence in Palestine as well. Each of the country's various regions left an indelible stamp on the nature and plans of local synagogue buildings, e.g., the Galilean- and Golan-types, and well as that of southern Judaea.[169]

Thus, the picture that emerges within Palestine is not unlike that which we have observed in the Diaspora. Morton Smith noted this phenomenon in passing over thirty-five years ago: "But the different parts of the country (i.e., Israel) were so different, such gulfs of feeling and practice separated Idumea, Judea, Caesarea, and Galilee, that even on this level there was probably no more agreement between them than between any one of them in a similar area in the Diaspora."[170]

Use of Jewish symbolism, particularly the menorah, shofar, *lulav, ethrog*, and Torah shrine, are another common phenomenon of Diaspora and Palestinian synagogues. What appears in third-century Dura is likewise evidenced in third-century Bet She'arim and Khirbet Shema'. The Jewish symbols of fourth-century Sardis, Stobi, and Ostia are matched at Ḥammat Tiberias, Susiya, and 'En Gedi. It has been claimed that the extensive use of Jewish symbols in Diaspora synagogues reflects the psychology of alienation among the Jews, a phenomenon specifically associated with Jewish minority status in the Diaspora.[171] This may be true; however, it can hardly be the sole reason, for we find that these very same symbols were being introduced into Palestine at about the same time, even in areas where the Jews were clearly the majority. Moreover, Diaspora minority status is far from an adequate explanation even for the Diaspora, since pre-70 Diaspora remnants, though meager, carry no representations of Jewish symbols. This is true of Hellenistic and early Roman inscriptions from Egypt and Cyrene, of the Delos synagogue remains, and of first-century inscriptions from Cyrene, Asia Minor, and the Crimea. If minority status had been the major impetus in the use of such symbolism, one might have expected to see examples of it even in the pre-70 era. In fact, such symbols were likewise extremely rare in Second Temple Palestine. Even the menorah appears in only a few places in Jerusalem and nowhere else in Judaea.

While the factor of alienation due to minority status may have, indeed, played a role in stimulating the use of such symbols, we ought to look elsewhere for more promising reasons for this phenomenon. The emergence of such symbolism may be related to more general developments of late antiquity, such as the increasing degree of sanctity accorded the synagogue (see above), the transference of Temple symbolism to it and other Jewish

---

169. Ma'oz, "Art and Architecture of the Synagogues of the Golan," 98–115. Regarding southern Judaea, see Amit and Ilan, "Ancient Synagogue at Ma'on," 115–25. Even within the Galilee, significant differences have been noted among the synagogues of the Upper and Lower Galilee. See E. M. Meyers, "Galilean Regionalism," 93–101.

170. M. Smith, "Palestinian Judaism," 67–81 (quotation from p. 81).

171. H. Krauss, "Jewish Art as a Minority Problem," 147–71. See also Fine and Zuckerman, "Menorah as Symbol," 24–31.

frameworks (including the cemetery), the eventual rise of and threat posed by a victorious Christianity, and, finally, the more widespread use of symbols.[172]

Interestingly, it is precisely with regard to these and other artistic motifs that some fascinating differences emerge between Palestinian and Diaspora synagogues, and in rather unexpected ways. The intensive use of Jewish symbols, whether on mosaic floors or in stone moldings, is, in fact, much greater in synagogues in Palestine than in the Diaspora. The many Jewish symbols appearing, for example, in a fixed pattern on the mosaic floors of Bet Shean, Ḥammat Tiberias, Bet Alpha, Naʿaran, and Susiya include the Torah shrine, menorah, shofar, *ethrog*, *lulav*, and incense shovel.[173] Such a cluster of symbols never appears in such a prominent fashion in any preserved Diaspora synagogue, with the exception, perhaps, of Dura Europos. The closest parallel to duplicating this set of symbols in any Diaspora context is found in the Jewish catacombs of Rome, and especially on the fragments of gold glass.[174]

At the same time, Palestinian synagogues show a much greater tendency to feature figural representations, even those with distinctly pagan associations, than do their Diaspora counterparts. Dura Europos, of course, is the classic example of the extensive use of figural art, albeit solely with respect to biblical scenes. Yet no Diaspora synagogue even begins to approximate the blatantly Hellenistic-Roman depictions of the four seasons, the zodiac signs, and particularly Helios found in a number of Palestinian synagogues. Amazing as it may appear, Diaspora synagogues, far from being more syncretistic and hellenized in this respect, were by and large much more conservative in their representations. Perhaps the security of living in their own land, among a largely Jewish population, allowed many Palestinian communities to indulge in artistic expressions that their Diaspora counterparts found objectionable or threatening.

CONCLUSIONS

Our knowledge of Jewish life in the Diaspora in late antiquity has been significantly augmented in the past century by a large number of archeological finds. Some of this material, particularly that relating to synagogues, has offered a rather different picture of these Jewish communities than had heretofore been assumed. The attraction of the synagogue for gentile sympathizers continued at least until the end of the fourth century, and a number of synagogues maintained a vigorous communal life well into the Byzantine period.[175] Sardis, of course, offers the most spectacular example of a synagogue flourishing right up until the destruction of the city in the seventh century.

---

172. See L. Levine, "Menorah."

173. Hachlili, *Art and Archaeology*, 347–65.

174. Goodenough, *Jewish Symbols*, II, 108–19.

175. Feldman, *Jew and Gentile*, 45–83, 342–415. See also Hengel, *Johannine Question*, 116–17.

This newly discovered archeological material is not all of one hue. We have noted evidence of some synagogues that were destroyed and others which were converted into churches, thus corroborating a number of literary sources which tell a similar story of persecution. Throughout this period, there was continuous pressure in certain church circles to limit, if not eliminate, Jewish practices, rights, and influence.[176] Thus, this very diverse data regarding the positive and negative dimensions of Jewish-Christian relations must be fully integrated in order to gain as accurate and balanced a portrayal as possible of Jewish life at the time. If the resulting picture is ambiguous, offering different assessments from place to place and from period to period, so be it; that in itself undoubtedly approximates what must have indeed been a complex situation in a period of transformation and realignment for all elements of Byzantine society.

We are left with the puzzling phenomenon of a Diaspora as united as it was diverse, utilizing symbols and reflecting values that were common to most synagogues throughout antiquity. Despite the often dramatically different historical, social, political, and cultural contexts within Diaspora Jewry, and between Diaspora and Palestinian Jewry, there may indeed be enough evidence to justify the assumption of a common and shared tradition which affected and influenced Jews everywhere, a heritage which found expression in similar communal and religious frameworks despite differences of language, culture, and immediate political and social contexts.[177]

Modern critical scholars, by their very nature, have spent much time analyzing and dissecting, differentiating and distinguishing. In our case, this tendency has been augmented by literary sources which are scattered, fragmentary, and often quite tendentious, as well as by archeological material which is reflective only of its immediate environs. No less important than these legitimate concerns is the need to balance such analyses by focusing on the unifying and common as well, the shared continuum—both the vertical continuum from the past and the horizontal continuum within the contemporary Jewish world. Only by weighing all these factors can one hope to achieve as comprehensive and in-depth an understanding of ancient Judaism as possible.[178]

---

176. See, for example, the many laws issued and re-issued for the protection of synagogues at the end of the fourth and in the early part of the fifth centuries (Linder, *Jews in Roman Imperial Legislation*, nos. 21, 25, 40, 46-49). To this must be added the famous *Novella* 146 of Justinian banning the use of the Mishnah in the synagogue; see ibid., no. 66; A. Baumgarten, "Justinian and the Jews," 37-44.

177. On the relation of Diaspora communities to their immediate geographical and social environments, see Gafni, *Land, Center and Diaspora*, 41-57.

178. On this larger question, see below, Chap. 18.

part II THE SYNAGOGUE
AS AN INSTITUTION

nine THE BUILDING

Archeological data constitute our main source of information regarding the physical features of the synagogue, although literary material has much to contribute as well.[1] The many scores of synagogue buildings throughout the Roman-Byzantine world known to date present a wide variety of examples regarding the location of the building as well as its external and internal appearance.

In this chapter, we shall examine the different parts of the synagogue building, beginning with its external features and components and moving inward, to its internal plan and organization.[2] Thus, we will first look at the synagogue's location in a community, its plan as a communal complex, its architecture and orientation, adjacent courtyard, water installations, and facade and then proceed to the elements of the building's interior, beginning with the entrances and culminating with the areas devoted to religious worship. The various types of artistic representation within the building will also be discussed. The chapter will conclude with some thoughts as to how the synagogue's main hall functioned liturgically. There will be an attempt to relate architectural elements to the liturgical functions of the ancient synagogue.

In describing the synagogue building from late antiquity, I am assuming that its major

1. See, for example, the wealth of material amassed in S. Krauss, *Synagogale Altertümer,* 267–364.
2. See also L. Levine, "Interior of the Ancient Synagogue," 36–84, as well as the sources marshaled in Z. Safrai, "Institution of the Synagogue," 33–70.

components were similar enough to warrant such a presentation and comparison. The ancient synagogue, like many public buildings of the time, might include a courtyard, entrances, a main hall, benches, columns, decorations, and some sort of unique internal arrangement. Except perhaps for the decorations, which often included a Torah shrine and possibly a menorah and other Jewish symbols, the synagogue building was not unique in its physical appearance. Nevertheless, regardless of whether it was unique, we shall examine those features found in most, if not all, ancient synagogues. As has already been noted, synagogues might differ sharply from one another in appearance. Regional or local influences often left their mark on the appearance of these buildings; yet, despite all the obvious variations, many common traits remain, and it is to the examination of this commonality, together with its many nuances, that this chapter is devoted.

There is little justification in this regard, or in other areas to be addressed in subsequent chapters, for differentiating between the Diaspora and Palestine. In both regions, synagogue art and architecture were influenced by the cultural currents of later antiquity, with each community adopting and adapting elements according to its own proclivities. Although some striking differences between buildings of the Diaspora and Byzantine Palestine do, in fact, exist, there are also some significant differences among the Palestinian synagogues as well as among those of the Diaspora (see above, Chap. 8). Given this variety, and the ultimate responsibility of each community to determine the appearance of its public building, there is little reason here to draw geographical distinctions between the Diaspora and Palestine.

LOCATION

Local Jewish communities seem to have had certain accepted preferences with regard to the location of their synagogue buildings, even though there was a considerable amount of variation. In Palestine, some communities chose to build their synagogues in the center of the village or town in order to afford easy access. This was clearly the case at Chorazim, Susiya, and Merot. However, some synagogues were not centrally located, as at Gamla and Arbel, or were placed at a considerable distance from town, as at Gush Halav.[3] In the reworking of a tannaitic source, the Bavli makes it clear that synagogues were known to be built outside the city's official boundaries: "Come and hear: the following are included in the Sabbath boundary of a town [i.e., a distance ca. one thousand meters beyond the town limits]: a funerary monument of the size of four by four cubits, a bridge or a cemetery that contains a dwelling chamber, a synagogue that has a dwelling house for the ḥazzan, a heathen temple that contains a dwelling house for priests, stables and storehouses in fields which have dwelling chambers, watchmen's huts in a field, and a house by the sea [on an island?]."[4]

---

3. A similar instance is mentioned in B Qiddushin 73b in a Babylonian setting.

4. B ʿEruvin 55b; see also T ʿEruvin 4:7 (p. 106).

The two synagogues in Bet Shean proper are quite different in this regard. One (whether Samaritan or Jewish) is located some two hundred meters north of the city wall, the other within the city, near its southwestern gate. In Gush Ḥalav there was almost certainly a synagogue inside the town, as well as one ca. three hundred meters to the north.

Many synagogues were located on an elevated spot, sometimes at the highest point of a town, per the dictum preserved in rabbinic literature.[5] Meiron and Kanaf in the Golan are classic examples of this phenomenon, perched as they are on the mountaintop, towering over the residential areas below. A similar instance of this practice can be found at Ḥammat Gader, while at Susiya, Merot, Capernaum, and Chorazim the synagogue's physical prominence was enhanced by its placement on an artificial podium. Whether this was done because of the rabbinic statement or because of Greco-Roman practice intended to give emphasis to public buildings (or both) is indeterminable. Nevertheless, not all synagogues were located at the highest local point, as, for example, at ʿEn Neshut in the Golan and Arbel and Gush Ḥalav in the Galilee.

Samaritan synagogues, for their part, appear to have been more consistently located on the outskirts of a town or village. The recently discovered synagogues at Khirbet Samara and el-Khirbe were built on the periphery of their respective settlements, and the above-noted synagogue located north of the Bet Shean city wall, if in fact Samaritan, would be another example of this tendency.[6] There is no obvious reason why the Samaritans would do this; purity concerns, political pressures, or their desire for social and religious isolation immediately come to mind, but the phenomenon remains an enigma.

In the Diaspora as well, as we have noted above, synagogues are located in diverse places within the various towns and cities. On the one hand, the synagogue at Sardis was very centrally located in the city, as were those in Apamea and Philippopolis (Plovdiv). The synagogue at Gerasa was also centrally positioned among the city's public buildings, just west of the Temple of Artemis and on one of the highest places in the city. On the other hand, the synagogue at Dura Europos was built on the outskirts of the city, as were those of Delos, Bova Marina, and Ostia. As we have seen, first-century literary sources make it quite clear that many Diaspora Jewish communities actually preferred having their synagogues outside the city and near a body of water, such as the *proseuche* at Philippi in Macedonia.[7] A second-century B.C.E. land survey from Arsinoe notes a synagogue by a canal on the outskirts of the town.[8]

---

5. T Megillah 3:23 (p. 360); see also Tanḥuma, B'ḥuqotai, 4 (p. 55b); B Shabbat 11a. On the placing of pagan shrines on high places, see Bowsher, "Architecture and Religion," 63.

6. Magen, "Samaritan Synagogues" (Eng.), 193-227. On the dispute regarding the identification of the northern synagogue at Bet Shean, see above, Chap. 7, note 19.

7. Acts 16:13. See also above, Chap. 4.

8. Tcherikover et al., *CPJ*, I, no. 134. See also the fascinating remark in Mekhilta of R. Ishmael, Bo, 1 (p. 2), which describes Moses in Egypt praying outside the city because of the latter's "abominations and idols." Might this reflect the contemporary attitudes of some communities?

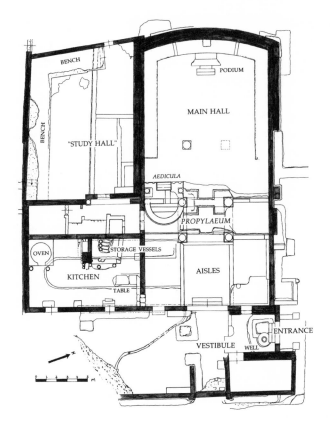

60. Ostia synagogue complex.

THE SYNAGOGUE COMPLEX

A synagogue often consisted of a complex of rooms, with a courtyard adjoining the main hall. Most of the Diaspora buildings explored to date designate the main sanctuary (or main hall) as the focal point of the complex. Dura Europos, Ostia (fig. 60), Stobi, and Naro are particularly developed in this regard; Dura, for example, has nine additional rooms, an entranceway, and a forecourt, while Naro has twelve such rooms in addition to a series of forecourts and a passageway. The synagogue buildings at Priene, Aegina, and Philippopolis (and presumably Elche and Bova Marina as well) had additional rooms, but very little remains. The Aphrodisias inscription makes note of a "memorial," a building whose function, however, is far from clear. Sardis is somewhat unusual in this regard, as its monumental main hall stands alone; other than the large adjacent 20-meter-long atrium, no other room appears to have been associated with this synagogue.

As for Palestine, the picture is less clear, as the main halls of many synagogue buildings were excavated, but not their immediate surroundings (e.g., Ḥorvat ʿAmmudim, Jericho, Eshtemoa, ʿEn Neshut, Khirbet e-Dikke, Barʿam). Nevertheless, there still remain many synagogues whose complexes of rooms have been revealed: Ḥammat Tiberias (last stage), Ma'on (Nirim), Ḥammat Gader, 'En Gedi, Khirbet Shema', Khirbet Rimmon, Gush Ḥalav, and Na'aran, among others. Some synagogue buildings, such as those at Meiron and Arbel, were constructed in unusual settings which, in effect, precluded the building of any significant additions.

In most cases, the specific function of these ancillary rooms remains unknown. Rarely have the results of archeological excavations offered sufficient information, and it is generally on the basis of literary sources that we have become aware of the potentially broad range of synagogue activities.[9] However, in several cases we do, in fact, possess epigraphical evidence regarding the nature of these rooms. An inscription found in the synagogue at Qatzrin reads: "[U]zi made this *revu'a[h]*."[10] The use of this term as a noun is rare; the verb, however, which is far more frequent, means "to lie down."[11] Thus, the several rabbinic sources in which the term *revu'ah* appears (usually with reference to the academy) seem to refer to a kind of *triclinium*, where festive meals were held. For example: "As was the case in the days of R. Judah b. Pazi. There was a *revu'ah* in the academy and they used to spread a curtain over four cubits on Friday [lit., from yesterday] and on the morrow [i.e., Shabbat] they would spread it out completely."[12] And, "R. Yonah and R. Yosi went to the academy of Bar 'Ulla, where there was a *revu'ah*, and there were beams there. They asked him: "Can these be carried [on the Sabbath]?"[13] Although not referring specifically to a *revu'ah*, R. Yoḥanan takes note of meals being held in synagogues on the New Moon and at other times, and such activity is attested elsewhere as well.[14] A number of Nabatean inscriptions also make reference to a *rab'ata*, which presumably has a similar connotation.[15]

Several Greek inscriptions, one from Caesarea and another from Stobi, refer to a *triclinium* as part of the synagogue complex,[16] while literary references from Josephus to the synagogues of Delos and Sardis note that communal meals were held there.[17] Actual kitchen facilities have been found only in Ostia, and these consist of an oven and a marble-topped table.[18]

In a number of synagogues, as at Ostia, Gamla, and Khirbet Shema', side rooms of

9. See the discussion of synagogue functions in Chaps. 5 and 10.

10. Naveh, *On Stone and Mosaic*, no. 110; Urman, "Jewish Inscriptions," 533–35.

11. Jastrow, *Dictionary*, 1444–45; Sokoloff, *Dictionary*, 514.

12. Y Shabbat 20, 1, 17c.

13. Ibid., 4, 2, 7a.

14. Y Sanhedrin 8, 2, 26a–b. See also the more oblique reference to food in the synagogue by R. Jeremiah in Y Pesaḥim 1, 1, 27b; Meitlis, "Significance of the 'Revua,'" 465–66; and below, Chap. 10.

15. See, for example, *CIS*, II/1, no. 160; and other references cited in Urman, "Jewish Inscriptions," 534–35. On *triclinia* and cultic meals among the Nabataeans generally, see Glueck, *Deities and Dolphins*, 163–91.

16. Lifshitz, *Donateurs et fondateurs*, nos. 10 and 66.

17. Josephus, *Antiquities* 14, 214; 16, 164.

18. Squarciapino, *Synagogue of Ostia*, 24.

varying sizes have been found with benches along one or more walls. Excavators have regularly—and usually quite arbitrarily—labeled these as places of study, as either schools for children or academies for adults. The remains of two rooms in the synagogue courtyard at Merot have likewise been identified as such.[19]

Finally, the use of synagogue premises as a hostel is clearly (though meagerly) attested in our sources. The Theodotos inscription makes specific mention of such a function, and this is corroborated by literary material as well.[20] On occasion, living quarters within the building were provided for functionaries; this is expressly noted in relation to the *ḥazzan*[21] but may have applied to others as well.

The second stage at Dura Europos, which joined the original premises to the adjacent House H, significantly expanded the area of communal activity.[22] Such was the case in Stobi as well. It will be recalled that this building was originally the home of a wealthy patron, Claudius Tiberius Polycharmos, who donated part of this home to the local community for use as a "holy place." Archeological data seem to indicate that, at one point, the synagogue was enlarged by joining it with a building next door.

The example of Dura Europos is indicative of another trait of Diaspora synagogues in that it was originally a private home which was then converted into a public building for the community at large.[23] Thus, even this type of facility was not just a hall for meetings, but had a number of ancillary rooms for other activities as well. The synagogues at Priene, Naro, Delos, and Stobi are similar to Dura in this respect. With the possible exception of the Leontis complex in Bet Shean, no extant synagogue from Roman-Byzantine Palestine appears to have been converted from a private home; all seem to have been intended as communal buildings from their inception.

ARCHITECTURE

As noted above, communities built their synagogues in many styles and shapes. Some were monumental and imposing (e.g., Sardis), others modest and unassuming (e.g., Dura Europos); some were long and basilical, with the focus on a short wall at one end of the hall (e.g., Meiron), others more compact (the broadhouse-type), focusing on the long wall (e.g., Susiya); some faced Jerusalem via their facades and main entrances (the Galilean-type), others via their apses, niches, or podiums, with their main entrances at

---

19. Z. Ilan, "Synagogue and Bet Midrash of Meroth," 275–85. The identification of one of these rooms has been aided by an inscription citing Deut. 28:6, which is interpreted as referring to academies and synagogues. On the *pronaos* mentioned in an inscription from Mantineia (Greece), see Frey, *CIJ*, I, no. 720; White, *Social Origins*, 359–60.

20. See Chaps. 3, 5, and 10.

21. B ʿEruvin 55b.

22. Kraeling, *Dura: Synagogue*, 10.

23. White, *Building God's House*, 60–101.

the opposite end of the hall (e.g., Bet Alpha); some were richly ornate (e.g., Capernaum), others completely undecorated (e.g., Meiron). In short, no two synagogues were identical in either shape, size or design, no matter how close they were to one another geographically or chronologically. One has only to compare the synagogues at Na'aran and Jericho, Khirbet Shema' and Meiron, Reḥov and Bet Alpha, or Dura Europos and Sardis to understand how striking these differences could be. This remarkable variety was an integral component of the synagogue scene throughout this period and, as noted, was as true of Palestine as it was of the Diaspora.

This last assertion is at odds with the widely accepted theory throughout much of this century regarding the architectural development of the synagogue, particularly in Roman-Byzantine Palestine. As already mentioned, archeologists since the publications of Kohl, Watzinger, and Sukenik have accepted as axiomatic a twofold and, later, threefold typological division of buildings based upon chronological considerations.[24] The early or Galilean synagogue (e.g., Chorazim or Capernaum) was dated to the late second and early third centuries), the transitional or broadhouse-type (e.g., Eshtemoa or Khirbet Shema') to the late third or fourth century, and the later or basilica-type (e.g., Bet Alpha) to the sixth and seventh centuries in the main.

This approach, articulated in several stages, first by Kohl and Watzinger, then by Sukenik, and later by Avi-Yonah and Goodenough, was based primarily on historical and artistic considerations. Kohl and Watzinger had argued that the most logical period in which to place the sometimes ornate, monumental Galilean synagogue was around the turn of the third century, at the time of R. Judah I. It was assumed that by that time the Jewish community had recovered from the traumatic repercussions of the previous century and a half and was in a position to erect such grandiose structures. R. Judah's political and religious stature, together with his apparently excellent relations with the Roman authorities, presumably facilitated this development. Such a supposition was strengthened, in these scholars' opinion, by the artistic similarities between these Galilean synagogues and contemporary pagan public buildings of second-century Syria and elsewhere.[25] With the discovery of Bet Alpha in 1928–29 and other synagogues by the early 1930s, Sukenik went a step further and, having noted the striking resemblance between the apsidal synagogue with its mosaic floors and the Byzantine basilical church, posited a second basilical type.[26] However, the discovery of a totally different model of the synagogue at Eshtemoa in 1934 eventually led to the suggestion of yet another, transitional phase (the broadhouse-type), which linked the two better-known ones.[27]

---

24. *Twofold:* Sukenik, *Ancient Synagogues,* 27; May, "Synagogues in Palestine," 231–37. *Threefold:* Goodenough, *Jewish Symbols,* I, 178–267; Avi-Yonah, "Synagogue Architecture," 65–82.

25. Kohl and Watzinger, *Antike Synagogen,* 138ff.

26. Sukenik, *Ancient Synagogues,* 27–37; idem, "Present State," 7–23.

27. For the most extensive explanation of this theory, see Goodenough and Avi-Yonah (above, note 24); see also above, Chap. 1.

61. Lintel from the sixth-century Nevoraya synagogue. Note the wreath and menorah in the center and the inscription across the entire width of the lintel.

However, this neat compartmentalized reconstruction—coupling typology with chronology—has been seriously undermined over this past quarter century by numerous archeological discoveries.[28] At first, the results of the Franciscan excavations at Capernaum placed this Galilean synagogue in the late fourth and fifth centuries.[29] Soon thereafter, the excavation findings from the synagogues at Khirbet Shemaʿ and Meiron—located some six hundred meters from each other as the crow flies—dated both of these structures to the latter half of the third century.[30] Each of these buildings represents a dramatically different architectural style according to the old theory; Meiron is a quintessentially Galilean-type structure, Khirbet Shemaʿ a broadhouse-type. Nevertheless, they were both built at the same time and in the same locale.

The excavation results from Nevoraya proved that the extant building, known for over a century as a Galilean-type structure, was, in fact, the third stage of a synagogue at the site and dates from the sixth century.[31] Such is the explicit attestation of its lintel inscription, which was found in the nineteenth century but deciphered by Avigad only in the mid-twentieth (fig. 61). The inscription reads as follows: "To the count of 494 years after the destruction of the Temple, (this synagogue) was built during the office of Ḥanina ben Lizar and Luliana bar Yudan."[32]

28. For some of the more recent critiques of an ever growing list, see E. M. Meyers, "Current State of Galilean Synagogue Studies," 127–37; Seager, "Recent Historiography," 85–92; Chiat and Mauck, "Using Archeological Sources," 69–73; L. Levine, in *NEAEHL*, IV, 1422; Groh, "Stratigraphic Chronology of the Galilean Synagogue," 51–69; Hachlili, "Synagogues in the Land of Israel," 99–102.

29. Loffreda, "Late Chronology," 52–56; idem, in *NEAEHL*, I, 292–94, and bibliography there, p. 296. Even before the Franciscan excavations, several scholars had already noted Byzantine elements in the Capernaum synagogue. Sukenik had suggested a Byzantine date for one of the synagogue inscriptions (*Ancient Synagogues*, 72), and Avi-Yonah a similar date for a number of capitals from this and other Galilean-type synagogues ("Synagogue Architecture," 70). See also the comments of Chen ("Chronology," 134–43) and Sharon ("Models for Stratigraphic Analysis," 277–83) supporting this dating and, on the other hand, Tsafrir's critique of the Franciscans' conclusions ("Synagogues of Capernaum and Meroth," 151–61).

30. *Khirbet Shemaʿ*: E. M. Meyers et al., *Excavations at Khirbet Shemaʿ*, 33ff.; E. M. Meyers, "Horvat Shemaʿ," 71–73. *Meiron*: Meyers et al., *Excavations at Ancient Meiron*, 16. See the reservations of Loffreda regarding the chronology of the Khirbet Shemaʿ synagogue ("Meyers et al., *Excavations at Khirbet Shemaʿ* [Review]," 75–79). Regarding Meiron, see the critiques in Foerster, "Ancient Meron," 262–69, esp. 264–65; Netzer, "Gush Halav and Khirbet Meiron," 453–54.

31. E. M. Meyers et al., "Second Preliminary Report on Excavations at en-Nabratein," 35, 43.

32. Avigad, "Dated Lintel," 49–56; Naveh, *On Stone and Mosaic*, 31–33. Similar usage of the word

Until these recent excavations, no one could accept this epigraphical evidence at face value—namely, that the synagogue was built in 564 C.E.—because of the regnant chronological assumptions of the time, and thus the term "built" was interpreted as "repaired." Now that archeological excavations have determined that this last stage was built several centuries after the earlier one; and according to a somewhat different plan, it is clear that much more than a repair was involved.

Throughout the 1970s and 1980s, several other excavations were conducted at already identified Galilean synagogues—Horvat ʿAmmudim, Gush Ḥalav, and Chorazim. The finds from the first two sites point to a mid to late third-century date of construction at the earliest; those from Chorazim indicate a fourth- to fifth-century date.[33] Moreover, the results of a number of excavations in the Golan in the 1980s date the time of construction of synagogues there to the fifth and sixth centuries C.E.[34] Finally, the discovery of a Galilean-type structure at Merot in the mid-1980s placed another nail in the coffin of the older theory, as the earliest stage of this building was clearly and unequivocally set in the late fourth or early fifth century.[35]

Thus, the linear approach equating each type of building to a specific historical period can rightly be put to rest.[36] Diversity reigned in synagogue architecture and art, as it did in other dimensions of synagogue life.[37] The social implications of this phenomenon are likewise clear. Local tastes and proclivities were the decisive factors in determining what a synagogue looked like and how it functioned.

"house" for synagogue with reference also to the term of office of an official appears at Dura Europos; see Kraeling, *Dura: Synagogue*, 263. On similarly dated inscriptions from the time of the destruction of the Temple, see the funerary evidence from Zoʿar in the southern part of the Dead Sea (Naveh, *On Sherd and Papyrus*, 203–5).

33. *Horvat ʿAmmudim:* L. Levine, "Excavations at the Synagogue of Horvat ʿAmmudim," 1–12; idem, "Excavations at Horvat ha-ʿAmudim," 78–81. *Gush Ḥalav:* E. M. Meyers, in *NEAEHL*, II, 547. *Chorazim: NEAEHL*, I, 304. At excavations now taking place at Barʿam (summer 1998), Motti Aviʿam reports (personal communication) that the synagogue dates to the fourth century; pottery and Constantinian coins found under the floor are cited as evidence.

34. Maʿoz, "Art and Architecture of the Synagogues of the Golan," 113; idem, in *NEAEHL*, II, 538–45. See also Ariel, "Coins from Synagogue at En Nashut," 156; and Hachlili, "Jewish Art from the Golan," 189–91.

35. Z. Ilan, "Synagogue and Bet Midrash of Meroth," 21, 37; idem, *Ancient Synagogues*, 41. Cf., however, the comments of Tsafrir, "Synagogues of Capernaum and Meroth," 151–61.

36. Other generally held conceptions relating to the Galilean-type synagogue have likewise been questioned of late—for example, original flagstone floors that were sometimes replaced by mosaic ones (contra those at Horvat ʿAmmudim and Merot), and the absence of fixed Torah shrines (see below). Avi-Yonah, one of the main proponents of the traditional linear theory, had already voiced reservations in this regard in an article published in 1973, shortly before his death: "Ancient Synagogues," 29–43. See also Chen, "Design of Ancient Synagogues in Judea," 38; and L. Levine, "Synagogues," *NEAEHL*, IV, 1421–24.

37. On the diversity in Palestinian synagogues, see Foerster, "Ancient Synagogues," 40–42.

Interestingly, the same diversity appears to have held for Samaritan synagogues. In several recently discovered buildings dating from the fourth and fifth centuries, the entrances of each differed radically. At el-Khirbe, the building's single portal faced southeast, toward Mt. Gerizim. Some eight kilometers westward, the synagogue at Khirbet Samara had a single entrance facing west; its eastern wall, later embellished with an apse, faced Mt. Gerizim.[38]

However, a synagogue was not merely an entity unto itself. The proliferation of synagogue finds over the past decades has enabled us to define certain regional characteristics ever more clearly. Much has been written about the Galilean-type, which usually featured monumental facades, occasionally with ornate stone moldings, one or three entrances facing Jerusalem (Arbel excepted), benches along two or three walls, flagstone floors (except at Horvat 'Ammudim), and relatively little figural representation (Capernaum and Chorazim aside) or Jewish symbolism.[39] Given the similarity in style among many of the Galilean synagogues, it is conceivable that a central authority such as the Patriarch may have had a hand in this renewed construction. From the evidence available, the Patriarchate was already a powerful institution and continued to function as such throughout the fourth century. To date, however, we have no hard evidence linking synagogue building in the Galilee with the Patriarch.[40] Regional traditions, rather than a central authority, may indeed provide an adequate explanation for this trend.

The Golan-type synagogue is in many respects similar to the Galilean-type; it also boasts a monumental and ornate facade. Nevertheless, the differences are quite striking. Golan buildings, traces of which have been found at twenty-five sites, were constructed of local basalt, contained many more Jewish and figural representations, had single entrances (with the exception of e-Dikke) in every conceivable direction, and were oriented consistently in the interior to either the south or the west.[41]

The four synagogues discovered to date in southern Judaea (Eshtemoa, Susiya, 'Anim, and Ma'on of Judaea), for all the differences among them, nevertheless share some noteworthy characteristics: they contain no Greek inscriptions, they have relatively little figural representation, the main hall has no columns, and their entrances are toward the east,

---

38. See above, note 6.

39. Even with the striking similarities, not all Galilean-type synagogues were identical. Some were more rectangular than others, with one or three entrances, more and less elaborate designs, and two or three rows of internal columns. The synagogue at Bar'am, with its entrance portico and possibly four rows of columns (per Motti Avi'am), was unique, as was the one at Capernaum with its side atrium, Arbel with its single entrance from the east and niche for the Torah ark, and Horvat 'Ammudim with its mosaic floor. Nevertheless, despite all the variations among these buildings, the impression of overall unity and commonality of plan predominates.

40. See below, Chap. 12.

41. Ma'oz, "Art and Architecture of the Synagogues of the Golan," 98–115; idem, *NEAEHL*, II, 539–45; Hachlili, "Jewish Art from the Golan," 183–212. On the issue of orientation, see below.

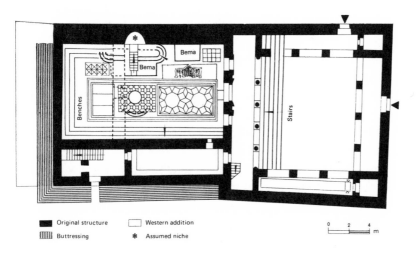

Original structure | Western addition
Buttressing | * Assumed niche

0 2 4 m

62. Plan of the Susiya synagogue. Note the broadhouse-type features, with *bima* and niche facing north and entrances and courtyard toward the east.

as recommended in Tosefta Megillah (fig. 62).[42] Other synagogues in the country, most of which are in or near major Roman cities (Gadara, Tiberias, Bet Shean, Caesarea, Ashkelon, and Gaza), followed the basilical model that was predominant in Byzantine society.

Thus, taking into account all of the above, synagogue art and architecture appear to have reflected a delicate balance between the individual community and its larger regional context. On the one hand, each synagogue reflected the economic resources, social configuration, and cultural as well as religious proclivities of the local community; on the other, it shared characteristics common to a given region or to other synagogues throughout the Roman world.[43]

The outward appearance of synagogues throughout the ages has been heavily influenced by their surrounding cultures. Scholars continue to argue over the origin of the Galilean-type building: Was it an offshoot of Hellenistic places of assembly (the *ecclesiasterion* or *bouleuterion*), of the Second Temple synagogue (e.g., Masada), of Roman basilical models, of earlier Herodian buildings, like that at Jericho (which themselves were probably influenced by foreign models), or of Nabatean temple courtyards from southern Syria?[44] Whatever one's preference in this regard, one matter is clear: the art and

42. On these as well as the synagogues listed below, see the relevant entries in *NEAEHL*. On the Judaean synagogues in particular, see Amit, "Architectural Plans," 129–56; and comments by S. Safrai, *In Times of Temple and Mishnah*, I, 154–58. On entrances to the east, see T Megillah 3:22–23 (p. 360): "One should build synagogue entrances only toward the east. . . . One should build them at the highest point of the town."

43. See above, Chap. 8.

44. Kohl and Watzinger, *Antike Synagogen*, 219ff.; and the articles of Avigad, Foerster, and Netzer, in *Ancient Synagogues Revealed*, 42–51.

architecture of the eastern Roman world were a significant source of inspiration in the construction of the Galilean-type synagogue buildings. All their architectural features point to Hellenistic-Roman models: the triportal entrance, decorated lintels, windows, gables, acroteria, etc.[45]

The same holds true with regard to the basilica-type synagogue. The Byzantine church basilica was clearly a major source of influence, and thus in these synagogues there is a greater emphasis on the building's interior, as opposed to its exterior, with mosaic floors rather than the facade as the focus for artistic display.

Whatever may have been the sources of influence for the different types of synagogues, the exterior was no different from that of other buildings which a pedestrian might pass by on a Roman-Byzantine street.[46] Archeological remains of synagogues throughout the Roman world have made this crystal clear. This very point is strikingly confirmed in a rabbinic discussion regarding the halakhic implications of a man who might walk along the street of a town and bow when passing a building he thought to be a synagogue but later discovered to be a pagan temple.[47] Of interest for our purposes are neither the details of the particular halakhic issue at hand, i.e., whether in such a situation one is guilty of an intentional transgression of idolatry, nor the fact that such a practice of bowing before a temple was common among pagans as well,[48] but rather the architectural reality behind this account. Clearly, the rabbis assumed that from a building's exterior one could not distinguish between a synagogue and a pagan temple. Especially in the Diaspora, where many synagogues were reconstructed private homes, they did not usually stand out from their surroundings. Owing to its unusual state of preservation, the synagogue at Dura Europos is a classic example of how a synagogue might blend in with other buildings on its street.

ORIENTATION

As already noted, synagogues were almost universally oriented toward Jerusalem. This custom, based perhaps on several scriptural references, was widely accepted throughout the Jewish world.[49]

---

45. Cf. the comments by Tsafrir ("Source of Architectural Design," 80–86), who argues for a uniquely Jewish adaptation of these foreign elements.

46. On the engaging though enigmatic reference of Epiphanius, that Jews built their synagogues like open-air theaters, see his *Panarion* 80, 1, 5.

47. B Shabbat 72b; see also B Sanhedrin 61b.

48. Apuleius, *Apologia* 56, 4; Minucius Felix, *Octavius* 2, 4.

49. I Kgs. 8:29–30; Is. 56:7; Dan. 6:11. See Landsberger, "Sacred Direction," 181–203. It is of interest that members of the Jewish-Christian sect the Elkesaites are reported by Epiphanius to have turned toward Jerusalem in prayer (*Panarion* 19, 3, 5). Cf., however, the somewhat problematic distinctions put forth in Wilkinson, "Orientation," 16–36. On synagogue orientation, see also Chap. 7.

A word is in order as to the term "orientation," as there has been much confusion in this regard. There are three possible ways to determine orientation: (1) the external direction of a building, indicated by its facade, doors, or adjacent atrium, thus following pagan models; (2) the internal design of the main hall, indicated by the placement of columns, benches, *bima*, and Torah shrine; and (3) the direction of prayer for the *'Amidah*, which with rare exception (see below) requires facing Jerusalem. Often scholars have used the direction of synagogue facades and doors to determine synagogue orientation. However, the positioning of these external architectural elements, which was often a matter of style or topographical necessity, seems to have been a consideration of secondary importance when compared with that of the internal design and usage of the main hall.[50] It would appear that the focus of attention and activity from within the hall should be the primary and decisive factor in determining orientation. With this in mind, and on the basis of the seating arrangements along the walls, we can conclude that the focus in all synagogues was both the center of the hall and the Jerusalem wall, where a Torah shrine, an apse, or a *bima* might be found. Only on occasion, as was the case with Galilean buildings, did the exterior of a building reflect this internal orientation as well. Finally, it can be assumed that the direction of prayer followed (or perhaps determined) the building's internal design.

This normativeness of orientation toward Jerusalem certainly holds true in the Diaspora. The Dura Europos and Gerasa synagogues faced west; Apamea south; Delos, Priene, Aegina, Stobi, Sardis, Ostia, and Naro east or southeast.[51] Moreover, such was the norm in Roman Palestine as well. Galilean synagogues faced south, those in the southern part of the country north, and those in the southern Shephelah northeast.

Nevertheless, we also know of some interesting "deviations." The Golan synagogues, as a group, are quite unusual in this regard. With the exception of the Gamla building, which is a pre-70 structure, all the Byzantine synagogues in this region faced either south or west.[52] None is oriented to the southwest, i.e., directly toward Jerusalem. The

---

50. See the comments of Amit, "Excavations at Ma'on and 'Anim," 26–34.

51. See Kraabel, "Diaspora Synagogue," foldout opposite p. 504; Foerster, "Survey of Diaspora Synagogues," 164–71; L. Levine, "Synagogue at Dura-Europos," 172–73; White, *Building God's House*, figs. 9–16.

52. See Z. Ilan, *Ancient Synagogues*, 63–113.

One possible explanation for the western or southern orientations of the Golan synagogues is that this region may have served as a destination for populations moving from the Galilee in the north of Palestine and from Peraea, east of the Jordan River. Those from the Galilee may have then continued to face south and those from the Transjordan area to face west, according to their former customs (we assume the Transjordan custom from the Gerasa structure). As intriguing as this theory may be, it remains speculative at best, although it is interesting to note that this phenomenon is evident in modern times. Central and eastern European synagogues faced east despite the fact that Jerusalem lies to the south. Presumably, this tradition originated in western Europe and was maintained in very different geographical circumstances.

There has been some confusion regarding the Gamla synagogue's orientation. On the one hand, the

southern and western directions adopted by Byzantine Golan architects are understandable: westward would indicate that the primary focus was toward the Holy Land, per the rabbinic injunction for Diaspora Jews;[53] facing south may have been justified by the fact that Jerusalem lies primarily in that direction. Nevertheless, to have so many synagogue buildings in this small area rather evenly divided between these two alternatives, with no apparent geographical, topographical, or urban-rural explanation, is puzzling.

A number of other synagogue buildings likewise exhibit a "deviant" orientation. The synagogue at Ḥorvat Sumaqa on the Carmel range was built along an east-west axis, with an undoubtedly eastward orientation.[54] Jerusalem, however, is located southeast of this site, and thus the building should have faced this latter direction, as did the nearby Ḥuseifa and Bet She'arim synagogues.[55] If this part of the coastal region was not considered part of the Holy Land, then facing east may have been considered as similar, perhaps, to the westward orientation of many Golan synagogues.[56] This is a possible, although admittedly inelegant explanation. The Lower Galilean synagogue of Yafia also lies on an east-west axis, and its excavators assume that it must have been oriented toward the east. Entrances, a focal apse, or a *bima*, however, have not been recovered, and it may very well be that we have here an example of a broadhouse-type building oriented toward the southern long wall.[57]

Whatever the merit of the above explanations in accounting for a number of apparent exceptions regarding orientation, there are two synagogues whose orientation is a total anomaly. The Bet Shean synagogue, built just north of the Byzantine city wall, faces northwest. Moreover, it will be remembered from a previous discussion that one of the side rooms contained a Samaritan (i.e., paleo-Hebraic) inscription.[58] Why did this com-

---

building itself is clearly on a southwest-northeast axis. However, this may have been for topographical, and not ideological, considerations. The building's interior focus is on the center of the hall, with four rows of columns and benches on each of its four walls. It is the latter consideration which, in our opinion, is decisive.

53. T Berakhot 3:15-16 (pp. 15-16); Sifre-Deuteronomy 29 (p. 47); Pesiqta Rabbati 33 (p. 149b); Tanḥuma, Vayishlaḥ, 21 (p. 87b). See also Gafni, *Land, Center and Diaspora*, 58-73.

54. Dar and Mintzer, "Synagogue of Horvat Sumaqa," 157-65.

55. Z. Ilan, *Ancient Synagogues*, 198-200, 231, 234; *NEAEHL*, loc. cit.

56. On the status of the Carmel range in late antiquity, see Z. Safrai, *Boundaries and Rule*, 42-45. On the rabbinic tradition ("The Baraita of Boundaries") which renders this region undefined in its halakhic status as part of Jewish Palestine, see Sussmann, "Boundaries," 227-29; Neeman, *Boundaries*, 39-51. Millar, who has referred to this area as the southern region of Phoenicia, describes it thusly: "this is an indication that we should see this coastal region as a border-zone of 'Phoenicia'—as well, of course, as an area of cities with Greek constitutions, a border-zone (as Tyre and Sidon were also) with the properly Jewish area, and the site of the second Roman *colonia* [i.e., Caesarea—L. L.) of the Near East" (*Roman Near East*, 270).

57. Z. Ilan, *Ancient Synagogues*, 213-14. See also Sukenik, "Synagogue at Yafia," 6-24.

58. On this Bet Shean synagogue, see above, Chap. 7, note 19.

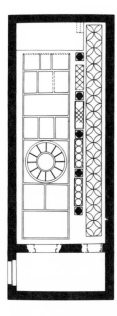

63. Plan of the Sepphoris synagogue,
which faces northwest.

munity so orient its building? Did the orientation have anything to do with the pagan
and Christian structures located on Tel Bet Shean to the immediate south? And even
were we to assume that this was a Samaritan building, the same problem would exist, for
the Samaritans would also have wanted to build their synagogue in a southerly direction,
toward Mt. Gerizim.

Recently, this synagogue at Bet Shean has been joined by another, similarly oriented
to the northwest, at Sepphoris. This structure is sui generis in many ways, from its artistic representations to its inscriptions, though these do not seem in any way related to
the building's unique orientation (fig. 63).[59] There is no way at present to determine why
these two synagogues faced northwest. Indeed, the explanation might not be based upon
ideological considerations, but rather on those much more mundane in nature: ignorance (however unlikely), indifference, convenience (topographical or otherwise), or the
need to accommodate some other factor. If the situation today (particularly in the Diaspora) is any barometer, any one of the above, or a combination thereof, may well have
played a role in creating this deviation in orientation. Nevertheless, despite these and the
other instances noted above, it should not be forgotten that the overwhelming majority
of synagogues discovered in Roman-Byzantine Palestine reflect the accepted practice of
orientation toward Jerusalem.

---

59. See Netzer and Weiss, *Zippori*, 58; and, for a fuller discussion, idem, *Promise and Redemption*, 12–
13. On the Sepphoris synagogue's artistic uniqueness, see many of the articles in L. Levine and Weiss,
From Dura to Sepphoris. For a recent discussion of different rabbinic conceptions as to where prayer
should be directed, see Ehrlich, "Place of the *Shekhina*," 315–29.

There can be no better example of Jewish particularism than the phenomenon of orientation. The facade of sacred buildings in antiquity—and thus their orientation—was eastward, toward the rising sun, and this was as true of pagan temples as it was of Christian churches.[60] Early Jewish tradition appears to have accommodated this practice with regard to both the desert Tabernacle and the two Jerusalem Temples. However, sometime during the Second Temple era, such obvious parallels with pagan worship became problematic, and a ceremony was reportedly introduced on the festival of Sukkot to emphasize the difference between pagan and Jewish practice with respect to orientation: "And two priests stood at the Upper Gate, which leads down from the Court of the Israelites to the Court of the Women, and they had two trumpets in their hands. When the cock crowed, they blew three blasts [תקעו והריעו ותקעו]. . . . They continued blowing until they came to the gate leading to the east. When they came to the gate leading to the east, they turned around and faced westward, saying: 'Our fathers who were at this place "had their backs to the Temple of God and they faced eastward, and they worshipped the sun toward the east" [Ezek. 8:16]. But we turn our eyes to God!' "[61]

It is probably not coincidental that the custom of orienting the synagogue hall toward Jerusalem became normative at about the same time that prayer was becoming a more dominant component in Jewish communal worship and the synagogue was assuming a more expanded and clearly defined religious character. Archeologically, we first encounter this phenomenon in the third century; in literary sources, it appears already in tannaitic literature.[62] Moreover, the memories of the Temple and Jerusalem, together with the introduction into the synagogue liturgy of expressions of hopes to return and rebuild the Temple and city, were undoubtedly additional forces that helped to create a distinct and significant synagogue orientation.

ATRIUMS AND WATER INSTALLATIONS

An atrium was often an integral part of the synagogue complex. In most cases, this area was located just outside the main entrance to the synagogue hall (e.g., at Bet Alpha and Susiya in Palestine; at Dura Europos, Sardis, and Gerasa in the Diaspora). The Capernaum synagogue was unusual in this regard because its courtyard was on the side of the building. On occasion, the courtyard bordered several sides of the building, as at Na'aran and Ma'on (Nirim).

The atrium might have served a number of functions. On the most basic level, it was

---

60. Stillwell, "Greek Temples," 3–8; Vogel, "*Sol aequinoctialis*," 155–211; idem, "Orientations," 1ff.; and the *Apostolic Constitutions* 2, 57. However, regarding Greek temples, cf. the remarks in Herbert, "Orientation of Greek Temples," 31ff.

61. M Sukkah 5:4.

62. See above, Chap. 6. See also B Bava Batra 25a–b.

a passage area from the street to the synagogue sanctuary. Such was the case at Sardis and Susiya, where the only entrance to the main synagogue hall was through the atrium, which might front on one street or, in the case of the former, two. At Capernaum, where the courtyard was off to the side of the building, one could enter the synagogue through it or through the three main portals to the south. In the early stage of the Dura synagogue building, the atrium, and subsequently the synagogue sanctuary and the other rooms of the building complex, was reached through an entrance hall. In its later stage, the atrium, which separated the main hall from the rest of the complex, could be reached only after passing through a number of rooms. This, too, was the way the Hammat Tiberias atrium functioned in the last, seventh- to eighth-century stage of the building. It was located west of the main hall and was reached through other rooms in the synagogue complex. It was this type of internal courtyard that may be reflected in the talmudic report about R. Abbahu, who once demonstratively crossed such a synagogue courtyard in order to make his presence known to a teacher who, in his opinion, was dealing too harshly with his students.[63] In the absence of an atrium, a synagogue may have had a hall leading into a number of rooms (e.g., at Ostia and 'En Gedi).

In addition to serving as a passageway, the atrium was probably also a place for spontaneous gatherings, perhaps before or after some more formal activity inside the building. However, it is also likely that the courtyard served as a meeting place for various synagogue functions. The courtyard at Capernaum, for instance, located next to the main hall, was probably used, inter alia, in this capacity. Lieberman has suggested that the comforting of mourners may have taken place in such a setting.[64] Finally, an atrium may have been divided into smaller units with the intention of serving a variety of purposes. Several rooms in the Merot courtyard have been identified, somewhat speculatively, as a bet midrash and a school.[65]

Generally speaking, few finds were discovered in such atriums; the most impressive one, however, is the remains of a krater from the atrium of the Sardis synagogue (fig. 64). A fountain is mentioned in a very fragmentary inscription, also from Sardis,[66] and may well refer to the one found in its atrium. Sundials were found in several synagogues in Hellenistic Egypt and Delos.[67] In at least one synagogue (Arbel), what has been inter-

---

63. Y Megillah 3, 4, 74a. Another source, from the very end of late antiquity or soon thereafter, raises the question about what to do if the prayer leader has to relieve himself in the middle of his recitation. One option was to clear the congregation from the synagogue hall into the atrium while he took care of his needs; another was for the leader to leave the hall and, upon his return, resume his prayer recitation from the beginning. See J. Mann, "Sefer Hama'asim," 7.

64. Lieberman, TK, I, 49.

65. Z. Ilan, "Synagogue and Bet Midrash of Meroth," 274ff.

66. Frey, CIJ, II, no. 751.

67. Horbury and Noy, Jewish Inscriptions, no. 115, and comments on pp. 196–99.

64. Sardis atrium, looking west toward the synagogue nave, with the "eagle table" in the background.

preted as a charity box (trough) was found in the outer courtyard at the northeastern corner of the building.[68]

Water installations seem to be the element most commonly found in the synagogue atrium. They stood outside the main hall of the synagogue, yet were clearly related to the ritual conducted inside. The most frequently encountered of such installations was the basin (כיור).[69] On the basis of our literary sources and archeological data, it would seem that it had two functions. The basin, or גורנה, as it is referred to in the Talmud, was used for the washing of hands and feet and was placed in the middle of the courtyard (atrium), just outside the main entrance to the synagogue, or in the hall, or narthex, leading from the street into the synagogue sanctuary.[70] Installations of this type were found at Gaza and 'En Gedi as well as Dura Europos, Ostia, Asia Minor (Sardis, Philadelphia in Lydia,

---

68. Z. Ilan, *Ancient Synagogues*, 116–17. Similar arrangements are known from Elche and from medieval synagogues as well; see Assis, "Synagogues throughout the Ages," 167.

69. At several sites (e.g., Priene and Bet She'arim), such installations were found inside the main hall of the synagogue; see below.

70. Brand, *Ceramics*, 96–97. The case that washing one's feet before prayer was already a well-known Jewish custom in late antiquity has been argued by Bar Ilan ("Washing Feet," 162–69).

Priene), Delos, and Gerasa.[71] The Yerushalmi speaks of a synagogue in Bet Shean that had a גורנה in its courtyard and was used by those coming to pray.[72]

The Theodotos inscription explicitly mentions water installations as part of the synagogue complex, although neither their specific function nor their location are ever made clear.[73] In an inscription from Sidé in Pamphylia, Asia Minor, it is reported that in the days of one Leontius, son of Jacob, a leader in the local synagogue, a fountain ($\kappa\rho\acute{\eta}\nu\eta$) was constructed in the synagogue courtyard.[74] In a number of locales, water installations were not artificially made objects, but rather natural cavities in the ground from which water was drawn.[75]

Water installations are known from the pagan and Christian world as well. Plutarch and Seneca attest to the fact that basins were standard temple equipment.[76] Upon entering the *temenos*, or sacred area, of a shrine or sanctuary, devotees would wash their hands and pray facing the deity. Eusebius, in describing the magnificent church in Tyre built by Constantine, notes that at the entrance to the sacred precincts in the east there were fountains to cleanse those entering.[77]

Several explanations for this practice of washing have been offered.[78] One such reason given by the author of the *Letter to Aristeas* is the need for purification at the time of prayer.[79] A Genizah fragment posits another reason; washing symbolizes the need to act in awe and holiness while in the synagogue, as was once the practice when entering the precincts of the Jerusalem Temple — "It is for this reason that our ancestors installed in all synagogue courtyards offering basins of fresh water for sanctifying the hands and feet."[80]

A very different type of water installation, found only on occasion close to synagogues,

---

71. *Gaza:* Ovadiah, "Synagogue at Gaza," 130. *'En Gedi:* Barag et al., "Synagogue at 'En-Gedi," 117. *Dura Europos:* Kraeling, *Dura: Synagogue,* 13 and 28; *Ostia:* Squarciapino, *Synagogue of Ostia,* 22. *Sardis:* Mitten, "Sardis Excavations," 46-47; Seager, "Building History," 425; Seager and Kraabel, "Synagogue and Jewish Community," 169; and S. Krauss, *Synagogale Altertümer,* 313-14. *Philadelphia:* Lifshitz, *Donateurs et fondateurs,* 31. *Priene:* Goodenough, *Jewish Symbols,* II, 77; III, no. 879. *Delos:* see above, Chap. 4. *Gerasa:* Crowfoot and Hamilton, "Discovery," 216. See also Goitein, *Mediterranean Society,* II, pp. 154-55. A fragmentary inscription found in Tiberias has been restored by Ben-Dov ("Fragmentary Synagogue Inscriptions," 80) to read "this basin" (הדן מש[קוליתא or [כילתא]מש הדן).

72. Y Megillah 3, 4, 74a.

73. See above, Chap. 3.

74. Lifshitz, *Donateurs and fondateurs,* no. 37.

75. As, for example, in the synagogues of Bet Alpha, Bet Shean, Susiya, Eshtemoa, Na'aran, and Khirbet Sumaqa; see *NEAEHL.*

76. Plutarch, *Sulla* 32; Seneca, *Ep.* 41, 1.

77. Eusebius, *Ecclesiastical History* 10, 4, 40.

78. See above, Chap. 4.

79. *Letter to Aristeas* 304-6. See also Alon, *Studies,* 202-3; E. P. Sanders, *Jewish Law,* 231, 258-71.

80. Margoliot, *Palestinian Halakhah from the Genizah,* 132. On entering a synagogue barefoot, see ibid., 131. There are also references in early Muslim literature to the Jewish practice of not wearing shoes when praying — Muslims were not to follow suit; see Kister, " 'Do Not Assimilate Yourselves,' " 335-49.

was the stepped cistern. Whether such a cistern is to be labeled a *miqveh* (ritual bath) is an open question. Three synagogues from pre-70 Judaea, i.e., at Masada, Herodium, and Gamla, had such cisterns nearby.[81] Given the highly charged religious and nationalistic fervor of the inhabitants in these three places in particular and the fact that these buildings were contemporoneous with the Temple and its purity requirements, the cisterns there may very well have served as *miqva'ot*.[82] For other Judaean synagogues we have no information, and it would be unwarranted to generalize what we know from these three sites and apply it to others.[83] Nevertheless, the custom of performing ablutions before engaging in sacred worship was well known in the ancient world. This is a clearly documented practice in the Second Temple; Jubilees, the Testament of Levi, and the Mishnah all describe the preparations of the high priest for the Yom Kippur ceremonies, alluding to the necessary ablutions preceding a sacred moment, often the sacrificial act itself.[84]

Following the destruction of the Second Temple, and throughout late antiquity, the number of *miqva'ot* in Jewish communities declined precipitously. Several criteria have been suggested which might indicate the use of a stepped cistern for ritual purposes in the Second Temple period; with but one exception, no post-70 stepped cistern meets any of these criteria. Moreover, even when a stepped cistern existed and may have been used for ritual purposes, communities were not always concerned about placing them near synagogues.[85] It would seem that the destruction of the Temple diminished the importance of ritual purification among the Jews, and there was thus less need for *miqva'ot*. There is nothing in Jewish law which indicates the use of such ritual baths with respect to the synagogue.[86] In most synagogue complexes of late antiquity, remains of such stepped

---

81. The buildings at Masada and Herodium did not become synagogues until the time of the first Jewish revolt, and the ritual baths there also date to that time. The northern *miqveh* at Masada is located in building VII, about 40 meters east of the synagogue; that of Herodium was adjacent to the synagogue hall. The Gamla synagogue was constructed several generations earlier, at the turn of the first century C.E., but its *miqveh* was added at the outbreak of the revolt. See Foerster, "Synagogues at Masada and Herodium," 26; Ma'oz, "Synagogue of Gamla and Typology of Second-Temple Synagogues," 36; idem, "Architecture of Gamla," 154. See also Reich, "Synagogue and Ritual Bath," 290–92.

82. E. P. Sanders, *Jewish Law*, 214–27.

83. It is impossible to determine with any degree of certitude what the water installations mentioned in the Theodotos inscription refer to. Their use as *miqva'ot* is certainly possible. One possible indication that not all Judaean synagogues had *miqva'ot* may be found in Qiryat Sefer (above, Chap. 3). To date, no stepped cistern has been found near this structure, though excavations continue.

84. 1QS 3:4–5; 5:13; CD 10, 10–13; Josephus, *War* 2, 129; see Leaney, *Rule of Qumran*, 141–42, 191–95; Jubilees 21:16; Testament of Levi 9:4; M Yoma 3:3.

85. Reich, "Synagogue and Ritual Bath," 292–97.

86. According to the Samaritan Chronicle, Baba Rabba built a ritual bath and synagogue at the foot of Mt. Gerizim. However, this ritual bath was undoubtedly built because of the holy mountain and not because of the presence of a synagogue; with regard to the other seven synagogues attributed to him, no mention is made of ritual baths. See J. M. Cohen, *Samaritan Chronicle*, 71–72.

cisterns have not been found. Exceptions to this would include Merot, Ma'on (Nirim), and Ma'on (Judaea).[87]

Whatever the purpose and frequency of these stepped cisterns, some communities may have used other already available installations for purification. One practice, well documented for the first century by Josephus and the New Testament and a century later by Tertullian, was to build the synagogue near a body of water, perhaps for this purpose.[88] Such was the case at Caesarea, Gaza, Delos, and Ostia.[89] Other communities may have taken advantage of the local bathhouse.[90]

ENTRANCES

Architecturally speaking, one of the most important components of the ancient synagogue building was its entranceway. With rare exceptions, all Galilean-type synagogues had their main entrances on the southern side of the building, in the direction of Jerusalem. In the basilica-type synagogue, the entrances were invariably in the opposite direction from the apse or *bima*, which faced Jerusalem. In the Golan, as noted, entrances had no consistent pattern and faced in any direction. The main entrances of the four synagogues discovered to date in southern Judaea (Susiya, Eshtemoa, Ma'on, and 'Anim) faced east (fig. 65).[91] In this region at least, the rabbinic dictum to place synagogue entrances in this direction appears to have been the rule: "They should place the entrances to synagogues only in the east, for thus we have found with the Tabernacle, that they oriented [its entrances] toward the east, as it is written: 'Those encamped before the Tabernacle [were located] eastward, before the Tent of Meeting eastward' [Num. 3:38]."[92]

Archeological discoveries attest to the enormous investment often made in decorating this part of the synagogue building. In many synagogues, especially those of the Galilee and Golan, the entrance facade was the building's most ornate feature. This was true both of smaller buildings having only one entrance and of larger ones boasting three.

---

87. Reich, "Synagogue and Ritual Bath," 292–95; Z. Ilan and Damati, *Meroth*, 45; Amit and Ilan, "Ancient Synagogue at Ma'on," 121–22; and Reich, "*Miqva'ot* (Jewish Ritual 'Immersion' Baths)," 325–40.

88. Josephus, *Antiquities* 14, 257–59; Acts 16:13; Philo, *Flaccus* 122–23; Tertullian, *Ad Nationes* 13. See also Lauterbach, "Tashlik," 234.

89. *Caesarea:* L. Levine, *Roman Caesarea*, 42. *Gaza:* Ovadiah, "Synagogue at Gaza," 129. *Delos:* Bruneau, "'Israélites de Délos,'" 465ff. *Ostia:* Squarciapino, *Synagogue of Ostia*, 20–21. On the sea as a place of ritual immersion in rabbinic literature, see M Miqva'ot 5:4; T Miqva'ot 6:3 (p. 658); on a river as such a place, see T Makhshirin 2:12 (p. 674); T Miqva'ot 4:5 (p. 656).

90. M Miqva'ot 6:10; T Miqva'ot 5:7–8 (p. 657); 6:3–4 (p. 658). There is a question as to whether the phrase "gentile *miqva'ot* outside of Eretz Israel" refers to bathhouses; see M Miqva'ot 8:1; T Miqva'ot 6:1 (p. 657).

91. Amit, "Architectural Plans," 136–55.

92. T Megillah 3:22 (p. 360); see also Lieberman, *TK*, V, 1200.

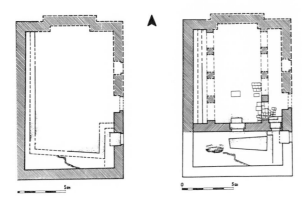

65. Stages of the Maʿon (Judaea) synagogue: stage 1 (left) and stage 2 (right).

The synagogue facade not only served as an entranceway but also demarcated the boundary between the outside world and the building's interior, where degrees of holiness prevailed. According to the Babylonian sage, R. Ḥisda, before a person begins to pray he must "enter two doors" into the sanctuary, which may be understood literally as going "through two openings" or, according to a later gloss, "the distance of two openings" (כשיעור שני פתחים).[93] In this vein, a later midrash makes the following statement: "What is the meaning of the phrase, 'to guard my doors' [Prov. 8:34]? The Holy One, Blessed be He, said: 'If you came to pray within a synagogue, do not stand by the outer portal to pray there, but rather you should intend to enter one door and then the other.' 'To guard my door' is not written here but 'my doors,' i.e., two doors. And why is that? The Holy One, Blessed be He, counts your steps and rewards you accordingly."[94]

It may not be coincidental that the basilica-type synagogue, so ubiquitous in the Byzantine period, usually had two separate entrances leading into the main sanctuary, one which led from the atrium into the narthex (the entrance corridor) and a second from the narthex into the main sanctuary. If this is indeed the saying's original *Sitz im Leben*, the above midrash seems to be encouraging one to enter not just the first door, into the narthex only, but to continue through the second portal into the prayer hall itself.

The synagogue gate is mentioned in a number of rabbinic traditions and probably refers to its entrance. An innkeeper, sent to find someone last seen in the synagogue, came to its gate and called out the person's name through the entire night.[95] Another tradition locates the well of Miriam in the Sea of Galilee (or the Sea of Tiberias), and according to R. Yoḥanan b. Maria, the well was located directly in front of the middle gate of the Saringit (or Sarongaia, Sarongin) synagogue.[96]

93. B Berakhot 8a.

94. Deuteronomy Rabbah 7:2; see also Deuteronomy Rabbah, Ki Tavo, 2 (p. 108).

95. Genesis Rabbah 92:6 (pp. 1144–45) and parallels.

96. Leviticus Rabbah 22:4 (p. 511). See also Y Ketubot 12, 3, 35b; Y Kilʾaim 9, 4, 32c; Ecclesiastes Rabbah 5:7. This town was presumably located southwest of the Kinneret; see S. Klein, *Sefer Hayishuv*, I, 113;

66. Inscription on a lintel
from the Barʿam synagogue.

Synagogue portals were often chosen as the place for displaying dedicatory inscriptions. Several inscriptions regarding the making of the portal or parts thereof, such as the lintel, were found at Dabbura, ʿAlma, Tiberias, Kokhav Hayarden, and Rama.[97] Because of its prominence, the portal was also chosen as the place for more general dedicatory inscriptions regarding the entire building or for those concerning the congregation or the artisan. Thus, we read the following on the lintel of the synagogue at Barʿam: "May peace be in this place and all the places of Israel. Yosi the Levite, son of Levi, made this lintel. May blessing come through his deeds. Shalom" (fig. 66).[98] Yosi the Levite was apparently the artisan who executed the work and perhaps donated his time and money as well. His status as artisan is confirmed by an inscription from nearby ʿAlma which spells out this same Yosi's profession: "May peace be in this place and all places of His people, Israel. Amen. Selah. I, Yosi b. Levi the Levite, the artisan who made [this lintel]."[99]

BENCHES AND COLUMNS

The interior furnishings of the synagogue may be divided into two categories: those elements which could be found in any public building, Jewish or not, and those unique to the synagogue setting. The former include, inter alia, benches and columns, which are among the most ubiquitous archeological findings (fig. 67). However, the location of stone benches within the synagogue building is not uniform. Generally, they were placed along two or three walls of the main assembly hall, although at ʿEn Gedi and ʿAnim

---

idem, *Galilee*, 113; Press, *Topographical-Historical Encyclopaedia*, III, 675; Avi-Yonah, *Gazetteer*, 96; Reeg, *Ortsnamen*, 463-64.

97. Naveh, *On Stone and Mosaic*, nos. 4, 11, 15, 21, 22, 42. Regarding a possible reference in an inscription from Ḥorvat ʿAmmudim, see the comments in ibid., no. 42; and Hüttenmeister, "Aramaic Inscription," 109-12. The inscription from Kokhav Hayarden reads as follows: "[May . . . be remembered for good] he who donated this lintel from . . . of God (lit., the compassionate one) and from his property. Amen. Amen. Selah" (Naveh, *On Stone and Mosaic*, no. 42).

98. Naveh, *On Stone and Mosaic*, no. 1.

99. Ibid., no. 3. On one occasion only does rabbinic literature mention the donation of a gate: it is reported that R. Abun donated the gates of the Great Academy of Tiberias; see Y Sheqalim 5, 6, 49b. Another source mentions a sage's donation to some unidentified building, as well as the fact that R. Ḥanania built the *bet midrash* in Sepphoris with money he earned from business dealings; see Y Peah 7, 4, 20b.

67. Interior of the Capernaum synagogue, looking north.

(southern Judaea) benches were found along only one side. In a number of instances, in Second Temple Gamla and Masada and in later Dura, stone benches lined each of the four walls. Only rarely were no traces of stone benches found, as, for example, at Sardis and Sepphoris.

Many, if not most, synagogues apparently also had wooden benches or mats in addition to the fixed stone benches.[100] Several accounts in the Bavli mention dragging benches on the Sabbath, and one specifically notes an *archisynagogos* of Bostra doing so in the presence of R. Jeremiah.[101] Clearly, then, some synagogues did have portable benches. It is hard to imagine that the synagogue generally accommodated only those who sat on the stone benches lining the walls. Moreover, in places where no stone benches were found, the congregation clearly employed alternative means of seating. Although the only literary source mentioning mats in a synagogue setting (אציפי דבי כנישתא) relates to fourth-

---

100. See B Shabbat 29a for an example of a movable—presumably wooden—bench. On the existence of non-permanent seats in a Jewish institutional setting (in this case, the academy), see Y Berakhot 4, 1, 7d; Y Ta'anit 4, 1, 67d; B Berakhot 28a. On benches for teachers, see T Kelim—Bava Batra 1:11 (p. 591). Y Sukkah 1, 11, 52c mentions mats of Usha and mats of Tiberas, but we have no idea how these mats were used.

101. B Shabbat 29b.

century Babylonia, it is reasonable to assume that they were used elsewhere as well.[102] If Byzantine churches are any example, then congregations may have sat in all parts of the assembly hall, in the nave as well as in the aisles—on stone benches, wooden benches, and mats.[103] Moreover, it should be noted that the practice among Greeks and Romans was to pray standing, often with arms outstretched toward the deity.[104]

Rabbinic literature mentions, en passant, two different scenarios for congregational seating. In one source, the Bavli probably refers to benches along the walls of the building when it speaks of an *av bet din* who died; when gathering in the synagogue, members altered their pattern of seating: "Those [accustomed to sitting] in the north [now] sit in the south; those [accustomed to sitting] in the south [now] sit in the north."[105] In the Tosefta, however, the following is recorded: "How did the elders sit? Facing the congregation and with their backs to the holy [i.e., Jerusalem and the Temple] . . . the *ḥazzan* of the synagogue faces the holy and the entire congregation faces the holy."[106] From this last tradition, it would seem that the congregation sat in rows facing the front of the synagogue, while the elders sat facing the congregation.[107] Not only does this source appear to contradict the former tannaitic tradition preserved in the Bavli, but both these sources stand in sharp contrast to the extant archeological remains. Benches have been found primarily on the western and eastern walls of synagogues, never on the north and south only. Moreover, only on rare occasions has an excavation revealed benches along the Jerusalem wall.

Benches or chairs may have been reserved on occasion for important personages. Rabbinic sources take note of seventy-one ornate chairs in an Alexandrian synagogue, as well as of a bench in the synagogue at Ma'on (a suburb of Tiberias) possibly reserved for charity donors from outside the city.[108] In other synagogues, as noted above, the Tosefta describes the elders of the congregation sitting on benches arranged against the wall facing Jerusalem, while a later source described them as sitting facing that wall with the rest of the congregation.[109]

---

102. B Bava Batra 8b; see S. Krauss, *Synagogale Altertümer*, 387.

103. Mathews, *Early Churches*, 117–37. Rabbinic literature also reports on benches in pagan sanctuaries; see T 'Avodah Zarah 6:3 (p. 469).

104. Alderink and Martin, "Prayer in Greco-Roman Religions," 125.

105. B Mo'ed Qatan 22b. On the problem of reconciling these sources with the archeological remains, see below, Chap. 13.

106. T Megillah 3:21 (p. 360). Those facing the holy could be those sitting along the side walls. However, this is not the simplest or most likely explanation of the phrase.

107. See Maimonides, *Laws of Prayer* 11:4.

108. T Sukkah 4:6 (p. 273); and above, Chap. 4; Y Megillah 3, 2, 74a, and commentaries, loc. cit.

109. *Differences in Customs*, no. 36 (p. 156). This apparent contradiction may possibly be resolved by interpreting the latter source as referring to the actual moment of recitation of the *'Amidah*, when the congregation turns toward Jerusalem, as was done centuries later under Muslim influence (see Wieder, *Islamic Influences*, 68). The problem remains, however, as to why the elders are described as facing the congregation and not changing their direction to face the holy, like everyone else.

Archeological evidence points to the arrangement of special seats for synagogue leaders at several sites. In the Diaspora, the apse at the western end of the building at Sardis was clearly reserved for prominent members of the congregation, and such may also have been the case at Naro.[110] An inscription on the side of the nave in the synagogue at Elche mentions elders and presbyters and seems to indicate the existence of such a bench for these leaders.[111] The Ḥammat Tiberias building, in its last stages (seventh to eighth centuries) also had a bench in its apse which may well have been reserved for congregational leaders.[112]

In some synagogues, special seats were reserved for prominent individuals. As noted elsewhere, in Phocaea (Asia Minor), a woman named Tation, "having erected the assembly hall [οἶκος] and the enclosure of the open courtyard [περίβολος] with her own funds, gave them as a gift to the Jews." This generous benefaction merited her a prominent seat (προεδρία) in the synagogue hall.[113] Synagogue leaders or important visitors also may have had occasion to sit on the Cathedra of Moses, examples of which may have been discovered at a number of sites in Palestine and the Diaspora (see below).

Columns to support the roof are an essential element of every building and were found in almost all excavations of ancient synagogues. Donors to the synagogue often inscribed their names and the names of others on these columns as dedicatory inscriptions, as they were readily visible to all and afforded maximum exposure and recognition. Such columns were found, inter alia, at Dabbura in the Golan and at Gush Ḥalav, Capernaum, and Khirbet Yitzhaqia (south of Bet She'arim).[114] One Shim'ai (?), son of Ocsantis, from Bet Guvrin purchased a column "in honor of the congregation [ליקרה דכנישתא]."[115]

Columns in synagogues are often noted in literary sources as a place for quiet meditation or for support when feeling ill.[116] In describing someone at the time of prayer, the Yerushalmi states: "Although He far transcends His world, [yet when] someone enters a synagogue and stands behind a column and prays in silence, the Holy One, Blessed be He, hears his prayer."[117] When R. Judah b. Pazi felt weak in the synagogue, he held his head and stood behind a column; in similar circumstances, however, R. El'azar is re-

---

110. *Sardis:* Seager, "Building History," 426–27; Seager and Kraabel, "Synagogue and Jewish Community," 169. *Naro:* Goodenough, *Jewish Symbols*, II, 91 and 93. On the Cathedra of Moses, see below.

111. See above, Chap. 8.

112. Even though preliminary publications dealing with this synagogue do not indicate the existence of a bench, visits to the site clearly show a course of stones protruding along the entire back wall of the apse—probably a bench for the elders of the synagogue.

113. Frey, *CIJ*, II, no. 738; Lifshitz, *Donateurs et fondateurs*, no. 13; Treblico, *Jewish Communities*, 110–11.

114. Naveh, *On Stone and Mosaic*, nos. 7, 12, 18, 40.

115. Ibid., no. 71. On a similar expression, "honor of the house of Caesar," in rabbinic literature, see L. Levine, "R. Abbahu," 66–69.

116. Lieberman, *TK*, IV, 890. On columns in synagogues of the later geonic era, see Goitein, "Women's Gallery," 314.

117. Y Berakhot 9, 13a.

ported to have simply left the premises.[118] In another instance, R. Shmuel bar R. Yitzḥaq noticed that the *meturgeman* leaned against the column and did not stand next to the Torah reader, as was customary.[119]

Besides their essentially functional role, the columns of a synagogue might have had a purely ornamental purpose. The four monumental columns in the entranceway to the Ostia sanctuary were clearly intended as a kind of *propylaeum*.[120] Moreover, an inscription from Sidé notes two main columns, together with two *menorot*, that perhaps flanked the Torah shrine.[121] There is no way of telling whether such columns were intended to represent the Joachim and Boaz columns, which graced the entrance to Solomon's Temple (I Kgs. 7:21).[122]

PARTITIONS AND BALCONIES

On the basis of archeological and literary data, it has become clear that the synagogue sanctuary had no permanent internal division; the term "partition" (מחיצה) appears only rarely in relation to the synagogue.[123] Partitions were erected for special occasions, as, for example, when a leper came to a synagogue.[124] Elsewhere, we know of a very general reference to a partition, but with no specific referent.[125] A partition is never mentioned in any dedicatory inscription, even though this type of inscription usually takes note of important architectural elements in the synagogue. Moreover, nothing has ever been found in any of the archeological excavations which might be interpreted as a partition.[126]

The one kind of partition that appears with some frequency was the chancel screen

---

118. Y Berakhot 5, 9b.

119. Y Megillah 4, 1, 74d. Columns are mentioned also in connection with the academy in Tiberias at the end of the third century. It is noted that R. Ami and R. Asi preferred to pray between the columns of the academy, instead of in one of the thirteen synagogues in the city. See B Berakhot 8a, 30b; ibid., 27b, which speaks of R. Ishmael b. R. Yose, who would pray next to a column every Friday night.

120. See above, Chap. 8.

121. Lifshitz, *Donateurs et fondateurs*, no. 36.

122. Several rabbinic descriptions of these two pillars may actually have been of synagogue representations: "These are the two silver-plated columns that stood before it [i.e., the ark] as a kind of stoa" (Numbers Rabbah 12:4; Song of Songs Rabbah 1:11).

123. On the structural and functional divisions within the Byzantine church, in contrast, see Mathews, *Early Churches*, 117–37.

124. M Negaʿim 13:12.

125. B Sotah 38b. On the use of the term *meḥitzah* in this source, see the comments in Bokser, "Wall Separating God and Israel," 349–74.

126. This subject—especially in relation to the women's gallery—has been addressed in a number of studies; see Löw, "Synagogale Rituus," 364–74; S. Safrai, "Was There a Women's Section?" 329–38; Goitein, "Women's Gallery"; and below, Chap. 14. On a "fence" or partition (גדר) reputedly in the Yavneh academy, behind which part of the audience stood, see Y Berakhot 4, 1, 7d; Y Taʿanit 4, 1, 67d.

that separated the area of the apse from the rest of the main hall.[127] In the Jerusalem Temple, a partition (referred to as סורג [soreg] in the Mishnah and ἑρκίον λίθινου by Josephus) separated that part of the Temple Mount which was open to all and the sacred Temple courtyards which only a ritually pure Jew could enter.[128] However, it is unlikely that this earlier usage directly influenced later synagogue practice. The appearance of the chancel screen in the Byzantine synagogue seems to be another example of Christian influence on this Jewish institution. In the Byzantine church, the chancel screen had a very definite purpose, i.e., to separate the congregation from the clergy, which functioned in and in front of the apse area, particularly around the altar. Although this kind of hierarchical division had no place in synagogue worship (see below), the chancel screen, nevertheless, was adopted into the synagogue context as part and parcel of the overall basilical model.

The chancel screen itself was composed of small columns (at times with capitals) between which marble plaques or slabs were placed. Sometimes these plaques bore inscriptions or symbols, the most frequently displayed being the menorah. Other motifs represented include the Torah shrine, clusters of grapes, pomegranates, geometric figures, and floral patterns, as well as birds, eagles, and lions (fig. 68). Remains of chancel screens have been found at sites around the Sea of Galilee (Ḥammat Tiberias, Ḥammat Gader), near Bet Shean (Maʿoz Ḥayyim, Reḥov), in southern Palestine (ʿEn Gedi, Susiya), and on the coastal plain (Caesarea, Ashdod, Ashkelon, and Gaza).[129] In a synagogue at Syracuse, a chancel screen appears to have been built around the bima itself,[130] while at Sardis, a railing separated the benches for synagogue leaders from the area for the rest of the congregation. This latter example is perhaps the closest approximation to church usage (i.e., a hierarchical separation) that we have among ancient synagogues.

The existence of balconies is indicated archeologically by the remains of different-sized columns, as a second story would require smaller columns than those which stood on the ground floor. In several instances, the remains of stairs were discovered, also indicating a second story.[131] The function of the second story is unclear. Some have opined that it served as a women's gallery, but there is no evidence to support this claim (see below, Chap. 14). An upper chamber of the synagogue is mentioned on occasion in rabbinic sources as a place where festive meals were held, but it also might have served as the residence of a ḥazzan or as a place for study and possibly for litigation.[132]

---

127. Crowfoot, *Early Churches*, 46–52; Xydis, "Chancel Barrier," 1–11; Foerster, "Decorated Marble Chancel Screens," 1809–20. See also Tsafrir, "Byzantine Setting," 147–57.

128. M Middot 2:3; *Antiquities* 15, 417; see also Hollis, *Archaeology of Herod's Temple*, 153–57; P. Segal, "Penalty of the Warning Inscription," 79–84.

129. See *NEAEHL*; Hachlili, *Art and Archaeology—Israel*, 187–91.

130. Lifshitz, *Donateurs et fondateurs*, no. 102.

131. As at Capernaum, Chorazim, and Susiya. See Hachlili, *Art and Archaeology—Israel*, 194–95.

132. See below, Chap. 10.

68. Chancel screen (*soreg*) from an Ashdod synagogue, with a wreath enclosing a menorah, shofar, and *lulav*, in addition to an inscription: "May . . . be remembered for good and for a blessing. Shalom."

BIMOT AND PLATFORMS (PODIUMS)

A primary focal point in the synagogue hall was the *bima*. The Tosefta, as will be recalled, mentions a *bima* made of wood located in the center of the synagogue in Alexandria.[133] Possibly owing to the perishable nature of wood, no such *bima* has ever been found among the archeological finds. In only one instance, in an inscription from Syracuse, is the term *bima* ($\beta\hat{\eta}\mu\alpha$) explicitly mentioned.[134] In two others, the Greek word *ambon* or *ambol* ($\check{\alpha}\mu\beta\omega\nu$) seems to indicate a similar installation, and in this case it was probably made of stone. In one instance, this term appears in a document from the Cairo Genizah with reference to a twelfth-century synagogue in Ashkelon.[135] Of more relevance, however, is an inscription from Sidé in Pamphylia in which the following is recorded: "[I, Is]aac, *phrontistes* of the most holy synagogue, have successfully invested in and completed the marble paving from the *ambon* to the *simma*, and I have refinished (or polished) the two *menorot* and the two main capitals [or columns]. The fifteenth year of the indiction, the fourth month."[136]

A platform ($\tau\grave{o}$ $\beta\acute{\alpha}\theta\rho o\nu$) is noted in an inscription from Tralles in Caria, and a marble table was found in the center of the hall at Sardis. At both Sardis and Dura, depressions

---

133. See the practice as codified by Maimonides (*Laws of Prayer* 11:3).

134. Lifshitz, *Donateurs et fondateurs*, no. 102.

135. Goitein, "Anbol-Bima," 162–67; idem, *Mediterranean Society*, II, 146–47. Rashi and others have interpreted the term *kursaya* (כורסיא) in B Megillah 26b to mean *bima*; however, the word has generally been taken to refer to a special type of seat, a *cathedra*; see Sokoloff, *Dictionary*, 254; Z. Safrai, "Dukhan, Aron and Teva," 77–78.

136. Frey, *CIJ*, II, no. 781; Lifshitz, *Donateurs et fondateurs*, no. 36; S. Krauss, *Synagogale Altertümer*, 351–52; Goodenough, *Jewish Symbols*, II, 81–83. There is some unclarity with regard to the terms *ambon* and *simma*, especially the latter. See comments in the above references and the bibliographies cited therein.

found in the floor in the center of the main hall may have once supported the legs of a table or platform.[137]

We have already had occasion to note that a wooden *bima* was placed in a public square or in the courtyard of Jerusalem's Second Temple for the purpose of reading the Torah.[138] Ezra read the Torah to the Jerusalem populace from a wooden platform (מגדל עץ),[139] and the high priest stood on a *bima* (ἐπὶ βήματος) and read from the Torah during the *Haqhel* ceremony.[140] In a parallel tradition, perhaps reflecting a different time frame, the Mishnah tells of King Agrippa I, who read a portion of the Torah (subsequently referred to as פרשת המלך) from "a wooden platform in the Temple courtyard."[141]

Even with these precedents in Jewish tradition, it is quite probable that the placement of a *bima* in the center of a Byzantine synagogue was influenced to an even greater degree by the church practice of having an *ambo* in the nave. In fact, these two dimensions—earlier Jewish and contemporary church practices—need not be considered mutually exclusive. Both factors may have been at play, with current Christian practice being given a measure of legitimacy and acceptability by the existence of an earlier Jewish precedent. Moreover, it is also possible that the church itself may have adopted this arrangement on the basis of earlier Temple practice, only to have it reappropriated later by the Jews in a more developed form.[142]

However, in contrast to the above-noted archeological data from the Diaspora of late antiquity, there is virtually no archeological evidence for a *bima* in the center of synagogues from Roman-Byzantine Palestine. Other than possible hints from Nevoraya and Kefar Ḥanania (i.e., depressions in the floor), there is little evidence that such an installation was located in the nave area.[143] Likewise, in synagogues having fully or almost fully

---

137. *Tralles:* Lifshitz, *Donateurs et fondateurs*, no. 30. *Sardis:* Seager, "Building History," 426; Seager and Kraabel, "Synagogue and Jewish Community," 169–70. *Dura Europos:* Kraeling, *Dura: Synagogue*, 17, 255–56.

138. See above, Chap. 2.

139. Neh. 8:4.

140. *Antiquities* 4, 209–11.

141. M Sotah 7:8. In describing the annual reading of the Torah on Yom Kippur by the high priest, no mention is made of a platform, although one was probably erected for such an occasion (M Yoma 7:1).

142. Goitein, *Mediterranean Society*, II, 147. See also Z. Safrai, "Dukhan, Aron and Teva," 74–77. See also the suggestive, though late, tradition according to which sermons were delivered from a *bima* in (the middle of?) the academy hall: "It is said that David the Righteous would set up a *bima* in the *bet midrash* and he would sit and expound to Israel good tidings and comfort, the laws of Passover on Passover, the laws of Shavuʿot on Shavuʿot, and the laws of Sukkot on Sukkot" (Midrash Hagadol, Exodus 35:1 [p. 723]).

143. According to the excavators of Nevoraya and Kefar Ḥanania, the depressions found in the floor of the main hall once fit the legs of a wooden *bima;* see E. M. Meyers et al., "Second Preliminary Report on Excavations at en-Nabratein," 40; Z. Ilan, "Kefar Hananya," 255. See also Seager, "Recent Historiography," 86. At Bet Alpha, remains of a small platform, perhaps a *bima*, were found against two southern columns at the eastern end of the hall; see *NEAEHL*, loc. cit.

preserved mosaic floors, there is no indication or trace of a *bima* in the center. This is as true of Palestinian synagogues such as Ḥammat Tiberias, Bet Alpha, Jericho, and Naʿaran as it is of the Diaspora synagogue at Naro or Aegina. The absence of a centrally located *bima* may not be surprising, given the fact that many synagogue floors were covered with often lavishly decorated mosaic floors containing figural and symbolic representations as well as dedicatory inscriptions. It is difficult to imagine that a community would have invested time and money in creating floors with such art and inscriptions if they were only to cover them, even partially, with a *bima*. Synagogues that did not have such rich decorations may well have had a *bima* in the center, but no indications of this have been discovered to date. Of course, if we assume that such *bimot* were made of wood (per the practice in the Second Temple and in the first-century Alexandrian basilica), then the absence of any remains would be most understandable. It may also be that in many cases, particularly in smaller towns and villages, such a *bima* was a portable wooden table or lectern, as has been the Yemenite tradition for centuries.[144] Nevertheless, in the absence of evidence it seems rather unlikely that a *bima* stood in the center of many, if not most, synagogue halls in Byzantine Palestine.[145]

Despite earlier precedents, and in contrast to widespread church practice at the time, the synagogue *bima* might also have been located elsewhere in the main hall of the synagogue. At some sites, for example, it seems to have been set in the back of the nave, against the wall opposite the Jerusalem orientation; such appears to have been the case at Ostia, Bet Sheʿarim, and Naro, and such an arrangement became quite normative later on in some synagogue traditions of the Middle Ages.[146] At Bet Alpha, a platform appears to have been located off to the side of the nave, adjacent to one of the columns; however, its apparently small size probably precluded its functioning as a *bima*.

The most widespread practice for making a *bima* or a platform for the Torah chest was to create an elevated area along the Jerusalem wall. While such a podium might have been very modest and may have been located by the side of the entranceway, it also could have been a much more impressive installation occupying a more central position along the Jerusalem wall. In places where there was only a small platform, as at Gush Ḥalav, ʿEn Gedi, and Chorazim (per the suggested reconstruction), there was no room for a Torah-reading ceremony to have taken place on such a podium, and thus the ceremony must have been held elsewhere, possibly toward the middle of the nave.

---

144. Muchawsky-Schnapper, *Jews of Yemen*, 112–13.

145. Z. Safrai, "Dukhan, Aron and Teva," 74–77.

146. *Ostia:* Squarciapino, *Synagogue of Ostia*, 24; Kraabel, "Diaspora Synagogue," 498; Goitein, *Mediterranean Society*, II, 144–47. *Bet Sheʿarim: NEAEHL*, loc. cit. *Naro:* Goodenough, *Jewish Symbols*, II, 91. See also the testimony of Maimonides (*Laws of Prayer* 11:3); and comments of Blidstein (*Prayer,* 210–11). That such an arrangement may have been true in eleventh-century France, in Rashi's time, may be reflected in his comment on the talmudic discussion of the *bima* in the Alexandrian synagogue (B Sukkah 51b).

Given these various options regarding the *bima*, I have deliberately distinguished between it and the raised podium at the front of the synagogue. At times they may have been one and the same, at times not. The *bima* is the place where the Torah was read, the *targum* translated, and probably the sermon delivered. It may have consisted merely of a table standing on the floor or, alternatively, a raised platform on which the lectern was placed. If the latter, then it is safe to assume that this podium was often where the Torah shrine was located.

A major difference between early synagogues (first centuries C.E.) and those of later antiquity (later third to eighth centuries C.E.), with but a few notable exceptions, was precisely the existence of such a fixed podium, which appeared regularly in the later buildings and was entirely absent from Second Temple buildings. Podiums built in the fourth century can be found in the northern part of the country at Bet Alpha, Reḥov, and Maʿoz Ḥayyim.[147] The excavators of Merot thought that one of the two small platforms found along the southern wall of the synagogue was the base of a Torah shrine, while the second was probably for reading the Torah.[148] Other possibilities are that the additional podium was for a large menorah, the prayer leader, or additional scrolls.[149] Finally, Yeivin has suggested that a second (alleged) podium found at Chorazim was for a Seat of Moses.[150]

Remains of stone platforms have likewise been preserved in a number of synagogues in southern Palestine. At a later stage at Eshtemoa, a stone foundation built adjacent to the northern wall may well have served as such a podium (fig. 69).[151] A similar raised structure was placed before the niche on the northern wall of the synagogue at ʿEn Gedi,[152] and two such installations were found before the northern wall of the synagogue at Susiya. Although their excavators refer to them as *bimot*, their precise function is not clear.[153] Moreover, other elements, such as the niche, apse, and *bima*, may have been added after the podium was built.

With the introduction of the podium, a place was allocated for the Torah, which had now become permanently ensconced within the hall.[154] This was indeed a decisive step in transforming the synagogue building into a holy place.[155] In fact, several synagogues

---

147. For these sites, see *NEAEHL*, loc. cit.

148. Z. Ilan, "Synagogue and Bet Midrash of Meroth," 258–59.

149. Seager and Kraabel, "Synagogue and Jewish Community," 170; Trebilco, *Jewish Communities*, 41; Meyers, "Torah Shrine," 318, 325.

150. Yeivin, "Synagogue of Chorazin," 274; idem, *NEAEHL*, I, 304.

151. Yeivin, "Synagogue at Eshtemoa," 44.

152. Barag, "Second Season of Excavations at En Gedi," 53.

153. Yeivin, "Khirbet Susiya," 93–97. At ʿAnim, the podium occupied fully one-fourth of the main hall.

154. Scholars have at times related this architectural development with the rabbinic phrase "to go down before the Torah chest" (לרדת לפני התיבה), often somewhat speculatively. See, for example, Elbogen, *Jewish Liturgy*, 704–5; I. Levy, *Synagogue*, 54; and, for a more comprehensive discussion, Weiss, "Location of *Sheliaḥ Tzibbur*," 8–21. See also the remarks in Hacohen and Rozenson, "Comments," 172–77.

155. On the prominence of the Torah ark in the Byzantine period inviting criticism and disparage-

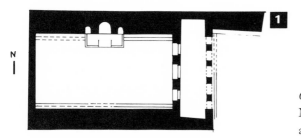

69. Plan of the Eshtemoa synagogue. Note niches and *bima* to the north and entrances and narthex to the east.

seem to have altered their original plans in order to replace entrances in walls facing Jerusalem with podiums and Torah shrines. Such changes appeared at Ḥammat Tiberias, ʿEn Gedi, and possibly Bet Sheʿarim.[156] There can be no doubt that such shrines were reflective of a major development in the religious status of the synagogue hall.

Nevertheless, it should be pointed out that not all synagogues had podiums. At a number of archeological sites no traces have been found (e.g., Horvat ʿAmmudim), and in some cases excavators have been hard pressed to identify such remains (e.g., Meiron, Chorazim).[157] It may well be that in these places the community continued the ancient custom of introducing the Torah scroll into the main hall for its public recitation and then removing it to another room upon completion of the reading (see below).

CATHEDRA OF MOSES

One of the few furnishings found in synagogue excavations in both Palestine and the Diaspora is a seat reserved for an honored personage.[158] This seat has been identified in several literary sources as the Cathedra or Seat of Moses. The earliest literary source in this regard is the New Testament:

> Then Jesus said to the crowds and to his disciples: "The scribes and the Pharisees sit on Moses' seat; therefore, do whatever they teach you and follow it; but do not do as they do, for they do not practice what they teach. . . . They love to have the place of honor at banquets and the best seats in the synagogues."[159]

---

ment on the part of a number of church fathers (and later on, the Karaites); see Lieberman, *Midreshei Teiman*, 24–25; idem, *Sheqiʿin*, 9.

156. At Merot, the podiums were in place from the beginning; just the entrances were changed from the south to the north.

157. *Meiron:* E. M. Meyers et al., *Excavations at Meiron*, 12–13. *Chorazim:* Yeivin, "Reconstruction of Southern Interior Wall," 268–76; *NEAEHL*, I, 304.

158. For the most recent review of this evidence, see the detailed study by Rahmani, "Stone Synagogue Chairs," 192–214.

159. Matt. 23:1–6. Cf., however, comments in S. J. D. Cohen, "Pharisees and Rabbis," 103–5.

The fifth or sixth century midrash, Pesiqta de-Rav Kahana, in describing Solomon's throne, notes a comment by R. Aḥa that the throne resembled the Cathedra of Moses.[160]

Other literary references to this seat are more oblique. The term "cathedra" alone appears in rabbinic literature in a number of different contexts. It will be recalled that the seventy-one magnificent seats in the Alexandrian synagogue described by the Tosefta are referred to as cathedrae but are not associated with Moses.[161] One midrash speaks of a seat reserved for a visiting sage which may well have been the synagogue cathedra: "R. Huna in the name of R. Yose said: 'Everywhere that this Jerusalemite goes they offer him a cathedra and they seat him on it so that they can listen to his wisdom.'"[162]

A later midrash may refer to this seat when describing Moses, who wrapped himself in his *talit* and sat as an elder while God stood. In reacting to such surprising behavior (i.e., that Moses sat while God remained standing), the midrash responds that it was a special chair that God made for Moses so that he could sit, yet seem to be standing: "R. Drusai said: 'He made him a chair as the chair of the lawyers [אסטליסטקין] who, when appearing before government officials, seem as if they are standing but in reality are sitting. Also, here we are talking of sitting which looks like standing. Thus it is written: "And I will sit on the mountain."'"[163]

In rabbinic society, a sage would sit in front of his students while teaching, but a Cathedra of Moses is never mentioned in this context. With regard to R. 'Aqiva and R. Judah, we read of a special seat (ספסל) on which they sat when teaching,[164] and, in a relatively late midrash, we learn of a stone on which R. Eli'ezer b. Hyrcanus of Yavneh used to sit in his academy. After R. Eli'ezer's death, R. Joshua came and kissed the stone, saying: "This stone is like Mt. Sinai, and he who sat on it was like the Ark of the Holy Covenant."[165] Might the association ascribed to R. Joshua, namely, that the chair is like Mt. Sinai and he who occupied it is like the Ark of the Covenant, explain why a similar type of seat had come to be associated with Moses in the synagogue context?[166]

---

160. PRK 1:7 (p. 12).

161. T Sukkah 4:6 (p. 273).

162. Lamentations Rabbah 1:1 (p. 23b). On sitting while teaching, see, for example, PRK 18:5 (p. 297)—R. Joshua b. Levi; Tanḥuma, Lech Lecha, 10 (p. 34b)—Yoḥanan b. Zakkai.

163. Exodus Rabbah 43:4; see Sperber, *Dictionary of Legal Terms*, 22.

164. B Yevamot 98a. See also the tradition about Yoḥanan b. Zakkai, who sat "on a stone under an olive tree while R. El'azar b. Arakh was teaching about the Chariot" (T Ḥagigah 2:1 [p. 380]; B Ḥagigah 14b); cf., however, the account in Y Ḥagigah 2, 1, 77a, which omits the reference to a stone. This type of mystical experience is likened to the Sinaitic revelation, as suggested in Urbach, "Traditions about Merkavah Mysticism," 2–11; Gruenwald, "Yannai's Piyyutim," 260–66; and Halperin, *Faces of the Chariot*, 11–37.

165. Song of Songs Rabbah 1:3, 1. See also Luke 4:20–22, where it is reported that Jesus, after concluding his haftarah-reading while standing, proceeded to sit and deliver a sermon. Another tradition regarding R. Eli'ezer's preaching in an academy setting while sitting in a chair (interestingly, with a *ḥazzan* standing next to him) and wrapped in a *talit* is preserved in Tanḥuma, Lech lecha, 10 (p. 35a).

166. The stone on which Moses sat in the battle against the Amalekites (Ex. 17:12) was regarded with

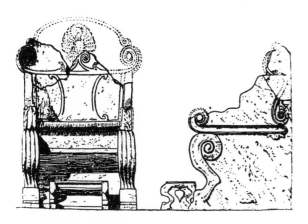

70. Magnificent chair from the
Delos synagogue, possibly a
Cathedra of Moses.

Let us turn now to the archeological evidence. Special seats identified as the Seat of
Moses have been found in a number of ancient synagogues. The earliest example comes
from first-century B.C.E. Delos (fig. 70), and another from third-century C.E. Dura Europos.[167] Three cathedrae, all dating to the fourth or fifth century C.E., have been found
in Roman-Byzantine Palestine: at Hammat Tiberias (in the Slousch excavations in the
early 1920s), Chorazim, and 'En Gedi.[168] The actual term "Cathedra of Moses," however,
has never been found on any archeological artifact; in a fragmentary inscription from
Dalton in the Upper Galilee the single word "cathedra" appears.[169]

Despite the limited number of archeological finds, the types of cathedrae and their appearance vary greatly. Sometimes the seat stood as an independent unit, as at Chorazim,
Hammat Tiberias, and Delos, and at times it was an integral part of the network of
benches in a synagogue, as at Dura and 'En Gedi. The simplest examples have been found
at Dura Europos and 'En Gedi, the most elaborate at Delos, and intermediate types at
Hammat Tiberias and Chorazim. Only at Chorazim does the cathedra bear a dedicatory
inscription, to one R. Judan bar Ishmael who made the stoa (columns?) and stairs of the

---

awe by later generations (B Berakhot 54a). See also the statements of the second-century B.C.E. trage-
dian Ezekiel on Moses and the heavenly throne (Holladay, *Fragments*, II, 363–67, and his comments,
438–51). See also van der Horst, "Moses' Throne Vision," 21–29; and, generally, Bar Ilan, "Stone, Seat,
and Cathedra," 15–23.

167. *Delos:* Sukenik, "Cathedra of Moses," 145–47; idem, *Ancient Synagogues*, 57–61; Foerster, "Survey
of Diaspora Synagogues," 166. Goodenough (*Jewish Symbols*, II, 85) has suggested a further reference
to a cathedra in an inscription from Hellenistic Egypt, where, he posits, the practice first arose. For the
inscription in question, see Horbury and Noy, *Jewish Inscriptions*, no. 28. *Dura Europos:* Kraeling, *Dura:
Synagogue*, 260. Sukenik (*Synagogue of Dura*, 46), however, interprets the top step in the Dura synagogue
as a *bima* for reading the Torah.

168. *NEAEHL*, loc. cit.; Sukenik, "Cathedra of Moses," 147–51.

169. Naveh, *On Stone and Mosaic*, no. 107; Hüttenmeister and Reeg, *Antiken Synagogen*, I, 97.

synagogue.[170] Perhaps R. Judan himself once sat on this seat, as Samuel, a presbyter and archon of the Dura Europos synagogue, undoubtedly did.[171]

Several cathedrae were found against the wall facing Jerusalem—the western wall by the Torah shrine at Dura Europos and the northern wall to the right of the Torah shrine at 'En Gedi. The cathedrae at Chorazim and Ḥammat Tiberias were not found in situ, although both were discovered at the southern end of the building and, more specifically, near the southeastern corner, close to the wall facing Jerusalem. The cathedra at Delos was located against its western wall, facing the eastern entrance and the direction of the Holy Land. Thus, at least with the Dura and 'En Gedi examples, elders sat facing the congregation with their backs to the holy per the Toseftan tradition.[172] In this context, it is worth noting the Samaritan account which speaks of a synagogue built by Baba Rabba at the foot of Mt. Gerizim; seven stones reputedly from the ancient Tabernacle were placed there, and on them sat seven members of the council.[173]

Many explanations have been put forth in an attempt to explain the precise purpose of this cathedra, with each explanation finding its support in a particular source or a specific archeological find. Roth and, more recently, Rahmani interpret the cathedra as the place where the Torah scroll was placed after it was read.[174] Most scholars, however, view the cathedra as the seat for a leader in the congregation, although opinions differ as to the precise role of that leader: judge, archisynagogue, or spiritual-religious figure such as a Pharisee, sage, preacher, or some honored guest.[175]

Special cathedra-like seats are known from pagan and Christian contexts as well, and the Jews thus appear to have adopted this practice from their surroundings, using it for any or all of the above-noted purposes. Pagan priests often sat on cathedrae in their temples, and bishops and other clergy sat on special seats in their churches.[176] However, to the best of our knowledge and in contrast with the pagan priest and the Christian bishop, there was no one particular person who might have been the logical candidate to

---

170. Naveh, *On Stone and Mosaic*, no. 17.

171. Kraeling, *Dura: Synagogue*, 17.

172. T Megillah 3:21 (p. 360).

173. J. M. Cohen, *Samaritan Chronicle*, 71.

174. Roth, " 'Chair of Moses,' " 100–11; Rahmani, "Stone Synagogue Chairs," 203–13. Support for this theory can be found in B Megillah 26b, where a *kursaya* (chair) is noted as a place in which a Torah scroll might be placed; see above, note 135.

175. Bacher, "Siège de Moïse," 299ff.; Elbogen, *Jewish Liturgy*, 361–62; S. Krauss, *Synagogale Alter-tümer*, 386; Sukenik, "Cathedra of Moses," 145–51; Bar Ilan, "Stone, Seat, and Cathedra," 22–23; Mack, "Seat of Moses," 3–12. Seats which famous sages once occupied were regarded with veneration as, for example, in the case of R. 'Aqiva (B Yevamot 98a). A cathedra in a synagogue might have been used to seat someone who took ill or for an elderly or infirm person; see J. Mann, "Sefer Hama'asim," 7.

176. *Pagans:* Richter, *Furniture*, 31–32, 101–2. See also *TDNT*, VI, 870–71; and T 'Avodah Zarah 6:3 (p. 469). *Christians: Didascalia Apostolorum* 12 (p. 119); Mango, *Art of the Byzantine Empire*, 24–25; and bibliography in Rahmani, "Stone Synagogue Chairs," 207 nn. 78–79.

occupy such a seat in the synagogue, where leadership was relatively decentralized. Thus, it is very likely that in many congregations more than one person might well have occupied the cathedra, depending upon the particular activity then taking place: prayers, a sermon, a teaching session, court proceedings, visits by special guests, etc.

Mention should also be made of another kind of chair (כורסיא) noted in a synagogue context. According to the Bavli, the fourth-century Babylonian sage Rava notes that a Torah scroll was regularly placed on such a chair, which was sometimes covered with a cloth.[177] In Rava's opinion, the chair thus acquired a degree of holiness which prohibited it from being sold for other purposes. Given this sanctity, it is unlikely that this chair also functioned as a cathedra.[178]

How widespread the use of the Cathedra of Moses was in the synagogue setting remains unknown.[179] Since cathedrae have not been found in most ancient synagogues excavated to date, it is wholly gratuitous to suppose that they were common in the repertoire of synagogue furniture.[180] As far as can be known, the Cathedra of Moses per se is never accorded any particular theological or ideological significance, nor does it appear to have had any particular religious or ritual function, unless, of course, we assume R. Joshua's lamentation for R. Eliʿezer and his seat was widely known and indeed referred to the synagogue cathedra. Barring this, it is more probable that the cathedra was merely a piece of furniture on which an important person sat, as was the case elsewhere in the ancient world. It found its way into a number of synagogues and became thoroughly judaized through association with Moses.

THE TORAH CHEST AND TORAH SHRINE

As was made clear in an earlier chapter, the chest or ark containing the Torah scroll was the undisputed religious focal point in the ancient synagogue. Referred to in rabbinic literature as *tevah* (תיבה) or *ʾaron* (ארון),[181] the ark is listed in the Mishnah's enumeration

---

177. B Megillah 26b. See Narkiss, "Heikhal, Bimah and Teivah," 45.

178. Contra Z. Safrai, "Dukhan, Aron and Teva," 77–78.

179. A Genizah fragment, nevertheless, refers to the cathedra as a known and familiar piece of furniture in synagogues; see J. Mann, "Sefer Ha-maʿasim," 7.

180. The synagogues in which remains of these seats have been found have no apparent common denominator. As indicated, they are geographically scattered throughout Palestine and the Diaspora, in cities and villages, in synagogues heavily influenced by the surrounding culture and as those which were more isolated and insulated.

181. These two terms are identical in meaning; the former is more widespread in tannaitic traditions, the latter in amoraic ones. So, for example, *tevah* is used in T Megillah 3:21 (p. 360), but *ʾaron* is used in the parallel source, Y Bikkurim 3, 3, 65c. See also M Taʿanit 2:1 as against Y Taʿanit 2, 1, 65a. Nevertheless, there are some exceptions to this rule; see B Shabbat 32a; and Z. Safrai, "Dukhan, Aron and Teva," 71–72.

The term *ʾarona* (ארונה) appears in inscriptions from Dura Europos and Naveh; see Kraeling, *Dura: Synagogue*, 269; Braslawski, "Hebrew Aramaic Inscription," 8–12.

of the degrees of sanctity within the synagogue as holier than the synagogue building but less so than the garments covering the Torah scrolls (מטפחות). The Torah scroll itself, of course, is ranked as the most sacred object of all.[182] In Jewish art, the Torah ark is often depicted as a chest with legs and—as in Roman glass representations—two doors opening outward; it was presumably made of wood.[183] The chest contained shelves which held the Torah scrolls. The upper part of the chest's exterior was often decorated with a gable, in the center of which was a conch. A *parokhet* may have covered the front of the chest, and it is often depicted as being drawn to either side, revealing the ark itself.

This *tevah* was reportedly brought outside for the public fast-day services,[184] and it was also introduced into the regular worship setting in a ceremonious fashion: "When they set the *tevah* down [in the synagogue hall], it faces the people and its back is to the holy."[185] Although Lieberman explains this last tradition in connection with a public fast-day ceremony, most commentators have rightfully argued for a regular Sabbath or holiday synagogue context.[186]

In early synagogue buildings, it would seem that the Torah chest was mobile and was introduced into the main hall only when it was to be read. There is no other way to explain the absence of a podium, niche, or apse in Second Temple synagogues. Even as late as the third and fourth centuries, several sources indicate that the Torah scroll was not always a permanent fixture in the synagogue hall, but was brought in only for reading and then subsequently removed: "When R. Dimi [early fourth century] came, he said: 'On one occasion they forgot and did not bring a Torah scroll the day before. The next day they spread a sheet over the columns and brought a Torah scroll and read from it.'

The term *taka* (Heb. תקא; Greek θήκη) occurs in several instances, at Ḥorvat ʿAmmudim and Dalton, and probably referred to an ark or chest; see Naveh, *On Stone and Mosaic*, nos. 20 and 107. Cf., however, Naveh's more recent comments regarding his former reading from Ḥorvat ʿAmmudim, in "Aramaic and Hebrew Inscriptions," 306-7.

182. M Megillah 3:1; and above, Chap. 6. See the discussion in Fine, *This Holy Place*, 112-21.

183. Goodenough, *Jewish Symbols*, IV, 99-144; and below, note 194. Gold glass, found primarily in funerary settings in the catacombs of Rome, provides the best illustrative material regarding the Torah chest (Goodenough, *Jewish Symbols*, II, 108-20; Rutgers, *Jews in Late Ancient Rome*, 81-85; see also Hachlili, *Art and Archaeology—Diaspora*, 292-304). The doors are open at times and then one can see scrolls placed on shelves. In Christian art from Ravenna as well, doors of a chest are at times open and boxes containing the gospels are displayed, as in the mausoleum of Galla Placidia; see Deichmann, "Frühchristliche Bauten," pls. 5-6. Two recently excavated Samaritan synagogues, at el-Khirbe and Khirbet Samara, feature Torah chests with their outer curtains tied to one side, thus revealing the Torah chest in its entirety; a somewhat similar phenomenon appears in Byzantine mosaics from Jordan and in the church of St. Apollonia at Ravenna; see Amit, "Curtain," 571-75; Piccirillo, *Mosaics of Jordan*, pls. 335, 370, 505; Deichmann, "Frühchristliche Bauten," 107-10.

184. M Taʿanit 2:1.

185. T Megillah 3:21 (p. 360).

186. Lieberman, *TK*, V, 1199-1200. Cf., however, Ginzberg, *Commentary*, III, 394; S. Safrai, "Synagogue," 941. See also Maimonides, *Laws of Prayer* 11:3.

And who permitted them to spread it out in the first place? Everyone admits that one should not make a temporary tent on Shabbat![187] Rather [thus should we formulate the tradition], they found sheets already spread over the columns and they brought a Torah scroll and read from it."[188]

The reality behind this source, especially the comment about the spreading of sheets over columns, is unclear. The reference may be to the columns of the synagogue court-yard, and R. Dimi may have been reporting a Palestinian custom of bringing the Torah scroll into the synagogue on the Sabbath. A similar situation may be alluded to in several statements attributed to the third-century R. Joshua b. Levi: "The prayer leader [שליח ציבור] is not permitted to remove [the mantels] from the Torah chest in public, owing to the honor due the congregation. 'The congregation may not leave until the Torah scroll is removed and put in its proper place.'"[189]

Finally, such a practice may be reflected in a source from late antiquity: "Those in the east [i.e., Babylonia] honor the Torah when it is introduced [into the synagogue]; those in Palestine [honor it] when it is introduced and taken out."[190]

Several scholars have speculated on the nature of the ceremony accompanying the introduction of the Torah ark into the main hall of the ancient synagogue. Ginzberg, for example, has opined that the song of the kine (I Sam. 6:12) appearing in the Bavli and midrashim was recited;[191] Gutmann has suggested that the middle panel at Dura Euro-pos, illustrating the ark in the wilderness and its fate when captured by the Philistines, was a visual parallel to the procession of introducing the Torah ark into the synagogue hall.[192] A ceremony—whatever it may have involved—appears to have continued into the Byzantine period, especially in the Galilee and the Golan, at sites which had no perma-nent place for the Torah chest, as at Horvat 'Ammudim, Huseifa, Meiron, e-Dikke, Umm el-Qanatir, Horvat Kanaf, 'Assalieh, and Nevoraya (the last stage).

Nevertheless, the last-mentioned synagogues are in a distinct minority when we con-

---

187. Such an activity is prohibited on the Sabbath. Who, then, permitted it? See B Shabbat 125b.

188. B 'Eruvin 86b; and *Diqduqei Soferim*, loc. cit.

189. B Sotah 39b. Interestingly, Rashi seems to explain this passage in light of the medieval reality, where there was a permanent ark. The Torah is brought in and placed in the ark and only later removed from it. "As long as the congregation is in the synagogue, where it was customary to bring the Torah scroll into the synagogue from another house [or room], where it was kept, they [the congregation] would spread beautiful garments around the Torah chest and place it [the Torah] in its midst [in the chest or ark]; when they were about to leave they would take the Torah scroll back to the house [or room] where it was kept; they would not remove the garments from the Torah chest in the presence of the congregation."

190. *Differences in Customs*, no. 49 (pp. 173–74).

191. B 'Avodah Zarah 24b; Genesis Rabbah 54:4 (pp. 581–82); Seder Eliyahu Rabbah 12 (p. 58); and Ginzberg, "Beiträge zur Lexikographie," 86–89. Cf., however, Kraeling (*Dura: Synagogue*, 105), who con-nects this song with the return of the ark from the land of the Philistines, or Scholem (*Jewish Gnosticism*, 24–25), who associates it with mystical circles.

192. Gutmann, "Programmatic Painting," 148.

71. Torah shrine from the
Ḥammat Tiberias synagogue.

sider the sum total of buildings in which a podium was found. At dozens of sites in Israel and throughout the Diaspora, the Torah chest was a permanent fixture in some sort of *aedicula*, or shrine, on a raised platform in the main sanctuary[193] and may have been found in one of the following contexts or a combination thereof.[194]

Podium. As noted above, the chest might be placed on a stone platform usually located along the wall facing Jerusalem. This podium was usually found in the center of the wall, as at Ḥorvat Rimon, Ḥammat Tiberias, Reḥov, Qatzrin, 'Anim, and elsewhere, or on one side of the main entrance, as at Gush Ḥalav and 'En Neshut.[195] We have seen that two such small podiums were built on both sides of the main entrance, at Nevoraya (the first and second stages), Sardis, and Merot.[196]

Aedicula. Made of stone, such an installation was either placed on a podium as a free standing element or built into the wall with steps leading up to it. It was often decorated

---

193. See Meyers, "Torah Shrine," 303–38; Weiss, "Location of *Sheliaḥ Tzibbur*," 16–19.

194. On an inscription referring to the Torah shrine at Sardis as a νομοφυλάκιον, "a place for safeguarding the Torah," see Seager and Kraabel, "Synagogue and Jewish Community," 170. Regarding the various contexts in which it was found, see Hachlili, "Niche and Ark," 43–53; idem, *Art and Archaeology—Israel*, 166–94. On the Diaspora, see Kraabel, "Social Systems," 82.

195. See *NEAEHL*, loc. cit.

196. *Sardis:* Seager, "Building History," 426; Seager and Kraabel, "Synagogue and Jewish Community," 169. *Merot:* Z. Ilan and Damati, *Meroth*, 49. On Nevoraya, see Meyers et al., "Second Preliminary Report on Excavations at en-Nabratein," 40–43. On the reconstruction of two such shrines flanking the entrance to the Chorazim synagogue, see Yeivin, "Synagogue of Chorazim," 274–75. Hachlili exaggerates the number of such attested finds in Galilean synagogues ("Synagogues in the Land of Israel," 105–6).

72. Torah shrine from the
Dura Europos synagogue.

with small columns, a gable, and other architectural elements. Fragments of *aediculae* are
rare and have been found in Palestine only at Nevoraya and perhaps Khirbet Shemaʿ,
although the Torah shrine depicted on the Ḥammat Tiberias mosaic floor may represent an *aedicula* par excellence (fig. 71). The Sardis synagogue seems to have had *aediculae*
on either side of its entrance, and Ostia boasted a magnificent *aedicula* on one side of
the synagogue hall's main entrance.[197] The second type of *aedicula*—built into the wall—
is well represented at Dura Europos, where the *aedicula* was located toward the middle
of the western wall facing Jerusalem (fig. 72).[198] In this type, columns and an arch surrounded the niche, affording the Torah shrine an elegant appearance.

Niche. The Torah chest might also have been placed within a much simpler setting,
i.e., in a semicircular or rectangular recess cut into the wall facing Jerusalem. Such niches
have been discovered at Apamea, Bova Marina, and Priene in the Diaspora, as well as at
Arbel, ʿEn Gedi (its later stage), and possibly also Eshtemoa and Susiya in Palestine.[199]

Apse. In the course of the Byzantine period, under the influence of the Christian
basilica, the apse was introduced into synagogues throughout Palestine, though less so in
the Galilee and Golan.[200] The apse was semicircular in shape and located at one end of
the main sanctuary; it is not clear how the apse itself was decorated, if at all. Synagogues

---

197. Squarciapino, *Synagogue of Ostia,* 23; Fine and Della Pergola, "Synagogue of Ostia," 50–57; see
also Kraabel, "Diaspora Synagogue," 498–500; and above, Chap. 8.

198. Kraeling, *Dura: Synagogue,* 16; see also Hachlili, *Art and Archaeology—Israel,* 167–87.

199. Hachlili, *Art and Archaeology—Israel,* 179–80; idem, "Niche and Ark," 43–53.

200. See Foerster, "Dating Synagogues with a 'Basilical' Plan," 173–79.

with apses were discovered at Ḥammat Gader, Ḥammat Tiberias (the last stage), Bet Shean (the northern synagogue), Bet Alpha, Maʿoz Ḥayyim, Jericho, Maʿon (Nirim), and possibly Gaza.[201] In the Diaspora, apses were found at Elche and Aegina.[202] In addition to being a place for setting the Torah chest, the apse served other functions. In several places a cavity was made in the apse floor for storage; coins were found in some of these cavities, possibly indicating that a community chest was stored there (e.g., Bet Alpha).[203]

All of the facilities intended to house the Torah scrolls were considered to some degree holy in themselves per M Megillah 3:1. The Ostia inscription of Mindius Faustus, noting his contribution of an "ark for the sacred Law," indicates this association, as does the Greek inscription for the Torah shrine in Sardis, which calls it a *nomophylakion*, a place where the Law is guarded.[204]

THE ETERNAL LIGHT AND THE MENORAH

Little is known about the eternal light (נר תמיד, *ner tamid*), which was suspended above the Torah shrine (and perhaps from the menorah) in late antiquity. It was an innovation in Judaism of this period and served as both a religious symbol and an artistic ornament. The *ner tamid* mentioned in the Torah was not a perpetually burning lamp, but rather one which burned from evening to morning.[205] Thus, it is noted in the story about Samuel that "the lamp of God had not yet gone out" in the sanctuary at Shiloh.[206]

Although alluded to in tannaitic *midrashim*,[207] the term *ner tamid* later came to mean "eternal light," referring to a continually lit lamp suspended over the Torah ark in the synagogue. Commenting on the peculiar name "Peʿultai" (I Chr. 26:5), but probably with an eye to contemporary practice, R. Yoḥanan explained it thusly: "He carried out an important task [פעל פעולה גדולה] [as commanded] in the Torah. And what did he carry

---

201. Hachlili, *Art and Archaeology—Israel*, 180–82; Ovadiah, "Mutual Influences," 163–66.

202. An apse is also mentioned in a Greek inscription from Khan-Khalde, less than twenty kilometers south of Beirut: "May they be remembered for good and for a great abundance of blessings, Yose Abamaris and his son Benjamin, who, for their salvation, donated and made the apse and laid the mosaic for the apse and the upper [part] in the year 686 [= 605 C.E.]." See Roth-Gerson, "Greek Inscription at Khan-Khalde," 193–200.

203. Sukenik, *Synagogue of Beth Alpha*, 13.

204. See Noy, *JIWE*, I, no. 13; Seager and Kraabel, "Synagogue and Jewish Community," 171.

205. Ex. 27:20, 30:7–8; Lev. 24:3. Thus, the word תמיד should be translated as "regularly." Similar use of this word is found with regard to the daily sacrifice (קרבן תמיד) in the Temple, which likewise must be understood as a sacrifice made on a regular basis. However, Josephus, allegedly following Hecataeus, reports that there was a perpetually burning light in the Second Temple (*Against Apion* 1, 199).

206. I Sam. 3:3.

207. Sifra 1:5 (ed. Finkelstein, p. 5); Sifre–Numbers 1 (pp. 1–2).

out [as commanded] in the Torah? He would light one candle before the ark [ארון] every morning and one every evening."[208]

A midrashic fragment from the Genizah clearly attests to the ritual function of lights in the synagogue framework: "Three sections of the Torah are prefaced by the word *tzav* [command] because they had been established immediately and for all generations: the sections on lights, sending away the impure, and the daily offering. As for the section on lights, whether in the Temple, the synagogues, or the academies, Jews [lit., Israel] are obligated [to use them ritually] since synagogues and academies are similar to the Temple, as it is written: I will be for you a lesser sanctuary [Ezek. 11:16]."[209]

At the very least, such a light (or lights) served as a reminder of the Temple's lights, although undoubtedly it soon acquired other meanings as well, such as symbolizing God's continued presence in the synagogue and His ongoing relationship with Israel.[210] The presence of this light in synagogues (and its association with the Temple and sanctity) became a controversial issue later on between the Karaites and the Rabbanites.[211]

Two pieces of archeological evidence that can be associated with the *ner tamid*—both sui generis—come from Nevoraya. Just to the south of the synagogue, several fragments of a black ceramic vessel were found on which there appeared a design of a Torah ark with what seems to be a suspended lamp. In the same excavations, as noted above, the pediment of what has been identified as a Torah shrine was found buried in the *bima* of phase III. It depicts two lions flanking a gable, beneath which is a shell with a hole through which probably passed a chain holding an eternal light (fig. 73).[212] Artistic depictions of what is undoubtedly the *ner tamid* were also found at Bet She'arim, Bet Alpha, and Bet Shean.[213]

The menorah is by far the most ubiquitous symbol in Jewish art of late antiquity, appearing on stone moldings, clay lamps, mosaic floors, and glass vessels.[214] *Menorot* are prominent in Palestinian synagogues and often appear together with other Jewish symbols; in many cases, the Torah shrine stands at the center and is flanked by two large

---

208. Midrash on Song of Songs 2:16 (ed. Dunesky, p. 62).

209. Ginzberg, *Geniza Studies*, I, 77. See also Midrash Hagadol, Leviticus 6:2 (p. 141); and Z. Safrai, "From Synagogue to 'Little Temple,'" 23-24.

210. B Shabbat 22b. See also the curious reference to "the bomos and the lantern-stand with the lantern" from second-century Pergamum. It appears that this dedication to the God of Israel ("God [is the] Lord [the one] who is forever") was intended for the local synagogue; see Trebilco, *Jewish Communities*, 163.

211. See Ta-Shma, "Synagogal Sanctity," 356-57.

212. E. M. Meyers and C. L. Meyers, "Finders of a Real Lost Ark," 24-36; idem, "Ark in Art," 176-85; E. M. Meyers, *NEAEHL*, III, 1077-79.

213. Hachlili, *Art and Archaeology—Israel*, 268-73, although compare her reservations on p. 272.

214. Ibid., 236-56. On the menorah of antiquity and the various meanings associated with it, see Sperber, "History of the Menorah," 135-59; Negev, "Chronology of Seven-Branched Menorah," 193-210; Goodenough, *Jewish Symbols*, IV, 71-98.

73. Stone fragment from the Nevoraya *aedicula* depicting the remains of two lions on a gable with a conch below.

and often lavishly ornamented *menorot* (e.g., Ḥammat Tiberias, Sepphoris, Bet Alpha, Bet Shean, Naʿaran, and Susiya). Parts of actual three-dimensional *menorot* were found in the synagogues at Merot, Tiberias, ʿEn Gedi, Ḥorvat Rimmon, Eshtemoa, Susiya, and Maʿon (Judaea).[215]

The menorah is often featured in Diaspora remains as well; large, centrally located *menorot* appear on mosaic floors at Bova Marina and Plovdiv and on the wall above the *aedicula* at Dura Europos. It is also a prominent feature on the gold glass fragments from Rome (fig. 74). The Sardis finds are particularly striking in this regard. Remains of some nineteen *menorot* have been found, one mentioned in an inscription, two three-dimensional examples, and sixteen incised in brick, stone, or ceramics.[216] An inscription from Sidé attests to the donations of two *menorot* to that synagogue.[217]

Issues related to making a menorah or donating one to the synagogue appear in rabbinic literature. One question concerns changing the purpose for which a menorah was donated while the name of the donor is still remembered: "[If one] makes a menorah and a lamp for the synagogue, as long as the name of the owner or donor is not forgotten, one cannot use them for another purpose; when the name of the donor has been forgotten, one can use them for another purpose."[218]

The term "menorah," of course, might also refer to any lamp or other kind of light fixture. However, the juxtaposition of a menorah and a lamp (נר) would seem to indicate that a candelabrum is intended, and not merely an ordinary light fixture. The fact

215. *Merot:* Z. Ilan and Damati, *Meroth,* 50. For the other sites, see *NEAEHL,* loc. cit.; as well as Yeivin, "Inscribed Marble Fragments," 209; Amit, "Marble Menorah," 155–68; Hachlili, *Art and Archaeology—Israel,* 236–56; Fine, *This Holy Place,* 114–21. Strauss reports that "two small bronze candlesticks" were discovered in Bet Shean ("History and Form," 12).

216. Seager and Kraabel, "Synagogue and Jewish Community," 176.

217. Lifshitz, *Donateurs et fondateurs,* no. 36.

218. T Megillah 2:14 (p. 352); and Lieberman, *TK,* V, 1154–55.

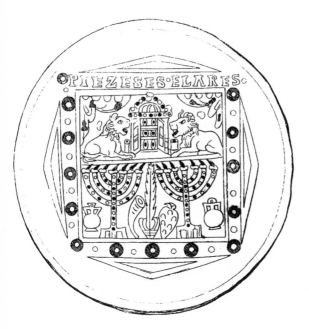

74. Gold glass from a Roman
catacomb depicting Jewish symbols
and an open Torah ark.

that a special donation to a synagogue is being discussed would also seem to indicate that this was not an ordinary object. Both *talmudim* address the issue of *menorot* given to a synagogue by Jews and by non-Jews; the Yerushalmi notes that an emperor named Antoninus, perhaps a reference to Caracalla (211-17 C.E.), donated one such menorah to a synagogue.[219] It has usually been assumed—and rightly so—that the menorah depicted in synagogue art represented, in one form or another, an object that was to be found in the actual synagogue setting. Dothan has gone so far as to claim that the depiction on the mosaic floor of Ḥammat Tiberias was, in fact, a replica of what stood in the front of the

219. Y Megillah 3, 2, 74a; B ʿArakhin 6b. On donations to the ancient synagogue by gentiles, see Bickerman, "Altars of Gentiles," 156–58; White, *Building God's House*, 77–85.

Providing light for a synagogue (ומי שנותנים נר למאור), per the medieval prayer following יקום פורקן) came to be considered a meritorious duty. See Midrash Hagadol, Exodus 27:21 (p. 613); ibid., Leviticus 6:2 (p. 141): "Even though the Temple has been destroyed and the lights abolished, nevertheless [we have] synagogues and academies wherein we light [lights] and they are called 'small sanctuaries.'"

Not a great deal is known about synagogue lighting in general. Windows were the main source of light (e.g., Barʿam), and buildings with clerestory windows were designed to provide an even greater amount of light. Reference to synagogue windows ([אמפומטה] חלונות אפומיות, bright or glass windows—see Jastrow, *Dictionary*, I, 78) can be found in Pirqei d'Rabbi Eliʿezer 10. See also PRK 11:13 (p. 188). Lamps and candelabra, remains of which have been found at Kefar Ḥanania, Reḥov, Maʿon (Judaea), Bet Shean, Jericho, Ḥorvat Rimmon, and Sepphoris, were used regularly to provide artificial light. See M Terumot 11:10; M Pesaḥim 4:4; T Megillah 2:14 (p. 352). On the use of lamps in pagan settings, see MacMullen, *Paganism*, 45; and see Goitein, *Mediterranean Society*, II, 150, regarding the medieval synagogue.

hall.[220] Whatever the case, there can be little doubt that the menorah played a major role in the internal decoration of most synagogues in antiquity.[221]

ART

Synagogue decorations were many, and they varied in both subject matter and artistic quality. Three types of ornamentation can be distinguished: (1) stone carvings, principally on the facade of the building but also inside the prayer hall, on friezes, architraves, capitals, and elsewhere; (2) mosaic floors, especially in the nave; and (3) frescoes on the interior walls of a building. Rarely, if ever, were all three types of decoration found together in one synagogue building; rather, only one type or, at the most, two were used at any one time and place.[222]

Stone Carvings. Widespread in the Galilean-type and Golan synagogues, this decoration was found on a building's exterior, i.e., on the door and window areas, featured on capitals, lintels, doorposts, and especially facades, which included friezes, pilasters, gables, and arches.[223] Although concrete data are lacking for the most part, it is reasonable to assume that when a permanent Torah shrine existed, it was often richly decorated, as may be inferred from the *aedicula* fragment from Nevoraya.[224]

Stone carvings were featured in a variety of designs executed in great detail and on a sophisticated technical level. Such carvings from Capernaum and Chorazim, for example, are especially notable for their wealth of motifs and generally impressive execution (fig. 75), and this stands in sharp contrast to those from synagogues at Meiron, Gush Ḥalav, Ḥorvat ʿAmmudim, Nevoraya, and Merot, where the decoration is much simpler and the level of execution often inferior.

In many respects, artistic expression in the Golan was unlike that in the Galilee. The repertoire of designs and symbols in the former tends to be different, with Jewish symbols and figural representations very much in evidence. While there are also considerable differences among the Golan synagogues, these variations are less extreme than among the Galilean synagogues.[225]

---

220. See Dothan, *Hammath Tiberias*, 38; as well as Goodenough, *Jewish Symbols*, IV, 75–76; Hachlili, *Art and Archaeology—Israel*, 253. Cf. however, Barag (*"Menorah,"* 46), who claims that depictions of the menorah at this time "do not imitate contemporary functional objects."

221. On the significance ascribed to the menorah in synagogue art, see below, Chap. 17. On its transformation into the Jewish symbol par excellence in late antiquity, see L. Levine, "Menorah."

222. See Vitto, "Interior Decoration," 290–300.

223. See Foerster, "Ancient Synagogues of the Galilee," 290ff.; Hachlili, *Art and Archaeology—Israel*, 143–66; as well as S. Krauss, *Synagogale Altertümer*, 358–61.

224. See above, note 212.

225. Maʿoz, "Art and Architecture of the Synagogues of the Golan," 98–115; Hachlili, "Jewish Art from the Golan," 183–212.

75. Frieze from the Capernaum synagogue with the representation of a wagon, often interpreted as a portable Torah shrine.

The decoration in the Galilean and Golan synagogues were generally geometric and floral, although, as noted, faunal and, more rarely, human representations also appear.[226] Animal representations appear on lintels (Ḥorvat ʿAmmudim, Safed, Gush Ḥalav, Capernaum, and Dabbura), gables (Chorazim), and an orthostat (ʿEn Samsam), while human or mythological figures adorn friezes (Chorazim) and lintels (Capernaum, Rama, and e-Dikke). In a number of synagogues from the Galilee (Merot, Qana, Barʿam, and Bet Sheʿarim) and the Golan (Dabbura and Rafid), figures appearing on stone have been interpreted arguably as vestiges of zodiac signs.[227] Generally speaking, human and faunal figures abound at Capernaum and Chorazim, yet they appear far less frequently in other Galilean-type synagogues.

Mosaic Floors. These floors were not as widespread in the Galilee or Golan as they were elsewhere, and the floors in these regions were often composed of earth or flagstones. The mosaic floors that have been discovered usually bear very simple designs, appearing only in the later stages of the buildings, with the exception of the Merot, and ʿAnim, and Ḥorvat ʿAmmudim synagogues, where the mosaic pavements were part of the original phase (fig. 76).[228] Nevertheless, the synagogues at Sepphoris and Ḥammat Tiberias featured the most elaborately decorated mosaic pavements as one might find anywhere.

From the Sea of Galilee southward, to Bet Shean, the Jordan Valley, Judaea, and the coastal region, mosaics constituted the main vehicle of decoration. As noted, a wide variety of motifs and designs are in evidence, from the simplest ones in Jericho, ʿEn Gedi, and Reḥov, to the more complex, featuring full-blown figural scenes (fig. 77).[229] The

---

226. See Kohl and Watzinger, *Antike Synagogen*, 138–203.

227. Regarding the zodiac signs on stone moldings, see Z. Ilan and Damati, *Meroth*, 47, and bibliography cited there.

228. L. Levine, "Excavations at the Synagogue of Horvat ʿAmmudim," 10–12.

229. See above, Chap. 7; and Ovadiah, "Mosaic Art," 185–203.

76. Depiction of a soldier from the
Merot synagogue, often identified
as David. The inscription to the left
reads: "Yudan bar Shimon mani [?]."

most striking example of the latter are Helios and the zodiac signs attested in at least six
synagogues in Byzantine Palestine to date: Ḥammat Tiberias, Bet Alpha, Ḥuseifa on the
Carmel, Naʿaran, Sepphoris, and probably Susiya.[230] Even more common than the zodiac
signs was the cluster of Jewish symbols which usually included the Torah shrine, menorah,
lulav, *ethrog*, shofar, and incense shovel. In sharp contrast to the Galilean-type buildings,
where there was a dearth of such representations (exceptional in this respect is a menorah
on a Capernaum capital; fig. 78), buildings elsewhere had many more Jewish symbols.

The earliest mosaic floors are dated to the third century (Ḥammat Tiberias, Ḥorvat
ʿAmmudim, and ʿEn Gedi), and the use of figural representation became widespread in
the fourth century and beyond. This conclusion, based on archeological finds, dovetails
neatly with the evidence from rabbinic sources: "In the days of R. Abun [fourth century]
they began drawing [figural images] on mosaic floors, and he did not object."[231]

Mosaic pavements were ubiquitous among Diaspora synagogues as well, and it appears
that almost every building discovered to date had such floors: Gerasa, Apamea, Sardis,
Delos, Aegina, Stobi, Plovdiv, Ostia, Bova Marina, Naro, and Elche. Two features are
particularly noteworthy: the degree to which mosaics dominated synagogue decorations
throughout the Diaspora and the relative absence of figural representation.[232] A few ran-

230. Hachlili, "Zodiac," 61–77; idem, *Art and Archaeology—Israel*, 301–9; Goodenough, *Jewish Symbols*, VIII, 167–218.

231. Y ʿAvodah Zarah 3, 3, 42d; and the Genizah fragment published in J. N. Epstein, "Yerushalmi Fragments," 20; and below, Chap. 13.

232. See above, Chap. 8.

77. Representation of an eagle with outstretched wings perched on double volutes incorporating a human head, from the Yafia synagogue.

78. Menorah on top of a capital from the Capernaum synagogue.

dom images have been found (e.g., the Noah story at Gerasa and the selection of animals, fish, and birds at Naro); Sardis presents a fascinating study of contrasts between its totally aniconic mosaic floor and wall revetments on the one hand and the lion statues and eagle reliefs on the other.[233]

Frescoes. In contrast to mosaic remains, we have very little evidence for wall decorations, from either archeological or literary sources. Walls were decorated with painted

233. Two other exceptions should be mentioned. It is reported in the Bavli that a synagogue in Nehardea had a statue inside and that, despite this, a number of sages continued to pray there; see B Rosh Hashanah 24b; B ʿAvodah Zarah 43b.

frescoes, as at Dura Europos and Acmonia, or with marble revetments (*skoutlosis*), as at Sardis.[234] At several sites in Byzantine Palestine, painted pieces of plaster, apparently remains of frescoes, were found among the debris.[235] An inscription from Susiya makes specific reference to the plastering of walls in a synagogue: "May he be remembered for good, the holy sage R. Isi, the priest, the honored one, son of a rabbi, who made this mosaic and plastered its walls."[236] The only source in the Talmud which relates to this phenomenon is the first part of the passage cited above: "In the days of R. Yoḥanan they began drawing [figural images] on the walls, and he did not object."[237]

Given the limited amount of preserved archeological material, it is difficult to determine what type of decoration appeared on these plastered synagogue walls. In the synagogue at Reḥov, there are clear signs of paint on the walls, but no design or representation was found. To date, magnificent wall paintings at the synagogue of Dura Europos constitute the sole example of Jewish art represented by frescoes, and there free use was made of human and animal representations. Such frescoes are well known throughout Dura Europos, in both religious and secular contexts.[238] Not surprisingly, the Duran Jews used this technique as well. Nevertheless, it is difficult to imagine that the rich artistic expression in Dura's synagogue could have been the result of local inspiration only — the product of what was, in effect, a small and relatively isolated Jewish community that had existed in the city for no more than a generation or two. The fact remains, however, that another instance of this type of Jewish fresco art has yet to be discovered elsewhere in the Roman world.

ICONOCLASM

Another issue, addressed only occasionally in the past, involves the destruction of figural art in ancient synagogues. Since the earliest discoveries of these buildings, scholars have noticed that, in many instances, figural images had been intentionally defaced, sometimes in a wholesale fashion, at other times selectively. In some cases, the figures destroyed were stone-molded representations found on architectural elements of the buildings; in others (e.g., Naʿaran and Susiya), mosaic floors likewise suffered vandalism (fig. 79). Opinions are divided as to when this occurred, who was responsible, and why.

Given the fact that this type of activity is almost impossible to date (for example, was it perpetrated after the building ceased to function as a synagogue or while it was still in

---

234. Majewski, "Interior Decoration," 46–50; and above, Chap. 8.

235. For example, at Reḥov; see Vitto, "Synagogue of Rehob," 215; idem, "Byzantine Synagogue," 166. On Merot, see Z. Ilan, "Synagogue and Beth Midrash of Meroth," 235.

236. Naveh, *On Stone and Mosaic*, no. 75.

237. See above, note 231.

238. Kraeling, *Dura: Synagogue*, 366ff.; Perkins, *Art of Dura*, 33–69.

79. Defaced mosaic floor
from the Naʿaran synagogue.

operation?), positing the time of destruction and the perpetrators becomes rather speculative. The following are some of the main suggestions offered to date.[239]

Watzinger, believing the Galilean synagogues were a gift from the Roman emperor,
claimed that zealous Jews, bolstered by rabbinic support, removed all objectionable figures in an attempt to eradicate all traces of pagan influence.[240] Klein, however, has dated
this phenomenon to the Byzantine period generally, viewing it as an aspect of the Christian persecution of the Jews and Judaism.[241] Sukenik and Ovadiah have posited a seventh-
century date, during the transition from Byzantine to Arab rule, assuming that the
destruction was perpetrated by zealous Jews under the influence of the iconoclastic movement then surfacing in the Byzantine and Arab worlds; Kitzinger views this Jewish iconoclasm as a reaction to the emergence of the Christian cult of images.[242] S. Stern has recently argued that this iconoclastic phenomenon was perpetrated by Jews and reflected a
major ideological shift in how figural representation was viewed by rabbis and laypeople
alike.[243] Avi-Yonah has concluded that this iconoclastic process was more than a onetime
occurrence; he posited several waves of Jewish iconoclastic zealotry, the first occurring
sometime in the early fourth century and the second in the seventh century, with the

239. See Amit, "Iconoclasm," 9–10; Wharton, "Erasure"; Fine, "Art and Iconoclasm."

240. Watzinger, *Denkmäler Palästinas*, 116; Kohl and Watzinger, *Antike Synagogen*, 203.

241. S. Klein, *History of Jewish Settlement*, 36–38.

242. Sukenik, *Synagogue of Beth Alpha*, 58; Ovadiah, "Mosaic Art," 199; idem, "Art of the Ancient
Synagogues," 308, 316; Kitzinger, "Cult of Images," 130 n. 204. See also Barber, "Truth in Painting,"
1019–36. On a Jewish polemic against Christian icons and a Christian response, see Baynes, "Icons before Iconoclasm," 93–106.

243. S. Stern, "Synagogue Art," 37; idem, "Figurative Art and *Halakha*," 416–18; and below, Chap. 13.

latter instance possibly linked in some way to Arab iconoclastic influences.[244] Finally, Mayer, Reifenberg, King, and Tsafrir have claimed that this vandalism was the work of Muslims in the eighth century, following a decree by the caliph Yazid II (721 C.E.) which led to the systematic destruction of Christian images and crosses in both the public and private domain.[245]

Amit has recently published a preliminary study on this subject wherein he presents evidence—primarily from Susiya, but also from Barʿam, Ashkelon, and Nevoraya—indicating that this destruction was selective in nature and was carried out while these synagogues were still in operation.[246] He thus concludes that Jews opposed to figural representation perpetrated these acts, viewing these figures as a breach of the second commandment.

The rapid rise in the number of excavated synagogues, along with the increased scholarly attention given the issue of iconoclasm, has heightened awareness regarding the evidence for this phenomenon. Thus, while Chiat and Schick listed twelve and thirteen such instances, respectively, Amit has recorded twice that number.[247] This more complete listing is intriguing. Half of the synagogues listed by Amit are to be found in the Galilee, while nine others are to be found in the Golan. Thus, twenty-one out of twenty-four examples, some 88%, are from these northern regions. The three remaining examples are from Judaea proper—Naʿaran, Susiya, and Eshtemoa. With the exception of Tiberias, all the sites not only are rural, but lie in areas relatively far removed from the large urban, hellenized centers. Such places generally tend to be more conservative in orientation, as attested by their minimal use of Greek and the limited amount of figural representations. The recent excavations in Sepphoris also bear out this distinction; the remains from this major urban site in the central Galilee show no sign of iconoclasm.

This pattern would seem to support the claim of Sukenik, Ovadiah, S. Stern, and Amit that domestic Jewish social and religious pressures, rather than the decrees of a ruling power imposing its will on the Jews, were at the root of much of this iconoclastic activity.[248] This, of course, does not preclude the possibility that these Jews were also

244. Avi-Yonah, "Synagogue Architecture," 79–80.

245. Mayer and Reifenberg, "Jewish Buildings," 1–8; King, "Islam, Iconoclasm," 266–77; Tsafrir, *Archaeology and Art*, 180. According to an eighth-century presbyter from Jerusalem named John, a Jewish sorcerer from Tiberias advised Yazid that if he wished to rule for thirty years, "every kind of pictorial representation, on boards or in wall-mosaic or on holy vessels or altar-cloths, or anything else of the sort that is found in all Christian churches, should be obliterated and entirely destroyed; not only these, but also all the effigies that are set up as decoration in the marketplaces of cities." See Schick, *Christian Communities*, 215. On the Islamic context of Byzantine and Jewish iconoclasm, see Crone, "Iconoclasm," 59ff.; as well as Vasiliev, "Iconoclastic Edict," 23–47; Grabar, *Formation of Islamic Art*, 75–103.

246. Amit, "Iconoclasm," 9–16.

247. Chiat, *Handbook of Synagogue Architecture*, 344. Schick, *Christian Communities*, 203; Amit, "Iconoclasm," 13.

248. In this regard, see also Avigad, *Beth Sheʿarim*, 281–82.

80. Representation of the Torah shrine in a mosaic floor from the Jericho synagogue.

influenced by outside phenomena—whether of Muslim or Christian origin.[249] Perhaps here, as elsewhere, it would be best not to fall into the trap of seeking one overriding, all-inclusive explanation. The forces at play may well have been many, spread over generations, stemming from a number of sources and expressing a varied agenda. Religious zealotry was not the monopoly of Jews only at this time, as the destructive forays of Barsauma, together with the destruction of images at the Ḥammat Gader baths and on the Madeba map, attest.[250] Given the limited and uncertain evidence at hand, other than tentative suggestions would be hazardous.[251]

A noteworthy and undoubtedly related phenomenon is the fact that synagogues built (or remodeled) in the seventh century and thereafter were invariably aniconic (e.g., ʿEn Gedi, Jericho [fig. 80], Reḥov, Maʿoz Ḥayyim, and Ḥammat Tiberias). Thus, Jewish art at the end of late antiquity clearly leaned toward a strict avoidance of figural representation, much as it had centuries earlier in the Hasmonean and Herodian eras. How the iconoclasm discussed above related to this new tendency—as cause, effect, or parallel development—must remain moot for the present.

249. See Schick, *Christian Communities*, 218-19; Ovadiah, "Art of Ancient Synagogues," 316-17. On the hostility to art among Christians, Jews, and Muslims in this period, see Grabar, *L'iconoclasme*, 93-112.

250. Tsafrir, *Archaeology and Art*, 113 and 427.

251. On a similarly nuanced explanation of the damage to churches in Palestine in the seventh to eighth centuries, see Schick, *Christian Communities*, 180-219.

A RABBINIC SOURCE ON THE SYNAGOGUE INTERIOR

The Yerushalmi, in the context of a discussion about the sanctity of various synagogue-related objects, preserves a source relating to the interior furnishings of the synagogue in some detail. We have already had occasion to discuss the mishnah which notes six items, each one holier than its predecessor: the plaza, the synagogue building, the Torah chest, the Torah coverings, the books of the Bible, and the Torah scrolls.[252] Most curious for our present purposes is the jump from the synagogue building to the Torah chest and the objects associated with it. Did the mishnah simply ignore other objects in the synagogue that might have been noted, or was there perhaps nothing else in the second-century synagogue that merited a sacred status? In any case, by the third century, a sacred status was ascribed to other objects found within the synagogue, and these are categorized by the Yerushalmi in one of two ways: their sanctity was compared either to the sanctity of the synagogue building or to that of the Torah ark. The tradition referred to reads as follows:

> All vessels [כלי: perhaps appurtenances] of the synagogue [have the same sanctity as that attributed to] the synagogue itself: the bench [ספסלה] and the *kaltira* [קלטירה] [are similar in their sanctity to] the synagogue; [however,] the mantle [כילה] over the ark [is similar to] the ark. R. Abbahu used to place a garment [גולתא] under that mantle. R. Judah in the name of Samuel [said]: The *bima* [בימה] and the *lukhin* [לווחין] do not have the sanctity of the ark but rather the sanctity of the synagogue.[253] *Inglin* [אינגלין] do not have the sanctity of the ark, but they do have the sanctity of the synagogue.
>
> R. Jeremiah went to the Golan,[254] where he saw people placing a *makusha* [מכושא] inside the ark. He came and asked R. Ami, and he [R. Ami] said to him: I tell you that they have made an agreement [lit., a condition] from the very outset [to act thusly]. R. Yonah made a tiered chest [מגדל] and stipulated the following regarding it, [namely] that the upper part [would be for] books and the lower [part] for vessels [or garments].[255]

The general thrust of this source is clear. Sanctity is indeed applicable to synagogue appurtenances not listed in the mishnah. The tradents of this source appear to have been minimalists. The opening statement assigns all synagogue "vessels" the sanctity of the synagogue itself. The objects in question are holy, but only to a distinctly lower degree; i.e., they have a status similar to but not greater than that of the synagogue building itself. The above source introduces an agreed-upon exception: the *kila*, which is expressly associated with the ark, bears the latter's sanctity. In three cases—*bima*, *lukhin*, and *inglin*—

---

252. M Megillah 3:1. See also above, Chap. 6.

253. According to a tradition in the Bavli, quoted in the names of R. Ze'ira and R. Mattenah, no sanctity whatsoever is attached to these objects (B Megillah 32a).

254. On the identification of the term גולנה, see S. Klein, *Transjordan*, 51; idem, "Estates of R. Judah Ha-Nasi," 549; Hüttenmeister and Reeg, *Antiken Synagogen*, I, 139–40.

255. Y Megillah 3, 1, 73d. See Ratner, *Ahavat Zion v'Yerushalayim*, loc. cit.

a difference of opinion is alluded to regarding their sanctity, though the Babylonian tradents (R. Judah in the name of Samuel) prefer the more limited option. To what extent this was an exclusively Babylonian issue or practice cannot be assessed. Finally, it is noteworthy that the objects in dispute generally seem to cluster around two foci of the synagogue interior, the *bima* and the Torah or Torah shrine.

Despite its apparent richness, this source nevertheless remains enigmatic. While there is a consensus regarding certain terms used, others are far from clear. In the former category we may include the *kila, gulta, bima, makusha,* and *migdal.*

It is possible to identify the terms *kila* and *gulta* owing to their connection with the ark and their frequent usage in other rabbinic sources. The *kila* is a curtain or canopy; there is little doubt that this refers to the *parokhet* on the ark's outside or inside.[256] It parallels another term, *perisah,* appearing in the Bavli.[257] The fact that this is the only exception agreed upon by our source as having a level of sanctity equal to that of the Torah ark is a clear indication of a close association with it. According to R. Abbahu, an additional covering—the *gulta*—was placed beneath the *kila,* perhaps as in the representation of the Torah shrine in Bet Shean.[258] Mentioned frequently in rabbinic literature, the *gulta* is some sort of cloak, often made of wool. Such a garment may denote high rank and honor, or it may have been the garment that a sage wore during prayer, or both.[259]

The other three objects listed in our source are likewise easily identifiable. We have already spoken of the *bima.* The *makusha* was an instrument for weaving or, more likely in this context, a bell or knocker, while a *migdal* was a storage chest.[260] The relevance of the latter two items will be discussed below.

More problematic are the *kaltira* (wooden *bima?* footstool? couch?), *lukhin* (boards on which the Torah scroll was placed [lectern?] or on which writing lessons were conducted), and *inglin* (poles for the mantel? pegs for the Torah chest? a lectern?). The fact that so many suggestions have been offered for each of these terms indicates the lack of clarity. In attempting to determine their interpretation, one must examine not only the source as a whole, but also each term in its immediate context. Since some terms are related directly to the sanctity of the synagogue and others to the sanctity of the ark, this

---

256. For this and subsequent identifications, the following have been consulted: the traditional commentators to the Yerushalmi, P'nei Moshe, and Qorban Ha-'edah; the *Arukh Hashalem* with Kohut's comments; Jastrow's and Sokoloff's dictionaries; and S. Krauss's *Synagogale Altertümer.* All the above agree that the *kila* is to be identified with the ark's curtain—with the exception of Krauss, who regards it as a canopy over the ark (p. 381).

257. See B Megillah 26b; see also Y Shabbat 20, 17c. For other uses of the *kila,* see Genesis Rabbah 36:1 (p. 334); and Leviticus Rabbah 5:1 (p. 99).

258. See *NEAEHL,* I, 234.

259. Y Berakhot 4, 7c; Y Ta'anit 4, 1, 67c; Y Sanhedrin 10, 28c. On using the *talit* in much the same way, see Y Bikkurim 3, 3, 65d; and L. Levine, *Rabbinic Class,* 52, 175.

260. Sokoloff, *Dictionary,* 289.

distinction might well facilitate the identification of the item in question as well as its possible location in the synagogue hall.

Benches were physically attached to the synagogue building, and therefore they were considered to have the same degree of sanctity as the synagogue.[261] It may not be coincidental that our source begins with two items about which there is no dispute; i.e., they are similar in sanctity to the synagogue building itself. The same appears to have been true with respect to the *kaltira*, which was probably one of the synagogue hall's permanent fixtures; its precise meaning, however, has not as yet been satisfactorily elucidated.

It would seem that one source in antiquity saw reason to define the *bima, lukhin*, and *inglin* as objects associated with the ark—if not their location, then at least in their liturgical function. It would be reasonable to assume that the *bima* in this source is a raised platform on which the Torah was read, and my preference is to interpret the term *lukhin* as a lectern on the *bima*.[262] These two items were thus considered one unit. If we assume that they were located toward the center of the hall, it would explain why this source associates them more with the synagogue's interior than specifically with the ark.

As for the *inglin*, although there was an opinion in antiquity which associated it with the ark, the above pericope associates it with the sanctity of the synagogue in general.[263] Therefore, it would appear more reasonable to interpret this term to mean poles for the mantel, that is, part of the synagogue interior near the ark though not related directly to it.[264]

Associating a number of the above objects with the ark further enhances the centrality of the Torah shrine in the synagogue building. Its importance is reflected in those mosaic floors where the ark is surrounded by symbols of Jewish religious practice. The Torah shrine itself is regularly depicted in great detail, with its doors, curtains, accompanying poles, decorations, etc. Thus, a number of items appearing in the above list—specifically those associated by some with the sanctity of the ark—were probably used in the context of Torah-related activities, either as accoutrements to the ark or as part of the Torah-reading liturgy.

---

261. P'nei Moshe and Sokoloff have suggested that the reference here to benches may, in fact, refer to footstools, although this is not the usual meaning of the term; nor do we know much about the use and placement of footstools in synagogues. Cf., however, Kraeling's identification of a raised part of the benches at Dura Europos as a footrest (*Dura: Synagogue*, 16). Alternatively, the term may refer to benches for important individuals, as we have noted above.

262. See Elbogen, *Jewish Liturgy*, 359-60. For another view, see the comments by M. Simon on B Megillah 32a (Soncino, p. 193 n. 3).

263. Identified as poles by Qorban ha-ʿedah; as pegs to hold the ark in place by P'nei Moshe, and as a lectern by Jastrow and Krauss.

264. See, however, Sukenik's somewhat far-fetched suggestion ("Designs of the Lection," 221-25) that the term refers to a lectern, an identification for which he claims to have found confirmation in certain objects appearing in synagogue art.

The last two objects listed in the source, *makusha* and *migdal*, are not related to the sanctity of the synagogue per se. The former indicates how the Torah chest might have been used for purposes other than housing the Torah. It seems clear that this chest may have been used to store other items as well, perhaps to safeguard them or possibly to keep them because they were in some way related to synagogue functions. Even though it is not clear how a *makusha* was used in a synagogue setting,[265] this object was important to the people of the Golan, as they saw fit to keep it in a holy place. According to R. Ami, the local population agreed upon this arrangement from the outset. In addition, other synagogue-related items were kept in a separate cabinet that stood in the synagogue hall. According to our source, R. Yonah once had a cabinet built, and presumably it was located in the synagogue. This sage further stipulated that holy books should be placed on the top shelves, while other items could be placed on the bottom ones, most probably in order to separate the holy and the profane or to distinguish between various degrees of holiness.

INSCRIPTIONS

Inscriptions were an integral part of the synagogue setting and might have been found in almost every part of the building—on its facade and throughout its interior, including the area around the Torah shrine. Columns and chancel screens were often used for inscriptions, but, for the most part, mosaic floors bore most of this epigraphical material.[266] Synagogue inscriptions are usually short, no more than ten to twenty words. We have already made extensive use of this form of epigraphical evidence throughout this volume; below is a brief overview of this important corpus of evidence.

Over five hundred inscriptions relate to the synagogue and its officials; some 60% of these come from the Diaspora and the remainder from Roman-Byzantine Palestine. Inscriptions were written in any one of the languages spoken by Jews in a given area; Greek and Aramaic generally predominated, while Hebrew constituted a minor, though not entirely insignificant, component in Palestine. At several sites in the Upper Galilee and southern Judaea, Hebrew appears to have occupied a fairly central role. In the western part of the Empire, Latin was sometimes used, and Iranian appears in some fifteen inscriptions from Dura Europos.[267]

Inscriptions served a number of purposes. At times they were used to identify specific

---

265. See S. Klein, "Estates of R. Judah Ha-Nasi," 549–50; Lieberman, *TK*, V, 1154; and Y Betzah 5, 2, 63a.

266. Only a few inscriptions state explicitly that the donation was for a synagogue. Ḥammat Gader (Naveh, *On Stone and Mosaic*, no. 34); Bet Guvrin (ibid., no. 71); Gerasa (Roth-Gerson, *Greek Inscriptions*, no. 10); and Jerusalem (ibid., no. 19).

267. Kraeling, *Dura: Synagogue*, 300–317. On evidence for the use of Hebrew in late antiquity, see de Lange, "Revival of Hebrew," 342–58.

artistic depictions, such as the Hebrew legends that invariably accompanied the representations of the various signs and seasons of the zodiac (e.g., Ḥammat Tiberias, Bet Alpha, Sepphoris, and Naʿaran).[268] Biblical scenes, though rare, almost invariably have accompanying inscriptions—usually in Hebrew—which identify the figures depicted, as was the case with the *ʿAqedah* mosaic in Bet Alpha and the representations of David in Gaza, Daniel in Naʿaran and Susiya, Noah's sons in Gerasa, and Aaron in Sepphoris. In the Dura synagogue, inscriptions identify nine figures appearing on its walls.[269] Moreover, the Jericho synagogue contains a biblical phrase (שלום על ישראל—Ps. 125:5) and the Merot synagogue a complete verse (Deut. 28:6).

Inscriptions also may have been instrumental in fostering memories of the past and hopes for the future. This is particularly true of the lists of the twenty-four priestly courses that have been found in both Palestine and the Diaspora. Their presence seems to have been intended to maintain and strengthen national-religious longings and aspirations.[270]

A number of inscriptions from the Diaspora serve as official communal documents attesting to decisions and actions taken by the community. The three inscriptions from Berenice are a case in point, as are the manumission inscriptions from the Bosphorus region.[271] The inscription from Stobi is a further example, as it records the contribution and transference of part of a building to the community by its owner, Claudius Tiberius Polycharmos. In Palestine, an inscription serving as a communal document comes from ʿEn Gedi. In its prefatory paragraph, the inscription lists the fathers of the world according to I Chr. 1, the zodiac signs, the months of the year, the names of the three biblical patriarchs, and the three friends of Daniel, then the names of three patrons. A series of vows by which members of the community were warned to abide appears next. The main section of this inscription instructs the members of the congregation in their relations with one another and with the outside world, particularly with respect to the "secret of the community."[272]

However, the overwhelming majority of synagogue inscriptions is dedicatory in nature. The wealthy would commemorate their gifts, which were a means of gaining prestige while, at the same time, fulfilling a religious vow and serving the common good.[273] As noted, these inscriptions could appear anywhere in the building and were often placed on the very object being donated. At times, the inscription itself specified what precisely had been contributed (e.g., Apamea); on other occasions, the contribution was unstated (e.g., Ḥammat Tiberias). Usually the donation was made by an individual or family, although

---

268. For these and other sites listed below, see *NEAEHL*, passim.

269. Kraeling, *Dura: Synagogue*, 269–72.

270. See above, Chap. 7.

271. See above, Chap. 4.

272. L. Levine, "Inscription in the ʿEn Gedi Synagogue," 140–45; and below, Chap. 10.

273. See Rajak, "Benefactors," 305–19.

more generally formulated inscriptions acknowledging the donations of a larger group of people, such as the community at large, are noted.

Inscriptions often contain a great deal of information: the language in use at that time and place, the prosopography of the donors, and the donors' professions and official titles. At times, a contribution was made in fulfillment of a vow; on occasion, the precise sum contributed is mentioned (e.g., Berenice) and, in other instances, the number of feet of mosaic floor contributed (e.g., Emesa and Apamea).

As might be expected, donors were almost always members of the local community.[274] There are also instances when people from one city took up residence elsewhere and donated to their new synagogue, although they continued to refer to themselves by their place of origin. We have had occasion to note this phenomenon in Rome and in Jerusalem, as well as in Byzantine Sepphoris, where communities of Jews from Tyre and Sidon lived but continued to refer to themselves in terms of their former residence.[275] Only rarely do we read of a synagogue supported by people from elsewhere, as at the mineral springs of Ḥammat Gader, where donors hailed from Arbel, Capernaum, Emmaus, Sepphoris, and Kefar 'Aqavia.[276]

Occasionally, the names of the artisans themselves are recorded in inscriptions, such as Marianos, Ḥanina, and Yosi Halevi. The first two—father and son—built the synagogues in Bet Alpha and Bet Shean; the last worked in 'Alma and Bar'am in the Upper Galilee.[277]

Precious, though rare, are inscriptions which mention the date of a building's construction or renovation. Such pieces of information have been retrieved from the synagogues of Nabratein, Bet Alpha, Ashkelon, and Gaza in Palestine and Stobi and Dura in the Diaspora.[278] The various eras invoked might include the reign of a given emperor (Dura, Bet Alpha), a municipal era (Gaza, Ashkelon), a famous event, such as the battle of Actium (Stobi), the Seleucid era (Dura), creation of the world (Susiya, Bet Alpha), sabbatical years (Susiya), and the time since the Temple's destruction (Nevoraya).

One unique inscription may be classified as literary in nature. The Reḥov halakhic inscription features laws relating to sabbatical year observances in northern Palestine (listing the areas to be included in this observance and the fruits and vegetables prohibited to Jews during this year).[279] Another unique inscription comes from the Jericho synagogue

---

274. Roth-Gerson (*Greek Inscriptions*, 67) has put forward the unlikely suggestion that some of the donors to the Ḥammat Tiberias synagogue were gentiles.

275. Ibid., no. 24.

276. Naveh, *On Stone and Mosaic*, no. 33.

277. Ibid., nos. 1 and 3; Roth-Gerson, *Greek Inscriptions*, nos. 4 and 5. See also the inscription from Tiberias mentioning "Abraham the marble-cutter," though it is unclear whether he ever worked in a synagogue setting (Roth-Gerson, *Greek Inscriptions*, no. 14).

278. On Palestinian sites, see *NEAEHL*, passim. *Stobi*: Hengel, "Synagogeninschrift von Stobi," 150–59. *Dura*: Kraeling, *Dura: Synagogue*, 263–68.

279. This inscription—the longest known from Palestine, containing 29 lines and 365 words—is sui

81. Aramaic inscription
from the Jericho synagogue.

and acknowledges the donations of congregants in very flowery, poetic language, amazingly reminiscent of later Jewish prayers which offer a blessing to the congregation as a whole (fig. 81).[280]

The unusual inscription from Aphrodisias almost certainly originated in a synagogue setting. As will be recalled, the list of 130 donors, including Jews and some proselytes and an almost equal number of God-fearers, is the longest synagogue inscription known to date. As noted, these people may have been donors to a soup kitchen, and the names which appear along with their titles and professions are most illuminating.[281]

A number of inscriptions from the Diaspora attest to the fact that non-Jews as well were deeply involved in synagogue affairs. Several pagan women, such as Julia Severa from Acmonia and Capitolina from Tralles in Asia Minor, were prominently mentioned as donors to synagogues. While Julia remained fully pagan, from the use of the term *theosebis* it appears that Capitolina was a God-fearer who was identified with the local Jewish community and actively involved in its affairs.[282] Finally, we learn that a number of Jewish donors were active in urban and provincial affairs. Several Sardis patrons are listed as city councillors, and we read of one Cosimus who was in charge of the customs station at Spondill.[283]

---

generis in its halakhic content, much of which also appears in rabbinic sources. The inscription itself was given prominent display in the building's narthex, next to the main entrance. Clearly, the Reḥov community was expressing its deep concern with such halakhic matters, reflecting a conservative bent which is further exhibited in the almost total absence of both figural representations and the use of Greek.

280. See Foerster, "Synagogue Inscriptions," 12–40; and below, Chap. 16.

281. Reynolds and Tannenbaum, *Jews and God-Fearers*, 93–123; and comments above, Chap. 8.

282. Lifshitz, *Donateurs et fondateurs*, nos. 30 and 33.

283. Ibid., nos. 22–25; Scheiber, *Jewish Inscriptions*, 29. Recently, Lapin has utilized synagogue inscriptions in an attempt to gauge the emerging ethnicity in Palestinian Jewish communities ("Palestinian Inscriptions").

LITURGY AND ARCHITECTURE:
THE WORSHIP SETTING

So far, the various components of the synagogue building have been described, with particular emphasis on its main hall. But what actually transpired there in a religious vein, and where? The worship framework regularly included a number of activities: the recitation of prayers; the priestly blessing; the ceremony of introducing the Torah scroll and returning it; the Torah-reading and its translation; the reading of the haftarah; the sermon; and the recital of *piyyutim*.[284] Not all of these activities were necessarily conducted from the same place in the synagogue sanctuary, and there may have been differences from one congregation to the next regarding where one or another of these activities occurred, much as is the case today. In late antiquity, i.e., from the fourth to the seventh centuries, we can point to two or perhaps three foci of synagogue worship, each with its own distinct role.

One focus was the raised platform on the wall facing Jerusalem, where there may have been a niche, *aedicula*, apse, or some other facility for housing the Torah ark. The presence of the ark clearly defined this area as sacred, a status that might have been enhanced by the addition of an eternal light. The priests ascended the podium to bless the congregation, standing with their backs to the Jerusalem wall and facing the congregation; this remained the custom throughout this period: "When the priests raise their hands [in blessing], their faces are toward the people and their backs toward the holy [the site of the Jerusalem Temple]."[285]

A description of the priestly blessing appearing in a later midrash is even more specific, noting explicitly that priests stood next to the ark: "The people behind the priests are not included in the blessing. Therefore, the priests should go up to the ark so that the entire congregation will then be [standing] in front of them. . . . R. Joshua b. Levi said: 'Any priest who does not make the effort to go up [lit., עוקר את רגליו] to the [Torah] chest during the blessing over the Temple sacrifice [ברכת עבודה—which precedes the priestly blessing] should not ascend again.' "[286]

Finally, a preacher or teacher may have sat on the podium when addressing the congregation, assuming that a Cathedra of Moses was used, inter alia, for this purpose. As mentioned above, four of the five archeological sites containing remains of such chairs (Dura Europos, Chorazim, Ḥammat Tiberias, and ʿEn Gedi) were located along the Jerusalem-oriented wall or close to it.

In many (most?) synagogues, the actual Torah-reading ceremony seems to have taken

---

284. On the worship components in the ancient synagogue, see below, Chap. 16.

285. T Megillah 3:21 (p. 360).

286. Numbers Rabbah 11:4. See also B Sotah 38b: "R. Joshua b. Levi said: 'Any priest who does not approach the platform [lit., *dukhan*] in the blessing over the Temple sacrifice may not approach later on [when the Temple is rebuilt].'" See also Safrai, "How Was the Ancient Synagogue Furnished?" 69–71.

place on this podium as well. Given the number of people involved in the reading at any one time (usually three or four—two *gabbaim*, a reader, and perhaps one called to the Torah) and the need for a table on which to set the Torah scroll, a sizable area would have been required.

Indeed, a number of synagogues—as noted—had a large, elevated platform in the front of the hall which may well have been the focus for this and other liturgical activities noted above. Some synagogues, however, had a single or double platform, which was quite small. This might have been adequate for a Torah shrine, menorah, or something of that order, but not for the activities just mentioned.

Thus, a second possible focus of ancient Jewish liturgy was the *bima* or a table in the center or back of the synagogue's main hall. The Torah scroll would then have been brought in and placed there for reading, the *targum* would have been rendered there, and the sermon would possibly have been delivered there. Byzantine churches often had a podium in the center, like the *ambo* in Aegean buildings and the semicircular *bema* in Syrian churches.[287] The location of a teacher or preacher in the center of the hall is possibly reflected in an inscription found near four stone slabs, in the very center of the nave at Sardis, referring to a "priest and *sophodidaskalos*." Seager and Kraabel have suggested that the structure resting on these slabs may have been some sort of platform from which this *sophodidaskalos* taught.[288]

The absence of a central *bima* at most synagogue sites, especially in Palestine, may be due to one of two reasons: either the *bima* was not all that ubiquitous or it was usually made of wood, a perishable material which leaves no remains over time and in normal (i.e., humid) climatic conditions. This last alternative should not be considered simply a convenient excuse for what has not been found. The fact is that biblical and Second Temple *bimot* are specifically noted as being made of wood, including the famous Alexandrian *bima* mentioned in the Tosefta.

There was a third focus of the synagogue liturgy, which, to date, has not found expression architecturally—presumably because it required no material props. The prayer leader—*hazzan* or *sheliah tzibbur*—seems to have stood in the nave, before the podium and Torah ark located along the Jerusalem-oriented wall, which the congregation faced during the recital of the *'Amidah* prayer.[289] The frequently recurring phrases in rabbinic literature "he who passes before the ark" (עובר לפני התיבה) and "he who goes down before the ark" (יורד לפני התיבה) refer to such a prayer leader.[290] This person apparently stood

---

287. Mathews, *Early Churches*, 120, 148–49.

288. Seager and Kraabel, "Synagogue and Jewish Community," 170. As noted above, the *bima* may also have been located elsewhere in the nave, possibly along the back wall, as at Bet She'arim, Ostia, and Naro. See Lifshitz, *Donateurs et fondateurs*, no. 36.

289. On a similar arrangement according to Maimonides, see his *Laws of Prayer* 11:4; and comments in Blidstein, *Prayer*, 211-12.

290. For an attempt to explain these various terms in specific chronological contexts, see Weiss,

on the floor of the synagogue below the ark and faced it. This may be the simplest way to understand the realia behind the phrase "to go down before the ark." Moreover, the above two terms also indicate the prayer leader's proximity to the podium on which the Torah shrine stood (i.e., לפני התיבה). This proximity is confirmed by the term קרב ("draw near"), used in describing the prayer leader or *ḥazzan* as he approached the ark before reciting the *'Amidah* prayer.[291] One tradition quotes R. Menaḥem as saying: "Do not say to one who is leading the *'Amidah* prayer [lit., passing before the ark], 'come and pray,' but rather 'come and draw near.'"[292]

A further emphasis on the setting of the prayer leader comes from later sources, where we learn of the custom of two people standing beside the *ḥazzan*, a practice probably derived from public fast-day ceremonies.[293] Tractate Soferim relates the following: "Similarly, it is not desirable that a *ḥazzan* should stand by himself in front of the Torah ark; rather, there should also be someone to his right and someone to his left, as against the [three] patriarchs."[294]

A parallel tradition is found in the almost contemporaneous eighth-century midrash Pirqei de R. Eliezer, which also relates that two people should stand beside the *ḥazzan*. The midrash attributes this custom to the war against the Amalekites, when Moses was flanked on either side by Aaron and Hur (Ex. 17:12): "from this you learn that the prayer leader should not pray unless there are two people standing [by his side]."[295] Finally, a fascinating tradition notes a very prominent role for—and most unusual image of—the *ḥazzan* on the Hoshanah Rabbah festivities (i.e., the last day of Sukkot): "and when the first day of the holiday (Sukkot) came, all Israel, adults and children, would take their *lulavim* in their right hands and *ethrogim* in their left, and all would know that Israel was victorious in judgment. And when Hoshanah Rabbah would come, they would take willow branches and make seven *haqafot* [encirclements], and the *ḥazzan* of the synagogue would stand like an angel of God with a Torah scroll in his arm, and the people would encircle him as they once did the altar."[296]

When the *piyyut* (liturgical poem) was introduced into the synagogue service in the fourth or fifth century, it was often intended to replace the regular service led by the

---

"Location of *Sheliaḥ Tzibbur*," 8–21, the bibliography cited there, and esp. nn. 6 and 7. See also Elbogen, "Studies in Jewish Liturgy," 704–11; Scholem, *Jewish Gnosticism*, 20; Gruenwald, "Song of the Angels," 479–81.

291. Leviticus Rabbah 23:4 (p. 531); Midrash on Psalms 19:2 (p. 82a).

292. Y Berakhot 4, 4, 8b; Genesis Rabbah 49:23 (pp. 506–7). See also Ginzberg, *Commentary*, III, 350–51.

293. Mekhilta of R. Ishmael, Beshalaḥ, 1 (pp. 180–81); Tanḥuma, Beshalaḥ, 27.

294. Tractate Soferim 14:9 (p. 263).

295. Pirqei de R. Eliʿezer 44. See also a similar tradition in what appears to be a late addition to PRK 3:1 (p. 36).

296. Midrash on Psalms 17:5 (pp. 64b–65a). See also Yalqut Shimʿoni, Psalms, 703.

ḥazzan or *sheliaḥ tzibbur* by incorporating the mandatory prayers into its composition.[297] At such times the *paytan* undoubtedly stood in the same place where the prayer leader stood. Some *piyyutim* contained choral elements (refrains, responses), and it has also been suggested that a chorus may have joined the *paytan* in this recitation. However, there is no way to determine where such a chorus might have stood.[298]

On the basis of the above, let us attempt to sketch the evolution of the synagogue from a liturgical-architectural perspective.

At the outset, i.e., in Second Temple times, there seems to have been only one liturgical focus within the synagogue building, i.e., in the middle of the hall where the Torah chest was brought and the Torah-reading ceremony was held. As was argued in an earlier chapter, regular communal prayer had not, as yet, been instituted in the ordinary pre-70 Judaean synagogue, nor is it probable that the priestly blessing was recited outside the Temple precincts in the pre-70 era.

According to Luke's description of Jesus' appearance in the Nazareth synagogue—and here it is immaterial whether what is reflected is, in fact, an early first-century Judaean setting or a late first-century Diaspora one—Jesus, upon concluding the haftarah, immediately sat down and preached, presumably while sitting near the lectern or table in the center of the synagogue hall.

Archeological remains from this early period, i.e., up to the mid-third century, appear to confirm this focus in the center of the hall. These synagogues often had a rectangular hall (Maʿoz Ḥayyim [Building I] or Delos), seats on all four sides (Gamla, Masada, and Dura), or, in the case of a monumental building, a *bima* in the center (Alexandria).[299]

A second stage in synagogue liturgy and architecture emerged in the course of the third century, when the earlier, almost exclusive Torah-reading focus was expanded to include other modes of worship. Evidence from rabbinic literature now begins to relate more and more to the prayer component in communal Jewish worship. To offer but one illustration of this shifting emphasis in rabbinic material: whereas early discussions of synagogue liturgy in tannaitic literature are found almost exclusively in Tractate Megillah, from the mid-third century onward such discussions are found to a great extent in Tractate Berakhot, which is devoted to issues of prayer.[300]

---

297. See below, Chap. 16.

298. Fleischer, *Hebrew Liturgical Poetry*, 133–36. See also idem, "Influence of Choral Elements," 18–48, where it is suggested that the two people on either side of the *ḥazzan* may have constituted the chorus (pp. 25–26).

299. On the basis of a preliminary report, it seems that the first stage (second century) of the Nevoraya building—a small rectangular room—had two platforms flanking its southern entrance. This would be exceptional.

300. Tractate Megillah in the *talmudim* has by no means been abandoned in this regard. Since many amoraic discussions elaborate or comment on mishnaic material, and most synagogue matters do, in fact, appear in Mishnah Megillah, it is only natural that many later traditions found their way into these tractates of the Yerushalmi and Bavli.

Archeologically, this new emphasis on prayer, and the need for a particular orientation toward Jerusalem in the 'Amidah prayer, finds expression in more elaborate synagogues oriented toward Jerusalem. Such an orientation is reflected, inter alia, in the facades of the Galilean buildings and the podiums of Khirbet Shemaʿ and Nevoraya.

A third and final stage in the evolution of the ancient synagogue's interior is clearly in evidence by the fourth century with the widespread introduction of a permanent Torah shrine on the Jerusalem wall of the synagogue's main hall. Several already existing synagogues now changed their mode of orientation dramatically: instead of doors in the direction of Jerusalem, as had been the case earlier, there was now a podium with either a niche or an apse in the Jerusalem wall. Moreover, at some point during this Byzantine era, a number of synagogues expanded their facilities, sometimes adopting a Christian basilical plan. Examples of such expansion are evident at Qatzrin, Ḥammat Tiberias (I), Maʿoz Ḥayyim, and Nevoraya.

How the nave itself was used in the synagogue setting is difficult to determine. It may well have been kept empty to allow for a shift of attention from one focus to another. This may well have been the case at Sardis, where, in addition to the *aediculae* in the eastern entrance, a stone table and some sort of additional installation (for a teacher?) were located in the nave. Thus, in the case of Sardis, it is doubtful whether ordinary members of the congregation occupied much, if any part, of the nave itself. Likewise, it is also difficult to imagine that the congregation occupied the central nave in synagogues having elaborate decorations of mosaic floors with intricate motifs, both ornate and symbolic, as are often found in Byzantine Palestine. Thus, it would appear that, in many cases, the seating of the congregation was confined, for the most part, to the side aisles.[301]

As might well be expected, liturgy and architecture went hand in hand in the synagogue of late antiquity to create a degree of architectural and liturgical balance. The

---

301. For very different reasons, the situation in many synagogues may have been similar to that described by Krautheimer (*Early Christian and Byzantine Architecture*, 159) with regard to the Hagia Sophia church: "However this revelation was reserved for the few admitted to the nave during services: the clergy led by the patriarch, and the Emperor accompanied by his court. The large mass of the faithful, gathered in aisles and galleries, saw only fragments of the building, just as the solemn celebration of the services was revealed to them only in fragments. It had long been liturgical custom in the Aegean coastlands to reserve the nave for the performance of the clergy. . . . The nave, then, was a stage on which the procession moved along a solemn path from the royal gate towards the solea, and along the solea into the *bima*. During much of the Mass, however, this stage remained empty." Yet, even here, there is no consensus with respect to the nave's usage in the church setting (Mathews, *Early Churches*, 124–25), and it may well be that different customs prevailed in different places.

The implication of such a limited seating arrangement in synagogues is enormous. Not many people could find a place on the stone benches, and even if mats and wooden benches were in the aisles, the number would not be large. We may be dealing with small communities, communities whose members did not always attend services, or a steady flow of people entering and leaving the synagogue (Tractate Soferim 10:6 [p. 217]). Finally, it is possible that most places had more than one synagogue (e.g., Barʿam) which has not yet been discovered.

building underwent a series of far-reaching changes. It acquired greater sanctity, and its liturgy developed, especially in the areas of prayer and *piyyut*. At the same time, it evolved a series of foci: the *bima* in the front of the hall, where the ark was located and the priests stood for the benediction, the place where the prayer leader stood, and a possible podium in the center or back of the hall. This range of foci gave expression to the various facets of the worship service, striking some sort of balance between various modes of worship while also emphasizing the corporate nature of the community.

The Torah-reading remained central. It was an activity conducted either on the platform at the end of the hall or in its center and was characterized by active participation of the congregation. The *ḥazzan* served not only as a prayer leader, but also as a surrogate for individuals unable to recite the prayers for themselves. He thus stood in the nave, on par with the congregation, yet close to the holy. In the part of the worship service which bore an entirely different character, the priests stood on the podium near the Torah ark, relatively removed from the congregation, and blessed the people in the name of God. Each of these varying modes found its particular setting within the synagogue building. No hierarchy governed these proceedings; no single set of divinely inspired individuals officiated. Whether during the Torah- and haftarah-readings, the recitation of the *targum*, sermon, prayer, *piyyut*, or priestly blessing, an ordinary Jew had the opportunity to actively participate in the synagogue ritual. The synagogue's often modest size as well as its multifocal liturgy articulated a message of inclusion and community.

ten THE COMMUNAL DIMENSION

T he synagogue was created by the local Jewish community in response to its need for a central institution which would provide it with a range of services. As a result, the synagogue became firmly rooted in Jewish communities of late antiquity as their communal institution par excellence. Synagogue officials, for the most part, do not appear to have been beholden to any outside authority.[1] The synagogue was referred to as a *bet 'am* ("house of a people"),[2] and it functioned in this capacity. The Mishnah views this communal dimension in the following fashion: "And what things belong to the town itself? For example, the plaza, the bath, the synagogue, the Torah chest, and [holy] books."[3]

COMMUNITY CONTROL

It was the townspeople or their chosen representatives who had ultimate authority in synagogue matters. Thus, in addressing the issue of whether or not to sell communal

---

1. On the relation of institutions such as the Patriarchate and the rabbinate to the synagogue, see below, Chaps. 12 and 13. On the organization of villages generally throughout the region at this time, see Graininger, "'Village Governernt,'" 179–95 and bibliography cited there.

2. B Shabbat 32a.

3. M Nedarim 5:5; see also B Betzah 39b. The communal dimension of the synagogue is also reflected in a later rabbinic interpretation of a Bet Hillel–Bet Shammai dispute; see T Tohorot 8:10 (p. 669).

property, the Mishnah states that it was the local population (בני העיר) that makes that decision, while the Tosefta (according to R. Judah) notes that appointed *parnasim* should act on the institution's behalf, but only after the local townspeople grant them the requisite authority.[4] In fact, the Yerushalmi makes it quite clear that synagogue officials were dependent upon the community at large: "The three [representatives] of the synagogue [act on behalf of] the [entire] synagogue; the seven [representatives] of the townspeople [act on behalf of] the [entire] town."[5] Thus, appointed synagogue officials had the full range of authority to act in matters pertaining to their institution; nevertheless, in the final analysis, they were only as strong as the power vested in them by the community. This point is clearly made by the Bavli in its discussion of the mishnah dealing with the sale of a synagogue or its holy objects. Rava notes that the restrictions recorded in this mishnah were in effect only when the seven town representatives acted on their own initiative. If, however, a decision had been made by the entire town (במעמד אנשי העיר), then any type of sale made by these representatives would be valid, even if the synagogue were to be converted into a tavern.[6]

The above traditions refer to the vast majority of congregations, those situated in rural as well as urban settings. However, we also read of synagogues that operated under the patronage of a wealthy individual, an oligarchy of wealthy members, or, as was sometimes the case in Babylonia, a rabbi.[7] In such instances, power and authority ipso facto became highly centralized. Whether these types of synagogues were primarily urban or rural, and how many did, in fact, operate in this latter fashion, is difficult to say.

The control exercised by the community included the hiring and firing of synagogue

---

4. M Megillah 3:1; T Megillah 2:12 (p. 351).

5. Y Megillah 3, 2, 74a. The existence of a body of seven at this time is clearly indicated by Josephus (*War* 2, 571). Moreover, if his descriptions in *Antiquities* 4, 214 and 287, are indeed anachronistic, then he may be alluding to such an institution there as well. According to one second-century tradition, three representatives of the congregation (שלשה בני הכנסת) had the authority to determine whether a maimed firstborn animal could be slaughtered; see M Bekhorot 5:5; T Bekhorot 3:25 (p. 538); B Bekhorot 36b. What the term בני הכנסת refers to here is unclear, but it may well be to some group other than a synagogue congregation. See also M Zavim 3:2.

6. B Megillah 26a-b; see also ibid., 27a. Attestation of extensive communal authority and responsibility occurs specifically in the Bavli. See above, Chap. 8, for a discussion of the synagogue in the Babylonian setting. The Toseftan tradition (Megillah 2:17 [p. 352]), in which R. El'azar bought a synagogue in pre-70 Jerusalem, is specifically noted in B Megillah 26a. Cf. above, Chap. 3.

A striking statement of the communal involvement of Jews throughout the Roman world is found in the biography of Alexander Severus in *Scriptores Historiae Augustae* (45, 6–7). Following Jewish and Christian practice, the emperor suggested that the names of candidates for Imperial appointments be announced beforehand in order to give everyone an opportunity to lodge a protest. See M. Stern, *Greek and Latin Authors*, II, no. 523.

7. B Megillah 26a-b. On synagogues associated with individuals, see below; there may have been an oligarchal setting at Ḥammat Tiberias. On "rabbinic" synagogues, see B Megillah 26a.

functionaries. One account notes that the synagogue community of Tarbanat[8] dismissed R. Simeon when the latter proved unwilling to comply with their requests: "The villagers said to him: 'Pause between your words [either when reading the Torah or rendering the *targum*], so that we may relate this to our children.'[9] He went and asked [the advice of] R. Ḥanina, who said to him: 'Even if they [threaten to] cut off your head, do not listen to them.' And he [R. Simeon] did not take heed [of the congregants' request], and they dismissed him from his position as *sofer*."[10]

Needless to say, such authority carried with it the responsibility of locating competent personnel, and such searches were undoubtedly a common occurrence. So, for example, the communities of Simonias and Bostra approached leading sages for help in this respect.[11] Around the turn of the third century, the former asked R. Judah I to find someone who could preach, judge, be a *ḥazzan* and teacher of children, and "do everything else for us."[12] The person recommended or appointed by R. Judah, Levi b. Sisi, made a somewhat less than memorable first impression. A similar request was made of R. Simeon b. Laqish in the third century while he was visiting Bostra.[13]

Given the centrality and importance of the synagogue, communities—or, in the case of large cities, individual congregations—would often judge themselves and others by how successful and impressive their respective institutions appeared. This sense of pride is reflected in an already noted exclamation made by R. Ḥanina bar Ḥama to R. Hoshaya while touring the synagogues of Lod: "How much [money] have my ancestors invested here [i.e., in these buildings]!" The response of R. Hoshaya is likewise of interest, reflecting his reservations regarding this "edifice complex": "How many souls have your ancestors lost here [by the wrong prioritization of values]? There is no one studying Torah!"[14]

---

8. Although at times disputed, it is generally agreed that Tarbanat was located on the border between the Lower Galilee and the Jezreel Valley, northwest of present-day ʿAfula, near Simonias (see below, note 11); see Press, *Topographical-Historical Encyclopaedia*, II, 380; S. Klein, "R. Simeon Sofer of Tarbanat," 96–99; idem, *Galilee*, 110; Avi-Yonah, *Gazetteer*, 99, 108; Reeg, *Ortsnamen*, 278–79. Other identifications include Tarichaeae (Horowitz, *Palestine and the Adjacent Countries*, I, 305) and Trachonitis (M. B. Schwartz, *Torah-Reading*, 288).

9. Alternatively: "so that they [i.e., our children] may recite this material to us."

10. Y Megillah 4, 5, 75b. The translation follows the traditional commentators. Sokoloff (*Dictionary*, 488), on the other hand, suggests that the reference here is specifically to the reading of the Decalogue.

11. *Simonias*: located in the southwestern sector of the Lower Galilee, on the periphery of the Jezreel Valley to the west of ʿAfula. See Neubauer, *Géographie*, 189; Möller and Schmitt, *Siedlungen Palästinas*, 174–75; Reeg, *Ortsnamen*, 456–57 and bibliography therein. See also Z. Safrai, *Pirqei Galilee*, 55–57. *Bostra*: Bowersock, *Roman Arabia*, passim; Kindler, *Coinage of Bostra*, 6–11.

12. Y Yevamot 12, 6, 13a; Genesis Rabbah 81:2 (pp. 969–72).

13. Y Sheviʿit 6, 1, 36d; Deuteronomy Rabbah, Vaʾethanan (p. 60). One can thus understand the irritation—if not outright anger—felt by the community of Cilicia, who saw their synagogue officials dismissed by the Patriarch's emissary, Joseph, in the early fourth century; see Epiphanius, *Panarion* 30, 11, 4.

14. Y Sheqalim 5, 6, 49a. On Lod and its Jewish community in this period, see J. J. Schwartz, *Lod (Lydda)*, 101–20.

Public buildings and their functionaries were often a cause of competition between neighboring communities, and at times envy motivated one to imitate and outdo the achievements of the other. Although clearly articulated only in a late midrash, such competition between communities is so well documented for the Roman world generally and the Galilee in particular as to imbue this source with a substantial degree of credibility. "[Regarding] a small town in Israel, they [the townspeople] built for themselves a synagogue and academy and hired a sage and instructors for their children. When a nearby town saw [this], it [also] built a synagogue and academy, and likewise hired teachers for their children." [15]

The local community was also responsible for the synagogue's ongoing maintenance. Salaries were undoubtedly a major expense. Some synagogue functions were covered by wealthy laymen or by officials such as the archisynagogue, presbyter, and archon. In all probability, these people as well as the ten *batlanim* (whatever their function) were not remunerated for their services.[16] Many individual participants in synagogue worship, such as prayer leaders, Torah readers, liturgical poets, and preachers, may have performed these services gratis, but of this we cannot be sure. Nevertheless, other functionaries—teachers (סופרים), *ḥazzanim*, *shamashim*, and *meturgemanim*—clearly received compensation, no matter how minimal.[17]

Construction or repair of the synagogue building was likewise a communal responsibility. The Tosefta makes it patently clear that the community at large could obligate its members in this regard: "Members of a town [can] force one another [כופין] to build themselves a synagogue and to purchase a Torah scroll and [books of the] Prophets." [18]

For this period we are fortunate to have a number of epigraphical sources which contribute immensely to an appreciation of this communal dimension. Almost all relevant epigraphical evidence stems from Byzantine Palestine.[19] Many of these inscriptions clearly attest to cases in which the community as a whole was acknowledged for its contributions to and support of the synagogue. All this, it should be noted, stands in sharp

---

15. Seder Eliyahu Rabbah 11 (pp. 54–55). Competition between neighboring cities is attested in Josephus, *Life* 35–39; Lamentations Rabbah 1:17 (p. 46a).

16. See below, Chap. 11.

17. See, for example, B Shabbat 56a; Midrash Hagadol, Exodus 21:1 (p. 454). For one of the rare references to a *shamash*, see Y Maʿaser Sheni 5, 2, 56a. See also Targum Pseudo-Jonathan of Gen. 25:27, referring to Jacob functioning in such a capacity in a school. An inscription from the Bet Sheʿarim synagogue may indeed refer to such a position; see Schwabe and Lifshitz, *Beth Sheʿarim*, II, no. 205; Roth-Gerson, *Greek Inscriptions*, 141. On the שומר (guard) with regard to a *bet midrash* setting, see B Yoma 35b (= Yalqut Shimʿoni, Genesis, 145 [p. 753].

18. T Bava Metzia 11:23 (p. 125); and Lieberman, *TK*, IX, 320–21. For a suggestion that a communal effort on the part of Sardis Jewry was responsible for the acquisition and remodeling of the local synagogue in the third and fourth centuries, see Bonz, "Differing Approaches to Religious Benefaction," 139–54.

19. Naveh, *On Stone and Mosaic*, 4–6.

contrast to the mode of church building in Byzantine Palestine, where church authorities (bishop, deacon, or others) were almost exclusively named.[20]

Jericho:
May they be remembered for good. May their memory be for good, the entire holy congregation, the old and the young, whom the King of the Universe has helped, for they have contributed to and made this mosaic.[21]

Bet Shean:
May they be remembered for good, all members of this holy association, who have supported the repair of the holy place and its well-being. May they be blessed. Amen . . . in great kindness and peace.[22]

Sometimes an inscription was intended not only to thank and bless members for past good deeds, but also to encourage them to do so in the future:

Hammat Tiberias:
May peace be with all those who have contributed in this holy place, and who will continue to give charity in the future. May that person be blessed. Amen, Amen, Selah. And to me, Amen.[23]

Almost without exception, these communal inscriptions were written in Aramaic, while wealthy donors were recorded almost exclusively in Greek.[24] Notable exceptions to this rule have been found at Na'aran and Hammat Gader, where Aramaic inscriptions cite individual donors, and at Caesarea, where a Greek inscription refers to the community at large.[25]

On occasion, an inscription offers a general blessing for the entire community:

Jericho:
May He who knows their names, [as well as] their children's and members of their house-

20. Di Segni, "Involvement," 312–17.

21. Naveh, *On Stone and Mosaic*, no. 69. Additional examples may be found at Susiya, perhaps Hammat Tiberias, and especially Huseifa on the Carmel. See ibid., nos. 76, 24, and 39, respectively.

22. Ibid., no. 46, and comments thereon, p. 10.

23. Ibid., no. 26. Cf. a similar formulation from the Na'aran synagogue, in ibid., no. 64.

24. On this and other distinctions between the Aramaic and Greek inscriptions, see Roth-Gerson, *Greek Inscriptions*, 147–52. The Hammat Tiberias synagogue provides us with an example of this contrast. Whereas the above-quoted Aramaic inscription thanks the entire congregation of this "holy place," a Greek inscription acknowledges a prominent individual for his contribution to this "holy place": "May Profutoros the *mizoteros* [the exact meaning of this term is unclear, but it is probably the title of an official] be remembered for good and for blessing, he who made this stoa of the holy place. May he be blessed. Amen. Shalom (ibid., no. 17 and p. 169)." The one Greek inscription which refers to the contribution of the people at large comes from Caesarea.

25. Ibid., no. 25.

holds, write them in the Book of Life together with all the righteous. All the people of Israel are brethren [חברין]. Peace. Amen.[26]

In some places, synagogue inscriptions indicate what matters are of primary concern to the congregation as a whole. The halakhic orientation and focus of the Reḥov community, for example, are reflected in its synagogue's inscriptions. Preliminary notices of as yet unpublished remains indicate that fragmentary blessings and prayers were written on the building's walls and columns. The monumental halakhic inscription placed near the entrance to the synagogue's main hall—a meticulous listing of forbidden foods and a delineation of the boundaries of Palestine within which such laws applied—is a powerful statement by the community of the importance it attached to the observance of sabbatical-year laws.[27]

A second example of concerns particular to a given community is reflected in a synagogue inscription from 'En Gedi (fig. 82). Located in the western aisle of the hall and written in Aramaic, the inscription addresses a number of important communal issues: "he who causes dissension within the community, or speaks slanderously about his friend to the gentiles, or steals something from his friend, or reveals the secret of the community to the gentiles—He, whose eyes observe the entire world and who sees hidden things, will turn His face to this fellow and his offspring and will uproot them from under the heavens. And all the people said: 'Amen, Amen, Selah.'"[28] Thus, the 'En Gedi community spelled out on the synagogue floor, for all to see and ponder, what kinds of behavior it found objectionable. The exact nature of the community's secret remains unknown. Theories abound, from the political and economic to the communal and religious, yet the secret remains to this day.[29] Here, as in the above examples, synagogue inscriptions were a main vehicle for expressing communal concerns and interests.[30]

In order to cover all the expenses of the institution, congregational donations were necessary, although far from sufficient. Larger individual donations were also required, and we are well informed about such contributions from the epigraphical evidence. Synagogue inscriptions mention numerous individuals who made donations for various parts of synagogue buildings:[31] lintels (Bar'am, 'Alma, Ḥammat Tiberias, Kokhav Hayarden), columns (Dabbura, Khirbet Yitzḥaqia, Bet Guvrin, Capernaum), portals (Rama, Dab-

---

26. Naveh, *On Stone and Mosaic*, no. 69. On the expression כל ישראל חברים, see Y Ḥagigah 3, 6, 79d.

27. Sussmann, "Inscription," 146–53.

28. L. Levine, "Inscription in the 'En Gedi Synagogue," 140–45.

29. For a summary of the various interpretations of the "secret of the community," see ibid.

30. For other examples of a synagogue inscription which served as a pronouncement of communal decisions, see below.

31. The following list is based on the epigraphical collections of Frey, Lifshitz, Naveh, and Roth-Gerson. On the issue of euergetism in later antiquity, see the cautious remarks of Rogers, "Gift and Society," 188–99.

82. 'En Gedi synagogue inscription.

bura, 'Ibilin), fountains or water basins (Philadelphia in Lydia, and Sidé—both in Asia Minor), a stoa or porticoes (Caesarea, Ḥammat Tiberias, Chorazim, Athribis, Xenephyris in Egypt, Phocaea), stairs (Chorazim), a Torah ark (Ostia, Ḥorvat 'Ammudim), perhaps a Torah shrine (Naveh), wall revetments and paintings (Tralles in Caria, Acmonia, Syracuse), chancel screens (Smyrna), mosaic floors or parts thereof (Sepphoris, Caesarea, Ḥorvat 'Ammudim, Apamea, Ḥammat Gader, Bet Shean, Maʿon [Nirim], Jericho, Susiya, Gaza, Smyrna, Emesa), a marble pavement (Sidé), a platform (Tralles), a vestibule (Mantinea), additional rooms, including a *triclinium* (Jerusalem, Caesarea, Naro, Stobi), a roof (Acmonia), and, finally, a *bima* and lamp (Pergamum).

In some cases, one or more wealthy individuals bore the entire expense of a building, as seems to have been the case in Jerusalem, Dura, Taphos (Syria), Teos, Phocaea, and Golgoi (Cyprus). At times, a community was spared much of the burden of building and maintaining a synagogue if it was part of a wealthy individual's house or building complex. This may have been the case with the Leontis complex in Bet Shean.[32] Alter-

32. Z. Ilan, *Ancient Synagogues*, 176.

natively, a wealthy person might donate a floor or building for use by the community, which would then bear the maintenance expenses. Such seems to have been the arrangement between Claudius Tiberius Polycharmos and the Stobi community.[33] In fact, the talmudic reference to "a synagogue of an individual" (בית הכנסת של יחיד) probably refers to this phenomenon.[34]

Rabbinic sources, too, have preserved a series of references to synagogue gifts. On several occasions, specific individuals are mentioned, such as the emperor Antoninus, who reputedly contributed a menorah, and an Arab merchant (?), es-Shazrak, who donated candles.[35] Luke's account of a Roman centurion who built a synagogue is well known.[36] Mention is also made of individual contributions involving a Torah chest and mantles, a menorah and candles, as well as a beam donated by a gentile.[37] It is difficult to say whether some of the above are indeed historical instances or whether they are fictitious examples invoked as part of a halakhic discussion.

Judging by the epigraphical remains, it would seem that wealthy and acculturated community members were responsible for the physical appearance of the synagogues in Ḥammat Tiberias, Sepphoris, Caesarea, Bet Shean, and other cities.[38] Greek was the predominant language used in these settings, as were the Greek names of the benefactors.[39] Even the related artistic motifs are best explained as reflecting the tastes and cultural proclivities (and perhaps religious tendencies) of the upper classes.[40] Not only was this stratum of society in large part responsible for most urban synagogue buildings, but it is more than likely that these people may also have had a decisive say in synagogue affairs in such communities.

Communal control of the synagogue is undoubtedly a crucial factor in explaining the wide diversity among synagogue buildings. Different sizes and shapes are, of course, to be expected and are directly related to the size of a community and to the physical location of the building. However, the shape and plan of a building are the function of other factors as well, such as local or regional traditions, or the desire to create a certain type of

---

33. Hengel, "Synagogeninschrift von Stobi," 159ff.; see above, Chap. 8.

34. Y Megillah 3, 1, 73b. See also T Megillah 2:17 (p. 352); and, for a specific example of this phenomenon, B Megillah 26a.

35. Y Megillah 3, 2, 74a; B ʿArakhin 6b. Antoninus is generally identified with Caracalla (211-17 C.E.); see Alon, *Jews in Their Land*, II, 682; Avi-Yonah, *Jews of Palestine*, 39-42; L. Levine, "Age of R. Judah I," 98-100; Oppenheimer, *Galilee*, 63-66. See also M. Stern, *Greek and Latin Authors*, II, 626-27.

36. Luke 7:5.

37. T Megillah 2:13-16 (pp. 351-52). See also B ʿArakhin 6b.

38. See Roth-Gerson, *Greek Inscriptions*, passim.

39. A corrective to Roth-Gerson's theory that this practice was basically linguistic, i.e., in Greek as against Semitic inscriptions, is that it may also be related to the urban-rural dichotomy. In truth, the correlation of Greek inscriptions to urban settings is predictably quite high. See ibid., 147-62; and idem, "Similarities and Differences," 133-46; as well as below, Chap. 11.

40. See J. Baumgarten, "Art in the Synagogue," 204-6; L. Levine, *Rabbinic Class*, 178-81.

worship experience.[41] While this last consideration is difficult to substantiate, it is equally hard to imagine that two synagogues (e.g., Meiron and Khirbet Shemaʿ), built at the same time and in the same area but according to two very different models, did not represent, inter alia, different notions of what a prayer hall should look like, how it should function, and what sort of ambience ought to be created therein. Similar thoughts arise when comparing two very disparate third-century Diaspora buildings, Sardis in the West and Dura Europos in the East. In this last instance it is clear that the general social and cultural matrix of each of these communities constituted a powerful influence in determining the size and interior arrangement of the buildings.

As noted above,[42] artistic tastes among various communities differed significantly, and this is clearly reflected in their preferences for the types of decorations (geometric, floral, figural), designs, and motifs they each used. Did they use Jewish symbols? If so, which? And where were they placed? Are biblical scenes or figures represented, or was the popular zodiac motif with Helios in the center used? Or were both of these elements perhaps placed side by side, as at Bet Alpha and Sepphoris? Were the choices of these communities based on economic considerations, aesthetic appeal, or, perhaps, religious proclivities? Whatever the case, ultimately each community shaped its own synagogue, and even where certain regional "models" existed (as, for example, with respect to the Galilean-type synagogue), there still remained a wide range of choices to make in the process of adoption and implementation.[43]

As already noted, epigraphical evidence attests to the fact that matters of fundamental concern to communities often found expression in prominently placed inscriptions in the synagogue buildings.[44] The agreement between Claudius Tiberius Polycharmos and the Stobi community over use of the synagogue building was inscribed on a column; the halakhic rules of the sabbatical year were written on a mosaic floor located just inside the main entrance of the Reḥov synagogue and again on one of its columns; and injunctions relating to the ʿEn Gedi community, along with the curses to be invoked if the injunctions were ignored, were written in a mosaic inscription prominently set in the forecourt of the synagogue building.[45]

At the outset of the chapter, we noted that there is no evidence during this period to suggest that anyone besides the local community determined the nature of the local syna-

---

41. As is the case in the Golan, where late antique synagogues are oriented either to the south or west, or in southern Judea, where the entrances to synagogues face east, following the Temple model. See T Megillah 3:22 (p. 360).

42. See above, Chap. 7.

43. Compare, for example, the degrees and types of decoration in Capernaum and Chorazim on the one hand and Meiron and Barʿam on the other.

44. See below, Chap. 9.

45. *Stobi:* Hengel, "Synagogeninschrift von Stobi," 145ff. *Reḥov:* Vitto, "Synagogue of Rehob," 90–94. *ʿEn Gedi:* L. Levine, "Inscription in the ʿEn Gedi Synagogue," 140–45.

gogue. Neither during the time of the Temple nor afterward do we have any hint of an office, person, or institution exercising such authority. At times, the sages suggested certain practices, but the final decision to implement them in a given community was rarely, if ever, in their hands.[46]

INSTITUTIONAL FUNCTIONS

The destruction of the Temple in 70 had little effect on the synagogue's range of activities[47] as the focal communal institution within the Jewish community.[48] Much like certain pagan temples and many churches in late antiquity, the synagogue functioned as a core institution.[49] Because of the relative paucity of evidence for the pre-70 era, we are much better informed about late antiquity, owing largely to the abundance of information culled from rabbinic literature and archeological data. Although the material preserved is rather uneven, with references to primary schools far outweighing references to other functions, there is nevertheless enough material in these sources to clearly indicate the wide variety of activities that might have taken place in any given synagogue. The needs of each community were many; on several occasions, rabbinic sources list those institutions considered essential to communal life: "A sage may not live in any town which does not have ten things. They are: a penal court [בין דין מכין ועונשין], a charity fund collected by two and distributed by three, a synagogue, a bathhouse, a privy, a doctor, a bloodletter, a scribe, a butcher, and a teacher of children."[50] While this tradition appears to differentiate between the synagogue and other communal services, there can be little question that many of the above-named functions were part of the synagogue's agenda. Witness, for example, the sources referred to above which describe the tasks of a synagogue appointee; such a person was to function as a preacher, judge, *ḥazzan*, teacher, and one who "does everything else for us."[51] Let us review the evidence for the various activities which are attested for the synagogues of late antiquity.

---

46. See below, Chap. 13.

47. For the functions of the pre-70 synagogue, see above, Chap. 5. Though mention will be made from time to time of the earlier material, the focus of this chapter is late antiquity. Chapter 16 is devoted to the synagogue as a worship setting.

48. Baron, *Social and Religious History of the Jews*, II, 280–86; S. Safrai, "Synagogue," 942–44; and esp. Z. Safrai, "Communal Functions," 181–204. The synagogue continued to function as the center of communal activities in the Middle Ages as well, see Goitein, *Mediterranean Society*, II, 155–70; Assis, "Synagogues in Medieval Spain," 23–26; Ben Sasson, "Appeal," 327–31.

49. MacMullen, *Paganism*, 10–12, 34–42.

50. B Sanhedrin 17b. See also Y Qiddushin 4, 12, 66b; Pirqei Derekh Eretz 1 (in Seder Eliyahu Zuta 1 [p. 13]).

51. See above, notes 12 and 13.

Meeting Place

The locus classicus for the synagogue as a forum for discussing community issues is, of course, Josephus' account of the deliberations in the Tiberias *proseuche* over whether or not to join the revolt in 66–67.[52] Another kind of meeting in the synagogue, though under very different circumstances, occurred in the early second century in Lydda. Bones from the nearby village of Kefar Tavi[53] were brought into the synagogue to determine whether they were pure or impure. As a decision in this matter depended on whether they belonged to one or more bodies, a number of doctors accordingly convened there to render an opinion.[54]

The third-century R. Yoḥanan, as quoted by R. Jacob b. Idi, is quite explicit in his claim that communal matters should be discussed in the synagogue, even on the Sabbath: "We determine matters of life and death and matters of common concern on the Sabbath, and we go to the synagogue to determine matters of public concern on the Sabbath."[55]

At times communal issues were discussed via the sermon delivered in the synagogue on the Sabbath. The question was posed by the preacher, at times forcefully and in a transparently tendentious way, thereby engendering on occasion extreme responses of either enthusiastic support or heated opposition. Since the traditions preserved in this regard are found in rabbinic sources, it is only natural that the spokespersons mentioned are rabbis, or those closely identified with them, and that the issues discussed involved the sages. In one instance, Jacob of Kefar Nevoraya delivered a homily at the Caesarean Maradata synagogue, inveighing against the wealthy (and indirectly against the Patriarch who appointed them) as unacceptable choices for judicial posts. Not unexpectedly, his words were enthusiastically received (וקילסוהו) by the sages present.[56]

In another instance, at the Maʿon synagogue near Tiberias, Yosi of Maʿon castigated the Patriarch (*Nasi*) in a public sermon because of a taxation policy which effectively reduced any support which the sages might have expected to receive from the people. The Patriarch's angry reaction to this harangue was predictable; Yosi fled the city in fear of a reprisal, and rabbinic mediation was invoked to try and resolve the crisis.[57] It is impossible to

---

52. See above, Chap. 3.

53. On the location of this village east of Lydda, see T Maʿaser Sheni 5:16 (p. 271); Neeman, *Encyclopedia*, II, 44.

54. T Oholot 4:2 (p. 600); Y Berakhot 1, 2, 3a; B Nazir 52a. See also Ginzberg, *Commentary*, I, 86–87.

55. B Shabbat 150a; see also B Ketubot 5a, with some variations.

56. Midrash on Samuel 7:10 (p. 34b); Y Bikkurim 3, 3, 65d.

57. Y Sanhedrin 2, 6, 20c–d; Genesis Rabbah 80:1 (pp. 950–53). Resh Laqish also delivered a harsh attack on the *Nasi*, which likewise evoked a sharp response. However, it is not stated in what context this statement was made; see Y Sanhedrin 2, 1, 19d–20a; Y Horayot 3, 2, 47a; Midrash on Samuel 7:5 (p. 34b). See also B Taʿanit 24a; as well as the remarks in Herr, "Synagogues and Theatres," 105–19.

assess how common this type of incident was; what is of greater significance, however, is that such political issues were raised for public discussion within the synagogue setting.[58]

We have already noted several rabbinic traditions which highlight the fact that the synagogue in Palestine served as a setting for discussion of serious communal matters. Following the Bar-Kokhba revolt and subsequent persecutions, an attempt was made by Hananiah, nephew of R. Joshua b. Hanania, to assert Babylonian religious supremacy over Palestine by proclaiming the calendar there (i.e., New Moons and leap years). The challenge was met by the Patriarch R. Simeon b. Gamaliel, who dispatched two Palestinian sages to Babylonia.[59] According to the Babylonian tradition, the public confrontation between these Palestinian representatives and Hanania took place in the academy, while in the Palestinian account the setting was the synagogue following the Torah-reading on the Sabbath, with the community in attendance. The historical veracity of these accounts is not of concern to us here; what is of interest is the venue depicted in each case. For those living in Palestine, the synagogue was the natural and recognized setting for such a gathering.[60]

Moreover, as we have seen, various professional and social groups held regular meetings in the synagogue in the pre-70 period.[61] The recently found Aphrodisias inscription attests to the existence of a benevolent society (*dekany*) which seems to have provided food for the poor and which was undoubtedly affiliated in some way with the local synagogue.[62] Instances are noted in which rabbis gathered for study in or near synagogues,[63] although generally they seem to have preferred their academies.

Public communal acts were invariably held in a synagogue setting. Not only were the declarations of the Cyrenian community to honor certain individuals publicly carried out in gatherings at the synagogue, but a stele honoring these people was erected on the

---

58. Interestingly, in matters of life and death or in discussions of important political issues (presumably involving Jews), some sages permitted attendance of theaters and stadiums, where such decisions were being made. See T ʿAvodah Zarah 2:7 (p. 462); B Shabbat 150a; B Ketubot 5a.

59. Y Sanhedrin 1, 19a; Y Nedarim 6, 40a; B Berakhot 63a-b.

60. Gafni, "Synagogues in Talmudic Babylonia," 226–27.

61. See above, Chap. 5. For example, burial and other societies may have met there, as was common in pagan and Christian settings of later antiquity; see, for example, Tcherikover et al., *CPJ*, I, no. 138; C. Roberts et al., "Gild of Zeus," 75ff.; Cameron, *Later Roman Empire*, 126–27; Herrin, "Ideals of Charity," 151–64. See also Malherbe, *Social Aspects*, 94ff.; Meeks, *First Urban Christians*, 109.

62. Reynolds and Tannenbaum, *Jews and God-Fearers*, 28–38. See also Rajak, "Jewish Community," 20–21.

An inscription found in the Bet Sheʿarim synagogue reads as follows: "Of R. Samuel, who wraps [in shrouds?] and Judah who lays to rest"; see Schwabe and Lifshitz, *Bet Sheʿarim*, II, 90–91. That such functionaries existed is not surprising, surely not in a major necropolis such as Bet Sheʿarim. The fact, however, that such people were noted in inscriptions found in the local synagogue may possibly indicate that meetings pertaining to their work were held there.

63. See, for example, Genesis Rabbah 33:3 (p. 305).

premises.[64] Similarly, epigraphical evidence from several Crimean synagogues refers to a public declaration of manumission being made in a synagogue setting, in one case with the actual involvement of the congregation per se as a signatory.[65]

Evidence regarding meals in synagogues has accumulated over the years, and they can now be regarded as a fairly ubiquitous feature of synagogue life in late antiquity. What blurred the issue at first was an often quoted rabbinic prohibition: "There is to be no eating, drinking, or sleeping in the synagogue."[66] Other sources as well appear to make a very clear distinction (perhaps polemically) between attending the synagogue on the one hand and eating and drinking on the other.[67]

Rabbinic sources themselves appear to offer contradictory evidence. It is clearly stated that either religious associations (חבורות מצווה) or the community at large held festive meals on synagogue premises.[68] Moreover, as noted above, guests staying at the synagogue hostel would obviously eat, drink, and sleep there, with rabbinic acquiescence.[69] A number of traditions tell of rabbis as well as priests who ate in the synagogue, and additions to the grace after meals were made on their behalf.[70]

One tradition speaks of a company of servants who would dine each Friday evening in the synagogue.[71] Meals were also held there just prior to a public fast. Before the Ninth of Av, the day marking the destruction of the two Temples, there appears to have been a custom among some Jews to eat (even to excess) in synagogues and academies and then proceed to recite the book of Lamentations and principal dirges prescribed for the occasion.[72] The ubiquitousness of the above kinds of meals during the year necessitated a careful search for leaven in the synagogues and academies before the Passover holiday.[73]

Archeological evidence in this regard, though limited, is likewise unequivocal. A Jewish dining club, in all likelihood functioning in a *proseuche* setting, is known from Hellenistic Egypt.[74] Inscriptions from synagogues at Caesarea, Qatzrin (Golan), and Stobi

---

64. See above, Chap. 4.

65. Levinskaya, *Acts in Its Diaspora Setting*, 231–42.

66. T Megillah 2:18 (p. 353); B Megillah 28a–b; and above, Chap. 6.

67. PRK 28:1 (p. 423); Seder Eliyahu Rabbah 1 (p. 4).

68. Y Mo'ed Qatan 2, 3, 81b; Y Sanhedrin 8, 2, 26a–b. Moreover, rabbinic sources make it eminently clear that academies as well may have had such dining areas, referred to as ריבעה; see Y Shabbat 4, 2, 7a; 20, 1, 17c; and comments in J. N. Epstein, *Studies in Talmudic Literature*, II/2, 870–71; Lieberman, *Ha-yerushalmi Kiphshuto*, 213; idem, *Studies in Palestinian Talmudic Literature*, 214; Meitlis, "Significance of the 'Revua,'" 465–66.

69. B Pesaḥim 100b–101a.

70. Y Berakhot 2,5d, where it is stated that sages ate in the upper chamber, or balcony, of a synagogue (עליה); cf. Ginzberg, *Commentary*, I, 412–13. On priests, see Y Berakhot 3, 6a; Y Nazir 7, 1, 56a.

71. Genesis Rabbah 65:15 (pp. 728–29).

72. Lamentations Rabbah, Proem 17 (p. 14).

73. Y Pesaḥim 1, 1, 27b.

74. Tcherikover et al., *CPJ*, I, no. 139.

83. Aramaic inscription from Qatzrin: "[U]zi made this *revuʿa.*"

record the presence of a *triclinium* or *revuʿa* (fig. 83);[75] the building at Ostia had a kitchen on its premises with an adjoining hall perhaps used, inter alia, for banqueting.[76] Finally, an inscription from Susiya in southern Judaea tells of a major donation to the local synagogue, which was made at a banquet quite possibly held on the synagogue premises.[77]

The above-noted evidence makes it quite clear that meals were a familiar feature of ancient synagogue life. This was true of the Diaspora as well as Palestine, and throughout all of late antiquity. Chrysostom, too, seems to have referred to such repasts in fourth-century Antioch when taking note of synagogues with their "table of demons."[78]

There are several possible interpretations regarding the rabbinic statements noted at the outset which prohibited such activity in the synagogue. These declarations either opposed prevalent practices (apparently unsuccessfully) or were directed to prohibit eating in specific areas within the synagogue building, such as the prayer hall. However, there is no indication of such specificity in these statements, and the rabbinic prohibition in the Tosefta passage is absolute and unreserved. Thus, the former alternative appears far more likely.

Court

The right of adjudication was of paramount importance for every Jewish community because it provided the basis for communal discipline and self-regulation. This

---

75. *Caesarea:* Roth-Gerson, *Greek Inscriptions*, 115–17. *Qatzrin:* Naveh, *On Stone and Mosaic*, 147; Urman, "Jewish Inscriptions," 533–34; idem, "Public Structures," 469–73. *Stobi:* Hengel, "Synagogeninschrift von Stobi," 165–69. On the term רבע in Nabatean contexts, see Urman, "Jewish Inscriptions," 534–35.

76. Squarciapino, *Synagogue of Ostia*, 24; Fine and Della Pergola, "Synagogue of Ostia," 43, 45; White, *Building God's House*, 69. On dining facilities in pagan and Christian contexts, see ibid., 40–41, 109, 122.

77. Naveh, *On Stone and Mosaic*, no. 75, 115–16. Perhaps relevant to this context is the parchment fragment discovered in the streetfill near the Dura synagogue containing a Hebrew text of *birkat hamazon* (the grace after meals). Whether this text was used for synagogue meals or for instruction in a local school (or perhaps for some other purpose) remains unknown. See Kraeling, *Dura: Synagogue*, 259.

78. *Homily* 1 (*PG* 48, 854).

is already attested for the Diaspora in several edicts relating to the first-century B.C.E. Sardis community.[79] In one of the edicts, the place of adjudication referred to is clearly the local *proseuche*. The holding of court proceedings within the synagogue in Judaea in the first century C.E. is confirmed by a number of New Testament references.[80]

With regard to late antiquity, both Epiphanius and rabbinic literature note that the synagogue served as a place for administering punishment, particularly flogging, and the *ḥazzan* is named as the official who carried this out.[81] A later source interprets the titles "judges and officers" in Deut. 16:18 as referring to judges and *ḥazzanim* in one place,[82] while in another it notes the judges' responsibility for the salary of the *ḥazzanim*.[83] The Yerushalmi states that R. Abbahu was the sole judge (and not part of the usual tribunal of three) in a court gathering convened in the Maradata synagogue of Caesarea.[84]

The status of Jewish communal courts, many, if not most, of which met in the synagogue of late antiquity, is difficult to assess, especially after 212, when Jews throughout the Empire were granted Roman citizenship.[85] In fact, the authority of these synagogue-based courts may have been anchored in moral, religious, and social suasion alone, which in village settings and even in urban communities was undoubtedly a powerful force. In many cities, particularly in Palestine, a number of court settings were available, of the municipal, rabbinic, Roman, and Patriarchal variety,[86] but we do not know which of these courts met in the synagogue. The Roman courts certainly did not, but those which included rabbinic participation often did.[87] The lack of a binding authority in many of these non-Roman judicial settings is reflected in an account of Tamar, whose case was adjudicated by three Tiberian rabbis. Dissatisfied with their decision, Tamar appealed to the Roman court in Caesarea. The three rabbis then approached their Caesarean colleague, R. Abbahu, to intercede, hoping to have the case dismissed or the appeal rejected. However, R. Abbahu failed in his efforts to persuade Tamar to agree.[88] The undermining effects on the Jewish court system of such appeals to Roman authorities can well be imagined.

Another kind of legal procedure which may have been held on synagogue premises

---

79. *Antiquities* 14, 235 and 260. This right was more fully spelled out in the latter edict (260), although it is implicit in the former (235) as well.

80. Matt. 10:7; Acts 22:19.

81. Epiphanius, *Panarion* 30, 11; M Makkot 3:12.

82. Midrash Hagadol, Deuteronomy 16:18 (p. 371).

83. Ibid., Exodus 21:1 (p. 454); and, indirectly, B Shabbat 56a.

84. Y Sanhedrin 1, 1, 18a. Cf. also Y Bikkurim 1, 4, 64a.

85. Juster, *Juifs*, II, 149ff.; Goodman, *State and Society*, 155–71.

86. Alon, *Jews, Judaism and the Classical World*, 385ff. Gafni has suggested that a rather unique situation existed in Sassanian Babylonia, i.e., that many court proceedings seem to have taken place in rabbinic academies; see his "Court Cases," 23–40.

87. On rabbis adjudicating in synagogues, see below, Chap. 13.

88. Y Megillah 3, 2, 74a.

involved the manumission of slaves. Such declarations, as noted above, are recorded for the communities of first-century c.e. Crimea.[89]

Charity

Both Jewish and non-Jewish sources attest to the fact that the Jewish communities of late antiquity had spawned a rather highly developed social welfare system. Rabbinic literature contains a plethora of traditions indicating a range of charities for the needy, the existence of officials charged with such responsibilities, and a system of taxation for such purposes.[90] The emperor Julian likewise took note of the Jewish community's care for its own. In complaining about pagan society's lack of attention to its needy, he stated: "For it is disgraceful that, when no Jew ever has to beg, and the impious Galileans [i.e., Christians] support not only their own poor but ours as well, all men see that our people lack aid from us."[91]

Charity was pledged and then given within the synagogue setting, and the former was often (if not regularly) carried out on the Sabbath. Various sources note this already in the first century, and even though some rabbis may have had reservations regarding certain situations, by late antiquity it had become an activity that was taken for granted.[92] The primary donation was aid for the poor (food and clothing), although there was also a matter of community dues, such as teachers' salaries.[93]

It appears that these communal funds were, in many—if not most—cases, kept on synagogue premises.[94] In a number of excavations, large caches of coins were recovered, which were probably designated, at least in part, for such purposes.[95] The sacred funds

89. See above, note 65; and Chap. 4.

90. See, inter alia, M Peah 8:7; T Peah 4:8–21 (pp. 57–61); T Demai 3:16–17 (pp. 77–78); Y Peah 8, 7, 21a; Y Demai 3, 1, 23b; Y Bava Batra 1, 6, 12d; B Bava Batra 8a–11a. See also Baron, *Jewish Community*, I, 131–32; L. Levine, *Rabbinic Class*, 162–67; Z. Safrai, *Jewish Community*, 62–76.

91. Julian, *Epistle* 22, 430D. While largely accurate, such care was not always forthcoming from the Jewish community, as is attested by a number of second-century Roman writers; see M. Stern, *Greek and Latin Authors*, I, no. 246; II, nos. 299, 395. On charity within the Byzantine church, see Herrin, "Ideals of Charity," 151–64.

92. *First century:* Matt. 6:2; T Shabbat 16:22 (p. 79); and above, Chap. 5. *Rabbinic reservations:* T Shabbat, 16:22 (p. 79); T Terumot 1:10 (p. 109) and parallels; and comments in Lieberman *TK*, I, 301, with respect to guardians donating the monies of orphans on the Sabbath. *Accepted activities:* B Shabbat 150a; B Ketubot 5a, where a synagogue venue is undoubtedly intended.

93. M Peah 8:7–8; T Peah 4:9 (p. 57); Y Peah 8, 7, 21a.

94. On communal funds deposited earlier in the Jerusalem Temple, see M Sheqalim 3–4; Josephus, *War* 2, 175; I Macc. 1:21–24; II Macc. 5:21. On pagan temples serving in such a capacity, see Thucydides, *Peloponnesian War* 1, 141; Stambaugh, "Functions of Roman Temples," 586.

95. So, for example, at Ḥammat Tiberias—see Dothan, *Hammath Tiberias*, 31; at Bet Alpha—see Sukenik, *Ancient Synagogues*, 13; at Merot—see Z. Ilan, "Synagogue and Beth Midrash of Meroth," 30–31. To date, some fourteen caches have been found in synagogue remains from Roman-Byzantine Palestine.

kept by Jews of Asia Minor in their synagogue halls or banquet rooms also may have been intended for charitable purposes, although some, if not most, of these funds may have been intended for the Jerusalem Temple in the pre-70 period.[96] The sacred funds referred to in the third-century Stobi inscription, however, were undoubtedly earmarked for local purposes, for either the synagogue building, synagogue activities, or other charitable causes.[97]

Rabbinic sources focus on the distribution of food to the needy, noting both a weekly allocation referred to as *kuppah* (lit., a charity box) and a daily one called *tamhui* (lit., a charity plate).[98] Those who did not have enough food for two meals a day could take advantage of the *tamhui*, which functioned as a public soup kitchen; those who did not have provisions for fourteen meals a week could avail themselves of the *kuppah*.[99] Collection for the latter was supervised by at least two persons and distribution was administered by at least three. Special arrangements were made for indigents.[100] In addition to food, clothing was donated and monies were collected for orphans, captives, and burial of the poor.[101] The early third-century inscription from Aphrodisias relates directly to the issue at hand, and the *dekany* noted therein seems to have been responsible for the maintenance of a *patella*, generally interpreted as some sort of soup kitchen.[102]

Then, as now, those known for their charitable benefactions were accorded special honors. They may have occupied special seats, as appears to have been the case at the Ma'on synagogue.[103] Other techniques as well were utilized for raising funds. A wealthy Bostran named Abun donated matching funds to charity, but only after the members of his congregation had made their pledges.[104] In another instance, R. Berekhia made a special appeal for funds for a poor itinerant immediately following his sermon; however, it is unclear whether this was in a synagogue or academy setting.[105] At times, charity officials did not limit their activity to synagogue premises, and we learn that on one occasion

---

96. *Antiquities* 16, 164.

97. See above, Chap. 8; and the Acmonia inscription, in White, *Social Origins*, 309–10.

98. T Peah 4:9 (p. 57) and parallels. See also Lieberman, *TK*, I, 184.

99. M Peah 8:7.

100. Ibid.

101. Baron, *Jewish Community*, I, 131–32. In the Arbel synagogue, recent excavations have uncovered what had been interpreted as the community *kuppah*, so placed as to allow for individual donations to be made from outside the building (Z. Ilan, *Ancient Synagogues*, 117).

102. See above, note 62.

103. Y Megillah 3, 2, 74a. From a *bet midrash* context, we learn of a major donor who was seated next to the leading sage of the institution, in this case R. Ḥiyya bar Abba; see Leviticus Rabbah 4:3 (p. 113); Deuteronomy Rabbah 4:8 (ed. Mirkin, p. 79); Exodus Rabbah 41:2.

104. Tanḥuma, Ki Tissa, 15.

105. Leviticus Rabbah 32:7 (pp. 752–53). See also Y Qiddushin 3, 14, 64c; as well as Y Megillah 3, 2, 74a, with regard to R. Ḥelbo in Sepphoris.

charity officials solicited a potential contributor in the marketplace for a donation to help an orphan.[106]

Place of Study

As has been spelled out above, the synagogue, from its earliest days, was a place for Torah study. At first, such study was conducted primarily within a liturgical context in conjunction with the regular Torah and haftarah readings. The Theodotos inscription seems to suggest that by the end of the Second Temple period, study within the synagogue may also have taken place independently of the liturgical framework.[107] Moreover, if communal schools were already in existence in this early period (see below), then they probably occupied synagogue premises.[108]

The development of an educational system within the Jewish community is shrouded in mystery. There were schools for the training of priests, scribes, and sages (i.e., wisdom schools) and, of course, the rigorous study programs associated with several religious sects, but nothing is known about educational frameworks for the public at large before the latter Second Temple period.[109] Often rabbinic sources retroject contemporary institutions and practices to biblical times. However, with respect to the matter at hand, several traditions date the development of some sort of a school system in Roman Judaea to the days of Simeon b. Shataḥ (first century B.C.E.) and the high priest Joshua b. Gamala (first century C.E.).[110]

There is every reason to believe that the development of an institutionalized educational system within the Jewish community was the product of influences from the surrounding Hellenistic world as well as internal religious and cultural factors.[111] Education was far too common a phenomenon in the Greco-Roman world to be ignored by the Jews. Moreover, in the absence of any evidence for comparable educational institutions

---

106. Leviticus Rabbah 37:2 (pp. 856–58).

107. Cf. above, Chap. 5.

108. This is clearly reflected in numerous rabbinic traditions which speak of schools in synagogue buildings. See, for example, Y Megillah 3, 1, 73d and Y Ketubot 13, 1, 35c (Jerusalem); B Gittin 58a (Betar). Cf. S. Safrai, "Education," 946–58.

109. See, inter alia, Schürer, *History*, II, 417–20; *EJ*, VI, cols. 381–403. See also Swift, *Education in Ancient Israel*; S. Greenberg, "Jewish Educational Institutions," 1254–87.

110. Y Ketubot 8, 11, 32c; B Bava Batra 21a. Identifying Joshua b. Gamala and clarifying the historicity and relationship of the above-noted traditions have been the subject of much scholarly discussion. See, for example, Schürer, *History*, II, 418–19; S. Safrai, "Education," 947–48; Hengel, *Judaism and Hellenism*, I, 81–82; Ebner, *Elementary Education*, 38–50.

111. Hengel, *Judaism and Hellenism*, I, 78–83; Rengstorf, in *TDNT*, IV, 415–41. See also Safrai, "Elementary Education," 148–49; Morris, *Jewish School*, 37ff. On primary schools in the Greco-Roman world, see Freeman, *Schools of Hellas*, 79ff.; Carcopino, *Daily Life*, 103–7; Bonner, *Education in Ancient Rome*, 34–46, 115–211; and, of course, the classic study of Marrou, *History of Education*.

in early Jewish history, the possible impact of the surrounding Hellenistic context ought to be given due weight.

Nevertheless, whatever stimuli may have been supplied by the non-Jewish milieu, it is clear that the educational curriculum was significantly different in a Jewish context. The subject matter, for example, would have been predominantly, if not exclusively, Jewish in content. Such an emphasis would have been strengthened by the fact that by late antiquity, schooling for the young had become a communal responsibility; it was no longer a private affair left in large measure to the initiative and means of each parent, an arrangement typical of Greco-Roman society generally.[112]

In the post-70 period, synagogue-based educational frameworks had thus become an integral feature of synagogue life, as is amply reflected in rabbinic literature. More specifically, it is the education of children on synagogue premises which is often noted in these sources. The importance of this activity in the eyes of the sages finds varied expression. R. Joshua's mother is said to have brought him to the synagogue when he was only a baby, so that he might become accustomed to hearing words of Torah;[113] when asked which group is most beloved by God, one sage answered: "Those teachers of Bible and Mishnah who have diligently given instruction to children will in the future sit to the right of God."[114] R. Simeon b. Yoḥai ventured an opinion that towns and villages become desolate because their inhabitants do not pay teachers enough for instructing their children. To this is appended a well-known story which stresses the importance of teachers ("guardians of the city," נטורי קרתא) as a crucial element in a city's functioning:

> R. Judah Nesiah sent R. Ḥiyya, R. Asi, and R. Ami to tour the towns of Palestine in order to establish for [or: assign] them teachers of Scriptures and teachers of Oral Law. In one place they found neither teachers of Scriptures nor teachers of Oral Law, whereupon they said to them [the residents]: "Bring us the guardians of the city." They brought them the sentries of the city. The sages responded: "These are not the guardians of the city, but rather its destroyers!" "And who are its guardians?" they [the people] asked. [The sages responded:] "The teachers of Scriptures and the teachers of Oral Law."[115]

Not only is Israel protected from within by the proper maintenance of these schools, but it is shielded from outside adversaries as well. According to another rabbinic tradi-

---

112. Marrou, *History of Education*, 199–222, 358–68. On this type of private arrangement, which seems to have been the norm in Babylonia, see Gafni, *Jews of Babylonia*, 107-9. This may explain why discussions regarding teachers' pay are to be found almost exclusively in Palestinian sources. It was there that these issues were public and communal matters, not private ones. See, for example, Y Peah 8, 7, 21a.

113. Y Yevamot 1, 6, 3a.

114. PRK 27:2 (p. 406).

115. Y Ḥagigah 1, 7, 76c; Sokoloff, *Dictionary*, 590. See also PRK 15:5 (p. 253); Lamentations Rabbah, Proem 2 (p. 1b); Midrash on Psalms 127 (pp. 256b–257a); Yalqut Shimʿoni, Psalms, 881; Midrash on Song of Songs 1 (p. 47).

tion, when asked by the nations of the world how the Jewish people could be overcome, the pagan philosopher Oenomus of Gadara replied: "Go and visit their synagogues and academies. If you find the voices of children chirping [i.e., reciting their lessons] you will not be able to overcome them; if not, you will be able to."[116] The belief that the divine presence hovers over schools is likewise reflected in the tradition that the *bat qol* ("heavenly voice") communicates via the recitation of children's lessons in schools.[117]

Sending children to a school in the synagogue appears to have been a nearly universal practice among the Jews.[118] As noted, the hiring of a well-known teacher may have served, inter alia, as a source of imitation and envy to others.[119] Children studying in synagogue schools on a daily basis must have been as impressive as it was typical. A number of rabbinic accounts commence by telling of a sage who, passing such a school, heard a verse being recited, which, in turn, triggered his own interpretation of the verse. Such occurrences are reported at the Babylonian synagogue in Sepphoris with regard to R. Ḥiyya bar Abba in the late third century, R. Tanḥum bar Ḥanilai in the early fourth, and R. Ḥaggai of Tiberias in that same century.[120] A late fictional account reports that Elishaʿ b. Abuya (אחר) went from synagogue to synagogue and heard different verses recited by children, all reflecting aspects of his personal predicament.[121] A gentile is reported to have had a similar experience.[122] Finally, one account tells of R. Simeon b. Yoḥai, who passed the Migdal synagogue and overheard a conversation between students and teacher regarding his (R. Simeon's) recent act of purifying Tiberias.[123]

Children would begin their studies at about the age of five. The Mishnah offers what appears to be a standardized division of subjects and ages: "At the age of five, Bible; at ten, Mishnah; at fifteen, Talmud."[124] This progression seems probable. Rabbinic sources

---

116. Genesis Rabbah 65:22 (pp. 734–35); PRK 15:5 (pp. 254–55); Lamentations Rabbah, Proem 2 (p. 1b); Midrash Hagadol, Genesis 27:22 (p. 474).

117. See Lieberman, *Hellenism in Jewish Palestine*, 194–99.

118. Y Sanhedrin 10, 29a; Tractate Soferim 18:7 (p. 319). See also the interesting comment of the sixth-century Christian pilgrim Antoninus of Piacenza, who states that in the Nazareth synagogue "there is the bench on which he [Jesus] sat with the other children" (Wilkinson, *Jerusalem Pilgrims*, 79). On the education of children in Roman Italy, see Dyson, *Community and Society*, 189–93.

119. See above, note 15.

120. *R. Ḥiyya:* Genesis Rabbah 52:4 (pp. 543–44); Yalqut Shimʿoni, Genesis, 87 (p. 402). *R. Tanḥum:* PRK 25:1 (pp. 380–81). *R. Ḥaggai:* Midrash on Psalms 93:8 (pp. 416–17).

121. B Ḥagigah 15a-b. See Liebes, *Elisha's Sin*, 71ff.

122. ʾAvot de R. Nathan, A, 15 (p. 31); Yalqut Shimʿoni, Exodus, 379 (p. 698). For a similar tradition, this time with respect to the academy, see B Shabbat 31a.

123. PRK 11:16 (p. 193) and parallels. On this tradition generally, see L. Levine, "R. Simeon b. Yoḥai," 143–85.

124. ʾAvot 5:21. The number five may be schematic. In contrast, the Bavli (Bava Batra 21a) notes the ages of six and seven. In Roman society, in comparison, schools generally were entered at the age of seven, and they emphasized reading, writing, and arithmetic during the primary years, until the students

indicate that the synagogue school focused on what we would call today primary or elementary education, with children studying the Bible and Mishnah.[125] An interesting description of Bible studies is offered by Eusebius, who, living in Caesarea, had every opportunity to be familiar with Jewish practice: "Moreover, they [the Jews] have certain teachers [*deuterotai*] of primary studies, for so they liked to call the interpreters of their Scriptures. They make clear those things, obscurely taught in riddles, by means of translation and interpretation." [126] Eusebius perhaps alludes here to the study of midrash or *targum*, which seems to have been an integral part of some schools' curricula per the following rabbinic tradition: "This teaches that fear leads one to [study] Scriptures, Scriptures leads one to [study] *targum*, *targum* leads one to [study] Mishnah, Mishnah leads one to [study] Talmud." [127]

Children appear to have studied the book of Leviticus first, the practice being explained thusly: just as the young are pure, so they begin with sacrifices, which are likewise pure ("Let the pure come and deal with things pure").[128] Studies beyond the elementary level probably required attendance at another school, which may have been associated with a rabbinic academy.[129] Nevertheless, one source speaks explicitly, and in detail, of the advanced subjects studied in the synagogue. We learn that a child begins with a scroll (perhaps intended for reading exercises; perhaps containing biblical texts) and then proceeds to study the Torah, Prophets, and Writings, moving on to the Talmud, Halakhah, and *Aggadah*.[130]

Information about the regular routine in these schools is extremely fragmentary. Studies appear to have continued throughout the day. Children would go to school in the morning, as is attested by Christian as well as Jewish sources.[131] The school day seems to have commenced with prayer and probably included the recitation of the *Hallel* on

---

were eleven or twelve (Marrou, *History of Education*, 207; Carcopino, *Daily Life*, 104). Secondary schools focused on literary works, first and foremost among which was Homer's *Iliad* (Marrou, *History of Education*, 369–80). For the earlier Greek period, see Freeman, *Schools of Hellas*, 79ff., 157ff.

125. Teachers are regularly referred to as סופרים ומשנים, i.e., teachers of the Bible and Mishnah (or Oral Law). See, for example, PRK 27:2 (p. 406); and below, Chap. 11. On Jewish primary education at this time, see Goldin, *Studies in Midrash*, 205–8.

126. *Praeparatio Evangelica* 513C, as quoted in York, "Targum in Synagogue and School." 84; see also Lieberman, *Hellenism in Jewish Palestine*, 57.

127. Sifre-Deuteronomy 161 (p. 212). See also 'Avot de R. Nathan, B, 12 (p. 29); B Qiddushin 49a.

128. Leviticus Rabbah 7:3 (p. 156); PRK 6:3 (p. 118); Tanhuma, Tzav, 14; Yalqut Shim'oni, Leviticus, 479 (p. 199). The study of Leviticus may also have been linked to the post-70 hopes for restoration of the Temple sacrifices; see Ebner, *Elementary Education*, 78–79.

129. B Berakhot 17a; Midrash Hagadol, Genesis 23:1 (p. 374). Cf. also B Qiddushin 30a; Yalqut Shim'oni, Exodus, 376 (p. 691); ibid., Genesis, 158 (pp. 836–37).

130. Deuteronomy Rabbah, Nitzavim 3 (p. 115). Notice the absence of the Mishnah in this listing as well the addition of *aggadah* at the end.

131. Epiphanius, *Commentary on Isaiah* 19:14; Yalqut Shim'oni, Lamentations, 1022.

holidays and the New Moon.[132] Studies often lasted until the evening hours,[133] and adults might study at night as well (see below).[134] Some children apparently returned home at noontime, either because they were very young and had a shortened day or because this was their midday break.[135]

Children from both wealthy and poor homes studied together, and at some point in the morning there was a break for food. In an engaging story, we learn of one child who brought meat, eggs, and most anything his heart desired. Another youngster brought only carobs, a food that was generally associated with the poor. Because of the differences, the latter child suffered; his father then made a special effort, bought meat, and proceeded to prepare a festive meal for his son.[136]

Elementary schoolteachers were often accused of excessive strictness, at times bordering on cruelty. Quintilian has left us a vivid description of such behavior: "Pain and fear [he sadly testifies] drive children into doing things which they cannot confess, and which soon cover them with shame. It is even worse where no one has taken the trouble to investigate the morals of the teachers and masters. I dare not speak of the abominable infamies to which men can be degraded by their right to inflict corporal punishment, nor of the assaults, for very fear of which the unfortunate children may sometimes provoke further assaults; I will have been sufficiently understood: *nimium est quod intellegitur.*"[137]

Jewish sources tell of similar behavior. A maidservant (שפחה) once passed the synagogue school and observed a teacher beating a child in an extreme fashion (יתיר מן צורכיה). She confronted the teacher, saying that he deserved to be ostracized (חרם). When the teacher consulted R. Aḥa as to the severity of this threat, he was told that he had good cause for worry.[138] Straps used for flogging might have become a memorable part of the school experience — the more distant the memory, perhaps, the better. Two students who had gone on to advanced studies once returned to their childhood school and began playing with the strap, reminiscing about their early experiences.[139]

---

132. Y Sotah 5, 6, 20c.

133. Exodus Rabbah 47:5; Pesiqta Rabbati 41 (p. 174a); Midrash on Psalms 14:6 (p. 114); and perhaps B Qiddushin 26a (= B Bava Qama 114b) as well. On this practice in antiquity, see Freeman, *Schools of Hellas*, 79–80.

134. B Pesaḥim 8b.

135. Pesiqta Rabbati 43 (p. 182b) (= Yalqut Shim'oni, I Samuel, 77). See also Freeman, *Schools of Hellas*, 80.

136. Deuteronomy Rabbah, 'Eqev (p. 78); the story continues thereafter in a different vein. Note here how the terms "school" and "synagogue" are used interchangeably.

137. Quintilian, *Institutio Oratoria*, 1, 3, 13–17; and below, Chap. 11, pp. 419–20. See also Marrou, *History of Education*, 220–22, 366–68.

138. Y Mo'ed Qatan 3, 1, 81d. In another case, this time from Babylonia, one sage attempted to dismiss a teacher for excessive cruelty, but was overruled by a colleague (B Gittin 36a and parallels).

139. Seder Eliyahu Rabbah 5 (p. 25).

At times, sages issued explicit instructions to curb teachers' excesses. R. Samuel and R. Isaac once told teachers not to forget to release the students after four hours' study in the hot summer season, and R. Yoḥanan warned teachers not to strike children during the three-week period before the fast of Av.[140] On another occasion, R. Abbahu purposely crossed the synagogue courtyard to remind a teacher, known to be a strict disciplinarian, to dismiss the children from school.[141]

Besides schooling for the young, the community was likewise concerned with adult education,[142] and the synagogue presumably served as a setting for this as well. The *dekany* of those committed to study (δεκανία τῶν φιλομαθῶν) referred to in the Aphrodisias inscription may well have been an organized adult education group.[143] Pagan temples in antiquity were often the setting for similar functions, providing visitors with the opportunity to attend lectures and classes, discuss issues with local priests and sages, and visit a public library.[144] Rabbinic sages urged people to stop in the synagogue on their way home from work at night to study for a while.[145] R. Yoḥanan asserted that one who studies in the synagogue would not easily forget what he has learned;[146] R. Yonatan b. R. Eli'ezer met someone in a marketplace who asked him for instruction, and the sage referred him to the *bet talmud* (probably located in the local synagogue), where he promised to teach him.[147] The rabbis lost no opportunity to emphasize among themselves as well as to others the importance of such study: he who teaches the public at large merits the Holy Spirit.[148] Moreover, they even imagined that schools were already in existence at the time of the biblical Patriarchs.[149]

Although based primarily in their academies, the sages often conducted study sessions in synagogues.[150] Thus, R. Judah I, who lived in Sepphoris the last seventeen years of his

140. Midrash on Psalms 91 (pp. 199a-b).

141. Y Megillah 3, 4, 74a.

142. Cf. Aberbach, *Jewish Education*, 14ff.; S. Safrai, "Education," 958-69.

143. One passage in a late midrashic collection highlights this type of congregational instruction on the Sabbath in the academy; in certain places this may have included the synagogue as well; see Yalqut Shim'oni, Exodus, 407.

144. MacMullen, *Paganism*, 11 and nn. 51-52.

145. 'Avot de R. Nathan, A, 2 (p. 14).

146. Y Berakhot 5, 9a.

147. Tanḥuma, Leviticus, B'ḥuqotai, 4 (p. 55a).

148. Song of Songs Rabbah 1:9 (ed. Dunesky, p. 8).

149. Yalqut Shim'oni, Genesis, 152 (p. 820).

150. In addition to these two principal locales, sages also taught at the Patriarch's home (B Ketubot 34a), at the city-gate (Midrash Hagadol, Genesis 25:8 (pp. 420-21), and in the fields (Yalqut Shim'oni, Genesis, 110 [p. 505]).

life, would sit and study in front of the city's Babylonian synagogue, as did R. Yoḥanan a generation later.[151]

Involvement in every level of education not only was an abstract value for the sages; it also guaranteed that their ranks would be replenished from generation to generation:

> If there are no small children, there will be no [future] disciples;
> If there are no disciples, there will be no sages;
> If there are no sages, there will be no Torah;
> If there is no Torah, there will be no synagogues and academies;
> If there are no synagogues and academies, the Holy One, Blessed be He, will no longer
>   allow His Presence [Shekhinah] to dwell in this world.[152]

Library

The Second Temple of Jerusalem apparently contained sacred books—not only Torah scrolls but also, as seems to be noted by both Josephus and the Mishnah, other holy books (perhaps a reference to the remainder of the biblical corpus).[153] Synagogues, in a far more modest fashion, appear to have had libraries as well. We read of a book of *aggadah* which was perused by sages on the Sabbath,[154] and Jerome alludes to books borrowed from the synagogue. His Jewish teacher appears to have overstepped his bounds in presenting him with scrolls he had taken from a synagogue.[155] How extensive such synagogue libraries may have been is impossible to know. Clearly, they differed from congregation to congregation, depending upon local economic resources and local intellectual and cultural proclivities. Synagogues in Alexandria, Antioch, and Tiberias were undoubtedly much more richly endowed in this regard than the average rural ones.

Pagan temples also had libraries or archives.[156] According to Cassius Dio, most Egyptian sanctuaries contained sacred books, a fact seemingly corroborated by Origen, who speaks of the wisdom of Egypt as reflected in its literature and of priests as the acknowledged experts.[157] Aristides tells of large collections of the wondrous deeds (*aretai*)

---

151. B Ketubot 103b–104a; Genesis Rabbah 33:3 (p. 305); Y Berakhot 5, 9a. For a more detailed discussion, see below, Chap. 13. On R. Judah's seventeen years in Sepphoris, see Y Kil'aim 9, 4, 32b (= Y Ketubot 12, 3, 35a).

152. Leviticus Rabbah 11:7 (p. 230).

153. See Sifre-Deuteronomy 356 (p. 423); Josephus, *Antiquities* 16, 164; M Megillah 3:1.

154. Yalqut Shim'oni, Leviticus, 481 (p. 202).

155. Jerome, *Letter* 36.

156. See Plato, *Timaeus* 23a: "And if any event has occurred that is noble and great, all such events are recorded from of old and preserved here in our temples." On the library in the Temple of Apollo on the Palatine, see Suetonius, *Augustus* 31; Galinsky, *Augustan Culture*, 218.

157. *Roman History* 76, 13, 1: "He [Septimius Severus] inquired into everything, including things that were very carefully hidden; for he was the kind of person to leave nothing, either human or divine, uninvestigated. Accordingly, he took away from practically all the sanctuaries all the books that he could

of Serapis that were kept in "sacred archives," while Augustine notes the existence of libraries in the temples of Cybele in North Africa.[158]

Place of Residence

One or more rooms in a synagogue complex might have served as a place of residence. This was certainly the case in situations where an individual had transferred property to the community for use as a synagogue; this was in all probability what is referred to in the Talmud as "a synagogue of an individual."[159] In Stobi, for instance, Claudius Tiberius Polycharmos designated part of his home for the congregation, stipulating specifically what was to remain for himself and his family.[160] If, indeed, the Leontis inscription from Bet Shean belongs to a private home, then there, too, we have an instance of a small prayer room within a private residence that was set aside for a congregation of worshippers.[161]

The synagogue may also have served as a place of residence for its *ḥazzan*;[162] in an anachronistic vein, the *targum* speaks of the biblical Jacob performing menial tasks in a school (משמש בית אולפנא) while actually living on the premises.[163] Interestingly, rabbinic authors themselves were aware of the fact that pagan temples also had rooms reserved for at least some of their priests.[164]

Finally, a third use of the synagogue as a residence was in its capacity as a hostel. Although sources in this regard are limited, those that do exist suggest a well-known practice. The earliest evidence, noted above, is the first-century Theodotos inscription from Jerusalem, which explicitly states that the synagogue served as a hostel for visitors from abroad.[165] Rabbinic literature is likewise unambiguous. The Bavli speaks of "people who eat, drink, and sleep in the synagogue" on Sabbath and holidays, and thus the need arose to recite the *Kiddush* (blessing over wine) at the conclusion of the evening synagogue service, a practice which continues in Diaspora synagogues to this day.[166]

Several third-century traditions refer to visitors who, upon arriving in Tiberias, first

---

find containing any secret lore." See also *Contra Celsum* 1, 12; Griffiths, "Egypt and the Rise of the Synagogue," 11–14.

158. Aristides, *Oracles* 8, 54; Augustine, *City of God* 2, 7. A library is noted in the Christian church of Cirta, Numidia, that dates from the early fourth century; see White, *Building God's House*, 122.

159. Y Megillah 3, 1, 73d.

160. See above, Chap. 8.

161. Zori, "House of Kyrios Leontis," 123–34.

162. B ʿEruvin 55b, 74b; and below, Chap. 9.

163. Targum Jonathan and Neofiti of Gen. 25:27.

164. T ʿEruvin 4:7 (p. 106).

165. See above, Chaps. 3 and 4.

166. B Pesaḥim 100b–101a. The term גני, "to lie down or sleep," however, does not appear in many manuscripts. Perhaps this custom became rarer, or more objectionable, at a later period.

went to the synagogue, perhaps to seek lodging. R. Ami instructed an official of the local synagogue that such people were to be welcomed only if they showed some knowledge of the Torah.[167] Whether this welcome involved an invitation to lodge in the building is not stated.

Presumably, soldiers were on occasion billeted in a synagogue—much to the consternation of its members. An edict from the time of Valentinian I (ca. 370 C.E.) declares that synagogues were to be considered *religionum loca* and were thus not to be used by soldiers seeking a place to stay (*hospitium*).[168]

Place of Individual Recourse

As might be expected, an individual member of the community would have recourse to the synagogue on special occasions during his lifetime. We read, for example, that nuptial matches (שידוכין) were made on the Sabbath, presumably in the synagogue.[169] Grooms were welcomed into the synagogue to be blessed and praised, and were then accompanied to their homes in a festive procession.[170]

The synagogue also appears to have been the mise-en-scène for a public eulogy (הספד של רבים) and is mentioned on a number of occasions, particularly with respect to several Babylonian sages.[171] To what extent this may have been the practice of the wider Jewish community, either regularly or occasionally, is unknown.

Several sources note that there were instances when a body was placed in one of the rooms of a synagogue prior to burial. Once, while teaching in the Maradata synagogue of Caesarea, R. Abbahu was confronted with a situation in which priests recited the priestly blessing during a worship service but were then hesitant to partake of a meal owing to the presence of a corpse. R. Abbahu chided them for being concerned about purity requirements with regard to food but not with respect to the priestly blessing.[172] In early

---

167. Y Megillah 3, 4, 74a. This story is reflective of certain rabbinic biases. Its fuller context remains elusive. Perhaps it is related (as the editor of the Yerushalmi supposed) to the subsequent account which makes an extreme claim regarding rabbinic prerogatives in the synagogue: "For thus R. Joshua b. Levi has said: 'Synagogues and academies are for the sages and their students.'" On the relationship between the sages and the synagogue, see below, Chap. 13.

168. Linder, *Jews in Roman Imperial Legislation*, no. 14, and comments, pp. 161–63. On the refraction of *hospitium* in rabbinic sources, see Oppenheimer, *Galilee*, 99.

169. B Shabbat 150a; B Ketubot 5a.

170. Tractate Soferim 19:9 (pp. 335–36).

171. T Megillah 2:18 (p. 353); B Megillah 28b. See also M Megillah 3:3. The Bavli interprets a "public eulogy" to be one at which an important personage is present among the living or the deceased. Perhaps it is the giving of eulogies upon Judah I's death that is being referred to with regard to the eighteen synagogues in the area of Sepphoris; see Y Kil'aim 9, 4, 32b; Y Ketubot 12, 3, 35a.

172. Y Berakhot 3, 6a; Y Nazir 7, 2, 56a. Similar circumstances may be referred to in incidents involving R. Ḥiyya bar Abba and R. Ze'ira (Y Berakhot 3, 1, 6a), as well as R. Yose (Y Bava Metzia 2, 9, 8d), although the context in the latter may be the academy.

fourth-century Babylonia, a similar question arose with regard to a synagogue of Roman (?) Jews.[173] Presumably, a corpse was lying in an adjacent room (אידרונה), and when the priests asked Rava what they should do about the priestly blessing, he instructed them to set a wooden chest in the doorway, thereby creating a partition.[174]

In the pre-70 era, public consolation of mourners is mentioned in connection with the southern entrances and passageways of the Temple Mount.[175] However, since most Jews did not have access to the Temple Mount, some form of public solace may have been offered to them within the context of the local community, perhaps in the city-gate area or in the early synagogue. Later on, however, in the post-70 period, a more formal custom seems to have crystallized within the synagogue. It is impossible to assess when this took place; one tradition dates this development to the Yavnean period, at the same time that a number of other Temple practices were in the process of being transferred to the synagogue.[176] In later antiquity, when mourners would come to the synagogue to be comforted, a special section was apparently reserved for them, either outside the synagogue door (i.e., in the courtyard) or in some corner of the main hall. Upon completion of the Sabbath *Mussaf* service, the *ḥazzan* would approach them, offer an appropriate blessing, and then recite the *Qaddish*.[177] A similar procedure was followed on weekdays as well.[178]

Aside from the universal life-cycle needs which the community addressed within the synagogue, individuals came there for help in moments of personal stress. One well-attested need was that of healing. Throughout the Greco-Roman period, Jews and Judaism were often associated with prowess in magic and supernatural powers.[179] The association of healing with a synagogue setting is clearly reflected in a number of gospel narratives, and a similar association held true of pagan temples as well.[180] In the fourth century, as noted, John Chrysostom was distressed by the large number of Christians flocking to the synagogue for healing, presumably confident of success through the use of

173. On the assumption that the reference is to "Roman" Jews in Babylonia, see S. Krauss, *Synagogale Altertümer*, 222.

174. B Megillah 26b.

175. M Middot 2:2.

176. Tractate Soferim 19:9 (pp. 335–36).

177. Ibid.; cf. Y Pesaḥim 8, 8, 36b. See also *TK*, I, 49. In Babylonia, mourners were greeted outside the synagogue in the town plaza (רחבה); see B Ketubot 8b; and comments in Lieberman, *TK*, V, 1180–81. See also Hezser, *Form, Function, and Historical Significance*, 80–81.

178. Pirqei d'Rabbi Eliezer 17 (end) as per Lieberman, *TK*, I, 49.

179. See, for example, Josephus, *Antiquities* 8, 46; and the overviews provided in Schürer, *History*, III, 342–79; Gager, *Moses*, 134–61; M. Smith, *Jesus the Magician*; Kee, *Miracle in the Early Christian World*; idem, *Medicine, Miracle and Magic*; as well as Crossan, *Historical Jesus*, 137–67. Cf. above, Chap. 8.

180. For example, Matt. 12:9ff.; Luke 13:10ff. See also E. P. Sanders, *Jesus and Judaism*, 157–73; Vermes, *Jesus the Jew*, 22–26, 58–82; as well as citations in the previous note. On pagan temples, see MacMullen, *Paganism*, 49–62.

Jewish amulets and incantations:[181] "What kind of excuse will we give if, when we suffer and undergo misfortunes because of fever or bodily hurts, we run to the synagogues."[182] And, "Yet if you have a minor illness, you immediately turn away from his authority and run to demons and flee to the synagogues."[183]

Most unusual is a practice associated by Chrysostom with the synagogue at Daphne near Antioch and also well documented in the temples of Asclepius in the late Empire, whereby people would spend the night in a holy precinct in the hope of recovery: "And I say this not only about the synagogue here in the city but also about the one in Daphne. For the pit of destruction there, which they call Matrona, is even more evil. For I have heard that many of the faithful have gone up there to practice incubation in the shrine. But I shall not be calling such people 'unfaithful.' Both the synagogue of Matrona and the temple of Apollo are equally impure to me."[184]

Jewish, specifically rabbinic, sources are relatively silent regarding this aspect of the synagogue, though stories dealing with the healing and magical powers of sages are numerous.[185] Nevertheless, the connection is made in several instances. In one curious statement, the synagogue is where the angel of death is said to have deposited his belongings when visiting a city; therefore, when a plague befalls a city no one should enter the synagogue unaccompanied.[186] The late magical tract "Sword of Moses," on the other hand, states very explicitly: "should you desire that people be fearful of you, then write on a lead slate . . . and bury it in a synagogue towards the west"; in a fragment of a magical text found in the Cairo Genizah, one is told to bury an amulet under the Torah ark in the synagogue.[187] Indeed, similar texts have been found in the excavations of the Merot and Ma'on (Nirim) synagogues.[188]

The same awe of the synagogue setting holds true with regard to the oaths and vows taken by individuals. Once again, Chrysostom provides us with dramatic testimony; he claims that ordinary Christians considered such oaths to be more effective if taken in a synagogue and not a church.[189] Such veneration for synagogue-associated oaths is attested by Justin Martyr and in several later rabbinic sources.[190]

A person might have taken the opportunity when the congregation met in the syna-

---

181. Wilken, *John Chrysostom and the Jews*, 83–94.

182. *Adv. Iud.* 8, 5, 6.

183. Ibid., 8, 8, 7–9.

184. Ibid., 1, 6, 2–3; 1, 8, 1.

185. See, for example, Goldin, "Magic," 115–47.

186. B Bava Qama 60b.

187. See Naveh, "Aramaic and Hebrew Inscriptions," 303.

188. Naveh and Shaked, *Amulets and Magical Bowls*, 16, 91–92; and below, Chap. 11.

189. Wilken, *John Chrysostom and the Jews*, 79–83.

190. *First Apology* 45; Pesiqta Rabbati 22 (p. 113a); Midrash Hagadol, Exodus 20:7 (pp. 410–11). Cf., however, Leviticus Rabbah 6:3 (p. 131), where a synagogue context is not mentioned.

gogue to demand that those who could testify on his or her behalf should come forward.[191] Moreover, the story is told of a father who was angry with his son for not providing for (i.e., feeding) him; R. Yonatan advised him to prevent his son from entering the synagogue (how, though, we are not told) and thus humiliate him publicly.[192]

People may have had recourse to a synagogue for far more prosaic reasons. Valuables left there or lost elsewhere were brought to the synagogue for reclamation.[193] We are told that petty thieves at times took advantage of such procedures by claiming items not their own.[194] Synagogues may have also been used for the safekeeping of monies, much the way a modern-day bank is used. The Jerusalem Temple appears to have once served in such a capacity, and this practice may well have been carried over to the synagogue.[195]

From the foregoing, we may assess the extent to which the synagogue filled a wide variety of functions required by the Jewish community. As noted, the synagogue in this sense was not sui generis within the ancient world; similar functions were being carried out in many pagan temples and, later on, by churches. Nevertheless, if there is some element of uniqueness to be found in the synagogue's communal dimension, it may be in its highly concentrated centrality. Neither the pagan temple nor the church appears to have combined so many communal activities under one roof, nor did either need to. Pagans before the fourth century and Christians thereafter had a range of institutions at their disposal which addressed non-liturgical needs. Most Jewish communities, excluding the academy which served the rabbinic elite, had but one address.[196] Thus, for example, the presence of a court was a very rare phenomenon in a pagan temple or church, and these institutions did not house schools for primary education. The pagan elite had special schools and private instructors for their youth, and, for want of a local institution, they often sent their children to nearby cities for instruction.[197] The church, likewise, did not pro-

---

191. M Shevuʿot 4:10.

192. Y Peah 1, 1, 15d; Y Qiddushin 1, 8, 61c; and A. Grossman, "Stopping-the-Service," 199–203.

193. B Bava Metzia 28b.

194. Y Bava Metzia 2, 9, 8d; see Hezser, *Form, Function, and Historical Significance*, 78–80, 307.

195. II Macc. 3:10–12. On synagogues where caches of money have been found (certainly public funds, but perhaps also money belonging to individuals), see above, as well as Chap. 9.

196. L. Levine, *Rabbinic Class*, 43ff. This was certainly the case for Jews living in small towns and villages as well as for those living in large urban centers. The Jews of Tiberias and Sepphoris would have had other "Jewish" institutions at their disposal.

197. See the fascinating story reported by Pliny the Younger (Letter IV, 13) in this regard. When he asked a father living in Como, a provincial town in northern Italy, why he had sent his son to Milan for schooling, the reply was: "We have no teachers here." Pliny's response was as follows: "How is that? . . . Surely it nearly concerns you who are fathers . . . that your sons should receive their education here rather than elsewhere. . . . Upon what easy terms might you by a general contribution procure teachers if you would apply toward raising a salary for them what you now pay for your son's lodgings, journeys,

vide for the schooling of the young, utilizing, for the most part, existing institutions.[198] Thus, studying, so characteristic of Judaism from the Second Temple era onward, was an activity absorbed by the synagogue, and it contributed significantly to the uniqueness of this institution in late antiquity.[199]

and whatever a man has to pay when away from home. . . . Why I, who have as yet no children, am ready to give a third part of any sum you think proper to raise for this purpose for the benefit of our commonwealth, which I regard as a daughter."

198. Marrou, *History of Education*, 397–99; Wilken, *John Chrysostom and the Jews*, 24.

199. Nevertheless, it should be noted that some of the above functions of the synagogue were to be found in rabbinic academies as well: collection for charity (Leviticus Rabbah 4:3 [p. 113]; Deuteronomy Rabbah 4:8 [ed. Mirkin, p. 79]; Exodus Rabbah 41:2); festive meals (Y Shabbat 20, 1, 17c); discussion of communal issues (B Shabbat 150a; B Ketubot 5a); court proceedings (B Yevamot 65b); and study. Presumably, classes for children were also held there on occasion (Y Ḥagigah 2, 1, 77b; 2, 3, 78a and parallels; B Shabbat 104a; Midrash Hagadol, Exodus 34:8 [p. 710]; Yalqut Shimʿoni, Genesis, 110 [pp. 519–20]). All this presupposes that there was no conflation of synagogue and academy functions by later editors.

eleven LEADERSHIP

The cadre of synagogue leadership that determined the policy of the institution and directed its affairs is an important aspect of ancient synagogue studies. Although the titles of officials and their roles have been only sporadically investigated over the past century, the dramatic increase in the publication of epigraphical material in recent decades has revitalized interest in this area.[1]

The study of leadership in the ancient synagogue is fraught with uncertainties. Although the primary epigraphical and literary sources in this regard are far from negligible (the latter including both Jewish and non-Jewish material), the historical reality behind these sources is often beclouded, resulting in strikingly diverse scholarly assessments. Moreover, the sources themselves may appear contradictory, as, for example, when comparing literary and epigraphical data, rabbinic and Christian material, or Roman and Byzantine legal sources and, not least, when attempting to make sense of the rabbinic and epigraphical material from Jewish Palestine on the one hand and the epigraphical evidence from the Diaspora on the other. However, these sources may, in fact, reflect a variety of organizational settings throughout the Roman world, and such an assumption may offer the best explanation for what often seems to be a bewildering range of titles.

The relevant data regarding synagogue leadership are geographically diffuse, deriving from almost every corner of the Roman world and beyond—from Babylonia to Spain,

---

1. Regarding epigraphical publications in recent decades, see above, Chap. 1.

from North Africa to central Europe and the Crimea. It has become clear with the passage of time and the accumulation of evidence that this material is unevenly spread, varying from region to region throughout the Empire. While some titles of officials appear in certain geographical regions quite often, they are negligible, if not almost entirely absent, in others. The chronological range is likewise broad, from as early as the Hellenistic period down to the end of late antiquity and beyond—a period of over one thousand years. To further complicate matters, some individuals bear more than one title, often leaving us to wonder what, in fact, the areas of responsibility of each office were.

Finally, these titles are recorded in the extant literary and epigraphical material with no explanation of their significance or meaning, thus offering little, if any, indication of the roles and functions involved. Even when we have an idea of the function of a given official, it remains unclear which communal framework this title refers to. For example, it is not always certain which titles relate directly to the synagogue and which to the Jewish community at large. Granted, an archon was a layman with some sort of administrative or political responsibility, often of a supervisory nature; but was he part of a community-wide board or did his title belong specifically to a synagogue context, presumably in reference to the governing body of that institution?

This last-mentioned consideration touches upon the fundamental question as to how Jewish communities were organized at the time and how the synagogue, with its leadership and administrative setup, fit into the overall communal framework. The issues here are many and complex. Was there a difference, for example, between Diaspora and Palestinian communities? Was there a different administrative framework for communities of different sizes or for those in a rural as against an urban setting? Did the communal structures in the urban settings where Jews constituted the majority (e.g., in Tiberias and Sepphoris) operate differently from communal structures in places where they were a minority, especially in the Diaspora? Or were there a variety of possible models in evidence throughout the larger Greco-Roman world from which each community might have chosen in order to suit its specific needs?

Over the course of the past century, there has been a decided shift in scholarly opinion regarding the question of Jewish communal organization. At first, there was a consensus that organizational patterns were largely the same for all Jewish communities throughout the Empire. While some differences surfaced regarding the nuances of definition and delineation, the fundamental assumption of a common communal pattern was nevertheless shared by virtually everyone.[2]

This consensus held that Jewish communities were governed by a *gerousia*, composed of archons and headed by a gerousiarch. All communal activities were controlled by this

---

2. Schürer, *History*, II, 429ff.; Juster, *Juifs*, I, 438ff.; Frey, *CIJ*, I, lxxxii ff.; S. Krauss, *Synagogale Altertümer*, 103ff.; La Piana, "Foreign Groups," 361ff. See also Elbogen, *Jewish Liturgy*, 368-74; Applebaum, "Organization of Jewish Communities," 464-503; Kasher, *Jews in Egypt*, 208-11, 289-309.

body, either directly or through appointed or elected officials charged with specific functions. The situation in Alexandria and, to a much lesser extent, Berenice played a significant role in forming this consensus. The situation in Rome, according to the catacomb inscriptions, was considered most unusual, as there appears to have been an emphasis on local synagogues and an apparent absence of any all-embracing communal organization.[3] Nevertheless, some scholars still claimed that a similar kind of overarching communal apparatus existed there.[4]

A significant conceptual change in this regard has taken place in recent decades. With the proliferation of studies relating to specific Jewish communities over the past half-century,[5] there is an increasing awareness of a wide range of Jewish communal practices and organizational forms which existed throughout the Roman Empire. Not only is it generally agreed that Rome and Alexandria present radically different organizational models, but we have further evidence for this diversity in Berenice and Asia Minor, as well as in Palestine. As with other aspects of the synagogue, so, too, the organizational structure of Jewish communities at large and the synagogue in particular were likely candidates to absorb and assimilate outside influences. This is evident since the very beginnings of Jewish history and continues to the present.[6] The influence of urban and regional patterns on a given Jewish community can often be easily detected in the social and political dimensions of communal life.

In light of the above, only those officials most directly associated with the synagogue institution will be discussed: the archisynagogue, archon, *pater* and *mater synagoges*, presbyter, *grammateus*, *phrontistes*, *ḥazzan*, and teacher. Other officials, whose direct association with the synagogue is far less certain (e.g., *parnas*, gerousiarch, and *prostates*),[7] will not be treated.

Inquiry into the nature and definition of Jewish communal leadership, especially synagogue leadership, has received increased scholarly attention over the past decade and a half.[8] Several contributions are noteworthy. The first is a monograph by Brooten (*Women*

---

3. Schürer, *Gemeindeverfassung*, 15ff.; Frey, *CIJ*, I, cii–cxi; Leon, *Jews of Ancient Rome*, 170.

4. Juster, *Juifs*, I, 418–24; Vogelstein, *Rome*, 32; S. Krauss, *Synagogale Altertümer*, 137ff.; La Piana, "Foreign Groups," 361ff.; Baron, *Jewish Community*, I, 99–107; Schürer, *History*, II, 199.

5. See the following studies relating to Diaspora communities: Rome (Vogelstein, Leon), Egypt (Tcherikover, Kasher), Antioch (Meeks and Wilken), Asia Minor (Trebilco), and the Diaspora generally (Smallwood, M. Stern, Feldman). On Jewish communities in Roman Palestine, see: Lydda (J. J. Schwartz, Oppenheimer), Jericho (J. J. Schwartz), Sepphoris (Miller), Caesarea (L. Levine, Ringel), Bet Shean (Fuks), and Tiberias (Avissar).

6. For an overview of this phenomenon in the course of Jewish history, see Baron, *Jewish Community*, I, 10–21, 95–107, 283–347.

7. In this regard, the evidence from Rome is exceptional, as every office there seems to have been connected with a synagogue. So, for example, we read of gerousiarchs of the Augustesian and Agrippesian synagogues (Noy, *JIWE*, II, nos. 96, 130).

8. Before that time, the basic studies in this respect included Juster, *Juifs*, I, 450–56; S. Krauss, *Syna-*

Leaders, 1982) which examines the evidence for female leadership in the ancient synagogue. In the course of this study, Brooten surveys a wide range of sources mentioning the various titles accorded synagogue officials generally. In volume IV of *New Documents Illustrating Early Christianity* (1987), G. H. R. Horsley addresses the issue of synagogue leadership. In 1992, Burtchaell published a monograph, *Synagogue and Church*, in which he espouses the theory that Jewish communal organization, and especially that of the synagogue, had a profound influence on the structure of the early church. In this context, Burtchaell accorded the former extensive treatment in order to account for the development of the latter. In the article "Archisynagogoi" (1993), Rajak and Noy examine the office of the archisynagogue in detail, arguing for a rather revolutionary understanding of this title (see below). Finally, Williams ("Structure," 1994) addresses the many leadership titles associated with the synagogues of Rome, arguing for a large measure of variation among them.[9]

ARCHISYNAGOGUE

The archisynagogue is the official most commonly associated with the synagogue and its operation. Our discussion will deal extensively with this office not only because of its prominence, but also because most of the central issues regarding synagogue leadership generally seem to revolve around this position.

Scholarly opinion regarding this office has varied greatly over the past century. In the dominant view this office was primarily, if not exclusively, spiritual and religious (e.g., Schürer, Juster, S. Krauss, Frey, and La Piana).[10] Opinions differ, however, with respect to the type of religious status enjoyed by the archisynagogue, whether he was the primary religious and spiritual figure within the synagogue or whether he was merely in charge of the worship setting—a kind of glorified attendant (*shamash*).[11] The powerful influence of New Testament depictions, often supported by rabbinic passages, has helped the above perception gain ascendancy.

A second approach, although basically in agreement with the first, nevertheless takes into consideration the epigraphical evidence which focuses on the archisynagogue as a benefactor, one who contributed to the construction of the facility or its repair and restoration. Thus, scholars holding this latter position have appended to the first view a further

---

gogale Altertümer, 112–59; Elbogen, *Jewish Liturgy*, 368–74; Frey, *CIJ*, I, lxxxii–ci; Leon, *Jews of Ancient Rome*, 165–94.

9. See also Feldman, "Diaspora Synagogues," 55–62, a recent overview; Levinskaya, *Acts in Its Diaspora Setting*, 185–93; van der Horst, *Ancient Jewish Epitaphs*, 89–101.

10. Schürer, *Gemeindeverfassung*, 27–28; idem, *History*, II, 434; Juster, *Juifs*, I, 450–53; S. Krauss, *Synagogale Altertümer*, 114–21; Frey, *CIJ*, I, xcviii; La Piana, "Foreign Groups," 359–60. See also Trebilco, *Jewish Communities*, 104–5; Vogelstein, *Rome*, 30–31.

11. See, for example, Marmorstein, "Synagogue of Theodotos," 24–25.

dimension which would account for the financial contributions made by the archisyna-gogue. Elbogen was the first to highlight this aspect, and he has since been joined by Leon, Schrage, and Linder.[12]

Only recently, however, has the pendulum come full swing, with the epigraphical evidence considered decisive for an understanding of this office.[13] According to Rajak and Noy, the archisynagogue was primarily a patron and benefactor whose title was honorary in nature. It was bestowed by Jewish communities only on those individuals who helped maintain and embellish the physical and material dimension of the synagogue.

The basic difference between the above views revolves primarily around the sources upon which each relies. The first position has traditionally been anchored in evidence from the New Testament, which highlights the religious role of the archisynagogue, and this is also the thrust of the relevant rabbinic and patristic sources. In contrast, Rajak and Noy rely exclusively on epigraphical data, dismissing the literary material as tendentious and historically unreliable. The intermediate approach noted above takes account of both the literary and epigraphical sources, thus amalgamating both the religious and financial components in its definition of the office.

There is, however, a fourth alternative, which recognizes the need to give due consideration to all the above-noted primary sources, even those which, at first glance, are polemical and historically problematic. This approach gives weight to the fact that a number of these sources indeed overlap and thus, in effect, reinforce the depiction found in each. It is thus posited that the archisynagogue often assumed not only religious and financial roles, but political and administrative ones as well. In short, the office of the archisynagogue involved overall responsibility for all facets of the institution, as, in fact, the title itself seems to convey. While several scholars have in the past attributed certain administrative and financial components to this office, these aspects, for the most part, have been alluded to only fleetingly. Leon, for example, mentions an additional administrative dimension en passant when discussing the archisynagogue as a representative of the institution before the larger community.[14] Brooten, following a remark by Juster, speaks of the archisynagogue, together with the elders, as being responsible for transferring monies to the Patriarch.[15] All this, of course, is in addition to the other functions clearly noted in the literary and epigraphical material; i.e., he is the one in charge of worship and a financial patron. Stern has the following very succinct, yet unequivocal, remark to make on the subject: "In the Roman period the *archisynagogus* had the most important function in the Jewish communities. The supervision of the synagogue was

---

12. Elbogen, *Jewish Liturgy*, 368–69; Leon, *Jews of Ancient Rome*, 171–72; Schrage, in *TDNT*, VII, 844–47; Linder, *Jews in Roman Imperial Legislation*, 137 n. 10. See also Juster, *Juifs*, I, 452–53.

13. Rajak and Noy, "*Archisynagogoi*," 75–93.

14. Leon, *Jews of Ancient Rome*, 172.

15. Juster, *Juifs*, I, 452–53; Brooten, *Women Leaders*, 28.

concentrated in his hands."[16] Burtchaell, too, gives expression to this more encompassing view, although he qualifies it by proposing a reconstruction of Jewish communal organization which is rather artificial and speculative.[17]

It is this last view of the archisynagogue which appears to be the most historically sound. Thus, in attempting to assess the nature and importance of the office, it is necessary to take into account all relevant sources and not exclude any simply because they appear to be polemical, tendentious, late, or seemingly incoherent in nature. Even these types of sources may reflect a historical reality in their details, especially if they appear as obiter dicta. We must never forget that polemical sources, too, must bear some modicum of truth if they are to be believed, as the authors clearly intended. The fact remains that such sources exist and thus must be regarded as evidence. Either they do, in fact, describe a historical reality as purported or, alternatively, a situation current in the author's day, or one which the author (for whatever reason) desired to project. Generally speaking, a source should be acknowledged to have at least some measure of historical value, unless a case can be made to completely disqualify it.

In examining the evidence itself, a number of aspects of this office become eminently clear. First and foremost is the extent to which the title *archisynagogos* was to be found throughout the Jewish world of late antiquity. This conclusion is based primarily, though not exclusively, on epigraphical material spanning the first six centuries of the Common Era and is attested in Palestine (Jerusalem, Caesarea, Sepphoris, Achziv, and presumably many Galilean settings, per rabbinic sources), Phoenicia (Beirut, Tyre, and Sidon), Arabia (Bostra), Syria (Antioch and Apamea), Asia Minor (Phrygia, Lycia, Caria, Ephesus, Teos, Myndos, Acmonia, Smyrna, and Sidé), Cyprus, Crete, Greece (Corinth and Aegina), Lower Moesia (Oescus), Italy (Rome, Ostia, Brescia, Venosa, Capua), Egypt (Alexandria), North Africa (Carthage, Naro-Ḥammam Lif), and Spain (Tarragona). In most of the above locales, the term *archisynagogos* appears just once. In Acmonia, Apamea, Venosa, Jerusalem, and Rome, the title appears anywhere from two to five times. Thus, only a few fringe regions of the Empire (the northwestern, southwestern, and northeastern prov-

---

16. M. Stern, *Greek and Latin Authors*, II, 630.

17. Burtchaell, *From Synagogue to Church*, 244: "What emerges from the evidence is an enduring perception from within the Jewish people that this officer, the *archisynagôgos*, was not simply a master of religious ceremonies. He was the executive of the local community, acting under the formal oversight of the elders but the more active superintendence of the notables. He presided over the community, he convened it for its activities, he superintended its staff. It was a position of some permanency, and one in which fathers might hope to see their sons succeed them. The community chief was, if not the most prestigious member of his community socially, the one who worked, often professionally, as the man at the forefront of his people. As broad as were the interest and the programs and services of his community, so broadly reached the breadth of his responsibility. If he presided at worship, it was because he presided at all community functions." See also G. H. R. Horsley, *New Documents*, IV, 218; Williams, "Structure of Roman Jewry," 135.

inces) are bereft of evidence for this office, just as they are for all other types of Jewish officeholders.

Nevertheless, it seems that the term *archisynagogos* was more popular in some areas than in others. It is almost totally absent from Egyptian and Cyrenian material (appearing only in one late third-century C.E. inscription in the former), and this is consistent with the fact that the term *synagoge* itself was not widely used in these regions. This correlation is true of Egypt, the Black Sea region, and the island of Delos. In all these places, the term *proseuche* was dominant.

In rabbinic literature, "archisynagogue" appears in its Hebrew equivalent (*rosh knesset*) about a dozen times in nine independent pericopae and is noted in connection with several specific locales—Achziv and Tiberias in Palestine, and Bostra in Provincia Arabia. In addition, the church fathers Justin and Epiphanius refer to the archisynagogue, and the title appears in a number of edicts in the Theodosian Code, as well as in several books of the *Scriptores Historiae Augustae*.

Let us review the evidence preserved in the six types of sources at our disposal: the New Testament, the writings of the church fathers, rabbinic literature, pagan literature, imperial legislative documents, and inscriptions.[18]

New Testament. The term *archisynagogos* appears in three books—Mark, Luke, and Acts. The two gospels take note of an archisynagogue named Jairos, whose daughter was healed by Jesus (Mark 5:22, 35, 36, 38; Luke 8:49). Of interest is Luke's usage of another term, "archon of the synagogue," in 8:41, which is parallel to Mark 5:22.[19] In Luke 13:10–17, an archisynagogue was reportedly angry with Jesus when the latter healed a woman on the Sabbath: "There are six days in which work ought to be done; so come during those days and be healed, but not on the Sabbath" (13:14).

"Archisynagogue" also appears in Acts, where the office is accorded a religious component; the archisynagogues in Antioch of Pisidia invited Paul to speak immediately following the Torah and haftarah readings (Acts 13:15). Moreover, Acts mentions two Corinthian archisynagogues by name—Crispus, who became a believer in Jesus (18:8), and Sosthenes, who apparently led the opposition to Paul (18:17). Both figures appear to have commanded respect within the community, the former by bringing with him other converts to the new faith (18:8), the latter by apparently organizing a protest on behalf of the local Roman governor against this perceived breach of the Law (18:12–17).[20]

It is worth noting a textual variant to Acts 14:2 found in Codex D. Instead of the

---

18. For a review of the evidence, see Juster, *Juifs*, I, 450–53; Brooten, *Women Leaders*, 15–27; Schrage, in *TDNT*, VII, 844–47; Burtchaell, *From Synagogue to Church*, 240–44; Roth-Gerson, *Greek Inscriptions*, 168–80; Rives, *Religion and Authority in Roman Carthage*, 221; and above, notes 9, 10, 13.

19. In Matt. 9:18 and 23, only the term "archon" appears.

20. Sosthenes here is probably the person of the same name in I Cor. 1:1; see *ICC*, loc. cit.; Haenchen, *Acts*, 536–37.

usual reading, "The Jews who did not believe," this text reads: "The archisynagogues of the Jews and the archons of the synagogue." This is indeed a very unusual phraseology; whether it reflects an actual, though sui generis, use of these titles, rather than a confusion in the mind of the tradent or scribe, is unclear.

In summary, the New Testament evidence attests to an office which was prestigious and was associated with a leadership role within the synagogue in the political and especially religious realms.

Church Fathers. Several patristic sources mention the archisynagogue, albeit cryptically. Justin notes that after prayer the archisynagogues taught the people to mock Jesus.[21] Here, too, this official is cast as an instructor of sorts in religious matters.

Epiphanius offers a somewhat more substantive picture. In describing the Ebionite sect, he takes note of the "presbyters and [or: who are] archisynagogues" who functioned as leaders of this sect and had a hand in arranging matrimonial relationships within their "synagogues."[22] Given the fact that this is a Jewish-Christian group, the use of Jewish names and titles may reflect a desire to imitate Jewish parlance. This might have applied not only to the title *archisynagogos*, but also to the nature of the position.

Of greater import is a second passage in which Epiphanius describes the officials in Diaspora synagogues, particularly those of Asia Minor.[23] In the context of the story of Joseph the Comes, who was sent to Cilicia by the Patriarch to oversee synagogue affairs, presumably in the time of Constantine, this church father names the following types of Jewish officials: archisynagogues, priests, presbyters, and *ḥazzanim* (whom he defines as *diakonoi* or *hyperetes*). There is really no compelling reason to dismiss this list as "a curious and scarcely coherent collection of seemingly token titles."[24] These are probably among the most prominent of the synagogue officials whom Epiphanius chose to identify, and each undoubtedly had some sort of religious and/or administrative responsibility.

The only other patristic comment of importance was made by Palladius in the early fifth century;[25] he notes a rumor ("it is said") that the Patriarch and archisynagogues make annual appointments on the basis of bribes received. The obviously hostile and polemical tone of this report, however, should not automatically lead us to assume that it has no historical value whatsoever. The fact that communal appointments were made regularly (whatever their nature, frequency, and reception) within the Jewish community by both Patriarchs and archisynagogues as part of their administrative responsibilities may certainly reflect contemporary practice. It is difficult to imagine why Palladius

---

21. Justin, *Dialogue with Trypho* 137, 2.

22. Epiphanius, *Panarion* 30, 18, 2; see Brooten, *Women Leaders*, 22; G. H. R. Horsley, *New Documents*, IV, 220.

23. *Panarion* 30, 11, 1.

24. Rajak and Noy, *"Archisynagogoi,"* 79.

25. *Dialogue on the Life of John Chrysostom* 15.

or anyone else would have invented such an accusation if there was absolutely no basis for such a practice. As noted above, even a distortion of reality has a kernel of truth. In fact, we have some indirect corroboration of Palladius' claim for regular appointments of certain synagogue officials in a late third-century Christian text, which speaks of Jewish archons who were appointed before every Jewish New Year.[26]

Finally, mention should be made of the apocryphal *Martyrdom of Peter and Paul*, which claims that Jewish archisynagogues, along with pagan priests, were responsible for opposing the apostles Peter and Paul in Rome.[27]

Thus, the above patristic sources make it quite clear that archisynagogues not only fulfilled some sort of religious function, but held political and administrative responsibilities as well.

Rabbinic Literature. Interestingly and perhaps surprisingly, rabbinic sources mention the archisynagogue only on occasion. The contexts in which the title appears are most often religious-liturgical, which is quite understandable given the interests and concerns of the sages. Nonetheless, even this evidence hints at a much wider role for this official, who, as noted, is referred to as *rosh knesset*. There has been some speculation as to which title, the Greek or the Hebrew, was the original and which was derivative.[28] As interesting and important as such a determination might be, it remains a moot question for the present. While the Greek term is well attested for the first century C.E., the Hebrew equivalent appears only in the Mishnah, around the turn of the third century; little can be said of its earlier history. If the mishnaic tradition regarding the *rosh knesset* in the Temple is authentic (see below), then, at the very least, a first-century C.E. date is called for; however, even such an assumption would hardly resolve the issue. To assume a correlation between the origin of a term and its first appearance in an extant source is unwarranted.

The earliest context in rabbinic literature associated with the *rosh knesset* relates to a Torah-reading ceremony in the Temple. Both a *ḥazzan* and a *rosh knesset* were part of the chain of officials who transferred the Torah scroll to the high priest or king for reading during the Yom Kippur and *Haqhel* ceremonies.[29] Despite the apparent anachronism in associating synagogue-related officials with Temple proceedings, there is nevertheless a possibility that this tradition was not entirely devoid of a historical basis. When the functions once located at the city-gate were moved elsewhere in the course of the Second Temple period, the Temple precincts and the Temple Mount area generally may well have incorporated some of the activities formerly associated with the gate area and would have included elements of religious worship that had taken place there.[30] As the *ḥazzan* and

---

26. Noy, *JIWE*, II, 61. See below, p. 403.

27. *Acta apostolorum apocrypha* (p. 128); see also Juster, *Juifs*, I, 452 n. 3.

28. G. H. R. Horsley, *New Documents*, IV, 220.

29. M Yoma 7:1; M Sotah 7:7–8.

30. See above, Chap. 2.

the *rosh knesset* may already have functioned at the city-gate in some religious capacity, the transference of the Torah-reading ceremony to the Temple, and to synagogues elsewhere, could have involved the participation of persons bearing these titles. Thus, on the rare occasions when the Torah was read in the Temple, it was with the participation of a *ḥazzan* and a *rosh knesset* who may have come from one of the Jerusalem synagogues or perhaps were directly associated with the Temple. Although the above line of reasoning is admittedly somewhat speculative, it may not be a wholly implausible reconstruction.

Whatever the case, the Toseftan tradition of the *ḥazzan* and the *rosh knesset* being in charge of the Torah-reading ceremony in the synagogue clearly points to a religious dimension of this position. On occasion, the *rosh knesset* also read from the Torah,[31] and this type of involvement dovetails neatly with the New Testament evidence.

A number of other second-century rabbinic sources reflect the generally prominent status of the archisynagogue. One tradition regarding burial customs notes the addition of three cups of wine at a funeral meal in honor of a *ḥazzan knesset*, a *rosh knesset*, and Rabban Gamaliel.[32] In a *baraita* listing those women who are preferred as wives, the highest consideration is accorded the daughter of a sage, followed by the daughter of one of "the great men of the generation" (גדולי הדור, i.e., wealthy communal leaders), the daughter of a *rosh knesset*, the daughter of a charity official, and, finally, the daughter of a schoolteacher.[33] Two second-century heads of synagogues are mentioned in connection with visiting sages: one Sagvion of Achziv, identified as a *rosh knesset*, addressed a halakhic question to Rabban Gamaliel II when the latter visited his town, and the *rosh knesset* of Nisibis, who invited R. Judah b. Bathyra to dine with him on the eve of Yom Kippur.[34]

From the late third century, we have the account of a *rosh knesset* in Bostra who is described as dragging a bench in the presence of R. Jeremiah.[35] In addition, some Galileans asked R. Ḥelbo about the proper order in which to call people to the Torah following the Cohen and Levi, to which he responded: "after them read sages who are appointed as *parnasim* in the community; after them, sages who are qualified to be appointed *parnasim*; after them, the sons of sages who function as *parnasim*; and after them, the *rashei knesset*; and after them, anyone else."[36]

---

31. T Megillah 3:21 (p. 359); and Lieberman, *TK*, loc. cit.

32. Y Berakhot 3, 1, 6a. See also Tractate Semaḥot 14:14 (p. 209) for a slightly different order; and B Ketubot 8b for a significantly different version, reading *parnas* instead of "archisynagogue." See also Ginzberg, *Commentary*, II, 63–80, esp. 65–66.

On the association of cups of wine in a banquet setting (festival of Muses) with the various types of teachers (*litterator, grammaticus*, and rhetor), see Apuleius, *Florida* 20 (pp. 168–69).

33. B Pesaḥim 49b.

34. T Terumot 2:13 (p. 115) and Lamentations Rabbah 3:17 (p. 130), respectively; on the latter, see the editor's comments, n. 75; and Beer, *Babylonian Exilarchate*, 21–22 n. 25.

35. B Shabbat 29b.

36. B Gittin 60a.

In reviewing these nine different rabbinic traditions, which are fairly evenly divided between Palestinian and Babylonian sources (with all but one referring to Palestinian settings), it is clear that the rabbis considered the *rosh knesset* a significant enough personage to be accorded recognition. Needless to say, his position was always considered inferior to that of the sage, but that is to be expected for any non-rabbinic figure mentioned in these sources. What is of significance is that of all synagogue-related officials, the archisynagogue was accorded the highest honors.

Of particular interest are the functions actually depicted, alluded to, or omitted in these reports. For example, nothing is said of the *rosh knesset* as a benefactor, unless being named right after "the great men of the generation" and before the charity officers is of significance in this respect, which is doubtful. Several traditions are quite explicit with respect to his religious functions. Even if we were to disregard the mishnaic testimony relating to the Temple, the Toseftan tradition about reading Scriptures and the halakhic query posed to Rabban Gamaliel in Achziv by the local *rosh knesset* are quite revealing. Of no less importance are other indications we have of the archisynagogue's administrative responsibilities. The arranging of seats by the *rosh knesset* in the synagogue in Bostra and the ranking of the *rosh knesset* between the community's most powerful members and its charity officers may well point to other administrative and political aspects of the archisynagogue's duties.

Pagan Literature. There are two pagan sources which relate to the archisynagogue, both found in the fourth-century collection of imperial biographies, *Scriptores Historiae Augustae.* In a letter allegedly written by Hadrian, the following statement is made: "those who worship Serapis are, in fact, Christians, and those who call themselves bishops of Christ are, in fact, devotees of Serapis. There is no chief of the Jewish synagogue [i.e., archisynagogue], no Samaritan, no Christian presbyter who is not an astrologer, a soothsayer, or an anointer."[37] As puzzling as this text may appear to be, several details are nevertheless noteworthy. The first is the fact that the archisynagogue is singled out from among all other Jewish officials; second is the implicit comparison of the archisynagogue with a Christian presbyter.

No less intriguing, however, is the well-known reference in the *Life of Alexander Severus* to a mob scene in Antioch or Alexandria (or both): "on the occasion of a certain festival, the people of Antioch, of Egypt, and of Alexandria had annoyed him with jibes as was their custom, calling him a Syrian archisynagogue and a high priest."[38] In contrast to the statement in the previous source, it is not impossible that such an incident, in one form or another, did, in fact, occur during the lifetime of Alexander Severus. As with other

---

37. *Life of Saturninus* 8 (*SHA*, III, 398–99); M. Stern, *Greek and Latin Authors*, II, 637–38. See also Rajak and Noy (*"Archisynagogoi,"* 81), who translate *aliptes* as "wrestling master" instead of "anointer." On this and the following source, see the comments in Isaac, "Orientals and Jews," 108–12.

38. *Life of Alexander Severus* 28, 7 (*SHA*, II, 234–35); M. Stern, *Greek and Latin Authors*, II, 630.

members of this dynasty, he, too, was known for his sympathies toward Jews and Judaism, as well as for trying to conceal his Syrian origins. Such an accusation would thus
have been especially poignant in both respects.[39] The selection of the title "archisynagogue" for such an insult (whether the source is an accurate third-century account or a
fabrication from the fourth century) would seem to reflect how well known—albeit in a
pejorative way—this title was among the pagan masses.

Imperial Legislation. The Theodosian Code makes it quite clear that the archisynagogue was a pivotal communal official, and not only in the religious realm. As early
as 330, Constantine issued several edicts which addressed the status of Jewish communal and religious officials: "The same Augustus to the priests, the archsynagogues [*sic*],
fathers of synagogues, and the others who serve in the same place. We order that the
priests, archsynagogues, fathers of synagogues, and the others who serve in synagogues
shall be free from all corporal liturgy."[40] Taken together with another edict issued several days earlier,[41] the intention of the emperor becomes quite clear. Jewish "clergy," i.e.,
those who held a leading role in synagogue affairs ("those who dedicated themselves with
complete devotion to the synagogues of the Jews"—ibid.), are to be exempt from certain
liturgies, as are their pagan and Christian counterparts.

A similar law exempting archisynagogues and others from liturgies was issued at the
end of the century by the emperors Arcadius and Honorius: "The Jews shall be bound
to their rites; while we shall imitate the ancients in conserving their privileges, for it
was established in their laws and confirmed by our divinity, that those who are subject
to the rule of the Illustrious Patriarchs, that is the Archsynagogues, the patriarchs, the
presbyters and the others who are occupied in the rite of that religion, shall persevere in
keeping the same privileges that are reverently bestowed on the first clerics of the vener-
able Christian Law."[42]

Finally, a third law notes a specific communal function ascribed to the archisynagogue: "It is a matter of shameful superstition that the Archsynagogues, the presbyters
of the Jews, and those they call apostles, who are sent by the Patriarch on a certain date
to demand gold and silver, exact and receive a sum from each synagogue, and deliver
it to him."[43] Although there seems to be ambiguity regarding the precise role of archi-

---

39. Momigliano, "Severo Alessandro Archisynagogus," 151–53.

40. *Cod. Theod.* 16, 8, 4 (Linder, *Jews in Roman Imperial Legislation*, 135).

41. *Cod. Theod.* 16, 8, 2 (ibid., 134).

42. *Cod. Theod.* 16, 8, 13 (ibid., 202).

43. *Cod. Theod.* 16, 8, 14 (ibid., 216). Moreover, there is every reason to believe that the term "Primates" in *Cod. Theod.* 16, 8, 8 (ibid., 187–88), a reference to the most prestigious personages in the local
Jewish community, may indeed mean the archisynagogues: "In the complaints of the Jews it was affirmed that some people are received in their sect on the authority of the judges, against the opposition
of the Primates of their Law, who had cast them out by their judgment and will. We order that this in-
jury should be utterly removed, and that a tenacious group in their superstition shall not earn aid from

synagogues and elders in this process of tax collection—i.e., they were not sent by the Patriarch to carry out this task, as may have been the case with the apostles—there is little justification in dismissing this report in its entirety. These synagogue officials were apparently also involved in the collection of monies from their communities, and thus this source has historical significance for our purposes.

Inscriptions. The largest corpus of material regarding the archisynagogue is to be found in inscriptions. Horsley as well as Rajak and Noy have conveniently listed all known examples, which, by their count, total more than thirty inscriptions containing names of about forty persons holding that title. Most of the inscriptions are funerary and thus usually only take note of the fact that the person being honored once held that position. Yet even from this limited context we may cull some additional information regarding this office.

Of especial importance are the dedicatory inscriptions from synagogues which tell us something about the functioning of the archisynagogue.[44] Eight such inscriptions exist— more than for any other synagogue-related post.[45] By way of comparison, seven dedicatory inscriptions mention presbyters, five (perhaps six) note an archon, and five a *phrontistes*.[46] The archisynagogues who are mentioned as donors hailed from North Africa, Greece, Asia Minor, Syria, and Palestine. Some are noted as having built or founded the synagogue (Jerusalem, Teos, Aegina) or as having restored it (Acmonia), others as having contributed a chancel screen (Myndos), a mosaic pavement (Naro), the entrance to the building (Apamea), or a *triclinium* (Caesarea).

Clearly, these inscriptions indicate that an archisynagogue was not infrequently an important donor to the synagogue. However, it is a major—and unwarranted—leap to assume, on the basis of this evidence, that this philanthropic dimension was a sine qua non for becoming an archisynagogue[47] or that an archisynagogue functioned only in this capacity. What may have been common and, in many cases, even expected was not necessarily the sole or determinant factor in defining one's position. It is entirely conceivable that many archisynagogues did not contribute to the synagogue building; otherwise, we might have expected to find many more such inscriptions, and not only eight. However, this last point is difficult to substantiate, as it rests on an *argumentum ex silentio*. More-

---

their undue readmission through the authority of judges or of ill-gotten rescript, against the will of their Primates, who are manifestly authorized to pass judgment concerning their religion, under the authority of the Most Renowned and the Illustrious patriarchs."

44. In addition to the above, see Lifshitz, *Donateurs et fondateurs*, 88 (ἀρχισυνάγωγος); Burtchaell, *From Synagogue to Church*, 243 n. 83; Brooten, *Women Leaders*, 23ff., 229-30 n. 93.

45. Rajak and Noy list nine, yet the Salamis inscription may be an epitaph. See also Lifshitz, *Donateurs et fondateurs*, no. 85 and esp. p. 76.

46. *Presbyter*: Lifshitz, *Donateurs et fondateurs*, nos. 14, 32, 37, 58, 82, 84, 101. *Archon*: ibid., nos. 11, 33, 37, 100, 101, and possibly 9a. *Phrontistes*: ibid., nos. 1, 2, 36, 37, 66.

47. Rajak and Noy, "*Archisynagogoi*," 84-89.

over, other synagogue officials and ordinary members also made substantial contributions toward synagogue-related projects, as did the community as a whole.[48] Thus, one need not have been an archisynagogue to contribute. Indeed, the distinction made in rabbinic literature between "the great men of the generation" and the *rosh knesset* may, in fact, indicate that the latter was not always the primary benefactor, at least in Palestinian circles.

These inscriptions likewise confirm the overall prominence of this office, as is evidenced in other sources as well. Not infrequently, a lavish honorific title accompanies the mention of an archisynagogue: ἀξιολογώτατος — "the most respected" (Teos); τιμιώτατος — "the most honored" (Apamea); and λαμπρότατος — "the most illustrious" (Sepphoris, twice). This evidence thus dovetails nicely with the report in *Scriptores Historiae Augustae*, noted above, of the pagan mob calling the emperor an archisynagogue, as well as indications in the Theodosian Code of the prominence of this office.

It is also noteworthy that an archisynagogue may have held more than just one title. This same person may also have been an archon, presbyter, rabbi, *didaskalos*, *phrontistes*, or priest.[49] Dual titles, however, were not unique to this office. A *phrontistes*, for example, could also have been a *pater synagoges*, archon, or presbyter.[50]

Moreover, the position of archisynagogue may have combined with another post, civilian or military, which related to the larger non-Jewish society. Two known instances of such a combination come from the Danube region. An inscription from Moesia identifies one Joses as an archisynagogue and *principales*, the latter term possibly referring to a military or civilian post.[51] From Intercisa, we know of an archisynagogue who was also head of a customs station.[52]

Furthermore, more than one person could have held the title of archisynagogue at any one time. At Apamea, three archisynagogues were honored by Ilasios, who was an archisynagogue in Antioch.[53] Acmonia had two archisynagogues and an archon who together undertook the restoration of the building.[54] The office may have been hereditary in some instances, or at least customarily transmitted from one generation to the next within a single family. Such was the case recorded in the Theodotos inscription from Jerusalem,

---

48. See in general Lifshitz, *Donateurs et fondateurs*, passim; for the Palestinian evidence in particular, see Roth-Gerson, *Greek Inscriptions*, 147–52, 168–74. See also the inscription from Reggio di Calabria; see Noy, *JIWE*, I, no. 139.

49. *Archon*: Noy, *JIWE*, II, no. 322 (Rome); ibid., I, no. 20 (Campania). *Presbyter*: Lifshitz, "Prolegomenon," 88, no. 731c (Crete). *Rabbi*: Frey, *CIJ*, II, no. 1414 (Jerusalem). *Didaskalos*: G. H. R. Horsley, *New Documents*, IV, no. 113 (Corinth). *Phrontistes*: Lifshitz, *Donateurs et fondateurs*, no. 1 (Aegina); ibid., no. 66 (Caesarea). *Priest*: ibid., no. 79 (Jerusalem).

50. See, for example, Noy, *JIWE*, II, nos. 164 and 540; Lifshitz, *Donateurs et fondateurs*, no. 37. See also ibid., no. 14.

51. Scheiber, *Jewish Inscriptions*, no. 10; see also G. H. R. Horsley, *New Documents*, IV, 215, no. 20.

52. Scheiber, *Jewish Inscriptions*, no. 3.

53. Lifshitz, *Donateurs et fondateurs*, no. 38.

54. Ibid., no. 33.

wherein it is stated that the same family retained leadership in the synagogue for at least three generations.[55] A similar situation, lasting two generations, is attested at Venosa.[56]

Finally, the title may have been used in an honorary sense—for instance, when it was bestowed on a child.[57] It is not clear whether "archisynagogue for life" (διὰ βίου) was an honorary title or whether its holder actually continued to function in this capacity until death.[58]

While the non-Jewish epigraphical material referring to *archisynagogoi*[59] points clearly to their role as patrons, other functions of this office are also noted. Eusebius, for example, refers to a pagan by the name of Macrianus, describing him as "a teacher and archisynagogue of Egyptian magicians";[60] Epiphanius relates that Ebionite leaders were called archisynagogues and presbyters and that these officials served as teachers and also arranged marriages within the community.[61]

In summary, our sources refer to the position of archisynagogue in ways that we might well have been able to anticipate. Sources with primarily religious concerns, such as rabbinic material, the New Testament, and the church fathers, all emphasize the religious dimension of the office. Even Imperial legislation, focusing as it does on the Jews as a religious community, addresses this aspect of Jewish life generally, the archisynagogue in particular. Inscriptions, on the other hand, relate mostly to the benefactions of such individuals. But over and above each source's specific concern, we have noted evidence time and again that this office was charged with more than religious and/or financial responsibilities. An archisynagogue was looked upon by Jews and non-Jews alike as a leader and representative of his community. Our sources' biases should not prevent us from trying to recapture the full scope of his responsibilities in the many far-flung Jewish communities of late antiquity.

The office of the Jewish archisynagogue is a fascinating example of adoption and adaptation. Whatever the origin or derivation of the Hebrew *rosh knesset* may have been, Jews clearly borrowed the term "archisynagogue" from their surroundings.[62] On the basis of the available evidence (heavily epigraphical, as noted), pagans appear to have used this term largely in a philanthropic vein, i.e., for one who was conspicuous in his contributions to an association or organization. Nevertheless, given the unique functions of

---

55. Ibid., no. 79.

56. Noy, *JIWE*, I, no. 70.

57. Ibid., no. 53. On other children who were given titles usually reserved for community officials, see ibid., II, nos. 288 and 337.

58. See, for example, Lifshitz, *Donateurs et fondateurs*, no. 16 (Teos); ibid., no. 33 (Acmonia). Both places are in Asia Minor.

59. Cf. the non-Jewish inscriptions cited in G. H. R. Horsley, *New Documents*, IV, 219-20; Rajak and Noy, "Archisynagogoi," 92–93.

60. Eusebius, *Ecclesiastical History* 7, 10, 4.

61. Epiphanius, *Panarion*, 30, 18, 2.

62. *TDNT*, VII, 844-45.

the synagogue as a communal organization and its all-encompassing role in the lives of the local Jewish population, the responsibilities of the Jewish archisynagogue were most probably broader and more comprehensive than those of his pagan namesake. It is doubtful whether such a role was influenced by previous Jewish communal history, since no comparable synagogue framework existed heretofore—either in Palestine or the Diaspora. The office of archisynagogue was therefore a phenomenon of the Greco-Roman world, but it was significantly redefined when brought into the Jewish context, thus attesting to both the responsiveness and the adaptiveness of these Jewish communities.

OTHER OFFICIALS

Archon

Evidence regarding the office of archon in a synagogue setting is spotty and uncertain.[63] While archons at the fore of Palestine's Jewish cities (e.g., Tiberias) and Diaspora communities are well attested,[64] there is also evidence, albeit restricted to Rome, that archons could be associated with particular synagogues as well. Of the forty-seven references to this office in Rome's catacomb inscriptions, sixteen include mention of specific synagogues: four are connected to that of the Siburesians, three to the Calcaresian synagogue, two each to the Augustesian, Vernaclesian, and Volumnesian synagogues, and one each to the Agrippesian, Hebrew, and Tripolitan synagogues. Thus, of the eleven known synagogues in Rome, eight had officials bearing the title "archon."[65]

Scholarly opinion has been divided as to whether the archon functioned as a community leader or as head of a synagogue board.[66] Extant evidence precludes any single all-embracing definition, and it seems that here, as in other cases, there was a great deal of local variation. It is also quite probable that in some places at least, there was little, if any, distinction between the two frameworks, community and synagogue. In Berenice, as we have seen, archons initiated a series of communal decisions and granted awards in a synagogue setting; these officials may well have headed both community and synagogue frameworks at one and the same time. No other official, and particularly no archisyna-

---

63. On this office generally, see Juster, *Juifs*, I, 443–47; Frey, *CIJ*, I, lxxxvii–lxxxix; Leon, *Jews of Ancient Rome*, 173–80.

64. On Tiberias, see Josephus, *War* 2, 599, 641; idem, *Life* 64, 134, 271, 294–96, 313, 381; and Schürer, *History*, II, 179–80. On Berenike, see above, Chap. 4. Regarding the archons of the Theban synagogue at Arsinoe, see Tcherikover et al., *CPJ*, II, 223. On an archon mentioned in an inscription from Utica, see Le Bohec, "Inscriptions juives," 65.

65. Leon, *Jews of Ancient Rome*, 173.

66. Schürer (*Gemeindeverfassung*, 18–20) and Frey (*CIJ*, I, lxxxvii) hold to the latter view, Juster (*Juifs*, I, 444–46) to the former.

gogue, is noted among those mentioned in the three long inscriptions from this Jewish community, and this, in itself, may be significant.[67]

Thus, although we have some interesting information about archons in general, it is impossible to know which refers to a synagogue setting and which to a communal one. For example, in a well-known homily by a Christian writer from around the turn of the fourth century, spuriously ascribed to John Chrysostom, we are told of the Jewish practice of choosing archons in September, on the eve of each Jewish New Year.[68]

Besides Rome, a handful of dedicatory inscriptions from the area of Greece and Asia Minor (Cyprus, Acmonia, Olbia, and Magnesia [?]) specifically mention archons in connection with synagogues.[69] At Elche, archons and presbyters are noted in an inscription on the synagogue's mosaic floor, which may indicate a special place of seating for both of these groups.[70]

Some interesting facts may be learned from the evidence in Rome, where, as noted, the archons were in all probability seen as part of the synagogue officialdom. People could serve as archons on more than one occasion, and there were those who held that position for two and three terms.[71] Special titles such as ἄρχων πάσης τιμῆς ("archon of all honors"), mellarchon, and exarchon are also noted.[72]

Furthermore, the archon is mentioned together with the archisynagogue, at times as an official functioning alongside the latter (e.g., at Acmonia).[73] On occasion, however, one and the same person held both titles (e.g., in Rome and Capua).[74] Several literary examples in the New Testament appear to confuse the two: Mark and Luke-Acts speak of an archisynagogue (see above), but Luke also uses the term "archon of the synagogue."[75] Matthew refers to Jairus simply as "archon," and Mark uses "archisynagogue."[76] Moreover, as noted above, Codex D of Acts 14:2 refers to "the archisynagogues of the Jews and the archons of the synagogue." Whether these discrepancies are the result of ignorance, sloppiness, or variant traditions, or whether the reality itself was as fluid as some of our sources seem to indicate, is difficult to ascertain. It may well be that in smaller

---

67. See above, Chap. 4.

68. *De solstitiis et aequinoctiis*, as referred to in Leon, *Jews of Ancient Rome*, 174; Talley, *Origins of the Liturgical Year*, 92–94; and Wilmart, "Homélies Latines de Chrysostome," 316–17.

69. Lifshitz, *Donateurs et fondateurs*, nos. 9, 11, 33, 85.

70. Noy, *JIWE*, I, no. 181.

71. See, for example, ibid., II, nos. 98, 164, 165, 540.

72. *"Archon of all honors"*: ibid., nos. 121, 164, 259; the precise meaning of this title remains unclear. *Mellarchon*: one designated to become an archon. The term appears six times; see ibid., 538. *Exarchon*: ibid., nos. 2, 4; on possible meanings, see ibid., 11–12.

73. Lifshitz, *Donateurs et fondateurs*, no. 33.

74. *Rome*: Noy, *JIWE*, II, no. 322. *Capua*: ibid., I, no. 20.

75. Luke 8:41, 49.

76. Matt. 9:18, 23; Mark 5:22, 38.

communities these various positions were combined, whereas in the cities they were generally designated as distinct positions.

Pater Synagoges

This term appears in only a few locales, most particularly in Rome, where it is mentioned in nine inscriptions.[77] It also occurs twice in Mauretania[78] and in the monumental inscription from Stobi. The title takes a somewhat different form elsewhere. In an inscription from Mantinea, Aurelius Elpidios is referred to as the "father of the people" ($\pi\alpha\tau\grave{\eta}\rho$ $\lambda\alpha o\hat{v}$) and is accorded this title for life ($\delta\iota\grave{\alpha}$ $\beta\acute{\iota}ov$), while in Smyrna, Irenopolos is called an "elder and father of the community."[79] The word *pater* appears alone in an inscription found near Ostia, and it almost assuredly refers to the *pater synagoges* (see below). In a deed of enfranchisement from Egypt dating to the year 291, one of the parties putting up the ransom money was Aurelius Justus, identified as a *pater synagoges* and city councillor from Ono in Roman Palestine.[80] Finally, the title *patres synagogarum* is mentioned in an edict dated to 330 in the Theodosian Code (see below).

There is general agreement that this title was essentially honorific, denoting a major patron and benefactor of the community,[81] and was used similarly in pagan contexts; Roman municipal governments and *collegia* also had their *patres*.[82] Moreover, the use of the term "father" as a title of honor and respect has deep roots in ancient Judaism. It appears in the Bible, most memorably in Elisha's cry to Elijah when the latter ascended to heaven, and the Maccabean martyr Razis is referred to as "father of his people."[83] Whether the use of this term with reference to specific sages has a similar honorific meaning or whether it is merely part of the actual name (e.g., Abba Saul, Abba Yosi, Abba Eli'ezer) is difficult to determine.[84] Surely the use of the term for the head of a rabbinic court, *av bet din*, not only carries with it an honorific dimension, but is also a clear indication of status and authority.[85]

Yet, despite the overwhelming consensus that we are essentially dealing here with a

---

77. Noy, *JIWE*, II, 538. See also Schürer, *Gemeindeverfassung*, 29–30; Juster, *Juifs*, I, 449 n. 2; Leon, *Jews of Ancient Rome*, 186–88.

78. Le Bohec, "Inscriptions juives," nos. 74, 79.

79. *Mantinea*: Lifshitz, *Donateurs et fondateurs*, no. 9; White, *Social Origins*, 359–60. *Smyrna*: ibid., no. 14.

80. Tcherikover et al., *CPJ*, III, no. 473.

81. Juster, *Juifs*, I, 448–49; Elbogen, *Jewish Liturgy*, 369; Leon, *Jews of Ancient Rome*, 186–88; Brooten, *Women Leaders*, 64ff.; Linder, *Jews in Roman Imperial Legislation*, 137 n. 11; Burtchaell, *From Synagogue to Church*, 249–50.

82. Schürer, *Gemeindeverfassung*, 29–30; White, *Building God's House*, 57–58, 174 n. 134; Noy, *JIWE*, I, 34, 91, 146; Di Segni, "Involvement," 325–26.

83. II Kgs. 2:12; 6:21; II Macc. 14:37.

84. See, for example, M Betzah 3:8; M 'Avot 2:8; M Middot 2:5–6; M Miqva'ot 2:10.

85. Mantel, *Studies*, 102ff.

position of honor, there are a number of sources which suggest that this may not always have been the case. The Stobi inscription, which mentions the *pater synagoges* Claudius Tiberius Polycharmos conveys the impression that this individual played a crucial and pivotal role in synagogue affairs generally. Truth to tell, the inscription itself never indicates this explicitly, and what is recorded could well fit the activities of any wealthy patron. Nevertheless, the tenor and tone of this inscription seem to imply the very broad involvement of Polycharmos in synagogue affairs.[86]

Another indication of the *pater*'s prominence in synagogue affairs is found in an inscription from Castel Porziano, near Ostia.[87] We learn that the transfer of property to the gerousiarch Gaius Julius Justus for purposes of building a family tomb was done through the efforts of three officials, the first of whom was one Livius Dionysius, *pater*. Although only the word *pater* is used here without the accompanying *synagoges*, this one word may, in fact, be a shortened form of this title. In any case, it seems that Livius' involvement was more than merely titular or honorary, and he presumably functioned as part of a local governing board charged with executing this transaction.

The most important source attesting to the role of the *pater* in synagogue affairs is the Theodosian Code. A decree reads as follows: "The same Augustus [Constantine] to the priests, the archsynagogues, fathers of synagogues, and the others who serve in the same place: We order that the priests, archsynagogues, fathers of synagogues, and the others who serve in synagogues shall be free from all corporate liturgy."[88] The mention of "fathers of synagogues" alongside other functionaries, such as the priests (see below, Chap. 15) and archisynagogues, would seem to indicate a position of responsibility for the *patres*. This inference is reinforced by the phrase "and the others who serve in the same place" and confirmed by the exemption of the aforementioned from all liturgies. Unless we dismiss this evidence as totally misconstrued, and this would appear to be a severe and unwarranted judgment, it must be conceded that such a title included, at least on occasion, a variety of administrative duties.

As noted, most of the epigraphical references to *pater* appear in connection with synagogues in Rome, specifically the synagogues of the Hebrews, Calcaresians, Vernaclesians, Elaeans, and Campesians.[89] It may be of significance that most titles connected with the last-named synagogue are either *pater* or *mater*. Might this mean that the heads of this particular institution bore these titles specifically?

---

86. On the Stobi inscription, see above, Chap. 8. Such an inference was made by White (*Building God's House*, 71): "Yet, Polycharmos himself continued to exercise leadership in both social and religious matters as *pater synagoges*." More generally, however, he notes: "Unlike other offices in the synagogue, *pater* and *mater* seem to have been positions of high status earned chiefly through conspicuous acts of generosity" (ibid., 81).

87. Noy, *JIWE*, I, no. 18. See also White, "Synagogue and Society," 42–48.

88. *Cod. Theod.* 16, 8, 4 (Linder, *Jews in Roman Imperial Legislation*, 135).

89. Leon, *Jews of Ancient Rome*, 187; Noy, *JIWE*, II, 538.

A *pater* may have held other communal positions at some point, such as one Domnus who was referred to as a *pater*, a three-time archon, and a two-time *phrontistes*.[90] On another occasion, a *pater* also served as an archon.[91] Mnaseas (Menasseh?) was noted as "a student of the wise" or "sage" ($\mu\alpha\theta\eta\tau\grave{\eta}s\ \sigma\sigma\phi\hat{\omega}\nu$) and "father of synagogues,"[92] and Pancharius, who died at the ripe old age of 110, was "father of the synagogue of Elea . . . who loved his people and the Law."[93] As noted, Aurelius Elpidios of Mantinea was referred to as a "father of his people, forever."[94]

Mater Synagoges

The same dilemmas regarding the term *pater synagoges* face us when considering the term *mater synagoges*. Was this an honorific term, or did it at times connote a position of substance within the community? This question is even more difficult to answer with regard to *mater*, owing to the fewer sources at our disposal. Let us review the evidence at hand.

Six inscriptions note this title in one form or another, three in Greek and three in Latin. All come from Italy: three from Rome, two from Venosa in the south, and one from Brescia in the north.[95]

[1] Here lies Simplica, mother of the synagogue, who loved her husband . . . the synagogue for his own spouse

[2] Here lies [. . .]ia Marcella, mother of the synagogue of the Augustesians. May [she?] be remembered [?]. In peace here sleep.

[3] Veturia Paula, place in her eternal home, who lived 86 years 6 months, a proselyte for 16 years under the name of Sarah, mother of the synagogues of Campus and Volumnius. In peace her sleep.

[4] Here lies Faustina the mother, wife of Auxanius the father and patron of the city.

[5] Here rests Alexandria the fatheress [*pateressa*], who lived more or less . . . years. Peace.

[6] For Coelia Paterna, mother of the synagogue of the Brixians.

The title *mater* appears to have taken one of a number of forms. A woman might be designated simply as *mater*, or *mater synagoges*, without any further identification. On the other hand, three women are given this title with respect to specific synagogues, that of the Augustesians, the Campesians, the Volumnesians, and the Brixians (nos. 2, 3, and 6). Most unusual is the case of Veturia Paula (no. 3), who was mother of two Roman synagogues. Given her advanced age at conversion, it would seem likely that her title was strictly honorary and did not reflect an active responsibility in either of the synagogues.

---

90. Noy, *JIWE*, II, no. 540.

91. Ibid., no. 210.

92. Ibid., no. 544.

93. Ibid., no. 576.

94. Lifshitz, *Donateurs et fondateurs*, no. 9.

95. Noy, *JIWE*, I, nos. 5, 63, 116; II, nos. 251, 542, 577.

Presbyter (Elder)

There is no question that the presbyter was an integral part of the synagogue officialdom in many locales. Some thirty inscriptions from sites stretching across the breadth
of the Empire take note of this office, from Elche in Spain to Dura Europos in Syria.[96]
Nevertheless, despite the geographical dispersion, use of the term tends to be concentrated in certain areas, for example, in the region of Asia Minor (including Cyprus and
Rhodes) and in southern Italy, particularly Venosa and Sicily. It is noticeably absent from
Rome and Egypt and appears only infrequently in North Africa, Syria, and Palestine.
The same holds true for references to women elders (*presbytera*). Four references come
from Venosa and Malta, one each from Crete, Thrace, and North Africa, and a possible,
though disputed, reference from Rome.[97] This title appears as early as the Theodotos inscription of first-century Jerusalem (referring in all probability to the first century B.C.E.)
and continues down to the end of antiquity.

Nevertheless, it is difficult to pinpoint precisely the function of this office. Was it
administrative, financial, religious-liturgical, all three, or perhaps a combination of any
two? The specific definition of this title may well have differed from place to place, as the
prominence of elders is attested in all societies from hoary antiquity. In Jewish tradition,
the term is equivalent to the Hebrew word *zaqen* (= elder), who is featured prominently
in biblical and post-biblical literature, including rabbinic sources.[98] In the last, the term
appears in a variety of contexts, but lacks specificity regarding definition and framework.
The looseness of this term may be compared to that of "archon," which, as noted, could
have applied to a number of roles. It has often been assumed that the council of elders
(presbyters) was the chief governing board of a community or congregation, from which
archons were selected to run day-to-day affairs.[99] However, there may also have been
situations where the governing council was composed of archons (as at Berenice), and
smaller communities may have dispensed with such a governing council. The case against
pressing for too neat a definition is vividly demonstrated in several inscriptions from
Dura Europos. One of the heads of the community, Samuel the priest, son of Yeda'ya, is
referred to as an archon in an Aramaic inscription and as a presbyter in a Greek one.[100]
Here, at least, these terms seem to have been interchangeable.

---

96. Frey, *CIJ*, II, nos. 790, 792, 800, 801, 931, 1137, 1277, 1404; Lifshitz, "Prolegomenon," nos. 731c,
731f; idem, *Donateurs et fondateurs*, nos. 14, 32, 37, 38, 58, 82, 84; Noy, *JIWE*, I, nos. 59, 62, 71, 75, 148, 149,
157, 163, 181; Robert, *Nouvelles inscriptions*, 57; Le Bohec, "Inscriptions juives," no. 4. On an inscription
found recently in Binyamina, near Caesarea, naming Judah the presbyter, see Herman, "Jewish Tombstone," 160–61.

97. Brooten, *Women Leaders*, 41–46; Noy, *JIWE*, I, nos. 59, 62, 163; for his reservations regarding
Rome, see ibid., II, no. 24.

98. *TDNT*, VI, 652–61; Brooten, *Women Leaders*, 46–52. For early Christian literature, see *TDNT*,
VI, 661–83.

99. See, for example, Baron, *Jewish Community*, I, 99.

100. Kraeling, *Dura: Synagogue*, 263–68, 277; Lifshitz, *Donateurs et fondateurs*, no. 58.

A presbyter could have been a benefactor of a synagogue and may have been one of its founders.[101] He or she simultaneously might have borne other titles as well, such as *pater*, *phrontistes*, or archisynagogue, as in the case of Sophia of Gortyn (see below, Chap. 14).[102] As a group, presbyters are listed alongside archisynagogues and archons and, as noted above, appear to have occupied special seats along with the archons in the Elche synagogue.[103]

One of the few rabbinic sources which places the elders firmly within a synagogue context concerns seating arrangements. The Tosefta has preserved several intriguing descriptions of the seating within a synagogue, wherein elders were accorded a special place. The elders in the first-century Alexandrian synagogue are said to have occupied seventy-one elaborately decorated chairs.[104] Another tradition speaks of elders seated with their backs to the Jerusalem-oriented wall while facing the congregation.[105] However, the precise role of these elders in the worship context—if any—is never spelled out.

Three edicts from the Theodosian Code clearly reveal that the presbyters held a recognized role in synagogue life. The first is dated to 330: "Those who dedicated themselves with complete devotion to the synagogues of the Jews, to the Patriarchs or to the Presbyters . . . it is they who preside over the law, [and they who] shall continue to be exempt from all liturgies, personal as well as civil." [106]

The second edict, issued by Arcadius in his and Honorius' name in 397, lists those who were subject to the Patriarch's rule and were devoted to Jewish rites. Presbyters are listed along with the archisynagogues and Patriarchs, and all three are granted exemptions similar to those enjoyed by the Christian clergy.[107] A third edict, from 399, mentions presbyters along with archisynagogues and apostles, who were charged with the collection of taxes from the Patriarch.[108]

Finally, in his famous *Novella* from 553, Justinian refers to synagogue leaders who might have attempted to hinder the implementation of his law. Among the three officials named, one was a presbyter.[109] One can thus safely assume from the above that in many places throughout the course of late antiquity presbyters played a central role in the religious and administrative life of the synagogue.

---

101. Lifshitz, *Donateurs et fondateurs*, nos. 32, 37; ibid., nos. 58, 79.

102. *Pater:* ibid., no. 14. *Phrontistes:* ibid., no. 37. *Archisynagogue:* Lifshitz, "Prolegomenon," no. 731c.

103. G. H. R. Horsley, *New Documents*, IV, 215, no. 23; Noy, *JIWE*, I, no. 181. On Elche, see above, Chap. 8. As noted (above, note 22), according to Epiphanius, leadership of the Ebionites was in the hands of archisynagogues and presbyters.

104. T Sukkah 4:6 (p. 273); and above, Chap. 4.

105. T Megillah 3:21 (p. 360).

106. Linder, *Jews in Roman Imperial Legislation*, 134, no. 9.

107. Ibid., no. 27.

108. Ibid., no. 30.

109. Ibid., no. 66.

Grammateus

Although some have defined the *grammateus* as a scholar of sorts, probably influenced in this interpretation by the Hebrew *sofer* (= scribe),[110] the title has generally been understood in a secretarial vein, as were similar titles of officials in a Greco-Roman context.[111] Possible tasks would have included responsibility for keeping records of official meetings and decisions, handling correspondence, managing the archives, keeping synagogue membership lists, and serving as a notary.

Our knowledge of this office is radically skewed, as practically all of our evidence comes from the Roman catacomb inscriptions. Of the twenty-seven inscriptions mentioning a *grammateus*, twenty-six derive from these epitaphs (the remaining one was found in Bithynia).[112] Six of the Roman *grammatei* are explicitly associated with a synagogue—two with the synagogue of the Siburesians and one each with those of the Vernaclesians, Augustesians, Calcaresians, and Secenians.

Of the more than one hundred inscriptions recorded by Lifshitz in his *Donateurs et fondateurs*, no *grammateus* is listed as a benefactor. Since evidence for this office stems from epitaphs, and not from dedicatory inscriptions, it may be concluded that, by and large, these officials were not among the wealthy members of the congregation. Yet, as elsewhere, one can find an exception to this rule. In the dedicatory inscription from Bithynia, the *grammateus* also served as a presbyter and as head of some sort of council of elders.[113]

The *grammateus* was not necessarily an older person, as the ages noted range from twenty-two to seventy.[114] On occasion, this title was passed down from generation to generation, with sons following in their fathers' footsteps. Children were also given the title, presumably because of their father's position and perhaps with the intention that they would one day have the title in their own right.[115] That such a title might be bestowed for this reason is attested in an inscription noting the death of a twenty-four-year-old referred to as a *mellogrammateus*, i.e., a future *grammateus*.[116] In one unusual case, the grandfather Honoratus was a *grammateus*, as were his son Petronius and his grandson (by his other son, Rufus), also named Honoratus.[117]

---

110. Schürer, *Gemeindeverfassung*, 30.

111. Juster, *Juifs*, I, 447–48; Frey, *CIJ*, I, xcii–xciv; Baron, *Jewish Community*, I, 102–3; Leon, *Jews of Ancient Rome*, 183–86; Burtchaell, *From Synagogue to Church*, 251–53.

112. Noy, *JIWE*, II, 538 (*grammateus*); see also Leon, *Jews of Ancient Rome*, 183 n. 2; Burtchaell, *From Synagogue to Church*, 252 n. 130. On the epitaph from Bithynia, see Frey, *CIJ*, I, no. 800.

113. Frey, *CIJ*, I, no. 800.

114. Leon, *Jews of Ancient Rome*, 185; Burtchaell, *From Synagogue to Church*, 252.

115. For example, see Noy, *JIWE*, II, no. 255.

116. Ibid., no. 231; see also no. 404.

117. Ibid., nos. 223, 256, 257.

Phrontistes

The office of *phrontistes* appears to have been administrative in nature, referring to one who manages or oversees some sort of facility.[118] The position is attested at a number of sites in Palestine (Caesarea, Jaffa), Egypt, Pamphylia, Porto, and Rome.[119] At times, this office, too, might be combined with another. Beryllos of Caesarea, for instance, was both *phrontistes* and archisynagogue; in Rome, Eupsychius was an archon on two occasions, an "archon of all honor" and a *phrontistes*.[120] In another Roman epitaph already mentioned, Domnus was a *phrontistes* for two terms, as well as an archon for three and the *pater synagoges* of the Vernaclesian synagogue.[121] A *phrontistes* could thus have made substantial contributions to the synagogue building, as attested in the above-noted dedicatory inscriptions.

Perhaps the best indication of the possible roles of this official is to be found in two inscriptions from Aegina.[122] Although the noun *phrontistes* is not used there, its verb form is invoked twice. The first reference is to the archisynagogue Theodoros, who served (*phrontisas*) the synagogue for four years and built the structure from its foundations. In the second inscription, Theodoros the Younger (a son?) oversaw (*phrontizon*) the laying of a mosaic floor in the synagogue.

Ḥazzan

The most prominent functionary in the Palestinian synagogue, as least as reflected in rabbinic literature, was the *ḥazzan*.[123] This is not to say that he was the most powerful or influential officer; he clearly was not. Nevertheless, the *ḥazzan*, although answerable to others, such as the archisynagogue, sage, or the community at large, was a pivotal figure in many synagogue-related activities. He himself had a wide variety of tasks, and often—especially within smaller communities—this position was combined with others. The account of the Simonias community asking R. Judah I to find someone who would serve as a preacher, judge, *ḥazzan*, teacher of Bible and Oral Law, and otherwise "attend to all our needs" is revealing.[124] A generation or two later, the Jewish community of Bostra similarly turned to Resh Laqish in the mid-third century in search of someone who could be a "preacher, judge, teacher of Bible, *ḥazzan*, and attend to all our other needs."[125] That a

---

118. Frey, *CIJ*, I, xcii.

119. Ibid., II, nos. 918, 919; Lifshitz, *Donateurs et fondateurs*, nos. 36, 37, 66; Horbury and Noy, *Jewish Inscriptions*, no. 146; Noy, *JIWE*, I, no. 17; ibid., II, nos. 164, 540.

120. Lifshitz, *Donateurs et fondateurs*, no. 66; Noy, *JIWE*, II, no. 164.

121. Noy, *JIWE*, II, no. 540.

122. Lifshitz, *Donateurs et fondateurs*, nos. 1, 2.

123. On the *ḥazzan* generally, see Schürer, *History*, II, 438; Juster, *Juifs*, I, 454; S. Krauss, *Synagogale Altertümer*, 121–31. See also Landman, *Cantor*, 3ff.; Sky, *Office of Hazzan*, 11–36.

124. Y Yevamot 12, 13a. A shorter version of this same tradition, which, however, excludes the word *ḥazzan*, is found in Genesis Rabbah 81:2 (p. 969).

125. Y Shevi'it 6, 1, 36d; Deuteronomy Rabbah, Va'ethanan (p. 60). Note the slightly different listing

room was often set aside in a synagogue building for a *ḥazzan*'s personal needs serves as a clear indication of the extended time he was expected to spend there.[126]

While a *ḥazzan* was crucial to the synagogue enterprise, he was considered in rabbinic sources as distinctly secondary in status. In one tradition, the *ḥazzan* is ranked after the sage and the teacher, ahead of only the *'am ha-'aretz*—not a complimentary position, in light of the rabbinic attitude toward this last-mentioned group.[127] Given his multifaceted role, it should not be surprising, then, that the *ḥazzan* was often perceived, by sages at least, as overstepping his authority. One rabbinic statement flatly states that the *ḥazzan* should not assume authority (אינו נוטל שררה לעצמו).[128] In one midrash, the following statement is ascribed to God: "Pay attention to the teachers of Bible, *ḥazzanim*, and police [guards] that stand before you, that they may not become arrogant, and don't raise their wages and thus place a burden on the community."[129]

Contrastingly, in what may be a more popular, rather than rabbinically inspired, tradition the *ḥazzan* is regarded with considerable deference. A tannaitic tradition (noted above) speaks of additional cups of wine that were to be added to a funerary meal in honor of a (local) *ḥazzan*, a *rosh knesset*, and Rabban Gamaliel.[130] Moreover, each of the synagogue inscriptions which names a *ḥazzan* notes that he either contributed to the building or held office when a certain repair or addition was made.[131] Thus, although such evidence is severely limited, it would appear that in some cases the *ḥazzan* enjoyed greater esteem in Jewish society than is often conveyed in rabbinic sources.

We know practically nothing about the individuals who served as *ḥazzanim*. On only

---

in the latter source: "teacher of Bible and Oral Law, *ḥazzan*, scribe (כתב), and involved (alternatively: expert) in all matters." See comments in Deuteronomy Rabbah (ed. Lieberman, n. 16) and particularly the reference found in Leviticus Rabbah 23:4 (pp. 531–32).

See also an inscription from Apamea where the *ḥazzan* also served as the local deacon (διάκονος); see Lifshitz, *Donateurs et fondateurs*, no. 40. See also Mouterde, *Inscriptions*, IV, no. 1321; Robert, "Epitaphes juives," 394.

126. B 'Eruvin 55b, 74b.

127. M Sotah 9:15; B Sotah 49a–b. Note the variants listed in the edition of the *Complete Israeli Talmud—Sotah*, II, 353–54; and comments in J. N. Epstein, *Introduction to the Mishnaic Text*, 976. Later on, these two categories (*ḥazzan* and teacher) are coupled in exegetical (e.g., Y Sanhedrin 13, 9, 23d; B Shabbat 56a) and theoretical (e.g., B Sanhedrin 17b) contexts.

128. Genesis Rabbah 79:20 (p. 950); Yalqut Shim'oni, Genesis, 133 (p. 682).

129. Midrash Hagadol, Exodus 21:1 (p. 454). In a similar vein, see also the comment by R. El'azar regarding a *ḥazzan*'s behavior (Y Berakhot 5, 9c). Relevant also is the instruction given to the *ḥazzan* by R. Yose on what to do when one or two Torah scrolls were available for separate readings; see below, note 132.

130. See above, note 32. Whether the *ḥazzan* had some specific function with regard to burial is unknown. See, however, Zlotnick (*Tractate "Mourning,"* 169), who suggests that the *ḥazzan* attended to the needs of the dead.

131. Naveh, *On Stone and Mosaic*, nos. 20, 28, and p. 12; Lifshitz, *Donateurs et fondateurs*, no. 40. See also Barag, "Second Season of Excavations at En Gedi," 53.

one occasion is the name of a particular *hazzan* mentioned in the sources.[132] In inscriptions, however, a number of names appear; Nemeas was a *hazzan* in Apamea, Yoʻezer at Horvat ʻAmmudim, Judah at Aphek, and Yohanan at ʻEn Gedi.[133] Not surprisingly, each of these names is of Jewish origin.[134] Presumably, Nemeas was important enough a personage that this inscription at least was dated to his ministry (ἐπὶ Νεμία), as was the case with "a very distinguished archisynagogue" in Apamea as well as a "presbyter, auditor, and administrator" in the synagogue of Sidé.[135] In the inscription from Aphek, the *hazzan* proclaims: "I am Judah the *hazzan*." Similar to other offices at the time, the position of *hazzan* may also have been hereditary, although evidence for this is only to be found in an eleventh-century divorce document stemming from the Jewish community in Jaffa.[136]

An official bearing the title *hazzan* is mentioned in a number of traditions relating to the pre-70 era; at this time at least, the position seems to parallel that of the attendant (νεωκόρος) in the pagan temple of the Hellenistic and pre-Hellenistic eras and the ὑπηρέτης and deacon of the early Empire.[137] The *hazzan* is mentioned as having functioned in a Temple setting, handing the Torah scroll to the *rosh knesset* on two different ceremonial occasions: (1) on Yom Kippur, before the high priest read the Torah portion pertaining to the day and (2) before the king read from the Torah at the *Haqhel* ceremony, at the close of a sabbatical year.[138] Moreover, this Temple *hazzan* was said to have attended to the priests' wardrobe on a daily basis, taken charge of *lulavim* left on the Temple premises overnight during the Sukkot festival, and generally kept order.[139] *Hazzanim* purportedly accompanied local delegations of priests (משמרות) and non-priests (מעמדות) to Jerusalem when the former were to officiate in the Temple ceremonies on a given week.[140] With regard to the first-century synagogue, Luke takes note of a ὑπηρέτης who took the book of Prophets from Jesus when the latter had finished reading.[141] Finally, the *hazzan*

---

132. One Bar ʻUlla (also referred to as R. ʻUlla) is mentioned as the *hazzan* of the Babylonian synagogue in Sepphoris (Y Yoma 7, 1, 44b; Y Megillah 4, 5, 75b; Y Sotah 7, 6, 22a; Tractate Soferim 11:3 [p. 220]).

133. See above, note 131.

134. The name "Nemeas," written in Greek, is undoubtedly equivalent to the Hebrew "Nehemiah."

135. Lifshitz, *Donateurs et fondateurs*, nos. 37, 38.

136. See Margoliot, *Palestinian Halakhah*, 122.

137. Dion, "Synagogues et temples," 68–72. See also Josephus' use of the term in referring to a Temple functionary in the time of Pompey (*War* I, 153). On the similarities between the synagogue *hazzan* on the one hand and the terms ὑπηρέτης and deacon (διάκονος) on the other, see *TDNT*, II, 89–93, esp. 91; VIII, 530–44. These titles are most often regarded as synonymous; see Schürer, *History*, II, 438; C. Roberts et al., "Gild of Zeus," 50; S. J. D. Cohen, *From Maccabees to Mishnah*, 217.

138. *Yom Kippur:* M Yoma 7:1; M Sotah 7:7; *Haqhel:* M Sotah 7:8.

139. M Tamid 5:3; M Sukkah 4:4; and ʼAvot de R. Nathan, A, 35 (p. 106).

140. T Bikkurim 2:8 (p. 292); and Lieberman, *TK*, II, 848. The term חזני בית הכנסת used here may indeed be anachronistic. The parallel in M Bikkurim 3:2 mentions a ממונה (appointee) instead of a *hazzan*.

141. Luke 4:20.

of this early period appears to have been in charge of other details of the Torah-reading ceremony, as already noted in the tradition regarding the Alexandrian synagogue, where the *ḥazzan* signaled the congregation with handkerchiefs when it was time for them to respond to the Torah benedictions.[142]

Since all of the above sources are themselves post-70 in origin, the question naturally arises as to whether they are historically reliable. Are we perhaps dealing with anachronistic traditions, which may tell us more about the tradents' post-70 setting or what they imagined to have been the case earlier, than what actually took place in the pre-70 years? To be sure, there can be little, if any, certitude of these traditions' historical reliability. Nevertheless, there may indeed be a historical basis for some, if not most, of the above traditions. Such a possibility stems from a number of considerations. First of all, this title — or parallels to it — appear in a wide variety of independent sources (rabbinic literature, the New Testament, and a Ptolemaic inscription), and this fact, in itself, may lend some credence to these traditions. In addition, the argument of anachronism is itself a double-edged sword. If a phenomenon is acknowledged to have existed from the second century on, why dismiss, a priori, evidence that it may have existed in the first century as well? Why assume that such an office (and consequently an "anachronistic" tradition) emerged in the post-70 period, if the institution with which it was associated existed beforehand?

As regards the Temple customs noted above, the situation is admittedly more complex. The appearance of a *ḥazzan* in such a context is indeed unexpected. Yet, the fact remains that it is mentioned, and here one would be hard pressed to make a case for anachronism. Nothing resembling these two ceremonies existed in the post-70 period, nor is the *ḥazzan* mentioned as having functioned in a later synagogue context in any way remotely like what is described with regard to the Temple. Moreover, why is it more cogent to assume that the term *ḥazzan* was retrojected from later synagogue usage onto the Temple setting, rather than posit that such an official may have also functioned in the Temple, as in parallel pagan contexts? We may thus conclude that there is some degree of probability in the historicity of these traditions; at the very least, they cannot be summarily dismissed as irrelevant for the early period.

Turning to the post-70 era, the centrality of the *ḥazzan* in synagogue worship is especially evident in the Torah-reading ceremony. At every stage of this ritual, which remained focal in the worship service, the *ḥazzan* played a key role. According to the Tosefta, the *ḥazzan* would choose the people who would read from the Torah, a task which he shared with the archisynagogue. The *ḥazzan* would then tell the Torah reader when to begin,[143] and during the reading itself, according to one tradition, he would recite each verse, after which the person selected to read from the Torah would repeat it. This, following Lieberman, is the meaning of the phrase אחד עומד ומחזין לו עד שעה שיקרא:

---

142. T Sukkah 4:6 (p. 273) and parallels.
143. T Megillah 3:21 (p. 359); and Lieberman, *TK*, V, 1196–97.

"one stands [next to the *ḥazzan*] and recites each verse beforehand as the *ḥazzan* was wont to do, until he has read [i.e., concluded the reading]."[144]

Neither the *ḥazzan* nor the archisynagogue would read from the Torah regularly. They would do so only under special circumstances, for they were, in essence, charged with distributing this honor among others present.[145] In addition, the *ḥazzan* was responsible for such tasks as taking the book of Prophets when the reader had finished and rolling a scroll or replacing one with another if the day's reading so required.[146]

In second-century sources, we read of the *ḥazzan* being called upon to orchestrate other public ceremonies as well. A special moment in the synagogue liturgy was the priestly blessing, and it was the *ḥazzan* who was to indicate to the priests when to commence (אמורו).[147] As in the Torah-reading ceremony, the *ḥazzan* would recite the priestly blessing in a low voice to aid the priests, as is still the practice to this day. In describing where and how the priests and *ḥazzan* were usually placed in the synagogue, the Tosefta relates: "And as the priests raised their hands [for the blessing], they face the people and their backs are turned to the holy [i.e., Jerusalem]. The *ḥazzan* of the synagogue faces the holy and all the people face the holy."[148]

In yet another public framework, during a fast in time of drought, the *ḥazzan* might announce to the assembled priests when they should sound the shofar. Such a fast-day ceremony took place in the early second-century Galilee under the auspices of several sages. However, this practice met with opposition from other rabbis, possibly because they found the emulation of certain Temple practices objectionable.[149]

By the early third century, the *ḥazzan* played an active role in public prayer. The Tosefta account of the *ḥazzan* facing the holy may also reflect the practice of his leading the congregation in the recitation of the *'Amidah*.[150] Other sources corroborate this role. One reports on a *ḥazzan* in the southern part of the country who served as a prayer leader and whose rendition of the opening paragraph was not to the liking of several visiting sages.[151] A later source reports that the *ḥazzan* is required to recite the *Qedushah* prayer

---

144. T Megillah 3:21 (p. 360); and comment to line 77 in Lieberman, *TK*, V, 1198–99. On a possible reference (albeit requiring a textual emendation) to a *ḥazzan* functioning as both reader and translator, see Y Megillah 4, 1, 74d; and comments in York, "Targum in Synagogue and School," 76 n. 6.

145. See above, note 143.

146. See above, note 141; Y Yoma 7, 1, 44b; Y Megillah 4, 5, 75b; Y Sotah 7, 6, 22a; Tractate Soferim 11:3 (p. 220). See Rashi's definition of a *ḥazzan* as a שמש הצבור ("one who serves the congregation") in his commentary to B Sukkah 51b.

147. Sifre–Numbers 39 (p. 43).

148. T Megillah 3:21 (p. 360).

149. T Taʿanit 1:13 (p. 327). See also B Rosh Hashanah 27a; B Taʿanit 16b; as well as Alon, *Studies*, I, 108; Miller, *Studies*, 103–15.

150. See above, note 149.

151. Y Berakhot 9, 1, 12d. See also Midrash on Psalms 19:2 (p. 82b); and below, Chap. 16.

in the *'Amidah* of minor festivals (i.e., Hanukkah, the New Moons, and the intermediate days of festivals).[152]

Also within the liturgical setting, the *ḥazzan* had occasion to ask others to lead in prayer. This was not always an easy task, particularly when someone refused and the *ḥazzan* became overly insistent.[153]

At the very end of late antiquity, we read of a *ḥazzan* approaching mourners following the *Mussaf* (Additional) service, reciting for them a special prayer followed by the recitation of the *Qaddish*.[154] About the same time, there appears to have been a custom of offering special praise for a groom, and it was the *ḥazzan* who may have officiated in this capacity as well. In any case, he is specifically mentioned as blessing the bride under the bridal canopy.[155] On several occasions, as reported in Tractate Soferim, a *ḥazzan* is referred to as one who recites prayers publicly and is duly instructed as to what to say on various occasions.[156] We have already noted above[157] the custom of posting two people on either side of the *ḥazzan* while the latter leads the congregation in prayer, a practice which may have evolved from the fast-day ceremonies first described in tannaitic literature. The significance of this practice remains elusive. Was it strictly a ceremonial gesture, or was there some functional purpose, as, for example, having people on hand to serve as prompters.[158]

Although certainty is elusive, it appears that the status and functions of the *ḥazzan* evolved significantly over these centuries. We have only snippets of information regarding his role, and thus any suggested reconstruction taking into account chronological and geographical distinctions is doomed from the outset to be largely speculative. Nevertheless, what we may safely claim is that the *ḥazzan*—at least in Jewish Palestine—remained the quintessential synagogue functionary throughout late antiquity. This appears to be reflected in an interesting parallel regarding the cups of wine used at funerary meals, referred to above. Whereas the Bavli tradition speaks of the town *ḥazzan* and the *parnas*, Palestinian sources (the Yerushalmi and Tractate Semaḥot) refer to the synagogue *ḥazzan* and the *rosh knesset*.[159] As the synagogue developed new liturgical expressions, so, also,

---

152. Tractate Soferim 20:5 (p. 345). See also the mention of a *super orans* dating back to fifth- or sixth-century Spain, which probably refers to a chief cantor of the local synagogue (Lifshitz, "Prolegomenon," 58, no. 665a).

153. Y Berakhot 5, 3, 9c.

154. Tractate Soferim 19:9 (p. 336).

155. Ibid.; Midrash Hagadol, Genesis 24:60 (p. 408).

156. Tractate Soferim 10:6 (p. 216); 20:5 (p. 345).

157. See above, Chap. 9.

158. Tractate Soferim 14:9 (p. 263). The recognized custom of having three people standing at certain times during the prayer service is well attested; see Mekhilta of R. Ishmael, Beshalaḥ, 1 (pp. 180–81); PRK 3 (p. 36); Pirqei de R. Eli'ezer 44. See also Büchler, *Jewish-Palestinian Piety*, 216–17.

159. See above, note 32. See also the later tradition explaining the practice of reciting twenty-two

did the *hazzan* assume additional functions. As prayer and *piyyut* began to occupy an ever greater role, the *hazzan* became instrumental in the implementation of these components.

Whether his role with regard to the Torah-reading remained the same in later antiquity is unclear. Significantly, perhaps, earlier sources emphasize the Torah-reading function; later ones focus more on the liturgical components of prayer and *piyyut*. Is this because the focus of the *hazzan*'s activities changed? Or did prayer and *piyyut* begin to replace the Torah-reading as the central worship component? Perhaps it was more a matter of editorial preference. Since these two forms of worship (prayer and *piyyut*) were the most recent developments in synagogue liturgy, they therefore may have commanded more attention in later sources. There is simply no way of making a determination, at least for the present.

Outside the liturgical framework, the *hazzan* was also charged with making various announcements before an assembly of people. He is explicitly reported to have done so in the rabbinic academy, although this is one of the very few times a *hazzan* is mentioned as having functioned in such a setting.[160] Two late sources report that the *hazzan* made announcements of public concern in the synagogue, such as acknowledging charitable donations or announcing a stolen object.[161] Regarding the latter, Judah, son of (?) R. Huna, reported that his sandals were once taken from the synagogue (while praying barefoot?): "If I had not gone to the synagogue, my sandals would not have gone [away, i.e., been taken]."[162] Continuing a practice from Second Temple Jerusalem, when priests would announce the onset and conclusion of the Sabbath and festivals by sounding a trumpet from the southwestern corner of the Temple Mount, in late antiquity it was the *hazzan*'s duty to similarly usher in these festive days from a high roof of the town.[163] He would sound

---

verses for the haftarah: twenty-one verses correspond with the seven people called to the Torah (three verses per person), and one additional verse is in honor of the synagogue *hazzan* (Tractate Soferim 13:15 [p. 250]).

160. As, for example, one R. Zenon at Yavneh around the turn of the second century; see Y Berakhot 4, 7d; Y Ta'anit 4, 1, 67d; as well as Tanhuma, Genesis, Lech Lecha, 10 (p. 35a).

161. *Announcing donations:* This late tradition, preserved in al-Nakawa's fourteenth-century *Menorat Ha-maor* (p. 27), is presumably based on early traditions. *Announcing a stolen object:* Yalqut Shim'oni, Leviticus, 471 (p. 157).

162. Y Bava Metzia 2, 9, 8d; and comments by Lieberman in Rosenthal, *Yerushalmi Neziqin*, 138.

163. *Second Temple Jerusalem:* Josephus, *War* 4, 582; M Sukkah 5:5; Tanhuma, Numbers, Matot, 2 (p. 79b); Y Shabbat 17, 16a. On priests sounding the shofar or trumpet on various occasions, see Sifre-Numbers 75 (p. 70) for Rosh Hashanah and Jubilees; T Sotah 7:15-16 (p. 196) (= Y Yoma 1, 38d) for *Haqhel;* M Ta'anit 2:5 for public fasts; Pirqei de R. Eli'ezer 38 for excommunication (see also Büchler, *Jewish-Palestinian Piety,* 227ff.); T Sukkah 4:11-12 (pp. 274-75); and Lieberman, *TK,* IV, 894-96, for later antiquity in a town setting. B Shabbat 35b makes a point of stressing that this was done from the roof of the *hazzan*'s house. See also Tanhuma, Numbers, Matot, 2 (p. 79b), where the number of blasts is reduced to three; see Margalioth, *Differences in Customs,* no. 54, and comments on p. 178; as well as the tradition in M Hullin 1:7; Y Shabbat 17, 1, 16a.

three blasts with his trumpet to signal the cessation of work and another three at the conclusion of preparations for the Sabbath. This practice (at least with regard to the advent of the Sabbath) continued in Palestine until the end of antiquity, though not in Babylonia.

Several other tasks are also associated with the *ḥazzan*. One mishnaic source indicates that the *ḥazzan* may also have served as a teacher for children.[164] This would not be surprising; just as the Simonias and Bostra communities mentioned above searched for a functionary who could fulfill a number of different tasks, it may well be that this was a regular component of the *ḥazzan*'s job description. The *ḥazzan* also may have been charged with the not always pleasant task of collecting outstanding pledges. The difficulty of this job, as well as its virtues, is reflected in the rabbinic reference to the *ḥazzan* as "an angel."[165]

In court proceedings in the synagogue the *ḥazzan* appears to have regularly filled two specific roles. One was the task of summoning litigants to the legal proceedings, and the other was the execution of the court's decision with specific reference to flogging.[166] There is no reason to assume that the *ḥazzan* mentioned in these court contexts was someone other than the official who fulfilled religious and liturgical roles within the synagogue. No distinction between two officials called by the same name but having different tasks is ever alluded to in our sources. The assumption that we are dealing with one and the same office is strengthened by the fact that all the above activities were clearly performed within the same institution, i.e., the synagogue.[167]

Teacher

Schoolteachers[168] are frequently mentioned in rabbinic literature as communal functionaries;[169] generally speaking, they conducted their lessons in the synagogue.[170] The term *sofer* may include any one (or more) of the following roles: scribe, teacher, early sage, community secretary (= *grammateus*), *meturgeman*, preacher. In one tradition, these teachers are ranked just higher than *ḥazzanim*.[171] A variation of this tradition places the

---

164. M Shabbat 1:3.

165. Leviticus Rabbah 16:5 (p. 357) and parallels.

166. *Summoning litigants:* T Sanhedrin 9:1 (p. 428); Y Sanhedrin 12, 4, 23a. *Executing court decisions:* M Makkot 3:12; T Makkot 5:2 (p. 444); B Makkot 23a.

167. Of interest in this regard is a late source which notes that it is the judge who is responsible for the behavior, attitude, and salary of the *ḥazzan* (and the police); see Midrash Hagadol, Exodus 21:1 (p. 454). See also ibid., Deuteronomy 16:18 (p. 371).

168. On the position in general, see Ebner, *Elementary Education*, 51–60; Aberbach, *Jewish Education*, 33–92; Arzt, "Teacher," 35–47. Other terms for teacher include מקרי דרדקי, מקרי ינוקי, קרא. See Aberbach, *Jewish Education*, 36–41.

169. See, for example, B Shabbat 56a; Y Sanhedrin 13, 9, 23d; B Sanhedrin 17b.

170. See above, Chap. 10. Classes may at times also have taken place in the homes of these teachers. See, for example, PRK 27:1 (p. 402); B Betzah 16a; Arzt, "Teacher," 44 n. 80.

171. See above, note 127.

teacher (= *sofer*) squarely between sages and pupils: "R. Eli'ezer the Great said: 'From the day the Temple was destroyed, sages began to be like the *soferim*, the *soferim* like the pupils, and the pupils like [ordinary] people.' "[172] These teachers were praised because of the important function which they played in the education of the young. Towns were uprooted, according to the second-century *tanna* R. Simeon b. Yoḥai, when citizens failed to support such teachers properly; another source relates an incident, which allegedly took place in the third century, wherein teachers are referred to as the true guardians of a city (נטורי קרתא).[173] According to one *amora*, these teachers are called "a beloved group" of God, and they will eventually occupy a place to His right.[174] Thus, in places where the teacher was a communal employee—and this seems to have been the case very often, at least in Palestine—an attempt was made to enhance his status. Private tutors, on the other hand, were often placed in demeaning and compromising situations in their quest for students, a situation common to the Greco-Roman world generally. Their pay was invariably poor, and more often than not they were forced to seek supplementary sources of income.[175]

Hiring and keeping good teachers were high on the agendas of many communities. According to one account, competition between cities and villages might focus on the success of each in building synagogues, establishing schools, and hiring teachers.[176] As noted above, the people of Simonias approached R. Judah I, and the Jewish community of Bostra approached Resh Laqish for help in filling this as well as other positions.[177] The obligation to pay taxes to cover tuition is reiterated time and again in Palestinian rab-

---

172. M Sotah 9:15. According to MS Lowe (p. 105), this statement is attributed to R. Joshua. The term *sofer* here refers to schoolteachers, as the context clearly demonstrates, and not to scribes as reflected the New Testament and early rabbinic traditions; see the comments in Albeck, *Six Orders*, loc. cit., 415–16. In one list from a Roman context, the teacher or schoolmaster is ranked after the shoemaker, barber, and fuller; see Carcopino, *Daily Life*, 298 n. 25.

173. Y Ḥagigah 1, 7, 76c. See also PRK 15:5 (p. 253); Lamentations Rabbah, Proem 2 (p. 1b); Midrash on Psalms 127 (pp. 256b–257a).

174. PRK 27:2 (p. 406); Leviticus Rabbah 30:2 (p. 693) and later parallels. It should be noted that rabbinic sources are far from uniform regarding teachers. While some sources are, for the most part, quite favorable (B Bava Batra 8b; B 'Avodah Zarah 3b; Yalqut Shim'oni, Exodus, 286 [pp. 441–42]), others were far more reserved, their remarks often bordering on disparagement (Y Berakhot 4, 1, 7c, and parallels; Ginzberg, *Commentary*, III, 141–43; B Pesaḥim 49b; B Sanhedrin 17b and 104b).

175. Marrou, *History of Education*, 203–5; Carcopino, *Daily Life*, 109. See also Freeman, *Schools of Hellas*, 81–82.

176. Seder Eliyahu Rabbah 11 (pp. 54–55). Compare this to the situation in northern Italy, where a not insignificant town like Como had no schools. Parents interested in educating their children had to send them to Milan (Pliny, *Letters IV*, 13).

Another expression of competition among Palestinian towns might revolve around the acquisition of the burial remains of a well-known sage. See, for example, PRK 11:23 (p. 199); B Bava Metzia 84b.

177. See above, notes 124 and 125.

binic sources. Certain taxes, obligatory after a twelve-month residency, were earmarked for teachers, and the rabbis offer the highest praise to a bachelor who pays these taxes, thus subtly hinting that no one ought be exempt.[178] According to one tradition, payment of taxes for such purposes is even more important than giving to charity.[179] Clearly, the rabbis were supportive of teachers, although it is no less certain that there were many people who tried to avoid such payments.

Little is noted in our sources regarding the requisite qualifications for becoming a teacher. In fact, only one mishnah addresses the issue, albeit in a negative fashion, i.e., by spelling out those who should not hold such a position. The issue in this particular case appears to have been one of modesty; a teacher should not be put in potentially compromising situations: "A bachelor may not teach children [lit., shall not learn subjects and skills associated with teachers], nor may a woman teach children. R. Eli'ezer says: One who is not married may not teach children." [180]

Sages further recommend what conduct would be appropriate or inappropriate for teachers; for example, one should not be irritable.[181] Use of a strap for punishment is associated with some teachers, and the fear they engendered in their pupils also finds expression in halakhic discussions.[182] Corporal punishment was endemic to the Roman world generally, and Quintilian, as noted, minced no words in upbraiding such behavior with regard to children.[183]

---

178. Y Peah 8, 7, 21a; see also B Bava Batra 8b; PRK 27:1 (p. 402); Leviticus Rabbah 27:2 (p. 624); PRK 9:9 (p. 150); Tanḥuma, Emor, 10 (p. 45a).

179. PRK 27:1 (p. 402) and parallels. On rabbinic attempts to justify such salaries, despite their claim that one should not derive material benefits from teaching the Torah, see Y Nedarim 4, 3, 38c; B Nedarim 37a (see also B Bekhorot 29a); Sifre–Deuteronomy 48 (p. 111); Leviticus Rabbah 30:1 (p. 688); Derech Eretz Zutta 4:3 (p. 38).

180. M Qiddushin 4:13. See the extension of the prohibition in T Qiddushin 5:10 (p. 297) and parallels; Lieberman, TK, VIII, 980. Later halakhah did not accept this addition as normative (Maimonides, Laws of Talmud Torah 2:4).

181. M 'Avot 2:6; see also B Ta'anit 24a.

182. On punishment: B Sukkah 29a; B Bava Batra 21a; see Sokoloff, Dictionary, 421; B Gittin 36a; B Makkot 16b. Regarding fear in pupils: B Shabbat 13a. For instances of excessive physical punishment, see the incidents recorded in Y Mo'ed Qatan 3, 1, 81d; Y Megillah 3, 74a.

183. Institutio oratoria 1, 3, 13–17: "I disapprove of flogging, although it is the regular custom and meets with the acquiescence of Chrysippus, because in the first place it is a disgraceful form of punishment and fit only for slaves, and is in any case an insult, as you will realize if you imagine its infliction at a later age. Secondly, if a boy is so insensible to instruction that reproof is useless, he will, like the worst type of slave, merely become hardened to blows. Finally, there will be absolutely no need of such punishment if the master is a thorough disciplinarian. As it is, we try to make amends for the negligence of the boy's paedagogus, not by forcing him to do what is right, but by punishing him for not doing what is right. And though you may compel a child with blows, what are you to do with him when he is a young man no longer amenable to such threats and confronted with tasks of far greater difficulty? Moreover, when children are beaten, pain or fear frequently have results of which it is not pleasant to speak and which are

An interesting discussion among Babylonian sages focuses on whether an unsuccessful teacher should be replaced by a better one. Rabba claimed that the latter would eventually be no better than the former; R. Dimi asserted that the latter would always be motivated to succeed for "jealousy [i.e., competition] among teachers increases wisdom [קנאת סופרים תרבה חכמה]." [184]

Since the primary task of teachers was to instruct the young, and such instruction invariably took place in the synagogue; the result was that teachers spent much time there. Thus, a teacher was once asked to greet certain visitors to the synagogue warmly. [185] Teachers, for their part, are known to have consulted with sages, presumably regarding issues connected with their instruction and perhaps on other matters as well. [186]

Teachers appear to have taken on additional roles within the synagogue. [187] On a number of occasions they functioned as translators of Scriptures (*meturgemanim*); [188] it has been suggested that translation may have been a regular—if not primary—assignment. [189] They also appear to have served as Torah readers and at times led in the recitation of the *Shema*ʿ. [190]

Only one inscription makes specific mention of a *sofer;* interestingly enough, the person holding that title appears to have been a recognized personality. In the inscription from the Susiya synagogue, it is noted that R. Asi, the holy teacher and honorable priest (קדושת מרי רבי איסי הכהן המכובד), made a substantial donation, possibly on the occasion of the marriage of his son, R. Yoḥanan, a *sofer.* [191] It is quite possible that this R. Yoḥanan was a teacher, although, as indicated, the word *sofer* may have referred to one of several positions.

---

likely subsequently to be a source of shame, a shame which unnerves and depresses the mind and leads the child to shun and loathe the light. Further, if inadequate care is taken in the choices of respectable governors and instructors, I blush to mention the shameful abuse which scoundrels sometimes make of their right to administer corporal punishment or the opportunity not infrequently offered to others by the fear thus caused in the victims. I will not linger on this subject; it is more than enough if I have made my meaning clear. I will content myself with saying that children are helpless and easily victimized, and that therefore no one should be given unlimited power over them." On the *Institutio* and the methods advocated therein, see Murphy, *Quintilian*, xviii–xxxiv. See above, p. 378.

184. B Bava Batra 21a.

185. Y Megillah 3, 4, 74a.

186. Ibid., 3, 6, 74b.

187. As did Roman teachers, as already noted.

188. Y Megillah 4, 1, 74d; 4, 5, 75b.

189. York, "Targum in Synagogue and School," 81–82.

190. *Torah readers:* Y Megillah 3, 8, 74b; Tractate Soferim 11:3 (pp. 226–27). *Shema*ʿ: Midrash Hagadol, Exodus 15:1 (p. 284).

191. Naveh, *On Stone and Mosaic*, no. 75.

Minor Officials

Each synagogue undoubtedly needed someone to take care of the physical facilities, a kind of building superintendent. This task may have been fulfilled by a *shamash*, a title mentioned only rarely in rabbinic sources. Such a position is reflected in the anachronistic reference to the Patriarch Jacob fulfilling such a role in an academy.[192] An inscription from the synagogue at Bet She'arim may refer to someone in charge of synagogue furnishings and, if so, would point to such a position.[193] A teacher may also have served as such an attendant; in fact, a teacher by the name of Nikkai, from Migdal Tzeva'aya near Tiberias, is referred to in the Yerushalmi as a *shamash*, while in later *midrashim* he is called a teacher (*sofer*).[194]

Another group associated with the synagogue is the *batlanim*. Determining the nature of this group has proven to be difficult, in part owing to the paucity of sources. The term *batlan* is usually understood as one unemployed, unoccupied. But it may refer to one who has no need to work,[195] i.e., a member of the community who has the time to tend to synagogue matters, particularly to help make up the necessary quorum of ten for certain prayers and Torah-reading. This is the activity which is often noted in rabbinic sources with respect to the *batlanim*. Naturally, not every village or town would have had the requisite number of persons, and the Mishnah thus defines a large village (עיר גדולה) as one having ten such citizens.[196] R. Joshua b. Levi in the third century suggests that it was because of these ten men that at least ten verses were required for the public reading of the Torah.[197]

SYNAGOGUE OFFICIALS IN JEWISH PALESTINE AND THE DIASPORA

We have already had occasion to note the surprisingly meager amount of material in rabbinic literature which deals with the archisynagogue. That there are about as many references to this most prominent synagogue official in Christian literature as there are in

---

192. See Targum Pseudo-Jonathan and Targum Neofiti of Gen. 25:27.

193. Roth-Gerson, *Greek Inscriptions*, 141; see also Schwabe and Lifshitz, *Beth She'arim*, II, 192-93.

194. Y Ma'aser Sheni 5, 2, 56a; Lamentations Rabbah 3 (p. 63b); Ecclesiastes Rabbah 10:8.

195. This interpretation is perhaps alluded to by the Babylonian R. Judah (third century C.E.) in Y Megillah 1, 6, 70b, where he claims that these people "are like ourselves, for we do not need to [always] attend to our studies." See Schürer, *History*, II, 438-39; S. Krauss, *Synagogale Altertümer*, 104 n. 1; and Reynolds and Tannenbaum, *Jews and God-Fearers*, 28-29.

196. M Megillah 1:3. The importance of this function is reflected in a statement of R. Yoḥanan: "Whenever God comes to a synagogue and does not find ten men for prayer, he immediately becomes angry" (B Berakhot 6b).

197. B Megillah 21b. In a later tradition, this group is honored by being included in the calculation of how one reaches the number 120 for a full court (Midrash Hagadol, Exodus 18:21 [p. 365]).

rabbinic sources calls for an explanation. Moreover, focusing on the subject of synagogue officials as a whole, we note a baffling incongruity. There seems to be a sizable gap between rabbinic material, on the one hand, and the epigraphical evidence, on the other. As we have seen, inscriptions tell us much about the archisynagogue, *pater* and *mater synagoges*, presbyter, *phrontistes*, archon, and *grammateus*—positions which were all connected in one way or another with the synagogue. Rabbinic literature, however, has preserved very little regarding most of these and instead offers information about a different set of synagogue officials: *ḥazzanim*, charity officers, teachers, and others. The epigraphical corpus is almost totally silent regarding these officials, and the amount of overlap is thus minimal.

How does one account for such incongruity? One approach is to view the two types of sources—rabbinic and epigraphical—as complementary corpora. One might assume that the epigraphical material deals with the external aspects of the synagogue, including those who constructed the building and contributed to its ornamentation and mosaic floors, or those who ran the institution administratively and socially and controlled its finances, etc. On the other hand, rabbinic material might be assumed to have focused on the educational and liturgical dimensions of the synagogue, including those who conducted the worship services, distributed charity, taught the children, and served as synagogue attendants. Such functionaries do not usually merit inscriptions or communal honors.[198]

However, as neat as the above solution might seem, it is not altogether satisfactory. In the first place, neither type of source adheres strictly to the above division. Moreover, the issue becomes more acute when we consider that the discrepancy is not merely between rabbinic and epigraphical sources, but also within the epigraphical evidence itself. When we examine the 130 or so Hebrew and Aramaic inscriptions found in Roman-Byzantine Palestine, we find no trace of the terms regularly found in Diaspora inscriptions. There is no mention of an archisynagogue, presbyter (*zaqen*), archon, *pater*, or *mater*. Instead, the offices that do appear dovetail rather neatly with those mentioned in rabbinic sources;

---

198. This approach—explaining contradictions by assuming that different aspects or dimensions of a phenomenon are being addressed—has been applied in other areas as well. For example, the case of the Second Temple that Herod built has received a great deal of scholarly attention over the years. Even the most cursory examination of Mishnah Middot and Josephus' descriptions of this building reveals some startling differences that have long baffled scholars. One of the more widespread approaches to this enigma in the past has been to claim precisely this dichotomy: Josephus focuses on the exterior aspects of the building while rabbinic literature deals primarily with its interior (see, for example, Avi-Yonah, "Second Temple," 396–97). Moreover, the approach has been used extensively when dealing with the issue of hellenization. Rather than simply denying the phenomenon, which has become increasingly difficult with the passage of time and the accumulation of data, a favorite approach of minimalists in this regard is to speak in terms of a shell and a kernel; i.e., Judaism may have been influenced by Hellenism in some of its externalities, but its "essential nature" (whatever that may have been) has been preserved intact and relatively undiluted. See, for example, Feldman, "How Much Hellenism?" 83–111; cf. L. Levine, *Judaism and Hellenism*, passim.

the titles which constitute the core of rabbinic discussions regarding the synagogue and related matters are the most prominent in Palestinian Semitic inscriptions. The *ḥazzan*, for example, is noted in three inscriptions, from Ḥorvat ʿAmmudim in the Galilee, Aphek in the Golan, and ʿEn Gedi. A *parnas* and priest are mentioned at Naʿaran, and the latter designation appears twice in the Susiya synagogue.[199] Even the title "rabbi," whatever its precise meaning, occurs some fifty times in these Palestinian inscriptions, as against only seven times in the Diaspora inscriptions.[200]

Moreover, in contrast to the Diaspora evidence, where the benefactors are invariably individuals and at times officials, most Palestinian inscriptions speak of communal efforts. In no fewer than ten inscriptions from every part of the country, it is the community as a whole which contributed to the building. Such was the case at Ḥammat Tiberias, Bet Shean, and Bet Alpha in the north; Jericho and Naʿaran in the Jordan Valley; Susiya (twice) and Maʿon in the south; and Ashkelon and Caesarea along the coast.[201]

This emphasis on communal efforts corresponds to the statement in one rabbinic source which addresses the issue of synagogue building directly: כופין בני העיר זה את זה לבנות להם בית הכנסת ולקנות להם ספר תורה ונביאים ("The villagers may compel one another to build a synagogue and buy a Torah scroll and [book of] Prophets").[202] According to one rabbinic tradition, synagogues belong to the community as a whole;[203] the phenomenon of communal contributions is thus readily understandable and existed side by side with individual contributions.[204] The opposite, however, is not the case. Communal contributions were almost unknown in Greek-speaking environs,[205] and individual contributions are exclusively in evidence.

However, a further distinction is required at this point and has to do with our use of the term "Jewish Palestine." What has been noted above as reflective of Palestine is restricted to the Hebrew and Aramaic material. When, however, we examine the seventy or so Greek inscriptions known to date,[206] the offices familiar to us from Diaspora material are clearly in evidence. Archisynagogues are mentioned on six occasions in Greek inscriptions from Palestine, once from Jerusalem (Theodotos) and once from Caesarea (Beryllos), twice from Bet Sheʿarim (Jacob of Caesarea, the archisynagogue of Pamphylia, and

199. Naveh, *On Stone and Mosaic*, nos. 20, 28, 58, 63, 75.

200. These appear in five different inscriptions; see S. J. D. Cohen, "Epigraphical Rabbis," 1–17.

201. *North:* Naveh, *On Stone and Mosaic*, nos. 26, 46, and 43. *Jordan Valley;* ibid., nos. 69 and 64. *South:* ibid., nos. 83, 84, and 57. *The coast:* ibid., no. 53; Roth-Gerson, *Greek Inscriptions*, no. 25.

202. T Bava Metzia 11:23 (p. 125); and Lieberman, *TK*, IX, 320–21.

203. M Nedarim 5:5.

204. See, for example, Naveh, *On Stone and Mosaic*, nos. 7, 12, 18, 20, 29, 35, 50, 59–63, 71, and 75. See also *NEAEHL*, II, 565–69; as well as Naveh, *On Stone and Mosaic*, no. 33, and, generally, pp. 54–64.

205. One exception is from Caesarea, where an inscription speaks of a donation of the people (τοῦ λαοῦ); see Roth-Gerson, *Greek Inscriptions*, no. 25.

206. See above, Chap. 6, note 9; and several other inscriptions from elsewhere in Tiberias.

Avitus), and twice from Sepphoris (Judah of Sidon and Suberianos Aphros from Tyre).[207] Other titles appear as well: presbyters in Caesarea and Jerusalem, a *phrontistes* in Caesarea, a *pronomenos* or *pronoetes* and *mizoteros* (?) from Tiberias, and a *comes* from Sepphoris.[208]

Thus, there is a marked discrepancy not only between Palestinian and Diaspora inscriptions, but also among those in Palestine itself, and the distinction appears to be sharp and clear. Palestinian Greek inscriptions bear a strong resemblance to those of the Diaspora, while the Hebrew-Aramaic ones correlate rather well with rabbinic evidence. Greek titles appear in Greek inscriptions, and this heavily hellenized nomenclature was undoubtedly dominant owing to the extensive contact of these Jewish communities with the surrounding Greco-Roman world. Since each of the terms appearing in Greek synagogue inscriptions of the Diaspora and Palestine has parallels in titles relating to Greek and Roman institutions, it would seem that these Jewish communities adopted not only the terminology of the Hellenistic world, but something of its organizational and administrative patterns as well. Rabbinic literature and the Hebrew-Aramaic inscriptions of Palestine, on the other hand, focus largely on a particular geographical location: the interior hill-country of Roman and Byzantine Palestine, particularly in the Galilee, with special reference to rural areas that were somewhat impervious to these influences.

Thus, this basically geographical distinction appears to be rather compelling. The Greek inscriptions of Palestine, with their Greek nomenclature, were all found in Hellenistic settings, either Greco-Roman cities, such as Caesarea or Ashkelon, or Jewish cities with a significant degree of acculturation. Moreover, almost all of the archisynagogues mentioned in Palestinian Greek inscriptions had well-documented ties with Diaspora communities. Such, for example, was the case with the archisynagogues of Tyre and Sidon at Sepphoris, with Beryllos of Caesarea, with Jacob of Pamphylia, resident of Caesarea, and, of course, Theodotos of Jerusalem, whose family hailed from Rome.

However, aside from the internal-external dimensions or the geographical distinction already noted, it is also possible to view this difference in synagogue nomenclature along urban-rural lines. The assumption, then, might be that much of rabbinic literature (especially the tannaitic material), together with the Palestinian epigraphical evidence (i.e., the Hebrew and Aramaic inscriptions), derives from (or reflects) in the main the rural areas of the country, while the Diaspora material and the Greek inscriptions from Palestine are more typically urban. Thus, the fact that in Jewish Palestine individuals rarely built synagogues (or large parts of them) and that communal efforts were much more predominant may argue for a rural rather than urban context. However, even this type of distinction is not foolproof. Some "congregational" inscriptions do, in fact, come from cities, such as Ḥammat Tiberias, Bet Shean, and Caesarea. Nevertheless, it cannot be

---

207. Roth-Gerson, *Greek Inscriptions*, nos. 19, 24, 27, and pp. 137 and 143.

208. *Presbyters:* ibid., no. 19. *Phrontistes:* ibid., no. 27. *Pronomenos* or *pronoetes*, and *mizoteros:* ibid., nos. 18 and 17. *Comes:* ibid., no. 24.

denied that villages often had modes of communal organization different from those in large cities, particularly when the cities were heavily influenced by Hellenistic patterns.

Although it might seem preferable to adopt one of the three positions noted above, each, in fact, has some measure of cogency. Clearly, the epigraphical evidence and the talmudic material offer different perspectives, as do the Palestinian Greek inscriptions in contrast to the Hebrew-Aramaic ones. To assume that inscriptions focus on the external appearance of a building and the rabbinic sources on its internal aspects is not altogether unreasonable, nor without parallel. Nevertheless, as noted, such a distinction is not fully satisfactory; rabbinic literature, for its part, is not totally oblivious to the physical aspects of the synagogue building or to contributions made to it. The sages in rabbinic literature seem to deliberately downplay prominent synagogue officials, such as the archisynagogue. This may stem not only from rabbinic disinterest in the position per se, but also from possible tensions between these two types of leadership.[209] Relations between the rabbis and the wealthy were often problematic during this period; if a wealthy individual was charged with running an institution that some rabbis, at least, wished to influence, the result may not have been entirely harmonious.[210]

Yet the geographical argument is no less compelling in light of the remarkable compatibility between rabbinic sources and Palestinian Aramaic-Hebrew inscriptions in what they both do and do not say. The weak link in this suggestion is that these two areas, the Diaspora and Palestine, were not totally unrelated. On the one hand, Jewish Palestine as reflected in rabbinic literature knows of the archisynagogue or the *rosh knesset*; on the other, the title *ḥazzan* appears in several Diaspora contexts.[211] Therefore, a theory based solely on geographical considerations is insufficient.

Finally, there can be no question that much of rabbinic (especially tannaitic) material reflects non-urban contexts, as do most of the extant non-Greek epigraphical remains. Before we can judge the cogency of the urban-rural dichotomy, however, we must account for some crucial missing components. For example, how were Jewish communities in the rural Diaspora organized? Did their synagogue dedicatory inscriptions and modes of operation parallel those of rural Palestine, their urban Diaspora coreligionists, or perhaps neither? It would appear unlikely that Diaspora rural practice was similar to that in Palestine (examples from Hellenistic and early Roman Egypt which are overwhelmingly rural would seem to bear this out), but we cannot be sure about this for late antiquity. Until we have more evidence in hand, this possibility of an urban-rural distinction must remain speculative. Only on rare occasions do we find evidence of some sort of urban-rural correlation, such as the inscription from urban Caesarea which speaks of a "contri-

---

209. On the tensions between the sages and communal leadership generally, see Büchler, *Political and Social Leaders*; L. Levine, *Rabbinic Class*, 98ff. and esp. 167–76.

210. L. Levine, "Sages and Synagogue," 201–22; and below, Chap. 13.

211. *Apamea*: Lifshitz, *Donateurs et fondateurs*, no. 40. *Alexandria*: T Sukkah 4:6 (p. 273).

bution of the people," using a phrase characteristic of Palestinian Semitic evidence. The existence of such evidence should caution against making any premature generalization.

Thus, given the limited sources available, it is impossible to embrace any one of the above positions without reservation. Perhaps this is the true value of the diverse material at our disposal. Just as our sources are complex, so, too, seems to have been the reality of late antiquity. Any kind of oversimplification or attempt to fit all evidence into one particular mold may well do injustice to both the sources and the historical reality behind them.

When all is said and done, however, one fact can be safely asserted. For whatever reason, be it cultural, geographical, or sociological, synagogue officialdom in Jewish Palestine appears to have been different from that of the Diaspora, as well as from that of the hellenized areas of Palestine. This is true of the titles used and presumably of the roles played as well. Some common threads indeed existed, but clearly there were regional differences, which, in turn, reflected a wide range of political, social, and cultural realities about which we are only very partially informed. The situation in Jewish Palestine was indeed unique, probably because remnants of earlier Jewish practices were more preserved there than in the Diaspora, where the pressures and attractions of acculturation were more intense.

CONCLUSIONS

Several aspects of synagogue leadership in antiquity have become clear from the above discussion. Most obvious, of course, is the wide variety of titles for these officials of the Jewish communities throughout the Empire.[212] Titles appearing with frequency in one region may have been entirely absent from another. Moreover, the combinations of titles assumed by officials in a given locale might differ considerably from those assumed elsewhere. It is clear that there was no fixed nomenclature for synagogue leadership throughout the Jewish world of late antiquity.

Thus, we may safely conclude, here as elsewhere, that local communities enjoyed a wide range of autonomy. This was expressed not only in how and where they built their synagogues and the types of activities conducted therein, but also in the form and nature of their leadership. This local contextual focus also serves to highlight the absence in Jewish life in late antiquity of any kind of overriding sacerdotal or communal authority in either Palestine or the Diaspora, with the possible exception of Babylonia. This pattern of locally based authority is somewhat similar to that found in pagan life and stands in contrast to that typical of Christianity, where the concentration of power in a dominant ecclesiastical framework tended to homogenize patterns of leadership.[213] Clearly, the synagogue evolved along very different lines.

---

212. On the heterogeneity of Roman synagogues, see Williams, "Structure of Roman Jewry," 129–41.
213. See Bradshaw, *Liturgical Presidency*, 21–27.

This having been said, certain qualifications ought to be made. While diversity is the dominant characteristic of synagogue leadership in antiquity, the situation was far from chaotic. Titles may have differed, but the menu of choices was fairly limited. The same titles often appeared in far-flung Jewish communities. The most prominent of these was "archisynagogue." While not used everywhere in the Jewish world, it was by far the most ubiquitous title of all, appearing in Jewish communities the length and breadth of the Empire.

A further conclusion to be drawn from our discussion is the extent to which the Jewish community borrowed from its Greco-Roman surroundings in choosing these titles. Some titles may have been mere translations of well-known ones used in earlier Jewish and contemporary non-Jewish societies, as, for example, presbyter for *zaqen*, or *grammateus* for *sofer*; others may have been generic enough to fit already existing leadership roles as well, as was probably the case with the title "archon." Nevertheless, even in these instances the very choice of these titles in their Greek form was clearly determined by the larger context of the Greco-Roman world in which the Jews lived.

However, with regard to other terms, chief among which was "archisynagogue," such equivocation is uncalled for. These terms were patently borrowed from the surrounding culture and were appropriated and adapted by the Jews for their own needs. The case of the archisynagogue is the most striking example of the remodeling of a foreign form into a Jewish context whereby the office itself seems to have been significantly altered in definition and status. The *phrontistes*, *pater* and *mater synagoges*, and even the *ḥazzan*, whose roots appear to have been in Assyrian and Babylonian cultures, are further instances of such adopted titles.

Finally, synagogue officials were products of their age in one further respect. Synagogues depended on the benefactions of their members, be they wealthy individuals or the community at large. There simply was not another source of revenue, neither an overriding Jewish institutional framework which might subsidize the building and maintenance of synagogues nor a way to tap into Imperial government funds. Thus, the entire financial burden fell on the local community. What we have seen above, both in this chapter and in earlier ones, is the degree to which the Jews adopted the practice of *philotimia*, or euergetism, from the Greco-Roman world. Private benefactions for cities, institutions, services, and countless amenities are a most salient characteristic of city life in Greco-Roman society. Temples, festivals, and other celebrations might merit support; in case of crises such as famines and plagues, wealthy individuals would help alleviate suffering.[214] Many contributions were made to the Temple in Jerusalem by affluent Diaspora Jews, even though the institution itself was well endowed by official sources (Hasmonean and later Herodian) and by the massive contributions of the half-sheqel by Jews everywhere.[215] The synagogues, however, enjoyed no such institutionalized international

214. White, *Building God's House*, 77–85; Rogers, "Gift and Society," 188–99.
215. See, for example, Josephus, *War* 5, 201–6.

support, and thus contributions of local individuals were indispensable. From what we have seen above, such contributions were forthcoming from synagogue officials and lay-people alike.

While the above discussion has been able to address a number of issues, some matters must remain unanswered owing to a lack of sufficient information. How are we to account for the selection of some titles and not others by a given community? The simplest answer would be that these were the titles most prominent in pagan life of that given area. Chances are that this explanation goes a long way in accounting for these differences, but, given the lack of supporting evidence from most surrounding contexts, there is no way of demonstrating this satisfactorily.

No less than for titles, functions, and organization, information about the synagogue officials themselves, on a personal level, is wanting. Who were these people? Which strata of the population—social, economic, religious—did they represent? What were their aspirations and motivations? What obstacles did they encounter? These questions go well beyond the scope of our sources. It is thus quite unusual, and indeed fortuitous, that an amulet containing a prayer of one Yosi, son of Zenobia, was found in the Merot synagogue in the Upper Galilee. He was clearly the leader of his community, and while he never called himself an archisynagogue or a *rosh knesset*, it appears quite certain that this, in fact, was his role. The text of this amulet gives expression to several aspects of synagogue leadership (or communal leadership, for that matter), i.e., the clash between leader and congregation, the former's resolve to prevail, and the accompanying feelings of frustration and isolation. We conclude this chapter with his personal prayer, which reads as follows:

> For Your lovingkindness and for Your truth [Ps. 115:1, 138:2]. In the name of God, we shall do and we shall succeed! Strong and mighty God! Blessed be Your name and blessed be Your kingdom! As You have conquered the sea with Your horses and You have crushed the earth with Your shoes, and as You suppress the trees in the winter days and the grass in the earth in the summer days, so may the people of this village be subdued before Yosi son of Zenobia. May my words and my authority be upon them. Just as the heavens are subdued before God, and the earth is subdued before men, and men are subdued before death, and death is subdued before God, so may the people of this village be subdued, broken, and fall before Yosi son of Zenobia. In the name of the angel Hatu'a'a, who was sent before Israel, I make this sign—Success, Success, Amen, Amen, Selah, Hallelujah.[216]

---

216. For a full discussion, see Naveh, "Good Subduing," 367–82. On the excavations at Merot, see Z. Ilan, "Synagogue and Beth Midrash of Meroth," 21–41.

twelve

THE PATRIARCH (*NASI*)
AND THE SYNAGOGUE

The status and authority of the Patriarch in late antiquity is a subject that has merited a great deal of scholarly attention over the past generation.[1] Assessments have ranged from those regarding the office as pivotal, affecting Jewish communities throughout the entire Roman Empire, to those assuming that the Patriarchate declined precipitously in the course of the third and fourth centuries, with a minimal and often deleterious influence on Jewish society.[2] Such dramatically varied assessments stem directly from the fact that the sources at our disposal are both limited and varied.[3] From rabbinic literature to the writings of the church fathers, from archeological remains to Roman legal codes, the depiction of the Patriarchate is riddled with diverse and often contradictory information. Depending on which of these sources one chooses to emphasize and how others are incorporated into a wider picture,

1. Mantel (*Studies*, 1–53, 175–253); L. Levine ("Jewish Patriarch," 649–88; "Status of the Patriarch," 1–32); J. Cohen ("Roman Imperial Policy," 1–29); S. J. D. Cohen ("Pagan and Christian Evidence," 170–75); Goodman (*State and Society*, 111–18; "Roman State and Jewish Patriarch," 127–39; "Roman Identity," 94*–99*); Stemberger (*Juden und Christen*, 184–213); Jacobs (*Jüdischen Patriarchen*); Rosenfeld ("Crisis of the Patriarchate," 239–57); S. A. Cohen (*Three Crowns*, 200–4); Hezser (*Social Structure*, 406–17).

2. See the assessments of Mantel, L. Levine, J. Cohen, S. J. D. Cohen, Goodman, Stemberger, and Jacobs as against those of Rosenfeld and S. A. Cohen (above, note 1).

3. For a review and discussion of these sources, see L. Levine, "Status of the Patriarch," 4–26; Jacobs, *Jüdischen Patriarchen*, passim.

very different conclusions can be drawn regarding this office and its authority within Jewish society. Given the centrality of the synagogue in Jewish communities throughout the Empire, it would seem that the degree of the Patriarch's prominence in Jewish communal affairs had a direct bearing on his involvement in and influence on this institution.

The sources relating specifically to the relationship between the Patriarchate and the synagogue are intriguing. Although they are preciously few in number, they point to the seemingly significant role of this office in synagogues. Let us begin by reviewing the material at our disposal and then attempt to place the sources in some sort of historical perspective.

RABBINIC LITERATURE

The rabbinic sources that make some sort of connection between the Patriarch (*Nasi*) and the synagogue can be divided into four categories: those in which the association is tangential and thus of limited value for our discussion; those which tell of Patriarchal involvement in appointing synagogue personnel; those relating to Patriarchal responsibilities and authority over activities which almost certainly took place in the synagogue; and, finally, one specific source which makes an explicit connection between the Patriarch and a range of communal institutions, particularly the synagogue.

This last-mentioned source, which happens to be the earliest, seems to have been the product of R. 'Aqiva's students in the mid-second century C.E. (i.e., the Ushan era).[4] In a discussion of vows between two people wishing to deprive each other of certain benefits, it is stated that one can ban another from deriving satisfaction not only from personal effects, but also from local institutions, such as the bathhouse, town plaza, and synagogue (together with its ark and books), since all residents are considered co-owners of these institutions.[5] Since such a situation could easily have led to total anarchy or to a general disregard of these regulations, the Mishnah also indicates a way to circumvent this type of ban:

> Yet one may assign his part [of the institution] to the *Nasi* [and then the other person could benefit from these institutions since the one making the ban is no longer a co-owner]. R. Judah says: "It makes no difference whether he assigns them to the *Nasi* or to any other private individual." What, then, is the difference between one who assigns [them] to the *Nasi* or one who assigns [them] to a private individual?[6] One who assigns [them] to the Patriarch would not have to formally grant him [the *Nasi*] title [to the building]. But the sages say:

---

4. J. N. Epstein, *Introduction to Tannaitic Literature*, 378–82.

5. B Betzah 39b.

6. On the literary form, "It makes no difference . . . What, then is the difference . . . ?" see B Shevu'ot 13b (also quoting R. Judah); M 'Arakhin 3:2; 7:2.

"In either case, formal title must be granted." And they spoke of the *Nasi* only with regard to existing items. R. Judah says: "Galileans do not have to assign [their shares], since their ancestors have already done so."[7]

While the possibility of assigning communal property to the Patriarch is certainly of importance, R. Judah (ben Ilai)'s statement, that such arrangements had already been made by Galileans is particularly engaging. The Bavli cites the following tannaitic tradition in the name of R. Judah: "The Galileans were cantankerous and would continuously vow not to benefit one another. Their ancestors [lit., fathers] then assigned their shares [i.e., title to their property] to the *Nasi*."[8] Taken at face value, this source has far-reaching implications, namely, that the second-century Galilean synagogue belonged, in some fashion, to the Patriarch. Assuming the veracity of R. Judah's statement (and its attribution), it is clear that such an arrangement was already in effect in his day, i.e., in the time of the Patriarch Rabban Simeon ben Gamaliel, following the Bar-Kokhba rebellion, and it may indeed go back even further, to the time of Rabban Gamaliel II in the Yavnean period (70–132 C.E.).[9]

However, the historical implications of such assignments to the *Nasi* remain unclear. Did everyone do so, or was the practice only in some places and by a small minority of the population (as reflected in this rabbinic pericope)? If the latter, then perhaps it was only within rabbinic circles of second-century Galilee that the Patriarch was a recognized leader who was assigned ownership of public property. This does not, at first glance, appear to be the intent of the source; what seems to be described here is a more general situation throughout the Galilee. Moreover, the question arises as to what precisely such an assignment meant. Was it to avoid the deleterious consequences of rash vows, thus making it merely a theoretical gesture, or was there some practical consequence in having the Patriarch own these properties? Was the office also involved, or made to be involved, in the operation of these institutions? Were synagogue officials or the townspeople at

---

7. M Nedarim 5:5. Although many medieval (and even some modern) commentators have suggested that the term *Nasi* refers to a local leader (see Albeck, *Six Orders*, III, 363; J. N. Epstein, *Introduction to the Mishnaic Text*, I, 361 n. 2), I am assuming that the Patriarch is intended. No local official bearing such a title is known from any other rabbinic source. See also Mantel (*Studies*, 45–49), who, apparently following Ginzberg, dates this tradition to the pre-70 era. For a messianic twist to this tradition (based on Ezekiel and Y Nedarim 5, 6, 39b), see Jacobs, *Institution*, 48–49.

8. B Nedarim 48a.

9. It has been noted on various occasions of late that there is no reliable historical tradition attesting to the fact that the title *Nasi* was used with regard to the Patriarchal house before the mid-second century (see S. Safrai, "Mantel, *Studies*," 70–71; idem, "Jewish Self-Government," 389; idem, *In Times of Temple and Mishnah*, II, 365 n. 1) or even the third (Goodblatt, *Monarchic Principle*, 184–93, esp. 192; see also idem, "The Title *Nasi*," 114–17). Our source seems to indicate a mid-second century use of the title and perhaps hints at its usage even earlier. Goodblatt, regrettably, does not discuss this mishnah.

large accountable to the Patriarch in some fashion? Unfortunately, the lack of additional information prevents us from formulating any firm answers to these questions.[10]

Thus, despite the potentially far-reaching implications of this source for the subject at hand, its historical value is severely limited by its vagueness as well as by the absence of corroborating evidence. A further complication lies in the fact that the picture emerging from this source seems to go against what we know from other sources about this period and the status of the Patriarch. The *communis opinio* is that the post–Bar Kokhba era witnessed a serious diminution in the political and economic position of Palestinian Jews generally and in the standing of the Patriarch in particular. It was at this time, for example, that Rabban Simeon b. Gamaliel was challenged from within the academy as well as by one Ḥananiah, who attempted to wrest control of calendrical authority from the Patriarch on behalf of Babylonia.[11] Therefore, even if we assume the basic historicity of the above account, the challenge of fitting it into the overall picture of this period in the history of the Galilee remains formidable. It may be for this reason that historians such as Alon, Oppenheimer, and Goodman have simply ignored this mishnah when discussing the Ushan period.[12]

A second type of rabbinic source attests to Patriarchal involvement in, and even control of, certain activities which regularly took place within the synagogue. At some point in the late third century, R. Judah II Nesiah dispatched three sages "to establish" (or "to assign," למתקנא) schoolteachers in towns throughout Palestine;[13] they presumably taught in the synagogue.[14] Patriarchal control of the judicial system is also well attested throughout rabbinic literature, and the courts undoubtedly convened in the synagogue.[15]

A third category deals with the appointment of synagogue functionaries. I have already had occasion to refer to the account in which the community of Simonias asked R. Judah I for help in finding someone who would fill a wide range of communal functions. The phrase used in this regard may be significant—"Give us [תתן לן] someone."[16] Another ac-

---

10. According to S. Safrai, the above source indicates that the *Nasi* was the initiator and owner of Galilean synagogues from the Ushan period onward; see Z. Safrai, *Jewish Community*, 186.

11. *Internal challenge:* Y Bikkurim 3, 65c; B Horayot 13b–14a. *Babylonia:* Y Nedarim 6, 40a; B Berakhot 63a–b.

12. Alon, *Jews in Their Land*, passim; Oppenheimer, *Galilee*, 45–59; Goodman, *State and Society*, 111–14.

13. Y Ḥagigah 1, 7, 76c; see also Lamentations Rabbah, Proem 2 (p. 1b); PRK 15:5 (p. 253); Midrash on Psalms 127:1 (pp. 256b–257a); Yalqut Shim'oni, Psalms, 881. It is possible that two other sages, R. Ḥanina (according to MS Rome) and R. Jonathan, were sent by R. Judah Nesiah II to the south "to make peace" (Y Berakhot 9, 1, 12d). Both of these sages were in the company of "Southerners" when at Ḥammat Gader (Y 'Eruvin 6, 23c), and R. Jonathan is mentioned as having spent time there with the Patriarch (Y Qiddushin 3, 14, 64c).

14. See above, Chap. 10.

15. See Mantel, *Studies*, 206–21; L. Levine, "Status of the Patriarch," 7–10.

16. Y Yevamot 12, 13a; Genesis Rabbah 81:1 (pp. 969–72); Tanḥuma, Tzav, 7 (p. 9a).

count, two generations later, tells of the Bostra community consulting with Resh Laqish on the same matter: "Show us [חמי לן] someone . . ."[17] Might we conclude that whereas the *Nasi* was asked to make appointments, Resh Laqish was asked merely to make recommendations? This is certainly a possibility, although the meager evidence at hand precludes conclusiveness.[18]

Finally, there are a number of sources that make a connection between the Patriarch and the synagogue but do not indicate the official standing of the former within the latter. So, for example, Rabban Gamaliel II once visited a synagogue in Tiberias and issued a decision contrary to local practice; in Achziv he was asked by the head of the local synagogue about a halakhic matter.[19] R. Gamaliel's son, R. Ḥanina, once told the *meturgeman* in the Kabul synagogue to translate only the last part of Gen. 35:22 of the Torah reading (thereby omitting the account of Reuben and Bilhah).[20] In reverence for a deceased Patriarch, there were elaborate mourning practices conducted in the synagogue: "Our rabbis have taught: If a sage dies, his academy suspends [its usual routine]. If the head of a court [*av bet din*] dies, all academies in his city are suspended, and they gather in the synagogue and change their seating: those who sit in the north sit in the south, those who sit in the south sit in the north. [When] a *Nasi* dies, academies everywhere are suspended, and the members of the congregation enter the synagogue and read seven portions from the Torah and depart."[21] Such unique behavior at the death of a *Nasi* may have been no more than a public display of mourning within this central Jewish institution for an acknowledged communal figure. However, it may also reflect a special standing that the *Nasi* held within the synagogue generally. Thus, it may not be entirely coincidental that several instances of public rabbinic condemnation of the Patriarch took place within the synagogue framework.[22]

---

17. Y Shevi'it 6, 1, 36d; Tanḥuma, Massa'ei, 1; Deuteronomy Rabbah, V'ethanan (ed. Lieberman, p. 60).

18. Indirect evidence of the Patriarch's authority in communal matters may be culled from the fact that a number of sages closely associated with the *Nasi* appear to have had significant authority. R. Yoḥanan, at one point described as "from the house of the *Nasi*" (B Sotah 21a), is said to have made judicial appointments (B Sanhedrin 14a, 30b; Y Bikkurim 3, 3, 65d; L. Levine, *Rabbinic Class*, 151–59), and R. Ḥiyya bar Abba, also in the service of the *Nasi* (Y Ḥagigah 1, 7, 76c, and parallels), is credited with appointing archons (Y Peah 8, 7, 21a). Moreover, he himself may have even served as a Patriarchal *apostolos* (Y Ḥagigah 1, 8, 76d). On Rabban Gamaliel's appointment of several sages to some sort of communal position, see Sifre-Deuteronomy 16 (p. 26); B Horayot 10a.

19. M 'Eruvin 10:10; T Terumot 2:13 (p. 115).

20. T Megillah 3:35 (p. 363); B Megillah 25b. Interestingly, the Tosefta seems to indicate that R. Ḥanina himself was reading the Torah, whereas the Bavli explicitly notes that the synagogue *ḥazzan* was reading. The reference to *ḥazzan*, however, is unattested in Bavli MSS and by the Rishonim.

21. B Mo'ed Qatan 22b–23a.

22. Genesis Rabbah 80:1 (pp. 950–53); Y Sanhedrin 2, 6, 20d; Y Bikkurim 3, 3, 65d.

ARCHEOLOGICAL EVIDENCE

Two excavated synagogues are specifically associated with the Patriarch, one from third-century Stobi, in the province of Macedonia, the other from fourth-century Tiberias, where the Patriarch resided.

The association of the Patriarch with Stobi appears in a monumental inscription prominently displayed on a synagogue column which records an agreement between one Claudius Tiberius Polycharmos and the Stobi Jewish community.[23] The precise formulation of the agreement—background information about the donor, a description of the premises, a clarification of the legal basis of Polycharmos' ownership, as well as the stipulation of a heavy fine to be imposed for breach of agreement ("Whosoever wishes to make changes beyond these decisions of mine will give the Patriarch 250,000 denarii. For thus have I agreed")—all attest to the importance of this inscription. That the Patriarch would be designated as the sole beneficiary of any violation of this contract is rather conclusive evidence of the prestige accorded his office.[24]

Of the eleven inscriptions discovered in the Ḥammat Tiberias synagogue, ten are dedicatory inscriptions in Greek.[25] Of these, the two most prominent ones name Severus "disciple [lit., one raised in the household] of the most Illustrious Patriarchs" [θρεπτὸς τῶν λαμπροτάτων πατριαρχῶν].[26]

[1] Severus, disciple of the most Illustrious Patriarchs, fulfilled [it]. Blessings upon him. Amen.

[2] Severus, disciple of the most Illustrious Patriarchs completed [it]. Blessings on him and on Ioullos, the supervisor [*pronoetes*].

Severus apparently not only was a wealthy individual, but was also proud to be associated with the Patriarch, a relationship which he took pains to note on both occasions. Un-

---

23. See above, Chap. 8; and L. Levine, "Status of the Patriarch," 13.

24. It has been suggested that the patriarch mentioned in the inscription is a local official noted on occasion in the Theodosian Code (e.g., 16, 8, 13). However, owing to the enormous sum involved, it is far more reasonable to assume that we are dealing here with the Patriarch of Palestine and not a local official. In any case, this local official may well have been in the service of the Palestinian Patriarch. See Hengel, "Synagogeninschrift von Stobi," 152–58.

Reynolds and Tannenbaum have suggested that the Aphrodisias inscription reflects Palestinian rabbinic influence, which could have been effected only by the Patriarch (*Jews and God-Fearers*, 80–83), a claim rightly rejected by Williams ("Jews and Godfearers," 297–310).

25. Dothan, *Hammath Tiberias*, 53–62; L. Levine, "Status of the Patriarch," 14. These numbers do not include the brief identifications of the zodiac signs and seasons of the year appearing in Hebrew.

26. The word θρεπτός may also be translated as "apprentice" or "pupil"; see Lifshitz, *Donateurs et fondateurs*, 64; Dothan, *Hammath Tiberias*, 57; Roth-Gerson, *Greek Inscriptions*, 68; Stemberger, *Juden und Christen*, 184. Other meanings for the word θρεπτός include "servant," "servant born to a master's household," "foundling"; see Frey, *CIJ*, I, 57; Cameron, "θρεπτός," 27–62; Nani, "ΘΡΕΠΤΟΙ," 45–84; Martin, "Construction of the Ancient Family," 46 n. 25. See also Di Segni, "Inscriptions of Tiberias," 92–94.

doubtedly, such a liaison afforded him an honorable position in the community. It is not surprising that the *Nasi* should appear in a fourth-century Tiberian synagogue, since in the previous century the office moved from Sepphoris to Tiberias, where it would remain until its disappearance in the early fifth century.[27]

EPIPHANIUS

Of all the church fathers who have had occasion to mention the Patriarch in one context or another, only Epiphanius did so extensively. In his narrative about Joseph the Comes, a once-loyal member of the Patriarch's entourage who converted to Christianity and subsequently devoted himself to building churches in the Galilee, Epiphanius describes the *Nasi*'s involvement in Diaspora synagogues.[28] Epiphanius' description of the Patriarch, however, is a problematic historical account. The *Panarion* was written between the years 374 and 376, and this particular account was told to Epiphanius by Joseph himself several decades earlier (when the latter was some seventy years old), about twenty-five to thirty years after the events described purportedly transpired.

Whatever the circumstances of this source, the section of primary interest to us may be the most reliable part of Epiphanius' account; it appears to be the least tendentious, as it describes Joseph's duties when he was sent by the Patriarch to the Diaspora:

> It happened that after the Patriarch Judah [that may have been his name], of whom we spoke, reached maturity, he gave Joseph in recompense the revenue of the apostleship. He was sent with letters to Cilicia, went up there, and started collecting the tithes and firstfruits from the Jews of the province in each of the cities of Cilicia. . . . Now because as an apostle [for that, as I said, is what they call the office] he [was] quite austere and upright in his manner, persisted in proposing measures to restore correct observance of the law, and deposed and removed from office any of those appointed synagogue rulers, priests, elders, and *hazzanim* [which in their language means "ministers" or "servants"], he angered many people, who as if in an attempt to avenge themselves made every effort to pry into his affairs and investigate all that he did.[29]

On the basis of this account, it would seem that the Patriarch wielded a good deal of authority among the Diaspora communities of Asia Minor. Armed with letters of introduction from the *Nasi*, Joseph was sent to Cilicia on his behalf to collect taxes, referred to here in Temple terminology, i.e., tithes and firstfruits. As an apostle, Joseph also took the initiative in trying to rectify religious practice, which he presumably found lax. How-

---

27. Y. Cohen, "When Did the *Nesiut* Move to Tiberias?" 114–22. It has also been suggested that there is archeological evidence for the *Nasi* from Hammat Gader. Habas (Rubin) claims that the reference to "the [spring] of the Patriarch" in a local inscription refers to the Jewish Patriarch ("Poem by Eudocia," 108–19).

28. See L. Levine, "Status of the Patriarch," 24–26; Rubin, "Joseph the Comes," 105–16.

29. Panarion, 30, 11, 1–4 (p. 100); cf. Jacobs, *Institution*, 308–12.

ever, his authority seems to have been restricted in this regard, if we can believe Epiphanius' formulation. Joseph was only able to persist "in proposing measures to restore correct observance of the law." Nevertheless, when it came to removing (and appointing?) synagogue officials, Joseph's authority appears to have been recognized and effective. Although he enraged many, it seems there was little that the communities could do other than harass him because of his status as representative of the Patriarch. This account clearly indicates that the power of the Patriarch was considerable and that, in some cases at least, local officials were replaced by his emissaries at will.

THE THEODOSIAN CODE

Published in 438 C.E. by the Emperor Theodosius II, this code contains decrees and decisions of the emperors since the time of Constantine. One section is devoted to minority groups, including Jews, and it is in this context that the Patriarch played a prominent role and his authority was emphasized time and again. He bore some of the most honored titles in contemporary Roman society (*spectabilis, illustris,* and *clarissimus et illustris*), and his rights included the promulgation of bans, exemption from public service, control over communal officials, Imperial protection from damage and insult, judicial and arbitrational rights, and permission to collect the *aurum coronarium* tax.

The following decrees focus specifically on the position and authority of the Patriarch within the synagogue.

> *(1) A decree of Arcadius and Honorius from 397*
> The Jews shall be bound to their rites; while we shall imitate the ancients in conserving their privileges, for it was established in their laws and confirmed by our divinity, that *those who are subject to the rule of the Illustrious Patriarchs, that is the Archsynagogues [sic—L. L.], the patriarchs, the presbyters and the others who are occupied in the rite of that religion* [emphasis mine—L. L.], shall persevere in keeping the same privileges that are reverently bestowed on the first clerics of the venerable Christian Law. For this was decreed in divine order also by the divine Emperors Constantine and Constantius, Valentinian and Valens. Let them therefore be exempt even from the curial liturgies, and obey their laws.[30]

> *(2) A decree of Arcadius and Honorius from 399*
> It is a matter of *shameful superstition that the Archsynagogues, the presbyters of the Jews, and those they call apostles, who are sent by the Patriarch on a certain date to demand gold and silver, exact and receive a sum from each synagogue, and deliver it to him* [emphasis mine—L. L.]. Therefore everything that we are confident has been collected when the period of time is considered shall be faithfully transferred to our Treasury, and we decree that henceforth nothing shall be sent to the aforesaid [this last order was canceled five years later—L. L.]. . . .[31]

---

30. Linder, *Jews in Roman Imperial Legislation,* no. 27; see also Jacobs, *Institution,* 280–84; L. Levine, "Status of the Patriarch," 17–18.

31. Linder, *Jews in Roman Imperial Legislation,* no. 30. Cf. Jacobs, *Institution,* 299–300.

(3) A decree of Honorius and Theodosius II from 415
Since Gamaliel supposed that he could transgress the law with impunity all the more because he was elevated to the pinnacle of dignities, Your Illustrious Authority shall know that Our Serenity has directed orders to the Illustrious Master of the Offices, that the appointment documents to the honorary prefecture shall be taken from him, so that he shall remain in the honour that was his before he was granted the prefecture; *and henceforth he shall cause no synagogues to be founded, and if there are any in deserted places, he shall see to it that they are destroyed, if it can be done without sedition* [emphasis mine—L. L.]. . . .[32]

The above three decrees are clear-cut evidence of the dominance of the Patriarch in a wide range of synagogue affairs. According to the first, he stands at the head of a network of officials, including archisynagogues, patriarchs, presbyters, and others, in charge of the religious dimension of the synagogue. The second describes the Patriarch utilizing some of these same officials to collect taxes from synagogues throughout the Empire. The last decree, while abolishing an earlier privilege, nevertheless gives evidence that, at least until 415, the Patriarch had a recognized role in the founding and building of synagogues. When the role began we do not know.

A fourth decree from the Theodosian Code, dating to the first part of the fourth century, speaks of the religious involvement of patriarchs and presbyters in synagogue affairs.

(4) A decree of Constantine from 330
Those who dedicated themselves with complete devotion to the synagogues of the Jews, to the patriarchs or to the presbyters, and while living in the above-mentioned sect, it is they who preside over the law, shall continue to be exempt from all liturgies, personal as well as civil; in such a way that those that happen to be decurions already shall not be designated to transportations of any kind, for it would be appropriate that people such as these shall not be compelled for whatever reason to depart from the places in which they are. Those, however, who are definitely not decurions, shall enjoy perpetual exemption from the decurionate.[33]

The above references to "patriarchs" is unclear, as is the syntax of the opening sentence. Does the phrase "devotion to the synagogues" refer to the Patriarch and presbyters, or did the emperor have two objects of devotion in mind: those devoted to the synagogue and those devoted to the patriarchs and presbyters? The former seems more likely. It thus appears that the decree relates specifically to these two officials who have dedicated themselves with complete devotion to the synagogue. The exemptions in the decree parallel those granted to the pagan priesthood and Christian clergy because of involvement in their respective religious institutions. It is unclear whether the reference to patriarchs points to local officials or to the Patriarchs of Palestine. Certainty in this matter is elusive, and very diverse interpretations have been offered.[34] Nevertheless, the

---

32. Linder, *Jews in Roman Imperial Legislation*, no. 41. Cf. Jacobs, *Institution*, 287–91.

33. Linder, *Jews in Roman Imperial Legislation*, no. 9. Cf. Jacobs, *Institution*, 277–80.

34. Linder, *Jews in Roman Imperial Legislation*, 133–34; S. J. D. Cohen, "Pagan and Christian Evi-

context of this law seems to point to local officials who may have been called patriarchs because they functioned—at least in part—under the auspices of the Palestinian Patriarch. Thus, it would appear that both titles used in this law, patriarchs and presbyters, refer to local communal officials who were granted exemptions from civil and Imperial liturgies. A suggestion to identify the presbyters ("elders") with members of the Sanhedrin is most problematic.[35] There is no basis for such an assumption; in fact, it is quite certain that no Sanhedrin existed in the third and fourth centuries.[36]

PATRIARCHAL INVOLVEMENT IN THE SYNAGOGUE

To assess the role of the Patriarch in the synagogue on the basis of the above sources is thus well-nigh impossible. The material is simply too limited and scattered to permit any type of meaningful generalization. The clearest attestations of a major role played by the Patriarch are, of course, the last-quoted sources, i.e., the decrees from the Theodosian Code. Major areas of synagogue life, from the religious to the administrative, are covered in these documents. However, since they derive from the very end of the fourth and the early fifth centuries, it is difficult to assess how reflective they are of an earlier period, or of the Empire as a whole. A number of scholars have posited a dramatic rise in Patriarchal prominence and authority under Theodosius I (379-95 c.e.) and his successors, and such an assumption would restrict the *Nasi*'s authority as reflected in these decrees to only a few brief decades.[37] In contrast, we have argued elsewhere that many of the Patriarchal prerogatives enumerated in the Theodosian Code are, in fact, attested in other sources for earlier periods as well. When all these various sources are taken into consideration, it becomes clear that the Patriarchate enjoyed a great deal of prominence throughout most of the third and fourth centuries. In other words, when viewing the status of this office in a broader perspective, we see that late fourth-century Patriarchal privileges appear to have been as much a continuation of past privileges as they were an innovation of the latter era. This observation holds true with respect to administrative, tax, and judicial matters in particular.[38]

As specifically regards synagogue involvement, supportive material is woefully limited. Other than Epiphanius' account and several possible allusions in rabbinic sources, no other third- or fourth-century literary source speaks of actual Patriarchal control of

---

dence," 171-72; Jacobs, *Institution*, 275-77. On the vagueness of synagogue titles appearing in the *Theodosian Code* generally, see Rajak and Noy, *"Archisynagogoi,"* 80.

35. Linder, *Jews in Roman Imperial Legislation*, 133.

36. L. Levine, *Rabbinic Class*, 76-83; Goodblatt, *Monarchic Principle*, 232-76; Jacobs, *Institution*, 93-99.

37. See, for example, S. J. D. Cohen and Goodman (above, note 1). Cf. also Brown, *Authority and the Sacred*, 47-48. J. Baumgarten ("Art in the Synagogue," 204-6) tends to maximize the influence of the Patriarch and his circles on the synagogue.

38. L. Levine, "Status of the Patriarch," 1-32.

or active intervention in local synagogues. Even the Stobi inscription tells us nothing about the nature of the Patriarch's involvement in synagogue life on an ongoing basis, nor does the mishnaic report of Galileans assigning public property to the *Nasi*. As for the "right" to build synagogues, implied in the edict of 415, this may be interpreted as a formal grant issued by the Patriarch, but without any fiscal or administrative responsibility or authority. Similarly, throughout the Byzantine period the formality of a provincial governor's confirmation was required for local initiatives.[39]

We are thus at a standstill in this matter. This is unfortunate not merely because the issue itself is of great importance to our understanding of Jewish communal life in late antiquity, but because positing the active involvement of the Patriarch in the ancient synagogue would help explain a number of other synagogue-related enigmas. It would go a long way toward explaining the emergence of synagogues in general and the Galilean-type synagogue in particular in the course of the third century, at a time when the office was accruing a large measure of power and prestige.[40] It might also help explain the construction of numerous Diaspora synagogues in the third and fourth centuries, because we could assume that these Jewish communities enjoyed the aid and support of a powerful office with considerable Imperial recognition. Finally, such an assumption might even account for some of the similarities among ancient synagogues everywhere, particularly in their use of common Jewish symbols and perhaps in their orientation. The above, unfortunately, must be relegated to mere speculation for the present.

We can only conclude at this juncture that there were times and places when the office of the Patriarch was a significant factor in synagogue affairs. Few can question that this was the case in many late fourth-century Diaspora locales and perhaps even in second-to third-century Galilee. However, the extent of this Patriarchal involvement, both geographical and chronological, is unclear. Ironically, it was not long before the disappearance of the office, ca. 425, that the Patriarch reached the apogee of his prestige and power, a status which might have allowed for considerable influence on the synagogue.

---

39. See Di Segni, "Involvement," 328–32. Imperial building initiatives in the Roman Empire are, of course, well known. However, there is no evidence, epigraphical or otherwise, that the Patriarch operated in a similar manner. See MacMullen, "Roman Imperial Building," 207–35; Mitchell, "Imperial Building," 18–25.

40. See L. Levine, "Jewish Patriarch," 649–88.

thirteen

THE SAGES AND
THE SYNAGOGUE

The nature and extent of rabbinic involvement in, and influence on, the synagogue in late antiquity are of cardinal importance not only for understanding how the synagogue functioned, but also for gaining a perspective on the status of the sages in Jewish society of this period.[1]

In studies of Jewish history in the Greco-Roman and Byzantine eras, it has often been assumed that the sages were the dominant religious and social force within Jewish society. This has been asserted with regard to the Pharisees in the pre-70 era as well as the talmudic sages in the post-destruction period of Roman Palestine.[2] Some have carried this assumption over to the Diaspora as well, applying it to such areas as the study of Torah in Rome and Aphrodisias and the art of the Dura Europos synagogue. Kraeling, followed

---

1. See, for example, L. Levine, "Sages and Synagogue," 201–22; and, more generally, idem, *Rabbinic Class*, 43–47; S. J. D. Cohen, "Place of the Rabbi," 157–73; Hezser, "Social Fragmentation," 234–51; idem, *Social Structure*, 214–24; as well as Urbach, *Sages*, I, 603–20; Beer, "Issachar and Zebulun," 167–80.

2. Alon, *Jews, Judaism and the Classical World*, 22 n. 11. While Alon makes this statement only with regard to the Pharisees, this viewpoint is assumed in all of his writings and by those who have adopted his approach. See, for example, idem, *Jews in Their Land*, I, 308; S. Safrai, "Recovery of the Jewish Community," 27–39. See also Oppenheimer, "Restoration of the Jewish Community," 80–92; idem, *Galilee*, passim. Such an assumption is likewise implicit in Urbach, "Rabbinical Laws of Idolatry," passim, which argues—contra Goodenough—that Jewish art was not antithetical to rabbinic Judaism but even had the sages' approval. See also the comments of Fine in this regard ("From Meeting House," 28; *Holy Place*, 147).

by Schubert and others, has assumed that the Dura artist (or artists) was influenced by rabbinic midrashic traditions; Reynolds and Tannenbaum detect the influence of rabbinic cultural values and institutions in the Aphrodisias inscription; and Feldman assumes that rabbinic Judaism was well known in Asia Minor.[3]

At the same time, there has been a countertrend these past decades advocating a more circumspect view with regard to rabbinic influence generally and on the synagogue in particular. Two important studies, appearing in the 1950s and coming from entirely different perspectives, have had a powerful influence on the discussion of Pharisaic and rabbinic status in antiquity. One was Smith's pathbreaking article claiming that the Pharisees were just one of a number of pre-70 sects, and not the dominant force in the religious life of the masses.[4] At the same time, Goodenough was publishing his multivolume *Jewish Symbols*, wherein he argued, on the basis of Jewish artistic remains from synagogues and cemeteries, that the rabbis of later antiquity were a marginal group with little or no impact on wider Jewish society.[5] The questions raised by these seminal studies have remained central to the scholarly agenda right up to the present.

However, the degree of rabbinic influence on the ancient synagogue is far more complex and varied than any sweeping and facile generalization of yes or no. First of all, not all rabbis were cut from the same cloth. They differed from one another in personality, socioeconomic standing, social context (including urban versus rural), and degree of religious stringency; some were more involved in the political and social issues or in communal life, others less so. Moreover, there were often varied attitudes among them toward the non-rabbinic world, be it Jewish or non-Jewish. Finally, the cataclysmic changes which affected the Jews at large in the first four or five centuries C.E. had major repercussions on the rabbinic class as well. For example, this period of time was distinguished by a major shift in the attitudes of many sages regarding their involvement in the wider Jewish community—e.g., between the second century on the one hand and the third and fourth on the other. This change relates not only to the rabbis' overall attitude toward communal affairs, but also to their actual participation in these areas.[6]

As regards the synagogue specifically, besides differences among the rabbis, one must distinguish between different aspects of this institution. Are we speaking of their influence on the actual physical building, its style, plan, and interior design, its administrative and political leadership, the responsibility for its many activities (educational, social, judicial, etc.), or the institution's religious dimension?

---

3. Kraeling, *Dura: Synagogue*, 351–60; Schubert, "Jewish Pictorial Traditions," 171–88; Reynolds and Tannenbaum, *Jews and God-Fearers*, 25–37; Feldman, *Jew and Gentile*, 69–74.

4. M. Smith, "Palestinian Judaism," 73–81.

5. See his summary statement, *Jewish Symbols*, XII, 184–98.

6. According to R. Jeremiah, "He who is involved in communal matters is like one who studies Torah" (Y Berakhot 5, 1, 8d). See also my *Rabbinic Class*, 23–42; Hezser, *Social Structure*, 240ff.

Finally, when speaking about the rabbis' influence on or involvement in the ancient synagogue, geographical distinctions must be borne in mind. Some areas may have been more affected by rabbinic values and practices than others. For example, are the Galilee or the areas of rabbinic activity in Babylonia comparable in this respect to other regions in Palestine or Babylonia? And what are we to make of regions where there is almost no evidence of rabbinic presence, such as the Roman Diaspora?

One further caveat should be considered in this regard, and that is the very different impression of rabbinic involvement in the synagogue that is gained from different sources. Rabbinic literature tells us a great deal about the institution and rabbinic activity therein. Based on these sources alone, it is all too easy to assume extensive rabbinic involvement in and influence on the synagogue. Sages are noted visiting, functioning, and at times determining policy for various synagogue activities. However, we must ask whether rabbinic involvement in the synagogue was indeed the norm or whether only a small number of sages were actually active in its affairs and, if so, when and where they lived.[7] Furthermore, what are the implications when no mention is made of rabbinic involvement? Are we to assume that it simply did not exist or that it was merely taken for granted? Of no less importance are instances when information culled from rabbinic literature contradicts evidence derived from other literary or archeological sources. How are these contradictions to be explained? Needless to say, these other non-rabbinic sources must be given a chance to speak for themselves, and not just viewed through the prism of rabbinic material. The more information that comes to light reflecting a social, cultural, or religious orientation different from that of the rabbis as a whole, the less likely it is that their influence was significant, much less pervasive. What is called for is an effort to gain a wider perspective, which is crucial in trying to draw any sort of historical conclusions. These are some of the issues at the heart of the discussion of the relationship between the rabbis and the synagogue.

NON-RABBINIC SOURCES

The information culled from non-rabbinic sources regarding rabbinic involvement in the synagogue, although mostly of negative import, is nevertheless of interest and merits presentation. Although in essence *ex silentio*, these sources nevertheless appear to make a forceful statement. Many other offices and titles are noted, administrative, religious, and honorary, but never with regard to the rabbis. Such sources can be divided into three categories: non-Jewish literary sources, archeological material, and Jewish non-rabbinic literary evidence. Let us examine each in turn.

The relevant non-Jewish sources are rather late, stemming from the fourth and early

---

7. For a similar methodological issue, this time with regard to Byzantine hagiography, see Brown, *Authority and the Sacred*, 59–65.

fifth centuries, and are primarily of three sorts: the writings of church fathers who comment on the synagogue, edicts preserved in the Theodosian Code, and fourth-century pagan sources which refer in passing to this institution.

A number of fourth- to fifth-century church fathers—John Chrysostom, Epiphanius, and Jerome—mention synagogue and other communal officials, albeit infrequently. On the one hand, they take note of various synagogue practices;[8] on the other hand, Jewish leaders or groups are rarely identified. Epiphanius notes the Pharisees, archisynagogue, hazzan, priests, presbyters, and the apostoli of the Patriarch, who had the authority to remove each of the above; Jerome, the magistrorum synagoge, Pharisees, praepositi sapientissimi, and priests.[9] However, the sages as such, either individually or collectively, are never mentioned in connection with the synagogue. The mention of Pharisees is enigmatic; does it refer to contemporary sages, or is it based on New Testament verses?

The Theodosian Code similarly addresses synagogue-related affairs on a number of occasions and notes specific offices. Edicts from the year 330 speak of Patriarchs, presbyters, archisynagogues, and fathers of synagogues; from 392, about primates of the Law; from 396, 404, and 415, about the Patriarchs; from 397, about Patriarchs, archisynagogues, patriarchs, presbyters, and others involved in the rite (sacramentum) of the religion; and from 399, about Patriarchs, archisynagogues, presbyters, and apostles.[10] Never are the sages per se mentioned as a factor in the synagogue. Other fourth-century pagan sources which make reference to Jews take note of Patriarchs, archisynagogues, and others, but here, as well, not the rabbis.[11] Thus, the above sources which relate first and foremost to the Roman Diaspora know nothing of the involvement of sages in any aspect of synagogue life.

Turning now to the archeological material, a similar picture emerges from the not inconsiderable amount of epigraphical data at hand. Of the hundreds of synagogue inscriptions known, none mentions any sage known to us from rabbinic literature. True enough, the title "rabbi" appears not infrequently, particularly in Palestinian inscriptions in Aramaic and Hebrew. However, as has been argued on a number of occasions, this title was

---

8. Wilken, *John Chrysostom and the Jews*, 97–127; S. Krauss, "Jews in the Works of the Church Fathers," part 1, 122; part 2, 82–99, 225–61.

9. *Epiphanius—Panarion* 30, 11, 4. *Jerome—magistrorum synagoge: In Zach.* II, 6, 9. Pharisees: *Letter* 112. *Praepositi sapientissimi: Letter* 121, 10, 19–20. The last reference in Jerome comes the closest to pointing to the rabbis. Jerome defines the *praepositi* as those who teach Pharisaic traditions (*deuterosis*, i.e., Mishnah). Such traditions, he claims, are binding on the Jews; those who do not accept them are liable to attack (*Comm. in Isa.* 59, 25). On the use of the above-mentioned titles throughout the Roman Diaspora, see Juster, *Juifs*, I, 442–56.

10. *Cod. Theod.* 16.8.2, 4, 8, 13, 14, 15. See Linder, *Jews in Roman Imperial Legislation*, nos. 9, 20, 24, 27, 30, 32, 41.

11. For example, Libanius (M. Stern, *Greek and Latin Authors*, II, 589–97); *SHA* (ibid., 630, 636–41); and Palladius (*Life of John Chrysostom* 15). Cf. Jacobs, *Jüdischen Patriarchen*, passim.

not limited to talmudic sages alone, but was used as an honorary designation for a wealthy donor, a learned individual, or one appointed as judge.[12] Thus, it would seem, according to the epigraphical evidence, that synagogues were built and run by Jews other than rabbis.

Moreover, synagogue art does not appear to reflect rabbinic attitudes of late antiquity. Art per se is not a major subject of discussion in rabbinic literature, and it is mentioned only with regard to questions of idolatry or the making and enjoyment of (or deriving benefit from) pagan images. The relatively few sources that address the subject of figural representation indicate that, with rare exceptions, rabbis were either opposed to or, at best, grudgingly accepting of this phenomenon (see below). Even depictions of the seven-branched menorah as it had once existed in the Temple were regarded as problematic;[13] symbols such as the globe, scepter, and bird were associated with pagan worship and hence forbidden.[14] Notwithstanding these rabbinic reservations, some of the above depictions appear with relative frequency in ancient Jewish art.[15]

In which synagogues might most rabbis have felt comfortable on the basis of the above? In the absence of any sort of embracement of figural art by a sage, I would hazard a guess that most would probably have preferred the artistically more conservative synagogues, those with little or no decoration, such as the ones at 'En Gedi, Jericho, Khirbet Shema', Meiron, and Qatzrin. The synagogue at Reḥov, with its aniconic art, almost exclusive use of Hebrew and Aramaic, and its halakhic inscriptions, would almost certainly have been to the liking of most.

Finally, we turn to the third type of source, the Jewish non-rabbinic literary material, of which we have a considerable amount at hand: late Byzantine apocryphal texts, Hekha-

---

12. See esp. S. J. D. Cohen, "Epigraphical Rabbis," 1–17; Shanks, "Title 'Rabbi,'" 337–45; idem, "Origins of the Title," 152–57; Zeitlin, "Reply," 345–49; idem, "Title Rabbi," 158–60.

13. B Rosh Hashanah 24a–b; B 'Avodah Zarah 43a; B Menaḥot 28b.

14. M 'Avodah Zarah 3:1; T 'Avodah Zarah 5:1 (p. 468); Y 'Avodah Zarah 3, 1, 42c. See Urbach, "Rabbinical Laws of Idolatry," 238–45.

15. On the menorah in archeological finds, see, inter alia, Goodenough, *Jewish Symbols*, IV, 71–77; Negev, "Chronology of Seven-Branched Menorah," 193–210; Hachlili, *Art and Archaeology—Israel*, 236–56; Hachlili and Merhav, "Menorah in First and Second Temple Times," 256–67. On the use of the zodiac, see Hachlili, *Art and Archaeology—Israel*, 301–9; idem, "Zodiac," 61–77. See also Dothan, *Hammath Tiberias*, 39–43. In other areas, the visual arts are not in sync with rabbinic behavior; e.g., there is no distinctive Jewish garb in the Dura paintings—see Revel-Neher, *Image of the Jew*, 96.

On the non-rabbinic character of some aspects of Jewish art, especially the zodiac and Helios scenes, see Urbach, "Rabbinical Laws of Idolatry," 238–45; J. Baumgarten, "Art in the Synagogue," 196–206. Foerster has argued that the zodiac signs are endemic to Jewish tradition from the Second Temple period onward. He is probably correct, although the real issue is not the zodiac signs per se (see Deuteronomy Rabbah 1:16 [p. 16]), but their non-Jewish artistic representation and, more particularly, the representation of Helios and his accoutrements, as at Ḥammat Tiberias; see his "Zodiac in Ancient Synagogues," 225–34.

lot mystical tracts, and books of magic, such as *The Book of Secrets* (*Sefer Harazim*) and the Sword of Moses (*Ḥarba de-Moshe*).[16] How these circles are related to the talmudic rabbis, if at all, is one of the many unresolved problems in the research of this period. Moreover, it is unclear as to how much of this material is relevant to the synagogue. Is there a connection, for example, between the role of Helios in *The Book of Secrets* and his depiction on the synagogue mosaic floor at Ḥammat Tiberias and elsewhere?[17] And how is the liturgical material in the Hekhalot texts related to contemporary synagogue practice?

One type of source, however, is unequivocally of synagogue provenance—the *targumim*. Scholars have long recognized discrepancies between targumic literature and rabbinic sources.[18] In fact, there are specific instances in which sages have objected to particular translations, yet these renditions often appear in Targum Pseudo-Jonathan.[19] One such discrepancy between the targumic tradition and the sages deals specifically with the use of figural representation in synagogues, with the *targum* reflecting a more forthcoming attitude, essentially allowing for figural representations to appear on synagogue mosaic floors: "You shall not make any idols for yourself and you shall not erect any statues or pillars, nor shall you place a figural stone in your land for the purpose of prostration, but you may place a stoa [here, probably a mosaic pavement] impressed with drawings and figures on the floors of your sanctuaries [מקדשיכון, i.e., floors of your synagogues],[20] though not to bow down to it [for purposes of worship], for I am the Lord your God."[21]

In addition, many of the targumic elaborations would seem to refer to popular customs, practices, and beliefs that were most probably not rabbinically inspired.[22] For the most part, and given the harmonizing proclivities characteristic of former generations, it has been assumed that the *targum* often might reflect either the personal opinion of a particular sage or *meturgeman* or, alternatively, an early stage of rabbinic halakhic opinion.[23]

---

16. Schürer, *History*, III, 343–79, with especial attention to Ibn Shmuel, *Midreshei Geulah*, and *Sepher Ha-Razim* (trans. Morgan).

17. A connection first suggested in J. Z. Smith, "Observations," 158–60. See L. Levine, "Ancient Synagogues—Historical Introduction," 9.

18. Not all *targumim* are similar in this regard. It is generally acknowledged that Onkelos and Neofiti are much more in line with the rabbinic corpora than Pseudo-Jonathan.

19. See, for example, the statement of R. Yose b. R. Abun in Y Berakhot 5, 3, 9c and Targum Pseudo-Jonathan of Lev. 22:28. For other examples, see Bacher, *JE*, XII, 58, s.v. "Targum"; Lieberman "Hazzanut Yannai," 222–23; Alexander, "Rabbinic Lists," 177–91.

20. Chilton, *Isaiah Targum*, 11. Cf., however, the interpretation in Fine, "Art and Iconoclasm."

21. Targum Pseudo-Jonathan of Lev. 26:2. See Ginzberg, *Commentary*, III, 116–23; Blidstein, "Prostration and Mosaics," 37–39; M. L. Klein, "Palestinian Targum," 44–45.

22. Shinan, *Embroidered Targum*, 104–67; and below, Chap. 16.

23. The former option was adopted in Albeck, "Apocryphal Halakha," 93–104. The latter has been advocated in Kahle, *Cairo Geniza*, 206; Diez-Macho, "Recently Discovered Palestinian Targum," 222–

Both of these approaches posit that rabbinic thought as reflected in talmudic literature was, as a matter of course, normative in the synagogue. However, in light of this discussion, it seems even more likely that the *targum* often reflects non-rabbinic conceptions and practices prevalent in Jewish society at that time.

Thus, our review of non-rabbinic evidence offers a distinctly different picture of the relationship between rabbis and synagogues than has ordinarily been assumed. On the basis of the above evidence, it would seem that in most areas concerning the synagogue—the building, art, donors, and leadership, and even some liturgical practices—rabbinic involvement was minimal, at best.

RABBINIC SOURCES

Rabbinic evidence itself is far from conclusive regarding the sages' relation to the synagogue. In fact, it offers a rather complex picture of their involvement in this institution. In some respects these sources confirm the picture gained from the non-rabbinic sources cited above; in others, however, they shed a rather different light.

Dissonance between the Sages and Synagogue Practices

There is a disparity between rabbinic descriptions of synagogues and the archeological remains. To cite but three examples:

(1) The Tosefta states that synagogue entrances should face east.[24] However, to date, few synagogues seem to have adhered to this guideline. Aside from four synagogues found in southern Judaea which were built in this manner,[25] only three or four of the remaining one hundred or so buildings in Roman-Byzantine Palestine have their main (or only) entrance to the east.

(2) One rabbinic tradition prescribes changing the usual seating arrangements within the synagogue in times of mourning: those sitting in the north should sit in the south and vice versa.[26] However, it is almost impossible to anchor this tradition in any known archeological reality, since entrances were almost always oriented toward or away from Jerusalem, i.e., to the north or to the south, and thus benches were invariably placed on the eastern and western sides of the building. Only in a small number of cases were benches also found on the building's northern or southern side. Thus, determining the *Sitz im Leben* of this rabbinic tradition is almost impossible.

45; Heinemann, "Early Halakhah," 114–22; Faur, "Targumim and Halakha," 19–26; and, generally, York, "Dating of Targumic Literature," 49–62; McNamara, "Targums," 856–61.

24. T Megillah 3:22 (p. 360).

25. In addition to the well-known examples at Susiya and Eshtemoa (see L. Levine, *Ancient Synagogues Revealed*, 120–28), two others from the same area have been discovered in recent years, at Maʻon and ʻAnim. See reports of Z. Ilan and Amit, in *NEAEHL*, passim.

26. B Moʻed Qatan 22b.

(3) The statement that the elders are to sit facing the congregation with their back to the holy (probably a reference to Jerusalem and the site of the Temple) does not find expression in most synagogue buildings of late antiquity.[27] Only in the extant pre-70 Judaean buildings and in several later ones did benches line the wall facing Jerusalem.[28]

In another vein, rabbinic literature itself has preserved a dramatic account of the practice in one synagogue setting that was contrary to rabbinic views. In a Caesarean synagogue, where it was customary to recite the *Shema* in Greek, we are told that two rabbis reacted in very different ways.[29] One was openly hostile, the other more tolerant—at least post facto. Levi bar Ḥiyta was incensed enough to consider bringing the service to a halt, while R. Yosi responded that it was better that the congregation recite the *Shema* in Greek than not at all. Ironically, neither statement of these third-century sages reflects the more lenient position of the Mishnah, which explicitly makes allowance for the *Shema* to be recited in any language.[30]

Rabbinic literature has also preserved a number of instances in which practices revolving around the delivery of the *targum* in the synagogue were at odds with rabbinic conceptions and dictates. The Yerushalmi, for example, relates a series of stories about local targumic practices which ran counter to rabbinic prescriptions. Three such instances involved R. Samuel b. R. Isaac: in the first, he rebuked a *meturgeman* for translating the scriptural reading while standing by a column (instead of next to the Torah reader); in the second, one and the same person read from the Torah and translated the Torah portion (instead of two different people); in the third, the *meturgeman* read the scriptural translation from a book, instead of giving a spontaneous translation.[31] The responses of these functionaries, or of the congregation generally, to these directives are not related.

The account regarding R. Simeon of Tarbanat demonstrates how one rabbi-*meturgeman* dared to defy the will of the congregation.[32] When asked by the congregation to break up each verse when translating, in order to allow time for the adults to explain what

---

27. T Megillah 3:21 (p. 360).

28. See the articles by Yadin, Foerster, Gutman, and Maʿoz in L. Levine, *Ancient Synagogues Revealed*, 19–41. Later examples would include Dura Europos and ʿEn Neshut; see Kraeling, *Dura: Synagogue*, 16–17, and *NEAEHL*, respectively.

29. Y Sotah 7, 1, 21b.

30. M Sotah 7:1. However, these sages' attitude corresponds to the view of R. Judah I quoted in the Yerushalmi just before the Caesarean account (see previous note), namely, that the *Shema* ought to be recited in Hebrew.

31. Y Megillah 4, 1, 74d. This same R. Samuel b. R. Isaac reportedly instructed teachers on other occasions as well; see Numbers Rabbah 12:3; Midrash on Psalms 91:3 (pp. 397–98). Rabbinic objections to the use of a written translation clearly indicate that *targumim* existed at this time, as we see, for example, in M Yadaim 4:5; T Shabbat 13:2 (p. 57); B Shabbat 115a; as well as in evidence from Qumran (Schiffman, *Reclaiming*, 214–15).

32. Y Megillah 4, 5, 75b.

84. Representation of Helios in a mosaic floor from the Ḥammat Tiberias synagogue. Note the halo and rays over his head, his right hand raised in triumph, and his left hand holding a sphere and a staff.

was being read to the children present, R. Simeon decided to consult with his teacher, R. Ḥanina. The latter affirmed the rabbinic dictum that each verse should be translated as a whole unit. When R. Simeon resumed his targumic activities in accordance with R. Ḥanina's advice, he was immediately fired by the congregation.[33]

A further example of synagogue practice defying rabbinic prescription, noted above, is evidenced in the fourth-century Ḥammat Tiberias building. In the middle of the zodiac mosaic is a depiction of Helios holding in his left hand a sphere (i.e., the earth) and a staff (i.e., a scepter; fig. 84). These very features were explicitly prohibited by the sages:

> All images are forbidden because they are worshipped [at least] once a year. So [says] R. Meir. But the sages say: "Only that is forbidden which holds a staff or bird or sphere in its hand." R. Simeon b. Gamaliel says: "A [statue] which holds any kind of object [is forbidden]."[34]

---

33. It is not entirely clear what R. Simeon was doing when he provoked the anger of the local community: translating a passage from the Torah? the haftarah? teaching children? The terminology is vague. Following this incident, the Talmud brings in the opinions of two other sages, one apparently siding with the congregation, the other praising R. Simeon for his tenacity.

34. M ʿAvodah Zarah 3:1. Cf. Urbach, "Rabbinical Laws of Idolatry," 238–39. The depiction of nudity

On not a few occasions, sages looked askance upon certain synagogue practices. The Mishnah lists a series of prayers recited in local synagogues which the rabbis found objectionable. For the sages, saying "we give thanks" (מודים) twice raised suspicions of dualism, as did adding a prayer for God's mercy on a bird's nest or that His name be associated only with good.[35] A prayer leader who insisted on wearing only white in the synagogue was declared unacceptable, as was the priest who insisted on standing barefoot. Any deviation from the prescribed way in which a man placed the phylacteries on his head and hand was declared invalid and termed sectarian (דרך החיצונים, דרך המינות).[36] R. Yoḥanan and R. Yose — the latter despite the vigorous objections of R. Aḥa — chose not to protest when the *Shemaʿ* was recited more than three hours after sunrise on a fast day, contrary to their practice.[37]

Some sages objected vehemently to synagogues belonging to ordinary people (*ʿammei ha-ʾaretz*), as well as to the latter's practice of referring to the holy ark as *ʾarona* and to the synagogue as *bet ʿam*.[38] In Babylonia as well, it was the custom in one particular synagogue to bow down; however, Rav, who had just arrived from Palestine and was unfamiliar with this practice, refused to do so.[39] We read of at least one instance in which dragging a bench in a synagogue violated rabbinic law; R. Jeremiah was involved in one such incident in Bostra.[40] Finally, Resh Laqish's comparison of a preacher in the synagogue to a theater mime entertaining the masses reflects a rather condescending attitude — to say the least — toward this aspect of synagogue worship.[41]

Synagogue versus *Bet Midrash*

In trying to understand and assess rabbinic involvement in the synagogue, it is important to bear in mind the communal nature of this institution, on the one hand, and the fact that the rabbinic world revolved primarily around the academy (*bet midrash*), on the other. These were in essence separate institutions, and several talmudic statements

---

on this synagogue's mosaic floor — including a male phallus — was clearly not to rabbinic liking; see Satlow, "Jewish Constructions of Nakedness," 429-54, esp. 435-36.

35. M Berakhot 5:3; M Megillah 4:9. On these rabbinic traditions, see A. F. Segal, *Two Powers in Heaven*, 98-108.

36. M Megillah 4:8. The distinction made by the sages between these two types of sectarianism is not altogether clear. See the comments by Rashi and the Rambam, loc. cit. Wearing white, (i.e., linen) clothing recalls Essene sectarian behavior; see Josephus, *War* 2, 123; S. Krauss, *Qadmoniot Ha-Talmud*, II/2, 89.

37. Y Berakhot 1, 5, 3c.

38. M ʾAvot 3:10; B Shabbat 32a. Such references to the ark have been found at Dura Europos and Naveh; see Kraeling, *Dura: Synagogue*, 269; Braslavski, "Hebrew-Aramaic Inscription," 8-12; Frey, *CIJ*, II, 93. Naveh first questioned this reading, but later retracted his reservations; see his *On Stone and Mosaic*, no. 37; idem, "Aramaic and Hebrew Inscriptions," no. 8.

39. B Megillah 22b.

40. B Shabbat 29b. A similar incident took place in Sepphoris in the presence of R. Isaac b. Elʿazar, but it is not clear whether this happened in a synagogue (ibid.).

41. Genesis Rabbah 80:1 (pp. 950-53). See Herr, "Synagogues and Theatres," 105-19.

do, in fact, imply that the academy was an autonomous rabbinic institution.[42] In describing Jerusalemite customs on the holiday of Sukkot, rabbinic literature makes a clear distinction between synagogue and academy, which was certainly reflective of the situation in later antiquity whatever the reality of the pre-70 period might have been.[43] R. Pappa claims that it is permissible to turn a synagogue into an academy but not vice versa, while R. Joshua b. Levi states that one can sell a synagogue in order to buy an academy but not vice versa.[44] In each dictum, a clear-cut distinction is maintained between these two institutions.

Although synagogue and academy are often mentioned together in rabbinic literature—and thus the tendency of some to identify them as one and the same institution—it is quite clear that each functioned autonomously. The Bavli distinguishes between a place where one promotes Torah study (מקום שמגדלין בו תורה), i.e., the academy, and a place where one promotes prayer (מקום שמגדלין בו תפילה), i.e., the synagogue.[45] A statement by R. Isaac is also indicative of this distinction: "Thus God moves from synagogue to synagogue, from academy to academy," as is the following statement in Midrash on Psalms: "Thus our sages taught us: Anyone who leaves the synagogue and enters the academy is referred to by the verse 'They will go from strength to strength' [Ps. 84:8]. Moreover, such a person is considered worthy of receiving the Divine Presence."[46]

Nevertheless, while some sages did frequent the synagogue, others seem to have studiously avoided it, preferring instead the *bet midrash*. The fact that some sages found the synagogue setting less congenial to their spiritual needs may be inferred from the repeated rabbinic statements urging colleagues to pray in a synagogue setting.[47] Indeed, it would have been natural and understandable for some sages to shy away from such public settings, preferring either the intimacy of their homes or the familiarity of the academy, where they spent most of their time. One rabbinic dictum that urges rabbis to arise and pray after studying halakhah apparently refers to the academy setting.[48] R. Isaac once asked R. Naḥman:

---

42. For example, Y Taʿanit 1, 2, 64a; Y Megillah 3, 4, 74a; B Megillah 29a; B Moʿed Qatan 22b; B Ketubot 5a. As to the differences of opinion regarding the character of the Babylonian academy in late antiquity (how public and institutionalized a framework it was), see Goodblatt, *Rabbinic Instruction*, 267–72, as against Gafni, "Yeshiva and Metivta," 22–37.

43. T Sukkah 2:10 (p. 265); see B Sukkah 41b.

44. B Megillah 26b–27a; Y Megillah 3, 1, 73d.

45. B Megillah 27a.

46. Midrash on Psalms 84:4 (p. 186a). Cf. also PRK 5:8 (p. 90). Against Hüttenmeister's suggestion to identify these two institutions ("Synagogue and Beth-Ha-midrash," 38–44), see the strong—and in my opinion, correct—reservations of Oppenheimer ("Beth Ha-midrash," 45–48) and S. Safrai ("Halakha," 49).

47. Y Berakhot 5, 1, 8d; B Berakhot 6b–8a; and below.

48. Y Berakhot 5, 1, 8d.

"Why does the master not come to the synagogue and pray?" He responded: "I am not able." He asked him: "Let the master assemble ten people and pray in their company [i.e., in a congregational setting]." He responded: "It is too much trouble for me [טריחא לי מלתא]." "Then why not ask the prayer leader to inform you when the congregation is praying [so you can do so at the same time]?" He responded: "Why [are you making] all this fuss?" He said: "For R. Yohanan said in the name of R. Simeon ben Yohai . . . 'When is an acceptable time?' When the congregation prays.' "[49]

Abbaye said: "At first I would study in my home and pray in the synagogue. Once I heard a statement of R. Ḥiyya bar Ami quoting 'Ulla: 'Since the day the Temple was destroyed, the Holy One Blessed be He has nothing in this world except the four cubits of the halakha alone'; I pray only in the place where I study." Although there were thirteen synagogues in Tiberias, R. Ami and R. Asi prayed only between the pillars where they were accustomed to study.[50]

The basic distinction between these two institutions did not preclude use of the synagogue by sages for their own purposes. There were clearly instances in which this communal building served their needs as well, and they utilized it for their own rabbinic agenda.[51]

The Sages and Figural Art

Rabbinic attitudes toward figural art seem to have varied considerably. The second century C.E. has given us several contrasting rabbinic viewpoints. Two tannaitic traditions offer widely differing assessments regarding the permissibility of figural images. One is Rabban Gamaliel's visit to the bathhouse of Aphrodite in Acco, wherein a rather liberal and flexible attitude toward figural art is reflected, one which allowed its use in almost all settings, except where idolatry was clearly involved.[52] How reflective Rabban Gamaliel's attitude was of all or most rabbis is impossible to determine; given his position and responsibilities as Patriarch at the time, and in light of the more cosmopolitan worldview his position undoubtedly required, there is every possibility that Rabban Gamaliel was far more liberal in these matters than most sages.

A statement perhaps more reflective of rabbinic views on this matter is contained in a tannaitic midrash on Exodus (the *Mekhilta*), which states unequivocally that no figural

---

49. B Berakhot 7b–8a; and the textual variant in MS Munich (see *Diqduqei Soferim*).

50. B Berakhot 8a and 30b. See, however, the statement attributed to Abbaye (B Megillah 29a): "At first I used to study at home and pray in the synagogue. When I realized [the implications] of what David said, 'O Lord, I loved your temple abode' [Ps. 26:8], I began studying in the synagogue." This statement not only contradicts the quotation in the text ("Abbaye said"), but would seem to stand in contrast with what we generally know regarding the role of the synagogue in amoraic Babylonia; see *Diqduqei Soferim*, Megillah, loc. cit.; and Gafni, "Synagogues in Talmudic Babylonia," 155–62. On Tiberian synagogues, see Miller, "Number of Synagogues," 55–58.

51. For example, Y Berakhot 3, 1, 6a (= Y Nazir 7, 1, 56a).

52. M 'Avodah Zarah 3:4; and above, Chap. 7.

representation is permissible in any way, shape, or form. In commenting on the Second Commandment, the following is recorded:

"You shall not make a sculptured image" [Ex. 20:4]. One should not make one that is engraved, but perhaps one may make one that is solid? Scripture says: "Nor any likeness" [ibid.]. One should not make a solid one, but perhaps one may plant something? Scripture says: "You shall not plant an *asherah*" [Deut. 16:21]. One should not plant something, but perhaps one may make it [i.e., an image] of wood? Scripture says: "Any kind of wood" [ibid.]. One should not make it of wood, but perhaps one may make it of stone? Scripture says: "And a figured stone" [Lev. 26:1]. One should not make it of stone, but perhaps one may make it of silver? Scripture says: "Gods of silver" [Ex. 20:20]. One should not make it of silver, but perhaps one may make it of gold? Scripture says: "Gods of gold" [ibid.]. One should not make it of gold, but perhaps one may make it of copper, tin, or lead? Scripture says: "Do not make molten gods" [Lev. 19:4]. One should not make an image of any of the above, but perhaps one may make an image of any sort of likeness? Scripture says: "Lest you act wickedly and make for yourselves a sculptured image in any likeness whatsoever" [Deut. 4:16]. One should not make an image in any likeness whatsoever, but perhaps one may make an image of cattle or a bird? Scripture says: "The form of any beast on earth, the form of any winged bird" [ibid., 17]. Perhaps one should not make an image of any of these, but perhaps one may make an image of a fish, locust, unclean animals or reptiles [שקצים ורמשים]? Scripture says: "The form of anything that creeps on the ground, the form of any fish that is in the waters" [ibid., 18]. Perhaps one should not make an image of any one of these, but one may make an image of the sun and moon, stars and planets? Scripture says: "Lest you lift your eyes toward heaven, etc." [ibid., 19]. One should not make an image of any of these, but perhaps one may make an image of angels, cherubim, and other heavenly creatures (אופנים וחשמלים)? Scripture says: "Which are in the heavens" [Ex. 20:4]. If in the heavens [is intended], perhaps one may make an image of the sun, moon, stars, and planets? Scripture says: "Above" [ibid.]—neither the images of angels, nor of cherubs, nor of heavenly creatures. One should not make an image of any of these, but perhaps one may make an image of the abyss, darkness, and deep darkness [אפלה]? Scripture says: "And that which is under the earth" [ibid.] "or in the waters under the earth" [ibid.]—this comes to include even the reflected image [בבואה], according to R. ʿAqiva. Others say it comes to include the *shavriri* [i.e., the spirit causing blindness]. Scripture goes to such great lengths in pursuit of the evil inclination so as not to leave any room for allowing it.[53]

The difference between these almost contemporaneous traditions regarding figural art is indeed striking. The *Mekhilta*'s total and absolute ban on the making of any sort of image most probably includes any contact with them, on the suspicion of potential idolatry.[54] It is thus advocating a distinctly conservative approach: that which had been

---

53. Mekhilta of R. Ishmael, Yitro, 6 (pp. 224–25).

54. I have interpreted this passage, as have Goodenough, B. Cohen, and Urbach, to mean that the ban includes all figural representation (Goodenough, *Jewish Symbols*, IV, 3–24; B. Cohen, "Art in Jewish Law," 168; Urbach, "Rabbinical Laws of Idolatry," 235). Blidstein ("Tannaim and Plastic Art," 19–20)

the practice among Jews for centuries should continue. Behind this assertion lies the assumption that the Jews should remove themselves as much as possible from the pagan world of images. Such a distancing from any sort of figural image is also reflected in a midrash which forbids any kind of representation—even for decorative purposes (נואי):

> Our sages have taught: "You shall not make [together] with Me gods of silver, nor should you make for yourselves gods of gold" [Ex. 20:20]. If, with respect to worshipping them, it has already been said, "You shall not make any sculptured image nor any likeness" [ibid., 4], how, then, should I interpret the verse: "You shall not make [together] with Me?" You should not say: "Just as others make decorations by placing a replica of the sun and moon and serpent [or dragon, דרקון] on the gates of the city and its entrances, so, too, will I act similarly." Scripture says: "You shall not make [together] with Me"—do not make them, even for decorative purposes." [55]

The account of Rabban Gamaliel implies a willingness to deal with each situation on its own merit, while he himself is inclined toward a lenient position. Since the absence of figural representation had heretofore constituted one of the cardinal distinctions between Jewish and non-Jewish societies,[56] these different viewpoints reflect the various ways in which the sages (and perhaps Jewish society in general) were now grappling with this reality. Rabban Gamaliel—perhaps because of the new historical reality of the post-70 period and the increased contact with non-Jewish society or because of his own prominent position or personal proclivity—advocated a reassessment of the previous prohibition with the purpose of allowing for greater leeway.[57] He interpreted the prohibition as

---

and S. Stern ("Figurative Art and *Halakha*," 408-9), on the other hand, suggest that only cultic objects are intended. See also Goodenough, "Rabbis and Jewish Art," 269-79.

55. Midrash Hagadol, Exodus 20:29 (p. 442). Although embedded in a late midrashic compilation, this source dovetails with the above-quoted source from the Mekhilta of R. Ishmael. Moreover, a similar prohibition appears elsewhere in Midrash Hagadol, Exodus 34:14 (p. 711), and has been assumed by Epstein to have been part of the tannaitic midrash Mekhilta of R. Simeon bar Yoḥai (see p. 222 in his edition). See also a similar tradition in Midrash Hagadol, Deuteronomy 5:8 (p. 105): "'You shall not make any sculptured image or any likeness' [Deut. 5:8]. This is a warning to one who would make an idolatrous object for himself, whether he actually makes it with his own hands or others make it for him. And even if he does not worship it, it still is prohibited." Hoffmann includes this tradition in his Midrash Tannaim (p. 20). Rabbinic tradition also knows of several individuals (referred to as holy) who refused to look at coins, which usually bore the images of rulers; see Y Megillah 3, 2, 74a; B ʿAvodah Zarah 50a; B Pesaḥim 104a.

56. Tacitus, *History* 5, 5, 4 (M. Stern, *Greek and Latin Authors*, II, 26, and comments on p. 43). On the aniconic nature of Jewish art at the end of the Second Temple period, see above, Chap. 7.

57. R. Gamaliel's more lenient attitude is reflected in the various representations of the moon which he would use when examining witnesses with regard to their testimony about seeing the New Moon (M Rosh Hashanah 2:8). Those sages ascribing to the Mekhilta's total ban undoubtedly would have looked askance at this practice. See B Rosh Hashanah 24a–b. Moreover, the statement ascribed to R. Gamaliel's son Ḥanina is likewise revealing: "In my father's house, they would use seals (or stamps) bearing (all sorts of) images" (T ʿAvodah Zarah 5:2 [p. 468]).

referring to images bearing cultic significance only, just as the Decalogue itself, as well as Deut. 4:15-19, might well be understood.[58]

Contrasting views as to how Jews were to relate to pagan images are reflected in the attitudes of R. Yoḥanan and Resh Laqish, two leading Palestinian *amoraim* of the third century.[59] When in Bostra, the capital of Provincia Arabia, Resh Laqish was asked whether it was permissible for a Jew to draw water from the local nymphaeum even though it displayed many statues, especially that of Aphrodite, and even though the place was used on occasion for idolatrous worship. Resh Laqish immediately forbade such usage, thus forcing observant Jews to walk a considerable distance to draw water. However, when he told his teacher and colleague, R. Yoḥanan, what had happened, the latter responded by ordering him to immediately return to Bostra and rescind his decision. R. Yoḥanan then ruled that any statue or image in the public domain (such as a nymphaeum, which often stood at a main intersection of a city) was not to be considered idolatrous. In other words, in order for Jews to function within a third-century Roman city, allowance had to be made for the many statues which inevitably graced its streets and plazas, the overwhelming majority of which were for aesthetic, and not overtly religious, purposes.

The above examples clearly indicate that rabbinic circles encompassed a broad range of attitudes and practices with regard to Jewish interaction with the outside world and its culture, particularly vis-à-vis figural representation.[60] This situation was in many ways similar to that confronted by the church fathers. While Clement could embrace the large Hellenistic-Roman world and mediate its seemingly conflicting claims, Tertullian tended to emphasize dichotomy and inherent irreconcilability.[61]

---

58. Josephus makes two statements which reflect this distinction. In *Antiquities* 3, 91, he summarizes the second commandment as forbidding the making of an "image of any living creature for adoration." In *Against Apion* 2, 75, however, he notes that Moses "forbade the making of images, alike of any living creature."

59. Y Shevi'it 8, 11, 38b-c; B 'Avodah Zarah 58b-59a; and comments in Lieberman, *Hellenism in Jewish Palestine*, 132-33; Blidstein, "R. Yohanan, Idolatry and Public Privilege," 154-61.

60. No more striking an example of the diversity within Patriarchal (rabbinic?) circles regarding figural representation can be found than in comparing catacombs 14 and 20 at Bet She'arim; the former has many human and animal depictions, the latter none.

61. Greer, "Alien Citizens," 39-56. In general, the attitude of the church fathers toward figural art was ambivalent. It is generally assumed that from Tertullian and Clement down to Epiphanius, Jerome, and Augustine, church leaders looked askance at such representations, although they were often willing (or compelled?) to make concessions to popular practice (see Chadwick, *Early Church*, 277-78). However, the degree of their fundamental antagonism toward this type of art remains unclear. While this position is generally assumed by most scholars, Murray ("Art and the Early Church," 303-45) has argued that the evidence affirming this hostility is, in reality, nonexistent. Although her position appears to be somewhat extreme, it does indicate that these leaders were as divided on this question as were their Jewish counterparts. See also Finney, *Invisible God*, 39-68, 86-93; Kitzinger, "Cult of Images," 85ff.; Barnard, *Background of Iconoclastic Controversy*, 89ff.

Another amoraic source, this time referring almost certainly to a synagogue setting, deals with the issue of bowing down on a mosaic floor containing images during a fast-day ceremony:

> Rav instructed the house of R. Aḥa, and R. Ami instructed his own household: "When you go [to the synagogue] on a [public] fast, do not recline [lit., lie down] as you are accustomed to [so as not to appear to be bowing to the images decorating the synagogue]." R. Yonah reclined sideways; R. Aḥa reclined sideways. R. Samuel said: "I saw R. Abbahu recline as usual." R. Yosi said: "I asked R. Abbahu: 'Is it not written, "And a figured stone you shall not place in our land to bow down upon it [Lev. 26:1]."'" [The difficulty concerning R. Abbahu's behavior] should be solved [by applying this verse to a situation] where one has a fixed place [in the synagogue] for bowing.[62]

Setting aside this last explanation, which the editor of the Yerushalmi provided, it appears that R. Abbahu, contrary to other sages, was not in any way troubled by prostrating himself (as was customary on public fast days) on a decorated synagogue floor, an attitude undoubtedly engendered by his Hellenistic acculturation.[63] On the other hand, several of his colleagues were clearly uncomfortable with such an arrangement, and each found a different way to sidestep the predicament.

The problematics of figural art are reflected in the following accounts in the Mishnah and Yerushalmi 'Avodah Zarah:

> If one finds objects upon which the figure of the sun or of the moon is engraved, he should get rid of them. R. Simeon b. Gamaliel says: "If the objects are ornamental they are forbidden; if plain, they are allowed."[64]

> R. Ḥiyya had a pitcher [or cup, pot][65] in which Tyche [Fortuna] of Rome was depicted. He came and asked R. Yohanan, who told him: "Since water covers her, it is considered an insult [and therefore it can be used]." Similarly with respect to a cup [or ladle]:[66] Since you dip it in water, it is considered an insult [and it also can be used].

> In the days of R. Yohanan, they began to make [figural] representations on the walls and he

---

62. Y 'Avodah Zarah 4, 1, 43d; Blidstein, "Prostration and Mosaics," 33–37; Steinfeld, "Prostration in Prayer," 59–65. On the custom of full prostration on public fasts, see Y Shevi'it 1, 7, 33b; Y Sukkah 4, 1, 54b.

63. See L. Levine, "R. Abbahu," 64. Whether prostration was forbidden, at least in part, in order to distinguish current Jewish practice from that of the Temple or from contemporary Christianity is an open question. In this particular case, however, the problem is directly linked to representations on the floor paving. See Ginzberg, *Commentary*, III, 116–23; Blidstein, "Prostration and Mosaics," 33–37. Regarding the issue of bowing in third-century Babylonia, customary in Sura but strange to Rav, who had recently arrived from Palestine, see B Megillah 22a.

64. M 'Avodah Zarah 3:3.

65. See Lieberman, *Greek in Jewish Palestine*, 171 (pitcher); idem, *Hellenism in Jewish Palestine*, 134 (cup); Sokoloff, *Dictionary*, 478 (pot).

66. Sokoloff, *Dictionary*, 492 (drinking cup); Jastrow, *Dictionary*, 371 (ladle).

did not object; in the days of R. Abun, they began making such representations on mosaic floors and he did not object.[67]

This last statement, regarding R. Yoḥanan and R. Abun, is quite revealing. These two sages were obviously far from enthusiastic about the phenomenon of figural representation on either walls or floors, and they certainly would never have lent their support to such initiatives. Nevertheless, Jews were beginning to decorate their buildings, presumably both public and private, in such a fashion, and this process could not easily, if at all, be reversed. These two rabbis, therefore, took the middle ground, neither supportive nor actively opposing, a position which might be described as one of benign neutrality (לא מחי בידיה).[68] They decided simply to ignore the phenomenon; although they did not like what they saw, they could live with it. Thus, most rabbinic sources display an attitude toward figural art which ranges from passive tolerance to hostile opposition. None embraces this phenomenon as positive or desirable.[69]

---

67. Y ʿAvodah Zarah 3, 3, 42d. This text follows the Genizah fragment published in J. N. Epstein, "Yerushalmi Fragments," 20.

68. On this term, see Jastrow, *Dictionary*, 759-60; Sokoloff, *Dictionary*, 300. A similar use of this term is found in M Pesaḥim 4:8; T Pesaḥim 3:19 (p. 157) and parallels; M Menaḥot 10:8; B ʿEruvin 96a and parallels.

69. S. Stern ("Figurative Art and *Halakha*," 397-419) has suggested a rather novel thesis, namely, that the sages viewed decorative figural art with equanimity down to the end of late antiquity and only reversed course at the time of an iconoclastic upsurge. However, in arguing his point, certain phenomena are ignored and several questionable assumptions are made: (1) Explicit historical and archeological data regarding the almost universal avoidance of figural art for a three-hundred-year period prior to the Bar Kokhba revolt are ignored. The Jews in the post-70 era (rabbis included) were, in fact, heirs to a strictly aniconic religious tradition which had been regnant in Jewish society for centuries. (2) Rabbinic silence regarding the phenomenon of figural art in the second and third centuries does not necessarily mean that they accepted this art form, but only that this phenomenon had not yet penetrated Jewish society to the extent to which it became an issue for them. (3) The second- to fourth-century sources attesting to the problematics of figural art for many sages are dismissed, and such evidence is relegated to the latest editorial stratum of the two *talmudim*. Thus, the absence of protestations to figural art is taken to indicate rabbinic approval of the practice. (4) A series of assertions are made which challenge common wisdom in a wide range of areas: the sages were more open and accommodating to figural art than most Jews; rabbis shared the same tolerant attitude for centuries; in the latter part of the sixth century, the sages changed their opinion, adopting a strict aniconic posture, and this occurred precisely at the time when paganism had almost totally disappeared.

Contrast this with Lieberman's formulation of the phenomenon of cultural influences on the masses and the response of the rabbis: "The cultural influence of Hellenism on the people was even larger and deeper than could be inferred from the facts recorded in Rabbinic literature. The middle class of the Jewish people lived together with heathens and Christians in the big cities of Palestine; they traded together and they worked together. The people could not help admiring the beautiful and the useful; they could not fail to be attracted by the external brilliance and the superficial beauty of Gentile life. The learned and pious Rabbis did their utmost to prevent the people from becoming thoroughly Hellenized; they persisted in stressing to the people the superiority of the spiritual over the physical and the final vic-

In light of the above, those scholars who claim to have found a reflection of rabbinic values and ideas in synagogue art now bear the burden of proof. The artistic material recovered from archeological excavations is neutral, and its meaning (assuming that there is some symbolic message) is open to many possible interpretations—to wit, the plethora of explanations for the Dura murals and for the zodiac and Helios depictions in Palestinian synagogues.[70] One cannot assume that the synagogue was an extension of rabbinic Judaism simply because a similar motif appears in both places.

In certain cases there seems to be a considerable gap between the appearance of certain symbols in archeological remains and their prominence in rabbinic sources. The menorah is a classic example of this phenomenon. Rarely addressed in its contemporary appearance by the sages (in contrast to numerous comments on the Tabernacle menorah described in the Torah), the menorah became the most widespread Jewish symbol and was reproduced in later antiquity in many hundreds of instances throughout Palestine and the Diaspora. The gap between rabbinic interest in this symbol and its universal appearance in Jewish communities the world over is striking. Moreover, the rabbinic opposition to replicating the Tabernacle-Temple menorah, with its seven branches, is simply ignored in the overwhelming majority of cases, as is attested by archeological finds. We have already commented on the clash between the image of Helios in Ḥammat Tiberias and the Mishnah's prescription ('Avodah Zarah 3:1).

Even when the same motif appears, there is often no indication that a particular idea was "rabbinic" in essence. It may well be that the rabbis were merely elaborating on a homily or biblical exegesis known to Jewish society generally from other sources. For instance, the flames in the six branches of the menorah at the Ḥammat Tiberias synagogue all face inward, with the central flame pointed upward—a pattern noted in the Bavli (fig. 85).[71] Does this mean that synagogue artists were influenced by rabbinic dicta? Or might it be that both rabbis and artists were harking back to a common tradition. For instance, the fact that the rabbis discussed the Temple and sacrifices does not mean that they controlled that institution or that sacrificial procedures in pre-70 Jerusalem were rabbinically mandated. Similarly, the existence of rabbinic discussions regarding the sanctity of certain books of the Bible does not necessarily mean that the sages were the decisive and determinant authority in the process of canonization. Likewise with respect

---

tory of the soul over the body. But it is hardly possible that the great masses of the Jewish people in the big towns conducted themselves in conformity with the idealistic views of the Rabbis. It is very unlikely that they kept consciously refusing to imitate the manners and life-pattern of their neighbors, so attractive at first sight. The ignorant people of the country, on the other hand, whose economic status made it impossible for them to emulate the middle class in the pursuit of pleasures and elegance, adopted their neighbors' belief in magic, astrology and all kinds of superstitions in defiance of Written and Oral Laws" (*Greek in Jewish Palestine*, 91). See also Schubert, "Jewish Pictorial Traditions," 147-59.

70. See below, Chap. 17.

71. B Menaḥot 98b.

85. Menorah from the Ḥammat
Tiberias synagogue with flames
turned inward, toward the center.

to the synagogue: to label everything "rabbinic" and thus to assume the sages' influence
on synagogue decoration is unjustified.

RABBINIC INVOLVEMENT IN THE SYNAGOGUE

Until now we have noted rabbinic traditions which reflect a gap between the sages
and the synagogue. We shall now examine those traditions which reveal another dimension of this relationship, one of support, identification, and active involvement. It should
be noted at the outset that throughout late antiquity rabbinic attitudes toward the synagogue were undeniably positive, and the sages evinced a great measure of respect for
this institution: "One is not to conduct oneself disrespectfully in synagogues; one should
not enter them in the heat because of the heat, nor in the cold because of the cold, nor
in the rain because of the rain, and one does not eat there, drink there, sleep there, or
stroll there."[72]

The second-century Abba Benjamin once remarked: "One's prayer is heard only in
the synagogue";[73] according to another rabbinic source, the synagogue is to be included
among the ten institutions vital to any town.[74] Tannaitic legislation explicitly mentions
the synagogue as the proper place for the fulfillment of a mitzvah, such as the use of

---

72. T Megillah 2:18 (p. 353); see also Y Megillah 3, 4, 74a; B Megillah 28a–b; as well as M Megillah 3:3.

73. B Berakhot 6a.

74. B Sanhedrin 17b.

the *lulav* on Sukkot and the recitation of the *Hallel* on holidays.[75] In the third and fourth
centuries, some rabbis would study near the entrance of a synagogue; both R. Judah I
and R. Yoḥanan are noted as having studied in front of the large Babylonian synagogue
in Sepphoris.[76] R. Isaac (late third century) claimed that God Himself was to be found
in the synagogue: "From where do we learn that the Holy One Blessed be He is to be
found in the synagogue? As it is written: 'God stands in the divine assembly' [Ps. 82:1]."[77]
In the fourth century, R. Zeʿira eulogized a colleague in a synagogue, while R. Pinḥas
compared prayer in the synagogue to a pure meal offering at the Temple. In a public sermon Jacob of Nevoraya applied the verse "And God is in His sanctuary" (Hab. 2:20) to
R. Isaac b. Elʿazar, who was adjudicating in a Caesarean synagogue.[78]

By the third and fourth centuries, the synagogue had assumed a much more central
role in rabbinic circles than before. The rabbis' emphasis on the synagogue and regular attendance reflects an identification with this communal institution, and this, in turn,
probably indicates that the worship conducted therein met with their approval, and perhaps even followed their dictates. Nevertheless, this point should not be overly exaggerated. The fact that some sages repeatedly emphasized their approval would seem to
indicate that there were others who disagreed. As noted above, some sages tended to shy
away from the synagogue, preferring instead either the intimacy of their homes or the
familiarity of the academy.[79]

The nature and extent of rabbinic contact with the synagogue in late antiquity were
not uniform. Some rabbis appear to have been regularly involved in synagogue affairs,
others not. This variety of attitudes vis-à-vis the synagogue is, of course, understandable
given the diversity of rabbinic opinion with respect to a plethora of synagogue-related
subjects.[80] What is clearly evident from rabbinic sources, however, is a marked increase
in rabbinic involvement in synagogue affairs from the mid-third century on.

Earlier, in the second century, rabbinic ties to the synagogue are rarely mentioned.
One well-known tradition speaks of R. Meir teaching in a synagogue at Ḥammat Tiberias
on Friday evenings. A woman who came regularly to hear his sermons incurred the wrath
of her husband, since her attendance meant that Sabbath meals were not prepared on
time.[81] Even if this report is historical (although the story appears only in the Yerushalmi,
which was redacted several centuries after R. Meir lived), it stands practically alone in

---

75. M Sukkah 3:13; T Pesaḥim 10:8 (p. 197).

76. Genesis Rabbah 33:3 (p. 305); Y Berakhot 5, 1, 9a; see also PRK 18:5 (p. 297).

77. B Berakhot 6a.

78. B Megillah 28b; Y Berakhot 5, 1, 8d; Y Bikkurim 3, 3, 65d.

79. See above, notes 49–50.

80. See L. Levine, *Rabbinic Class*, 83–97.

81. Y Sotah 1, 4, 16d. Cf., however, Leviticus Rabbah 7:11 (pp. 191–92) and Deuteronomy Rabbah 5:15,
which either do not mention where this happened or refer to the *bet midrash* instead of the synagogue.

attributing an active synagogue role to a sage.[82] The only other source which might be invoked in this regard is found in the fifth- to sixth-century midrashic compilations. Leviticus Rabbah and Pesiqta de-Rav Kahana both refer to R. El'azar b. R. Simeon, teacher of Bible and Oral Law, reciter of different types of poetry (פייטס/פוייטיו, קרוב),[83] and expounder of Scriptures. If this report is accurate, and not simply a retrojection from the Byzantine period, R. El'azar may have functioned in the above capacities in the synagogue, although a *bet midrash* setting remains a possibility. The limited contact between the sages and the synagogue in the second century seems also to be reflected in the Mishnah itself, which mentions the institution on only twelve occasions, often with regard to issues which have no particular relevance to the sages.[84] Moreover, each of the tannaitic *midrashim* (Mekhilta, Sifra, and Sifre) mentions the synagogue only once.[85] Even when discussing prayer, these sources do so in general terms, with only rare references to a synagogue setting (see Chap. 16).

One conclusion from the evidence at hand—despite the fact that we are primarily invoking an *argumentum ex silentio* and dealing with largely halakhically oriented tannaitic sources—is that this dearth of information may be far from coincidental, but may, in fact, reflect the historical reality of the times. It would appear that there was a minimal involvement of the sages in the workings of the second-century Palestinian synagogue.

In contrast, from the mid-third century through the fourth century, the number of sources attesting to rabbinic activity within the context of the synagogue increases dramatically.[86] The third-century Tosefta specifically mentions the synagogue in twenty-five instances, although it discusses synagogue-related matters on many other occasions. The

---

82. R. Meir is also said to have preached in a Tiberian academy on the Sabbath (Y Ḥagigah 2, 1, 77b). According to R. Yoḥanan, his public discourses were usually divided into three parts: halakhah, *aggadah*, and parables.

83. Leviticus Rabbah 30:1 (p. 690); PRK 27:1 (pp. 403–4); and Song of Songs Rabbah 3:5, 7 omit the word דרש. See also PRK 28 (Buber, p. 179a n. 23); and Lieberman, "Hazzanut Yannai," 223. See J. N. Epstein (*Introduction to the Mishnaic Text*, 688), who interprets תנא to mean a public reciter (שליח צבור) of oral tradition.

84. See, for example, M Nedarim 5:5. For additional references, see Kasovsky, *Thesaurus Mishnae*, s.v. "bet knesset."

85. Mekhilta of R. Ishmael, Yitro, 11 (p. 243); Sifra, Vayiqra, 11, 8, 6 (ed. Weiss, p. 22b); Sifre-Deuteronomy 306 (p. 342).

86. This increased involvement of sages is evidenced not only by the greater number of attestations in this respect, but also by the wide variety of areas which their activity encompassed. The greater number of sources include those directly mentioning a rabbi functioning in a synagogue setting, as well as those noting rabbinic involvement in an activity that undoubtedly took place there (even though a synagogue is not explicitly mentioned). This last category would include, for example, rabbinic contacts with teachers, schoolchildren, prayer leaders, and *meturgemanim*. Moreover, as noted above, only for this period do we read of instances of sages utilizing synagogue premises for "rabbinic" activities and not only for communal ones (e.g., a Sabbath sermon).

Yerushalmi and later aggadic *midrashim* are infinitely richer in synagogue-related material than earlier tannaitic sources.[87] However, despite this increase in source material and the documentation of stepped-up rabbinic involvement, it should be noted that some aspects of this synagogue-related activity appear sporadic, and the focus was often on particular sages.

There seem to have been three major areas of rabbinic involvement in the ancient synagogue. The first is preaching, and several sages are singled out in this regard. Most notable is the third-century *amora* R. Yohanan, who appears to have preached regularly in the synagogue of Sepphoris: "R. Yohanan was sitting and expounding in the great synagogue of Sepphoris . . . a seafaring *min* [one who deviated from rabbinic norms] spoke up." On another occasion, a *min* found R. Yohanan sitting and expounding on the same matter."[88] Most telling of all is a Yerushalmi account attesting to R. Yohanan's popularity (albeit in an academy setting): "R. Hanina was leaning on R. Hiyya bar Ba in Sepphoris and saw all the people running. He said to him: 'Why are these [people] running?' He said: 'R. Yohanan is preaching in the academy of R. Benaya and the people are running to hear him.' He said: 'Blessed be the Merciful one Who has shown me the fruits [of my labor] while I am still alive.' "[89]

R. Yohanan's student R. Abbahu, likewise a noted speaker, was often found at the Maradata synagogue in Caesarea and elsewhere.[90] Another Caesarean, R. Isaac b. R. El'azar, functioned in a judiciary capacity in this same synagogue and, as noted above, was compared on one occasion to "God in His holy sanctuary" (Hab. 2:20).[91] R. Samuel b. R. Nahman preached in the Tarsian synagogue (alternatively, Synagogue of the Weavers [or Coppersmiths]) in Lod.[92]

On one occasion in the fourth century, R. Jeremiah expounded the Scriptures (דרש) in the Tiberian Synagogue of the Boule while, at the same time, R. Aha did so in the academy.[93] This account is reminiscent of the well-known story regarding R. Abbahu and R. Hiyya b. Abba. Upon arriving in a certain town, the latter spoke on halakhah while the former focused on *aggadah*. People flocked to hear R. Abbahu, leaving R. Hiyya with practically no audience and bruised feelings. R. Abbahu subsequently sought to console

---

87. See the various Kasovsky concordances, the *Bar-Ilan Responsa Project*, or *Davka*.

88. PRK 18:5 (pp. 297-98). On the presence of a *min* in the synagogue and the nature of his exchange with R. Yohanan, see the comments in Urbach, "Heavenly and Earthly Jerusalem," 170; Kimelman, *R. Yohanan of Tiberias*, 175ff. and esp. 187-88. On the term "seafaring" (*prs*), see Lieberman, *TK*, I, 54 n. 84.

89. Y Bava Metzia 2, 12, 8d. See also Y Horayot 3, 7, 48c; as well as Hirshman, "Preacher and His Public," 112; Hezser, *Form, Function, and Historical Significance*, 83-88.

90. See, for example, Y Nazir 7, 2, 56a; Pesiqta Rabbati, Appendix 2 (p. 196b).

91. Y Bikkurim 3, 3, 65d; Midrash on Samuel 7:6 (p. 68); Midrash Hagadol, Exodus 20:20 (p. 443).

92. Leviticus Rabbah 35:12 (pp. 830-31).

93. Y Ta'anit 1, 2, 64a.

his colleague by according him the respect due to a great teacher.[94] Although not specifically indicated, the settings of their talks may well have been the *bet midrash* and the synagogue.

A striking confirmation of the success of many sages in public forums comes from Jerome, who has the following to say about people's reaction: "They say one to another: 'Come let us listen to this or that rabbi who expounds the divine law with such marvelous eloquence. Then they applaud and make a noise and gesticulate with their hands.'"[95]

A second aspect of rabbinic activity within the synagogue involved adjudication of halakhic matters. On one level, rabbis were asked to make decisions in many areas of law, but whether this was done in some sort of official capacity is unclear. So, for example, R. Yohanan was questioned on halakhic issues in the synagogue of Maʿon near Tiberias and in a Caesarean synagogue.[96] Sages also served in courts that convened in synagogues, as was the case with R. Abbahu in the Maradata synagogue of Caesarea.[97]

A third area of rabbinic involvement concerned the education of the young. We have already noted that elementary school education took place primarily, if not exclusively, in the synagogue. Rabbinic involvement in this area was twofold. On the one hand, sages such as R. Yohanan, R. Ami, and R. Samuel b. R. Isaac issued directives to teachers;[98] these teachers, in turn, would often consult them on various matters, as was the case with R. Jeremiah, R. Isaac, and R. Mana.[99] In one instance, R. Abbahu attempted to discreetly convey a message to a teacher through his own personal example.[100] The clearest statement of rabbinic involvement in the education of the young, which presumably took place in synagogues, comes from the later third century: "R. Judah Nesiah II sent R. Hiyya, R. Asi, and R. Ami to tour the towns of Palestine in order to establish for (or: assign) them teachers of Scriptures and teachers of Oral Law. In one place they found neither teachers of Scriptures nor teachers of Oral Law, whereupon they said to them [the residents]: 'Bring us the guardians of the city.' They brought them the sentries of the city. The sages responded: 'These are not the guardians of the city, but rather its destroyers!' 'And who are its guardians?' they [the people] asked. 'The teachers of Scriptures and the teachers of Oral Law.'"[101]

Two important points ought to be highlighted with regard to this tradition. First of all,

---

94. B Sotah 40a.

95. Jerome, *In Ezek.* 33, 33, per S. Krauss, "Jews in the Works of the Church Fathers," 234.

96. *Maʿon:* B Bava Qama 99b; B Yevamot 64b; B Hullin 97a. *Caesarea:* B Yevamot 65b.

97. Y Sanhedrin 1, 1, 18a, and elsewhere.

98. Y Megillah 3, 4, 74a; Midrash on Psalms 91:3 (pp. 199a-b).

99. Y Megillah 3, 6, 74b.

100. Y Megillah 3, 4, 74a. According to York, the ספרא (*safra*) was (primarily?) in charge of Torah-reading and also served as *meturgeman*; see his "Targum in Synagogue and School," 74-86.

101. Y Hagigah 1, 7, 76c, and other references listed in chap. 10 n. 115. See also L. Levine, *Rabbinic Class*, 159-62.

sages were at times involved in the educational activities of Jewish communities, at least throughout Roman Palestine. Secondly, sages who functioned in this capacity, according to the above pericope, served under the auspices of the Patriarch as his representatives and emissaries.

The educational functions of a synagogue were often filled by sages or those close to them. This is indicated in two third-century accounts. In one instance, from the turn of the century, the inhabitants of Simonias solicited the help of R. Judah I in finding someone to serve their community as a "preacher, judge, ḥazzan, teacher of Bible and Oral Law, and one who would attend to all our needs," whereupon R. Judah recommended a student, Levi b. Sisi.[102] On another occasion, from the mid-third century, Resh Laqish recommended a Babylonian (sage?) when approached by the people of Bostra for someone to fill a similar position.[103]

Besides the above three areas, there were issues about which third-century sages were consulted. The residents of Migdal sought the advice of Resh Laqish regarding re-using the stones of a synagogue from one city in order to build a synagogue in another, and a generation later, the Jews of Bet Shean asked R. Ami about re-using stones of a synagogue within the same town.[104] In the mid-fourth century, the inhabitants of Sinbarri asked R. Yonah and R. Yosi about using a defective Torah scroll, which may have been damaged during the Gallus Revolt.[105]

In fact, several Babylonian sources point to situations in which rabbis actually built or owned synagogue property.[106] Rabina owned an unused synagogue and wanted to tear it down and plant a field, while Rami bar Abba wanted to build a new synagogue from the wood and bricks taken from a vacated one. Rav Ashi claimed he had the right to sell a particular synagogue since it was only because of him that it was so well known. From Palestine, we have the intriguing—and enigmatic—statement of R. Berekhiah (quoting the third-century R. Joshua b. Levi) uttered when he has taken aback by ordinary people washing their hands and feet in a synagogue courtyard in Bet Shean. His response was: "Synagogues and academies belong to the sages and their disciples!"[107]

---

102. Y Yevamot 12, 7, 13a.

103. Y Shevi'it 6, 1, 36d; Deuteronomy Rabbah, V'ethanan (pp. 60–61).

104. Y Megillah 3, 1, 73d.

105. Y Megillah 3, 1, 74a. On the debate surrounding the effects of the Gallus Revolt, see Avi-Yonah, *Jews of Palestine*, 176–84; Lieberman, "Palestine in the Third and Fourth Centuries," 335–41 (= *Texts and Studies*, 118–124); Geiger, "Gallus Revolt," 202–8; Schäfer, "Aufstand gegen Gallus," 184–201.

106. B Megillah 26a–b.

107. Y Megillah 3, 4, 74a.

RABBIS AND LITURGY

What was the extent of rabbinic influence within the synagogue's worship context?[108] The fact that the sages were involved in the above-noted areas does not necessarily indicate whether and to what extent they played a role in the religious life of the institution. In an official liturgical capacity, rabbis did not begin to function as religious leaders within the synagogue until the later Middle Ages.[109]

To offer an answer to the above question is far from a simple task, since the liturgical components within the synagogue of late antiquity were many: the Torah- and haftarah-readings, *targum*, prayer, sermon, and *piyyut*. The nature and extent of the information available for each of these activities differ, and in most cases we are dealing with limited direct evidence. Moreover, what we have has almost always been filtered through a rabbinic lens, with little chance of gaining a perspective from other quarters.[110]

It appears that rabbinic involvement might well have varied from one liturgical context to another. For example, the Torah- and haftarah-readings, as well as the sermon, had been integral parts of the synagogue liturgy since the Second Temple period, long before there was ever an issue of rabbinic influence;[111] as we have seen above, these elements were the main components of Jewish liturgy in the Diaspora as well. Therefore, how much the rabbis influenced this part of the service in late antiquity is difficult to gauge. True enough, we have rabbinic discussions about which Torah portions should be read on holidays and special occasions,[112] but it is unclear whether the rabbis were merely attempting to choose one of several current practices, or whether they were in the process of actually creating a new sequence of readings which had not existed beforehand.

The very fact that there were a number of traditions for the reading of the Torah in Roman-Byzantine Palestine[113] seems to argue against any type of overall control from a religious elite such as the sages, unless, of course, we were to assume—as is entirely possible—that this group itself was divided in its opinion. But about this, we have no information. We do have one interesting tradition which indicates a rabbinic desire to acquire a conspicuous role in the public Torah-reading ceremony. In this instance, a group referred to as Galileans turned to R. Ḥelbo, who then referred the question to R. Isaac

---

108. The ensuing section presages to some extent the discussion in Chap. 16. Here, however, the focus is on rabbinic involvement in synagogue liturgy.

109. Bonfil, *Rabbis and Jewish Communities*, 100–102.

110. For a full picture of rabbinic impact on the synagogue, the following discussion should be read in conjunction with that relating to synagogue liturgy (below, Chap. 16). An attempt has been made to eliminate unnecessary repetition; nevertheless, given the close interrelation of these two topics, some overlap is unavoidable.

111. See above, Chap. 5.

112. M Megillah 3:4–6; T Megillah 3:1–9 (pp. 353–55); Y Megillah 3, 5–8, 74a–c; B Megillah 29a–32a.

113. Elbogen, *Jewish Liturgy*, 132–33. See now Naeh, "Torah Reading Cycle," 167–87.

Nappha, regarding the proper order in which to call people to the Torah following the Cohen and Levi: "After them we call [to the Torah] sages who are *parnasim*; after them, sages worthy of being *parnasim*; after them, sages whose ancestors were *parnasim*; and after them, heads of the synagogue and anyone else."[114] Who precisely these Galileans were is difficult to say. Perhaps they hailed from the non-urban areas of the Galilee; maybe they were similar to those whom Josephus refers to as Galileans.[115] In any case, this source is quite self-serving, as it grants the sages a distinct preference in this realm. It is thus difficult to know how acceptable such a prioritization was in the community at large or what was in fact practiced.

Rabbinic influence in the area of *targum* is likewise unclear. The Yerushalmi relates a series of instances, noted above, in which R. Samuel b. R. Isaac corrected the practices of a *meturgeman:* One should not lean against a column when translating, nor should one and the same person read from the Torah and then translate, nor read the *targum* from a book.[116] Very little can be concluded from these episodes regarding rabbinic influence. Clearly, these practices were out of consonance with rabbinic (or at least R. Samuel's) wishes, but we have no evidence that his criticism was heeded. Moreover, we have already had occasion to note one striking instance in which a rabbinic practice was opposed by the local community. As will be recalled, when R. Simeon of Tarbanat insisted on translating the Torah-reading verse by verse against the wishes of the community, and even after he sought and received the backing of his teacher, R. Ḥanina, he found himself without a job.[117] Finally, the targumic tradition (Pseudo-Jonathan) of Lev. 26:2 varies considerably from most rabbinic attitudes toward figural art.

Rabbinic literature preserves numerous examples of rabbinic sermons, but how representative they are of what actually transpired in synagogues is difficult to say. Did rabbis always, sometimes, or only rarely sermonize publicly? The homilies, although not inconsequential in number, do not offer an adequate indication.[118]

While the impact of the rabbis on the prayer dimension of the ordinary synagogue is likewise difficult to assess, it is nevertheless clear that sages took a great interest in this component of the worship service throughout late antiquity. As will be argued below,[119] prayer as a religious obligation for every Jew was first conceived by the Yavnean sages,

---

114. B Gittin 59b–60a.

115. See Freyne, *Galilee,* 241–45; idem, *Galilee, Jesus and the Gospels,* 213–18; Oppenheimer, *'Am Ha-Aretz,* 201–18.

116. Y Megillah 4, 1, 74d. See York, "Targum in Synagogue and School," 75–78.

117. Y Megillah 4, 5, 75b.

118. Heinemann, *Public Sermons,* 7–28; and below, Chap. 16. It is interesting to point out in this regard that books of *aggadah,* to which some sages were opposed, circulated among the Jews and in the synagogues as well; see Y Shabbat 16, 1, 15c.

119. See below, Chap. 16.

and subsequent generations of sages never ceased to emphasize the obligatory nature of worship.

But of more importance to our present discussion are not rabbinic comments on this or that aspect of prayer, but their actual participation in what was happening in the synagogue service itself. A number of accounts in the Talmud do, indeed, reflect rabbinic involvement in the prayers and prayer settings of the synagogue. Two sources are of particular consequence regarding synagogue practices of the third century, as well as the place of rabbis and their prayer forms in the synagogue setting:

> R. Ḥiyya bar Abba said: R. Yoḥanan directs [מפקד] those in the synagogue of Kafra [a suburb of Tiberias] to try and enter [the synagogue] while it is still daytime [on the thirtieth of the month] so that [the required prayers] may be recited at their proper time.[120]

> R. Yoḥanan and Yonatan went to make peace [context unknown] in the towns in the south (of Palestine), and they came to a place where they found the ḥazzan chanting: "The great, strong, awesome, mighty, and courageous God." They silenced him and said to him: "You have no right to add to the [prayer] formulas that the sages have established."[121]

The first source indicates that R. Yoḥanan was able to be quite directive in telling the people of the Kafra synagogue what they should be doing on *Rosh Ḥodesh*. However, it might be claimed that, given his prominent position within Patriarchal and rabbinic circles, and given the fact that he himself was a resident of Tiberias, Yoḥanan's influence on the local community may not be all that surprising. The second account, therefore, is perhaps much more revealing for our purposes, for a number of reasons: (1) the alleged incident took place in the south, far from R. Yoḥanan's (though not R. Yonatan's) home community; (2) the rabbis here simply silenced the ḥazzan, who was being particularly effusive and expansive in reciting the *'Amidah*; (3) they claimed rabbinic prerogative in setting the proper prayer formulas to be used in synagogues; and (4) in this place, at least, the basic rabbinic formula for the *'Amidah* was known (or at least these two sages presumed so), although the local ḥazzan felt free to improvise on and supplement it. Thus, we can only conclude that the rabbinic ban on such additions was either unknown or disregarded. Here, then, is the earliest evidence we have of a specific synagogue setting in which rabbinic formulas were assumed to have been known and accepted, but where sages attempted to further impose their norms, clearly assuming that they had authority in such matters.[122]

---

120. Y Taʿanit 4, 5, 68b.

121. Y Berakhot 9, 1, 12d.

122. One might claim that the fact that these sages were sent on such a mission to these communities is an indication that the communities were predisposed to accept their authority. This is undoubtedly true, and such an assumption in itself would argue for rabbinic standing and influence in somewhat distant communities.

Such involvement is mentioned elsewhere as well. On one occasion, another third-century sage saw fit to remove a prayer leader who bowed for too long a time.[123] Several incidents are likewise known from the fourth century. R. Yosi instructed bar ʿUlla, the *ḥazzan* of a synagogue of Babylonians, as to the proper practice for reading from one or two Torah scrolls when two separate scriptural readings were required.[124] Similarly, R. Abun was consulted regarding the proper procedure when a prayer leader named Batit(ay) suddenly stopped in the middle of the *Qedushah* and a replacement had to be found for him.[125]

One area in which rabbinic involvement is quite well documented involves the public fast. With only sparse evidence from the second century and a plethora of material from the third and fourth, later antiquity witnessed active rabbinic involvement in this particular ceremony that was acknowledged by the community at large.[126] Sages are reported to have ordained fast days, offered prayers, and composed fast-day sermons calling for repentance and introspection. The tannaitic period has preserved such traditions regarding Shmuel Haqatan, R. Eliʿezer b. Hyrcanus, R. ʿAqiva, R. Ḥalafta, and R. Ḥanina b. Teradion.[127] Later on, we have a series of traditions similarly attesting to sages from almost every generation who took the lead in pronouncing fast-day ceremonies or offering prayers for the occasion. Babylonian sages include Rav, R. Judah, R. Naḥman, Samuel b. Naḥman, Rabba, Rava, and R. Pappa.[128] It is reported that on one occasion, the last-named sage called a fast upon arriving at the synagogue of Be Govar.[129] Palestinian sages from this period include the Patriarch on a number of occasions, specifically Rabbi Judah I, R. Ḥanina bar Ḥama, R. Joshua b. Levi, R. Ḥiyya, R. Aḥa, R. Yosi, and R. Berekhiah.[130] On one occasion, we are told that a local community approached R. Tanḥuma, requesting him to ordain a fast.[131]

In general, the communal setting is very much at the forefront of the Yerushalmi's public fast accounts; the sages often chose ordinary people to lead in the fast-day prayers, such as an ass driver or one who did menial work in a Caesarean theater; communities

---

123. Y Berakhot 1, 5, 3d. See Ginzberg, *Commentary*, I, 89.

124. *R. Yoḥanan:* Y Rosh Hashanah 4, 4, 59c; Y Taʿanit 4, 5, 68b. *R. Yosi:* Y Yoma 7, 1, 44b; Y Megillah 4, 5, 75b; Y Sotah 7, 6, 22a; Tractate Soferim 11:3 (p. 220).

125. Y Berakhot 5, 3, 9c.

126. Earlier, in the pre-70 period, others in Jewish society may have taken the lead in such ceremonies, such as one Ananias of Tiberias (Josephus, *Life* 290) or Jerusalem elders (M Taʿanit 3:6).

127. B Taʿanit 25b; Y Taʿanit 3, 4, 66c-d; T Taʿanit 1:13 (p. 328).

128. B Taʿanit 8b, 24a–25b.

129. Ibid., 26a. See Oppenheimer, *Babylonia Judaica*, 68–70.

130. Y Taʿanit 2, 1, 65a–b; 3, 4, 66c–d; Genesis Rabbah 31:19 (p. 287); B Taʿanit 23a–25b.

131. Genesis Rabbah 33:3 (p. 304); Leviticus Rabbah 34:14 (pp. 806–7). See also Lapin's interesting analysis of a number of the above traditions ("Rabbis and Public Prayers," 105–29).

could be rather critical of sages who did not produce the desired results.[132] Moreover, a number of studies have demonstrated how rabbinic tradition developed earlier accounts of rainmakers, particularly of Ḥoni the Circlemaker, recasting them as rabbinic prototypes.[133] This dimension is absent from the Bavli, maybe owing to its generally more focused attention on the rabbinic class.[134]

To conclude this discussion of the sages and the prayer setting, with all the ambiguities inherent in the talmudic material, it is nevertheless clear that by the sixth to eighth centuries, rabbinic influence upon the prayer liturgy appears to have been well established. Our primary source in this regard is Tractate Soferim, which outlines synagogue liturgical procedures. Not only was the ritual itself quite crystallized by this time, but the sages were very often cited as authorities in such matters. Many pericopae specifically note the directives regarding proper procedure given by both individual rabbis and the sages in general.[135]

Rabbinic influence on the *piyyut*, first introduced in the Byzantine period, is clearer. These liturgical compositions were created to correlate with the prayers as we know them from rabbinic literature, particularly the *'Amidah*. The *piyyut* for the weekday *'Amidah* assumes eighteen benedictions; for Shabbat and holidays, seven. Those *piyyutim* incorporating the *Shema'* also include accompanying benedictions, two before and one (in the morning) or two (in the evening) afterward, per rabbinic prescriptions. The *geulah* prayer before the *'Amidah*, as reflected in *piyyutim*, also contained the verses from Ex. 15 and was integral to the daily prayers prescribed in rabbinic literature.[136] Now it may be argued that perhaps it was only those *piyyutim* which conformed with rabbinic liturgy that survived into the Middle Ages, while all others were abandoned at one stage or another. At this moment, however, such an assumption appears to be unwarranted; there simply are no known *piyyutim* that reflect another type of liturgy.

Thus, despite the sometimes ambiguous evidence reviewed above, there seems to be enough material to indicate a significant amount of rabbinic influence on synagogue worship by the end of antiquity. This influence differed from one liturgical form to another and undoubtedly from one geographical location to another, but we can detect a growing

---

132. Y Ta'anit 1, 4, 64b; and Lieberman, *Greek in Jewish Palestine*, 30–33. The more rabbinically focused discussions of fast-day ceremonies are described in the Bavli, which attributes the success of various Babylonian sages in bringing rain to the different agendas of each generation of sages (B Ta'anit 24a–b). In commenting on the mishnaic statement that in the first stages of a new dry spell "individuals" (יחידים) should fast (M Ta'anit 1:4), the Yerushalmi (Y Ta'anit 1, 4, 64b) identifies these people as communal *parnasim*, while the Bavli (B Ta'anit 10a) claims the word refers to sages. My thanks to D. Levine ("Public Fasts") for calling my attention to the above distinctions.

133. See, for example, Green, "Palestinian Holy Men," 619–47.

134. See D. Levine, "Public Fasts."

135. See below, Chap. 16.

136. Fleischer, *Hebrew Liturgical Poetry*, 23–40.

rabbinic involvement in, and influence on, many phases of liturgical worship in Palestine and probably Babylonia. What may have been only partial and sporadic in the second and early third centuries evolved and expanded in late antiquity.

CONCLUSIONS

In trying to delineate the nature and degree of rabbinic involvement in the ancient synagogue generally, it has become clear that the rabbis were far from being in control of this institution. Nevertheless, we have noted that their involvement in synagogue affairs increased during the third and fourth centuries in a number of areas, and several factors appear to have been at play here. On the most immediate level, this trend may have been linked in some way to the figure of the most outstanding Palestinian *amora*, R. Yoḥanan (died ca. 280), who is prominently mentioned in almost every area of rabbinic involvement in synagogue life. A wider perspective, however, would view rabbinic penetration into the synagogue as part of the sages' increasing involvement in Jewish communal institutions generally from the turn of the third century on. As noted elsewhere, from the time of Rabbi Judah I the rabbinic class underwent a transformation from a relatively isolated elite centered in Judaean villages to one based in the major Galilean cities and much more active in the Jewish community at large.[137]

It is also possible, however, that increased rabbinic involvement was connected to the gradual transformation of the synagogue in the first centuries C.E. from a multipurpose communal institution into one with a more prominent religious profile, as has already been discussed.[138] This transformation is in all likelihood part of an overall pattern well known in late antiquity, i.e., the concern for the holy (be it a person, place, or object) and its impact on daily life.[139] The existence of Christian communities in third-century Palestine and their rapid expansion from the fourth century on, with bishops and other religious figures playing a prominent role in this process, would not have gone unnoticed by Jews; these developments may have affected both rabbinic attitudes regarding the synagogue and the community's increased receptivity to, and acceptance of, the sages as sources of religious authority.

Nevertheless, when all is said and done, the rabbis maintained a distinct religious and social identity that differentiated them from the surrounding society. Their way of life was essentially elitist; they adhered to unique patterns of behavior and had a deep commitment to learning and piety that could not be expected of the community at large. The chasm between elite and masses, the sophisticated and the superstitious, the learned

---

137. See L. Levine, *Rabbinic Class*, 23–42; S. J. D. Cohen, "Place of the Rabbi," 157–73; as well as below, Chap. 16.

138. See above, Chap. 7.

139. Brown, *Society and the Holy*, 163–65; idem, *World of Late Antiquity*, 49–57.

and the ignorant, could be minimized or exacerbated, but it was always there. For many, disparagement, even scorn, for those outside the elite was never far below the surface; Christian and pagan intellectual and religious elites shared the same prejudice—sometimes more, sometimes less.[140] The rabbis were most comfortable with their own kind, even though tensions were far from rare among them. The academy was their home; the synagogue was a place to frequent on occasion and in which to participate selectively.[141]

However, with their religious involvement on the rise, some sages naturally began to help shape and mold the liturgical components of the synagogue. It appears that many of their discussions about prayer in the second to fourth centuries eventually found expression in one form or another in the synagogues of Palestine and Babylonia in late antiquity. Only when the sages gained undisputed ascendancy within the Jewish community in religious matters, a process which culminated only in the early Middle Ages, was there a distinct and normative rabbinic stamp on the synagogue's religious dimension.

---

140. Idem, "Art and Society," 23.

141. Of interest is the remarkable correlation of a rabbinic midrash with the 'En Gedi inscription. In both, two sets of names (Abraham, Isaac, and Jacob; Hananiah, Mishael, and 'Azariah) are given. The rabbinic sources describe these men as "pillars of the world," a phrase which may explain their appearance in the inscription (Midrash on Psalms 1:15 [p. 8a]).

fourteen # WOMEN IN THE SYNAGOGUE

Much has been written of late about the role of women in ancient Jewish society. While the picture in this regard is not entirely negative, it is nevertheless clear that a woman's place was conceived to be primarily domestic and was often depicted in rather disparaging and uncomplimentary terms. Josephus, for one, has the following to say: "The woman, says the Law, is in all things inferior to the man. Let her accordingly be submissive, not for her humiliation, but that she may be directed; for the authority has been given by God to the man."[1] A woman was to appear in public as little as possible, but when she did she was to cover her hair and minimize her conversation.[2] In his Letter to the Corinthians, Paul demands the silence of women in churches, and in II Timothy, written early in the second century, Paul writes that women are "silly . . . laden with sins, led away with diverse lusts, ever learning, and never able to come to the knowledge of the truth."[3] Women were gener-

---

1. *Against Apion* 2, 201.
2. Philo, *Special Laws* 3, 169–74; M Ketubot 7:6.
3. This idea, in I Cor. 14:34, was often reiterated by various church fathers, like, for instance, Cyril of Jerusalem (*Procatechesis* 14, cited in Slusser, "Reading Silently," 499). Timothy (II Tim. 3:6–7), followed by Jerome several centuries later, traces in a derogatory fashion the female role in instances of heresy from the outset of Christianity up to his own day (Letter 33, 4). See also Kraemer, *Her Share of Blessings*, 157–73.

ally expected to remain at home, and the public sector was largely closed to them.[4] Such attitudes were not limited to a particular class, region, or era, but seem to have been the norm throughout antiquity.

Nevertheless, there were exceptions. Some literary works feature remarkably positive depictions of female biblical figures and of women who were public leaders and benefactors. The Hasmonean Queen Salome, Queen Helena of Adiabene, and Bruria, wife of R. Meir, are striking examples of Jewish women who reached the pinnacles of political power, social recognition, and intellectual-religious achievement within Jewish society in Roman Palestine.[5] However, such achievements by women were clearly not the rule, neither among Jews nor in the surrounding Greco-Roman milieu.[6] The reality of marginality in the public sector, punctuated on occasion by the prominence of particular individuals, also aptly describes of the role and status of women in the ancient synagogue.

Until recently, scholarly discussion of women in the ancient synagogue was limited. Only on rare occasions did scholars devote an article to one aspect or another of this issue (Löw, Friedmann, S. Safrai), while others wrote only several lines, paragraphs, or part of a chapter on the subject (e.g., S. Krauss, Schürer, Schechter, Elbogen, Rosenthal, and Zeitlin). In most instances, these authors discussed either women leaders or mixed seating.[7] More recently, a spate of articles have addressed the issue of women and the synagogue, often within the framework of their role and status in Jewish life generally.[8]

We shall divide our discussion on women in the synagogue into the following five topics: (1) synagogue attendance; (2) seating in the synagogue; (3) liturgical roles; (4) women as benefactors; and (5) women as synagogue officials. The first three categories relate to women in the context of the synagogue as a religious institution; the latter two, to the political and social standing of women in the synagogue generally.

ATTENDANCE

A number of sources from the first to the seventh centuries C.E. and from Palestine as well as the Diaspora indicate that women were regularly present in the synagogue dur-

---

4. Wegner, "Image and Status," 68–93; idem, *Chattel or Person?* 145–67; T. Ilan, *Jewish Women,* 122–34. See also Hauptman, "Women," 160–69; MacMullen, "Women in Public," 208–18.

5. Van der Horst, *Hellenism-Judaism-Christianity,* 73–95; Schürer, *History,* I, 229–32; III, 163–64.

6. T. Ilan, "Women's Studies," 168–73.

7. *Articles or chapters:* Löw, "Synagogale Rituus," 364–74; Friedmann, "Mitwirkung von Frauen," 511–23; S. Safrai, *In Times of Temple and Mishnah,* I, 159–68. *Shorter references:* S. Krauss, *Synagogale Altertümer,* 149, 356; Schürer, *History,* II, 435–36; 447–48; S. Schechter, "Women in Temple and Synagogue, 317–20; Elbogen, *Jewish Liturgy,* 357–58; Zeitlin, "Historical Study," 305–8.

8. H. Safrai, "Women and the Ancient Synagogue," 39–49; Kraemer, *Her Share of Blessings,* 117–23; idem, "Jewish Women in the Diaspora," 48–49; T. Ilan, "Window into the Public Realm," 56.

ing worship. In the mid-first century, Paul traveled throughout much of the Diaspora, and he invariably went to local synagogues, where he often spoke to women. He and his followers went "from there to Philippi, the first of the cities of the Macedonian province, and it is an independent city, and we dwelt in the city for a number of days. And on the Sabbath we went out of the city to the banks of the river, where there was a place of prayer [*proseuche*], as was their custom, and we sat there and we spoke to the women who were gathered there."[9] In Thessalonica and in nearby Berea, the presence of women in synagogues is noted.[10] Philo speaks of Therapeutae women and men who attended a "sacred place" (ἱερόν) on the Sabbath—in all probability a reference to their synagogue.[11] The fact that pagan women in Damascus were especially attracted to Judaism seems to be an almost certain indication that they attended the synagogue regularly;[12] otherwise, it would be hard to imagine how this attraction would have been effected, expressed, and maintained.

A series of rabbinic traditions allegedly relating to the second century and later indicate that women regularly attended the synagogue. One source tells of a woman in Tiberias who attended the synagogue every Friday night to hear R. Meir's sermons.[13] A tannaitic tradition speaks of a halakhic ruling allowing a non-Jewish woman to help prepare the meal while the Jewish woman of the household attended the synagogue.[14] Another mentions the right of women and minors to be included among the seven people called to read from the Torah on the Sabbath; the obvious assumption here, at the very least, is that these participants were regular attendees of the synagogue (see below).[15] A late midrash tells of an elderly woman who, when consulting with the second-century R. Yose b. Ḥalafta, mentioned that she attended the synagogue every morning.[16]

Some rabbinic traditions purportedly concerning the third and fourth centuries likewise speak of the presence of women in synagogues. R. Yoḥanan is said to have asked

---

9. Acts 16:12–13. See also Luke 13:10–14.

10. Acts 17:1–4, 10–12.

11. *Contemplative Life* 66–82. See, in this regard, Kraemer, "Monastic Jewish Women," 342–70.

12. Josephus, *War* 2, 560. On the growing religious piety of women in times of crisis in late antiquity, see Hunt, "St. Stephen in Minorca," 112.

13. Y Sotah 1, 4, 16d; Leviticus Rabbah 9:9 (pp. 191–93); Numbers Rabbah 9:20; Deuteronomy Rabbah 5:15; Midrash Hagadol, Numbers 5:31 (p. 73). Interestingly, in the course of relating this incident, mention is made of other women who likewise attended the synagogue regularly.

14. B 'Avodah Zarah 38a–b: "A [Jewish] woman may set a pot on a stove, and have a gentile woman come and stir it until she returns from the bathhouse or synagogue, and she [the Jewish woman] has no reason to be concerned." This ruling, however, may be mitigated by the fact that MS Munich reads "from the marketplace" instead of "from the synagogue," a reading confirmed by several other medieval authorities.

15. T Megillah 3:11 (p. 356).

16. Yalqut Shim'oni, Deuteronomy, 871; ibid., Proverbs, 943.

a woman who prayed daily in his academy why she did not attend the synagogue in her neighborhood instead.[17] Regarding the question as to who should recite "Amen" in synagogues where all the men were priests and took part in reciting the priestly blessing, it was decided that it should be recited by the women and children present.[18] One Yerushalmi tradition discusses the issue of whether a woman could enter a synagogue in the company of someone with whom she was suspected of having sexual relations.[19] Finally, Tractate Soferim speaks of women who regularly attended the synagogue on Tish'a b'Av:

> If he [the reader of Lamentations] knows how to translate it, this is preferred, and if not, he gives it to someone who knows how to translate it well, and he translates so that the rest of the people [i.e., the men] and women and children will understand, for women, like men, are obligated to hear the reading of the book, and certainly males [are obligated] to do so. And they [i.e., women] are obligated to read the *Shema'* and to recite the Prayer [i.e., the *'Amidah*] and the grace after meals, and [are obligated to put] a *mezuzah* [on their home]. And if they do not know Hebrew, we teach them in any language so that they can hear and learn. And that is the reason it was said, "He who recites the blessing must raise his voice for the benefit of his sons, his wife, and his daughters."[20]

The normal presence of women in Jewish congregations is dramatically confirmed by a Christian source from the Diaspora. Toward the end of the fourth century, John Chrysostom claimed, among other things, that synagogues were places of abomination, the proof of which lay in the fact that men and women gathered there together.[21] In his diatribe against the Jews, Chrysostom further remarked that some of the women in his congregation were judaizers, an indication that they regularly attended the synagogue.[22]

Given the fact that women were regularly present in the Jerusalem Temple until the year 70, and considering the not inconsequential evidence that they attended synagogues after that year, there can be no doubt that their presence in synagogues was a recognized and accepted phenomenon throughout late antiquity.[23]

---

17. B Sotah 22a.

18. Y Berakhot 5, 5, 9d. See also Ginzberg, *Commentary*, IV, 279; as well as B Sotah 38a.

19. Y Sotah 1, 2, 16c.

20. Tractate Soferim 18:5 (pp. 316–17).

21. *Adv. Iud.* 3, 1; 3, 2; 7, 4; and Wilken, *John Chrysostom and the Jews*, 121–22.

22. *Adv. Iud.* 2, 3, 4–6. See also 4, 7, 3. The Samaritans also seem to have included women in their worship frameworks. This is clear not only from the various Samaritan synagogues excavated to date which bear no evidence of any kind of a division or partition between men and women, but also from explicit statements relating to their sects that women attended services (Fossum, "Sects and Movements," 347).

23. On women in the Temple, see Grossman, "Women and the Jerusalem Temple," 15–37; H. Safrai, "Women and Processes of Change," 63–76.

SEATING

Having established that women attended the synagogue regularly, the question arises as to where they sat. A generation or two ago, this would not have been an issue, as it was generally assumed that the tradition reaching the modern era via the Middle Ages, i.e., that there was a separate section for women in all synagogues, reflected accepted Jewish practice from time immemorial. That this, too, had been the case for antiquity is presumably borne out in Josephus' *War*, which speaks of a strict division between the sexes in the Jerusalem Temple, noting that a special place for women to worship was walled off and had its own entrances.[24] Philo's description of the monastic Therapeutae in Alexandria could also be mobilized for this purpose; it appears that the men and women of this sect followed parallel but separate routines throughout the week, and when they congregated in their sanctuary on the Sabbath, they sat separately, with some sort of partition between them.[25]

This consensus was shaken in 1963, when S. Safrai argued that men and women did not sit apart in the ancient synagogue,[26] basing his claim on two factors. The first was the steady accumulation of archeological evidence from both Palestine and the Diaspora dating from the first seven centuries of the Common Era. From the farthest reaches of the Roman Empire and throughout Roman-Byzantine Palestine, no traces were found of a separate area that might be labeled a women's section; nor have any inscriptions noting such accommodations for women come to light. This absence is significant in light of the fact that many synagogue inscriptions do, in fact, name various parts of the synagogue. True enough, some excavation reports continue to identify one room or another as a place reserved for women, but these identifications are products of the excavators' preconceptions and rest on no solid evidence whatsoever.[27]

The majority of these synagogue buildings had only a single prayer room or hall where

---

24. *War* 5, 198–99.

25. *Contemplative Life* 32–33, 69; Kraemer, *Her Share of Blessings*, 113–16. See also Richardson and Heuchan, "Jewish Voluntary Associations," 239–46, with some suggestions regarding origins.

26. "Was There a Women's Section?" 329–38; reprinted in his collection of articles, *In Times of Temple and Mishnah*, I, 159–68; followed by Brooten, *Women Leaders*, 103–38; idem, "Were Women and Men Segregated?" 33–39.

27. E.g., Bet Alpha (*NEAEHL*, I, 191), Khirbet Shemaʿ (E. M. Meyers et al., *Excavations at Khirbet Shemaʿ*, 80–81), and, with reservations, Ḥammat Tiberias (Dothan, *Hammath Tiberias*, 24). This issue has been joined particularly with reference to Dura Europos and room 7 there. In his official publication, Kraeling (*Dura: Synagogue*, 31) identified this room as a place for women. Goodenough (*Jewish Symbols*, IX, 30–37) offered another interpretation, that it served as a storeroom for sacred objects, foremost among which was the Torah scroll. More recently, other reservations to Kraeling's suggestions have been voiced by Brooten (*Women Leaders*, 126–28), while White (*Building God's House*, 95) has generally followed Goodenough's suggestion. See also the comments of S. Schechter, "Women in Temple and Synagogue," 317–18; Archer, "Role of Women," 281–82.

the congregation gathered, and no trace of a balcony.[28] Even when a building had a balcony, indicated archeologically by a stairway or by columns of a different size from those of the first story, there is no reason to assume that it served as a women's gallery. Such areas might well have been used for meetings, court sessions, festive meals, study, or a place of residence for the ḥazzan; according to rabbinic sources, the synagogue was used for all these purposes.[29]

The second factor supporting Safrai's argument for reevaluating the question of separate seating is the silence of the rabbinic sources regarding such an arrangement. As we have had occasion to note, this vast corpus addresses the synagogue in a myriad of ways, in both halakhic and aggadic contexts. Nowhere in the four hundred or so pericopae dealing with the synagogue is mention made of a women's section, even though many other parts of a synagogue are noted in these sources.[30]

The sources often quoted from Josephus and Philo, according to whom Jews made a gender distinction in their public places of worship, e.g., the Temple and synagogue, are far from clear-cut. Josephus, in fact, contradicts himself on this very matter, in both *Against Apion* and *Antiquities*. In the former, he specifies four different courtyards: the first was open to all, including non-Jews, the second only to Jews, including women; the third to male Jews only, and the fourth to priests. In *Antiquities*, he notes an outer courtyard that both men and women entered, yet only men were permitted to proceed into the sacred Court of the Israelites.[31] Philo's description of the Therapeutae relates to a group so unique in its religious behavior as to preclude any assumption that they reflected normative Jewish practice at the time. In any case, the historical accuracy of Philo's highly idealized account is somewhat dubious.

Rabbinic sources, on the other hand, attest to the fact that men and women were together in what is referred to as the "Women's Court." In describing the preparations

---

28. According to J. Rosenthal (*Studies*, II, 652–56), there was no partition (מחיצה) in the ancient synagogue, but women nevertheless sat separately from men in the main hall. Such a separation between the sexes at festive meals is attested in a Genizah fragment from late antiquity (Lewin, "Eretz Israel 'Ma'asim,' " 97).

29. See above, Chap. 10.

30. See S. Safrai, *In Times of Temple and Mishnah*, I, 159–68. It is sometimes claimed that Y Sukkah 5, 5, 55b is an exception to this rule. This tradition states that Roman soldiers once killed the Jewish males in an Egyptian community while the women cried out, "What you have done to those below, do to those above [i.e., to us]," and has often been taken to reflect the local synagogue setting, where the men were to be found below and the women above, in the balcony. However, there is no indication that a synagogue setting was intended, and the story's setting may have been a wall or tower to which the Jews had fled. Moreover, in a parallel version found in Lamentations Rabbah 1:45, the women are reputed to have said just the opposite: "Do to those below [i.e., to us] what you have done to those above." Therefore, this source cannot be used as proof of separate seating in the synagogue.

31. *Against Apion* 2, 103–4; *Antiquities* 15, 418–19.

required for the Water-Drawing Festival (*Simḥat Bet Hasho'evah*) on Sukkot, tannaitic literature describes the construction of a special balcony around the "Women's Court" to separate the sexes, built because of the frivolity accompanying these particular cere-monies.[32] From this source it is crystal clear that on the other fifty-one weeks of the year, no such separation was in evidence. Furthermore, several rabbinic sources seem to indi-cate that women might have also entered the Israelites' Court, which Josephus claimed was restricted to men only.[33] When women brought sacrifices, as, for example, after child-birth, as part of the *sotah* ceremony (when a woman was accused of being adulterous), at the conclusion of a period of Nazirite vows, or when bringing firstfruits, they, too, would enter the sacred precincts.[34]

One striking example of a woman sitting among men is found in an inscription from the synagogue of Phocaea, in Asia Minor. In response to Tation's generous gift, the syna-gogue community accorded her several honors, including *prohedria*, sitting in the front row of the congregation.[35] There is no reason to assume that this refers to the front row of a women's section or to some sort of non-liturgical gathering of the community. Thus, it appears that, in this community at least, for women to sit among men was an accepted practice.

On the basis of the above, therefore, there can be little doubt that throughout late antiquity, Jews gathered in the synagogue for ritual purposes without making any dis-tinctions in seating arrangements for males and females.[36]

---

32. M Middot 2:5; T Sukkah 4:1 (p. 272); B Sukkah 51b–52a; Y Sukkah 5, 2, 55b. See Grossman, "Women and the Jerusalem Temple," 22–24; and, more generally, Rubenstein, *History of Sukkot*, 131–45.

33. *Antiquities* 15, 419; *War* 5, 198–99. On this and other contradictions between Josephus and rab-binic literature regarding the Temple, and within the sources themselves, see my "Josephus' Description of the Jerusalem Temple," 233–46.

34. See, for example, M Kritot 1:7; M Qinim 1:4 (and Maimonides' commentary to the mishnah, loc. cit.); Sifra–Tazria 4 (ed. Weiss, p. 59b); T 'Arakhin 2:1 (p. 544); M Bikkurim 1:5; and Maimonides, *Sacrifices—Laws of Ḥagigah* 3:2; as well as S. Safrai, *In Times of Temple and Mishnah*, I, 161–62; Grossman, "Women and the Jerusalem Temple," 20–27; H. Safrai, "Women and Processes of Change," 63–76.

35. Lifshitz, *Donateurs et fondateurs*, no. 13; Trebilco, *Jewish Communities*, 110–11; Rajak, "Jews as Bene-factors," 31. For further comments on this inscription, see below.

36. The earliest indication of a partition is found in sixth- or seventh-century Pirkei Mashiaḥ (Even-Shmuel, *Midreshei Geula*, 341), where it is written that women bringing their children to study (presum-ably in a synagogue) would stand behind a partition of reeds which served as a fence (מחיצת הקנים העשויים כגדר). On this source, see Fine, "At the Threshold." See also Zeitlin, *Studies*, I, 50–53. See the recent study of Mattila ("Where Women Sat," 276–83), who claims that there was separate seating in synagogues pri-marily on the basis of pagan and Christian parallels. Since there is no direct evidence for this, resorting to cross-cultural leveling is problematic, leaving little room for ethnic, cultural, and religious diversity. See below.

LITURGICAL ROLES

Women may have attended the synagogue, but did they actually play a role in the synagogue ritual — in prayers, sermons, or Torah-reading? Evidence here is almost totally absent, and, given the woman's generally inferior status in antiquity, one would be hard pressed to make a case for women's having any kind of active leadership in or responsibility for congregational worship in general.

Only one source, found in the Tosefta,[37] addresses this issue in some way; unfortunately, however, it is both ambiguous and ambivalent:

[A] Everyone is included [הכל עולין] in the counting of seven [people to be called up to read from the Torah on the Sabbath], even a woman, even a child.

[B] One does not bring [אין מביאין] a woman to read to the public [לרבים].

[C] If a synagogue has only one person who is able to read, he stands, reads, and sits; stands, reads, and sits; stands, reads, and sits — even seven times.

The apparent contradiction between (A) and (B) is clear. The pericope begins with what seems to be carte-blanche permission for a woman to read from the Torah ("Everyone is included . . . even . . . even . . ."). However, this allowance is immediately denied, by either a retraction (B) or severe limitation (C). By interpreting these three halakhot as a unit, and therefore as integrally related, Lieberman assumes that the first part of the Tosefta was never intended as a blanket endorsement of women's participation, but rather only as a reference to the Torah-reading following the first three ʿaliyot. Following the mainstream of medieval rabbinic interpretation, he posits that the first three ʿaliyot were regarded in rabbinic literature as Mosaic in origin (תקנת משה) and were thus reserved for adult males. It follows that the first part of the above source (A) allows a woman to be counted only among the remaining four ʿaliyot (עולין להשלים). The next statement (B) restricts a woman's participation in the sense that she is not to be called upon to read in public when there are males present. Moreover, if there is only one male who knows how to read, he is to continue reading the entire Torah portion (C).[38] In effect, then, according to Lieberman's understanding, a woman was really never permitted to read. What was granted (A) was immediately revoked (B, C).

If this was indeed the position taken by the author of this tradition, then the first formulation (A) is rather surprising. Why say a woman can do something if, indeed, the intention is to disqualify her from doing so? Moreover, the Tosefta speaks inclusively of all seven ʿaliyot, and any distinction between the first three and the last four appears to be completely alien to its literal meaning. In addition, this supposed attitude toward a woman certainly does not apply to a minor, who is mentioned in the same context; the Mishnah

---

37. T Megillah 3:11–12 (p. 356).
38. Lieberman, *TK*, V, 1176–77.

explicitly grants a minor permission to read from the Torah and haftarah.[39] In the case of a minor, it would be difficult to merely assume a contradiction between the Mishnah and the Tosefta, for surely one or both of the *talmudim* would have commented on it. Thus, to assume that the blanket statement of (A) granted permission to a minor but did not grant permission to a woman is difficult to reconcile. Moreover, if Lieberman is correct in his interpretation of the Tosefta, i.e., that it excludes women, then why did the Bavli comment on this tradition by saying, "But we do not act thusly because of the honor [or dignity] of the congregation"?[40] Clearly, the Bavli thought that permission was being granted to women for some sort of participation, which it then proceeded to rescind.

We thus must conclude that the Tosefta statement (A) was indeed intended to allow a woman to read, but that this permission was gradually diminished, first by restrictions made by the Tosefta itself, presumably later in the second century (B, C), and then by the general prohibition laid down by the Bavli.[41] It would seem, therefore, that what we have here are three independent traditions that were arranged contiguously in the Tosefta but were originally separate and independent pericopae.[42]

The question thus remains as to whether the Tosefta statement (A) allowing women to participate actually reflected a reality of second-century Palestine (and perhaps earlier), or was a purely theoretical statement. The second Tosefta pericope (B) also seems to indicate that at some point it was thought that a woman could be called to read; otherwise, a categorical statement denying this possibility would have been superfluous. However, at this point we reach a dead end. In the absence of any additional evidence, literary or otherwise, there is no way of making a final determination.[43]

BENEFACTORS

The evidence for philanthropic activity in antiquity is almost entirely epigraphical, as the purpose of most synagogue inscriptions was to record the names of donors and the contributions made toward the construction of a building or toward refurbishing it.[44]

---

39. M Megillah 4:6; and comments of Faur, "Aliyah for a Minor," 123–26.

40. B Megillah 23a interprets this phrase as a Bavli addition, and not as part of the original tannaitic tradition (*baraita*). See Lieberman, *TK*, V, 1177; Golinkin, "Aliyot," 14; and H. Safrai, "Women and the Ancient Synagogue," 42–44.

41. Elbogen, *Jewish Liturgy*, 139; Golinkin, "Aliyot for Women," 13–19. On the attitude of the Mishnah to women in the public sphere, see Wegner, *Chattel or Person?* 145–67; with respect to earlier traditions preserved in the Tosefta which appear to have been more inclusive of women, see Hauptman, "Women's Voluntary Performance," 161–68.

42. The very different formulations of each pericope might also point to the fact that these were originally independent traditions.

43. See the comments of S. and Ch. Safrai, "All Are Invited to Read," 399–401.

44. This and the following section rely heavily on the material gathered in Lifshitz, *Donateurs et fon-*

Women donors are recorded throughout the Empire.[45] This epigraphical evidence spans almost every century from the Hellenistic era down to the close of late antiquity, and while many inscriptions do not specify what was contributed, others do spell out exactly what was given and by whom. A woman, either by herself or together with her spouse, may have made a donation for an entire building, wall decorations, mosaics, a portico, a chancel screen or supporting posts, or a basin for ablutions.[46]

Thus, of the eighteen members of the Berenice synagogue who contributed toward the repair of the building, many of whom were communal officials, two were women— Isadora, daughter of Serapeion, and Zosima, daughter of Terpolius.[47] Elsewhere in North Africa, in Naro, Margarita, daughter of Riddeus, made a contribution together with Asterius, son of the archisynagogue Rusticus, who was no apparent relation.[48] In a dozen cases equally divided between Asia Minor and Syria, women made contributions together with their husbands; in only half of these cases is the wife's name mentioned.[49] On one occasion, a brother and sister made a joint donation, and on another a father made a contribution with his daughter.[50] Finally, an inscription from Apamea mentions a donation made on behalf of a wife (ὑπὲρ σωτηρίας), and one from Egypt mentions a contribution made on behalf of a woman by an unidentified donor.[51]

Three rather remarkable contributions from Asia Minor merit special attention.[52] The first, dating from the mid-first century C.E., has already been discussed, i.e., the contribution of a building to the Jewish community of Acmonia by the pagan Julia Severa.[53] The second records the construction of an entire synagogue building together with an adjacent courtyard for the Jewish community of Phocaea by one Tation, mentioned above, in the second or, more likely, third century C.E. It is worth citing this last inscription in full:

> Tation, the daughter of Straton, son of Emphedon, built out of her own [money] the synagogue building [τὸν ὄικον] and the colonnade of the courtyard, and gave them to the Jews. The community of Jews has honored Tation, daughter of Straton, son of Emphedon, with a gold crown and a front seat [in the synagogue].[54]

---

dateurs; Naveh, *On Stone and Mosaic;* Brooten, *Women Leaders;* and Roth-Gerson, *Greek Inscriptions.* See also M. S. Collins, "Money, Sex and Power," 7–22.

45. Brooten, *Women Leaders,* 157–65. More generally, see van Bremen, "Women and Wealth," 223–42.

46. See Lifshitz, *Donateurs et fondateurs,* nos. 16, 20, 28, 29, 41–43, 46, 48, 50, 53, 57, 96.

47. Lifshitz, *Donateurs et fondateurs,* no. 100.

48. Goodenough, *Jewish Symbols,* II, 90; Brooten, *Women Leaders,* 164, no. 38.

49. Brooten, *Women Leaders,* 161–63.

50. Lifshitz, *Donateurs et fondateurs,* nos. 28 and 67. An inscription from Sepphoris also names a father and daughter as donors (see below).

51. Ibid., nos. 39, 56, 91.

52. See in this regard Rogers, "Women at Ephesus," 215–23.

53. See above, Chap. 4.

54. See above, note 35. See also G. H. R. Horsley, *New Documents,* I, 111–12.

This inscription is remarkable not only for the generous gift of this apparently wealthy woman, but also for the very conspicuous acknowledgment she received. A gold crown was, of course, a common gift of recognition in the Roman world, and within the synagogue context such an acknowledgment is paralleled by a similar honor offered in Cyrene.[55] What is most unusual here is the prominent seat ($\pi\rho o\epsilon\delta\rho\acute{\iota}a$) accorded Tation in the synagogue, in a place usually reserved for the most honored patrons and elders.[56]

Finally, the third benefactor, one Capitolina, hailed from Tralles in Caria, Asia Minor:

> I, Capitolina, worthy and a fearer of God [$\theta\epsilon o\sigma\epsilon\beta\acute{\eta}s$], have made the entire platform and the inlay of the stairs in fulfillment of a vow to myself and my children and my grandchildren. Blessings.[57]

Of interest in this third-century inscription is not only the gift of a *bima* and the decoration for some stairs (whether the reference is to the stairs of the *bima* or somewhere else is unclear), but that, like Julia Severa, Capitolina hailed from a prominent local pagan family and was clearly of advanced years when she made this contribution. In contrast to Julia Severa, who remained pagan, and Tation, who was apparently Jewish,[58] Capitolina seems to have involved herself in local synagogue affairs and identified with the community to the extent that she was referred to as a "fearer of God."

It is noteworthy that pagan women are mentioned in two of these inscriptions. This not only seems to reflect the good relations between Jewish and pagan communities in Asia Minor in the first centuries C.E.,[59] but also provides concrete instances of one of the ways in which this pagan practice whereby women made donations penetrated the consciousness of local Jewish communities.

---

55. See above, Chap. 4.

56. A similar instance was noted with regard to a priestess of Athena, Chrysis of Delphi. In acknowledgment of her commendable execution of the office, *proxenia* was accorded "to her and to her descendants from the city, and the right to consult the oracle, priority of trial, safe conduct, freedom from taxes, and a front seat at all the contests held in the city" (Kraemer, *Maenads*, no. 78). See also MacMullen, *Roman Social Relations*, 76.

57. Lifshitz, *Donateurs et fondateurs*, no. 30; Trebilco, *Jewish Communities*, 157–58.

58. Opinions differ sharply as to whether Tation was Jewish. On the one hand, the phrases "gave them to the Jews" and "the community of Jews has honored" would seem to indicate that Tation was pagan. On the other hand, allotting her a front seat whenever the community assembled, which would basically be on Sabbaths and holidays, seems to indicate that she was Jewish. It would make little sense for a pagan to be accorded a front seat in a Jewish liturgical setting, unless, perhaps, she was a God-fearer. While certitude in the matter is impossible, the second alternative appears the most likely. See also White, *Social Origins*, 325 n. 69.

59. Kraabel, *Diaspora Jews and Judaism*, 237–55; Sheppard, "Jews, Christians and Heretics," 169–80; van der Horst, "Juden und Christen," 125–43; Trebilco, *Jewish Communities*, 173–85.

OFFICIALS

Women may have had some part in the leadership of the ancient synagogue. This topic has merited a great deal of scholarly attention recently, especially since the pioneering study by Brooten.[60] The available evidence appears to be quite clear: women are identified by the titles *archisynagogos/archisynagogissa* (Smyrna, Crete, Myndos), *archegissa* (Thessaly), *presbytera* (Crete, Thrace, Venosa [three times], Tripolitania, Rome, Malta), *mater* (Rome [three times], Venosa, Venetia), *pateressa* (Venosa), and priestess (Egypt, Rome, Jerusalem, Bet She'arim). To this we should add the single reference in rabbinic literature to a woman treasurer (*gizbarit*).[61] What, in fact, do these terms mean? Were these essentially honorific titles (granted to the woman either on her own merit or by virtue of her being the wife of an official), or were they actual official positions?[62]

Until the appearance of Brooten's monograph, it had been generally assumed that these titles were honorific. Such an interpretation seemed to correspond nicely with the thrust of rabbinic legislation and comments at the time, which, as noted, accorded women minimal opportunities in the public sphere. Nevertheless, it has been argued that rabbinic literature is the product of a religious elite in Palestine and Babylonia, and the degree to which this elite influenced or reflected society in general, even in its immediate environs, is open to debate. Whatever the case, rabbinic influence on Jewish communities with which the rabbis had little—if any—contact, is even less likely. Thus, the evidence from rabbinic sources is interesting, but may be somewhat irrelevant to our discussion. Having undermined a common assumption of previous scholarship, Brooten succeeded in reopening the question of women synagogue officials to review and reevaluation. However, she did not succeed in providing convincing proof that such official positions were indeed open to women and that these titles were therefore anything but honorific.[63]

Following the publication of Brooten's book, Kraemer analyzed a previously published inscription from Malta that appears to provide compelling evidence in favor of Brooten's

---

60. Brooten, *Women Leaders;* and idem, "Female Leadership." See also Kraemer, "New Inscription from Malta," 431–38; idem, *Her Share of Blessings,* 117–27; S. J. D. Cohen, "Women in the Synagogue," 23–29; van der Horst, *Ancient Jewish Epitaphs,* 105–9; and comments in Rajak, "Jewish Community," 22–24. On Megiste, the priestess in Jerusalem, see T. Ilan, "New Ossuary Inscriptions," 157. Cf., however, the reservations in Feldman, "Diaspora Synagogues," 56–58. On women functionaries in the early church, see, for example, *Didascalia Apostolorum* 3:8, 9, 12 (pp. 138–43, 146–50); La Porte, *Role of Women,* 109–32; Bradshaw, *Liturgical Presidency,* 20.

61. B Shabbat 62a.

62. See, for example, the dispute around the Marin (or Marion) inscription. Horbury and Noy (*Jewish Inscriptions,* no. 84) interpret the term ἱέρισα to mean "of priestly family"; Richardson and Heuchan ("Jewish Voluntary Associations," 234–39) interpret it to mean "priestess," one who functioned within the temple of Leontopolis.

63. Note the reservations in Rajak, "Jewish Community," 22–23.

theory.[64] The inscription records the titles of a man (gerousiarch) and his wife (*presbytera*). It would seem quite logical to assume that this latter title was not given to the woman owing to her husband's role, nor does it appear to have been simply an honorary designation. It is difficult to make a cogent case that a title which we would automatically assume reflects an actual communal office with regard to a man would be honorary simply because it was now attached to a woman. The same holds true for a recently discovered inscription from southern Italy cited by Brooten, which lists Myrina the elder (*presbytera*) along with her husband, Pedeneious, the scribe (*grammateus*).[65]

In sum, there is certainly a possibility that most, if not all, the titles that appear in over a score of Diaspora inscriptions are those of functioning women officials. The challenge, however, is finding a way to substantiate this claim and not merely assert it. I shall return to this issue below.

SOME IMPLICATIONS

So far we have surveyed the primary areas in which women were involved in the ancient synagogue and highlighted the most salient evidence for each. What, then, can be deduced from this data as regards the role of women and the dynamics of Jewish society at the time?

In the past, discussion has often been carried out on an "either-or" basis, often with sweeping generalizations in one direction or another: mixed seating in the ancient synagogue—yes or no? women officials—yes or no? True enough, there appear to be some areas where it seems possible to assume a great deal of uniformity among most, if not all, synagogues in the Roman world, including those in Palestine. For example, from everything we know to date—and, as mentioned, the data in this regard is far from inconsequential—it seems that the presence of women in the synagogue was a recognized and accepted occurrence.

On the other hand, the question of mixed seating is somewhat ambiguous, for although the data appear to be rather persuasive, they are nevertheless largely negative in essence. No evidence has been found on the architectural, epigraphical, or literary plane attesting to segregation by gender. Explicit evidence regarding mixed seating, such as Chrysostom's reference to the situation in Antiochan synagogues, is rare. His remarks make it clear that men and women sat together and not in self-contained groups next to one another; if the latter were the case, it would be difficult to understand why Chrysostom's reaction was negative. After all, even in churches, people sat in the same hall according to sex or other criteria (see below). One could, of course, ask whether Antiochan practice

---

64. Kraemer, "New Inscription from Malta," 431–38.
65. Brooten, "Female Leadership."

was, in fact, indicative of Diaspora patterns in general or those in Palestine itself. Chances are that it was not a local "Syrian" phenomenon, but there is no way of being absolutely sure of this at present. Perhaps the absence of explicit rabbinic sources with regard to special seating patterns, as well as the precedent of the Temple, where men and women were together in the Women's Court (except perhaps for a brief period just prior to the year 70 per Josephus' *War*—see above), might tilt the balance in favor of mixed seating, but there is no certainty of this. On the other hand, any assumption that women sat in a room next to the main hall (as has been suggested for the synagogues in Gamla and Dura), or that a balcony was reserved for their use (as posited for Galilean buildings), is wholly gratuitous in light of the evidence, or lack thereof, in literary and archeological sources.

However, it is when we turn to the other three areas noted above that we must exercise far more caution in making any sweeping generalizations, and in some of these cases chronological and geographical distinctions are called for. Regarding the liturgical involvement of women, we have noted the possibility, that the Tosefta may indicate that women were included in the Torah-reading ceremony, at least in some locales in first- or second-century Palestine.[66] In truth, this is not the only rabbinic source that alludes to a more active role of women at the time, whether theoretically or in practice. The tannaitic midrash Sifre–Numbers includes an opinion that women should be obligated to wear *tzitziot* (fringes on their garments), and the Bavli interprets several phrases in the Mishnah and the Tosefta (and also quotes the Palestinian *amora* R. Joshua b. Levi in this regard) as including women in the obligation to read the Megillah on Purim; this would thus put women in the rabbinic halakhic category of those who could read for others.[67] However, even should we wish to pursue this line of reasoning and assume that there might have been some sort of participation of women in the first centuries C.E., it is nevertheless clear that such a practice was at best very limited in scope. Not only are rabbinic sources silent regarding this phenomenon, but all references to liturgical titles in late antiquity, in both literary and epigraphical sources (e.g., *hazzan, sofer, super orans, psalmodos, sophodidaskalos*), are associated with the names of men; not one women's name is noted in this regard.[68]

In the last two areas mentioned above, women as benefactors and as synagogue officials, some very clear geographical distinctions can be made. Regarding benefactors, let us look more closely at the following geographical areas: the Roman Diaspora, Palestine, and, in the East, Dura Europos.

We know of over one hundred names of donors to synagogues in the Roman Diaspora.

66. See above, note 43.

67. *Tzitziot:* Sifre–Numbers 115 (p. 124); see also, B Menaḥot 43a. *Megillah:* B 'Arakhin 2b–3a. See Hauptman, "Women's Voluntary Performance," 161–68.

68. See above, Chap. 11.

Of these, approximately 29% were women.[69] More often than not, the women are named, but on several occasions they are referred to merely as spouses.[70] In Apamea, for example, fourteen of the nineteen inscriptions discovered in the fourth-century synagogue building mention women donors, either alone (nine) or together with their husbands (five).

However, we find a significantly different picture in Palestine. The Greek inscriptions have preserved almost seventy names associated with some sort of contribution; only three of these (about 4%) mention women. These three inscriptions were found in two large cities in the southern coastal region, one in Gaza and two in Ashkelon, all dating to the Byzantine period.[71] The data in the Aramaic and Hebrew inscriptions in Palestine are remarkably similar to those derived from the Greek inscriptions.[72] Close to 125 names are noted as synagogue benefactors; of these, all but five are males. One inscription mentions an anonymous female donor.[73] Thus, six inscriptions, or about 5%, mention women benefactors. As with the Palestinian Greek inscriptions, the data are concentrated in several locations. Three women's names appear in the synagogue at the hot springs resort of Ḥammat Gader, two in the synagogue at Naʿaran, and one in the synagogue at Sepphoris.[74]

To complete the spectrum of material in this regard, we must travel further east, to the Dura Europos synagogue, where there are numerous inscriptions in Greek, Aramaic, and Iranian. Four people are noted as having made contributions to the building. About a dozen other names appear as graffiti and apparently refer to visitors. All of the names are men's.[75]

In summary, then, there seem to have been three different patterns of women's participation as donors, each in a different region. Women are least represented as synagogue benefactors at Dura Europos, located in the far reaches of the Roman East and under Parthian control for centuries before the Roman conquest of the city in the mid-second

---

69. The percentages offered here and in what follows are only approximations. Some inscriptions are fragmentary and the readings uncertain, and in some cases it is not always clear whether the reference is to a man or to a woman. In a few instances, the same name appears more than once, and it is not clear whether it refers to the same person.

70. Lifshitz, *Donateurs et fondateurs*, nos. 40 and 50.

71. Roth-Gerson, *Greek Inscriptions*, nos. 2, 3, 23, and pp. 190–91.

72. For a comparison of Greek and Semitic inscriptions generally from Roman-Byzantine Palestine, see Roth-Gerson, *Greek Inscriptions*, 147–62.

73. Naveh, *On Stone and Mosaic*, no. 34. Some, however, read here the name Entolia; see Naveh's discussion on p. 61.

74. *Ḥammat Gader and Naʿaran*: ibid., nos. 32 and 34. *Sepphoris*: Weiss and Netzer, *Promise and Redemption*, 41. Not included here is an inscription from Ḥuseifa as interpreted by Hüttenmeister and Reeg (*Antiken Synagogen*, I, 183–84), an interpretation followed by Brooten (*Women Leaders*, 160, no. 18). The reading, however, was corrected in Naveh, *On Stone and Mosaic*, no. 39.

75. Kraeling, *Dura: Synagogue*, 261–317. See also Naveh, *On Stone and Mosaic*, nos. 88–104.

century C.E. Only a slightly different picture emerges from the Greek and Aramaic material from Palestine, where some 4–5% of the names refer to women donors. Finally, the most extensive involvement of women as synagogue benefactors was in the Roman Diaspora, where close to 30% of the names are women's.

The geographical factor is no less evident with respect to women as synagogue officials. In light of the fact that there is a concentration of evidence from Asia Minor and its immediate surroundings, how can one explain this phenomenon? Is it purely a local one, or might it point to a more widespread practice? We have noted above that the issue of women officials cannot be satisfactorily resolved solely on the basis of the primary evidence. However, one possible approach would be to see if the larger social context could provide data to support the assumption that women did, in fact, hold communal offices. If we can verify that women's participation in religious institutions was an accepted practice in a given area, it would lend credence to the claim that Jewish women in that particular region likewise participated.

We are best informed in this regard by comparative material from Asia Minor and the surrounding area. Since the submission of Kraabel's doctoral thesis in 1968, and down to Trebilco's 1991 monograph, a number of studies have included material indicating the extent to which pagan women generally played active roles in this region.[76] Trebilco notes ten women in six cities who held the title *demiourgos*, forty-eight in twenty-three cities who were called gymnasiarchs, twenty-eight in eight cities who received the title *prytanis*, thirty-seven in seventeen cities who held the title *stephanephoros*, eighteen women in fourteen cities who were called *agonothete*, and five who were referred to as *hipparchos*. A few women were members of a *gerousia*, and others held the positions of panegyriarch, *strategos*, and *dekaprotos*.[77] Trebilco also calls attention to an inscription from Phocaea that acknowledges a very accomplished woman thusly: "The Teuthadeos tribe, [to or for] Flavia Ammion, daughter of Moschos, who is called Aristios, chief-priestess of the Temple of Asia in Ephesus, *prytanis*, twice *stephanephoros*, priestess of the Massalia, *agonothete*, wife of Flavius Hermocrates, on account of excellence and propriety regarding conduct and purity."[78]

Another inscription, from Aphrodisias, speaks of another accomplished woman:

> The council and the people and the senate have granted first honors to Tata, daughter of Diodoros, son of Diodoros [by adoption], son of Leon by birth; holy priestess of Hera for life; mother of the city; who became and remained wife of Attalos, son of Pytheas, *stephanephoros*; [who is] also herself of foremost and illustrious stock; who served as priestess of the

76. For example, Brooten, "Iael," 156–62; Kraemer, *Her Share of Blessings*, 118–23; and, regarding the Montanist sect, ibid., 177–78.

77. Trebilco, *Jewish Communities*, 113–26. See also MacMullen, *Paganism*, 146 n. 52; van Bremen, "Women and Wealth," 223–42.

78. Trebilco, *Jewish Communities*, 119.

emperors for the second time; who twice supplied oil most abundantly for small vessels running from the bathing tubs even for the greater part of the night; who [herself] functioned as *stephanephoros*; who sacrificed during the course of entire years for the health of the emperors; who sponsored feasts for the people which were both frequent and involved reclining dinners for the whole populace; who primarily on her own maintained the top performances in Asia in both musical and theatrical competitions and who offered to [her] native city for the neighboring towns to assemble together for the display of the performances and to celebrate [the festival] together; who spared expenses on no one's wife; loving glory; adorned with virtue [and] prudence.[79]

Given these accolades, as well as the number of women who held titles and offices in this region, it is not difficult to assume that nearby Jewish communities might well have been affected. It appears that the concentration of titles for Jewish women in this part of the world was far from coincidental.

Assuming that the above-noted titles for Jewish women do, in fact, point to many cases of women's leadership in the Jewish community generally, and in the synagogue in particular, it is also important to note that this situation was not the norm for all communities of late antiquity. Focusing for a moment on the term "archisynagogue," we note that women are mentioned in that role on only three occasions. All three cases come from the area of the Aegean and Asia Minor, i.e., Smyrna, Crete, and Myndos. Altogether, the title "archisynagogue" appears in ancient inscriptions in connection with some forty people, including eight from Palestine. Women bearing this title in the Diaspora synagogue are about 10% of those mentioned.[80] However, statistics from the catacombs of Rome would caution us against too facile a conclusion with regard to women officeholders. In inscriptions there, only five women bear official titles, as compared to 117 men, i.e., only slightly over 4%.[81] Here, as elsewhere, the local context—internal and external—appears to have been decisive.

The above discussion, especially with regard to the last two areas, makes a patently clear case for the extent to which various Jewish communities were influenced by the surrounding culture. Not only were women in the Roman Diaspora particularly active as benefactors, but, like their husbands, they preserved this information via inscriptions,

---

79. Brooten, "Iael," 157. See also Kraemer, *Maenads*, no. 81; Gordon, "Veil of Power," 228-30; Torjesen, *When Women Were Priests*, 89-109.

80. Whether the name "Iael" (or Jael), president or patron of a Jewish *dekany* in Aphrodisias, is that of a man or woman has been argued over the past decade, and certitude in the matter remains elusive, although a growing consensus tends toward the latter alternative. The identification as a woman's name has been maintained in the revised edition of Schürer, *History*, III, 25-26; Brooten, "Iael," 156-62; Rajak, "Jews and Christians," 255; Williams, "Jews and Godfearers," 300. Reynolds and Tannenbaum (*Jews and God-Fearers*, 41, 101) prefer to consider it a man's name; see also Mussies, "Jewish Personal Names," 261-69.

81. Rutgers, *Jews in Rome*, 135. Cf. also Kraemer, "Non-Literary Evidence," 90-91.

which in itself was a decidedly Roman practice—what MacMullen refers to as "the epigraphic habit."[82]

The external influence is no less evident with regard to women officials; as we have seen, this phenomenon was most pronounced in the Jewish context precisely in those areas where it applied to pagan and Christian women as well. Moreover, it must be remembered that the presence of women officials was indeed a departure from earlier Jewish practice. Except for certain charismatic biblical figures, such as Miriam and Deborah, in neither the First or the Second Temple periods can one find any trace of women holding defined communal positions. Thus, when such a phenomenon occurs, it clearly is due to synchronic forces impacting on the local Jewish communities.

Jewish communities may have been responsive to their immediate social and religious contexts, but there were some issues on which they stood apart from their surrounding culture. One such area concerns the seating arrangements which seem to have been prevalent within the synagogues of both Palestine and the Diaspora. In order to fully appreciate the uniqueness of this practice, it is important to view the phenomenon in the context of the wider culture. Roman society regularly practiced segregation in public arenas, along class, ethnic, or gender lines.[83] This separation was adopted by the early church, and while there assuredly were differences from one tradition and locale to another, the main thrust was one of a division between clergy and laypeople, men and women, and full-fledged Christians and catechumens.[84] The *Didascalia Apostolorum*, a Syriac document originally written in Greek sometime in the third century (and translated into Syriac in the fourth), has the following to say in this regard: "And for the presbyters let there be assigned a place in the eastern part of the house; and let the bishop's throne be set in their midst, and let the presbyters sit with him. And again, let the lay men sit in another part of the house toward the east. For so it should be, that in the eastern part of the house, the presbyters sit with the bishops, and next the lay men, and then the women."[85]

---

82. MacMullen, "Epigraphic Habit," 233–46.

83. See above, Chap. 4, note 88.

84. See, for example, Kraemer, *Her Share of Blessings*, 107.

85. *Didascalia Apostolorum* 12 (p. 119). See also the more detailed exposition of seating arrangements in the *Apostolic Constitutions* 2, 57: "But if any one be found sitting out of his place, let him be rebuked by the deacon, as a manager of the foreship, and be removed into the place proper for him; for the Church is not only like a ship, but also like a sheepfold. For as shepherds place all the brute creatures distinctly, I mean goats and sheep, according to their kind and age, and still every one runs together, like to his like; so is it to be in the Church. Let the young persons sit by themselves, if there be a place for them; if not, let them stand upright. But let those that are already stricken in years sit in order. For the children which stand, let their fathers and mothers take them to them [i.e., the children to their parents—L.L.] Let the younger women also sit by themselves, if there be a place for them; but if there be not, let them stand behind the women. Let those women which are married, and have children, be placed by themselves; but let the virgins and the widows, and the elder women stand or sit before all the rest; and let the deacon be

Why did the synagogue continue to maintain this practice, which was exceptional in the world of late antiquity? Perhaps it was owing to the absence of an earlier tradition to the contrary, the apparent equality of women in many ritual ceremonies, as set forth in Deuteronomy,[86] or to the fact that no kind of hierarchical system existed within Jewish society in the post-70 era (unlike the situation in the Roman, Byzantine, and Christian worlds). Alternatively, it may have been because, when all is said and done, the synagogue was essentially a communal institution, and thus any kind of division between its members was foreign—and perhaps such an attitude carried over into the liturgical setting. Whatever the reason, the reality seems to have been the continuation of open seating within the synagogue framework, a situation which brought on the ridicule and disparagement of detractors such as Chrysostom.

Sometime in the early Middle Ages, for reasons unknown to us, this practice changed, and separate seating was finally introduced into the synagogue. By the eleventh and twelfth centuries, as is evident from the Cairo Genizah material and Maimonides, the custom of separate seating, in Egypt at least, was already well in place. The above sources explicitly note a separation or partition (*meḥitzah*).[87] Thus, at some point between the seventh century (our last-dated sources, archeological and literarary, for late antiquity) and eleventh century (the sources from Egypt) this division was adopted by Jewish communities, owing to either Islamic or Christian influence, to newly developing religious stringencies regarding the impurity of women, or perhaps to both these external and internal considerations.[88]

A second area in which Jewish communities appear to have resisted contemporary

---

the disposer of the places, that every one of those that come in may go to his proper place, and may not sit at the entrance."

86. Weinfeld, *Deuteronomy*, 291. Cf. also Tigay, *Deuteronomy*, 499–502; and Mathews, *Clash of Gods*, 170–71.

87. Goitein, *Mediterranean Society*, II, 144; see also idem, "Women's Gallery," 314.

88. See Z. Safrai ("Dukhan, Aron and Teva," 78–79), who suggests a sixth- to eighth-century date and assumes that this separation was ultimately due to religious developments among the Jews themselves: "In Christian churches built during this time [the sixth to the eighth centuries] balconies were built to serve as women's galleries. Nevertheless, it does not necessarily follow that the churches influenced the building of the synagogue or, for that matter, that practices of modesty prevalent in Muslim society influenced Jewish society. On the contrary, it would appear that internal Jewish instincts tended towards increased strictness regarding ritual purity and these instincts also brought about the adoption of stricter laws of modesty which found expression in the construction of a separate balcony for women in the synagogue."

On the increased strictness regarding the impurity of the menstruant and its effect on women in the synagogue, see S. J. D. Cohen, "Purity and Piety," 107–9; idem, "Menstruants and the Sacred," 284–87, 291; Ta-Shma, "Synagogal Sanctity," 356–64. Swartz ("'Like the Ministering Angels,'" 165–66) suggests that this increasing concern with impurity stemmed from pietist groups and not necessarily from rabbinic circles, but Karaite influence may also have been a factor here.

influences was in the denial of any liturgical function to women. In the Greco-Roman world women played both important and secondary roles in cultic settings. They served as priests and took other kinds of roles in the temple worship of a wide variety of deities, as well as in temples devoted to emperor worship and the provincial cults (for example, that of the Asiarchs). Perhaps because of the plethora of gods and goddesses in the Greco-Roman pantheon, paganism accorded a prominent role to women in many facets of the temple cult: they were present in the temple, guarded and maintained the premises, offered sacrifices on a regular basis, and sometimes organized the major festivals.[89]

Similarly, women played important roles within early Christianity, at first within the early church and later within a number of prominent sects. Whether because of the challenge of early Christian ideology to many of the social and religious assumptions of the age, the emphasis on asceticism, communal living, the downplaying of marriage and family, heightened spirituality, or a strong apocalyptic orientation, some Christian settings allowed women to free themselves from the shackles of society and tradition and make their contribution.[90] As long as these sects flourished (until the fourth century), women were a well-recognized and influential factor in such frameworks. In certain locales—for example, in Asia Minor—these sects even posed a serious threat to the more normative Christianity then crystallizing.

In this respect as well, Jewish society was quite different from its social environs. To the best of our knowledge, women did not play any kind of liturgical role in the synagogue. The reasons for this have yet to be fully explored. Perhaps it was the Semitic, Near Eastern roots of Israelite tradition which might explain why Jews looked askance upon women's cultic participation, often associating it with temple prostitution. Or perhaps it was because of the monotheistic nature of Judaism: at the center was one God, of masculine gender. Interestingly, as Christianity developed in late antiquity, and as the sects disappeared (or were eliminated), so, too, did the role of women as communal liturgical figures.[91] Moreover, with the rise of Islam, investiture of religious leadership exclusively in the hands of males became the accepted pattern. Whatever may have been the reason, the fact remains that in monotheistic settings an official liturgical role for women was always peripheral, if not almost negligible.

---

89. See Kraemer, *Her Share of Blessings*, 80–92; idem, *Maenads*, nos. 78–83. For a late reference to women as working in academies as custodians (משמשין), see Targum Jonathan of Judg. 5:24.

90. Meeks, "Image of the Androgyne," 165–208; Witherington III, *Women in Earliest Churches*, 183–210; Fiorenza, *In Memory of Her*, parts II–III; Kraemer, *Her Share of Blessings*, 157–90. See, however, the comments of Cameron, " 'Neither Male nor Female,' " 60–68.

91. Cf. Cameron, *Mediterranean World*, 148–51; Torjesen, *When Women Were Priests*, 155–76.

fifteen   PRIESTS

The destruction of the Jerusalem Temple in 70 brought an end to a millennium of priestly political and religious dominance. For an elite which had been accorded the highest status in Jewish society and which had shouldered the bulk of the ritual, cultural, judicial, and political responsibilities for many centuries, the sudden absence of its base of power was undoubtedly traumatic.[1]

It has generally been assumed that in the post-70 era, the priesthood became a mere vestige of its former self, a kind of honorary caste among the Jews, enjoying no real standing, bearing no authority of significance, and opposed by the sages (as was the case before 70).[2] Rabbinic protestations regarding certain second-century fast-day ceremonies in the Galilee may have been due, inter alia, to the prominent role played by priests in this ritual, as in pre-70 days.[3] Similarly, the silence of rabbinic literature regarding Julian's plan to rebuild the Temple in 363 has been interpreted as an indication

---

1. On the role of priests in the days of the Temple, see de Vaux, *Ancient Israel*, 245–474; Schürer, *History*, II, 237–308; Jeremias, *Jerusalem in the Time of Jesus*, 147–221; M. Stern, "Aspects of Jewish Society: Priesthood," 561–612; Burtchaell, *From Synagogue to Church*, 253–56.

2. See, for example, B Yoma 71b; T Sotah 13:8 (pp. 233–34); T Menahot 13:21 (p. 533); B Rosh Hashanah 29b; Büchler, *Political and Social Leaders*, 69–70; Alon, *Jews in Their Land*, I, 99–103; Aderet, *From Destruction to Restoration*, 280–89; Miller, *Studies*, 88–103.

3. T Ta'anit 1:13 (p. 327–28); Lieberman, *TK*, V, 1075; Miller, *Studies*, 103–15.

of the sages' reservations about the return of the priesthood to a position of power and authority among the Jews.[4]

Of late, however, this picture of an eclipsed priestly class has undergone some serious reevaluation. Goodblatt has argued that the Bar Kokhba revolt was in fact motivated by priestly ideology and involved extensive priestly participation.[5] Kimelman has claimed that there was a strong priestly presence in Sepphoris and that this class was well entrenched in the leadership of the city, opposing much of the rabbinic activity there.[6] Archeological material has brought to light a half-dozen inscriptions on display in synagogues that listed the priestly courses (see below). Trifon has gathered a number of sources from Byzantine Palestine which seem to point to a central role played by priests in Jewish affairs of the Galilee in general and in Tiberias in particular.[7] It has also been noted that priests were amply represented among the sages throughout much of the talmudic period. The Yavnean period (70–132), as well as the third and fourth centuries, witnessed a large number of prominent sages who were priests.[8] Moreover, it has been suggested that the anti-priestly rabbinic polemics should be taken not only as an indication of rabbinic antipathy, but also as evidence of continued priestly influence within Jewish society.[9] Thus, it is clear today that the issue of the place of priests and the priesthood in Jewish life of late antiquity merits reconsideration; furthermore, this reality was probably complex, as it deals with a formerly powerful group in transition.[10]

One of the most striking expressions of priestly group consciousness in the post-70 era is the fact that many, if not most, priests continued to remain a separate and distinct entity throughout late antiquity. Organized into twenty-four priestly courses scattered throughout Judaea for centuries prior to the loss of Jerusalem, they appear to have retained this framework even afterward.[11] Sometime in the century or so following 70, the priestly courses took up residence in the central and eastern Galilee. Opinion differs as to when this actually occurred, and a number of suggestions have been put forth: immedi-

---

4. Avi-Yonah, *Jews of Palestine*, 196–98. Goodman's comments ("Minim," 501–10, esp. 507), although addressing a different issue, may be equally valid here—namely, what did not interest the sages, they simply ignored.

5. Goodblatt, "Title *Nasi*," 113–32; idem, *Monarchic Principle*, 228–29. See also Trifon, "Aspects of Internal Politics," 24–26; S. Schwartz, *Josephus and Judaean Politics*, 72–82.

6. Kimelman, "Conflict between Priestly Oligarchy and Sages," 135–47. See, however, the reservation of Miller ("Cantankerous Sepphoreans") regarding this thesis.

7. Trifon, "Jewish Priests," 130–276.

8. Ibid., 141, 175; 219; L. Levine, "R. Simeon b. Yohai," 173–74; Kimelman, "Conflict between Priestly Oligarchy and Sages," 142–43.

9. S. A. Cohen, *Three Crowns*, 158–63.

10. Ibid., 158–63; L. Levine, "Caesarea's Synagogues," 670–73.

11. The pioneering works in this regard have been those of S. Klein: *Beiträge; Sefer Hayishuv*, 162–65; *Galilee*, 62–68, 177–92. See also Urbach, "Mishmarot," 304–27; Kahane, "Priestly Courses." 9–29.

ately after the first revolt against Rome (66–74); after the Bar-Kokhba revolt of 132–135; or somewhat later in the third century.[12] Whichever theory one adopts—and perhaps each contains some truth, and we are, in fact, dealing with a process that transpired over a number of generations—the presence of priests in some twenty-five Galilean villages and cities by late antiquity is clearly attested in both literary and archeological data. Most of the locales noted were almost assuredly small settlements, and thus the priests may have constituted a majority in each, or at least a very recognizable minority.[13] But even in a place as large as Sepphoris, priestly influence might have been significant, and, in fact, the priests are singled out on several occasions as having been particularly wealthy.[14]

Priestly involvement in the synagogue could have assumed one of a number of expressions: they might have been benefactors or synagogue officials or had a role in synagogue liturgy. The first two categories have little to do with priestly lineage per se, and the role of a priest as benefactor or synagogue leader was probably acquired for other reasons (personality, family ties, wealth, or wisdom).[15] In most cases, these people just happened to be priests. The third category, however, is quite different, and any role played by priests in synagogue liturgy was directly connected to their Aaronic ancestry. Let us briefly discuss each of these categories.

BENEFACTORS

The striking example of a synagogue founded and headed by a priestly family over a number of generations, as evidenced in the pre-70 Theodotos inscription from Jerusalem, finds no parallel elsewhere, either in the first century or in later antiquity.[16] The

---

12. *After 70:* S. Klein, *Galilee*, 66–67. *After 135:* Kahane, "Priestly Courses," 14; Miller, *Studies*, 132; Z. Safrai, *Pirqei Galil*, 271–74; idem, "Priestly Courses," 287–92; Oppenheimer, *Galilee*, 53–57. Urbach, on the other hand, dates the main transition from Judaea to the Galilee, presumably that of the priests as well, to the post-115–117 era; see his "From Judaea to Galilee," 66–69. *Third century:* Trifon, "Priestly Courses," 77–93.

13. See what appears to have been a tomb reserved expressly for priests at Bet She'arim; see Schwabe and Lifshitz, *Beth She'arim*, II, no. 14.

14. *Sepphoris:* Meyers et al., "Sepphoris," 17–18; Hoglund and E. Meyers, "Residential Quarter," 39–42. *Wealthy priests:* Sifre–Deuteronomy 352 (p. 409)—"Most priests are wealthy"; B Pesaḥim 49a; Midrash Hagadol, Leviticus 22:13 (p. 618)—"R. Yoḥanan said: 'One who wishes to become rich should cling to a descendent of Aaron.'" See also the comment of Lieberman (*TK*, VIII, 762): "And know that the most wealthy *tannaim* [except for the Patriarchs] were all priests."

15. Even in rabbinic circles, when the deposition of Rabban Gamaliel II and the appointment of R. El'azar b. Azariah are discussed, the priestly factor is one of a number of possible considerations in choosing a successor (B Berakhot 27b; Y Berakhot 4, 1, 7d). I am assuming that the reference to R. El'azar's descent from Ezra is intended to highlight his priestly lineage and not his "rabbinic" connections.

16. See above, Chap. 3.

86. Inscription from the Susiya synagogue noting a donation by R. Asi the priest at a feast for his son, R. Yoḥanan the *sofer.*

only other instance of a donation by a priest in the first century comes from Berenice, where one of the contributors listed, Cartisthenes, son of Archias, is so identified.[17]

Three inscriptions from the Judaean region of Byzantine Palestine name priests as donors. An Aramaic inscription from Eshtemoa reads as follows: "May he be remembered for good, Lazar the priest and his sons, who gave one tremissis [one-third of a gold dinar] from his assets [or property]."[18] Another Aramaic inscription, from neighboring Susiya, is more elaborate and was likewise found as part of a mosaic floor in the synagogue's atrium: "May he be remembered for good, the holy master, R. Asi the priest [who is also honored with the title of] *biribbi,* who made this mosaic and plastered the walls, [a contribution] which he donated at a [wedding?] banquet for his son, R. Yoḥanan the priest and scribe *biribbi.* Peace on Israel. Amen" (fig. 86).[19] In the Naʿaran synagogue near Jericho, a centrally placed inscription reads as follows: "May he be remembered for good, Pinḥas the priest, son of Justus, who gave the cost of the mosaic from his own resources and property [?]." Next to this is an inscription naming his wife: "May she be remembered for good, Rebecca the wife of Pinḥas."[20] Presumably, Rebecca made a contribution of her own. It may not be coincidental that these "priestly" inscriptions were found adjacent to the menorah, a symbol which might easily have been associated with the Temple.

The only other inscription noting a donor priest in fifth-century Byzantine Palestine was discovered in the Galilee, in the recently discovered Sepphoris synagogue: "May he be remembered for good, Yudan, son of Isaac the priest, and Paregri his daughter. Amen. Amen."[21]

---

17. See above, Chap. 4.

18. Naveh, *On Stone and Mosaic,* no. 74.

19. Ibid., no. 75. S. Safrai (*In Times of Temple and Mishnah,* I, 157–58) has suggested that the R. Asi mentioned in this inscription is to be identified with the amoraic sage R. Asi of Tiberias.

20. Naveh, *On Stone and Mosaic,* nos. 58–59.

21. Weiss and Netzer, *Promise and Redemption,* 41.

OFFICIALS

Once again, the pre-70 Theodotos inscription is worthy of mention. Therein three generations of priests are recorded as having held the title *archisynagogos*, a most unusual occurrence anywhere in the Roman or Byzantine eras.

Two examples of priestly leadership from the Diaspora of later antiquity are noteworthy. One comes from Dura Europos, where the most important member of the community was Samuel the priest, who functioned as the governing presbyter and archon. It was in his term of office that the elaborate second stage of this synagogue building was erected. His name appears in no fewer than three Aramaic inscriptions and one Greek inscription, all appearing on ceiling tiles.[22] The Aramaic texts are basically the same, giving the date of the building and the auspices under which the work was carried out. To cite the longest: "This house was built in the year 556, this corresponding to the second year of Philip Julius Caesar; in the eldership [קששותה] of the priest Samuel, son of Yeda'aya the archon. Now those who stood in charge of this work were . . ." The Greek inscription is even shorter: "Samuel, son of Idaeus, elder [πρεσβύτερος] of the Jews, built it."

The second example of priestly leadership in the Diaspora comes from Sardis, where one Samoe was identified as a priest and *sophodidaskalos*. The inscription is prominently displayed in the middle of the synagogue's main hall, perhaps in the very place where Samoe sat and instructed the community.[23]

Priests who occupied official positions are noted elsewhere in the Diaspora as well: in Aphrodisias, the only priest mentioned was also a *presbeutes* (= elder); and in Rome, several priests were archons and one was an archisynagogue.[24]

The Theodosian Code preserves one decree which, at first glance, appears to refer explicitly to priests. Constantine issued the following edict in 330: "The same Augustus to the priests, the archsynagogues [*sic*], fathers of synagogues and the others who serve in the same place. We order that the priests, archsynagogues, fathers of synagogues, and the others who serve in synagogues shall be free from all corporal liturgy."[25] Although from the above it might seem that the place of the priest was of cardinal importance in the functioning of the early fourth-century synagogue, this source's value is mitigated by two factors. First of all, no other source, except for Epiphanius, mentions priests in a functional role within the synagogue. This is not an insignificant omission, at least insofar as the Theodosian Code is concerned. We have had occasion to note the many synagogue officials mentioned in edicts from the end of the fourth century, and nowhere is a priest named.[26] Secondly, the meaning of the term "priest" in the above source is not as clear as

---

22. Kraeling, *Dura: Synagogue*, 263–68, 277.

23. Kraabel, "Impact of the Discovery," 183–84, 189–90.

24. *Aphrodisias:* Reynolds and Tannenbaum, *Jews and God-Fearers*, 5. *Rome:* Noy, *JIWE*, II, 538.

25. Linder, *Jews in Roman Imperial Legislation*, no. 9.

26. So, for example, ibid., nos. 27, 30.

it may seem at first; indeed, the title may well refer to any type of Jewish official whose role is analogous to that of an official in a pagan or Christian context; it may not necessarily refer to a person from the seed of Aaron.[27] Thus, there is little to derive from this last source as regards the role of priests in the synagogue of late antiquity.[28]

PRIESTS IN SYNAGOGUE RITUAL

The prominence of priests within the liturgical setting of the synagogue was expressed in a variety of ways. First, as noted, contemporary priestly communities are mentioned on stone plaques attached to the walls of many synagogues. To date we have remains of six such plaques throughout Palestine and the Diaspora. Fragments of these plaques were found in the Galilee (Nazareth), the Bet Shean area (Reḥov), the coastal region (Caesarea [fig. 87], Ashkelon), and quite possibly in the southern Shephelah (Kissu-fim). The longest and most complete fragment was found in Yemen.[29] There can be little doubt that many other synagogues had such lists as well. These plaques attest to both the shared memories of the Temple and the common hope that it would be rebuilt sometime in the future.

The liturgy of the synagogue service often highlighted elements of earlier Temple worship, with which the priests were thoroughly identified. These elements included the sacrificial service on Sabbaths and holidays, which found expression in the 'Amidah and/ or Torah-reading, and the detailed description of the atonement ceremony held in the Temple which became an integral part of the Yom Kippur liturgy.[30] Yahalom has suggested that priests may have been responsible for transmitting (if not composing) liturgical poetry memorializing the Temple throughout late antiquity.[31] Commencing in the Byzantine period, the *piyyut* not only featured memories of the Temple, but often focused on the twenty-four priestly courses.[32] Thus, in a continuous, though indirect, way the

---

27. In this regard, one must be careful when using Pharr's translation of the Theodosian Code, where "presbyter" is often rendered as "priest." See also *SHA:* "For, he used to say, it was unjust that, when Christians and Jews observed this custom in announcing the names of those who were to be ordained priests, it should not be similarly observed in the case of governors of provinces." See M. Stern, *Greek and Latin Authors,* II, no. 523; R. Lane Fox, *Pagans and Christians,* 497.

28. The situation among the Samaritans appears to have been quite different. Among the reforms of Baba Rabba (himself identified in Chronicle II as a priest) was the appointment of a governing council of seven, of whom three were priests (Abu 'l-fath [p. 43]; *Chronicle* II, 5 [pp. 66–67]). Moreover, priests were assigned to various regions in Samaritan territory (ibid., 9 [pp. 72–74]).

29. Naveh, *On Stone and Mosaic,* nos. 51, 52, 56, 106; H. Eshel, "Fragmentary Hebrew Inscription?" 159–61; *NEAEHL,* IV, 1273.

30. See above, Chap. 6.

31. Yahalom, *Priestly Palestinian Poetry,* 56–58.

32. See S. Klein, *Galilee,* 177–92. Much work has been done in this regard over the past decades by

משמרת ראשונה יהויריב מסרביי מרון
משמרת שניה ידעיה עמוק צפורים
משמרת שלישית חרים מפשטה
משמרת רביעית שעורים עיתהלו
משמרת חמשית מלכיה בית לחם
משמרת ששית מימין יודפת
משמרת שביעית הקוץ עילבו
משמרת שמינית אביה כפר עוזיה
משמרת תשיעית ישוע ארבל
משמרת עשירית שכניה זבדות כבול
משמרת אחת עשרה אלישיב כהן קנה
משמרת שתים עשרה יקים פשחור צפת
משמרת שלוש עשרה חופה בית מעון
משמרת ארבע עשרה ישבאב בית דצפ תשיחן
משמרת חמש עשרה בלגה מעריה מריה הבלג הזיונית
משמרת שש עשרה אמר פרנמרה
משמרת שבע עשרה חזיר ג... עליה
משמרת שמונה עשרה הפיצץ נצרת
משמרת תשע עשרה פתחיה אכלה ערב
משמרת עשרים יחזקאל ב עולא
משמרת עשרים ואחת יכין כפר יוחנה
משמרת עשרים ושתים גמול בית חריה
משמרת עשרים ושלוש דליהו הגנתון צלמין
משמרת עשרים וארבע מעזיהו חמת אריח

87. Three fragments of a plaque from Caesarea listing the twenty-four priestly courses.

central role of the priests, past and future, was brought to the attention of synagogue worshippers.

Priests were accorded priority in the Torah-reading ceremony. Already in the Mishnah, the first to read from the Torah was a priest, and even if a priest was willing to cede this right, he was not allowed to do so.[33] By the amoraic period, there was an attempt by some rabbis to set an order for the 'aliyot, but the first two were universally reserved for a priest and Levite.[34]

One particular mishnaic source may allude to a custom whereby a priest might have played a central role in synagogue liturgy. The following is recorded: "Whoever reads the prophetic passages also leads in the recitation of the *Shema'*, leads in the *'Amidah*, and

Fleischer; see his "New Shiv'atot," 30-55; "Regarding the Courses," 141-61; and the recent "Additional Data," 47-60. See also L. Levine, "Caesarea's Synagogues," 671.

33. M Gittin 5:8; B Ketubot 25b.
34. B Gittin 59b-60a.

raises his hand [as part of the priestly blessing]."[35] Although both *talmudim* try to explain away the implications of this passage or to move the discussion in another direction, the plain meaning is that very often (usually?) priests would function in these capacities. Since only the priests were empowered to bless the congregation, it is they who may well be referred to as reading from the Prophets and leading the prayer service as well. If this was the case either at a particular time or in certain locales, it would be an important piece of evidence pointing to priestly prominence in some second-century synagogues.[36]

Finally, the priests played a significant role during the *'Amidah* service, with the recitation of the priestly blessing. This custom was apparently transferred to the synagogue following the destruction of the Temple, although some have claimed that it was practiced in synagogues beforehand as well.[37] The moment of reciting this blessing was considered holy, and a number of procedures transferred directly from Temple practice were introduced to emphasize its sanctity. The blessing concluded the *'Amidah* recitation, just as in the pre-70 days it concluded the daily Tamid sacrifice, and on certain days it was also recited just before the locking of the Temple gates.[38] R. Yoḥanan b. Zakkai decreed that priests should offer these blessings barefoot, as had been done in the Temple.[39] Likewise, following Temple practice, priests would wash before blessing.[40] They would recite a special benediction before blessing the congregation and would spread their fingers when blessing, apparently as had been Temple practice.[41]

The prayer leader would formally invite the priests to commence the ceremony,[42] whereupon they recited one special prayer before leaving their seats and another at the conclusion of the ceremony.[43] The place where the priests stood when blessing the people was called the *dukhan* (presumably, as in the Temple), and often this ceremony was referred to, primarily in Babylonian sources, as simply "ascending the *dukhan*."[44] The congregation would face the priests, although by late antiquity an interesting difference between Palestinian and Babylonian practices had crystallized. In the former, priests would

---

35. M Megillah 4:5. See also the comments in Albeck, *Mishnah—Mo'ed*, 503–4.

36. Cf., however, the explanation in Elbogen, *Studies*, 599: whoever is capable of the one is capable of doing the others as well. It is likewise engaging to consider the rabbinic prohibitions on wearing white and removing one's shoes when leading services (M Megillah 4:8), perhaps a reference to priestly norms as attested by earlier Temple practices.

37. See, for example, Elbogen, *Jewish Liturgy*, 62–66; Alon, *Jews in Their Land*, I, 114; S. Safrai, *Pilgrimage*, 8 n. 10. See also Schürer, *History*, II, 453–54; and above, Chap. 5.

38. M Tamid 5:1; M Ta'anit 4:1.

39. B Sotah 40a; B Rosh Hashanah 31b.

40. B Sotah 39a; M Tamid 1:2; 2:1.

41. B Sotah 39a–b; Targum Jonathan of Num. 6:23.

42. Sifre-Numbers 39 (p. 43).

43. B Sotah 39a–b.

44. B Rosh Hashanah 31b; B Ḥagigah 16a; B Sukkah 51a; Tanḥuma, Noah, 20 (p. 24a). See also Z. Safrai, "Dukhan, Aron and Teva," 69–71. With regard to Levites, see B Ta'anit 29a.

face the ark (with their backs to the congregation), while in the latter, priests would face the congregation, as had been the practice earlier.[45] Some magical effect seems to have been associated with this ritual in Babylonia. We read of a sage advising people who had dreams but did not know their meaning: they were to stand in front of the priests at the time of the benediction and ask God for favor, optimally concluding their request at the termination of the priestly blessing so that the congregation would answer both blessing and request with "Amen."[46] In the third century, it was the custom not to look at priests at the moment of blessing, presumably owing to the sanctity of the moment.[47] Moreover, as was the case with other central components of the liturgy—namely, recitation of the *'Amidah*, the *Qaddish*, and the reading of the Torah—the priestly blessing could be offered only in the presence of ten males.[48] It was important that priests recite this blessing even when they were the only males in the congregation. In response to the query as to precisely whom they were to be blessing, it is stated that they were blessing Jews everywhere (lit., to the north, south, east, and west). And to the further question, who would respond "Amen" to these blessings, the answer was, the women and children.[49]

Whatever the similarities between synagogal and Temple practice with respect to the priestly blessing, there were also some substantial differences, which served to preserve some distinction between the original setting and its later continuation. In the Temple, the priestly blessings were recited without interruption; outside the Temple, each blessing was said separately.[50] As a result, following each of the blessings, special responses were introduced into the synagogue ritual for the congregation to recite.[51] It seems that a number of different customs crystallized, each emphasizing certain phrases or verses; this, then, led to attempts by the rabbis to limit the number of responses and to determine how and when such verses were to be said.

The importance of the priests themselves for the recitation of these blessings is preserved in Palestinian practice, but not in Babylonian. In the latter, if no priests were present, then the prayer leader would recite these verses (which is the accepted practice to this day). However, such was not the case in Palestine: if no priests were present, then the priestly benediction was not said at all.[52]

Priests seem to have been particularly active as *paytanim* in late antiquity. The first known *paytan* was Yose b. Yose, who referred to himself as a "high priest." Other prominent priestly *paytanim* include Shim'on Megas, Yohanan the priest, son of Joshua the

---

45. T Megillah 3:21 (p. 360); *Differences in Customs*, no. 36 (p. 156).
46. B Berakhot 55b.
47. B Ḥagigah 16a.
48. M Megillah 4:3; B Megillah 23b.
49. Y Berakhot 5, 5, 9d.
50. M Tamid 7:2.
51. Y Berakhot 1, 2c; B Sotah 39b. See Elbogen, *Jewish Liturgy*, 63–64.
52. *Differences in Customs*, no. 29 (pp. 145–46), and Margalioth's comment on p. 145 in n. 1.

priest, Pinḥas the priest of Kafra, and Haduta. The fact that many *piyyutim* deal with Temple issues and the twenty-four priestly courses may be due, in part, to the priestly lineage of so many synagogue poets.[53] Certainly, the very positive portrayal of the priests and priestly cultic functions in many *piyyutim* could not but enhance priests' status within the congregation.[54]

One other possible connection between priests and synagogue liturgy should be noted. It has often been claimed that priestly traditions stand behind many of the mystical Hekhalot sources, and that this mystical literature, which focuses on heavenly ascent, emanated from priestly circles in later antiquity. Moreover, many of the prayers which constitute an integral part of these mystical experiences are strikingly similar to those familiar in synagogue liturgy. The question often debated is whether these mystical circles influenced synagogue practice or whether they appropriated known liturgical excerpts from the synagogue context. No consensus has yet emerged. Were one to assume a connection between priestly traditions and Hekhalot literature, on the one hand, and the influence of Hekhalot prayers on synagogue liturgy, on the other, then an avenue of profound priestly influence on the synagogue of late antiquity would be opened up. For the moment, however, this option remains moot.[55]

Still, enough evidence has accumulated of late to posit a far more prominent role for priests in the synagogue setting than has been heretofore assumed. Whether such prominence was always there but came to the attention of scholars studying the Byzantine period only recently, as a result of additional sources of information, or whether it was indeed something rather new in synagogue life, the product of changed circumstances in late antiquity (especially the emergence of Christianity and its clergy), remains to be clarified.

---

53. Mirsky, *Yosse ben Yosse*, 10; Fleischer, "Early Paytanim of Tiberias," 368–71; Yahalom, *Priestly Palestinian Poetry*, 56–57. In addition to the liturgy itself, it has been suggested of late that priestly views found expression in the Sepphoris synagogue mosaic; see the forthcoming articles by J. Yahalom ("Sepphoris Synagogue mosaic") and E. Kessler ("Art Leading the Story").

54. Swartz, "Ritual about Myth about Ritual," 135–55; idem, "Sage, Priest, and Poet."

55. The literature on this issue is extensive; see, for example, Gruenwald, *From Apocalypticism*, 125–73; idem, "Impact of Priestly Traditions," 65–120; Elior, "From Earthly Temple to Heavenly Shrines," 217–67. For a different and somewhat controversial connection between this literature and the synagogue, see Halperin, *Faces of the Chariot*; and the reviews of Elior ("Merkabah Mysticism," 233–49) and Wolfson ("Halperin's *Faces*," 496–500).

sixteen LITURGY

T here is no dimension more reflective of the growth and evolution of the
synagogue in antiquity than its liturgy.[1] From constituting one of many activities in its early stages, the ritual component of the synagogue eventually
became a dominant and definitive element. At first it included the reading
of Scriptures, a translation of the reading, and some sort of homily or instruction;[2] by
late antiquity, the liturgy had evolved into a rich and varied worship setting which included not only these three components, but also regular communal prayers and poetic
renditions (*piyyutim*), especially on Sabbaths and holidays.

The development of synagogue liturgy was far from linear. Some practices appeared

---

1. The term "liturgy" will be used with regard to public religious rituals within the context of the
synagogue. Clearly, rituals may have been performed elsewhere as well: in the home, academy, or other
religious settings; a community may have held its public ritual, for instance, in an outdoor plaza in times
of drought. The term has a long and varied history. In the Greco-Roman world it usually meant some
sort of public service (although at times it could have had a cultic association), and in the early church it
was often limited to the Eucharist celebration. The Hebrew equivalent to the Greek *leitourgia* is *'avodah*,
meaning "the service of God." Originally this referred specifically to Temple sacrifice (M 'Avot 1:2), but
later it was applied to prayer as well (Sifre–Deuteronomy 41 [pp. 87–88]; and Goldin, *Studies in Midrash*,
27–38; see also Tanḥuma, Vayishlaḥ, 9). On the term "liturgy," see, inter alia, Martimort, *Church at
Prayer*, 7–18; Jones et al., *Study of Liturgy*, passim; Reif, *Judaism and Hebrew Prayer*, 71–72.

2. See Neh. 8:5–8; and above, Chap. 5.

for a time and were then suppressed, sometimes with relative success, as was the case with the recitation of the Decalogue;[3] at other times, prayers were eventually incorporated into the liturgy, though not always in the place for which they had been originally intended. In amalgamating two competing versions of the same prayer, one was often relegated to a different prayer service, as happened with alternative versions of several of the blessings surrounding the *Shema'* (see below). Finally, some periods appear to have been characterized by vigorous liturgical creativity and others by less dramatic consolidation. Not all worship components underwent growth and development at the same time or at the same pace.

In the tannaitic period, for example, the Yavneh generation of sages engaged in intensive religious creativity, especially in the area of prayer. This is attributable to the recent loss of Jerusalem and its Temple, and the concomitant need to find adequate substitutes for a community which still vividly remembered the myriad of religious and ethnic functions fulfilled by that institution. Daily sacrificial worship at the Jerusalem Temple, like that practiced by the pagans in their temples,[4] was a well-known phenomenon, and Jewish life now needed a substitute. The synagogue became the logical setting for this communal expression.

Another reason for this intensive Yavnean activity was the strong leadership of Rabban Gamaliel, whose vigorous pursuit of his declared goals provided the impetus and framework for sustained efforts in this regard.[5] Moreover, only such a strong-willed person could deal with the reservations, if not outright opposition, of sages who either were not comfortable with the pace or direction of his program or remained unconvinced of its correctness. While rabbinic liturgical activities continued throughout the second century, these appear to have been undertaken at a much slower pace and to have dealt more with clarifying alternative traditions resulting from the breakthroughs of the Yavnean period. This slackened pace may also be accounted for by the upheavals of the Bar Kokhba revolt, the ensuing persecution, and the large-scale migration of Jews (sages included) from Judaea to the Galilee.

By the third century, the enhanced significance of the prayer component was reflected in synagogue architecture. Galilean-type buildings, beginning in the latter half of the century, regularly had ornate facades and entranceways facing in the direction of Jerusalem, and their interior plans likewise reflected this orientation. Other synagogues in the Galilee at this time, such as the one at Khirbet Shema', also emphasized the direction

---

3. See B Berakhot 12a; Y Berakhot 1, 5, 3c; and comments in Urbach, "Role of Ten Commandments," 161–84; Fleischer, *Prayer and Prayer Rituals*, 259–74.

4. As in the temple of Dionysius at Teos, or of Asclepius in Athens and Pergamum; see MacMullen, *Paganism*, 149 n. 78. See also Lieberman, *Hellenism in Jewish Palestine*, 164–79.

5. R. Yohanan ben Zakkai began this process immediately following the Temple's destruction, but his measures were limited in scope and probably in their impact as well. See Alon, *Jews, Judaism and the Classical World*, 314–43.

toward Jerusalem. Moreover, first at Dura Europos and then with increasing frequency throughout the course of late antiquity, synagogues utilized religious symbols and motifs (e.g., the menorah), while some of the scenes at Dura have been interpreted as reflecting the synagogue liturgical experience.[6]

In what follows, we shall discuss synagogue worship as it evolved in two separate stages. The first is the tannaitic period (ca. 70–225), and the second, the period of late antiquity (the third through seventh centuries). These stages are posited on the basis of a number of factors. Firstly, the relevant rabbinic sources change from one era to the next. The corpus of tannaitic works, together with the tannaitic traditions embedded in the *talmudim* (i.e., the *baraitot*), serve as sources of information for the earlier time frame. The amoraic material—essentially the two *talmudim* and the aggadic *midrashim*— in addition to *piyyutim*, *targumim*, and several post-talmudic compilations, i.e., the *Differences between Those of the East and the Inhabitants of Eretz-Israel* and Tractate Soferim, constitute the second set of sources. This latter group is far greater not only in quantity, but in scope as well. Thus, with regard to the earlier tannaitic period, this discussion will, of necessity, be limited to rabbinic literature and to what the rabbis legislated and presumably practiced within their own circles. We have no evidence, neither literary nor archeological, as to how rabbinic discussions and decisions impacted on the community at large. On the other hand, for the period of later antiquity, there are both rabbinic and non-rabbinic literary sources, which, combined with inscriptions and other archeological finds, offer some information about what was actually happening in at least some synagogues in Roman-Byzantine Palestine and Sassanian Babylonia.

Of no less consequence for the proposed division is the fact that each group of sources appears to reflect a decidedly different stage in the evolution of synagogue liturgy. This is particularly evident with respect to the two new components of this liturgy which made their appearance during these centuries: communal prayer and *piyyut*. Regarding the former, the first period can generally be characterized as one of conceptualization and preliminary composition, the second as one of consolidation and amplification; by the end of late antiquity or, at most, a century or so later, there was a further stage of development, that of amalgamation and standardization.[7] The latter liturgical form, *piyyut*, was introduced into synagogue worship only in the second stage, toward the end of late antiquity (i.e., the fifth or sixth century) and constituted an entirely new genre in synagogue worship. These and other developments in the realm of synagogue worship are considered in the present chapter.[8]

---

6. See Levine, "Menorah"; Gutmann, "Programmatic Painting," 137–54.

7. One could add a further stage of codification and institutionalization primarily under the aegis of the Babylonian gaonate in the ninth and tenth centuries C.E.; see Baron, *Social and Religious History of the Jews*, VII, 62–134; L. A. Hoffman, *Canonization*, 1–9; Reif, *Judaism and Hebrew Prayer*, 122–206; Petuchowski, "Liturgy of the Synagogue," 47; and below.

8. In what follows the focus will be on worship as it developed in the synagogue context. The litera-

METHODOLOGICAL CONSIDERATIONS

Before commencing the discussion, it is necessary to address a number of methodological concerns. The study of liturgy, whether Christian or Jewish, is fraught with pitfalls.[9] First and foremost, standardized Jewish liturgical texts made their appearance only toward the end of the first millennium. Until then, liturgical traditions, particularly prayer, were transmitted orally in the main. All that is available to us before that time are snippets of information regarding specific prayers and practices. If our task were only to try and fit these pieces together into some sort of coherent picture, matters might be manageable. But the issues are far more complex.

In the first place, we are faced with the problem of the reliability of the texts at hand. In not a few cases, there are textual variants in the phraseology of prayers of greater and lesser degrees of importance. This is true not only of a major prayer such as the ʿAmidah, but also of shorter blessings such as "Who has not made me a gentile, . . . an ignoramus, . . . a woman."[10]

Secondly, our sources indicate that liturgical practice was far from fixed. Alternative versions of prayers and supplications were in use for some time, with new ones constantly being added and others being eliminated. When the sources themselves speak about competing versions, we are often left wondering what exactly they are referring to. Do they reflect practices in a given locale or in different geographical regions? Or are they chronological distinctions reflecting earlier and later periods? Was one of the practices normative for most Jewish communities, while the other was much more localized? In another vein, we might ask whether the plethora of variations reflect later stages of development that evolved from a more or less standardized "original," as earlier generations of scholars had posited, or perhaps the opposite was the case, namely, that there were initially a plurality of versions, and these underwent a gradual process of standardization and unification. This latter possibility, presented by Baumstark as one of his so-called laws, has been widely accepted in current scholarship.[11] Furthermore, Baumstark's second "law" also seems to apply to the Jewish liturgical context—namely, that very fre-

---

ture on Jewish worship generally in this period is vast, and no attempt will be made to deal with many of the philological, textual, and theological issues connected with individual prayers; otherwise, the presentation would quickly become unwieldy.

9. Much has been written on methodology in the study of liturgy. See, for example, Heinemann, *Prayer*, 1–12; Fiensy, *Prayers Alleged to Be Jewish*, 1–10, 209–42; Sarason, "Use of Method," 97–172; Zahavy, "New Approach," 45–60; Reif, "Liturgical Difficulties," 99–122; idem, "Jewish Liturgical Research," 161–70; idem, *Judaism and Hebrew Prayer*, 1–21, 88–95; idem, "Jewish Liturgy—Methodological Considerations," 1–8; and the instructive remarks in Bradshaw, "Ten Principles," 10–21.

10. T Berakhot 6:18 (p. 38); and comments in Lieberman, *TK*, I, 119–21. One of the versions recorded in B Menaḥot 43b substitutes "slave" for "ignoramus" (בור). See also Wieder, "On the Blessings 'Gentile-Slave-Woman,'" 97–115.

11. Baumstark, *Comparative Liturgy*, 16–19.

quently, though not always, there is a movement from simpler to more elaborate forms in the course of standardization.[12] In short, assessing the dynamics of liturgical practice, given the piecemeal nature of this evidence, is a formidable task.

Let me offer but two illustrations of this fragmentary documentation. Sometimes we are simply uninformed of the halakhic status of a particular prayer. As we shall see below, the evening *'Amidah* prayer was a major subject of halakhic controversy among the sages of Yavneh: Was it to be considered obligatory or optional? We are never informed as to how this particular dispute was resolved. From a series of references to this prayer in the third and fourth centuries, it becomes quite clear that most rabbis assumed that it was a required practice. But because this is never explicitly stated, the de jure status of the evening *'Amidah*—as against the de facto practice—has remained anomalous to this day.

A second example relates to the *Qedushah*. On the basis of rabbinic literature alone, we would know next to nothing about this prayer; yet other sources seem to indicate that it had been, and continued to be, an important component of Jewish worship. How, then, does one explain the silence of rabbinic sources? Was it a matter of indifference or opposition, or is it simply a manifestation of woefully incomplete evidence?

Discussion of Jewish liturgy in later antiquity is, of necessity, heavily reliant upon the wealth of data preserved in rabbinic literature, yet this material is rife with problems. Beyond the textual issues noted above, there is the question of the degree of acceptance of rabbinic formulations and decisions in these centuries. That rabbinic prayer eventually became standardized in Jewish life is well known, but that came about only in the ninth and tenth centuries, under the aegis of the Babylonian *geonim*.[13] What, then, was the situation in the second to sixth centuries? Even if we are inclined to posit some sort of correlation between rabbinic dicta and actual synagogue practice, the questions remain as to whether this was true with each liturgical component, whether it was valid everywhere, and whether it was consistent throughout these centuries. In other words, how authoritative and effective was rabbinic legislation in shaping Jewish liturgical practice in the synagogues of the late Roman and Byzantine periods?

In other words, when the sages supported or opposed a liturgical practice, was their opinion generally followed, or can we only conclude in such an instance that more than one practice existed? As we try to answer these questions, caution must be exercised before accepting the explanations, for certain practices as related in rabbinic literature, and this is certainly true when competing explanations are offered. In such cases, there can be no certitude, for the sages themselves were unsure of the matter.

One final issue, which we have had occasion to address above, involves problems related to the first mention of a phenomenon in our sources. Does this indicate that something new had crystallized, or is it possible that this phenomenon had existed earlier in one

12. Ibid., 19–21.
13. See above, note 7.

form or another and was only now mentioned? Does the absence of explicit references to certain liturgical practices necessarily mean that they did not exist? At times this seems to have been the case. All of the above, of course, are issues which one encounters in every area of historical research; the situation with respect to the study of liturgy is no different.

THE SECOND CENTURY

There is no question that a major shift in the nature of religious worship in the synagogues of Palestine was precipitated by the destruction of the Temple.[14] For all the controversy which surrounded this central institution in the late Second Temple period—as reflected in contemporary sectarian literature, the writings of Josephus, the New Testament, and rabbinic literature—the Temple, down to its very end, remained the central and preeminent religious framework of Jewish life. Thus, it is no wonder that, with its disappearance, there was an urgent need to fill the vacuum by incorporating certain Temple practices within the synagogue framework, as well as by creating additional avenues of religious expression.[15] Under the leadership of Rabban Yoḥanan b. Zakkai and especially Rabban Gamaliel, the sages at Yavneh (70-135) addressed this issue in a variety of ways; their work was continued in subsequent generations, at Usha (ca. 140-80) and in the era of R. Judah I (ca. 180-225). Together, this period of approximately 150 years produced the first clear-cut evidence of a synagogue prayer liturgy, which eventually evolved into what has become normative Jewish worship.

Torah-Reading

Let us commence our discussion with the one worship element that was clearly carried over from the pre-70 worship context: the Torah-reading. Evidence from throughout the entire first millennium has shown that Palestinian practice involved a triennial cycle, which, however, was loosely defined and might have varied from one locale to the next in its specific implementation.[16] Evidence from the second half of the millennium indicates that a triennial cycle may have been divided into 141, 154, 167, or even 175 portions

---

14. We have no idea how the destruction affected the Diaspora because we know so little about synagogue liturgy beforehand or afterward.

15. Besides liturgical developments, other behavior was now being recognized as of the highest religious order as well, even on a part with the now defunct sacrifices, e.g., repentance, the practice of good deeds, and the study of Torah; see, for example, PRK 24:7 (p. 355); ʾAvot de R. Nathan, A, 4 (pp. 9b, 11a); B Berakhhot 10b; B Sukkah 49b. See also Aderet, *From Destruction to Restoration*, 37-170; Reif, *Judaism and Hebrew Prayer*, 95-102; Viviano, *Study as Worship*, passim.

16. See above, Chap. 5. On the Torah-reading generally during this period, see Elbogen, *Jewish Liturgy*, 129-42; Wacholder, "Prolegomenon," xvii-xx; Perrot, "Reading of the Bible," 137-49; Gilat, "*Derasha* and Reading of the Torah," 266-78.

(*sedarim*).[17] The annual Torah-reading cycle, associated primarily with Babylonia in late antiquity, is evidenced in late Byzantine Palestine as well, but appears to have been either limited to Babylonian Jews living there or reflective of a period in which Babylonian customs began making inroads into Palestine.[18] Two statements from later antiquity explicitly relate to the Palestinian triennial cycle. One appears in the Bavli: "those in the west [i.e., Palestine] who finish reading the Torah in three years."[19] The second is from the *Differences in Customs*, which reflects the very end of late antiquity: "Those in the east (Babylonia) celebrate Simḥat Torah [marking the conclusion of the reading of the Torah] every year, those in Eretz-Israel [celebrate the holiday once] every three and a half years."[20]

Despite this rather clear-cut evidence, we are nevertheless ill informed as to precisely how the triennial cycle worked. Several tannaitic statements give us some idea of the many times during the year the regular reading was suspended:

> When the New Moon [*Rosh Ḥodesh*] of Adar falls on the Sabbath, we read *Parashat Sheqalim*. When it falls in midweek, we move [the reading] up to the previous [Sabbath] and skip [i.e., suspend the usual reading for] the following Sabbath. On the second [Sabbath, we read] *Zachor* [Deut. 25:17]; on the third, the "Red Heifer" [Num. 19:1]; on the fourth, "This month will be to you" [Ex. 12:1]; on the fifth, we return to the regular order. For all [special occasions] we interrupt [the regular order]: for New Moons, for Hanukkah, and for Purim, for fast days and *ma'amadot*, and for Yom Kippur.[21]

Although the Bavli records a dispute between two Palestinian sages originally from Babylonia over what the phrase "regular order" refers to—the reading of the Torah or of the haftarah—it seems rather clear that the subject of this mishnah is the Torah-reading. Postponing the regular readings so frequently could never work out if an annual cycle was being practiced,[22] and, indeed, it may have been the Babylonian annual cycle that prompted R. Jeremiah to interpret the above tradition as referring to the haftarah cycle.

Another tannaitic tradition, this one ascribed to R. Simeon b. El'azar, adds two more special Sabbaths, when the regular reading is suspended:

---

17. These numbers derive from lists of *sedarim* found in Genizah manuscripts and early Torah scrolls (Joel, "Bible Manuscript," 126-29), as well as Tractate Soferim 16:8 (pp. 291-92). On the number 175, see Elbogen, *Jewish Liturgy*, 133. Shinan ("Sermons, Targums and Reading from Scriptures," 97-110) argues that many more variations are reflected in midrashic homilies. Cf., however, Naeh, "Torah Reading Cycle," 167-87.

18. Fleischer, "List of Yearly Holidays," 343-44; D. Rosenthal, "Annual Torah Reading," 147-48. Cf., however, Steinfeld's reservations ("Qaliri's Partition," 266-67). See also Chap. 5, notes 83-85.

19. B Megillah 29b.

20. *Differences in Customs*, no. 48 (pp. 172-73).

21. M Megillah 3:4.

22. According to the opinion of R. Ami (B Megillah 30b). See Ginzberg, *Commentary*, III, 132-35; Albeck, *Mishnah—Mo'ed*, II, 501-2; Lieberman, *TK*, IV, 1166; and Fleischer, "Annual and Triennial Torah Reading," 47.

It [i.e., a tannaitic tradition] has been taught: R. Simeon b. El'azar said: "Ezra established for Israel that they should read the curses in Leviticus before 'Atzeret [i.e., Shavu'ot], and those of Deuteronomy before Rosh Hashanah." [23]

Although this source has been interpreted by Fleischer as evidence for an annual Torah-reading cycle in second-century Palestine, it seems best explained as adding two further instances when the triennial Torah-reading was to be interrupted.[24] To interpret the source otherwise, i.e., that it is intended to promote an annual cycle, is problematic. In the first place, it would stand alone as evidence for a Palestinian annual cycle (in contrast to those noted above). Moreover, on the assumption that an annual cycle existed, there would be little reason to make such a statement. These particular portions would have been read as a matter of course at about the same time as the two holidays mentioned. Thus, on the assumption that an annual cycle existed, it is hard to imagine why R. Simeon would have had to make such a statement or, for that matter, why later generations would have wished to preserve it. Finally, as in other cases in rabbinic literature, the enactment was considered to be of such significance that it was attributed to Ezra, whom the sages associate with a variety of liturgical innovations.[25]

With regard to the Torah-reading, the Tosefta fills out the picture sketchily drawn by the Mishnah. For example, it adds the *haftarot* to be recited on special Sabbaths and holidays and spells out the Torah-readings for the intermediate days of the Passover and Sukkot festivals.[26] Of more interest, however, is the fact that the Tosefta also notes Torah-reading customs alternative to those listed in the Mishnah. For Shavu'ot, for example, instead of the selection from Deut. 16, another custom of reading Ex. 19–20 is noted; with regard to Rosh Hashanah, some replaced the reading in Lev. 23 with Gen. 21–22.[27] The difference between these alternative practices is far from insignificant, as the contents of each varies greatly; knowing the *Sitz im Leben* of each custom would be an enormous aid to understanding the different emphases among various second-century congregations. On the one hand, according to the Mishnah and the main tradition cited in the Tosefta, the Torah selections are what we might have expected for special occasions, namely, passages which address these particular holidays. The alternative readings, however, introduced by the phrase "Others say," [28] focus on a very different type of read-

---

23. B Megillah 31b.

24. Fleischer, "Annual and Triennial Torah Reading," 38–40; idem, "Inquiries Concerning the Triennial Reading," 43–61.

25. See, Bar-Ilan, "Interpreting a Baraita," 126–34. For other traditions attributed to Ezra, see Y Megillah 4, 1, 75a; B Bava Qama 82a.

26. T Megillah 3:1–7 (pp. 353–55).

27. Ibid., 3:5–6 (p. 354).

28. This term is ambiguous, and rabbinic traditions are both laconic and contradictory; see, for example, Z. Frankel, *Darkei Hamishnah*, 165 n. 5; Hyman, *Toldot Tanaim V'amoraim*, 138; Yashar, "'יש אחרים' and 'אומרים,'" 380–81. My thanks to David Golinkin for these references.

ing, namely, narrative portions: the revelation on Mt. Sinai in one case and the story of Abraham and his seed in the other. Was this choice based on ideological or religious considerations, or were these readings simply more appealing and popularly oriented? We have no way of knowing.

Tannaitic material knows of other instances of competing customs revolving around the reading of the Torah. For example, R. ʿAqiva and R. Ishmael differ on the number of people who are to be called to the Torah on Yom Kippur and the Sabbath. R. Ishmael accorded the Sabbath preeminence and allotted it seven ʿaliyot and Yom Kippur six; R. ʿAqiva advocated the opposite.[29] More important is the difference of opinion between two Ushan sages, R. Meir and R. Judah, regarding the weekday Torah-readings. According to the former, each reading is to be consecutive. Thus, the reading on Monday morning picks up where the Saturday afternoon Torah-reading left off, and the readings on Thursday and the following Sabbath follow suit. R. Judah, on the other hand, was of the opinion that the readings on these three occasions should repeat themselves, and then on the following Sabbath this same portion would once again be read and more added to it.[30] The implication of these different procedures might well be that different synagogues were reading at varying paces and reading different sections of the Torah on any given Sabbath, not to speak of a weekday.

It is difficult to say how much the sages themselves had a hand in shaping the Torah-reading service at this stage. Many customs practiced in the second century C.E. probably originated in the pre-70 era, rendering the sages' influence on synagogue worship unknown (and likely minimal). Moreover, one is hard put to gauge the degree to which the Mishnah and Tosefta simply recorded common practices or, alternatively, recorded rulings which the sages themselves were making.[31]

Finally, it is impossible to determine how much change took place in the second cen-

---

29. T Megillah 3:11 (p. 356).

30. Ibid., 3:10 (p. 355); B Megillah 31b. The Mishnah itself (3:6) simply gives R. Judah's opinion, and, as a result, this has been the normative Jewish practice to the present day. These two sages are purported to have disagreed on how the Torah blessings should be recited—with the scroll opened or closed; see B Megillah 32a.

31. An interesting case of the sages shaping earlier practices is reflected in M Megillah 4:4 and M Taʿanit 4:3. In the former source, the sages clearly legislated that at least three verses must be read for each ʿaliyah. Yet the procedure noted in the latter source for the week of the maʿamad ceremony, which quite clearly reflects pre-70 practice (see above, Chap. 2), does not require this number of verses. For two days during that week, only eight verses were prescribed. Either fewer than three verses were read for each ʿaliyah or fewer than three people were called up. Regarding the latter instance, see above, Chap. 2. In either case, the practice advocated by the tannaim was different, and later rabbis had difficulty explaining the discrepancy. See Wacholder, "Prolegomenon," xviii–xix. On the issue of short Torah-readings (fewer than three verses), see Sperber, "Note on Palestinian Division," 119–20.

Another instance of rabbinic adaptation of Temple practices is the blessing for the Torah taken from the high priest's Yom Kippur blessings; see M Yoma 7:1; T Kippurim 3:18 (p. 247).

tury in the area of Torah-reading. Most relevant traditions are anonymous (in sharp distinction to the prayer component; see below), and most pericopae seem to describe known practices, without much deliberation regarding change, tension, or conflict. We may thus assume that the practices noted were widespread customs which aroused relatively little controversy and related not only to rabbinic circles, but to the community at large (at least in Palestine).

The 'Amidah

The rabbinic role in the shaping of the Torah-reading ceremony may be ambiguous, but not so in the second major area of Jewish liturgy: communal prayer. The role of the sages in formulating the prayer liturgy is clearer, although there is no gainsaying that even here greater clarity would have been welcomed. The key prayer formulated at this time was the 'Amidah. Ironically, only a lone statement refers explicitly to this event: ת״ר: שמעון הפקולי הסדיר י״ח ברכות לפני רבן גמליאל על הסדר ביבנה ("Our sages taught: Simeon Hapaquli arranged eighteen benedictions before Rabban Gamaliel according to [their] order at Yavneh").[32]

Most scholars have assumed that Simeon's task involved some sort of editing or reworking of already existing material that had been in use in one form or another in the pre-70 Judaean synagogue. What is unclear, and indeed has been debated throughout this century, is whether Simeon's work in Yavneh was basically editorial in nature or whether it involved some more creative integration of the contents, patterns, and structure of these prayers. Since there was a general consensus that public prayer existed before 70, it was assumed that Simeon's task, under Gamaliel's aegis, involved (re)arranging earlier material, perhaps adding some elements, and then editing the final product. Over the years, various suggestions have been made regarding traces of these earlier strata of the 'Amidah in a plethora of biblical and Second Temple sources, from Psalms and Nehemiah through Ben Sira, the Psalms of Solomon, the Dead Sea Scrolls, to, finally, pre-70 rabbinic traditions.[33] On the other hand, several scholars have suggested that the catalyst for the formulation of this prayer stemmed from Hellenistic influences: Baer claims to have found a Greek parallel to many of the themes in the 'Amidah, and Bickerman points to Hellenistic civic prayers that resemble paragraphs in Ben Sira and the later 'Amidah.[34] Few scholars, however, ever questioned the assumption that a central public prayer existed before 70.

---

32. B Berakhot 28b; B Megillah 17b; Midrash Hagadol, Exodus 40:32 (p. 790). This prayer is referred to in three ways: (1) the Eighteen Benedictions (Shemoneh 'Esreh); (2) the Prayer (Hatefillah); (3) the Standing Prayer ('Amidah). On the importance of standing in prayer, see Ehrlich, " 'When You Pray,' " 38–50.

33. See above, Chap. 5; and, inter alia, Elbogen, Jewish Liturgy, 21–34; Alon, Jews in Their Land, I, 266–69; Heinemann, Prayer, 21–24; Petuchowski, "Liturgy of the Synagogue," 51.

34. Baer, Israel among the Nations, 32–36; Bickerman, "Civic Prayer," 163–85.

Over the past decade and a half, this consensus has been shaken by a series of polar positions on the subject. An extremely minimalistic position has been adopted by N. Cohen, who claims that the editorial work carried out by Simeon Hapaquli at Yavneh was virtually nil.[35] According to her, the word הסדיר in the above statement should be understood as "set forth" or "recite" (and not "edit" or "organize"); i.e., Simeon simply recited these prayers before Rabban Gamaliel. Cohen thus severely restricts the contribution of the Yavnean sages in the crystallization of what had already developed into the central Jewish prayer. She assumes that this prayer achieved its present form before 70, a view not far from that already expressed by Alon, Blidstein, and Fox, who view the primary achievement of Yavneh as one of redefining a known communal prayer as obligatory for individuals as well.[36]

In the late 1980s and early 1990s, three scholars adopted a view that was radically different than that of Cohen and others. Fleischer, who is of the opinion that no organized communal Jewish prayer existed prior to 70, claims that the institution of fixed public communal prayer, as well as compulsory prayer for the individual, were conceived and created ex nihilo by Rabban Gamaliel and his colleagues in Yavneh; he refers to this effort as "the special institution established by Rabban Gamaliel."[37]

At about the same time that Fleischer made his views known, Zahavy published several articles and a monograph also claiming that Jewish prayer, as it is first encountered in the Mishnah and Tosefta, was the creation of the Yavnean sages. However, Zahavy goes one step further in attempting to identify the distinct groups that contributed to this enterprise and whose ideologies are incorporated into the fixed prayers established in Yavneh: according to him, both the *'Amidah* and the *Shema'* and its blessings were products of the priestly and scribal classes, respectively.[38]

Finally, Kugelmass has adopted a similar position, namely, that the *'Amidah* was fashioned by the post-70 sages. Noting that the destruction of the Temple constituted a major turning point in Jewish history, he interprets the *'Amidah* as "a guilt-laden admission that

---

35. N. Cohen, "Shim'on Hapakuli's Act," 547–55.

36. Alon, *Jews in Their Land*, I, 267–71; Blidstein, "Individual and Communal Prayer," 256; M. Z. Fox, "Responses," 170. See also Heinemann, *Prayer*, 15–17; idem, *Studies*, 171–72.

37. Fleischer, "Beginnings of Obligatory Jewish Prayer," 426–41. On pre-70 worship, see above, Chap. 5.

38. Zahavy, "Three Stages," 233–65; idem, "Politics of Piety," 42–68; and esp. idem, *Studies in Jewish Prayer*. See also idem, "New Approach," 45–60. The above-noted theories of Cohen and Zahavy (on Fleischer, see below) are engaging but unconvincing. Cohen has no proof that such a prayer existed largely in its present form in Second Temple Judaea, and her understanding of the word הסדיר is conceivable, though far from compelling. Zahavy's theory, on the other hand, is an artificial distinction with no basis in the sources. There is simply no clear evidence of scribal or priestly activity having functioned thusly in Yavneh, nor is the connection between such hypothetical groups and the content of these prayers at all persuasive. One could just as easily make a case for the priestly origins of the *Shema'*, since these paragraphs were recited daily by priests in the Jerusalem Temple (M Tamid 5:1).

they [i.e., the Jews—L. L.] had recklessly abandoned the stipulations of the covenant that are expressed so vividly in the *Shemaʿ* that precedes it." [39]

Recent efforts notwithstanding, it appears that, in trying to fathom a complex reality in light of admittedly diffuse pieces of information, scholars are drawing conclusions far too sharply. It is therefore most refreshing that in the midst of this recent spate of studies which have tended to stake out rather unilateral positions, Reif has charted a more balanced and nuanced historical approach. Reckoning with the rich mosaic in public and private expressions of prayer in the first century C.E., Reif points to the delicate balance between variety and uniformity as well as continuity and creativity in the evolution of Jewish prayer from the Second Temple to the tannaitic eras.[40]

What is called for is an approach which takes into account not only the primary data that have been brought to bear on the subject, but also the ostensibly contradictory claims by scholars for the existence of a pre-70 communal prayer on the one hand and the purportedly far-reaching measures adopted in Yavneh on the other. Needless to say, an attempt to synthesize such data is not merely a question of setting them down side by side and somehow trying to create an amalgam; these views, in their present formulation, are clearly irreconcilable. However, recognizing the valid points in each of the approaches may enable us to integrate them into a plausible theory.

What, then, are these basic points of reference? First of all, there is no question that public prayer existed in pre-70 Judaea, but, as we have seen, the instances were restricted to specific circles.[41] Such was the case in Qumran, in the morning service of the priests in the Jerusalem Temple, perhaps among the Pharisees on Sabbaths and holidays, and, one might add, among the Therapeutae of Egypt, per Philo.[42] On the other hand, it is equally clear that public prayer (as distinct from prayer recited in public) did not exist in the ordinary community synagogue of pre-70 Judaea—whether in Jerusalem or the Galilee, or whether we consider Josephus, rabbinic literature, the New Testament, or archeological finds.

The sages of Yavneh did not work in a vacuum. The similarities between earlier Jewish literature and many motifs, sequences of ideas, and even overall structure in certain sections of the *ʿAmidah* make it crystal clear that the rabbis (or, should we say, Simeon Hapaquli) drew on a reservoir of earlier traditions and practices. Adopting phrases and ideas borrowed from scriptural verses (Neh. 9 or Ps. 103:2–6), perhaps from earlier Pharisaic practice (e.g., the dispute between Bet Hillel and Bet Shammai),[43] or from Ben

---

39. Kugelmass, "Jewish Liturgy," 289–301.

40. Reif, *Judaism and Hebrew Prayer*, 53–87.

41. See above, Chap. 5.

42. See his *Contemplative Life*.

43. T Berakhot 3:13 (p. 15); T Rosh Hashanah 2:17 (pp. 320–21); but see below, note 71. On the various theories regarding the origin of the *ʿAmidah*, see above, Chap. 5.

Sira was not a problem for the Yavnean sages. Interestingly, however, not all of the traditions which may have constituted potential sources for the 'Amidah stem from settings or groups with whom the rabbis would necessarily have wished to associate themselves. The priestly liturgy from the Temple and Qumran are cases in point.[44] How some of these ideas and formulations reached Yavneh is impossible to determine, though the fact that so many threads of different origins appear to have been interwoven is intriguing. It is reminiscent of the selection of very diverse books for inclusion in the Bible, or the confluence of so many contradictory opinions in R. Judah's Mishnah. Thus, we can assuredly posit a great deal of continuity in Jewish liturgy if we understand that this corpus evolved as a result of rabbis drawing significantly from earlier literary and nonliterary traditions. In other words, what they created was in some sense as much a continuation as it was an innovation.

Nevertheless, there is little question that something very new (for Palestine, at least) was developing in Yavneh as a result of the new circumstances and historical exigencies of the post-destruction period. However, it would be wholly gratuitous to assume that Rabban Gamaliel's initiatives brought about a sudden and total revolution by creating ex nihilo an obligatory prayer liturgy for individuals and community alike. It is most improbable that the prayers discussed by the rabbis took shape all at once or that they immediately became the normative practice among Jews. We will argue below that the creation of an obligatory daily worship framework in Yavneh was a dramatic initiative which required decades, even centuries, to reach some sort of final form.

On what basis can one claim, then, that a major breakthrough in the development of Jewish worship came in the post-70 period? Let us review the evidence leading to this conclusion.

Two sources attest explicitly to the innovative activity at Yavneh. The first is the above-quoted statement about Rabban Gamaliel and Simeon Hapaquli. It must be noted, however, that the rabbinic sources themselves have preserved conflicting traditions on this subject.[45] Thus, after reporting on Simeon Hapaquli's achievement, the Bavli itself questions the originality of that achievement, citing an alternative tradition claiming that the exact same work was carried out centuries earlier by 120 elders.[46] The response to this claim is revealing; after a digression, the Talmud reaffirms that Simeon's achievement was still revolutionary, for what had once existed had been completely forgotten, and Hapaquli restored the earlier practice.

---

44. On the liturgical elements from Qumran, see Weinfeld, "Traces of Qedushat Yoser," 15–26; idem, "Prayers for Knowledge, Repentance and Forgiveness," 186–200; idem, "Heavenly Praise," 427–37; idem, "Morning Prayers in Qumran," 481–94; Schiffman, "Dead Sea Scrolls and Jewish Liturgy," 33–48; idem, *Reclaiming*, 292–97.

45. See, for example, Sifre–Deuteronomy 343 (pp. 394–95); Y Berakhot 7, 4, 11c; B Berakhot 26b, 33a.

46. B Megillah 17b.

The second source deals with a dispute between Rabban Gamaliel and other Yavnean sages regarding what components of the *Amidah*, if any, ought to be considered fixed:

> Rabban Gamaliel says: "One must recite the *Shemoneh 'Esreh* [i.e., the *Amidah*] daily"; R. Joshua says: "[It suffices to recite] a shortened *Shemoneh 'Esreh* [מעין שמונה עשרה]." R. 'Aqiva says: "If one knows the prayer well [שגורה בפיו], he should recite the [entire] *Shemoneh 'Esreh*; if not, a shortened *Shemoneh 'Esreh*. R. Eli'ezer says: "One who makes his prayer fixed [קבע], his prayer is no longer a supplication."[47]

The span of ideas reflected in this source is wide. Rabban Gamaliel wished to institute a full recitation of the *Amidah*'s eighteen blessings, with set themes and a fixed order. R. Joshua advocated a shortened version of the above. What precisely he had in mind is unclear. The fact that, over a century later, sages had differing opinions regarding what exactly was meant by a "shortened *Shemoneh 'Esreh*" indicates the continued ambiguity.[48] R. 'Aqiva took a middle-of-the-road approach: recitation of a complete or shortened version should be dependent upon the knowledge of the particular individual. R. Eli'ezer, however, adopted a radically different position, opposing any imposition of a set framework.[49] The statement attributed to him juxtaposes two different, and seemingly contradictory, elements: fixed prayer and prayer as supplication. According to his view, the two do not mix. Prayer requires spontaneity, and any attempt at regimentation is self-defeating. This view is articulated by another Yavnean sage, R. Simeon b. Netanel, a student of R. Yoḥanan b. Zakkai, who is quoted as saying: "And when you pray, do not make your prayers fixed, but rather [a plea for mercies and] supplications before God."[50] Thus, between Rabban Gamaliel on the one hand and R. Eli'ezer and R. Simeon on the other, and taking into account the two middle positions, we have a wide spectrum of attitudes regarding this innovation, and little consensus appears to have existed at this juncture.

In addition to the above two sources, a number of discussions about prayers held by Rabban Gamaliel and his colleagues are best interpreted in light of the fact that the institution of obligatory prayer had been introduced only recently. These discussions appear

---

47. M Berakhot 4:3–4a.

48. See below, note 131.

49. M Berakhot 4:4a. Interpreting R. Eli'ezer's statement in conjunction with the previous mishnah was first suggested by R. Yehosef Ashkenazi in his commentary *Melekhet Shelomo*, loc. cit., and commented on by Lieberman, in *TK*, I, 31–32. Another statement by R. Eli'ezer reflects this same view as well: "Whenever you pray, know before Whom you stand" (B Berakhot 28b). See also the story of R. Eli'ezer, who appointed two students to lead the service; one was criticized for being brief (קצרן), the other for being long-winded (מארכן). R. Eli'ezer's reputed defense of his students was: "there is a time to be brief and there is a time to be expansive" (Mekhilta of R. Ishmael, Beshalaḥ, 1 [p. 155]). See also the anonymous statement in M Menaḥot 13:11 with regard to sacrifices: "Whether one brings a costly sacrifice or a modest one, what is important is that a person thinks of [God in] heaven."

50. M 'Avot 2:13.

to be a working-out of the implementation and ramifications of the new framework. Here are some examples.

(1) The dramatic dispute recorded in both the Yerushalmi and the Bavli between Rabban Gamaliel and R. Joshua in which the former was temporarily deposed is a case in point. The issue was whether the evening ʿAmidah should be considered obligatory[51] and can be best explained as having arisen in the context of deliberations over setting a fixed liturgy. The morning and afternoon prayers were less of an issue; they were to be considered substitutes for the Temple sacrifices and thus obligatory. However, in view of the fact that there was no evening sacrifice, the question naturally arose as to its obligatory nature, even though the precedent of praying three times a day was already known from biblical traditions.[52]

(2) Another disagreement between two of the above-noted Yavnean sages, R. Eliʿezer and R. Joshua, over the relationship between personal petitions and the regular ʿAmidah, is also best explained as the kind of issue that would surface with the institutionalization of the ʿAmidah: "It was taught: R. Eliʿezer says: 'One should first pray for his own needs and then pray [i.e., recite the ʿAmidah]. . . .' But R. Joshua says: 'One should first pray [i.e., recite the ʿAmidah] and then ask for his own needs. . . .' And the sages say: 'Neither according to the one or the other; rather, one should ask for his personal needs in the [ʿAmidah] benediction "Who hears prayer." ' "[53] Thus, both sages agreed that the ʿAmidah and prayers for personal needs should be said but not mixed; they disagreed, however, about the proper order: R. Eliʿezer preferred beginning with the personal supplication and ending with the ʿAmidah; R. Joshua, the opposite.[54] The sages carved out a different course, advocating that the two elements be combined: the personal requests should be integrated into the final, open-ended, petitionary blessing of the ʿAmidah's middle section.[55]

(3) The disagreement between Rabban Gamaliel and his colleagues over the primacy

---

51. B Berakhot 27b–28a; Y Berakhot 4, 1, 7c–d; Y Taʿanit 4, 1, 67d; and the analysis in Goldenberg, "Deposition of Rabban Gamaliel," 167–90.

52. Ps. 55:18; Dan. 6:11.

53. B ʿAvodah Zarah 7b–8a. See also Blidstein, "Individual and Communal Prayer," 257–61. The emphasis on more spontaneous, personal prayer is related to the issue of kavanah (כוונה, loosely understood as fixed attention or intent) in prayer, about which the rabbis were quite concerned. See the statement of R. Meir, "The validity of the words depends on the intent of the heart" (B Berakhot 15a); as well as Kadushin, Rabbinic Mind, 212–14; Heschel, Quest for God, 11–14.

54. There is no necessary contradiction between this source, in which R. Eliʿezer accepts the institution of the ʿAmidah, and the earlier tradition cited (above, note 47), where he objects to a fixed version. R. Eliʿezer's objection was not to reciting the ʿAmidah per se, but rather to the degree of standardization to which R. Gamaliel aspired.

55. An anonymous tradition in T Berakhot 3:6 (p. 13) agrees with R. Joshua: "No words [of praise and supplication; see Lieberman, TK, I, 31] should be said after the 'True and certain' blessing [i.e., גאולה]; but one may recite such words after the ʿAmidah, even as much as the Yom Kippur confession."

of the public or private recitation of the *'Amidah* likewise reflects a still inchoate state of affairs. Rabban Gamaliel claimed that the prayer leader's rendition of the *'Amidah* was the crucial recitation, while the sages claimed that the prayer of the individual was the decisive component, and the leader's recitation was intended only for those unable to pray on their own.[56]

(4) Rabban Gamaliel is reported to have turned to Samuel Haqatan, requesting him to compose a special prayer, or reformulate an existing one, that would curse informers and sectarians.[57] Presumably, with the framework of the *'Amidah* now fixed, the absence of such a reference was noted, and Rabban Gamaliel directed a member of his circle to deal with this issue.

(5) The additional *'Amidah* (*Mussaf*) appears to have had a rather unusual status at this early stage. R. Eli'ezer b. 'Azariah claimed that it should be recited only in an official communal framework (i.e., in the *ḥever ha-'ir*). Other sages disagreed, saying this prayer should be recited anywhere. R. Judah offered a third alternative: whenever it is said by the *ḥever ha-'ir*, individuals in the same locale are exempt from saying it.[58] Thus, the first stage of introducing an obligatory *'Amidah* seems the most logical backdrop to the ambiguous status of the *Mussaf 'Amidah*; details still had to be fully worked out.

(6) The third-century R. Joshua b. Levi (or, in a parallel tradition: the sages) offers the explanation that the thrice-daily recitation of the *'Amidah* was intended as a substitute for sacrificial worship at the Temple. Though almost two centuries removed from the Temple's destruction, this view attests to an amoraic tradition that communal prayer was created in the Yavnean period.[59] Moreover, Sifre–Deuteronomy explicitly compares prayer (i.e., the *'Amidah*) to sacrifices; just as the latter are referred to as worship (*'avodah*), so, too, are the former.[60] Perhaps this view of the *'Amidah* is likewise based on the assumption that it served as a substitute for sacrifices, thus pointing to a date soon after 70 for its creation.[61]

---

56. M Rosh Hashanah 4:9; and esp. T Rosh Hashanah 2:18 (p. 321). See also the comments in Blidstein, "Sheliach Tzibbur," 69–77. The difference between R. Gamaliel and his colleagues parallels the contrasting emphases in pagan and Christian prayer; the former tended to be public and spoken aloud, the latter private and personal (per Matt. 6:6).

57. B Berakhot 28b. On the problematic historicity of this attribution, see Kimelman, "Birkat Ha-Minim," 226–44; Hirshman, "Shmuel ha-Katan," 165–72.

58. M Berakhot 4:7. *Ḥever ha-'ir* seems to have disappeared by the third century. It is rarely mentioned in material relating to the amoraic period, and R. Yoḥanan explicitly says that it did not exist in Sepphoris in his day (Y Berakhot 4, 6, 8c).

59. B Berakhot 26b; Y Berakhot 4, 1, 7b. Other suggestions link the *'Amidah* with (1) the biblical patriarchs—Genesis Rabbah 68:9 (pp. 778–80); 69:4 (p. 793); Y Berakhot 4, 3, 8a; Y Ta'anit 2, 2, 65c; Midrash Hagadol, Genesis 28:13 (p. 505); and (2) Ps. 29—T Berakhot 3:25 (pp. 17–18). For further explanations, see Midrash Hagadol, Exodus 40:32 (p. 789); Midrash on Psalms 19:22 (p. 82b).

60. Sifre–Deuteronomy 41 (p. 88).

61. Alternatively, this statement might be interpreted as reflecting a pre-70 setting, emphasizing the

Assuming such a revolutionary attempt on the part of Rabban Gamaliel is consistent with what we know of the man and his vigorous leadership;[62] this would not be the only instance in which he and his colleagues demonstrate an active and creative posture in liturgical matters. Let me cite two instances of Yavnean initiative.

The first concerns Passover. Together with his Yavnean colleagues, Rabban Gamaliel appears to have been largely responsible for creating the Passover *seder* ritual we know today. Little of what appears in the *seder* liturgy as reflected in the last chapters of Mishnah and Tosefta Pesaḥim or the Passover Haggadah (which, of course, was redacted much later)[63] is known to have existed prior to the year 70. An analysis of the above-noted sources indicates that the Yavnean sages were the ones who gave shape and substance to this liturgical home ceremony, which was created to fill the void resulting from the destruction of the Temple.[64] The Passover celebration in the Second Temple period had been intimately connected with the paschal sacrifice, which was eaten in a family setting either within the Temple precincts or elsewhere in Jerusalem. With the Temple's destruction, a vacuum was created, and the Yavnean sages aimed to fill it by implementing a newly reconstituted liturgy, parts of which were known from before but which now underwent extensive revision and enlargement—as was the case with the *'Amidah*.

The second instance of Yavnean liturgical creativity is evident in the High Holiday liturgy, which also appears to have been crafted under rabbinic auspices. Little is known about a Rosh Hashanah liturgy in the pre-70 period, and the entire ritual of Yom Kippur seems to have revolved around the Temple and the high priest. The core of the rabbinic High Holiday liturgy was in the *Mussaf 'Amidah*, where the themes of kingship, remembrance, and *shofarot* (i.e., redemption) are highlighted. There is every reason to believe that the latter two themes were known earlier and may have even functioned liturgically in certain Jewish contexts. If the fast-day ceremonies described in Mishnah Ta'anit reflect Second Temple practice, then we have evidence of the themes of remembrance and redemption in this early period.[65] These same two themes appear elsewhere in Second Temple sources. Jubilees knows of the remembrance theme associated with the first day of the seventh month and the figure of Noah (thus anticipating later rabbinic High Holiday liturgy), and Philo emphasizes the redemption motif when discussing Rosh Hasha-

---

importance of prayer even while sacrifices were still being offered. See Acts 3:1.

The account of the second-century R. Eli'ezer Ḥismeh learning how to lead public prayers is as fascinating as it is problematic. The story appears in a later midrash (Leviticus Rabbah 23:4 [pp. 531-32]) and is clearly etiological in character. Thus, its historical value for the second century is considerably mitigated.

62. See Alon, *Jews in Their Land*, I, 119-322; Goodblatt, *Monarchic Principle*, 176-231.

63. On the later redaction of the Haggadah, see L. A. Hoffman, *Canonization*, 10-23; Goldschmidt, *Passover Haggadah*, passim.

64. See Alon, *Jews in Their Land*, I, 262-65 and esp. n. 32; S. Stein, "Influence of Symposia Literature," 13-44. See also Bokser, *Origins of the Seder*, 67-100.

65. M Ta'anit 2:3-4.

nah.[66] The Yavnean sages seem to have incorporated these themes into their High Holiday liturgy, adding the third component, kingship, to form a trilogy.[67]

On the basis of the above evidence, there can be little doubt that obligatory daily prayer —both personal and communal—was first conceived in the post-70 period under the auspices of Rabban Gamaliel. On the one hand, as noted, these prayers were not created ex nihilo. There were many precedents, and the Yavnean *tannaim* incorporated earlier materials,[68] reworking, reformulating, and restructuring them so as to fashion a prayer which they sought to make obligatory for Jews everywhere, as a community and as individuals.

On the other hand, as has been recognized for generations, and has received particular emphasis in the writings of Heinemann, the prayer formulas of the *'Amidah* and *Shema'* benedictions (on the latter, see below) which began in Yavneh were not etched in stone. As regards the *'Amidah*, for example, what was promulgated in Yavneh involved the overall framework, sequential topics, and the number of blessings.[69] These elements were fleshed out over time; the Tosefta says that certain competing themes should be combined, thus indicating that various combinations of themes were still being recited: "The eighteen benedictions that the sages fixed are parallel to [the use of the Divine name in Psalm 29], "Give praise to the Lord, sons of gods. . . ." One should incorporate [the reference to] heretics [מינים] in [the blessing about] sectarians [פרושין], proselytes in [the blessing relating to] elders, and David in 'He Who builds Jerusalem.' "[70]

Before concluding this discussion of the *'Amidah* prayer, let us consider several important caveats. In the first place, for all the innovation of the Yavnean generation of sages, we must remember that what has been discussed in these sources was the daily prayer— the *Shemoneh 'Esreh*, or eighteen benedictions. In terms of the Pharisaic-rabbinic tradition, the Sabbath and holiday *'Amidah* may have already been known and practiced by Bet Hillel and Bet Shammai in the first century, although the tradition attesting to this is problematic.[71] If its historicity is granted, then within their own Pharisaic-rabbinic

---

66. Jubilees 6:23-31; Philo, *Special Laws* 2, 188-92.

67. In this we follow the opinion of Finkelstein ("Development of the Amidah," 17-18; idem, *Akiba*, 312), Gilat (*R. Eliezer ben Hyrcanus*, 284-86), and Heinemann, in his early writings (the Hebrew version of his *Prayer*, 61-62; "Melekh ha-'olam," 177-79; *Studies*, 55 n. 6). This would go hand in hand with the suggested addition of the word "king" (מלך) to benedictions in the post-70 era. In support of an earlier, Second Temple origin of the kingship motif, see Büchler, *Jewish Palestinian Piety*, 241ff.; and the later Heinemann, *Studies*, 44-53; idem, *Prayer*, 94-95.

68. See Blenkinsopp, "Second Temple as House of Prayer," 109-22.

69. Heinemann, *Prayer*, 23-30.

70. T Berakhot 3:25 (pp. 17-18). See also Shinan, "Literature of the Ancient Synagogue," 143-44. Toward the end of the third century, R. Abbahu, in the name of R. El'azar, defines the proper place in the High Holiday liturgy for the inclusion of a certain prayer (Y Rosh Hashanah 4, 6, 59c). On the internal logic of the *'Amidah*, most scholars have adopted Maimonides' distinction of praise-request-thanks (*Laws of Prayer* 1:2 and 4); cf., however, Kimelman, "Daily 'Amidah," 165-97, and the bibliography cited therein.

71. T Rosh Hashanah 2:17 (p. 320): "When the New Year holiday falls on the Sabbath, Bet Shammai

circles, Rabban Gamaliel and his colleagues expanded a known practice to the weekday—
a not insignificant move, yet, at the same time, one that was not totally revolutionary.

Having said this, however, let me say that it is also true that vis-à-vis Jewish society
generally, these Yavnean sages were taking a very significant step in obligating every
Jew to recite weekday prayers, and this certainly meant (although it was admittedly not
stated) Sabbath and holiday prayers as well. Moreover, much of the discussion in Mishnah
Berakhot seems to deal with the obligation of prayer, regardless of where it was carried
out. Very little is said of prayer in a public setting. One might, therefore, gain the impression that synagogue worship was almost entirely irrelevant or superfluous. It is only
in other tannaitic sources that the importance and centrality of public prayer, presumably in the synagogue, are emphasized.[72]

---

says, 'One is to recite ten [blessings in the *'Amidah*],' and Bet Hillel says, 'One is to recite nine.' When a
festival falls on the Sabbath, Bet Shammai says: 'One is to recite eight, and [the blessing] of the Sabbath
[is to be said] separately, and that for the festival separately, and one begins with that of the Sabbath.'
And [conversely] Bet Hillel says: 'One is to recite seven, and begins with the Sabbath and ends with the
Sabbath, and says the "Sanctification of the Day" in the middle.'"

"Bet Hillel said to Bet Shammai: 'And was it not in the presence of all of you, Elders of Bet Shammai, that Ḥoni Haqatan went down [i.e., led the *'Amidah*] and said seven [blessings, i.e., thus following
our opinion], and everyone there [lit., all the people] said to him: 'You did well [lit., you should be sat-
isfied]?'"

"Bet Shammai said to them [Bet Hillel]: 'It was a time when one should have been brief.' Bet Hillel said
to them: 'If indeed it was a time to be brief, he [Ḥoni Haqatan] should have abbreviated all of the blessings
(and not have omitted one blessing, which then would have followed your opinion).'" See also T Berakhot
3:13 (p. 15); and comments in Lieberman, *TK*, I 41; V, 1062–63; Neusner, *Rabbinic Traditions*, II, 181–82.

The case for the historical reliability of the above tradition rests on the following: (1) the dispute
is clearly attributed to Bet Hillel and Bet Shammai; (2) it is highlighted by the repartee between the
two schools; and (3) the reference is to a specific event involving the main issue under discussion. On
the other hand, there is no attestation to this tradition: (1) it is quoted anonymously, and the only sage
mentioned is R. Judah I (ca. 200 C.E.), at the end of the Berakhot version (Ḥoni Haqatan does not appear in this context); (2) the exchange between the two schools is very likely a late addition; (3) no
similar discussion involving liturgical issues is ever noted for Pharisaic circles in the pre-70 era; (4) the
questions addressed (Sabbath, holiday, and High Holiday *'Amidah*, blessings, Sanctification of the Day,
"descending" to lead in prayer) are issues and terms which figure prominently only in second-century
C.E. tannaitic discussions (see above, note 67); and (5) as J. N. Epstein has shown, in several instances,
disputes or opinions of Yavnean sages (e.g., R. Joshua and R. Eli'ezer) were recast and attributed to Bet
Hillel and Bet Shammai (*Introduction to Tannaitic Literature*, 60–61). See also the comments in Urbach,
World of the Sages, 68 n. 7. Thus, this text either preserves a unique and important tradition reflecting the
existence of the Sabbath and holiday *'Amidah* in the pre-70 era within Pharisaic circles, or it is an anachronistic tradition, attributing to Bet Hillel and Bet Shammai the concerns and disputes of the Yavnean
generation. At present, the issue remains moot.

72. See below, notes 106 and 107. See also Fleisher, "Annual and Triennial Torah Reading," 35–37, 43.

The *Shema*

The second basic component of Jewish prayer at this time was the *Shema* and its accompanying blessings.[73] The rabbis in this case adopted a tradition that was clearly Temple-based. However, the sages were not satisfied with mere adoption; they set about to supplement, amplify, and even eliminate some of the paragraphs preceding and following the three biblical passages which constitute the *Shema*.[74] As noted above, the Mishnah reports that the prayer service recited in the Temple every morning was composed of four parts: (1) a call for reciting a blessing and its recitation; (2) recitation of the Decalogue; (3) three paragraphs from Deuteronomy and Numbers; and (4) three blessings for the people. The mishnah reads as follows: "He who was in charge said to them [the priests], "Recite one blessing," and they recited it. They [then] read the Decalogue, "*Shema*" [Deut. 6:4–9], "And it will be if you listen" [ibid., 11:13–21], "And He said" [Num. 15:37–41]. They blessed the people with three blessings: "True and certain," the Temple service, and the priestly blessing. On the Sabbath, they added a blessing for the outgoing [priestly] course."[75]

Assuming the veracity of this report,[76] the sages consciously reworked this Temple-prayer unit, transforming it into an integral part of the daily prayer ritual they were promoting. The three Pentateuchal paragraphs retained their centrality, although why precisely these three passages had been selected in the first place and why they were presented in this particular order is unclear.[77] No fully satisfactory explanation has been offered thus far.

The relationship between the three paragraphs according to the Mishnah is both ideological and technical. The ideological component characterizes the link between the first two paragraphs: a person first accepts the yoke of God's kingdom and then the yoke of His commandments. The tie between the second and third is more technical in nature; the second paragraph deals with commandments relevant to both day and night, the third

---

73. Some traditions clearly gave priority to the recitation of the *Shema* over other prayers; see, for example, M Shabbat 1:2; Y Sheqalim 3, 4, 47c. See also T Berakhot 3:19 (p. 16).

74. See Avery-Peck, "Judaism without Temple," 416–17. For another example of adapting Temple practice, see above, note 31.

75. M Tamid 5:1. According to one rabbinic tradition, whose historical accuracy in this regard is questionable, priests would also recite Deut. 32 at the Sabbath *Mussaf* sacrifice (B Rosh Hashanah 31a; see also Y Megillah 3, 7, 74b; Tractate Soferim 12:7 [pp. 231–32]).

76. For a skeptical view regarding the reliability of this tradition, see Fleischer, "Beginnings of Obligatory Jewish Prayer," 420–21.

77. It is not even clear whether all three paragraphs were selected at the same time or on different occasions. The Nash papyrus preserves only the first two sentences of the *Shema* (Deut. 6:4–5) in addition to the Decalogue (an apparent composite of the Exodus and Deuteronomy versions); see M. Z. Segal, "Nash Papyrus," 27–36. It is also not clear whether this papyrus reflects liturgical practice; perhaps it was intended for inclusion in a *mezuzah* or *tefillin*. Cf. Fleischer, *Prayer and Prayer Rituals*, 259 n. 1.

only to daytime commandments.[78] A widely accepted view today is that the three blessings preceding and following the *Shema'* focus on the three basic themes of creation, revelation, and redemption, and some have gone further to suggest that the three biblical paragraphs may be understood in this light as well.[79]

Thus, building on the Temple liturgy as described in Mishnah Tamid, the sages added a second blessing before the *Shema'* (and possibly changed the content of the first, which is left undefined in the Mishnah) while developing the above-noted three basic themes. Moreover, the Decalogue was eliminated—possibly by the sages themselves, but of this we cannot be sure—despite the fact that the Decalogue-*Shema'* combination appears to have been widely used in the late Second Temple period. They appear together (though not always contiguously), first in Deuteronomy (5–6) and then in the Nash papyrus from Hellenistic Egypt (fig. 88), *tefillin* from Qumran, and the above-noted morning priestly prayer from the Temple.[80] The coupling of the *Shema'* and the Decalogue remains enigmatic. Weinfeld opines that they parallel ancient Near Eastern loyalty oaths and vassal treaties, similar to those found in connection with Nabonidus and Esarhaddon, while Goldstein suggests that they are similar to the oath (*sacramentum*) taken by a Roman soldier in allegiance to the emperor.[81] Although later, amoraic explanations attribute the elimination of the Decalogue to an attempt to counter sectarian polemics, the associa-

---

78. M Berakhot 2:2; B Berakhot 14b. Nevertheless, M Berakhot 1:5 seems to indicate that the third paragraph was related to the Exodus theme or, if you will, redemption. See the rationale of descending importance offered by R. Simeon Bar Yoḥai in Sifre–Numbers 115 (p. 126). See also Mekhilta of R. Ishmael, Baḥodesh 6 (pp. 222–23); B Berakhot 14b. Maimonides (*Laws of Torah-Reading* 1:2), on the other hand, suggests that the third paragraph (Num. 15:38–41) is intended to serve as a reminder to fulfill all the commandments (via the fringes noted therein), a suggestion that makes a great deal of sense. We would add, from a literary point of view, that this section concludes with verse 41, which is very reminiscent of the opening of the Decalogue (Ex. 20:2; Deut. 5:6). Perhaps for this reason as well it was chosen to conclude the four-part series of Torah selections. See also the comments of Levenson, *Sinai and Zion*, 80–86.

79. Heinemann, *Prayer*, 33–36; Petuchowski, "Liturgy of the Synagogue," 49; Heinemann and Petuchowski, *Literature of the Synagogue*, 15–21; and Rotenstreich, *Jewish Philosophy*, 186–215; and especially Kimelman, "Šĕma' and Its Blessings," 73–86; idem, "Case for Creation, Revelation, and Redemption," 170–92; idem, "Shema' and Its Rhetoric," 111–56, and literature cited therein. For reservations regarding this triad of themes in the blessings section, see Shinan, "Redeemer and Redemption," 61–63. For attempts to see these themes as already existent in the biblical passages, and thus influencing the selection of the *Shema'* paragraphs, see Liebreich, "Impact of Nehemiah 9:5–37," 228–32 (Neh. 9:6–11); Mirsky, *Piyyut*, 11–17 (Ps. 19).

80. Albright, "Biblical Fragment," 145–76; Tcherikover et al., *CPJ*, I, 107 n. 48; Yadin, *Tefillin from Qumran*, 23–29; E. P. Sanders, *Jewish Law*, 68–70. On the question whether the *Shema'* and the Decalogue may have been part of early Christian liturgy in Bithynia, see Kimelman, "Note on Weinfeld's 'Grace After Meals'," 695–96, and literature cited therein.

81. Weinfeld, *Deuteronomy*, 352–54; Goldstein, *I Maccabees*, 133 n. 171. Kohler (*Origins of Synagogue and Church*, 56–57), focusing on the *Shema'* passage alone (Deut. 6:4), suggests that it was used as a protest against Persian dualism. See also Weinfeld, "Uniqueness of the Decalogue," 27–34.

88. Nash Papyrus containing
part of the Ten Commandments
and the *Shemaʿ*.

tion of the *Shemaʿ* with the Decalogue nevertheless continues in a number of rabbinic expositions, as well as in later Palestinian synagogue traditions.[82]

The formulation of the three paragraphs surrounding the *Shemaʿ* was far from fixed either in tannaitic times or later. A number of versions seem to have been in circulation. For example, although the benediction following the *Shemaʿ* was to deal with redemption, its central theme was not set at the outset, and a number of different historical references were being used by the turn of the third century: "He who reads the *Shemaʿ* must mention the Exodus from Egypt in [the paragraph] 'True and certain.' Rabbi [Judah I] says: 'He must mention [God's] sovereignty.' Others say: 'He must mention the slaying of the firstborn and the splitting of the sea.'"[83]

---

82. B Berakhot 12a; Y Berakhot 1, 5, 3c; and Ginzberg, *Commentary*, I, 166–67; Baron, *Social and Religious History of the Jews*, II, 134–35. See also Kimelman, "Shemaʿ and Its Rhetoric," 135–43; idem, "Shema and Amidah," 110. For later rabbinic references, see Y Megillah 3, 8, 74b; 4, 2, 75a; as well as comments in Urbach, "Role of Ten Commandments," 182–89; Vermes, "Decalogue and Minim," 232–40. On the Decalogue in early Christianity, see R. M. Grant, "Decalogue," 1–17; and, in later Jewish tradition, Fleischer, *Prayer and Prayer Rituals*, 259–74. The elimination of the Decalogue may have something to do with internal Jewish polemics; see Yalqut Shimʿoni, Numbers, 752 (p. 327).

83. T Berakhot 2:1 (p. 6); Y Berakhot 1, 6, 3d; Exodus Rabbah 22:3. For other examples of variant customs practiced at this time, see T Berakhot 1:5 (p. 3).

Just as the *'Amidah* was to be recited in a very particular way, first by individuals and then by the prayer leader, so, too, the *Shema'* was to be recited in a fixed way: antiphonally, or responsively—what is referred to in rabbinic literature as פרס על [את] שמע. This practice is noted in several sources, particularly in the context of a tannaitic discussion about the singing of the Song of the Sea by the Israelites fleeing Egypt. All the discussants agree that the song itself was recited responsively, but they differ as to how this was done.[84] The Tosefta describes the various proposals as follows: the Israelites would repeat Moses' words phrase by phrase as would a pupil reciting the *Hallel* in school (R. 'Aqiva); the people would repeat the opening refrain each time as would one reciting the *Hallel* in the synagogue (R. El'azar, son of R. Yosi the Galilean); they would respond as would the people reciting the *Shema'* in the synagogue, where the congregation and prayer leader recite alternate verses aloud (R. Nehemiah).[85] To complicate matters, however, the Bavli describes these views differently, particularly with regard to the *Shema'* analogy: R. Nehemiah is of the opinion that the recitation of the Song of the Sea was like that of a teacher reciting the *Shema'* in the synagogue (with his pupils)—he begins and they reply after him. The Talmud understands this to mean that after reciting the opening section of the *Shema'* (including its blessings?) responsively, they recite everything else in unison.[86]

Thus, much remains unclear. How many of these paragraphs were recited responsively we do not know—only the first verse, i.e., the *Shema'* itself? the entire first paragraph? all three biblical sections? Or were they perhaps recited together with the accompanying blessings?[87] Furthermore, it is not clear how the recitation was to be carried out—responsively verse by verse or by half verses, or perhaps with the congregation repeating what the reader said. Nor is it clear whether this responsive recitation was intended for Sabbaths and holidays only (as seems likely) or for weekdays as well.[88]

Other Liturgical Developments

In other areas, synagogue ritual appears to have been enriched in the late first century and later by the transference to its domain of a series of customs formerly associated primarily, if not exclusively, with the Temple. R. Yoḥanan b. Zakkai's famous *taqqanot* (enactments) were intended, in part, to universalize certain Temple practices in order to perpetuate that institution's memory and fill the ritual void left by its destruction. This is

---

84. Bacher, "L'expression 'פרס על שמע,' " 100–102; Elbogen, "Studies in Jewish Liturgy," 587–99, 229–34; idem, *Jewish Liturgy*, 24, 392 n. 24; Finkelstein, "Meaning of the Word פרס (1)," 387–406; ibid. (2), 29–48; Fleischer, "Clarification of 'Poreis 'al Shema','" 133–44; Knohl, "Accepting the Kingdom of Heaven," 11–15; Kimelman, "Case for Creation, Revelation, and Redemption," 182–84. Cf., however, Kohler, *Origins of Synagogue and Church*, 58.

85. T Sotah 6:2–3 (pp. 183–84); and Lieberman, *TK*, VIII, 667–68.

86. B Sotah 30b. Y Sotah 5, 6, 20c, does not mention R. Nehemiah's opinion at all.

87. See above, note 84.

88. On congregational responses generally, see Werner, *Sacred Bridge* (1959 ed.), 508–20; and below.

the reason behind the blowing of the shofar on the Sabbath of Rosh Hashanah, using the *lulav* for the entire Sukkot holiday, and having the priests bless the synagogue congregation—all were once performed in the Temple.[89] Major holidays, including *Rosh Ḥodesh* and Hanukkah, were celebrated with the recitation of the *Hallel* (Pss. 113-18), a custom originating in the levitical Temple service.[90]

One major issue largely overlooked (or perhaps taken for granted) in the past is the relationship between these rabbinic enactments and actual synagogue practice. We have already considered this question with regard to Torah-reading, which had been well ensconced in the Jewish world for generations, and we may likewise address this issue with regard to obligatory prayers, whose introduction was clearly spearheaded by the second-century sages: Were these rabbinic dicta immediately implemented in local synagogue practice, or did they penetrate only very gradually? That rabbinic circles themselves were affected by these decisions is obvious; beyond this, however, we are hard pressed to make any assured determination.

Recent studies have indicated that there is little evidence that rabbinic authority was widely recognized during this period, or that second-century sages usually addressed major social, political, or religious issues or institutions of their day.[91] In fact, rabbinic sources make no claim, either directly or indirectly, that the sages had any significant influence whatsoever over synagogue practice. The Mishnah and Tosefta mention the synagogue only infrequently, a most surprising fact given the institution's centrality in Jewish life. When the synagogue is noted, however, it is often in connection with its communal role; only a minority of references to the synagogue in the Mishnah deal with ritual (four out of nine), and of these, only two relate to prayer.[92] The Tosefta reflects a similar situation. Eleven out of twenty-five pericopae deal with ritual, and only four of these deal directly with prayer.[93]

Moreover, when prayer and its content, structure, and setting are, in fact, discussed, the synagogue is almost entirely ignored. Rabbinic references to prayer in the Mishnah and Tosefta clearly address religious acts to be practiced by either the individual or

---

89. M Rosh Hashanah 4:1, 3; M Sukkah 3:12; B Rosh Hashanah 31b. In contrast to the usual historical credibility accorded these traditions, see the thoughtful remarks of Jaffee on the *taqqanah* as a literary genre and its use in the Mishnah ("Taqqanah," 204-25, and the comprehensive bibliography cited there). Nevertheless, with regard to Yoḥanan b. Zakkai (in contrast to earlier Second Temple figures mentioned by Jaffee), it would appear that such traditions, however stylized their formulation, probably reflect the reality of the immediate post-70 period and the goals of many, if not most, rabbis (see ibid., 210).

90. On the inclusion of the *Hallel* in post-70 holiday worship, see M Rosh Hashanah 4:7; T Pesaḥim 10:6-8 (p. 197); T Sukkah 3:2 (p. 266); T Sotah 6:3 (p. 183); see also M Taʿanit 4:4.

91. Goodman, *State and Society*, 93-118; S. J. D. Cohen, "Place of the Rabbi," 157-73; L. Levine, *Rabbinic Class*, 23-33.

92. Kasovsky, *Thesaurus Mishnae*, I, 366-67.

93. Kasovsky, *Thesaurus Thosephthae*, II, 102.

the community through specific formulas, at a proper time, and in some cases almost anywhere, e.g., when a worker finds himself laboring in a tree or erecting a wall.[94] It is interesting to note that the sages were rather flexible regarding the language in which these prayers were to be recited. The two central prayers, the ʿAmidah and Shemaʿ, could be recited in any language; only the priestly benediction had to be rendered in Hebrew. The Torah and haftarah seem to have been translated into the vernacular as a matter of course.[95]

Moreover, even were we to assume that second-century rabbinic sources correlate with contemporary synagogue ritual, it is not at all clear who was ultimately responsible for these practices. As with the Torah-reading ceremony, were the rabbis reacting to some generally observed practices, or were these developments, in fact, rabbinic initiatives in an as yet uncharted sea? An example of rabbinic involvement in a well-known communal setting may be reflected in the fast-day ceremony depicted in Mishnah Taʿanit. The events described appear to have been "popular" in nature, with no particular rabbinic standing or authorization required. Fast-day ceremonies were universal in different cultures, and not a few practices described in the Mishnah are strikingly reminiscent of other peoples and places.[96] The prayers as described were led not by a sage (חכם), but by an "elder and one used to functioning in this manner [זקן ורגיל]." [97]

Two incidents cited by the Yerushalmi give us some sense of this amorphous state within the general community regarding obligatory prayer. The passage reads as follows: "Rabbi [Judah I] ordered Avadan, his amora [one who related the sage's words to those assembled]: 'Tell the audience, "Whoever is wont to pray should say the evening ʿAmidah while it is still day."' R. Ḥiyya b. Vava ordered his amora: 'Announce to the audience: "Whoever is wont to pray should say the evening ʿAmidah while it is still day."'"[98] The setting of the above incidents, whether the academy or the synagogue, is not at all certain. What is clear, however, is that the recitation of the evening ʿAmidah was not practiced by all, thus necessitating the announcement. As noted above, the evening ʿAmidah had an ambiguous status among the rabbis, as the controversy between R. Joshua and Rabban Gamaliel clearly demonstrates, and this situation may have led to alternative practices. Nevertheless, all other rabbinic sources in this regard seem to posit that whatever its ha-lakhic status, the evening ʿAmidah was an accepted practice, at least in rabbinic circles.[99] Thus, these announcements would seem to indicate that not everyone followed rabbinic behavior in this regard.

---

94. M Berakhot 2:4; B Berakhot 6ob.

95. M Sotah 7:1–2.

96. See, for example, the description in Tertullian, *On Fasting* 16. See also Josephus, *Against Apion* 2, 282.

97. M Taʿanit 2:1–2.

98. Y Berakhot 4, 1, 7c.

99. B Berakhot 4b (R. Yoḥanan and R. Joshua b. Levi); B Yoma 87b (Rav).

Moreover, tannaitic sources make mention of synagogues that were not at all responsive to rabbinic teachings. On several occasions, the Mishnah protests synagogue practices which, in rabbinic eyes, were aesthetically unbecoming or religiously problematic. Forms of dress, deviant liturgical formulations, and the shape and use of *tefillin* are among the issues criticized by the sages.[100] Presumably, these practices were serious and widespread enough to evoke rabbinic responses and to be mentioned in the Mishnah. Even within rabbinic circles, differing practices might become a source of friction and irritation. Several second-century Galilean sages, R. Ḥalafta and R. Ḥanina b. Teradion, adopted one or more fast-day practices which clearly offended their colleagues.[101]

Despite all the significant innovations over these generations, it would seem that the prayer component, and not just the *'Amidah*, was still, in many respects, rather fluid. The structure of the special additions to the High Holiday liturgy remained a subject of controversy throughout this period, and these differences might not have been just local but regional as well.[102] Even the status of Rosh Hashanah as a one- or two-day holiday seems to have been an issue, and there may have been varying customs in this regard in different locales or at different times.[103]

At some point in the course of the second century, there appears to have been a move toward combining the *Shema'* and *'Amidah* into one prayer service in both morning and evening.[104] Here, however, the sages made a clear-cut distinction. While they were willing to consider the recitation of the morning *Shema'* in the synagogue as fulfilling one's obligation of saying it upon awaking, this was not true with regard to the evening *Shema'*, which had to be recited upon retiring.[105] It was left to the third-century R. Yoḥanan to take a further step, advocating that the evening *Shema'* be combined with the *'Amidah* as well (see below).

The contours of synagogue liturgy as it evolved in the second century may well be reflected in several tannaitic sources which speak of those liturgical elements requiring a quorum of ten men, a *minyan*. The Mishnah speaks in the following vein: "We do not recite the *Shema'* responsively [as a congregation], nor [have the prayer leader] pass be-

---

100. M Berakhot 5:3; M Megillah 4:8–9; T Berakhot 6:20 (p. 39).

101. M Ta'anit 2:5; T Ta'anit 1:13 (pp. 327–28).

102. T Rosh Hashanah 2:11 (pp. 316–17); Y Rosh Hashanah 4, 6, 59c.

103. *One day:* M Megillah 3:5; T Megillah 3:6 (p. 354); B Megillah 31a; Tractate Soferim 17:5 (p. 302). *Two days:* M 'Eruvin 3:7–9; Y 'Eruvin 3, 21c. See Zeitlin, *Rise and Fall of the Judaean State*, I, 236–37; idem, "Second Day of Rosh Ha-Shanah," 326–29; Petuchowski, "Liturgy of the Synagogue," 53–54; as well as the interchange between Fleischer ("List of Yearly Holidays," 249–53; idem, "Celebration of *Rosh Hashana*," 293–95) and Herr ("Matters of Palestinian Halakha," 76–80; idem, "Two Days of *Rosh Hashanah*," 142–43).

104. See Elbogen, *Jewish Liturgy*, 202–5. On the theme of redemption which may unite these two units, see Kimelman, "Literary Structure," 214–16.

105. Y Berakhot 1, 1, 2a.

fore the ark [i.e., recite the *Amidah*], nor [have the priests] lift their hands [in blessing], nor read the Torah, nor recite the haftarah . . . with fewer than ten." [106]

A *baraita* expands on this list in a somewhat different vein: "As was taught [in the Mishnah]: We do not recite the *Shemaʿ* responsively with fewer than ten men [present]. If we begin with ten and some leave, one completes [the recitation]. We do not recite the *Amidah* congregationally with fewer than ten; if we begin with ten and some leave, one completes [the *Amidah*]. We do not recite the priestly blessing with less than ten; if we begin [with ten] and some leave, one completes [the benediction]. We do not read the Torah with less than ten; if we begin [with ten] and some leave, one completes [the reading]. We do not recite the haftarah with less than ten; if we begin [with ten] and some leave, we complete [the reading]." [107]

Thus, by the end of the second century, the rabbinic Sabbath and holiday liturgy seems to have featured five elements, three of which occurred daily, one weekly, and one several times a week. The *Shemaʿ*, *Amidah*, and priestly blessing (included as part of the *Amidah* but singled out owing to its uniqueness and importance) constituted the basic liturgical framework, with the Torah-reading supplementing this basic ritual twice on the Sabbath (morning and afternoon) and once on Monday and Thursday. Reading the haftarah was a Sabbath and holiday addition. Elsewhere in the Mishnah, a similar listing appears, minus the reading of Scriptures, which was dealt with in previous and subsequent paragraphs. The following mishnah seems to imply that one could often fulfill all the above functions at any one service: "He who recites the passage from the Prophets leads in the recitation of the *Shemaʿ* and leads the congregation in the *Amidah*, and raises his hands [in blessing]." [108]

To these lists we should add prayers such as the *Hallel* for holidays as well as private penitential prayers, which, in rabbinic circles at least, appear to have been fairly widespread.[109] Moreover, there were a number of short responses which were used in the liturgy, although we cannot be sure of their precise context. Sifre–Deuteronomy lists a number of these. Following the formal call to prayer, "Praise the Lord Who is blessed"

---

106. M Megillah 4:3. See also Tractate Soferim 10:6 (pp. 212–14); Yalqut Shimʿoni, Leviticus, 643 (p. 700).

107. Y Megillah 4, 4, 75a. Pesiqta Rabbati 40 (p. 167b) adds one further element: "When one arises, he immediately goes to the synagogue and recites the *Shemaʿ*, the *Amidah*, listens to the Torah, and listens to the elder [preach]."

108. M Megillah 4:5. What is most unusual in this listing is the reference to the priestly benediction. Since only priests could offer this blessing, either this mishnah assumes that priests usually led the prayers, or the intent here is that the prayer leader would recite the priestly benediction along with the priest. Elbogen interprets this source as indicating that one capable of doing one thing can do the others as well, an interesting but not persuasive interpretation ("Studies in Jewish Liturgy," 599).

109. See above, note 90. On private prayers, see Y Berakhot 1, 5, 3d; B Berakhot 16b–17a, 60b; see also T Berakhot 3:5–6 (pp. 12–13); and comments in Lieberman, *TK*, I, 29, 31.

[ברכו את ה׳ המבורך], the congregation responded, "Praised is the blessed Lord forever" [ברוך ה׳ המבורך לעולם ועד]; "Amen" was said after every benediction; "Blessed be the name of His glorious kingdom forever" [ברוך שם כבוד מלכותו לעולם ועד] was recited, presumably following the opening verse of the *Shemaʿ*; some said, "May His great name be praised" [יהא שמו הגדול מבורך], and others responded, "Forever and ever" [לעולם ולעולמי עולמים].[110] The former praise ["May His great name . . ."], which eventually became the central refrain in the *Qaddish* prayer, is reported elsewhere in connection with the second-century R. Yosi (b. Ḥalafta) as being regularly recited in synagogues and academies.[111]

Early Christian and Rabbinic Liturgies

On the assumption that the early church borrowed heavily from Jewish precedents in the first century C.E., Christian scholars have long shown an interest in Jewish liturgy. Since many of these studies appeared a generation or so ago, in the mid-twentieth century, before the explosion in the study of Second Temple literature and particularly the Qumran scrolls, these scholars drew most of their analogies from rabbinic literature. Sharing the same basic assumption as those who specialized in the study of Jewish liturgy, they assumed that the prayers finding expression in rabbinic literature existed well before the destruction of Jerusalem in 70 and thus served as the background, and in many cases the source of inspiration, for Christian liturgical initiatives in the first century.[112]

While there can be little question that the Jewish liturgical context of the first century was indeed a powerful influence on the fledgling Christian community, in light of the above remarks we may conclude that this did not include the unique rabbinic prayer forms that appear in tannaitic literature. Use of the *ʿAmidah*, as crystallized at Yavneh and in subsequent generations, to explain first-century Christian prayer formulas, would be anachronistic. Thus, any reference to early synagogue prayer (in contrast to that of the Temple or sectarian groups), to the Torah-reading, or to sermons (which were clearly components already existing in the first century C.E. but whose particulars are unknown) in order to explain Christian liturgy in the New Testament era is unjustified.[113]

Our suggested reconstruction of the early development of synagogue prayer in the late first and second centuries has led to a very different point of reference. It appears that both Christians and the sages developed new forms of liturgical expression in light of the dramatic events of the first century. Christians were responding to the divinity of

---

110. Sifre-Deuteronomy 306 (p. 342).

111. B Berakhot 3a. See also ibid., 21b; Midrash on Proverbs 14 (p. 112), where the context given is that of a *bet midrash*. On this last source, as well as on the *Qaddish* proper in later antiquity, see below.

112. Oesterley, *Jewish Background*, 111–236; Dugmore, *Influence of the Synagogue*, passim; Gavin, *Jewish Antecedents*, passim; Bouley, *From Freedom to Formula*, 13–28, 33–36. Cf., however, Bradshaw, *Origins of the Daily Office*, 1–11; idem, *Search for Origins*, 1–29; idem, *Daily Prayer*, passim.

113. See in this regard Fiensy, *Prayers Alleged to Be Jewish*, passim; Bradshaw, *Search for Origins*, 30–55.

Jesus, his passion, and his resurrection, with all the theological ramifications associated with these events as expounded by Paul and others. The Jews, for their part, were reacting to the Temple's destruction. Thus, not only did Christian worship stem from a very different religious, social, and political context than Jewish worship did, but it began at least a generation earlier.

Thus, our needs would be better served were we to focus on the parallel development of Christian and rabbinic prayer modes in the realization that both stemmed from common Second Temple worship and ritual configurations.[114] Common roots should probably be assumed for the appearance of similar phenomena in the first centuries, and only secondarily should we assume any sort of direct borrowing from one tradition to the other, except perhaps in the case of Jewish Christians and the like (e.g., the Quartodecimans).[115] Use of Scriptures, sermons, the benediction (ברכה), and biblical and other hymns containing the *sanctus* (see below) were well established in parts of Second Temple Jewish society, and thus it is not surprising to find these forms well entrenched in these two traditions from the outset.

A striking parallel between Christian and rabbinic liturgy in these first centuries is the degree to which public prayer was extemporaneous and spontaneous. At first, many of these prayers were regularly improvised following a few very loose guidelines. In the Christian tradition this phenomenon is most understandable, given the fact that Jesus' prayer was largely private, and thus there were no fixed liturgical precedents on which Christian communities could base their services. Moreover, since the liturgy was first articulated in churches which were created through the missionary activity of itinerants preaching the gospel, oral tradition played a decisive role in giving shape to the earliest forms of Christian prayers, and thus few fixed patterns are in evidence. "We may conclude, therefore, that the New Testament provides ample evidence that many prayer elements of primitive Christian worship were marked by spontaneity and freedom of expression though their origins are often to be found in the forms and spirit of Jewish prayer. Fully liberated by the example, person and the saving mystery of Christ their Lord, impelled by the Spirit and their new faith, the followers of Jesus christianized what they borrowed from the past. They did not shatter the old models, but according to the spirit or even in keeping with the generic framework of the models, Christians freely constructed the stuff of their own worship as it grew and developed."[116]

The central Christian prayer, the Eucharist, is an instructive example of a liturgical rite evolving from a largely spontaneous prayer into one with a number of fixed formu-

---

114. Beckwith, "Jewish Background," 68–80.

115. See the provocative and engaging studies by Yuval ("Haggadah," 5–28) and Liebes ("Mazmiaḥ Qeren," 313–48). On Christian worship in early second-century Asia Minor as reflected in a letter of Pliny, see van Beeck, "Worship of Christians," 121–31.

116. Bouley, *From Freedom to Formula*, 87.

las in the course of the first four to five centuries c.e.[117] The Eucharist was originally an integral part of the *agape* meal and not an independent liturgical unit. By all indications, the blessings over bread and wine were said at different points during the meal. Moreover, originating in a house setting, the early Eucharist did not require or acquire a fixed formula, for it was geared to domestic celebration only. By the second century, however, Justin attests that the Eucharist had become divorced from its original supper assembly, taking on the form of an independent worship unit recited over bread and wine. Nevertheless, it was still performed in a largely free and extemporaneous manner.[118]

In the third century, Hippolytus' *Apostolic Tradition* and the *Disdascalia Apostolorum* report on a much more expansive Eucharist; together, these sources appear to reflect a prayer configuration that was widespread in both Rome and the East. Here, too, no fixed prayer formula is in evidence. However, owing to Hippolytus' stature, the anaphoric formulation was eventually to have a major impact on written texts in subsequent generations.[119] Quasten and others have viewed the *Apostolic Tradition* as a watershed in moving from improvisation to fixed formula.[120]

In the fourth century, with the rapid expansion of Christianity, the amount of extant liturgical material burgeoned. As the church became public and prominent, so, too, did Christian worship become more refined and structured. The Eucharist liturgy had become much less fluid, and written anaphoras were linked to it and other rituals, giving rise to prayer settings in the West and East (including the seven known liturgical traditions in the latter) with similar formulas—yet not without significant regional differences.[121]

Thus, the similarities between early Christian and Jewish liturgies in the second and third centuries are apparent. First of all, the process of formalizing these new liturgies was slow and gradual. Both drew heavily on earlier Jewish liturgical traditions and biblical texts, both featured scriptural readings and expositions, both invoked praise, petition, thanksgiving, and doxologies[122] in their prayers, and both had the Sabbath as a focal institution. Spontaneity and improvisation existed side by side with generally ac-

---

117. See the comprehensive study in Mazza, *Origins of Eucharist Prayer*, as well as Bradshaw, *Search for Origins*, 131–60, and Jones, "New Testament," 184–209.

118. Justin, *First Apology* 65, 67, and possibly also *Didache* 9–10, if indeed a Eucharist setting was intended.

119. Jones et al., "Apostolic Tradition," 87–89; Cobb, "Apostolic Tradition," 213–16.

120. Quasten, *Patrology*, II, 189; Jungmann, *Early Liturgy*, chap. 6; Cuming, "Eucharist," 39–51. Cf., however, Willis, *History of Early Roman Liturgy*, 9–16.

121. Baldovin, "Christian Worship," 165–72; Bouley, *From Freedom to Formula*, 159–253; Bradshaw, *Search for Origins*, 161–84.

122. *Didache* 9–10; Origen, *Contra Celsum* 8, 34; 1 Clement 59, 3–4; and the *Didascalia Apostolorum* 9:25 (p. 86): "instead of the sacrifices which then were, offer now prayers and petitions and thanksgivings." See also Dix, *Shape of Liturgy*, 214–18; Oesterley, *Jewish Background*, 130–47; Baldovin, "Christian Worship," 157–65.

cepted guidelines. At the same time, however, when circumstances warranted it, regional and local differences once again coalesced. This is what happened during the enormous growth of the church from the fourth century on, and this is what began to happen in Jewish liturgy with the emergence of a second rabbinic center in Babylonia.

LATE ANTIQUITY

Our knowledge of Jewish liturgy increases immeasurably in late antiquity, when a much larger and more variegated array of sources became available, not only from within rabbinic circles as before, but from other sources as well. The Yerushalmi and Bavli replace the Mishnah and Tosefta, and amoraic *midrashim*, almost exclusively aggadic in nature, replace their tannaitic predecessors, which were far more focused on halakhic issues. Even within rabbinic literature itself, we can detect traces of liturgical poetry, which some sages seem to have been inclined to produce. This expanded rabbinic agenda reflects internal rabbinic literary proclivities and also seems to be a response to the external needs of the Jewish community. These types of intellectual-religious endeavors would appeal to a wider public. A statement by the third-century R. Isaac is most revealing in this regard: "Once, when money was available, a person would want to study mishnah and talmud. Now, when there is no money, and especially when we suffer from the [rule of the wicked] kingdom, a person prefers to study Scriptures and *aggadah*."[123] It may not be coincidental, therefore, that late antiquity witnessed increased rabbinic activity: rabbis delivered public sermons and, later, compiled much of their midrashic material into literary corpora.

There were a number of significant and dramatic developments in Jewish communal worship in late antiquity. On one level, there was the continued crystallization and amplification of the basic communal liturgical frameworks. The cluster of blessings and prayers around the *Shema'* and the *'Amidah* was further refined, and new components were added, either to the body of these prayers or as prefatory and concluding sections.

At the same time, an entirely new liturgical genre—the *piyyut*—made its appearance in Byzantine Palestine, stemming from circles not necessarily identical with the sages. By the turn of the fifth century, the sages were no longer heard of as a definable group, and it is not clear what—if any—role their successors played on the religious and social landscape of Palestine at the end of late antiquity. Another group which was active in Palestine and seems to have had some connection with the liturgical practices of the time were the mystics, whose traditions, taking form between the fourth and seventh centuries, are recorded in the Hekhalot literature.

At any rate, by the third century, some rabbis were becoming more involved in communal life generally and in the synagogue in particular, which opened numerous lines of

---

123. PRK 12:3 (p. 205); see also Song of Songs Rabbah 2:5, 1.

communication between them and the people at large.[124] A by-product of this increased involvement may well have been that, on the one hand, the sages were more responsive to congregational needs and proclivities while, on the other, the community was more sympathetic to rabbinic opinion, thus enabling rabbinic liturgical traditions to impact more readily on their lives.

With the emergence of a rabbinic center in Babylonia, rabbinic forms of worship evolved in more than one locale, affording us an opportunity to compare and contrast developments there as well as in Palestine. Tannaitic initiatives now proceed to evolve and consolidate along parallel tracks, with some striking instances of the accommodation of liturgical practices to local conditions and of the adoption of certain forms due to different historical contexts. In speaking of liturgy in general, Baumstark makes the following remark, which is applicable to our subject as well: "But if the movement of liturgical evolution is in the direction of a more and more pronounced uniformity, the latter is quite consistent with certain local peculiarities which give the impression of a retrograde movement. It seems to be of the nature of Liturgy to relate itself to the concrete situations of times and places. No sooner had the vast liturgical domains come into being than they began to be divided up into smaller territories whose several forms of worship were adapted to local needs."[125]

The Third Century

The third century witnessed a surge of liturgical activity in both Babylonia and Palestine, particularly in the area of prayer. Not only were the sages active in commenting upon what, where, and how prayers should be said, but, as noted above, a number of accounts purporting to relate incidents which occurred in liturgical settings make it quite clear that the rabbis at this time wielded some sort of authority in these matters.[126] Naturally, the material which has been preserved in rabbinic sources is tendentious, and undoubtedly there were many places which may not have responded sympathetically to rabbinic exercises of authority. The instance of a Caesarean congregation reciting the *Shema'* in Greek—to the consternation of one sage and the acquiescence of another—may be a case in point.[127]

While there are scores of third- and fourth-century sages who contributed to the evolving liturgical tradition, two pairs of rabbis, in Babylonia and in Palestine, stand out as having been unusually active in this area. Both pairs lived in the third century, Rav

---

124. L. Levine, *Rabbinic Class*, 23–42, 98–133; idem, "Sages and Synagogue," 201–22; and above, Chap. 13.

125. Baumstark, *Comparative Liturgy*, 18–19.

126. See above, Chap. 13.

127. Y Sotah 7, 1, 21b; see L. Levine, "Synagogue Officials," 392–400.

and Samuel in Babylonia in the first part of the century and the slightly younger *amoraim* R. Joshua b. Levi and R. Yoḥanan in Palestine in the middle of the century.[128]

Rav and Samuel addressed a plethora of issues in their liturgical rulings. Regarding daily prayer, Samuel identified the second blessing before the *Shemaʿ* as "With abounding love" [אהבה רבה], while Rav required the recitation of "True and certain" [אמת ויציב] in the morning and "True and trustworthy" [אמת ואמונה] in the evening for the third benediction after the *Shemaʿ*.[129] Each sage had his own response when the prayer leader came to the paragraph "We thank you" [מודים],[130] and each had his own interpretation of what the abbreviated *ʿAmidah* advocated by R. Joshua a century earlier should comprise. Rav claimed that what was intended was a shortened version of the full *ʿAmidah*; Samuel understood it to mean a one-paragraph summary of that prayer.[131] Rav composed a prayer for the conclusion of the *ʿAmidah* (which is still used today on the Sabbath preceding *Rosh Ḥodesh*), and he is quoted in several contradictory traditions as to when private prayers could be introduced into the *ʿAmidah*, if at all.[132]

Regarding the Sabbath, both sages knew of differing versions for the *havdalah* benediction,[133] but they disagreed as to whether the *Mussaf ʿAmidah* should be innovative: Rav required it, Samuel did not.[134] Rav was particularly active regarding the High Holiday liturgy, noting several expressions of sovereignty to incorporate ("the king of justice," "the holy king"), suggesting several additions in the *Mussaf* service, and perhaps composing the *ʿAlenu* (עלינו) prayer.[135] Both Rav and Samuel composed confessional prayers for Yom Kippur.[136] They also addressed the timing of the two kinds of prayer for rain, both when mention should first be made and when the formal request should commence.[137] Finally, Rav declared that any benediction which did not include the name of God was not valid.[138] Whether Rav or Samuel was indeed responsible for the actual com-

---

128. On the correspondence between R. Yoḥanan and his Babylonian colleagues, see B Ḥullin 95b. See also Kimelman, *Rabbi Yohanan of Tiberias*, 156–58. Of interest is the fact that Samaritan liturgy apparently underwent a dramatic development at this time regarding both prayer and religious poetry; see J. M. Cohen, *Samaritan Chronicle*, 68–69.

129. B Berakhot 11b–12a.

130. B Sotah 40a.

131. B Berakhot 29a. Cf., however, the different formulation in Y Berakhot 4, 3, 8a; Y Taʿanit 2, 2, 65c.

132. *Composing prayer:* B Berakhot 16b. *Private prayer:* B Berakhot 31a; B ʿAvodah Zarah 8a.

133. B Pesaḥim 102b.

134. Y Berakhot 4, 6, 8c.

135. *Kingship:* B Berakhot 12b. *Mussaf:* Leviticus Rabbah 29:1 (p. 668); PRK 23:1 (p. 333); Y Rosh Hashanah 1, 3, 57a; Y ʿAvodah Zarah 1, 2, 39c; Tanḥuma, Haʾazinu, 4; B Rosh Hashanah 27a. On the *ʿAlenu* prayer, see Elbogen, *Jewish Liturgy*, 119–20, 220; and the reservations of Heinemann in his notes to ibid.

136. B Yoma 87b. See Abrahams, "Lost Confession," 377–85.

137. B Taʿanit 4b–5a, 10a.

138. B Berakhot 40b.

position of the various prayers noted above is a moot issue. It may very well be that, in many instances, they were simply taking note of already existing prayers or practices. However, in most cases, we can assume with a great measure of probability that most of these traditions were brought from Palestine by this generation of sages.

These sages also addressed several Torah-reading issues, although far less extensively and often in connection with the matters discussed in the Mishnah. They disagreed, for example, on which reading was appropriate for the Sabbath of *Sheqalim* and which Sabbath should be designated the Sabbath of Remembrance when Purim falls on a Friday.[139]

Assuming that this concentration of source material indeed reflects the unusually extensive involvement of these two Babylonian sages in liturgical innovation, we might ask why this was so. Both these sages were, in essence, the founders of Babylonian rabbinic tradition, and it was they who in large part transmitted rabbinic culture from Palestine to Babylonia, establishing academies which were to become the backbone of rabbinic culture there for a millennium. Given this pioneering context, it is not at all surprising that they would take the lead in commenting upon synagogue practices in a place whose congregations had heretofore probably been only minimally affected by rabbinic forms and customs. This first encounter with local tradition is reflected in Rav's introduction to Babylonian synagogue practices with which he was not familiar. In one instance, he was surprised by a particular custom of prostration, and in another, by the recitation of the *Hallel* on *Rosh Ḥodesh*.[140]

In third-century Palestine, R. Yoḥanan was far and away the dominant rabbinic personality, and, as might be expected, his comments on the two major components of the prayer liturgy are legion. He is quoted as having addressed all aspects of the *Shema'*— when, where, and how it ought to be recited.[141] To the *'Amidah*, R. Yoḥanan added introductory and concluding verses (Pss. 51:17; 19:15), which are an accepted part of the liturgy even today.[142] He established that every blessing should have a reference to God's sovereignty (מלכות), and commented on the priestly benediction, the *Hallel* psalms, and, quite extensively, on the fast-day ritual.[143] R. Yoḥanan reaffirmed the importance of a *minyan* of ten for reciting certain parts of the service and offered midrashic support for the public recitation of a minimum of ten verses of the Torah.[144] He also adopted a rather strident position regarding the exclusive use of Hebrew in prayer: "The ministering angels pay

---

139. B Megillah 29b–30a.

140. *Prostration:* B Megillah 22a. *Hallel:* B Taʿanit 28b.

141. Y Berakhot 2, 3, 4b–c; B Berakhot 13b, 14a–b, 16a, 24b (= B Rosh Hashanah 34b).

142. B Berakhot 4b, 9b.

143. *Sovereignty:* B Berakhot 40b. *Priestly benediction:* B Megillah 24b. *Hallel:* B Taʿanit 28b. *Fast-day ritual:* ibid., 4b, 14b, 19b, 22b, 29b.

144. *Minyan:* B Megillah 23b. *Torah-reading:* ibid., 21b.

no attention to whoever makes personal requests in Aramaic, since angels do not understand Aramaic."[145]

Another important opinion associated with R. Yoḥanan appears in the context of an exchange between him and an older colleague, R. Joshua b. Levi: "R. Yoḥanan has said: 'Who merits the future world? Whoever juxtaposes [the prayer for] redemption to the evening *Amidah*.' R. Joshua b. Levi says: 'The *Amidot* [to be recited each day] were established to be in the middle [i.e., between the two recitations of the *Shemaʿ*, in the morning and evening].'"[146] Clearly, R. Yoḥanan was trying to establish a new norm linking the evening *Shemaʿ* with the *Amidah*, as was already customary in the morning,[147] thus forming a full evening service which would serve as the liturgical focus at the end of the day. R. Joshua b. Levi seems to have maintained a more conservative posture, claiming that the evening *Shemaʿ* should be said only upon retiring for the night, which would mean that the three daily *Amidot* were to be recited between the morning and evening *Shemaʿ*. As noted above, the obligatory nature of the evening *Amidah* had been a subject of dispute since the days of Rabban Gamaliel; R. Yoḥanan was advocating its importance and obligatory nature here by linking it with the recital of the *Shemaʿ*.

Both R. Yoḥanan and R. Joshua b. Levi asserted that the proper recitation of prayer was tantamount to offering a sacrifice, and the latter went even further by claiming that the *Amidah* was established in place of the Temple sacrifices.[148]

Finally, it was Joshua b. Levi who first determined that all the traditions declared by various *tannaim* to be the essence of the redemption paragraph following the *Shemaʿ* should be included.[149] This policy of preserving alternative traditions as much as possible was followed in many other instances as well, particularly when it came to rival Palestinian and Babylonian ones. One way to do this was to divide competing versions between the morning and evening services. Indeed, this is what eventually was done with the two versions of the second blessing before the *Shemaʿ* (אהבת עולם and אהבה רבה), the two versions of the paragraph following the *Shemaʿ* (אמת ויציב and אמת ואמונה), and, much later, with the two final paragraphs of the *Amidah* (שים שלום and שלום רב).[150] When confronted with a series of versions of the silent thanksgiving prayer (מודים דרבנן), which was recited by the congregation during the reader's repetition of the *Amidah*, R. Pappa declared: "Therefore, let us say them all."[151]

---

145. B Sotah 33a; B Shabbat 12b. See also Yahalom, "Angels Do Not Understand Aramaic," 33–44.

146. B Berakhot 4b.

147. Already recorded in T Berakhot 1:2 (pp. 1–2).

148. B Berakhot 15a, 26b.

149. Y Berakhot 1, 6, 3d.

150. See the material, much of which is liturgical, collected in Sperber, *Jewish Customs*, I, 29–35; II, 23–75.

151. B Sotah 40a; see also Y Berakhot 1, 5, 3d.

It may not be coincidental that it is precisely at this time that we read with far greater frequency of sages remarking on the virtues of reciting prayers in the synagogue.[152] By the third and fourth centuries, the synagogue was assuming a more central role in rabbinic circles than before. The repeated emphasis on the synagogue and regular attendance may serve as an indication of their support for and identification with the institution, and this, in turn, may mean that the worship conducted there met with their approval. Nevertheless, even here, one should not exaggerate. As noted, the fact that some sages emphasized their approval probably shows that there were others who had reservations. Not only would it have been natural and understandable for some sages to have shied away from a public forum such as the synagogue, preferring either the intimacy of their homes or the familiarity of the academy, where they spent much of their time, but such behavior is explicitly documented.[153]

Differences between Palestine and Babylonia

Although the liturgies of Palestine and Babylonia derived from a common source (i.e., second-century Palestine), the differences between them became increasingly pronounced in the course of late antiquity.[154]

These differences were manifest in the main body of the liturgy as well as in its ancillary customs. For example, the Babylonian sages expanded the *'Amidah* from eighteen to nineteen prayers by creating a separate one for the seed of David (lit., "plant of David," צמח דויד).[155] Whether this was a gesture made toward the Exilarch, who claimed to have descended from the Davidic line, or merely an expression of theological yearnings for redemption, which the Babylonians wished to further emphasize, is impossible to tell. In the area of Torah-reading, the Babylonians instituted (or exclusively adopted) an annual cycle, which stood in sharp contrast to the Palestinian triennial one; they also added readings for the extra festival days.[156] These are probably three of the most salient differences between Babylonian and Palestinian synagogue practice, but there were others as well:

(1) Babylonians would sit when reciting the *Shemaʿ*; in Palestine, the congregation would stand.[157] Such were also the respective practices with regard to one of the

---

152. See above, Chap. 13.

153. B Berakhot 7b–8a; and above, Chap. 13.

154. A trait noted by Baumstark; see above, note 125.

155. Elbogen, *Jewish Liturgy*, 34–35, 48–49. On Liebes' theory that the ending of this blessing, "Mazmiaḥ Qeren Yeshuʿah," is of Jewish-Christian origin dating from the first century, see his "Mazmiaḥ Qeren," 313–48; as well as the comments of Ta-Shma ("Liebes, ʿMazmiaḥ Qeren Yeshuʿahʾ " [review], 181–89) and Kister ("Horn of David," 191–207), as well as Liebes' rejoinders ("Responses," 209–17).

156. *Torah-reading: Differences in Customs*, no. 48 (pp. 172–73); B Megillah 29b. *Additional festival days: Differences in Customs*, no. 41 (pp. 161–64); B Megillah 31a; Y Demai 4, 2, 23d; Y ʿEruvin 3, 9, 21c, and elsewhere.

157. *Differences in Customs*, no. 1 (pp. 91–94); see R. Yoḥanan's remark in B Berakhot 13b.

blessings following the haftarah which the congregation would recite aloud; in Babylonia the custom was to sit, in Palestine to stand.[158]

(2) Babylonian elders would face the congregation, as had been the practice in the tannaitic period, whereas in Palestine, the elders would face the ark along with the rest of the congregation.[159]

(3) Babylonians would conclude the blessing following the *Shema'* with the phrase "Who has redeemed Israel" (past tense); in Palestine the concluding phrase was in the present tense: "Rock of Israel and its Savior."[160]

(4) Babylonians would recite the daily *'Amidah* silently, while Jews in Palestine would do so aloud, so as "to familiarize the people."[161]

(5) Babylonians would conclude the middle benediction of the Sabbath *'Amidah* with the words "He who sanctified the Sabbath," while in Palestine, following an earlier custom, the congregation would conclude with the blessing "He who sanctified Israel and the Sabbath."[162]

(6) The *Qedushah* prayer was recited every day in Babylonia, while in Palestine it was recited on the Sabbath only (see below).[163]

(7) Both the Torah reader and the congregation in Babylonia would read the *parashah* (Torah portion) every week; in Palestine the congregation would read the *parashah* (following Babylonian custom), but the Torah reader would read according to the order of the triennial cycle (*sidrah*).[164]

(8) Babylonians would pay homage to the Torah scroll when it was introduced (lit., brought in), whereas in Palestine the congregation would honor it when it was introduced and removed (lit., taken out).[165]

(9) Babylonians would recite the priestly benediction even when the prayer leader was not a priest; in Palestine the blessing was recited only by a prayer leader who was a priest.[166]

(10) Babylonians would not allow bareheaded priests to bless the congregation; in Palestine the practice was allowed.[167]

---

158. Tractate Soferim 13:9 (pp. 245–46).

159. *Differences in Customs*, no. 36 (p. 156).

160. Elbogen, *Jewish Liturgy*, 210; Shinan, "Redeemer and Redemption," 49–66.

161. *Differences in Customs*, no. 43 (pp. 165–67).

162. Ibid., no. 32 (pp. 150–51).

163. Pirqoi ben Baboi, in Ginzberg, *Geniza Studies*, II, 555–56.

164. *Differences in Customs*, no. 47 (pp. 169–72). This rather strange Palestinian practice apparently stems from the very end of antiquity, when Babylonian customs were beginning to penetrate Palestine. See Fleischer, *Prayer and Prayer Rituals*, 298–300.

165. *Differences in Customs*, no. 49 (pp. 173–74).

166. Ibid., no. 29 (pp. 145–46).

167. Ibid., no. 42 (pp. 164–65).

(11) Babylonians would recite the priestly blessing in the evening as well as the morning of a fast day; in Palestine the blessing was recited only in the morning, except on Yom Kippur.[168]

(12) In Babylonia, priests would recite the priestly blessing three times on Yom Kippur; in Palestine they would recite it four times, following an older custom.[169]

(13) In Babylonia, a mourner would enter a synagogue every day; in Palestine, only on the Sabbath.[170]

Even with regard to the recitation of certain central prayers, there were differences between Palestine and Babylonia in late antiquity. A controversial instance concerns the third paragraph of the *Shemaʿ* and whether it should be recited at night, when the phrase "And you shall *see* it [referring to the fringes of the *tzitzit*]" could not be fulfilled. As a result, a number of alternative customs were developed. In Babylonia, for example, this paragraph was not recited, but if someone nevertheless began it, then it had to be concluded. In Palestine, on the other hand, the first, but not the latter, part of the paragraph would be read.[171] Neither of these positions may have been in accordance with the Mishnah, which has been understood to mean that the third paragraph (יציאת מצרים) was recited at night.[172] Again, it is unclear whether what is being discussed here is general synagogue procedure or only the customs of rabbinic circles in late antiquity. To further complicate matters, it is reported that on coming to Babylonia, R. Abba bar Aḥa discovered that the practice there was to routinely begin and end the paragraph.[173] These differences appear to have continued for some time.

Taking into account some of the above differences, together with other related issues, we can see emerging a rather sharp distinction between a more fluid Palestinian practice and a more fixed and standardized Babylonian one. The Babylonians concluded the Torah-reading cycle in one year, whereas in Palestine it took anywhere between three and three and a half years. Thus, in Palestine the length of the reading in various synagogues might differ on any given Sabbath, as would the particular section being read. Moreover,

---

168. Ibid., no. 22 (pp. 135–36). Margalioth, in his comments (ibid.), points out that this is the one instance in which later Palestinian practice contradicted not only an explicit mishnaic ruling (Taʿanit 4:1), but also what appears to have been an earlier custom in Palestine (Y Taʿanit 4, 1, 67b). Nevertheless, this later Palestinian practice was labeled an alternative custom in T Taʿanit 3:1 (p. 336). It is also worth pointing out that customs other than the one noted in *Differences in Customs* are mentioned with respect to Babylonia (B Taʿanit 26b).

169. *Differences in Customs*, no. 55 (p. 179).

170. Ibid., no. 14 (pp. 122–23).

171. Y Berakhot 1, 6, 3d.

172. M Berakhot 1:5. I follow the interpretation of medieval commentators, as against Ginzberg (*Commentary*, I, 207–8) and Lieberman (*TK*, I, 12), who interpret this mishnah as referring to the third blessing, i.e., that following the three paragraphs of the *Shemaʿ*.

173. Y Berakhot 1, 6, 3d.

the choice of Prophetic readings (*haftarot*) often varied among Palestinian communities, as, of course, did the languages in use. When added to the range of Palestinian customs regarding the *targum*, sermon, and *piyyut*—practices unknown in the Babylonian setting (see below)—this distinction becomes even more striking.[174] To what extent Babylonian practice was indeed homogeneous, and whether the perceived difference between Babylonia and Palestine depends in large measure on the multifaceted sources available for the latter, is difficult to determine.

Prayer

A number of sages aired reservations about the ever-increasing formalization of prayer. Commenting on R. Eli'ezer's emphasis on spontaneity as a necessary component of prayer (M Berakhot 4:3-4), some third- and fourth-century sages commented as follows: "R. Abbahu, quoting R. Eli'ezer [b. Pedat; third century], states: "[One should pray] so as not to appear to be reading a letter." R. Aha, in the name of R. Joseph, [said]: "One must say something new [לחדש דבר] every day." Ahitophel would recite three new prayers each day."[175]

Moreover, the Yerushalmi describes the way in which some sages actually expressed this spontaneity. R. Eli'ezer (b. Pedat) would recite a new prayer (תפילה חדשה) each day, and R. Abbahu a new blessing (ברכה חדשה).[176] Other sages sought alternative ways: R. Yohanan would add two verses, one at the beginning and one at the end of the *'Amidah*, while R. Judan would recite these verses before the *'Amidah*.[177] Many *amoraim* composed individual prayers, usually of a personal supplicatory nature, which they would recite regularly. At first, such personal appeals seem to have been recited at different points in and around the *'Amidah* (see above), but as time went on, there was a tendency to concentrate them at the end of that prayer; at a later stage, a fixed liturgy of supplication replaced these individual outpourings. An interesting example of this process may be found in the following: "R. Ze'ira asked R. Yosi: 'How does one add a new thought to it [the *Mussaf 'Amidah*]?' He said to him: 'Even if one says, "And may we offer before You our obligatory daily sacrifices and the additional [*Mussaf*] sacrifice," one has fulfilled the obligation [to add something new].'"[178] Thus, what was arguably a private prayer of R. Yosi eventually became the accepted norm for the *Mussaf 'Amidah*; it was subsequently fleshed out with a fuller statement regarding the loss of the Temple and the longing to renew its mode of worship.

---

174. Shinan, "Literature of the Ancient Synagogue," 136–37, 152.

175. Y Berakhot 4, 3, 8a.

176. Ibid.

177. Ibid.

178. Y Berakhot 4, 6, 8c; see Hoffman, "Surprising History of Musaf 'Amidah," 41–45.

Qedushah

The complexity of Jewish prayer at this time, the variant customs that may have coexisted, and the fact that not all prayers were rabbinic in origin are all reflected in the *Qedushah* (sanctification) prayer of late antiquity.[179] While there can be no question as to the importance of this prayer, its origins and its stages of institutionalization in synagogue liturgy nevertheless present intriguing and vexing questions. Built around Isa. 6:3 (referred to as the *trisagion* in Christian liturgy) and Ezek. 3:12, which describe the angelic adoration of God, these verses appear in a variety of contexts and combinations throughout the liturgy, often together with other verses and always in a different form. When fully developed, this imitation of the praise of God by the angels was recited in three different places in the morning liturgy (and again during the *Mussaf* service on the Sabbath and festivals), before, during, and after the *'Amidah:* in the first blessing preceding the *Shema'*, known as the "*Qedushah* of the Creator" (קדושת היוצר; also referred to as the "*Qedushah* while sitting," קדושה דמיושב); within the third benediction of the *'Amidah* (referred to as the "standing *Qedushah*," קדושה דעמידה); and toward the end of the service ("*Qedushah de-Sidra*," קדושה דסדרא—i.e., the "*Qedushah* following the study sessions").[180]

A cluster of intriguing problems connected with this prayer relates to where it came from, when it was incorporated into the liturgy, and whether its components were introduced at more or less the same time. Was it originally a Palestinian or a Babylonian innovation, and how widespread did it become in late antiquity? Let us examine the evidence at hand.

One major issue relates to the time that the *Qedushah* of the Creator was introduced into the synagogue liturgy; many early medieval orders of prayer, including those of R. 'Amram and Sa'adiah Gaon (ninth and tenth centuries), do not include it. Moreover, the evidence of Pirqoi ben Baboi (ca. 800 C.E.), a fervent supporter of Babylonian traditions as against Palestinian ones, is noteworthy: "Until now the *Qedushah* and *Shema'* are said in Palestine only on Sabbath and holidays and only in the morning service [*Shaḥarit*], with the exception of Jerusalem and all cities where there are Babylonians who pressed [lit., caused controversy and dispute] until they [the Palestinians] took upon themselves [the custom of] saying the *Qedushah* daily. But in the other cities and towns of Eretz-Israel, where there are no Babylonians, they only recite the *Qedushah* on Sabbath and holidays."[181]

For many years, this statement led scholars to believe that the entire *Qedushah* entered

---

179. On this prayer generally, see Elbogen, *Jewish Liturgy*, 54–62; Werner, "Doxology," 292–307; idem, *Sacred Bridge*, I, 282–91; II, 108–26; Heinemann, *Prayer*, 230–33; Bar-Ilan, "Basic Issues of the Qedushah," 5–20; Fleischer, "Qedusha," 301–50.

180. The last term, *Qedushah de-Sidra*, is unclear and may refer to prayers or a study session which preceded it. See B Sotah 49a; Elbogen *Jewish Liturgy*, 70–71; Sokoloff, *Dictionary*, 368–69.

181. See above, note 163. See also Baron, *Social and Religious History of the Jews*, VII, 76–78.

the Jewish liturgical framework in the Middle Ages, and following Bloch's pathbreaking study a century ago, it was assumed to have originated in contemporary mystical circles. More recent research, however, has pointed unequivocally in another direction. The theme of angelic praise of God was well known in Second Temple sectarian circles, and this motif was integrated into the Qumran liturgy, as the Songs of the Sabbath Sacrifice scroll vividly describes.[182] The verse from Isaiah appears in Enoch and Revelation as well.[183] Moreover, the *sanctus* is evidenced by Clement of Rome, Ignatius, Clement of Alexandria, and perhaps also Tertullian.[184]

The most salient Christian use of the *Qedushah* verses as an emulation of heavenly angels is found in the *Apostolic Constitutions*, a work edited in the fourth century C.E. in which the *trisagion* appears in a context praising God as creator and redeemer: "And the bright host of angels and the intellectual spirits say to Palmoni [Dan. 8:13], 'There is but one holy being.' And the holy seraphim, together with the six-winged cherubim, who sing to Thee their triumphal song, cry out with never-ceasing voices: 'Holy, holy, holy Lord God of hosts, heaven and earth are full of Your glory' [Isa. 6:3]. And the other multitudes of the orders, angels, archangels, thrones, dominions, principalities, authorities, and powers cry aloud and say: 'Blessed be the glory of the Lord out of his place' [Ezek. 3:12]."[185] This theme is repeated in several other early Christian liturgies as well.[186]

Thus, there can be no question that a *Qedushah* was recited regularly in certain Christian circles, that this practice was influenced by earlier Jewish tradition, and that it perhaps paralleled contemporary Jewish usage as well.[187]

Solid evidence for the centrality of the *Qedushah* in Jewish liturgy of late antiquity may be found in the *piyyut*. In these poems, which reflect elements of the Sabbath and holiday worship services, the *Qedushah* is integrated into the *Shemaʿ* and *ʿAmidah* contexts regularly. *Yotzerot* and *Qerovot*—*piyyutim* composed for recitation in the Creator blessing before the *Shemaʿ* and within the *ʿAmidah*, respectively—indicate the extent to which the

---

182. Flusser, "Jewish Roots," 37–43; Strugnell, "Angelic Liturgy," 318–45; Newsom, *Songs of the Sabbath Sacrifice*, 23–38; Weinfeld, "Heavenly Praise," 427–37; Schiffman, *Reclaiming*, 355–60.

183. Enoch 39:12–14: "Those who do not slumber but stand before your glory, did bless you. They shall bless, praise, and extol [you], saying, 'Holy, Holy, Holy Lord of the Spirits; the spirits fill the earth.' And at that place [under his wings] my eyes saw others who stood before him sleepless [and] blessed [him], saying, 'Blessed are You and blessed is the name of the Lord of the Spirits forever and ever'" (Charlesworth, *Old Testament Pseudepigrapha*, I, 31). See also Rev. 4:8–11. On Flusser's suggestion that the *Qedushah* is mirrored in the *Gloria* (Luke 2:14), see his "Sanktus und Gloria," 129–52, as well as Dan. 7:10.

184. Werner, *Sacred Bridge*, II, 115–16; Weinfeld, "Heavenly Praise," 432.

185. *Apostolic Constitution* 7, 35; see also ibid., 8, 12. See Fiensy, *Prayers Alleged to Be Jewish*, 66–73, 98–109, 176–81. Like Jewish liturgy, Christian liturgy describes the angels as joining mortals in prayer at the time of the Eucharist ceremony; cf. Markus, *End of Ancient Christianity*, 21–22.

186. For other examples, see the liturgies of James and Mark, in A. Roberts et al., *Ante-Nicene Fathers*, VII, 538, 544, 552–53, 557.

187. Taft, *Beyond East and West*, 176–77; Jones et al., *Study of Liturgy*, passim.

Qedushah was a fixture in the synagogue liturgy. It was clearly a fundamental component of these prayers in fifth- and sixth-century Byzantine Palestine.

The centrality of the *Qedushah* in the mystical prayers of Hekhalot literature has long been recognized.[188] These traditions seem to have coalesced sometime in late antiquity, between the fourth and sixth or seventh centuries, and not in the Middle Ages as heretofore believed.[189]

The nature of the relationship between Hekhalot prayers and those of rabbinic and synagogue circles has been disputed for some time. Much has been written about the centrality of prayer in Hekhalot mysticism, and a number of prayers identical or similar to those of the synagogue were recorded in these various traditions. Clearly, some sort of connection existed. Although certain scholars have assumed that these prayers were originally composed by mystics and only later impacted on the synagogue,[190] others have suggested precisely the opposite, that mystical circles flourishing in the post-talmudic period adopted some of the prayers known from synagogue contexts and adapted them to fit their needs.[191] Although the latter approach appears to be more accurate, there is no way of knowing for sure. In any case, differences of opinion over the ultimate origin of the *Qedushah* are irrelevant. Because there were so many possible channels through which these prayer formulas might have been conveyed to both the synagogue and mystical circles, stretching back many centuries, any suggestion positing a causal relationship between them is, at best, mere speculation.

In the Hekhalot literature, the angels are said to recite the *Qedushah* three times a day near the Seat of Glory (כסא הכבוד).[192] God occupies this throne while Israel recites its prayers; furthermore, only when the *Qedushah* is recited in the synagogues and academies by mortal beings do the angels recite this hymn in His honor.[193] Thus, for the mystics, synagogue prayer was a crucial dimension, bringing God closer to His angelic and mortal (i.e., mystic) admirers. However, in contrast to what seems to have been the accepted

---

188. See, for example, Fleischer, "Diffusion of Qedushot," 255–84; Schäfer, *Synopse*, nos. 179, 188; idem, *Hekhalot-Studien*, 285–89; Swartz, *Mystical Prayer*, s.v. "Qedushah."

189. Swartz, *Mystical Prayer*, 223; Elior, "Merkabah Mysticism," 235.

190. See, for example, L. A. Hoffman, "Censoring In and Censoring Out," 19–37; Goldberg, "Service of the Heart," 205; Bar-Ilan, *Mysteries of Jewish Prayer*, 15–38, 84–140. Also at issue is whether these mystics are to be identified or associated with rabbinic Judaism. Scholem's classic view claiming such a tie (*Jewish Gnosticism*, 9–30) has come under much attack of late. See, inter alia, Schäfer, *Hekhalot-Studien*, 289–95; Halperin, *Faces of the Chariot*, 447–55.

191. Swartz, "'Alay Le-Shabbeah," 179–90; idem, *Mystical Prayer*, 217, as well as 122–25; idem, "Like the 'Ministering Angels,'" 166; Schäfer, "Jewish Liturgy and Magic," 544–53.

192. According to B Ḥullin 91b, there are different traditions stating how many times angels recite the *Qedushah*, from once a day to once in the course of history.

193. Schäfer, *Synopse*, no. 180.

Palestinian synagogue practice at the time—i.e., that the *Qedushah* of the Creator was recited only on Sabbaths and holidays—the mystics clearly said it every day.[194]

Although, as we have established, the *Qedushah* was firmly ensconced in the Jewish liturgy of late antiquity, little information about this prayer has been preserved in rabbinic literature. It is first mentioned in the Tosefta, but in a very different context from the one we might have expected. In discussing blessings in general, and those associated with the *Shema'* specifically, the Tosefta notes the following: "And one does not respond to someone reciting a blessing. R. Judah [mid-second century] would respond to one reciting a blessing [by saying,] 'Holy, holy, holy, etc.' and 'Blessed be, etc.' All these R. Judah would say together with one reciting a blessing."[195] Not much can be extrapolated from this brief notation, nor is it clear which blessing is being referred to.[196] Was this just the practice of R. Judah, or did others (sages? the people generally?) follow suit? Did his response consist only of these two verses, or were there others as well?

In the first part of the third century, R. Joshua b. Levi is quoted as saying that if someone comes to the synagogue late and can manage to begin and finish the *'Amidah* before the prayer leader reaches the *Qedushah*, he is permitted to do so.[197] Here we seem to be on solid ground in assuming that, by this time at least, the *Qedushah* was part and parcel of the synagogue liturgy, although it still is not clear which *Qedushah* is meant, the third benediction of the *'Amidah* or the *Qedushah* before the *Shema'*. From the context, the former seems probable, but we have no way of being certain. We may be on somewhat more solid ground with a fourth-century source, a description in the Yerushalmi of an incident from the time of R. Abun:

> Batitay [presumably the name of a prayer leader] became silent at [the point when he was about to recite] the "And the heavenly creatures" [lit., "the wheels," the beginning of a sentence in the *Qedushah*; see Ezek. 1:19]. They went and asked R. Abun [what to do]. R. Abun said to them in the name of R. Joshua b. Levi: "He who passes [before the ark] in his stead begins from the point where he stopped." He then said to them: "Since you have already answered with the *Qedushah* [קדושתא], it is as if [we are at] the beginning of a benediction [and you may proceed from there].[198]

We are clearly dealing here with the public recitation of a section of the *Qedushah*. Again, the question arises regarding which *Qedushah* this is referring to. This story con-

---

194. See Gruenwald, "Song of the Angels," 475–76.

195. T Berakhot 1:9 (pp. 3–4). It is not entirely clear whether R. Judah responded at the same time that the prayer leader recited the blessing (Elbogen, *Jewish Liturgy*, 55) or following the blessing, reciting it together with the prayer leader (Lieberman, *TK*, I, 11).

196. Gruenwald, "Song of the Angels," 478.

197. B Berakhot 21b.

198. Y Berakhot 5, 3, 9c. On the custom of worshippers standing on their tiptoes when reciting the *Qedushah* in imitation of the angels, see Tanḥuma, Tzav, 13.

tains a number of contradictory hints. On the one hand, the term "wheels" fits the *Qedushah* of the Creator, at least in its later formulation. On the other hand, the phrase "pass (before the ark)" is used exclusively for the *'Amidah*, and thus we are left in a quandary. The only certainty here is that by later antiquity the *Qedushah* had indeed become an integral part of some morning service.

What, then, was the origin of this prayer? The *Qedushah* clearly was not a rabbinic creation, nor did the sages ever discuss its recitation in any halakhic context. In all probability, it stemmed from circles outside the rabbinic sphere, presumably at first among Second Temple Jewish sectarians. In fact, Second Temple traditions may well hold the key to the manifold appearances of the *Qedushah* among Christians, Jews, Jewish mystics, and *paytanim* in late antiquity. Its benign neglect by the rabbis may indicate their lack of enthusiasm, due perhaps to its mystical, sectarian, or Christian overtones.

Archeological Evidence for Prayer

Regarding Jewish prayer generally in late antiquity, our knowledge may be elucidated by archeological finds as well. A number of the Hebrew-Aramaic dedicatory inscriptions found in synagogues in Byzantine Palestine acknowledge contributions made by individuals or the congregation as a whole.[199] Such acknowledgments are often accompanied by wishes for peace and for the well-being of the donors, sometimes in simple, straightforward language and sometimes in a flowing poetic style. We have already had occasion to note several such inscriptions.[200] The synagogue at Na'aran offers the following example:

> May they be remembered for good everyone who donated and gave or will give to this holy place, whether it be gold or silver or anything else. Amen. May their portion be in this holy place. Amen.[201]

The fullest inscription in this respect, however, was found in the nearby Jericho synagogue:

> May they be remembered for good. May their memory be for good. The entire holy congregation, the old and the young, whom the King of the Universe has helped, have contributed and made this mosaic. He who knows their names, their children's, and [those] of the members of their households will inscribe them in the Book of Life [with all] the righteous. All Israel are brethren [חברין לכל ישראל]. Shalom. Amen.[202]

Not infrequently, as the above inscriptions indicate, the ending of an inscription was taken from prayers and psalms concluding with "Amen" or "Selah." This practice is par-

---

199. See above, Chap. 9.

200. See above, Chap. 11.

201. Naveh, *On Stone and Mosaic*, no. 64.

202. Ibid., no. 69. For the phrase כל ישראל חברים, see Y Ḥagigah 3, 6, 79d; and esp. Wieder, "Jericho Inscription," 572-79.

ticularly pronounced in a series of inscriptions from Ḥammat Gader; two inscriptions conclude with "Amen. Amen. Selah," one with "Amen. Amen. [Selah]. Shalom," and a fourth with "Amen. Selah. Shalom."[203] More than these individual terms have been adopted; the phraseology of the Jericho inscription is remarkably similar to prayer formulas that emerged much later in Jewish liturgy. As early as 1942, Schwabe pointed out the striking similarities between this inscription (and several Greek ones as well) and the יקום פורקן or מי שברך prayers of the Jewish prayerbook. Weinfeld, Foerster, and Wieder have expanded on this comparison.[204] Thus, it may well be that these inscriptions echo prayers familiar to the congregation which, although not noted in ancient literary sources, were already in existence in one form or another and continue to be recited down to our own day.

Torah Ceremony

The second focus of synagogue liturgy in late antiquity was the Torah-reading ceremony. This component continued to be rich and varied and included readings from the Torah and the Prophets (haftarah), the *targum*, and sermons. None of these activities was new by this time; all had existed within the synagogue setting for centuries. Nevertheless, the overwhelming majority of sources relating to these dimensions of synagogue worship date back to late antiquity, and thus our knowledge of each of these components is far greater for this period than for earlier ones. Ironically, very little new information is available with regard to the pivotal component, the Torah-reading itself. Both *talmudim*, our primary sources in this regard, essentially relate to mishnaic and toseftan discussions, and little new material has been added. The additional readings required for the second day of a holiday in the Babylonian Diaspora (and possibly elsewhere as well, although this cannot be verified) are one notable exception to this rule. Moreover, as mentioned, *Differences in Customs* spells out a number of contrasting Palestinian and Babylonian customs with regard to the Torah-reading ceremony.[205]

Torah- and Haftarah-Readings. We have already suggested that the Torah-reading component of synagogue liturgy seems to have been the least susceptible to rabbinic influence. Rabbinic prescriptions aside, we hear of Torah-readings where no blessings were recited[206] or where only eight verses were read. In the latter case, sages were hard pressed to bring this practice into line with their requirement of at least ten verses. One approach was to read a verse twice; another was to split one verse into two and thus artificially cre-

---

203. Naveh, *On Stone and Mosaic*, nos. 32–35.

204. Schwabe, "Ancient Synagogue," 92; Weinfeld, "Synagogue Inscriptions," 288–95; Foerster, "Synagogue Inscriptions," 12–40; Wieder, "Jericho Inscription," 557–79.

205. B Megillah 31a; *Differences in Customs*, nos. 47, 49 (pp. 169–74).

206. Y Megillah 4, 1, 75a: "R. Samuel bar Naḥman said: 'R. Jonathan passed a *sidra* [a place of study or a synagogue; see Sokoloff, *Dictionary*, 369] and heard voices reading [the Torah], but without [reciting] blessings.' He said to them: 'How long will you make the Torah bald [קרחות קרחות, i.e., bereft of accompanying blessings]?' "

ate the required number.[207] There also seem to have been some radically different practices regarding the reading of the haftarah; some synagogues required twenty-one verses
to be read (three for each of the seven people called to the Torah),[208] but there also appears to have been a custom of reading only three verses. The Yerushalmi's explanation
for this difference was that in places where there was a *targum* recitation, only three verses
were read; otherwise, the number was twenty-one.[209] While the Yerushalmi notes that in
the presence of R. Yoḥanan only three verses of the haftarah were normally recited, the
Bavli records ten.[210] Tractate Soferim, on the other hand, mentions at least four different practices; "When are these rules applicable? When there is no translation or homily.
But if there is a translator or a preacher, then the *maftir* reads three, five, or seven verses
[instead of twenty-one] in the Prophets, and that is sufficient."[211] Given its lesser sanctity, the haftarah reading was a much more flexible component than the Torah-reading;
verses could be drawn from two different sources, on different subjects, or even from
several books.[212]

Targum. The targum was a widespread, if not universal, practice in the synagogues of
late antiquity, and certainly in Palestine and Babylonia, for which our information is relatively abundant. The Roman-Byzantine Diaspora remains an enigma in this regard, nor
do we know whether the Torah was read in Hebrew or Greek in these communities (or if
both, then the extent of each). Thus, the degree to which a *targum* was needed remains an
open question. After Justinian's *Novella* 146 of 553 C.E., the use of the vernacular apparently increased, but to what extent remains unknown.[213] There is even an opinion voiced
in the Yerushalmi that *targumim* are not indispensable, but translations, if implemented,
must be made properly.[214] The haftarah was translated along with the Torah-reading,
but, as noted above, the rabbis were much less stringent about the former.[215] The system
of translation preserved in rabbinic literature is as follows: A translation must be made
orally (although targumic texts seem to have existed) immediately following the Torah-
reading; the translation is to be made verse by verse with regard to the Torah, but as many
as three verses at a time for the haftarah. The goal was to render a passage as faithfully
as possible, but not too slavishly. As the second-century R. Judah b. 'Ilai says: "He who

---

207. Y Megillah 4, 2, 75a; B Megillah 21b–22a.
208. B Megillah 23a.
209. Y Megillah 4, 3, 75a.
210. B Megillah 23b.
211. Tractate Soferim 13:15 (pp. 250–51).
212. M Megillah 4:4; B Megillah 24a.
213. On this law generally, see Linder, *Jews in Roman Imperial Legislation*, no. 66. See also A. Baumgarten, "Justinian and the Jews," 37–44.
214. Y Megillah 4, 1, 74d.
215. M Megillah 4:4; T Megillah 3:18–20 (pp. 358–59); B Megillah 21b. See also Zevin, in *Talmudic
Encyclopedia*, X, 26–27.

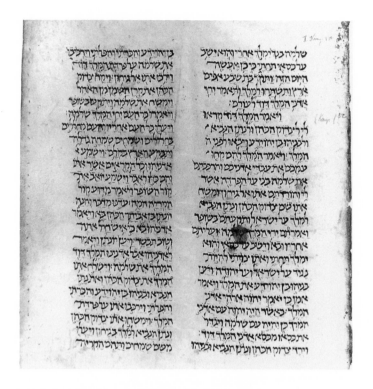

89. Genizah fragment of Targum-Pseudo-Jonathan.

translates a verse according to its plain meaning [כצורתו] is a liar, and he who adds [to it] is a blasphemer."[216]

Most *targumim* which have come down to us have a great deal in common and seem to reflect, to a greater or lesser degree, a common targumic tradition as well as what was actually delivered in the synagogue setting.[217] The various *targumim* are roughly of the same length, both in relation to one another and in relation to the original Torah-reading, thus reflecting a balance between the Hebrew and Aramaic renditions.[218] The major exception in this regard is Pseudo-Jonathan, which is distinguished by the number of its additions (about six thousand), which are both interpolated in the verses and prefatory to them (fig. 89).[219] Some are much more than explanatory comments and often incorporate

---

216. T Megillah 3:41 (p. 364); B Qiddushin 49a.

217. Shinan, "Aggadah of Palestinian Targums," 73; idem, *Embroidered Targum*, 20–35; idem, "Targumic Additions," 139–45; idem, "Echoes from Ancient Synagogues," 353–64; Alexander, "Targumim and Rabbinic Rules," 14–28; Bowker, *Targums and Rabbinic Literature*, 14–15; Flesher, "Mapping the Targums," 247–53; idem, "Targumim in Context," 626–29; as well as McNamara, "Targums," 857–58, 860. See also M. L. Klein, *Geniza Manuscripts*, I, xxix–xxxiv.

218. Shinan, "Targumic Additions," 142.

219. Ibid., 145–55; idem, *Embroidered Targum*, 46–60.

aggadic traditions which expand upon the text, as in *midrashim*.[220] These targumic additions also refer to popular traditions, daily life and habits, and a full range of folk beliefs, including witchcraft, superstitions, miracles, angelology, and "popular" theology (e.g., simple and direct Divine retribution).[221] It has been suggested that Pseudo-Jonathan, more than any other *targum*, is a literary creation in which the editor incorporated the traditions at his disposal into a basic running commentary on the biblical text.[222] At times, as Shinan has pointed out, the editor was guilty of repetition and contradiction in carrying out his massive compilation.[223] In this area, too, significant differences are evident between Palestine and Babylonia; in the former there is a considerable variation in the degree of literalness as well as in the inclination to include additional material, while Babylonia's one targumic tradition, Onqelos, is literal and straightforward.

One particular targumic tradition which has a direct bearing on the synagogue and its art is to be found in Pseudo-Jonathan of Leviticus 26:1: "Nor shall you place a figured stone in your land for the purpose of prostration, but you may place a stoa [here, a mosaic pavement] impressed with drawings and figures in the ground of your sanctuaries [i.e., the floors of your synagogues], though not to bow down to [for purposes of worship], for I am the Lord your God."

The reality of Byzantine synagogues in Palestine, as we have seen above, is that many featured figural representations, ranging from birds, fish, and humans all the way to zodiac signs and Helios. However, in contrast to the sages, who, at best, took a rather dim view of this phenomenon, the author of this targumic tradition appears to have come to terms with this widespread, popular development, even granting it the sanction of the Torah.[224]

Sermon. From our earliest records of synagogue liturgy in the first century C.E., the sermon, or homily, constituted an integral part of the Torah-reading ceremony.[225] For late antiquity we have a great deal of material in this regard, in the form of both sermons and accounts of actual homiletical settings.[226]

---

220. Shinan, *Embroidered Targum*, 46–103; Alexander, "Jewish Aramaic Translations," 229–34; Hirschberg, "On the Place of Aramaic Targums," 21–23.

221. Shinan, *Embroidered Targum*, 104–67; idem, "Live Translation," 45–47. See also Hayward, "Targum Pseudo-Jonathan," 177–88.

222. See, for example, Maher, "Targum Pseudo-Jonathan," 264–90.

223. Shinan, "Aggadah of Palestinian Targums," 72–87; idem, "Targumic Additions," 149.

224. Klein, "Targum and Mosaics," 33–45; Fine, "Iconoclasm"; and above, Chap. 13.

225. See above, Chap. 5.

226. See Zunz, *Haderashot*, 163–75; Heinemann, *Public Sermons*, 7–28; Y. Frankel, *Darkei Ha-aggadah*, 16–26. This increase—and shift—in available source material may not be just a matter of different types of sources, but, as noted above, a matter of changes in the political, social, economic, and religious climate of third-century Palestine and later. These changes seem to have led to a different or, at least, additional religious emphasis among the sages vis-à-vis the general population. This is what seems to be

Although rabbinic involvement in targumic activity remains somewhat enigmatic, there is little question that a number of sages delivered sermons in synagogues. Rabbinic literature has preserved a number of interesting references in this regard, as we have noted above.[227] Besides known rabbis, we hear of itinerant preachers who would travel from place to place and address congregations.[228] We are told of one such preacher, identified simply as a *ḥaver*, who came to a synagogue and, having expounded a scriptural lesson, was accorded respect and material support.[229]

Sometimes such a transitory arrangement caused temporary embarrassment, for there were many different local customs. Thus, when visiting a community, R. Ḥanina b. R. Aḥa had to find out where the reading for that week began and then quickly improvise a sermon.[230] In general, sages were urged to have some teaching material ready at hand, so as to be able to respond to a spontaneous situation, and on at least one occasion, a congregation was said to have reacted negatively to such an improvisation.[231] Sermons appear to have been delivered from a raised platform so the speaker could be seen more readily, as was the custom with rhetors who spoke in a public setting.[232]

Since a synagogue audience may have been heterogeneous and included the more learned along with the less sophisticated, preachers were well advised to utilize whatever rhetorical talents and techniques were at their disposal in order to gain and hold the audience's attention.[233] These might include humor, the use of anecdotes, and other ploys.[234] R. Judah I, for example, is said to have always waited for the audience to assemble before he made his entrance.[235] Another way of engaging the congregation was to ask less important figures, often students, to deliver prefatory remarks; having been given a warm-

---

reflected in R. Isaac's well-known remark about changing times and the need for *aggadah* and not halakhah (PRK 12:3 [p. 205]). See my *Rabbinic Class*, 23–42, 98–133.

227. See above, Chap. 13. On the identification of a preacher as a sage, see Ecclesiastes Rabbah 9:17.

228. See M 'Eruvin 3:5 regarding the redefinition of the area covered by an *'eruv* to enable one to hear a visiting sage on the Sabbath. Paul may also have been perceived thusly in Antioch-in-Pisidia (Acts 13:14–15).

229. Tanḥuma, Terumah 1 (p. 45a). On preaching in the Byzantine church, see Cunningham, "Preaching and Community," 29–47.

230. Leviticus Rabbah 3:6 (p. 69).

231. Exodus Rabbah 40:1; Genesis Rabbah 28:3 (p. 261).

232. See, for example, Genesis Rabbah, 81:1 (p. 969); Midrash Hagadol, Exodus 35:1 (p. 723). On rhetors as noted by the midrash, see Sifre–Deuteronomy 343 (p. 394). See also above, Chap. 9.

233. See generally Lieberman, *Hellenism in Jewish Palestine*, 47–82; and, more specifically, Bregman, "Darshan," 19; Hirshman, "Preacher and His Public," 108–16; Mack, *Aggadic Midrash*, 38–56.

234. *Humor:* Genesis Rabbah 30:8 (p. 275). See also the statement in PRK 12:25 (p. 223), where "a laughing countenance" is associated with *aggadah*. *Other ploys:* Lamentations Rabbah 2:47 (p. 50b).

235. Deuteronomy Rabbah 7:8. See also ibid., Ki Tavo, 8 (ed. Lieberman, p. 111). Note the two versions: in one, the setting was a synagogue; in the other, an academy.

up, the audience was assumed to be primed for the main lecture,[236] although it is unclear whether the setting for such arrangements was the academy or the synagogue, or perhaps both. We are told that audiences fell asleep at times, requiring the preacher to display ingenuity in regaining their attention.[237]

Resh Laqish, in trying to appease the *Nasi* after a scathing attack on his office in a public sermon by Yosi of Ma'on, compares the role of the preacher in the synagogue to that of a theater performer, for whom the entertainment factor is of prime importance.[238] In the same vein, Jerome says the following about preachers' techniques: "The preachers make the people believe that the fictions which they invent are true; and after they have, in theatrical fashion, called forth applause . . . they arrogantly step forward, speak proudly, and usurp the authority of rulers.[239]

Sermons were delivered primarily, if not exclusively, on Sabbaths and holidays and, with rare exception, always in conjunction with the Torah- or haftarah-reading.[240] As early as the first century, Jesus and Paul were said to have delivered sermons following the reading of the haftarah; in the case of the former at least, the sermon was based on the Prophetic reading.[241] Rabbinic literature has preserved a different genre of sermons: those delivered before the Torah-reading and linked with its opening verse.[242] This type of sermon might take one of several forms. The most widespread is the *Petiḥta*, of which a very large number have been identified to date, in which a preacher begins with a verse far removed from the Torah portion (often from the Writings) and then makes his way from topic to topic through associative reasoning, until finally reaching the opening verse of the Torah-reading. In the meantime, he has managed to touch on a variety of themes,

236. Genesis Rabbah 98:13 (pp. 1261–62); Y Sukkah 5, 1, 55a.

237. Stories are told of R. 'Aqiva and R. Judah I in this regard; see Song of Songs Rabbah 1:15, 3; Yalqut Shim'oni, Genesis, 102 (p. 464). Chrysosotom has some interesting things to say regarding his church's audience: "Here in church there is great disturbance and confusion, and it is as bad as a tavern. There is so much laughing and tumult, with everyone chattering and making a noise, just as they do at the baths or the market" (I Cor. 36:5, as quoted in Kallistos, "Meaning of Divine Liturgy," 13–14).

238. Genesis Rabbah 80:1 (pp. 950–53); see also Y Sanhedrin 2, 6, 20c-d; Lamentations Rabbah, Proem 17 (p. 14); and Herr, "Synagogues and Theatres," 105–19.

239. Jerome, *In Ezek.* 34, 3, as quoted in S. Krauss, "Jews in the Works of the Church Fathers," 234.

240. The only exceptions noted in our sources are the account of R. Meir, who preached on Friday nights (Y Sotah 1, 4, 16d), and a late tradition which speaks of a Saturday afternoon sermon (Midrash on Proverbs 31 [p. 121 and n. 4]; Yalqut Shim'oni, Proverbs, 964). On a Babylonian custom of reading the haftarah on the Sabbath afternoon, following the *Minḥah* service, see B Shabbat 24a; and Sperber, *Jewish Customs*, I, 25; IV, 69.

241. *Jesus:* Luke 4:16–30. *Paul:* Acts 13:14–41. See also Bregman, "Triennial Haftarot," 74–84.

242. On these and other types of sermons, see Heinemann, *Public Sermons*, 11–24. Compare these types of sermons and the concern for the audience at which sermons were directed with the remarks of MacMullen regarding Chrysostom's audience ("Preacher's Audience," 503–11).

and at least part of the audience's interest has been held captive by curiosity as they have wondered how the preacher would get to the point everyone knew he must reach.[243]

A variation of this form, though far less ubiquitous in extant sources, is the *Tanḥuma-Yelamdenu* type, in which a relatively simple halakhic issue is posed at the beginning (by the preacher, a student, or a member of the congregation); in the course of addressing the issue the preacher must also work his way toward the opening verse of the Torah portion.[244]

Despite the apparent wealth of midrashic material in the various rabbinic compilations, it is not at all clear whether these texts are refined literary creations by a series of editors or are, in fact, testimony to what was actually said in front of a synagogue (or academy) audience. There is much evidence pointing to the careful literary crafting of much of this material, which would seem to indicate that it is more a literary than an oral tradition.[245] Thus, it may be that these homilies are more the product of editors organizing earlier traditions (and adding something of their own) than of what actually transpired in the synagogue. Even were we to assume that some of these homilies may indeed have been public sermons, it is not at all clear whether they were delivered in an academy (and therefore geared to a relatively closed rabbinic audience) or in a synagogue (i.e., addressed to the wider community).[246] Thus, extreme caution ought to be exercised before drawing too hasty an inference as to what was actually said before a synagogue audience in late antiquity.

As with every aspect of liturgical practice, we must remember that this discussion regarding sermons relates primarily to the Palestinian setting. There is little or no evidence for such rabbinic involvement in the Babylonian or Roman-Byzantine Diaspora. As for Diaspora liturgy generally, only scant traces have been identified in Christian and papyrological sources.[247] These Jewish communities appear to have nurtured customs and practices that had evolved over centuries with no apparent rabbinic input.

---

243. Heinemann, "Proem," 100–122; Mack, *Aggadic Midrash*, 57–69; Shinan, "Literature of the Ancient Synagogue," 140–43.

244. For example, B Shabbat 30a–b. See also Strack and Stemberger, *Introduction to Talmud and Midrash*, 329–33.

245. Bregman, "Circular Proems," 34–51; Sarason, "Petihtot," 557–65; idem, "Toward a New Agendum," 55–73; Hirshman, *Rivalry of Genius*, 23–30; Meir, "The Term 'Midrash,'" 103–10.

246. Heinemann, *Public Sermons*, 7–28. It is interesting to point out in this regard that books of *aggadah* to which the sages were opposed clearly circulated among the Jews and in the synagogues; see Y Shabbat 16, 1, 15c.

247. On the *Apostolic Constitutions*, see Simon, *Verus Israel*, 53–60; Fiensy, *Prayers Alleged to Be Jewish*, passim. On Papyrus Egerton 2, see Bell and Skeat, *Fragments*, 1–41; van der Horst, "Greek Evidence," 277–96. Regarding a Hebrew prayer from Byzantine Egypt, see Harding, "A Hebrew Congregational Prayer," 145–47.

Piyyut

The third basic component of Jewish liturgy in the Byzantine era, and the one entirely new element in synagogue worship at the time, was the *piyyut*. Derived from the Greek ποιήτης, the *piyyut* was a liturgical poem that may have been introduced into any one of a number of worship frameworks: in the *Shemaʿ* section (*yotzer*), in the morning *ʿAmidah* (*qerovah*, especially the one featuring the *Qedushah*, i.e., the *qedushta*), on Sabbath and festival evening services (*shivʿata*), in the *Mussaf ʿAmidah*, and on special occasions, such as the *ʿAvodah* service on Yom Kippur and on Tishʿa b'Av.[248] Written in Hebrew for the most part, the *piyyut* draws heavily on biblical and midrashic literature in its rich and often complex poetic presentation. Besides these sources, Hekhalot traditions played a role in setting the religious, intellectual, and literary framework for the compositions, as did the contemporary Christian liturgical tradition.[249]

We know very little about who the poets (*paytanim*) of these early compositions were or what their social and religious standing was within the communities in which they lived and functioned. In contrast to the belief of earlier generations, who dated the beginnings of *piyyut* to anywhere between the second and ninth centuries, there is a general consensus today that this form of religious expression emerged in Palestine sometime during the Byzantine era.[250]

More controversial, however, is the source of the *piyyut* form. Scholarly opinion in this matter is divided. Many have viewed the *piyyut* as a continuation of an earlier Jewish religious expression, although here opinions differ as to precisely which one: prayer, midrash, homily, biblical and post-biblical Hebrew poetry, or private supplication.[251] Other scholars assume a Byzantine setting for the origin of the *piyyut*, but here, too, there are a variety of suggestions. The classical explanation, deriving from several twelfth-century sources, is that the *piyyut* developed as a result of the persecution of Jews when their regular worship services were prohibited. It offered a liturgical form to substitute for the regular prayers (Samauʾal b. Yaḥya al-Magribi) or to replace study (Judah b. Barzillai al-Barceloni). Often these reports have been connected with Justinian's famous *Novella* or a

---

248. For a listing of various types of *piyyutim*, see Fleischer, *Hebrew Liturgical Poetry*, 67–76; Heinemann and Petuchowski, *Literature of the Synagogue*, 212–13.

249. P. Bloch, "Die יורדי מרכבה," 18–25, 69–74, 257–66, 305–11; Gruenwald, "Yannai's Piyyutim," 257–77; Yahalom, "*Piyyut* as Poetry," 112. On the Christian context, see below.

250. Fleischer, "Problems Related to Liturgical Function," 60–63; Lerner, "Origin of Piyyut," 13–34. For an early, second-century dating, see Schirmann, "Hebrew Liturgical Poetry," 129–33. On poetic renditions of the Yom Kippur *ʿAvodah* service which preceded Yosi b. Yosi, see Yahalom, *Priestly Palestinian Poetry*, 21–55; as well as the earlier comments in Roth, "Ecclesiasticus," 171–78.

251. Elbogen, *Jewish Liturgy*, 219–25 (prayer, *aggadah*); Zunz, *Literaturgeschichte*, 22–29 (midrash and *targum*); Mirsky, *Piyyut*, 7–85; idem, *Beginnings of Piyyut*, 18–29 (midrash, Hebrew poetry); Ta-Shma, "Beginning of *Piyyut*," 285–88 (prayer). See also Yahalom, *Priestly Palestinian Poetry*, 21–30.

Sassanian persecution.[252] Fleischer, who views the *piyyut* as a strictly internal Jewish development, considers this genre to have been a form of rebellion against fixed prayer and
a means by which the rabbinically ordained prayer framework could be kept intact while,
at the same time, instilling it with creativity and freshness.[253]

Other scholars have emphasized the elements common to the *piyyut* and the poetry of
surrounding cultures and have posited the influence of the latter on the former, in form
and possibly also in content. When the assumption was that the *piyyut* stemmed from the
Middle Ages, it was thought that Muslim poetry was a decisive factor.[254] When it became
clear that a Byzantine setting was indicated, Werner made a case for Christian liturgical
influence on Jewish forms.[255] Schirmann also recognized the common elements in both,
but since he dated the Jewish evidence quite early, i.e., to the second century c.e., he
therefore assumed that Jewish practice influenced Christian practice, and not the other
way around.[256]

The *piyyut* focused on the basic components of the service (the *Shema‘* and *'Amidah*);
in fact, this is a further indication as to what constituted the formal public prayer service
at the time. The *piyyut* was intended from the outset for public recital by the *hazzan*. We
know of no such poetry for private use. As a matter of fact, the silent recitation of the
'Amidah probably was retained even when the *piyyut* replaced the usual oral repetition of
the *'Amidah*.

It is far from clear what sort of reality lay behind this liturgical phenomenon. For
example, how many synagogues would have had such a poetic recitation on any given
Sabbath, and how often would this occur in any particular place? While thousands of
piyyutim have already been identified, it is not clear how widespread or frequent such
recitations were. While Fleischer's theory that the early *piyyut* (in contrast to its later
forms and the *piyyut* today) was intended to replace the public prayer service for a particular morning has often been quoted,[257] it is far from clear whether this was always the
case or whether there might have been different concurrent practices in this regard.

Of more consequence is the issue of comprehension, noted above. Even today, when

---

252. Heinemann and Petuchowski, *Literature of the Synagogue*, 206–7. See also the comments of Pirqoi
ben Baboi, in Ginzberg, *Geniza Studies*, II, 551–52; J. Mann, "Changes in the Divine Service," 251–59;
Baron, *Social and Religious History of the Jews*, VII, 94–96; Linder, *Jews in Roman Imperial Legislation*,
404–5.

253. Fleischer, "Problems Related to Liturgical Function," 52–55; idem, *Hebrew Liturgical Poetry*, 41–
46. Recently Elior, following Gruenwald ("Priestly Traditions"), has emphasized the priestly background
of Hekhalot traditions; "From Earthly Temple to Heavenly Shrines," 352–63, 369–79. See also Ta-Shma,
"Beginning of Piyyut," 285–88.

254. See, for example, Graetz, *History of the Jews*, III, 111–18.

255. Werner, *Sacred Bridge*. See also his "Hebrew and Oriental Christian Metrical Hymns," 397–432.

256. Schirmann, "Hebrew Liturgical Poetry," 123–61.

257. Fleischer, *Yozer*, 11–15.

studying the *piyyut* and utilizing the various apparatuses available, one does not find it an easy task to understand the language of these poems or their allusions, metaphors, and nuances. If the intended audience was the ordinary synagogue congregant, then comprehension of this genre speaks wonders for the intellectual level of the typical Jewish worshipper. Perhaps, however, *piyyutim* were to be enjoyed primarily for their aesthetic value, i.e., the melodies in which they were sung. Barring the latter, are we to assume that these compositions were recited when only a very few in attendance could understand their language? Alternatively, were the *piyyutim* intended primarily for certain types of audiences in which the participation of the learned was more pronounced (for example, an academy setting)?[258] Whatever the case, the contrast between the attempt to make the Torah-reading and sermon comprehensible to a wider audience, on the one hand, and the complexity of most *piyyutim*, on the other, is puzzling. We are not in a position at present to answer the above questions. While the *piyyut* has led to a new understanding of the variety of components in Jewish worship in late antiquity, it has also left us with a series of intriguing questions to ponder.

It is interesting to note that a number of themes which frequently appear in *piyyutim* also found expression in other synagogue media in Byzantine Palestine, and there may well be a correlation between some of these phenomena. For example, six synagogues located all over the country display zodiac signs, and the use of the zodiac theme is also quite frequent in these compositions.[259] In the latter, the theme is often introduced when they address the change of season in the spring and fall. Thus, prayers for dew (on the first day of Passover) or for rain (on Shemini 'Atzeret at the conclusion of the Sukkot holiday) utilize this theme, as do *piyyutim* marking the New Moon. Moreover, the zodiac motif appeared when a *paytan* wished to involve the entire creation in the mood he was trying to capture: sadness at the loss of the Temple on Tish'a b'Av and joy on Yom Kip-

258. Goitein, *Mediterranean Society*, II, 159-61; Fleischer, *Hebrew Liturgical Poetry*, 273-75; and, for greater detail, Elizur, "Congregation in the Synagogue," 171-90.

The same intellectual disparity seems to have surfaced with regard to some of the learned sermons of the church fathers. There, too, it is impossible to know exactly how many in the congregation really understood what was being said. A rather negative assessment of this problem with regard to preaching is offered in Maguire, *Art and Eloquence*, 6:

"Many of the church sermons were written in a highly complicated, affected, and archaizing style, which may have been as far from the everyday speech of a Byzantine in the Middle Ages as Chaucerian English is from the average English of today. The medieval preachers who continued to compose in this style were members of a tiny elite who had received their higher education in the schools of Constantinople. Their homilies may have been all but incomprehensible to provincial audiences if they were delivered in the style in which they were written."

For a more positive assessment of the early Byzantine era, see Cunningham, "Preaching and Community," 29-45.

259. Yahalom, "Zodiac Signs," 313-18; idem, "*Piyyut* as Poetry," 119-20; idem, "Synagogue Inscriptions," 54-55; Shinan, "Synagogues in the Land of Israel," 148.

pur when the *'Avodah* service concluded, with the high priest emerging unscathed from
his prayer in the Holy of Holies.

The twenty-four priestly courses is another motif in many *piyyutim*, especially those
intended for Tish'a b'Av. The most famous of Byzantine *paytanim*, Eli'ezer ha-Qallir (or
Qillir), excelled in this regard, as did Hadutaha and Pinḥas, who also resorted to this
theme regularly, even on ordinary Sabbaths. In this last instance, the *piyyut* was appended to the last blessing of the *'Amidah* and became part of the priestly benediction.[260]
It is tempting to speculate that much of the impetus for composing such poetry came
from priestly circles wishing to maintain the memory of the Temple and, indirectly, their
own standing in the community. These *piyyutim* go hand in hand with the five inscriptions naming the priestly courses which were found in Byzantine synagogues in Palestine
(a sixth was discovered in Yemen). Such plaques were presumably affixed to the wall of
the synagogue and, as noted above, listed the names of the twenty-four priestly courses
and where they resided in the Galilee.[261]

Piyyutim, however, may also have had contemporary relevance in some of the themes
they developed. These compositions would often reflect the difficulties and pressures
felt by Jews living under Byzantine-Christian rule. Both the Imperial government and
the church are reflected in a sometimes critical, sometimes defensive posture assumed
by various *paytanim*.[262] A very powerful and touching expression of such sentiments is
offered by the *paytan* Yannai to the verse "And the Lord saw that Leah was hated" (Gen.
29:30). Playing on the contrast of love (Rachel) and hate (Leah), the poet turns to God
in despair and anguish, saying:

> Our eyes are weak with longing for your love,
> O loving One,
>   for we are hated by the hating enemy;
> Look how afflicted we are from within,
> See how hated we are from without—
>   as You looked on Lea's affliction
> and saw her tormented by hate.
> Within the house she was hated
> and from without detested.
> But not every loved one is loved
> nor every hated one hated:
>   there are some who are hated below
> and yet loved above.
> Those whom You hate are hated;

---

260. Fleischer, "Regarding the Courses," 142–61; idem, "Piyyutim of Yannai," 176–84.
261. See above, Chap. 15.
262. Maier, "Piyyut and Anti-Christian Polemics," 100–110; Mirsky, *Beginnings of Piyyut*, 46–53.

those whom You love are loved.
The hatred against us is because
we love You, O Holy One.[263]

To reinforce this attempt to reach the masses, we may refer to a corpus of some fifty Aramaic *piyyutim*, which may have been intended for the large number of congregants who would best understand this language.[264]

On the basis of the material at hand, all the *piyyutim* we have come from Palestine. Babylonia does not seem to have produced any such compositions in late antiquity, and judging from the attitude of several *geonim* from ensuing centuries, there was not a great deal of enthusiasm for this genre, at the least within Babylonian rabbinic circles.[265] As noted, our information is woefully scanty regarding the rest of the Diaspora. Two inscriptions, one from Rome and another from Aphrodisias, speak of psalm singers, who may have been synagogue functionaries who recited hymns similar to *piyyutim*.[266] The *super orans* (chief cantor) noted in an inscription from Emerita, Spain, may also have recited *piyyutim* along with the regular prayers, but of this we cannot be sure.[267] Finally, a fragmentary Hebrew papyrus, dating to the third or fourth century C.E., was found in Oxyrhynchus in Egypt. The text appears to be some sort of *piyyut*, and on the basis of the small fragment preserved, it has been interpreted as a theme appropriate for commemorating the destruction of the Temple or perhaps the holiday of Shavu'ot.[268]

BEYOND LATE ANTIQUITY

The end of late antiquity and the few centuries thereafter (fifth to ninth centuries C.E.) were characterized by efforts to compile and consolidate a wide variety of oral and literary traditions. It was during this period that both *talmudim* were edited, Hekhalot traditions coalesced, midrashic works were compiled, and new halakhic and apocryphal books were composed.[269]

---

263. Yahalom, "*Piyyut* as Poetry," 125.

264. See Sokoloff and Yahalom, "Aramaic Piyyutim," 309–21.

265. See, for example, Pirqoi ben Baboi, in Ginzberg, *Geniza Studies*, II, 544–54, and comments of the editor, 508–27; Baron, *Social and Religious History of the Jews*, VII, 100–105; Heinemann and Petuchowski, *Literature of the Synagogue*, 209–11.

266. Noy, *JIWE*, II no. 502; Reynolds and Tannenbaum, *Jews and God-Fearers*, 5, 9.

267. Lifshitz, "Prolegomenon," no. 665a.

268. De Boer, "Notes," 49–57.

269. On these cultural developments generally, see Dan, "Byzantine Rule," 323–48. A series of fragments known collectively as *Sifrut Ha-ma'asim* (Law-Case Literature) has been gradually accumulating over the past half-century as a result of the publication of Genizah materials. A number of these fragments relate to the synagogue and the worship context therein. See Margaliot, *Hilkhot*, 1–16.

Liturgical matters likewise received much attention: targumic traditions, such as Targum Pseudo-Jonathan, were redacted, the *piyyut* flourished, sermonic material was gathered (or created) in a number of midrashic compilations, and two works were composed at the outset of the Middle Ages (seventh to eighth centuries) to record the various liturgical practices then in vogue. We have already referred to both of these works on many occasions: (1) *Differences in Customs between the People of the East and the People of Eretz-Israel*, which includes some fifty-six halakhic divergencies between Palestine and Babylonia, of which 25% are related to the synagogue and its liturgy, and (2) Tractate Soferim, which has an eclectic agenda. The first nine chapters describe the writing of Torah scrolls, from laws relating to the writer, to discourses on the scroll itself, to textual variants and readings of particular verses. Chapters 10–17 deal with the Torah-readings, especially those intended for particular situations, from festivals and New Moons to Purim. The last four chapters (18–21) deal with the prayer setting, focusing on the psalms and liturgical matters connected with holidays and holy days. This section also contains smatterings of *aggadah*.

These last-mentioned works were a natural and necessary development given the accumulation of customs and practices from late antiquity, as well as the ever more intensive contact (or, should we say, conflict) between Babylonia and Palestine. Such divergent customs evoked a response of either elucidation (*Differences in Customs*) or some sort of synthesis (Tractate Soferim). However, external factors also may have played a role in hastening this process of consolidation: the persecutions of late antiquity; the influence of liturgical developments in the Christian and Islamic worlds; and competing ideologies, such as those of the Samaritans and Karaites. Whatever the case, the effects were aided by new developments in the Jewish world, which included increased migration, easier opportunities for communication, and ever greater political and religious centralization in Babylonia.[270]

The need for such consolidation at this time seems to have been quite apparent, and a statement by Sa'adiah Gaon makes this fact quite clear: "it is thus necessary to gather the prayers and blessings of our time, i.e., the period of the Exile, especially because of what is happening owing to three things, neglect, additions, and deletions, and because of them one should be concerned about forgetting and making changes. . . . with respect to our people's traditions regarding prayers and blessings, there are matters that have been so neglected that they have become completely forgotten except by select individuals; others were either so amplified or truncated that they have become completely changed and lost their original meaning."[271]

Tractate Soferim is the earliest compilation of Jewish liturgical practices. It focuses

---

270. Baron, *Social and Religious History of the Jews*, VII, 64–73.
271. *Siddur R. Saadja Gaon*, 10–11.

on those traditions discussed in the Mishnah and *talmudim*, not infrequently adding de-tails not otherwise documented.[272] As indicated above, very little is said about the regular weekly Torah-readings, as most of the material relates to special occasions. Prayer, too, is clearly ancillary in the compiler's agenda. There is almost total silence regarding the *'Amidah* and *Shema'*, but preliminary and concluding hymns and psalms are spelled out, in some instances for the first time in any extant source.[273] A second recitation of the *Barkhu* introductory call to prayer is introduced for latecomers, and it is here that the *Qaddish* prayer is first mentioned.[274]

The *Qaddish* prayer appears as an integral part of the service. It was to be recited, on two occasions, once at the conclusion of the Torah-reading ceremony and once as part of the afternoon (and presumably the morning) service.[275] The earlier history of this prayer is shrouded in mystery.[276] The central verse, taken from Ps. 113:2 and Dan. 2:20, was recited regularly in synagogues as early as the second century.[277] It is mentioned on a number of occasions as a refrain at the conclusion of a public-oriented study session.[278] Another key phrase—the opening words of the *Qaddish* (יתגדל ויתקדש ויתברך ויתרמם שמך מלכנו)—is noted in the Yerushalmi as prefacing a prayer for rain.[279] Also, the similarity between various phrases and terms in the *Qaddish* and Jesus' *pater nostrum* prayer has long been noted (Matt. 6:9-15; Luke 11:2-4).

While it has generally been assumed, since the time of Zunz, that the *Qaddish* was originally associated with study, this may not have been the case.[280] The other instances noted would seem to indicate that various phrases were used in different contexts, and the prayer we know as the *Qaddish* was a composite created apparently toward the close of late antiquity.

As had been the case for centuries, the main parts of the service required a quorum of ten for public recitation: the *Shema'*, the *'Amidah*, the priestly blessing, the Torah-and haftarah-readings, and the *Qaddish* and *Barkhu* prayers.[281] This last-mentioned call

---

272. See, for example, Tractate Soferim 11:4-6 (pp. 220-24).

273. Ibid., 18:1 (pp. 308-10); and Liebreich, "Compilation of Pesuke De-Zimra," 255-67; idem, "*Pesuke De-Zimra* Benedictions," 195-206.

274. Tractate Soferim 10:6 (pp. 216-17).

275. *Torah-reading:* ibid., 14:6 (pp. 259-60); 21:5 (pp. 357-58). *Afternoon service (Minhah):* ibid., 18:10 (p. 322).

276. The classic work on this subject is that of de Sola Pool, *Kaddish.* See also Elbogen, *Jewish Liturgy,* 80-84.

277. See above, note 111.

278. B Sotah 49a; Midrash on Proverbs 10 (p. 57 and n. 38); Ecclesiastes Rabbah 9:15, 7. See also Jellinek, *Bet Midrash,* V, p. 46.

279. Y Berakhot 9, 2, 14a; Y Ta'anit 1, 3, 64b.

280. Zunz, *Haderashot,* 483 n. 64; Elbogen, *Jewish Liturgy,* 80; Heinemann, *Prayer,* 266-67.

281. Tractate Soferim 10:6 (pp. 216-17).

to prayer (*Barkhu*) required only seven (and according to some, only six) people in Palestinian practice.

Despite the generally accepted practice to combine the two key segments of the prayer service (i.e., the *Shemaʿ* and the *ʿAmidah*) without interruption, it seems that, in Palestine at least, this was not always done. Although R. Yoḥanan had advocated joining the blessing of redemption (גאולה) with the *ʿAmidah*, the custom recorded in Tractate Soferim differs somewhat: "And the sages directed the *ḥazzanim* to recite after the redemption blessing the *Qaddish* ["May the name of God be blessed from now and forever more"], and after this 'Blessed is God who is blessed' [i.e., the *"Barkhu"*]."[282] Thus, the flow of the service between these two sections, so important according to a number of talmudic sources, was broken by additional elements. Moreover, the prominence and special status of this *Shemaʿ* section is expressed not only by the form of recitation, but also by the fact that this prayer was said standing,[283] a not uncommon practice with certain prayers in the Palestinian setting. As far back as the first century C.E., Bet Shammai insisted on standing for the morning recitation of the *Shemaʿ*, and the debate continued into the second century.[284] Later on, in the amoraic period, different practices are attested.[285]

The Palestinian custom of standing for important prayers was not restricted to the *Shemaʿ* and *ʿAmidah*. We read, for example, of the congregation standing at one point during the blessings following the reading of the haftarah, on Passover when reciting the *Hallel*, after the Torah-reading when saying the *Qaddish*, and at other times.[286] In the *seder* (i.e., order of prayer) of the Babylonian R. ʿAmram Gaon (ninth century) specific mention is made of this practice, albeit in a distinctly critical tone: "As for those who pretend to be rigorous in their religious behavior by accepting the yoke of the kingdom [i.e., the *Shemaʿ*] standing, this is a mistake and [this is nothing more than] simplemindedness, ignorance, and foolishness."[287]

By this time, the daily service regularly included a special psalm for each day of the week; and the holiday liturgy—including the three festivals, Hanukkah, Purim, the High Holidays, and Tishʿa b'Av—was elaborated as well.[288]

With respect to the synagogue liturgy, it is clear that there was constant development throughout the period of seven hundred or so years that we have been tracing. Begin-

---

282. Ibid.

283. *Differences in Customs*, no. 1 (pp. 91–94). On the significance of standing in prayer, see Ehrlich, "'When You Pray,'" 38–50.

284. M Berakhot 1:3; T Berakhot 1:4 (p. 2).

285. Y Berakhot 2, 1, 4a; cf., however, PRK 9:5 (pp. 155–56).

286. *Haftarah:* Tractate Soferim 13:9 (pp. 245–46). *Passover Hallel:* ibid., 18:3 (p. 314). *Qaddish:* ibid., 21:5 (pp. 356–58). *Other times: Differences in Customs*, no. 1 (pp. 92–93).

287. Seder R. ʿAmram Gaon 1, 21 (p. 15).

288. Tractate Soferim 18:2 (pp. 310–13); 19:5 (pp. 327–28); 20:5–9 (pp. 345–52).

ning with an almost exclusive focus on the reading of Scriptures (at least in Second Temple Judaea), along with other activities intended to enhance this experience, synagogue liturgy expanded over the course of late antiquity to include other important components. The prayer dimension was crystallized in the second and third centuries, while the *piyyut* emerged as a significant element in the fifth to seventh centuries.

The liturgical dimension, like the halakhah, was exposed to centripetal and centrifugal forces. There were periods of consolidation and others of increasing differences and variation. The non-sacrificial component of Jewish worship during the Second Temple period appears to have been diffuse and largely dependent on local initiative. This was certainly the case with respect to the prayer component in Palestine, but only within certain circles, such as the Temple priesthood or sectarian groups. On the other hand, the tannaitic period witnessed a serious rabbinic effort to create a new framework which would integrate some of what had existed earlier, while adding new material as well. This effort, which lasted about a century, seems to have created a degree of unity while still allowing for a wide range of diversity.

With the growth of a second rabbinic center in Babylonia in the third century, some significant variations emerged in synagogue liturgy. Each tradition not only developed within its own religious and social setting, but also was influenced by its immediate non-Jewish historical context. This is particularly evident in the homily, the *piyyut*, and an expanded targumic tradition (Pseudo-Jonathan) which developed in Byzantine Palestine, and this is in contrast to the Babylonian liturgy, which exhibited little of these last-mentioned components. The Babylonian Targum Onqelos, as against the Targum Pseudo-Jonathan of Palestine, is a case in point; the former has a more focused rabbinic agenda.

Thus, by late antiquity, the pendulum had swung in the opposite direction, and this situation called for a renewed period of consolidation. This process was to continue for a number of centuries, reaching its apogee in the ninth and tenth centuries with the appearance of the first *siddurim*, composed by ʿAmram and Saʿadiah Gaon.[289]

---

289. Baron, *Social and Religious History of the Jews*, VII, 111-18; L. A. Hoffman, *Canonization*, 160-71.

seventeen

ICONOGRAPHY: THE LIMITS
seventeen OF INTERPRETATION

J ewish art is a relatively new field in Jewish studies. It was only in the first half of the twentieth century that scholars began addressing this subject in one form or another; the pioneering works are by Kohl and Watzinger (1916), Schwarz (1928), Cohn-Wiener (1929), Sukenik (1932), Wischnitzer (1934), Landsberger (1935), and M. Narkiss (1939), among others.[1] However, it was the discovery of a series of sensational archeological remains (the Na'aran and Bet Alpha mosaics in 1919–21 and 1928–29, respectively, the wall frescoes of Dura Europos in 1932, and the remains of the Bet She'arim necropolis in 1936–40) which catapulted this field into the forefront of scholarly interest. In the following years, these finds and their ramifications were discussed by Rostovtzeff, Grabar, Hopkins, Cumont, de Mesnil de Buisson, Goodenough, and others.[2] However, given the time required to digest these revolutionary findings fully, together with the disruption brought about by World War II, it was not until the late forties and fifties that sustained attention was focused on these and other finds—earlier ones (such

1. For a survey of the development of the field of Jewish art with specific reference to many of these scholars, see Sabar, "Development," 264–75. To Sabar's listing I would add Kohl and Watzinger, *Antike Synagogen*; Sukenik, *Synagogue of Beth Alpha*. See also Baron, *Social and Religious History of the Jews* (1937 ed.), III, 51–53 n. 15.

2. See the bibliography for these years at the end of Sukenik's *Synagogue of Dura*, 193–96; as well as Goodenough, "Symbolism in Hellenistic Jewish Art," 103–14.

as the catacombs of Rome and Galilean-type synagogues) and others which had come to
light in the 1930s (Gerasa, Jericho, Ḥuseifa, and Apamea). Landsberger, Wischnitzer, and
Narkiss are among the most prominent scholarly figures of the immediate postwar era.[3]

The study of Jewish art was given an enormous boost in the fifties and sixties by
the publication of Goodenough's monumental thirteen-volume study of ancient Jewish
symbols (1953–68) and Kraeling's meticulous final report of the Dura synagogue finds
(1956). Roth's collection of essays by leading figures in the field (*Jewish Art*, 1961) was
another landmark, as were Mayers' *Bibliography of Jewish Art* (1967), the inauguration of
the *Journal of Jewish Art* (1974, subsequently renamed *Jewish Art*), and the establishment
of the Center for Jewish Art (1979) at the Hebrew University of Jerusalem. Moreover,
these past decades have witnessed both the discovery of a plethora of archeological finds,
which have immensely enhanced the repertoire of Jewish artistic remains, and a broad
spectrum of scholarly treatments. In the former category, mention should be made of
the mosaic floors of Ḥammat Tiberias, Sardis, Susiya, and Sepphoris and the carved
stone fragments from Sardis and the Golan synagogues; in the latter category is a host
of articles as well as full-length monographs on Jewish art, especially those of Gutmann,
Weitzmann, H. Kessler, Sed-Rajna, Revel-Neher, and Hachlili.[4]

METHODOLOGICAL CONSIDERATIONS

We have had occasion to refer to synagogue artistic remains in the previous chapters—actual sites, different types of depictions, and their relationship to extant literary
sources. However, we have yet to look at the meanings of these depictions, their iconography, and the possible uses of this material for a fuller understanding of Jewish society,
and its historical and social contexts, and of the synagogue and its religious traditions in
particular.

In what follows I do not intend to present new material, offer additional interpretations
of specific material, or summarize past research. My aim is essentially methodological.
I wish to pose a number of questions regarding the cogency and feasibility of offering
interpretations of Jewish artistic remains given our present knowledge. Although many
art historians have been inclined to invest these artistic remains with heavy overlays of
symbolic and iconographic significance, such interpretations more often than not remain
unconvincing. To identify the specific subject matter of a particular panel or scene is
not usually a problem; biblical scenes as well as symbols and motifs drawn from Jewish
tradition are usually readily identifiable and at times are even labeled with an appropri-

---

3. See Sabar, "Development," 268–71.

4. See the bibliographies listed in Gutmann, "Synagogue and Catacomb Art," 1339; Weitzmann and
H. Kessler, *Frescoes*, 194–95; Sed-Rajna, *Jewish Art*; Revel-Neher, *L'arche d'alliance*; idem, *Image of the Jew*;
Hachlili, *Art and Archaeology—Israel*; idem, *Art and Archaeology—Diaspora*. A listing of recently published
articles and monographs in the field appears at the end of each volume of *Jewish Art*.

ate inscription (e.g., at Dura Europos, Bet Alpha). The problem arises, however, when one sets out to interpret these depictions. What does a particular scene or sequence of scenes mean? What messages are being conveyed by the artist, the donors, or the community at large by these depictions? Here, the literary evidence is indispensable for the interpretation of art. It can provide the cultural-historical context of the artist and the congregation, and it can help us understand what beliefs and views were being expressed.

Let me make the nature of these reservations quite clear at the outset. I have few qualms about a working assumption that many narrative and figural depictions, as well as representations of Jewish religious artifacts in synagogues, may well have had symbolic implications. This holds true for biblical representations, the Helios and zodiac motifs, and for most, if not all, depictions of Jewish religious symbols. It is hard to imagine, for example, that mosaic floors in synagogues were simply "decorated," or that a panel with zodiac motifs was chosen merely for its aesthetic value and placed at random next to one containing a cluster of Jewish symbols or a biblical scene fraught with religious significance (as is evidenced in literary sources).[5]

This does not mean, of course, that all depictions were necessarily imbued with symbolic meaning. It is not at all clear whether each of the dozens of biblical scenes from Dura Europos had some sort of meaning or significance, or whether their arrangement in a given register or wall was meant to invoke an overall message. The various explanations offered in response to the above questions have been quite diverse and often mutually exclusive. While some arguments appear more compelling than others—and some may even be on the mark—certainty in this regard is well nigh impossible.

This brings us to the crux of the matter. Given the limited array of archeological material at our disposal (even after a half-century of discovery and publication), together with the minimal amount of literary data that may in some way relate to these artistic motifs and their possible meanings, our hands are in effect tied when it comes to pinning down a specific interpretation. There simply is not enough of a historical context to offer a degree of assuredness in determining what a particular symbol or representation might have meant at a specific time or place. This is certainly true with regard to a site such as the Dura synagogue. Despite the synagogue's unparalleled array of biblical scenes, we have no independent source which can shed light on the beliefs and practices of this Jewish community located on the Euphrates River on the eastern frontier of the Roman Empire in the first half of the third century. Rabbinic texts—most often Palestinian *midrashim* or *targumim* invoked to reinforce one or another interpretation of these frescoes—are inevitably plucked from a world far removed from Dura itself. The assumption of a common tradition behind these midrashic and artistic expressions is possible, but becomes increasingly problematic as the chronological and geographical gap between the two bodies of evidence widens.

---

5. Cf., however, Hachlili, "Synagogues in the Land of Israel," 128.

Moreover, all-encompassing theories such as messianism (Wischnitzer, Goldstein), mysticism (Goodenough), and, more recently, the Jewish-Christian polemic (H. Kessler) have been suggested as capable of explaining the various figural and non-figural representations appearing throughout this synagogue.[6] Such attempts, as well as less ambitious ones, are intriguing but, in the end, unconvincing. Whereas some panels might fit one or another theory quite nicely, in many instances the theory is not especially persuasive, and in still others the interpretations are forced. As a result, none has won general acclaim.

One need not single out Dura Europos in this respect. The impressive mosaic floors of Bet Alpha, Ḥammat Tiberias, and Sepphoris, which include zodiac signs and representations of Helios, do not, in and of themselves, provide a cultural or religious context in which to interpret these scenes. Even were we to draw from similar examples in Jewish and non-Jewish art, these remains would still require interpretation. Rabbinic literature, with its vast variety of traditions spanning a millennium, can likewise be ambiguous, and targumic traditions, ancient *piyyutim*, and Jewish liturgy are no less enigmatic with regard to the dating and interpretation of these remains.

The last-noted issue of interpretation is, however, still more complicated. Even were we to arrive at some sort of satisfactory explanation, to whom would it apply? To the artisan who actually executed the work? To the one who produced the supposed copybook from which the artisan drew his inspiration? To the donors or synagogue leaders, who undoubtedly had a decisive say in the choice of artistic patterns? Or, perhaps, to the community at large, who may also have had some input—although this very likely varied from place to place? And to which Jewish community are we referring—those living when the synagogue was built or those living fifty or a hundred years later? That a motif as rich as the ʿAqedah or Helios would have conveyed different meanings to different people, even at one and the same time, not to speak of different generations, should be rather self-evident (see below).

Moreover, symbolic and representational interpretations were not necessarily constant in varying historical contexts. An urban setting may have given rise to an interpretation which would have been unknown or unacceptable in a rural context, and the same holds true of a community in the Roman East as against one in the West, or one in a Greek-speaking (and presumably more acculturated and sophisticated) environment as opposed to one in which Aramaic was the lingua franca. Changes in interpretation were inevitable over the centuries, if not over generations. The facade of the Temple or representations

---

6. Wischnitzer, *Messianic Theme*; Goldstein, "Judaism of the Synagogues"; Goodenough, *Jewish Symbols*; Weitzmann and H. Kessler, *Frescoes*. For a suggestion that the art of the baptistry at the Dura church could be understood as a Christian polemic in favor of the primacy of Sunday as the proper day of worship, see Goranson, "Battle over Holy Day," 23–33. For another instance of a Jewish-Christian polemic involving art forms, see H. Kessler, "Through the Temple Veil," 53–77; see also Maser, "Synagoge und Ecclesia," 9–26.

of Jewish symbols may not have meant the same thing in third-century Dura that they did in fourth-century Rome, fifth-century Sepphoris, or sixth-century Bet Alpha. Likewise, Helios in fourth-century Tiberias may have evoked a set of beliefs and associations different from those evoked in rural Naʿaran or Bet Alpha in the sixth century.[7] As Elsner has argued in his work on Roman and Byzantine artistic perspectives, "People relate to works of art in different ways, depending upon different contexts and at different times."[8]

COMPARISONS WITH CHRISTIAN ART

Christian art, so often invoked by students of Jewish art, is in many ways of an entirely different order. Owing to the wealth of Christian art that had accumulated by the fifth and sixth centuries, internal artistic comparisons and the relation of art to contemporary customs and to the ideology articulated by church fathers living at the time were made possible. This allowed for comparison and the creation of ever more inclusive theories. In addition, there are a number of Christian literary sources which actually describe and interpret church decorations in these centuries. Both Paulinus of Nola and Prudentius discuss scenes depicted in their churches in Italy, as does Choricius of Gaza with regard to the mosaics of that city's church.[9] Thus, when Mathews suggests that the "processional convergence on an axially organized core image provided a formula for the program of the Early Christian church,"[10] he is relying upon the following data: "A confluence of figures toward Christ is prominent in the art of the catacombs and sarcophagi, and this composition governs a surprising number of church programs of the widest diversity in size, shape, and function. Over sixty percent of the apse compositions catalogued by Ihm include centripetal processions. All of the mosaicked churches of Ravenna fall in this class, including basilicas, baptisteries, and the octagon of Saint Vitalis."[11]

The remains of Jewish art known to us today are far more modest. There is no Jewish equivalent of the Ravenna churches. Besides the Dura synagogue, no other Diaspora building has anywhere near the same kinds of figural remains, and the six Palestinian synagogues with the Helios and zodiac design, in addition to about the same number featuring a biblical personality (Gaza, Susiya, Naʿaran, Sepphoris, and perhaps Merot) or a biblical scene (Bet Alpha and Sepphoris), are a distinct minority of the synagogue remains

---

7. See the comments by Frend ("Town and Countryside," 25–42) with respect to Christian communities in late antiquity.

8. Elsner, *Art and the Roman Viewer*, 1. See also Ovadiah, "Art in the Ancient Synagogue," 308.

9. Davis-Meyer, *Early Medieval Art*, 17–23 (Paulinus), 25–33 (Prudentius); Grabar, *Christian Iconography*, 100–101. My thanks to Professor Z. Amishai-Maisels for referring me to these sources. See also Mango, *Art of the Byzantine Empire*, 32–39.

10. Mathews, *Clash of Gods*, 176.

11. Ibid., 150. In this regard, see also Miles, "Santa Maria Maggiore's Mosaics," 155–75.

discovered throughout Israel. Most synagogues appear to have had minimal decorations, and these contain, for the most part, only floral and geometric designs of greater or lesser sophistication.[12] Thus, in the overwhelming majority of synagogues from late antiquity, the possible functions of art—to stimulate historical memory, to highlight ritual symbols and through them certain Jewish religious observances, to complement the instruction that took place in religious institutions, and to instill messianic hopes—could hardly be realized.[13]

Comparison of Jewish and Christian art with a view toward their connection with liturgical function, a topic that has merited much consideration of late, is likewise fraught with difficulties. Much of the concern of church art historians in relating artistic material to liturgical ritual is often explained by the need to illustrate and concretize highly complex theological issues. The didactic function of art in the church setting is assumed to be of great importance. In discussing apsidal imagery, Hellemo has the following to say:

> During the liturgical introductory invocation (Sursum corda), the congregation's attention is called upon and mental concentration is requested. As the celebration of the Eucharist involves complicated chains of thought, the participants need all the help they can get in order to understand the depths of meaning contained in the act. To the overall synthesis of the various chains of thought which contribute to the meaning of the Eucharist, the visible pictorial programs are of the greatest value. Imagery's most important quality is to recapitulate in synthesis that which words and ritual acts take such time to present. Thus, all additional elements entering the liturgy as it progresses can be retained by the congregation. In our opinion, apsidal imagery unifies and summarizes the central content of the eucharistic prayer. By doing this it furnishes a certain support for members of the congregation in their participation and understanding of the ritual celebration itself.[14]

The inclination to relate Christian practice to the Jewish context needs to be carefully examined, given the striking differences in the nature of the liturgy of each. One would be hard pressed to make a case for comparable complex doctrines among Jews which might have required the assistance of narrative or symbolic art. Admittedly, it has been suggested at times that synagogue art might have been intended to illustrate one or another aspect of Jewish liturgy (e.g., the zodiac signs mentioned in some *piyyutim*, the *'Aqedah* narrative read at least several times annually, or an eschatological theme). Even

---

12. See Hachlili, *Art and Archaeology—Israel*, 370–75; Vitto, "Interior Decoration," 297–99. This is based on extant artistic remains, primarily of mosaic floors. What the walls of synagogues might have displayed is, with rare exception, unknown (ibid., 299–300).

13. On the possible didactic role of the Dura frescoes, see the recent Moon, "Nudity and Narrative," 590, and on p. 588, the quotation brought from Pope Gregory the Great: "Pictures are used in church so that those who are illiterate may, by looking at the walls, read there what they are unable to read in books."

14. Hellemo, *Adventus Domini*, 281. See also Sinding-Larsen, *Iconography and Ritual*, passim; Mathews, *Clash of Gods*, 142–80. With regard to the Byzantine world generally, see MacCormack, *Art and Ceremony*; and Maguire, *Art and Eloquence*, 109–11.

if such a claim is entertained, it would be of an entirely different order than the situation envisioned for the contemporary Christian context. Thus, any comparison between Christian and Jewish practice in this regard requires much scrutiny, along with a rigorous rationale as to why such art would have been deemed necessary in a synagogue context.

THE USE AND ABUSE OF LITERARY SOURCES

The attempt to use rabbinic sources to corroborate iconographic interpretation is a natural and understandable exercise. After all, such a rich corpus of material spanning centuries, including those to which the extant archeological material is dated, is a most inviting trove to explore and exploit. As a result, rabbinic sources have been invoked for every conceivable artistic motif or interpretation, from the menorah to Helios, and from the Torah shrine to the zodiac, and for places as diverse as Capernaum and Bet Alpha, Dura and Sepphoris.[15]

Rarely, however, have the necessary controls for the use of such sources been properly exercised. And here I am not referring to the important issue regarding the use of critical editions or the best manuscripts available as a basis for citation. My focus is far broader. For instance, is a ninth-century (the assumed date of editing) midrash relevant to third-century Dura?[16] Or an eighth-century targumic translation to a fourth- or fifth-century mosaic depiction?[17] While such connections are often made, they rest on assumptions which often require a stretch of the imagination. Moreover, not only is the chronological factor an issue, but so, too, are the geographical disparities. Thus, the appearance of a particular tradition in one or another rabbinic collection does not necessarily mean it was known to the founders of a particular synagogue or to the artist who employed a particular motif. For example, it cannot be automatically assumed that views expressed in

15. See, for example, Kraeling, *Dura: Synagogue*, 346–56; Schubert, "Jewish Pictorial Traditions," 177; Klagsbald, "Menorah as Symbol," 126–34. Brilliant's remarks regarding Goodenough appear to be applicable in our context as well: "the explanatory texts he provided for his 'mute' images too often failed to account for the independence of the visual evidence, which had its own frames and routes of reference. Too often he relied on a tendentious choice of contemporary texts" (*Commentaries*, 242).

16. For a general statement in this regard, see Kraeling, *Dura: Synagogue*, 351–56. Specific examples can be found throughout his volume, for example, on pp. 78, 83–84, 107, 121, 140, 179, 191.

17. For example, the *targum* of Lev. 26:1 regarding figural images on mosaic floors, or Pirqei d'Rabbi Eli'ezer 6 with respect to the Helios depictions. On Kraeling's use of targumic material for Dura, see his *Dura: Synagogue*, 85, 92, 156–57. In a similar vein, see the rather speculative suggestion of Moon ("Nudity and Narrative," 599): "Instead, I propose that the synagogue paintings derive from a more popular tradition, from sets or series of hand-held pinakes or placards, which may have been used by a *meturgeman* as he paraphrased the Torah and other lessons for a Jewish community that was multilingual but, probably, scarcely familiar with Hebrew. Compositional aspects within the scenes themselves and the repetition of the main character, frame to frame, suggest placards; these stylistic features are preserved on placards from other later art-historical traditions." See also ibid., 609–14.

rabbinic traditions were always, or even usually, widely publicized. Nor is it clear whether such views, even if known, were invariably adopted by a particular community. Behind any such correlation—whether between rabbinic sources and artistic remains, or with regard to an identical interpretation of a motif appearing in several places—lies the assumption of a set of common beliefs and values among the Jewish communities of late antiquity. Such an assumption at this stage of our knowledge is gratuitous.

Since literary sources could conceivably hold the key to a persuasive interpretation of artistic remains, let us examine this dimension in greater detail. What would be an ideal situation for utilizing literary material for iconographic purposes? The existence of synagogal art remains together with a contemporary commentary of its iconography would probably provide a sound—although still not necessarily conclusive—basis from which to draw conclusions. However, even in such ideal circumstances, a good deal of caution is yet required. The sixth-century rhetor Choricius of Gaza describes the decorations of a church in his city, but Grabar terms his description "a piece of rhetoric" and goes on to say that "we cannot eliminate the possibility that the text, while not necessarily contradicting the images of Gaza, interpreted and enriched their iconography in the direction of drama and narrative."[18] In any case, to the best of my knowledge, no comparable correlation between a contemporary literary text and a specific artistic representation exists within a Jewish context.

A somewhat less ideal situation would be a source from the time and place of a specific synagogue building which comments generally on a theme appearing in that synagogue's art. In this case at least, one could make a claim that the ideas articulated in that source were then current. However, not only is this type of evidence not easy to find, but there is no way of being sure that the opinion expressed by the author mirrors the views of those who determined the synagogue decorations. Thus, to link the comments of the fourth-century R. Ze'ira regarding the relationship between the rule of a governor, a cosmocrator (presumably the emperor), and God with the Helios depictions on synagogue floors (even that of fourth-century Hammat Tiberias) may be interesting, but it is far from compelling.[19]

While contemporaneity should be considered a factor in lending some degree of cogency to a literary reference, whether it is sufficient in and of itself is another question. Other considerations may restrict our use of such a source, as in the case of *The Book of Secrets (Sefer Harazim)*, a handbook of practical magic usually dated to the fourth century. Reference therein to Helios as an archangel knowing the secrets of the universe is a case in point.[20] Since this composition is more or less contemporaneous with the

---

18. Grabar, *Christian Iconography*, 101.

19. Y 'Avodah Zarah 3, 1, 42c. See Weiss and Netzer, *Promise and Redemption*, 38–39. See also the reservations in S. Schwartz, "Program and Reception."

20. Margolioth, *Sepher Ha-Razim*, 99.

Hammat Tiberias synagogue, the link between this literary reference and the mosaic depiction of Helios may be self-evident. Even here, however, we have no idea of the extent to which the beliefs expressed in *Sefer Harazim* permeated Jewish society. Moreover, the implications of such a linkage are far-reaching, even revolutionary, given the "unorthodox" beliefs reflected in this book.

A second contemporary reference is Epiphanius' description of the Pharisees, wherein it is stated that the latter used Hebrew names not only for astrological terms (i.e., sun, moon, and planets), but also for the zodiac signs.[21] It is rather obvious that this description has nothing to do with the pre-70 Pharisees, as there is no other attestation for such speculation in Pharisaic circles. More likely, Epiphanius had in mind current (synagogue?) practice; however, the particular connection between such usage and the Pharisees (or should we say, rabbis) remains most enigmatic.

Finally, it goes without saying that extreme caution must be exercised when utilizing much earlier materials to explain artistic remains of late antiquity. Both Philo and Josephus have at times been invoked in attempts to explain the significance of the zodiac and other symbols.[22] Other than the fact that these earlier Jewish writers related to such phenomena, which, of course, is interesting in its own right, there is probably little to learn from them regarding the use of artistic motifs centuries later.

One might, of course, claim that all current theories are relevant, and that the various interpretations suggested to date may in some way reflect a similar range of associations in antiquity; multiple and simultaneous interpretations for any given symbol undoubtedly existed. However, such a line of reasoning is of limited value, telling us everything and nothing; it is, in the end, wholly speculative, and we are left with no indication of what, if any, was a primary or more accepted interpretation.

Still, this may be all that we can aspire to at the moment. The desire to fathom the meaning and significance of artistic remains is deeply embedded in modern scholarship, and many of the suggestions raised may indeed reflect ideas and opinions current in antiquity. Beyond this supposition, however, there may be little more to say.

LIMITATIONS IN THE INTERPRETATION OF JEWISH ART

What, then, can be determined about the significance of Jewish art vis-à-vis the ancient synagogue and its community?[23] On the most basic level, it is clear that the subject

---

21. Epiphanius, *Panarion* 16, 2, 1–5.

22. See Goodenough, *Jewish Symbols*, VIII, 209–14; 224–32; Wilkinson, "Beit Alpha Mosaic," 23–24, 26. On the other hand, according to Josephus, the zodiac signs were omitted from the heavenly signs portrayed on the Temple curtain (*War* 5, 213–14).

23. I am using the term "Jewish art" with reference not only to uniquely Jewish symbols and motifs

matter depicted gives us some idea of the religious and cultural topics of interest within a particular Jewish community. What biblical scenes are represented and which Jewish symbols appear? Which motifs are more ubiquitous than others, in what contexts (urban or rural), and in which geographical areas? When do motifs appear, and do they disappear at any point? Determining the "what" is relatively easy to achieve, but the "why" often remains elusive.

No less intriguing is the simultaneous use of Jewish and pagan symbols in synagogue art. As we have had occasion to note, this occurs time and again on mosaic floors from Byzantine Palestine, where a panel of Jewish symbols (Torah shrine, menorah, *lulav*, *ethrog*, and incense shovel) appears alongside one depicting Helios and the zodiac signs (Ḥammat Tiberias, Bet Alpha, Naʿaran, Sepphoris, and Ḥuseifa). At Bet Alpha, the zodiac-Helios panel is also flanked by the *ʿAqedah* scene; at Sepphoris, it is bordered on one side by the *ʿAqedah* and on the other by unusually detailed Tabernacle-Temple imagery and an additional panel displaying Jewish symbols. The intertwining of Jewish and pagan motifs is thus well evidenced in Palestine; such a combination (or anything analogous) is, however, strikingly absent in Diaspora synagogues.[24]

Let us examine three examples of the iconography most frequently addressed in the study of Jewish art in order to ascertain what may and may not be determined with any degree of certainty. Taken together, these examples exemplify some of the cardinal issues relating to the interpretation of synagogue art.

Menorah

No Jewish symbol is more ubiquitous in late antiquity than the menorah, but on artistic remains dating back to the time before the third century C.E., *menorot* are few and far between. The menorah appears on a coin of Mattathias Antigonus and on several plaster fragments and a sundial found in the Jewish Quarter and Temple Mount excavations, respectively, as well as on the walls of Jason's tomb in the Reḥavia section of Jerusalem. In the period following the destruction of the Temple, the menorah was depicted on the Arch of Titus and on several ossuaries and a number of oil lamps of the "Darom" type.[25]

However, it is only in the third and especially the fourth centuries that the menorah became the most frequently depicted Jewish symbol, appearing in a wide variety of contexts—burial sites and synagogues, glass vessels, household objects, lamps, amulets,

---

(e.g., the menorah), but also to all artistic representations used in Jewish religious settings where one might expect to find an articulation of ideas and values. In late antiquity, this would include synagogues and cemeteries.

24. On the other hand, Diaspora synagogues found many other ways of incorporating influences from their surrounding cultures: in architecture, art, inscriptions, and synagogue and communal organization. See above, Chap. 8; and below, Chap. 18.

25. Meshorer, *Ancient Jewish Coinage*, I, 92–94; Avigad, *Discovering Jerusalem*, 147–50; B. Mazar, "Excavations," 82; Rahmani, *Catalogue*, 51–52, and nos. 815, 829; Sussman, *Ornamental Oil-Lamps*, 20.

90. Depiction of a menorah on part of a chancel screen found at Ashkelon.

91. Bronze menorah found at 'En Gedi.

and seals. In synagogues, it appears on capitals, a column, column bases, lintels, chancel screens (fig. 90), and mosaic floors, often together with one or more other ritual symbols.[26] Remains of freestanding *menorot* have been discovered in Ḥammat Tiberias, 'En Gedi (fig. 91), Sardis, Susiya, Eshtemoa, and Ma'on (Judaea).

Matters appear to be relatively clear-cut on the descriptive plane. However, when we discuss the menorah's function and meaning, the issues begin to become clouded. Whether *menorot* were actually used in the synagogue and, if so, whether they were intended to be decorative or functional, is an open question, although most opinions incline toward the decorative alternative.[27] Moreover, there is little agreement as to what, in fact, the menorah in the synagogue setting was supposed to represent—the Tabernacle or Temple menorah or a menorah in the synagogue hall itself? In other words, was it

---

26. Goodenough, *Jewish Symbols*, IV, 72–77; Yarden, *Tree of Light*, 29–38; Hachlili, *Art and Archaeology—Israel*, 236–56; idem, *Art and Archaeology—Diaspora*, 316–44; Barag, "Menorah," 45–46.

27. Sukenik (*Synagogue of Beth Alpha*, 34), Goodenough (*Jewish Symbols*, IV, 74–76), Negev ("Chronology of Seven-Branched Menorah," 197), Yeivin ("Synagogue of Chorazim," 272), Hachlili (*Art and Archaeology—Israel*, 253), and Amit ("Marble Menorah," 58) believe they were actually used; Barag ("Menorah," 46) and Foerster ("Allegorical and Symbolic Motifs," 546) assume they were merely decorative.

intended to convey memories of the past or to remind the congregation of present circumstances?[28]

The subject of even greater dispute is the meaning accorded this symbol. Goodenough has suggested that it represented the heavenly spheres and was "a true symbol of God, the source of their Light, their Law, the Tree of Life, the astral path to God."[29] Smith expands Goodenough's interpretation, associating the image of the cosmos and the saints with the menorah symbol.[30] Both Barag and Hachlili opine that the menorah symbolized the yearning of Jews for the Temple and their hopes for its renewal, as well as providing a countersymbol to the Christian cross,[31] while a number of other scholars have focused exclusively on the menorah's reputedly messianic and eschatological significance.[32] Fine and Zuckerman call attention to the menorah as a symbol of minority status.[33]

As the most ubiquitous representation in Jewish art, the menorah undoubtedly served as a symbol; as such, it bore a wide range of meanings, as attested by extant literary sources (viz., Zechariah, Philo, Josephus, and rabbinic literature). As noted, scholars have been creative to date in positing what this symbol may have meant, and other suggestions will surely surface in the future. Whether the menorah's meanings changed over time or varied in different locales and historical settings cannot be determined. As the quintessential Jewish symbol, the menorah was certainly associated with a wide range of meanings, and, indeed, its popularity was probably due, at least in part, to the fact that it was amenable to varying interpretations. Thus, the most that can be said is that at any one time and in any specific context the menorah's significance was undoubtedly multifaceted.[34]

Helios and the Zodiac Signs

The discovery of zodiac signs in a half-dozen synagogues across the length and breadth of Byzantine Palestine dating from the fourth to sixth centuries has been one of the most riveting of all iconographic issues of this past half-century, owing, of course, to its blatantly pagan overtones. Little or no consensus, however, has been reached with regard to why these signs or the figure of Helios were so popular. We have already taken note of the range of interpretations accorded the figure of Helios: the Godhead; the arch-

---

28. See above, Chap. 7.

29. Goodenough, *Jewish Symbols*, IV, 96. See also C. L. Meyers, *Tabernacle Menorah*, 187.

30. M. Smith, "Image of God," 508.

31. Barag, "*Menorah*," 44–47; Hachlili, *Art and Archaeology—Israel*, 254–55.

32. See, for example, Roth, "Messianic Symbols," 151–64; Wirgin, "Menorah as Symbol of Judaism," 140–42; idem, "*Menorah* as Symbol of After-Life," 102–4; Namenyi, *Essence of Jewish Art*, 64; Sperber, "History of the Menorah," 155.

33. Fine and Zuckerman, "Menorah as Symbol," 24–31. For an example of the extensive use of rabbinic sources in determining the meaning of the menorah as a symbol of Jewish spirituality, see Klagsbald, "Menorah as Symbol," 126–34.

34. For a more detailed treatment of the menorah, see my "Menorah."

angel of *Sefer Harazim;* a symbol of God's power as the creator of the universe; the "day" in a panel depicting the yearly calendar, which included months and seasons; a decorative element. As noted with respect to Ḥammat Tiberias,[35] two factors have made this particular Helios depiction so intriguing. First, the motif was being used by pagans and Christians in the fourth century, when the Ḥammat Tiberias synagogue was erected. In other words, Helios was a live symbol that was being mobilized by emperor and church alike to represent the cosmocrator, with each tradition providing its own interpretation.[36] Second, the globe and scepter accompanying Helios at Ḥammat Tiberias are symbols explicitly forbidden in the Mishnah, which had been edited in the previous century.[37]

In the absence of relevant data from contemporary Jewish society, we have no choice but to grapple with a conception of what Judaism would and would not permit at this time. Should we expect these remains to fit into a rabbinic scheme and thus be reflected in some way in rabbinic literature? If so, then perhaps these remains should be assigned a less significant interpretation. However, those advocating cleavages in what had been considered "normative" rabbinic Judaism tend to emphasize more revolutionary implications. Goodenough and Smith have articulated the latter position, Urbach and Avi-Yonah the former.[38] To force such remains into a rabbinic mold owing to certain preconceptions is unjustified. It is more probable that, because so many different expressions of Judaism and Jewish art were current at the time, there is no way to posit any one rabbinic conception which might have enjoyed a monopoly at the time.[39]

The search for the meaning of this motif has been enriched (or, should we say, complicated) by discoveries over the past three decades. First, in 1967, was the publication of *Sefer Harazim,* which featured a prayer to the angel Helios.[40] Soon thereafter, a list of the names of the zodiac (but not representations of the signs) was discovered in the synagogue of ʿEn Gedi. Helios is not mentioned in this list, nor is his figure elsewhere

---

35. See above, Chap. 7.

36. MacMullen, *Paganism,* 84–94; Athanassiadi, *Julian,* 113–14, 176–81; Dothan, "Representation of Helios," 99–104; L'Orange, *Likeness and Icon,* 325–44.

37. M ʿAvodah Zarah 3:1.

38. Goodenough, *Jewish Symbols,* IV, 215–18; XII, 152–56; M. Smith, "Observations," 142–60, and esp. 158–60; Urbach, "Rabbinical Laws of Idolatry," 149–65, 229–45; Avi-Yonah, "Caesarea Inscription," 56–57. For a comprehensive review of the literature on the zodiac in the synagogue context (especially publications in Hebrew), see Mack, "Mosaic and Midrashim."

39. For an interpretation of Helios as a reflection of a mystical-gnostic dimension in ancient Judaism, see L. A. Hoffman, "Censoring In and Censoring Out," 19–37; on the zodiac as representing the presence and power of God, see Ness, "Astrology and Judaism," 126–31.

40. Following Margalioth, *Sepher Ha-Razim,* 99: "I adore you, Helios, who rises in the east, good mariner, trustworthy guardian, trustworthy [or: exalted] leader of the sun's rays, reliable [witness], who of old did establish the mighty [or: heavenly] wheel, holy orderer [of the stars], ruler of the axes [of the heavens], lord, brilliant leader, king, establisher of the stars." For a slightly different rendition, see Morgan, *Sepher Ha-Razim,* 71.

92. Zodiac panel from Sepphoris. Note the column and sun rays where the figure of Helios usually appears in other synagogues.

ever accompanied by an identifying inscription—unlike the zodiac signs. The Sepphoris mosaic adds a significant variant: the figure of Helios is strikingly absent from the chariot, with only the sun and its rays represented (fig. 92). Presumably, this congregation was less conservative in its artistic tastes than the one at ʿEn Gedi, although more so than in other places, at least with respect to the display of Helios.

The importance of the Helios-zodiac motif cannot be underestimated. As noted, it appears at a wide range of sites (i.e., urban and rural, and in all parts of the country), among them the two most important cities of Jewish Palestine, and invariably at the very center of the mosaic floor.[41] This motif always appears in conjunction with other panels containing well-known ritual symbols or depictions of clear religious significance (the ʿAqedah, the Tabernacle sacrifices, and other offerings). Quite obviously, the zodiac-Helios motif bore an appealing message. But what precisely that was, and whether it was always the same from place to place and from one era to the next, are as yet unresolved

41. On the zodiac in antiquity generally, see Gundel, *Zodaikos*, passim.

issues. We find ourselves here at the limits of what can be said with any degree of certainty. In such a situation, we have no recourse but to leave the issue open until further discoveries or insights might allow us to progress further.[42]

Programmatic Explanations

In most instances, scholars have focused on specific images or panels in analyzing Jewish artistic forms. On rarer occasions, an attempt has been made to explain two or more contiguous representations (such as Jewish symbols and the zodiac motif), each of which seems to be of consequence both religiously and symbolically.

Three sites have attracted attention in this regard, since panels and registers with motifs rich in associations and apparently laden with meaning have been found therein. The best known is Dura Europos, with its walls covered with biblical scenes, while in the center of its focal western wall is a series of scenes flanked by four large figures which have drawn much attention since their discovery. We have had several occasions to note the richness of these scenes, as well as the variety of interpretations offered.

Some have attempted to interpret all the scenes with one all-encompassing theory (e.g., Goodenough, Wischnitzer, and Goldstein), while others have interpreted each of the three registers as representing a different theme, the three together forming a trilogy of ideas found also in rabbinic literature (e.g., Sonne, Grabar, and du Mesnil de Buisson). More recently, H. Kessler has suggested that a Jewish-Christian polemic is reflected in many of these scenes. On the other hand, many scholars have disavowed the existence of any overriding theme, contenting themselves with the view that what is represented here is simply a series of biblical accounts of Israel's history and the salvational deeds of God (e.g., Kraeling, Bickerman).[43]

Until recently, the only site in Byzantine Palestine that had merited the application of this type of all-encompassing theory is the Bet Alpha synagogue. Its mosaic floor is unusual in that all three panels bear significant depictions. From north to south, i.e., in the direction of the apse, panels are devoted to the following: the *Aqedah;* Helios and the zodiac signs; and a full array of Jewish symbols, namely, the Torah shrine, and pairs of *menorot, shofarot, lulavim, ethrogim,* and incense shovels. Goodenough was the first to attempt an overall explanation, viewing the three panels as representative of the mystical ascent through sacrifice (the *Aqedah*), then through the upper regions of heaven (the zodiac), and finally through the curtains of the Temple to the true heaven.[44] This sugges-

---

42. See in this regard the insightful statements in Goodenough, "Symbolism in Hellenistic Jewish Art," 108–14.

43. See above, Chap. 8 on Dura, as well as Kraeling, *Dura: Synagogue,* 346–48; Gutmann, "Programmatic Painting," 137–54; and esp. idem, "Early Synagogue and Jewish Catacomb Art," 1313–34, with accompanying bibliography. On Goodenough's thesis and reactions to it, see M. Smith, "Goodenough's *Jewish Symbols,*" 53–68; Neusner, "Studying Judaism through Art," 29–57.

44. Goodenough, *Jewish Symbols,* I, 246–53.

tion was developed by Goldman, who placed special emphasis on the scene which represents, as he interprets it, a portal to the celestial regions; it is "the architectural symbol of the door as the celestial abode."[45] In another vein, Wischnitzer has interpreted these panels as reflective of the Sukkot holiday and the blessings of the harvest, while Wilkinson, aided by the writings of Philo, Josephus, and the mystical tract *Sefer Yetzirah*, interprets the three panels as references to the Temple precincts: the *'Aqedah* symbolizes the altar; the zodiac, the *Hekhal*; and the Torah Shrine and related ritual objects, the *Devir*, or Holy of Holies.[46] Whatever ingenuity and creativity one might wish to ascribe to any or all of the above opinions, none has succeeded in winning much support over the years.

The exciting discovery of the Sepphoris synagogue in 1993 revealed a mosaic floor with no fewer than seven horizontal bands (some divided into two or three panels) bearing rich and at times unusual motifs (fig. 93). Several of these motifs were new to the synagogue scene, and even when a theme is known from elsewhere, the Sepphoris example is often different in important and striking ways. On the floor, moving from the entrance toward the *bima* (panel 7 to panel 1), we can see the following. Two panels presumably deal with the Abraham story (the angels' visit to Abraham and Sarah and the story of the *'Aqedah*); one panel is devoted to the Helios-zodiac motif, with a number of important differences from other such representations (the use of Hebrew for the names of the months, the inclusion of a Greek dedicatory inscription, the use of Greek names for the seasons, and, most of all, the representation of Helios by the sun and its rays only); two panels detail the Tabernacle-Temple, some of their appurtenances (shofar, meal offering, and oil), daily sacrifices (with the relevant biblical verses), the showbread table, firstfruits, and the figure of Aaron; the next panel depicts the familiar cluster of Jewish symbols surrounding the Torah shrine; and, finally, the last panel depicts two pairs of lions flanking a wreath with a partially preserved Greek inscription.[47] The synagogue's excavators suggest dividing the floor bands into three main foci and then including these under one all-encompassing theme of promise and redemption. The Abraham stories represent the former, the Tabernacle-Temple panels the latter, while the Helios-zodiac motif reflects the power of the God of Israel, which will facilitate this redemption.[48] It is an interesting suggestion; alternatively, the different panels may just as well represent a number of separate and independent ideas.[49]

In summary, there can be little question that Jewish art includes many symbolic rep-

---

45. Goldman, *Sacred Portal*, 103; see also p. 124.

46. Wischnitzer, "Beit Alpha Mosaic," 133–44; Wilkinson, "Beit Alpha Mosaic," 27. For an attempt to fit the three panels of the zodiac mosaic into one, all-encompassing rubric, see Roussin, "Zodiac," 83–96.

47. Weiss and Netzer, *Promise and Redemption*, 16–32.

48. Ibid., 34–39.

49. See, for example, Fine, "Art and Liturgical Context"; idem, *This Holy Place*, 121–25. An indication of the plethora of opinions surrounding the meaning of the Sepphoris mosaic can be found in L. Levine and Z. Weiss, *From Dura to Sepphoris*.

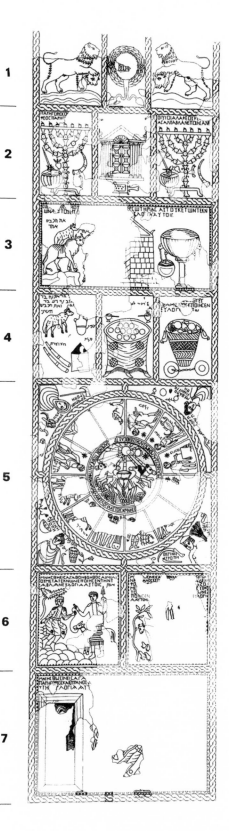

93. Plan of the Sepphoris mosaic floor.

resentations, and any one motif or depiction may well have a multiplicity of meanings, not only over the generations but even at any one time. However, given the limitations of our literary and archeological sources at present, any explanation necessarily remains largely speculative. If the issue is only what these depictions signify to us, their viewers and interpreters, some fifteen hundred years later, then all the above theories are engaging and welcome. If, however, the goal is to determine what the original intent was of those who made, paid for, or simply gazed at the images, then we simply do not know enough to determine the truth of the matter.

CONCLUDING PERSPECTIVES

In dealing with the interpretation of Jewish art, we are inevitably caught on the horns of a dilemma. Given the limited amount of material available, we are heavily dependent on literary sources and Christian artistic parallels to try and make some sense of the material. But this approach carries with it the danger of imposing external agendas on Jewish art remains. In addition, it assumes, rather than argues, that such influences did exist. And even if we do assume some sort of connection between the literary and artistic evidence, for example, there is also the possibility that it worked in the opposite direction, namely, that artistic remains—what E. Kessler has referred to as "artistic midrash"[50]—influenced the literary midrash of the rabbis. Thus, much clarity and caution is required to argue for one or another interpretation.

The case of Jewish art is further complicated by its localized nature; in fact, it is quite analogous to what we have seen with regard to other aspects of the synagogue—its architecture, plan, liturgy, officials, etc. In contrast to contemporary Christendom, there was no political or ecclesiastical authority which might have determined, or at least seriously influenced, such selections. An example of such intervention in the Christian framework is reflected in the account of Mark the Deacon with regard to the building of the Gazan cathedral, which was to replace the pagan temple, the Marneion: "The holy Bishop had engaged the architect Rufinus from Antioch, a dependable and expert man, and it was he who completed the entire construction. He took some chalk and marked the outline [thesis] of the holy church according to the form of the plan [skariphos] that had been sent by the most pious Eudoxia. And as for the holy Bishop, he made a prayer and a genuflexion, and commanded the people to dig. Straightaway all of them, in unison of spirit and zeal, began to dig, crying out, "Christ has won!" . . . And so in a few days all the places of the foundations were dug out and cleared."[51]

In Jewish society of late antiquity, local communities constructed their buildings on their own. Only when one compares a Galilean-type or Golan synagogue with one from

---

50. E. Kessler, "Art Leading the Story."

51. Mark the Deacon, *Life of Porphyry* 78, as quoted in Mango, *Art of the Byzantine Empire*, 31.

southern Judaea and one from an urban center in Palestine, or, alternatively, the Diaspora synagogues at Ḥammam Lif, Sardis, and Dura, can one appreciate the almost infinite range of architectural and artistic expression among Jewish communities. No two mosaic floors are identical; Jewish art, like Jewish liturgy, was still very much in flux. Thus, determining influences in such circumstances is well nigh impossible.

From the aniconic to the figural, a vast array of combinations of human, animal, floral, and geometric patterns are in evidence. Jewish communities demonstrated a large degree of autonomy in choosing the types of decorations and symbols to grace their public buildings. Discussions of Jewish art have understandably focused on the sensational and exceptional—the zodiac signs, the image of Helios—as well as biblical figures and episodes. Studies on Dura, Bet Alpha, Ḥammat Tiberias, and now Sepphoris have quite naturally always held center stage. However, these spectacular examples constitute only a small percentage of the totality of synagogue art. The simplicity of the majority should be of no less consequence than the designs and motifs among the more lavishly decorated.

Recognition of this enormous diversity among synagogues is inversely proportional to the chance of reaching any sort of satisfactory iconographic interpretation. Local autonomy, when wedded to the absence of contextual evidence, creates, for the moment at least, an almost insurmountable obstacle in this regard.

DIACHRONIC AND
eighteen SYNCHRONIC DIMENSIONS—
THE SYNAGOGUE IN CONTEXT

O n numerous occasions throughout the course of this volume, we have commented on the extent to which the synagogue was shaped by larger social,
material, cultural, and religious contexts. The present chapter will focus
upon this dimension, bringing together many of the themes which have
already been discussed and incorporating other evidence in order to gain a more comprehensive understanding of the growth and development of this institution.

There is no doubt that the study of hellenization, i.e., the impact of the larger surrounding culture on the Jews in the Greco-Roman and Byzantine worlds, has been one
of the most fruitful areas of inquiry over the past several generations. The term addresses
the cultural vortex of classical antiquity and includes eastern as well as western components; it thus refers to the overall effect that this larger cultural matrix—the synchronic
dimension—had on Jewish life, not always on a conscious level. Byzantine Christianity is
included as well, since it embraced the classical tradition in a myriad of ways. Often these
dynamics involved a complex process of adopting and adapting various components of
this culture as they impacted on the material, social, cultural, and religious realms. No
area of Jewish life was immune to such influences.[1]

Nevertheless, certain distinctions must be made in this regard. Not all areas of Jewish
life were equally affected (e.g., physical remains as against religious matters), nor were

---

1. For a more detailed treatment of this topic, see L. Levine, *Judaism and Hellenism*, chap. 1.

all strata of society equally exposed or influenced; the wealthy, for example, were usually more amenable to such influences than the poor. Nor did hellenization affect all places in a similar fashion. Cities were more intensively exposed to cosmopolitan trends than were villages, Diaspora urban communities more so than Jewish cities of the Galilee, while certain regions in Palestine were more isolated geographically and were thus less affected than others.

The importance of the diachronic dimension in Jewish history should never be lost, of course. The power of tradition and the status quo are crucial components to bear in mind at all times, for much of Jewish life at any given moment is composed (in varying degrees) of these elements. This is the case even though many of these "Jewish" elements might, at some point in the past, have been considered innovations, perhaps even of foreign origin; nevertheless, they had become so much a part of Jewish behavior and practice as to be considered authentically Jewish by later generations.

In examining the variety of diachronic and synchronic influences on the synagogue, three phenomena become clear: the degree to which the synagogue was shaped by its surroundings; the ways in which its Jewish components found expression; and, finally, the seemingly infinite variety of syntheses effected at different times and in different places. Let us begin by examining the major areas of outside influence as manifested in this institution.

ARCHITECTURAL EVIDENCE

The Jewish people never possessed an independent architectural tradition either in their private or in their public domain, and, as a result, they borrowed heavily from the regnant architectural styles of contemporary society. A visit to the Museum of the Diaspora at Tel Aviv University offers a striking demonstration of this fact in its exhibit of miniature replicas of a score or so synagogue buildings from various periods, each constructed and decorated in the tradition and style of the predominant culture of the time.

Thus, while many Galilean and Golan synagogues boasted a monumental facade with a single tripartite entrance, as well as lintels, doorposts, friezes, Syrian gables, windows, and arches with stone reliefs, such elements are also well attested in Roman public buildings and especially temples of second- and third-century Syria, as well as in a number of Byzantine churches from that region (fig. 94).[2] Given the extensive imitation of external architectural models, it was nearly impossible to distinguish a synagogue from a non-Jewish edifice merely by its exterior, a fact not only corroborated by archeological remains, but also reflected in a rabbinic tradition.[3] According to this source, the sages

---

2. Foerster, "Art and Architecture," 139–46; Tchalenko, *Villages antiques*, II, pl. xi.

3. B Shabbat 72b.

94. Suggested reconstruction of the Meiron synagogue facade.

debated whether one who bowed in deference before a pagan temple, thinking it was a synagogue, was guilty of committing an intentional or an unintentional sin. While the halakhic aspects of this rabbinic discussion are not relevant to our purposes, the historical reality behind the example is most germane. The rabbis clearly imagined a situation in which someone walking in the streets of a town or city would be unable to differentiate between a pagan temple and a synagogue on the basis of the building's exterior. This story thus confirms what is patently evident from archeological finds, namely, the striking similarity in the external features of Jewish and non-Jewish buildings. This, in fact, was the assumption of Kohl and Watzinger and others who have attempted to reconstruct the facades and interiors of Galilean synagogues.[4]

This assumption likewise governs most suggestions regarding the models which influenced Second Temple and Judaean synagogue buildings. Debate has generally revolved around which non-Jewish precedent served as the source of inspiration. With regard to the Masada synagogue, for example, Yadin has suggested that it followed the

---

4. See, for example, Kohl and Watzinger, *Antike Synagogen*, 138–203; Meyers et al., *Excavations at Ancient Meiron*, 9–16; *NEAEHL*, I, 149, 292. For the reconstruction of the interior of a synagogue, see Yeivin, "Reconstruction," 268–76.

95. Remains of the Bar'am synagogue portico and facade.

plan of the Hellenistic council hall (i.e., the *bouleuterion*), Foerster that it followed that of the pagan *pronaos* found in a number of Dura Europos temples, and Ma'oz that it had an Alexandrian prototype.[5] A similar range of opinion has been advanced regarding the architectural origins of the Galilean synagogue: Roman basilicas; Nabatean temple courtyards; Herodian palaces as attested in Jericho, themselves a product of Hellenistic-Roman models; the earlier Masada-type synagogue.[6] Even those who have proposed according greater weight to Jewish architectural creativity in the shaping of the Galilean-type synagogue still recognize the dominance of Greco-Roman architectural elements in these buildings (fig. 95).[7]

The same indebtedness to contemporary architectural models holds true with respect to the plans of basilica-type Byzantine synagogues. Patterned after contemporary Christian churches, many of these synagogues featured a courtyard (atrium), tripartite en-

5. See above, Chap. 3.

6. See Kohl and Watzinger, *Antike Synagogen*, 219 (followed by Krauss, *Synagogale Altertümer*, 337–38; Goodenough, *Jewish* Symbols, I, 181; Avi-Yonah, "Synagogue Architecture," 69; and others); as well as the articles of Avigad, Foerster, and Netzer, in *ASR*, 42–51.

7. Tsafrir, *Archaeology and Art*, 165–89.

trances leading into a narthex, and then three portals into a main hall, with a nave, two side aisles, and an apse (or *bima*) positioned in the direction of the building's orientation. Such borrowing is clearly attested by the adoption of the church's chancel screen in synagogue architecture. In its Christian milieu, the chancel screen served as a parapet; built of stone slabs fitted into the grooves of posts, it was intended to separate the clergy, altar, and presbyterium from the congregation. But the screen had no discernible function in the synagogue, where there was no comparable division between clergy (i.e., prayer leaders, preachers, or Torah readers) and congregation (see below). Thus, the appearance of the chancel screen in a Jewish context seems to be a striking example of the incorporation of a foreign architectural element which, as far as we know, had no practical purpose within the synagogue setting. Once borrowed, however, the synagogue chancel screen was often decorated like its Christian counterpart, but with Jewish symbols, floral and geometric decorations, and dedicatory inscriptions. Whether the synagogue chancel screen subsequently acquired its own symbolic meaning, e.g., as marking off sacred space in imitation of the Temple balustrade, is debatable.[8]

The same architectural dependence holds true with respect to Diaspora synagogues. To the best of our knowledge, it would seem that Jewish communities built their synagogues in consonance with local tastes and regnant styles. It will be remembered that the well-established and highly-integrated Sardis community established its monumental synagogue building on the main street of the city, in a structure that had originally been built as a wing of the local *palaestra* and was later converted into a civic basilica. The synagogue building that had taken shape by the fourth century was a reworking of this earlier basilica.[9]

In contrast, the community at Dura Europos located its far more modest synagogue on the western fringes of the city, in a private home that had been converted for communal use. Such was the case with the nearby church and mithraeum as well.[10] The pattern of using private homes as synagogues recurred in a number of other Diaspora communities, e.g., Delos, Priene, and Stobi.[11] The Dura building, whose urban surroundings have been revealed through the extensive excavations carried out in the 1930s, provides a striking example of significant contextual influence. The synagogue, particularly in its second phase, adopted and adapted patterns drawn from nearby pagan shrines. Its hall and courtyard, as well as the series of adjacent rooms, are reminiscent of a number of Duran temples. The synagogue *aedicula* housing the Torah was a close approximation

---

8. On parallels with contemporary churches, see idem, "Byzantine Setting," 147-57. See also Chiat, "Synagogue and Church Architecture," 6-24. For a discussion of the significance of the chancel screen in Christian and Jewish contexts, see Branham, "Vicarious Sacrality," 319-45.

9. Seager and Kraabel, "Synagogue and Jewish Community," 168-90; and above, Chap. 8.

10. Kraeling, *Dura: Synagogue*, 7-33; idem, *Dura: Christian Building*, 3-5; Perkins, *Art of Dura*, 23-32.

11. White, *Building God's House*, 60-101.

of Duran temple *aediculae*, the significant distinction being that the former contained a Torah scroll and not the statue of a deity.[12]

ART

Owing to the extensive artistic remains from both Byzantine Palestine and the Diaspora, the information relating to synagogue art in late antiquity is rich and varied, ranging from instances of slavish imitation of foreign models to those of remarkable originality. In terms of technique (mosaics, frescoes, stone moldings) and general types of categories (floral, faunal, geometric, human), the Jewish communities had only a limited repertoire in their own tradition from which to draw. Thus, outside influence was considerable. Jewish creativity often expressed itself in the selection of motifs to adopt. Blatantly pagan representations were, for the most part, eschewed, while more neutral patterns were easily assimilated. As a result, geometric and floral patterns were especially common in synagogues, although figural representations of animals, birds, and fish were also quite ubiquitous.[13]

Three specific instances of artistic borrowing in Byzantine Palestine synagogues are particularly instructive. The first is the remarkable similarity between the mosaic floors of the synagogues in Gaza and nearby Maʿon (Nirim), on the one hand, and that of the Shellal church, on the other, all three dating to the sixth century C.E. (figs. 96–97). The sites are so close to one another geographically, and their patterns and motifs so similar (an amphora with vine tendrils flanked by birds and animals, forming rows of medallions containing depictions of animate and inanimate objects), that Avi-Yonah has suggested that all three floors may have originated in the same Gazan workshop. Although this particular suggestion has met with some reservations, there is little disagreement as to the remarkable resemblance between these floors.[14] A second example of a motif in common is that of the Temple facade appearing in a sixth-century church on Mount Nebo. Foerster has suggested that the artisan of the synagogue at Susiya in southern Judaea may have borrowed the architectural representation of the facade from this church (or, we may add, from a pattern book).[15] Finally, Bregman has argued persuasively that the ram motif which appears in the *ʿAqedah* scene in the Bet Alpha synagogue was borrowed

---

12. Kraeling, *Dura: Synagogue*, 16.

13. Goodenough, *Jewish Symbols*, V–VIII, passim; Narkiss, "Pagan, Christian and Jewish Elements," 183–88; Hachlili, *Art and Archaeology—Israel*, 199–382; Ovadiah, "Art of the Ancient Synagogues," 301–18; Foerster, "Allegorical and Symbolic Motifs," 545–52. See also M. Smith, "Image of God," 473–512.

14. Avi-Yonah, *Art in Ancient Palestine*, 389–95; idem, "Mosaic Pavement of Maʿon Synagogue," 25–35; Hachlili, "Gaza School of Mosaicists," 46–58; idem, *Art and Archaeology—Israel*, 310–16; N. Stone, "Shellal Mosaic," 207–14; Ovadiah, "Mosaic Workshop," 367–72.

15. Foerster, "Allegorical and Symbolic Motifs," 545–52. For other examples from Byzantine Palestine, see Rutgers, *Jews in Late Ancient Rome*, 89–92.

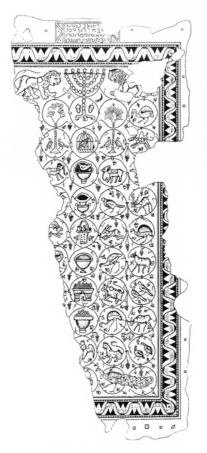

96. Mosaic floor from the
Ma'on (Nirim) synagogue.

97. Remains of the mosaic floor
from the Shellal church.

from a Christian exemplar; the "hanging" ram was originally intended as a prefiguration of Jesus on the cross.[16]

However, not all borrowing can be viewed as a judicious selection of more or less neutral motifs, and several had an unsettling effect when first discovered. Such was the case with the mosaics in the House of Leontis at Bet Shean, which feature scenes from Homer's *Odyssey*, a depiction of Alexandria, and a Nilotic scene including a semiclad god of the Nile. To date, it is still an open question whether the Leontis hall was part of a Jewish private home, a communal building complex, or—less likely—a synagogue hall.[17] Another instance is the zodiac-Helios motif about which much has been written; here, too, indebtedness to Greco-Roman models is unquestionable.

In fact, one can readily generalize that, with the exception of a limited number of distinctly Jewish symbols (see below), all the artistic motifs and styles in the ancient synagogues of Palestine and the Diaspora were in one way or another borrowed from the surrounding culture. As was the case with the architectural dimension, Jewish culture never developed an independent artistic tradition from which the communities of late antiquity might draw. When it came to figural representations, the three or so centuries (the mid-second century B.C.E. through the second century C.E.) of Jewish aniconic art left later generations with a minimal repertoire. Even biblical scenes within the synagogue context were heavily indebted to non-Jewish paradigms when it came to their form and style of representation.

The convergence of Jewish and non-Jewish elements is nowhere more vividly expressed than in synagogue art. The varieties and permutations of motifs are as numerous as the number of synagogues themselves. We have had occasion to note that Palestinian communities, ironically, appear to have been more liberal in their use of pagan motifs than were their Diaspora counterparts (the zodiac, as noted, never appears in Diaspora synagogues). Yet even within Palestine, signs of conservatism and liberalism in art forms are also discernible—not only between different regions of the country but also within the same urban setting.

In light of archeological data, rabbinic sources afford some insight into the dramatic changes in artistic expression that occurred within Jewish society, changes that were clearly wrought under the influence and attraction of foreign models. One of the most revealing sources in this regard—which we have already had occasion to cite—describes the reactions of several rabbis to the progressive introduction of figural representation into Jewish society:

---

16. Bregman, "Riddle of the Ram," 127–45, esp. 140–44. For further discussion of Jewish-Christian parallels, see the articles by Friedman, Talgam, and Habas in L. Levine and Z. Weiss, *From Dura to Sepphoris.*

17. Foerster, "Allegorical and Symbolic Motifs," 547–50; Hachlili, *Art and Archaeology—Israel*, 301; Roussin, "Beit Leontis Mosaic," 6–19.

> In the days of R. Yoḥanan [third century C.E.], they began depicting [figural representations] on walls, and he did not protest; in the days of R. Abun [fourth century C.E.], they began depicting [such figures] on mosaic floors, and he did not protest.[18]

The widespread introduction of figural representation on mosaic floors throughout the East followed the above-noted pattern; the fourth century witnessed the increased use of such depictions on mosaic floors in civic and private buildings, a process which had begun already a century earlier. The Jews were clearly following suit, as we have clear-cut evidence from both literary and archeological sources for the penetration of Greco-Roman artistic patterns into Jewish society generally, and into the synagogue in particular.

If we are able to trace synagogue decorations in Palestine to pagan and Christian models, the situation in the Diaspora is even clearer. Given the sometimes substantial amount of comparative material from the synagogue's immediate surroundings, we can confidently assert that synagogue decoration invariably reflected the styles and patterns of its immediate context.[19] So, for example, the mosaics at the Elche synagogue are similar to those of Roman villas in the region. The different building styles used over the centuries in Roman Ostia, i.e., *opus reticulatum*, *opus vittatum*, and *opus listatum*, are evidenced in the local synagogue's walls and provide, inter alia, valuable evidence for dating. The Naro mosaics feature motifs common in Roman Africa.[20]

The plethora of articles and books written on Dura Europos have made clear the extent to which synagogue wall decorations were indebted to Parthian, Roman, and local Syrian artistic traditions. While Rostovtzeff emphasized Parthian art, and Goodenough the Roman parallels, Moon has recently suggested that Roman commemorative art was a decisive factor in shaping synagogue paintings.[21] While Gates highlights the Syro-Mesopotamian context, Perkins focuses mainly on the Duran context, as represented by this town's temples, mithraeum, church, and private houses, to explain the synagogue's art.[22] Having noted the salient characteristics of local Duran art, she attempts to trace the wider artistic strands that have gone into this particular series of representations:

---

18. Y 'Avodah Zarah 3, 3, 42d; and Genizah fragment published in J. N. Epstein, *Studies in Talmudic Literature*, II, 251–52. See also above, Chap. 13.

19. See above, Chap. 4.

20. See above, Chap. 8. On the influence of North African mosaics in the East generally, see Dunbabin, *Mosaics of Roman North Africa*, 222–33; and on the mosaics of Roman Sepphoris in this regard, see Roussin, "Birds and Fishes," 125.

21. Rostovtzeff, "Dura and Parthian Art," 155–301; Goodenough, *Jewish Symbols*, IX, 124–74, inter alia; and Moon, "Nudity and Narrative," 589–90: "This paper will identify in the paintings some Graeco-Roman conventions of representation and arrangement which a patron or group of planners manipulated more or less intentionally to facilitate narrative comprehension and to advertise by way of comparison their own commitment to God and status within the congregation itself."

22. Gates, "Dura-Europos," 166–81; Perkins, *Art of Dura*, 33–69.

In summary, the Durene style in painting and relief is characterized by frontal, two-dimensional, static, schematically drawn figures set in the available space with little or no meaningful visual connection. Costumes, coiffures, attributes, and poses are drawn from the repertoires of Greece, Rome, Iran, and Western Asia; and it is the amalgam of these varied elements which is the major identifying feature of the style. . . . The style of the Durene paintings and sculptures, then, is fundamentally an Asiatic one, with an admixture of Western elements which the local artists adapt and combine to suit their own tastes. . . . While there are specific motifs and formal elements in Durene art which are found nowhere else and may well be Durene in origin . . . it is the combination of disparate features which is the major characteristic of the Durene style.[23]

The evidence from Sardis is likewise self-evident in this regard. The very location of the synagogue, in what was formerly a civic basilica next to the city's *palaestra*, is indicative of the Jews' comfortableness in the Sardis environment. The synagogue mosaics and revetments are similar to those found elsewhere in the city. Especially noteworthy is the "eagle table" in the synagogue nave, presumably used for the reading of the Torah. Next to this table, it will be remembered, were two pairs of stone lions, and outside the synagogue atrium was a massive Lydian lion (or perhaps a pair of lions, as inside the synagogue). Just as the eagle was, among other things, a symbol of Rome, so, too, was the lion a figure which loomed large in Sardis mythology.[24]

The accessibility of non-Jewish workshops for the creation of synagogue decorations facilitated Jewish dependency upon pagan and Christian models. This appears to have been a common occurrence in many areas boasting a mixed population. We have noted this possibility above with respect to the synagogues of Gaza and Ma'on (Nirim), and Rutgers has argued that Jewish and Christian art and artifacts in fourth- and fifth-century Rome owe much to common local workshops. This finds expression in the plans and decorations of catacombs and hypogea and in the types of sarcophagi, gold glass, lamps, and amulets found there.[25]

COMMUNAL CENTER

We have noted above that Diaspora synagogues functioned, and indeed were often referred to, as associations; they followed one of several Greco-Roman models.[26] Here,

---

23. Perkins, *Art of Dura*, 117, 126.

24. Seager and Kraabel, "Synagogue and Jewish Community," 184–85; Kraabel, "Paganism and Judaism," 242–46.

25. Rutgers, *Jews in Late Ancient Rome*, 50–99. It would seem that not a few Byzantine workshops for producing oil lamps and glass jars served both Christians and Jews; crosses appear on the same types of objects on which *menorot* were found. See Y. Israeli, *Light of the Menorah*, 139, 143; Barag, "Glass Pilgrim Vessels (1)," 35–63; ibid. (2), 45–63.

26. See above, Chap. 4.

too, whenever comparative material is available, influences of the immediate milieu are striking. In Egypt, for example, such influences found expression in the various components of the *proseuche* complex, as well as in the Ptolemaic practice of dedicating buildings to the king and queen. Not only do the Cyrene synagogue inscriptions contain names typical of the region, but two of them refer to the synagogue as an amphitheater.

Close ties between Jews and their surroundings are revealed in several inscriptions, and these ties were mutual; Jews were involved in the life of the city, and members of the general community participated in activities of the Jewish community. The Julia Severa inscription highlights the contribution of a prominent Acmonian to the local synagogue, and an inscription from fourth-century Panticapaeum in the Bosphorus indicates that the synagogue was built by a high Imperial official. In another Bosphoran city, Olbia, the local *proseuche* was repaired by the city's archons,[27] and non-Jewish participation in Jewish community affairs is dramatically expressed in the Aphrodisias inscription. Jewish involvement in civic life is reflected in the many Sardis inscriptions which refer to members of the community as *Sardianoi* ("citizens of Sardis"), *bouleutes* (members of the city council), *comes* and *procurator* (both Imperial offices).[28]

A number of first-century C.E. Bosphoran communities have produced documents of manumission similar to those found in Delphi from the second century B.C.E. and elsewhere.[29] In the Bosphoran examples, not only was the synagogue the venue of these ceremonies, but the congregation served on occasion as an official signatory of the transaction. These documents of manumission are similar to pagan documents known from the Greek world; Westermann lists seven ways in which these Jewish manumission documents and procedures follow those of the Greeks: (1) the manumission itself, for the release of any slave, especially a non-Jew, was not acknowledged by Jewish law; (2) the language, terminology, and sequence of clauses in these documents; (3) the form of the documents as consecrations; (4) the continuation by the freed slave of some part of his (or her) former service; (5) an oath naming Zeus, the earth, and the sun; (6) assent to the new status by heirs of the former owner; and (7) the use of three cardinal clauses: legal freedom (*eleutheria*), no unwarranted seizure or harassment, and unhampered travel.[30]

One of the social functions of synagogues, as with pagan temples, was to serve as a place of dining and banqueting. Temples served this purpose not only if the meal was part of some sort of religious context, but even if it was purely secular in nature. As a result, professional, social, and religious associations often used these premises for such purposes, and the many rooms surrounding the courtyards of Duran temples appear to

---

27. Levinskaya, *Acts in Its Diaspora Setting*, 113–14.

28. Seager and Kraabel, "Synagogue and Jewish Community," 184.

29. *Bosphoran kingdom:* Levinskaya, *Acts in Its Diaspora Setting*, 231–42. *Delphi:* Frey, *CIJ*, I, nos. 709–11. *Egypt:* Tcherikover, *CPJ*, III, no. 473.

30. Westermann, *Slave Systems*, 125.

have been used for banqueting. Evidence from Hellenistic-Roman Egypt, as well as inscriptions from Stobi and Caesarea and several rabbinic traditions, point to similar usage in synagogues.[31]

INSCRIPTIONS

Epigraphical data likewise make clear the extent to which the synagogue was attuned to the dominant norms of the surrounding culture. This is expressed first and foremost in the language of the inscriptions, which, with rare exceptions in the Diaspora and only in a small minority of cases in Palestine, was the language of the region. Greek and Latin dominated in the West, Greek and Aramaic in the East (fig. 98). Moreover, with the exception of rural Palestine and Dura, names of synagogue donors are overwhelmingly Greek.[32]

The titles of synagogue officials were almost always taken from the Greek. Whether we encounter an archisynagogue, archon, *prostates, pater* or *mater synagoges*, or *phrontistes*, Jewish usage often correlates with the titles used by the non-Jews in the same area.[33]

Furthermore, the dedicatory formulas like the manumission declarations, are patterned after current pagan and Christian models. Thus, the Greek "May he be remembered" is found in pagan and Christian inscriptions, while the Aramaic "May so-and-so be remembered for good" (דכיר לטב) is recurrent in Syrian and Nabataean Aramaic inscriptions.[34]

LITURGY

There can be little question that the Jews of the Diaspora worshipped in the vernacular, although evidence in this regard is largely inferential. Some prayers with an apparently Jewish orientation have been preserved in early church documents, although we cannot be certain that their source was synagogue liturgy.[35] Clear-cut evidence for the use of Greek is preserved in Justinian's famous *Novella* 146 from 553 C.E., wherein it is stated that Jews read the Torah in Greek:

---

31. See C. Roberts et al., "Gild of Zeus," 72–87; and above, Chaps. 4 and 10.

32. Rabin, "Hebrew and Aramaic," 1007–39; Mussies, "Greek in Palestine and the Diaspora," 1040–64; E. M. Meyers and Strange, *Archaeology, Rabbis and Christianity*, 62–91; van der Horst, *Ancient Jewish Epitaphs*, 22–39.

33. See above, Chap. 11.

34. Naveh, *On Stone and Mosaic*, 8–9; Foerster, "Synagogue Inscriptions," 18–22, 37–40. On some similarities and differences between Jewish and non-Jewish inscriptions with regard to donors, see Rajak, "Benefactors," 305–19.

35. On possible Diaspora prayers, see Charlesworth, "Jewish Hymns, Odes and Prayers," 411–36; Darnell and Fiensy, "Hellenistic Synagogal Prayers," 671–97; and esp. Fiensy, *Prayers Alleged to Be Jewish*.

98. Greek dedicatory inscriptions from the Ḥammat Tiberias synagogue.

We decree, therefore, that it shall be permitted to those Hebrews who want it to read the Holy Books in their synagogues and, in general, in any place where there are Hebrews, in the Greek language before those assembled and comprehending, or possibly in our ancestral language (we speak of the Italian language), or simply in all the other languages, changing language and reading according to the different places; and that through this reading the matters read shall become clear to all those assembled and comprehending, and that they shall live and act according to them. We also order that there shall be no license to the commentators they have, who employ the Hebrew language to falsify it at their will, covering their own malignity by the ignorance of the many. Furthermore, those who read in Greek shall use the Septuagint tradition, which is more accurate than all the others, and is preferable to the others particularly in reason of what happened while the translation was made, that although they divided by twos, and though they translated in different places, nevertheless they presented one version.[36]

Rabbinic literature as well has preserved some evidence in this regard, although how much of it applies to the Diaspora setting, rather than to the more hellenized parts of Roman Palestine, is uncertain. One source specifically addresses itself to a congregation

36. Linder, *Jews in Roman Imperial Legislation*, 408. See also A. Baumgarten, "Justinian and the Jews," 37–44; de Lange, "Hebrew Language," 132–34.

reciting prayers in a language other than Hebrew: "In a synagogue of non-Hebrew (probably Greek) speakers [לעוזות—*sic*], if there is someone among them who can read [the Torah] in Hebrew, he should commence and conclude in Hebrew [reading the middle part in Greek so that the congregation can understand]."[37] Tannaitic material is quite clear in its assertion that the important components of Jewish liturgy may be recited in any language (though not optimally, according to some rabbis), and this passage seems to be referring to at least Greek.[38] The Yerushalmi, it will be recalled, preserves a most revealing anecdote about two rabbis who, around the turn of the fourth century C.E., entered a Caesarean synagogue wherein Jews were reciting the most basic of prayers—the *Shemaʿ*—in Greek. Astounded by this scene, one sage wished to stop the entire service, while the other replied that it was preferable for the congregation to recite these prayers in Greek than not at all.[39] There can be little question that in synagogues such as this one, sermons and the expounding of the Scriptures were likewise in Greek.[40]

Although Greek successfully penetrated into synagogue worship in the hellenized centers of the Diaspora and Palestine, it does not appear to have played any kind of role in the worship context of either the Galilee or Babylonia. This, at least, is the inference one may draw from rabbinic sources, assuming, of course, that they reflect contemporary practice. Everything in this literature seems to indicate that prayer was conducted, and some sermons, at least, were delivered, in Hebrew, although the latter may have been presented in an academy setting or may be merely literary creations. The most significant evidence for the importance of Aramaic in the liturgy is the *targum*, which was used in most, if not all, Palestinian synagogues throughout late antiquity. There can be no more eloquent a testimony of the linguistic status of Jewish society in both Palestine and Babylonia than the need for translations of the Scriptures into Aramaic.[41] A few Aramaic prayers, at least one of which eventually became central to the liturgical context (i.e., the *Qaddish*), were incorporated into the service, and Aramaic *piyyutim* were being composed in Byzantine Palestine alongside the more predominant Hebrew compositions.[42] Many *midrashim* have been preserved in Aramaic, and some of this material may have been delivered initially in the form of a sermon within a synagogue setting.

---

37. T Megillah 3:13 (p. 356); and Lieberman, *TK*, V, 1179–80.

38. M Sotah 7:1; T Sotah 7:7 (pp. 192–93).

39. Y Sotah 7, 1, 21b.

40. On the influence of Greek on the pronunciation of the Hebrew prayers in various towns and cities of late Roman Palestine, there is interesting textual and archeological evidence. According to the Yerushalmi, people from Bet Shean, Haifa, and Tivʿon were not qualified to serve as prayer leaders because their pronunciation was faulty. The mistakes noted also appear in a Bet Shean synagogue inscription (Y Berakhot 2, 4, 4d; Naveh, *On Stone and Mosaic*, no. 47).

41. For a very different view on the function of Aramaic *targumim* in the synagogue, cf. Fraade, "Rabbinic Views on the Practice of Targum," 253–86.

42. On Aramaic prayers, *piyyutim*, and targumic material, see Shinan, "Hebrew and Aramaic," 224–32; Sokoloff and Yahalom, "Aramaic Piyyutim," 309–21.

A further area of inquiry relates not to the language of Jewish worship, but to its form. How much of Jewish worship in late antiquity was derived directly from Jewish precedents, and how much was a product of outside influences impacting upon earlier Jewish forms? Such a question arises because synagogue liturgy did not crystallize until the Greco-Roman era, and thus many of its forms, and perhaps its content, may have been influenced by the wider religious context. Influence in this case might have taken one of several forms: adopting a foreign worship component in both form and content (an unlikely occurrence); borrowing a form but utilizing traditional material; or being stimulated by outside models to create something new.

Among the wide range of components of Jewish worship, some appear uniquely Jewish in form and content, while others may well have derived from external stimuli. The former category is represented by the Torah-reading and its accompanying study. This, as noted, was the earliest and most unique form of Jewish worship. While it is true that there are sporadic indications of the study and recital of sacred texts in temples and other pagan religious contexts, such activity usually involved priests or, at most, a limited coterie of initiates. Nowhere in the ancient world is there evidence that the primary mode of religious expression for a community was this type of reading and study of sacred texts performed on a regular basis.[43] The church comes closest to this model, but in this particular case, it appears to have been influenced by the synagogue.

At the other end of the spectrum are liturgical forms reflecting some sort of outside influence, such as the *piyyut*, which had become part of the synagogue's liturgical repertoire by the fifth or sixth century. This was an entirely new element in synagogue worship, and those who account for its origins only on the basis of earlier Jewish liturgical forms are hard put to explain how such forms evolved into the *piyyut* precisely at this time.[44] In the final analysis, the evidence seems to point in but one direction, i.e., the influence of contemporary Christian practice.

About this time, the church was introducing the liturgical poem into its worship settings. The poets Ephrem and Romanus were pioneers in this regard, and certain similarities to the latter's liturgical pieces have been detected in early Jewish *piyyut*.[45] The

---

43. Momigliano, *On Pagans, Jews and Christians*, 89–91. On study and learning within pagan religious contexts, see Griffiths, "Egypt and the Rise of the Synagogue," 7–14; MacMullen, *Paganism*, 10–12.

44. See, for example, Rabinowitz, *Halakha and Aggada*, 12–23; Mirsky, *Piyyut*, 1–76. See, however, Fleischer (*Hebrew Liturgical Poetry*, 63–97), who discounts any substantial outside influence on the development of this genre.

45. Schirmann, "Hebrew Liturgical Poetry," 123–61; Werner, *Sacred Bridge*, I, 212–46; Yahalom, "*Piyyut* as Poetry," 111–26. See the careful distinction made by Werner (*Sacred Bridge*, I, 246) on this subject: "Concerning the interchange of ideas, it may be said that Syrian, Byzantine and Armenian hymnody unfolded from a nucleus of Hebrew style and conceptions; the Byzantine and Syrian hymns show even faint traces of early rabbinic ideas. But stylistically and poetically, the Synagogue learned more from the old Oriental Churches and their poetry, since Judaism admitted hymnody only at a time when it was already well developed in Christianity." See also Mitsakis, *Language of Romanos*, passim; and Werner's fascinat-

fact that this liturgical form appeared in the synagogue context at this time, that the same term is used for this genre (the Hebrew *piyyut*, deriving from the Greek ποίημα or ποίησις, and the Hebrew *paytan* from the Greek ποιήτης), that similarities in formal characteristics (meter, acrostic, and rhyme), style, content, and use of choruses appear in both, and that the similarities arose in the context of Jewish borrowing of church architectural, artistic, and even epigraphical patterns are powerful arguments for claiming Jewish adoption and adaptation of this Byzantine church model.[46] The fact that most *piyyutim* are in Hebrew and that their themes derive from the Bible and *midrashim* should not be surprising.[47] This reflects the creative process of borrowing (as against slavish imitation) that is characteristic of cultural transmission generally. As a result of these dynamics, a new liturgical form was created which has constituted an integral part of Jewish worship (in varying degrees, depending on the particular tradition) from late antiquity down to the present.

Between these polar examples—Torah-reading and *piyyut*—can be located other elements of Jewish worship. As we have seen, communal prayer, which had become a basic component of Palestinian Jewish worship in the post-70 era, is an intriguing and as yet enigmatic phenomenon with regard to its Jewish and possibly non-Jewish origins. Jewish communal prayer was negligible in the biblical era, and even at the end of the Second Temple period it was quite peripheral to the daily ritual of the Jerusalem Temple. Whereas Torah-reading was an early component of synagogue ritual, and *piyyut* was a late liturgical development, communal prayer seems to have first appeared in the Hellenistic Diaspora (to wit, the term *proseuche*, "place of prayer") and was included in the Palestinian synagogue worship context only later on.[48] Therefore, questions of why and how such developments took place are quite natural.

There seems to be little doubt that regular communal prayer developed in post-70 C.E. Roman Palestine in order to fill the vacuum created by the destruction of the Temple. It has usually been assumed that the *'Amidah* incorporated a range of earlier traditions—private and public, literary and oral. Thus, although scholars have attempted to isolate liturgical patterns or clusters of ideas of pre-70 vintage which are reminiscent of later rabbinic prayer formulations, only a few have paid attention to the wider context and its possible role in such a process.

In the Greco-Roman era, organized prayer and the recital of hymns were well-recog-

---

ing discussion of the parallel (possibly Byzantine) between the Jewish High Holiday prayer, *Unetaneh toqef*, and the Christian *Dies irae* (*Sacred Bridge*, I, 252–55).

46. Interestingly, religious poetry among the Samaritans likewise makes its first appearance as early as the fourth century; see J. A. Cohen, *Samaritan Chronicle*, 68–69; MacDonald, *Theology of the Samaritans*, 26, 43; Crown, "Samaritan Religion," 43.

47. For an emphasis on the unique aspects of the *piyyut* genre, viewing it almost exclusively in diachronic terms, see Fleischer, "Early Hebrew Liturgical Poetry," 63–97.

48. See above, Chaps. 5 and 16.

nized components of pagan temple worship. Morning prayers were offered in the temple of Dionysius in Teos and the temples of Asclepius in Athens and Pergamum. Often such worship settings would include professional singers, choruses, and instrumental accompaniment, as well as the use of incense during the recitation of the prayers and hymns.[49] In a short but provocative article, M. Smith has suggested that many Jewish prayers praising God in abstract, otherwordly terms which include epithets of praise reflect a Hellenistic prayer mode. This type of prayer, he claims, stands in contrast to the earlier, Deuteronomic form of prayer, which focused on historical memory.[50] Moreover, several studies on the two basic Jewish prayers—the *Shema*ʿ and the *ʿAmidah*—have suggested that the form and content of each might well have been influenced by Hellenistic patterns. Regarding the former, Knohl has noted that the *Shema*ʿ prayer and its accompanying blessings were structured and recited much as were Hellenistic royal decrees, with their *acclamatio*, antiphony, and emphasis on observing the king's commands.[51] With regard to the *ʿAmidah*, Bickerman has opined that its source was originally a civic prayer for Jerusalem which derived from Ben Sira and was parallel to and influenced by the daily civic prayers offered in other Hellenistic cities.[52]

With regard to late antiquity, a number of striking parallels between Christian and Jewish liturgy have been noted by Werner. These include not only the reading and study of the Scriptures, but various prayer forms such as the use of psalms, hymns, and the Doxology.[53]

Besides the prayer mode, actual instruction through discourses, sermons, and more general expositions were also known in pagan contexts. Such expositions may have been of a more popular or theological nature, and were to be found both in pagan temple settings and among various religious associations. As we have already noted, synagogue worship of the pre-70 era had already incorporated this component.[54] Whether the sermon in the ancient synagogue was indebted in any way to its pagan counterpart is impossible to assess at present. All substantive literary material regarding Jewish practice is relatively late, while pagan evidence is, at best, meager.

---

49. Nilsson, "Pagan Divine Service," 63–69; MacMullen, *Paganism*, 16–17, 149 n. 78.

50. M. Smith, "On the *Yôṣēr*," 87–95.

51. Knohl, "Accepting the Kingdom of Heaven," 11–31.

52. Bickerman, "Civic Prayer," 163–85. For an interesting though somewhat speculative theory regarding the influence of a Jewish-Christian blessing on Jewish liturgy, see Liebes, "Mazmiaḥ Qeren," 313–48. In the same vein, Yuval ("Haggadah," 5–28) has suggested that much of the seder ritual is a result of rabbinic reactions to the Jewish-Christian Passover celebration.

53. Werner, *Sacred Bridge*, passim. Cf. also Markus, *End of Ancient Christianity*, 21–22.

54. Regarding the pagans, see above, note 43. On such activities in a synagogue setting, see, for example, Luke 4:20–21; Acts 13:15; Philo, *On Moses* 2, 215; idem, *Hypothetica* 7, 13. See also Wills, "Form of the Sermon," 277–99; Black II, "Rhetorical Form of the Sermon," 1–18; and above, Chap. 5.

SANCTITY

A prominent feature of the synagogue in late antiquity was the sanctity which the institution had acquired. As we have seen, this sacred dimension was not inherent in the synagogue, which at first had been a "neutral" communal institution par excellence. The impetus for sacred status appeared first in the Diaspora synagogue and apparently came in response to a variety of needs and especially the desire for an enhanced self-identity and self-image to serve as a counterbalance to the ubiquitous pagan temple and other reminders of pagan worship. This might also explain why Diaspora Jews tended to call their central communal building by a religious term, *proseuche* (place of prayer), instead of *synagoge* (place of assembly), which was used with rare exceptions in Second Temple Judaea. The fact that many Hellenistic temples (and cities) were acquiring the title "holy and inviolable" undoubtedly contributed to this Diaspora phenomenon.[55]

The emergence of the Palestinian synagogue's sanctity, however, is a complex issue. On the one hand, one could easily ascribe its growing sacredness to the destruction of the Jerusalem Temple. As the synagogue began to incorporate more and more religious practices and symbols, particularly those associated with the Temple, a holy status might have evolved quite naturally. Several other developments undoubtedly contributed to this sacrality, as, for example, the permanent presence of Torah scrolls within most synagogues and the gradual institutionalization of communal prayer as an integral part of synagogue worship.[56] However, there is also the possibility that the adoption of such symbols and practices may have been the result, and not the cause, of synagogue sanctity.

The above factors are necessary, but perhaps insufficient, to account for the ever increasing sanctity of the Palestinian synagogue. Together with these internal factors, it should be borne in mind that many pagan and Christian ideologies and worship settings were also moving in this direction in late antiquity. "Holiness" as a religious category characterizing place, people, and objects was becoming a major concern in a wide variety of religious circles.[57] The intensive Christian interest in Palestinian holy places, beginning with Constantine's building of churches in Jerusalem, was undoubtedly a phenomenon of which the Jews of the country could not help but be aware.[58] Might these developments have in any way influenced the Jews of Palestine and their attitude toward the synagogue? As we have already had occasion to note,[59] Byzantine synagogues clearly owed a great deal to their Christian counterparts, both externally and internally. With the

---

55. See Rigsby, *Asylia*, 1–29.

56. See above, Chap. 6.

57. See, for example, Brown, *Society and the Holy*; Wilken, *Land Called Holy*; Walker, *Holy City, Holy Places?*; and above, Chap. 7.

58. Wilken, *Land Called Holy*, 82–100; Tsafrir, "Development of Ecclesiastical Architecture," 1–16; Wilkinson, Constantinian Churches," 23–27.

59. See above, Chap. 7.

dramatic penetration of Christianity into Byzantine Palestine—particularly the Judaean region—in the fourth century, Jews may have felt the need to respond, inter alia, by endowing their central religious institution with an aura of sanctity, thereby countering in some way the erection of sacred buildings under Christian auspices. The appearance of Jewish symbols and biblical figures and scenes in synagogues may also have served a similar function. Such contextual factors undoubtedly played a significant role in the creation of a sacred dimension in the Byzantine synagogue and in transforming the institution into a "miniature Temple."[60]

DEGREES OF HELLENIZATION

The wealth of synagogue data thus afford the opportunity to make a number of interesting distinctions regarding the question of hellenization. In the first place, one is struck by the sheer variety of artistic and architectural forms found in ancient synagogues. As noted above, synagogues in the more remote areas of Byzantine Palestine were clearly less affected by outside influences (e.g., 'En Gedi), while urban Jewish communities were generally more cosmopolitan than their rural counterparts. Thus, there is less evidence of hellenization (e.g., the use of Greek or figural representations) in the Upper Galilee, as opposed to the Lower Galilee, or in southern Judaea and the Golan, in contrast to Jewish communities in the large hellenized cities along the coast of Roman Palestine.[61] All inscriptions from the coastal area, for example, are in Greek, and thus the story of the Caesarea congregation reciting the *Shemaʿ* in that language is not at all surprising. Similarly, the synagogues discovered in Sepphoris and Tiberias, the two large Jewish urban centers of the Lower Galilee, were hellenized in a number of significant ways, not the least of which was the use of the zodiac and of Greek inscriptions.[62]

We must be careful, nevertheless, not to overstate the case. While urban Jews were generally more inclined toward cosmopolitanism than those living in rural settings, within the cities there were many different types of synagogues. Some congregations tended to be more conservative and less inclined to incorporate cosmopolitan modes of expression, while others were more receptive to outside influences. We have already had occasion to note the diversity among sixth-century synagogues in the Bet Shean area, and this holds true of synagogues within the same geographical area, such as those in Jericho and nearby Naʿaran.[63]

---

60. B Megillah 29a.
61. E. M. Meyers, "Galilean Regionalism," 93–101; idem, "Galilean Regionalism: A Reappraisal," 115–31; Roth-Gerson, *Greek Inscriptions*, passim.
62. Weiss and Netzer, *Promise and Redemption.* See also Roth-Gerson, *Greek Inscriptions*, 58–75, 105–10.
63. See above, Chap. 7.

UNIQUE JEWISH COMPONENTS

Until now we have been focusing primarily on the universal dimensions of the ancient synagogue. In order to strike some sort of balance that will afford a more complete
picture of the nature and character of this institution, it is also important to take note
of the synagogue's uniquely Jewish dimensions. While in their architecture, most synagogues followed the regnant styles of the time, there are some notable instances of both
independence and creative adaptation, even in this domain. One striking example of the
former is in the orientation of the synagogue, which differed from that of other contemporary religious buildings. Whereas pagan temples and Christian churches invariably
faced eastward, synagogues located outside of Israel were oriented toward the Holy Land
and those located within Israel toward Jerusalem. This norm, which was undoubtedly
based on biblical verses noting that prayer was to be directed toward Jerusalem, may have
been liberally interpreted at times, but was rarely ignored.[64]

Regarding the creative use of pagan models, we may make mention of the internal
layout of the Galilean synagogues, with benches and columns usually on three (in the
smaller buildings, only two) sides and the focus on the fourth wall, facing Jerusalem.
This internal plan is sui generis. Roman basilicas had either two or four rows of columns;
the use of three rows of columns, with the fourth side serving as the focus of the worship service, is characteristic of Galilean synagogues, although it may be seen in several
Nabatean temple courtyards and in some Byzantine churches in Syria as well.[65]

Independence and creative adaptation are also evident in artistic representation. We
find the uniquely Jewish symbols (*lulav, ethrog*, shofar, and incense shovel) ubiquitous
both individually and collectively among communities throughout Byzantine Palestine
and the Diaspora. The menorah was especially popular, and appears in a wide range of
sizes and shapes, including three-dimensional representations. Examples of the creative
use of borrowed patterns include a design such as the zodiac, which, while adopted from
pagan precedents, was given a centrality and importance in Byzantine synagogues unmatched in contemporary Byzantine settings.

In the use of religious motifs on mosaic floors, about which we are best informed, Jewish and Christian practices in the Byzantine period appear to have been moving in two
very different directions. While Christians increasingly avoided the depiction of religious
scenes or symbols on their floors (use of the cross in this context was officially banned in
427),[66] Jews did not. Throughout this period, in fourth-century Ḥammat Tiberias, fifth-
century Sepphoris, and sixth-century Bet Alpha alike, Jewish symbols and representa-

---

64. See above, Chap. 9.

65. Foerster, "Synagogues of the Galilee," 289–319; idem, "Art and Architecture," 139–46.

66. Despite this official ban, crosses continue to appear on church mosaic floors, especially in rural
districts, such as the western Upper Galilee.

tions of holy artifacts (e.g., the Torah shrine), as well as biblical scenes and characters, were to be found on mosaic floors throughout Palestine. Interestingly, and perhaps significantly, such depictions on floors are unknown in contemporary Diaspora synagogues. Perhaps these communities were influenced by Christian norms in this regard.[67]

Another area of unique Jewish expression was to be found in the way Jewish liturgy functioned within the synagogue setting. In late antiquity, the synagogue offered a very different architectural-liturgical conception from that prevalent in Byzantine Christianity. The focus in the Byzantine church was almost exclusively on the altar and apse area (presbyterium), which by the fifth century was augmented by two flanking rooms: the *diaconicon*, a dressing room for officiants as well as a place for votive offerings, and the *prothesis*, where the Eucharist was prepared. The clergy generally remained in the apse area, and it was from there that the Eucharist was offered. Although customs and architecture varied among churches in different regions, the nave—with its *ambo* and *solea*—generally played a secondary role in this liturgy.[68]

As noted above, the contemporary synagogue appears to have been quite different.[69] Synagogue liturgy was usually not concentrated in any one area, but rather spread over several foci throughout the nave, each place reserved for a specific mode of worship: the Torah ark was placed against the wall facing Jerusalem, the prayer leader (and presumably the *paytan*) stood on the floor of the nave before the ark, and the Torah-reading ceremony appears to have taken place either on the *bima* in the front of the hall or in its center. The priestly blessing was offered from the front of the hall, but the *targum* and perhaps sermon were delivered near or on the *bima*, where the Torah was read. The focus thus shifted from center to front center and to the Jerusalem wall, depending on which component of Jewish worship was then taking place.

The Byzantine church's seemingly strict division between various groups within the congregation, i.e., clergy, laymen, laywomen, catechumens, and penitents, was unknown in the ancient synagogue, and the Byzantine synagogue remained much more congre-

---

67. Why these developments took place is more or less clear, at least on the Jewish side. For Christians, the cross was clearly becoming a more important and sacred symbol, and was being intimately associated with the divinity of Jesus as well as acquiring a host of other associations. Besides, with the lavish outlays of money for artistic decoration in many churches, there were other options open to Christian communities for depicting this symbol, as, for example, on walls and apses. On the Jewish side, however, other than from Dura, we know very little about artistic representation in other parts of the synagogue besides the mosaic floors. If, indeed, the mosaic floor was the primary vehicle for artistic expression for Jews, then the increasing use of symbols there clearly reflects the needs of these communities to have such depictions in front of them both for aesthetic reasons and, of more consequence, for religious edification and inspiration. There can be little question that the triumphant presence of Christianity in the Holy Land proved to be unsettling for some (many?) Jews, and this created the need for symbols of reaffirmation and self-identity. See also L. Levine, "Menorah."

68. Mathews, *Early Churches*, 105–37.

69. See above, Chap. 9.

gational in orientation. The emphasis within the Byzantine church toward hierarchical sanctification of space was shared only very partially, if at all, by the contemporary synagogue, and Jewish worship was far more participatory than its Christian counterpart.

CONCLUSIONS

The study of the ancient synagogue thus offers a rich and variegated panorama of the encounter between Judaism and Hellenism.[70] The large number of archeological remains, together with the rich trove of literary references, afford a nuanced appraisal of the creative encounter of these two cultures. It is hard to imagine another subject besides the synagogue offering such a detailed and comprehensive view of this phenomenon, in both Diaspora and Palestinian settings, in urban as well as rural areas, and in both the external and the internal physical features of the institution. In certain aspects of the ancient synagogue, the hellenizing component was pervasive; in others it was markedly ancillary. Even within a given area, the degree of influence differed from one community to another. On the other hand, the Jewish component of the synagogue, architecturally, artistically, and liturgically, likewise found expression in many ways, but was rarely the same in any two places. If diversity was a hallmark among the synagogues of late antiquity, then this was largely owing to the different ways in which each community related to the models and influences stemming from the outside world.[71]

For a millennium, Jews found themselves in the vortex of those ancient cultures that shaped the Greco-Roman and Byzantine worlds. The *oikumene,* or inhabited world, of that era was indeed multifaceted, though the Greek tradition, mediated by the Hellenistic, Roman, and Byzantine worlds, remained dominant. The thrust of the discussion in the present chapter has been to transcend an oversimplification of the question "Hellenism—yes or no?" This type of question, which was of interest to scholars a generation or two ago, ought now be regarded as settled; contact between Jews and the outside world was ongoing and often intensive. Like other peoples living under Roman and Byzantine domination, the Jews could in no way remain oblivious to the cultural and social, as well as the political and economic, forces at work throughout the Empire, and they reacted to them in various ways: by choosing suitable features for incorporation into their own culture, adopting regnant patterns without giving much thought to selectivity, or simply rejecting elements as foreign and undesirable. But whatever their reaction, Hellenism served at all times as a stimulant and goad, and even the act of rejection often created a new and unforeseen reality. Moreover, in not a few instances, Hellenistic models

---

70. For a fuller treatment of this subject, see L. Levine, *Judaism and Hellenism.*

71. Such influence is evident in other aspects of Jewish life as well; see, for example, Rutgers, *Jews in Ancient Rome,* passim; Williams, "Organization," 173, 177–78. See also the nicely nuanced presentation of Rutgers regarding the Jews of Sicily ("Interaction and Its Limits," 245–56).

served to enhance particularistic developments. In this respect, Bowersock has proposed a useful formulation in noting that through its wide range of cultural expression in art, language, and thought, Hellenism offered the East "an extraordinarily flexible medium of both cultural and religious expression. It was a medium not necessarily antithetical to local and indigenous traditions. On the contrary, it provided a new and more eloquent way of giving voice to them."[72]

72. Bowersock, *Hellenism*, 7.

nineteen EPILOGUE

In the thousand years leading up to the end of late antiquity, Jewish society and its institutions underwent a total transformation. What had crystallized by the seventh century C.E. was a far cry from what had been normative during the Hellenistic period. Earlier religious frameworks were radically altered or abandoned: holidays, such as those listed in Megillat Ta'anit, were dropped, others, such as Passover and Yom Kippur, were significantly revamped, and still others, such as Hanukkah and Simḥat Torah, were added to the Jewish calendar. New political and religious frameworks (the synagogue) now replaced older ones (the Temple), and new leadership roles evolved (rabbis replaced the priests, and *paytanim* the Temple Levites). Concepts such as the Oral Law and resurrection of the dead, which had been associated with one or more sects, had by now become mainstream. Jewish art developed to a degree which might have been thought unimaginable in the later Second Temple period. A series of Jewish symbols had been created, while foreign motifs—often daring and revolutionary—were being appropriated. The image of an eagle, for instance, regarded by many as anathema in Herod's day, had become a widespread decoration in synagogues of late antiquity; and the concept of sacred literature had been greatly expanded. Alongside the books of the Bible, rabbinic compilations began occupying an important place in Jewish consciousness. Demographically, the Jews were dispersed more than ever before, and while a large Jewish population remained in the Holy Land throughout this period, in the course of time this prominence was being increasingly challenged, both de jure and de facto.

There is no example more illustrative of these far-reaching changes than the ancient synagogue. First crystallized in the course of the Second Temple period, the synagogue was the communal center of each Jewish settlement, the Jewish public building par excellence. During late antiquity, however, while maintaining its status as a communal center, the synagogue began to acquire an enhanced measure of sanctity. Its liturgy expanded enormously, and its main hall assumed a dimension of holiness. Far from being a period of decadence and decline, late antiquity constituted a period of dynamic growth and continued development within Jewish communities in general, and with regard to the synagogue in particular.

The "exuberant diversity" referred to at the outset of our study as characterizing the ancient synagogue is evident throughout this period. It makes little difference whether the discussion has focused on the nomenclature of the synagogue, officials, architecture, art, inscriptions, or liturgy; in each and every one of these areas the ancient synagogue reflects a kaleidoscope of styles, shapes, customs, and functions that is best accounted for by two complementary factors: the degree of influence of the non-Jewish social and religious milieux on the synagogue and the fact that the institution was first and foremost a local one. The tastes and proclivities of each and every community or congregation governed all aspects of the local synagogue—physical, functional, cultural, and religious.

With the possible exception of the Patriarchate, and even then only at certain times and not necessarily in all places, no one political or religious institution determined the manifold aspects of synagogue practice and policy. It has often been assumed that a larger framework, such as the rabbinic class, gave direction and supervision to the various Jewish communities in both Palestine and the Diaspora. However, this was rarely the case in late antiquity. While rabbinic influence may have made itself felt in certain liturgical areas and in certain places in both Palestine and Babylonia—and even then it was dependent upon the willingness of the sages to guide and of the communities to be so guided—for much of this period and in most locales, rabbinic leadership does not appear to have been of consequence.

As a communal institution, the synagogue was all inclusive. The entire range of communal needs was met within its framework, and, in turn, the synagogue mirrored the community's wishes in its physical appearance, functions, and leadership.

Yet the synagogue's inclusiveness went far deeper. Because of its centrality, it brought together and integrated into one framework a wide range of forces and tendencies— often seemingly contradictory. On some occasions these elements simply coexisted; on others they were more fully integrated. Thus, for example, the tension between unity and diversity among Jewish communities gains fascinating expression in synagogue remains, not only among those in the same geographical area, but also among those throughout Palestine and the far-flung Diaspora. The various ways in which these two tendencies are incorporated is clearly demonstrated in the rich evidence associated with the institution. Balancing the sacred and secular was yet another challenge of the synagogue, as liturgical and religious interests existed alongside the many communal functions fulfilled by that institution. Finally, the integration of the particular and the universal is vividly attested in almost every aspect of the ancient synagogue. Uniquely Jewish elements coexisted alongside those drawn from the outside world. In this regard, the synagogue demonstrated a resiliency in what was incorporated as well as rejected. This balance between universal and particular is especially evident in Jewish art. It was in part borrowed and adapted and in part distinctly Jewish, both in content and in the selection of forms to emulate. This inclusive role within the community was itself a unique phenomenon in antiquity. Rarely do we hear of as broadly based an agenda for either a pagan or a Christian institution.

But the very essence and singularity of the synagogue was in its twin focus on the communal and religious dimensions. On the one hand, the former came to be dominated and shaped by religious concerns; whereas the main hall of the building was once neutral in decoration and function, it eventually came to be regarded as a sacred area, with its art highlighting ritual objects and symbols. On the other hand, this religious emphasis was rooted in the community which created it, and the religious functions were anchored in the will, participation, and resources of the community at large.

Herein lies a cardinal difference between the church and the synagogue of late antiquity. The former aspired not only to be holy, but even to acquire a divine status. The Byzantine church was often considered a *domus dei* and not merely a *domus ecclesiae*. The description of the church building by the eighth-century bishop Germanus is classic: "The church is heaven on earth, where the God of heaven dwells and moves. It images forth the crucifixion and burial and resurrection of Christ. It is glorified above the tabernacle of the testimony of Moses with its expiatory and holy of holies, prefigured in the patriarch, founded on the apostles, adorned in hierarchs, perfected in the martyrs."[1]

A century earlier, Maximus also wrote about the symbolism of the church building as expressed in its liturgy and architecture. The building represented a two-tiered arrangement: the sanctuary ($\iota\epsilon\rho\bar{\alpha}\tau\epsilon\hat{\iota}o\nu$) and nave ($\nu\alpha\acute{o}s$), with priests and bishops occupying the former, the congregation the latter. This setting reflects the entire universe: the angelic world and the human one, heaven and earth, soul and body.[2] Hand in hand with this concept of the church as an otherworldly edifice was the status of the bishop, who was considered the focus of the community, the representative of God, the mediator, high priest, and earthly father of his flock.

No comparable descriptions are known to have existed regarding the synagogue. No hierarchy governed its proceedings and no set of divinely inspired individuals officiated. Whether during the Torah- and haftarah-readings, the *targum*, sermons, prayers, or *piyutim* (with the sole exception of the priestly blessings), every Jew had the opportunity

---

1. Quoted in Taft, "Liturgy of the Great Church," 72. On the distinction between *domus dei* and *domus ecclesiae*, see Turner, *From Temple to Meeting House*, 11–12, 304–45.

2. Mathews, *Early Churches*, 121.

to actively participate in any aspect of the synagogue ritual. From its usually modest size to its multifocal liturgy, the Byzantine synagogue, in contradistinction to its Christian counterpart, expressed a message of inclusion and involvement, where the congregation per se was of primary importance. In this sense, the Christian church more closely approximates the hierarchical stratification that once existed in the Jerusalem Temple. The Jews of late antiquity appear to have shied away from too close an approximation; the Temple was the house of God, whereas the synagogue was a communal framework with a modicum of sanctity.

In a larger context, the synagogue's primary historical significance was that it provided Jewish life of late antiquity with an essential unity.[3] Despite its many geographical, linguistic, cultural, and religious variations, this communal institution, with its ever more prominent religious component, provided a common framework for Jewish communities everywhere. The function fulfilled by the Jerusalem Temple in the pre-70 era was now achieved, mutatis mutandis, by this locally based—yet universally present—institution that Jews created wherever they lived, a "diminished sanctuary" that served their corporate needs throughout late antiquity, and beyond.

---

3. See comments in Davies, *Paul and Rabbinic Judaism*, 6–8.

GLOSSARY

Plural forms are shown in parentheses.

aedicula	small shrine composed of columns supporting a pediment
aggadah	non-halakhic rabbinic literature
ʿaliyah	act of going up to read from the Torah or recite the Torah blessings
ʿAmidah	lit., "standing"; central prayer in Jewish liturgy, recited thrice daily
amora(im)	sage who lived after the compilation of the Mishnah and who was active in the period of the *talmudim* (ca. 200–500)
amphora	vase with a large oval body, a neck, and two handles reaching the top of the vessel
apse	a semicircular recess in a hall, found mainly in a basilica
ʿAqedah	story of the Binding of Isaac (Gen. 22)
atrium	courtyard before the entrance to a basilica
av bet din	head of a rabbinic court
ʿAvodah	Temple cultic service
baraita	"external" tannaitic tradition, one not included in the Mishnah of R. Judah I
basilica	large Roman civic building
Bavli	Babylonian Talmud
bet midrash	house of study, usually a rabbinic academy
bima (*bimot*)	raised platform in a synagogue or a church
birkat hamazon	grace after meals

boule	city council of a *polis*
bouleuterion	meeting place of a city council (*boule*)
cardo maximus	main north-south street in a Roman city
Cathedra of Moses	seat of honor in a synagogue
chancel screen	partition around the *bima* consisting of stone posts and panels; see also *soreg*
chora	Egyptian countryside outside of Alexandria
collegia	religious or professional voluntary association
conch	shell pattern, often decorating the top of a niche
diakonos	synagogue official, similar to a church deacon
Diaspora	Jewish settlement outside of Judaea or Palestine
ethrog (*im*)	citron used on the Sukkot holiday
exedra	semicircular or rectangular recess
Exilarch	political and communal leader of Babylonian Jewry
fresco	wall painting composed by the application of watercolors to wet plaster
gable	triangular end of a roof above a building's facade
gaon	head of a Babylonian academy in the early Middle Ages
gerousia	governing council of elders
haftarah	reading from the Prophets following the Torah-reading on Sabbaths and holidays
Hallel	Pss. 113–18, recited on holidays
Haqhel	ceremonial Torah-reading ceremony held every seven years on the Sukkot holiday (per Deut. 31:10–13)
Hekhalot	mystical traditions composed in Palestine in late antiquity
Helios	Greco-Roman sun god
lintel	horizontal beam above a doorway or window
lulav (*im*)	palm branch used on the Sukkot holiday
maftir	last person to be called to the Torah, who recites the haftarah-reading
meturgeman (*im*)	translator of the Torah-reading into the vernacular
miqveh (*miqva'ot*)	stepped cistern used as a ritual bath
Mussaf	"Additional" *'Amidah* recited on Sabbaths and holidays
naos	central chamber (*cella*) in a Greek temple, where the statue of a deity was placed
narthex	entrance hall leading into the nave and aisles of a synagogue
nave	central hall of a basilica separated from the side aisles by a row of columns or pillars
ner tamid	eternal light used in synagogues
niche	rectangular or curved recess in a wall
nymphaeum	public water facility, usually decorated with statues
opus listatum	another term for *opus vittatum*
opus reticulatum	a facing composed of small square stones laid diagonally
opus vittatum	a facing composed of courses of small square stones alternating with one or more courses of bricks

parashah	weekly portion of the Torah-reading following the Babylonian cycle
parnas(im)	Jewish community leader
parokhet	a covering or a veil for a sacred space or for holy objects in the Tabernacle, the Temple, or the synagogue
paytan	composer of synagogue liturgical poetry (*piyyut*)
piyyut(im)	liturgical poetry composed for synagogue use
polis	Greek city
politeuma	autonomous political body in a *polis* granted by civil or Imperial authorities
pronaos	entrance room in front of the *naos*
propylaeum	monumental entranceway
proseuche (*proseuchae*)	"house of prayer"; synonym for "synagogue," used primarily in the Diaspora
Qaddish	prayer of praise that punctuates the worship service
Qedushah	central prayer built around verses from Is. 6:3 and Ezek. 3:12; see also *trisagion*
qerovah	*piyyut* for the *'Amidah*
Qiddush	blessing over wine, recited on Sabbaths and holidays
Rosh Ḥodesh	special day celebrating the appearance of the new moon
sebomenoi	lit., "God-fearers," i.e., pagan sympathizers of Judaism
sheliaḥ tzibbur	prayer leader in a synagogue
Shema'	central prayer in Jewish liturgy (per Deut. 6:4–9)
Shemoneh 'Esreh	another term for *'Amidah*
Shephelah	coastal area of Palestine, west of the Judaean hills
shiv'ata	*piyyut* for Sabbaths and festival evenings
shofar (*shofarot*)	ram's horn used on New Year's Day (Rosh Hashanah)
siddur	Jewish prayerbook
sidrah	weekly portion of the Torah-reading following the Palestinian cycle
skoutlosis	marble panels (revetments) decorating the walls of a hall
sofer(im)	teacher or scribe who often functioned as the translator of the Torah-reading (*meturgeman*)
soreg	chancel screen or partition used in the Jerusalem Temple and in Byzantine churches and synagogues
stoa	public building with multiple colonnades open on one side (= Latin *porticus*)
stylobate	row of hewn stones used to support columns
tabula ansata	rectangular frame flanked by "ear"-shaped triangles on its short sides, usually containing an inscription
tanna(im)	sage who lived up to the time of the compilation of the Mishnah (ca. 200 C.E.)
taqqanah (*taqqanot*)	rabbinic enactment
targum(im)	translation of the Torah into Aramaic or Greek
temenos	sacred site of a temple

triclinium	dining hall
trisagion	lit., "thrice holy"; verse from Is. 6:3 constituting the core of a central prayer in Judaism and Christianity
Yerushalmi	Jerusalem, or Palestinian, Talmud
yotzer	*piyyut* for the blessing preceding the *Shema*

ABBREVIATIONS

AJA	*American Journal of Archaeology*
AJP	*American Journal of Philology*
AJSL	*American Journal of Semitic Languages and Literatures*
AJS Review	*Association for Jewish Studies Review*
ANRW	*Aufstieg und Niedergang der römischen Welt*
ASR	*Ancient Synagogues Revealed* (L. Levine, 1981)
B	Bavli (Babylonian Talmud)
b.	ben, bar (son of)
BA	*Biblical Archaeologist*
BAR	*Biblical Archaeology Review*
BASOR	*Bulletin of the American Schools of Oriental Research*
BCH	*Bulletin de Correspondance Hellénique*
BIOSCS	*Bulletin of the International Organization for Septuagint and Cognate Studies*
BJPES	*Bulletin of the Jewish Palestine Exploration Society*
BJRL	*Bulletin of the John Rylands Library*
BMC	*British Museum Catalogue*
CAD	*Chicago Assyrian Dictionary*
CBQ	*Christian Biblical Quarterly*
CD	Codex Damascus
CIJ	*Corpus Inscriptionum Judaicarum* (Frey, 1936–52; reprint II, 1975)
CIRB	*Corpus Inscriptionum Regni Bosporani*

CIS	*Corpus Inscriptionum Semiticarum*
CJ	*Conservative Judaism*
CPJ	*Corpus Papyrorum Judaicarum* (Tcherikover et al., 1957–64)
DOP	*Dumbarton Oaks Papers*
EI	*Eretz-Israel*
EJ	*Encyclopaedia Judaica*
FJB	*Frankfurter Judäistische Beiträge*
HSCP	*Harvard Studies in Classical Philology*
HTR	*Harvard Theological Review*
HUCA	*Hebrew Union College Annual*
ICC	*International Critical Commentary*
IDB	*The Interpreter's Dictionary of the Bible*
IEJ	*Israel Exploration Journal*
INJ	*Israel Numismatic Journal*
JA	*Jewish Art*
JAAR	*Journal of the American Academy of Religion*
JBL	*Journal of Biblical Literature*
JE	*Jewish Encyclopedia*
JGS	*Journal of Glass Studies*
JHS	*Journal of Hellenic Studies*
JIWE	*Jewish Inscriptions of Western Europe* (Noy, 1993–95)
JJA	*Journal of Jewish Art*
JJS	*Journal of Jewish Studies*
JPOS	*Journal of the Palestine Oriental Society*
JQR	*Jewish Quarterly Review*
JRA	*Journal of Roman Archaeology*
JRH	*Journal of Religious History*
JRS	*Journal of Roman Studies*
JSJ	*Journal for the Study of Judaism*
JSNT	*Journal for the Study of the New Testament*
JSP	*Journal for the Study of Pseudepigrapha*
JSQ	*Jewish Studies Quarterly*
JSS	*Jewish Social Studies*
JTS	*Journal of Theological Studies*
LCL	Loeb Classical Library
MAMA	*Monumenta Asiae Minoris Antiqua*
MGWJ	*Monatsschrift für Geschichte und Wissenschaft des Judentums*
NEAEHL	*New Encyclopedia of Archaeological Excavations in the Holy Land* (E. Stern, 1993)
NTS	*New Testament Studies*
Or.	*Orientalia* (Rome)
PAAJR	*Proceedings of the American Academy for Jewish Research*
PBSR	*Papers of the British School at Rome*

PEFQSt	*Palestine Exploration Fund Quarterly Statement*
PEQ	*Palestine Exploration Quarterly*
PG	*Patrologia Graeca*
PL	*Patrologia Latina*
PO	*Patrologia Orientalis*
PPTS	*Palestine Pilgrim Text Society*
PRK	Pesiqta de Rav Kahana
R.	Rabbi
RA	*Rabbinical Assembly*
RB	*Revue Biblique*
REG	*Revue des Etudes Grecques*
REJ	*Revue des Etudes Juives*
RHPR	*Revue d'Histoire et de Philosophie Religieuses*
RPh	*Revue Philologique*
RQ	*Revue de Qumran*
RSR	*Recherches de Science Religieuse*
SCI	*Scripta Classica Israelitica*
SH	*Scripta Hierosolymitana*
SHA	*Scriptores Historiae Augustae*
SL	*Studia Liturgica*
T	Tosefta
TDNT	*Theological Dictionary of the New Testament*
TK	*Tosefta Ki-Fshutah* (Lieberman, 1955–88)
VC	*Vigiliae Christianae*
VT	*Vetus Testamentum*
Y	Yerushalmi (Jerusalem, or Palestinian, Talmud)
ZAW	*Zeitschrift für die Alttestamentliche Wissenschaft*
ZDPV	*Zeitschrift des Deutschen Palästina-Vereins*
ZNW	*Zeitschrift für die Neutestamentliche Wissenschaft*
ZPE	*Zeitschrift für Papyrologie und Epigraphik*

BIBLIOGRAPHY

MODERN LITERATURE

Aberbach, M., "The Conflicting Accounts of Josephus and Tacitus Concerning Cumanus' and Felix' Terms of Office," *JQR* 40 (1949–50).

———, *Jewish Education in the Mishnaic and Talmudic Period* (Jerusalem: R. Mass, 1982). Hebrew.

Abrahams, I., "The Lost Confession of Samuel," *HUCA* 1 (1924).

Aderet, A., *From Destruction to Restoration: The Mode of Yavneh in the Re-Establishment of the Jewish People* (Jerusalem: Magnes, 1990). Hebrew.

Adler, E. N., "Une nouvelle chronique samaritaine," *REJ* 45 (1902).

Albeck, Ch., "Apocryphal Halakha in the Palestinian Targum and the Aggada," *B. Lewin Jubilee Volume*, ed. J. L. Fishman (Jerusalem: Mosad Harav Kook, 1939). Hebrew.

———, "Midrash Wayyiqra Rabba," *Louis Ginzberg Jubilee Volume* (New York: American Academy of Jewish Research, 1945). Hebrew.

———, *Six Orders of the Mishnah*, 6 vols. (Jerusalem & Tel Aviv: Bialik & Dvir, 1952–58). Hebrew.

———, *Introduction to the Mishnah* (Jerusalem & Tel Aviv: Bialik & Dvir, 1959). Hebrew.

Albright, W. F., "A Biblical Fragment from the Maccabean Age: The Nash Papyrus," *JBL* 56 (1937).

Alderink, L. J., and Martin, L. H., "Prayer in Greco-Roman Religions," *Prayer from Alexander to Constantine: A Critical Anthology* (London & New York: Routledge, 1997).

Alexander, P. S., "The Targumim and Early Exegesis of 'Sons of God' in Genesis 6," *JJS* 23 (1972).

———, "The Rabbinic Lists of Forbidden Targumim," *JJS* 27 (1976).

———, "The Targumim and the Rabbinic Rules for the Delivery of the Targum," *Congress Volume—Salamanca 1983*, Supplement to *VT* 36, ed. J. A. Emerton (Leiden: Brill, 1985).

————, "Jewish Aramaic Translations of Hebrew Scriptures," *Mikra*, ed. M. J. Mulder (Assen: Van Gorcum, 1988).

————, "Jerusalem as the *Omphalos* of the World: On the History of a Geographical Concept," *Jerusalem: Its Sanctity and Centrality to Judaism, Christianity and Islam*, ed. L. I. Levine (New York: Continuum, 1998).

Alon, G., *Studies in Jewish History*, 2 vols. (Tel Aviv: HaKibbutz Hameuchad, 1957-58). Hebrew.

————, *Jews, Judaism and the Classical World* (Jerusalem: Magnes, 1977).

————, *The Jews in Their Land in the Talmudic Age*, 2 vols. (Jerusalem: Magnes, 1980).

Amit, D., "A Marble Menorah from the Synagogue at Maʿon-Judea," *Studies in Judea and Samaria — Proceedings of the Seventh Conference, 1997*, ed. Y. Eshel (Qedumim-Ariel: College of Judea and Samaria, 1998). Hebrew.

————, " 'The Curtain Would Be Removed for Them' (*Yoma* 54a) in Ancient Synagogue Depictions," *Tarbiz* 61 (1992). Hebrew.

————, "Excavations at Maʿon and ʿAnim: Their Contribution to the Study of Ancient Synagogues in Southern Judea," *Cathedra* 68 (1993). Hebrew.

————, "Reactions and Comments," *Qadmoniot* 26/101-2 (1993). Hebrew.

————, Iconoclasm in the Ancient Synagogues in Eretz-Israel," *Proceedings of the Eleventh World Congress of Jewish Studies*, B/1 (Jerusalem: World Union of Jewish Studies, 1994).

————, "Architectural Plans of Synagogues in the Southern Judean Hills and the 'Halakah,' " *Ancient Synagogues: Historical Analysis and Archaeological Discovery*, I, ed. D. Urman and P. V. M. Flesher (Leiden: Brill, 1995).

Amit, D., and Ilan, Z., "The Ancient Synagogue at Maʿon in Judah," *Qadmoniot* 23/91-92 (1990). Hebrew.

Anderson, G., *Sage, Saint and Sophist: Holy Men and Their Associates in the Early Roman Empire* (London: Routledge, 1994).

Anderson, H., "Broadening Horizons: The Rejection at Nazareth Pericope of Luke 4:16-30 in Light of Recent Critical Trends," *Interpretation* 18 (1964).

Applebaum, S., "The Jewish Community of Hellenistic and Roman Teucheria in Cyrenaika," *SH* 7 (1961).

————, "A New Jewish Inscription from Berenice in Cyrenaica," *Yediʿot* 25 (1961). Hebrew.

————, "The Legal Status of the Jewish Communities in the Diaspora," *The Jewish People in the First Century*, I, ed. S. Safrai and M. Stern (Philadelphia: Fortress, 1974).

————, "The Organization of the Jewish Communities in the Diaspora," *The Jewish People in the First Century*, I, ed. S. Safrai and M. Stern (Philadelphia: Fortress, 1974).

————, *Jews and Greeks in Ancient Cyrene* (Leiden: Brill, 1979).

Arav, R., *Settlement Patterns and City Planning in Palestine during the Hellenistic Period. 322-37 B.C.E.* (New York: New York University Press, 1986).

Archer, L. J., "The Role of Women in Graeco-Roman Palestine," *Images of Women in Antiquity*, ed. Av. Cameron and A. Kuhrt (London: Routledge, 1993).

Ariel, D. "Coins from the Synagogue at En Nashut," *IEJ* 37 (1987).

Arzt, M., "The Teacher in Talmud and Midrash," *Mordecai Kaplan Jubilee Volume* (New York: Jewish Theological Seminary, 1953).

Assis, Y. T., "Synagogues in Medieval Spain," *JA* 18 (1992).

———, "Synagogues throughout the Ages," *And I Shall Dwell among Them: Historic Synagogues of the World*, ed. N. Folberg (New York: Aperture, 1995).

Athanassiadi, P., *Julian: An Intellectual Biography* (London: Routledge, 1992).

Aune, D. E., "Orthodoxy in First Century Judaism? A Response to N. J. McEleney," *JSJ* 7 (1976).

———, "Magic in Early Christianity," *ANRW*, II, 23.2, ed. H. Temporini and W. Haase (Berlin & New York: de Gruyter, 1984).

Avery-Peck, A. J., "Judaism without the Temple: The Mishnah," *Eusebius, Christianity and Judaism* (Leiden: Brill, 1992).

Avigad, N., "A Dated Lintel-Inscription from the Ancient Synagogue of Nabratein," *Bulletin of the Louis M. Rabinowitz Fund for the Exploration of Ancient Synagogues*, III (Jerusalem: Hebrew University, 1960).

———, "On the Form of Ancient Synagogues in Galilee," *All the Land of Naphtali*, ed. H. Hirshberg (Jerusalem: Israel Exploration Society, 1967). Hebrew.

———, *Beth She'arim*, III (New Brunswick: Rutgers University Press, 1976).

———, *Discovering Jerusalem* (Nashville: Thomas Nelson, 1983).

———, "Samaria (City)," *NEAEHL*, IV, ed. E. Stern (Jerusalem: Carta, 1993).

Avissar, O., ed., *Sefer Teveria* (Jerusalem: Keter, 1973). Hebrew.

Avi-Yonah, M., "The Second Temple," *Sefer Yerushalayim*, ed. M. Avi-Yonah (Jerusalem & Tel Aviv: Bialik & Dvir, 1956). Hebrew.

———, "The Mosaic Pavement of the Ma'on Synagogue," *Bulletin of the Louis M. Rabinowitz Fund for the Exploration of Ancient Synagogues*, III (Jerusalem: Hebrew University, 1960).

———, "The Mosaic Floor of the Ma'on Synagogue," *EI*, VI (Jerusalem: Israel Exploration Society, 1961). Hebrew.

———, *Oriental Art in Roman Palestine* (Rome: University of Rome, 1961).

———, "Synagogue Architecture in the Late Classical Period," *Jewish Art: An Illustrated History*, ed. C. Roth (Greenwich: New York Graphic Society, 1961).

———, *In the Days of Rome and Byzantium* (Jersalem: Bialik, 1962). Hebrew.

———, "The Caesarea Inscription of the Twenty-Four Priestly Courses," *The Teacher's Yoke: Studies in Memory of Henry Trantham*, ed. E. J. Vardamon and J. L. Garrett (Waco: Baylor University Press, 1964).

———, "The Founding of Tiberias," *All the Land of Naphtali*, ed. H. Hirshberg (Jerusalem: Israel Exploration Society, 1967). Hebrew.

———, "Tiberias in the Roman Period," *All the Land of Naphtali*, ed. H. Hirshberg (Jerusalem: Israel Exploration Society, 1967). Hebrew.

———, "Ancient Synagogues," *Ariel* 32 (1973).

———, "Jewish Art and Architecture in the Hasmonean and Herodian Periods," *The World History of the Jewish People: The Herodian Period*, ed. M. Avi-Yonah (Jerusalem: Massada, 1973).

———, *Gazetteer of Roman Palestine*, Qedem 5 (Jerusalem: Institute of Archaeology, Hebrew University, 1976).

———, *The Jews of Palestine* (New York: Schocken, 1976).

———, *Art in Ancient Palestine* (Jerusalem: Magnes, 1981).

———, "The Mosaics of Mopsuestia—Church or Synagogue?" *Ancient Synagogues Revealed*, ed. L. I. Levine (Jerusalem: Israel Exploration Society, 1981).

———, "Ancient Synagogues," *NEAEHL*, IV, ed. E. Stern (Jerusalem: Carta, 1993).

Avi-Yonah, M., and Kloner, A., "Maresha," *NEAEHL*, III, ed. E. Stern (Jerusalem: Carta, 1993).

Ayali, M., *Workers and Artisans: Their Work and Status in Rabbinic Literature* (Givatayim: Massada, 1987). Hebrew.

Bacher, W., "Siège de Moïse," *REJ* 34 (1897).

———, "Synagogue," *JE*, XI (New York & London: Funk & Wagnalls, 1901–6).

———, "Targum," *JE*, XII (New York & London: Funk & Wagnalls, 1901–6).

———, "L'expression 'פרס על שמע'," *REJ* 57 (1909).

———, *Die exegetische Terminologie der jüdischen Traditionsliteratur*, reprint (Hildesheim: G. Olms, 1965).

Baer, Y. F., *Israel among the Nations* (Jerusalem: Bialik, 1955). Hebrew.

Baillet, M., *Qumran Grotte 4 (4Q482–4Q520)*, Discoveries in the Judaean Desert, VII (Oxford: Clarendon, 1982).

Baldovin, J. F., "Christian Worship—The Eve of the Reformation," *The Making of Jewish and Christian Worship*, ed. P. F. Bradshaw and L. Hoffman (Notre Dame: University of Notre Dame Press, 1991).

Barag, D., "Glass Pilgrim Vessels from Jerusalem," *JGS* 12 (1970); 13 (1971).

———, "The Second Season of Excavations at En Gedi," *Qadmoniot* 5/18 (1972). Hebrew.

———, "The *Menorah* in the Roman and Byzantine Periods: A Messianic Symbol," *Bulletin of the Anglo-Israel Archaeological Society* (1985–86).

———, "A Silver Coin of Yohanan the High Priest and the Coinage of Judea in the Fourth Century B.C.," *INJ* 9 (1986–87).

———, "A Coin of Bagoas with a Representation of God on a Winged-Wheel," *Qadmoniot* 25/99–100 (1992). Hebrew.

Barag, D., et al., "The Synagogue at 'En-Gedi," *Ancient Synagogues Revealed*, ed. L. I. Levine (Jerusalem: Israel Exploration Society, 1981).

Barber, C., "Truth in Painting: Iconclasm and Identity in Early Medieval Art," *Speculum* 72 (1997).

Barclay, J. M. G., *Jews in the Mediterranean Diaspora: From Alexander to Trajan (323 B.C.E.–117 C.E.)* (Edinburgh: T. & T. Clark, 1996).

Bar-Ilan, M., "Stone, Seat, and Cathedra on Which Moses Sat," *Sidra* 2 (1986). Hebrew.

———, *The Mysteries of Jewish Prayer and Hekhalot* (Ramat Gan: Bar Ilan University Press, 1987). Hebrew.

———, "Basic Issues in the Formation and Crystallization of the Qedushah," *Da'at* 25 (1990). Hebrew.

———, "Blessings and Curses Are Read Prior to Rosh Hashana," *Sinai* 110 (1992). Hebrew.

———, "Washing Feet before Prayer," *Mahanaim* 1 (1992). Hebrew.

———, "Interpreting a Baraita Dealing with the Torah-Reading," *Sinai* 112 (1993). Hebrew.

Bar Ilan University Responsa Project: The Data Base for Jewish Studies (Ramat Gan: Bar Ilan University, n.d.).

Barnard, L. W. *The Graeco-Roman and Oriental Background of the Iconoclastic Controversy* (Leiden: Brill, 1974).

Barnes, J. T. D., *Constantine and Eusebius* (Cambridge: Harvard University Press, 1981).

Barnett, R. D., "Bringing the God into the Temple," *Temples and High Places in Biblical Times*, ed. A. Biran (Jerusalem: Hebrew Union College, 1981).

Baron, S. W., *A Social and Religious History of the Jews*, 3 vols. (New York: Columbia University Press, 1937).

———, *The Jewish Community: Its History and Structure to the American Revolution*, 3 vols. (Philadelphia: Jewish Publication Society, 1942).

———, *A Social and Religious History of the Jews*, 2d ed., 18 vols. (New York: Columbia University Press, 1952–83).

Baumgarten, A., "Justinian and the Jews," *Rabbi Joseph H. Lookstein Memorial Volume*, ed. L. Landman (New York: KTAV, 1980).

———, "Torah as a Public Document in Judaism," *Studies in Religion* 14/1 (1985).

———, "Literary Evidence for Jewish Christianity in the Galilee," *The Galilee in Late Antiquity*, ed. L. I. Levine (New York & Jerusalem: Jewish Theological Seminary, 1992).

———, "City Lights: Urbanization and Sectarianism in Hasmonean Jerusalem," *The Centrality of Jerusalem: Historical Perspectives*, ed. M. Poorthuis and Ch. Safrai (Kampen: Pharos, 1996).

———, "Invented Traditions of the Maccabean Era," *Geschichte-Tradition-Reflexion: Festschrift für Martin Hengel zum 70. Geburtstag*, I: *Judentum*, ed. P. Schäfer (Tübingen: J. C. B. Mohr, 1996).

Baumgarten, J., "Art in the Synagogue: Some Talmudic Views," *Judaism* 19/2 (1970).

Baumstark, A., *Abendländische Palästinapilger des ersten Jahrtausends und ihre Berichte* (Cologne: Bachem, 1906).

———, *Comparative Liturgy* (London: Mowbray, 1958).

Bauer, G. L., *Beschreibung der gottesdienstlichen Verfassung der alten Hebräer*, 2 vols. (Leipzig: Weygand, 1805–6).

Baynes, N. H., "The Icons before Iconoclasm," *HTR* 44 (1951).

Beckwith, R. T., "The Jewish Background to Christian Worship," *The Study of Liturgy*, ed. C. Jones et al. (London: SPCK, 1992).

Beeck, F. J. van, "The Worship of Christians in Pliny's Letter," *SL* 18 (1988).

Beek, G. van, and Beek, O. van, "Canaanite-Phoenician Architecture: The Development and Distribution of Two Styles," *EI*, XV (Jerusalem: Israel Exploration Society, 1981).

Beer, M., "Issachar and Zebulun," *Bar Ilan Studies* 6 (1968). Hebrew.

———, *The Babylonian Amoraim: Aspects of Economic Life* (Ramat Gan: Bar Ilan University Press, 1974). Hebrew.

———, *The Babylonian Exilarchate in the Arsacid and Sassanian Periods* (Tel Aviv: Dvir, 1976). Hebrew.

———, "The Hereditary Principle and Jewish Leadership," *Bar Ilan Studies* 13 (1976). Hebrew.

———, "Sons of Eli in Rabbinic Aggadah," *Bar Ilan Annual* 14–15 (1977). Hebrew.

Bell, H. I., and Skeat, T. C., *Fragments of an Unknown Gospel and Other Early Christian Papyri* (London: British Museum, 1935).

Belz, C., *Marine Genre Mosaic Pavements of Roman North Africa* (Ann Arbor: University Microfilms, 1983).

Ben Dov, M., "Fragmentary Synagogue Inscriptions from Tiberias," *Qadmoniot* 9/34–35 (1976). Hebrew.

Ben-Sasson, H. H., *Trial and Achievement: Currents in Jewish History* (Jerusalem: Keter, 1974).

Ben-Sasson, M., "Appeal to the Congregation in Islamic Countries in the Early Middle Ages,"

Knesset Ezra: Literature and Life in the Synagogue—Studies Presented to Ezra Fleischer, ed. S. Elizur et al. (Jerusalem: Yad Izhak Ben Zvi, 1994). Hebrew.

Bergman, Y., *Charity in Israel: History and Institutions* (Jersalem: Tarshish, 1944). Hebrew.

Bickerman, E. J., "On the Sanhedrin," *Zion* 3 (1937-38). Hebrew.

———, "Les Maccabées de Malalas," *Byzantion* 21 (1951).

———, "The Altars of Gentiles: A Note on the Jewish 'ius sacrum,'" *Revue Internationale des Droits de l'Antiquité* 5 (1958).

———, "The Civic Prayer of Jerusalem," *HTR* 55 (1962).

———, "Symbolism in the Dura Synagogue: A Review Article," *HTR* 58 (1965).

———, *The Jews in the Greek Age* (Cambridge: Harvard University Press, 1988).

Biebel, F. M., "The Mosaics of Hammam Lif," *Art Bulletin* 18 (1930).

Biran, A., "Tel Dan: Five Years Later," *BA* 13 (1980).

———, "'To the God Who Is in Dan,'" *Temples and High Places in Biblical Times*, ed. A. Biran (Jerusalem: Hebrew Union College, 1981).

———, "Dan," *NEAEHL*, I, ed. E. Stern (Jerusalem: Carta, 1993).

———, *Biblical Dan* (Jerusalem: Israel Exploration Society, 1994).

Black, M., "Aramaic Studies and the Language of Jesus," *In Memoriam Paul Kahle*, ed. M. Black and G. Fohrer (Berlin: Toepelmann, 1968).

———, *The Scrolls and Christian Origins: Studies in the Jewish Background of the New Testament* (Chico, Calif.: Scholars, 1983).

Black, C. C., II, "The Rhetorical Form of the Hellenistic Jewish and Early Christian Sermon: A Response to Lawrence Wills," *HTR* 81 (1988).

Blenkinsopp, J., "The Second Temple as House of Prayer," *"Où demeures-tu?" (Jn. 1, 38): La maison depuis le monde biblique*, ed. J. C. Petit (Quebec: Fides, 1994).

Blidstein, G. J., "Sheliach Tzibbur: Historical and Phenomenological Observations," *Tradition* 12/1 (1971).

———, "The Tannaim and Plastic Art," *Perspectives in Jewish Learning*, V, ed. B. L. Sherwin (Chicago: Spertus College of Judaica, 1973).

———, "Prostration and Mosaics in Talmudic Law," *Bulletin of the Institute of Jewish Studies* 2 (1974).

———, "R. Yohanan, Idolatry and Public Privilege," *JSJ* 5 (1974).

———, "Between Individual Prayer and Communal Prayer," *Sinai* 106 (1990). Hebrew.

———, *Prayer in Maimonidean Halakha* (Jerusalem: Bialik & Ben Gurion University Press, 1994). Hebrew.

Bloch, P., "Die מרכבה יורדי, die Mystiker der Gaonenzeit und ihr Einfluss auf die Liturgie," *MGWJ* 37 (1893).

Bloch, R., "Methodological Note for the Study of Rabbinic Literature," *Approaches to Ancient Judaism: Theory and Practice*, ed. W. S. Green (Missoula: Scholars, 1978).

Bloedhorn, H., "The Capitals of the Synagogue of Capernaum—Their Chronological and Stylistic Classification with Regard to the Development of Capitals in the Decapolis and in Palestine," *Ancient Synagogues in Israel*, ed. R. Hachlili, B.A.R. International Series 499 (Oxford: B.A.R., 1989).

Boer, P. A. H. de, "Notes on an Oxyrhynchus Papyrus in Hebrew," *VT* 1 (1951).

Boethius, A., and Ward-Perkins, J. B., *Etruscan and Roman Architecture* (Harmondsworth: Penguin, 1970).

Bohec, Y. le, "Inscriptions juives et judaïsantes de l'Afrique romaine," *Antiquités Africaines* 17 (1981).

Boid, R., "Use, Authority and Exegesis of Mikra in the Samaritan Tradition," *Mikra*, ed. M. J. Mulder (Assen: Van Gorcum, 1988).

Bokser, B., "Rabbinic Responses to Catastrophe: From Continuity to Discontinuity," *PAAJR* 50 (1983).

———, "The Wall Separating God and Israel," *JQR* 73 (1983).

———, *Origins of the Seder: The Passover Rite and Early Rabbinic Judaism* (Berkeley: University of California Press, 1984).

———, "Todos and Rabbinic Authority in Rome," *New Perspectives on Ancient Judaism*, I: *Religion, Literature, and Society in Ancient Israel: Formative Christianity and Judaism*, ed. J. Neusner et al. (Atlanta: Scholars, 1990).

Bonfil, R., *Rabbis and Jewish Communities in Renaissance Italy* (London: Littman, 1993).

Bonner, S. F., *Education in Ancient Rome: From the Elder Cato to the Younger Pliny* (London: Methuen, 1977).

Bonz, M. P., "The Jewish Community of Ancient Sardis: A Reassessment of Its Rise to Prominence," *HSCP* 93 (1990).

———, "Differing Approaches to Religious Benefaction: The Late Third-Century Acquisition of the Sardis Synagogue," *HTR* 86 (1993).

———, "The Jewish Donor Inscriptions from Aphrodisias: Are They Both Third-Century, and Who Are the *Theosebeis?*" *HSCP* 96 (1994).

Bottermann, H., "Die Synagoge von Sardis: Eine Synagoge aus dem 4. Jahrhundert?" *ZNW* 81 (1990).

Bouley, A., *From Freedom to Formula: The Evolution of the Eucharistic Prayer from Oral Improvisation to Written Texts* (Washington, D.C.: Catholic University Press, 1981).

Bousset, W., and Gressmann, H., *Die Religion des Judentums im späthellenistischen Zeitalter* (Tübingen: J. C. B. Mohr, 1926).

Bowersock, G. W., *Roman Arabia* (Cambridge: Harvard University Press, 1983).

———, *Hellenism in Late Antiquity* (Cambridge: Cambridge University Press, 1990).

Bowker, J., "Speeches in Acts: A Study in Proem and Yelammedenu Form," *NTS* 14 (1967).

———, *The Targums and Rabbinic Literature* (Cambridge: Cambridge University Press, 1969).

Bowsher, J. M., "Architecture and Religion in the Decapolis: A Numismatic Survey," *PEQ* 119 (1987).

Bradbury, S., ed. and trans., *Severus of Minorca: Letter on the Conversion of the Jews* (Oxford: Clarendon, 1996).

Bradshaw, P. F., *The Origins of the Daily Office* (London: SPCK, 1978).

———, *Daily Prayer in the Early Church: A Study of the Origin and Early Development of the Divine Office* (London: SPCK, 1981).

———, *Liturgical Presidency in the Early Church* (Bramcote: Grove, 1983).

———, "Ten Principles for Interpreting Early Christian Liturgical Evidence," *The Making of Jewish and Christian Worship*, ed. P. F. Bradshaw and L. Hoffman (Notre Dame: University of Notre Dame, 1991).

———, *The Search for the Origins of Christian Worship: Sources and Methods for the Study of Early Liturgy* (New York: Oxford University Press, 1992).

———, "The Influence of Jerusalem on Christian Liturgy," *Jerusalem: Its Sanctity and Centrality to Judaism, Christianity and Islam*, ed. L. I. Levine (New York: Continuum, 1998).

Brändle, R., "Christen und Juden in Antiochien in den Jahren 386/87," *Judaica* 43 (1987).

Brand, Y., *Ceramics in Talmudic Literature* (Jerusalem: Harav Kook, 1953). Hebrew.

Branham, J., "Sacred Space under Erasure in Ancient Synagogues and Early Churches," *Art Bulletin* 74 (1992).

———, "Vicarious Sacrality: Temple Space in Ancient Synagogues," *Ancient Synagogues: Historical Analysis and Archaeological Discovery*, I, ed. D. Urman and P. V. M. Flesher (Leiden: Brill, 1995).

Braslawski (Braslavi), Y., "A Hebrew-Aramaic Inscription from Naveh," *Yedi'ot* 4 (1936). Hebrew.

———, "Symbols and Mythological Figures in Ancient Galilean Synagogues," *All the Land of Naphtali*, ed. H. Hirshberg (Jerusalem: Israel Exploration Society, 1969). Hebrew.

Braun, T., "The Jews in the Late Roman Empire," *SCI* 17 (1998).

Braun, W., "Were the New Testament Herodians Essenes? A Critique of an Hypothesis," *RQ* 14/1 (53) (June 1989).

Brawley, R. L., *Luke-Acts and the Jews: Conflict, Apology and Conciliation* (Atlanta: Scholars, 1987).

Bregman, M., "Circular Proems and Proems Beginning with the Formula 'Zo hi shene'emra beruah haq-qodesh,'" *Studies in Aggadah, Targum and Jewish Liturgy in Memory of Joseph Heinemann*, ed. J. J. Petuchowski and E. Fleischer (Jerusalem: Magnes, 1981). Hebrew.

———, "The Triennial Haftarot and the Perorations of the Midrashic Homilies," *JJS* 32 (1981).

———, "The Darshan: Preacher and Teacher of Talmudic Times," *The Melton Journal* 14 (Spring 1982).

———, "The Riddle of the Ram in Genesis Chapter 22: Jewish-Christian Contacts in Late Antiquity," *The Sacrifice of Isaac in the Three Monotheistic Religions*, ed. F. Manns (Jerusalem: Franciscan Printing, 1995).

Bremen, R. van, "Women and Wealth," *Images of Women in Antiquity*, ed. Av. Cameron and A. Kuhrt (London: Routledge, 1993).

Brenk, B., "Die Umwandlung der Synagoge von Apamea in eine Kirche: Eine mentalitätsgeschichtliche Studie," *Tesserae: Festschrift für Josef Engemann*, Jahrbuch für Antike und Christentum. Ergänzungsband 18 (Münster: Aschendorff Verlag, 1991).

Brent, B., "Die Christianisierung des jüdischen Stadtzentrums von Kapernaum," *Byzantine East, Latin West: Art-Historical Studies in Honor of Kurt Weitzmann*, ed. C. Moss and K. Kiefer (Princeton: Department of Art and Archaeology, Princeton University Press, 1995).

Brilliant, R., *Commentaries on Roman Art: Selected Studies* (London: Pindar, 1994).

Brinkman, J. A., "The Literary Background of the 'Catalogue of the Nations' (Acts 2, 9–11)," *CBQ* 25 (1963).

Brion, M., *Pompeii and Herculaneum: The Glory and the Grief* (New York: Crown, 1960).

Broadie, A., *A Samaritan Philosophy: A Study of the Hellenistic Cultural Ethos of the Memar Marqah* (Leiden: Brill, 1981).

Brooten, B. J., *Women Leaders in the Ancient Synagogue*, Brown Judaic Studies 36 (Chico: Scholars, 1982).

———, "Were Women and Men Segregated in Ancient Synagogues?" *Moment* 14/7 (1989).

———, "Iael προστάτης in the Jewish Donative Inscription from Aphrodisias," *The Future of Early Christianity: Essays in Honor of H. Koester*, ed. B. Pearson (Minneapolis: Fortress, 1991).

——, "Female Leadership in the Ancient Synagogue," *From Dura to Sepphoris: Studies in Jewish Art and Society in Late Antiquity*, ed. L. I. Levine and Z. Weiss (Ann Arbor: *Journal of Roman Archaeology* Supplementary Series, forthcoming).

Brown, P. R. L., *The World of Late Antiquity: From Marcus Aurelius to Muhammad* (London: Thames & Hudson, 1971).

——, "Art and Society in Late Antiquity," *The Age of Spirituality: Late Antique and Early Christian Art, Third to Seventh Century*, ed. K. Weitzmann (New York: Metropolitan Museum of Art, 1979).

——, *Society and the Holy in Late Antiquity* (London: Faber & Faber, 1982).

——, "The Saint as Exemplar in Late Antiquity," *Representations* 1/2 (1983).

——, *Authority and the Sacred: Aspects of the Christianisation of the Roman World* (Cambridge: Cambridge University Press, 1995).

Brownlee, W. H., "The Habakkuk Midrash and Targum of Jonathan," *JJS* 7 (1956).

Bruce, F. F., *Commentary on the Book of Acts* (Grand Rapids: Eerdmans, 1954).

——, *The Acts of the Apostles*, reprint (Grand Rapids: Eerdmans, 1970).

Bruneau, P., *Recherches sur les cultes de Délos à l'époque hellénistique et à l'époque impériale* (Paris: E. de Boccard, 1970).

——, "'Les Israélites de Délos' et la juiverie délienne," *BCH* 106 (1982).

Büchler, A., "The Reading of the Law and Prophets in a Triennial Cycle," *JQR* 5 (1893); 6 (1894).

——, *Die Tobiaden und Oniaden im II. Makkabäerbuche und in der verwandten jüdisch-hellenistischen Literatur* (Vienna: Israelitisch-Theologische Lehranstalt, 1899).

——, *The Political and Social Leaders of the Jewish Community of Sepphoris in the Second and Third Centuries* (London: Jews' College, 1909).

——, "The Levitical Impurity of the Gentiles in Palestine before the Year 70," *JQR* 17 (1926–27).

——, *Types of Jewish-Palestinian Piety from 70 B.C.E. to 70 C.E.: The Ancient Pious Men*, reprint (New York: KTAV, 1968).

Bull, R., "The Mithraeum of Caesarea Maritima," *Textes et Mémoires* 4 (1978).

Bultmann, R. K., *History of the Synoptic Tradition*, rev. ed. (New York: Harper & Row, 1963).

Burgos, F. Cantera Y, *Sinagogas españolas* (Madrid: Instituto "Arias Montano," 1955).

Burkert, W., "Oriental Symposia: Contrasts and Parallels," *Dining in a Classical Context*, ed. W. J. Slater (Ann Arbor: University of Michigan Press, 1991).

Burtchaell, J. T., *From Synagogue to Church: Public Services and Offices in the Earliest Christian Communities* (Cambridge: Cambridge University Press, 1992).

Busink, T. A., *Der Tempel von Jerusalem von Salomon bis Herodes: Eine archäologisch-historische Studie unter Berücksichtigung des westsemitischen Tempelbaus*, 2 vols. (Leiden: Brill, 1970).

Cadbury, H. J., *The Book of Acts in History* (New York: Harper, 1955).

Cameron, A., "θρεπτός and Related Terms in the Inscriptions of Asia Minor," *Anatolian Studies Presented to William H. Buckler*, ed. W. M. Calder and J. Keil (Manchester: Manchester University Press, 1939).

Cameron, Av., "'Neither Male nor Female,'" *Greece and Rome* 27 (1980).

——, *The Later Roman Empire, A.D. 284–430* (Cambridge: Harvard University Press, 1993).

——, *The Mediterranean World in Late Antiquity, A.D. 395–600* (London: Routledge, 1993).

Cantineau, J., *Le Nabatéen* (Paris: E. Leroux, 1930–32).

Caputo, G., "Nota sugli edifici teatrali della Cirenaica," *Anthemon: Scritti di archeologia e di antichità classiche in onore di C. Anti* (1955).

Carcopino, *Daily Life in Ancient Rome: The People and the City at the Height of the Empire*, reprint (New Haven: Yale University Press, 1963).

Cassuto, M. D., *Commentary on Exodus* (Jerusalem: Magnes, 1969). Hebrew.

Chadwick, H., *The Early Church* (New York: Penguin, 1967).

———, *History and Thought of the Early Church* (London: Variorum, 1982).

Charles, R. H., *The Apocrypha and Pseudepigrapha of the Old Testament in English*, 2 vols., reprint (Oxford: Clarendon, 1963).

Charlesworth, J. H., ed., "A Prolegomenon to a New Study of the Jewish Background of the Hymns and Prayers in the New Testament," *JJS* 33 (1982).

———, *The Old Testament Pseudepigrapha*, 2 vols. (New York: Doubleday, 1983–85).

———, "Jewish Hymns, Odes and Prayers (ca. 167 B.C.E.–135 C.E.)," *Early Judaism and Its Modern Interpreters*, ed. R. A. Kraft and G. W. E. Nickelsburg (Atlanta: Scholars, 1986).

Chazon, E. G., "On the Special Character of Sabbath Prayer: New Data from Qumran," *Journal of Jewish Music and Liturgy* 15 (1992–93).

———, "Prayers from Qumran and Their Historical Implications," *Dead Sea Discoveries* 1 (1994).

Chen, D., "The Design of the Ancient Synagogues in Judea—Masada and Herodium," *BASOR* 230 (1980).

———, "On the Chronology of the Ancient Synagogue at Capernaum," *ZDPV* 102 (1986).

Chiat, M. J., "First-Century Synagogue Architecture: Methodological Problems," *Ancient Synagogues: The State of Research*, ed. J. Gutmann (Chico: Scholars, 1981).

———, *Handbook of Synagogue Architecture*, Brown Judaic Studies 29 (Chico: Scholars, 1982).

———, "Synagogue and Church Architecture in Antiquity: A Comparative Study," *Proceedings of the Eighth World Congress of Jewish Studies*, IV (Jerusalem: World Union of Jewish Studies, 1982–84).

Chiat, M. J., and Mauck, M. B., "Using Archeological Sources," *The Making of Jewish and Christian Worship*, ed. P. F. Bradshaw and L. A. Hoffman (Notre Dame: University of Notre Dame Press, 1991).

Chilton, B. D., "Announcement in Nazara: An Analysis of Luke 4:16–21," *Gospel Perspectives—Studies of History and Tradition in the Four Gospels*, II, ed. R. T. France and P. Wenham (Sheffield: Sheffield Academic, 1981).

———, *God in Strength: Jesus' Announcement of the Kingdom* (Sheffield: Sheffield Academic, 1987).

———, *The Isaiah Targum: Introduction, Translation, Apparatus and Notes*, The Aramaic Bible 11 (Wilmington: Michael Glazier, 1987).

Churgin, P., "The Targum and the Septuagint," *AJSL* 50 (1933–34).

Clermont-Ganneau, C., "Découverte à Jérusalem d'une synagogue de l'époque hérodienne," *Syria* 1 (1920).

Cobb, P. G., "The *Apostolic Tradition* of Hippolytus," *The Study of Liturgy*, ed. C. Jones et al. (London: SPCK, 1992).

Cohen, B., *Mishnah and Tosefta: A Comparative Study*, I: *Shabbat* (New York: Jewish Theological Seminary, 1935).

———, "Art in Jewish Law," *Judaism* 3 (1954).

Cohen, J., "Roman Imperial Policy toward the Jews from Constantine until the End of the Palestinian Patriarchate (ca. 429)," *Byzantine Studies* 3 (1976).

Cohen, J. M., *A Samaritan Chronicle: A Source-Critical Analysis of the Life and Times of the Great Samaritan Reformer, Baba Rabbah* (Leiden: Brill, 1981).

Cohen, N., "Shim'on Hapakuli's Act Regarding the Eighteen Blessings," *Tarbiz* 52 (1983). Hebrew.

———, "Earliest Evidence of the Haftarah Cycle for the Sabbaths between בתמוז י"ז and סוכות in Philo," *JJS* 48 (1997).

Cohen, S. A., *The Three Crowns: Structures of Communal Politics in Early Rabbinic Jewry* (Cambridge: Cambridge University Press, 1990).

Cohen, S. J. D., *Josephus in Galilee and Rome: His Vita and Development As a Historian* (Leiden: Brill, 1979).

———, "Women in the Synagogues of Antiquity," *Conservative Judaism* 34 (1980).

———, "Epigraphical Rabbis," *JQR* 72 (1981–82).

———, "The Significance of Yavneh: Pharisees, Rabbis and the End of Jewish Sectarianism," *HUCA* 55 (1984).

———, "The Temple and the Synagogue," *The Temple in Antiquity: Ancient Records and Modern Perspectives*, ed. T. G. Madsen (Provo: Religious Study Center, Brigham Young University, 1984).

———, *From the Maccabees to the Mishnah* (Philadelphia: Westminster, 1987).

———, "Pagan and Christian Evidence on the Ancient Synagogue," *The Synagogue in Late Antiquity*, ed. L. I. Levine (Philadelphia: Jewish Theological Seminary & American Schools of Oriental Research, 1987).

———, "Respect for Judaism by Gentiles According to Josephus," *HTR* 80 (1987).

———, "Crossing the Boundary and Becoming a Jew," *HTR* 82 (1989).

———, "Menstruants and the Sacred in Judaism and Christianity," *Women's History and Ancient History*, ed. S. B. Pomeroy (Chapel Hill: University of North Carolina Press, 1991).

———, "The Place of the Rabbi in Jewish Society of the Second Century," *The Galilee in Late Antiquity*, ed. L. I. Levine (New York & Jerusalem: Jewish Theological Seminary, 1992).

———, "Purity and Piety: The Separation of Menstruants from the Sancta," *Daughters of the King: Women and the Synagogue*, ed. S. Grossman and R. Haut (Philadelphia: Jewish Publication Society, 1992).

———, "Was Judaism in Antiquity a Missionary Religion?" *Jewish Assimilation, Acculturation and Accommodation: Past Tradition, Current Issues and Future Prospects*, ed. M. Mor (Lanham: University Press of America, 1992).

———, "Were Pharisees and Rabbis the Leaders of Communal Prayer and Torah Study in Antiquity? The Evidence of the New Testament, Josephus, and the Church Fathers," *The Echoes of Many Texts: Reflections on Jewish and Christian Traditions—Essays in Honor of Lou H. Silberman*, ed. W. G. Dever and J. E. Wright (Atlanta: Scholars, 1997).

Cohen, Y., "When Did the Nesiut Move to Tiberias?" *Zion* 39 (1974). Hebrew.

Collins, J. J., "The Jewish Apocalypses," *Semeia* 14 (1979).

———, "Apocalyptic Literature," *Early Judaism and Its Modern Interpreters*, ed. R. A. Kraft and G. W. E. Nickelsburg (Atlanta: Scholars, 1986).

———, "L. H. Feldman, *Jew and Gentile in the Ancient World*" (review), *JBL* 113 (1994).

Collins, M. S., "Money, Sex and Power: An Examination of the Role of Women as Patrons of the Ancient Synagogue," *Recovering the Role of Women: Power and Authority in Rabbinic Jewish Society*, ed. P. J. Haas (Atlanta: Scholars, 1992).

Combrink, H. J. B., "The Structure and Significance of Luke 4:16–30," *Neotestamentica* 7 (1973).

Conzelmann, H., *The Theology of St. Luke* (Philadelphia: Fortress, 1961).

———, *Acts of the Apostles* (Philadelphia: Fortress, 1987).

Cook, M., *Mark's Treatment of Jewish Leaders* (Leiden: Brill, 1978).

Corbo, V. C., *The House of St. Peter at Capharnaum* (Jerusalem: Franciscan Printing, 1972).

———, *Cafarnao: Gli edifici della città* (Jerusalem: Franciscan Printing, 1975).

———, "La città romana di Magdala," *Studia Hierosolymitana in onore del P. B. Bagatti*, Studium Biblicum Franciscanum Collectio Maior 22 (Jerusalem: Franciscan Printing, 1976).

———, "Resti della sinagoga del primo secolo a Cafarnao," *Studia Hierosolymitana* 3 (1982).

Costamagna, L., "Seminari di archeologia cristiana," *Rivista di Archeologia Cristiana* 68 (1992).

Crawford, J. S., *The Byzantine Shops at Sardis* (Cambridge: Harvard University Press, 1990).

———, "Multiculturalism at Sardis," *BAR* 22/5 (1996).

Crockett, L., "Luke IV:16–30 and the Jewish Lectionary Cycle: A Word of Caution," *JJS* 17 (1966).

Crone, P., "Islam, Judeo-Christian and Byzantine Iconoclasm," *Jerusalem Studies in Arabic and Islam* 2 (1980).

Cross, F. M., *The Ancient Library of Qumran* (Garden City: Doubleday, 1961).

Crossan, J. D., *The Historical Jesus: The Life of a Mediterranean Jewish Peasant* (New York: Harper-Collins, 1992).

Crowfoot, J. W., *Churches at Jerash* (London: Palestine Exploration Fund, 1931).

———, *Early Churches in Palestine* (London: British Academy, 1941).

Crowfoot, J. W., and Hamilton, R. W., "The Discovery of a Synagogue at Jerash," *PEFQSt* 61 (1929).

Crowfoot, J. W., Kenyon, K. M., and Sukenik, E. L., *The Buildings in Samaria* (London: Palestine Exploration Fund, 1942).

Crown, A. D., "The Samaritans in the Byzantine Orbit," *BJRL* 69 (1980).

———, "Samaritan Religion in the Fourth Century A.D.," *Nederlands Theologisch Tijdschrift* 4 (1987).

———, "The Byzantine and Moslem Period," *The Samaritans*, ed. A. Crown (Tübingen: J. C. B. Mohr, 1989).

Cuming, G., "The Eucharist," *Essays on Hippolytus*, ed. P. W. Bradshaw et al. (Bramcote: Grove, 1978).

Cunningham, M. B., "Preaching and the Community," *Church and People in Byzantium*, ed. R. Morris (Birmingham: Centre for Byzantine, Ottoman and Modern Greek Studies, University of Birmingham, 1990).

Damerji, M., *The Development of the Architecture of Doors and Gates in Ancient Mesopotamia* (Tokyo: Institute for Cultural Studies of Ancient Iraq, Kokushikan University, 1987).

Dan, J., *On Sanctity: Religion, Ethics and Mysticism in Judaism and Other Religions* (Jerusalem: Magnes, 1998). Hebrew.

Dan, Y., *The City in Eretz-Israel during the Late Roman and Byzantine Periods* (Jerusalem: Yad Izhak Ben Zvi, 1984). Hebrew.

———, "Byzantine Rule (395–640)," *The Mishnaic and Talmudic Period and Byzantine Rule*, ed. M. D. Herr (Jerusalem: Keter, 1985). Hebrew.

Daniel, J. L., "Antisemitism in the Hellenistic-Roman Period," *JBL* 98 (1979).

Daniel-Nataf, S., *Philo of Alexandria—Writings*, 2 vols. (Jerusalem: Bialik & Israel Academy of Sciences and Humanities, 1986–91). Hebrew.

Danov, C., "Neues aus der Geschichte von Philippopolis und Altthrakien in der Spätantike," *Römische Geschichte, Altertumskunde und Epigraphik: Festschrift für A. Betz zur Vollendung seines 80. Lebensjahres*, ed. E. Weber and G. Dobesch (Vienna: Österreichische Gesellschaft für Archäologie, 1985).

Danov, C., and Kesjakova, E. "Unique Finding—An Ancient Synagogue in the City of Plovdiv (New Pages from the History of Plovdiv and Thrace during the Late Antiquity)," *Annual of the Social, Cultural and Educational Association of the Jews in the People's Republic of Bulgaria* 19 (1984).

Dar, S., and Mintzer, Y., "The Synagogue of Horvat Sumaqa, 1983–1993," *Ancient Synagogues: Historical Analysis and Archaeological Discovery*, I, ed. D. Urman and P. V. M. Flesher (Leiden: Brill, 1995).

Darmon, J. P., "Les mosaïques de la synagogue de Hamman Lif: Un réexamen du dossier," *Fifth International Colloquium on Ancient Mosaics*, ed. R. Ling (Ann Arbor: Journal of Roman Archaeology, 1995).

Darnell, D. R., and Fiensy, D. A., "Hellenistic Synagogal Prayers (Second to Third Century A.D.), *The Old Testament Pseudepigrapha*, II, ed. J. H. Charlesworth (Garden City: Doubleday, 1985).

Davies, W. D., *Paul and Rabbinic Judaism: Some Elements in Pauline Theology* (Philadelphia: Fortress, 1980).

Davis-Meyer, C., *Early Medieval Art, 300–1150* (Toronto: University of Toronto, 1986).

Davka CD-ROM Judaic Classics Library (www.davka.com, 1996).

Déaut, R. le, *Introduction à la littérature targumique* (Rome: Institut Biblique Pontifical, 1966).

Degan, R., "An Inscription of the Twenty-Four Priestly Courses from Yemen," *Tarbiz* 42 (1973). Hebrew.

Deichmann, F. W., *Frühchristliche Bauten und Mosaiken von Ravenna* (Wiesbaden: F. Steiner, 1958).

Deissmann, A., *Light from the Ancient East* (New York: G. H. Doran, 1927).

Delcor, M., "Repas cultuels esséniens et thérapeutes: Thiases et Haburoth," *RQ* 6 (1968).

Denton, W., *A Commentary on the Acts of the Apostles*, 2 vols. (London: Bell, 1876–88).

Dever, W. G., *Recent Archaeological Discoveries and Biblical Research* (Seattle: University of Washington Press, 1990).

Diamond, E., "Hunger Artists and Householders: The Tension between Asceticism and Family Responsibility among Jewish Pietists in Late Antiquity," *Union Theological Quarterly Review* 48 (1994).

Diez-Macho, A., "The Recently Discovered Palestinian Targum: Its Antiquity and Relationship with the Other Targums," supplement to *VT* 7 (1960).

Dimant, D., "Qumran Sectarian Literature," *Jewish Writings of the Second Temple Period*, ed. M. Stone (Assen: Van Gorcum, 1984).

Dion, P.-E., "Synagogues et temples dans l'Egypte hellénistique," *Science et Esprit* 29 (1977).

Dix, G., *The Shape of Liturgy* (London: Dacre, 1945).

Donner, H., "Argumente zur Datierung des 74. Psalms," *Wort, Lied und Gottesspruch: Beiträge zu Psalmen und Propheten—Festschrift für Joseph Ziegler,* ed. J. Schreiner (Würzburg: Echter, 1972).

Dothan, M., "The Representation of Helios in the Mosaic of Hammath-Tiberias," *Tardo antico e alto medioevo: La forma artistica nel passaggio dall'antichità al medioevo* (Rome: Accademia Nazionale dei Lincei, 1968).

———, "The Fortifications of Ptolemais," *Qadmoniot* 9/34-35 (1976). Hebrew.

———, *Hammath Tiberias: Early Synagogues and the Hellenistic and Roman Remains* (Jerusalem: Israel Exploration Society, 1983).

Downey, G., *A History of Antioch in Syria* (Princeton: Princeton University Press, 1961).

Drijvers, H. J. W., "Syrian Christianity and Judaism," *The Jews among Pagans and Christians in the Roman Empire,* ed. J. Lieu et al. (London: Routledge, 1992).

Dugmore, C. W., *The Influence of the Synagogue upon the Divine Office* (London: Oxford University Press, 1944).

Dunbabin, K. M. D., *The Mosaics of Roman North Africa: Studies in Iconography and Patronage* (Oxford: Clarendon, 1978).

Duval, N., "Art paléochrétien," *Bulletin Monumental* 150 (1992).

Dyson, S. L., *Community and Society in Roman Italy* (Baltimore: Johns Hopkins University Press, 1992).

Ebner, E., *Elementary Education in Ancient Israel* (New York: Bloch, 1956).

Edmondson, J. C., "Dynamic Arena: Gladiatorial Presentations in the City of Rome and the Construction of Roman Society during the Early Empire," *Roman Theater and Society: E. Togo Salmon Papers,* I, ed. W. J. Slater (Ann Arbor: University of Michigan Press, 1996).

Edwards, D., "The Socio-Economic and Cultural Ethos of the Lower Galilee in the First Century: Implications for the Nascent Jesus Movement," *The Galilee in Late Antiquity,* ed. L. I. Levine (New York & Jerusalem: Jewish Theological Seminary, 1992).

Efron, J., *Studies on the Hasmonean Period* (Leiden: Brill, 1987).

Ehrlich, U., "The Place of the *Shekhina* in the Consciousness of the Worshipper," *Tarbiz* 65 (1996). Hebrew.

———, " 'When You Pray, Know before Whom You Are Standing' (b Ber. 28b)," *JJS* 49 (1998).

Eitan, A., "The Menora as a Symbol," *Israel Museum News* 3/1-2 (1968).

Elbogen, I., "Studies in Jewish Liturgy," *JQR* (old series) 18 (1906); 19 (1907).

———, *Studien zur Geschichte des jüdischen Gottesdienstes* (Berlin: Mayer & Müller, 1907).

———, *Der jüdische Gottesdienst in seiner geschichtlichen Entwicklung* (Leipzig: G. Fock, 1913).

———, *Jewish Liturgy: A Comprehensive History,* trans. R. P. Scheindlin (Philadelphia: Jewish Publication Society, 1993).

Eliav, Y. Z., *Sites, Institutions and Daily Life in Tiberias during the Talmudic Period,* Mi'tuv T'veria 10 (Tiberias: Center for the Study of Tiberias, 1995). Hebrew.

Elior, R., "Merkabah Mysticism, a Critical Review," *Numen* 37 (1990).

———, "From Earthly Temple to Heavenly Shrines: Prayer and Sacred Song in the Hekhalot Literature and Its Relation to Temple Traditions," *JSQ* 4 (1997).

Elizur, S., "The Congregation in the Synagogue and the Ancient Qedushta," *Knesset Ezra: Lit-

erature and Life in the Synagogue, ed. S. Elizur et al. (Jerusalem: Yad Izhak Ben Zvi, 1994). Hebrew.

Elsner, J., *Art and the Roman Viewer: The Transformation of Art from the Pagan World to Christianity* (Cambridge: Cambridge University Press, 1995).

Eph'al, I., and Naveh, J., "The Jar of the Gate," *BASOR* 289 (1993).

Epstein, A., *Meqadmoniot Hayehudim* (Jerusalem: Mossad Harav Kook, 1957). Hebrew.

Epstein, J. N., "Yerushalmi Fragments," *Tarbiz* 3 (1932). Hebrew.

———, *Introduction to Tannaitic Literature: Mishna, Tosephta and Halakhic Midrashim* (Jerusalem: Magnes, 1957). Hebrew.

———, *Introduction to the Mishnaic Text*, 2d ed., 2 vols. (Jerusalem: Magnes, 1964). Hebrew.

———, *Studies in Talmudic Literature and Semitic Languages*, 2 vols. (Jerusalem: Magnes, 1983–88). Hebrew.

Eshel, E., "An Incised Hebrew Inscription from a Synagogue in Chersonesus in the Crimean Peninsula," *Tarbiz* (in press). Hebrew.

Eshel, H., "A Fragmentary Hebrew Inscription of the Priestly Courses?" *Tarbiz* 61 (1991). Hebrew.

Evans, C. A., *Luke—New International Biblical Commentary* (Peabody: Hendrickson, 1990).

Evans, G., " 'Coming' and 'Going' at the City Gate—A Discussion of Professor Speiser's Paper," *BASOR* 150 (1958).

———, " 'Gates' and 'Streets': Urban Institutions in Old Testament Times," *The Journal of Religious History* 2 (1962).

Falk, D. K., "Jewish Prayer Literature and the Jerusalem Church in Acts," *Book of Acts*, ed. R. Bauckham (Grand Rapids: Eerdmans, 1995).

———, *Daily, Sabbath, and Festival Prayers in the Dead Sea Scrolls* (Leiden: Brill, 1998).

Faur, J., "The Targumim and Halakha," *JQR* 66 (1975–76).

———, "The Aliya for a Minor to Read from the Torah," *Festschrift to R. I. Nissim*, I, ed. M. Benayahu (Jerusalem: R. Nissim, 1985). Hebrew.

Feldman, L. H., "How Much Hellenism in Jewish Palestine?" *HUCA* 57 (1987).

———, "Proselytes and 'Sympathizers' in the Light of the New Inscription from Aphrodisias," *REJ* 148 (1989).

———, "Some Observations on the Name of Palestine," *HUCA* 61 (1990).

———, "Was Judaism a Missionary Religion in Ancient Times?" *Jewish Assimilation, Acculturation and Accommodation: Past Tradition, Current Issues and Future Prospects*, ed. M. Mor (Lanham: University Press of America, 1992).

———, *Jew and Gentile in the Ancient World: Attitudes and Interactions from Alexander to Justinian* (Princeton: Princeton University Press, 1993).

———, "Diaspora Synagogues: New Light from Inscriptions and Papyri," *Sacred Realm: The Emergence of the Synagogue in the Ancient World*, ed. S. Fine (New York: Oxford University Press, 1996).

Fernandez, R. Ramos, *La ciudad romana de Ilici: estudio arqueológico* (Alicante: Instituto de Estudios Alicantinos, 1975).

Fiensy, D. A., *Prayers Alleged to Be Jewish: An Examination of the Constitutiones Apostolorum* (Chico: Scholars, 1985).

———, "The Hellenistic Synagogal Prayers: One Hundred Years of Discussion," *JSP* 5 (1989).

Figueras, P., "Epigraphic Evidence for Proselytism in Ancient Judaism," *Immanuel* 24–25 (1990).

Fine, S., "Did the Synagogue Replace the Temple?" *Bible Review* 12/2 (1996).

———, "From Meeting House to Sacred Realm: Holiness and the Ancient Synagogue," *Sacred Realm: The Emergence of the Synagogue in the Ancient World*, ed. S. Fine (New York: Oxford University Press, 1996).

———, *This Holy Place: On the Sanctity of Synagogues during the Greco-Roman Period* (Notre Dame: University of Notre Dame Press, 1997).

———, "Art and the Liturgical Context of the Sepphoris Synagogue Mosaic," *Galilee: Confluence of Cultures, Proceedings of the Second International Conference in Galilee*, ed. E. M. Meyers et al. (Winona Lake: Eisenbrauns, forthcoming).

———, "At the Threshold of the *Beit Midrash:* On the Place of Women in Rabbinic Study Houses in Late Antique Palestine" (forthcoming).

———, "Art and Iconoclasm in the Late Antique Palestinian Synagogue," *From Dura to Sepphoris: Studies in Jewish Art and Society in Late Antiquity*, ed. L. Levine and Z. Weiss (Ann Arbor: *Journal of Roman Archaeology* Supplementary Series, forthcoming).

Fine, S., and Della Pergola, M., "The Synagogue of Ostia and Its Torah Shrine," *The Jewish Presence in Ancient Rome*, ed. J. G. Westenholz (Jerusalem: Bible Lands Museum, 1995).

Fine, S., and Rutgers, L. V., "New Light on Judaism in Asia Minor during Late Antiquity: Two Recently Identified Inscribed Menorahs," *JSQ* 3 (1996).

Fine, S., and Zuckerman, B., "The Menorah as Symbol of Jewish Minority Status," *Fusion in the Hellenistic East*, ed. S. Fine (Los Angeles: University of Southern California, 1985).

Finkel, A., "Jesus' Sermon at Nazareth," *Abraham unser Vater—Festschrift für Otto Michel zum 60. Geburtstag*, ed. O. Betz et al. (Leiden: Brill, 1963).

———, "The Prayer of Jesus in Matthew," *Standing before God: Studies in Prayer in Scriptures and in Tradition with Essays in Honor of J. M. Oesterreicher*, ed. A. Finkel and L. Frizzell (New York: KTAV, 1981).

———, "Jesus' Preaching in the Synagogue on the Sabbath (Luke 4:16–28)," *The Gospels and the Scriptures in Israel*, ed. C. A. Evans and W. R. Stegner (Sheffield: Sheffield Academic, 1994).

Finkelstein, L., "The Development of the Amidah," *JQR* 16 (1925–26).

———, "Origin of the Synagogue," *PAAJR* 1 (1928–30).

———, "The Meaning of the Word פרס in the Expression פורס על שמע, בפרוס העצרת, בפרוס הפסח and בפרוס החג," *JQR* 32 (1941–42); 33 (1942–43).

———, *Akiba: Scholar, Saint and Martyr* (Cleveland: World Publishing, 1962).

———, *The Pharisees: The Sociological Background of Their Faith*, 3d ed., 2 vols. (Philadelphia: Jewish Publication Society, 1962).

Finney, P. C., *The Invisible God: The Earliest Christians on Art* (New York: Oxford University Press, 1994).

Fiorenza, E. S., *In Memory of Her: A Feminist Theological Reconstruction of Christian Origins* (New York: Crossroad, 1994).

Fischer, M. L., *Das korinthische Kapitell im Alten Israel in der hellenistischen und römischen Periode: Studien zur Geschichte der Baudekoration im Nahen Osten* (Mainz: Philipp von Zabern, 1990).

Fishbane, M. A., *Biblical Interpretation in Ancient Israel* (Oxford: Clarendon, 1985).

FitzGerald, G. M., "Theodotus Inscription," *PEFQSt* 53 (1921).

Fitzmyer, J. A., "The Genesis Apocryphon and the Targums," *The Genesis Apocryphon of Qumran Cave I* (Rome: Biblical Institute, 1966).

———, "Languages of Palestine in the First Century A.D.," *CBQ* 32 (1970).

———, *The Gospel according to Luke (I–IX)* (Garden City: Doubleday, 1981).

Fleischer, E., "New Shiv'atot of the Paytan R. Pinchas on Priestly Courses," *Sinai* 61 (1967). Hebrew.

———, "Regarding the Courses in Piyyutim," *Sinai* 62 (1968). Hebrew.

———, "The Diffusion of the *Qedushot* of the *'Amida* and the *Jozer* in the Palestinian Jewish Ritual," *Tarbiz* 38 (1969). Hebrew.

———, "The Piyyutim of Yannai the Ḥazzan on the Priestly Courses," *Sinai* 64 (1969). Hebrew.

———, "Studies on the Problems Related to the Liturgical Function of the Early Piyyut," *Tarbiz* 40 (1970). Hebrew.

———, "Towards a Clarification of the Expression 'Poreis 'al Shema'' ('פורס על שמע')," *Tarbiz* 41 (1972). Hebrew.

———, "Early Paytanim of Tiberias," *Sefer Teveria*, ed. O. Avissar (Jerusalem: Keter, 1973). Hebrew.

———, "Qaliric Compositions for 'Tisha B'Av," *HUCA* 45 (1974). Hebrew.

———, "Studies on the Influence of Choral Elements on the Configuration and Development of Types of Piyyut," *Yuval* 3 (1974). Hebrew.

———, *Hebrew Liturgical Poetry in the Middle Ages* (Jerusalem: Keter, 1975). Hebrew.

———, "Haduta-Hadutahu-Chedweta: Solving an Old Riddle," *Tarbiz* 53 (1983). Hebrew.

———, "A List of Yearly Holidays in a Piyyut by Qiliri," *Tarbiz* 52 (1983). Hebrew.

———, "Concerning the Celebration of *Rosh Hashana* in Eretz Israel," *Tarbiz* 53 (1984). Hebrew.

———, *The Yozer: Its Emergence and Development* (Jerusalem: Magnes, 1984). Hebrew.

———, "Additional Data Concerning the Twenty-Four Priestly Orders," *Tarbiz* 55 (1985). Hebrew.

———, *Eretz-Israel Prayer and Prayer Rituals as Portrayed in the Geniza Document* (Jerusalem: Magnes, 1988). Hebrew.

———, "On the Beginnings of Obligatory Jewish Prayer," *Tarbiz* 59 (1990). Hebrew.

———, "Inquiries Concerning the Triennial Reading of the Torah in Ancient Eretz-Israel," *HUCA* 62 (1991). Hebrew.

———, "The Annual and Triennial Torah Reading in the Early Synagogue," *Tarbiz* 61 (1992). Hebrew.

———, "Early Hebrew Liturgical Poetry in Its Cultural Setting (Comparative Experiments)," *Moises Starosta Memorial Lectures: First Series*, ed. J. Geiger (Jerusalem: Hebrew University, 1993). Hebrew.

———, "The *Qedusha* of the *'Amida* (and Other *Qedushot*): Historical, Liturgical and Ideological Aspects," *Tarbiz* 67 (1998). Hebrew.

Flesher, P. V. M., "Palestinian Synagogues before 70 C.E.: A Review of the Evidence," *Approaches to Ancient Judaism*, VI, ed. J. Neusner and E. Frerichs (Atlanta: Scholars, 1989).

———, "Mapping the Synoptic Palestinian Targums of the Pentateuch," *The Aramaic Bible: Targums in Their Historical Context*, ed. D. R. G. Beattie and M. J. McNamara (Sheffield: Sheffield Academic, 1994).

————, "The Targumim in the Context of Rabbinic Literature," *Introduction to Rabbinic Literature*, ed. J. Neusner (New York: Doubleday, Anchor, 1994).

Flusser, D., "Sanktus und Gloria," *Abraham unser Vater: Festschrift für Otto Michel*, ed. O. Betz, M. Hengel, and P. Schmidt (Leiden: Brill, 1963).

————, "Jewish Roots of the Liturgical Trishagion," *Immanuel* 3 (1973–74).

————, "The Jewish Religion in the Second Temple Period," *The World History of the Jewish People: Society and Religion in the Second Temple Period*, ed. M. Avi-Yonah and Z. Baras (Jerusalem: Massada, 1977).

————, "Psalms, Hymns and Prayers," *Jewish Writings of the Second Temple Period*, ed. M. Stone (Assen: Van Gorcum, 1984).

————, "The Second Benediction of the *Amida* and a Text from Qumran," *Tarbiz* 64 (1995). Hebrew.

Foakes-Jackson, F., and Lake, K., *The Beginnings of Christianity: The Acts of the Apostles*, II: *Prolegomena II: Criticism*, reprint (Grand Rapids: Baker Book House, 1979).

Foerster, G., "Ancient Synagogues in Eretz-Israel," *Qadmoniot* 5/18 (1972). Hebrew.

————, "Art and Architecture in Palestine," *The Jewish People in the First Century*, II, ed. S. Safrai and M. Stern (Philadelphia: Fortress, 1976).

————, "Remains of a Synagogue at Corinth," *Ancient Synagogues Revealed*, ed. L. I. Levine (Jerusalem: Israel Exploration Society, 1981).

————, "A Survey of Ancient Diaspora Synagogues," *Ancient Synagogues Revealed*, ed. L. I. Levine (Jerusalem: Israel Exploration Society, 1981).

————, "The Synagogues at Masada and Herodium," *Ancient Synagogues Revealed*, ed. L. I. Levine (Jerusalem: Israel Exploration Society, 1981).

————, "Synagogue Inscriptions and Their Relation to Liturgical Versions," *Cathedra* 19 (1981). Hebrew.

————, "Representations of the Zodiac in Ancient Synagogues and Their Iconographic Sources," *EI*, XVIII (Jerusalem: Israel Exploration Society, 1985). Hebrew.

————, "The Fifth Century Synagogue in Leptis Magna," *Proceedings of the Ninth World Congress of Jewish Studies* II/I (Jerusalem: World Union of Jewish Studies, 1986). Hebrew.

————, "A Basilical Plan (Including Apsis) as a Chronological Criterion in Synagogues," *Synagogues in Antiquity*, ed. A. Kasher et al. (Jerusalem: Yad Izhak Ben Zvi, 1987). Hebrew.

————, "Excavations at Ancient Meron" (review article), *IEJ* 37 (1987).

————, "The Zodiac in Ancient Synagogues and Its Place in Jewish Thought and Literature," *EI*, XIX (Jerusalem: Israel Exploration Society, 1987). Hebrew.

————, "Decorated Marble Chancel Screens in Sixth Century Synagogues in Palestine and Their Relation to Christian Art and Architecture," *Actes du XIe Congrès d'Archéologie Chrétienne* (Rome: Ecole Française de Rome, 1989).

————, "Allegorical and Symbolic Motifs with Christian Significance from Mosaic Pavements of Sixth-Century Palestinian Synagogues," *Christian Archaeology in the Holy Land—New Discoveries: Essays in Honour of V. F. Corbo, OFM*, ed. G. T. Bottini et al. (Jerusalem: Franciscan Printing, 1990).

————, "The Ancient Synagogues of the Galilee," *The Galilee in Late Antiquity*, ed. L. I. Levine (New York & Jerusalem: Jewish Theological Seminary, 1992).

———, "Dating Synagogues with a 'Basilical' Plan and an Apse," *Ancient Synagogues: Historical Analysis and Archaeological Discovery*, I, ed. D. Urman and P. V. M. Flesher (Leiden: Brill, 1995).

Fortis, U., *Jews and Synagogues* (Venice: Edizioni Storti, 1973).

Fossum, J., "Sects and Movements," *The Samaritans*, ed. A. Crown (Tübingen: J. C. B. Mohr, 1989).

Fowden, G., "Bishops and Temples in the Eastern Roman Empire, A.D. 320-435," *JTS* 29 (1978).

———, "The Pagan Holy Man in Late Antique Society," *JHS* 102 (1982).

Fox, M. Z., "Responses to Two Revolutionaries," *Sinai* 114 (1994). Hebrew.

Fox, R. Lane, *Pagans and Christians* (New York: Knopf, 1987).

Fraade, S. D., *From Tradition to Commentary: Torah and Its Interpretation in the Midrash Sifre to Deuteronomy* (Albany: State University of New York Press, 1991).

———, "Rabbinic Views on the Practice of Targum, and Multilingualism in the Jewish Galilee of the Third-Sixth Centuries," *The Galilee in Late Antiquity*, ed. L. I. Levine (New York & Jerusalem: Jewish Theological Seminary, 1992).

———, "Interpretive Authority in the Studying Community at Qumran," *JJS* 44 (1993).

Frankel, Y., *Darkei Ha-aggadah V'Hamidrash*, 2 vols. (Jerusalem: Massada, 1991). Hebrew.

Frankel, Z., *Vorstudien zu der Septuaginta* (Leipzig: Vogel, 1841).

———, *Über den Einfluss der palästinischen Exegese auf die alexandrinische Hermeneutik* (Leipzig: Barth, 1851).

———, *Darkei Hamishnah*, reprint (Tel Aviv: Sinai, 1959). Hebrew.

Fraser, P. M., "Inscriptions of Cyrene," *Berytus* 12/2 (1958).

———, *Ptolemaic Alexandria*, 3 vols. (Oxford: Clarendon, 1972).

Freehof, S. B., "The Structure of the Birchos Hashachar," *HUCA* 23 (1950–51).

Freeman, K. J., *Schools of Hellas: An Essay on the Practice and Theory of Ancient Greek Education from 600 to 300 B.C.*, 3d ed. (London: Macmillan, 1932).

Frend, W. H. C., "Town and Countryside in Early Christianity," *The Church in Town and Countryside*, ed. D. Baker (Oxford: Blackwell, 1979).

Freudenthal, J., *Die Flavius Josephus beigelegte Schrift über die Herrschaft der Vernunft (IV. Makkabäerbuch)* (Breslau: Schletter, 1869).

Frey, J.-B., "Les communautés juives à Rome aux premiers temps de l'église," *RSR* 20 (1930); 21 (1931).

———, *Corpus Inscriptionum Judaicarum* [*CIJ*], 2 vols. (Rome: Pontificio Istituto di Archeologia Cristiana, 1936-52), II, reprint (New York: KTAV, 1975).

Freyne, S., *Galilee from Alexander the Great to Hadrian: A Study of Second Temple Judaism* (Wilmington: Glazier & Notre Dame University Press, 1980).

———, *Galilee, Jesus and the Gospels: Literary Approaches and Historical Investigations* (Dublin: Gill & MacMillan, 1988).

———, "Urban-Rural Relations in First-Century Galilee: Some Suggestions from the Literary Sources," *The Galilee in Late Antiquity*, ed. L. I. Levine (New York & Jerusalem: Jewish Theological Seminary, 1992).

Frick, F. S., *The City in Ancient Israel*, SBL Dissertation Series 36 (Missoula: Scholars, 1977).

Fried, N., "List of the Sedarim for Numbers According to the Tri-Annual Cycle," *Textus* 7 (1969).

Friedländer, M., *Synagoge und Kirche in ihren Anfängen* (Berlin: Reimer, 1908).

Friedman, M., "An Eschatological Motif in Byzantine and Jewish Art," *From Dura to Sepphoris: Studies in Jewish Art and Society in Late Antiquity*, ed. L. Levine and Z. Weiss (Ann Arbor: *Journal of Roman Archaeology* Supplementary Studies, forthcoming).

Friedmann, M., "Mitwirkung von Frauen beim Gottesdienste," *HUCA* 8–9 (1931–32).

Fritz, V. *The City in Ancient Israel* (Sheffield: Sheffield Academic, 1995).

Frova, A., *Scavi di Caesarea Maritima* (Rome: "L'Erma" di Bretschneider, 1966).

Fuks, G., *Scythopolis—A Greek City in Eretz-Israel* (Jerusalem: Yad Izhak Ben Zvi, 1983). Hebrew.

Gabba, E. *Iscrizioni greche e latine per lo studio della bibbia* (Turin: Marietti, 1958).

Gafni, I. M., "Yeshiva and Metivta," *Zion* 43 (1978). Hebrew.

———, "Court Cases in the Babylonian Talmud," *PAAJR* 49 (1982). Hebrew.

———, "Pre-Histories of Jerusalem in Hellenistic, Jewish and Christian Literature," *JSP* 1 (1987).

———, "Synagogues in Talmudic Babylonia," *Synagogues in Antiquity*, ed. A. Kasher et al. (Jerusalem: Yad Izhak Ben Zvi, 1987). Hebrew.

———, *The Jews of Babylonia in the Talmudic Era: A Social and Cultural History* (Jerusalem: Shazar Center, 1990). Hebrew.

———, "Public Sermons in Talmudic Babylonia: The *Pirqa*," *Knesset Ezra—Literature and Life in the Synagogue: Studies Presented to Ezra Fleischer*, ed. S. Eliezer et al. (Jerusalem: Yad Izhak Ben Zvi, 1994). Hebrew.

———, "Concepts of Periodization and Causality in Talmudic Literature," *Jewish History* 10 (1996).

———, "Punishment, Blessing or Mission—Jewish Dispersion in the Second Temple and Talmudic Period," *The Jews in the Hellenistic-Roman Worlds: Studies in Memory of Menahem Stern*, ed. I. M. Gafni et al. (Jerusalem: Shazar Center & Historical Society of Israel, 1996). Hebrew.

———, *Land, Center and Diaspora: Jewish Constructs in Late Antiquity* (Sheffield: Sheffield Academic, 1997).

Gager, J. G., *Moses in Greco-Roman Paganism* (Nashville: Abingdon, 1972).

———, *The Origins of Anti-Semitism: Attitudes toward Judaism in Pagan and Christian Antiquity* (New York: Oxford University Press, 1983).

———, "Jews, Gentiles, and Synagogues in the Book of Acts," *HTR* 79 (1986).

Galinsky, K., *Augustan Culture* (Princeton: Princeton University Press, 1996).

Gartner, B., *The Temple and the Community in Qumran and the New Testament* (Cambridge: Cambridge University Press, 1965).

Gaster, T. H., *The Dead Sea Scriptures* (Garden City: Doubleday, 1956).

Gates, M. H., "Dura-Europos: A Fortress of Syro-Mesopotamian Art," *BA* 47 (1984).

Gavin, F., *The Jewish Antecedents of the Christian Sacraments* (New York: KTAV, 1969).

Geiger, J., "The Gallus Revolt," *Eretz Israel from the Destruction of the Second Temple to the Muslim Conquest*, I, ed. Z. Baras et al. (Jerusalem: Yad Izhak Ben Zvi, 1982). Hebrew.

Gelston, A., "Note on Psalm lxxiv 8," *VT* 34 (1984).

Georgi, D., *The Opponents of Paul in Second Corinthians: Study of Religious Propaganda in Late Antiquity* (Edinburgh: Clark, 1985).

Gera, D., and Cotton, H., "A Dedication from Dor to a Governor of Syria," *IEJ* 41 (1991).

Gerkan, A. von, "Eine Synagoge in Milet," *ZNW* 20 (1921).

Gibbon, E., *The Decline and Fall of the Roman Empire*, 3 vols. (New York: Heritage, 1946).

Gilat, Y. D., *R. Eliezer ben Hyrcanus: A Scholar Outcast* (Ramat Gan: Bar Ilan University Press, 1984).

———, "The Development of the *Shevuth* Prohibitions of Shabbat," *Tenth World Congress of Jewish Studies*, C/I (Jerusalem: World Union of Jewish Studies, 1990). Hebrew.

———, "The *Derasha* and the Reading of the Torah in the Synagogue on the Sabbath," *Jews and Judaism in the Second Temple, Mishna and Talmud Period: Studies in Honor of Shmuel Safrai*, ed. I. Gafni et al. (Jerusalem: Yad Izhak Ben Zvi, 1993). Hebrew.

Ginzberg, L., *Geniza Studies*, 3 vols. (New York: Jewish Theological Seminary, 1928–29). Hebrew.

———, "Beiträge zur Lexikographie des Jüdisch-Aramäischen III," *Essays and Studies in Memory of Linda R. Miller*, ed. I. Davidson (New York: Jewish Theological Seminary, 1938).

———, *A Commentary on the Palestinian Talmud*, 4 vols. (New York: Jewish Theological Seminary, 1941–61). Hebrew.

———, *The Legends of the Jews*, 7 vols. (Philadelphia: Jewish Publication Society, 1955).

———, *On Jewish Law and Lore* (New York: Atheneum, 1970).

Glueck, N., *Deities and Dolphins* (New York: Farrar, Straus & Giroux, 1965).

Goitein, S. D., "Anbol—Bima of the Synagogue," *EI*, VI (Jerusalem: Israel Exploration Society, 1961). Hebrew.

———, "A Women's Gallery in the Synagogue Building in the Gaonic Period," *Tarbiz* 33 (1964). Hebrew.

———, *A Mediterranean Society: The Jewish Communities of the Arab World as Portrayed in the Documents of the Cairo Geniza*, 6 vols. (Berkeley: University of California Press, 1967–93).

Goldberg, A., "Die Heiligkeit des Ortes in der frühen rabbinischen Theologie," *FJB* 4 (1976).

———, "Service of the Heart: Liturgical Aspects of Synagogue Worship," *Standing before God: Studies in Prayer in Scriptures and in Tradition with Essays in Honor of J. M. Oesterreicher*, ed. A. Finkel and L. Frizzell (New York: KTAV, 1981).

Goldberg, A., "The Mishna—A Study Book of Halakha," *The Literature of the Sages*, I, ed. S. Safrai (Assen: Van Gorcum, 1987).

———, "The Palestinian Talmud," *The Literature of the Sages*, I, ed. S. Safrai (Assen: Van Gorcum, 1987).

———, "The Tosefta—Companion to the Mishna," *The Literature of the Sages*, I, ed. S. Safrai (Assen: Van Gorcum, 1987).

Goldenberg, R., "The Deposition of Rabban Gamaliel II: An Examination of the Sources," *JJS* 23 (1972).

———, "The Broken Axis: Rabbinic Judaism and the Fall of Jerusalem," *JAAR* 45 (1977).

———, "History and Ideology in Talmudic Narrative," *Approaches to Ancient Judaism*, IV, ed. W. S. Green (Chico: Scholars, 1983).

Goldin, J., "The Magic of Magic and Superstition," *Aspects of Religious Propaganda in Judaism and Christianity*, ed. E. S. Fiorenza (Notre Dame: University of Notre Dame Press, 1976).

———, *Studies in Midrash and Related Literature* (Philadelphia: Jewish Publication Society, 1988).

Goldman, B. M., *The Sacred Portal: A Primary Symbol in Ancient Judaic Art* (Detroit: Wayne State University Press, 1966).

Goldschmidt, E. D., *The Passover Haggadah: Its Sources and History* (Jerusalem: Bialik, 1960). Hebrew.

———, *Mahzor for the High Holidays*, 2 vols. (Jerusalem: Koren, 1970). Hebrew.

Goldstein, J. A., *I Maccabees: A New Translation* (Garden City: Doubleday, 1976).

———, "The Judaism of the Synagogues (Focusing on the Synagogue of Dura-Europos)," *Judaism in Late Antiquity*, II, ed. J. Neusner (Leiden: Brill, 1995).

Golinkin, D., "Aliyot for Women," *Responsa of the Va'ad Halacha of the Rabbinical Assembly of Israel* 3 (5748–49). Hebrew.

Golvin, J.-C., *L'amphithéâtre romain: Essai sur la théorisation de sa forme et de ses fonctions*, 2 vols. (Paris: E. de Boccard, 1988).

Goodblatt, D., *Rabbinic Instruction in Sasanian Babylonia* (Leiden: Brill, 1975).

———, "Towards a Rehabilitation of Talmudic History," *History of Judaism: The Next Ten Years*, ed. B. Bokser (Chico: Scholars, 1980).

———, "The Title *Nasi* and the Ideological Background of the Second Revolt," *The Bar-Kokhva Revolt: A New Approach*, ed. A. Oppenheimer and U. Rappaport (Jerusalem: Yad Izhak Ben Zvi, 1984). Hebrew.

———, *The Monarchic Principle: Studies in Jewish Self-Government in Antiquity* (Tübingen: J. C. B. Mohr & Siebeck, 1994).

Goodenough, E., "Symbolism in Hellenistic Jewish Art," *JBL* 56 (1937).

———, *Jewish Symbols in the Greco-Roman Period*, 13 vols., Bollingen Series 37 (New York: Pantheon, 1953–68).

———, "Bosphorus Inscriptions and the Most High God," *JQR* 47 (1957).

———, "The Rabbis and Jewish Art in the Greco-Roman Period," *HUCA* 32 (1961).

Goodman, M., *State and Society in Roman Galilee, A.D. 132–212* (Totowa: Rowman & Allenheld, 1983).

———, "Jewish Proselytizing in the First Century," *The Jews among Pagans and Christians in the Roman Empire*, ed. J. Lieu et al. (London: Routledge, 1992).

———, "The Roman State and the Jewish Patriarch in the Third Century," *The Galilee in Late Antiquity*, ed. L. I. Levine (New York: Jewish Theological Seminary, 1992).

———, *Mission and Conversion: Proselytizing in the Religious History of the Roman Empire* (Oxford: Clarendon, 1994).

———, "The Function of Minim in Early Rabbininc Judaism," *Geschichte-Tradition-Reflexion: Festschrift für Martin Hengel zum 70. Geburtstag*, I: *Judentum*, ed. P. Schäfer (Tübingen: J. C. B. Mohr, 1996).

———, "The Roman Identity of Roman Jews," *The Jews in the Hellenistic-Roman Worlds: Studies in Memory of Menahem Stern*, ed. I. M. Gafni et al. (Jerusalem: Shazar Center & Historical Society of Israel, 1996).

———, "Sacred Space in Diaspora Judaism," *Studies on the Jewish Diaspora in the Hellenistic and Roman Periods*, Te'uda 12, ed. B. Isaac and A. Oppenheimer (Tel Aviv: Ramot, 1996).

Goranson, S., "The Battle over the Holy Day at Dura-Europos," *Bible Review* 12/4 (1996).

Gordon, H. L., "The Basilica and the Stoa in Early Rabbinical Literature," *Art Bulletin* 13 (1931).

Gordon, R., "The Veil of Power: Emperors, Sacrificers and Benefactors," *Pagan Priests: Religion and Power in the Ancient World*, ed. M. Beard and J. North (Ithaca: Cornell University Press, 1990).

Goshen-Gottstein, M. H., "The *Psalms Scroll* (11QPs²): A Problem of Canon and Text," *Textus* 5 (1966).

———, "Aspects of Targum Studies," *Proceedings of the Ninth World Congress of Jewish Studies—Panel Sessions: Bible Studies and the Ancient Near East,* ed. M. H. Goshen-Gottstein (Jerusalem: World Union of Jewish Studies & Magnes, 1988).

Grabar, A., "Le thème religieux des fresques de la synagogue de Doura (245–256 après J.C.)," *Revue de l'Histoire des Religions* 123 (1941); 124 (1942).

———, *L'iconoclasme byzantin: Dossier archéologique* (Paris: Collège de France, 1957).

———, *Christian Iconography: A Study of Its Origins* (Princeton: Princeton University Press, 1968).

———, *The Formation of Islamic Art* (New Haven: Yale University Press, 1973).

Grabbe, L. L., "The Jannes/Jambres Tradition in Targum Pseudo-Jonathan," *JBL* 98 (1979).

———, "Synagogues in Pre-70 Palestine: A Re-Assessment," *JTS* 39 (1989).

———, *Judaism from Cyrus to Hadrian,* 2 vols. (Philadelphia: Fortress, 1992).

Graetz, H., *History of the Jews,* 6 vols. (Philadelphia: Jewish Publication Society, 1956).

Graininger, J. D., " 'Village Government' in Roman Syria and Arabia," *Levant* 27 (1995).

Grant, F. C., "Modern Study of the Jewish Liturgy," *ZAW* 65 (1953).

Grant, R. M., "The Decalogue in Early Christianity," *HTR* 40 (1947).

———, *Historical Introduction to the New Testament* (New York: Harper & Row, 1963).

Green, W. S., "Palestinian Holy Men: Charismatic Leadership and Rabbinic Tradition," *ANRW*, II, 19.2, ed. H. Temporini and W. Haase (Berlin & New York: de Gruyter, 1979).

———, "Context and Meaning in Rabbinic 'Biography,' " *Approaches to Ancient Judaism,* II, ed. W. S. Green (Chico: Scholars, 1980).

Greenberg, M., "On the Refinement of the Conception of Prayer in Hebrew Scriptures," *AJS Review* 1 (1976).

———, "Tefilla," *Encyclopedia Biblica,* VIII (Jerusalem: Bialik, 1982). Hebrew.

———, *Biblical Prose Prayer as a Window to the Popular Religion of Ancient Israel* (Berkeley: University of California Press, 1983).

Greenberg, S., "Jewish Educational Institutions," *The Jews: Their History, Culture and Religion,* ed. L. Finkelstein (Philadelphia: Jewish Publication Society, 1960).

Greer, R., "Alien Citizens: A Marvelous Paradox," *Civitas: Religious Interpretation of the City,* ed. P. S. Hawkins (Atlanta: Scholars, 1986).

Gregg, R. C., and Urman, D., *Jews, Pagans and Christians in the Golan Heights: Greek and Other Inscriptions of the Roman and Byzantine Eras* (Atlanta: Scholars, 1996).

Griffiths, J. G., "Egypt and the Rise of the Synagogue," *JTS* 38 (1987).

Groh, D. E., "The Stratigraphic Chronology of the Galilean Synagogue from the Early Roman Period through the Early Byzantine Period (ca. 420 C.E.), *Ancient Synagogues: Historical Analysis and Archaeological Discovery,* I, ed. D. Urman and P. V. M. Flesher (Leiden: Brill, 1995).

Grossberg, A., "Reactions," *Qadmoniot* 26/101-2 (1993). Hebrew.

Grossfeld, B., "Targum Onqelos, Halakha and the Halakhic Midrashim," *The Aramaic Bible: Targums in Their Historical Context,* ed. D. R. G. Beattie and M. J. McNamara (Sheffield: Sheffield Academic, 1994).

Grossman, A., "The Origins and Essence of the Custom of 'Stopping-the-Service,' " *Milet: Studies in Jewish History and Culture* 1 (1983). Hebrew.

Grossman, S., "Women and the Jerusalem Temple," *Daughters of the King: Women and the Synagogue*, ed. S. Grossman and R. Haut (Philadelphia: Jewish Publication Society, 1992).

Grossman, S., and Haut, R., eds., *Daughters of the King: Women and the Synagogue* (Philadelphia: Jewish Publication Society, 1992).

Gruen, E., "The Origins and Objectives of Onias' Temple," *SCI* 16 (1997).

Gruenwald, I., "Yannai's Piyyutim and the Literature of יורדי מרכבה," *Tarbiz* 36 (1967). Hebrew.

———, "The Song of the Angels, the *Qedushah* and the Composition of the *Hekhalot* Literature," *Jerusalem in the Second Temple Period: Schalit Memorial Volume*, ed. A. Oppenheimer et al. (Jerusalem: Yad Izhak Ben Zvi, 1980). Hebrew.

———, "The Impact of Priestly Traditions on the Creation of Merkabah Mysticism and the Shiur Komah," *Proceedings of the First International Conference on the History of Jewish Mysticism — Early Jewish Mysticism*, ed. J. Dan, Jerusalem Studies in Jewish Thought 6 (Jerusalem: Hamakor, 1987).

———, *From Apocalypticism to Gnosticism* (Frankfurt: P. Lang, 1988).

Guilding, A., *Fourth Gospel and Jewish Worship* (Oxford: Clarendon, 1960).

Gundel, H. G., *Zodaikos: Tierkreisbilder im Altertum* (Mainz: Philipp von Zabern, 1992).

Gundry, R. H., "The Language Milieu of First-Century Palestine: Its Bearing on the Authenticity of the Gospel Tradition," *JBL* 83 (1964).

Gutman, S., "The Synagogue at Gamla," *Ancient Synagogues Revealed*, ed. L. I. Levine (Jerusalem: Israel Exploration Society, 1981).

———, "Gamala," *NEAEHL*, II, ed. E. Stern (Jerusalem: Carta, 1993).

Gutmann, J., "The Origin of the Synagogue," *Archäologischer Anzeiger* 87 (1972).

———, ed., *The Dura-Europos Synagogue: A Re-Evaluation (1932–72)*, (Missoula: American Academy of Religion & Society of Biblical Literature, 1973).

———, "Programmatic Painting in the Dura Synagogue," *The Dura-Europos Synagogue: A Re-Evaluation (1932–72)*, ed. J. Gutmann (Missoula: American Academy of Religion & Society of Biblical Literature, 1973).

———, *The Synagogue: Studies in Origins, Archaeology and Architecture* (New York: KTAV, 1975).

———, ed., *Ancient Synagogues: The State of Research*, Brown Judaic Studies 22 (Chico: Scholars, 1981).

———, "Synagogue Origins: Theories and Facts," *Ancient Synagogues: The State of Research*, ed. J. Gutmann, Brown Judaic Studies 22 (Chico: Scholars, 1981).

———, "Early Synagogue and Jewish Catacomb Art and Its Relation to Christian Art," *ANRW*, II, 21.2, ed. H. Temporini and W. Haase (Berlin & New York: de Gruyter, 1984).

———, "Sherira Gaon and the Babylonian Origin of the Synagogue," *Occident and Orient: A Tribute to the Memory of A. Scheiber*, ed. R. Dan (Budapest & Leiden: Akademiai Kiado & Brill, 1988).

———, "Ancient Synagogues: Archaeological Fact and Scholarly Assumption," *Bulletin of the Asia Institute* 9 (1997).

Habas (Rubin), E., "A Poem by the Empress Eudocia: A Note on the Patriarch," *IEJ* 46 (1996).

Habas, L., "The Eschatological Theme in Jewish Chancel Screen Art and Its Origins," *From Dura to Sepphoris: Studies in Jewish Art and Society in Late Antiquity*, ed. L. Levine and Z. Weiss (Ann Arbor: *Journal of Roman Archaeology* Supplementary Studies, forthcoming).

Hachlili, R., "The Niche and the Ark in Ancient Synagogues," *BASOR* 223 (1976).

————, "The Zodiac in Ancient Jewish Art: Representation and Significance," *BASOR* 228 (1977).

————, "On the Gaza School of Mosaicists," *EI*, XIX (Jerusalem: Israel Exploration Society, 1987). Hebrew.

————, *Ancient Jewish Art and Archaeology in the Land of Israel* (Leiden: Brill, 1988).

————, ed., *Ancient Synagogues in Israel*, B.A.R. International Series 499 (Oxford: B.A.R., 1989).

————, "The State of Ancient Synagogue Research," *Ancient Synagogues in Israel*, ed. R. Hachlili, B.A.R. International Series 499 (Oxford: B.A.R., 1989).

————, "Late Antique Jewish Art from the Golan," *The Roman and Byzantine Near East: Some Recent Archaeological Research*, ed. J. Humphrey (Ann Arbor: Cushing-Malloy, 1995).

————, "The Origin of the Synagogue: A Reassessment," *JSJ* 28 (1997).

————, *Ancient Jewish Art and Archaeology in the Diaspora* (Leiden: Brill, 1998).

Hachlili, R., and Merhav, R., "The Menorah in the First and Second Temple Times in the Light of the Sources and Archaeology," *EI*, XVIII (Jerusalem: Israel Exploration Society, 1985). Hebrew.

————, "Synagogues in the Land of Israel: The Art and Architecture of Late Antique Synagogues," *Sacred Realm: The Emergence of the Synagogue in the Ancient World*, ed. S. Fine (New York: Oxford University Press, 1996).

Hacohen, A., and Rozenson, I., "Comments on Z. Weiss' 'Goes Down before the Ark,'" *Cathedra* 64 (1992). Hebrew.

Haenchen, E., *The Acts of the Apostles: A Commentary* (Oxford: Blackwell, 1982).

Hahn, R. R., "Judaism and Jewish Christianity in Antioch: Charisma and Conflict in the First Century," *JRH* 14 (1986–87).

Halivni (Weiss), D., "The Location of the Bet Din in the Early Tannaitic Period," *PAAJR* 29 (1960–61).

————, *Midrash, Mishnah and Gemara: The Jewish Predilection for Justified Law* (Cambridge: Harvard University Press, 1986).

Hall, B. W., *Samaritan Religion from John Hyrcanus to Baba Rabba* (Sydney: Mandelbaum Trust, 1987).

————, "Samaritan History: From John Hyrcanus to Baba Rabbah," *The Samaritans*, ed. A. D. Crown (Tübingen: J. C. B. Mohr, 1989).

Halperin, D. J., *The Faces of the Chariot* (Tübingen: J. C. B. Mohr, 1988).

Halperin, D. A., *The Ancient Synagogues of the Iberian Peninsula* (Gainesville: University of Florida Press, 1969).

Hammer, R., "What Did They Bless? A Study of Mishnah Tamid 5, 1," *JQR* 81 (1991).

Hanfmann, G. M. A., et al., "The Roman and Late Antique Period," *Sardis from Prehistoric to Roman Times*, ed. G. M. A. Hanfmann (Cambridge: Harvard University Press, 1983).

Hanson, P. D., *The People Called: The Growth of Community in the Bible* (San Francisco: Harper & Row, 1986).

Haran, M., "Priest, Temple and Worship," *Tarbiz* 48 (1979). Hebrew.

————, "Torah Scrolls and Biblical Scrolls in the First Centuries C.E.," *Shnaton: An Annual for Biblical and Ancient Near Eastern Studies* 10 (1986–89). Hebrew.

Harding, M., "A Hebrew Congregational Prayer from Egypt," *New Documents Illustrating Early Christianity*, VIII, ed. S. R. Llewelyn (Grand Rapids: Eerdmans, 1998).

Harkins, P. W., trans., "Prolegomenon," *Saint John Chrysostom: Discourses against Judaizing Christians* (Washington, D.C.: Catholic University Press, 1979).

Harrill, J. A., *The Manumission of Slaves in Early Christianity* (Tübingen: J. C. B. Mohr, 1995).

Harrison, J. R., "Benefaction Ideology and Christian Responsibility for Widows," *New Documents Illustrating Early Christianity*, VIII, ed. S. R. Llewelyn (Grand Rapids: Eerdmans, 1998).

Harvey, G., "Synagogues of the Hebrews: 'Good Jews' in the Diaspora," *Jewish Local Patriotism and Self-Identification in the Graeco-Roman Period*, ed. S. Jones and S. Pearce (Sheffield: Sheffield Academic, 1998).

Hauptman, J., "Women and the Conservative Synagogue," *Daughters of the King: Women and the Synagogue*, ed. S. Grossman and R. Haut (Philadelphia: Jewish Publication Society, 1992).

———, "Women's Voluntary Performance of Mitzvot from Which They Are Exempt," *Proceedings of the Eleventh World Congress of Jewish Studies*, C/1 (Jerusalem: World Union of Jewish Studies, 1994). Hebrew.

Hayward, R., "Targum Pseudo-Jonathan to Genesis 27:31," *JQR* 84 (1993–94).

———, "The Date of Targum Pseudo-Jonathan—Some Comments," *JJS* 40 (1989).

Heinemann, J., "The Formula melekh ha-ʿolam," *JJS* 11 (1960).

———, "The Triennial Lectionary Cycle," *JJS* 19 (1968).

———, *Public Sermons in the Talmudic Period* (Jerusalem: Bialik, 1970). Hebrew.

———, "The Proem in the Aggadic Midrashim: A Form-Critical Study, *SH* 22 (1971).

———, "Early Halakhah in the Palestinian Targumim," *JJS* 25 (1974).

———, *Prayer in the Talmud: Forms and Patterns* (Berlin: de Gruyter, 1977).

———, *Studies in Jewish Liturgy* (Jerusalem: Magnes, 1981). Hebrew.

Heinemann, J., and Petuchowski, J. J., eds., *Literature of the Synagogue* (New York: Behrman House, 1975).

Hellemo, G., *Adventus Domini: Eschatological Thought in Fourth-Century Apses and Catecheses* (Leiden: Brill, 1989).

Hengel, M., "Die Synagogeninschrift von Stobi," *ZNW* 57 (1966).

———, *Judaism and Hellenism: Studies in Their Encounter in Palestine during the Early Hellenistic Period*, 2 vols. (London: SCM, 1974).

———, "Proseuche und Synagoge," *The Synagogue: Studies in Origins, Archaeology and Architecture*, ed. J. Gutmann (New York: KTAV, 1975).

———, *The Johannine Question* (London: SCM, 1989).

———, *The Pre-Christian Paul* (London: SCM, 1991).

———, "The Scriptures and Their Interpretation in Second Temple Judaism," *The Aramaic Bible: Targums in Their Historical Context*, ed. D. R. G. Beattie and M. J. McNamara (Sheffield: Sheffield Academic, 1994).

Hengel, M., and Deines, R., "E. P. Sanders' 'Common Judaism,' Jesus, and the Pharisees," *JTS* 46 (1995).

Herbert, S., "The Orientation of Greek Temples," *PEQ* 116 (1984).

Herford, R. T., *The Pharisees* (London: G. Allen, 1924).

Herman, G., "Jewish Tombstone from Binyamina," *SCI* 11 (1991–92).

Herr, M. D., "The Conception of History among the Sages," *Proceedings of the Sixth World Congress of Jewish Studies* (Jerusalem: World Union of Jewish Studies, 1977). Hebrew.

———, "Matters of Palestinian Halakha during the Sixth and Seventh Centuries C.E.," *Tarbiz* 49 (1979–80). Hebrew.

———, "More on Two Days of *Rosh Hashanah* in the Land of Israel," *Tarbiz* 53 (1983). Hebrew.

———, "From the Destruction of the Temple to the Bar-Kosiba Revolt," *The History of Eretz Israel*, IV, ed. M. Stern (Jerusalem: Keter, 1984). Hebrew.

———, "Synagogues and Theatres (Sermons and Satiric Plays)," *Knesset Ezra—Literature and Life in the Synagogue: Studies Presented to Ezra Fleischer*, ed. S. Eliezer et al. (Jerusalem: Yad Izhak Ben Zvi, 1994). Hebrew.

Herrin, J., "Ideals of Charity, Realities of Welfare: The Philanthropic Activity of the Byzantine Church," *Church and People in Byzantium*, ed. R. Morris (Birmingham: Centre for Byzantine, Ottoman and Modern Greek Studies, University of Birmingham, 1990).

Herzog, Z., "The City-Gate in Eretz-Israel and Its Neighboring Countries," Ph.D. dissertation (Tel Aviv University, 1976). Hebrew.

———, *Das Stadttor in Israel und in den Nachbarländern* (Mainz: Philipp von Zabern, 1986).

———, "Settlement and Fortification Planning in the Iron Age," *The Architecture of Ancient Israel from the Prehistoric to the Persian Periods*, ed. A. Kempinski and R. Reich (Jerusalem: Israel Exploration Society, 1992).

———, *Archaeology of the City: Urban Planning in Ancient Israel and Its Social Implications* (Tel Aviv: Yass Archaeology Press, 1997).

Heschel, A. J., *Quest for God: Studies in Prayer and Symbolism*, reprint (New York: Crossroad, 1987).

Hezser, C., *Form, Function, and Historical Significance of the Rabbinic Story in Yerushalmi Neziqin* (Tübingen: J. C. B. Mohr, 1993).

———, "Social Fragmentation, Plurality of Opinion, and Nonobservance of Halakhah: Rabbis and Community in Late Roman Palestine," *JSQ* 1 (1993–94).

———, *The Social Structure of the Rabbinic Movement in Roman Palestine* (Tübingen: J. C. B. Mohr, 1997).

Hildesheimer, I., "Die Beschreibung der herodianischen Tempels im Tractate Middoth und bei Flavius Josephus," *Jahresbericht des Rabbiner-Seminars für das orthodoxe Judenthum* (Berlin: Driesner, 1876–77).

Hirschberg, H. Z., "On the Place of Aramaic Targums in the Life of the People," *Bar Ilan* 1 (1963). Hebrew.

———, *A History of the Jews in North Africa*, 2d ed., 2 vols. (Leiden: Brill, 1974–81).

Hirschfeld, Y., "Holy Sites in the Vicinity of the Monastery of Chariton," *Early Christianity in Context*, ed. F. Manns and E. Alliata (Jerusalem: Franciscan Printing, 1993).

Hirshman, M., "The Preacher and His Public in Third-Century Palestine," *JJS* 42 (1991).

———, "Shmuel ha-Katan," *Jews and Judaism in the Second Temple, Mishna and Talmud Period: Studies in Honor of Shmuel Safrai*, ed. I. Gafni et al. (Jerusalem: Yad Izhak Ben Zvi, 1993). Hebrew.

———, *A Rivalry of Genius: Jewish and Christian Biblical Interpretation in Late Antiquity* (Albany: State University of New York Press, 1996).

Hoehner, H., *Herod Antipas* (Cambridge: Cambridge University Press, 1972).

Hoenig, S. B., "The Supposititious Temple-Synagogue," *JQR* 54 (1963–64).

———, "The Ancient City-Square: The Forerunner of the Synagogue," *ANRW* II, 19.1, ed. H. Temporini and W. Haase (Berlin & New York: de Gruyter, 1979).

Hönigman, S., "The Birth of a Diaspora: The Emergence of a Jewish Self-Definition in Ptolemaic Egypt in the Light of Onomastics," *Diasporas in Antiquity*, ed. S. J. D. Cohen and E. S. Frerichs (Atlanta: Scholars, 1993).

Hoffman, J., "The Surprising History of the Musaf 'Amidah," *CJ* 42/1 (1989).

Hoffman, L. A., *The Canonization of the Synagogue Service* (Notre Dame: University of Notre Dame Press, 1979).

———, "Censoring In and Censoring Out: A Function of Liturgical Language," *Ancient Synagogues: The State of Research*, ed. J. Gutmann, Brown Judaic Studies 22 (Chico: Scholars, 1981).

Hoglund, K. G., and Meyers, E. M., "The Residential Quarter on the Western Summit," *Sepphoris in Galilee: Crosscurrents of Culture*, ed. R. M. Nagy et al. (Raleigh: North Carolina Museum of Art, 1996).

Holladay, C. R., *Fragments from Hellenistic Jewish Authors*, 2 vols. (Atlanta: Scholars, 1983–89).

Hollis, F. J., *The Archaeology of Herod's Temple* (London: J. M. Dent & Sons, 1934).

Holum, K., et al., eds., *King Herod's Dream: Caesarea on the Sea* (New York: Norton, 1988).

———, "Hadrian and St. Helena: Imperial Travel and the Origins of Christian Holy Land Pilgrimage," *The Blessings of Pilgrimage*, ed. R. Ousterhoot (Urbana: University of Illinois Press, 1990).

Horbury, W., and Noy, D., *Jewish Inscriptions of Greco-Roman Egypt* (Cambridge: Cambridge University Press, 1992).

Horowitz, G., "Town Planning of Hellenistic Marisa: A Reappraisal of the Excavations after Eighty Years," *PEQ* 112 (1980).

Horowitz, I. S., *Palestine and the Adjacent Countries* (Vienna: A. Horowitz, 1923). Hebrew.

Horsley, G. H. R., *New Documents Illustrating Early Christianity*, 7 vols. (North Ryde, N.S.W.: MacQuarie University, 1981–94).

Horsley, R. A., *Jesus and the Spiral of Violence: Popular Jewish Resistance in Roman Palestine* (San Francisco: Harper & Row, 1987).

———, *Galilee: History, Politics, People* (Valley Forge: Trinity, 1995).

———, *Archaeology, History, and Society in Galilee: The Social Context of Jesus and the Rabbis* (Valley Forge: Trinity, 1996).

Horst, P. W. van der, "Moses' Throne Vision in Ezekiel the Dramatist," *JJS* 34 (1983).

———, "Juden und Christen in Aphrodisias," *Juden und Christen in der Antike*, ed. J. van Amersfoort and J. van Oort (Kampen: Pharos, 1990).

———, *Ancient Jewish Epitaphs* (Kampen: Pharos, 1991).

———, *Hellenism-Judaism-Christianity: Essays on Their Interaction* (Kampen: Pharos, 1994).

———, "Was the Synagogue a Place of Sabbath Worship before 70 C.E.?" (forthcoming).

———, "Neglected Greek Evidence for Early Jewish Liturgical Prayer?" *JSJ* 29 (1998).

Hruby, K., *Die Synagoge: Geschichtliche Entwicklung einer Institution* (Zurich: Theologischer Verlag, 1971).

Humphrey, J. H., "Amphitheatrical Hippo-Stadia," *Caesarea Maritima: A Retrospective after Two Millennia*, ed. A. Raban and K. G. Holum (Leiden: Brill, 1996).

Hüttenmeister, F. G., "The Aramaic Inscription from the Synagogue at H. 'Ammudim," *IEJ* 28 (1978).

———, "Synagogue and Beth Ha-Midrash and Their Relationship," *Cathedra* 18 (1981). Hebrew.

Hüttenmeister, F. G., and Reeg, G., *Die antiken Synagogen in Israel*, 2 vols. (Wiesbaden: L. Reichert, 1977).

Hunt, E. D., *Holy Land Pilgrimage in the Later Roman Empire, A.D. 312–460* (Oxford: Clarendon, 1982).

———, "St. Stephen in Minorca: An Episode in Jewish-Christian Relations in the Early Fifth Century A.D.," *JTS* 33 (1982).

Hyman, A., *Toldot Tanaim V'amoraim* (London: Express, 1910).

Ilan, T., "New Ossuary Inscriptions from Jerusalem," *SCI* 11 (1991–92).

———, "A Window into the Public Realm: Jewish Women in the Second Temple Period," *A View into the Lives of Women in Jewish Societies: Collected Essays*, ed. Y. Azmon (Jerusalem: Shazar Center, 1995). Hebrew.

———, *Jewish Women in Greco-Roman Palestine* (Peabody: Hendrickson, 1996).

———, "Women's Studies and Jewish Studies," *JSQ* 3 (1996).

Ilan, Z., "A Broken Slab Containing the Names of the Twenty-Four Priestly Courses Discovered in the Vicinity of Kissufim," *Tarbiz* 43 (1974). Hebrew.

———, Kefar Hananya—Its History and Remains," *Teva V'aretz* 22 (1980–81). Hebrew.

———, "Fragments from Nave," *'Et-mol* 14/5 (1985) (June 1989). Hebrew.

———, "The Synagogue and Bet Midrash of Meroth," *Ancient Synagogues in Israel*, ed. R. Hachlili, B.A.R. International Series 499 (Oxford: B.A.R., 1989).

———, *Ancient Synagogues in Israel* (Tel Aviv: Ministry of Defense, 1991). Hebrew.

Ilan, Z., and Damati, E., *Meroth: The Ancient Jewish Village* (Tel Aviv: Society for the Protection of Nature in Israel, 1987). Hebrew.

The Interpreter's Dictionary of the Bible [*IDB*], 5 vols., ed. G. A. Buttrick (New York: Abingdon, 1962).

Isaac, B., "Orientals and Jews in the Historia Augusta: Fourth-Century Prejudice and Stereotypes," *The Jews in the Hellenistic-Roman Worlds: Studies in Memory of Menahem Stern*, ed. I. M. Gafni et al. (Jerusalem: Shazar Center & Historical Society of Israel, 1996). Hebrew.

Israeli, Y., ed., *By the Light of the Menorah: The Evolution of a Symbol—Israel Museum Catalogue* (Jerusalem: Israel Museum, 1998).

Isser, S., *The Dositheans: A Samaritan Sect in Late Antiquity* (Leiden: Brill, 1976).

Isserlin, B., "Israelite Art during the Period of the Monarchy," *Jewish Art: An Illustrated History*, ed. C. Roth (Greenwich: New York Graphic Society, 1961).

Jacobs, M., *Die Institution des jüdischen Patriarchen* (Tübingen: J. C. B. Mohr, 1995).

Jacoby, R., "Responses," *Qadmoniot* 2/103–4 (1993). Hebrew.

Jaffee, M. S., "The Taqqanah in Tannaitic Literature: Jurisprudence and the Construction of Rabbinic Memory," *JJS* 41 (1990).

———, *Early Judaism* (Upper Saddle River: Prentice Hall, 1997).

Janssen, E., *Juda in der Exilszeit* (Göttingen: Vandenhoeck & Ruprecht, 1956).

Jastrow, M., *A Dictionary of the Targumim, the Talmud Babli and Yerushalmi, and the Midrashic Literature*, reprint (New York: Judaica Press, 1971).

Jeremias, J., *The Prayers of Jesus* (London: SCM, 1967).

———, *Jerusalem in the Time of Jesus: An Investigation into Economic and Social Conditions during the New Testament* (Philadelphia: Fortress, 1969).

Joel, I., "A Bible Manuscript Written in 1260 (with Two Facsimiles)," *Qiryat Sefer* 38 (1962). Hebrew.

Johnson, N. B., *Prayer in the Apocrypha and Pseudepigrapha: A Study of the Jewish Concept of God* (Philadelphia: Society of Biblical Literature and Exegesis, 1948).

Jones, C. P. M., "The New Testament," *The Study of Liturgy*, ed. C. Jones et al. (London: SPCK, 1992).

Jones, C. P. M., et al., "The Apostolic Tradition," *The Study of Liturgy*, ed. C. Jones et al. (London: SPCK, 1992).

———, eds., *The Study of Liturgy* (London: SPCK, 1992).

Jost, I. M., *Geschichte des Judenthums und seiner Sekten*, 3 vols. (Leipzig: Doerffling & Franke, 1857–59).

Jungmann, J. A., *Early Liturgy to the Time of Gregory the Great* (Notre Dame: University of Notre Dame Press, 1959).

Juster, J., *Les juifs dans l'empire romain*, 2 vols. (Paris: Geuthner, 1914).

Kadushin, M., *The Rabbinic Mind* (New York: Jewish Theological Seminary, 1952).

Kahane, T., "The Priestly Courses and Their Geographical Settlements," *Tarbiz* 48 (1979). Hebrew.

Kahle, P. E., *Masoreten des Westens*, 2 vols. (Stuttgart: W. Kohlhammer, 1927–30).

———, *The Cairo Geniza* (London: British Academy, 1947).

Kallistos of Diokloa, Bishop, "The Meaning of the Divine Liturgy for the Byzantine Worshipper," *Church and People in Byzantium*, ed. R. Morris (Birmingham: Centre for Byzantine, Ottoman and Modern Greek Studies, University of Birmingham, 1990).

Kalmin, R., "Christians and Heretics in Rabbinic Literature of Late Antiquity," *HTR* 87 (1994).

Kane, J. P., "The Mithraic Cultic Meal in Its Greek and Roman Environment," *Mithraic Studies* 2 (1975).

Kanof, A., *Jewish Ceremonial Art and Religious Observance* (New York: H. N. Abrams, 1970).

Kant, L. H., "Jewish Inscriptions in Greek and Latin," *ANRW* II, 20.2, ed. H. Temporini and W. Haase (Berlin & New York: de Gruyter, 1987).

Kasher, A., "Three Jewish Communities of Lower Egypt in the Ptolemaic Period," *SCI* 2 (1975).

———, "The *Isopoliteia* Question in Caesarea Maritima," *JQR* 68 (1978).

———, "Jewish Migration and Settlement in the Diaspora in the Hellenistic-Roman Period," *Migration and Settlement among Jews and the Nations*, ed. A. Shinan (Jerusalem: Shazar Center, 1982).

———, *The Jews in Hellenistic and Roman Egypt: The Struggle for Equal Rights* (Tübingen: J. C. B. Mohr, 1985).

———, "The Aramaic Targumim and Their *Sitz im Leben*," *Proceedings of the Ninth World Congress of Jewish Studies — Panel Sessions: Bible Studies and the Ancient Near East*, ed. M. H. Goshen-Gottstein (Jerusalem: World Union of Jewish Studies & Magnes, 1988).

———, "The Founding of Tiberias and Her Functioning as the Capital of the Galilee," *Tiberias: From Her Founding to the Muslim Conquest*, ed. Y. Hirschfeld (Jerusalem: Yad Ben Zvi, 1988). Hebrew.

———, "Synagogues as 'Houses of Prayer' and 'Holy Places' in the Jewish Communities of

Hellenistic and Roman Egypt," *Ancient Synagogues: Historical Analysis and Archaeological Discovery*, I, ed. D. Urman and P. V. M. Flesher (Leiden: Brill, 1995).

———, *Flavius Josephus, Against Apion*, 2 vols. (Jerusalem: Shazar Center, 1996). Hebrew.

Kasovsky, C. Y., *Thesaurus Thosephthae*, 6 vols. (Jerusalem: HaKohen, Bamberger & Wahrmann, 1932–61). Hebrew.

———, *Thesaurus Mishnae*, 4 vols. (Jerusalem: Israel Academy of Sciences and Humanities & Jewish Theological Seminary, 1956–60). Hebrew.

Katz, S., "Pope Gregory the Great and the Jews," *JQR* 24 (1933–34).

Katz, S., "Issues in the Separation of Judaism and Christianity after 70 C.E.: A Reconsideration," *JBL* 103 (1984).

Kaufman, S. A., "On Methodology in the Study of the Targums and Their Chronology," *JSNT* 23 (1985).

———, "Dating the Language of the Palestinian Targums and Their Use in the Study of First Century C.E. Texts," *The Aramaic Bible: Targums in Their Historical Context*, ed. D. R. G. Beattie and M. J. McNamara (Sheffield: Sheffield Academic, 1994).

Kaufman, S., *The Akkadian Influences on Aramaic*, Assyriological Studies 19 (Chicago: University of Chicago, 1974).

Kaufmann, Y., *The Religion of Israel: From the Beginnings to the Babylonian Exile* (Chicago: University of Chicago Press, 1960).

Kee, H. C., *Miracle in the Early Christian World: A Study in Sociohistorical Method* (New Haven: Yale University Press, 1983).

———, *Medicine, Miracle and Magic in New Testament Times* (Cambridge: Cambridge University Press, 1988).

———, "The Transformation of the Synagogue after 70 C.E.: Its Import for Early Christianity," *NTS* 36 (1990).

———, "Early Christianity in the Galilee: Reassessing the Evidence from the Gospels," *The Galilee in Late Antiquity*, ed. L. I. Levine (New York: Jewish Theological Seminary, 1992).

———, "The Jews in Acts," *Diaspora Jews and Judaism: Essays in Honor of, and in Dialogue with, A. Thomas Kraabel*, ed. J. A. Overman and R. S. McLennan, South Florida Studies in the History of Judaism 41 (Atlanta: Scholars, 1992).

Kenyon, K., *Royal Cities of the Old Testament* (New York: Schocken, 1973).

Kessler, E., "Art Leading the Story: The Akedah in Early Synagogue Art," *From Dura to Sepphoris: Studies in Jewish Art and Society in Late Antiquity*, ed. L. I. Levine and Z. Weiss (Ann Arbor: *Journal of Roman Archaeology* Supplementary Series, forthcoming).

Kessler, H., "Through the Temple Veil: The Holy Image in Judaism and Christianity," *Kairos* 32–33 (1990–91).

Kimelman, R., *R. Yohanan of Tiberias: Aspects of the Social and Religious History of Third Century Palestine* (Ann Arbor: University Microfilms, 1978).

———, "*Birkat Ha-Minim* and the Lack of Evidence for an Anti-Christian Jewish Prayer in Late Antiquity," *Jewish and Christian Self-Definition*, II, ed. E. P. Sanders et al. (Philadelphia: Fortress, 1981).

———, "The Conflict between the Priestly Oligarchy and the Sages in the Talmudic Period (on Explication of PT Shabbat 12:3, 13C = Horayot 3:4, 48C)," *Zion* 48 (1983). Hebrew.

———, "The Šĕmaʿ and Its Blessings: The Realization of God's Kingdom," *The Synagogue in Late Antiquity*, ed. L. I. Levine (Philadelphia: Jewish Theological Seminary & American Schools of Oriental Research, 1987).

———, "The Daily ʿAmidah and the Rhetoric of Redemption," *JQR* 89 (1988–89).

———, "The Case for Creation, Revelation and Redemption in the Shemaʿ: A Study in the Rhetoric of Liturgy," *RA Proceedings—1990 Convention* (New York: Rabbinical Assembly, 1991).

———, "The Shemaʿ and Its Rhetoric: The Case for the Shemaʿ Being More Than Creation, Revelation and Redemption," *Journal of Jewish Thought and Philosophy* 2 (1992).

———, "A Note on Weinfeld's 'Grace after Meals in Qumran,'" *JBL* 112 (1993).

———, "The Literary Structure of the Amidah and the Rhetoric of Redemption," *The Echoes of Many Texts: Reflections on Jewish and Christian Traditions—Essays in Honor of Lou H. Silberman*, ed. W. G. Dever and J. E. Wright (Atlanta: Scholars, 1997).

———, "The Shema and the Amidah: Rabbinic Prayer," *Prayer from Alexander to Constantine: A Critical Anthology*, ed. M. Kiley et al. (London & New York: Routledge, 1997).

Kindler, A., *The Coinage of Bostra* (Warminster: Aris & Phillips, 1983).

King, G., "Islam, Iconoclasm, and the Declaration of Doctrine," *Bulletin of the School of Oriental and African Studies* 48 (1985).

Kippenberg, H. G., *Garizim und Synagoge: Traditionsgeschichtliche Untersuchungen zur samaritanischen Religion der aramäischen Periode* (Berlin: de Gruyter, 1971).

———, "Die Synagoge," *Die Samaritaner*, ed. F. Dexinger and R. Pummer (Darmstadt: Wissenschaftliche Buchgesellschaft, 1992).

Kirschner, R., "Apocalyptic and Rabbinic Responses to the Destruction of 70," *HTR* 78 (1985).

Kister, M., "The Horn of David and the Horn of Salvation (Mazmiah Qeren Yeshuʿah)," *Jerusalem Studies in Jewish Thought* 4 (1984–85). Hebrew.

———, "'Do not assimilate yourselves . . .'—'La tashabbu . . . ,'" *Jerusalem Studies in Arabic and Islam* 12 (1989).

Kitzinger, E., "A Survey of the Early Christian Town of Stobi," *DOP* 3 (1946).

———, "The Cult of Images in the Age before Iconoclasm," *DOP* 8 (1954).

Klagsbald, V. A., "The Menorah as Symbol: Its Meaning and Origin in Early Jewish Art," *JA* 12 (1987).

Klein, M. L., "Palestinian Targum and Synagogue Mosaics," *Immanuel* 11 (1980).

———, "Geniza Manuscripts of Palestinian Targum to the Pentateuch," 2 vols. (Cincinnati: Hebrew Union College, 1986).

Klein, S., *Beiträge zur Geographie und Geschichte Galiläas* (Leipzig: R. Haupt, 1909).

———, "The Estates of R. Judah Ha-Nasi and the Jewish Community in the Trans-Jordanic Region," *JQR* 2 (1911–12).

———, *Transjordan* (Vienna: "Menorah," 1925). Hebrew.

———, *The History of Jewish Settlement in Palestine* (Tel Aviv: Mizpeh, 1935). Hebrew.

———, "R. Simeon the Sofer of Tarbanat," *Minhah L'David: Festschrift for D. Yellin* (Jerusalem: R. Mass, 1935). Hebrew.

———, *Sefer Hayishuv* (Tel Aviv: Dvir, 1939). Hebrew.

———, *The Galilee* (Jerusalem: Harav Kook, 1946). Hebrew.

Klil-Hahoresh, H., ed., *Synagogues in Eretz Israel* (Tel Aviv: Israel Defence Forces Educational Division, 1993). Hebrew.

Klinghardt, M., "The Manual of Discipline in the Light of Statutes of Hellenistic Associations," *Methods of Investigation of the Dead Sea Scrolls and the Khirbet Qumran Site: Present Realities and Future Prospects*, ed. M. O. Wise et al. (New York: New York Academy of Sciences, 1994).

Kloner, A., "Ancient Synagogues in Israel: An Archeological Survey," *Ancient Synagogues Revealed*, ed. L. I. Levine (Jerusalem: Israel Exploration Society, 1981).

Kloppenborg, J. S., "Collegia and *Thiasoi:* Issues in Function, Taxonomy and Membership," *Voluntary Associations in the Graeco-Roman World*, ed. J. S. Kloppenborg and S. G. Wilson (London & New York: Routledge, 1996).

———, "Early Synagogues as Collegia in the Diaspora and Palestine," *Voluntary Associations in the Graeco-Roman World*, ed. J. S. Kloppenborg and S. G. Wilson (London & New York: Routledge, 1996).

Knohl, I., "A Parasha Concerned with Accepting the Kingdom of Heaven," *Tarbiz* 53 (1983). Hebrew.

———, *The Sanctuary of Silence: The Priestly Torah and the Holiness School* (Minneapolis: Fortress, 1995).

———, "Between Voice and Silence: The Relationship between Prayer and Temple Cult," *JBL* 115 (1996).

Köhler, L., *Der hebräische Mensch* (Tübingen: J. C. B. Mohr, 1953).

Kohl, H., and Watzinger, C., *Antike Synagogen in Galilaea* (Leipzig: Heinrichs, 1916).

Kohler, K., "The Origin and Composition of the Eighteen Benedictions with a Translation of the Corresponding Essene Prayers in the Apostolic Constitutions," *HUCA* 1 (1924).

———, *The Origins of the Synagogue and the Church* (New York: Macmillan, 1929).

Kohut, A., *Sefer Arukh Ha-shalem*, 10 vols. (Vienna: G. Breg, 1878–92). Hebrew.

Kon, M., "Jewish Art at the Time of the Second Temple," *Jewish Art: An Illustrated History*, ed. C. Roth (Greenwich: New York Graphic Society, 1961).

Konikoff, A., *Sarcophagi from the Jewish Catacombs of Ancient Rome: A Catalogue Raisonné* (Stuttgart: Steiner, 1986).

Koranda, C., "Menorah-Darstellungen auf spätantiken Mosaikpavimenten," *Kairos* 30–31 (1988–89).

Kraabel, A. T., "Judaism in Western Asia Minor under the Roman Empire," Ph.D. dissertation (Harvard University, 1968).

———, "*Hypsistos* and the Synagogue at Sardis," *Greek, Roman and Byzantine Studies* 10 (1969).

———, "Melito the Bishop and the Synagogue at Sardis: Text and Context," *Studies Presented to George M. A. Hanfmann*, ed. D. G. Mitten et al. (Cambridge: Fogg Art Museum, Harvard University Press, 1971).

———, "The Diaspora Synagogue: Archaeological and Epigraphic Evidence since Sukenik," *ANRW* II, 19.1, ed. H. Temporini and W. Haase (Berlin & New York: de Gruyter, 1979).

———, "Jews in Imperial Rome: More Archaeological Evidence from an Oxford Collection," *JJS* 30 (1979).

———, "Paganism and Judaism: The Sardis Evidence," *Paganisme, judaïsme, christianisme: Influ-*

ences et affrontements dans le monde antique—Mélanges offerts à Marcel Simon, ed. A. Benoit et al. (Paris: de Boccard, 1979).

———, "The Disappearance of the 'God-Fearers,'" *Numen* 28 (1981).

———, "Social Systems of Six Diaspora Synagogues," *Ancient Synagogues: The State of Research*, ed. J. Gutmann (Chico: Scholars, 1981).

———, "The Excavated Synagogues of Late Antiquity from Asia Minor to Italy," XVI. Internationaler Byzantinisten-Kongress, Akten II/2, *Jahrbuch der Österreichischen Byzantinistik* 32/2 (1982).

———, "Impact of the Discovery of the Sardis Synagogue," *Sardis from Prehistoric to Roman Times*, ed. G. M. A. Hanfmann (Cambridge: Harvard University Press, 1983).

———, "The Roman Diaspora: Six Questionable Assumptions," *Essays in Honour of Yigael Yadin*, ed. G. Vermes and J. Neusner (Totowa: Allanheld & Osmun, 1983).

———, "New Evidence of the Samaritan Diaspora Has Been Found on Delos," *BA* 47 (1984).

———, "*Synagoga Caeca*: Systematic Distortion in Gentile Interpretations of Evidence for Judaism in the Early Christian Period," *"To See Ourselves as Others See Us": Christians, Jews, "Others" in Late Antiquity*, ed. J. Neusner and E. Frerichs (Chico: Scholars, 1985).

———, "Unity and Diversity among Diaspora Synagogues," *The Synagogue in Late Antiquity*, ed. L. I. Levine (Philadelphia: Jewish Theological Seminary & American Schools of Oriental Research, 1987).

———, *Diaspora Jews and Judaism: Essays in Honor of, and in Dialogue with, A. Thomas Kraabel*, ed. J. A. Overman and R. S. McLennan, South Florida Studies in the History of Judaism 41, (Atlanta: Scholars, 1992).

———, "*Pronoia* at Sardis," *Studies on the Jewish Diaspora in the Hellenistic and Roman Periods*, ed. B. Isaac and A. Oppenheimer, Teʻuda 12 (Tel Aviv: Ramot, 1996).

Kraeling, C. H., "The Jewish Community at Antioch," *JBL* 51 (1932).

———, ed., *Gerasa: City of the Decapolis* (New Haven: American Schools of Oriental Research, 1938).

———, *The Excavations at Dura-Europos*, VIII, Part I: *The Synagogue* (New Haven: Yale University, 1956; reprint, New York: KTAV, 1979).

———, *The Excavations at Dura-Europos*, VIII, Part II: *The Christian Building* (New Haven: Yale University Press, 1967).

Kraemer, R. S., "A New Inscription from Malta and the Question of Women Elders in Diaspora Jewish Communities," *HTR* 78 (1985).

———, "Non-Literary Evidence for Jewish Women in Rome and Egypt," *Helios* 13 (1986).

———, ed., *Maenads, Martyrs, Matrons, Monastics* (Philadelphia: Fortress, 1988).

———, "Monastic Jewish Women in Greco-Roman Egypt: Philo on the Therapeutrides," *Signs: Journal of Women in Culture and Society* 14 (1989).

———, "Jewish and Christian Fish: Identifying Religious Affiliation in Epigraphic Sources," *HTR* 84 (1991).

———, "Jewish Women in the Diaspora World of Late Antiquity," *Jewish Women in Historical Perspective*, ed. J. S. Baskin (Detroit: Wayne State University Press, 1991).

———, *Her Share of Blessings: Women's Religions among Pagans, Jews and Christians in the Greco-Roman World* (New York: Oxford University Press, 1992).

Krauss, H., "Jewish Art as a Minority Problem," *Journal of Jewish Sociology* 2 (1960).

Krauss, S., "The Jews in the Works of the Church Fathers," *JQR* (old series) 5 (1843); 6 (1894).

———, "Antioche," *REJ* 45 (1902).

———, *Qadmoniot Ha-Talmud*, II/2 (Tel Aviv: Dvir, 1945). Hebrew.

———, *Synagogale Altertümer* (Hildesheim: G. Olms, 1966).

Krautheimer, R., "The Constantinian Basilica," *DOP* 21 (1967).

———, *Early Christian and Byzantine Architecture*, 3d ed. (Harmondsworth: Penguin, 1979).

Krinksy, C. H., *Synagogues of Europe: Architecture, History, Meaning* (Cambridge: MIT Press, 1985).

Kühnel, B., "Jewish Symbolism of the Temple and the Tabernacle and Christian Symbolism of the Holy Sepulchre and the Heavenly Tabernacle: A Study of Their Relationship in Late Antique and Early Medieval Art and Thought," *JA* 12–13 (1986–87).

———, *From the Earthly to the Heavenly Jerusalem: Representations of the Holy City in Christian Art of the First Millennium* (Rome: Herder, 1987).

Kümmel, W. G., *Introduction to the New Testament* (Nashville: Abingdon, 1975).

Kugel, J. L., and Greer, R. A., *Early Biblical Interpretation* (Philadelphia: Westminster, 1986).

Kugelmass, H. J., "Jewish Liturgy and the Emergence of the Synagogue as House of Prayer in the Post-Destruction Era," *'Où demeures-tu?' (Jn. 1, 38): La maison depuis le monde biblique*, ed. J. C. Petit (Quebec: Fides, 1994).

Kuhn, K. G., "The Lord's Supper and Communal Meal at Qumran," *The Scrolls and the New Testament*, ed. K. Stendahl (New York: Crossroad, 1992).

Kutscher, E. Y., *The Language and Linguistic Background of the Isaiah Scroll* (Leiden: Brill, 1974).

Lacheman, E. R., "A Matter of Method in Hebrew Paleography," *JQR* 40 (1949–50).

Lagrange, M.-J., *L'évangile de Jésus Christ* (Paris: J. Gabalda, 1954).

Landman, L., *The Cantor: An Historic Perspective* (New York: Yeshiva University, 1972).

———, "The Origin of the Synagogue," *Essays on the Occasion of the Seventieth Anniversary of the Dropsie University (1909–79)*, ed. A. Katsh and L. Nemoy (Philadelphia: Dropsie University, 1979).

Landsberger, F., "The House of the People," *HUCA* 22 (1949).

———, "The Sacred Direction in Synagogue and Church," *HUCA* 28 (1957).

Lange, N. de, "The Hebrew Language in the European Diaspora," *Studies on the Jewish Diaspora in the Hellenistic and Roman Periods*, ed. B. Isaac and A. Oppenheimer, Te'uda 12 (Tel Aviv: Ramot, 1996).

———, "The Revival of the Hebrew Language in the Third Century C.E.," *JSQ* 3 (1996).

Lapin, H., "Rabbis and Public Prayers for Rain in Later Roman Palestine," *Public and Private Prayers in the Ancient Near East*, ed. A. Berlin (Potomac: CDL, 1996).

———, "Palestinian Inscriptions and Jewish Ethnicity in Late Antiquity," *Galilee: Confluence of Cultures, Proceedings of the Second International Conference in Galilee*, ed. E. M. Meyers et al. (Winona Lake: Eisenbrauns, forthcoming).

Lattanzi, E., *Neapolis: Atti del venticinquesimo convegno di studi sulla Magna Grecia* (Taranto: Istituto per la Storia e l'Archeologia della Magna Grecia, 1986).

Lauterbach, J. Z., "Tashlik: A Study in Jewish Ceremonies," *HUCA* 11 (1936).

———, *Rabbinic Essays* (Cincinnati: Hebrew Union College Press, 1951).

Leaney, A. R. C., *A Commentary on the Gospel According to St. Luke* (New York: Harper & Row, 1963).

———, *The Rule of Qumran and Its Meaning* (London: SCU, 1966).

Lehmann, M. R., "1 Q Genesis Apocryphon in the Light of Targumim and Midrashim," *RQ* 1 (1958).

Leon, H. J., *The Jews of Ancient Rome* (Philadelphia: Jewish Publication Society, 1960).

Lerner, M. B., "On the Origin of the Piyyut: Midrashic and Talmudic Clarifications," *Sidra* 9 (1993). Hebrew.

Leszynsky, R., *Die Sadduzäer* (Berlin: Mayer & Müller, 1912).

Levenson, J. D., "From Temple to Synagogue: 1 Kings 8," *Tradition in Transformation*, ed. B. Halpern and J. D. Levenson (Winona Lake: Eisenbrauns, 1981).

———, *Sinai and Zion: An Entry into the Jewish Bible* (Minneapolis: Winston Press, 1985).

Lévi, I., "Les dix-huit bénédictions et les Psaumes de Salomon," *REJ* 32 (1896).

Levick, B. M., *Roman Colonies in Southern Asia Minor* (Oxford: Clarendon, 1967).

Levine, D., "Public Fasts in Talmudic Literature: Halakhah and Practice," Ph.D. dissertation (Hebrew University, 1998).

Levine, L. I., "The Jewish-Greek Conflict in First Century Caesarea," *JJS* 25 (1974).

———, *Caesarea under Roman Rule* (Leiden: Brill, 1975).

———, "Rabbi Abbahu of Caesarea," *Christianity, Judaism and Other Greco-Roman Cults: Studies for Morton Smith at Sixty*, IV, ed. J. Neusner (Leiden: Brill, 1975).

———, *Roman Caesarea: An Archeological-Topographical Study*, Qedem 5 (Jerusalem: Institute of Archaeology, Hebrew University, 1975).

———, "R. Simeon b. Yohai and the Purification of Tiberias: History and Tradition," *HUCA* 49 (1978).

———, "The Jewish Patriarch (Nasi) in Third Century Palestine," *ANRW*, II, 19.2, ed. H. Temporini and W. Haase (Berlin & New York: de Gruyter, 1979).

———, ed., *Ancient Synagogues Revealed* (Jerusalem: Israel Exploration Society, 1981).

———, "Ancient Synagogues—A Historical Introduction," *Ancient Synagogues Revealed*, ed. L. I. Levine (Jerusalem: Israel Exploration Society, 1981).

———, "Excavations at Horvat ha-'Amudim," *Ancient Synagogues Revealed*, ed. L. I. Levine (Jerusalem: Israel Exploration Society, 1981).

———, "The Inscription in the 'En Gedi Synagogue," *Ancient Synagogues Revealed*, ed. L. I. Levine (Jerusalem: Israel Exploration Society, 1981).

———, "The Synagogue at Dura Europos," *Ancient Synagogues Revealed*, ed. L. I. Levine (Jerusalem: Israel Exploration Society, 1981).

———, "The Age of R. Judah I," *Eretz-Israel from the Destruction of the Second Temple to the Muslim Conquest*, I, ed. Z. Baras et al. (Jerusalem: Yad Izhak Ben Zvi, 1982). Hebrew.

———, "Excavations at the Synagogue of Horvat 'Ammudim," *IEJ* 32 (1982).

———, "Palestine in the Third Century C.E.," *Eretz-Israel from the Destruction of the Second Temple to the Muslim Conquest*, I, ed. Z. Baras et al. (Jerusalem: Yad Izhak Ben Zvi, 1982). Hebrew.

———, "The Finds from Beth-Shearim and Their Importance for the Study of the Talmudic Period," *EI*, XVIII (Jerusalem: Israel Exploration Society, 1985). Hebrew.

———, ed., *The Synagogue in Late Antiquity* (Philadelphia: Jewish Theological Seminary & American Schools of Oriental Research, 1987).

———, "The Second Temple Synagogue: The Formative Years," *The Synagogue in Late Antiquity*, ed. L. I. Levine (Philadelphia: Jewish Theological Seminary & American Schools of Oriental Research, 1987).

——, *The Rabbinic Class of Roman Palestine in Late Antiquity* (Jerusalem & New York: Yad Izhak Ben Zvi & Jewish Theological Seminary, 1989).

——, "The Interior of the Ancient Synagogue and Its Furnishings: From Communal Center to 'Lesser Sanctuary,'" *Cathedra* 60 (1990). Hebrew.

——, "Judaism from the Destruction of Jerusalem to the End of the Second Jewish Revolt, 70-135 C.E.," *Christianity and Rabbinic Judaism: Parallel History of Their Origins and Early Development*, ed. H. Shanks (Washington, D.C.: Biblical Archaeology Society, 1992).

——, "The Sages and the Synagogue in Late Antiquity: The Evidence of the Galilee," *The Galilee in Late Antiquity*, ed. L. I. Levine (New York & Jerusalem: Jewish Theological Seminary, 1992).

——, "Caesarea's Synagogues and Some Historical Implications," *Biblical Archaeology Today, 1990: Proceedings of the Second International Congress on Biblical Archaeology, Jerusalem, June–July 1990* (Jerusalem: Israel Exploration Society, 1993).

——, "Josephus' Description of the Jerusalem Temple: *War, Antiquities*, and Other Sources," *Josephus and the History of the Greco-Roman Period*, ed. F. Parente and J. Sievers (Leiden: Brill, 1994).

——, "Diaspora Judaism of Late Antiquity and Its Relationship to Palestine: Evidence from the Ancient Synagogue," *Studies on the Jewish Diaspora in the Hellenistic and Roman Periods*, ed. B. Isaac and A. Oppenheimer, Te'uda 12 (Tel Aviv: Ramot, 1996).

——, "The Nature and Origin of the Palestinian Synagogue Reconsidered," *JBL* 115 (1996).

——, "The Status of the Patriarch in the Third and Fourth Centuries: Sources and Methodology," *JJS* 47 (1996).

——, "Synagogue Officials: The Evidence from Caesarea and Its Implications for Palestine and the Diaspora," *Caesarea Maritima: A Retrospective after Two Millennia*, ed. A. Raban and K. Holum (Leiden: Brill, 1996).

——, *Judaism and Hellenism in Antiquity* (Seattle: University of Washington Press, 1998).

——, "The History and Significance of the Menorah in Antiquity," *From Dura to Sepphoris: Studies in Jewish Art and Society in Late Antiquity*, ed. L. I. Levine and Z. Weiss (Ann Arbor: *Journal of Roman Archaeology* Supplementary Series, forthcoming).

Levine, L., and Weiss, Z., eds., *From Dura to Sepphoris: Studies in Jewish Art and Society in Late Antiquity* (Ann Arbor: *Journal of Roman Archaeology* Supplementary Series, forthcoming).

Levinskaya, I. A., "A Jewish or Gentile Prayer House? The Meaning of ΠΡΟΣΕΥΧΗ," *Tyndale Bulletin* 41 (1990).

——, *The Book of Acts in Its Diaspora Setting* (Grand Rapids: Eerdmans, 1996).

Levinskaya, I. A., and Tokhtas'yev, S. R., "Jews and Jewish Names in the Bosporan Kingdom," *Studies on the Jewish Diaspora in the Hellenistic and Roman Periods*, ed. B. Isaac and A. Oppenheimer, Te'uda 12 (Tel Aviv: Ramot, 1996).

Levy, E., *Foundations of Prayer* (Jerusalem: Horev, 1948). Hebrew.

Levy, I., *The Synagogue* (London: Vallentine, Mitchell, 1963).

Levy, J. H., *Studies in Jewish Hellenism* (Jerusalem: Bialik, 1960). Hebrew.

Lewin, B., "Eretz Israel 'Ma'asim,'" *Tarbiz* 1 (1930). Hebrew.

Liber, M., "Structure and History of the *Tefilah*," *JQR* 40 (1950).

Licht, J., *The Rule Scroll: A Scroll from the Wilderness of Judaea 1QS, 1QSa, 1QSb* (Jerusalem: Bialik, 1965). Hebrew.

Lichtenberger, H., "Organisationsformen und Ämter im antiken Griechenland und Italien," *Jüdische Gemeinden und Organisationsformen von der Antike bis zur Gegenwart*, ed. R. Jütte and A. P. Kustermann (Vienna: Böhlau, 1996).

Lieberman, S., *Hayerushalmi Kiphshuto* (Jerusalem: Darom, 1934). Hebrew.

———, "Hazzanut Yannai," *Sinai* 4 (1939). Hebrew.

———, *Sheqi'in* (Jerusalem: Mercaz, 1939; reprint, Jerusalem: Wahrmann, 1970). Hebrew.

———, *Midreshei Teiman* (Jerusalem: Mercaz, 1940). Hebrew.

———, *Greek in Jewish Palestine* (New York: Jewish Theological Seminary, 1942).

———, "Palestine in the Third and Fourth Centuries," *JQR* 36–37 (1946).

———, "The Discipline in the So-Called Dead Sea Manual of Discipline," *JBL* 71 (1952).

———, *Tosefta Ki-Fshutah: A Comprehensive Commentary on the Tosefta* [*TK*], 10 vols. (New York: Jewish Theological Seminary, 1955–88). Hebrew.

———, *Hellenism in Jewish Palestine*, reprint (New York: Jewish Theological Seminary, 1962).

———, *Texts and Studies* (New York: KTAV, 1974).

———, "Persecution of the Jews," *S. Baron Jubilee Volume* (New York: American Academy of Jewish Research, 1975). Hebrew.

———, *Studies in Palestinian Talmudic Literature* (Jerusalem: Magnes, 1991). Hebrew.

Liebes, Y., "Mazmiah Qeren Yeshu'ah," *Jerusalem Studies in Jewish Thought* 3 (1983–84). Hebrew.

———, "Responses to I. M. Ta-Shema and M. Kister," *Jerusalem Studies in Jewish Thought* 4 (1984–85). Hebrew.

———, *Elisha's Sin* (Jerusalem: Hebrew University, 1986). Hebrew.

Liebeschuetz, J. H. W. G., *Antioch: City and Imperial Administration in the Late Roman Empire* (Oxford: Clarendon, 1972).

Liebreich, L. J., "The Compilation of the Pesuke De-Zimra," *PAAJR* 18 (1948–49).

———, "The *Pesuke De-Zimra* Benedictions," *JQR* 41 (1950).

———, "The Impact of Nehemiah 9:5–37 on the Liturgy of the Synagogue," *HUCA* 32 (1961).

Lifshitz, B., *Donateurs et fondateurs dans les synagogues juives*, Cahiers de la *Revue Biblique* 7 (Paris: Gabalda, 1967).

———, "Prolegomenon," in Frey, J.-B., *Corpus Inscriptionum Judaicarum*, I (New York: KTAV, 1975).

———, "Jewish History in the Bosphorean Kingdom," *The Diaspora in the Hellenistic-Roman World*, ed. M. Stern (Jerusalem: Am Oved, 1983). Hebrew.

Lightstone, J. N., *The Commerce of the Sacred: Mediation of the Divine among Jews in the Graeco-Roman Diaspora* (Chico: Scholars, 1984).

Linder, A., *The Jews in Roman Imperial Legislation* (Detroit: Wayne State University Press, 1987).

Lipiński, E. "Le repas sacré à Qumrân et à Palmyre," *EI*, XX (Jerusalem: Israel Exploration Society, 1989).

Liver, Y., *Chapters in the History of the Priests and Levites* (Jerusalem: Magnes, 1969). Hebrew.

Llewelyn, S. R., *New Documents Illustrating Early Christianity*, VIII (Grand Rapids: Eerdmans, 1998).

Llewelyn, S. R., and Kearsley, R. A., *New Documents Illustrating Early Christianity*, VI (Marrickville, Australia: Southwood, 1992).

Löw, L., "Der synagogale Rituus," *MGWJ* 33 (1884).

———, *Gesammelte Schriften*, 5 vols. (Szegedin: A. Bava, 1889–1900).

Loffreda, S., "The Late Chronology of the Synagogue of Capernaum," *IEJ* 23 (1973).

———, "Meyers et al., *Ancient Synagogue Excavation at Khirbet Shemaʿ*" (review), *BASOR* 244 (1981).

L'Orange, H. P., *Likeness and Icon: Selected Studies in Classical and Early Mediaeval Art* (Odense: Odense University Press, 1973).

Lüderitz, G., *Corpus jüdischer Zeugnisse aus der Cyrenaika*, Beihefte zum Tübinger Atlas des Vorderen Orients, Series B, No. 53 (Wiesbaden: L. Reichert, 1983).

———, "What Is the *Politeuma?*" *Studies in Early Jewish Epigraphy*, ed. J. W. van Henten and P. W. van der Horst (Leiden: Brill, 1994).

Lund, J., "A Synagogue at Carthage? Menorah-Lamps from the Danish Excavations," *JRA* 8 (1995).

MacCormack, S., *Art and Ceremony in Late Antiquity* (Berkeley: University of California Press, 1981).

———, "Loca Sancta: The Organization of Sacred Topography in Late Antiquity," *The Blessings of Pilgrimage*, ed. R. Ousterhoot (Urbana: Illinois University Press, 1990).

MacDonald, J., *The Theology of the Samaritans* (Philadelphia: Westminster, 1964).

Mack, H., *The Aggadic Midrash Literature* (Tel Aviv: Ministry of Defence, 1989).

———, "The Seat of Moses," *Cathedra* 72 (1994). Hebrew.

———, "The Unique Character of the Zippori Synagogue Mosaic and Eretz Israel Midrashim," *Cathedra* 88 (1998). Hebrew.

MacLennan, R. S., "In Search of the Jewish Diaspora," *BAR* 22/2 (1996).

MacLennan, R. S., and Kraabel, A. T., "The God-Fearers—A Literary and Theological Invention?" *BAR* 12 (1986).

MacMullen, R., "Roman Imperial Building in the Provinces," *HSCP* 64 (1959).

———, *Roman Social Relations, 50 B.C. to A.D. 284* (New Haven: Yale University Press, 1974).

———, *Roman Government's Response to Crisis, A.D. 235–237* (New Haven: Yale University Press, 1976).

———, "Women in Public in the Roman Empire," *Historia* 29 (1980).

———, *Paganism in the Roman Empire* (New Haven: Yale University Press, 1981).

———, "The Epigraphic Habit in the Roman Empire," *AJP* 103 (1982).

———, *Christianizing the Roman Empire, A.D. 100–400* (New Haven: Yale University Press, 1984).

———, "The Preacher's Audience (A.D. 350–400)," *JTS* 40 (1990).

———, "The Unromanized in Rome," *Diasporas in Antiquity*, ed. S. J. D. Cohen and E. S. Frerichs, Brown Judaic Studies 228 (Atlanta: Scholars, 1993).

Magen, Y., "Mount Gerizim—The Temple-City," *Qadmoniot* 23/91–92 (1990). Hebrew.

———, "Samaritan Synagogues and Their Liturgy," *Studies of Judaea and Samaria*, ed. E. Ehrlich and H. Eshel (Qedumim: Ariel, 1992). Hebrew.

———, "Samaritan Synagogues," *Early Christianity in Context: Monuments and Documents*, ed. F. Mann and E. Alliata (Jerusalem: Franciscan Printing, 1993).

———, "Samaritan Synagogues," *Qadmoniot* 25/99–100 (1993). Hebrew.

Magie, D., *Roman Rule in Asia Minor to the End of the Third Century after Christ*, 2 vols. (Princeton: Princeton University Press, 1950).

Maguire, H., *Art and Eloquence in Byzantium* (Princeton: Princeton University Press, 1981).

Maharshen, I., "The Daily Psalm," *V'zot L'yehuda: Festschrift for J. A. Blau* (Budapest: Union, 1926). Hebrew.

Maher, M., "Targum Pseudo-Jonathan of Deuteronomy 1.1–8," *The Aramaic Bible: Targums in Their Historical Context*, ed. D. R. G. Beattie and M. J. McNamara (Sheffield: Sheffield Academic, 1994).

Maier, J., "The Piyyut '*Ha'omrim le-khilay shoa*' and Anti-Christian Polemics," *Studies in Aggadah, Targum and Jewish Liturgy in Memory of Joseph Heinemann*, ed. J. J. Petuchowski and E. Fleischer (Jerusalem: Magnes, 1981). Hebrew.

Majewski, L. J., "Evidence for the Interior Decoration of the Synagogue," *BASOR* 187 (1967).

Malbon, E. S., "The Jewish Leaders in the Gospel of Mark: A Literary Study of Marcan Characterization," *JBL* 108 (1989).

Malherbe, A. J., *Social Aspects of Early Christianity* (Philadelphia: Fortress, 1983).

———, *Moral Exhortation: A Greco-Roman Sourcebook* (Philadelphia: Westminster, 1989).

Mango, C., *The Art of the Byzantine Empire, 312–1453: Sources and Documents* (Englewood Cliffs: Prentice Hall, 1972).

Mann, J., "Sefer Hama'asim for Palestinian Jewry," *Tarbiz* 1 (1920). Hebrew.

———, "Changes in the Divine Service of the Synagogue Due to Religious Persecution," *HUCA* 4 (1927).

———, *The Bible as Read and Preached in the Old Synagogue*, 2 vols. (Cincinnati: J. Mann, 1940–66).

Mann, V. B., *Gardens and Ghettoes: The Art of Jewish Life in Italy* (Berkeley: University of California Press, 1989).

Mano-Zissi, D., "Stratigraphic Problems and Urban Development of Stobi," *Studies in the Antiquities of Stobi*, I, ed. J. Wiseman (Belgrade: Titov Veles, 1973).

Mantel, H., *Studies in the History of the Sanhedrin* (Cambridge: Harvard University Press, 1961).

Ma'oz, Z. U., "The Art and Architecture of the Synagogues of the Golan," *Ancient Synagogues Revealed*, ed. L. I. Levine (Jerusalem: Israel Exploration Society, 1981).

———, "The Synagogue of Gamla and Typology of Second-Temple Synagogues," *Ancient Synagogues Revealed*, ed. L. I. Levine (Jerusalem: Israel Exploration Society, 1981).

———, "Architecture of Gamla and Her Buildings," *Z. Vilnay Jubilee Volume*, II, ed. E. Shiller (Jerusalem: Ariel, 1987). Hebrew.

———, *Jewish Art in the Golan* (Haifa: Reuben and Edith Hecht Museum, 1987).

———, "The Judaean Synagogues as a Reflection of Alexandrine Architecture," *Alessandria e il mondo ellenistico-romano*, Atti del II Congresso Internazionale Italo-Egiziano (Rome: "L'Erma" di Bretschneider, 1995).

———, "When Were the Galilean Synagogues First Constructed?" *EI*, XXV (Jerusalem: Israel Exploration Society, 1996). Hebrew.

Marcus, R., trans., *Josephus: Jewish Antiquities*, LCL 7 (Cambridge: Harvard University Press, 1961).

Margoliot, M., *Palestinian Halakhah from the Genizah* (Jerusalem: Harav Kook, 1973). Hebrew.

Margalioth, M., *Sepher Ha-Razim: A Newly Recovered Book of Magic from the Talmudic Period* (Jerusalem: Yediot Achronot, 1966). Hebrew.

Markus, R. A., *Christianity in the Roman World* (London: Thames & Hudson, 1974).

———, *The End of Ancient Christianity* (Cambridge: Cambridge University Press, 1990).

———, "How on Earth Could Places Become Holy? Origins of the Christian Idea of Holy Places," *Journal of Early Christian Studies* 2 (1994).

Marmorstein, A., "Studien zum Pseudo-Jonathan Targum, I: Das Targum und die apokryphe Literatur," Ph.D. dissertation (Pozsony, 1905).

———, "The Synagogue of Theodotos at Jerusalem," *PEFQSt* 53 (1921).

———, "The Synagogue of Claudius Tiberius Polycharmus in Stobi," *JQR* 27 (1936–37).

———, "The Oldest Form of the Eighteen Benedictions," *JQR* 34 (1943–44).

Marrou, H. I., *A History of Education in Antiquity* (London: Sheed & Ward, 1956).

Martimort, A. G., *The Church at Prayer*, I: *Principles of the Liturgy* (Collegeville: Liturgical, 1987).

Martin, D., "The Construction of the Ancient Family: Methodological Considerations," *JRS* 86 (1996).

Martin, R. P., "The Pericope of the Healing of the 'Centurion's' Servant/Son (Matt. 8:5–13 par. Luke 7:1–10): Some Exegetical Notes," *Unity and Diversity in New Testament Theology: Essays in Honor of G. E. Ladd*, ed. R. A. Guelich (Grand Rapids: Eerdmans, 1978).

Maser, P., "Synagoge und Ecclesia—Erwägungen zur Frühgeschichte des Kirchenbaus und der christlichen Bildkunst," *Kairos* 32–33 (1990–91).

Mason, S., "Greco-Roman, Jewish, and Christian Philosophies," *Approaches to Ancient Judaism*, IV, ed. J. Neusner (Atlanta: Scholars, 1993).

Mathews, T. F., *The Early Churches of Constantinople: Architecture and Liturgy* (University Park: Pennsylvania State University Press, 1971).

———, *Clash of Gods: A Reinterpretation of Early Christian Art* (Princeton: Princeton University Press, 1993).

Mattila, S. L., "Where Women Sat in Ancient Synagogues: The Archaeological Evidence in Context," *Voluntary Associations in the Graeco-Roman World*, ed. J. Kloppenborg and S. G. Wilson (London & New York: Routledge, 1996).

May, H. G., "Synagogues in Palestine," *BA* 7 (1944).

Mayence, F., "La quatrième campagne de fouille à Apamée (rapport sommaire)," *L'Antiquité classique* 4 (1935).

Mayer, G., *Index Philoneus* (Berlin: de Gruyter, 1974).

Mayer, L. A., and Reifenberg, A., "The Jewish Buildings of Naveh," *BJPES* 4 (1936). Hebrew.

Mazar, A., *Archaeology of the Land of the Bible, 10,000–586 B.C.E.* (New York: Doubleday, 1990).

Mazar, B., "Excavations near the Temple Mount," *Qadmoniot* 5/19–20 (1973). Hebrew.

Mazur, B. D., *Studies on Jewry in Greece*, I (Athens: "Hestia," 1935).

Mazza, E., *The Origins of the Eucharistic Prayer* (Collegeville: Liturgical, 1995).

McCown, C. C., "City," *IDB*, I (Nashville: Abingdon, 1962).

McKay, H. A., *Sabbath and Synagogue: The Question of Sabbath Worship in Ancient Judaism* (Leiden: Brill, 1994).

McKenzie, D. A., "Judicial Procedure at the Town Gate," *VT* 14 (1964).

McKnight, S., *A Light among the Gentiles: Jewish Missionary Activity in the Second Temple Period* (Minneapolis: Fortress, 1991).

McNamara, M. J., "Some Early Rabbinic Citations and the Palestinian Targum to the Pentateuch," *Rivista degli studi orientali* 41 (1966).

———, "Targums," *IDB*, supplementary volume (Nashville: Abingdon, 1976).

———, *The New Testament and the Palestinian Targum to the Pentateuch* (Rome: Pontificio Istituto Biblico, 1978).

———, *Palestinian Judaism and the New Testament* (Wilmington: M. Glazier, 1983).

Meeks, W. A., "The Image of the Androgyne: Some Uses of a Symbol in Earliest Christianity," *History of Religions* 13 (1974).

———, *The First Urban Christians: The Social World of the Apostle Paul* (New Haven: Yale University Press, 1983).

Meeks, W. A., and Wilken, R. L., *Jews and Christians in Antioch in the First Four Centuries of the Common Era* (Missoula: Scholars, 1978).

Meiggs, R., *Roman Ostia* (Oxford: Clarendon, 1973).

Meir, O., "The Problem of the Term 'Midrash' in the Studies of Midrashim," *Proceedings of the Eleventh World Congress of Jewish Studies*, C/1 (Jerusalem: World Union of Jewish Studies, 1994). Hebrew.

Meitlis, I., "The Significance of the 'Revua' in Katzrin," *Tarbiz* 53 (1984). Hebrew.

Mendelson, A., *Secular Education in Philo of Alexandria* (Cincinnati: Hebrew Union College Press, 1982).

Menzel, B., *Assyrische Tempel* (Rome: Pontificio Istituto Biblico, 1981).

Meshorer, Y., "Sepphoris and Rome," *Greek Numismatics and Archaeology: Essays in Honor of Margaret Thompson*, ed. O. Morkholm and N. M. Waggoner (Wetteren: Cultura, 1979).

———, *Ancient Jewish Coinage*, 2 vols. (Dix Hills: Amphora, 1982).

———, *A Treasury of Jewish Coins* (Jerusalem: Yad Izhak Ben Zvi, 1997). Hebrew.

Meslin, M., "Convivialité ou communion sacramentelle? Repas mithraïque et eucharistie chrétienne," *Paganisme, judaïsme, christianisme: Influences et affrontements dans le monde antique — Mélanges offerts à Marcel Simon*, ed. A. Benoit et al. (Paris: de Boccard, 1979).

Mesnil de Buisson, R. du, *Les peintures de la synagogue de Doura-Europos, 245–256 après J.-C.* (Rome: Pontificio Istituto Biblico, 1939).

Meyers, C. L., *The Tabernacle Menorah: A Synthetic Study of a Symbol from the Biblical Cult* (Missoula: Scholars, 1976).

Meyers, C. L., and Meyers, E. M., "The Ark in Art: A Ceramic Rendering of the Torah Shrine from Nabratein," *EI*, XVI (Jerusalem: Israel Exploration Society, 1982).

Meyers, E. M., "Galilean Regionalism as a Factor in Historical Reconstruction," *BASOR* 221 (1976).

———, "The Synagogue at Horvat Shema," *Ancient Synagogues Revealed*, ed. L. I. Levine (Jerusalem: Israel Exploration Society, 1981).

———, "Galilean Regionalism: A Reappraisal," *Approaches to the Study of Ancient Judaism*, V, ed. W. S. Green (Chico: Scholars, 1985).

———, "The Current State of Galilean Synagogue Studies," *The Synagogue in Late Antiquity*, ed. L. I. Levine (Philadelphia: Jewish Theological Seminary & American Schools of Oriental Research, 1987).

———, "The Torah Shrine in the Ancient Synagogue: Another Look at the Evidence," *JSQ* 4 (1997).

Meyers, E. M., and Meyers, C. L., "Finders of a Real Lost Ark," *BAR* 7/6 (1981).

Meyers, E. M., and Strange, J. F., *Archaeology, the Rabbis and Early Christianity* (Nashville: Abingdon, 1981).

Meyers, E. M., et al., *Ancient Synagogue Excavations at Khirbet Shemaʿ, Upper Galilee, Israel, 1970– 1972* (Durham: American Schools of Oriental Research & Duke University, 1976).

———, *Excavations at Ancient Meiron, Upper Galilee, Israel, 1971–72, 1974–75, 1977* (Cambridge: American Schools of Oriental Research, 1981).

———, "Second Preliminary Report on the 1981 Excavations at en-Nabratein, Israel," *BASOR* 246 (1982).

———, "Sepphoris, 'Ornament of All Galilee,' " *BA* 49 (1986).

———, eds., *Galilee: Confluence of Cultures, Proceedings of the Second International Conference in Galilee* (Winona Lake: Eisenbrauns, forthcoming).

Miles, M., "Santa Maria Maggiore's Fifth-Century Mosaics: Triumphal Christianity," *HTR* 86 (1993).

Millar, F., "Paul of Samosata, Zenobia and Aurelian: The Church, Local Culture and Political Allegiance in Third-Century Syria," *JRS* 61 (1971).

———, "The Jews of the Graeco-Roman Diaspora between Paganism and Christianity, A.D. 312– 438," *The Jews among Pagans and Christians in the Roman Empire*, ed. J. Lieu et al. (London: Routledge, 1992).

———, *The Roman Near East, 31 B.C.–A.D. 337* (Cambridge: Harvard University Press, 1993).

Miller, S. S., *Studies in the History and Traditions of Sepphoris* (Leiden: Brill, 1984).

———, "Cantankerous Sepphoreans Revisited," *Ki Baruch Hu: Ancient Near Eastern, Biblical and Judaic Studies in Honor of Baruch A. Levine*, ed. R. Chazan et al. (Warsaw, Ind.: Eisenbrauns, 1998).

———, "On the Number of Synagogues in the Cities of 'Erez Israel," *JJS* 49 (1998).

Mimouni, S. C., "La synagogue judéo-chrétienne de Jérusalem au Mont Sion," *Proche-Orient Chrétien* 40 (1990).

Minns, E. H., *Scythians and Greeks*, 2 vols. (New York: Biblo & Tannen, 1965).

Mirsky, A., *The Beginnings of Piyyut* (Jerusalem: Jewish Agency, 1965). Hebrew.

———, *Yosse ben Yosse: Poems* (Jerusalem: Bialik, 1977). Hebrew.

———, *The Piyyut: The Development of Post-Biblical Poetry in Eretz Israel and the Diaspora* (Jerusalem: Magnes, 1990). Hebrew.

Mitchell, S., "Imperial Building in the Eastern Roman Provinces," *Roman Architecture in the Greek World*, ed. S. Macready and F. H. Thompson (London: Society of Antiquaries, 1987).

Mitsakis, K., *The Language of Romanos the Melodist* (Munich: Beck, 1967).

Mitten, D. G., "Sardis Excavations—The Synagogue," *BASOR* 170 (1963).

Modrzejewski, J. M., "How to Be a Jew in Hellenistic Egypt," *Diasporas in Antiquity*, ed. S. J. D. Cohen and E. S. Frerichs, Brown Judaic Studies 228 (Atlanta: Scholars, 1993).

———, *The Jews of Egypt: From Ramses II to Emperor Hadrian* (Philadelphia: Jewish Publication Society, 1995).

Moe, D. L., "The Cross and the Menorah," *Archaeology* 30 (1977).

Moehring, H. R., "*Acta pro Judaeis* in the *Antiquities* of Flavius Josephus: A Study in Hellenistic and Modern Apologetic Historiography," *Christianity, Judaism and Other Greco-Roman Cults: Studies for Morton Smith at Sixty*, IV, ed. J. Neusner (Leiden: Brill, 1975).

Möller, C., and Schmitt, G., *Siedlungen Palästinas nach Flavius Josephus* (Wiesbaden: L. Reichert, 1976).

Momigliano, A., "I nomi delle prime sinagoghe romane, e la condizione giuridica delle comunità in Roma sotto Augusto," *La Rassegna mensile di Israel* 6 (1931).

——, Severo Alessandro Archisynagogus," *Athenaeum* 12 (1934).

——, *On Pagans, Jews and Christians* (Middletown: Wesleyan University Press, 1987).

Monshouwer, D., "The Reading of the Prophet in the Synagogue at Nazareth," *Biblica* 72 (1991).

Montgomery, J. A., *The Samaritans*, reprint (New York: KTAV, 1968).

Moon, W. G., "Nudity and Narrative: Observations on the Frescoes from the Dura Synagogue," *JAAR* 60 (1992).

Moore, C. A., *Daniel, Esther and Jeremiah: The Additions* (Garden City: Doubleday, 1977).

Moore, G. F., *Judaism in the First Centuries of the Christian Era: The Age of the Tannaim*, 2 vols. (Cambridge: Harvard University Press, 1927).

Mor, M., *The Bar-Kochba Revolt: Its Extent and Effect* (Jerusalem: Yad Izhak Ben Zvi & Israel Exploration Society, 1991). Hebrew.

Morgan, M. A., trans., *Sepher Ha-Razim (The Book of Mysteries)* (Chico: Scholars, 1983).

Morgenstern, J., "The Origin of the Synagogue," *Studi Orientalistici* 2 (1956).

Morris, N., *The Jewish School: An Introduction to the History of Jewish Education* (London: Eyre & Spottiswoode, 1937).

Mouterde, R., and Jalabert, L., *Inscriptions grecques et latines de la Syrie*, IV (Paris: P. Geuthner, 1929-).

Muchawsky-Schnapper, E., *The Jews of Yemen: Highlights of the Israel Museum Collection* (Jerusalem: Israel Museum, 1994).

Murphy, J. J., ed., *Quintilian: On the Teaching of Speaking and Writing* (Carbondale: Southern Illinois University Press, 1987).

Murray, C., "Art and the Early Church," *JTS* 28 (1977).

Mussies, G., "Greek in Palestine and the Diaspora," *The Jewish People in the First Century*, II, ed. S. Safrai and M. Stern (Philadelphia: Fortress, 1976).

——, "Jewish Personal Names in Some Non-Literary Sources," *Studies in Early Jewish Epigraphy*, ed. J. W. van Henten and P. W. van der Horst (Leiden: Brill, 1994).

Naeh, S., "The Torah Reading Cycle in Early Palestine: A Re-Examintion," *Tarbiz* 67 (1998). Hebrew.

Namenyi, E., *The Essence of Jewish Art* (New York: T. Yoseloff, 1960).

Nani, T. G., "ΘΡΕΠΤΟΙ," *Epigraphica* 5-6 (1943-44).

Narkiss, B., "The Image of Jerusalem in Art: Symbolic Representations of the Temple," *Ha-universita* 13 (1968). Hebrew.

——, "The Scheme of the Sanctuary from the Time of Herod the Great," *JJA* 1 (1974).

——, "Representational Art," *Age of Spirituality*, ed. K. Weitzmann (New York: Metropolitan Museum of Art, 1979).

———, "Pagan, Christian and Jewish Elements in the Art of the Ancient Synagogues," *The Synagogue in Late Antiquity*, ed. L. I. Levine (Philadelphia: Jewish Theological Seminary & American Schools of Oriental Research, 1987).

———, "The Heikhal, Bimah and Teivah in Sephardi Synagogues," *JA* 18 (1992).

Narkiss, M., "Origins of the Spice Box," *JJA* 8 (1982).

Nau, F., *Un martyrologe et douze ménologes syriaques* (Paris: Firmin-Didot, 1915).

———, "Deux épisodes de l'histoire juive sous Théodose II (423 et 438) d'après la vie de Barsauma le Syrien," *REJ* 83 (1927).

Naveh, J., *On Stone and Mosaic: The Aramaic and Hebrew Inscriptions from Ancient Synagogues* (Jerusalem: Israel Exploration Society & Carta, 1978). Hebrew.

———, "A Good Subduing: There Is None Like It," *Tarbiz* 54 (1985). Hebrew.

———, "Aramaic and Hebrew Inscriptions from Ancient Synagogues," *EI*, XX (Jerusalem: Israel Exploration Society, 1989). Hebrew.

———, *On Sherd and Papyrus: Aramaic and Hebrew Inscriptions from the Second Temple, Mishna and Talmudic Periods* (Jerusalem: Magnes, 1992). Hebrew.

Naveh, J., and Shaked, S., *Amulets and Magical Bowls: Aramaic Incantations of Late Antiquity* (Jerusalem: Magnes, 1985).

———, *Magic Spells and Formulae: Aramaic Incantations of Late Antiquity* (Jerusalem: Magnes, 1993).

Neeman, P., *Encyclopedia of Talmudical Geography*, 2 vols. (Tel Aviv: J. Chachik, 1971–72). Hebrew.

———, *Boundaries of Erez-Israel According to Hasal* (Jerusalem: R. Mass, 1979). Hebrew.

Negev, A., "The Chronology of the Seven-Branched Menorah," *EI*, VIII (Jerusalem: Israel Exploration Society, 1967). Hebrew.

———, "The Nabataean Necropolis of Mampsis," *IEJ* 21 (1971).

Ness, L. J., "Astrology and Judaism in Late Antiquity," *The Ancient World* 26 (1995).

Netzer, E., "Did the Water Installation in Magdala Serve As a Synagogue?" *Synagogues in Antiquity*, ed. A. Kasher et al. (Jerusalem: Yad Izhak Ben Zvi, 1987). Hebrew.

———, *Masada — The Yigael Yadin Excavations, 1963–1965, Final Reports*, III: *The Buildings: Stratigraphy and Architecture* (Jerusalem: Israel Exploration Society & Hebrew University, 1991).

———, "The Synagogues of Gush Halav and Khirbet Meiron," *EI*, XXV (Jerusalem: Israel Exploration Society, 1996). Hebrew.

———, "A Synagogue from the Hasmonean Period Recently Exposed in the Western Plain of Jericho," *Qadmoniot* (forthcoming). Hebrew.

Netzer, E., and Weiss, Z., *Zippori* (Jerusalem: Israel Exploration Society, 1994).

Neubauer, A., *La géographie du Talmud* (Hildesheim: G. Olms, 1967).

Neusner, J., "The Fellowship (*Haburah*) in the Second Jewish Commonwealth," *HTR* 53 (1960).

———, *A History of the Jews in Babylonia*, 5 vols. (Leiden: Brill, 1965–70).

———, *The Rabbinic Traditions about the Pharisees Before 70*, 3 vols. (Leiden: Brill, 1971).

———, *Talmudic Judaism in Sasanian Babylonia: Essays and Studies* (Leiden: Brill, 1976).

———, *Formative Judaism: Religious, Historical and Literary Studies*, III (Chico: Scholars, 1983).

———, "Studying Ancient Judaism through the Art of the Synagogue," *Art as Religious Studies*, ed. D. Adams and D. A. Cappadona (New York: Crossroad, 1987).

———, *Judaism and Its Social Metaphors: Israel in the History of Jewish Thought* (Cambridge: Cambridge University Press, 1989).

———, *The City of God in Judaism and Other Comparative and Methodological Studies* (Atlanta: Scholars, 1991).

———, *Judaism in the Matrix of Christianity* (Atlanta: Scholars, 1991).

Newsom, C., *Songs of the Sabbath Sacrifice: A Critical Edition* (Atlanta: Scholars, 1985).

Nibley, H., "Christian Envy of the Temple," *JQR* 50 (1959–60).

Nicholson, E. W., *Preaching to the Exiles: A Study of the Prose Tradition in the Book of Jeremiah* (New York: Schocken, 1970).

Nickelsburg, G. W. E., *Jewish Literature between the Bible and the Mishnah: A Historical and Literary Introduction* (Philadelphia: Fortress, 1981).

———, "Stories of Biblical and Early Post-Biblical Times," *Jewish Writings of the Second Temple Period*, ed. M. E. Stone (Assen: Van Gorcum, 1984).

Nijf, O. M. van, *The Civic World of Professional Associations in the Roman East* (Amsterdam: Gieben, 1997).

Nilsson, M. P., "Pagan Divine Service in Late Paganism," *HTR* 38 (1945).

Nitzan, B., *Qumran Prayer and Religious Poetry* (Leiden: Brill, 1994).

Nock, A. D., *Conversion* (Oxford: Oxford University Press, 1933; reprint, 1965).

———, *Early Gentile Christianity and Its Hellenistic Background* (New York: Harper & Row, 1964).

Noy, D., "A Jewish Place of Prayer in Roman Egypt," *JTS* 43 (1992).

———, *Jewish Inscriptions of Western Europe* [*JIWE*], 2 vols. (Cambridge: Cambridge University Press, 1993–95).

———, "Writing in Tongues: The Use of Greek, Latin and Hebrew in Jewish Inscriptions from Roman Italy," *JJS* 48 (1997).

———, "Letters Out of Judaea: Echoes of Israel in Jewish Inscriptions from Europe," *Jewish Local Patriotism and Self-Identification in the Graeco-Roman Period*, ed. S. Jones and S. Pearce (Sheffield: Sheffield Academic, 1998).

Obermann, J., "The Sepulchre of Maccabean Martyrs," *JBL* 50 (1931).

O'Dell, J., "The Religious Background of the Psalms of Solomon," *RQ* 3 (1961).

Oesterley, W. O. E., *The Jewish Background of the Christian Liturgy* (London: Oxford University Press, 1925).

On, A., and Rafyunu, Y., "Jerusalem–Khirbet a-Ras, *Hadashot Arkheologiyot* 100 (1993). Hebrew.

Oppenheimer, A., *The ʿAm-Ha-aretz: A Study in the Social History of the Jewish People in the Hellenistic-Roman Period* (Leiden: Brill, 1977).

———, "Beth Ha-Midrash—An Institution Apart," *Cathedra* 18 (1981). Hebrew.

———, "The Restoration of the Jewish Community in the Galilee," *Eretz Israel from the Destruction of the Second Temple to the Muslim Conquest*, I, ed. Z. Baras et al. (Jerusalem: Yad Izhak Ben Zvi, 1982). Hebrew.

———, *Babylonia Judaica in the Talmudic Period* (Wiesbaden: L. Reichert, 1983).

———, "Jewish Lydda in the Roman Era," *HUCA* 59 (1988).

———, *Galilee in the Mishnaic Period* (Jerusalem: Shazar Center, 1991). Hebrew.

———, "Babylonian Synagogues with Historical Associations," *Ancient Synagogues: Historical Analysis and Archaeological Discovery*, I, ed. D. Urman and P. V. M. Flesher (Leiden: Brill, 1995).

Oppenheimer, A., et al., "The Jewish Community in the Galilee in the Yavnean and Bar-Kokhba Period," *Cathedra* 4 (1977). Hebrew.

———, eds., *Synagogues in Antiquity* (Jerusalem: Yad Izhak Ben Zvi, 1987). Hebrew.

Oster, R., Jr., "Supposed Anachronism in Luke-Acts' Use of ΣΥΝΑΓΩΓΗ: A Rejoinder to H. C. Kee," *NTS* 39 (1993).

Ovadiah, A., "Mutual Influences between Synagogues and Churches in Byzantine Palestine," *Between Hermon and Sinai—Memorial to Amnon*, ed. M. Broshi (Jerusalem: Yedidim, 1977). Hebrew.

———, "Ancient Synagogues in Asia Minor," *Proceedings of the Tenth International Congress of Classical Archaeology, 1973* (Ankara: Türk Tarih Kurumu, 1978).

———, "The Synagogue at Gaza," *Ancient Synagogues Revealed*, ed. L. I. Levine (Jerusalem: Israel Exploration Society, 1981).

———, "Ancient Synagogues from Magna Grecia," *From Then to Now: Cathedra Lectures*, ed. Z. Ankori (Tel Aviv: Tel Aviv University, 1984). Hebrew.

———, "Mosaic Art in Ancient Synagogues of Eretz-Israel," *Synagogues in Antiquity*, ed. A. Kasher et al. (Jerusalem: Yad Izhak Ben Zvi, 1987). Hebrew.

———, "Art of the Ancient Synagogues in Israel," *Ancient Synagogues: Historical Analysis and Archaeological Discovery*, II, ed. D. Urman and P. V. M. Flesher (Leiden: Brill, 1995).

———, "The Mosaic Workshop of Gaza in Christian Antiquity," *Ancient Synagogues: Historical Analysis and Archaeological Discovery*, II, ed. D. Urman and P. V. M. Flesher (Leiden: Brill, 1995).

Overman, J. A., and MacLennan, R. S., eds., *Diaspora Jews and Judaism: Essays in Honor of, and in Dialogue with, A. Thomas Kraabel*, South Florida Studies in the History of Judaism 41 (Atlanta: Scholars, 1992).

Parkes, J., *The Conflict of the Church and the Synagogue: A Study in the Origins of Antisemitism* (Philadelphia: Jewish Publication Society, 1961).

Patte, D., *Early Jewish Hermeneutic in Palestine* (Missoula: Society of Biblical Literature, 1975).

Payne Smith, R., *Thesaurus Syriacus* (Oxford: Clarendon, 1903; reprint, 1967).

Penna, R., "Les juifs à Rome au temps de l'apôtre Paul," *NTS* 28 (1982).

Perkins, A. L., *The Art of Dura-Europos* (Oxford: Clarendon, 1973).

Perrot, C., *La lecture de la Bible dans la synagogue: Les anciennes lectures palestiniennes du Shabbat et des fêtes* (Hildesheim: Gerstenberg, 1973).

———, "Luc 4:16-30 et la lecture biblique de l'ancienne synagogue," *RSR* 47 (1973).

———, "Jésus à Nazareth, Mc 6, 1-6," *14e Dimanche Ordinaire—Assemblées du Seigneur* 45 (1974).

———, "La lecture de la Bible dans la diaspora hellénistique," *Etudes sur le Judaïsme Hellénistique, Congrès de Strasbourg (1983)*, ed. R. Kuntzmann and J. Schlosser (Paris: Cerf, 1984).

———, "The Reading of the Bible in the Ancient Synagogue," *Mikra*, ed. M. J. Mulder (Assen: Van Gorcum, 1988).

Peters, F. E., *Jerusalem: The Holy City in the Eyes of Chroniclers, Visitors, Pilgrims and Prophets from the Days of Abraham to the Beginning of Modern Times* (Princeton: Princeton University Press, 1985).

Petuchowski, J. J., "The Liturgy of the Synagogue," *The Lord's Prayer and Jewish Liturgy*, ed. J. J. Petuchowski and M. Brocke (New York: Seabury, 1978).

Pfeiffer, R. H., and Speiser, E., *One Hundred Newly Selected Nuzi Texts* (New Haven: American Schools of Oriental Research, 1935).

Phillips, C. R., "The Sociology of Religious Knowledge in the Roman Empire to A.D. 284," *ANRW* II, 16.3 (Berlin & New York: de Gruyter, 1983).

Piana, G. La, "Foreign Groups in Rome during the First Centuries of the Empire," *HTR* 20 (1927).

Picard, G. C., *L'établissement des Poseidoniastes de Bérytos* (Paris: de Boccard, 1921).

Piccirillo, M., *Mt. Nebo* (Jerusalem: Franciscan Printing, 1988).

———, *The Mosaics of Jordan* (Amman: American Center of Oriental Research, 1993).

Plassart, A., "La synagogue juive de Délos," *RB* 23 (1914).

Platner, S. B., and Ashby, T., *A Topographical Dictionary of Ancient Rome* (London: Oxford University Press, 1929).

Ploeg, J. P. M. van der, "The Meals of the Essenes," *Journal of Semitic Studies* 2 (1957).

Poehlman, W., "The Polycharmos Inscription and Synagogue I at Stobi," *Studies in the Antiquities of Stobi*, III, ed. B. Aleksova and J. Wiseman (Titov Veles: Macedonian Review Editions, 1981).

Poland, F., *Geschichte des griechischen Vereinswesen* (Leipzig: Teubner, 1960).

Porte, J. La, *The Role of Women in the Early Church* (New York: Mellen, 1982).

Porter, J. R., "The Pentateuch and the Triennial Lectionary Cycle: An Examination of a Recent Theory," *Promise and Fulfilment: Essays Presented to S. H. Hooke*, ed. F. F. Bruce (Edinburgh: T. & T. Clark, 1963).

Press, I., *A Topographical-Historical Encyclopaedia of Palestine*, 4 vols. (Jerusalem: R. Mass, 1951–55). Hebrew.

Price, J., "The Jewish Diaspora of the Graeco-Roman Period," *SCI* 13 (1994).

Pucci Ben-Zeev, M., "Caesar and Jewish Law," *RB* 102 (1995).

———, "Jewish Rights in the Roman World: New Perceptions," *Studies on the Jewish Diaspora in the Hellenistic and Roman Periods*, ed. B. Isaac and A. Oppenheimer, Te'uda 12 (Tel Aviv: Ramot, 1996).

———, "Who Wrote a Letter Concerning Delian Jews?" *RB* 103 (1996).

Pummer, R., *The Samaritans* (Leiden: Brill, 1987).

———, "Samaritan Rituals and Customs," *The Samaritans*, ed. A. D. Crown (Tübingen: J. C. B. Mohr, 1989).

———, "How to Tell a Samaritan Synagogue from a Jewish Synagogue," *BAR* 24/3 (1998).

Quasten, J., *Patrology*, 4 vols., reprint (Westminster: Christian Classics, 1993-94).

Rabello, A. M., "The Legal Condition of the Jews in the Roman Empire," *ANRW*, II, 13, ed. H. Temporini and W. Haase (Berlin & New York: de Gruyter, 1980).

———, "Le iscrizioni ebraiche della Spagna Romana e Visigotica," *Studi in onore di C. San Filippo* (Milan: Giuffre, 1985).

———, "The Situation of the Jews in Roman Spain," *Studies on the Jewish Diaspora in the Hellenistic and Roman Periods*, ed. B. Isaac and A. Oppenheimer, Te'uda 12 (Tel Aviv: Ramot, 1996).

Rabin, Ch., *Qumran Studies* (New York: Schocken, 1957).

———, "Hebrew and Aramaic in the First Century," *The Jewish People in the First Century*, II, ed. S. Safrai and M. Stern (Philadelphia: Fortress, 1976).

Rabinowitz, Z. M., *Halakha and Aggada in the Liturgical Poetry of Yannai* (Tel Aviv: Greenberg, 1965). Hebrew.

Rahmani, L. Y., "Stone Synagogue Chairs: Their Identification, Use and Significance," *Israel Exploration Journal* 40 (1990).

———, *A Catalogue of Jewish Ossuaries in the Collections of the State of Israel* (Jerusalem: Israel Antiquities Authority, 1994).

Rajak, T., "Was There a Roman Charter for the Jews?" *JRS* 74 (1984).

———, "Jewish Rights in the Greek Cities under Roman Rule: A New Approach to Ancient Judaism," *Studies in Judaism and Its Greco-Roman Context*, V, ed. W. S. Green (Atlanta: Scholars, 1985).

———, "Jews and Christians as Groups in a Pagan World," *"To See Ourselves as Others See Us": Christians, Jews, "Others" in Late Antiquity*, ed. J. Neusner and E. Frerichs (Chico: Scholars, 1985).

———, "The Jewish Community and Its Boundaries," *The Jews among Pagans and Christians in the Roman Empire*, ed. J. Lieu et al. (London: Routledge, 1992).

———, "Inscriptions and Context: Reading the Jewish Catacombs of Rome," *Studies in Early Jewish Epigraphy*, ed. J. W. van Henten and P. W. van der Horst (Leiden: Brill, 1994).

———, "Benefactors in the Greco-Jewish Diaspora, *Geschichte-Tradition-Reflexion: Festschrift für Martin Hengel zum 70. Geburtstag*, I: *Judentum*, ed. P. Schäfer (Tübingen: J. C. B. Mohr, 1996).

———, "Jews as Benefactors," *Studies on the Jewish Diaspora in the Hellenistic and Roman Periods*, ed. B. Isaac and A. Oppenheimer, Teʿuda 12 (Tel Aviv: Ramot, 1996).

Rajak, T., and Noy, D., "*Archisynagogoi*: Office, Title and Social Status in the Greco-Jewish Synagogue," *JRS* 83 (1993).

Ramsay, W., *The Cities and Bishoprics of Phrygia*, 2 vols. (Oxford: Clarendon, 1967).

Rappaport, S., *Agada und Exegese bei Flavius Josephus* (Vienna: A. Kohut Memorial Foundation, 1930).

———, *Erech Millin*, 2 vols., reprint (Jerusalem: Makor, 1970). Hebrew.

Rappaport, U., "Les iduméens en Egypte," *RPh* 43 (1969).

Ratner, B., *Ahavat Zion v'Yerushalayim*, 12 vols., reprint (Jerusalem: n.p., 1967). Hebrew.

Rawson, E., "Discrimina Ordinum: The Lex Julia Theatralis," *PBSR* 55 (1987).

Reeg, G., *Die Ortsnamen Israels nach der rabbinischen Literatur* (Wiesbaden: L. Reichert, 1989).

Reich, R., "Synagogue and Ritual Bath during the Second Temple and the Period of the Mishna and Talmud," *Synagogues in Antiquity*, ed. A. Kasher et al. (Jerusalem: Yad Izhak Ben-Zvi, 1987). Hebrew.

———, "*Miqwaʾot* (Jewish Ritual 'Immersion' Baths) in Eretz-Israel in the Second Temple and the Mishnah and Talmud Periods," Ph.D. dissertation (Hebrew University, 1990). Hebrew.

Reif, S. C., "Liturgical Difficulties in Geniza Manuscripts," *Studies in Judaism and Islam*, ed. S. Morag et al. (Jerusalem: Magnes, 1981).

———, "Jewish Liturgical Research: Past Present and Future," *JJS* 35 (1983).

———, *Judaism and Hebrew Prayer: New Perspectives on Jewish Liturgical History* (Cambridge: Cambridge University Press, 1993).

———, "Jewish Liturgy in the Second Temple Period—Some Methodological Considerations," *Proceedings of the Eleventh World Congress of Jewish Studies*, C/1 (Jerusalem: World Union of Jewish Studies, 1994).

———, "*Sabbath and Synagogue: The Question of Sabbath Worship in Ancient Judaism*, by H. McKay" (review), *JTS* 46 (1995).

Rengstorf, K. H., "μονθάνω," *TDNT*, IV (Grand Rapids: Eerdmans, 1969).

Revel-Neher, E., *L'arche d'alliance dans l'art juif et chrétien du second au dixième siècles* (Paris: Association des Amis des Etudes Archéologiques Byzantino-Slaves et du Christianisme Oriental, 1984).

———, *The Image of the Jew in Byzantine Art* (Oxford: Vidal Sassoon International Center for the Study of Antisemitism, 1992).

———, "From Dura to Sepphoris: Evolution and Continuity in Jewish Art," *From Dura to Sepphoris: Studies in Jewish Art and Society in Late Antiquity*, ed. L. Levine and Z. Weiss (Ann Arbor: *Journal of Roman Archaeology* Supplementary Series, forthcoming).

Reviv, H., "Early Elements and Late Terminology in the Descriptions of Non-Israelite Cities in the Bible," *IEJ* 27 (1977).

Reynolds, J., "Inscriptions," *Excavations at Sidi Khrebish Benghazi (Berenice)*, I, ed. J. A. Lloyd (Tripoli: Department of Antiquities, 1977).

Reynolds, J., and Tannenbaum, R. F., *Jews and God-Fearers at Aphrodisias: Greek Inscriptions with Commentary*, Proceedings of the Cambridge Philological Society, Supplement 12 (Cambridge: Cambridge University Press, 1987).

Rhoads, D. M., and Michie, D., *Mark as Story: An Introduction to the Narrative of the Gospel* (Philadelphia: Fortress, 1982).

Richardson, P. "Augustan-Era Synagogues in Rome," *Judaism and Christianity in First-Century Rome*, ed. K. P. Donfried and P. Richardson (Grand Rapids: Eerdmans, 1998).

Richardson, P., and Heuchan, V., "Jewish Voluntary Associations in Egypt and the Roles of Women," *Voluntary Associations in the Graeco-Roman World*, ed. J. Kloppenborg and S. G. Wilson (London & New York: Routledge, 1996).

Richter, G. M. A., *The Furniture of the Greeks, Etruscans and Romans* (London: Phaidon, 1966).

Riesner, R., "Synagogues in Jerusalem," *The Book of Acts in Its Palestinian Setting*, ed. R. Bauckham (Grand Rapids: Eerdmans, 1995).

Rigsby, K. J., *Asylia: Territorial Inviolability in the Hellenistic World* (Berkeley: University of California Press, 1996).

Ringe, S. H., *Jesus, Liberation and the Biblical Jubilee: Images for Ethics and Christology* (Philadelphia: Fortress, 1985).

Rives, J. B., *Religion and Authority in Roman Carthage from Augustus to Constantine* (Oxford: Clarendon, 1995).

Rivkin, E., "Ben Sira and the Non-Existence of the Synagogue," *In the Time of Harvest: Essays in the Honor of Abba Hillel Silver*, ed. D. J. Silver (New York: Macmillan, 1963).

Robert, L., *Les gladiateurs dans l'Orient Grec* (Paris: H. Champion, 1940).

———, "Inscriptions grecques de Sidé en Pamphylie," *RPh* 32 (1958).

———, "Epitaphes juives," *Hellenica* 11–12 (1960).

———, *Nouvelles inscriptions de Sardes* (Paris: A. Maisonneuve, 1964).

Roberts, A., et al., eds., *The Ante-Nicene Fathers*, VII, reprint (Grand Rapids: Eerdmans, 1975).

Roberts, C., et al., "The Gild of Zeus Hypsistos," *HTR* 29 (1936).

Rogers, G., "The Constructions of Women at Ephesos," *ZPE* 90 (1992).

————, "The Gift and Society in Roman Asia: Orthodoxies and Heresies," *SCI* 12 (1993).

Rosenfeld, B.-Z., "The Crisis of the Patriarchate in Eretz-Israel in the Fourth Century," *Zion* 53 (1988). Hebrew.

Rosenthal, D., "On the Annual Torah Reading in Eretz Israel," *Tarbiz* 53 (1983–84). Hebrew.

Rosenthal, E. S., *Yerushalmi Neziqin* (Jerusalem: Israel Academy of Sciences and Humanities, 1984). Hebrew.

Rosenthal, J., *Studies*, II (Jerusalem: R. Mass, 1966). Hebrew.

————, "The Four Commemorative Fast Days," *The Seventy-Fifth Anniversary Volume of the Jewish Quarterly Review* (Philadelphia: Jewish Quarterly Review, 1967).

Rostovtzeff, M., "Dura and the Problem of Parthian Art," *Yale Classical Studies* 5 (1935).

————, *Dura-Europos and Its Art* (Oxford: Clarendon, 1938).

Rotenstreich, N., *Jewish Philosophy in Modern Times: From Mendelssohn to Rosenzweig* (New York: Holt, Rinehart & Winston, 1968).

Roth, C., "The 'Chair of Moses' and Its Survivals," *PEQ* 81 (1949).

————, "Ecclesiasticus in the Synagogue Service," *JBL* 71 (1952).

————, "Messianic Symbols in Palestinian Archaeology," *PEQ* 87 (1955).

Roth-Gerson, L., *The Greek Inscriptions from the Synagogues in Eretz-Israel* (Jerusalem: Yad Izhak Ben Zvi, 1987). Hebrew.

————, "Similarities and Differences in Greek Inscriptions of Eretz-Israel and the Diaspora," *Synagogues in Antiquity*, ed. A. Kasher et al. (Jerusalem: Yad Izhak Ben Zvi, 1987). Hebrew.

————, "A Greek Inscription at Khan-Khalde," *Zion* 56 (1991). Hebrew.

————, "Anti-Semitism in Syria in the Hellenistic-Roman Period," *The Jews in the Hellenistic-Roman Worlds: Studies in Memory of Menahem Stern*, ed. I. M. Gafni et al. (Jerusalem: Shazar Center & Historical Society of Israel, 1996). Hebrew.

Rouèche, C., *Aphrodisias in Late Antiquity* (Oxford: Society for the Promotion of Roman Studies, 1989).

Roussin, L., "The Beit Leontis Mosaic: An Eschatological Interpretation," *JJA* 8 (1981).

————, "The Zodiac in Synagogue Decoration," *Archaeology and the Galilee: Texts and Contexts in the Graeco-Roman and Byzantine Periods*, ed. D. Edwards and C. T. McCollough (Atlanta: Scholars, 1997).

————, "The Birds and Fishes Mosaic," *Sepphoris in Galilee: Crossroads of Culture*, ed. R. M. Nagy et al. (Raleigh: North Carolina Museum of Art, 1996).

Roux, G., and Roux, J., "Un décret du politeuma des juifs de Bérénikè en Cyrénaïque," *REG* 62 (1949).

Rowley, H. H., *Worship in Ancient Israel: Its Form and Meaning* (Philadelphia: Fortress, 1967).

Rubenstein, J., *The History of Sukkot in the Second Temple and Rabbinic Periods* (Atlanta: Scholars, 1995).

Rubin, Z., "Christianity in Byzantine Palestine—Missionary Activity and Religious Coercion," *The Jerusalem Cathedra*, III, ed. L. I. Levine (Jerusalem: Yad Izhak Ben Zvi, 1983).

————, "Joseph the Comes and the Attempts to Convert the Galilee to Christianity in the Fourth Century C.E.," *Cathedra* 26 (1983). Hebrew.

Runia, D., "The Structure of Philo's Allegorical Treatises," *VC* 38 (1984).

————, "Further Observations of the Structure of Philo's Allegorical Treatises," *VC* 41 (1987).

Rutgers, L. V., "Überlegungen zu den jüdischen Katakomben Roms," *Jahrbuch für Antike und Christentum* 33 (1990).

———, "Archeological Evidence for the Interaction of Jews and Non-Jews in Late Antiquity," *AJA* 96 (1992).

———, *The Jews in Late Ancient Rome: Evidence of Cultural Interaction in the Roman Diaspora* (Leiden: Brill, 1995).

———, "Diaspora Synagogues: Synagogue Archaeology in the Greco-Roman World," *Sacred Realm: The Emergence of the Synagogue in the Ancient World*, ed. S. Fine (New York: Oxford University Press, 1996).

———, "Interaction and Its Limits: Some Notes on the Jews of Sicily in Late Antiquity," *ZPE* 115 (1997).

Sabar, S., "The Development of the Study of Jewish Art," *Maḥanaim* 11 (1995). Hebrew.

Safrai, H., "Women and the Ancient Synagogue," *Daughters of the King: Women and the Synagogue*, ed. S. Grossman and R. Haut (Philadelphia: Jewish Publication Society, 1992).

———, "Women and Processes of Change in the Temple in Jerusalem," *A View into the Lives of Women in Jewish Societies: Collected Essays*, ed. Y. Azmon (Jerusalem: Shazar Center, 1995). Hebrew.

Safrai, S., "Was There a Women's Section (עזרת נשים) in the Ancient Synagogue?" *Tarbiz* 32 (1963). Hebrew.

———, "H. Mantel, *Studies in the History of the Sanhedrin*," (review), *Qiryat Sefer* 39 (1964). Hebrew.

———, *Pilgrimage at the Time of the Second Temple* (Tel Aviv: Am Hassefer, 1965). Hebrew.

———, "Jewish Self-Government," *The Jewish People in the First Century*, I, ed. S. Safrai and M. Stern (Philadelphia: Fortress, 1974).

———, "Relations between the Diaspora and the Land of Israel," *The Jewish People in the First Century*, I, ed. S. Safrai and M. Stern (Philadelphia: Fortress, 1974).

———, "Education and the Study of the Torah," *The Jewish People in the First Century*, II, ed. S. Safrai and M. Stern (Philadelphia: Fortress, 1976).

———, "The Synagogue," *The Jewish People in the First Century*, II, ed. S. Safrai and M. Stern (Philadelphia: Fortress, 1976).

———, "Halakha and Reality," *Cathedra* 18 (1981). Hebrew.

———, "The Recovery of the Jewish Community in the Yavnean Generation," *Eretz Israel from the Destruction of the Second Temple to the Muslim Conquest*, I, ed. Z. Baras et al. (Jerusalem: Yad Izhak Ben Zvi, 1982). Hebrew.

———, *In Times of Temple and Mishnah: Studies in Jewish History*, 2 vols. (Jerusalem: Magnes, 1996). Hebrew.

Safrai, S., and Safrai, Ch., "All Are Invited to Read," *Tarbiz* 66 (1997). Hebrew.

Safrai, Z., "Samaritan Synagogues in the Roman-Byzantine Period," *Cathedra* 4 (1977). Hebrew.

———, *Boundaries and Rule in Eretz-Israel in the Period of the Mishnah and Talmud* (Tel Aviv: Hakibbutz Hameuchad, 1980). Hebrew.

———, *Pirqei Galil* (Maʿalot: Shorashim, 1981). Hebrew.

———, ed., *The Ancient Synagogue: Selected Studies* (Jerusalem: Shazar Center, 1986). Hebrew.

———, "Dukhan, Aron and Teva: How Was the Ancient Synagogue Furnished?" *Ancient Synagogues in Israel*, ed. R. Hachlili, B.A.R. International Series 499 (Oxford: B.A.R., 1989).

———, "From the Synagogue to 'Little Temple,'" *Proceedings of the Tenth World Congress of Jewish Studies* B/II (Jerusalem: World Union of Jewish Studies, 1990).

———, "The Origins of Reading the Aramaic Targum in Synagogue," *Immanuel* 24–25 (1990).

———, "Did the Priestly Courses (*Mishmarot*) Transfer from Judaea to Galilee after the Bar Kokhba Revolt?" *Tarbiz* 62 (1993). Hebrew.

———, "The Institution of the Synagogue and Its Functions," *Synagogues in Eretz Israel*, ed. H. Klil-Hahoresh (Tel Aviv: Israel Defence Forces Educational Division, 1993). Hebrew.

———, "The Communal Functions of the Synagogue in the Land of Israel in the Rabbinic Period," *Ancient Synagogues: Historical Analysis and Archaeological Discovery*, I, ed. D. Urman and P. V. M. Flesher (Leiden: Brill, 1995).

———, *The Jewish Community in the Talmudic Period* (Jerusalem: Shazar Center, 1995). Hebrew.

Saldarini, A. J., *Pharisees, Scribes and Sadducees in Palestinian Society: A Sociological Approach* (Wilmington: M. Glazier, 1988).

———, "The Gospel of Matthew and the Jewish-Christian Conflict in the Galilee," *The Galilee in Late Antiquity*, ed. L. I. Levine (New York & Jerusalem: Jewish Theological Seminary, 1992).

Saller, S. J., *The Second Revised Catalogue of the Ancient Synagogues of the Holy Land* (Jerusalem: Franciscan Printing, 1972).

Samuel, A. E., *From Athens to Alexandria: Hellenistic and Social Goals in Ptolemaic Egypt*, Studia Hellenistica 26 (Leuven: Université Catholique de Louvain, 1983).

Sanders, E. P., *Paul and Palestinian Judaism* (Philadelphia: Fortress, 1977).

———, *Jesus and Judaism* (Philadelphia: Fortress, 1985).

———, *Jewish Law from Jesus to the Mishnah: Five Studies*, 2 vols. (London: SCM, 1990–92).

———, *Judaism: Practice and Belief, 63 B.C.E.–66 C.E.* (London: SCM, 1992).

———, *The Historical Figure of Jesus* (London: Penguin, 1993).

Sanders, J. T., "From Isaiah 61 to Luke 4," *Christianity, Judaism and Other Greco-Roman Cults: Studies for Morton Smith at Sixty*, II, ed. J. Neusner (Leiden: Brill, 1975).

———, *The Jews in Luke-Acts* (Philadelphia: Fortress, 1987).

Sandmel, S., *Judaism and Christian Beginnings* (New York: Oxford University Press, 1978).

Sarason, R. S., "On the Use of Method in the Modern Study of Jewish Liturgy," *Approaches to Ancient Judaism: Theory and Practice*, ed. W. S. Green (Missoula: Scholars, 1978).

———, "Toward a New Agendum for the Study of Rabbinic Midrashic Literature," *Studies in Aggadah, Targum and Jewish Liturgy in Memory of Joseph Heinemann*, ed. J. J. Petuchowski and E. Fleischer (Jerusalem: Magnes, 1981).

———, "The Petihtot in Leviticus Rabba: 'Oral Homilies' or Redactional Constructions?" *JJS* 33 (1982).

Sarna, N., *Exploring Exodus* (New York: Schocken, 1987).

Satlow, M., "Jewish Constructions of Nakedness in Late Antiquity," *JBL* 116 (1997).

Schäfer, P., *Synopse zur Hekhalot-Literatur* (Tübingen: J. C. B. Mohr, 1981).

———, "Der Aufstand gegen Gallus Caesar," *Tradition and Re-Interpretation in Jewish and Early Christian Literature: Essays in Honour of J. C. H. Lebran*, ed. J. W. van Henten et al. (Leiden: Brill, 1986).

———, *Hekhalot-Studien* (Tübingen: J. C. B. Mohr, 1988).

———, "Jewish Liturgy and Magic," *Geschichte-Tradition-Reflexion: Festschrift für Martin Hengel zum 70. Geburtstag*, I: *Judentum*, ed. P. Schäfer (Tübingen: J. C. B. Mohr, 1996).

Schatkin, M., "The Maccabean Martyrs," *VC* 28 (1974).

Schechter, S., "Women in Temple and Synagogue," *Studies in Judaism: First Series* (Philadelphia: Jewish Publication Society, 1915).

Scheiber, A., *Jewish Inscriptions in Hungary from the Third Century to 1686* (Leiden: Brill, 1983).

Schick, R., *The Christian Communities of Palestine from Byzantine and Islamic Rule: A Historical and Archaeological Study* (Princeton: Darwin, 1995).

Schiffman, L., "The Dead Sea Scrolls and the Early History of Jewish Liturgy," *The Synagogue in Late Antiquity*, ed. L. I. Levine (Philadelphia: Jewish Theological Seminary & American Schools of Oriental Research, 1987).

———, *The Eschatological Community of the Dead Sea Scrolls: A Study of the Rule of the Congregation*, Society of Biblical Literature Monograph Series 38 (Atlanta: Scholars, 1989).

———, *Reclaiming the Dead Sea Scrolls* (Philadelphia: Jewish Publication Society, 1994).

Schirmann, J., "Hebrew Liturgical Poetry and Christian Hymnology," *JQR* 44 (1953).

Scholem, G. G., *Jewish Gnosticism, Merkabah Mysticism and Talmudic Tradition* (New York: Jewish Theological Seminary, 1960).

Schubert, K., "Jewish Pictorial Traditions in Early Christian Art," *Jewish Historiography and Iconography in Early and Medieval Christianity*, ed. H. Schreckenberg and K. Schubert (Assen: Van Gorcum, 1992).

Schürer, E., *Die Gemeindeverfassung der Juden in Rom in der Kaiserzeit nach den Inschriften dargestellt* (Leipzig: J. C. Hinrichs'sche, 1879).

———, *The History of the Jewish People in the Age of Jesus Christ*, rev. ed., 3 vols. (Edinburgh: T. & T. Clark, 1973–87).

Schurmann, H., *Das Lukasevangelium* (Freiburg: Herder, 1969).

Schwabe, M., "The Ancient Synagogue in Apamea in Syria," *Qedem* 1 (1942). Hebrew.

———, "Greek Inscriptions from Jerusalem," *Sefer Yerushalayim*, ed. M. Avi-Yonah (Jerusalem & Tel Aviv: Bialik & Dvir, 1956). Hebrew.

Schwabe, M., and Lifshitz, B., *Beth She'arim*, II: *Greek Inscriptions* (New Brunswick: Rutgers University Press, 1974).

Schwartz, D. R., "Josephus and Philo on Pontius Pilate," *The Jerusalem Cathedra*, III, ed. L. I. Levine (Jerusalem: Yad Izhak Ben Zvi, 1983).

———, "On Drama and Authenticity in Philo and Josephus," *SCI* 10 (1989–90).

———, *Agrippa I: The Last King of Judaea*, Texte und Studien zum antiken Judentum 23 (Tübingen: J. C. B. Mohr & Siebeck, 1990).

———, "Law and Truth: On Qumran-Sadducean and Rabbinic Views of Law," *The Dead Sea Scrolls: Forty Years of Research*, ed. D. Dimant and U. Rappaport (Leiden: Brill, 1992).

———, *Studies in the Jewish Background of Christianity* (Tübingen: J. C. B. Mohr, 1992).

———, "Felix and Isopoliteia, Josephus and Tacitus," *Zion* 58 (1992–93). Hebrew.

Schwartz, J. J., *Jewish Settlement in Judaea after the Bar-Kochba War and the Arab Conquest* (Jerusalem: Magnes, 1986).

———, "The *Encaenia* of the Church of the Holy Sepulchre, the Temple of Solomon and the Jews," *Theologische Zeitschrift* 43 (1987).

———, *Lod (Lydda), Israel: From Its Origins through the Byzantine Period, 5600 B.C.E.–640 C.E.*, B.A.R. International Series 571 (Oxford: B.A.R., 1991).

Schwartz, M. B., *Torah-Reading in Ancient Synagogues* (Ann Arbor: University Microfilms, 1985).

Schwartz, S., *Josephus and Judaean Politics* (Leiden: Brill, 1990).

———, "On the Program and Reception of the Synagogue Mosaics," *From Dura to Sepphoris: Studies in Jewish Art and Society in Late Antiquity*, ed. L. Levine and Z. Weiss (Ann Arbor: *Journal of Roman Archaeology* Supplementary Series, forthcoming).

Schwartzman, S., "How Well Did the Synoptic Evangelists Know the Synagogue?" *HUCA* 24 (1952–53).

Schweitzer, A., *The Quest of the Historical Jesus* (New York: Macmillan, 1964).

Seager, A. R., "The Building History of the Sardis Synagogue," *AJA* 76 (1972).

———, "The Architecture of the Dura and Sardis Synagogues," *The Dura-Europos Synagogue: A Re-Evaluation (1932–1972)*, ed. J. Gutmann (Missoula: University of Montana Press, 1973).

———, "The Synagogue at Sardis," *Ancient Synagogues Revealed*, ed. L. I. Levine (Jerusalem: Israel Exploration Society, 1981).

———, "The Recent Historiography of Ancient Synagogue Architecture," *Ancient Synagogues in Israel*, ed. R. Hachlili, B.A.R. International Series 499 (Oxford: B.A.R., 1989).

——— and Kraabel, A. T., "The Synagogue and the Jewish Community," *Sardis from Prehistoric to Roman Times*, ed. G. M. H. Hanfmann (Cambridge: Harvard University Press, 1983).

——— et al., eds., *The Synagogue and Its Setting* (Cambridge: Harvard University Press, in press).

Sed-Rajna, G., *Jewish Art* (New York: H. N. Abrams, 1997).

Segal, A. F., *Two Powers in Heaven* (Ann Arbor: University Microfilms International, 1976).

———, *Paul the Convert* (New Haven: Yale University Press, 1990).

Segal, J. B., *Edessa "The Blessed City"* (Oxford: Clarendon, 1970).

Segal, L. A., "R. Matiah Ben Heresh of Rome on Religious Duties and Redemption: Reacting to Sectarian Teaching," *PAAJR* 58 (1992).

Segal, M. Z., "Nash Papyrus," *Lešonenu* 15 (1947). Hebrew.

Segal, P., "The Penalty of the Warning Inscription from the Temple of Jerusalem," *IEJ* 39 (1989).

Segni, L. Di, "Inscriptions of Tiberias," *Tiberias: From Its Founding to the Muslim Conquest*, ed. Y. Hirschfeld (Jerusalem: Yad Izhak Ben Zvi, 1988). Hebrew.

———, "The Involvement of Local, Municipal and Provincial Authorities in Urban Building in Late Antique Palestine and Arabia," *JRA* 14 (1995).

Shanks, H., "Is the Title 'Rabbi' Anachronistic in the Gospels?" *JQR* 53 (1962–63).

———, "Origins of the Title 'Rabbi,'" *JQR* 59 (1968–69).

———, *Judaism in Stone: The Archaeology of Ancient Synagogues* (Washington, D.C.: Biblical Archaeology Society, 1979).

Sharon, I., "Phoenician and Greek Ashlar Construction Techniques at Tel Dor, Israel," *BASOR* 267 (1987).

———, "The Fortification of Dor and the Transition from the Israeli-Syrian Concept of Defence to the Greek Concept," *Qadmoniot* 24/95–96 (1991). Hebrew.

———, "Local Traditions and the Process of Hellenization and Dor—Archaeological Perceptions," *Twentieth Archaeological Conference in Israel* (Jerusalem: Israel Exploration Society, 1994). Hebrew.

———, "Models for Stratigraphic Analysis of Tell Sites," Ph.D. dissertation (Hebrew University, 1995).

Shatzman, I., "Artillery in Judaea from Hasmonean to Roman Times," *The Eastern Frontier of the Roman Empire*, ed. D. H. French and C. S. Lightfoot, B.A.R. International Series 553 (Oxford, B.A.R., 1989).

———, "Ballistra Stones from Tel Dor and the Artillery of the Greco-Roman World," *Qadmoniot* 24/95–96 (1991). Hebrew.

Sheppard, A. R. R., "Jews, Christians and Heretics in Acmonia and Eumenia," *Anatolian Studies* 29 (1979).

Shinan, A., *The Aggadah in the Aramaic Targums to the Pentateuch*, 2 vols. (Jerusalem: Makor, 1979). Hebrew.

———, "Live Translation: On the Nature of the Aramaic Targums to the Pentateuch," *Prooftexts* 3 (1983).

———, "Sermons, Targums and the Reading from Scriptures in the Ancient Synagogue," *The Synagogue in Late Antiquity*, ed. L. I. Levine (Philadelphia: Jewish Theological Seminary & American Schools of Oriental Research, 1987).

———, "Hebrew and Aramaic in Synagogue Literature," *Tura—Studies in Jewish Thought: Simon Greenberg Jubilee Volume* (Tel Aviv: Hakibbutz Hameuchad, 1989). Hebrew.

———, "Dating Targum Pseudo-Jonathan: Some More Comments," *JJS* 41 (1990).

———, "The 'Numerical Proem' Type in the Palestinian Aramaic Targum of the Pentateuch and Its Contribution to the Study of the Division of the Torah into Sedarim," *Jerusalem Studies in Hebrew Literature* 12 (1990). Hebrew.

———, "Echoes from Ancient Synagogues: Vocatives and 'Emendations' in the Aramaic Targums to the Pentateuch," *JQR* 81 (1991).

———, "Targumic Additions in Targum Pseudo-Jonathan," *Textus* 16 (1991).

———, "The Aramaic Targum as a Mirror of Galilean Jewry," *The Galilee in Late Antiquity*, ed. L. I. Levine (New York & Jerusalem: Jewish Theological Seminary, 1992).

———, *The Embroidered Targum: The Aggadah in Targum Pseudo-Jonathan of the Pentateuch* (Jerusalem: Magnes, 1992). Hebrew.

———, "The Aggadah of the Palestinian Targums of the Pentateuch and Rabbinic Aggadah: Some Methodological Considerations," *The Aramaic Bible: Targums in Their Historical Context*, ed. D. R. G. Beattie and M. J. McNamara (Sheffield: Sheffield Academic, 1994).

———, "Redeemer and Redemption in the Prayer Book," *Varieties of Opinion and Views in Jewish Culture*, ed. D. Kerem (Jerusalem: Department of Settlement Education, 1994). Hebrew.

———, "Synagogues in the Land of Israel: The Literature of the Ancient Synagogue and Synagogue Archaeology," *Sacred Realm: The Emergence of the Synagogue in the Ancient World*, ed. S. Fine (New York: Oxford University Press, 1996).

———, "Seventy Names of Jerusalem in Midrash and Cognate Literatures," *The Sanctity and Centrality of Jerusalem in Judaism, Christianity and Islam*, ed. L. I. Levine (New York: Continuum, 1998).

Siegert, F., *Drei hellenistisch-jüdische Predigten*, II (Tübingen: J. C. B. Mohr, 1986).

Sievers, J., " 'Where Two or Three . . . ': The Rabbinic Concept of *Shekhinah* and Matthew 18:20,"

Standing before God: Studies in Prayer in Scriptures and in Tradition with Essays in Honor of J. M. Oesterreicher, ed. A. Finkel and L. Frizzell (New York: KTAV, 1981).

Siker, J. S., "'First to the Gentiles': A Literary Analysis of Luke 4:16–30," *JBL* 111 (1992).

Silber, M., *The Origin of the Synagogue* (New Orleans: Steeg, 1915).

Simon, M., *Recherches d'histoire judéo-chrétienne* (Paris: Mouton, 1962).

———, *Verus Israel: Etude sur les relations entre chrétiens et juifs dans l'empire romain (135–425)* (Paris: de Boccard, 1964).

———, "Theos Hypsistos," *Ex Orbe Religionum*, ed. J. Bergman et al. (Leiden: Brill, 1972).

Simons, J. J., *Jerusalem in the Old Testament: Researches and Theories* (Leiden: Brill, 1952).

Sinding-Larsen, S., *Iconography and Ritual: A Study of Analytical Perspectives* (Oslo: Universitetsforlaget, 1984).

Sivan, H., "Pilgrimage, Monasticism and the Emergence of Christian Palestine in the Fourth Century," *The Blessings of Pilgrimage*, ed. R. Ousterhout, Illinois Byzantine Studies 1 (Urbana: University of Illinois Press, 1990).

Sky, H. I., *Redevelopment of the Office of the Hazzan through the Talmudic Period* (San Francisco: Mellon Research, 1992).

Slusser, M., "Reading Silently in Antiquity," *JBL* 111 (1992).

Small, D. B., "Social Correlations to the Greek Cavea in the Roman Period," *Roman Architecture in the Greek World*, ed. S. Macready and F. H. Thompson (London: Society of Antiquaries, 1987).

Smallwood, E. M., *The Jews under Roman Rule: From Pompey to Diocletian* (Leiden: Brill, 1976).

———, "Philo and Josephus as Historians of the Same Events," *Josephus, Judaism, and Christianity* ed. L. H. Feldman and G. Hata (Leiden: Brill, 1987).

Smelik, K. A. D., "John Chrysostom's Homilies against the Jews," *Nederlands Theologisch Tijdschrift* 39 (1985).

Smith, J. Z., "Observations on *Hekhalot Rabbati*," *Biblical and Other Studies*, ed. A. Altmann (Cambridge: Harvard University Press, 1963).

———, *To Take Place: Toward Theory in Ritual* (Chicago: University of Chicago Press, 1987).

———, *Map Is Not Territory: Studies in the History of Religions* (Chicago: University of Chicago Press, 1993).

Smith, M., "Palestinian Judaism in the First Century," *Israel: Its Role in Civilization*, ed. M. Davis (New York: Jewish Theological Seminary, 1956).

———, "The Image of God: Notes on the Hellenization of Judaism, with Especial Reference to Goodenough's Work on Jewish Symbols," *BJRL* 40 (1958).

———, "Goodenough's 'Jewish Symbols' in Retrospect," *JBL* 86 (1967).

———, *Jesus the Magician* (New York: Harper & Row, 1978).

———, "Jewish Religious Life in the Persian Period," *Cambridge History of Judaism*, I, ed. W. D. Davies and L. Finkelstein (Cambridge: Cambridge University Press, 1984).

———, "On the *Yôṣēr* and Related Texts," *The Synagogue in Late Antiquity*, ed. L. I. Levine (Philadelphia: Jewish Theological Seminary & American Schools of Oriental Research, 1987).

Sokoloff, M., ed. and trans., *The Targum to Job from Qumran Cave XI* (Ramat Gan: Bar Ilan Studies in Near Eastern Languages and Culture, 1974).

————, *Dictionary of Jewish Palestinian Aramaic of the Byzantine Period* (Ramat Gan: Bar Ilan University Press, 1990).

Sokoloff, M., and Yahalom, J., "Aramaic Piyyutim from the Byzantine Period," *JQR* 75 (1985).

Sola Pool, D. de, *The Kaddish* (Leipzig: R. Haupt, 1909).

Solin, H., "Juden und Syrer im westlichen Teil der römischen Welt," *ANRW* II, 29.2 (Berlin & New York: de Gruyter, 1983).

Sonne, I., "The Paintings of the Dura Synagogue," *HUCA* 20 (1947).

Speiser, E., " 'Coming' and 'Going' at the 'City' Gate," *BASOR* 144 (1956).

Sperber, D., "The History of the Menorah," *JJS* 16 (1965).

————, "Mishmarot and Maʿamadot," *EJ*, XII (Jerusalem: Macmillan, 1971).

————, *Roman Palestine 200–400—The Land: Crisis and Change in Agrarian Society as Reflected in Rabbinic Sources* (Ramat Gan: Bar Ilan University Press, 1978).

————, *A Dictionary of Greek and Latin Legal Terms in Rabbinic Literature* (Ramat Gan: Bar Ilan University Press, 1984).

————, "A Note on the Palestinian Division of the Reading of the Levitical Curses," *Sidra* 6 (1990). Hebrew.

————, *Jewish Customs: Sources and History*, 5 vols. (Jerusalem: Harav Kook, 1990–95). Hebrew.

Squarciapino, M. F., "The Synagogue at Ostia," *Archaeology* 16 (1963).

————, *La sinagoga di Ostia—The Synagogue of Ostia* (Rome: n.p., 1964).

————, "Plotius Fortunatus archisynagogus," *La Rassegna Mensile di Israel* 36 (1970).

Stambaugh, J. E., "The Functions of Roman Temples," *ANRW* II, 16.1, ed. W. Haase and H. Temporini (Berlin & New York: de Gruyter, 1978).

Stavroulakis, N. P., and DeVinney, T. J., *Jewish Sites and Synagogues of Greece* (Athens: Talos, 1992).

Stein, S., "The Influence of Symposia Literature on the Literary Form of the Pesaḥ Haggadah," *JJS* 8 (1957).

Steinfeld, Z. A., "Qaliri's Partition of the Reading of the Torah," *Tarbiz* 55 (1986). Hebrew.

————, "Prostration in Prayer and the Prohibition of the Paving Stone," *Sidra* 3 (1987). Hebrew.

Stemberger, G., *Juden und Christen im Heiligen Land* (Munich: C. H. Beck, 1987).

————, "Non-Rabbinic Literature," *Judaism in Late Antiquity*, I: *The Literary and Archaeological Sources*, ed. J. Neusner (Leiden: Brill, 1995).

Stenhouse, P., "Baba Rabba: Historical or Legendary Figure? Some Observations," *New Samaritan Studies: Essays in Honour of G. D. Sexdenier*, ed. A. D. Crown and L. Davey (Sydney: Mandelbaum & University of Sydney, 1995).

————, "Fourth-Century Date for Baba Rabba Re-Examined," *New Samaritan Studies: Essays in Honour of G. D. Sexdenier*, ed. A. D. Crown and L. Davey (Sydney: Mandelbaum & University of Sydney, 1995).

Stern, E. "The Excavations at Tell Mevorakh and the Late Phoenician Elements in the Architecture of Palestine," *BASOR* 225 (1977).

————, "The Walls of Dor," *IEJ* 38 (1988).

————, "Hazor, Dor and Megiddo in the Time of Ahab and under Assyrian Rule," *IEJ* 40 (1990).

————, ed., *The New Encyclopedia of Archaeological Excavations in the Holy Land* [*NEAEHL*], 4 vols. (Jerusalem, Carta, 1993).

————, *Dor: Ruler of the Seas* (Jerusalem: Israel Exploration Society, 1994).

Stern, E., and Sharon, I., "Tel Dor, 1986: Preliminary Report," *IEJ* 37 (1987).

———, et al., *Excavations at Dor, Final Report*, 2 vols., Qedem 1-2 (Jerusalem: Hebrew University & Israel Exploration Society, 1995).

———, "Cities of the Persian Period," *The Oxford Encyclopedia of Archaeology in the Near East*, II, ed. E. M. Meyers (New York: Oxford University Press, 1997).

———, "Fortifications of the Persian Period," *The Oxford Encyclopedia of Archaeology in the Near East*, II, ed. E. M. Meyers (New York: Oxford University Press, 1997).

Stern, M., "The Jewish Diaspora," *The Jewish People in the First Century*, I, ed. S. Safrai and M. Stern (Philadelphia: Fortress, 1974).

———, "The Reign of Herod and the Herodian Dynasty," *The Jewish People in the First Century*, I, ed. S. Safrai and M. Stern (Philadelphia: Fortress, 1974).

———, *Greek and Latin Authors on Jews and Judaism*, 3 vols. (Jerusalem: Israel Academy of Sciences and Humanities, 1974-84).

———, "Aspects of Jewish Society: The Priesthood and Other Classes," *The Jewish People in the First Century*, II, ed. S. Safrai and M. Stern (Philadelphia: Fortress, 1976).

———, "Jewish Community and Institutions," *The Diaspora in the Hellenistic-Roman World*, ed. M. Stern (Jerusalem: 'Am Oved, 1983). Hebrew.

———, "Jews of Italy," *The Diaspora in the Hellenistic-Roman World*, ed. M. Stern (Jerusalem: 'Am Oved, 1983). Hebrew.

———, "Sympathy for the Jews in Roman Senatorial Circles in the Early Empire," *Studies in Jewish History: The Second Temple Period*, ed. M. Amit et al. (Jerusalem: Yad Izhak Ben Zvi, 1991). Hebrew.

Stern, S., "Synagogue Art and Rabbinic Halakhah," *Le'ela* 38 (1994).

———, "Figurative Art and *Halakha* in the Mishnaic-Talmudic Period," *Zion* 61 (1996). Hebrew.

Steudel, A., "The Houses of Prostration *CD* XI, 21–XII, 1—Duplicates of the Temple," *RQ* 16 (1993).

Stillwell, R., "The Siting of Classical Greek Temples," *Journal of the Society of Architectural Historians* 13 (1954).

Stone, M., "Apocalyptic Literature," *Jewish Writings of the Second Temple Period*, ed. M. Stone (Assen: Van Gorcum, 1984).

Stone, N., "Notes on the Shellal Mosaic ('Ein Ha-Besor) and the Mosaic Workshops at Gaza," *Jews, Samaritans and Christians in Byzantine Palestine*, ed. D. Jacoby and Y Tsafrir (Jerusalem: Yad Izhak Ben Zvi, 1988). Hebrew.

Strack, H. L., and Stemberger, G., *Introduction to Talmud and Midrash* (Minneapolis: Fortress, 1992).

Strange, J., and Shanks, H., "Synagogue Where Jesus Preached Found at Capernaum," *BAR* 9 (1983).

Strauss, H., "The History and Form of the Seven-Branched Candlestick of the Hasmonean Kings," *Journal of the Warburg and Courtauld Institutes* 22 (1959).

Strugnell, J., "The Angelic Liturgy at Qumran—4QSerek Sirôt 'Ôlat Hassabbat," *Congress Volume: Oxford, 1959* (Leiden: Brill, 1960).

Sukenik, E. L., "Three Ancient Jewish Inscriptions from Palestine," supplement to *Zion* 1 (1926). Hebrew.

———, "'Cathedra of Moses' in Ancient Synagogues," *Tarbiz* 1 (1929). Hebrew.

————, *The Ancient Synagogue of Beth Alpha* (Jerusalem: Hebrew University, 1932).

————, "Designs of the Lection (αυλογειον) in Ancient Synagogues in Palestine," *JPOS* 12 (1933).

————, *Ancient Synagogues in Palestine and Greece* (London: Milford, 1934).

————, *The Synagogue of Dura Europos and Its Frescoes* (Jerusalem: Bialik, 1947). Hebrew.

————, "The Present State of Ancient Synagogue Studies," *Bulletin of the Louis M. Rabinowitz Fund for the Exploration of Ancient Synagogues*, I (Jerusalem: Hebrew University, 1949).

————, "The Mosaic Inscriptions in the Synagogue at Apamea on the Orontes," *HUCA* 23 (1950–51).

————, "The Ancient Synagogue at Yafia near Nazareth, Preliminary Report," *Bulletin of the Louis M. Rabinowitz Fund for the Exploration of Ancient Synagogues*, II (Jerusalem: Hebrew University, 1951).

Sussman, V., *Ornamental Jewish Oil-Lamps* (Warminster: Aris & Phillips, 1982).

Sussmann, J., "The Boundaries of Eretz-Israel," *Tarbiz* 45 (1976). Hebrew.

————, "The Inscription in the Synagogue at Rehob," *Ancient Synagogues Revealed*, ed. L. I. Levine (Jerusalem: Israel Exploration Society, 1981).

————, "Once Again Yerushalmi Neziqin," *Mehqerei Talmud*, I, ed. J. Sussmann and D. Rosenthal (Jerusalem: Magnes, 1990). Hebrew.

Swartz, M. D., "'Alay Le-Shabbeah: A Liturgical Prayer on Ma'aseh Merkabah," *JQR* 77 (1986–87).

————, *Mystical Prayer in Ancient Judaism: An Analysis of Ma'aseh Merkavah* (Tübingen: J. C. B. Mohr, 1992).

————, "'Like the Ministering Angels': Ritual and Purity in Early Jewish Mysticism and Magic," *AJS Review* 19 (1994).

————, "Ritual about Myth about Ritual: Towards an Understanding of the *Avodah* in the Rabbinic Period," *Journal of Jewish Thought and Philosophy* 6 (1997).

————, "Sage, Priest, and Poet: Typologies of Religious Leadership in Mishnaic and Liturgical Literatures," *Jews, Christians and Polytheists in the Ancient Synagogue*, ed. S. Fine (London: Routledge, forthcoming).

Swift, F. H., *Education in Ancient Israel, from Earliest Times to 70 A.D.* (Chicago: Open Court, 1919).

Tabory, J., *Jewish Prayer and the Yearly Cycle—A List of Articles*, *Kiryat Sefer* supplement to Vol. 64 (Jerusalem: Jewish National and University Library, 1992–93). Hebrew and English.

Taft, R., "Liturgy of the Great Church: An Initial Synthesis of Structure and Interpretation on the Eve of Iconoclasm," *DOP* 34–35 (1980–81).

————, *Beyond East and West: Problems in Liturgical Understanding* (Washington, D.C.: Pastoral, 1984).

Talbert, C. H., *Literary Patterns, Theological Themes, and the Genres of Luke-Acts* (Missoula: Scholars, 1974).

Talgam, R., "Similarities and Differences between Synagogue and Church Mosaics in Palestine during the Byzantine and Umayyad Periods," *From Dura to Sepphoris: Studies in Jewish Art and Society in Late Antiquity*, ed. L. Levine and Z. Weiss (Ann Arbor: *Journal of Roman Archaeology* Supplementary Studies, forthcoming).

Talley, T. J., *The Origins of the Liturgical Year* (New York: Pueblo, 1986).

Talmon, S., "The Manual of Benedictions of the Sect of the Judean Desert," *RQ* 2 (1959–60).

———, *The World of Qumran from Within: Collected Studies* (Jerusalem & Leiden: Magnes & Brill, 1989).

Ta-Shma, I. M., "On the Beginning of the *Piyyut*," *Tarbiz* 53 (1984). Hebrew.

———, "Y. Liebes, 'Mazmiaḥ Qeren Yeshu'ah'" (review), *Jerusalem Studies in Jewish Thought* 4 (1984–85). Hebrew.

———, "Synagogal Sanctity—Symbolism and Reality," *Knesset Ezra: Literature and Life in the Synagogue—Studies Presented to Ezra Fleischer*, ed. S. Elizur et al. (Jerusalem: Yad Izhak Ben Zvi, 1994). Hebrew.

Taylor, J. E., *Christians and the Holy Places: The Myth of Jewish-Christian Origins* (Oxford: Clarendon, 1993).

Tchalenko, G., *Villages antiques de la Syrie du Nord*, 3 vols. (Paris: Geuthner, 1953–58).

Tcherikover, V., *Hellenistic Civilization and the Jews* (Philadelphia: Jewish Publication Society, 1959).

———, "Prolegomenon," *CPJ*, by V. Tcherikover et al., I (Cambridge: Harvard University Press, 1957).

Tcherikover, V., Fuks, A., and Stern, M., *Corpus Papyrorum Judaicarum [CPJ]*, 3 vols. (Cambridge: Harvard University Press, 1957–64).

Temple, P. J., "The Rejection at Nazareth," *CBQ* 17 (1955).

Terrien, S., "The Omphalos Myth and Hebrew Religion," *VT* 20 (1970).

Thackeray, H., *The Septuagint and Jewish Worship: A Study in Origins*, 2d ed. (London: Oxford University Press, 1923).

Tigay, J. H., *The JPS Torah Commentary: Deuteronomy* (Philadelphia: Jewish Publication Society, 1996).

Toaff, A., "Matia ben Cheresh e la sua accademia rabbinica di Roma," *Annuario di studi ebraici* 2 (1964).

Tobler, T., and Molinier, A., eds. *Itinera hierosolymitana et descriptiones terrae sanctae*, I/2 (Geneva: Fick, 1880).

Torjesen, K. J., *When Women Were Priests* (San Francisco: Harper, 1995).

Trebilco, P. R., *Jewish Communities in Asia Minor* (Cambridge: Cambridge University Press, 1991).

Trifon, D., "Some Aspects of Internal Politics Connected with the Bar-Kokhva Revolt," *The Bar-Kokhva Revolt: A New Approach*, ed. A. Oppenheimer and U. Rappaport (Jerusalem: Yad Izhak Ben Zvi, 1984). Hebrew.

———, "The Jewish Priests from the Destruction of the Second Temple to the Rise of Christianity," Ph.D. dissertation (Hebrew University, 1985). Hebrew.

———, "Did the Priestly Courses (*Mishmarot*) Transfer from Judaea to Galilee after the Bar Kokhba Revolt?" *Tarbiz* 49 (1989). Hebrew.

Trombley, F. R., *Hellenic Religion and Christianization, c. 370–529*, 2 vols. (Leiden: Brill, 1992–94).

Tsafrir, Y., *Eretz Israel from the Destruction of the Second Temple to the Muslim Conquest*, II: *Archaeology and Art* (Jerusalem: Yad Izhak Ben Zvi, 1984). Hebrew.

———, "The Byzantine Setting and Its Influence on Ancient Synagogues," *The Synagogue in Late Antiquity*, ed. L. I. Levine (Philadelphia: Jewish Theological Seminary & American Schools of Oriental Research, 1987).

———, "The Development of Ecclesiastical Architecture in Palestine," *Ancient Churches Revealed*, ed. Y. Tsafrir (Jerusalem: Israel Exploration Society, 1993).

———, "On the Source of the Architectural Design of the Ancient Synagogues in the Galilee: A New Appraisal," *Ancient Synagogues: Historical Analysis and Archaeological Discovery*, I, ed. D. Urman and P. V. M. Flesher (Leiden: Brill, 1995).

———, "The Synagogues of Capernaum and Meroth and the Dating of the Galilean Synagogue," *The Roman and Byzantine Near East: Some Recent Archaeological Research*, ed. J. Humphrey, *Journal of Roman Archaeology* Supplementary Series 14 (Ann Arbor: Cushing-Malloy, 1995).

———, "Some Notes on the Settlement and Demography of Palestine in the Byzantine Period: The Archaeological Evidence," *Retrieving the Past: Essays on Archaeological Research and Methodology in Honor of Gus W. van Beek* (Winona Lake: Eisenbrauns, 1996).

Tsafrir, Y., and Foerster, G., "On the Date of the 'Sabbatical Year Earthquake,'" *Tarbiz* 58 (1989). Hebrew.

Turner, V., *From Temple to Meeting House* (The Hague: Mouton, 1979).

Tyson, J. B., *Images of Judaism in Luke-Acts* (Columbia: University of South Carolina Press, 1992).

Urbach, E. E., "The Rabbinical Laws of Idolatry in the Second and Third Centuries in the Light of Archaeological and Historical Facts," *IEJ* 9 (1959).

———, "Class Status and Leadership in the World of the Palestinian Sages," *Proceedings of the Israel Academy of Sciences and Humanities* 2 (1966).

———, "Traditions about Merkavah Mysticism in the Tannaitic Period, *Studies in Mysticism and Religion Presented to Gershom G. Scholem*, ed. E. E. Urbach et al. (Jerusalem: Magnes, 1967). Hebrew.

———, "Heavenly and Earthly Jerusalem," *Jerusalem through the Ages: The Twenty-Fifth Archaeology Convention* (Jerusalem: Israel Exploration Society, 1968). Hebrew.

———, "Mishmarot U'Ma'amadot," *Tarbiz* 42 (1973). Hebrew.

———, "From Judaea to the Galilee," *Festschrift Y. Friedman*, ed. S. Pines (Jerusalem: Hebrew University, 1974). Hebrew.

———, *The Sages: Their Concepts and Beliefs*, 2 vols. (Jerusalem: Magnes, 1979).

———, *The World of the Sages: Collected Studies* (Jerusalem: Magnes, 1988). Hebrew.

———, "The Role of the Ten Commandments in Jewish Worship," *The Ten Commandments in History and Tradition*, ed. B. Z. Segal (Jerusalem: Magnes, 1990).

Urman, D., "Jewish Inscriptions from Kefar Dabura in the Golan," *Tarbiz* 40 (1971). Hebrew.

———, "On the Question of the Location of the Academy of Bar Kappara and R. Hoshayah Rabbah," *Nation and Its History*, ed. M. Stern (Jerusalem: Shazar Center, 1983). Hebrew.

———, *The Golan: A Profile of a Region during the Roman and Byzantine Periods*, B.A.R. International Series 269 (Oxford: B.A.R., 1985).

———, "The House of Assembly and the House of Study: Are They One and the Same?" *Ancient Synagogues: Historical Analysis and Archaeological Discovery*, I, ed. D. Urman and P. V. M. Flesher (Leiden: Brill, 1995).

———, "Public Structures and Jewish Communities in the Golan Heights," *Ancient Synagogues: Historical Analysis and Archaeological Discovery*, II, ed. D. Urman and P. V. M. Flesher (Leiden: Brill, 1995).

Urman, D., and Flesher, P. V. M., eds., *Ancient Synagogues: Historical Analysis and Archaeological Discovery*, 2 vols. (Leiden: Brill, 1995).

Valantasis, R., *Spiritual Guides of the Third Century: A Semiotic Study of the Guide-Disciple Relationship in Christianity, Neoplatonism, Hermetism, and Gnosticism* (Minneapolis: Fortress, 1991).

Vasiliev, J. A. A., "The Iconoclastic Edict of the Caliph Yazid II, A.D. 721," *DOP* 9–10 (1956).

Vaux, R. de, "Les patriarches hébreux et les découvertes modernes," *RB* 56 (1949).

———, *Ancient Israel: Its Life and Institutions*, 2 vols. (New York: McGraw-Hill, 1961).

Vermes, G., "A propos des commentaires bibliques découverts à Qumran, la Bible et l'Orient," *RHPR* 35 (1935).

———, "Essenes and Therapeutai," *RQ* 12 (1962).

———, "The Decalogue and the Minim," *In Memoriam Paul Kahle*, ed. M. Black and G. Fohrer (Berlin: Töpelmann, 1968).

———, *Jesus the Jew: A Historian's Reading of the Gospels* (London: Fontana-Collins, 1973).

———, *The Dead Sea Scrolls in English*, 4th ed. (London: Penguin, 1995).

Vermes, G., and Goodman, M., *The Essenes According to the Classical Sources* (Sheffield: JSOT, 1989).

Vincent, L.-H., "Chronique—Découverte de la 'Synagogue des Affranchis' à Jérusalem," *RB* 30 (1921).

Vincent, L.-H., and Stève, P. M.-A., *Jérusalem de l'Ancient Testament: Recherches d'archéologie et d'histoire*, 2 vols. (Paris: J. Gabalda, 1954–56).

Visotzky, B., "Anti-Christian Polemic in Leviticus Rabbah," *PAAJR* 56 (1990).

———, *The Midrash on Proverbs* (New Haven: Yale University Press, 1992).

———, *Fathers of the World: Essays in Rabbinic and Patristic Literatures* (Tübingen, J. C. B. Mohr, 1995).

Vitto, F., "A Byzantine Synagogue in the Beth Shean Valley," *Temples and High Places in Biblical Times*, ed. A. Biran (Jerusalem: Hebrew Union College Press, 1981).

———, "Synagogue of Rehob," *NEAEHL*, IV, ed. E. Stern (Jerusalem: Carta, 1993).

———, "The Interior Decoration of Palestinian Churches and Synagogues," *Byzantinische Forschungen*, XXI, ed. A. M. Hakkert and W. E. Kaegi, Jr. (Amsterdam: Am M. Hakkert, 1995).

Viviano, B. T., *Study as Worship: Aboth and the New Testament* (Leiden: Brill, 1978).

Vogel, C., "*Sol aequinoctiales*," *RSR* 36 (1962).

———, "Orientations vers l'est," *L'Orient Syrien* 9 (1964).

Vogelstein, H., *Rome* (Philadelphia: Jewish Publication Society, 1940).

Vryonis, S., Jr., "Hellas Revisited," *The Transformation of the Roman World*, ed. L. White, Jr. (Berkeley: University of California Press, 1966).

Wacholder, B. Z., "Prolegomenon," *The Bible as Read and Preached in the Old Synagogue*, I, ed. J. Mann, reprint (New York: KTAV, 1971).

Walbank, F. W., "The Hellenistic World: New Trends and Direction," *SCI* 11 (1991–92).

Waldow, H. E. von, "The Origin of the Synagogue Reconsidered," *Essays in Honor of Donald G. Miller*, Pittsburgh Theological Monograph Series 31 (Pittsburgh: Pickwick, 1979).

Walker, P. W. L., *Holy City, Holy Places? Christian Attitudes to Jerusalem and the Holy Land in the Fourth Century* (Oxford: Clarendon, 1990).

Waltzing, J. P., *Etude historique sur les corporations professionnelles chez les romains depuis les origines jusqu'à la chute de l'empire d'occident*, 4 vols. (Leuven: n.p., 1895–1900).

Ward-Perkins, J. B., *Cities of Ancient Greece and Italy: Planning in Classical Antiquity* (New York: G. Braziller, 1974).

Wasserstein, A., "Rabban Gamliel and Proclus the Philosopher (Mishna Aboda Zara 3, 4)," *Zion* 45 (1980). Hebrew.

Waterman, L., *Royal Correspondence of the Assyrian Empire*, 4 vols. (Ann Arbor: University of Michigan Press, 1930).

Watzinger, C., *Denkmäler Palästinas*, II (Leipzig: J. C. Hinrichs'sche, 1935).

Wegner, J. R., *Chattel or Person? The Status of Women in the Mishnah* (New York: Oxford University Press, 1988).

———, "The Image and Status of Women in Classical Rabbinic Judaism," *Jewish Women in Historical Perspective*, ed. J. R. Baskin (Detroit: Wayne State University Press, 1991).

Weinfeld, M., *Deuteronomy and the Deuteronomic School* (Oxford: Clarendon, 1972).

———, "Traces of Kedushat Yozer and Pesukey De-Zimra in the Qumran Literature and in Ben Sira," *Tarbiz* 45 (1976). Hebrew.

———, "The Prayers for Knowledge, Repentance and Forgiveness in the 'Eighteen Benedictions'—Qumran Parallels, Biblical Antecedents and Basic Characteristics," *Tarbiz* 48 (1979). Hebrew.

———, "Synagogue Inscriptions and Jewish Liturgy," *Annual for the Bible and the Study of the Near East* 4 (1980). Hebrew.

———, "The Heavenly Praise in Unison," *Meqor Hajjim: Festschrift für Georg Molin zum 75. Geburtstag* (Graz: Akademische Druck- u. Verlagsanstalt, 1983).

———, *The Organizational Pattern and the Penal Code of the Qumran Sect: A Comparison of Guilds and Religious Associations of the Hellenistic-Roman Period*, Novum testamentum et orbis antiquus 2 (Fribourg: Editions Universitaires, 1986).

———, "The Morning Prayers (Birkoth Hashachar) in Qumran and the Conventional Jewish Liturgy," *RQ* 13 (1988).

———, "The Uniqueness of the Decalogue and Its Place in Jewish Tradition," *The Ten Commandments in History and Tradition*, ed. B. Z. Segal (Jerusalem: Magnes, 1990).

———, *Deuteronomy 1–11* (New York: Doubleday, 1991).

———, "Prayer and Liturgical Practice in the Qumran Sect," *The Scrolls of the Judaean Desert: Forty Years of Research*, ed. M. Broshi et al. (Jerusalem: Bialik, 1992). Hebrew.

———, "The Biblical Roots of the Standing Prayer on the Sabbath and Festivals," *Tarbiz* 65 (1996). Hebrew.

Weingreen, J., "Origin of the Synagogue," *Hermathena* 98 (1964).

Weisberg, D., *Guild Structure and Political Allegiance in Early Achaemenid Mesopotamia* (New Haven: Yale University Press, 1967).

Weiss, Z., "The Location of the *Sheliah Tzibbur* during Prayer," *Cathedra* 55 (1990). Hebrew.

Weiss, Z., and Netzer, E., *Promise and Redemption: A Synagogue Mosaic from Sepphoris* (Jerusalem: Israel Museum, 1996).

Weitzmann, K., and Kessler, H. L., *The Frescoes of the Dura Synagogue and Christian Art* (Washington, D.C.: Dumbarton Oaks, 1990).

Welch, K., "Roman Amphitheatres Revived," *JRA* 4 (1991).

———, "The Arena in Late-Republican Italy: A New Interpretation," *JRA* 7 (1994).

Wellhausen, J., *Geschichte der christlichen Religion mit Einleitung in die israelitisch-jüdische Religion* (Berlin: B. G. Teubner, 1909).

Werner, E., "The Doxology in Synagogue and Church—A Liturgico-Musical Study," *HUCA* 19 (1945–46).

———, "Hebrew and Oriental Christian Metrical Hymns: A Comparison," *HUCA* 23 (1950–51).

———, *Sacred Bridge: Liturgical Parallels in Synagogue and Early Church* (London: Dobson, 1959).

———, *Sacred Bridge: Liturgical Parallels in Synagogue and Early Church*, I (New York: Schocken, 1970); II (New York: KTAV, 1984).

Westenholz, J. G., "The Synagogues of Rome," *The Jewish Presence in Ancient-Rome*, ed. J. G. Westenholz (Jerusalem: Bible Lands Museum, 1995).

Westermann, W. L., *The Slave Systems of Greek and Roman Antiquity* (Philadelphia: American Philosophical Society, 1955).

Wevers, J. W., "Barthélemy and Proto-Septuagint Studies," *BIOSCS* 21 (1988).

Wharton, A. J., "Good and Bad Images from the Synagogue of Dura Europos: Contexts, Subtexts, Intertexts," *Art History* 17 (1994).

———, *Refiguring the Post-Classical City: Dura Europos, Jerash, Jerusalem and Ravenna* (Cambridge: Cambridge University Press, 1995).

———, "Erasure: Eliminating the Space of Late Antique Judaism," *From Dura to Sepphoris: Studies in Jewish Art and Society in Late Antiquity*, ed. L. I. Levine and Z. Weiss (Ann Arbor: *Journal of Roman Archaeology* Supplementary Series, forthcoming).

White, L. M., "The Delos Synagogue Revisited: Recent Fieldwork in the Graeco-Roman Diaspora," *HTR* 80 (1987).

———, *Building God's House in the Roman World: Architectural Adaptation among Pagans, Jews, and Christians* (Baltimore: Johns Hopkins University Press, 1990).

———, *The Social Origins of Christian Architecture*, II: *Texts and Monuments for the Christian Domus Ecclesiae in Its Environment* (Valley Forge: Trinity, 1997).

———, "Synagogue and Society in Imperial Ostia: Archaeological and Epigraphical Evidence," *HTR* 90 (1997).

Wieder, N., *Islamic Influences on Jewish Worship* (Oxford: East & West Library, 1947). Hebrew.

———, "The Habakkuk Scroll and the Targum," *JJS* 4 (1953).

———, "On the Blessings 'Gentile-Slave-Woman,' 'Animal' and 'Ignoramus,'" *Sinai* 85 (1979). Hebrew.

———, "The Jericho Inscription and Jewish Liturgy," *Tarbiz* 52 (1983). Hebrew.

Wiegand, T., and Schrader, H., *Priene: Ergebnisse der Ausgrabungen und Untersuchungen in den Jahren 1895–1898* (Berlin: G. Reimer, 1904).

Wilcox, M., "The Aramaic Background of the New Testament," *The Aramaic Bible: Targums in Their Historical Context*, ed. D. R. G. Beattie and M. J. McNamara (Sheffield: Sheffield Academic, 1994).

Wilken, R. L., *John Chrysostom and the Jews: Rhetoric and Reality in the Late Fourth Century* (Berkeley: University of California Press, 1983).

———, *The Land Called Holy: Palestine in Christian History and Thought* (New Haven: Yale University Press, 1992).

Wilkinson, J., *Jerusalem Pilgrims before the Crusades* (Jerusalem: Ariel, 1977).

———, "The Beit Alpha Synagogue Mosaic: Towards an Interpretation," *JJA* 5 (1978).

————, "Orientation, Jewish and Christian," *PEQ* 116 (1984).

————, "Jewish Holy Places and the Origins of Christian Pilgrimage," *The Blessings of Pilgrimage*, ed. R. Ousterhoot (Urbana: University of Illinois Press, 1990).

————, "Constantinian Churches in Palestine," *Ancient Churches Revealed*, ed. Y. Tsafrir (Jerusalem: Israel Exploration Society, 1993).

Williams, M. H., "The Jews and Godfearers Inscription from Aphrodisias—A Case of Patriarchal Interference in Early Third Century Caria?" *Historia* 41 (1992).

————, "The Organisation of Jewish Burials in Ancient Rome in the Light of Evidence from Palestine and the Diaspora," *ZPE* 101 (1994).

————, "The Structure of Roman Jewry Re-Considered—Were the Synagogues of Ancient Rome Entirely Homogeneous?" *ZPE* 104 (1994).

Willis, G. G., *A History of Early Roman Liturgy to the Death of Pope Gregory the Great* (London: Boydell, 1994).

Wills, L., "The Form of the Sermon in Hellenistic Judaism and Early Christianity," *HTR* 77 (1984).

Wilmart, A., "Homélies latines de Saint Jean Chrysostome," *JTS* 19 (1918).

Wilson, S. G., *Related Strangers: Jews and Christians 70–170 C.E.* (Minneapolis: Fortress, 1995).

————, "Voluntary Associations: An Overview," *Voluntary Associations in the Graeco-Roman World*, ed. J. Kloppenborg and S. G. Wilson (London & New York: Routledge, 1996).

Windisch, H., "Die ältesten christlichen Palästinapilger," *ZDPV* 48 (1925).

Winter, F. E., *Greek Fortifications* (London: Routledge & K. Paul, 1971).

Wirgin, W., "The Menorah as a Symbol of Judaism," *IEJ* 12 (1962).

————, "The *Menorah* as a Symbol of the After-Life," *IEJ* 14 (1964).

Wischnitzer, R., *The Messianic Theme in the Paintings of the Dura Synagogue* (Chicago: University of Chicago Press, 1948).

————, "The Beth Alpha Mosaic: A New Interpretation," *JSS* 17 (1955).

————, *The Architecture of the European Synagogue* (Philadelphia: Jewish Publication Society, 1964).

Witherington, B., III, *Women in the Earliest Churches* (Cambridge: Cambridge University Press, 1988.

Wolfson, E. R., "Halperin's *The Faces of the Chariot*," *JQR* 81 (1991).

Wolfson, H. A., *Philo: Foundations of Religious Philosophy*, 2 vols. (Cambridge: Harvard University Press, 1948).

Xydis, S. G., "The Chancel Barrier, Solea and Ambo of Hagia Sophia," *The Art Bulletin* 29 (1947).

Yadin, Y., *Masada: Herod's Fortress and the Zealots' Last Stand* (London: Weidenfeld & Nicolson, 1966).

————, *Tefillin from Qumran (XQ PHYL 1–4)* (Jerusalem: Israel Exploration Society, 1969).

————, "The Synagogue at Masada," *Ancient Synagogues Revealed*, ed. L. I. Levine (Jerusalem: Israel Exploration Society, 1981).

Yahalom, J., "Synagogue Inscriptions in Palestine—A Stylistic Classification," *Immanuel* 10 (1980).

————, "Zodiac Signs in the Palestinian Piyyut," *Jerusalem Studies in Hebrew Literature* 9 (1986). Hebrew.

————, "The Sepphoris Synagogue Mosaic and Its Story," *From Dura to Sepphoris: Jewish Art and Society in Late Antiquity*, ed. L. Levine and Z. Weiss (Ann Arbor: *Journal of Roman Archaeology* Supplementary Series, forthcoming).

——, "*Piyyût* as Poetry," *The Synagogue in Late Antiquity*, ed. L. I. Levine (Philadelphia: Jewish Theological Seminary & American Schools of Oriental Research, 1987).

——, "Angels Do Not Understand Aramaic: On the Literary Use of Jewish Palestinian Aramaic in Late Antiquity," *JJS* 47 (1996).

——, *Priestly Palestinian Poetry: A Narrative Liturgy for the Day of Atonement* (Jerusalem: Magnes, 1996). Hebrew.

Yarden, L., *The Tree of Light: A Study of the Menorah* (Upsala: Skriv Service AB, 1972).

Yashar, B., "'יש אומרים' and 'אחרים'," *Sinai* 42 (1958). Hebrew.

Yeivin, Z., "The Synagogue of Chorazim," *All the Land of Naphtali*, ed. H. Hirschberg (Jerusalem: Israel Exploration Society, 1969). Hebrew.

——, "The Synagogue at Eshtemoa," *Qadmoniot* 5/18 (1972). Hebrew.

——, "Inscribed Marble Fragments from the Khirbet Susiya Synagogue," *IEJ* 24 (1974).

——, "Reconstruction of the Southern Interior Wall of the Khorazin Synagogue," *EI*, XVIII (Jerusalem: Israel Exploration Society, 1985). Hebrew.

——, "Khirbet Susiya—The *Bema* and Synagogue Ornamentation," *Ancient Synagogues in Israel*, ed. R. Hachlili, B.A.R. International Series 499 (Oxford: B.A.R., 1989).

——, "Susiya, Khirbet," *NEAEHL*, IV, ed. E. Stern (Jerusalem: Carta, 1993).

York, A., "The Dating of Targumic Literature," *JSJ* 5 (1974).

——, "The Targum in the Synagogue and in the School," *JSJ* 10 (1979).

Yuval, I. J., "The Haggadah of Passover and Easter," *Tarbiz* 65 (1995). Hebrew.

Zahavy, T., "A New Approach to Early Jewish Prayer," *History of Judaism: The Next Ten Years*, ed. B. M. Bokser (Chico: Scholars, 1980).

——, "Three Stages in the Development of Early Rabbinic Prayer," *From Ancient Israel to Modern Judaism: Intellect in Quest of Understanding: Essays in Honor of Marvin Fox*, I, ed. J. Neusner et al. (Atlanta: Scholars, 1989).

——, *Studies in Jewish Prayer* (Lanham: University Press of America, 1990).

——, "The Politics of Piety: Social Conflict and the Emergence of Rabbinic Liturgy," *The Making of Jewish and Christian Worship*, ed. P. F. Bradshaw and L. A. Hoffman (Notre Dame: University of Notre Dame Press, 1991).

Zeitlin, S., "Origin of the Synagogue," *PAAJR* 1 (1928–30).

——, "An Historical Study of the First Canonization of the Hebrew Liturgy," *JQR* 38 (1947–48).

——, "The Morning Benediction and the Readings in the Temple," *JQR* 44 (1953–54).

——, "The Second Day of Rosh Ha-Shanah in Israel," *JQR* 44 (1953–54).

——, *The Rise and Fall of the Judaean State*, 3 vols. (Philadelphia: Jewish Publication Society, 1962–78).

——, "A Reply," *JQR* 53 (1963–64).

——, "The Tefillah, the Shemoneh Esreh: An Historical Study of the First Canonization of the Hebrew Liturgy," *JQR* 54 (1964).

——, "The Title Rabbi in the Gospels Is Anachronistic," *JQR* 59 (1968–69).

——, *Studies in the Early History of Judaism*, I (New York: KTAV, 1973).

Zevin, S. J., *Talmudic Encyclopedia*, I (Jerusalem: Talmudic Encyclopedia & Mosad Harav Kook, 1947). Hebrew.

Zlotnick, D., *The Tractate "Mourning"* (New Haven: Yale University Press, 1966).

Zori, N., "The House of Kyrios Leontis at Beth-Shean," *IEJ* 16 (1966).

——, "The Ancient Synagogue at Beth-Shean," *EI*, VIII (Jerusalem: Israel Exploration Society, 1967). Hebrew.

Zuckerman, C., "Hellenistic *Politeumata* and the Jews: A Reconsideration," *SCI* 8–9 (1985–88).

Zulay, M., "Studies on Yannai," *Bulletin of the Institute for the Study of Hebrew Poetry* 2 (1936). Hebrew.

——, "On the History of the Piyyut in Eretz-Israel," *Bulletin of the Institute for the Study of Hebrew Poetry* 5 (1939). Hebrew.

Zunz, L., *Die gottesdienstlichen Vorträge der Juden, historisch Entwickelt: Ein Beitrag zur Alterthums-kunde und biblischen Kritik, zur Literatur und Religionsgeschichte* (Berlin: Asher, 1832).

——, *Literaturgeschichte der synagogalen Poesie* (Berlin: Gerschel, 1865).

——, *Haderashot B'Yisrael* (Jerusalem: Bialik, 1954). Hebrew.

CRITICAL EDITIONS

On occasion two different editions are used for the same source. Unless otherwise specified, pages indicated in the notes refer to the edition asterisked in the Bibliography.

Abu l'fath, in *Samaritan Documents*, ed. J. Bowman (Pittsburgh: Pickwick, 1977).

Avot de R. Nathan, ed. S. Schechter (New York: Feldheim, 1945). Hebrew.

Bet Hamidrash, ed. A. Jellinek, reproduction, 6 parts (Jerusalem: Wahrmann, 1967). Hebrew.

Derech Eretz Zutta, ed. D. Sperber, 2d ed. (Jerusalem: Tzur-Ot, 1982). Hebrew.

Deuteronomy Rabbah (Midrash Debarim Rabbah), ed. S. Lieberman (Jerusalem: Wahrmann, 1964). Hebrew.

——, XI, ed. A. Mirkin, 2d ed. (Tel Aviv: Yavneh, 1975). Hebrew.

Didascalia Apostolorum, ed. R. H. Connolly (Oxford: Clarendon, 1929).

Differences in Customs between the People of the East and the People of Eretz-Israel, ed. M. Margalioth (Jerusalem: R. Mass, 1938). Hebrew.

——, ed. B. M. Lewin, reprint (Jerusalem: Makor, 1973). Hebrew.

Genesis Rabbah, ed. Y. Theodor and Ch. Albeck, 2 vols. (Jerusalem: Wahrmann, 1965). Hebrew.

Genesis Rabbati, ed. Ch. Albeck (Jerusalem: Meqitzei Nirdamim, 1967). Hebrew.

Iggeret Harav Sherira Gaon, ed. B. M. Lewin (Haifa: n.p., 1921). Hebrew.

Itinerary of Rabbi Benjamin of Tudela, trans. and ed. A. Asher, 2 vols. (London & Berlin: A. Asher, 1840–41).

Josephus, LCL, 9 vols. (Cambridge: Harvard University Press, 1958–65).

Kitab al-Tarikh, ed. P. Stenhouse (Sydney: Mandelbaum Trust, 1985).

Lamentations Rabbah, ed. S. Buber (Vilna: Romm, 1899). Hebrew.

Leviticus Rabbah, ed. M. Margulies, 5 vols. (Jerusalem: Jewish Theological Seminary, 1953–60). Hebrew.

Malalas, *Chronicle* (Melbourne: Australian Association for Byzantine Studies, 1986).

*Mekhilta of R. Ishmael, ed. H. Horowitz and I. Rabin (Jerusalem: Bamberger and Wahrmann, 1960). Hebrew.

————, ed. J. Lauterbach, 3 vols. (Philadelphia: Jewish Publication Society, 1949).

Mekhilta of R. Simeon b. Yoḥai, ed. J. N. Epstein and E. Z. Melamed (Jerusalem: Meqitzei Nirdamim, 1956). Hebrew.

Midrash Hagadol, Genesis, ed. M. Margaliot (Jerusalem: Mosad Rav Kook, 1967). Hebrew.

Midrash Hagadol, Exodus, ed. M. Margaliot (Jerusalem: Mosad Rav Kook, 1957). Hebrew.

Midrash Hagadol, Leviticus, ed. A. Steinsaltz (Jerusalem: Mosad Rav Kook, 1976). Hebrew.

Midrash Hagadol, Numbers, ed. Z. M. Rabinowitz (Jerusalem: Mosad Rav Kook, 1967). Hebrew.

Midrash Hagadol, Deuteronomy, ed. S. Fisch (Jerusalem: Mosad Rav Kook, 1973). Hebrew.

Midrash Mishlei (*The Midrash on Proverbs*), ed. B. Visotzky (New Haven: Yale University Press, 1992).

Midrash on Psalms, ed. S. Buber (New York: Om, 1948). Hebrew.

Midrash on Samuel, ed. S. Buber (Cracow: Fischer, 1893; reprint, Jerusalem: n.p., 1965). Hebrew.

*Midrash on Song of Songs, ed. A. Greenhut and A. Wertheimer (Jerusalem: Ktav Yad Vasefer Institute, 1971). Hebrew.

————, ed. S. Dunesky (Jerusalem: Dvir, 1980). Hebrew.

Midrash Tannaim, ed. D. Hoffman, 2 vols. (Berlin: Itzkowski, 1909). Hebrew.

Philo, LCL, 11 vols. (Cambridge: Harvard University, 1949–62).

*Pesiqta de Rav Kahana, ed. B. Mandelbaum, 2 vols. (New York: Jewish Theological Seminary, 1962). Hebrew.

————, ed. S. Buber, 2d ed. (New York: Om, 1949). Hebrew.

Pesiqta Rabbati, ed. M. Friedmann (Tel Aviv: Esther, 1963). Hebrew.

Pirqei Derekh Eretz, in Seder Eliyahu Zuta, ed. M. Friedmann (Vienna: Achiasaf, 1904; reprint, Jerusalem: Bamberger and Wahrmann, 1960). Hebrew.

Pirkei Mashiaḥ, in *Midreshei Geula*, ed. Y. Even-Shmuel, 2d ed. (Jerusalem: Bialik, 1954). Hebrew.

Samaritan Chronicle, ed. J. M. Cohen (Leiden: Brill, 1981).

The Scriptores Historiae Augustae, LCL, 3 vols. (Cambridge: Harvard University Press, 1967–68).

Seder R. ʿAmram Gaon, ed. N. N. Coronel (Jerusalem: Qiryah Neemanah, 1964–65). Hebrew.

Seder Eliyahu Rabbah, ed. M. Friedmann (Jerusalem: Bamberger & Wahrmann, 1960). Hebrew.

Seder Eliyahu Zuta, ed. M. Friedmann (Jerusalem: Bamberger & Wahrmann, 1960). Hebrew.

Seder ʿOlam Rabbah, ed. D. B. Ratner (New York: Orot, 1966). Hebrew.

Siddur Abudraham, ed. Wertheimer (Tel Aviv: Zion, 1970). Hebrew.

Siddur R. Saadja Gaon, ed. I. Davidson et al. (Jerusalem: Meqitzei Nirdamim, 1941). Hebrew.

Sifra, ed. I. H. Weiss (New York: Om Publishing, 1946). Hebrew.

Sifra on Leviticus, ed. L. Finkelstein, 5 vols. (New York: Jewish Theological Seminary, 1989–91). Hebrew.

Sifre-Deuteronomy, ed. L. Finkelstein (New York: Jewish Theological Seminary, 1969). Hebrew.

Sifre-Numbers, H. Horowitz (Jerusalem: Wahrmann, 1966). Hebrew.

Song of Songs Rabbah, ed. S. Dunesky (Jerusalem & Tel Aviv: Dvir, 1950). Hebrew.

Tanḥuma, ed. S. Buber, reproduction (Jerusalem: Ortsel, 1964). Hebrew.

Tosefta (Orders Zeraʿim–Neziqin [through Bava Batra]), ed. S. Lieberman (1955–1988). Hebrew.

————, (Orders Neziqin [from Sanhedrin]–Tohorot), ed. M. Zuckermandel (Jerusalem: Bamberger & Wahrmann, 1937). Hebrew.

Tractate Semaḥot, ed. M. Higger, reprint (Jerusalem: Makor, 1970). Hebrew.

Tractate Soferim, ed. M. Higger, reprint (Jerusalem: Makor, 1970). Hebrew.

Yalqut Shim'oni, Genesis, ed. Y. Shiloni (Jerusalem: Mosad Rav Kook, 1973). Hebrew.

Yalqut Shim'oni, Exodus, ed. D. Hyman (Jerusalem: Mosad Rav Kook, 1984). Hebrew.

Yalqut Shim'oni, Leviticus, ed. D. Hyman (Jerusalem: Mosad Rav Kook, 1977–80). Hebrew.

ILLUSTRATION CREDITS

Courtesy of the Biblical Archaeology Society
Fig. 12. R. S. MacLennan, "In Search of the Jewish Diaspora," 46. Photo by R. S. MacLennan.
Fig. 38. H. Shanks, *Judaism in Stone*, 89.
Fig. 97. H. Shanks, *Judaism in Stone*, 122.

Courtesy of E. M. Meyers
Fig. 15. E. M. Meyers et al., *Excavations at Ancient Meiron*, 13.
Fig. 17. E. M. Meyers, C. L. Meyers, and J. F. Strange, *Excavations at the Ancient Synagogue of Gush Ḥalav* (Winona Lake: American Schools of Oriental Research, 1990), 66.
Fig. 34. E. M. Meyers et al., *Excavations at Khirbet Shemaʻ*, 59.
Fig. 94. E. M. Meyers et al., *Excavations at Ancient Meiron*, 12.

Drawn by Ḥani Davis
Fig. 36.

Courtesy of Yale University Press
Fig. 37. C. H. Kraeling, *Dura: Synagogue*, Plan VI.

Courtesy of Aschendorff Verlag
Fig. 42. B. Brenk, "Synagoge von Apamea," Seite 11.

Courtesy of C. Danov
Fig. 51. C. Danov, "Neues aus der Geschichte von Philippopolis," Pl. 2, 2.

Courtesy of R. Hachlili
Fig. 53. R. Hachlili, *Art and Archaeology—Diaspora*, 232.

Courtesy of the Bible Lands Museum Jerusalem
Figs. 54, 60.
Fig. 59. Drawn by J. Rosenberg.

Courtesy of E. Lattanzi
Fig. 56.

Courtesy of Z. Weiss and E. Netzer
Fig. 63. Z. Weiss and E. Netzer, *Promise and Redemption*, 12.
Fig. 92. Z. Weiss and E. Netzer, *Promise and Redemption*, 26–27.
Fig. 93. Z. Weiss and E. Netzer, *Promise and Redemption*, 14. Drawn by Pnina Arad.

Courtesy of the Jewish Theological Seminary of America
Fig. 89.

SOURCE INDEX

Zechariah

8	23
8:16	28

Psalms

7:8	78
17:14	78
19:15	534
24:7–9	30
26:8	451
29	516
51:17	534
55:18	515
69:13	28
74:8	22, 39
82:1	182, 459
84:8	450
90:1	21
103:2–6	512
113–18	524
113:2	558
115:1	428
125:5	348
138:2	428

Proverbs

1:21	183
31:23	28
31:31	28

Ruth

3:11	28
4:1–2	28

Daniel

2:20	558
6:11	152, 182, 302, 515
7:10	541
8:13	541

Nehemiah

2–3	33
8:1	30
8:4	320
8:5–8	501

8–10	21
9	512

I Chronicles

1	348
24:1–18	36
26:5	332

II Chronicles

6:32	180
6:34	182
6:38	180, 182
32:6	28, 29

SECOND TEMPLE JEWISH WRITINGS (LISTED ALPHABETICALLY)

Ben Sira

Prologue	143

Enoch

39:12–14	541

Jubilees

6:23–31	518
21:16	310

Judith

8:6	90
8:18	210

Letter of Aristeas

12–14	75
92	155
95	155
176–77	135
304–6	106, 281, 309
305	154
305–8	146
308–21	135
310	82, 148

I Maccabees

1:21–24	372
1:41–64	38

TARGUMS

Targum Jonathan

Targum Neofiti

CLASSICAL LITERATURE
(LISTED ALPHABETICALLY)

Apuleius

SUBJECT INDEX